MW01357418

MCSE™
Windows® 2000
Security Design

Phillip G. Schein

MCSE™ Windows® 2000 Security Design Exam Cram

Limits of Liability and Disclaimer of Warranty

The author and publisher of this book have used their best efforts in preparing the book and the programs contained in it. These efforts include the development, research, and testing of the theories and programs to determine their effectiveness. The author and publisher make no warranty of any kind, expressed or implied, with regard to these programs or the documentation contained in this book.

The author and publisher shall not be liable in the event of incidental or consequential damages in connection with, or arising out of, the furnishing, performance, or use of the programs, associated instructions, and/or claims of productivity gains.

Trademarks

Trademarked names appear throughout this book. Rather than list the names and entities that own the trademarks or insert a trademark symbol with each mention of the trademarked name, the publisher states that it is using the names for editorial purposes only and to the benefit of the trademark owner, with no intention of infringing upon that trademark.

The Coriolis Group, LLC
14455 N. Hayden Road
Suite 220
Scottsdale, Arizona 85260

(480)483-0192
FAX (480)483-0193
www.coriolis.com

Library of Congress Cataloging-in-Publication Data
Schein, Phillip G.
    MCSE Windows 2000 security design exam cram / by Phillip G. Schein.
        p.   cm.
    Includes index.
    ISBN 1-57610-715-9
    1. Electronic data processing personnel--Certification.   2. Microsoft software--Examinations--Study guides.   3. Microsoft Windows (Computer file) 4. Computer security--Examinations--Study guides.
I. Title.
QA76.3.S35   2000
005.8--dc21   00-058992
                                                            CIP

President and CEO
Keith Weiskamp

Publisher
Steve Sayre

Acquisitions Editor
Lee Anderson

Marketing Specialist
Brett Woolley

Project Editor
Meredith Brittain

Technical Reviewer
Jason A. Appel

Production Coordinator
Carla J. Schuder

Cover Designer
Jesse Dunn

Layout Designer
April Nielsen

Printed in the United States of America
10 9 8 7 6 5 4 3 2 1

The Coriolis Group, LLC • 14455 North Hayden Road, Suite 220 • Scottsdale, Arizona 85260

ExamCram.com Connects You to the Ultimate Study Center!

Our goal has always been to provide you with the best study tools on the planet to help you achieve your certification in record time. Time is so valuable these days that none of us can afford to waste a second of it, especially when it comes to exam preparation.

Over the past few years, we've created an extensive line of *Exam Cram* and *Exam Prep* study guides, practice exams, and interactive training. To help you study even better, we have now created an e-learning and certification destination called **ExamCram.com**. (You can access the site at **www.examcram.com**.) Now, with every study product you purchase from us, you'll be connected to a large community of people like yourself who are actively studying for their certifications, developing their careers, seeking advice, and sharing their insights and stories.

I believe that the future is all about collaborative learning. Our **ExamCram.com** destination is our approach to creating a highly interactive, easily accessible collaborative environment, where you can take practice exams and discuss your experiences with others, sign up for features like "Questions of the Day," plan your certifications using our interactive planners, create your own personal study pages, and keep up with all of the latest study tips and techniques.

I hope that whatever study products you purchase from us—*Exam Cram* or *Exam Prep* study guides, *Personal Trainers*, *Personal Test Centers*, or one of our interactive Web courses—will make your studying fun and productive. Our commitment is to build the kind of learning tools that will allow you to study the way you want to, whenever you want to.

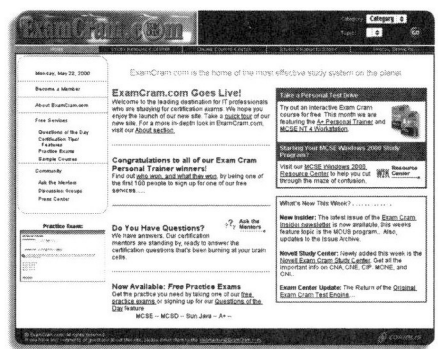

Visit ExamCram.com now to enhance your study program.

Help us continue to provide the very best certification study materials possible. Write us or email us at **learn@examcram.com** and let us know how our study products have helped you study. Tell us about new features that you'd like us to add. Send us a story about how we've helped you. We're listening!

Good luck with your certification exam and your career. Thank you for allowing us to help you achieve your goals.

Keith Weiskamp
President and CEO

Look for these other products from The Coriolis Group:

**MCSE Windows 2000 Accelerated
Exam Prep**
By Lance Cockcroft, Erik Eckel,
and Ron Kauffman

MCSE Windows 2000 Server Exam Prep
By David Johnson and Dawn Rader

**MCSE Windows 2000 Professional
Exam Prep**
By Michael D. Stewart, James Bloomingdale,
and Neall Alcott

MCSE Windows 2000 Network Exam Prep
By Tammy Smith and Sandra Smeeton

**MCSE Windows 2000 Directory Services
Exam Prep**
By David V. Watts, Will Willis,
and Tillman Strahan

**MCSE Windows 2000 Security Design
Exam Prep**
By Richard Alan McMahon and Glen Bicking

**MCSE Windows 2000 Network Design
Exam Prep**
By Geoffrey Alexander, Anoop Jalan,
and Joseph Alexander

**MCSE Migrating from NT 4
to Windows 2000
Exam Prep**
By Glen Bergen, Graham Leach,
and David Baldwin

**MCSE Windows 2000
Directory Services Design
Exam Prep**
By J. Peter Bruzzese and Wayne Dipchan

**MCSE Windows 2000 Core Four
Exam Prep Pack**

**MCSE Windows 2000 Server
Exam Cram**
By Natasha Knight

**MCSE Windows 2000 Professional
Exam Cram**
By Dan Balter, Dan Holme, Todd Logan,
and Laurie Salmon

**MCSE Windows 2000 Network
Exam Cram**
By Hank Carbeck, Derek Melber,
and Richard Taylor

**MCSE Windows 2000 Directory Services
Exam Cram**
By Will Willis, David V. Watts,
and J. Peter Bruzzese

**MCSE Windows 2000 Network Design
Exam Cram**
By Kim Simmons, Jarret W. Buse,
and Todd B. Halpin

**MCSE Windows 2000
Directory Services Design
Exam Cram**
By Dennis Scheil and Diana Bartley

**MCSE Windows 2000 Core Four
Exam Cram Pack**

and...
MCSE Windows 2000 Foundations
By James Michael Stewart and Lee Scales

To the grandmother I never met. You have visited me on many of these long, dark nights since our walks along the banks of the Genesee River. Promises have been kept.

❧

About the Author

Phillip G. Schein is a specialist in technical training whose expertise is in Web application development, courseware design and publishing, and in-house training programs. He has written articles about the computer industry for a regional publication (circ. 35,000) in Westchester/Rockland counties, New York. Phil has led corporate training seminars for Fortune 100 publishing companies, agricultural research firms, insurance reinvestment concerns, and business leaders in the insurance industry.

In addition to being a Microsoft Certified Systems Engineer/Trainer (MCSE/MCT) and Novell Certified Network Engineer (CNE), Phil is also recognized by The Chauncey Group International as a Certified Technical Trainer (CTT). He has CompTIA A+ certification in both Windows/DOS and Macintosh, as well as the latest CompTIA i-Net+ certification. In addition, he is a Certified Internet Webmaster (CIW-Site Designer). Phil is also a Microsoft Office User Specialist (MOUS) and Product Specialist (MCP+I) in several Microsoft products.

Phil's experience extends beyond the classroom; he hosts his own Web site, has developed in-house and commercial software, has served as a Unix administrator, and has done consulting work for more than 15 years. As for training, Phil has taught in both corporate and retail environments. His course list includes basic through advanced levels of all Microsoft operating systems, Novell OS, Macintosh OS, Web application development and Internet-related subjects, relational database management systems, leading mail systems, most of the popular accounting packages, and all Microsoft Office applications.

A native New Yorker, Phil completed undergraduate studies at the University of Rochester, NY, and graduate course requirements for a doctoral degree in physiological psychology at Indiana University in Bloomington. Formerly a staff instructor and interim network administrator at a local college, Phil is currently the Site Manager/Advanced Technology Trainer of a 78-seat training facility located in lower Manhattan in New York City. Prior to his career in the computer industry, Phil spent more than 10 years as an accounting manager in the transportation industry. He has served on the Board of Trustees for two not-for-profit organizations, owns a male chow named Marcus and a female keeshond named Cleo, and is an enthusiastic supporter of the dramatic arts.

You can reach the author for comment, correction, or criticism by email at **pschein@tchouse.com**, his personal home page at **www.tchouse.com/pgsbio.htm**, or through his Web site, The Clearing House Web Site, at **www.tchouse.com**.

Acknowledgments

Books are the original virtual machine. Like any Windows 2000 operating system, they have a user mode and a kernel mode. These brief paragraphs acknowledge the many service providers who run in that privileged area, the kernel mode. Without their invisible support, user mode activities would either run poorly or cease to function at all. The author is the keyboard, the monitor, the mouse. The services that drive the graphic device interface on which you read this text expend boundless energy, especially during development. A service provider (a.k.a. copyeditor) named Bonnie Trenga has incessantly, though correctly, returned a stream of error messages to the monitor: "Please specify... Please specify". Said the keyboard to the mouse, "She's made you a better writer ('rather than xx')!" Another service provider (a.k.a. technical reviewer), Jason A. Appel, is responsible for fault management. Said the keyboard to the mouse, "His insights turned background to foreground, his gentle nudges were in the right directions." Said the mouse to the keyboard, "Don't forget Lee Anderson (a.k.a. acquisitions editor) for giving me the opportunity to do the project, Carla Schuder (a.k.a. production coordinator) for making it flow; April Nielsen (a.k.a. interior designer) for turning words into pictures; and Jesse Dunn (a.k.a. cover designer) for guaranteeing the book will be favorably judged by its cover."

Other more peripheral, albeit no less significant, service providers never were aware they provided a service. To the instructors who arrived at my training center on time to work on mornings after my all-night vigils, thank you. I didn't want to have to cover a class at the last minute! Thank you, Arthur Epstein, for providing me with a black couch on which to sleep and a bird's-eye view of a 300-year-old cemetery on which to reflect. Though you didn't realize it, I couldn't have completed this project without either one providing much-needed background support. Thank you Evan Benjamin, Tharon Clausen, and David Safford for making yourselves available and waiting for a remote call. To friends who go unnamed, please forgive a driven individual—a Sisyphus who is, when writing, more often than not, less than communicative, unnaturally intense, and typically in need of a shave. Said the mouse to the keyboard, "And what of the ones you haven't mentioned?" Said the keyboard to the mouse, "There will be other server sessions."

A change in metaphor and a final thank you. It is written that the Buddha shows favor on the slowest horse even as the horse feels the stinging lash of the whip. That whip, in the hands of a wise equestrian, is a tool that shapes the performance of this strong, recalcitrant beast of burden—a performance that ranges from pulling plowshares through the fields in student's minds to clearing hurdles and finishing races. There is no horse without a rider and no rider without a horse. In the heat, sweat and pain of the race, the two are as one. Thank you, Meredith Brittain, project editor, for knowing when and when not to use the whip. We make a great team.

Contents at a Glance

Chapter 1   Microsoft Certification Exams   1

Chapter 2   Security Overview   25

Chapter 3   Public Key Infrastructure (PKI)   59

Chapter 4   Kerberos Security   87

Chapter 5   IP Security Architecture   125

Chapter 6   Remote Connectivity Issues   153

Chapter 7   Other Network Issues   183

Chapter 8   Constructing a Security Policy   213

Chapter 9   Identity Management Issues   251

Chapter 10   Group Policy   275

Chapter 11   Security and Configuration Tools   299

Chapter 12   Other Technical Issues   325

Chapter 13   Sample Test   361

Chapter 14   Answer Key   389

Table of Contents

Introduction xxi

Self-Assessment xxxiii

Chapter 1
Microsoft Certification Exams 1
Assessing Exam-Readiness   2
The Exam Situation   3
Exam Layout and Design: New Case Study Format   4
　　Multiple-Choice Question Format   5
　　Build-List-and-Reorder Question Format   7
　　Create-a-Tree Question Format   8
　　Drag-and-Connect Question Format   10
　　Select-and-Place Question Format   11
Microsoft's Testing Formats   13
Strategies for Different Testing Formats   15
　　The Case Study Exam Strategy   15
　　The Fixed-Length and Short-Form Exam Strategy   16
　　The Adaptive Exam Strategy   17
Question-Handling Strategies   18
Mastering the Inner Game   19
Additional Resources   20

Chapter 2
Security Overview 25
The Key Questions   26
Required Technical Background   27
IT Controls and Corporate Objectives   28
　　IT Security Controls   28
　　Corporate Objectives   30
　　Physical and Logical Access   30
　　System Security Audits   31

Risk Management   32

Security Requirements   33

Deployment of a Security System   34

Problems with Procedural Paradigms   34

A Microsoft Historical Perspective   35

Key Historical Trends   36

Active Directory   38

Integrating Security Account Management   41

Physical Organization   42

A Layered Security Paradigm   43

Evaluating Risks   45

Documenting Nontechnical Procedures   48

Using Security Protocols   49

Mapping Security Technologies   49

Competencies   50

Practice Questions   53

Need to Know More?   58

Chapter 3
Public Key Infrastructure (PKI) 59

Applying the Basic Security Scheme   61

Encrypted Exchanges   62

Symmetric Key Encryption   63

Cryptanalysis   65

Distribution Problems   66

Asymmetric Key Encryption   66

Active Interception   68

Authentication and Integrity Controls   68

One-Way Hash Functions   69

The Windows 2000 Implementation   70

Entity Authentication through Proof of Possession   70

Secret Key Agreements   71

Bulk Data Encryption   71

Digital Envelope   71

Certificates and Key
Management Services   72

Digital Signatures   73

Extensibility   73

Certificates   74

The PKI Suite   76
Microsoft CryptoAPI   78
Global Encryption Policies   79
Practice Questions   80
Need to Know More?   85

Chapter 4
Kerberos Security 87
MIT Kerberos: The Basis for
Microsoft's Implementation   88
Goals and Requirements   88
Assumptions   89
Components of the Protocol   89
Version 5 Enhancements   90
Microsoft's Implementation of
Kerberos 5   91
Public Key Infrastructure (PKI)   92
Ticket Structure   92
Other Enhancements   92
KDC   94
Cross-Domain Authentication   98
Delegation of Authentication   100
Account Database   101
Kerberos Policy   101
Interoperability   102
Kerberos and Alternative Protocols   103
The Big Picture   103
SSPs   104
A Kerberos Case Study   110
ExamCram Ltd.: Sharing Resources with
Other Companies   110
Commentary   112
Practice Questions   114
Need to Know More?   123

Chapter 5
IP Security Architecture 125
IP and Security   126
Examples of IPSec Deployment   128

Building upon IPSec   129
Industry Standards   131
    Security Protocols   131
    IPSec Architecture   132
    Encryption Techniques   133
    Key Management Protocols   134
TCO   135
    Software Upgrades   135
    Training   135
    Cryptographic Key Management   136
Deployment Strategy   136
    Analyze Information   136
    Create Communications Scenarios   136
    Determine Security Levels   137
    Build Security Policies   137
An IP Security Architecture Case Study   141
    ExamCram Ltd.: Considering Network Layer
      Security Solutions   141
    Commentary   142
Practice Questions   144
Need to Know More?   150

Chapter 6
Remote Connectivity Issues 153
An Overview of VPN   154
    Security Protocols   155
    Basic Remote Access Models   156
    Tunneling   158
    NAT   159
VPN Security Protocols   159
    Design Considerations   160
    IPSec Tunnel and Transport Modes   162
    Security Protocols Compared   162
VPN Management Policies   164
    Remote Access Policy Management   164
    Client Management   165
Firewall Technologies   165
    Firewall Components   166

Firewall Architectures   167

Firewall Policies   171

Practice Questions   173

Need to Know More?   180

Chapter 7
Other Network Issues 183

IIS 5   185

Network Addressing and Domain Name Security   185

IIS Authentication Security   186

IIS Permissions   189

Combining NTFS and IIS Permissions   189

Other Security Methods   190

Secure Channel (SChannel) Protocols   191

SSL3/TLS1   192

Deployment of SSL   192

Certificate Services   193

Deploying Security for
Distributed Services   194

SSL in Windows 2000   195

Application Standards and Policies   195

Authenticode   196

Secure Multipurpose Internet Mail Extensions (S/MIME)   197

Permission Management   197

Identity Management   198

Requirements for Identity Management   199

Deployment of Identity Management   200

Practice Questions   205

Need to Know More?   211

Chapter 8
Constructing a Security Policy 213

Steps in Planning Network Security   214

Identifying the User Population   216

Determining the Scope, Sizing, and Placement of IT Resources   217

Scoping Physical Assets   217

Scoping Logical Assets   218

Assessing Network Security Risks   220

Attack Modalities   220

Ring Model   221
Creating Secure Boundaries: Physical Scoping   224
Creating Secure Boundaries: Protocol Scoping   225
Creating Secure Boundaries: Application Scoping   225
Creating Secure Boundaries: Policy Scoping   225
Preparing a Support Team   226
Monitoring and Auditing   227
Help Desk Support   228
Developing a Security Deployment Plan   228
Creating and Publishing a Security Policy   228
Developing Strategies for Secure
Network Connections   228
Deploying Network Strategies for the Everyone Group   229
Deploying Network Strategies for Staff Members   229
Deploying Network Strategies for Users
and Applications   232
Deploying Network Strategies for Business Partners   233
A Security Policy Case Study   234
ExamCram Ltd. Reformulates Its Plans   234
Commentary   236
Practice Questions   243
Need to Know More?   248

Chapter 9
Identity Management Issues 251

Basic Directory Services   252
The X.500 Standard   253
LDAP v3   254
AD Directory Services   254
Objects and Attributes   255
Names/Name Resolution   256
Terms and Components   257
Access Control   262
Limiting Authenticated Access   262
Managing Access Control Lists   264
Managing Security Administration   264
Establishing Trust Relationships   266

Resources   267

    EFS   267

Practice Questions   269

Need to Know More?   274

Chapter 10
Group Policy 275

The Concept of Group   276

    Enhancements   277

    Policies and Settings   278

Securing the Desktop Environment   281

Securing Access and Permissions   281

    Policy Scoping: Secured Boundaries   282

    Types of Policy Management   283

    Group Policy Administration   284

    Group Policy Processing   286

Permission Management Tools   290

Practice Questions   292

Need to Know More?   296

Chapter 11
Security and Configuration Tools 299

Centralized Administration Tools   301

    WMI   301

    WSH   302

    TSA   302

    RIS   303

    AD   303

    MMC   303

Desktop Management with IntelliMirror   304

The Security Configuration (SC) Tool Set   306

    Security Areas   306

    Security Settings   307

    Tool Set Components   308

    Security Templates   309

    The secedit.exe Tool   310

Other System and Security Tools   312

    IPSec Monitoring Tool   313

    Certificate Services CLI Tools   313

Support Security Management Tools   314
Tools from the *Windows 2000 Server Resource Kit* CD   317
Practice Questions   319
Need to Know More?   323

Chapter 12
Other Technical Issues 325
Centralized Identity Management   326
Identity Administration   327
Community Management   328
Identity Integration   329
Standardizing Access for Users   330
Single Sign-On (SSO)   331
Securing Access for Users   333
Enhancement: Smart Cards   334
Terminal Services Uses   339
RIS   340
SNMP   341
SMB Signing   342
OS Migration vs. Coexistence   343
Interoperability/Migration: NetWare   343
Interoperability/Migration: Unix   345
Interoperability/Migration: Apple Macintosh   349
Extensibility: COM+   350
Distributed Services   351
Security and RBAC   353
Practice Questions   354
Need to Know More?   358

Chapter 13
Sample Test 361

Chapter 14
Answer Key 389

Glossary 409

Index 421

Introduction

Welcome to *MCSE Windows 2000 Security Design Exam Cram*! Whether this is your first or your fifteenth *Exam Cram* book, you'll find information here and in Chapter 1 that will help ensure your success as you pursue knowledge, experience, and certification. This book aims to help you get ready to take—and pass—Microsoft certification Exam 70-220, titled "Designing Security for a Microsoft Windows 2000 Network." This Introduction explains Microsoft's certification programs in general and talks about how the *Exam Cram* series can help you prepare for Microsoft's Windows 2000 certification exams.

Exam Cram books help you understand and appreciate the subjects and materials you need to pass Microsoft certification exams. *Exam Cram* books are aimed strictly at test preparation and review. They do not teach you everything you need to know about a topic. Instead, I present and dissect the questions and problems I've found that you're likely to encounter on a test. I've worked to bring together as much information as possible about Microsoft certification exams.

Nevertheless, to completely prepare yourself for any Microsoft test, I recommend that you begin by taking the Self-Assessment included in this book immediately following this Introduction. This tool will help you evaluate your knowledge base against the requirements for an MCSE under both ideal and real circumstances.

Based on what you learn from that exercise, you might decide to begin your studies with some classroom training or some background reading. On the other hand, you might decide to pick up and read one of the many study guides available from Microsoft or third-party vendors on certain topics, including The Coriolis Group's *Exam Prep* series. I also recommend that you supplement your study program with visits to **ExamCram.com** to receive additional practice questions, get advice, and track the Windows 2000 MCSE program.

I also strongly recommend that you install, configure, and acquire significant "seat time" with the software that you'll be tested on, because nothing compares with hands-on experience and familiarity when it comes to understanding the questions you're likely to encounter on a certification test. Book learning is essential, but hands-on experience is the best teacher of all!

The Microsoft Certified Professional (MCP) Program

The MCP Program currently includes the following separate tracks, each of which boasts its own special acronym (as a certification candidate, you need to have a high tolerance for alphabet soup of all kinds):

➤ *MCP (Microsoft Certified Professional)*—This is the least prestigious of all the certification tracks from Microsoft. Passing one of the major Microsoft exams qualifies an individual for the MCP credential. Individuals can demonstrate proficiency with additional Microsoft products by passing additional certification exams.

➤ *MCP+SB (Microsoft Certified Professional + Site Building)*—This certification program is designed for individuals who are planning, building, managing, and maintaining Web sites. Individuals with the MCP+SB credential will have demonstrated the ability to develop Web sites that include multimedia and searchable content and Web sites that connect to and communicate with a back-end database. It requires one MCP exam, plus two of these three exams: "70-055: Designing and Implementing Web Sites with Microsoft FrontPage 98," "70-057: Designing and Implementing Commerce Solutions with Microsoft Site Server 3.0, Commerce Edition," and "70-152: Designing and Implementing Web Solutions with Microsoft Visual InterDev 6.0."

➤ *MCSE (Microsoft Certified Systems Engineer)*—Anyone who has a current MCSE is warranted to possess a high level of networking expertise with Microsoft operating systems and products. This credential is designed to prepare individuals to plan, implement, maintain, and support information systems, networks, and internetworks built around Microsoft Windows 2000 and its BackOffice Server 2000 family of products.

To obtain an MCSE, an individual must pass four core operating system exams, one optional core exam, and two elective exams. The operating system exams require individuals to prove their competence with desktop and server operating systems and networking/internetworking components.

For Windows NT 4 MCSEs, the Accelerated exam, "70-240: Microsoft Windows 2000 Accelerated Exam for MCPs Certified on Microsoft Windows NT 4.0," is an option. This free exam covers all of the material tested in the Core Four exams. The hitch in this plan is that you can take the test only once. If you fail, you must take all four core exams to recertify. The Core Four exams are: "70-210: Installing, Configuring and Administering Microsoft Windows 2000 Professional," "70-215: Installing, Configuring and Administering Microsoft

Windows 2000 Server," "70-216: Implementing and Administering a Microsoft Windows 2000 Network Infrastructure," and "70-217: Implementing and Administering a Microsoft Windows 2000 Directory Services Infrastructure."

To fulfill the fifth core exam requirement, you can choose from three design exams: "70-219: Designing a Microsoft Windows 2000 Directory Services Infrastructure," "70-220: Designing Security for a Microsoft Windows 2000 Network," or "70-221: Designing a Microsoft Windows 2000 Network Infrastructure." You are also required to take two elective exams. An elective exam can fall in any number of subject or product areas, primarily BackOffice Server 2000 components. The two design exams that you don't select as your fifth core exam also qualify as electives. If you are on your way to becoming an MCSE and have already taken some exams, visit **www.microsoft.com/ trainingandservices/** for information about how to complete your MCSE certification.

In September 1999, Microsoft announced its Windows 2000 track for MCSE and also announced retirement of Windows NT 4.0 MCSE core exams on 12/31/2000. Individuals who wish to remain certified MCSEs after 12/31/ 2001 must "upgrade" their certifications on or before 12/31/2001. For more detailed information than is included here, visit **www.microsoft.com/ trainingandservices/**.

New MCSE candidates must pass seven tests to meet the MCSE requirements. It's not uncommon for the entire process to take a year or so, and many individuals find that they must take a test more than once to pass. The primary goal of the *Exam Prep* series and the *Exam Cram* series test preparation books is to make it possible, given proper study and preparation, to pass all Microsoft certification tests on the first try. Table 1 shows the required and elective exams for the Windows 2000 MCSE certification.

➤ *MCSD (Microsoft Certified Solution Developer)*—The MCSD credential reflects the skills required to create multitier, distributed, and COM-based solutions, in addition to desktop and Internet applications, using new technologies. To obtain an MCSD, an individual must demonstrate the ability to analyze and interpret user requirements; select and integrate products, platforms, tools, and technologies; design and implement code, and customize applications; and perform necessary software tests and quality assurance operations.

To become an MCSD, you must pass a total of four exams: three core exams and one elective exam. Each candidate must choose one of these three desktop application exams—"70-016: Designing and Implementing Desktop Applications with Microsoft Visual C++ 6.0," "70-156: Designing and Implementing

Table 1   MCSE Windows 2000 Requirements

Core

If you have not passed these 3 Windows NT 4 exams	
Exam 70-067	Implementing and Supporting Microsoft Windows NT Server 4.0
Exam 70-068	Implementing and Supporting Microsoft Windows NT Server 4.0 in the Enterprise
Exam 70-073	Microsoft Windows NT Workstation 4.0
then you must take these 4 exams	
Exam 70-210	Installing, Configuring and Administering Microsoft Windows 2000 Professional
Exam 70-215	Installing, Configuring and Administering Microsoft Windows 2000 Server
Exam 70-216	Implementing and Administering a Microsoft Windows 2000 Network Infrastructure
Exam 70-217	Implementing and Administering a Microsoft Windows 2000 Directory Services Infrastructure
If you have already passed exams 70-067, 70-068, and 70-073, you may take this exam	
Exam 70-240	Microsoft Windows 2000 Accelerated Exam for MCPs Certified on Microsoft Windows NT 4.0

5th Core Option

Choose 1 from this group	
Exam 70-219*	Designing a Microsoft Windows 2000 Directory Services Infrastructure
Exam 70-220*	Designing Security for a Microsoft Windows 2000 Network
Exam 70-221*	Designing a Microsoft Windows 2000 Network Infrastructure

Elective

Choose 2 from this group	
Exam 70-019	Designing and Implementing Data Warehouse with Microsoft SQL Server 7.0
Exam 70-219*	Designing a Microsoft Windows 2000 Directory Services Infrastructure
Exam 70-220*	Designing Security for a Microsoft Windows 2000 Network
Exam 70-221*	Designing a Microsoft Windows 2000 Network Infrastructure
Exam 70-222	Migrating from Microsoft Windows NT 4.0 to Microsoft Windows 2000
Exam 70-028	Administering Microsoft SQL Server 7.0
Exam 70-029	Designing and Implementing Databases on Microsoft SQL Server 7.0
Exam 70-080	Implementing and Supporting Microsoft Internet Explorer 5.0 by Using the Internet Explorer Administration Kit
Exam 70-081	Implementing and Supporting Microsoft Exchange Server 5.5
Exam 70-085	Implementing and Supporting Microsoft SNA Server 4.0
Exam 70-086	Implementing and Supporting Microsoft Systems Management Server 2.0
Exam 70-088	Implementing and Supporting Microsoft Proxy Server 2.0

This is not a complete listing—you can still be tested on some earlier versions of these products. However, we have included mainly the most recent versions so that you may test on these versions and thus be certified longer. We have not included any tests that are scheduled to be retired.

* The 5th Core Option exam does not double as an elective.

Desktop Applications with Microsoft Visual FoxPro 6.0," or "70-176: Designing and Implementing Desktop Applications with Microsoft Visual Basic 6.0"—*plus* one of these three distributed application exams—"70-015: Designing and Implementing Distributed Applications with Microsoft Visual C++ 6.0," "70-155: Designing and Implementing Distributed Applications with Microsoft Visual FoxPro 6.0," or "70-175: Designing and Implementing Distributed Applications with Microsoft Visual Basic 6.0." The third core exam is "70-100: Analyzing Requirements and Defining Solution Architectures." Elective exams cover specific Microsoft applications and languages, including Visual Basic, C++, the Microsoft Foundation Classes, Access, SQL Server, Excel, and more.

➤ *MCDBA (Microsoft Certified Database Administrator)*—The MCDBA credential reflects the skills required to implement and administer Microsoft SQL Server databases. To obtain an MCDBA, an individual must demonstrate the ability to derive physical database designs, develop logical data models, create physical databases, create data services by using Transact-SQL, manage and maintain databases, configure and manage security, monitor and optimize databases, and install and configure Microsoft SQL Server.

To become an MCDBA, you must pass a total of three core exams and one elective exam. The required core exams are "70-028: Administering Microsoft SQL Server 7.0," "70-029: Designing and Implementing Databases with Microsoft SQL Server 7.0," and "70-215: Installing, Configuring and Administering Microsoft Windows 2000 Server."

The elective exams that you can choose from cover specific uses of SQL Server and include "70-015: Designing and Implementing Distributed Applications with Microsoft Visual C++ 6.0," "70-019: Designing and Implementing Data Warehouses with Microsoft SQL Server 7.0," "70-155: Designing and Implementing Distributed Applications with Microsoft Visual FoxPro 6.0," "70-175: Designing and Implementing Distributed Applications with Microsoft Visual Basic 6.0," and two exams that relate to Windows 2000: "70-216: Implementing and Administering a Microsoft Windows 2000 Network Infrastructure," and "70-087: Implementing and Supporting Microsoft Internet Information Server 4.0."

If you have taken the three core Windows NT 4 exams on your path to becoming an MCSE, you qualify for the Accelerated exam (it replaces the Network Infrastructure exam requirement). The Accelerated exam covers the objectives of all four of the Windows 2000 core exams. In addition to taking the Accelerated exam, you must take only the two SQL exams—Administering and Database Design.

> ➤ *MCT (Microsoft Certified Trainer)*—Microsoft Certified Trainers are deemed able to deliver elements of the official Microsoft curriculum, based on technical knowledge and instructional ability. Thus, it is necessary for an individual seeking MCT credentials (which are granted on a course-by-course basis) to pass the related certification exam for a course and complete the official Microsoft training in the subject area, and to demonstrate an ability to teach.
>
> This teaching skill criterion may be satisfied by proving that one has already attained training certification from Novell, Banyan, Lotus, the Santa Cruz Operation, or Cisco, or by taking a Microsoft-sanctioned workshop on instruction. Microsoft makes it clear that MCTs are important cogs in the Microsoft training channels. Instructors must be MCTs before Microsoft will allow them to teach in any of its official training channels, including Microsoft's affiliated Certified Technical Education Centers (CTECs) and its online training partner network. As of January 1, 2001, MCT candidates must also possess a current MCSE.

Microsoft has announced that the MCP+I and MCSE+I credentials will not be continued when the MCSE exams for Windows 2000 are in full swing because the skill set for the Internet portion of the program has been included in the new MCSE program. Therefore, details on these tracks are not provided here; go to **www.microsoft.com/trainingandservices/** if you need more information.

Once a Microsoft product becomes obsolete, MCPs typically have to recertify on current versions. (If individuals do not recertify, their certifications become invalid.) Because technology keeps changing and new products continually supplant old ones, this should come as no surprise. This explains why Microsoft has announced that MCSEs have 12 months past the scheduled retirement date for the Windows NT 4 exams to recertify on Windows 2000 topics. (Note that this means taking at least two exams, if not more.)

The best place to keep up with the MCP Program and its related certifications is on the Web. The URL for the MCP program is **www.microsoft.com/trainingandservices/**. But Microsoft's Web site changes often, so if this URL doesn't work, try using the Search tool on Microsoft's site with either "MCP" or the quoted phrase "Microsoft Certified Professional" as a search string. This will help you find the latest and most accurate information about Microsoft's certification programs.

Taking a Certification Exam

Once you've prepared for your exam, you need to register with a testing center. Each computer-based MCP exam costs $100, and if you don't pass, you may retest for an additional $100 for each additional try. In the United States and Canada, tests are administered by Prometric and by Virtual University Enterprises (VUE). Here's how you can contact them:

➤ *Prometric*—You can sign up for a test through the company's Web site at **www.prometric.com**. Or, you can register by phone at 800-755-3926 (within the United States or Canada) or at 410-843-8000 (outside the United States and Canada).

➤ *Virtual University Enterprises*—You can sign up for a test or get the phone numbers for local testing centers through the Web page at **www.vue.com/ms/**.

To sign up for a test, you must possess a valid credit card, or contact either company for mailing instructions to send them a check (in the U.S.). Only when payment is verified, or a check has cleared, can you actually register for a test.

To schedule an exam, call the number or visit either of the Web pages at least one day in advance. To cancel or reschedule an exam, you must call before 7 P.M. pacific standard time the day before the scheduled test time (or you may be charged, even if you don't appear to take the test). When you want to schedule a test, have the following information ready:

➤ Your name, organization, and mailing address.

➤ Your Microsoft Test ID. (Inside the United States, this means your Social Security number; citizens of other nations should call ahead to find out what type of identification number is required to register for a test.)

➤ The name and number of the exam you wish to take.

➤ A method of payment. (As I've already mentioned, a credit card is the most convenient method, but alternate means can be arranged in advance, if necessary.)

Once you sign up for a test, you'll be informed as to when and where the test is scheduled. Try to arrive at least 15 minutes early. You must supply two forms of identification—one of which must be a photo ID—to be admitted into the testing room.

All exams are completely closed-book. In fact, you will not be permitted to take anything with you into the testing area, but you will be furnished with a blank sheet of paper and a pen or, in some cases, an erasable plastic sheet and an erasable pen. I suggest that you immediately write down on that sheet of paper all the information you've memorized for the test. In *Exam Cram* books, this information appears on a tear-out sheet inside the front cover of each book. You will have some time to compose yourself, record this information, and take a sample orientation exam before you begin the real thing. I suggest you take the orientation test before taking your first exam, but because they're all more or less identical in layout, behavior, and controls, you probably won't need to do this more than once.

When you complete a Microsoft certification exam, the software will tell you whether you've passed or failed. If you need to retake an exam, you'll have to schedule a new test with Prometric or VUE and pay another $100.

 The first time you fail a test, you can retake the test the next day. However, if you fail a second time, you must wait 14 days before retaking that test. The 14-day waiting period remains in effect for all retakes after the second failure.

Tracking MCP Status

As soon as you pass any Microsoft exam (except Networking Essentials), you'll attain Microsoft Certified Professional (MCP) status. Microsoft also generates transcripts that indicate which exams you have passed. You can view a copy of your transcript at any time by going to the MCP secured site and selecting Transcript Tool. This tool will allow you to print a copy of your current transcript and confirm your certification status.

Once you pass the necessary set of exams, you'll be certified. Official certification normally takes anywhere from six to eight weeks, so don't expect to get your credentials overnight. When the package for a qualified certification arrives, it includes a Welcome Kit that contains a number of elements (see Microsoft's Web site for other benefits of specific certifications):

➤ A certificate suitable for framing, along with a wallet card and lapel pin.

➤ A license to use the MCP logo, thereby allowing you to use the logo in advertisements, promotions, and documents, and on letterhead, business cards, and so on. Along with the license comes an MCP logo sheet, which includes camera-ready artwork. (Note: Before using any of the artwork, individuals must sign and return a licensing agreement that indicates they'll abide by its terms and conditions.)

➤ A subscription to *Microsoft Certified Professional Magazine*, which provides ongoing data about testing and certification activities, requirements, and changes to the program.

Many people believe that the benefits of MCP certification go well beyond the perks that Microsoft provides to newly anointed members of this elite group. I'm starting to see more job listings that request or require applicants to have an MCP, MCSE, and so on, and many individuals who complete the program can qualify for increases in pay and/or responsibility. As an official recognition of hard work and broad knowledge, one of the MCP credentials is a badge of honor in many IT organizations.

How to Prepare for an Exam

Preparing for any Windows 2000 Server-related test (including "Designing Security for a Microsoft Windows 2000 Network") requires that you obtain and study materials designed to provide comprehensive information about the product and its capabilities that will appear on the specific exam for which you are preparing. The following list of materials will help you study and prepare:

➤ The Windows 2000 Server product CD includes comprehensive online documentation and related materials; it should be a primary resource when you are preparing for the test.

➤ The exam preparation materials, practice tests, and self-assessment exams on the Microsoft Training & Services page at **www.microsoft.com/trainingandservices/ default.asp?PageID=mcp**. The Testing Innovations link offers samples of the new question types found on the Windows 2000 MCSE exams. Find the materials, download them, and use them!

➤ The exam preparation advice, practice tests, questions of the day, and discussion groups on the **ExamCram.com** e-learning and certification destination Web site (**www.examcram.com**).

In addition, you'll probably find any or all of the following materials useful in your quest for Security Design expertise:

➤ *Microsoft training kits*—Microsoft Press offers training kits that target specific exams. For more information, visit: **http://mspress.microsoft.com/findabook/ list/series_ak.htm**. This training kit contains information that you will find useful in preparing for the test.

➤ *Microsoft TechNet CD*—This monthly CD-based publication delivers numerous electronic titles that include coverage of Security Design and related topics on the Technical Information (TechNet) CD. Its offerings include product facts, technical notes, tools and utilities, and information on how to access the Seminars Online training materials for Security Design. A subscription to TechNet costs $299 per year, but it is well worth the price. Visit **www.microsoft.com/ technet/** and check out the information under the "TechNet Subscription" menu entry for more details.

➤ *Study guides*—Several publishers—including The Coriolis Group—offer Windows 2000 titles. The Coriolis Group series includes the following:

  ➤ *The Exam Cram series*—These books give you information about the material you need to know to pass the tests.

➤ *The Exam Prep series*—These books provide a greater level of detail than the *Exam Cram* books and are designed to teach you everything you need to know from an exam perspective. Each book comes with a CD that contains interactive practice exams in a variety of testing formats.

Together, the two series make a perfect pair.

➤ *Multimedia*—These Coriolis Group materials are designed to support learners of all types—whether you learn best by reading or doing:

➤ *The Exam Cram Personal Trainer*—Offers a unique, personalized self-paced training course based on the exam.

➤ *The Exam Cram Personal Test Center*—Features multiple test options that simulate the actual exam, including Fixed-Length, Random, Review, and Test All. Explanations of correct and incorrect answers reinforce concepts learned.

➤ *Classroom training*—CTECs, online partners, and third-party training companies (like Wave Technologies, Learning Tree, Data-Tech, and others) all offer classroom training on Windows 2000. These companies aim to help you prepare to pass Exam 70-220. Although such training runs upwards of $350 per day in class, most of the individuals lucky enough to partake find it to be quite worthwhile.

➤ *Other publications*—There's no shortage of materials available about Security Design. The resource sections at the end of each chapter should give you an idea of where I think you should look for further discussion.

By far, this set of required and recommended materials represents a nonpareil collection of sources and resources for Security Design and related topics. I anticipate that you'll find that this book belongs in this company

About this Book

Each topical *Exam Cram* chapter follows a regular structure, along with graphical cues about important or useful information. Here's the structure of a typical chapter:

➤ *Opening hotlists*—Each chapter begins with a list of the terms, tools, and techniques that you must learn and understand before you can be fully conversant with that chapter's subject matter. I follow the hotlists with one or two introductory paragraphs to set the stage for the rest of the chapter.

➤ *Topical coverage*—After the opening hotlists, each chapter covers a series of topics related to the chapter's subject title. Throughout this section, I highlight topics or concepts likely to appear on a test using a special Exam Alert layout, like this:

 This is what an Exam Alert looks like. Normally, an Exam Alert stresses concepts, terms, software, or activities that are likely to relate to one or more certification test questions. For that reason, I think any information found offset in Exam Alert format is worthy of unusual attentiveness on your part. Indeed, most of the information that appears on The Cram Sheet appears as Exam Alerts within the text.

Pay close attention to material flagged as an Exam Alert; although all the information in this book pertains to what you need to know to pass the exam, I flag certain items that are really important. You'll find what appears in the meat of each chapter to be worth knowing, too, when preparing for the test. Because this book's material is very condensed, I recommend that you use this book along with other resources to achieve the maximum benefit.

In addition to the Exam Alerts, I have provided tips that will help you build a better foundation for Security Design knowledge. Although the information may not be on the exam, it is certainly related and will help you become a better test-taker.

 This is how tips are formatted. Keep your eyes open for these, and you'll become a Security Design guru in no time!

➤ *Practice questions*—Although I talk about test questions and topics throughout the book, a section at the end of each chapter presents a series of mock test questions and explanations of both correct and incorrect answers.

➤ *Details and resources*—Every chapter ends with a section titled "Need to Know More?". This section provides direct pointers to Microsoft and third-party resources offering more details on the chapter's subject. In addition, this section tries to rank or at least rate the quality and thoroughness of the topic's coverage by each resource. If you find a resource you like in this collection, use it, but don't feel compelled to use all the resources. On the other hand, I recommend only resources I use on a regular basis, so none of my recommendations will be a waste of your time or money (but purchasing them all at once probably represents an expense that many network administrators and would-be MCPs and MCSEs might find hard to justify).

The bulk of the book follows this chapter structure slavishly, but there are a few other elements that I'd like to point out. Chapters 2 through 4 present key concepts used to analyze a case study, such as methodology, vocabulary, and tools. Practice questions at the end of Chapters 2 and 3 target topical discussions with both traditional multiple-choice questions and questions in some of Microsoft's new testing formats (see Chapter 1 for details). At the end of Chapter 4 and subsequent chapters, I use actual case studies to simulate an examination experience.

Chapter 13 includes a case-study–based sample test that provides a good review of the material presented throughout the book to ensure you're ready for the exam. Chapter 14 is an answer key to the sample test that appears in Chapter 13. In addition, you'll find a handy glossary and an index.

Finally, the tear-out Cram Sheet attached next to the inside front cover of this *Exam Cram* book represents a condensed and compiled collection of facts and tips that I think you should memorize before taking the test. Because you can dump this information out of your head onto a piece of paper before taking the exam, you can master this information by brute force—you need to remember it only long enough to write it down when you walk into the test room. You might even want to look at it in the car or in the lobby of the testing center just before you walk in to take the test.

How to Use this Book

I've structured the topics in this book to build on one another. Therefore, some topics in later chapters make more sense after you've read earlier chapters. That's why I suggest you read this book from front to back for your initial test preparation. If you need to brush up on a topic or you have to bone up for a second try, use the index or table of contents to go straight to the topics and questions that you need to study. Beyond helping you prepare for the test, I think you'll find this book useful as a tightly focused reference to some of the most important aspects of Security Design.

Given all the book's elements and its specialized focus, I've tried to create a tool that will help you prepare for—and pass—Microsoft Exam 70-220. Please share your feedback on the book, especially if you have ideas about how it can be improved for future test-takers.

Send your questions or comments to Coriolis at **learn@examcram.com**. Please remember to include the title of the book in your message. Also, be sure to check out the Web pages at **www.examcram.com**, where you'll find information updates, commentary, and certification information.

Thanks, and enjoy the book!

Self-Assessment

The reason I included a Self-Assessment in this *Exam Cram* book is to help you evaluate your readiness to tackle MCSE certification. It should also help you understand what you need to know to master the topic of this book—namely, Exam 70-220, "Designing Security for a Microsoft Windows 2000 Network." But before you tackle this Self-Assessment, let's talk about concerns you may face when pursuing an MCSE for Windows 2000, and what an ideal MCSE candidate might look like.

MCSEs in the Real World

In the next section, I describe an ideal MCSE candidate, knowing full well that only a few real candidates will meet this ideal. In fact, my description of that ideal candidate might seem downright scary, especially with the changes that have been made to the program to support Windows 2000. But take heart: Although the requirements to obtain an MCSE may seem formidable, they are by no means impossible to meet. However, be keenly aware that it does take "seat time," involves some expense, and requires real effort to get through the process.

Increasing numbers of people are attaining Microsoft certifications, so the goal is within reach. You can get all the real-world motivation you need from knowing that many others have gone before, so you will be able to follow in their footsteps. If you're willing to tackle the process seriously and do what it takes to obtain the necessary experience and knowledge, you can take—and pass—all the certification tests involved in obtaining an MCSE. In fact, *Exam Preps*, the companion *Exam Crams*, *Exam Cram Personal Trainers*, and *Exam Cram Personal Test Centers* are designed to make it as easy on you as possible to prepare for these exams. Coriolis has also greatly expanded its Web site, **www.examcram.com**, to provide a host of resources to help you prepare for the complexities of Windows 2000.

Besides MCSE, other Microsoft certifications include:

➤ MCSD, which is aimed at software developers and requires one specific exam, two more exams on client and distributed topics, plus a fourth elective exam drawn from a different, but limited, pool of options.

➤ Other Microsoft certifications, whose requirements range from one test (MCP) to several tests (MCP+SB, MCDBA).

The Ideal Windows 2000 MCSE Candidate

Just to give you some idea of what an ideal MCSE candidate is like, here are some relevant statistics about the background and experience such an individual might have. Don't worry if you don't meet these qualifications, or don't come that close—this is a far from ideal world, and where you fall short is simply where you'll have more work to do.

➤ Academic or professional training in network theory, concepts, and operations. This includes everything from networking media and transmission techniques through network operating systems, services, and applications.

➤ Three-plus years of professional networking experience, including experience with Ethernet, token ring, modems, and other networking media. This must include installation, configuration, upgrade, and troubleshooting experience.

Note: The Windows 2000 MCSE program is much more rigorous than the previous NT MCSE program; therefore, you'll really need some hands-on experience. Some of the exams require you to solve real-world case studies and network design issues, so the more hands-on experience you have, the better.

➤ Two-plus years in a networked environment that includes hands-on experience with Windows 2000 Server, Windows 2000 Professional, Windows NT Server, Windows NT Workstation, and Windows 95 or Windows 98. A solid understanding of each system's architecture, installation, configuration, maintenance, and troubleshooting is also essential.

➤ Knowledge of the various methods for installing Windows 2000, including manual and unattended installations.

➤ A thorough understanding of key networking protocols, addressing, and name resolution, including TCP/IP, IPX/SPX, and NetBEUI.

➤ A thorough understanding of NetBIOS naming, browsing, and file and print services.

➤ Familiarity with key Windows 2000-based TCP/IP-based services, including HTTP (Web servers), DHCP, WINS, DNS, plus familiarity with one or more of the following: Internet Information Server (IIS), Index Server, and Proxy Server.

➤ An understanding of how to implement security for key network data in a Windows 2000 environment.

➤ Working knowledge of NetWare 4.x and 5.x, including IPX/SPX frame formats, NetWare file, print, and directory services, and both Novell and Microsoft client software. Working knowledge of Microsoft's Client Service For NetWare (CSNW), Gateway Service For NetWare (GSNW), the NetWare Migration Tool (NWCONV), and the NetWare Client For Windows (NT, 95, and 98) is essential.

➤ A good working understanding of Active Directory. The more you work with Windows 2000, the more you'll realize that this new operating system is quite different than Windows NT. New technologies like Active Directory have really changed the way that Windows is configured and used. I recommend that you find out as much as you can about Active Directory and acquire as much experience using this technology as possible. The time you take learning about Active Directory will be time very well spent!

Fundamentally, this boils down to a bachelor's degree in computer science, plus three years' experience working in a position involving network design, installation, configuration, and maintenance. I believe that well under half of all certification candidates meet these requirements, and that, in fact, most meet less than half of these requirements—at least, when they begin the certification process. But because all the people who already have been certified have survived this ordeal, you can survive it too—especially if you heed what our Self-Assessment can tell you about what you already know and what you need to learn.

Put Yourself to the Test

The following series of questions and observations is designed to help you figure out how much work you must do to pursue Microsoft certification and what kinds of resources you may consult on your quest. Be absolutely honest in your answers, or you'll end up wasting money on exams you're not yet ready to take. There are no right or wrong answers, only steps along the path to certification. Only you can decide where you really belong in the broad spectrum of aspiring candidates.

Two things should be clear from the outset, however:

➤ Even a modest background in computer science will be helpful.

➤ Hands-on experience with Microsoft products and technologies is an essential ingredient to certification success.

Educational Background

1. Have you ever taken any computer-related classes? [Yes or No]

   If Yes, proceed to question 2; if No, proceed to question 4.

2. Have you taken any classes on computer operating systems? [Yes or No]

   If Yes, you will probably be able to handle Microsoft's architecture and system component discussions. If you're rusty, brush up on basic operating system concepts, especially virtual memory, multitasking regimes, user mode versus kernel mode operation, and general computer security topics.

   If No, consider some basic reading in this area. I strongly recommend a good general operating systems book, such as *Operating System Concepts, 5th Edition*, by Abraham Silberschatz and Peter Baer Galvin (John Wiley & Sons, 1998, ISBN 0-471-36414-2). If this title doesn't appeal to you, check out reviews for other, similar titles at your favorite online bookstore.

3. Have you taken any networking concepts or technologies classes or any classes that deal with security-related topics? [Yes or No]

   If Yes, you will probably be able to handle both Microsoft and generic networking terminology, concepts, and technologies (brace yourself for frequent departures from normal usage). If you're rusty, brush up on basic networking and Internet-related concepts and terminology, especially networking media, transmission types, the OSI Reference Model, and networking technologies such as Ethernet, token ring, FDDI, and WAN links.

   If No, you might want to read one or two books in this topic area. If you haven't purchased it already, the *MCSE Training Kit, Networking Essentials Plus, 3rd Edition*, by Microsoft Corporation (Microsoft Press, 1999, ISBN 1-57231-902-X) is the official documentation for the self-study course of the same name. Two other books that I know of are *Computer Networks, 3rd Edition*, by Andrew S. Tanenbaum (Prentice-Hall, 1996, ISBN 0-13-349945-6) and *Computer Networks and Internets, 2nd Edition*, by Douglas E. Comer (Prentice-Hall, 1998, ISBN 0-130-83617-6).

   For those of you specifically interested in security issues and Internet-related topics, consider *Practical Unix & Internet Security, 2nd Edition*, by Simson Garfinkel and Genee Spafford (O'Reilly, 1996, ISBN 1-56592-148-8) and *Network Security Essentials*, by William Stallings (Prentice-Hall, 1996, ISBN 0-13-016093-8). Although security is discussed in the context of the Unix environment, both books provide a comprehensive treatment of topics I encounter every day dealing with Microsoft operating systems. Differences in cultural viewpoint between the two network operating systems (Unix as opposed to Microsoft) when describing the same problems the IT professional faces daily is often insightful.

   Skip to the next section, "Hands-on Experience."

4. Have you done any reading on operating systems or networks? [Yes or No]

   If Yes, review the requirements stated in the first paragraphs after questions 2 and 3. If you meet those requirements, move on to the next section. If No, consult the recommended reading for both topics. A strong background will help you prepare for the Microsoft exams better than just about anything else.

Hands-on Experience

The most important key to success on all of the Microsoft tests is hands-on experience, especially with Windows 2000 Server and Professional, plus the many add-on services and BackOffice components around which so many of the Microsoft certification exams revolve. If I leave you with only one realization after taking this Self-Assessment, it should be that there's no substitute for time spent installing, configuring, and using the various Microsoft products upon which you'll be tested repeatedly and in depth.

5. Have you installed, configured, and worked with:

   ➤ Windows 2000 Server? [Yes or No]

   If Yes, make sure you understand basic concepts as covered in Exam 70-215. You should also study the TCP/IP interfaces, utilities, and services for Exam 70-216, plus implementing security features for Exam 70-220.

 You can download objectives, practice exams, and other data about Microsoft exams from the Training and Certification page at **www.microsoft.com/ trainingandservices/default.asp?PageID= mcp/**. Use the "Exams" link to obtain specific exam information.

If you haven't worked with Windows 2000 Server, you must obtain one or two machines and a copy of Windows 2000 Server. Then, learn the operating system and whatever other software components on which you'll also be tested.

In fact, I recommend that you obtain at least three computers (two servers and one workstation), each with a network interface, and set up a three-node network on which to practice. With generic Windows 2000-capable computers selling for about $500 to $600 apiece these days, this personal investment is small compared to the potential financial rewards and career satisfaction Microsoft certification can bring you in future years. To reduce your total cost of ownership (TCO), also consider a KVM (keyboard, video, mouse) device to consolidate your machine connections to a reliable monitor and keyboard. You should also consider yet another inexpensive "spare" machine with the fastest possible Internet access speed. I personally consider 24/7 Internet connectivity to be an essential part of my work environment and my "computer lab" when I am preparing to take an exam or when I am teaching a class. No matter what the state of my "lab" machines, I can always use the "spare" machine to reference online technical material, download software, or email a friend for help.

You may have to scrounge to come up with the necessary software, but if you scour the Microsoft Web site and ftp site (**ftp://ftp.microsoft.com/ bussys/winnt/winnt-public/reskit/**) you can usually find low-cost options to obtain evaluation copies of most of the software that you'll need. A more expensive but excellent investment is a professional subscription to the Microsoft Developer Network (**http://msdn.microsoft.com**), which provides software subscription programs, technical information, Web sites, and other material, including evaluation copies of the latest server products. You do not have to be a certified IT professional to subscribe to this subscription service.

➤ Windows 2000 Professional? [Yes or No]

If Yes, make sure you understand the concepts covered in Exam 70-210.

If No, you will want to obtain a copy of Windows 2000 Professional and learn how to install, configure, and maintain it. You can use *MCSE Windows 2000 Professional Exam Cram* to guide your activities and studies, or work straight from Microsoft's test objectives if you prefer.

For any and all of these Microsoft exams, the Resource Kits for the topics involved are a good study resource. You can purchase softcover Resource Kits from Microsoft Press (search for them at **http:// mspress.microsoft.com/**), but they also appear on the TechNet CDs (**www.microsoft.com/technet**). Along with *Exam Crams* and *Exam Preps*, I believe that Resource Kits are among the best tools you can use to prepare for Microsoft exams.

6. For any specific Microsoft product that is not itself an operating system (for example, SQL Server), have you installed, configured, used, and upgraded this software? [Yes or No]

If the answer is Yes, skip to the next section. If it's No, you must get some experience. Read on for suggestions on how to do this.

Experience is a must with any Microsoft product exam, be it something as simple as FrontPage 2000 or as challenging as SQL Server 7.0. For trial copies of other software, search Microsoft's Web site using the name of the product as your search term. Also, search for bundles like "BackOffice" or "Small Business Server."

 If you have the funds, or your employer will pay your way, consider taking a class at a Certified Training and Education Center (CTEC) or at an Authorized Academic Training Partner (AATP). Not all certified training facilities are the same; you should evaluate each candidate facility careful based on the kind of classroom equipment, the size of the classes, the frequency and reliability of class offerings, the experience of the certified instructors, and, most important, available lab time. In addition to classroom exposure to the topic of your choice, you get a copy of the software that is the focus of your course, along with a trial version of whatever operating system it needs, with the training materials for that class.

Before you even think about taking any Microsoft exam, make sure you've spent enough time with the related software to understand how it may be installed and configured, how to maintain such an installation, and how to troubleshoot that software when things go wrong. This will help you in the exam, and in real life!

Testing Your Exam-Readiness

Whether you attend a formal class on a specific topic to get ready for an exam or use written materials to study on your own, some preparation for the Microsoft certification exams is essential. At $100 a try, pass or fail, you want to do everything you can to pass on your first try. That's where studying comes in.

I have included a practice exam in this book, so if you don't score that well on the test, you can study more and then tackle the test again. There are also exams that you can take online through the **ExamCram.com** Web site at **www.examcram.com**. If you still don't hit a score of at least 70 percent after these tests, you'll want to investigate the other practice test resources I mention in this section.

For any given subject, consider taking a class if you've tackled self-study materials, taken the test, and failed anyway. The opportunity to interact with an instructor and fellow students can make all the difference in the world, if you can afford that privilege. For information about Microsoft classes, visit the Training and Certification page at **www.microsoft.com/education/partners/ctec.asp** for Microsoft Certified Education Centers or **www.microsoft.com/aatp/default.htm** for Microsoft Authorized Training Providers.

If you can't afford to take a class, visit the Training and Certification page anyway, because it also includes pointers to free practice exams and to Microsoft Certified Professional Approved Study Guides and other self-study tools. And even if you can't afford to spend much at all, you should still invest in some low-cost practice exams from commercial vendors.

7. Have you taken a practice exam on your chosen test subject? [Yes or No]

If Yes, and you scored 70 percent or better, you're probably ready to tackle the real thing. If your score isn't above that threshold, keep at it until you break that barrier.

If No, obtain all the free and low-budget practice tests you can find and get to work. Keep at it until you can break the passing threshold comfortably.

 When it comes to assessing your test readiness, there is no better way than to take a good-quality practice exam and pass with a score of 70 percent or better. When I'm preparing myself, I shoot for 80-plus percent, just to leave room for the unexpected questions that sometimes show up on Microsoft exams. We all know about Murphy's Law: What can go wrong invariably will. Based on my real-world experiences, I suggest you also remember O'Brian's Law: Murphy was an optimist!

Assessing Readiness for Exam 70-220

In addition to the general exam-readiness information in the previous section, there are several things you can do to prepare for the Designing Security for a Microsoft Windows 2000 Network exam. As you're getting ready for Exam 70-220, visit the Exam Cram Windows 2000 Resource Center at **www.examcram.com/ studyresource/w2kresource/**. Another valuable resource is the Exam Cram Insider newsletter. Sign up at **www.examcram.com** or send a blank email message to **subscribe-ec@mars.coriolis.com**. I also suggest that you join an active MCSE mailing list. One of the better ones is managed by Sunbelt Software. Sign up at **www.sunbelt-software.com** (look for the Subscribe button).

You can also cruise the Web looking for "braindumps" (recollections of test topics and experiences recorded by others) to help you anticipate topics you're likely to encounter on the test. The MCSE mailing list is a good place to ask where the useful braindumps are, or you can check Shawn Gamble's list at **www.commandcentral.com**.

 You can't be sure that a braindump's author can provide correct answers. Thus, use the questions to guide your studies, but don't rely on the answers in a braindump to lead you to the truth. Double-check everything you find in any braindump.

Microsoft exam mavens also recommend checking the Microsoft Knowledge Base (available on its own CD as part of the TechNet collection, or on the Microsoft Web site at **http://support.microsoft.com/support/**) for "meaningful technical support issues" that relate to your exam's topics. Although I'm not sure exactly what the quoted phrase means, I have also noticed some overlap between technical support questions on particular products and troubleshooting questions on the exams for those products.

Onward, through the Fog!

Once you've assessed your readiness, undertaken the right background studies, obtained the hands-on experience that will help you understand the products and technologies at work, and reviewed the many sources of information to help you prepare for a test, you'll be ready to take a round of practice tests. When your scores come back positive enough to get you through the exam, you're ready to go after the real thing. If you follow our assessment regime, you'll not only know what you need to study, but when you're ready to make a test date at Prometric or VUE.

By the way, there is no shame in failing an exam; it is a rite of passage for all of us. But your diligence in following the recommendations set out here and in using the material in this book should all but eliminate that possibility. I wish you good luck and remind you to enjoy the excitement of living the adventure!

Microsoft
Certification Exams

Terms you'll need to understand:

✓ Case study
✓ Multiple-choice question formats
✓ Build-list-and-reorder question format
✓ Create-a-tree question format
✓ Drag-and-connect question format
✓ Select-and-place question format
✓ Fixed-length tests
✓ Simulations
✓ Adaptive tests
✓ Short-form tests

Techniques you'll need to master:

✓ Assessing your exam-readiness
✓ Answering Microsoft's varying question types
✓ Altering your test strategy depending on the exam format
✓ Practicing (to make perfect)
✓ Making the best use of the testing software
✓ Budgeting your time
✓ Guessing (as a last resort)

Exam taking is not something that most people anticipate eagerly, no matter how well prepared they may be. In most cases, familiarity helps offset test anxiety. In plain English, this means you probably won't be as nervous when you take your fourth or fifth Microsoft certification exam as you'll be when you take your first one.

Whether it's your first exam or your tenth, understanding the details of taking the new exams (how much time to spend on questions, the environment you'll be in, and so on) and the new exam software will help you concentrate on the material rather than on the setting. Likewise, mastering a few basic exam-taking skills should help you recognize—and perhaps even outfox—some of the tricks and snares you're bound to find in some exam questions.

This chapter, besides explaining the exam environment and software, describes some proven exam-taking strategies that you should be able to use to your advantage.

Assessing Exam-Readiness

I strongly recommend that you read through and take the Self-Assessment included with this book (it appears just before this chapter, in fact). This will help you compare your knowledge base to the requirements for obtaining an MCSE, and it will also help you identify parts of your background or experience that may be in need of improvement, enhancement, or further learning. If you get the right set of basics under your belt, obtaining Microsoft certification will be that much easier.

Once you've gone through the Self-Assessment, you can remedy those topical areas where your background or experience may not measure up to an ideal certification candidate. But you can also tackle subject matter for individual tests at the same time, so you can continue making progress while you're catching up in some areas.

Once you have worked through an *Exam Cram*, read the supplementary materials, and taken the practice test, you'll have a pretty clear idea of when you should be ready to take the real exam. Although I strongly recommend that you keep practicing until your scores top the 75 percent mark, 80 percent would be a good goal to give yourself some margin for error in a real exam situation (where stress will play more of a role than when you practice). Once you hit that point, you should be ready to go. But if you get through the practice exam in this book without attaining that score, you should keep taking practice tests and studying the materials until you get there. You'll find more pointers on how to study and prepare in the Self-Assessment. But now, on to the exam itself!

The Exam Situation

When you arrive at the testing center where you scheduled your exam, you'll need to sign in with an exam coordinator. He or she will ask you to show two forms of identification, one of which must be a photo ID. After you've signed in and your time slot arrives, you'll be asked to deposit any books, bags, or other items you brought with you. Then, you'll be escorted into a closed room.

All exams are completely closed book. In fact, you will not be permitted to take anything with you into the testing area, but you will be furnished with a blank sheet of paper and a pen or, in some cases, an erasable plastic sheet and an erasable pen. Before the exam, you should memorize as much of the important material as you can, so you can write that information on the blank sheet as soon as you are seated in front of the computer. You can refer to this piece of paper anytime you like during the test, but you'll have to surrender the sheet when you leave the room.

You will have some time to compose yourself, to record this information, and to take a sample orientation exam before you begin the real thing. I suggest you take the orientation test before taking your first exam, but because they're all more or less identical in layout, behavior, and controls, you probably won't need to do this more than once.

Typically, the room will be furnished with anywhere from one to half a dozen computers, and each workstation will be separated from the others by dividers designed to keep you from seeing what's happening on someone else's computer. Most test rooms feature a wall with a large picture window. This permits the exam coordinator to monitor the room, to prevent exam-takers from talking to one another, and to observe anything out of the ordinary that might go on. The exam coordinator will have preloaded the appropriate Microsoft certification exam—for this book, that's Exam 70-220—and you'll be permitted to start as soon as you're seated in front of the computer.

All Microsoft certification exams allow a certain maximum amount of time in which to complete your work (this time is indicated on the exam by an on-screen counter/clock, so you can check the time remaining whenever you like). All Microsoft certification exams are computer generated. In addition to multiple choice, you'll encounter select and place (drag and drop), create a tree (categorization and prioritization), drag and connect, and build list and reorder (list prioritization) on most exams. Although this may sound quite simple, the questions are constructed not only to check your mastery of basic facts and figures about Security Design, but also to require you to evaluate one or more sets of circumstances or requirements. Often, you'll be asked to give more than one answer to a question. Likewise, you might be asked to select the best or most effective solution to a problem from a range of choices, all of which technically are correct. Taking the exam is quite an adventure, and it involves real thinking. This book shows you what to expect and how to deal with the potential problems, puzzles, and predicaments.

In the next section, you'll learn more about how Microsoft test questions look and how they must be answered.

Exam Layout and Design: New Case Study Format

The format of Microsoft's Windows 2000 exams is different from that of its previous exams. For the design exams (70-219, 70-220, 70-221), each exam consists entirely of a series of case studies, and the questions can be of six types. For the Core Four exams (70-210, 70-215, 70-216, 70-217), the same six types of questions can appear, but you are not likely to encounter complex multiquestion case studies.

For design exams, each case study or "testlet" presents a detailed problem that you must read and analyze. Figure 1.1 shows an example of what a case study looks like. For each case study, you will be presented with a dialog box with a series of tabs that contain geographical information, network topologies, current network composition and configuration, expansion plans, and specific interviews by key members of an organization. While you're taking the exam, click on the All tab to recast the set of separate items on one scrollable page.

Following each case study is a set of questions related to the case study; these questions can be one of six types (which are discussed next). Careful attention to details provided in the case study is the key to success. Be prepared to toggle frequently between the case study and the questions as you work. Some of the case studies also include diagrams, which are called *exhibits*, that you'll need to examine closely to understand how to answer the questions.

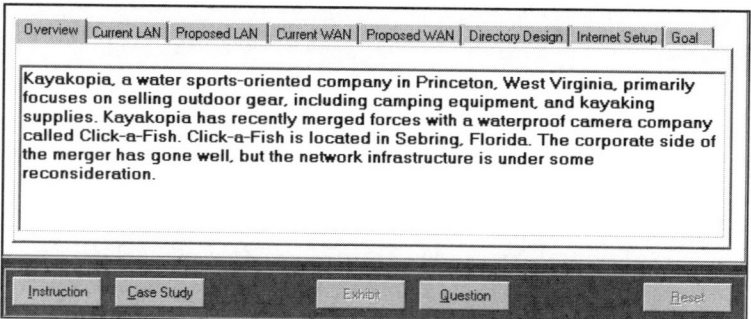

Figure 1.1   This is how case studies appear.

Once you complete a case study, you can review all the questions and your answers. However, once you move on to the next case study, you may not be able to return to the previous case study and make any changes.

 It is possible that two or more case studies or scenarios on a Microsoft exam will use the same or similar names during the same test session. Therefore, this book will also use the same or similar names and details in different case studies. Always read the case study carefully and assume that whatever is stated takes precedence over any statements made in earlier case studies.

The case study format is probably the most natural way to present and analyze security issues because it mirrors a real-world situation. One would typically base a security plan on information gathered in interviews with several key members of an organization. This book approaches the analysis of such case studies in a manner appropriate to both the certification candidate and the IT practitioner. For example, the security analysis discussed in Chapter 8 could easily be delivered to a client in a real-world situation.

The six types of question formats are:

➤ Multiple choice, single answer

➤ Multiple choice, multiple answers

➤ Build list and reorder (list prioritization)

➤ Create a tree

➤ Drag and connect

➤ Select and place (drag and drop)

Note: Exam formats may vary by test center location. Although most design exams consist entirely of a series of case studies or testlets, a test-taker may occasionally encounter a strictly multiple-choice test. You may want to call the test center or visit ExamCram.com to see if you can find out which type of test you'll encounter.

Multiple-Choice Question Format

Some exam questions require you to select a single answer, whereas others ask you to select multiple correct answers. The following multiple-choice question requires you to select a single correct answer. Following the question is a brief summary of each potential answer and why it is either right or wrong.

Question 1

> What factor guarantees message confidentiality?
>
> ○ a. Proper social attitudes in the user community
>
> ○ b. Length of the message
>
> ○ c. Length of the key
>
> ○ d. Authenticity of the sender

Answer c is correct. Length of the key guarantees message confidentiality. Proper social attitudes in the user community, length of the message, and authenticity of the sender do not guarantee confidentiality. Therefore, answers a, b, and d are incorrect.

This sample question format corresponds closely to the Microsoft certification exam format—the only difference on the exam is that questions are not followed by answer keys. To select an answer, you would position the cursor over the radio button next to the answer. Then, click the mouse button to select the answer.

Let's examine a question where one or more answers are possible. This type of question provides checkboxes rather than radio buttons for marking all appropriate selections.

Question 2

> Which of the following are encryption technologies? [Check all correct answers]
>
> ❑ a. Asymmetric key encryption
>
> ❑ b. Symmetric key encryption
>
> ❑ c. Hash function
>
> ❑ d. All of the above

Answers a and b are correct. Asymmetric key encryption and symmetric key encryption are encryption technologies. Hash functions convert a message to some hash value for comparison, not for decryption or reading, so answers c and d are incorrect.

For this particular question, two answers are required. Microsoft sometimes gives partial credit for partially correct answers. For Question 2, you have to check the boxes next to items a and b to obtain credit for a correct answer. Notice that picking the right answers also means knowing why the other answers are wrong!

Build-List-and-Reorder Question Format

Questions in the build-list-and-reorder format present two lists of items—one on the left and one on the right. To answer the question, you must move items from the list on the right to the list on the left. The final list must then be reordered into a specific order.

These questions can best be characterized as "From the following list of choices, pick the choices that answer the question. Arrange the list in a certain order." To give you practice with this type of question, some questions of this type are included in this study guide. Here's an example of how they appear in this book; for a sample of how they appear on the test, see Figure 1.2.

Question 3

From the following list of famous people, pick those that have been elected President of the United States. Arrange the list in the order that they served.

Thomas Jefferson

Ben Franklin

Abe Lincoln

George Washington

Andrew Jackson

Paul Revere

The correct answer is:

George Washington

Thomas Jefferson

Andrew Jackson

Abe Lincoln

On an actual exam, the entire list of famous people would initially appear in the list on the right. You would move the four correct answers to the list on the left, and then reorder the list on the left. Notice that the answer to the question did not include all items from the initial list. However, this may not always be the case.

To move an item from the right list to the left list, first select the item by clicking on it, and then click on the Add button (left arrow). Once you move an item from one list to the other, you can move the item back by first selecting the item and

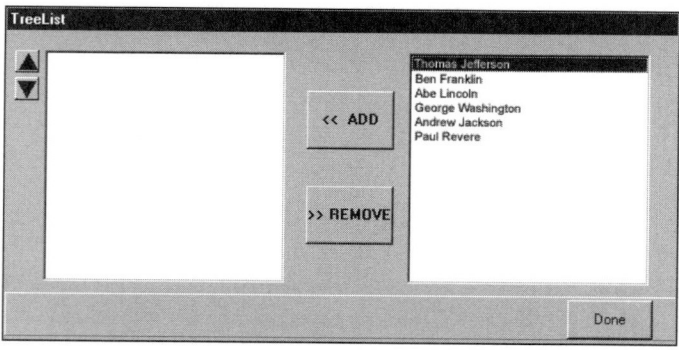

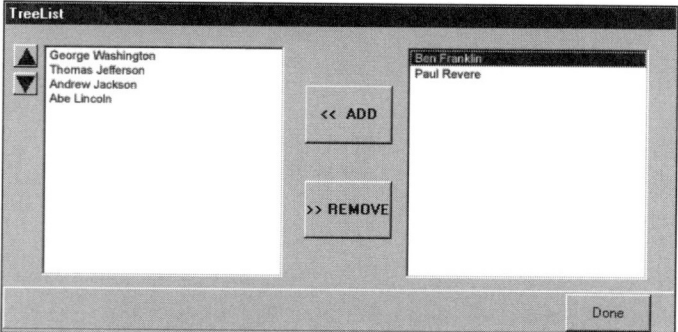

Figure 1.2 This is how build-list-and-reorder questions appear.

then clicking on the appropriate button (either the Add button or the Remove button). Once items have been moved to the left list, you can reorder an item by selecting the item and clicking on the up or down button.

Create-a-Tree Question Format

Questions in the create-a-tree format also present two lists—one on the left side of the screen and one on the right side of the screen. The list on the right consists of individual items, and the list on the left consists of nodes in a tree. To answer the question, you must move items from the list on the right to the appropriate node in the tree.

These questions can best be characterized as simply a matching exercise. Items from the list on the right are placed under the appropriate category in the list on the left. Here's an example of how they appear in this book; for a sample of how they appear on the test, see Figure 1.3.

Question 4

The calendar year is divided into four seasons:

Winter

Spring

Summer

Fall

Identify the season when each of the following holidays occurs:

Christmas

Fourth of July

Labor Day

Flag Day

Memorial Day

Washington's Birthday

Thanksgiving

Easter

The correct answer is:

Winter

Christmas

Washington's Birthday

Spring

Flag Day

Memorial Day

Easter

Summer

Fourth of July

Labor Day

Fall

Thanksgiving

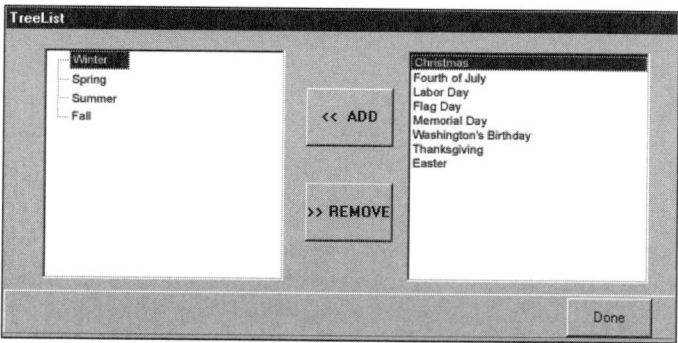

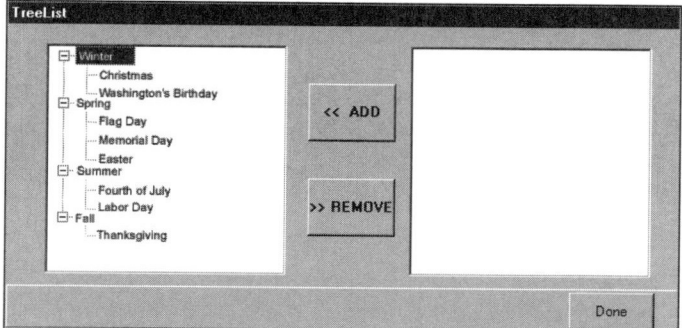

Figure 1.3 This is how create-a-tree questions appear.

In this case, all the items in the list were used. However, this may not always be the case.

To move an item from the right list to its appropriate location in the tree, you must first select the appropriate tree node by clicking on it. Then, you select the item to be moved and click on the Add button. If one or more items have been added to a tree node, the node will be displayed with a "+" icon to the left of the node name. You can click on this icon to expand the node and view the item(s) that have been added. If any item has been added to the wrong tree node, you can remove it by selecting it and clicking on the Remove button.

Drag-and-Connect Question Format

Questions in the drag-and-connect format present a group of objects and a list of "connections." To answer the question, you must move the appropriate connections between the objects.

This type of question is best described using graphics. Here's an example.

Question 5

The following objects represent the different states of water:

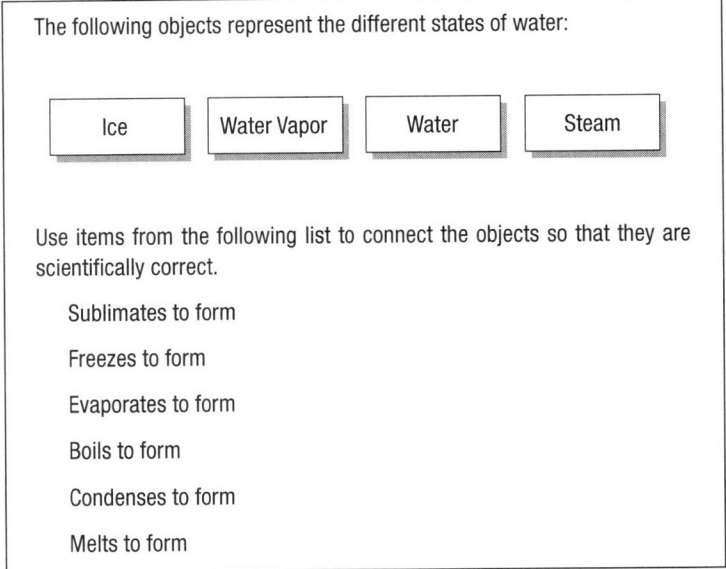

Use items from the following list to connect the objects so that they are scientifically correct.

Sublimates to form

Freezes to form

Evaporates to form

Boils to form

Condenses to form

Melts to form

The correct answer is:

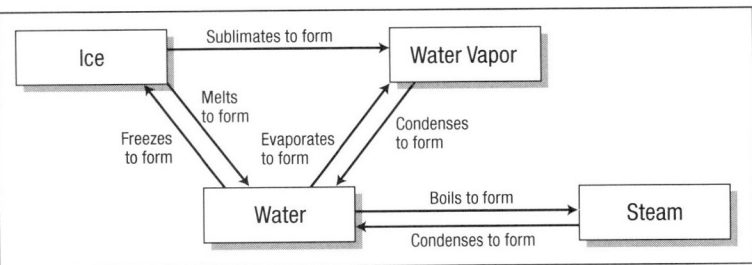

For this type of question, it's not necessary to use every object, and each connection can be used multiple times.

Select-and-Place Question Format

Questions in the select-and-place (drag-and-drop) format present a diagram with blank boxes, and a list of labels that need to be dragged to correctly fill in the blank boxes. To answer the question, you must move the labels to their appropriate positions on the diagram.

This type of question is best described using graphics. Here's an example.

Question 6

Place the items in their proper order, by number, on the following flowchart. Some items may be used more than once, and some items may not be used at all.

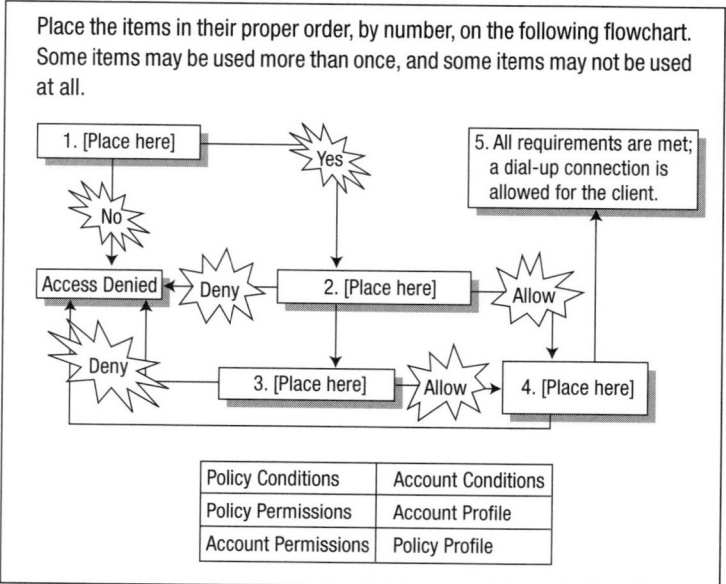

Policy Conditions	Account Conditions
Policy Permissions	Account Profile
Account Permissions	Policy Profile

The correct answer is:

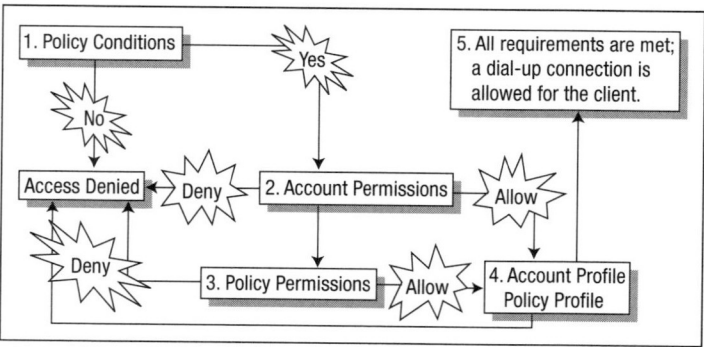

Microsoft's Testing Formats

Currently, Microsoft uses four different testing formats:

➤ Case study

➤ Fixed length

➤ Adaptive

➤ Short form

As I mentioned earlier, the case study approach is used with Microsoft's design exams, such as the one covered by this book. These exams consist of a set of case studies that you must analyze to enable you to answer questions related to the case studies. Such exams include one or more case studies (tabbed topic areas), each of which is followed by 4 to 15 questions. The question types for design exams and for Core Four Windows 2000 exams are multiple choice, build list and reorder, create a tree, drag and connect, and select and place. Depending on the test topic, some exams are totally case-based, whereas others are not.

Other Microsoft exams employ advanced testing capabilities that might not be immediately apparent. Although the questions that appear are primarily multiple choice, the logic that drives them is more complex than older Microsoft tests, which use a fixed sequence of questions, called a *fixed-length test*. Some questions employ a sophisticated user interface, which Microsoft calls a *simulation*, to test your knowledge of the software and systems under consideration in a more or less "live" environment that behaves just like the original. The Testing Innovations link at **www.microsoft.com/trainingandservices/default.asp?PageID=mcp** includes a downloadable practice simulation.

For some exams, Microsoft has turned to a well-known technique, called *adaptive testing*, to establish a test-taker's level of knowledge and product competence. Adaptive exams look the same as fixed-length exams, but they discover the level of difficulty at which an individual test-taker can correctly answer questions. Test-takers with differing levels of knowledge or ability therefore see different sets of questions; individuals with high levels of knowledge or ability are presented with a smaller set of more difficult questions, whereas individuals with lower levels of knowledge are presented with a larger set of easier questions. Two individuals may answer the same percentage of questions correctly, but the test-taker with a higher knowledge or ability level will score higher because his or her questions are worth more.

Also, the lower-level test-taker will probably answer more questions than his or her more-knowledgeable colleague. This explains why adaptive tests use ranges of values to define the number of questions and the amount of time it takes to complete the test.

Adaptive tests work by evaluating the test-taker's most recent answer. A correct answer leads to a more difficult question (and the test software's estimate of the test-taker's knowledge and ability level is raised). An incorrect answer leads to a less difficult question (and the test software's estimate of the test-taker's knowledge and ability level is lowered). This process continues until the test targets the test-taker's true ability level. The exam ends when the test-taker's level of accuracy meets a statistically acceptable value (in other words, when his or her performance demonstrates an acceptable level of knowledge and ability), or when the maximum number of items has been presented (in which case, the test-taker is almost certain to fail).

Microsoft also introduced a short-form test for its most popular tests. This test delivers 25 to 30 questions to its takers, giving them exactly 60 minutes to complete the exam. This type of exam is similar to a fixed-length test, in that it allows readers to jump ahead or return to earlier questions, and to cycle through the questions until the test is done. Microsoft does not use adaptive logic in this test, but claims that statistical analysis of the question pool is such that the 25 to 30 questions delivered during a short-form exam conclusively measure a test-taker's knowledge of the subject matter in much the same way as an adaptive test. You can think of the short-form test as a kind of "greatest hits exam" (that is, the most important questions are covered) version of an adaptive exam on the same topic.

Note: Some of the Microsoft exams can appear as a combination of adaptive and fixed-length questions.

Microsoft tests can come in any one of these forms. Whatever you encounter, you must take the test in whichever form it appears; you can't choose one form over another. If anything, it pays more to prepare thoroughly for an adaptive exam than for a fixed-length or a short-form exam: The penalties for answering incorrectly are built into the test itself on an adaptive exam, whereas the layout remains the same for a fixed-length or short-form test, no matter how many questions you answer incorrectly.

The biggest difference between an adaptive test and a fixed-length or short-form test is that on a fixed-length or short-form test, you can revisit questions after you've read them over one or more times. On an adaptive test, you must answer the question when it's presented and will have no opportunities to revisit that question thereafter.

Strategies for Different Testing Formats

Before you choose a test-taking strategy, you must know if your test is case study based, fixed length, short form, or adaptive. When you begin your exam, you'll know right away if the test is based on case studies. The interface will consist of a tabbed Window that allows you to easily navigate through the sections of the case.

If you are taking a test that is not based on case studies, the software will tell you that the test is adaptive, if in fact the version you're taking is an adaptive test. If your introductory materials fail to mention this, you're probably taking a fixed-length test (50 to 70 questions). If the total number of questions involved is 25 to 30, you're taking a short-form test. Some tests announce themselves by indicating that they will start with a set of adaptive questions, followed by fixed-length questions.

You'll be able to tell for sure if you are taking an adaptive, fixed-length, or short-form test by the first question. If it includes a checkbox that lets you mark the question for later review, you're taking a fixed-length or short-form test. If the total number of questions is 25 to 30, it's a short-form test; if more than 30, it's a fixed-length test. Adaptive test questions can be visited (and answered) only once, and they include no such checkbox.

The Case Study Exam Strategy

Most test-takers find that the case study type of test used for the design exams (70-219, 70-220, and 70-221) is the most difficult to master. When it comes to studying for a case study test, your best bet is to approach each case study as a standalone test. The biggest challenge you'll encounter is that you'll feel that you won't have enough time to get through all of the cases that are presented.

Each case provides a lot of material that you'll need to read and study before you can effectively answer the questions that follow. The trick to taking a case study exam is to first scan the case study to get the highlights. Make sure you read the overview section of the case so that you understand the context of the problem at hand. Then, quickly move on and scan the questions.

As you are scanning the questions, make mental notes to yourself so that you'll remember which sections of the case study you should focus on. Some case studies may provide a fair amount of extra information that you don't really need to answer the questions. The goal with this scanning approach is to avoid having to study and analyze material that is not completely relevant.

When studying a case, carefully read the tabbed information. It is important to answer each and every question. You will be able to toggle back and forth from case to questions, and from question to question within a case testlet. However, once you leave the case and move on, you may not be able to return to it. You may want to take notes while reading useful information so you can refer to them when you tackle the test questions. It's hard to go wrong with this strategy when taking any kind of Microsoft certification test.

The Fixed-Length and Short-Form Exam Strategy

A well-known principle when taking fixed-length or short-form exams is to first read over the entire exam from start to finish while answering only those questions you feel absolutely sure of. On subsequent passes, you can dive into more complex questions more deeply, knowing how many such questions you have left.

Fortunately, the Microsoft exam software for fixed-length and short-form tests makes the multiple-visit approach easy to implement. At the top-left corner of each question is a checkbox that permits you to mark that question for a later visit.

Note: Marking questions makes review easier, but you can return to any question by clicking the Forward or Back button repeatedly.

As you read each question, if you answer only those you're sure of and mark for review those that you're not sure of, you can keep working through a decreasing list of questions as you answer the trickier ones in order.

There's at least one potential benefit to reading the exam over completely before answering the trickier questions: Sometimes, information supplied in later questions sheds more light on earlier questions. At other times, information you read in later questions might jog your memory about Security Design facts, figures, or behavior that helps you answer earlier questions. Either way, you'll come out ahead if you defer those questions about which you're not absolutely sure.

Here are some question-handling strategies that apply to fixed-length and short-form tests. Use them if you have the chance:

➤ When returning to a question after your initial read-through, read every word again—otherwise, your mind can fall quickly into a rut. Sometimes, revisiting a question after turning your attention elsewhere lets you see something you missed, but the strong tendency is to see what you've seen before. Try to avoid that tendency at all costs.

➤ If you return to a question more than twice, try to articulate to yourself what you don't understand about the question, why answers don't appear to make sense, or what appears to be missing. If you chew on the subject awhile, your subconscious might provide the details you lack, or you might notice a "trick" that points to the right answer.

As you work your way through the exam, another counter that Microsoft provides will come in handy—the number of questions completed and questions outstanding. For fixed-length and short-form tests, it's wise to budget your time by making sure that you've completed one-quarter of the questions one-quarter of the way through the exam period, and three-quarters of the questions three-quarters of the way through.

If you're not finished when only five minutes remain, use that time to guess your way through any remaining questions. Remember, guessing is potentially more valuable than not answering, because blank answers are always wrong, but a guess may turn out to be right. If you don't have a clue about any of the remaining questions, pick answers at random, or choose all a's, b's, and so on. The important thing is to submit an exam for scoring that has an answer for every question.

At the very end of your exam period, you're better off guessing than leaving questions unanswered.

The Adaptive Exam Strategy

If there's one principle that applies to taking an adaptive test, it could be summed up as "Get it right the first time." You cannot elect to skip a question and move on to the next one when taking an adaptive test, because the testing software uses your answer to the current question to select whatever question it plans to present next. Nor can you return to a question once you've moved on, because the software gives you only one chance to answer the question. You can, however, take notes, because sometimes information supplied in earlier questions will shed more light on later questions.

Also, when you answer a question correctly, you are presented with a more difficult question next, to help the software gauge your level of skill and ability. When you answer a question incorrectly, you are presented with a less difficult question, and the software lowers its current estimate of your skill and ability. This continues until the program settles into a reasonably accurate estimate of what you know and can do, and takes you on average through somewhere between 15 and 30 questions as you complete the test.

The good news is that if you know your stuff, you'll probably finish most adaptive tests in 30 minutes or so. The bad news is that you must really, really know your stuff to do your best on an adaptive test. That's because some questions are so convoluted, complex, or hard to follow that you're bound to miss one or two, at a minimum, even if you do know your stuff. So the more you know, the better you'll do on an adaptive test, even accounting for the occasionally weird or unfathomable questions that appear on these exams.

 Because you can't always tell in advance if a test is fixed length, short form, or adaptive, you will be best served by preparing for the exam as if it were adaptive. That way, you should be prepared to pass no matter what kind of test you take. But if you do take a fixed-length or short-form test, remember the tips from the preceding section. They should help you improve on what you could do on an adaptive test.

If you encounter a question on an adaptive test that you can't answer, you must guess an answer immediately. Because of how the software works, you may suffer for your guess on the next question if you guess right, because you'll get a more difficult question next!

Question-Handling Strategies

For those questions that take only a single answer, usually two or three of the answers will be obviously incorrect, and two of the answers will be plausible—of course, only one can be correct. Unless the answer leaps out at you (if it does, reread the question to look for a trick; sometimes those are the ones you're most likely to get wrong), begin the process of answering by eliminating those answers that are most obviously wrong.

Almost always, at least one answer out of the possible choices for a question can be eliminated immediately because it matches one of these conditions:

➤ The answer does not apply to the situation.

➤ The answer describes a nonexistent issue, an invalid option, or an imaginary state.

After you eliminate all answers that are obviously wrong, you can apply your retained knowledge to eliminate further answers. Look for items that sound correct but refer to actions, commands, or features that are not present or not available in the situation that the question describes.

If you're still faced with a blind guess among two or more potentially correct answers, reread the question. Try to picture how each of the possible remaining answers would alter the situation. Be especially sensitive to terminology; sometimes the choice of words ("remove" instead of "disable") can make the difference between a right answer and a wrong one.

Only when you've exhausted your ability to eliminate answers, but remain unclear about which of the remaining possibilities is correct, should you guess at an answer. An unanswered question offers you no points, but guessing gives you at least some chance of getting a question right; just don't be too hasty when making a blind guess.

Note: If you're taking a fixed-length or a short-form test, you can wait until the last round of reviewing marked questions (just as you're about to run out of time, or out of unanswered questions) before you start making guesses. You will have the same option within each case study testlet (but once you leave a testlet, you may not be allowed to return to it). If you're taking an adaptive test, you'll have to guess to move on to the next question if you can't figure out an answer some other way. Either way, guessing should be your technique of last resort!

Numerous questions assume that the default behavior of a particular utility is in effect. If you know the defaults and understand what they mean, this knowledge will help you cut through many Gordian knots.

Mastering the Inner Game

In the final analysis, knowledge breeds confidence, and confidence breeds success. If you study the materials in this book carefully and review all the practice questions at the end of each chapter, you should become aware of those areas where additional learning and study are required.

After you've worked your way through the book, take the practice exam in the back of the book. Taking this test will provide a reality check and help you identify areas to study further. Make sure you follow up and review materials related to the questions you miss on the practice exam before scheduling a real exam. Only when you've covered that ground and feel comfortable with the whole scope of the practice exam should you set an exam appointment. Only if you score 80 percent or better should you proceed to the real thing (otherwise, obtain some additional practice tests so you can keep trying until you hit this magic number).

 If you take a practice exam and don't score at least 80 to 85 percent correct, you'll want to practice further. Microsoft provides links to practice exam providers and also offers self-assessment exams at **www.microsoft.com/trainingandservices/**. You should also check out **ExamCram.com** for downloadable practice questions.

Armed with the information in this book and with the determination to augment your knowledge, you should be able to pass the certification exam. However, you need to work at it, or you'll spend the exam fee more than once before you finally pass. If you prepare seriously, you should do well. I am confident that you can do it!

The next section covers other sources you can use to prepare for the Microsoft certification exams.

Additional Resources

A good source of information about Microsoft certification exams comes from Microsoft itself. Because its products and technologies—and the exams that go with them—change frequently, the best place to go for exam-related information is online.

If you haven't already visited the Microsoft Certified Professional site, do so right now. The MCP home page resides at **www.microsoft.com/trainingandservices** (see Figure 1.4).

Note: This page might not be there by the time you read this, or may be replaced by something new and different, because things change regularly on the Microsoft site. Should this happen, please read the sidebar titled "Coping with Change on the Web."

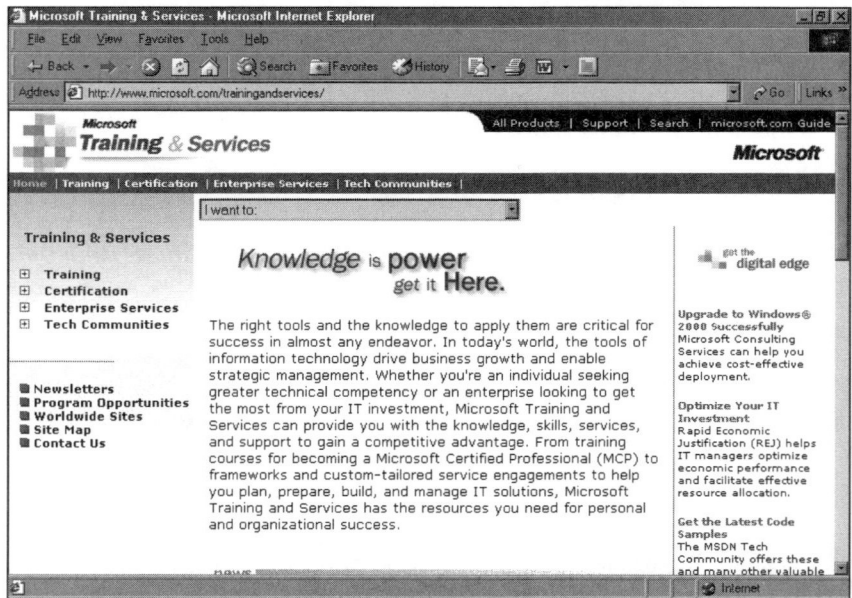

Figure 1.4   The Microsoft Certified Professional home page.

Other key military, government, and private sites you can consult for information about Security Design are as follows:

➤ *ftp://ftp.isi.edu/in-notes/rfcxxx.txt*—To use this URL, replace *xxx* with an RFC number

➤ *ftp://ftp.microsoft.com/*—Microsoft FTP Site for service packs

➤ *http://csrc.ncsl.nist.gov/topics/welcome.html*—National Institute of Standards and Technology Computer Security Resource Clearinghouse

➤ *http://ntbugtraq.ntadvice.com/*—NTBugTraq mailing list home page

➤ *http://web.mit.edu/is/help/mink/#overview*—The MIT Kerberos home page

➤ *www.alw.nih.gov/Security/security.html*—Advanced Laboratory Workstation System Computer Security Information page, CIT/NIH

➤ *www.armadillo.huntsville.al.us/*—The Fortezza Department of Defense home page

➤ *www.austinlinks.com/Crypto/*—Cryptography Archives page

➤ *www.boran.com/security/*—IT Security Cookbook

➤ *www.cerias.purdue.edu/*—Center for Education and Research in Information Assurance and Security page

➤ *www.cert.org/*—The Carnegie Mellon CERT Coordination Center

➤ *www.cryptography.com/resources/index.html*—Cryptographic Resources, Inc.'s Resource Library

➤ *www.cryptography.org/*—Cryptography.org's Crypto Archives page

➤ *www.cs.auckland.ac.nz/~pgut001/links.html*—Encryption and Security Related Resources Crypto-link farm

➤ *www.faqs.org/rfcs*—An Request For Comments search page

➤ *www.hideaway.net/index.html*—Hacker Libraries page

➤ *www.ietf.cnri.reston.va.us/*—The Internet Engineering Task Force home page

➤ *www.ietf.org/html.charters/ipsec-charter.html*—The Internet Engineering Task Force's page on IPSec

➤ *www.infosecnews.com/*—The InfoSecurity News home page

➤ *www.infosyssec.org/infosyssec/index.html*—Security Portal for Information Security Professionals

➤ *www.intelbrief.com/*—Intelligence Briefing; Computer Security page

➤ *www.iso.ch/search.html*—International Organization for Standardization Search Engine

➤ *www.microsoft.com/windows2000/upgrade/compat/default.asp*—Windows 2000 Hardware Compatibility List

➤ *www.nsa.gov/*—National Security Agency home page

➤ *www.nsi.org/*—National Security Institute's Security Resource Net page

➤ *www.pca.dfn.de/dfnpca/pki-links.html*—The PKI Page

➤ *www.pgp.com/*—Pretty Good Privacy home page

➤ *www.radium.ncsc.mil/tpep/library/rainbow/index.html*—Rainbow Series Library, Department of Defense page

➤ *www.sans.org/newlook/resources/glossary.htm*—National Security Agency Glossary page

➤ *www.setco.org/*—Secure Electronic Transaction LLC home page

➤ *www.vpnc.org/*—The VPN Consortium home page

Coping with Change on the Web

Sooner or later, all the information I've shared with you about the Microsoft Certified Professional pages and the other Web-based resources mentioned throughout the rest of this book will go stale or be replaced by newer information. In some cases, the URLs you find here might lead you to their replacements; in other cases, the URLs will go nowhere, leaving you with the dreaded "404 File not found" error message. When that happens, don't give up.

There's always a way to find what you want on the Web if you're willing to invest some time and energy. Most large or complex Web sites—and Microsoft's qualifies on both counts—offer a search engine. On all of Microsoft's Web pages, a Search button appears along the top edge of the page. As long as you can get to Microsoft's site (it should stay at **www.microsoft.com** for a long time), use this tool to help you find what you need.

The more focused you can make a search request, the more likely the results will include information you can use. For example, you can search for the string

```
"training and certification"
```

to produce a lot of data about the subject in general, but if you're looking for the preparation guide for Exam 70-220, "Designing Security for a Microsoft Windows

2000 Network," you'll be more likely to get there quickly if you use a search string similar to the following:

```
"Exam 70-220" AND "preparation guide"
```

Likewise, if you want to find the Training and Certification downloads, try a search string such as this:

```
"training and certification" AND "download page"
```

Finally, feel free to use general search tools—such as **www.search.com**, **www.altavista.com**, and **www.excite.com**—to look for related information. Although Microsoft offers great information about its certification exams online, there are plenty of third-party sources of information and assistance that need not follow Microsoft's party line. Therefore, if you can't find something where the book says it lives, intensify your search.

Security Overview

Terms you'll need to understand:

✓ Total cost of ownership (TCO)

✓ System security plan and audit

✓ Competency Model

✓ Information Technology (IT) security controls

✓ Risk management

✓ Encryption algorithms

✓ Hash function

✓ Message digest

✓ Digital signature

✓ Open Systems Interconnection (OSI) seven-layer model

✓ Department of Defense four-layer model

✓ Microsoft's four-layer model

Techniques you'll need to master:

✓ Identifying the major steps in risk management

✓ Applying the network reference models to security design

✓ Understanding the public/private key exchanges

✓ Identifying security attack modalities

✓ Mapping security protocols to the OSI Reference Model

New ideas are rare; most are repetitions of an old theme with slight twists and variations. When we view new concepts and "cutting-edge" technologies from a historical perspective, these ideas seem more familiar and easier to grasp. Recurring patterns help us immediately recognize common mechanisms. We visualize trends from these patterns and formulate a predictive model that helps us better understand trends and changes in information technology (IT). Many Windows 2000 concepts are actually built upon NT 4 core technologies and procedures. They are not a result of a radical mutation, but instead subtle shifts that lead to new forms of differentiation and specialization.

The Key Questions

You need to leverage your knowledge of NT4 security to develop an understanding of Windows 2000 security features. The procedural steps outlined in the following chapters will form a framework for efficient problem solving and reliable maintenance. Any approach to analyzing Windows 2000 security issues requires a broad, structured methodology because Windows 2000 distributed and network services are broad and relatively unstructured. Windows 2000 works in either a mixed legacy NT 4 domain model or in a native mode with Active Directory (AD) and Microsoft's version of Kerberos protocol. An enhanced Security Support Provider Interface (SSPI) now accommodates many distributed application services by supporting installable third-party security technologies. To efficiently analyze, compare, or design these systems, the security professional needs a flexible reference like the Open Systems Interconnection (OSI) model to add organizational structure to these interconnecting subsystems. Similarly, technical expertise is more easily acquired and maintained if similarities can be drawn quickly to well-known legacy systems. Procedural steps outlined in the following chapters will force you to systematically examine case studies, or real-world situations, to determine how to detect, protect, or correct a security vulnerability. Any security overview should ask the following questions:

➤ Who are the principal parties?

➤ What are the methods of exchange?

➤ What are the security objectives?

➤ What are the areas of risk?

➤ What are the security countermeasures?

This structured methodology will be applicable to both a system security audit (discussed in the "IT Controls and Corporate Objectives" section later in this chapter) or a Microsoft exam case study. It will help us identify, design, and troubleshoot security technologies as they relate to corporate objectives or a set of specific business rules. Furthermore, any methodology that makes it easier to identify sources of security risk in the planning stages of both distributed and network system security will continue to prove a valuable tool in the real world.

Required Technical Background

A major theme in Microsoft literature is the concept of total cost of ownership (TCO). The TCO, estimated at about four times the cost of a single workstation, includes:

➤ Cost of hardware/software

➤ Cost of system upgrades

➤ System maintenance

➤ System training

➤ Technical support

Of these cost components, system maintenance, training, and support vary the most. They are featured prominently in discussions of costs, benefits, and risk reduction. Other benefits less often cited but which are of similar significance and are more functional are streamlining workflow and increased productivity. This book is about achieving technical expertise in Windows 2000 security systems. The proper technical background when applied correctly impacts the most variable of the TCO cost components: productivity and the corporate "bottom line." This book is about achieving that technical expertise in Windows 2000 security systems. Thus, an effective system security plan is the synergy of three complementary factors:

➤ Appropriate security technologies

➤ Technical expertise for properly supporting and maintaining those technologies

➤ Proper social attitude and compliance of the user community

Experts seek out signs to help choose the most efficient direction toward some short-term objective or long-term goal. This book also uses Microsoft's Windows 2000 Competency Model to list those topics the exam candidate or security professional should give the closest scrutiny. The model ranks topics in security policy management, monitoring, planning, and administration in order of importance to specific job levels: IT executive, IT management, and IT workforce. The target audience of this book most likely has or will assume a role in IT management. The assumption in using this specific Competency Model is that if, in Microsoft's view, these topical areas rank high in required knowledge, they could be considered the most relevant areas on Microsoft certification examinations. It is also likely that these areas of expertise will be called upon most often for design, implementation, and support of security systems in the real world.

IT Controls and Corporate Objectives

In general, effective security management ensures confidentiality, integrity, and availability of information. It is both procedural and technical in nature. In fact, an organization's corporate security "culture" can sometimes be the critical factor in making security policy effective; firewall technologies are only as effective as the policy and administration that run them. You must thoroughly understand the fundamental relationships between corporate business objectives and IT security controls *before* you can formulate a system security plan or design a security infrastructure.

IT Security Controls

Corporate business objectives and IT security controls are found in departmental objectives in relation to some cumulative set of business rules or corporate business objectives. To formulate sound and reasonable policies, it is crucial to collect these departmental objectives with surveys. When you read these surveys, you will notice that specific themes define security concerns within a particular level of the organizational structure. The cumulative corporate business objectives determine the final implementation of a security system and how a company actually allocates financial resources.

Examples of IT security controls include:

➤ Availability of services or resources

➤ Optimized use of resources

➤ Compliance

➤ Reliability

➤ Integrity

➤ Confidentiality

These IT security controls can be categorized in more functional terms as preventing, detecting, and correcting breaches in security. For example, digital signatures prevent alteration or fabrication of information exchanged between two computer users on a network. One IT security control relevant here is the integrity of the message's content. If the receiver of the message detects some change in the message's content through comparison of hash values accompanying the message, the correct message can be re-sent. Security attack techniques might intercept and modify, or impersonate and fabricate, a message. Examples of security attack techniques include:

➤ *Brute force attack (or crack)*—One of the interception attack modalities. This type of attack applies all possible character combinations, one at a time, using the same encryption algorithm as the target from an appropriate character set to decrypt a password. The permutations involved limit the practicality of this attack method. A dictionary password attack, alternatively, uses a more limited list of dictionary words to either break the password or encrypt to the same one-way hash value used to authenticate a principal. The more sophisticated dictionaries offer mutation filters that change "idiot" to, for example, "1d10t", using the same word list.

➤ *Denial of service (DOS)*—One of the interference attack modalities. This type of attack overwhelms a service provider with legitimate requests for service beyond its operational capacity to service those requests in its intended manner. Normal use or management of the service provider is either prevented or totally inhibited. For example, a random crash of an application server is forced by a DOS attack following modification of logs showing evidence of penetration by an unauthorized, unauthenticated intruder.

➤ *Man-in-the-middle attack*—One of the impersonation attack modalities. In this type of attack, a consumer believes it is exchanging information *directly* with some other party when, in fact, the exchange is unknowingly passed through some intermediary intruder. An example of an active attack is when the intruding third party intercedes in the exchange on behalf of one of the conversing principals without the knowledge of the other. An example of a passive attack is when the intruding third party, masquerading as some legitimate service provider or other consumer, actively solicits information that is intended for the falsely portrayed legitimate party. The ability to actively solicit information distinguishes this attack from an interception attack modality.

➤ *Replay attack*—One of the impersonation attack modalities. This type of attack is an unauthorized, out-of-sequence retransmission of some previously intercepted service request or sequence of data. The replay attack is an attempt to actively impersonate an authenticated, authorized principal from whom the data stream was intercepted. Without appropriate IT security controls, such as using sequence numbers and timestamps to guarantee at least partial sequence integrity, the targeted service provider has no choice other than to respond to the request.

➤ *Spoof*—One of the impersonation attack modalities. This type of attack is an attempt to gain access or utilize some service as an authorized principal. This technique is often used as a legitimate network management tool to reduce bandwidth consumption, especially across wide-area network connections. Often, routers and other network devices "spoof" replies from remote sites to decrease network traffic across slow or metered data links.

The attack techniques here could involve a combination of two different attack modalities—namely, interception to crack the password, then impersonation. A security attack is typically launched in three separate, distinct phases: reconnaissance, penetration, and then control. These different modalities cause security violations during various phases of a security attack that must be prevented, detected, or corrected.

Corporate Objectives

The corporate security objectives are often documented in a disaster recovery plan because the IT security objective of availability of services is a key security issue. The plan details how countermeasures will be implemented in response to some disaster or security incident. When you define a disaster recovery procedure, you implicitly make a policy statement that defines critical business assets. The disaster plan typically describes which areas, functions, or services must be reestablished before others and which assets need to be repaired or replaced first. It is necessary, though often quite difficult, to assess the risk of exposure to loss or misuse of these assets during some disaster or security disruption. For insurance and investment purposes, these probabilities are often converted to monetary value commensurate with the probability of loss. These costs are, in turn, compared to the benefit a capital investment would garner in securing the particular asset from risk. The formulation of any broad corporate policy of this nature requires the careful balancing of accessibility, security, investment, and profit. Thus, risk assessment supports a cost/benefit analysis of investment in each IT security control, as well as relative priority and importance of any one risk with respect to overall corporate objectives.

The case study exam format simulates actual interviews or survey responses. Learn to identify in these case studies or in actual interviews what are the IT corporate objectives and areas of perceived risk. Remember, however, that the success of an effective security design lies not just in its agreement with corporate business objectives, but also in technical support and employee compliance.

Physical and Logical Access

Security policies describe corporate roles and responsibilities; employee rights; and methods of management, review, and auditing. An effective policy is one that encourages employee awareness and commitment in supporting the corporate objectives; in effect, it defines, reflects, and fosters a positive corporate cultural attitude toward security in the organization. You must consider two key areas under the umbrella of effective security management: physical access and logical access to corporate assets and resources. Both areas require some form of security policy statement. The physical area includes:

➤ *Physical access to system resources*—Network and data communication equipment as well as removable storage devices must be removed from unauthorized employee access.

➤ *Backup, restore, and disaster recovery procedures*—These as well as the backup media must be in place.

Similarly, access to assets and resources through a network or standalone computer system also requires a security policy statement. This area of logical access includes:

➤ *Auditing and monitoring of system resources*—Tracking of logical access includes an audit of access to assets such as files and directories, the Registry, print services, and remote access.

➤ *Access through interactive or external network connections*—The ability to locally log on at a server console as compared to access to a server across a network.

➤ *Security management of users, groups, and resources*—The use of built-in instead of user-defined groups, the assignment of permissions and rights to different groups.

➤ *Domain account policies*—Password policies such as expiration, length, history, and intruder detection.

 Notice the classification across a physical/logical dimension. For the purposes of analysis and study, try to determine a common dimension across lists of apparently related objects that helps associate and differentiate them from one another.

System Security Audits

Security objectives are defined on paper and implemented by a mixture of people with varying degrees of responsibility and hardware/software technologies with equally varying degrees of effectiveness. Superior security technologies can be totally compromised if a company administers procedures poorly. Conversely, the best administrative procedures will fail if a company improperly installs and maintains technology. Finally, comprehensive procedural planning as well as superior security technologies are subverted if the corporate culture or social practices foster noncompliance. It is a regrettable fact that security breeches are more likely to come from within an organization than from an outside source. Breaching security of an unauthorized area by an authenticated "rogue user" is an example of a security violation that uses an impersonation attack modality. These breeches may be intentional and a result of malice (with a clear aim to remove or destroy sensitive information), or they may be unintentional (due to poor training or inexperience with established procedures). A good security design detects, prevents, and corrects such breaches. It does not as much restrict as it directs "authorized" access; it should protect and facilitate legitimate use as transparently as possible, with as little required maintenance as possible and the lowest possible TCO.

An assessment of how well security controls detect, prevent, and correct breaches is called a *system security audit*, which consists of collecting background and support documentation, including:

➤ A disaster recovery plan

➤ Registration numbers

➤ License numbers

➤ The key network address

➤ Passwords

➤ Other background information about the IT organization

The company defines scopes of responsibility to determine key personnel, backup, chains of command, and communication procedures. Both technical and procedural security controls are reviewed, and findings are reported directly to the highest level of management.

 Exam case studies may include comments by key personnel (such as the CEO, CFO, CIO, VP of Marketing, VP of Sales, and VP of HR) that state specific corporate objectives. List specific IT objectives as you read the case study. Look for keywords such as "confidentiality," "integrity," and "availability" when they are applied to users, business services, or corporate assets. When suggesting an appropriate response, remember to classify security technologies as primarily involved with prevention, detection, and correction.

Risk Management

Security must be part of a dynamic process rather than an infrequent static survey. Risk represents only the *perceived* possibility of suffering loss, denial of access, or interception of privileged information—not the actual event itself. In fact, both the probability that such a situation will occur and its impact can vary over time. Detecting risk, however, leads to correction, which leads to routine prevention.

Microsoft's five-step proactive risk management process can be condensed into the following three steps:

1. *Risk identification and analysis.* There is a need to identify a risk as both a risk condition that could occur and as a consequence of what might happen; this leads to better control (detection, prevention) and management (correction). The condition(s) leading to some probability that a risk can occur and the impact of it happening are incorporated into an action plan.

2. *Risk action planning.* Security strategies and business objectives are integrated into an implementation plan.

3. *Risk tracking and control.* The action plan is regularly monitored to assess its effectiveness, and risk management is subsumed under daily project management.

Security Requirements

Let's simplify Windows 2000 security by distinguishing two possibilities: the simplest one, a distributed security system dealing exclusively with security issues within the enterprise, and the more complicated possibility, an enterprise that deals with both an internal distributed system and external network security requirements resulting from Internet-access (which I will discuss in greater detail in the "Using Security Protocols" section later in this chapter). Use the three risk management steps listed previously in an analysis of a distributed security:

➤ *Security risks*—Identify both perceived risk probability and risk impact or consequence as described in the risk identification and analysis step of the risk management process

➤ *Security strategies*—Risk action plans as described in the risk action planning step of the risk management process

➤ *Security group descriptions*—Determine the mapping of users, groups, and group policies, the use of templates and need, if any, for user-defined "functional adaptations" of Microsoft's built-in categories

➤ *Group policies*—Management of Microsoft's Group Policy security features

➤ *Network logon and authentication strategies*—Administration of local, remote, and smart card logons

➤ *Information security strategies*—Management of secured information transmission and the identification of cost/benefits in the use of various forms of encryption, digital signatures, and trusts among Certificate Authorities (CAs)

➤ *Administrative policies*—Management, monitoring, and auditing of administrative and system-related tasks

Deployment of a Security System

To deploy an enterprise security system, follow these steps:

1. Identify security risks.

2. Plan the size and capacity of the system.

3. Formulate a document that details security policies and procedures.

4. Create a methodology to deploy your security technologies.

5. Train the support staff.

6. Plan and deploy equipment.

7. Identify user groups and their needs.

Notice that procedural tasks precede technical tasks and that security systems are deployed *before* user groups are identified and individuals are assigned user accounts. Microsoft recommends that you formulate a detailed plan using project methodology to deploy network security technologies. In the context of network security strategies, developing secured boundaries—referred to as "hardening the boundaries"—is essential because network traffic will reach beyond an enterprise's namespace. The most conservative network security strategy considers penetration of security from within the enterprise namespace just as likely as from outside it. Effectively deploying security technologies means that those technologies will work in as broad a security context as permitted by the corporate security objectives to maintain a practical TCO.

Strategic planning may or may not include quantitative and qualitative growth projections. In other words, you can have a healthy growth rate of IT resources without the need for Internet access. This would be a noteworthy and valid corporate business objective with a subtle but perhaps important effect on how the business implements a security policy. The corporate business objectives, not the consultant, determine the scope of IT within an enterprise.

Problems with Procedural Paradigms

The Microsoft paradigm is procedural in approach. It does not provide a framework within which to understand and apply security technologies in a systematic and organized way. You need to identify security risk areas in relation to the scope of a set of business objectives. Troubleshooting techniques need similar reference models so that you can isolate, define, correct, test, and retest security breaches. A methodology that identifies key components and, thus, areas of risk would be a valuable tool for analyzing and studying a security system. Isolating key components or features often reveals how a function relates to both physical and logical structure. Just as the study of animal physiology provides a rationale for many peculiar behaviors, you better understand functional adaptations in a business workflow when you explore the limitations in the underlying structure that caused it. For example, an IT workforce adopts superstitious behavior in performing one task on a "special" workstation because of poor training or poorly understood installation procedures. This favored machine becomes a workflow bottleneck because of little or no support for concurrent user access to enterprise resources.

Procedural paradigms mentioned in system documentation work best for software installation and administrative tasks; they do not help organize objects with common characteristics across similar security technologies. In recent years, programming languages have evolved from the procedural business languages of the 1970s to the contemporary object-oriented paradigms, profoundly affecting software engineering and especially quality assurance methods. Procedural approaches have been replaced by more structured, concept-oriented tools. Perhaps an object-oriented approach to designing and implementing security systems in Windows 2000 would offer similar advantages.

A security practitioner analyzes corporate business objectives to reveal functional adaptations of that particular corporate body. Although it's critical to understand both the underlying physical and logical IT structures, a client's corporate "culture" actually determines how, within the greatest strengths and weaknesses of its security policy, corporate business objectives are finally implemented. This "social" layer will interpret the policy statements and carry out all or part of the policy within the context of some group consensus. Once you have described the physical, logical, and social layers of an organization, you should systematically compile organizational data in the following order:

1. Classify relevant IT objects.

2. Map objects to the some layered network reference model.

3. Identify attack modalities—the "who," "where," and "when"—associated with these objects within a layered reference model.

4. Select appropriate security technologies to detect, prevent, or correct the impact and consequences of some identified risk.

A Microsoft Historical Perspective

The ability to classify animal and plant life comes from studying both anatomy and physiology in the real world. Many "new concepts" in Windows 2000 are as easy to classify based upon trends in information technologies over the last 25 years. The following historical trends focus on the logical progression of changes in features now available in Windows 2000. Beginning with the standalone machines in the early 1980s, several themes are noteworthy:

➤ User-related data requires a growing, disproportionate share of the Registry.

➤ Greater differentiation of "named objects" requires greater organization.

➤ More services run in their own process space in the operating system.

➤ Services are delegated to specialized servers.

➤ Specialization requires more specific functional management areas.

➤ Security information is more widely distributed across the enterprise.

➤ Distribution of security information improves performance and fault tolerance.

These themes help identify trends that will continue to affect the "anatomy" and "physiology" of IT systems in the future. Security systems are fundamental to the IT "body." As security professionals analyze a case study or listen to a CIO describe her IT security objectives, they must train themselves to recognize where structure supports function and where it forces functional adaptation. Especially in Windows 2000, most corporate business objectives are fully realized through the use of built-in structures or templates, further reducing the variable cost components of TCO: training, support, and maintenance.

Key Historical Trends

In the beginning, there was just a local machine with text-file scripts that initialized various software drivers and environmental parameters. The transition from standalone personal computer to workgroup, and from workgroup to domain, represented the first leap in specialization, specifically from disk operating system to network operating system. The fundamental structural change from a flat-file Registry in Windows 3.x to the hierarchical though nonrelational database in Windows 95 formed the substrate for all subsequent IT expansion and development.

Windows for Workgroups managed to carry the additional overhead of a bloated user.dat, but more scalable, networked resources required an evolutionary change in system architecture. Two especially significant characteristics of Microsoft software development have been the use of interface specifications and the abstraction of functional areas in the operating system and the network environment. Microsoft has proposed a four-layer model similar to one proposed in the late 1960s by the Department of Defense. Both Microsoft and DoD models, depicted in Figure 2.1, simplify the seven layers described in the International Organization for Standardization (ISO) Open Systems Interconnection Reference Model (OSI model). The layers in the Microsoft model are Application Programming Interface (API), Transport Driver (sometimes called "Transport

OSI Model	Department of Defense (TCP/IP) Model	Microsoft Model
Application Presentation Session	Application	Application Programming Interface
Transport	Transport	Transport Driver Interface
Network	Internet	Network Device Interface Specification
Data Link Physical	Network Interface	Physical

Figure 2.1   A comparison of reference models.

Device") Interface (TDI), and Network Device (sometimes called "Network Driver") Interface Specification (NDIS). The layers in the DoD model are Application, Transport, Internet, Network, and Interface.

We will use the twin themes of identifying boundaries through the definition of interface specifications and the abstraction and isolation of functional areas to discuss security systems throughout this book. By creating a layered architectural model that emphasizes boundary interfaces and specific functional areas, NT architecture can be described in terms of virtualized or abstracted components— for example, the Hardware Abstraction Layer (HAL) and the Local Security Authority (LSA). Microsoft has successfully applied a component object model to the network operating system itself.

Learn to cross-reference the three major layered architectural models: the OSI model, the TCP/IP (DoD) model, and Microsoft's four-layer adaptation (MS model). Use the Microsoft layered model to organize the hierarchical relationships across the protocols and services mentioned in documentation. Use the OSI model to map these protocols to physical/logical layers in network architecture.

The "new technology" of Windows NT not only supported multiple client service subsystems, but also centralized the user administration in one primary domain controller. This domain controller stored a hierarchical, nonrelational directory database that contains unique information about every authenticated user. This directory database is called the Windows Registry. The logon process required the user or principal to enter a name and password at their local machine, which, through the LSA, was somehow matched to stored information on some domain controller. The domain controller returned a token to the LSA authorizing the user to access services within the domain namespace.

Secondary backup units that supported the primary domain controller partially solved the inherent physical limitations of one machine in supporting user authentication. As a result, organizational systems scaled the number of users to within the primary domain controller's physical capacity. The increased responsibility of administering the directory database for the organization literally pushed other IT services off the domain controller onto other "member" servers in the domain.

In the NT 4 world, greater specialization of one IT object—the domain controller—led to differentiation of other kinds of servers, defined by the directory database, as member servers in that domain namespace. More users created a greater need for some logical organization. With server differentiation comes greater differentiation of services accessible to more users. Clearly, the constraint on increased users/services lies within the design of the primary domain controller and directory database; NT 4 reached its capacity at about 40,000 objects. Creating a Metabase in Internet Information Server 4, a separate directory database exclusively for Web services, was an interesting example of differentiation of structure and specialization of services. However, the Metabase object doesn't support scalability of users and services necessary to scale to a million-object enterprise namespace.

Active Directory

NT 4 system architecture supports a single primary domain controller as the definitive source of authentication for all users accessing a domain's resources and services. Copies of this directory database are replicated to a secondary, backup domain controller. The accessibility to this data store for logon authentication is thus balanced across all domain controllers. Although the security design offers a degree of fault tolerance, it is nevertheless constrained by the primacy of one definitive user accounts directory database. As you scale IT to the level of an enterprise, you reach limits in your ability to efficiently access/replicate one common, central store. Thus, as NT evolves, one can't expect primary domain controllers to multiply. One can, however, assume that security-related processes will further differentiate and specialize in some specific security service support. One can expect a more efficient distribution of user data, greater fault tolerance, and greater security associated with accessing these user stores given the fundamental role they play in consumer-to-provider interactions.

The hallmark of Windows 2000 is Active Directory Services (ADS), a single, consistent, relational database of objects in a uniform namespace scalable to the level of an enterprise spanning multiple domains.

Throughout this book, I use certain icons in the figures to denote specific Active Directory concepts; Figure 2.2 shows the icons and their descriptions. One product of ADS is greater granularity in permissions, not only across a broader ranges of objects and across a wider range of domains, but deeper into the object's attribute sets. Figure 2.3 depicts an AD forest of domain trees, organized into a layered structure of parent domains branching into child domains. Across the entire enterprise, one uniform interface stores information about millions of objects. With greater choices of "named" objects, you must seek greater control and organization of groups spanning across legacy flat NT 4 domain namespaces.

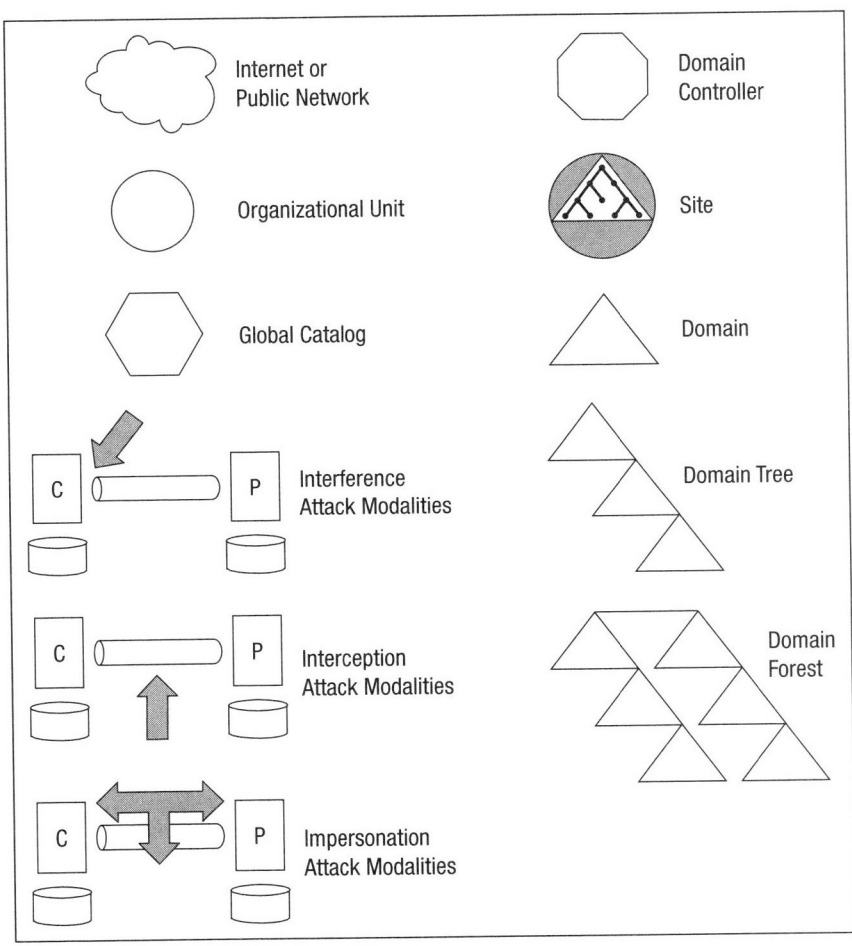

Figure 2.2   Commonly used icons and AD terms.

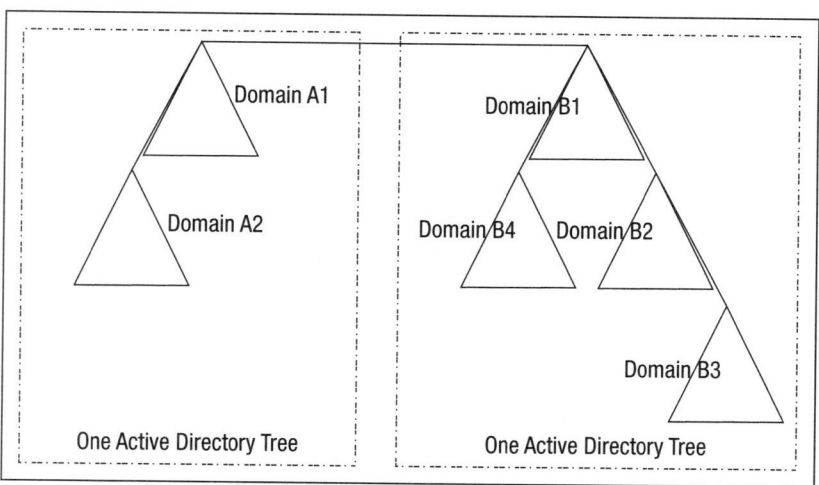

Figure 2.3 An example of an AD forest.

From a historical perspective, forces of differentiation lead not just to specialization, but also to the need for locating simple resources among specialty service providers. In fact, ADS provides a hierarchically arranged directory database and a mechanism to organize the objects within its namespace called the organizational unit (OU). Windows 2000, through its concept of group policies, can create and assign restricted "spheres of responsibility" across domain namespaces by using these logical OUs.

Group Policy usage and tools like OUs dramatically decrease the TCO of a Windows-based enterprise. Users and resource objects, now called *principals*, along with their rights and permissions, are mapped more closely to the way businesses operate, not by artificial constraints in hardware and system software. Microsoft describes ADS as "a single, consistent, open set of interfaces for performing common administrative tasks" that relates to named objects such as users, printers, and file resources across the enterprise. Resources are located in domains, trees, and forests. Just as with any other database, this hierarchical data store can be customized forest-wide through a central schema. ADS uses a multimaster replication model resulting in improved fault tolerance and accessibility; a complete copy of a common data store is replicated to every domain controller.

What is noteworthy here is that ADS is a directory service provider of information about named, network resources; ADS is not the directory database itself. In comparison to the practical 40,000-user limit of the flat NT 4 namespace, ADS will scale more than one million objects. The directory services it provides are a standards-based protocol called Lightweight Directory Access Protocol (LDAP). Using a nonproprietary protocol has security implications because a "well-known" interface allows access to directory stores. A stated goal of ADS is to provide a unified view of directories and namespaces regardless of location or operating system platform.

 Given the huge capacity of ADS, Microsoft suggests that in Windows 2000, many enterprises can adopt a single domain model and further reduce their TCO. A single domain model is important in many security schemes.

Integrating Security Account Management

Much like with the Metabase, specialization of directory services has led to ADS and a host of other system, file, and Registry features that support a single namespace containing millions of objects. The greater need for authentication, authorization, and auditing (AAA) has led to the Kerberos protocol, public key infrastructure (PKI), and server differentiation of what are generically referred to as AAA servers. The Kerberos protocol builds on the limitations of the propri-etary NT LAN Manager (NTLM) challenge/response authentication service. By adding a "multiheaded" gatekeeper, the NTLM authentication service has been replaced by a well-known, industry-standard design that efficiently delivers distributed security services within a native Windows 2000 environment. Single-user sign-on is enhanced through evolving APIs such as the SSPI, an adaptation of the *de jure* standard General Security Services API (GSS-API). Further scalability in authentication services leads to smart card logons and certificate mapping. In typical Microsoft tradition, backward compatibility rules implemen-tation of system designs. LAN Manager and NTLM authentication servers will remain highly visible in most corporate environments for several years due to the integration of NT 4 and Windows clients. The pure Windows 2000 security system will *not* be the default configuration in most real-life scenarios.

You might assume that because of the increase in use of the Distributed Com-ponent Object Model (DCOM) in software development and the emphasis on software interoperability across non-Microsoft "cultures" (e.g., Novell, Unix, and Macintosh), a major Windows 2000 theme is a scalable organizational structure. Similarly, the process of authentication of users and authorization to use both services and resources will also change with the organizational scheme. The relational structure of the AD database in these AAA servers supports even greater granularity by storing more access control information. Just like the software engineer can develop programming objects that have associated methods and attributes, every object in the AD database, including the direc-tory database itself, has associated with it a collection of access control entries (ACEs) that together form an access control list (ACL).

ACLs are either controlled by the system (system ACLs [SACLs]) or are user-defined Discretionary ACLs (or DACLs). Both provide a greater granularity of support in assigning permissions to objects like files, folders, printers, and the Registry than the hierarchical, nonrelational Registry found in NT 4. Such enhancements are necessary, for example, to authenticate and authorize remote users accessing the enterprise namespace. Security technologies included in Windows 2000, such as the PKI, offer a mechanism to secure mail and support new demands outside the boundaries of the enterprise. These security enhancements are discussed in the next chapter.

Physical Organization

Differentiation and specialization have occurred on the system side of the Registry. The local machine has evolved into virtual machine and client subsystems. The Windows 2000 enterprise, administering millions of objects, is still fundamentally a dichotomy of user and system data. The "physical" organization of sites may not reflect the "logical" organization of user objects and resources. Sites and domains still organize users and resources in a more physical dimension. With differentiation comes the need for enhancements in organization. Since the introduction of NT 4, there has been less emphasis on the individual user and growing administrative emphasis on groups. Group Policy spans both the physical and logical enterprise namespace. Workstation clients have names, printers have names, and files have names; all have ACLs.

A fundamental feature of a Microsoft domain model is that the system administrator can assign:

➤ Users to global groups

➤ Global groups to local groups

➤ Resource permissions to local groups

Windows 2000 builds on this schema but scales it to accommodate the enterprise; it places greater emphasis on the group and its policies than the legacy NT 4 domain model does. Group Policy Microsoft Management Console (MMC) snap-in dramatically expands upon the older System Policy Editor in NT 4. Whereas the legacy System Policy Editor specified both user and computer configurations, Group Policy, in association with the AD, centrally manages computers and users without additional administrative overhead. This topic is discussed in greater detail in Chapter 10. A more comprehensive, more accessible, more easily managed organizational structure with greater granularity at the object level has evolved. Tools such as MMC act as common, scalable administrative interfaces that allow you to add on tools such as the Security Template or the Security Configuration And Analysis snap-in to support both objects and policies.

Finally, specialization of individual component objects has also been scaled to accommodate the needs and breadth within *and* across enterprises. DCOM, in order to support increasing numbers of users *and* services, has forced differentiation of new kinds of inter-enterprise services (such as Microsoft Transaction Server, Microsoft Message Queue Server, and Distributed Transaction Coordinator) and has increased the need to both manage *and* audit the secured access to these services.

The majority of real-world corporate business objectives, and most likely the case studies in the Microsoft certification examination, will begin with e-commerce issues and will thus require you to analyze accessing services across enterprises. As suggested in the "A Microsoft Historical Perspective" section earlier in this chapter, you need to map business objectives to features that reflect recurring IT trends, not static system tools. Moore's Law states that because the number of transistors in integrated circuits has doubled every year since the integrated circuit was invented, the capacity to support data doubles approximately every 18 months. Technical experts must understand trends in order to efficiently map corporate business objectives to maintain or even reduce TCO.

 The key characteristic across all Microsoft competency areas for IT management is that you must understand the benefits, impact, and rationale for Windows 2000 features and areas. It is likely that the commonly perceived ambiguity of exam questions is testing this particular competency. Identify and map business objectives to IT objects, trends, and current system features. Select an implementation using the most "effective" security technology at the lowest TCO.

A Layered Security Paradigm

Technicians, Microsoft Certified Systems Engineers (MCSEs), and network managers troubleshoot by systematically applying a generic paradigm:

1. Collect data about some event.

2. Isolate the event by identifying conditions and consequences.

3. Resolve the event.

4. Replicate and confirm the resolution of the event.

5. Document the incident, its consequences, and the fix.

Technical personnel rely on layered network-system models to isolate an event. Efficient troubleshooting identifies and isolates only one layer at a time in order to resolve and replicate that event. Replication is the critical step in this process; if you can re-create the event on demand, you identify, isolate, and control all conditions necessary and sufficient to create that event. Layer boundaries are critical in both troubleshooting and design because they define the scope of the event. Notice the similarities here between this troubleshooting methodology and risk management mentioned earlier in this chapter. Basic troubleshooting includes problem identification, an action plan, and resolution. Security controls identified in an organization's corporate objectives are identified and mapped to specific functional areas, layers or interfaces in Windows 2000. To resolve or troubleshoot a particular security incident, it is advantageous to have a generic schema that helps to identify required security components in relation to these areas.

You can consider workstations, member servers, and domain controllers as different "species" of computers with different Registry configurations that support different characteristic workloads—for example, client workstations, file servers, application servers, and domain controllers. Likewise, it might be useful to consider the client workstation as a consumer, and a server as a service provider. Based upon different workload characterizations, service providers offer services (for example, application servers) or resources (for example, files, printers, and so on). Thus, as the number of users/consumers increases, providers supporting both resources and services become more differentiated and specialized. Fundamental to all systems is the asset itself. A generic file server is a service provider; it provides files, an asset. The consumer seeks authentication in order to use services or retrieve resources that a host/provider offers; a consumer requests and accesses or retrieves a file. The domain controller or AAA provider supports the specialized security services of authentication, authorization, and auditing. Finally, a channel of communication or virtual pipe represents the physical connection or logical session that exists at some point in time between consumer and provider when services are requested or delivered. The pipe may not directly connect to the consumer or provider. Instead, it may require an interface layer, as did the old telecommunications model, which connected the session pipe to data terminal equipment (DTE) through some data circuit interface (DCE).

Figure 2.4 shows a security component schema. The benefit of the schema, originally borrowed from a telecommunications model, is that you can easily identify key security components within any OSI layer of a network. Reliance on the OSI model helps to strengthen your security design, analysis, and troubleshooting and force a systematic and replicable way to analyze security scenarios. Any object in the enterprise namespace having some account information and login username is a *principal*. This principal-to-principal (consumer-to-provider) schema thus supports comparisons of different security technologies at different OSI layers to help quantify the cost effectiveness of any security implementation.

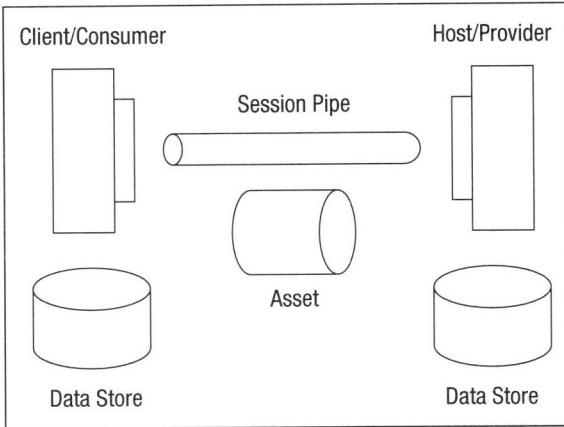

Figure 2.4 A consumer/provider interaction.

 You can simplify all design scenarios as consumer/provider, provider/ provider, or consumer/consumer interactions across a session pipe. Note that each component has a data store that may contain special security information used during the session. The simplest interaction involves a consumer, such as a client or user, who is requesting some asset (such as a file), from some provider (such as a file server).

Evaluating Risks

For the purposes of study and analysis, you must simplify the list of IT objectives and the many possible security exposures (any form of malicious program, denial of service attacks, spoofing, replay attacks, brute force attacks, and so on) that are detailed in numerous security references. In the real world, though, it is more advantageous to evaluate security designs in terms of generic kinds of security exposure, not in terms of security services. It is easier to conceptualize a denial of service, replay, or spoof directed at a service provider than discuss IT security control themes of availability and access. In fact, you can categorize security incidents as threats to one of the following:

➤ Users

➤ Assets

➤ Services

➤ Integrity of an object

You can determine the most effective security technologies by applying an attack modality to objects in your schema. Conceptualizing a security issue as an attack modality in this way helps to understand an issue and more readily translates that issue to the real world. Doing so helps to limit your scope of investigation and optimize your troubleshooting efforts when a security breach has occurred.

You can simplify the six IT security controls—namely, access, availability, integrity, authenticity, confidentiality, and nonrepudiation—by categorizing them into three attack modalities, each with an active and passive dimension. Figure 2.5 shows examples of three attack modalities staged against some service provider. In the remainder of the book, I will use this schema to explain security technologies at various levels of the OSI model. The three attack modalities are:

➤ *Interference*—Any form of security attack that renders an asset or service unavailable or unusable.

　➤ *Active*—An active interference attack specifically targets an asset or service with the programmed intention to either disable or destroy it. Examples of active interference attacks are classic boot sector viruses that rewrite the master boot record on a local hard drive or DOS attacks that overwhelm the capacity of a service provider, rendering it functionally useless.

　➤ *Passive*—Passive interference attacks, such as a virus, bacterium, or rabbit, do not target the asset or service directly but work to subvert accessibility through indirect activities. They are designed to exhaust all local resources and thereby prevent access to or use of an asset or service through indirect means.

➤ *Interception*—Any form of attack that covertly captures a data stream through either direct monitoring or redirection.

　➤ *Active*—An active interception attack intercepts a message flow and performs analysis of message content. Because the message content is known, the attack can include alteration or fabrication of data, which is

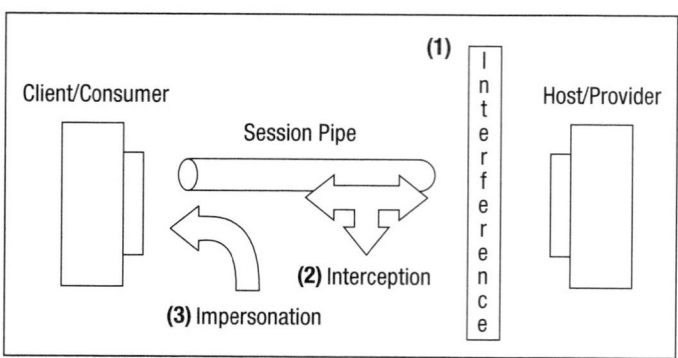

Figure 2.5 Applying attack modalities—three attacks on a provider.

then redirected to either subvert existing information or produce some unauthorized effect. An example is the unauthorized alteration of a DNS namespace.

➤ *Passive*—A passive interception attack intercepts a message flow and performs an analysis of the characteristics of the data stream, not its content. Examples are wire taps and network traffic analysis.

➤ *Impersonation*—Any form of attack that permits an intruding third party to intercede for one principal in the exchange of information or services without the knowledge of the other.

➤ *Active*—An active impersonation involves a third party spoofing or faking the IP address of one of the principals. The spoof impersonates either principal online without the other's knowledge.

➤ *Passive*—A passive impersonation does not directly target the session pipe or data stream but works indirectly to produce some unauthorized effect. A passive impersonation attack would involve the renaming of DNS namespace so that legitimate DNS lookup responses point to illegitimate hosts. Other forms of impersonation involve the creation of a secret trapdoor that allows unauthenticated, unauthorized access by a third party to system services.

A distinguishing factor between active and passive impersonation is the interactive nature and response time of the exchange of information between parties. An example would be a spoof logon screen requesting reentry of both username and password.

IT security controls like compliance are primarily procedural and attitudinal, so they cross attack modality boundaries. Similarly, many attacks include subversive techniques from all three modalities. Nevertheless, the classification scheme helps to identify areas of risk impact and their consequences. The different attack modalities and appropriate IT security controls for detection, prevention, and correction are summarized in Table 2.1.

Applying an attack modality to an asset, consumer, provider, or session pipe helps you identify the risk involved in losing accessibility to, the integrity of, or credibility in that particular object. Table 2.2 lists examples of security breaches within

Table 2.1 Three attack modalities and appropriate IT security controls.			
Dimension	**Interference**	**Interception**	**Impersonation**
Active	Access control	Integrity	Authenticity
Passive	Availability	Compliance, nonrepudiation	Confidentiality

Table 2.2 Examples of security breaches.			
Dimension	**Interference**	**Interception**	**Impersonation**
Active	Denial of service	Web page redirection	Spoof, replay, crack
Passive	Active viruses, bacteria	Wire taps	Trap doors, Trojan horse

the context of the three attack modalities. Security technologies need to support distributed application services in the context of e-commerce across enterprise borders. Especially outside the enterprise, authenticity applies to assets, consumers, and providers. Access control and integrity more clearly apply to asset providers. Confidentiality applies data flows through the session pipe between consumer and provider.

Familiarity with this schema helps you more readily:

1. Map the corporate business objectives to specific security objects within specific reference model layers.

2. Apply attack modalities to identify areas of security exposure.

3. Apply security technologies to detect, prevent, or correct any risk consequences.

This relatively simple analysis is useful when you are planning, troubleshooting, and building a security model. In the remainder of this book, you will use this security schema and these attack modalities to study and analyze security technologies. In Chapters 3 and 4, respectively, I discuss PKI and the Kerberos protocol at great length. In Chapter 5, you will apply this schema to design and analyze an actual network security plan. More important, though, is how to use the same simple schema at different OSI layers to correlate and compare different security technologies.

Documenting Nontechnical Procedures

Even though you can evaluate risks and apply security technologies, a critical part of a disaster recovery plan is thoroughly documenting nontechnical procedures associated with detecting, preventing, and correcting a security incident. Many times, the appropriate "paper trail" (compliance with a published auditing policy, the proper use of legal notices, proper disposal procedures, and so on) is carelessly overlooked or ignored. Sloppy administrative procedures sometimes undermine a company's ability to resolve a security incident. In Chapter 5, we will refine a network security policy and quantify the cost benefits/risk analysis so that financial decisions can be reached in an actual business context.

Using Security Protocols

I have already simplified designs by identifying scenarios that might deal just with distributed security within the enterprise. The unique factor facing network security issues is exposure to the Internet. Now, in addition to security threats to assets, services, and the integrity of objects, you have risks associated with impersonation from outside the enterprise namespace. For example, there are at least three active impersonation attacks:

➤ An unauthenticated person can impersonate or masquerade as a legitimate user (a *spoof*)

➤ An authenticated user (a *rogue user*) can access unauthorized areas

➤ An unauthenticated user (a *cracker* or *bogie*) can totally subvert security systems

Most corporate business objectives include e-commerce issues, so it's particularly relevant to understand the security ramifications of accessing services outside the enterprise. Chapter 3, which describes the PKI, and Chapter 4, which contains a discussion of the Kerberos protocol, deal with security issues that apply to both a distributed and Internet-aware security structure.

 Expect the majority of case studies to include Internet access as a key security issue. It may be advantageous to first address distributed security concerns. You can address many network security issues by adding specialized servers (such as a proxy server), implementing security technologies (such as firewalls), and redesigning network topology (such as constructing a demilitarized zone—DMZ—within the enterprise).

Mapping Security Technologies

The hardening of layered boundaries applies more closely to adding and changing configurations at or below the TDI than above the TDI. The acronyms and services are overwhelming. When you categorize them by, for example, Microsoft interface layers, a clearer picture for study and analysis emerges. Typically, service providers occupy the API layer or are found at the API/TDI interface. Below the TDI, most security technologies are involved with either the session pipe itself or the data flow within the pipe. In fact, PKI, by definition, is neither a protocol nor a service provider; but rather a system of technologies that includes digital signatures and Certificate Authority service providers. Notice how the hierarchical listing in Table 2.3 maps to the seven-layer OSI model, with the Application layer (layer 7) corresponding to Microsoft's API layer, the Transport layer (layer 4) corresponding to the TDI, and layers 3 (Network) and 2 (Data Link) corresponding to NDIS. You can apply each technology to address specific attack modalities. It is obvious

Table 2.3	A hierarchical listing of key security protocols as they relate to the OSI and Microsoft models.		
Layer Number	Layer Name (OSI)	Layer Name (Microsoft)	Security Protocols
7 6 5	Application Presentation Session	API	Secure Multipurpose Internet Mail Extensions (S/MIME); Kerberos protocol and other AAA servers; Proxy services; Secure Electronic Transaction (SET) service; IPSec: Internet Key Exchange Protocol (formerly ISAKMP/Oakley)
4	Transport	TDI	SOCKS (Sockets for Unix compatibility); Secure Sockets Layer/Transport Layer Security (SSL3/TLS1)
3	Network	NDIS	IPSec: Authentication Header (AH), Encapsulated Security Payload (ESP); packet filtering; Point-To-Point Tunneling Protocol (PPTP); Challenge Handshake Authentication Protocol (CHAP); Password Authentication Protocol (PAP); Microsoft CHAP (MS-CHAP)
2 1	Data Link Physical	Physical	PPP, L2TP, Hardware CSP

that implementing an effective security technology depends upon boundary interactions with other security technologies or server services.

Competencies

This chapter ends with a checklist of areas that Microsoft considers most relevant to anyone in a management role in the IT industry. What connotes technical expertise in this particular job role is always difficult to define. An objective of this book is that you will successfully pass the Microsoft Windows 2000 security exam, an area as widespread as the operating system itself. Even if you are not planning on taking a certification exam, the methodology and information in this book will offer valuable support in the analysis, design, and troubleshooting of Windows 2000 security systems. The areas Microsoft considers as requiring some competency are just as relevant to you as the certification exam candidate.

The Competency Model is a study guide that prioritizes topics in terms of their importance to particular IT support roles. Microsoft's list of required competencies are ranked from the lowest, 1, to the highest, 4. It is used in this book primarily as a checklist. As you review the various areas of study, you should note not only what is most significant, but also what is considered of lesser importance with regard to IT management. Unlike the competencies of the executive role, none of those for the management role received less than a 2 out of 4 ranking. In other words, all the areas listed in this section are relevant to the IT manager. You can assume that if these topics are considered relevant, they will somehow be included on a Microsoft examination.

Here is a list of the competencies and a description of each. These areas of competency are considered most relevant to an IT manager. Exam candidates should make certain they are thoroughly familiar with the topics listed prior to taking the security certification exam:

➤ *Security versus productivity issue*—This process requires that you maintain a balance between productivity and the security policy.

➤ *Security model*—This includes understanding the model's benefits, impact, and design rationale.

➤ *Compliance*—This IT objective, critical to the success of a security plan, is a procedural, legal, and social issue.

➤ Definition, rationale, and benefits of the following:

> ➤ Single Sign-On capability

> ➤ Active Directory

> ➤ Security Configuration Manager

> ➤ Remote access

> ➤ Smart card infrastructure

> ➤ IPSec protocol

> ➤ Group policies

> ➤ Access control lists

> ➤ Public key

> ➤ Certification server

> ➤ Encrypting file system and asset protection

> ➤ Kerberos 5

This book will discuss all topics included in the Microsoft Competency Model for Security but will focus especially on the areas Microsoft considers most relevant to IT management. One would expect that these areas are more likely to appear on a Microsoft certification exam and, therefore, require more than a casual understanding.

In the next few chapters, I will introduce more terms and concepts. Consumer-provider interactions will help you to conceptualize Windows 2000 security technologies. I will then apply these concepts to case studies. In addition, you will construct an actual network security plan using all techniques discussed in this chapter. As I discuss new technologies in subsequent chapters, I will introduce additional case studies to reinforce the Microsoft certification experience and security analysis in the real world.

Practice Questions

Question 1

Which of the following are components of TCO? [Check all correct answers]

❑ a. Cost of system upgrades

❑ b. System maintenance

❑ c. Cost of toner

❑ d. Technical support

Answers a, b, and d are correct. TCO (total cost of ownership) includes cost of system upgrades, system maintenance, and technical support. Cost of toner is not a component of TCO, so answer c is incorrect.

Question 2

An effective security plan is the synergy of which complementary factors? [Check all correct answers]

❑ a. Proper social attitudes in the user community

❑ b. A redundant array of independent drives (RAID) tower

❑ c. Technical expertise for proper support

❑ d. Appropriate security technologies

Answers a, c, and d are correct. Proper social attitude and compliance of the user community, technical expertise for proper support and maintenance, and the appropriate security technologies are all complementary factors. A RAID tower would most likely be included in a disaster recovery plan. Therefore, answer b is incorrect.

Question 3

> Which of the following are examples of IT security objectives? [Check all correct answers]
>
> ❑ a. Confidentiality
>
> ❑ b. Training
>
> ❑ c. Integrity
>
> ❑ d. Firewall technology

Answers a and c are correct. Examples of IT (information technology) security objectives include confidentiality and integrity. Training is not a typical security objective. Therefore, answer b is incorrect. Firewall technologies are, in isolation, not security objectives. Therefore, answer d is incorrect.

Question 4

> There are two categories of security policies:
>
> Logical
>
> Physical
>
> Identify whether each of the following key security policies is logical or physical. Categorize each item under the proper heading.
>
> Auditing and monitoring
>
> Backup and restore procedures
>
> Domain account policies
>
> Security management of users, groups, and resources

The correct answer is:

Physical

Backup and restore procedures

Logical

Auditing and monitoring

Domain account policies

Security management of users, groups, and resources

Only backup and restore procedures in this list have a physical component—that is, access to either the physical tape backup unit or to the actual backup media set(s).

Question 5

Which of the following items are included in a system security audit? [Check all correct answers]

❑ a. Phone numbers of key personnel

❑ b. List of domain controller IP addresses

❑ c. Software license numbers

❑ d. Serial numbers of all printers

❑ e. Passwords

❑ f. Birth dates of key personnel

❑ g. Weekly backup tapes

❑ h. List of vendor telephone numbers

Answers a, b, c, d, e, and h are correct. A system security audit is a collection of all relevant background and support documentation including a disaster recovery plan. Telephone numbers to contact key personnel are important, but their ages aren't. Therefore, answer f is incorrect. Weekly backup tapes would not be an actual part of the audit. Therefore, answer g is incorrect.

Question 6

When you are compiling a list of corporate business objectives for a security plan, the Chief Information Officer will supply the most relevant information.

○ a. True

○ b. False

Answer b, false, is correct. Corporate business objectives reflect the business mission of the entire organization. The objectives usually are based upon a survey of many departments within the organization.

Question 7

> Create an action plan for deploying an enterprise security system based upon the appropriate tasks listed below. Arrange all appropriate steps in the proper order.
>
> Plan and deploy equipment.
>
> Train your staff.
>
> Plan for size and capacity of the system.
>
> Create mandatory roaming profiles for all users.
>
> Formulate a security policy and procedures document.
>
> Identify user groups and their needs.
>
> Identify security risks.
>
> Create a methodology to deploy security technologies.

The correct answer is:

Identify security risks.

Plan for size and capacity of the system.

Formulate a security policies and procedures document.

Create a methodology to deploy security technologies.

Train your staff.

Plan and deploy equipment.

Identify user groups and their needs.

Note that the item "Create mandatory roaming profiles for all users" is not part of the action plan. The use of a mandatory or personal roaming profile might be documented in a comprehensive security policy statement, but it would typically be delegated to a system administrator or account operator.

Question 8

> Interference, impersonation, integrity, and interception are all examples of security attacks.
>
> ○ a. True
>
> ○ b. False

Answer b, false, is correct. Interference, impersonation, and interception are examples of security attacks; integrity, on the other hand, is an IT objective.

Question 9

Which security protocol(s) are parts of the TDI layer in the Microsoft four-layer model? [Check all correct answers]

❏ a. Proxy services

❏ b. IPSec IKE protocol

❏ c. S/MIME

❏ d. SET

❏ e. All of the above

❏ f. None of the above

Answer f is correct. None of these protocols is part of the TDI layer. The four protocols listed are found in the API layer. Examples of TDI protocols are SOCKS, SSL3, and TLS1.

Question 10

The Microsoft Windows 2000 Competency Model for security can be used for what purpose? [Choose the best answer]

○ a. A source of information about Windows 2000 features

○ b. A selling tool

○ c. A checklist

○ d. A study guide

Answer d is correct. The Microsoft Competency Model helps prioritize topical areas for each role member, so it functions as a study guide. It also ranks topical areas as least to most relevant for IT executives, IT management, and the IT workforce. The Microsoft Competency Model is specific to security issues; it is not a source of information about Windows 2000 features. Therefore, answer a is incorrect. The model is neither a selling tool nor simply a checklist of topics. Therefore, answers b and c are incorrect.

Need to Know More?

 McLean, Ian. *Windows 2000 Security Little Black Book*. The Coriolis Group, Scottsdale, Arizona, 2000. ISBN 1-57610-387-0. In addition to covering Windows 2000 security issues in a concise yet comprehensive manner, the author follows topical discussions with Immediate Solutions sections that explain, in a step-by-step format, how to implement the specific security techniques.

 Murhammer, Martin W. et al. *TCP/IP Tutorial and Technical Overview, Sixth Edition*. Prentice Hall, Upper Saddle River, New Jersey, 1998. ISBN 0-13-020130-8. Part 2, "Special Purpose Protocols and New Technologies," contains information about security breaches, cryptography, firewalls, network address translation, and IPSec.

 Search the TechNet CD (or its online version through **www.microsoft.com**) and the *Windows 2000 Server Resource Kit* CD using the keywords "competency", "security", "TCO", and "risk".

 **http://web.mit.edu/kerberos/www/dialogue.html** offers a fictitious account that Bill Bryant wrote in February 1988 about the design of the Kerberos protocol as implemented in the MIT Athena project.

Public Key Infrastructure (PKI)

· ·

Terms you'll need to understand:

✓ Public key infrastructure (PKI)

✓ Symmetric/asymmetric encryption algorithm

✓ Cryptanalysis

✓ Hash function

✓ Message digest

✓ Digital signature

✓ Bulk data encryption

✓ Digital envelope

✓ Certificate Authority (CA)

✓ Microsoft Cryptographic Application Programming Interface (CAPI)

Techniques you'll need to master:

✓ Identifying the hierarchical organization of security-provided services

✓ Describing the differences between symmetric and asymmetric encryption algorithms

✓ Discussing major issues in key management

✓ Describing how Certificate Authority hierarchies are organized

✓ Discussing major issues in successful key deployment

✓ Summarizing the features in the PKI Suite

✓ Outlining CAPI-supported features

✓ Describing the standard certificate stores in a Certificate Authority

This chapter begins with a discussion of secret and public key encryption, which address issues of confidentiality and authenticity. The next topic, key management, is a critical issue for deployment of security controls across unsecured namespaces. This topic is especially relevant in the area of e-commerce, where authentication of some service provider and confidentiality of the information exchange is critical to completing a business transaction. Finally, the various components of the public key infrastructure (PKI) are outlined to provide a foundation for Chapter 9.

In Chapter 2, I described key questions relating to any security analysis—namely, who is involved, what is happening, what are the objectives, where are the risks, and what are the security countermeasures. I then proceeded to describe how I would deploy a security system based on a set of corporate security objectives. You should use these corporate objectives to establish assumptions, definitions, priorities, and goals. Within the scope of these corporate objectives, you should attempt to identify predisposing risk conditions as well as the ramifications of a risk's impact on the business organization and its operations. The structured organization of the OSI and Microsoft reference models are helpful for systematically examining the different layers of the network structure. You need to begin the identification process by reducing each risk situation to one of the following:

➤ *Three basic components*—Namely, a consuming agent (consumer), a service providing agent (service provider), and a virtual pipe (session pipe) through which a dedicated transaction occurs between the two principal agents.

➤ *One or some combination of any three basic security attack methods or modalities*—Namely, interference, interception, and impersonation.

The identification process, especially with regards to Windows 2000, requires a level of competency in understanding the rationale for both design and implementation of several security substructures. Unlike NT 4 with its simpler domain model and NT LAN Manager (NTLM) challenge/response security protocol, Windows 2000 incorporates security subsystems like PKI, Kerberos protocol, IP Security (IPSec), and several remote connectivity designs. These all require a basic understanding before even the simplest security scenarios and basic components can be applied for comparison studies. The Windows 2000 competencies stress the need to understand the rationale for both design and implementation issues, because subsystems like PKI and IPSec support multiple installable cryptographic service providers (CSPs) and security protocols (Authentication Header Protocol and Encapsulated Security Payload Protocol), respectively. The understanding of these core components ought to precede the development of an actual security plan so you can better assess methods and costs of deployment.

Thus, in this chapter, I will begin by applying the basic security scheme proposed in Chapter 2 to a real-life security scenario. Specific requirements and goals will be described in the context of a business. You will often observe that the deployment costs of any security countermeasure can be measured only in terms relative to corporate security objectives and an organization's total cost of ownership (TCO). In the next four chapters, more technology is discussed to better gauge the cost of deployment and TCO. In Chapter 8, I return to a scenario-based discussion and complete the steps in the deployment of a security system—namely, plan the size of the system, formulate a securities policy, and create a methodology for deploying a security system.

Applying the Basic Security Scheme

A consumer-provider system can be compared to two people speaking, and the security issues that arise in computer networks have counterparts in this example. In normal discourse, one person (the consumer) speaks directly to another (the provider), and each person can see and hear the other. There is no passive interference from outside sources. The speaker can see that the listener is paying attention; outside tasks do not actively interfere with the conversation. Similarly, the speaker can be reasonably sure that his or her words are communicated in the intended manner and that the conversation is not overheard. Finally, because one party sees the other, there is little question of active impersonation.

 In a case study situation, compile a list of corporate business objectives before dealing with the technical issues of the data exchange. The consumer or service provider determines objectives for the exchange and establishes business rules that apply to how the exchange is conducted.

In this scenario, you can identify the following security components:

➤ Participatory roles as consumer and provider

➤ The session characteristics

➤ Relevant attack modalities based upon the security schema

How would the conversation change if one or both parties were threatened by outside forces seeking to learn about the exchanged information, interrupt the meeting, or discredit one or both parties in the exchange? IT security objectives would be established in anticipation of any one particular attack modality. Areas of risk and associated consequences of the attack would be systematically identified and evaluated in terms of the costs and benefits in this specific environment. Security breaches would be closed where appropriate. For businesses, the cost/benefits analysis, shaped by the business mission of the organization, becomes the security corporate objectives.

Table 3.1 A comparison of security objectives, controls, and countermeasure examples.		
Corporate Security Objective	**IT Security Control**	**Security Countermeasure**
The picture ID card must be a credible source of authentication.	Authentication	Certificate Authority
The picture ID card cannot show evidence of tampering or forgery.	Integrity	HMAC or message digest
Both parties have agreed to keep the exchange of information confidential.	Confidentiality	Symmetric or asymmetric encryption
The location of the conversation is not prearranged but made known to the intended listener only moments before the scheduled meeting.	Authentication, confidentiality	Session secret keys
As the conversation progresses, the parties move in some random direction to further minimize the effectiveness of some long-distance listening device.	Authentication, confidentiality	Subsession secret keys

For example, possible corporate security objectives for the above meeting are described in Table 3.1. Some of these security countermeasures will be discussed in this chapter and in Chapter 4.

Encrypted Exchanges

Corporate security objectives delineate business needs both within and outside the boundaries of an enterprise. This chapter introduces terms and concepts that are the foundation for security technologies discussed throughout the remainder of this book. The concepts are fundamental to both distributed and network security designs. PKI is a collection of tools and technologies that provide a secured exchange of information within and outside an enterprise. These security technologies are a prominent feature in e-commerce activities, which occur every minute somewhere on the Internet. Confidence in the authenticity of speaker and listener as well as consumer and provider is fundamental to securely exchanging information and assets. That exchange's privacy or confidentiality is equally important. PKI verifies authenticity and confidentiality between parties in an electronic information exchange.

Three basic cryptographic technologies generate a security component:

➤ Symmetric key encryption algorithms

➤ Asymmetric key encryption algorithms

➤ Secured one-way hash functions or hash message authentication code (HMAC)

Each provides countermeasures against one or several attack modalities, as summarized in Table 3.2 and discussed in more detail later in this chapter.

If the scenario I described at the beginning of this chapter had included corporate business objectives, the most obvious theme to emerge would be the meeting's confidentiality. Then again, business objectives and the "corporate culture" dictate what is required. For example, especially rigorous efforts to establish authenticity of either party could, in fact, have been detrimental to the exchange's progress. More simply, proof of possession or verification without specific knowledge of a secret code might prove more expedient in a given situation. Thus, applying technologies is a balance among several factors: the security objectives, the cost and implementation of resources (including licensing of patented technology), the network proximity of parties, and the exchange's time frame.

Symmetric Key Encryption

If privacy is a security objective, encrypting messages using a single, secret key has been—and still remains—the most common method of securing the contents of a message transmitted between two parties. Figure 3.1 shows a symmetric encryption exchange.

In the figure, the sender uses a unique key composed of a string of characters to transform data (or *cleartext*) into some scrambled message (or *ciphertext*). This is the *encryption phase*. The receiver uses the same key to decrypt or unscramble the transformed data (or ciphertext) back into the original message (or cleartext). This is the *decryption phase*. When the encryption and decryption phases use the same key, both the key and the encryption process are described as *symmetric* or

Table 3.2	Three methods for authentication/integrity.		
Feature	**Symmetric Key**	**Asymmetric Key**	**Hash Function**
Key management	Must be distributed	Publicly available	Not necessary
Execution	Fast	Slow	Fastest
Encryption	Just digital signature	Just digital signature	None
IT objectives	Authenticity, integrity, nonrepudiation	Authenticity, integrity, nonrepudiation	Integrity
Attack modalities	Interception, impersonation	Interception, impersonation	Interception, impersonation
Export restrictions	Yes	Yes	No

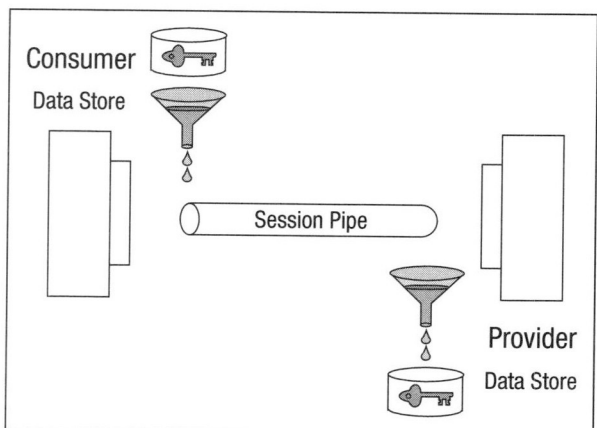

Figure 3.1 Applying symmetric encryption to a consumer/provider exchange.

conventional. In fact, the encryption algorithm and the ciphertext can both be publicly distributed. The guarantee of message confidentiality lies in the following:

➤ The secrecy of the symmetric key

➤ The length of the symmetric key

A strong encryption algorithm, by definition, cannot be used to generate a secret key even when the algorithm, ciphertext, and cleartext are known. In practice, however, as techniques to boost computational power—such as symmetric and massive multiprocessing (SMP and MMP, respectively)—improve, the resistance of a symmetric key to brute-force attack is decreasing.

The data encryption standard (DES) was developed in 1975 and standardized by American National Standards Institute (ANSI) in 1981. ANSI X3.92 uses 64 bits, a 56-bit key, and an 8-bit parity block. However, it is no longer considered secure because of its key length. A hardened version—called triple DES (TDES or 3DES), which uses three 128-bit keys—is available in a special upgrade High Encryption Pack as a Windows 2000 service pack add-on. You can also implement DES at the hardware level in the form of low-cost chips, especially for bulk encryption needs. However, using multiple keys in this algorithm increases the necessary computational time to generate the key. Nevertheless, symmetric key algorithms remain popular because you can implement them quickly. In Chapter 4, I will further discuss these encryption algorithms, along with such techniques as Cipher Block Chaining (CBC).

The following are prerequisites for symmetric encryption to work:

➤ Both parties must have the same symmetric key.

➤ The symmetric key must be secret—that is, known only to the intended parties.

➤ The encryption/decryption process must use a strong encryption algorithm.

Cryptanalysis

Going back to the security object schema shown in Figure 3.1, you can further refine the cryptographic operations performed on the message flowing through the session pipe. *Cryptography* describes how:

➤ The key is used in the symmetric or asymmetric encryption operation.

➤ The encryption operation—namely, substitution or transformation of a message's characters—is performed on the message before it enters the session pipe.

➤ The cleartext is encrypted, in blocks of bits or as individual bits.

Cryptanalysis is the interception and attempted recovery of a key or some specific cleartext from a secured exchange. *Passive interception* surreptitiously gathers any kind of information that flows through the pipe, such as traffic patterns and recurring blocks of encrypted code. Alternatively, an *active interception* attack uses a compromised secret key to reintroduce altered or newly fabricated information back into the session pipe. The method used to perform any cryptanalysis or code cracking depends on where the system security is breached; for example, copies of different cleartext can be captured in the data store prior to encryption, ciphertext can be intercepted in the session pipe, samples of known cleartext and its corresponding ciphertext can be captured through impersonation, and so on. Ciphertext interception through, for example, a network sniffer, typically provides just ciphertext, assuming that the attacker knows of the kind of encryption algorithm used. If the attacker does not have additional information about the nature of the cleartext source, such as file type, language, and so on, it is unlikely—though not impossible—that a key will be exposed. Success of a brute-force attack on any encryption algorithm is a function of the attacker's computing power and the encryption key length. In fact, Windows 2000 uses both the weaker DES 56-bit variation and the more hardened 3DES or TDES.

Statistical patterns in the traffic and recurring characteristics in the ciphertext flow increase the possibility that an attacker can decrypt ciphertext or discover a key. Once a session pipe is compromised, an attacker, through passive interception, will most likely scrutinize frequencies of pattern occurrence (e.g., a probable-word attack). To thwart statistical and structural analyses, you can convert cleartext blocks to ciphertext blocks (block cipher processes) so that there is a less predictable stream, eliminating the possible statistical regularities and pattern correlation.

Logically speaking, as the cost/benefit of uncovering a key increases, and/or the window of opportunity to use "cracked" ciphertext decreases due to the information's useful lifetime, the likelihood of an interception attack also increases. What is noteworthy, however, is that security attacks may not be motivated by logic. Nevertheless, because conventional symmetric encryption is computationally faster than asymmetric encryption, and because strong encryption algorithms are commercially available, symmetric encryption algorithms remain the most common security countermeasure to attacks against confidentiality or privacy.

Distribution Problems

If you look back at Figure 3.1, you can see that both parties share the secret key in the symmetric encryption method to exchange the encrypted information. Doing so is both a strength and a weakness. If the secret key is compromised, the secured exchange is breached. Issuing that key to some party, however, creates the opportunity for an on-demand, confidential virtual communication channel across public namespaces. Furthermore, frequently issuing a key to that same party shortens the time that secured information might be exposed to, for example, passive interception, if a key is compromised. Due to the computational speed of symmetric key distribution, it will always remain part of a comprehensive security strategy.

Distribution problems arise if the two parties are not within physical proximity. The most secure way to distribute a symmetric key is to deliver it physically. But in most case studies on an examination or in the real-world deal outside an enterprise, doing so is not a practical or cost-effective option. One alternative is to establish a specialized server, called a *key distribution center*, as a trusted third party to deliver keys (I will discuss this kind of server, which offers scalable authentication services that the NT 4 primary domain controller has been unable provide, in Chapter 4). A second alternative is to transmit the secret key in a secured fashion without the need for yet another secret key.

Asymmetric Key Encryption

Secret key distribution is a critical part of a comprehensive security plan, so a simple way to deploy those secret keys would be advantageous for a scalable network of distributed consumers and providers. The objective is to secure a session pipe between two parties to exchange confidential information. The process requires:

➤ A strong encryption algorithm

➤ A key that uniquely identifies the owner as a party to privileged data

➤ A key that can be distributed across unsecured namespaces

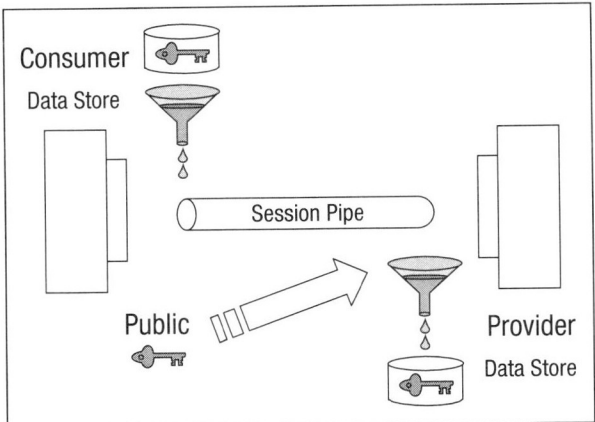

Figure 3.2   Applying asymmetric encryption to a consumer/provider exchange.

As shown in Figure 3.2, a possible solution is to break the key into two comple-mentary parts: a private complement on the encryption side of the session pipe and another complement on the opposite decryption side. One complement key component, like the symmetric key, is secret; the other complement, like the strong encryption algorithm itself, can be publicly known. By definition, a strong en-cryption algorithm cannot be used to generate a key even when the algorithm, ciphertext, and cleartext are known. In a similar context, access to the cleartext, ciphertext, encryption algorithm, or the well-known, public key complement does not reveal the value of the private key complement. The advantage of two comple-mentary but different—or *asymmetric*—keys is that you can publish or exchange the well-known public key across unsecured namespaces. The public key creates ciphertext that can be decrypted only by the complementary private key of the intended receiver.

Thus, asymmetric key encryption uses a set of complementary but different keys—one private and secret, the other public—and a strong encryption algorithm to securely exchange information across unsecured namespaces. The encryption al-gorithm requires greater processing time and hence is operationally slower than a symmetric key encryption scheme. The de facto public key standard, RSA (an acronym formed from the last names of the three inventors: Ron Rivest, Adi Shamir, and Leonard Adelman), uses asymmetric keys that are functions of two very large prime numbers. Unlike DES, which has a fixed-length key, RSA can continue to resist a brute force attack by increasing its key length. The ability to distribute a public key without compromising the integrity of a secret, private key is critical in the development of message confidentiality in distributed security systems. Public keys and asymmetric key encryption algorithms provide more scalable key management, confidentiality, authenticity, and nonrepudiation. How-ever, asymmetric encryption algorithms are several orders of magnitude slower than symmetric algorithms, so they are not typically used for bulk encryption. In addition, they are more vulnerable than symmetric algorithms to cryptoanalytic or code breaking attacks. A good security design would thus use an asymmetric algorithm to establish a secured session (authentication and key transfer) and a symmetric algorithm for encrypting the message.

Active Interception

Asymmetric and symmetric encryption algorithms protect against any passive interception attack modality like wiretaps or traffic analysis. *Active interception* (surreptitiously modifying or fabricating exchanged data) requires a different form of protection. Possession of a secret key implies that you are the chosen participant in a secured exchange of information. But if the secret key is compromised and a message is modified, the integrity of the message will have been compromised unbeknownst to the receiving party. A countermeasure against active interception attack modalities requires authentication of the asset being exchanged. Implementing this security control is more complicated than passive interception countermeasures because this attack strategy raises questions regarding:

➤ Integrity of the asset

➤ Authenticity of the source

➤ Timing of the exchange

In general, if one assumes a secret key is secure, possessing that key and using it in the exchange of information implicitly authenticate the source and confirm the integrity of the asset exchanged. In fact, using a secret key in an exchange also supports claims of nonrepudiation, especially when a timestamp is included in the message. Timing issues for the most part are handled by the transport and network protocols. In fact, IPSec architecture uses sequence numbers instead of timestamps to protect against impersonation attack modalities.

However, sometimes, the receiver of some message or other asset needs to confirm not just the identity of the sender through a shared, secret key but something about the exchanged object itself. If corporate business objectives require separate corroborative evidence of authenticity and integrity, the company needs to implement independent countermeasures against active interception of an asset or message.

Authentication and Integrity Controls

You can apply a symmetric key to a message digest to generate an HMAC just before data is exchanged. This calculated HMAC block, like a checksum, is sent along with the asset to the receiving party. When the receiving party gets the asset or message, it applies its copy of the symmetric key to the asset and generates its own HMAC tag. If the two generated tags or message digests agree, the integrity of an asset or message was not compromised during the exchange process. I will further discuss these and similar topics in Chapter 9.

One-Way Hash Functions

The hash function or message digest takes a variable-length message and, like a meat grinder, converts it into a fixed-length output string or hash value. A mathematical algorithm, similar to but not the same as an encryption algorithm, generates a 128-bit to 256-bit number or message digest derived from the message contents when a hash value is created. There is no easy way to reconstruct the pieces of "meat" from the extruded meat "pâté" because the meat grinding is a one-way process. The identity of the meat, however, is uniquely defined by the contents of the generated pâté. Similarly, the hash value is considered an electronic fingerprint of the variable-length message. A good hash function is considered collision resistant when it's not very likely that two different variable-length messages will converge on the same hash value—a collision—no matter how small that hash output is.

This hash value or authentication block (which is independent of the message or content) can prove authentication through comparison. You can independently generate a second hash function when you receive either a message or a demand for verification, and compare the two authentication blocks. If one character in the message has changed since the message was created, you know the hash values are no longer identical and thus the authenticity of the message or asset is questioned. As shown in Figure 3.3, the receiver of a message compares the results of the second hash function to the hash value sent with the message. If the two values agree, the message has not been modified during the exchange.

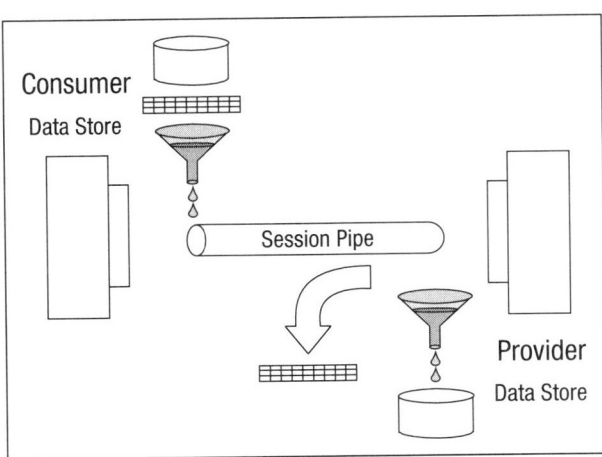

Figure 3.3   A hash function exchange.

The Windows 2000 Implementation

Microsoft uses two industry-standard cryptographic algorithms for creating message authentication code or digests—Message Digest 5 (MD5) and Secure Hash Algorithm (SHA-1)—to generate an HMAC. MD5 converts 512-bit blocks of cleartext to 128-bit-long tags. SHA-1 was designed for use with the Digital Signature Standard (DSS) by the National Institute of Standards and Technology (NIST) and the National Security Agency (NSA). It is slower than MD5 because it converts the same-size cleartext block into a larger, more secure 160-bit message digest.

Comparing hash values does not reveal the content of the actual message. For example, a personal banking or automatic teller machine (ATM) generates and compares hash values of the password keyed into its console with the personal identification number (PIN) it reads from the magnetic strip on the swiped smart card. If the two hash values agree, a transaction can proceed. The PIN password is never actually revealed in the authentication process. The NT LAN Manager (NTLM) challenge/response security service works in a similar way. The computational processing in encryption/decryption is, thus, eliminated. More significantly, information is never compromised because it is never revealed.

Sometimes, you can satisfy business objectives without using encryption. Generating asymmetric keys is more processor intensive and therefore slower than generating symmetric keys; using both encryption algorithms is slower than generating a hash number. In fact, when server workload or the processing of bulk messaging is an issue, it is not always necessary to encrypt a message. A message digest does not first have to be decrypted to prove authenticity.

Often, however, the hash function is keyed or encrypted to produce a digitally signed Message Authentication Code (MAC). As shown in Figure 3.4, the receiver can authenticate this digital signature by comparing his or her own generated hash number with the signed hash number from the sender using the receiver's copy of the shared, secret key. If a message were intercepted and modified during an exchange, the value of the signed, encrypted message digest would not necessarily be revealed. In a subsequent comparison of the two message digests, any discovered differences would indicate tampering.

Entity Authentication through Proof of Possession

One way the receiving party can determine the authenticity of the sending party is to send a cleartext challenge to that party. If the sending party possesses the private key complementing the public key that the receiving party is using to key the cleartext challenge, the sending party demonstrates proof of possession of that particular private key. The receiver initiates the exchange session and spontaneously creates the cleartext challenge, so impersonation attack modalities are not likely.

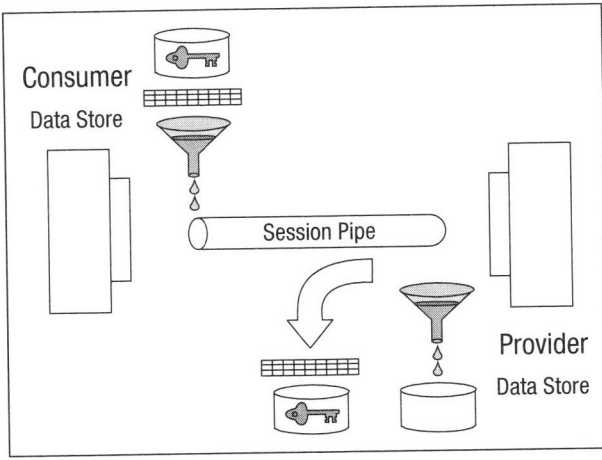

Figure 3.4 Applying a secured hash function or MAC to a consumer/provider exchange.

Secret Key Agreements

You can trade mutually complementary portions of secret keys using asymmetric encryption. Each participant creates and exchanges a random number encrypted with the public key of the other. The two random numbers are exchanged and, based on prior agreement, combined to form a secret, symmetric key that can be used henceforth in symmetric exchanges of information.

Bulk Data Encryption

Symmetric encryption algorithms are several orders of magnitude faster than asymmetric encryption. Furthermore, these encryption algorithms (like DES) can also be implemented at the hardware level in the form of low-cost chips for greater scalability and lowered total cost of ownership (TCO). The fundamental problem is the exchange of the secret key across the nonsecured channel. A secret key for the session encrypts the message. To compensate for the increased computational overhead of asymmetric encryption, only the session key is encrypted with the receiver's public key. Only the intended party can decrypt the public key to unlock the storage.

Digital Envelope

When two layers of encryption to protect a message are used, the resulting package is called a *digital envelope*. First, the message itself is encoded using symmetric encryption; then, the key to decode the message is encrypted using public encryption. Thus, only the key is protected with public-key encryption. Encoding this smaller block of data dramatically reduces the computational overhead associated with asymmetric encryption.

Certificates and Key Management Services

In many commercial exchanges, a signature provides the most common level of integrity and nonrepudiation. The three algorithms that support a digital counterpart to the written signature are:

➤ Hash-based signature

➤ DSS

➤ RSA signature

Hash signatures use a cryptographically secure hash function (such as MD5 or SHA-1) to produce a single value from the file. By hashing together the file and an appended a secret key, you generate a single value in the form of a tag or code block. The file is shipped with the authenticating code block (but without the secret key) to a second party, who also possesses the same secret key. The receiver adds the secret key and recalculates the hash value. If the hash values are identical, the signatures are valid. As mentioned earlier, using a hash signature requires less computational overhead than using other signature technologies. A disadvantage of this technique, however, is that you use conventional encryption. The shared, secret key must be distributed to all who are participating in the secured information exchange. The greater the number of participants in the secured exchange, the greater the number of secret keys exposed to possible attack, and the more likely any one secret key will be compromised.

Both DSS and RSA use an asymmetric encryption algorithm that solves the problem of distributing and storing keys. DSS, developed in conjunction with the NSA, is a signature-only system designed to avoid using encryption algorithms. In fact, although the U.S. government heavily restricts software that involves general encryption, security technology that exclusively provides an authentication function like DSS is openly exported outside the United States. RSA signatures, unlike those of DSS, can encrypt data as well as prove authenticity.

Making keys with longer-bit strings to resist attacks hardens both hash-based and public-key algorithms. Sharing a secret key doubles the possibility of a security breach when you are using hash-based algorithms. An asymmetric encryption algorithm is more secure than conventional symmetric encryption because, even though there are many published public keys available in an unsecured namespace, there is only one secret key for every public/private key pair. However, in a hostile environment, publishing a public key can also increase the probability of impersonation.

Digital Signatures

Distributing a public key solves the problem of exchanging the more computationally efficient symmetric, secret key used in conventional encryption algorithms. In addition, it offers a way to potentially authenticate parties exchanging messages. A *digital signature*, like an electronic fingerprint, uniquely identifies the package as originating from the party possessing the key that complements the easily accessible public key. Unfortunately, there is no guarantee—especially outside an enterprise's boundary—that the public key in use really belongs to the intended party. Active impersonation through forgery of a public key can be prevented only if some trusted authority vouches for that public key's authenticity.

A Certificate Authority (CA) is a certifying third party that vouches for the public key's authenticity. It applies its "universally" trusted digital signature to a public key and some ID of the key owner. This certificate is then made available much like the original public key. Now, however, the CA manages the key's distribution. The issued certificate conforms to the International Telecommunications Union (ITU) Telecommunication Standardization (ITU-T) X.509 version 3 standard, which I discuss in more detail in Chapter 7. The certificate contains the following:

➤ The public key of the key holder

➤ The certificate's date of expiration

➤ Detailed information about the holder of that key

Extensibility

Each certificate, although primarily invented to validate the authenticity of a public key, also has associated with it an extensible set of data fields. These certifications are similar to the access control lists (ACLs) associated with resources in the NT file system (NTFS); the extensible fields store an object's attributes much like ACLs contain access control entries (ACEs). The extensible fields delineate not only group membership but also object permissions. It is important to consider that a CA provides the following key-management services:

➤ Public operations for a consumer and quick access to a valid, authentic public key

➤ Privileged operations for a service provider and a certificate corroborating that provider's authenticity

Creating strong certification structures depends upon these extensible data fields and how both consumer and service provider use them. This concept as well as certification services will continue to be major trends in the future development of distributed security systems.

Certificates

Certificates contain the private key of a CA, which publishes its public key in the form of a root certificate. As long as the key holder has a certificate maintained by a CA, the CA's public key opens its digital certificate that corroborates the key holder's authenticity. An organization or provider installs the root certificate of some trusted CA outside the enterprise in a certificate data store. The private key in that root certificate is used to open and confirm certificates issued by the CA outside the enterprise to validate key holders. Likewise, a CA within an enterprise publishes its root certificate outside its boundaries. When properly installed within other organizations, the root certificate provides the private key that will open certificates associated with public keys of enterprise users and services.

CA Hierarchies

Typically, a hierarchy of authorities is deployed. As shown in Figure 3.5, Windows 2000 provides for both a root and subordinate CA. The root CA is the first CA in an organization and, hence, the most trusted when multiple CAs are deployed. The root certificate authority either certifies itself or secures certification from some worldwide commercial organization. A CA that is not a root CA is

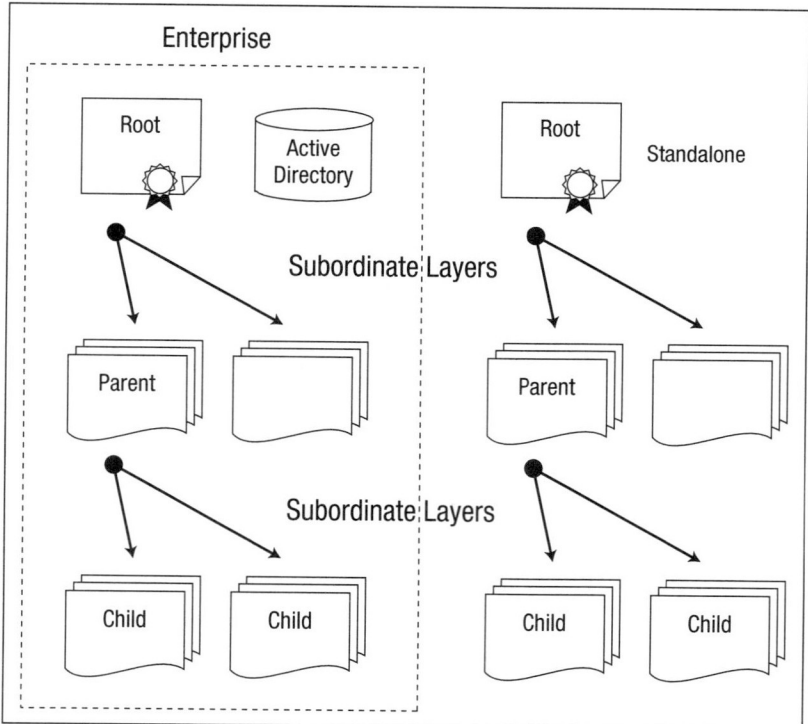

Figure 3.5 Certificate authority hierarchies.

subordinate to either the root or to another subordinate CA. A subordinate can issue its own certificates, but these are certified by its parent CA. A subordinate CA may act as a bridge that serves only to create certificates for other subordinate CAs. Finally, an enterprise CA is part of the Active Directory (AD); a standalone CA is not.

An organization might implement a hierarchy of CAs to achieve its corporate objectives. In fact, it is possible to have multiple CA hierarchies within an organization. Deploying multiple CAs offers:

➤ Structural support of organizational or administrative functions

➤ Separation of specific security technologies (e.g., smart card logons)

➤ Distribution of subordinate CAs on different sides of slow WAN links to facilitate access

➤ Redundancy and maintenance

Similarly, CA-based trust relationships can be created within or across organizations. An administrator can create a trust and select specific certificate purposes (such as client authentication, server authentication, time stamping, and so on) of that trusted CA. For example, to separate a specific security or administrative function, an administrator can configure a trusted root certificate authority to validate only certificates issued by a CA for smart card logons. Likewise, if two different organizations are subordinates under the same root CA, the two organizations implicitly trust each other. In addition to trust relationships and inheritance, Windows 2000 supports automatic certification enrollment defined through group policy at specific organizational levels.

The following factors can affect successful key deployment:

➤ Replication issues regarding authenticating information

➤ Verifying group policy and the effects of auto-enrollment

➤ Verifying certificate templates

➤ Effect of certificate revocation and certification revocation list (CRL) lifetimes

➤ Maintenance of CAs

➤ Certificate publisher's group membership

Providing Certificate Services

The CA's authority lies in the fact that it issues, renews, and revokes valid public key certificates for members of a specific user community. The community trusts the CA to validate the identity of the holder with a public/private key pair. The public key's authenticity lies in the credibility of the issuer of that certificate form. Auditing security, managing public keys, and maintaining the certification lists have become services of the certificate services provider. Because of these administrative roles, CAs maintain two databases: one that lists the certificate holders and one that lists the revoked certificates. The planned expiration as well as unplanned revocation of a certificate—published in a CRL—are parts of the provided certificate services.

Certificates are granted to and recognized by users of a specific community. The corporate business objectives usually define the criteria that requesters of this authentication must meet to receive certification by the CA. Thus, certificate authorities are policy independent. Likewise, a certificate can be requested and distributed through a variety of transport mechanisms. CAs are also transport independent. Certificate enrollment is standards based and uses message formats that support Public Key Cryptography Standards (PKCS) and the more recent Internet Engineering Task Force (IETF) Public Key Infrastructure X.509 (PKIX) draft standards. A CA typically accepts the PKCS #10 request package and issues an X.509 version 3 certificate in a PKCS #7 digital envelope. An exported certificate and key pair are encrypted as a PKCS #12 message. An Internet Architecture Board (IAB) draft standard called *Certificate Request Syntax* refines certificate enrollment.

The PKI Suite

Windows 2000 PKI is a suite of technologies and services that are relatively invisible to the consumer. Table 3.3 summarizes the standards that Microsoft included in its PKI suite.

Paralleling the historical theme of system architecture supporting increased scalability, PKI in Windows 2000 provides the security platform on which the Active Directory Services Interfaces (ADSI) can support million-user enterprises. It is noteworthy that these security technologies are nonproprietary and standards-based protocols. The goal of the ADSI, which I discuss in greater detail in Chapter 9, is to provide a unified view of directories and namespaces regardless of location or operating system platform. Windows 2000 PKI, the security platform for AD, reflects that theme.

In Figure 3.6, a user/consumer within the security context of logon services (provided by the NTLM domain/Kerberos protocol) uses network resources as defined by the organization and policies of AD.

Table 3.3 A summary of Windows 2000 PKI standards-based features.	
Standard	**Description**
Authenticode	Digital signatures that verify software origin, authenticity, and integrity
Certificate Revocation List v2 (CRL)	Part of PKIX (X.509); cited in RFC 2459
IP Security (IPSec)	Support for network encryption at the Internet Protocol (IP) protocol layer
Personal computer/smart card	Specifications based on International Organization for Standardization (ISO) 7816 standards
Public Key Cryptography for Initial Authentication in Kerberos (PKINIT)	PK-based authentication using Kerberos 5
Public Key Cryptography Standards (PKCS)	Certificate message standards and formats
Public Key Infrastructure X.509 (PKIX)	IETF draft for interoperable PKI (RFC 2459)
Secure Sockets Layer (SSL) v3	HTTP-based authentication, integrity, and confidentiality
Server Gateway Cryptography (SGC)	Similar to TLS, this SSP requires a 128-bit session key and authorized CA certificates
Transport Layer Security (TLS)	Implemented by the SChannel SSPI along with SSL v3

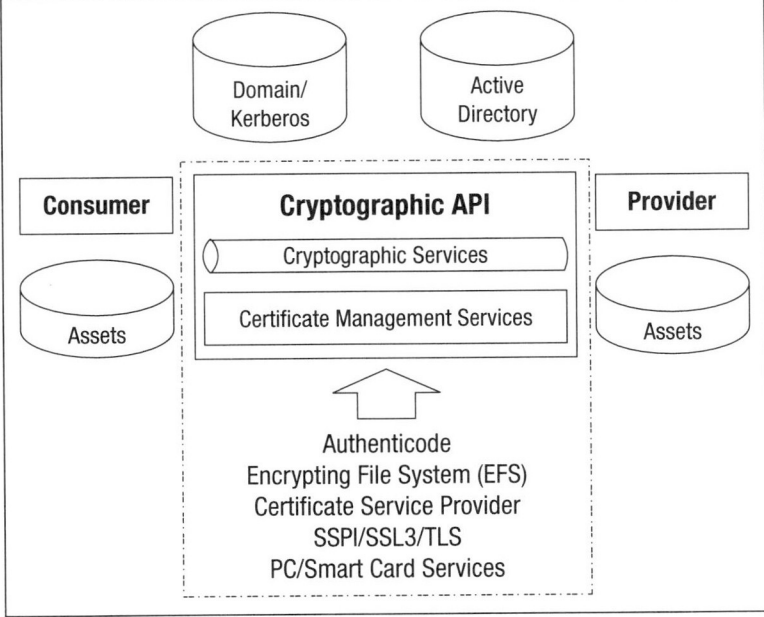

Figure 3.6 Microsoft PKI.

Microsoft CryptoAPI

To support exchanges between consumers (user/user) or consumers and providers—the generic scenario in this book—PKI provides services for the entire ranges of information technology (IT) security objectives in a distributed and scalable manner. Compatible with either legacy domain controllers or the Kerberos protocol, the Microsoft Cryptographic Application Programming Interface (CAPI) supports cryptographic service providers (CSPs) and certificate management services. The variety of services that CAPI supports is hierarchically shown in Table 3.4.

Security Support Provider Interface (SSPI) supports these primary security support provider protocols:

➤ *NTLM/Kerberos*—User authentication

➤ *SChannel security support providers*—Secured network exchanges

➤ *Server Gateway Cryptography (SGC)*—HTTP-based authentication

➤ *Distributed Password Authentication (DPA)*—Internet-based membership authentication

CAPI supports both cryptographic services and certificate management services. The Cryptographic Services layer must integrate with the domain administration/enterprise policy model as well as support potentially different providers of public-key algorithms. CAPI supports installable CSPs, each of which manages its own security material. Similarly, the certificate management services administer specific certificate stores or repositories for certificates and associate data in the "Providing Certificate Services" section earlier in this chapter. Table 3.5 shows standard certificate stores. Note that these certificate stores are logical representations of credentials available on a system-wide basis supporting authentication services in the AD namespace.

Table 3.4 CAPI-supported services.	
Services	**Description**
Smart cards	User authentication
Authenticode	Origin and integrity; code-signing
SSPI	Security context management
DES hardware and RSA-based CSP	Encryption algorithms
EFS	Directory- and file-level security

Table 3.5 Standard certificate stores.	
Certificate Store	**Contents**
ROOT	Self-signed CA certificates for trusted root CAs
TRUST	Certificate Trust Lists (CTLs) that describe the CA hierarchy
CA	Certification verification chains, including issuing CA certificates and intermediate CA certificates that show certification-verification chains
MY	User or computer certificates for the related private key
UserDS	Logical schema of the certificate repository stored in the AD

Global Encryption Policies

Even though security keys can be encrypted using different algorithms and technologies, the primary issue is key length. The most common commercially available encryption algorithms are provided by RSA, Inc., and use key lengths of up to 128 bits. However, encryption algorithms impact issues of national and international security. Different countries have restricted the importation/exportation of 128-bit encryption algorithms, whereas weak encryption systems using 40-bit keys are freely traded. Likewise, it is common for the banking industry to use DES products globally. Cryptography, formerly considered munitions, is now under the control of the U.S. Department of Commerce. Until 1999, the United States prohibited exportation of such software technology. France has even stricter licensing policies that control the marketing of cryptography in that country. A global policy has been proposed; it would create an international key-escrow system where copies of keys 128 bits or greater in length used by consumers and/or providers around the world would be stored. Access to these keys would be made available to authorities only through the written order of an international court.

Practice Questions

Question 1

> Which of the following are encryption technologies? [Check all correct answers]
>
> ❑ a. Asymmetric key encryption
>
> ❑ b. Symmetric key encryption
>
> ❑ c. Hash function
>
> ❑ d. All of the above

Answers a and b are correct. Asymmetric key encryption and symmetric key encryption are encryption technologies. Hash functions convert a message to some hash value for comparison, not for decryption or reading, so answers c and d are incorrect.

Question 2

> What factor guarantees message confidentiality?
>
> ○ a. Proper social attitudes in the user community
>
> ○ b. Length of the message
>
> ○ c. Length of the key
>
> ○ d. Authenticity of the sender

Answer c is correct. Length of the key guarantees message confidentiality. Proper social attitudes in the user community, length of the message, and authenticity of the sender do not guarantee confidentiality. Therefore, answers a, b, and d are incorrect.

Question 3

> Confidentiality, using symmetric encryption, depends on what conditions?
> [Check all correct answers]
>
> ❏ a. Both parties have the secret key.
>
> ❏ b. Secret keys are secure.
>
> ❏ c. A strong encryption algorithm is used.
>
> ❏ d. The receiver has been authenticated.

Answers a, b, c, and d are correct. Symmetric encryption algorithms depend upon parties sharing the same secret key, ensuring that the security of that key has not been compromised, and using a strong encryption algorithm. Only the intended receiver has a copy of the shared secret key, so possessing the key is evidence of authenticity.

Question 4

> What is the procedural order in using symmetric encryption to exchange a message? Arrange all appropriate steps in the proper order.
>
> Create the message.
>
> Apply your private key to the message.
>
> Apply your intended receiver's public key to the message.
>
> Send the message.

The correct answer is:

Create the message.

Apply your private key to the message.

Send the message.

In symmetric encryption, public keys are not used. Therefore, "Apply your intended receiver's public key to the message" should not be included in the ordered list.

Question 5

> Which item correctly describes asymmetric encryption?
>
> ○ a. The algorithm is faster than symmetric encryption.
>
> ○ b. The algorithm is slower than both a hash function and symmetric encryption.
>
> ○ c. The private key can be exchanged in an unsecured namespace.
>
> ○ d. The public key must be protected from exposure to unauthorized parties.

Answer b is correct. The asymmetric encryption algorithm is slower than hash functions and symmetric encryption. Answer a is incorrect because asymmetric encryption is slower than symmetric encryption. The private key is kept in a secured data store, whereas the public key is published across unsecured namespaces. Therefore, answers c and d are incorrect.

Question 6

> You should always use an asymmetric public key when performing bulk encryption to facilitate exchanges across unsecured namespaces.
>
> ○ a. True
>
> ○ b. False

Answer b, false, is correct. Asymmetric encryption requires greater computational resources and time to encrypt data; symmetric encryption is the method of choice when performing bulk encryption.

Question 7

> What is the procedural order when you are receiving an asymmetric encrypted message? Arrange all appropriate steps in the proper order.
>
> Open the message.
>
> Apply your public key to the message.
>
> Apply your private key to the message.
>
> Apply the sender's public key to the message.
>
> Apply the sender's private key to the message.

The correct answer is:

Open the message.

Apply your private key to the message.

The sender used your public key to encrypt the message, so only your private key will decrypt the ciphertext. Neither the sender's public nor the sender's private key will decrypt the message.

Question 8

Both symmetric and asymmetric encryption provide solutions to the issue of nonrepudiation.

○ a. True

○ b. False

Answer a, true, is correct. Unless the secret key is compromised, only an intended party can send or receive an encrypted message with a specific private key. Therefore, answer b is incorrect.

Question 9

What service(s) are supported by CAPI?

○ a. CSPs

○ b. DSS

○ c. DES

○ d. SSPI

○ e. 3DES

○ f. All of the above

○ g. None of the above

Answer f is correct. CAPI (Microsoft Cryptographic Application Programming Interface) supports Cryptographic Service Providers (CSPs), Digital Signature Standard (DSS), Data Encryption Standard (DES), Security Service Provider Interface (SSPI), and triple Data Encryption Standard (3DES). All answers are correct, so answer g is incorrect.

Question 10

> Your client develops software and wants to markedly improve its market
> share. It has added one new Windows 2000 server to a legacy NT 4 domain
> with two domain controllers and an application member server to improve
> production. You want to improve customers' confidence in the authenticity
> and integrity of the software that they purchase online from this company.
> What course of action should you suggest? [Choose the best answer]
>
> ○ a. You suggest installing an enterprise CA.
>
> ○ b. You suggest installing a standalone CA.
>
> ○ c. You suggest contacting VeriSign or Thawte.
>
> ○ d. None of the above.

Answer c is correct. The configuration stated in the question is a legacy domain
model, so the servers will not use Active Directory Services (ADS). You can
install only a standalone CA (Certificate Authority) in this environment. Answer b
however, does not adequately address the stated objective to improve customer
confidence in both authenticity and integrity. Although software certification by
the developer will ensure integrity of the exchanged package, it does not address
the level of trust in the authenticator, especially in a global market. The best
answer is c, which is to seek authentication from some validating third party that
has worldwide name recognition and reputation. Answers a, b, and d are not the
best courses of action, so they are incorrect.

Need to Know More?

 Stallings, William. *Network Security Essentials: Applications and Standards.* Prentice Hall, Upper Saddle River, New Jersey, 1999. ISBN 0-13-016093-8. This vendor-neutral overview of cryptography, system security, and network security applications describes and references the major security themes in a clear, technical style. Its balanced approach and broad range of topics offer a necessary perspective to texts specifically discussing Windows 2000 security design.

 Search the TechNet CD (or its online version through **www.microsoft.com**) and the *Windows 2000 Server Resource Kit* CD using the keywords "DES", "CA", "Kerberos", and "PKI".

 **http://microsoft.com/windows2000/library/planning/security/pki.asp** is the location of Microsoft's Windows 2000 White Paper, titled *Microsoft Windows 2000 Public Key Infrastructure,* originally posted in April 1999. This technical paper is the primary source of information for the Windows 2000 implementation of the public key infrastructure.

 **www.itl.nist.gov/fipspubs/fip46-2.htm** is the location of the DES 1993 standard. *Data Encryption Standard 1993* specifies a cryptographic algorithm that federal organizations can use to protect sensitive data. To maintain the confidentiality and integrity of the information represented by the data, it may be necessary to protect data during transmission or while in storage.

Kerberos Security

. . . .

Terms you'll need to understand:

✓ Kerberos protocol

✓ Authentication, authorization, and auditing (AAA) server

✓ Symmetric and asymmetric encryption algorithms

✓ Kerberos Authentication Service (AS) exchange

✓ AS request/reply

✓ Ticket-granting ticket (TGT)

✓ Kerberos ticket-granting service (TGS) exchange

✓ TGS request/reply

✓ Client/server (CS) authentication exchange

✓ Kerberos application request/reply

✓ Key Distribution Center (KDC)

✓ Hash function

✓ Cross-domain exchanges

✓ Security Support Provider Interface (SSPI)

Techniques you'll need to master:

✓ Describing the Microsoft Kerberos enhancements

✓ Describing the steps in the Kerberos AS exchange

✓ Describing the steps in the Kerberos TGS exchange

✓ Describing the steps in the Kerberos CS authentication exchange

✓ Describing the steps in cross-domain authentication of a service request

This chapter deals with the information technology (IT) security controls of authentication (who?) and authorization (what?). I begin by presenting an overview of the Massachusetts Institute of Technology (MIT) Kerberos protocol because it is the foundation for Microsoft's implementation of the protocol. Next, I discuss Microsoft's enhancements to the MIT Kerberos protocol. This information builds a foundation for the discussion of interoperability later in this chapter and a rationale for future enhancements in Microsoft's Multiple Authentication Architecture implemented through Security Support Provider Interface (SSPI), mentioned in Chapter 2. I then describe how Kerberos fits into the security protocol picture as a whole. Lastly, I describe common Security Support Providers (SSPs) that this interface supports: NT 4 NT LAN Manager (NTLM) and the Windows 2000 Kerberos authentication protocols. Chapter 7 discusses other supported SSPs: Secure Channel (SChannel) protocols.

This chapter also represents a turning point in how material is presented. As discussed in Chapter 1, my objectives are to prepare you for both simulated case studies on a Microsoft exam and real-life case studies. In Chapters 2 and 3, I introduced terms and definitions that provided the foundation for the fundamental IT security controls: authentication, confidentiality, and integrity. In this chapter, you will begin dealing with real-life problems you might encounter as an independent consultant.

MIT Kerberos: The Basis for Microsoft's Implementation

The Kerberos protocol, the default authentication protocol in Windows 2000, was proposed and first used in Project Athena conducted at MIT in the 1980s. The name "Kerberos" is a reference to the mythological three-headed dog that guarded the gates to Hades. The original proposed protocol in 1983 was to have provided the "triple A" services of authentication, authorization, and auditing (AAA). Of the three AAA services, MIT implemented only authentication services.

Goals and Requirements

The goals and requirements of the MIT Kerberos protocol are:

➤ Easy access that requires minimal information such as a username and password

➤ Strong authentication across an unsecured environment

➤ Scalability across a large, modular, distributed server architecture

➤ Reliable accessibility to security services in a scalable, distributed server architecture

➤ Prevention of an impersonation attack where one of the following occurs:

   ➤ A legitimately authenticated user attempts to request unauthorized resources or services (a rogue user)

   ➤ An outside intruder (a cracker or bogie) impersonates an authenticated, authorized user (a spoof)

   ➤ An outside intruder gains unauthorized, illegitimate access to the network and obtains confidential information

➤ The Kerberos server itself is both physically and logically secured

Assumptions

The MIT Kerberos protocol makes several assumptions:

➤ *AAA servers are always accessible.* There is no countermeasure to interference attack modalities, specifically denial of service (DOS) attacks, where the AAA server is actively prevented from fully participating in legitimate exchanges with clients.

➤ *Secret keys are secured.* It is the responsibility of the principal (discussed later in this chapter) to store secret keys in a secure manner and to replace them as quickly as possible if a possible breach in that security occurs.

➤ *Symmetric keys are prone to attack.* There is no countermeasure to impersonation attack modalities, specifically password-guessing attacks where techniques are applied offline to solve the character combination in the secret key.

➤ *Timing is loosely synchronized.* There must be some clock-synchronization scheme across all participating network servers to differentiate slight discrepancies in timestamps from impersonation attack modalities such as replay attacks, where messages are intercepted and replayed out of temporal sequence to impersonate some authenticated principal or service.

➤ *Security identifiers (SIDs) are not reused.* Recycling of SIDs could evoke stale access control lists (ACLs), lists that describe how a user or group can manipulate properties of the specific resource object. An outdated ACL could permit new, potentially unauthorized consumers to have access to resources and services for which they have no authorization.

Components of the Protocol

MIT Kerberos uses a symmetric encryption protocol with appropriate data stores in some KDC. This encryption technique is discussed in Chapter 3. In Windows 2000 native mode, domain controllers (DCs) that run the Kerberos services are also referred to as KDCs. KDCs are discussed in more detail later in this chapter.

Kerberos security services can be divided into three exchanges, sometimes referred to as *subprotocols*. In this case, the term *protocol* refers to predetermined steps in any of the exchange procedures:

➤ *Authentication Service (AS) exchange*—The consumer requests authentication services in the form of a Kerberos Authentication Service Request (KRB_AS_REQ) from some AAA server. This consists of both the consumer's registered user ID and some encrypted preauthentication data that proves the knowledge of some secret key. The key response is a ticket-granting ticket (TGT) in the form of a Kerberos Authentication Service Reply (KRB_AS_REP).

➤ *Ticket-granting service (TGS) exchange*—The Kerberos client that is running on the workstation requests services in the form of a Kerberos Ticket-Granting Service Request (KRB_TGS_REQ). This request consists of a user ID, authenticator of that ID, targeted service provider, and TGT. The response is a Kerberos Ticket-Granting Service Reply (KRB_TGS_REP).

➤ *Client/server (CS) authentication exchange*—The Kerberos client that is running on the workstation requests services from a service provider in the form of a Kerberos Application Request (KRB_AP_REQ). This request consists of an encrypted authenticator, keyed with a session key common to consumer and provider, the TGS ticket, and a flag requesting mutual authentication. If the flag that indicates mutual authentication is set (during Kerberos configuration, not by the user), the service provider uses the session key to decrypt the time in the consumer's authenticator. The service provider then returns that time in a Kerberos Application Reply (KRB_AP_REP) to the consumer as a security control against a replay attack.

Note: The use of the term "protocol" or "subprotocol" to describe the separate Kerberos exchanges refers to the specific procedural steps that the ticket exchanges must follow, not to some packet design specification such as Transmission Control Protocol (TCP), User Datagram Protocol (UDP), or Internet Protocol (IP).

Version 5 Enhancements

The current version of Kerberos, version 5, is a standards-based distributed security protocol described in Request For Comments (RFC) 1510 that uses a symmetric key to mutually authenticate servers/servers and clients/servers. Some significant Kerberos 5 enhancements described in RFC 1510 are as follows:

➤ *Replaceable encryption systems*—Ciphertext is tagged with an encryption type identifier to allow you to specify different encryption algorithms. Kerberos 4 uses only data encryption standard (DES).

➤ *Replaceable network protocols*—Network addresses are tagged, allowing you to specify different network address types. Kerberos 4 required exclusively IP, a part of the TCP/IP network protocol suite.

➤ *Standardized messaging*—All message structures in Kerberos 5 are unambiguously defined using Abstract Syntax Notation One (ASN.1) and Basic Encoding Rules (BER). Kerberos 4, which incorporated a "receiver makes right" philosophy, allowed a user to define the byte ordering in the message.

➤ *Time To Live (TTL)*—Timestamping includes explicit start and end times that permit arbitrarily long lifetimes for Kerberos validated program execution. Kerberos 4, which used an 8-bit field, counted five-minute units of time and thus imposed a maximum ticket lifetime of 21.25 hours.

➤ *Authentication forwarding*—In a scalable, distributed server architecture, to achieve efficient and transparent exchanges of services and information, it is necessary to be able to forward a service request on behalf of some consumer to other trusted service providers. Kerberos 4 did not allow this forwarding to occur.

➤ *Principal naming schemes*—Identifiers are multicomponent names that can accommodate as many components as are necessary to identify the principal. The naming convention follows the standard ASN.1 GeneralStrings. In the Unix culture, these identifiers are written exclusively in uppercase. In Windows 2000, they appear in all lowercase. Kerberos 4 did not support this standardized naming scheme feature.

➤ *Subsession keys*—The session key between consumer and provider is likely to be replayed often, so it is vulnerable to impersonation attack modalities. Both the consumer and service provider can renegotiate and exchange a secured subsession key with an especially short lifetime for one-time session exchanges. A new subsession key could be generated for each exchange. Kerberos 4 did not support this feature.

Microsoft's Implementation of Kerberos 5

The discussion of MIT Kerberos offers a historical perspective in which to better understand Microsoft's implementation of the Kerberos protocol. Microsoft's immediate objective was to leverage its well-established system of access authorization with a more scalable authentication protocol. As already mentioned, only one of the three heads—authentication—works in the MIT implementation. Microsoft has brought life to the remaining two heads of the mythological gatekeeper—authorization and auditing. In this section, I'll discuss the enhancements that Microsoft made to Kerberos 5, specifically in the use of public key infrastructure, ticket structure, and in providing security support services to the Active Directory (AD) through the KDC. I'll explain how the Microsoft process works by providing an annotated look at it. I'll also cover cross-domain authentication, delegation of authentication, account database, and Kerberos policy.

Public Key Infrastructure (PKI)

PKI, discussed in Chapter 3, differs from the Kerberos 5 protocol in that it uses an asymmetric encryption algorithm, which requires a pair of keys, and certificate-management services for authentication. Microsoft has enhanced MIT Kerberos 5 by incorporating public-key encryption in the authentication phase to support PC/smart card technology. The smart card offers an alternative password logon for domain authentication. These enhancements, described in an Internet draft of Public Key Cryptography for Initial Authentication in Kerberos (PKINIT), are examples of the flexibility of the Microsoft Cryptographic Application Programming Interface (CAPI) and the implementation of an installable CSP. PKINIT integrates transparently with the distributed authentication and authorization services of Kerberos and AD.

Ticket Structure

Kerberos protocol specifically adds a series of flags that can be set in an exchanged ticket, different time settings (start, expiration, and renewal), and a *nonce* (a random value used as a countermeasure against impersonation attack modalities during both the AS and TGS exchanges). These changes primarily increase the flexibility of the Kerberos structure and are specific countermeasures to impersonation attack modalities.

These flags, stored as a bit string in a 32-bit field, are significant in controlling message flow or, for example, in signaling the need for mutual authentication. In the exchange between consumer and service provider, not only can the principals negotiate the use of a subsession key for one-time encryption of messages, but they can also sequentially number each message that is exchanged. It is also noteworthy that the mutual authentication flag must be set when you are configuring Kerberos; the user cannot set it.

Other Enhancements

Microsoft has enhanced Kerberos 5 in several other ways:

➤ Microsoft relies heavily on extensible fields in the Kerberos tickets and its integration with the AD to manage additional credentials (such as global and universal group membership) to help determine authorization.

➤ Through the AD, Group Policy Objects (GPOs), and the use of Microsoft Management Console (MMC) snap-ins such as Local Computer Policy, you can easily implement system-wide audit and tracking policies.

In effect, Microsoft has, through integration with AD, added authorization and auditing, the two originally planned, but never implemented, Kerberos security services.

Microsoft's enhancements make possible the following characteristics of Windows 2000:

➤ *Efficient authentication of consumers and service providers*—The consumer presents credentials directly to a distributed architecture of service providers. Authentication no longer depends on repeated calls to some DC, so it is faster and impacts network bandwidth less than the recurring legacy NT 4 exchanges between the Local Security Authority (LSA) and the Security Accounts Manager (SAM) on the DC. Principal credentials are stored either on the client workstation in a data store called the *credentials cache* or in the "cloud" of the AD spread across every DC in the enterprise.

➤ *Mutual authentication of both principals in a distributed services environment*— The (security) down-level NT 4 domain model was conceived of in the context of a secure intranet architecture; neither services nor the server architecture were distributed. NTLM, the down-level security protocol, assumes that all servers are known and therefore authentic. The only unknown principal that requires authentication is the consumer who is logging in with some registered user ID and password. Kerberos challenges both principals in an exchange of information or services.

 Microsoft uses the hierarchical concept of *up-level* (AD and Kerberos) and *down-level* (directory database and NTLM) in its seminars and technical literature. Remember that the default setup configuration is the deployment of Windows 2000 servers and legacy NT 4 DCs in an enterprise structure (a mixed mode organization). AD and Kerberos are not enabled in mixed mode by default; they are enabled in native mode.

➤ *Delegation of authentication*—NTLM uses local impersonation to access resources; it does not pass-through client data to support many service providers distributed across the enterprise. Kerberos uses a ticket for pass-through to a back-end server (a *proxy ticket*) to impersonate the client and support requests to distributed services on remote servers.

➤ *Scalable and easy trust management*—NTLM offers one-way trust relationships across domains; Kerberos establishes by default the more flexible two-way transitive trust relationship. This transitive trust structure supports the building of chains or trees in which some parent domain spawns a child domain. Credentials supplied by some trusted authority can apply to all branches in the tree and—when the tree trusts other trees—to all trees in the forest.

➤ *Interoperability across heterogeneous platforms*—Kerberos is a standards-based protocol, and the Microsoft enhancements are part of an Internet draft recommended to the IETF. Therefore, Windows 2000 security is not only extensible but scalable to other networks that also use the Kerberos security protocol, specifically the Unix operating system.

KDC

The Kerberos protocol is physically mapped to a Kerberos client service that is running on some workstation supporting the consumer, some server supporting the service provider, and the trusted third-party Kerberos server service. This third-party intermediary is known as the KDC. In the Unix culture, it manages the database directory of all principals in the Kerberos realm. In the Windows 2000 culture, the KDC is integrated with AD, where principal records and credentials are stored, and the KDC runs as a service on the DC. The KDC manages, among other things, the collection of secret keys called *long-term keys*, derived from the user logon password. KDC functions are divided between the AS function (which issues authenticating TGTs) and the TGS function (which grants session tickets).

The KDC is thus implemented, along with Active Directory Services (ADS), as a domain service running on DCs throughout the enterprise. It uses AD as its directory database or data store and retrieves information about principals through the Global Catalog. These topics and access authorization are discussed in more detail in Chapters 6 and 7. Both KDC and ADS are started by and run in the trusted process space of the LSA. It is significant that neither service can be stopped. DCs in Windows 2000 are considered peers, so the AS and TGS functions of the KDC security service are redundant.

An Annotated Look at the Microsoft Process

Microsoft Kerberos services that run on the KDC are differentiated into two separate security functions: the AS and TGS functions. The actual authentication process is completed in one exchange of messages between a consumer and the AS portion of the KDC. Once the AS authenticates a consumer, the consumer does not have to exchange information again with the AS. A reusable "pass" or TGT is repeatedly presented to the now separate TGS function for new service requests.

Note: This single AS exchange feature of Kerberos both decreases bandwidth consumption and minimizes any exposure of exchanged security credentials. Even though the NTLM authentication protocol exchanges a hash value, not actual security credentials, for authentication purposes, it does require a new authentication exchange for each additional service a consumer requests during a logon session. The authentication portion of Microsoft's Single Sign-On (SSO) feature is actually just that—a one-time authentication exchange of information between consumer and KDC.

This TGT is stored for the consumer on the client workstation in the credentials cache. When the consumer presents an authentic copy of the TGT to the TGS, it generates and returns to the consumer a service-granting ticket that is presented to the service provider whenever a service request is made.

To securely exchange a plaintext message over an unsecured session pipe to the KDC/AS during the initial request for authentication, you send a hash function of the consumer's password to the KDC/AS. Here are the protocol steps in the exchange:

1. a. The LSA on the client, through WinLogon, queries the consumer for his or her user ID and converts it to a hash value that it stores in the credentials cache in a secured memory area. In native mode, the Kerberos client sends a copy of this hash, along with a TGS ID request for TGS services, to the KDC/AS (refer to Step 1a in Figure 4.1). This message, called KRB_AS_REQ, contains critical preauthentication data, typically a keyed timestamp encrypted with a symmetric key shared by the consumer and KDC/AS. This timestamp proves knowledge of the consumer's secret, long-term password to the KDC/AS.

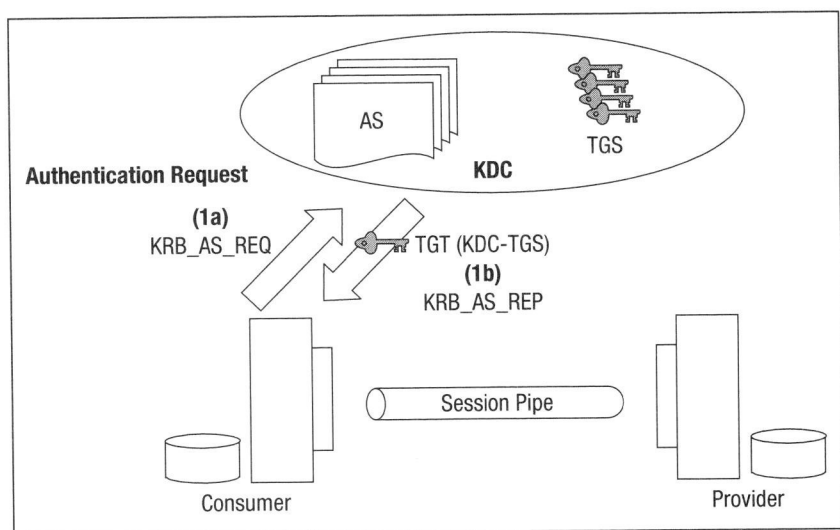

Figure 4.1   The flow of the Kerberos AS exchange.

b. The KDC/AS, upon validating the authenticity of the keyed timestamp, returns a TGT encrypted with a hash key derived from the user's archived password. The TGT is actually a timestamped digital envelope encrypted with a secret key shared by the KDC/AS and KDC/TGS. The KDC/AS also returns a secured session key specifically for the consumer using its copy of the secret, long-term password. In addition, a copy of the session key is included inside the TGT; it can be read only by the KDC/TGS to which the consumer directs his or her service requests. Both the ticket and session keys are encrypted with a hash derived from the consumer's password. It also contains the consumer's ID, the network address of the client on which the consumer is requesting service, and the TGS ID. This is the KRB_AS_REP (refer to Step 1b in Figure 4.1). Note the secret key, TGT (KDC-TGS), that is sent back to the consumer.

2. a. When the client receives this encrypted ticket, the client queries the consumer for his or her password. Using a hash key derived from the password, the client attempts to decrypt the incoming message. If the derived hash key can decrypt the ticket, the TGT is successfully recovered. The ticket includes a timestamp that indicates when it was issued and its lifetime or TTL (refer to Step 2a in Figure 4.2). The logon session key and the TGT are stored in the credentials cache. Using a copy of the stored TGT, the consumer requests a service-granting ticket from the KDC/TGS in a message called the KRB_TGS_REQ, which is encrypted with the secured session key (refer to Step 2a in Figure 4.2). This message

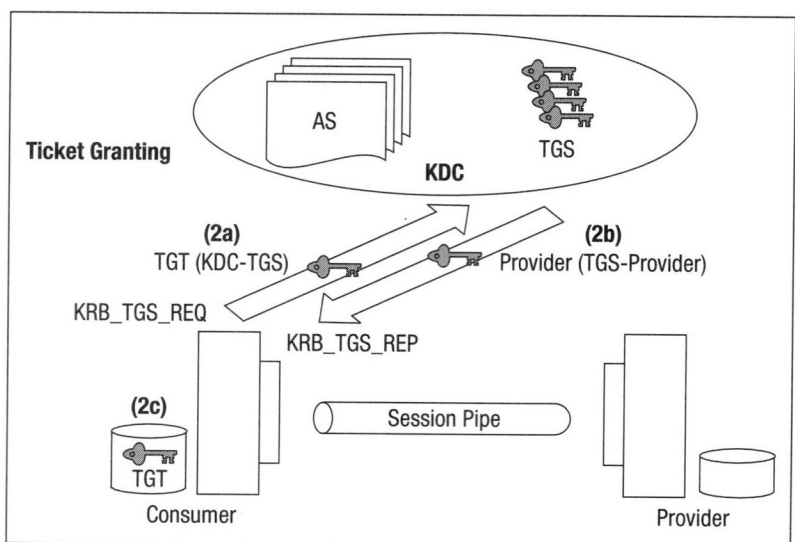

Figure 4.2 The flow of the Kerberos TGS exchange.

contains the consumer's name, a copy of the TGT, the ID of the targeted service provider, and an authenticator encrypted with the consumer's logon session key. The short-lived authenticator proves the identity of the consumer who is requesting the service at that moment in time. This proof is a countermeasure to an impersonator using a replay attack.

b. The KDC/TGS can verify the authenticity of the service request by decrypting its own TGS ID with a secret key that only it and the KDC/AS hold. It confirms the TGT's TTL. It compares the encrypted user ID and client network address with the incoming message. It decrypts the authenticator using its copy of the logon session key. If the user is authenticated, the KDC/TGS generates a service-granting ticket, the KRB_TGS_REP, for the requested service. It sends it back to the consumer with credentials, including the service provider ID and a new session key to be shared exclusively between the consumer and that targeted service provider. The service-granting ticket is encrypted with a secret key shared by the KDC/TGS and the service provider (refer to Step 2b in Figure 4.2).

c. The client receives the KRB_TGS_REP and, on behalf of the consumer, uses the logon session key to decrypt the new session key and the keyed service-granting ticket it will use for requesting the specific service. These credentials are also stored in the cache. The session keys, transferred to both consumer and service provider in a secured manner, create a secured session pipe for future exchanges of services (refer to Step 2c in Figure 4.2).

3. a. The consumer sends a KRB_AP_REQ that contains his or her user ID, a keyed authenticator, the service-granting ticket, and a preconfigured flag requesting mutual authentication to the service provider (refer to Step 3a in Figure 4.3). The authenticator is keyed with the new session key shared exclusively between the consumer and service provider. The service provider uses its secret key to decrypt the service-granting ticket and authenticate the consumer's ID. If the two coincide, the service provider determines whether the mutual authentication flag is set. If it is set, it uses the shared session key to encrypt the timestamp from the consumer's authenticator and returns it to the consumer in a KRB_AP_REP.

b. Upon receipt of the KRB_AP_REP, the client decrypts the returned timestamp and compares it with its cached copy to determine mutual authenticity. The session now proceeds using the shared secret key or a mutually agreed subsession key (refer to Step 3b in Figure 4.3).

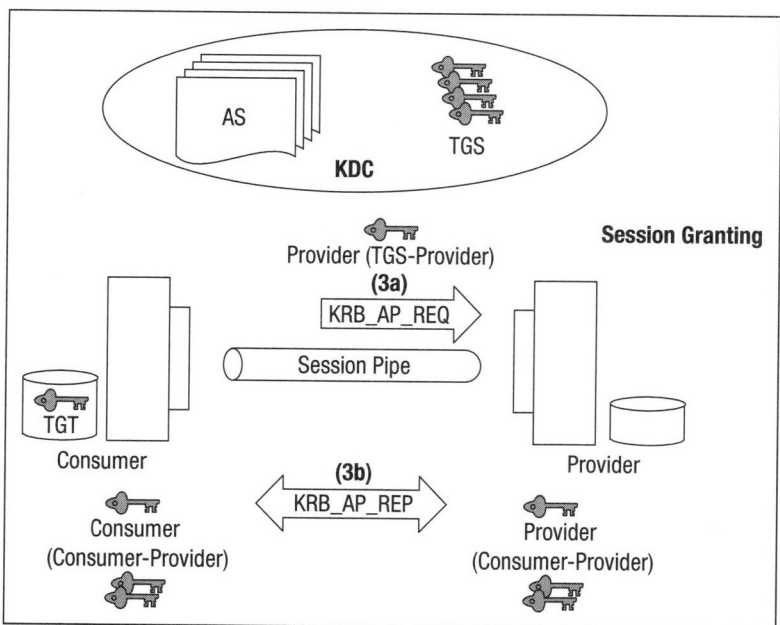

Figure 4.3   The flow of the Kerberos session-granting exchange.

The KDC/AS authenticates and authorizes the consumer. The ticket contains the network address of the client workstation on which the consumer has made his or her request. This prevents a spoof from some other client different from the workstation on which the request was originally made. The actual holder of the TGT who initiates requests for service is validated. To prevent reuse by some impersonator, the authenticator's TTL is for a very short period of time. Similarly, the service-granting ticket is symmetrically encrypted to prevent interception and alteration by all except the KDC/AS and the service provider.

Cross-Domain Authentication

Cross-domain authentication is the typical situation in a distributed server environment. A consumer requests services from some service provider in some other trusted domain. Figure 4.4 shows the more complex flow of exchanges in such a scenario. When you have multiple sites on different local area network (LAN) segments or subnets, you can arrange them in a hierarchical tree-like structure with a root domain (**examcram.com**) and child domains like **east.examcram.com**. If the domains are *well connected*—a term Microsoft uses to suggest that a reliable, high-speed connection interconnects the two domains—Windows 2000 transparently establishes a transitive, two-way trust that supports the sharing of TGTs across the domains. A transitive Kerberos trust is automatically created when you join a child

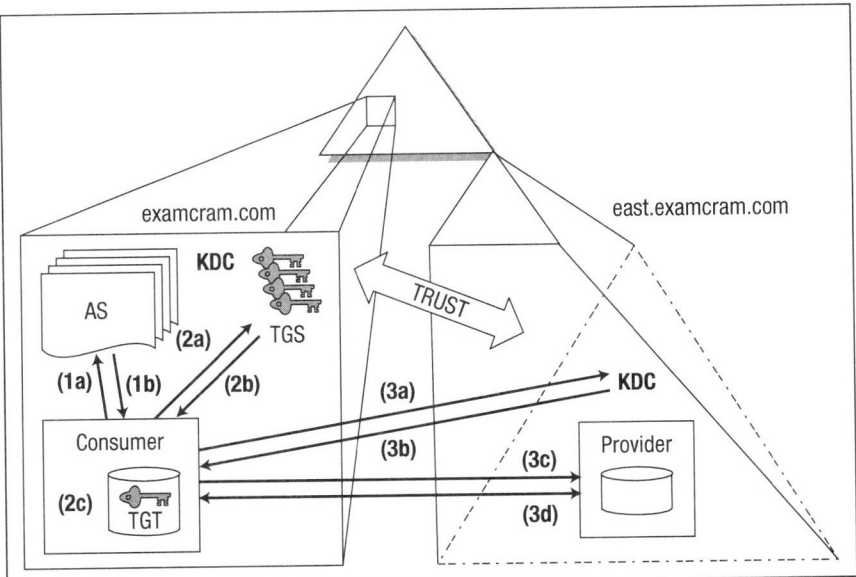

Figure 4.4 ExamCram Ltd. wants to expand its operations.

domain to a root or parent domain using the Active Directory Wizard (also referred to as DCPromo). The security relationships between parent and child domains are discussed in Chapters 9 and 10. You can define Kerberos policy in the
default Domain Group Object in each domain.

The division of a KDC into two security services—AS and TGS services—is
especially useful when services are distributed across domains or, in Unix terminology, Kerberos *realms*. KDCs in multiple Kerberos realms share a secret interrealm
key, so their TGS components are, in effect, security principals in each other's
realm. Referrals by local TGSs to some remote TGS provide session tickets to
remote service providers; during their session, authenticated consumers can thus
request a service anywhere in a Windows 2000 enterprise running in native mode.

Following authentication in Step 1 of Figure 4.4, the consumer in **examcram.com**
needs services from a provider in **east.examcram.com**, a child domain. The consumer first requests a session ticket from its local TGS in the form of a
KRB_TGS_REQ in Step 2. The local TGS first confirms the authenticity of the
consumer. It then determines that the service provider is, in fact, not part of its local
realm but, instead, is located in the child domain, **east.examcram.com**. Instead of
replying with a session-granting ticket to a local service provider, the TGS issues
the consumer a referral ticket to the TGS in **east.examcram.com** in Step 2c. This
referral ticket is keyed with the secret interrealm key shared only by TGSs that
trust each other. The consumer sends a request for services (KRB_AP_REQ) with
the referral ticket to the KDC/TGS in **east.examcram.com**, as shown in Step 3a.

The remote TGS validates the referral ticket with its own copy of the interrealm key and returns a session ticket to the consumer that the remote targeted service provider can validate in Step 3c. If the service provider validates the session ticket, and if mutual authentication is flagged, it returns a key timestamp in the KRB_AP_REP to the **examcram.com** consumer to confirm its identity. Following successful completion of that exchange, the consumer can receive services from the provider in **east.examcram.com** over a secured session pipe, as shown in Step 3d.

Delegation of Authentication

In NT 4, services typically impersonated consumers when accessing other resources on the same client platform. The impersonation functioned within the security context of the consumer. This security context, however, could not be created on other servers that offered distributed services. Windows 2000, through Kerberos delegation, can, in fact, offer to other service providers on remote servers a proxy ticket and the security context of that ticket holder. This delegation of authentication is especially important in N-tier architectures and for when you are accessing Web service providers. For this delegation of authority to occur:

➤ All client platforms and service processes must be running native Windows 2000 in a Windows 2000 domain.

➤ The consumer's account must be enabled for delegation.

➤ The service provider's account must be enabled for delegation.

By default, principal account properties are not enabled for delegation. In addition to properly configuring these properties, you must also be aware that the account type under which the service provider runs is an issue. If the service provider runs under a domain user account, the Account Options list in the object's property sheet must indicate that the account is trusted for delegation.

Delegation of authentication can be implemented in two ways. The first way is that the consumer requests a service from some back-end server to which it has no direct access. The consumer then presents its proxy ticket to a front-end server.

If the consumer cannot determine or is not aware of the existence of some back-end server, he or she can instead present the front-end server with a TGT that can be used on the consumer's behalf to request services as needed. This ticket, generated from the consumer credentials, is called a *forwarded TGT*. Kerberos policy, discussed later in this chapter, determines whether you can implement either proxy tickets or forwardable TGTs.

Account Database

The data store that holds credentials and other related security information is provided as part of the domain's AD directory services. The AS portion of the KDC accesses this store to obtain credentials data that will authenticate consumers and build message components in the TGT. By definition, a principal is represented in this data store as an account object. Keys are attributes of these objects and are covered in more detail in Chapter 6. DCs are both KDC and AD servers, so they share replicas of the account database through a proprietary multimaster replication protocol over a secured channel. You can thus consider DCs as AAA servers that integrate the three IT security controls of authentication, authorization, and auditing in a somewhat amorphous cloud of services that span the boundaries of the enterprise.

Like other resources in the NT File System (NTFS), AD objects contain ACLs that delineate specific access permissions. The granularity for AD objects, however, is finer than that for files and folders; there are ACLs for each attribute associated with an AD object. Thus, with AD objects, you have greater control over access to account attributes. One of these attributes is the encryption key used to communicate with a consumer, a client computer, or service provider. Even though only the encryption key derived from the actual password (and not the password itself) is stored in the object, access is restricted to the account holder and processes such as the LSA with the Trusted Computer Base privilege.

On Windows 2000 clients, the credentials cache holds the tickets and keys obtained from the KDC. This secured area in volatile memory is protected by the LSA. Because of the sensitivity of the cache's contents, they are never paged to disk. Similarly, when you shut down the client machine or log in as a new principal, this cache is destroyed. The LSA calls upon the Kerberos SSP (discussed later in this chapter) to perform management functions related to tickets or keys. The Kerberos SSP, which runs in the security context of the LSA process space on the client machine, manages this cache.

Kerberos Policy

Kerberos policy, along with other account policies regarding password and intruder detection lockouts, is defined by the default domain GPO in Windows 2000. By default, the right to modify these settings is assigned to members of the Domain Administrators security group. Features such as mutual authentication and the use of proxy and forwardable tickets are determined by Kerberos policy here. The user cannot configure them. Local policies dealing with auditing, user rights, and other security options for the DC are defined in the default DC GPO. It is noteworthy that settings defined in the default DC GPO have a higher precedence for DCs than settings defined in the default domain GPO.

According to Microsoft documentation, Kerberos session tickets are sometimes called *service tickets* because session tickets are used to authenticate connections to services. Kerberos TGTs are called *user tickets* for the same reason; they authenticate connections to users. This confusing naming convention may change in future releases of the software. Some elements of the Kerberos policy include:

➤ Enforcement of user logon restrictions

➤ Maximum lifetime for the service ticket

➤ Maximum lifetime for the user ticket

➤ Maximum lifetime for user ticket renewal

➤ Maximum tolerance for computer clock synchronization

The KDC does not notify consumers when session tickets or TGTs expire; it does not maintain any record of these expiration times. If an expired session ticket is presented to the service provider, it returns an error message. The consumer must then request a new session ticket from the KDC for additional services.

Interoperability

A Windows 2000 design goal is for ADS to provide a consistent, uniform name-space for principals in the enterprise. Interoperability requires that the namespace accommodate objects outside the boundaries of the enterprise. Microsoft's implementation of Kerberos through SSPI (discussed later in this chapter) offers that promised seamless, out-of-the-box interoperability. Users can authenticate anywhere in an AD forest because the Kerberos authentication services in each domain trust the tickets issued by other KDCs in the forest. This is an example of the advantages of transitive trusts and their effect on simplifying domain administration.

When you are working from a Microsoft KDC to other Kerberos implementations, you will find several scenarios. The primary variables are:

➤ Kerberos services running on the client that requests authentication and services

➤ Kerberos services running on the KDC that provides those authentication services

➤ Targeted service providers that provide the requested services

Although implementation methods vary depending on how Kerberos technologies are implemented, they typically include the following scenarios:

➤ *Native mode*—Both principals use Windows 2000 Kerberos security; the Kerberos client exchanges information with a KDC.

➤ *Client configuration*—The Kerberos client is configured to access a particular KDC for authentication.

➤ *One-way trust*—A trust relationship has been established between a Microsoft domain and a non-Microsoft Kerberos realm such that tickets generated by one KDC are recognized and accepted by the other and its resource services.

➤ *Service account*—You can represent a non-Microsoft Kerberized service in a Windows 2000 domain by creating an AD service account object for that one specific service.

➤ *Account mapping*—When a trust exists between a Kerberos realm and a Windows 2000 domain, you can map non-Microsoft Kerberized accounts to Microsoft Kerberized account objects.

Non-Microsoft Kerberos clients can authenticate to a Windows 2000 KDC; conversely, Windows 2000 systems can authenticate to a KDC in a Kerberos realm. Windows 2000 client applications require General Security Services Application Programming Interface (GSS-API), on which SSPI is based, to run on non-Microsoft systems and authenticate to Kerberos server services. Non-Microsoft systems that are GSS-API compatible can authenticate on Microsoft Kerberos server services. Finally, both Microsoft and Kerberos 5 can establish cross-trusts and thus account mapping.

Kerberos and Alternative Protocols

This section discusses how Kerberos relates to and compares with the other SSPs available in Windows 2000. But first, let's look at the big picture, showing how the appropriate security service is negotiated as part of an exchange of information between a consumer and a service provider.

The Big Picture

Information exchanges occur between at least two parties that have named accounts; the parties have some account record and some logon password. Microsoft refers to these named accounts generically as *principals*. I typically use the generic scenario of a consumer and a service provider to identify a message flow. In the security schema used in Chapter 2, I assume that the two parties either exchange information or that one requests/delivers some service to the other. Every principal, by definition, has account information regarding its specific identity, group memberships, and some associated password in some data store. In a down-level, legacy NT 4 model, this is the directory database. The up-level, Windows 2000 platform integrates AD and Kerberos services to facilitate both the scalability of and accessibility to this data store.

A Windows 2000 DC could consequently be referred to as a generic *AAA server* because:

➤ AD-Kerberos security services together support authentication and authorization.

➤ Group Policy, as applied through the GPO, configures local and system-wide security settings.

Introducing cross-cultural terminology such as *principals* and *AAA servers* here will help you to see commonalties among security models (such as the AAA security models described in Chapters 7 and 8), regardless of operating system platform or "culture." For example, in the Unix culture, a Kerberos ticket is valid for only a finite time interval or *lifetime*. I interchange that term with the cross-cultural term *TTL* to help you grasp concepts more rapidly by drawing analogies with concepts you already understand.

The historical trend toward a Unix-style distributed server architecture model is apparent in the design trends of both Microsoft Windows 2000 and Novell NetWare 5 when compared to their earlier designs: NT 4.x/3.x and NetWare 4.x/3.x. Such a historical trend is suggested by:

➤ The adoption of standards-based security protocols such as Kerberos and Novell Directory Services (NDS)

➤ The adoption of a nonproprietary network protocol (TCP/IP)

➤ The adoption of scalable directory services such as AD and NDS

➤ The scalable enterprise support provided by the AD forest and NDS multiple trees

The use of cross-cultural terminology will enhance your understand of these evolving cultures in dealing with future issues of interoperability.

SSPs

A *security support provider* is fundamentally an installable library of security features. Windows 2000 can install several standards-based SSPs that provide distributed authentication services on any service provider. The three primary SSPs currently supported are:

➤ NTLM challenge/response protocol (discussed in more detail later in this chapter)

➤ Microsoft Kerberos (discussed in more detail later in this chapter)

➤ SChannel security protocols (discussed in Chapter 7)

Windows 2000 uses three other network SSPs to provide authentication services by using digital certificates, to authenticate users across the Internet:

➤ *Distributed Password Authentication (DPA)*—An Internet membership authentication protocol that is like triple Data Encryption Standard (3DES) in that it must be purchased as a separate add-in product. DES and its variants, like 3DES, are discussed in Chapter 3.

➤ *Extensible Authentication Protocol (EAP)*—Cited in RFC 2284 this extends the communication protocol Point-to-Point Protocol (PPP) to allow installable authentication services on both sides of the communication channel.

➤ *Public key-based protocols*—These are SChannel services specifically using public keys and are discussed in more detail in Chapter 7. They include Secure Sockets Layer (SSL) version 3, Transport Layer Security v1 (TLS1), and Private Communications Technology (PCT).

All the authentication services are implemented as separate SSPs working through a common interface—SSPI. This Win32 system API interface offers a uniform set of "hooks" on which current and future security providers can attach their technologies.

Principals in an exchange "negotiate" the use of a particular SSP, which, in turn, determines the use of a specific security protocol in the exchange.

 SSPI, based on RFC 2078 and the standards-based GSS-API, provides multiple authentication architectural support for installable software or hardware cryptographic service providers (CSPs). Principals negotiate with SSPs for security services provided through these installable CSPs. Kerberos is the default SSP in Windows 2000 native mode.

Windows 2000 negotiations for a particular SSP are mediated by one of the many protocols defined by IETF: Security Negotiation Mechanism (SNEGO) for GSS-API (RFC 2478). Although Kerberos is the default SSP, SNEGO and SSPI extend the range of possible SSPs, allowing both future scalability and interoperability across current heterogeneous operating systems.

Of the SSPs discussed, Kerberos and the generic SChannel services focus primarily on authentication, integrity, and confidentiality. These technologies focus on the exchange of information through the session pipe as opposed to access management to resources or services. Authorization, alternatively, is based on a consumer's rights and the permissions associated with the requested resource; it is defined by specific attributes that either principal possesses.

As discussed previously, MIT Kerberos 5 does not provide authorization services; Microsoft enhanced MIT Kerberos 5 by integrating the Kerberos protocol with AD. Windows 2000 has leveraged a standards-based, well-known secured authentication protocol, Kerberos, with authorization services provided by the NT 4 legacy directory database using SIDs and ACLs. The NT 4 authorization system that manages these resources has not changed in Windows 2000. The SSPI uses a special pass-through SSP called *Negotiate* to match supportable security "levels" among its installable security providers, with those on the service provider to whom it has made a request. The Negotiate SSP applies the "strongest" available security services to the consumer/service provider exchange. In mixed mode, Negotiate may negotiate down-level to the NTLM challenge/response protocol and the directory database; in Windows 2000 native mode, Negotiate defaults to the Kerberos SSP. Microsoft designed Windows 2000 in native mode to seek the most restrictive security systems, typically Kerberos protocol.

To secure resources, there must be discretionary control over those securable objects. An object's security descriptor, a unique binary value, contains a discretionary access control list (DACL), and a system access control list (SACL). Activities associated with the use of many of these attributes can be audited. Both DACLs and SACLs are lists of individual access control entries that specify principal, specific rights that can be performed on the resource, as well as a description of how the right is activated. In addition to ACLs, the descriptor contains a listing of security attributes such as its SID and any associated group IDs. The SID is used to identify the principal or the group. A nonunique SID identifies the logon session.

NTLM Authentication Services

In Windows 2000, the basic NTLM exchange involves impersonation of a principal by using that principal's access token. A principal or consumer submits a request, with validating security identification data (including unique SIDs), to some provider for services. When NTLM authentication is used, passwords are never transmitted across unsecured namespaces. The principal and AAA server (DC) use a handshake method that encodes a random challenge. The principal encrypts random data that the challenging AAA server passes to it. If the AAA server can decrypt the random data, its challenge has been answered. Thus, passwords are never transmitted across unsecured channels.

When the LSA receives valid data, it generates an authorizing security access token based on the principal's SID. The provider, on behalf of the consumer, fulfills whatever requested services it can within the scope or security context of the issued token. The token's scope is limited by the resource's ACLs. An ACL, as previously described, is a list of individual access control entries (ACEs) that describe how a user, or more typically a group, can manipulate properties of the specific resource object. If the token's scope of authorization matches one or more specific ACEs, the service provider, on behalf of the consumer, performs the requested service. If any one ACE limits or denies a specific or required manner of manipulation, the provider is prevented from completing its task. For example, defining only the Read ACE in some ACL prevents a consumer from writing over that particular object. Thus, the security access token bestows authorization on its holder. Impersonation by operating system services is the most common method of providing distributed services to consumers in the enterprise. It is especially important that the token be exchanged in as secure a manner as possible in the scalable AD namespace.

Compared to Microsoft Kerberos, NTLM:

➤ Uses a slower one-way authentication process.

➤ Establishes trust relationships that are one way and nontransitive.

➤ Is proprietary and not standards based.

➤ Does not scale well.

Security services in Windows 2000 support scalable services through the use of impersonation; you can think of this as a form of distributed account authentication. The security services must also provide more flexible, transitive trust relationships to simplify administration while maintaining a major end-user feature: SSO.

Unlike with NT 4 and the security accounts manager, Windows 2000 security systems are integrated with directory services and hence are distributed system wide. The AD stores both account information and security policy in multilevel, hierarchical domain trees. With Kerberos protocol, trusts can be built across trees that are two way and transitive. Implicit relationships are established between parent domains and child domains. Finally, the granularity of security attributes has deepened within an object. In addition, because of AD, granularity now extends across logical organizational boundaries, transcending the legacy global groups, local groups, and users in the NT 4 domain model.

Note: NTLM is still necessary in Windows 2000 for establishing legacy one-way trusts with NT domains and the authentication of legacy or down-level NT 4 clients. In fact, the default installation is mixed node to accommodate Microsoft's current embedded customer base.

In a mixed-mode environment, NTLM authentication services are used instead of the Kerberos protocol.

Kerberos as an Installable SSP

Even though Kerberos protocol is the default provider of security features in Windows 2000, it is implemented as a dynamic link library (DLL). In fact, Microsoft has designed a security infrastructure that is truly extensible—SSPI.

This is where the Workstation service on the client communicates with an installed security service library, otherwise referred to as an SSP, to request services. The selection of any one specific DLL and hence a specific security protocol is negotiated between consumer and service provider. SSPI offers an API through which an extensible selection of these security libraries can be accessed. NTLM and the SChannel security protocols are, in addition to Kerberos, examples of security service libraries currently available as DLLs in Windows 2000. Figure 4.5 shows how SSPI supports multiple authentication protocols in addition to Kerberos security services.

When the key combination of Ctl+Alt+Delete (the Secure Attention Sequence) is pressed upon bootup, the Windows Logon (WinLogon) service is launched. It calls the LSA, which in turn loads both Kerberos and NTLM libraries using the Kerberos SSP by default. Negotiate, a pass-through SSP, seeks to establish up-level SSPs (like Kerberos) before falling back to down-level SSPs (such as NTLM). The consumer on the remote side of the session pipe determines which SSP is implemented based on the service provider ID it requests. If this were the logon sequence to a native Windows 2000 Server, the LSA, upon receiving a plaintext password from WinLogon, would do the following to subsequently secure session tickets through the TGS:

➤ Hash the password.

➤ Save a copy in the credentials cache.

➤ Forward a copy to the Kerberos SSP on the KDC for validation and a TGT.

Kerberos security services can be loaded as an instance within the security context of some user, by some process that requires, for example, the secured exchange of some messages. In fact, any system services and transport-level

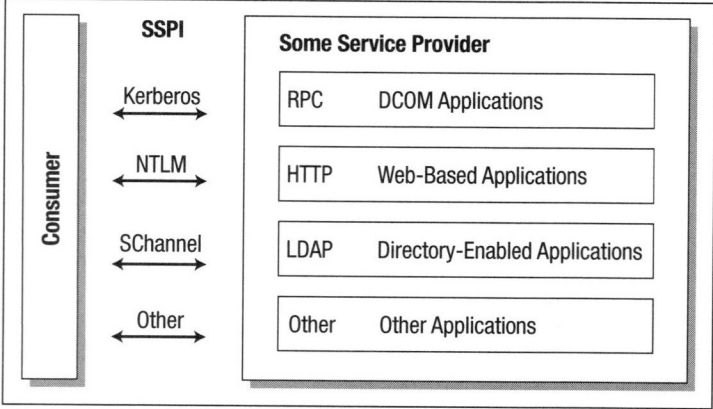

Figure 4.5 Security services available through SSPI.

applications can access any SSP through SSPI. The interface obtains authenticated connections based on the availability of SSPs and on the demands of the client/server applications that are attempting to establish a secure session.

As a security interface, SSPI contains methods that are called by applications running on the consumer side of the interface. For example, a consumer can send Kerberos credentials to a service provider using the SSPI method **InitializeSecurityContext** to generate a Kerberos Application Request message. The service provider responds with the SSPI method **AcceptSecurityContext**, which returns a Kerberos Application Response message back to the consumer. Once the consumer is authenticated, the LSA uses credentials in the consumer's ticket to build an access token on the service provider. It invokes the SSPI method **ImpersonateSecurityContext** to attach the token to an impersonation process thread to execute the service.

All Windows 2000 distributed services use SSPI to access the Kerberos SSP. A partial range of service requests involving Kerberos security includes:

➤ Print spooler services

➤ Common Internet File System (CIFS)/Server Message Block (SMB) file access

➤ Lightweight Directory Access Protocol (LDAP) queries in AD

➤ Intranet authentication to Internet Information Server (IIS)

➤ Remote management using authenticated remote procedure calls (RPCs)

➤ Certificate requests to the Microsoft Certificate Server

Table 4.1 summarizes the differences between NTLM and the Kerberos protocol.

Table 4.1	A comparison of NTLM and Kerberos.	
Feature	NTLM	Kerberos
Scalability	No	Yes
Execution	Slow	Fast
Encryption	Secured hash	Symmetric key
Open source	No	Yes, standards-based
Trusts	One-way, nontransitive	Two-way, transitive
Mutual authentication	No	Yes

A Kerberos Case Study

Note: To expand on the topics discussed in this chapter and to allow you to practice working with case studies, I have provided an annotated case study here. Some of the later chapters in this book also have an annotated case study in the body of the chapter; each deals with the same company but involves different circumstances.

ExamCram Ltd.: Sharing Resources with Other Companies

ExamCram Ltd., a publishing company in AnyTown, Arizona, focuses primarily on developing and selling advanced technical training materials. ExamCram Ltd. works with a consulting firm company called MyCompany Inc., located in the same building as ExamCram Ltd.

MyPartner Inc., located in SomeOtherPlace, New York, works with MyCompany Inc. MyPartner Inc. and MyCompany Inc. have a long-term business alliance. Discussions about merging ExamCram Ltd. with MyCompany Inc. are in progress. At the moment, neither group of attorneys has arranged a meeting.

Company Goal

ExamCram Ltd. runs Windows 2000 AD. Its immediate objective is to understand how security policies will be written and deployed. Its stated goal is to develop scalable, security services that provide mutual authentication across unsecured, distributed server environments. In addition, confidentiality of information must be maintained at all times. There is a high incidence of impersonation attacks on the network, specifically where legitimate users are gaining access to unauthorized services. ExamCram Ltd. also wants MyCompany Inc. to share its network resources.

Take careful note of subtle nuances in a case study's stated goals or objectives. The inclusion of a single keyword that corresponds to an IT security control could radically change the proposed design or spoil the expected results. Some case studies actually state that a particular attack modality either has happened recently or is a specific risk outlined in the corporate business objectives.

Exhibit

Exhibit 1 shows a diagram that might accompany this case study on a Microsoft exam.

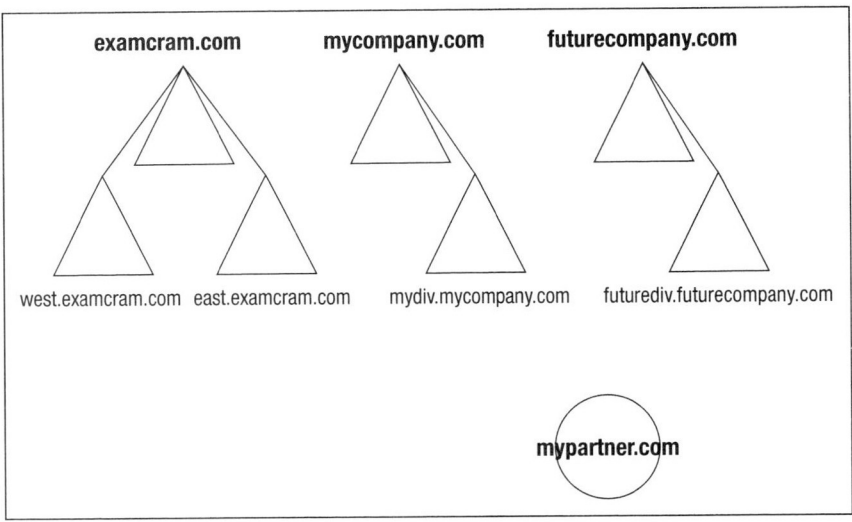

Exhibit 1   ExamCram Ltd. plans to expand operations.

 Pay particular attention to depictions of AD trees, forests, OUs, and trusts. Remember that although Kerberos supports transitive, two-way trusts, you can still construct a one-way trust for security reasons.

Current LAN/Network Structure

All 100-client machines are running native mode Windows 2000 configured as a root domain with two child domains: **west.examcram.com** and **east.examcram.com**. Each system is connected to a 10Mbps hub through 10Mbps LAN cards, although Category 5 Unshielded Twisted Pair (UTP) cabling connects each system and hub in a star topology. The network protocol is TCP/IP.

MyCompany Inc. has 20 users running native mode Windows 2000 with a root domain, **mycompany.com**, and a child domain, **mydiv.mycompany.com**. Both trees, **examcram.com** and **mycompany.com**, are internally well connected.

Proposed LAN/Network Structure

The Network Manager from ExamCram Ltd. says, "Give me some examples of possible security relationships if we were to merge with MyCompany Inc. The companies are in the same building, so we can add another router and have them connected over a weekend. Show me how I can scale the security structure to support this merger and future acquisitions. By the way, I don't want any of MyCompany Inc.'s business partners using ExamCram Ltd. resources. In fact, the only heavy users of our resources will be the Sales division at MyCompany Inc. I don't want to hear these users complaining to our CEO."

Current WAN Connectivity

Both companies have T1 connections and use Internet access to communicate.

Proposed WAN Connectivity

No changes in the current structure are proposed at this time.

Design Commentary

No changes in the current structure are proposed at this time.

Current Internet Positioning

ExamCram Ltd. is registered as **examcram.com**. Its IP address is 201.101.1.1. MyCompany Inc. is registered as **mycompany.com** at IP address 198.2.4.6. Both companies use a Class C private network address range for their internal networks. The ExamCram Marketing group is in a separate domain, **east.examcram.com**, and uses 192.168.3.x/24; the group will have the greatest contact with Sales in the mydivision domain in MyCompany Inc.

Future Internet Plans

No changes in the current structure are proposed at this time.

Commentary

Figure 4.6 shows a diagram I would give the Network Manager of ExamCram Ltd. Compare this with Exhibit 1. In this annotated diagram, I show a variety of possible scenarios that will allow scalability (namely, **futurecompany.com**) and exclusivity (specifically, the one-way trust between **mycompany.com** and its own extranet business partner, **mypartner.com**).

Here is a brief explanation of what's in the figure:

➤ **examcram.com** and **mycompany.com** are roots of two separate trees in the same forest; they share a transitive, two-way trust.

➤ **west.examcram.com** and **east.examcram.com** are child domains under **examcram.com**; **mydiv.mycompany.com** is a child under **mycompany.com**.

➤ **east.examcram.com** trusts **mydiv.mycompany.com**; this is a one-way short-cut trust that improves performance by reducing hops and allows **mydiv.mycompany.com** users to access **east.examcram.com** resources easily. The Network Manager specifically stated that the greatest workload will come from this division, so this shortcut is important.

➤ **mypartner.com** is a business partner of MyCompany Inc. It shares resources with the MyCompany Inc. Sales department in **mydiv.mycompany.com**. This is a one-way, nontransitive trust, so users in **mypartner.com** have limited

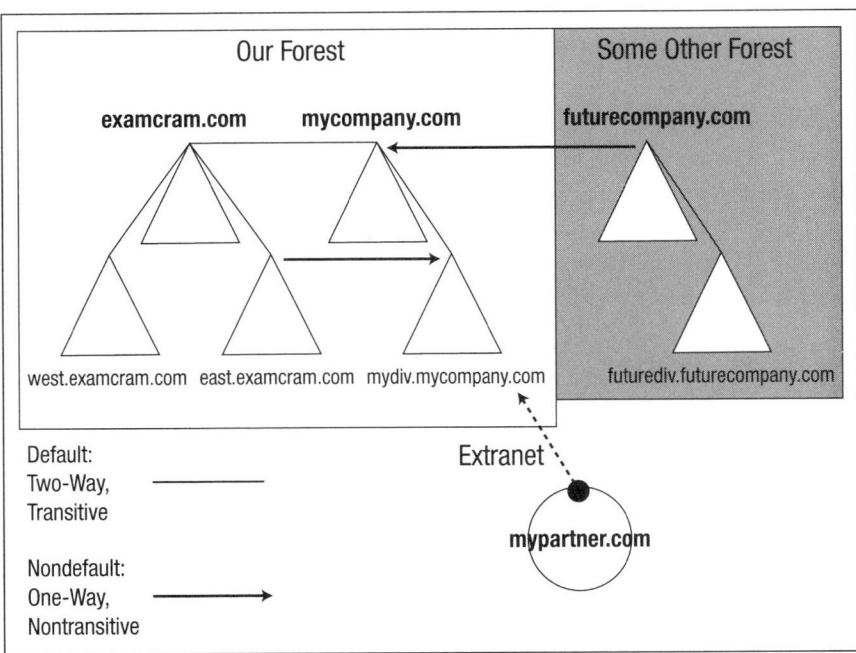

Figure 4.6   ExamCram Ltd. plans to expand operations.

access to the mydiv domain in MyCompany Inc. Users in **mypartner.com** cannot access ExamCram Ltd. resources.

➤ If a **futurecompany.com** tree were to merge with ExamCram Ltd., **futurecompany.com**'s domain users would, like those of **mycompany.com,** have access to all resources in both forests with a minimal amount of administrative maintenance. If, alternatively, **futurecompany.com** remains a root domain in its own forest, an explicit, one-way trust would allow **mycompany.com** domain users access to only **futurecompany.com** resources; access to any **futurecompany.com** child domains from **mycompany.com** or from its tree would not be allowed. Similarly, in a one-way trust, there would be no access from **futurecompany.com** into the ExamCram Ltd. forest.

Practice Questions

Case Study

4Sale, an online bartering company in ThatPlaceThere, North Dakota, focuses primarily on selling inexpensive, odd-lot items. 4Sale has recently merged forces with a smaller company, Got-a-Deal. Got-a-Deal rents space in the same office building. The corporate side of the merger has gone well, but the network infrastructure is under some reconsideration.

Current LAN/Network Structure

4Sale is presently running NT Server 4 on three machines:

➤ A primary domain controller

➤ A backup domain controller that serves as the Exchange (Simple Mail Transfer Protocol—SMTP) server

➤ A member server that is running IIS 4 (Hypertext Transfer Protocol [HTTP] server) and Proxy Server (packet filtering/caching/Network Address Translation—NAT)

All 100-client machines are configured in a single-domain model. The client systems are running Windows NT Workstation 4, with Office 97 being utilized as an applications package. Each system is connected to a 10Mbps hub through 10Mbps LAN cards running Category 5 UTP cabling in a star topology.

Got-a-Deal is undergoing changes to upgrade from its Ethernet bus topology, which uses coaxial cabling, to a more modern configuration. Got-a-Deal is using an NT Server in a 22-person-workgroup configuration as a file and print server. The network is stable but does not provide scalability.

Proposed LAN/Network Structure

4Sale would like to move forward towards Windows 2000 and develop its online barter/trading business. Some of the security features would help leverage development of its e-commerce plans and future corporate goals. In addition, 4Sale would like to improve the network's speed by implementing newer cards and hubs that support 100Mbps.

Got-a-Deal would also like to upgrade to Windows 2000 under a domain arrangement but has concerns regarding performance, deployment costs, maintenance, and training. The company will be hiring an in-house network engineer to be part of a newly formulated IT team that administers the resources of both companies. Got-a-Deal needs a faster network infrastructure in place within the next two months. It will depend on 4Sale for most of its network services.

Current WAN Connectivity

4Sale has a T1 connection to an Internet Service Provider (ISP) in OverHere, North Dakota. Got-a-Deal has 56Kbps dial-up networking connectivity through the same ISP.

Proposed WAN Connectivity

No changes are planned at this time.

Directory Design Commentary

Network Manager at 4Sale says, "We currently need personal password policies to be enforced and would like to retain as much control as possible over our portion of the directory."

Owner-Network Manager at Got-a-Deal says, "We would rather keep our password security at a minimum level, which will keep our current employees, some of whom we've had for five years, feel more comfortable about this merger of interests."

Current Internet Positioning

4Sale is registered as **4sale.com**. Got-a-Deal has been selling its goods through local companies and through the **4sale.com** Web site.

Future Internet Plans

No changes in the current structure are proposed at this time.

Company Goal with Windows 2000

4Sale has hired you as an outside consultant to get both companies up and running. You will try to accommodate each company's needs, but you've been given strict orders by 4Sale that there should be a higher level of control than what each company is individually proposing. You will help develop the standards and procedures that the newly formulated IT team will implement.

You have been told that 4Sale would like to utilize Windows 2000 AD by using the default schema that exists. 4Sale is expecting some growth and would like that growth to be facilitated through AD. It would also like to utilize some of the newer security features but does not understand all the possible options that will be available once Windows 2000 is implemented.

Question 1

Owner-Network Manager at Got-a-Deal says, "I've heard stories about how slow NT authentication runs on NT 4. I don't want my people turning on their machines in the morning and waiting 15 minutes. Why should I upgrade to Kerberos authentication on Windows 2000 when I have NT 4 anyway?"

Identify the two factors from the following list that you would use to formulate a reply:

PC/smart card technology

Kerberos

NT LAN Manager

SChannel

Next, group whichever of the following statements are applicable under the two headings you chose above:

Uses a slower one-way authentication process

Uses a faster authentication process

Is designed for distributed server architectures

Does not scale well

Is a proprietary standard

Is a standards-based protocol

The correct answer is:

Kerberos

Uses a faster authentication process

Is designed for distributed server architectures

Is a standards-based protocol

NT LAN Manager

Uses a slower one-way authentication process

Does not scale well

Is a proprietary standard

Question 2

Owner-Network Manager at Got-a-Deal says, "I'm still not convinced. I've done some more reading and it sounds to me like MIT Kerberos 5 supports the three key functions of authentication, authorization, and auditing. I think I am going to compile some pricing information about possible Unix operating systems."

What is your response? Is the Owner-Network Manager correct?

○ a. Yes

○ b. No

Answer b, no, is correct. Your client is misinformed. Microsoft's own implementation of Kerberos 5, not MIT Kerberos 5, integrates with Active Directory in Windows 2000 to deliver all three information technology security controls. In addition, when you compare Windows 2000 to other operating systems with regard to total cost of ownership, Windows 2000 provides both integrated, easy to manage services and a low total cost of ownership (TCO) as compared to other competitive operating systems.

Question 3

Owner-Network Manager at Got-a-Deal says, "I've been hearing about Unix and how Windows 2000 offers interoperability across the two system platforms. Explain to me how security works in native Windows 2000."

You need to first explain the specific Kerberos subprotocols.

There are three Kerberos subprotocols:

Client/server (CS) authentication exchange

Authentication Service (AS) exchange

Ticket-granting service (TGS) exchange

Identify the correct order of the three Kerberos subprotocols and group the following elements in the correct sequential order under their appropriate subprotocol:

The consumer requests a service-granting ticket.

The client requests service.

TGS returns the service-granting ticket.

The client requests a TGT.

The correct answer is:

> Authentication Service (AS) exchange
>
>> The client requests a ticket-granting ticket.
>
> Ticket-granting service (TGS) exchange
>
>> The consumer requests a service-granting ticket.
>
>> TGS returns the service-granting ticket.
>
> Client/Server (CS) authentication exchange
>
>> The client requests service.

Question 4

Network Manager at 4Sale says, "I've been reading about the Unix implementation of Kerberos in magazines. Where can I go for more detailed information?"

You cite RFC 1510 as the source document for the protocol enhancements. You want to help the Network Manager, so you mention some of the major improvements. You also want to identify features that are not part of the specification. Which of the following are not Kerberos 5 enhancements as specified in RFC 1510? [Check all correct answers]

- ❏ a. Authentication forwarding
- ❏ b. Subsession keys
- ❏ c. A more flexible principal-naming scheme
- ❏ d. Replaceable network protocols
- ❏ e. Public-key authorization

Answers a, b, c, and d are correct. Authentication forwarding, subsession keys, a more flexible principal-naming scheme, and replaceable network protocols were all added with Kerberos version 5. Public-key authorization is part of the Public Key Cryptography for Initial Authentication in Kerberos draft proposal submitted to the Internet Engineering Task Force, not part of Request For Comments 1510. Therefore, answer e is incorrect.

Question 5

> VP of Marketing at 4Sale says, "I am negotiating with **Mississippi.com**, the online bookstore, to provide us with banner space on its home page. I want to investigate how we can leverage its authentication systems."
>
> Given 4Sale's plans for e-commerce, which Security Support Providers should you research for your next meeting?
>
> ☐ a. PPP
>
> ☐ b. DPA
>
> ☐ c. EAP
>
> ☐ d. PCT

Answers b, c, and d are correct. Distributed Password Authentication is used by online services for Internet membership authentication. Extensible Authentication Protocol enhances Point-To-Point Protocol by allowing installable authentication services on both sides of the communication channel. Private Communications Technology is one of the Secure Channel Security Support Providers along Secure Sockets Layer version 3 and Transport Layer Security version 1. PPP is a communications protocol. Therefore, answer a is incorrect.

Question 6

> Network Manager at 4Sale says, "I can balance the authentication services load on my KDC by running just the TGS portion of the KDC on a separate domain controller."
>
> Is this statement true or false?
>
> ○ a. True
>
> ○ b. False

Answer b, false, is correct. Both authentication services and ticket-granting services are functions of Key Distribution Center services. They can be neither separated nor shut down on the domain controller. The division of Authentication Service (AS) and ticket-granting service (TGS) function supports interrealm requests for session tickets, not load balancing.

Question 7

> Network Manager at 4Sale asks, "Where are all the credentials like ticket-granting ticket or a service-granting ticket stored on the client computer?" [Choose the best answer]
>
> ○ a. In the credentials cache in the LSA
>
> ○ b. In the credentials subbranch in the Registry
>
> ○ c. In the credentials cache in RAM
>
> ○ d. In the credentials cache

Answer c is correct. Tickets and keys obtained from the Key Distribution Center are stored in a special area in volatile memory called the credentials cache. It is not located in the Local Security Authority nor in the Registry. Therefore, answers a and b are incorrect. Answer d is not as complete as answer c. Therefore, answer d is incorrect.

Question 8

> Owner-Network Manager at Got-a-Deal says, "Give me an example of how native Windows 2000 lowers cost of maintenance and training."
>
> Your client is concerned about TCO. Your discussions at the moment concern security, so you want to describe how Kerberos policy can be easily managed. Kerberos policy, defined in the default Domain Group Object, along with the password (length, expiration, and so on), IP security, and public key, includes what element(s)?
>
> ○ a. Maximum service ticket lifetime
>
> ○ b. Maximum TGT lifetime
>
> ○ c. Maximum TGT renewal lifetime
>
> ○ d. Maximum user ticket lifetime
>
> ○ e. All of the above
>
> ○ f. None of the above

Answer e is correct. Kerberos policy includes maximum service ticket lifetime, maximum TGT (ticket-granting ticket) lifetime, maximum TGT renewal lifetime, and maximum user ticket lifetime. Note that Microsoft calls the session key the service ticket and the ticket-granting ticket the user ticket. Use Microsoft's terminology to minimize confusion.

Question 9

Owner-Network Manager at Got-a-Deal says, "You are starting to convince me that deployment of Windows 2000 is a good business decision. But, if I did want to ever use the Unix platform, what are the important themes I should remember?"

You want to inform your client about key interoperability themes. Which theme is not relevant?

○ a. Windows 2000 mode of operation

○ b. Client configurations

○ c. Organization and trust relationships

○ d. Network protocol

○ e. All of the above

○ f. None of the above

Answer d is correct. Network protocol is not relevant in relation to interoperability themes. Answers a through c are all relevant with regard to interoperability, so they are incorrect answers. Windows 2000 must run in native mode for Kerberos to be the default security protocol; NT LAN Manager is a proprietary security protocol and does not work with other operating systems. Kerberos client services must run on a workstation for the security protocol to function. If trust relationships can be established, there are several ways two different systems can interoperate. Two possibilities are accounting mapping across the two systems; another is the possibility of cross-domain exchanges. Your client is not discussing legacy systems that might use proprietary network protocols.

Question 10

Considering the case study, what type of domain structure do you, as the consultant, visualize as an enterprise design with the lowest TCO?

○ a. Two distinct forests with an extended trust connecting them

○ b. An empty root domain with one domain in place and two OUs: one for 4Sale and one for Got-a-Deal

○ c. One domain with the root **4sale.com** with a lower domain being **got-a-deal.4sale.com**

○ d. One domain called **4sale.com** with two OUs: one for 4Sale and one for Got-a-Deal

Answer c is correct. This selection provides one of the solutions that would address the relevant concerns. For example, the company already has **4sale.com** registered and plans to continue with this naming convention for both companies when merged. Having two separate domains allows for distinct password structures, yet having 4Sale as the root still provides a way of implementing strong control. Another solution might have been an empty root with two distinct domains beneath, but this was not an option. Answer a is incorrect because it offers two distinct forests, and this provides a poor solution of unification and control. Answer b is incorrect because it offers an empty root, but then provides Organizational Units, which will not handle the issue of control over password security between the two locations. Answer d is incorrect for similar reasons as answer b; it provides a good root but does not allow for individual security policy control.

Need to Know More?

 McLean, Ian. *Windows 2000 Security Little Black Book*. The Coriolis Group, Scottsdale, AZ, 2000. ISBN 1-57610-387-0. Chapter 4 details the subprotocols, tickets, and configuration of Kerberos policies.

 Stallings, William. *Network Security Essentials: Applications and Standards*. Prentice Hall, Upper Saddle River, NJ, 1999. ISBN 0-13-016093-8. Chapter 4 discusses the Kerberos protocol and the rationale behind the development of the version 5 enhancements. Although this book deals specifically with the Unix operating system, it provides insights that are applicable to the Microsoft implementation of the security protocol.

 Search the TechNet CD (or its online version through **www.microsoft.com**) and the *Windows 2000 Server Resource Kit* CD using the keywords "Kerberos", "KDC", "SSPI", and "interoperability". This online source is Microsoft's most current collection of available technical bulletins and papers.

 ftp://athena-dist.mit.edu/pub/kerberos/doc/krb_evol.lpt Here, you can find the following paper: Kohl, John T., B. Clifford Neuman, and Theodore Y. Ts'o, *The Evolution of the Kerberos Authentication Service*. In Distributed Open Systems, pages 78-94. IEEE Computer Society Press, 1994. This highly technical paper discusses the development of the protocol and goes into the mechanism of key exchanges. It is an excellent source for Unix style terminology and definitions as well as a comprehensive discussion of the limitations of version 4 of Kerberos. It presents solutions provided by version 5.

 ftp://ftp.isi.edu/in-notes/rfc1510.txt Here, you can find the following paper: Kohl, John and B. Clifford Neuman, *The Kerberos Network Authentication Service (Version 5). Internet Request for Comments RFC-1510*. September 1993. This highly technical paper is the actual Internet RFC 1510 citation. This is how an Internet standards track protocol is specified for the Internet community and how technical requests for discussion and suggestions are solicited. It discusses improvements to the Kerberos protocol in version 5. It provides an overview and specification of version 5 of the protocol for the Kerberos network authentication system.

 **http://web.mit.edu/kerberos/www/papers.html#k5-papers** This home page hosted by MIT contains citations and references to information about Kerberos and related systems. It includes papers and technical discussions of Kerberos 4, Kerberos 5, and variants and derivatives of Kerberos. Each section includes tutorials, papers, protocol specifications, proposed protocol extensions, a discussion of APIs, and other material. Some of these papers are the original documentation that was released in the early 1990s.

 **www.isi.edu/gost/gost-group/products/kerberos/** This is the home page for the Kerberos Network Authentication Service. This site is hosted by the Global Operating Systems Technology Group, an informal group consisting of faculty, staff, and students of the Computer Networks Division of the Information Sciences Institute of the University of Southern California. It lists Kerberos-related materials, projects, and software products such as Sesame and NetCheque. It also provides links to documentation on areas such as RFC 1510 revision, PKINIT, and Public Key Cross-Realm authentication (PKCROSS) open issues.

 **www.isi.edu/gost/publications/kerberos-neuman-tso.html** Here, you can find *Kerberos: An Authentication Service for Computer Networks* by B. Clifford Neuman and Theodore Ts'o, reprinted, with permission, from *IEEE Communications Magazine*, Volume 32, Number 9, pages 33-38, September 1994. This well-written magazine article traces traditional authentication methods, discusses the use of strong authentication methods, and describes the Kerberos authentication system.

 **www.microsoft.com/windows2000/library/howitworks/security/ kerberos.asp** Here, you can find *Microsoft Windows 2000 Server White Paper—Windows 2000 Kerberos Authentication*. One of the Microsoft Windows 2000 resources under "How It Works," this paper provides a technical introduction to the Windows 2000 implementation of the Kerberos 5 authentication protocol. Starting with a nontechnical overview, it includes detailed explanations of important concepts, architectural elements, and authentication service features. The paper concludes with a discussion of interoperability with other implementations.

IP Security Architecture

· ·

Terms you'll need to understand:

✓ International Organization for Standardization (ISO) Open Systems Interconnection (OSI) Reference Model

✓ Symmetric and asymmetric encryption algorithms

✓ Hash message authentication code (HMAC)

✓ Data Encryption Standard (DES)- Cipher Block Chaining (CBC)

✓ Internet Key Exchange (IKE)

✓ Internet Security Association Key Management Protocol (ISAKMP)

✓ Oakley Key Determination Protocol

✓ Security association (SA)

✓ Tunneling

✓ Diffie-Hellman (DH) encryption algorithm

✓ Perfect Forward Secrecy (PFS)

✓ IP addressing scheme

Techniques you'll need to master:

✓ Describing different encryption techniques

✓ Discussing the impact of IP Security on total cost of ownership (TCO)

✓ Describing communication scenarios where IPSec enhances security

✓ Outlining the steps involved in deploying security protocols

✓ Listing the security services offered by IPSec security protocols

✓ Describing the components of IPSec policies

✓ Outlining the steps in a typical IPSec-secured exchange of information

Traditional network security draws analogies and terminology from the architecture of medieval castles and the way war was waged before field artillery was introduced. A long time ago, castles were built with high walls, moats, parapets, and drawbridges to thwart barbarian attacks. Terms like *bastion* (the strongest, most defensible part of a castle), and *choke* point (a narrow passage through which all traffic passes and can be monitored) are derived in part from the study of strategic warfare. Unfortunately, in the 21st century, sophisticated network attacks are more insidious than medieval battles. Although attacks are planned from outside the enterprise "walls," forces are now often unleashed from within the castle keep and its ring of authentication. Firewall technologies, secure routers, and foreign token authentication are ways to defend an enterprise from outside attack. The "hardened" bastion walls and moat, however, prove useless against an assault launched from within the boundaries of the enterprise. Unlike security technologies working at the Open Systems Interconnection (OSI) Application layer, Internet Protocol Security (IPSec) protects enterprise resources from both internal and external security breaches without increasing total cost of ownership (TCO); there are typically no extra costs for maintenance, training, or architectural changes.

IPSec, as defined by the Internet Engineering Task Force (IETF), uses two low-level, OSI Network layer security protocols: an Authentication Header (AH) and an Encapsulated Security Payload (ESP). AH provides source authentication and integrity; ESP offers confidentiality, authentication, and integrity. IPSec performs these services in such a way that only the principals know the key used in the information exchange. If the authentication data is validated while the exchange is taking place, the recipient of the message is assured that the information was not changed in transit.

Microsoft has enhanced IPSec by mixing asymmetric encryption algorithms with conventional symmetric cryptography and by providing automatic key management, which maximizes security and increases data throughput. Thus, information exchanges through the session pipe are guaranteed to be a combination of authentication, integrity, anti-replay, and (optionally) confidentiality. Working below the Microsoft Transport Driver (sometimes called "Device") Interface (TDI), IPSec provides the enterprise with a self-negotiating, transparent mechanism that supports strong network security.

IP and Security

With the proliferation of the Internet and the growing sophistication of users, IP as a network protocol has come under a variety of attacks. Table 5.1 lists some examples of IP attacks.

Table 5.1   Examples of IP attacks categorized by attack modality.

Involvement	Interception	Impersonation
Active	Connection hijacking: Active sessions (e.g., Telnet sessions) are seized.	IP (address) spoofing: Impersonation of an authenticated IP address.
Passive	Protocol analyzers (a.k.a. network sniffers): Information is captured in transit.	Data man-in-the-middle spoofing: Data is inserted into an active session pipe. An intruder between two parties can monitor and capture data.

The lack of protection at the OSI Network layer, although identified as a problem years ago, has never been addressed comprehensively because:

➤ Even though IP was designed for a distributed server architecture, the original architects did not anticipate how hostile the environment would become, nor the scale, number of participants, and sophistication of the user population.

➤ The IP protocol was not designed to provide any form of security services.

➤ Though designed to be an evolving protocol, IP clearly supports functions today for which it was never originally intended.

The stated objective of IP is to move data packets from one host computer to another on some network. No assumptions are made about what other computers or external devices are doing on the same network. When a third party intercepts and reads packets in realtime on that network pipe or on any data link, this activity (an example of a passive interception attack modality) is called *packet sniffing* or *eavesdropping*. In fact, Request for Comments (RFC) 1636 addresses architectural weakness in the Internet and recommends greater security for the exchange of information through the use of authentication and encryption. Susceptibility to passive interception varies with differences in protocol structure and the packet design. Table 5.2 compares the risk of a passive interception attack across different data links. It is obvious that most common channels that exchange information are highly susceptible to some form of attack.

The primary way to thwart interception and/or impersonation attack modalities is to encrypt the data stream. Several available methods are:

➤ *Link-level encryption*—This method is used in radio networking products. The packet stream is automatically encrypted upon transmission over unsecured channels and then decrypted at the receiving end.

➤ *End-to-end encryption*—This method is used in exchanges between encrypting routers. The packet stream is automatically encrypted upon transmission and then decrypted at the remote router.

Table 5.2	Potential of passive interception across various data links.	
Data Link	Risk	Comments
Ethernet	High	This is a bounded, broadcast-based protocol. Protocol analyzers are common diagnostic tools.
Fiber Distributed Data Interface (FDDI) (token ring)	High	Ring networks, although deterministic with regard to the token path, still have packets pass through, on average, half the nodes in the ring before reaching their destination.
IP over cable TV	High	Physical access to the TV cable is necessary; packet streams passed through Radio Frequency (RF) modems are unencrypted.
Microwave and radio	High	This is an unbounded, broadcast-based protocol. Any radio receiver will intercept the transmission.
Telephone	Medium	Physical access to telephone lines is necessary; packet streams over high-speed modems are more difficult to tap because data is transmitted across many frequencies.

➤ *Application-level encryption*—Packet encryption is done at the OSI Application layer.

It is noteworthy that, similar to IP, Domain Name System (DNS), an important component in Windows 2000, was not designed as a secure protocol either. Both IP and DNS were designed primarily to move data as quickly and efficiently as possible. Neither IP nor DNS is assumed to support any form of authentication or other security service. However, many network designs commonly use hostnames and IP addresses for authentication purposes. This has led to many kinds of security vulnerabilities such as client flooding (impersonation of a DNS nameserver that overwhelms a client with invalid DNS lookup responses), bogus nameserver cache loading (another impersonation of a DNS server), and rogue DNS server attacks (actual modification of the DNS namespace). Although strategies exist to minimize these attack modalities (e.g., double reverse DNS lookups and firewall technologies), reliance on IP addressing or hostnames for authentication opens a breach in any security design.

Examples of IPSec Deployment

The increasing frequency of IP spoofing and other impersonation attack modalities has resulted in the recommendation that authentication and encryption be included in the next generation of IP: IPng or IPv6. Wide deployment of the

128-bit addressing scheme and other IPv6 features will take several years, so many OSI Network layer security enhancements have been designed for the current version (IPv4) as well. Most discussions of IPSec apply to both the current IPv4 datagrams and IPv6 packets. In fact, IPSec is already providing enhanced security in information exchanges across unsecured Internet namespaces in a variety of scenarios, such as:

➤ *Remote site connectivity*—An organization can leverage Internet connectivity yet maintain intranet security and secured channels of communication through Virtual Private Networks (VPNs), discussed in greater detail in Chapter 6.

➤ *Remote access*—The advantages of Routing and Remote Access Service (RRAS), using proper client software, over a dedicated telephone line are now available through remote dialup to Internet Service Providers (ISPs).

➤ *Extranet connectivity*—Key exchange and management as well as authenticity and confidentiality provide virtually on-demand secured connectivity with new business partners outside an organization's enterprise boundaries.

➤ *E-commerce security*—Online businesses demand security enhancements, especially in authentication, confidentiality, and the ability to establish secured session pipes. Reliable key exchanges across unsecured namespaces are a prerequisite for such security technologies.

 Look for these deployment themes in either the "Objectives" or "Goals" section of exam case studies. IPSec is easier to implement than most other security technologies, which greatly enhances the security in the exchange of information and adds little to the TCO.

Building upon IPSec

IPSec provides comprehensive security management, including industry-standard encryption algorithms. These provide secured exchanges of information when TCP/IP is used on both ends of the session pipe between authenticated principals within the enterprise or across the corporate firewall. Microsoft's stated objective is end-to-end security strategies that prevent both external and internal attack modalities.

It is significant that IPSec comes with few or no deployment costs. Coordinating security at the Application layer of the OSI Reference Model is trivial because IPSec is deployed below the OSI Transport layer. Windows 2000 provides enterprise-wide protection and security subsystem safeguards that software applications automatically inherit. The encryption support of IPSec also extends to VPNs.

Advantages of IPSec include:

➤ *Full support for open industry (IETF) standards*—Interoperability is guaranteed by providing an open industry-standard alternative to proprietary IP encryption technologies.

➤ *Flexible security protocols and policies*—These policies can be implemented through easy-to-use Microsoft Management Console (MMC) snap-ins.

➤ *Transparency through flexible negotiation*—IPSec, invisible to both applications and users, is mediated through the IP Network layer with user intervention.

➤ *Authentication*—Both symmetric and asymmetric strong encryption algorithms block many interception attack modalities.

➤ *Confidentiality*—Information technology (IT) security controls that implement confidentiality prevent unauthorized access to data during exchanges.

➤ *Data integrity*—IP authentication headers and variations of hash message authentication code (HMAC) ensure data integrity during information exchanges.

➤ *Dynamic rekeying*—Dynamic rekeying during exchanges over unsecured session pipes thwarts most interception and impersonation attack modalities.

➤ *Secure end-to-end links*—Secure end-to-end links are provided for private network users within or across the enterprise boundary.

➤ *Easy implementation and centralized management*—Security policies and filters provide appropriate security levels while reducing administrative overhead and lowering TCO.

➤ *Scalability*—Security policies have a granularity that scales from a single workstation to the entire enterprise.

A historical theme shows the direct relationship between increased user demand for resources and services and a similar need for scalable security systems. The primary security concern in the NT 4 domain model was protection of resources from outside attack. With Active Directory (AD) now supporting distributed, enterprise-wide services, IPSec in Windows 2000 follows the Kerberos assumption (as discussed in Chapter 4) of *not making any assumption about authenticity*. IPSec protects information exchanges not just from outside attacks but from the more likely unauthorized rogue user inside the enterprise. Most technologies discussed in this chapter are invisible to the OSI Application layer and the user; they focus primarily on the packaging and exchanging of data below the OSI Transport layer and the analogous Microsoft TDI layer.

Industry Standards

Building on industry-standard cryptographic algorithms and security protocols, Windows 2000 is compliant with the latest IETF drafts proposed by the IPSec Working Group. IPSec, actually considered a protocol suite, provides not only an assortment of security techniques, but also a mechanism that negotiates, selects, and implements security services before engaging in a specific information exchange between two principals (such as a consumer and a service provider). Figure 5.1 uses a diagram published in RFC 2411 to show the interrelation among various IPSec component parts. It will serve as a reference model in the subsequent discussion.

Security Protocols

Secure Channel (SChannel) services at the OSI Transport layer provide, for example, security services to specific applications like browsers and Web applications. On the other hand, two other security protocols (AH and ESP) provide even lower-level security services of a similar nature. AH provides integrity, authentication, and anti-replay through partial sequence integrity checks by using an algorithm to compute a keyed message hash (HMAC) for each IP packet. AH does not offer confidentiality as a security service. ESP offers the same services as AH as well as provides confidentiality using the Data Encryption Standard (DES)-Cipher Block Chaining (CBC) algorithm, described in the "Encryption Techniques" section later in this chapter.

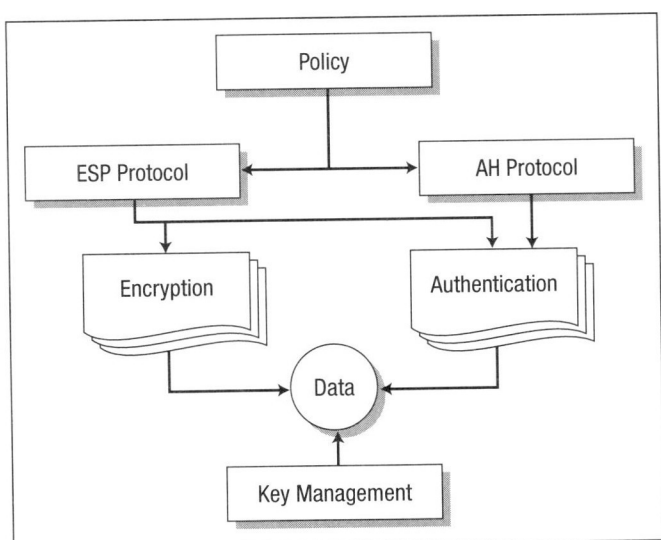

Figure 5.1   A modified IPSec overview from RFC 2411.

IPSec provides authentication, integrity, and confidentiality on both sides of a session pipe at the OSI Network layer, whether inside or outside a corporate firewall. Table 5.3 summarizes AH and ESP. ESP offers selectable features (e.g., encryption can be selected independent of authentication), so it is listed as two distinct variants of the same protocol.

The IPSec suite, as implemented in Windows 2000, is divided into AH, ESP, and Internet Key Exchange (IKE). IKE—the mechanism for exchanging keys between parties to ensure authenticity, integrity, and confidentiality—is further subdivided into two protocols:

➤ Internet Security Association and Key Management Protocol (ISAKMP)

➤ Oakley Key Determination Protocol

ISAKMP and Oakley are discussed in more detail in the "Key Management Protocols" section later in this chapter.

IPSec Architecture

In order for two client workstations to establish an IPSec connection, they must negotiate and agree on some arrangement of encryption algorithms, key generation methods, and security protocols. This arrangement is a Security Association (SA) between the two clients. ISAKMP defines the framework in which these security associations are established. Both SA and tunneling are two important concepts in IPSec architecture.

SA

An SA is a logical connection between two IPSec systems that defines, in unidirectional terms, the specific security protocol to be used when datagrams are passed to some destination IP address. This security descriptor or vector assumes one of two modes depending on the selected security protocol: transport or tunnel. SAs describe one-way relationships, so a bidirectional session pipe requires

Table 5.3 A comparison of IPSec security services by protocol.					
Protocol	Access Control	Integrity	Authentication	Partial Sequence Integrity*	Confidentiality
AH	Yes	Yes	Yes	Yes	No
ESP (encryption only)	Yes	No	No	Yes	Yes
ESP (encryption plus authentication)	Yes	Yes	Yes	Yes	Yes

* The rejection of packets not in sequence protects against replay attacks.

two SAs, one for each of the two directions. An SA indicates in which direction a specific security protocol carries a specific encryption service in the session pipe. An SA indicates only one security service carried by one protocol in one direction at one time.

When a session pipe carries two protocols, the SAs form an SA bundle. These SAs do not necessarily have to have the same destination IP address or target. One SA vector in an SA bundle, in other words, might specify that the AH protocol is supported up to a corporate firewall; another SA vector in the same bundle would extend ESP directly to some host behind that same firewall. Information about the SA vector, such as its source, destination, and whether it is inbound or outbound, is contained in some kind of security policy database. This data store assumes the form of an ordered list of policy entries separated according to inbound/outbound directions.

Tunneling

Tunneling or encapsulation consists of conceptually wrapping one packet inside another. A new header, in fact, is attached to the front of some existing datagram. This functionally changes the original packet header into a "data" payload of that leading or "encapsulating" header. Tunneling is a common technique used to carry some "unintelligible" protocol datagram over a network that does not "understand" that particular protocol directly. It is common practice, for example, to encapsulate Network Basic Input/Output System (NetBIOS) or Internet Protocol Exchange (IPX) in IP for transmission over a local area network (LAN)/wide area network (WAN) link. Using IPSec, you can hide the internal addressing scheme of a private network because the encrypted packet carrying that data is encapsulated in another IP datagram. Packets exchanged across hostile or unsecured namespaces in this way are never actually read; they remain payloads of other IP packets.

IPSec tunneling was originally designed for Mobile IP (RFC 2003), where a mobile host uses its home IP address for all transmissions regardless of its attachment to a remote network or foreign subnet. This topic is discussed in further detail in Chapter 6.

Encryption Techniques

Microsoft uses the following industry-standard cryptographic algorithms and authentication techniques:

➤ Diffie-Hellman (DH)

➤ Variations of HMAC

➤ DES-CBC

DH

The DH technique is a public-key algorithm invented by Whitfield Diffie and Martin Hellman. It allows two communicating principals to negotiate the sharing of a secret key over an unsecured namespace. DH is initiated when the two entities begin exchanging public information. Each entity combines the other's public information along with its own secret information to generate a shared-secret value.

HMAC

HMAC is a secret-key algorithm that provides integrity and authentication, and thus offers a defense to impersonation attack modalities. Authentication using keyed hash produces a digital signature for the packet that the receiver can verify. If the message changes in transit, the hash value is different and the IP packet is rejected. Message Digest 5 (MD5), sometimes referred to as HMAC-MD5, is a hash function that produces a 128-bit value. Secure Hash Algorithm (SHA), developed by the National Institute of Standards and Technology (NIST) and published as a federal information processing standard (FIPS PUB 180) in 1993, is a hash function that produces a 160-bit value. It was revised in 1995 as FIPS PUB 180-1, or SHA-1. Although somewhat slower than HMAC-MD5, SHA-1 is more secure.

DES-CBC

DES involves CBC, a secret key algorithm used for confidentiality. This key algorithm is a generated random number used with the secret key to encrypt the data.

 IPSec uses state-of-the-art cryptographic algorithms. The term *transform* is used to describe the specific implementation of an algorithm by an IPSec protocol. For example, when ESP invokes the DES algorithm, it is commonly called the ESP DES-CBC transform.

Key Management Protocols

Windows 2000 supports the standards-based protocols published by the IETF. IPSec complies with the latest IETF proposals, which include the ISAKMP/Oakley drafts. IPSec implements ISAKMP using the Oakley key determination protocol, which allows for dynamic rekeying.

ISAKMP

An SA must be established before IP packets can be transmitted. It is defined by a set of parameters that describe the security services and techniques, such as keys, that a security protocol uses to protect the exchange of information. An SA must be established between two principals using IPSec. ISAKMP defines a common, generic framework to support the establishment of these security associations. It does not define any one encryption algorithm, key-generation method, or security protocol.

Oakley

Oakley, a key determination protocol, uses the DH key exchange algorithm and supports Perfect Forward Secrecy (PFS). PFS ensures that if a single key is compromised, it permits access only to data protected by a single key. It does not reuse the key that protects communications to compute additional keys, nor does it use the original key-generation material to compute another key.

TCO

The principle of least privilege states that a (security) system is most robust when it is structured to demand the least privilege from its components. RFC 1636, as mentioned earlier in this chapter, suggests that the principle of least privilege might be in contradiction to the principle of least cost. Corporate security objectives very often fail to balance security needs, such as data protection, with the high costs of implementation and maintenance. In fact, the cost of a properly administered security policy—namely, the recurring costs of software upgrades, training, and cryptographic key management—typically exceeds the capital investment in original hardware. These recurring cost items are all variable components of TCO.

IPSec is a protocol suite that does not force the same investment of time or money as other security technologies, especially those working at the OSI Application layer. When correctly implemented, it is designed for interoperability because it is application independent. It does not affect networks or host machines that do not support it. It is fully compatible with IPv4 and will accommodate new cryptographic algorithms as they become available. It is a mandatory component of IPv6. In terms of TCO, IPSec is probably the most cost-effective security subsystem.

Software Upgrades

IPSec is deployed at the transport level, so it is transparent to software applications. These applications inherit the security without code modifications. Network-level security provides immense savings by eliminating the need for the upgrade of software applications to accommodate changes in the security structure.

Training

No user training is required because IPSec is transparent to users; this expense is eliminated.

Cryptographic Key Management

Manual key management, the regular changing of cryptographic keys, becomes extremely time-consuming and prone to intentional or unintentional noncompliance. Keys or passwords are often not changed or are changed on only some computers, in direct violation of corporate security policy. Windows 2000 IPSec, however, automatically handles key management and eliminates the maintenance costs associated with manual key management. TCO is lowered while compliance issues and stronger security are guaranteed across the enterprise.

Deployment Strategy

Windows 2000, through its selection of security protocols, provides scalable, enterprise-wide information security at a low TCO. There is both greater flexibility and granularity in security, permission management, and system-wide administration and policies as compared to earlier versions of NT. Security policies can be applied hierarchically, across the enterprise, or at the level of a single user, workstation, or group; there is minimal administrative overhead, redesign, or retraining. Furthermore, internal application programming interfaces (APIs) like the Security Support Provider Interface (SSPI) and the Cryptographic API (CAPI) provide extensible software interfaces that will accommodate future installable security libraries with minimal changes to the OSI Application layer.

I will go into greater detail about building a network security policy in Chapter 8. In brief, an administrator performs several steps in deploying security protocols:

1. Analyze the kind of information exchanged.

2. Create communications scenarios.

3. Determine security needs for each scenario.

4. Build the specific security policies.

Analyze Information

All information sent over networks or over the Internet is subject to, at the very least, interception attack modalities, including examination and modification. An administrator can determine which kinds of information are most valuable and what communications scenarios are most vulnerable.

Create Communications Scenarios

Organizations often follow specific, predictable operational steps in their business processes or information workflows. For example, a remote sales office sends daily business data to one of several different data stores in a centralized home office. Each communications scenario (e.g., operations information to a warehouse, daily payroll data and new hires to Human Resources, contracts to the Legal department) has different IP security policies associated with the confidentiality of the data. A policy needs to state, for example, that all communications to and from the HR department must be authenticated and confidential. Furthermore, required security levels will change, depending upon the sensitivity of exchanged information, operational procedures, and the relative vulnerability of the data link. IPSec configuration and deployment also relates to AD and Group Policy. You build a policy that can be applied to a forest, a tree, a domain, or a single computer, based on some scenario, in order to deploy IPSec in your enterprise.

Determine Security Levels

As with any security technology, it is necessary to adjust to changes in network infrastructure, the nature of the information exchanged, its level of sensitivity, and the vulnerabilities of the session pipe through which the message is sent. You need to assess the value of a resource in terms of its loss or unavailability over the short, medium, and long term, and categorize security levels based on an assessment of this loss. For example, information that could cause irreparable damage to your organization if it were publicly disclosed should be kept the most secured. Windows 2000 wizards and MMC snap-ins simplify the addition or modification of security options in any one security policy. For example, the IP Security Rule Wizard assists you in building a security rule that will control how and when security techniques are deployed based on a user-defined IP filter list. The wizard helps you compile a collection of actions that are activated when specific, user-defined criteria in this filter list, such as packet source, destination, and type, are met. These actions include IP tunneling attributes, authentication methods, and filter actions.

Build Security Policies

An administrator using Windows 2000 wizards and MMC snap-ins configures security attributes into what are called *security policies*, collections of associated negotiation policies and IP filter lists. Probably the simplest way to view the default IP security polices is in the IP Security Policy Management MMC snap-in.

During daily exchanges of information, negotiation policies determine the appropriate security services for any one particular communication scenario. Each negotiation policy sets multiple security methods so that appropriate security services are chosen. If the first method is not acceptable for the security association, the ISAKMP/Oakley negotiation service continues to look for a service until it finds one that it can use to establish the association.

An IP security policy can be assigned to the default domain policy, the default local policy, or a user-defined, customized local policy. During the logon process, computers automatically load these security policies. This lowers TCO by eliminating the need to configure or maintain each individual machine. Each security policy may contain one or more security rules, which are in turn related to filter lists and filter actions.

Rules, Filter Lists, and Filter Actions

A rule has six components:

➤ *IP filter list*—Target packets are defined by IP type or address with this rule

➤ *Filter actions*—Specific actions—namely, permit, block, and negotiate—are triggered when the target packet matches filter criteria in the filter list.

➤ *Security methods*—Computers secure an exchange of information using a high, medium, and custom method. The high method, which uses ESP, applies confidentiality (encrypted), authentication (authentic), and integrity (unmodified) security controls. The medium method, which uses AH, applies only confidentiality (encrypted) and integrity (unmodified) controls. The data in the medium method is not encrypted. The custom method allows the user to define an integrity algorithm without encryption, integrity with encryption, and session key settings.

➤ *Authentication methods*—This rule defines how trust is established between computers. Either the Windows 2000 default (Kerberos v5), a X.509 digital certificate from some specific certificate authority (CA), or a secret, preshared key can be specified. If a method cannot be negotiated, the next method in the list will be applied in descending order.

➤ *Tunnel settings*—This rule includes specification of transport or tunnel mode. Transport mode is the default method that provides end-to-end security between consumer and service provider on the same network, RAS, or intranet routers. It is not, however, recommended for exchanges of information across unsecured namespaces like the Internet. Tunnel mode is appropriate for information exchanges outside the boundaries of the enterprise. This topic is covered in Chapter 6.

➤ *Connection types*—This rule specifies whether network traffic will pass over all networks, the local area network, or remote access connections.

Security rules are applied to target computers matching specific criteria in an IP filter list. The filter list defines specific network traffic to which specific rules will apply. Filtering allows Windows 2000 to apply different security policies to different target machines. This filtering can include source and/or destination IP addresses; either individual host clients, network IDs, or subnet IDs that represent a scope of host IP addresses; or a specific DNS name. It also allows screening of the

IP protocol type—e.g., exterior gateway protocol (EGP), Internet Control Message Protocol (ICMP), host monitor protocol (HMP), and so on—and IP protocol port. By default, all IP or ICMP traffic—primarily Packet Internet Groper (Ping) packets—is targeted for IPSec rules. IP filters determine which actions to take, based upon the destination and protocol of individual IP packets.

A specific filter action is applied to a connection when communications are established through any of the filtered addresses or protocols. The default or customized action is then triggered. Actions are applied in the order in which they are listed. If an action cannot be negotiated, the next action in the list will be applied in descending order.

The three filter action options are:

➤ *Permit*—No IP security is applied to exchanges of information.

➤ *Block*—All packet traffic specified in the filter list is rejected.

➤ *Negotiate Security*—All packet traffic specified in the filter list must negotiate a compatible security protocol.

IPSec Policies

An IPSec policy is thus composed of IP security rules, IP filter lists, and IP filter actions. There are three built-in IPSec policies:

➤ *Client (respond only)*—Communications are normally unsecured. The default response rule is applied to secure connections that request security. Only the requested protocol and port traffic are secured.

➤ *Secure Server (require security)*—Secured connections must use Kerberos protocol for the exchange of information. Unsecured incoming packets from untrusted clients are rejected.

➤ *Server (request security)*—Secured connections are always requested but do not need to use Kerberos protocol for the exchange of information. Unsecured communications with untrusted clients are allowed. There is also an option to accept unsecured communications but respond with IPSec and thus negotiate a secured channel.

IPSec can significantly impact the flow of data. Although the built-in Server policy is IPSec aware and seeks the more preferred secured connection, it is flexible enough to exchange information with non-IPSec principals in the common Windows 2000 mixed-mode environment. Secure Server policy in a mixed-mode environment can cause major disruptions in the flow of services; those services that unsuccessfully negotiate security policies will fail to execute.

A typical exchange of information using IPSec occurs as follows:

1. A consumer sends a message to a service provider.

2. The consumer's IPSec driver attempts to match the outgoing packet's address or the packet type against the IP filter list.

3. The IPSec driver notifies ISAKMP to initiate security negotiations with the service provider.

4. The service provider's ISAKMP receives the security negotiations request.

5. Both principals initiate a key exchange, establishing an ISAKMP SA and a shared secret key.

6. Both principals negotiate the security level for the information exchange, establishing both IPSec SAs and keys.

7. The consumer's IPSec driver transfers packets to the appropriate connection type for transmission to the service provider.

8. The provider receives the packets and transfers them to the IPSec driver.

9. The provider's IPSec uses the inbound SA and key to check the digital signature and begin decryption.

10. The provider's IPSec driver transfers decrypted packets to the OSI Transport layer for further processing.

The IPSec security suite operates below the Transport layer, so neither application software nor user is aware of the additional security steps dealing with authentication, key exchanges, and encryption during the transmission of data. Routers and switches, in addition to workstations, ignore IPSec packet information. To ensure compatibility in heterogeneous environments, Windows 2000 IPSec-aware clients send data packets without encryption to non-Windows 2000 clients. Firewalls, security gateways, and proxy servers, however, require special configuration to avoid rejection of packets because they read and sometimes alter parts of the packet as it travels from its source to its destination—that is, end-to-end. Some devices, such as firewalls, translate the network addresses as they forward a packet from an external network to an internal network. Other times, the device will alter a header in a packet. In both cases, this network address translation (NAT) process either rejects the packet or causes the packet to fail an integrity check at its destination. Another problem with IPSec is in the exchange of key and dynamic rekeying between two parties that have their addresses translated; the outside party never really "knows" the IP address of the internal party, so the key exchanges to an "authentic" address always fail. These issues limit the use of IPSec, especially across public networks.

An IP Security Architecture Case Study

ExamCram Ltd.: Considering Network Layer Security Solutions

ExamCram Ltd., a publishing company in AnyTown, Arizona, primarily focuses on developing and selling advanced technical training materials. The Legal department at ExamCram Ltd. is expanding operations as the company accepts more clients. MyCompany Inc. does business with ExamCram Ltd. and is located in the same building.

Current LAN/Network Structure

All 100 client machines are configured in a single Windows 2000 root domain. The client systems are running Windows 2000 Professional, with Office 2000 being utilized as an applications package. Each system is connected to a 10Mbps hub through 10Mbps LAN cards, although Category 5 Unshielded Twisted Pair (UTP) cabling is connecting each system and hub in a star topology.

A centralized Legal department requires that communications:

➤ Within the department be secure but not confidential

➤ Between the Legal department and other departments within the organization be both secure and confidential

The Legal department runs on network 192.168.2.0/24. A network outside the department runs on 192.168.3.0/24.

MyCompany Inc. has 22 Windows 2000 Professional computers in a single child domain. The client systems are running Office 2000 as an applications package. Each system is connected to a 10Mbps hub through 10Mbps LAN cards, although Category 5 UTP cabling is connecting each system and hub in a star topology. A professional IT person administers the network.

Proposed LAN/Network Structure

No changes in the current structure are proposed at this time.

Current WAN Connectivity

No changes in the current structure are proposed at this time.

Proposed WAN Connectivity

No changes in the current structure are proposed at this time.

Design Commentary

It is assumed that IPSec is applied to all communications initiated by the Legal department. The VP of Sales at ExamCram Ltd. says, "We need to have our contracts signed, sealed, and delivered as quickly as possible to beat our competition. I don't want good authors getting away from us."

Current Internet Positioning

ExamCram Ltd. is registered as **examcram.com**. The Marketing department is registered as **mrkt.examcram.com**. MyCompany Inc. is registered as **mycompany.com**.

Future Internet Plans

No changes in the current structure are proposed at this time.

Company Goal

The only concern at the moment is the Legal department. All legal correspondence is considered top secret. Only top management and the Legal department need to know the actual terms of a book contract.

Commentary

Figure 5.2 shows the implementation plan, which is as follows:

1. Create a security policy in the IPSec Security Polices on Active Directory node in your MMC snap-in, which is assigned to the default domain policy with the following two negotiation policies and IP filters:

   ➤ *LegalPol1*—Provides confidentiality for all communications outside the Legal department. Under Edit Rule Properties, in the Security Method, select High (ESP). The caption reads: Data Will Be Encrypted, Authentic, And Unmodified.

   ➤ *LegalPol2*—Provides authentication and integrity for all communications within the Legal department. Under Edit Rule Properties, in the Security Method, select Medium (AH). The caption reads: Data Will Be Authentic And Unmodified, But Will Not Be Encrypted.

2. Create an IP filter associated with one of the negotiation policies listed in Step 1. The Legal department runs on network 192.168.2.0/24. A network outside the department runs on 192.168.3.0/24.

   ➤ *LegalFilt1*—Is for communications outside the Legal department and is associated with LegalPol1. The filter's source IP address is 192.168.2.0/24, its destination IP address is 192.168.3.0/24, and its protocol type is ALL.

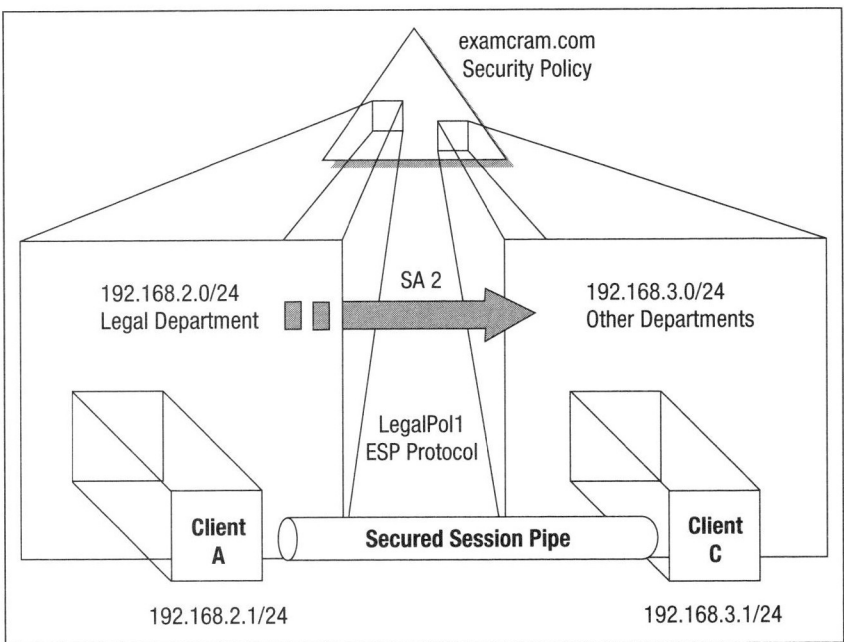

Figure 5.2   An example of IPSec deployment.

➤ *LegalFilt2*—Is for communications within the Legal department and is associated with LegalPol2. The filter's source IP address is 192.168.2.0/24, its destination IP address is 192.168.2.0/24, and its protocol type is ALL.

For communications outside the Legal department, both source and destination IP addresses are checked against the IP filters in the legal security policy. The IPSec level for the communication is determined by the associated negotiation policy assigned to an IP address range in the filter list.

For example, if a client in the Legal department with 192.168.2.1/24 as an IP address sends data outside the department, LegalFilt1 is triggered. The communication is sent according to the security level that LegalPol1 specifies. Thus, the authentication, integrity, and confidentiality IT security controls are applied using the ESP protocol to the information exchange, as you saw in Figure 5.2.

Practice Questions

Case Study

4Sale, an online bartering company in ThatTherePlace, North Dakota, primarily focuses on selling inexpensive, odd-lot items. The merger between 4Sale and Got-a-Deal has been finalized, and both companies have merged office space in the same office building.

Current LAN/Network Structure

4Sale is presently running Windows 2000 Server in native mode. One member server supports Exchange, and another member server is running Internet Information Server (IIS) 5, and Proxy Server 2. All 100 client machines are configured in a single domain model. The client systems are running Windows 2000 Professional, with Office 97 being utilized as an applications package. Each system is connected to a 10Mbps hub through 10Mbps LAN cards running Category 5 UTP cabling in a star topology.

Got-a-Deal has undergone changes. It is running all 22 client machines in a single child domain under the 4Sale root domain. The client systems are running Windows 2000 Professional, with Office 97 being utilized as an applications package. Each system is connected to a 10Mbps hub through 10Mbps LAN cards running Category 5 UTP cabling in a star topology. These hubs are on the same backbone as 4Sale but have a different subnet.

Proposed LAN/Network Structure

4Sale is developing its online barter/trading business through business alliances. It wants secure communications among specific departments. For example, the exchange of bids must be authenticated and kept confidential.

Current WAN Connectivity

4Sale has a T1 connection to an ISP in OverThere, North Dakota. Got-a-Deal has 56Kbps dial-up networking connectivity through the same ISP.

Proposed WAN Connectivity

No changes are planned at this time.

Directory Design Commentary

The Network Manager at 4Sale says, "We want to establish a firm security foundation that will be application independent. Our major IT concern is confidentiality within the company. In the future, I will be coming back to you with questions about remote connectivity."

Current Internet Positioning

4Sale is registered as **4sale.com**. Got-a-Deal has been selling its goods through local companies and through the **4sale.com** Web site.

Future Internet Plans

No changes in the current structure are proposed at this time.

Company Goal with Windows 2000

4Sale puts you on retainer. You will spend most of your time answering questions to help top management compile the company's long-term objectives.

Question 1

The CEO of 4Sale tells you, "We need security, but I don't want to overspend on technology." What TCO component is affected by deploying IPSec? [Choose the best answer]

○ a. Software upgrades

○ b. Training

○ c. Hardware

○ d. All of the above

○ e. None of the above

Answer e is correct. IP Security works at the OSI Transport layer. Software upgrades, training, and hardware are not directly affected. In other words, IPSec adds features like strong encryption without affecting the TCO specifically in terms of software upgrades, training, and hardware. Therefore, answers a, b, and c are incorrect. A feature like manual key management is an example of what is affected during deployment of IPSec; in other words, its maintenance is eliminated.

Question 2

The Network Manager at 4Sale asks, "From a technical point of view, what do I gain from using IPSec?" [Check all correct answers]

❑ a. Dynamic suballocation

❑ b. Confidentiality

❑ c. Flexible security protocols

❑ d. Flexible negotiation

❑ e. Data integrity

Answers b, c, d, and e are correct. Confidentiality, flexible security protocols, flexible negotiation, and data integrity, along with dynamic rekeying of sessions, are all advantages of IPSec. Dynamic suballocation applies to storage. Therefore, answer a is incorrect.

Question 3

The Network Manager at 4Sale asks, "How does IPSec actually work?" List the following elements in the correct sequential order:

Secured packets are exchanged.

The consumer's IPSec driver matches the outbound IP address to the filter list.

Security association is established.

The consumer's IPSec driver notifies ISAKMP to initiate security negotiations.

The service provider's ISAKMP receives the request and initiates the key exchange.

The correct answer is:

The consumer's IPSec driver matches the outbound IP address to the filter list.

The consumer's IPSec driver notifies ISAKMP to initiate security negotiations.

The service provider's ISAKMP receives the request and initiates the key exchange.

Security association is established.

Secured packets are exchanged.

Question 4

The Network Manager at 4Sale asks, "I mentioned to you my long-term plans to connect to other locations throughout the country. How does IPSec help us get closer to that goal?" Select the scenarios that would benefit from IPSec. [Check all correct answers]

❑ a. Remote site connectivity

❑ b. Remote access through TCP/IP

❑ c. Extranet connectivity

❑ d. All of the above

Answer d is correct. Remote site connectivity, remote access through Transmission Control Protocol/Internet Protocol, and extranet connectivity would all benefit from IP Security.

Question 5

The Network Manager at 4Sale says, "I've been reading *MCSE Windows 2000 Security Design Exam Prep.* I think I understand now: IPSec, like Kerberos, assumes that servers in the enterprise are authenticated; only the sender in a message exchange needs to be authenticated." Is the Network Manager correct?

○ a. Yes

○ b. No

Answer b, no, is correct. The Network Manager is incorrect. Neither IP Security nor Kerberos makes any assumptions about the authenticity of machines in the enterprise. Keys expire and need to be renewed. Also, the recipient of a message requests verification of the sender's authenticity when the mutual authentication flag is set during the setup of Kerberos policy.

Question 6

The Network Manager at 4Sale asks, "How do I organize IPSec's suite of protocols to better understand what each one does?"

List the components and subcomponents of the IPSec suite. Create an ordered list of only the appropriate components/subcomponents, and group each subcomponent under the correct component.

Internet Key Exchange

Oakley Key Determination Protocol

Internet Security Association

Key Management Protocol

Encapsulated Security Payload

Authentication Header Protocol

Security protocols

The correct answer is:

> Security protocols
>
>> Authentication Header Protocol
>>
>> Encapsulated Security Payload
>
> Internet Key Exchange
>
>> Internet Security Association
>>
>> Key Management Protocol
>>
>> Oakley Key Determination Protocol

Question 7

The Network Manager at 4Sale says, "Let me know whether I have this straight. An example of tunneling is simple: A data packet is encapsulated in a network protocol and exchanged across unsecured namespaces. Nothing else." Is the Network Manager correct?

○ a. Yes

○ b. No

Answer a, yes, is correct. The Network Manager is correct. Tunneling occurs at the Open Systems Interconnection (OSI) Network layer when one protocol datagram or packet is "wrapped" or encapsulated in another. You can tunnel packets without encrypting them.

Question 8

The Network Manager at 4Sale asks, "When I build security policies, what protocols do I need to know about?" You tell him he needs to be aware of OSI Network layer protocols. Which of the following are such protocols? [Check all correct answers]

❑ a. Authentication Header Protocol

❑ b. Authentication Header Payload

❑ c. Encapsulated Security Protocol

❑ d. Encapsulated Security Payload

Answers a and d are correct. The correct names are Authentication Header Protocol and Encapsulated Security Payload. Therefore, answers b and c are incorrect.

Question 9

> The Network Manager at 4Sale asks, "When I build a security policy, it asks me to choose between AH and ESP. What security services does AH provide?" [Check all correct answers]
>
> ❑ a. Access control
>
> ❑ b. Integrity
>
> ❑ c. Authentication
>
> ❑ d. Partial sequence integrity
>
> ❑ e. Confidentiality
>
> ❑ f. All of the above
>
> ❑ g. None of the above

Answers a, b, c, and d are correct. Authentication Header (AH) provides access control, integrity, authentication, and partial sequence integrity. Because AH doesn't offer encryption, it doesn't provide confidentiality. Therefore, answer e is incorrect, as are answers f and g.

Need to Know More?

 Garfinkel, Simson and Gene Spafford. *Practical Unix and Internet Security, Second Edition.* O'Reilly & Associates, Sebastopol, CA, 1996. ISBN 1-56592-148-8. Chapter 16 provides a very general, nontechnical discussion of IPSec. The authors briefly discuss link-level and end-to-end encryption in the context of TCP/IP networks. Chapter 17 deals specifically with TCP/IP services.

 Murhammer, Martin W. et al. *TCP/IP Tutorial and Technical Overview, Sixth Edition.* Prentice Hall, Upper Saddle River, NJ, 1998. ISBN 0-13-020130-8. Section 5.5 provides a technical review of IPSec architecture, the various protocols, the combination of IPSec protocols, and IKE. Section 5.4, Network Address Translation and NAT Limitations, is especially relevant in a discussion of incompatibilities within the IPSec suite. This book describes these protocols from a Unix perspective but is relevant to Windows 2000 topics.

 Shinder, Thomas W., Debra Littlejohn Shinder, and D. Lynn White. *Configuring Windows 2000 Server Security.* Syngress Media, Inc., Rockland, MD, 2000. ISBN 1-928994-02-4. Chapter 7 provides an excellent discussion that begins with network encroachment methodologies. The authors provide a comprehensive and technical discussion of IPSec architecture. They conclude with sections on how to evaluate levels of security, build rules, and configure policy.

 Stallings, William. *Network Security Essentials: Applications and Standards.* Prentice Hall, Upper Saddle River, NJ, 1999. ISBN 0-13-016093-8. Chapter 6 provides a detailed and technical discussion of the IPSec protocol suite. There is also a section on key management. This text discusses the protocols from a Unix perspective. Nevertheless, most topics are relevant in the Windows 2000 environment.

 Search the TechNet CD (or its online version through **www.microsoft.com**) and the *Windows 2000 Server Resource Kit* CD using the keywords "IPSec", "AH", "ESP", "DES", and "SA".

 **www.faqs.org/rfcs/** This is the RFC search page. Relevant RFCs found at this site include:

> RFC 2401: An overview of a security architecture. This memo specifies the base architecture for IPSec-compliant systems. Replaces RFC 1825.

> RFC 2402: Description of a packet authentication extension to IPv4 and IPv6. This memo describes the IP Authentication Header (AH) used to provide connectionless integrity and data origin authentication for IP datagrams, and to provide protection against replays. Replaces RFC 1826.

> RFC 2406: Description of a packet encryption extension to IPv4 and IPv6. This memo describes the Encapsulated Security Payload (ESP) header that is designed to provide a mix of security services in IPv4 and IPv6. Replaces RFC 1827.

> RFC 2408: Specification of key management capabilities. This memo describes a protocol utilizing security concepts necessary for establishing Security Associations (SAs) and cryptographic keys in an Internet environment.

 **www.ietf.cnri.reston.va.us/html.charters/ipsec-charter.html** This is the IETF's IPSec Web site. It offers links to draft papers and RFCs related to IPSec.

 **www.microsoft.com/windows2000/library/howitworks/security/ ip_security.asp** This site offers the Windows 2000 Server White Paper, *IP Security for Microsoft Windows 2000 Server*. This technical paper provides a clear overview of IPSec as well as a scenario that describes in general terms how security policies are configured. It supplies many of the terms associated with this particular security suite and thus provides a good introduction to this area.

Remote
Connectivity Issues

Terms you'll need to understand:

✓ Network Address Translation (NAT)

✓ Secure Sockets Layer/Transport Layer (or Level) Security (SSL/TLS)

✓ Hypertext Transfer Protocol (HTTP)

✓ Secure Hypertext Transfer Protocol (S-HTTP)

✓ Virtual Private Network (VPN) client

✓ VPN server

✓ Tunneling protocol

✓ IP Security (IPSec) protocol suite

✓ Security Parameter Index (SPI)

✓ Tunneled data

✓ Firewall technologies

✓ Demilitarized zone (DMZ)

✓ Screened-host architecture

✓ Screened-subnet architecture

Techniques you'll need to master:

✓ Describing how different IPSec components support remote access

✓ Understanding the basic remote access deployment scenarios

✓ Describing different tunneling modes

✓ Discussing feature differences in VPN-related security protocols

✓ Describing the three general firewall topologies

In this chapter, I explore the technologies used to exchange information with re-mote sites. The topic of remote connectivity begins with a discussion of Virtual Private Networks (VPNs). Microsoft has integrated VPN solutions with Routing and Remote Access Service (RRAS) because of the critical role this technology plays in supporting telecommuting, the designs of remote branch office enterprises, and off-site enterprise partnerships. This form of remote connectivity uses a secure tunneled connection within which only authenticated messages are exchanged. This chapter discusses several protocols emphasizing the OSI Link Layer and end-to-end security, including Layer 2 Tunneling Protocol (L2TP) and Point-To-Point Tunneling Protocol (PPTP). I also discuss a variety of topologies that involve the transmission of secured information over an unsecured namespace.

The chapter describes in greater detail IP Security (IPSec) and other security pro-tocols associated with VPN, providing the critical security controls: encryption, authentication, and integrity. L2TP and IPSec together provide strong security solutions. IPSec, discussed in Chapter 5, is especially relevant in discussions of information authenticity and confidentiality, not just in an e-commerce scenario but also in daily interoffice communications.

Then, I discuss three general firewall architectures in the context of remote con-nectivity. This topic provides a foundation for Chapter 7. Finally, this chapter ends with a variety of VPN scenarios that show various remote access features of Windows 2000.

An Overview of VPN

A VPN is created when a private channel, extended typically across an unsecured public network like the Internet, connects two computers. The private communi-cation channel creates, in effect, a "virtualized network" within which both these computers can work. From the consumer's viewpoint, this virtual network provides the same functionality found within the physical boundaries of the enterprise by delivering point-to-point private data links through a private tunnel. Figure 6.1 shows a VPN for ExamCram Ltd. A client workstation in **east.examcram.com** connects with a client workstation in **west.examcram.com** across the Internet. The connection travels through a tunnel that extends from client to server (more commonly referred to as end to end). The nature of the internetwork is irrelevant to both consumers, neither of which can tell the differ-ence between a VPN connection and a physical connection to another workstation across the room. VPN connections may sometimes be appropriate between, for example, subnets on the same local area network to provide strong authentication and confidentiality.

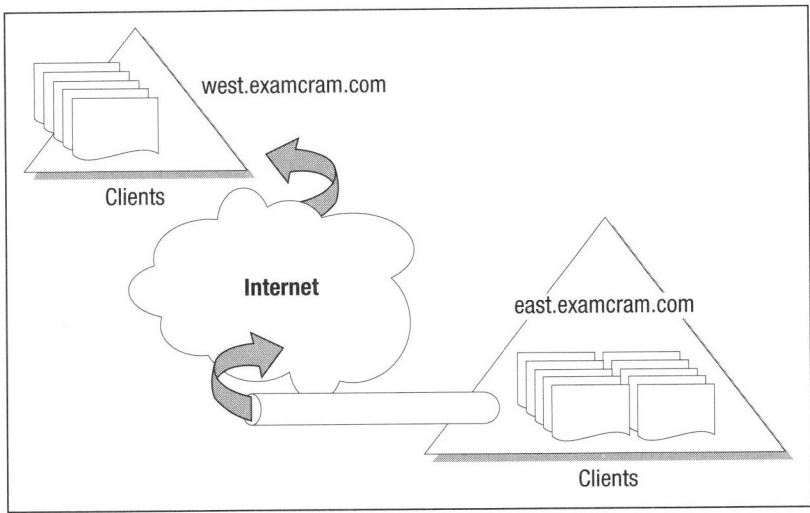

Figure 6.1 Representation of a virtual private network.

Before I can delve into the topic of VPNs, I need to give you a little background. This section provides the technical foundation for the rest of the chapter. I then go on to discuss tunneling and Network Address Translation (NAT).

Security Protocols

Windows 2000 supports the following new security protocols that verify a user's security credentials when connecting to network services:

➤ *Layer 2 Tunneling Protocol (L2TP)*—Discussed in the "VPN Security Protocols" section later in this chapter, this OSI Link layer protocol is a combination of PPTP and Layer 2 Forwarding (L2F, described in RFC 2341) and was originally created by Cisco Systems.

➤ *Extensible Authentication Protocol - Transport Layer (or Level) Security (EAP-TLS)*—The EAP protocol (RFC 2284), especially with TLS (RFC 2246), supports two-factor authentication through application programming interface (API) extensions and uses Message Digest 5 (MD5) as an encryption method.

➤ *Bandwidth Allocation Protocol (BAP)*—This control protocol enhances the ability of Point-To-Point Protocol (PPP) Multilink Protocol to bundle multiple physical connections in a single virtual connection of greater bandwidth.

➤ *Remote Authentication Dial-In User Service (RADIUS)*—A vendor-independent distributed user authentication service and dial-in security solution (RFC 2058 and 2138).

These security protocols lend support to legacy NT 4 authentication protocols such as PPTP, Password Authentication Protocol (PAP), Challenge Handshake Authentication Protocol (CHAP), Microsoft Challenge Handshake Authentication Protocol (MS-CHAP), and Shiva Password Authentication Protocol (SPAP, used in mixed environments that support Shiva LAN Rover software). Most noteworthy of the legacy protocols is PPTP, which was originally created by the PPTP Industry Forum. I will reference different components of the IPSec protocol suite, discussed in Chapter 5 of this book and described in RFCs 2401-2409, throughout this chapter.

Basic Remote Access Models

Windows 2000 supports three basic remote access models for a networked enterprise:

➤ Transport layer security technologies

➤ Private or trusted network infrastructures

➤ End-to-end network security

Many in the computer industry consider these three models to be examples of VPNs, but Microsoft has a more restricted view of VPNs, especially in relation to Windows 2000, which I will also address.

Transport Layer Security Technologies
Secure Sockets Layer/Transport Layer Security (SSL/TLS), Unix Sockets (SOCKS), and Secure Hypertext Transfer Protocol (S-HTTP)—among others—provide security to applications interfacing directly with the OSI Transport layer. SSL/TLS applications are typically written for the personal computer market and tend to scale poorly because of the specificity in their design. SOCKS, developed for the non-Windows market, is an authenticated firewall traversal protocol that provides both extensible authentication for distributed server architectures and sufficient granularity to control authorization of inbound/outbound transport sessions. SSL/TLS and SOCKS are complementary services that provide Transport layer security within VPNs and extranets. S-HTTP is an extension to the HTTP protocol that supports secured exchanges of information. SSL/TLS and S-HTTP use different technologies. SSL/TLS creates a secure connection by authenticating two computers; S-HTTP secures the transmission of individual messages.

Private or Trusted Network Infrastructures
Companies that physically deploy internal or outsourced data communication infrastructures for wide area networks (WANs) achieve their security objectives through true physical isolation. This method of deployment, however, does not

avoid the problems common to other forms of deployment (such as passive interception or impersonation). Once the capital investment is made, though, these private infrastructures are less likely to adapt to newer technologies or to provide the plasticity necessary to cope with future business objectives. This is because these infrastructures are typically expensive physical devices with structural limitations to installation, modification, extensions, and scalability, not to mention the training needed to maintain them. There is thus a twofold disadvantage to this kind of security deployment method: First, just like other technology, the investment experiences almost immediate obsolescence once it is deployed, and second, the cognitive dissonance experienced by management over the perceived return on investment increases in relation to the total cost of the infrastructure.

End-to-End Network Security

Security systems working end to end are a more functional approach to deployment than a private, physical infrastructure because the end-to-end systems transparently negotiate appropriate technologies and protocols from installed support services at each layer of the network. One example of end-to-end remote connectivity is when a person telecommuting from home or working on the road transmits data over a dedicated private link directly to some corporate server. The dial-up networking technology on the telecommuter's machine establishes secure connections with the branch office VPN server just as easily as employees communicating from one end of the office to another. The possible support service selections are controlled by remote access policies, which simplifies administration and maintenance. This approach to security is more centered on the network infrastructure (that is, more network-centric) and adopts a more restricted use of the VPN category as a support technology that provides security services across a public or untrusted network infrastructure.

VPN and RRAS

Although many in the computer industry consider the three models just mentioned to be distinct VPN categories, Windows 2000 integrates a secured end-to-end remote connectivity solution within its operating system design. It incorporates VPN into its RRAS and refines the definition to include:

➤ Any secured access from some remote client to some gateway through a public (Internet) infrastructure or within some private or outsourced one

➤ Any secured gateway-to-gateway connections across public, private, or outsourced networks

With the service integrated, both IPSec and Active Directory (AD) directory services provide the foundation for secured access to enterprise resources. Thus, remote access services have been fully incorporated into the network operating system and can benefit from centralized administration and policy-managed control.

Tunneling

A *VPN client* (for example, a remote user or consumer) connects to a *VPN server* (some service provider) through a *tunnel* (session pipe) using a *tunneling protocol*. *Tunneling* is a technique where a data packet is transferred inside the frame or packet of another protocol and thus uses the infrastructure of one network to travel across another network. Data packets are called the *payload*. The tunneling protocol encapsulates the data frame by appending an additional header on the front of the tunneling protocol's data packet. The new header provides routing information and conceals the true nature of the payload. The encapsulated packets are routed between tunnel endpoints over some other network. The logical path along which the encapsulated packet is routed is called the *tunnel*. At the end of the tunnel, the encapsulated payload is stripped of its wrapper and is forwarded to its final destination. Tunneling describes the entire process: encapsulate the data packet at the source, transmit the data packet through the tunnel, and unencapsulate the data packet at the destination.

When confidentiality is required, you need a private tunnel. To emulate that private link, you encrypt the packet for confidentiality before encapsulating it. Then, if some third party intercepts a packet in transit, that party would not be able to decipher the message. The private link in which encrypted data is encapsulated and transmitted is the VPN connection. When you create and send data without encryption, you are using a tunnel but not a VPN connection.

Note: A VPN connection sends encrypted data through the tunnel. If the data must be encrypted, the connection must be private.

Both the tunnel client and tunnel server must use the same OSI (Open Systems Interconnection) Layer 2 Data Link or OSI Layer 3 Network-based tunneling protocol. When an OSI Layer 2 protocol is used, frames are exchanged between client and server; packets connote an OSI Layer 3 exchange. Both PPTP and L2TP, working with frames at OSI Layer 2, create tunnels that are similar to sessions between the two endpoints. The tunnel and various configuration variables (such as address assignments, encryption, and compression variables) are negotiated. In addition, the L2TP over IP uses User Datagram Protocol (UDP) port 1701 to send control messages that provide tunnel maintenance.

There are two kinds of tunnels:

➤ *Voluntary tunnels*—When a client or a user requests to be a tunnel client, you can configure and create a voluntary tunnel where the client is the tunnel endpoint.

➤ *Compulsory tunnels*—With a compulsory tunnel, some device other than the client, such as a VPN-capable dial-up access server, is the tunnel endpoint and acts as the tunnel client. Such an endpoint is commonly known as a Front End Processor (FEP) in PPTP, an L2TP Access Concentrator (LAC) in L2TP, or an IPSec gateway in IPSec. An FEP must be able to support and negotiate establishing a tunnel when a client attempts to connect to it.

A virtual interface on which all VPN connections are made is created when a VPN server is configured. Both the client and server interfaces must have IP addresses assigned. The VPN server can obtain either statically assigned or DHCP (Dynamic Host Configuration Protocol)-leased IP address ranges for all VPN clients.

NAT

NAT reassigns the private IP addresses of, usually, a small number of client machines inside a network to published—and therefore accessible—IP addresses on the Internet. The internal, typically nonrouteable IP addresses are translated to a scope or range of IP addresses from a pool that the NAT administers. An advantage of using a NAT is that fewer published or officially assigned IP addresses are required because the NAT can reuse the same IP addresses at different times. Another advantage is security; the internal IP address ranges are never made known outside the enterprise.

A disadvantage of NATs is the size of the pool; the number of addresses in the NAT's assignable pool limits the number of concurrently used addresses. Other disadvantages arise from the inability of some protocols (such as L2TP and IPSec) to pass-through the translation process. The Internet Key Exchange (IKE) protocol, a component of the IPSec security suite, does not function properly when actual IP source or destination addresses are unknown. Thus, both L2TP/IPSec and IPSec tunnel mode (discussed later in this chapter) cannot engage in the automated exchange of keys across a NAT. The Internet Engineering Task Force (IETF) IPSec workgroup is currently working on correcting these and other incompatibilities.

VPN Security Protocols

Among the authentication protocols mentioned at the beginning of this chapter, several protocols are categorized by Microsoft specifically as VPN tunneling protocols—namely, PPTP and L2TP, based on PPP or IPSec. Although these specific protocols generally perform the same functions and are considered competing technologies, each offers different features particularly suited for different situations. You must therefore consider what features each protocol offers in relation to design goals before you choose which one to deploy.

Design Considerations

When planning VPN deployment, especially across a public network, security protocol features must be evaluated in terms of the three design approaches to the exchange process:

➤ Addressing each intermediate node link to link between the source and destination

➤ Viewing the deployment from end to end

➤ Dealing with security controls at the OSI Application layer

Now, I'll discuss PPP, PPTP, L2TP, and IP Sec in terms of these design considerations.

PPP

PPP is a widely supported communication protocol, so it benefits from multiprotocol support from such diverse network architectures as Novell Internet Protocol Exchange (IPX) and Apple (AppleTalk). PPP also offers a wide range of user authentication options that support smart card authentication, including CHAP, MS-CHAP, MS-CHAP2, and EAP. As mentioned earlier in this chapter, Microsoft implements PPTP and L2TP with EAP-TLS, a strong authentication protocol based on public key certificates. The TLS component is used for two-factor authentication technologies like smart cards.

PPTP

PPTP is a common protocol for both client-to-gateway and gateway-to-gateway VPN scenarios. PPTP not only passes through NATs but also supports mutual authentication based on consumer passwords and encryption keys. Thus, PPTP is inexpensive to install and simple to maintain. It uses a Transmission Control Protocol (TCP) connection for tunnel maintenance and Generic Routing Encapsulation (GRE) encapsulated PPP data frames for tunneled data. Payloads can be both encrypted and compressed.

L2TP

L2TP is a mature IETF standards-based protocol. PPP packet frames are encapsulated in L2TP for transmission across a variety of network and communications protocols like IP, X.25, Frame Relay, or asynchronous transfer mode (ATM). It was specifically designed for client-to-gateway and gateway-to-gateway connections with broad tunneling and security interoperability. L2TP has wide vendor support because it addresses the IPSec shortcomings of client-to-gateway and gateway-to-gateway connections.

L2TP tunneled in IP using UDP port 1701 is used as the VPN tunneling protocol over the Internet for tunnel maintenance. Compressed or encrypted PPP frames encapsulated in L2TP also use UDP to transmit tunneled data. L2TP tunnels appear as IP packets, so IPSec transport mode provides authenticity, integrity, and confidentiality security controls.

A security design calling for the encapsulation of an L2TP packet in IPSec leverages the authentication and encryption security controls of the IPSec wrapper with the protocol interoperability of the PPP payload. This combination is commonly referred to as L2TP/IPSec.

 Microsoft recommends the L2TP/IPSec combination as the best multivendor, standards-based client-to-gateway VPN solution.

IPSec

As mentioned in Chapter 5, the IPSec protocol suite consists of two security protocols—Authentication Header (AH) and Encapsulated Security Payload (ESP)—and key management provided by a variety of mechanisms and features. To review, the two protocols provide varying amounts of security services; ESP provides encryption and a combination of encryption and authentication, whereas AH provides just authentication. A security association (SA) between the sending and receiving parties provides access control based on the distribution of a cryptographic key and traffic management relative to these two protocols. This SA is either one one-way relationship or two one-way relationships in complementary directions. A Security Parameter Index (SPI) uniquely distinguishes each SA from other SAs.

IPSec is controlled specifically by a security policy of both sender and receiver and one or more SAs negotiated between them. The security policy consists of a filter list and associated actions. If some packet's IP address, protocol, or port matches the criteria, a specific security action is applied.

Key management involves the manual or automatic determination and distribution of secret keys between sender and receiver for both AH and ESP. The default protocol, referred to as IKE and previously known as ISAKMP/Oakley, supports automated SA negotiations and the automatic generation of keys. Internet Security Association and Key Management Protocol (ISAKMP) generically defines the management of SAs and keys. Oakley Key Determination Protocol uses public key encryption (sometimes referred to as the Diffie-Hellman encryption algorithm) to exchange and update key materials for the SAs.

IPSec Tunnel and Transport Modes

IPSec is deployed in *tunnel mode*—in which one packet is encapsulated or tunneled in another—or *transport mode*, which secures the packet exchange from end to end, source to destination. IPSec tunnel mode is used primarily for link-to-link packet exchanges between intermediary devices like routers and gateways; transport mode provides the security service between the two communicating endpoints.

IPSec provides different security controls by using the two protocol packet types:

➤ *IP 50 (ESP) packet type*—Offers authentication, integrity, and confidentiality

➤ *IP 51 (AH) packet type*—Offers authentication and integrity

Either mode can employ ESP or AH packet types. Both modes require that the two clients engage in a complex negotiation involving the IKE protocol and PKI certificates for mutual authentication.

IPSec tunnel and transport modes as well as L2TP/IPSec encounter incompatibility issues when dealing with NATs. Neither L2TP/IPSec nor IPSec tunnel mode functions when the IKE protocol is used across a NAT. Microsoft is actively encouraging the development of IPSec Remote Access (IPSRA) solutions for this IKE compatibility problem as well as integration with DHCP and other IETF standards for extensible authentication using EAP and General Security Services API (GSS-API).

 Microsoft recommends that you choose PPTP in scenarios that require NAT-capable VPN connectivity or where security that requires IPSec or PKI is not a major factor. It supports mutual authentication based on passwords and encryption keys.

Security Protocols Compared

PPP is actually a set of standardized authentication protocols (RFC 1334) that support interoperability among the various kinds of remote access software available. Thus, we can discuss a general PPP dial-up sequence in which various operations, including link configuration and authentication, are performed following the initial connection to some remote PPP server from some PPP client machine. Technical differences among the authentication protocols discussed in the previous sections are summarized in Table 6.1.

Table 6.1 Feature differences among network security protocols.					
Feature	**PPTP**	**L2TP**	**L2TP/IPSec**	**IPSec Transport**	**IPSec Tunnel**
Consumer authentication	Yes	Yes	Yes	Under development[1]	Under development[1]
Client authentication	Yes[2]	Yes	Yes	Yes	Yes
Packet authentication	No	No	Yes	Yes	Yes
Encryption	Yes	Yes	Yes	Yes	Yes
PKI support	Yes	Yes	Yes	Yes	Yes
NAT capable	Yes	Yes	No	No	No
Multiprotocol support	Yes	Yes	Yes	No	Under development[1]
Dynamic tunnel address assignment	Yes	Yes	Yes	N/A	Under development[1]
Multicast support	Yes	Yes	Yes	No	Yes

[1] Support is under development by the IETF IPSec working group.

[2] The user is authenticated when used as a client VPN; the machine is authenticated in a gateway-to-gateway connection.

 You should be able to arrange components (for example, PPP client, PPP server, RADIUS server, Web Server, Domain Controller) and protocols (for example, TCP/IP, PPP, L2TP, L2TP/IPSec) in some logical order and then connect components with the appropriate protocols. Not all components and protocols will be relevant in the context of the specific situation.

VPN Support

Microsoft currently says that IPSec tunnel mode by itself is a poor choice for most client-to-gateway VPN solutions. Although interoperability problems exist, gateway-to-gateway solutions are functional in tunnel mode. On the other hand, IPSec transport mode effectively delivers end-to-end authenticity and encryption within the network. In client-to-gateway and gateway-to-gateway VPN situations, user authentication and internal address configuration are critical but problematic because most aspects of this part of the VPN technology are either proprietary to the IPSec specifications or are weakly adopted extensions of them.

Note: The IETF IPSec working group is currently developing user authentication and internal (NAT) address features in both tunnel and transport modes. Microsoft has not announced plans to provide IPSec to legacy NT 4 or Windows 9x.

Windows 2000 includes L2TP/IPSec support for packet encryption from client-to-gateway or gateway-to-gateway scenarios and has tested interoperability with a variety of vendor-implemented VPN scenarios. Microsoft supports

L2TP/IPSec only on Windows 2000; it has not announced plans to bring this protocol to legacy operating systems like NT 4 or Windows 9x.

Windows 2000 includes PPTP support for password-based and public-key authentication (the latter through EAP) for both client-to-gateway and gateway-to-gateway configurations across most Windows operating system platforms, including down-level systems like NT 4 and Windows 9x.

Table 6.2 compares network security protocol differences among various VPN connection types.

VPN Management Policies

When an enterprise deploys a remote networking solution, it supports controlled access to resources and assets such as information. This access is provided by both roaming and remote users. In an enterprise, remote offices are just as common as remote users and assume a similar role. The remote local area network (LAN) connects to and shares resources; whether it's doing so across the internal enterprise or an unsecured network like the Internet, the same security controls are necessary because the security demands are the same. Thus, a VPN solution must provide:

➤ User authentication and auditing

➤ Address management

➤ Data encryption

➤ Key management

➤ Multiprotocol support

Remote Access Policy Management

In addition to the issues of encryption, Windows 2000 provides an extensive set of administrative policies in both the client-to-gateway and gateway-to-gateway scenarios. These access policies control consumer remote access to network

Table 6.2 VPN effectiveness of the network security protocols.					
Connection Type	PPTP	L2TP	L2TP/IPSec	IPSec Transport	IPSec Tunnel
End-to-end (no NAT)	Good	Good	Good	Good	Good
End-to-end (NAT)	Good	Good	Not good	Not good	Not good
Client-to-gateway	Good	Good	Good	Good	Not good
Gateway-to-gateway	Good	Good	Good	Good	Fair

resources through dial-up connections (RRAS), PPTP, and L2TP/IPSec connections. Access and authorization are granted or denied based on a variety of factors, including user ID calling/called station ID, day and time restrictions, TCP/UDP port number, tunnel type, encryption level, and so on. It is noteworthy that these policies are available in both native mode using the AD environment and mixed mode using a legacy NT 4 PDC directory database through the RADIUS protocol. A RADIUS server can also provide proxy services where authentication requests are forwarded to other RADIUS servers in remote locations. Internet Service Providers (ISPs) use this design to provide uninterrupted support services to roaming subscribers. Finally, RADIUS provides call-accounting services for auditing.

Other remote access policy management issues involve the design and placement of calling and answering routers, especially when dealing with a persistent branch office connectivity scenario. If a VPN answering router is deployed to support some remote branch office, it should be dedicated to remote access services and, depending on business needs, typically supports 24/7 access to the local network. VPN calling routers, on the other hand, do not require that guaranteed level of service. Consider hardware, maintenance, and support issues when formulating your remote access policy.

Client Management

The IPSec suite as well as security systems like Kerberos and PKI depend on AD for the definition of security policy. Windows 2000 by default installs the PPTP, L2TP, and IPSec protocols. Client configurations are accomplished in two ways:

➤ *Client side*—The New Connections Wizard guides the user through a series of dialog boxes to configure the client machine.

➤ *Administration side*—The Connection Manager Administration Kit and Connection Point Services deliver customized remote access configurations for both direct-dial and VPN client installations.

Firewall Technologies

Windows 2000 divides its security into distributed security within the enterprise and network security, which extends outside the enterprise perimeter. The simplest way to protect a computer system is through physical isolation from outside agents. However, electronic commerce and the need for remote access for mobile computing have forced the opening of the enterprise to outside forces and a hostile unsecured environment. Physical isolation is all but impossible in most network situations. One compromise approach is to allow partial connectivity through some managed bidirectional control or choke point. With this solution—as with a medieval castle—traffic moving to and from the interior of the fortress is forced through a narrow gate with extra-thick walls called the bastion. This heavily fortified central gateway can be closed and defended against attack. The gateway itself is not the security device; it provides an especially defensible setting that complements the military forces housed within the stronghold. Firewall technologies do not replace network security systems; they complement already hardened technologies.

Thus, firewall technologies separate the internal, distributed security network from outside, external namespaces like the Internet. Quite often, a specific topology called a demilitarized zone (DMZ), which physically separates data packet flows, is deployed. This middle area is designed to break the physical continuity between internal data packets and external ones. Just as a brick wall that separates office suites or apartments in large buildings retards or prevents the spread of fires, firewalls can limit network damage through physical containment.

Firewall Components

Firewall technology consists of chokes and various gates. *Chokes* are computers or communication devices that selectively restrict data flows among networks. Although these are often implemented using relatively expensive routers, a simple alternative is a multihomed server built using any computer with two or more network interface cards (NICs). This type of server is inexpensive to install and easy to implement.

Gates, such as packet filter routers and proxy servers, are specially designed software, devices, or computers that handle one or more firewall services or functions. A single computer designated to handle all firewall services is called a *bastion host*. Alternatively, one or more gates that support different functions are positioned inside a middle area or DMZ, as mentioned earlier in this chapter.

Packet Filter Routers

A *packet filter* is a device that examines a datagram or packet for some predefined contents; it is typically a router. Normally, this function is performed at some external router that interfaces with some other network or specifically the Internet. Packet filters work at the OSI Data Link, Network, or Transport layers. Therefore, any implementation requires that you formulate a policy and configure the filter to recognize inbound/outbound IP addresses or TCP/UDP source/destination ports.

Proxy Servers

These service providers act as intermediaries between the host machines within the enterprise and the hosts outside the enterprise namespace. The proxy server plays a significant role in managing IP address ranges by effectively replacing internal address ranges with its own address. This feature, NAT, provides significant protection from the outside attacks by, in effect, hiding the internal network address ranges from outside view. At the same time, it disrupts security protocols that authenticate to those internal addresses from the outside. This topic is discussed in more detail in the "Basic Remote Access Models" section earlier in this section and in Chapter 5. Its caching services improve response time for repeatedly requested Internet information, reduce the need to download material from remote Internet hosts, and reduce the amount of traffic on the Internet. Instead of filtering packets or protocol types, you can achieve higher-level filtering more logically by combining the use of specific Uniform Resource Locators (URLs) with domain names. In addition, you can permit or deny the passage of URL pattern matching, domain names, and host names through the proxy gate. Finally, some applications such as browsers are specifically configured to work exclusively through proxy servers to further control the flow of data to and from the enterprise.

Proxies come in two basic forms:

➤ *Circuit-level gateway*—Working at the OSI Transport layer, this separates the end-to-end TCP flow of packets by acting as a forwarding agent. The internal host sends its packet to the circuit-level gateway, and the packet is forwarded to the outside target from the gateway. The gateway, in relaying the packets across its own isolated address space, can apply filter rules regarding inbound/outbound TCP/IP addressing.

➤ *Application-level gateway*—Also called a proxy server, this relays OSI Application-level protocol traffic such as Simple Mail Transfer Protocol (SMTP), HTTP, and File Transfer Protocol (FTP) services. The filtering is application specific, so the application clients must be configured to access the gateway. This type of gateway is more secure than a packet filter gateway because Application-level gateways scan for specific applications, not IP addresses and TCP/UDP port numbers. Alternatively, these gateways add processing overhead to each transmission because all traffic must be examined and then forwarded to its target destination.

Firewall Architectures

A key to good firewall design is to create one choke point through which all outbound and inbound traffic must pass. This single portal, especially when isolated within a separate subnet, offers a defensible embattlement as well as an easily administered focal point for the deployment of network authentication, authorization, and auditing (AAA) services.

It is a conservative assumption that, given enough time and processor/memory firepower, someone will find a method to circumvent *any* firewall technology or topology. However, a well-designed multilayered security system offers sustainable resistance to any attack long enough to do the following:

➤ Detect and implement some corrective actions.

➤ Exhaust, at least temporarily, the attacker's resources long enough to implement some corrective actions.

You cannot truly deter an attack because, ethically speaking, there is no acceptable counterattack or form of retaliation outside of some form of legal prosecution. In practical terms, there is only a sustainable defense. You should view with suspicion any suggestion that an attack is unlikely due to some cost/benefit or "logical" argument; the motivation behind a security attack may have little to do with either practicality or logic.

Firewall architectures or choke point designs generally assume one of three topologies: packet filter, screened-host, and screened-subnet architectures.

Packet Filter Architecture

The packet filter topology is the most common option and the simplest. It uses a router as both a firewall component and outside, or external, network interface. The router, acting as a choke, relays inbound and outbound packets after inspecting packet IP addresses and TCP/UDP port numbers. Advantages of this option are its cost-effectiveness and low maintenance. Disadvantages include a lack of auditing features, vulnerability as a single-line-of-defense firewall strategy, and the success of the filter rules in rejecting rogue (authenticated but unauthorized) or bogus (unauthenticated) packets. Attacks to a packet filter router include:

➤ IP address spoofs that impersonate legitimate source IP addresses

➤ Source routing attacks in which specific routes across source-routing bridges are specified in an attempt to bypass inspection

➤ Tiny fragment attacks that circumvent the TCP filtering rules by sending illegally sized packets

Figure 6.2 shows a packet-filtering router architecture.

Screened-Host Architecture

This topology uses a computer (the host) as a gateway behind the packet-filtering (screening) external network interface. Figure 6.3 shows a screened-host architecture with a single-homed bastion.

A single-homed host or server has only one NIC and one IP address. When more than one NIC is added to the screened-host firewall, the bastion is considered a dual-homed (or multihomed) host or server. These servers are also sometimes

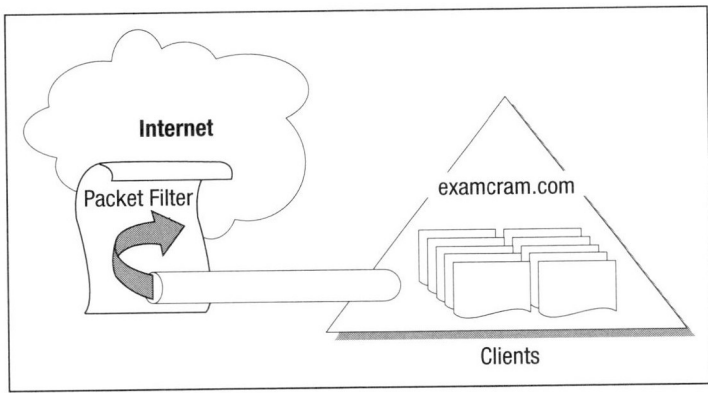

Figure 6.2   A packet-filtering (screening) router.

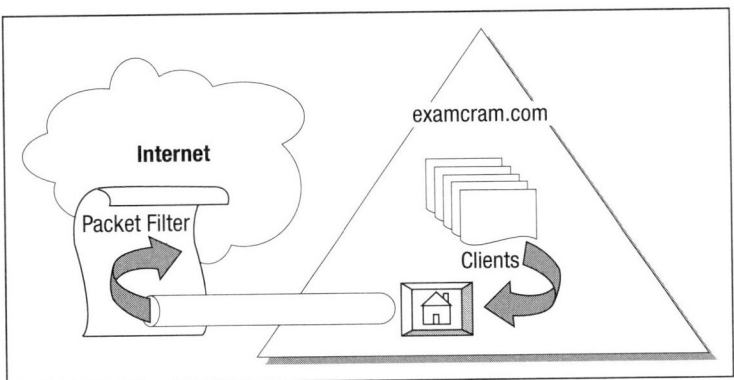

Figure 6.3   A screened-host (single-homed server) firewall.

called *dual-ported hosts*. IP packet forwarding must be disabled so that rules and policies determine which packets are relayed across the two or more NIC cards and the IP subnet spaces. Similarly, network users should be prevented from logging on to this server. Figure 6.4 shows a screened-host architecture with a dual-homed bastion.

The packet filter sends inbound packets directly to the bastion host and, similarly, accepts only outbound traffic from the bastion host. Thus, the bastion host is a choke point through which all outbound traffic must be directed. In addition to serving as a circuit-level gateway, the bastion typically functions as an Application-level gateway behind which externally accessible SMTP and HTTP application service providers can, in effect, hide. Advantages of dual-homed servers include a more sophisticated firewall technology than single-homed servers because the bastion, physically separate from the packet filter, also supports circuit-level and Application-level gateway services. The firewall now

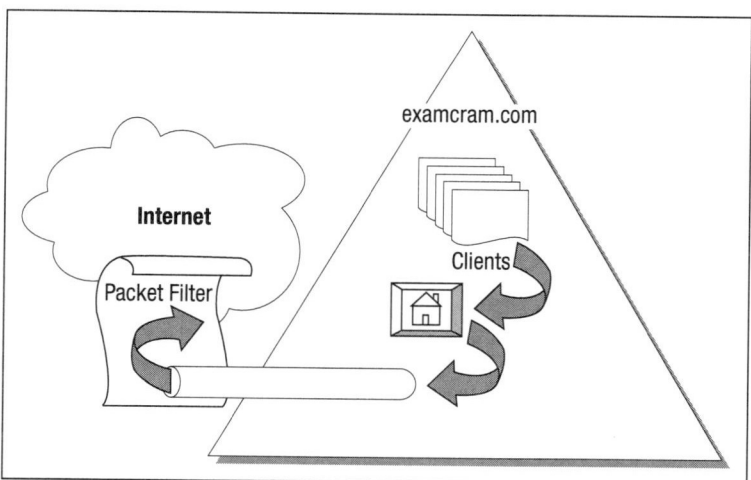

Figure 6.4 A screened-host (dual-homed server) firewall.

has a second line of defense that is technologically different from the first line of defense (the packet filter). With the addition of a multihomed server, the physical separation of IP address ranges adds a further level of complexity and hides the internal IP address ranges, thwarting, for example, the spoofing that can defeat a packet filter. Disadvantages of a bastion include increased cost, increased overhead, and reduced performance (as compared to packet filters) because packets must pass through at least two distinct firewall layers. With the increase in rules and policies, users typically experience a decrease in provided services. For example, policies may disallow some online services such as inbound Telnet.

Screened-Subnet Architecture (DMZ)

The last and most secure design is to isolate a subnet between two screening packet filters. Figure 6.5 shows a picture of this topology.

In this DMZ located between the two packet filters, the multihomed bastion host supports client-level and Application-level gateways. In addition, however, the externally accessible application service providers (such as SMTP, FTP, and HTTP servers) are deployed in this subnet. Both external and internal screening packet filters direct inbound and outbound traffic, respectively, through the bastion host. Application servers must also direct their traffic through the bastion because the external packet filter rejects outbound packets from any other source. Advantages of the DMZ architecture include three distinct lines of defense; two perimeter packet filters and one multihomed bastion. The DMZ physically separates the internal network from the outside world. The bastion host is not only a choke point for both inbound and outbound traffic but also effectively conceals private IP address ranges. Neither inbound nor outbound packets can bypass this

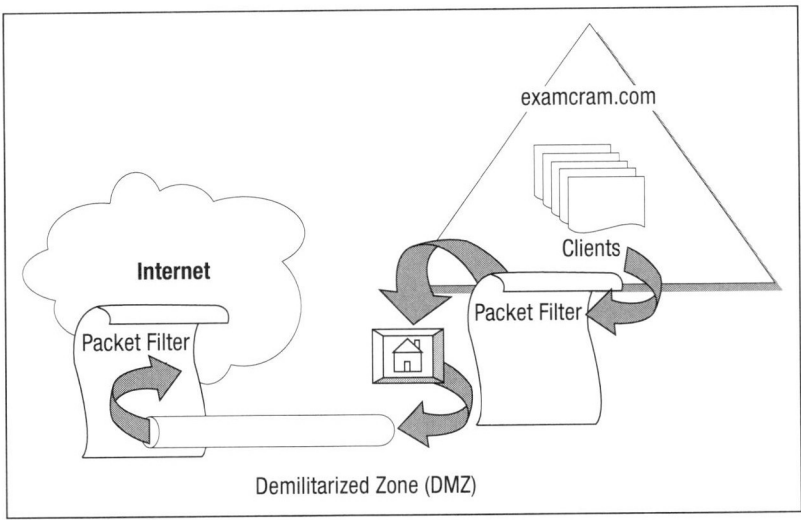

Figure 6.5   A screened-subnet firewall (DMZ) architecture.

security topology, so no a priori assumptions are made regarding the possible staging area for some security attack.

Of the three firewall architectures—packet filtering, screened hosts, and screened subnets—the screened-subnet firewall (or DMZ) topology is the most secure and makes the fewest assumptions regarding the origins of a security attack.

Firewall Policies

Just as with any other security technology, policy precedes implementation. Corporate objectives must define what will pass and what will be blocked at the firewall choke point for both inbound and outbound data. These rules, like IP filters (defined in Chapter 5), determine how the firewall mechanism operates. The firewall operates according to one of two basic strategies:

➤ *Default permit*—What is not expressly prohibited is, by default, permitted.

➤ *Default deny*—What is not expressly permitted is, by default, prohibited.

The two strategies differ primarily in the degree of management; a default permit strategy requires that you explicitly list hosts or protocols that are considered security threats; otherwise, it offers a relatively open gateway to and from the enterprise namespace. Alternatively, a default deny strategy enables pass-through only upon request for that passage case by case; it requires much more management but is more conservative in its restrictive approach to the data flows. It is noteworthy that the default deny strategy errs administratively on the side of greater, more restrictive, security. This is, however, a safer defensive posture when an enterprise borders on any public network, including the Internet. Even the most restrictive firewall policies are not panaceas, nor should you view them as turnkey security solutions when defending a network from any attack modality.

 Firewall technologies and IPSec can be considered first-line defenses in securing the enterprise from a hostile assault. It is important to realize that these technologies can be deployed without any assumption regarding from which direction the attack will take place—from outside or inside the secured enterprise namespace.

Positioning firewalls at network choke points can:

➤ Block access to specific Internet sites by host address, address range, or protocol type (for example, FTP or Telnet).

➤ Audit inbound and outbound data flows or protocol type; an example is corporate-sanctioned passive interception or eavesdropping.

➤ Provide the basis for secured information exchanges across unsecured namespaces using a VPN.

➤ Simplify the authentication process within an especially secured subnet within the enterprise namespace.

Practice Questions

Case Study

4Sale, an online bartering company in ThatTherePlace, North Dakota, focuses primarily on selling inexpensive, odd lot items. A merger between 4Sale and Got-a-Deal has been finalized and both companies have merged office space in the same office building. The corporate side of the merger has gone well and the staff is fully adjusted. The IT department, though well staffed, still needs your help.

Current LAN/Network Structure

4Sale is presently running Windows 2000 Server in native mode; one member server supports Exchange, whereas another is running Internet Information Server 5 and Proxy Server 2. All 100 client machines are configured in a single-domain model. The client systems are running Windows Professional, with Office 97 being utilized as an applications package. Each system is connected to a 10Mbps hub through 10Mbps LAN cards running Category 5 UTP cabling in a star topology.

Got-a-Deal is running all 22 client machines in one child domain under the 4Sale root domain. The client systems are running Windows Professional, with Office 97 being utilized as an applications package. Each system is connected to a 10Mbps hub through 10Mbps LAN cards running Category 5 UTP cabling in a star topology. These hubs are on the same backbone as 4Sale but have a different subnet.

Proposed LAN/Network Structure

4Sale is developing its online barter/trading business through business alliances. It is now investigating the use of remote access for employees and secured private networks for branch offices and business alliances.

Current WAN Connectivity

4Sale has a T1 connection to an ISP in OverHere, North Dakota. Got-a-Deal has 56Kbps dial-up networking connectivity through the same ISP.

Proposed WAN Connectivity

No changes are planned at this time.

Directory Design Commentary

Network Manager at 4Sale says, "We are negotiating with several companies on the West coast. How can we give them limited access to our network?"

Current Internet Positioning

4Sale is registered as **4sale.com**. Got-a-Deal has been selling its goods through local companies and through the **4sale.com** Web site.

Future Internet Plans

No changes in the current structure are proposed at this time.

Company Goal with Windows 2000

4Sale has put you on retainer and has given you strict orders that there should always be a higher level of control than what any one department or division individually proposes. You continue to help develop the standards and procedures that the IT department will implement.

Question 1

Considering the case study provided, what issue might be a major concern if you want to use L2TP/IPSec? Give a simple answer that emphasizes the key points of the case study.

○ a. UDP filtering policy

○ b. Authentication and encryption

○ c. Client-to-gateway connections

○ d. All of the above

○ e. None of the above

Answer d is correct. Answer a is correct because Layer 2 Tunneling Protocol tunneled in Internet Protocol uses User Datagram Protocol port 1701 for tunnel maintenance. Answer b is correct because compressed or encrypted Point-To-Point Protocol frames are encapsulated in L2TP; IP Security provides authenticity, integrity, and confidentiality. Answer c is correct because L2TP was specifically designed for client-to-gateway connections. Because all the answers are correct, answer d is the best choice.

Question 2

Network Manager for 4Sale asks, "If we install a proxy server, what protocols can we use?" You must consider the impact of Network Address Translation (NAT) in answering this question. Which protocols can pass through a NAT? [Check all correct answers]

❑ a. PPTP

❑ b. L2TP/PPP

❑ c. IPSec transport mode

❑ d. IPSec tunnel mode

Answers a and b are correct. PPTP and L2TP/PPP can both pass through a NAT, so they can be used in conjunction with a proxy server. IP Security, because of incompatibilities with the automated exchange of keys, does not function properly when network addresses are translated. Therefore, answers c and d are incorrect.

Question 3

Network Manager for 4Sale asks, "Do I have to leave the RRAS server up all the time?" For future growth projections, distinguish between answering routers (RRAS servers enabled for VPN) and calling routers or local RRAS servers that are calling, for example, a home office. Choose the correct statements from the following options.

❑ a. Answering routers must be dedicated.

❑ b. Calling routers must be dedicated.

❑ c. Answering routers do not have to be dedicated.

❑ d. Calling routers do not have to be dedicated.

Answers a and d are correct. Answering routers must be dedicated, and calling routers do not have to be dedicated. Answer b is incorrect because it doesn't matter whether the calling router is dedicated. A client or calling router makes requests either on demand or on a fixed schedule. The answering router however, must be accessible 24/7 to handle incoming requests. Answer c is incorrect because answer a is correct.

Question 4

Network Manager says, "What configuration provides the least exposure to internal IP addresses ranges?" The Network Manager is asking several question at once. He mentions internal IP addresses, which suggests that there are external and internal addresses. This, in turn, implies the use of a NAT, which implies that the VPN is located in such as way that it protects the integrity of the internal network addressing scheme.

Place the following in their proper order to indicate the flow of a packet through a firewall. Start at the highest level and work toward the bottom, with the bottom being the strongest applied.

External source

Bastion server

External packet filter router

Internal network

VPN server

Internal packet filter

The correct order is:

External source

External packet filter router

Bastion server

VPN server

Internal packet filter

Internal network

Question 5

Network Manager for 4Sale says, "What is the most flexible protocol that can be both encrypted and compressed?"

○ a. L2TP

○ b. PPTP

○ c. Both are the same in terms of encryption and compression

○ d. Neither can be encrypted or compressed

Answer a is correct. Layer 2 Tunneling Protocol is the most flexible protocol that can be both encrypted and compressed. Although both Layer 2 Tunneling Protocol and Point-To-Point Tunneling Protocol use Transmission Control Protocol connections for tunnel maintenance and generic routing encapsulation (GRE) to encapsulate Point-To-Point Protocol frames for tunneled data, they are not the same in terms of encryption and compression. PPTP is not as flexible as L2TP because PPTP requires IP, whereas L2TP requires only that tunnel media provide point-to-point connectivity. PPTP supports only a single tunnel, but L2TP allows the use of multiple tunnels. L2TP uses 4 bytes of overhead when compression is enabled; PPTP uses 6. L2TP alone provides tunnel authentication; PPTP does not.

Question 6

Network Manager of 4Sale says, "We have a static IP address on the Internet. In simple terms, what kinds of scenarios are we talking about for remote access for our offices and staff?" You want to suggest no more than three scenarios. The Network Manager suggests two. The best two scenarios to use in this conversation with the Network Manager are:

Remote access for employees

Persistent branch office

Place the following items in the appropriate scenarios (the design flow is from the remote client end coming into the 4Sale internal network):

VPN calling server

VPN client

VPN answering server

T1

Internet cloud

ISP

The correct answer is:

    Remote access for employees

        VPN client

        ISP

        Internet cloud

        VPN answering server

Persistent branch office

VPN calling server

T1

ISP

Internet cloud

VPN answering server

Question 7

Network Manager of 4Sale says, "If we really involve ourselves in remote access, is there a scalable approach that might incorporate long-term management features like auditing and accounting?" You need to discuss RADIUS. What is its key feature?

○ a. Ability to authenticate users through methods other than Windows 2000

○ b. Support for multiple VPN and/or RRAS servers configured with a common policy

○ c. Centralized call-accounting services

○ d. Proxy service to forward authentication

○ e. All of the above

Answer e is correct. Remote Authentication Dial-In User Service offers the ability to authenticate both Windows 2000 and non-Windows users, support for multiple Virtual Private Network and/or Routing and Remote Access Service (RRAS) servers configured with a common policy, centralized call-accounting services, and proxy service to forward authentication to other RADIUS servers.

Question 8

Network Manager for 4Sale says, "What are the advantages of using Layer 2 protocols?" You want to explain that Layer 2 protocols inherit authentication methods from PPP. Which of the following authentication methods are inherited? [Check all correct answers]

❏ a. PAP

❏ b. CHAP

❏ c. SPAP

❏ d. EAP-TLS

Answers a, b, c, and d are correct. Microsoft Virtual Private Networks support all these Data Link layer (OSI Layer 2) authentication protocols. PAP (Password Authentication Protocol), a weak method, uses a clear-text authentication scheme. CHAP (Challenge Handshake Authentication Protocol) does not transmit the actual password and is thus a stronger scheme than PAP. Remote consumers use a Message Digest 5 hash of their credentials in response to a challenge by a network access server. SPAP (Shiva Password Authentication Protocol) is used in mixed environments that support Shiva Local Area Network Rover software. Finally, EAP-TLS (Extensible Authentication Protocol - Transaction Level Security) is a Microsoft implementation of a strong authentication method that uses public-key certificates.

Need to Know More?

 Garfinkel, Simson and Gene Spafford. *Practical Unix and Internet Security, Second Edition.* O'Reilly & Associates, Sebastopol, CA, 1996. ISBN 1-56592-148-8. Chapter 21 of this book contains a detailed discussion of firewall technology. Chapter 22 discusses wrappers and proxies, as well as SOCKS. A separate section offers a 90-page discussion on how to handle security incidents. Although this book is specifically about the Unix architecture, these sections are well written and relevant to Windows 2000.

 McLean, Ian. *Windows 2000 Security Little Black Book.* The Coriolis Group, Scottsdale, AZ, 2000. ISBN 1-57610-387-0. The author discusses VPNs in Chapter 11 and follows topical discussions with "Immediate Solutions" sections that explain, in a step-by-step format, how to implement the specific security technique. Chapter 11 concisely discusses how to configure VPN servers and clients. This book is designed primarily as a quick reference and resource for immediate solutions to problems that you encounter in the field.

 Murhammer, Martin W., et al. *TCP/IP Tutorial and Technical Overview, Sixth Edition.* Prentice Hall, Upper Saddle River, NJ, 1998. ISBN 0-13-020130-8. Part 2, "Special Purpose Protocols and New Technologies," contains information about security breaches, cryptography, firewalls, NAT, and IPSec. This book, though written from a Unix perspective and focusing on both transport and network protocols, describes many security aspects in great detail. Most topics are relevant to the Windows 2000 environment.

 Search the TechNet CD (or its online version through **www.microsoft. com**) and the *Windows 2000 Server Resource Kit* CD using the keywords "VPN", "PPTP", "L2TP", and "EAP". This is Microsoft's definitive online resource for technical papers and bulletins.

 **www.microsoft.com/ISN/ind_solutions/virtual_private_ networking.asp?RLD=90** This is the home page for Microsoft Internet Services Network, a subscription service. It offers featured articles, technical and strategic white papers, and downloads like the Internet Services Connection for RAS, Commercial Edition. This is a subscription service. When using this or other technical resources, I strongly recommend that you disregard papers that refer to Windows 2000 as NT 5 or papers that are more than a year old. Using the NT 5 abbreviation sug-

gests that the material is seriously dated and might misrepresent or inadequately describe actual Windows 2000 features and configurations.

 **www.microsoft.com/windows2000/library/howitworks/communications/remoteaccess/vpnoverview.asp** This is the location of Microsoft's Windows 2000 White Paper, titled *Virtual Private Networking: An Overview,* originally posted in April 1999. This paper describes VPN technology used on Microsoft Windows 2000 Server and provides an overview of VPNs, describing basic requirements and key technologies that permit private networking to be provided over public internetworks.

 **www.vpnc.org/ietf-ipsec** is the Virtual Private Network Consortium (VPNC) Web site. This home page points to many important collections of material that relates to VPN and IPSec. It also offers RFCs and Internet drafts on related topics. Tables describe many features supported by VPNC's members in their software and hardware. There is a section on interoperability issues and a separate section on VPN terms, which is particularly useful when you are learning relevant terminology that pertains to remote connectivity issues.

Other Network Issues

Terms you'll need to understand:

- ✓ Principals
- ✓ UUEncoding
- ✓ Secure Channel (SChannel) security protocols
- ✓ Secure Hypertext Transfer Protocol (S-HTTP)
- ✓ Application Specifications For Windows 2000
- ✓ Secure Multipurpose Internet Mail Extensions (S/MIME)
- ✓ Fortezza Crypto Card technology
- ✓ Lightweight Directory Access Protocol (LDAP) version 3
- ✓ Meta-directory
- ✓ Directory consolidation technologies
- ✓ Active Directory Connector (ADC)
- ✓ Microsoft Directory Synchronization Services (MSDSS)
- ✓ Certificate practices statement

Techniques you'll need to master:

- ✓ Deploying security methods for intranet, Internet, and extranet Web sites
- ✓ Describing different Internet Information Server (IIS) authentication security methods
- ✓ Describing Secure Sockets Layer (SSL) in combination with X.509 v3 client certificates
- ✓ Describing differences between e-commerce and intranet connectivity issues
- ✓ Developing strategies for consolidating directory services

This chapter shows you how to configure and use Internet Information Server (IIS) and Secure Sockets Layer (SSL). With the default installation of IIS as part of the Windows 2000 operating system, Web security is not only relevant in real life but also figures prominently in any series of case studies that Microsoft will present in an examination setting. As I explain later in this chapter in the context of identity management, the Windows 2000 enterprise goes far beyond what the legacy NT 4 domain model would typically support.

The basic dichotomy of distributed and network security services, as described in Chapter 6, was useful in the NT 4 domain model to determine the initial scope of a security plan. With the integration of Web access and remote access in Windows 2000, however, an enterprise scenario now includes many forms of network connectivity outside the boundaries of the enterprise. You will see that the Internet and remote connectivity radically change the scope of your enterprise as well as its security requirements. I will distinguish these different service areas with regard to control and responsibility as well as design and deployment; each kind of connectivity contributes specific costs and benefits to the total cost of ownership (TCO).

Historical trends cited in Chapter 2 suggest a gradual differentiation in the distributed server architecture with increased specialization. I use Chapter 8 to describe how the boundary of distributed services inside an internal network is dissolving and how the dichotomy of distributed and networked services is losing significance in the Windows 2000 enterprise. In an Active Directory (AD) of over a million objects, there is, in relative terms, literally a universe of resources from which a consumer can request services. In Chapter 2, I describe the primary information technology (IT) security controls: identification, authentication, and authorization. In a corporate environment, identification is restricted to a limited namespace of known users or principals. However, you should pay more immediate attention to authentication and authorization, because both form the substrate on which all exchanges of digital information are made. In the AD of over a million objects, identification must come first. Confidentiality and non-repudiation always complement these primary security controls. The last two sections of this chapter, "Permission Management" and "Identity Management," suggest important developmental trends that Microsoft claims, are already works in progress. The discussion of these technologies and trends in Chapter 8 will help you design a security infrastructure that accommodates the breadth of Windows 2000 enterprise services, heterogeneous environments that demand interoperability, and the constantly evolving forces that drive e-commerce and network connectivity.

IIS 5

In Windows 2000, IIS 5 provides a scalable environment for hosting Internet, intranet, and extranet Web sites. Services include access to virtual servers, virtual directories, or published documents. Granting a request for IIS services depends upon passing sequentially through four separate security control layers:

1. *Internet Protocol (IP) address and domain name security*—Access based on network address or domain name regardless of group membership.

2. *IIS authentication security*—Access based on authentication method regardless of group membership.

3. *IIS permissions*—Access determined on the basis of Web-clients assigned permissions to published resources regardless of group membership.

4. *NT File System (NTFS) security permissions*—Access to physical data stores is determined by the access control list (ACL) of the specific resource. The ACL provides greater granularity in control than IIS permissions, specifically in differentiating group membership. The other three methods apply to all consumers regardless of group membership.

Note: IIS 5 uses two layers of access control: Web (IIS) permissions and NTFS permissions. The Web permissions define how the web clients accesses resources; NTFS permissions define how individual accounts access server resources

Network Addressing and Domain Name Security

By configuring IP address ranges or Domain Name System (DNS) domain names, the IIS server grants or denies access to resources. This gross, low level security setting acts as a gate that controls access to all resources exclusively on the basis of network addressing as opposed to a more granular control based on user identity or group membership. Methods for configuring these security restrictions vary depending on the kind of resource:

➤ *To configure virtual servers, directories, or subdirectories*—Right-click on the object's node in the Internet Services Manager and select Properties|Directory Security|Edit.

➤ *To configure file restrictions*—Right-click on the object's node in the MMC and select Properties|File Security|Edit.

Similar to firewalls, the restrictions with regard to the network addresses and domain names are based on one of the following basic strategies:

➤ *Default permit*—That which is not expressly prohibited is, *by default*, permitted.

➤ *Default deny*—That which is not expressly permitted is, *by default*, prohibited.

For example, by applying the principle of least privilege ("only enough access to get the job done"), the *default deny* strategy prohibits all external, public network access except for access expressly permitted, such as traffic to and from a business partner's extranet. Similarly, only the traffic from one particular subnet in an intranet is allowed access to some virtual directory; all other traffic is denied.

IIS Authentication Security

Four IIS authentication schemes are available:

➤ *Anonymous access*—An Everyone user category that allows access to all resources.

➤ *Basic authentication*—A valid Windows 2000 user account and password are required to request services.

➤ *Digest authentication for Windows domain servers*—Valid only in Windows 2000 domains. With an Internet Explorer browser version 5 or higher, a password's hash value (rather than the password itself) is transmitted across a network, firewall, or proxy server.

➤ *Integrated Windows authentication*—An example of Single Sign-On (SSO) where authentication of an account during the logon process is transparently applied during subsequent requests for service and access to resources. Integrated Windows authentication uses a cryptographic exchange between browser and server to confirm the user.

 You should use Integrated Windows authentication only when anonymous access is disabled or anonymous access is denied because the Windows file system permissions require a user to provide logon information before a connection can be established.

Access control extends to all Web content, virtual servers (individually hosted Web sites), virtual directories, and physical subdirectories and their contents on the host Web server. A default authentication setting for all virtual servers (Web sites) on a physical Web server can be applied through Computer Management in Administrative Tools. Under Internet Information Services, in the WWW Service Master Properties dialog box as well as an Inheritance Overrides option, which allows some virtual servers to have their own authentication methods independent of default settings. By default, all virtual servers inherit settings in the WWW Service Master Properties dialog box.

Anonymous Access

Upon installation, IIS creates an Internet Guest account, IUSR_*Servername*, where *Servername* is the machine name of the physical Web server. This account is a member of the Guests local group (assuming IIS services are running on a member server), has a nonexpiring password that cannot be changed, and has been assigned the user right to Log On Locally. By default, Allow Anonymous Access is enabled on the Authentication Methods dialog box. Regarding deployment strategies, this setting is acceptable in the following scenarios:

➤ For Web sites that are low-risk, public Internet areas

➤ Within an intranet, where this account simplifies administration

 IUSR_*Servername* is a member of the Guests group, so this account inherits any changes to rights or permissions made to that group during or sometime after installation of the Web server. You should periodically test the security scope of this group account with respect to outside Internet connectivity.

Basic Authentication

Basic authentication is the standard Hypertext Transfer Protocol (HTTP) user authentication method that most browsers support. Any consumer who requests Web services encounters an Enter Network Password dialog box that requests a username and password. An intruder detection feature is associated with the dialog box; after three unsuccessful attempts, an error message (401.1 Unauthorized Logon Failed) is returned to the consumer.

This form of authentication, however, is not secure because the username and password are encoded using a technique called *UUEncoding*, which translates the message into an easily decipherable string of American Standard Code for Information Interchange (ASCII) characters. This encoded string is placed in the HTTP Get Request Packet and sent to the server that provides the Web services. You can strengthen basic authentication, however, by combining it with SSL encryption to provide a secure method of authentication in heterogeneous environments. The disadvantage, however, is that the stronger encryption negatively impacts on server performance.

Regarding deployment strategies, basic authentication is useful in the following situations:

➤ Where security is low and non-Windows authentication is required

➤ Where browsers do not support integrated Windows authentication methods (discussed shortly)

➤ In extranet scenarios where security is needed and the information can be considered confidential but has no security classification (sensitive but unclassified—SBU—as discussed in Chapter 8).

Digest Authentication

Though not an Internet standard and currently supported only by Internet Explorer version 5 while accessing a Windows 2000 domain controller (DC), digest authentication (RFC 2069) improves upon basic authentication by passing the security credentials in a hashed format. A Windows 2000 domain must be specially configured to use digest authentication, as follows:

➤ The Web server must be running IIS 5 and must be in a Windows 2000 domain.

➤ The Save Password As Encrypted Clear Text must be enabled in the User account property sheet in the AD Users And Computers MMC snap-in.

Regarding deployment strategies, within a Windows 2000 intranet, this method provides greater security than basic authentication. It is a hashed value, so it passes through firewalls and proxy servers.

Integrated Windows Authentication

This method is the most secure of the authentication schemes because the consumer exchanges encrypted packets with the server. At no time is the actual password exchanged. Although all Microsoft browser software versions 2 or higher support this authentication method, no version of Netscape Navigator does. SSO depends upon which Windows platform you use to access the IIS server:

➤ *If you are a Windows 2000 domain user*—All exchanges involving the Web server are transparent. The only requirement here is that the initial authentication has taken place.

➤ *If you are requesting services from a non-Windows 2000 system*—The Enter Network Password dialog box is displayed. The initial authentication must again take place before Web-related services are rendered.

Regarding deployment strategies, with integrated Windows authentication, it is necessary to enforce the appropriate account policy, especially regarding passwords, through the Domain Security Policy MMC snap-in. With the policy in place and a written network security policy distributed to all users, this method is appropriate in high-security situations where domain users access Web resources. Similarly, both Windows 2000 and 98 clients benefit from SSO.

Combination Authentication Methods

If you use the Anonymous account in combination with some other authentication method, such as basic or integrated authentication, anonymous access to the resource is attempted first. If, for whatever reason, this access attempt fails (see the "IIS Permissions" and "NTFS Permissions" sections coming up shortly), a second, stronger authentication method that requires a username and password is used. In other combinations, integrated Windows authentication has precedence over all other methods.

IIS Permissions

The Web server can control access to the resources it hosts through global security settings for each object. These settings, done through the property sheets within the Context menus of the specific objects, affect access regardless of group membership. Access permissions such as Read, Write, and Execute, which involve exclusively running scripts or both scripts and executables, are enabled for a virtual directory through these settings. Conversely, you can configure a condition where no executables are allowed to run in a directory.

Combining NTFS and IIS Permissions

The access to physical directories and files on the Web server is based on how you configure NTFS. This access method, available only if the storage medium is formatted using NTFS, allows granularity that is unavailable with any of the other methods described in the "IIS Authentication Security" section earlier in this chapter. You can assign different permissions on the basis of user and group. This topic is discussed in greater detail in Chapter 9.

Regarding deployment strategies, always confirm that the Everyone group has been removed from ACLs on any virtual directories or Web pages. Assign the built-in Users group Read access permission to the specific sites. To minimize administration, consider a policy that what is not expressly prohibited is permitted (default permit). Restrict access by assigning problem users to a No Access group, which overrides the individual's effective permissions to the resource.

A more secure strategy than using NTFS permissions alone is to combine NTFS with IIS permissions. A possible strategic combination would be to assign IIS Read permission for directory browsing, NTFS Read permission to a local Users group, and Full Control to a local Administrators group. Using an NTFS No Access permission would deny access to any user or group to even browse the directory. In such a situation, explicitly denying access overrides permissions that explicitly grant access. Also apply the rule of least privilege, where access is allowed only to resources necessary and sufficient to complete the assigned job function. You should enable the execution of scripts as opposed to binary executables to control a user's range of activities in or outside the accessible virtual directory.

Other Security Methods

Besides the security methods mentioned previously, there are three other noteworthy methods of securing IIS servers, as follows:

➤ Disabling services, protocols, and bindings

➤ Disabling directory browsing

➤ Logging and auditing

In this section, I discuss each one in turn.

Disabling Services, Protocols, and Bindings

Disabling services, protocols, and bindings offers you several benefits. When you disable unnecessary services, you immediately see an increase in performance because of the decrease in demands on system resources. If a service or protocol is not available, a mistake in configuration that might otherwise impact performance is less likely to occur. However, the most important detail in disabling services is to minimize access to resources that an intruder might exploit in a security attack.

Regarding deployment strategies, by disabling the Server service on a dedicated Web server, you stop supporting shares, a potential point of entry to your Web server. Make certain, however, that you understand *all* dependencies that exist among services before you take such an action. A less radical strategy is to build a multihomed server with a second network interface card (NIC) (see the discussion of firewalls in Chapter 6). This design not only helps secure the Web server and your internal network but can segregate services on either the internal or external networks via the two network interfaces. Similarly, if you unbind or eliminate unnecessary protocols on either one of these two NICs, you not only improve the efficiency of your protocol stack, but you also minimize configuration errors in some network or system setting.

If the Server service, which uses the Server Message Block (SMB) protocol, is allowed to function over the Internet, you are in violation of the Microsoft licensing agreement that applies to the SMB protocol; you need to obtain additional licensing for Windows 2000 Server.

Disabling Directory Browsing

It is especially important to disable the ability to browse directories in a virtual server, virtual directory, or folder. This is one of the IIS permissions, mentioned earlier in this chapter, that you can configure through the property sheets within the Context menus of the specific objects. Make certain that the checkbox control for Directory Browsing Allowed is clear (disabled).

Logging and Auditing

One of the least expensive and probably most important tools in securing your IIS server is logging all IP activity. Both baseline and regular monitoring provide diagnostic tools to help analyze typical workloads, as well as indicate unusual external and internal activity. Periodic review of logs should include monitoring authenticated users, especially those making frequent visits to unusual internal areas. Such atypical behavior could indicate some security breach in your internal network. In fact, the combination of IIS logging with NTFS auditing and the Everyone group provides the most comprehensive security view of your Web server.

Auditing successful and failed logons and logoffs provides information about users and possible intruders, respectively. The failure of File And Object Access can similarly alert you to attempts to use unauthorized resources. Although using auditing impacts your system performance, the benefits of detecting an attack early can easily outweigh the performance penalties. You must remember, though, that to detect a breach in security, you must systematically review logs on a timely and consistent basis.

Secure Channel (SChannel) Protocols

In Chapter 2, I used the generic scenario of consumer and service provider to describe the various attack modalities. In the context of a Web server like IIS, we can again focus on the possible targets of a security attack, namely:

➤ Client browser

➤ Web server

➤ Traffic through the session pipe

The issue of traffic security rests upon authentication of client browser (consumer), Web server (Hypertext Transfer Protocol (HTTP) service provider), and the connection between the two, especially across public networks. Collectively, the issue of traffic security rests on a secure end-to-end service. The security of that service begins with confirming the authenticity of the two ends followed by securing the session between them. Both SSL and Transport Layer Security (TLS) protocols rely on public-key–based authentication and session key negotiations. They are associated with another common security protocol, Secure Hypertext Transfer Protocol (S-HTTP), although they operate at the Open Systems Interconnection (OSI) Transport layer (discussed in the "Transport Layer Security Technologies" section in Chapter 6) and have a different security focus. S-HTTP secures the transmission of individual messages; SSL/TLS creates a secure connection by authenticating two computers. This section describes how that is done.

SSL3/TLS1

Originally developed by Netscape, SSL3 allows you to encrypt information between a browser client and a Web server by using public key cryptography (see Chapter 4) and digital certificates (see Chapters 3 and 4). TLS, published as Request for Comments (RFC) 2246, represents a common proposed standard that incorporates SSL3 features. Though the two protocols are functionally the same, architectural differences between them are significant enough to raise interoperability issues. TLS1, however, can negotiate back down to SSL3. When used in conjunction with a browser, SSL/TLS, and a secure protocol designated as S-HTTP, use Transmission Control Protocol (TCP) to provide a secured end-to-end pipe between consumer and service provider. (Enterprise Integration Technologies developed S-HTTP in 1995.)

Deployment of SSL

A typical SSL session between a consumer and a Web server occurs as follows:

1. A certificate is issued to the Web server and installed on the Web server.

2. SSL is enabled on a virtual server or directory on that Web server using the Directory Security panel in the specific object's property sheet.

3. You must have stored on your browser a Certificate Authority (CA) certificate that contains the CA's public key to decrypt issued certificates.

4. You access the SSL-enabled virtual server using a secured Uniform Resource Locator (URL) such as **https://myweb.mysecuredserver.com** across TCP. You then encounter a security alert message that notifies you that you are about to view pages over a secured connection. If you do not have a copy of the CA's public key, a message saying the certificate issuer is untrusted appears. At this point in the exchange, you can install the CA certificate in the trusted root (certificate) store in your browser using the Certificate Import Wizard.

5. When your browser can read the server's digital certificate, the session pipe between you and the SSL-enabled Web site is established, keys are exchanged, and the encryption of information provides secured data.

Certificate Services

A *digital certificate* is a text file issued by some trusted certificate service provider (or Certificate Authority—CA) that corroborates the identity and credentials of the application or consumer. It usually also contains the public key in a digital envelope encrypted with the CA's private key. In fact, the only requirement of a CA is that it accurately bind security credentials to a public key. The authority of a CA is based on the namespace from which the identifying credentials are chosen. The CA must guarantee that all the security attributes that make up the credentials are accurate and that the list of endorsed account names are current. Only the CA's public key decrypts the envelope, so you can be confident that the certificate is authentic and unaltered.

The CA is a trusted service provider and is very often an outside third party such as VeriSign (www.verisign.com) and its subsidiary, Thawte (www.thawte.com). VeriSign provides global enterprise certificates, whereas Thawte caters to the global small-business market that requires entry-level SSL solutions. VeriSign, for example, offers a Class 1 certificate, which requires filling out an application form, through a Class 3 certificate, where credentials are notarized. A CA documents its practices in a certification practices statement. IIS can use third-party services or Microsoft Certificate Services, discussed later in this chapter, as an internally managed, private provider of these certificate services.

Certificates play an important role in Windows 2000 by providing three IT security controls: integrity, confidentiality, and nonrepudiation. These were briefly discussed in Chapter 2 and are involved in the Encrypting File System (EFS) (discussed in Chapter 9). These controls are a critical component of smart cards (discussed in Chapter 12), and you need them when verifying the parties in Web exchanges. The certificate identifies and encrypts information exchanged between consumer and service provider. It contains the holder's public key; an expiration date; and credentials about the holder such as name, address, and so on.

These certificates are widely used throughout the enterprise and are thus a critical component of Windows 2000 public key infrastructure (PKI), which runs transparently in the OSI Application layer. In general terms, a client (client digital certificate), a server (server digital certificate), and an application (application digital certificate) are all considered authentic principals because the same trusted CA corroborates their credentials. The first CA installed in an enterprise is called the *root CA*; it signs its own site or CA certificate. Certificates are issued to many objects in the enterprise, including:

➤ EFS Recovery Agent

➤ Basic EFS

➤ DCs

> Web servers

> Client machines

> Users

> Subordinate CAs

> Administrators

Certificate Server Tools

A Certificate Server provides several services: administration (creating certificates), logging (tracking requests for certificates), and revocation (maintaining lists of revoked certificates). Both Internet Explorer version 2 or higher and Netscape Navigator version 3 or higher support these certificates. A database logs the life cycle (the request, issuance, and revocation) of each certificate. The Certificate Services Manager MMC provides certificate services. There are four nodes, located under the root certificate authority, in the Certificate Authority MMC snap-in:

> Revoked Certificates

> Issued Certificates

> Pending Certificates

> Failed Certificates

Deploying Security for Distributed Services

You can address network security in general and Web security in particular at several OSI layers. One strategic approach is to deploy security technologies at the OSI Network layer by using IP Security (IPSec), discussed in Chapter 5. These gross, low-level techniques screen traffic flowing through the session pipe on the basis of network address schemes. Another more focused approach is at the OSI Transport layer using SSL/TLS technologies. Both are application independent and transparent to the consumer. An example of an OSI Application layer technique would be the use of S-HTTP.

Yet another category of technologies is application specific and therefore most readily customized to any specific business or user need. Assuming proper installation and administration, this last category of technologies provides high security protection because the technologies have been customized to a specific set of conditions. At the same time, because they are customized, they are the least adaptable of the technologies to changes in those conditions. Even a slight change can totally compromise what was a strong security infrastructure. Application-specific systems therefore incur greater administrative costs than security at lower network levels such as SSL/TSL and IPSec because of their need for maintenance and support. In a distributed services environment, you will see a mixture of all three strategies that each add their own individual costs and benefits to the TCO.

SSL in Windows 2000

The use of SSL/TLS, as a multivendor standard, to provide security services for distributed applications will remain an efficient and common practice because it provides authentication services. The application itself handles authorization. However, SSL/TLS cannot by itself support a Windows 2000 logon because it does not provide credentials to determine a user's levels of authorization. It needs help from AD directory services.

When Microsoft Certificate Services creates a digital certificate, an extended attribute field contains the special credentials called the User Principal Name (UPN). You can use this field to locate the account records in AD. When these records are located, authorization information is returned to the server. Similarly, if the certificate is from a third-party CA, the issuer's and holder's names are used as lookup keys to search the AD account database for security credentials. In the latter case, however, you must do some mapping of the issuer's and holder's name to valid account records for an association to take place.

The primary differences between SSL/TLS and Kerberos arise when you compare application-level security with networking security systems. SSL/TLS use public keys as opposed to directly or indirectly shared Key Distribution Centers (KDCs) across domains or realms. SSL/TLS scales more efficiently than Kerberos and can work in heterogeneous environments. The Kerberos protocol is more efficient than SSL/TLS in a homogeneous environment and is the default protocol in a Windows 2000 enterprise. Web-based applications determine their own authorization, so the need for AD directory services is actually redundant; SSL/TLS remains the security technology of choice in these situations.

Application Standards and Policies

It is important to remember that a secured enterprise doesn't remain secured; it grows and changes over time. General-purpose security technologies like IPSec and SSL/TLS provide wide-spectrum solutions without administrative overhead; secure applications provide granularity and a narrow security scope without administrative overhead. Applications that have security-enabled features integrate well with Microsoft's SSO theme for authenticated network connections. The

Application Specifications For Windows 2000 defines these technical requirements to earn the Certified For Microsoft Windows logo. Using secure applications that conform to this specification is an important factor in controlling an
organization's TCO. The minimum requirements for a secure application include
support for:

➤ Running on Windows 2000 servers

➤ Use of Kerberos and support of SSO

➤ Use of client impersonation to support access control mechanisms using permissions and security groups

➤ Application services run by using more limited service accounts rather than
full privileged local system accounts

Although the Microsoft specification does not state the need to properly design
the application so that it provides services as originally designed, I discuss this
need in Chapter 8. If there is a design issue in some application component caused
by faulty logic or some unusual boundary condition that in turn causes a buffer
overflow, you will eventually discover it. You must anticipate that some intruder
will exploit any security weakness in the enterprise to gain access to the security
context within which the application runs. Although outside the Microsoft specification, these subtle design weaknesses compromise the strongest security infrastructures because they remain relatively invisible until *after* the security attack
has been launched.

Authenticode

A way to control the deployment of software components and applications is by
using Authenticode, Microsoft's digitally signed technology that works through
Internet Explorer. A network policy statement is hardened when it prohibits the
execution of any software component or application, especially one downloaded
from a foreign Internet site. Authenticode allows developers to digitally sign an
application using the standard X.509 public key certificate (see Chapter 3). Any
consumer can verify not only a developer's identity but also the integrity of the
downloaded package. You can use Microsoft Certificate Services to issue digital
certificates to application software prior to distributing them through an intranet
or enterprise. Creating these digitally signed packages and using administrative
kits such as those for Internet Explorer, Outlook, and Connection Manager impact administration and maintenance of remote users and TCO tremendously.
You can enable Authenticode-based screening for trusted digital signatures in
Internet Explorer and then lock them down through the Group Policy snap-in in
MMC. Group Policy is discussed in Chapter 10.

Secure Multipurpose Internet Mail Extensions (S/MIME)

Another significant Internet draft that uses X.509 digital certificates and public key technology is an enhancement of the traditional email format standard, MIME, specified in RFC 822. S/MIME provides open-standard interoperability at the OSI Application layer among third-party secure email applications. Significant features of S/MIME are:

➤ Signed receipts that provide proof of delivery to the message originator

➤ Security labels that you can use for access control

➤ Secured mail lists where a mail list agent handles the administrative overhead

This technology provides for data integrity, authentication, and nonrepudiation, all features that PKI typically provides. In addition, senders can encrypt email messages to provide confidentiality. An example of a hardware solution that provides secured email exchanges is Fortezza Crypto Card technology. This security technology, originally developed by the National Security Agency for Department of Defense (DoD), has been incorporated into the Defense Message System (DMS) especially for SBU information. Another security technology that offers similar security services is Pretty Good Privacy (PGP), but it was not developed by, nor is it under the control of, any governmental agency or standards organization.

Permission Management

In a corporate environment, identification is simplified because it is restricted to the universe of known principals in the organization. Security is also simplified; you are either "known" or "unknown." Most IT security controls begin with the assumption that you are known and focus on proving that you are who you say you are. As enterprises scale to cover entire geographical continents and as a hierarchical AD structure composed of over a million objects replaces the flat domain model of NT 4, identity will become another major issue. This section and the "Identity Management" section at the end of this chapter discuss these issues and future trends in the context of Microsoft's current works in progress.

Within the enterprise, authentication, authorization, and auditing come before permissions are granted and services are rendered. When I expand my enterprise borders to include distributed services on the Internet, identification becomes a major focus of permission management. Web services, especially in a public network or e-commerce scenario, are all fundamentally based on identification.

In Chapters 9 and 10, I discuss in great detail how to handle permission management within the enterprise or any intranet. This chapter deals with various network issues, so it is appropriate to mention a few topics that relate to e-commerce and Web services. As already mentioned, identity management is a key issue. If the identity of the consumer is somehow validated, permissions will most likely flow out of specific distributed application software that is designed to deliver predetermined services. How you build, install, and manage the software dictates the scope of security. E-commerce security issues between consumer and service provider were compiled in the Secure Electronic Transaction (SET) specification that MasterCard and Visa originally proposed in 1996. This suite of security protocols and formats is based on data exchanges between a consumer, a merchant, and a host of service providers, all separated into independent yet codependent transactions that are coordinated over both time and space.

In addition to the need for a secure session pipe, trust between parties, and confidentiality, security controls must extend to transaction integrity. Any one transaction includes secure exchanges between customer/cardholder, vendor/ merchant, bank/issuer, and payment acquirer. Other intermediate agents (such as a payment gateway) could be involved. Permission management is integrated here with transaction management divided across several different parties into purchase request/response, payment authorization, and payment capture. Although the full details of this simplified e-commerce event are beyond the scope of most case studies (especially those presented in an exam environment), this scenario is one a consultant will encounter in real life. It requires specialized and detailed knowledge, not just of Windows 2000 security subsystems, but also of the specific objectives and rules of the e-commerce business involved.

 It is significant that although the design and security requirements of e-commerce exchanges are radically different from intranet/extranet network connectivity issues, the security solutions are based on the same technologies outlined for intranet exchanges.

Identity Management

In Chapter 2, I suggested that it would be useful to view current IT trends from a historical perspective. I will now outline how to construct a security plan for a Windows 2000 environment. The focus of this plan, however, is not on complex technical aspects but rather on architectural layers and the issue of identity management.

Any IT enterprise is fundamentally a heap of resources and a collection of information about the people that can use it. Software applications connect people to resources, or resources to other resources, to provide useful information functions or services. In previous chapters, I often replaced the term *user* with *consumer*, and *server* with *service provider*, to emphasize a more functional relationship between these two named entities. Scalable network operating systems like Windows 2000 require dedicated services to administer the credentials that identify legal member entities in its namespace. Microsoft now uses standards-based directory services that offer a uniform application interface, providing identity management that handles a variety of identity issues, such as:

➤ *SSO*—SSO initiatives manage object name, security password, and user rights across the entire enterprise namespace. This is an important Microsoft theme.

➤ *Global address book services*—Address book services synchronize collaborative or communicative information, especially across electronic mail systems.

➤ *"Hire & fire" scenarios*—This category deals with propagation issues of a newly hired or terminated employee's access permissions to company resources and services.

➤ *E-commerce applications*—Web-based applications require identity management, including the use of digital certificates that authenticate extranet partners and users outside the enterprise namespace.

Historical trends suggest that as namespaces expand and merge in a distributed server architecture, the need to manage distributed identity datastores will increase. Interoperability issues have already forced the migration of major operating systems like Novell and Microsoft to adopt a common standards-based protocol, Lightweight Directory Access Protocol (LDAP). In addition to maintaining account records and security credentials, directory services need to provide housekeeping services that manage duplicated information and issues of referential integrity across many different datastores throughout their namespaces.

Requirements for Identity Management

The goal of having one single, uniform enterprise directory that holds an organization's universe of principals and their associated security credentials does not seem achievable for a variety of reasons. Boundaries in a namespace will always exist; political, technical, and functional divisions will never totally disappear. Thus, at least for the foreseeable future, heterogeneous identity data in scattered locations throughout the enterprise will be a common occurrence. Furthermore, some datastores will either never be exposed or will never be accessible to a directory services interface. Issues of redundancy and referential integrity due to stale ACLs or other drifts in timestamp synchronization used, for example, in the exchange of secret keys, will also be common. In fact, one might predict that any centralized or composite view of credentials across identity datastores will be increasingly unlikely because of the increasing trend in distributed services.

Directory services and identity management are at the heart of the Windows 2000 enterprise. Therefore, to make the identity data accessible, you need a compromise strategy to transparently link disparate directory datastores in some easily managed way. This compromise approach must provide:

➤ *Connectivity*—The negotiation of secured exchanges of identity data includes interfacing with heterogeneous directory service providers, datastores, repositories, warehouses, and application programming interfaces (APIs). Two examples here are the standards-based directory services provided by LDAP version 3 and database access via Structured Query Language (SQL).

➤ *Brokering features*—These internal services manage the flow of identity data between datastores. These services detect changes in information and update repositories, aggregate data in central locations, and track object histories. An ordered propagation of changes to multiple repositories is especially important to maintain data consistency.

➤ *Integrity checks*—These internal services monitor any brokered exchanges of identity data for consistency, ownership, and referential integrity. These integrity checks determine proper execution of business rules applied during the brokering process and confirm or reject changes to the data.

Deployment of Identity Management

Based on the list of requirements in the previous section and the current heterogeneity in application and system software, the management of directory services will most likely be distributed across many different service providers and operating system platforms, even, perhaps, within the same enterprise. To support the previous list of service features, any one service provider is forced to use some combination of technologies, including:

➤ *Multidirectory access technologies*—These applications utilize published interface specifications to interact directly with data in the datastore that is relevant to some management operation. The technologies help simplify application development by providing a minimum number of API data access paradigms.

➤ *Synchronization connectors*—These software agents act as readers/distributors that are programmed to recognize changes in the state of data in a repository and then propagate those changes to other data sites.

➤ *Meta-directory technologies*—These technologies can maximize performance by collecting identity data from various repositories and offering a single access/distribution point and security model.

➤ *Directory consolidation technologies*—These technologies, under intense development, require minimal maintenance. For example, a consolidated directory does not need synchronization, multiple data access paradigms, or synchronization connectors. An example of this trend is Exchange 2000, which uses AD instead of its own data repository.

Microsoft has recognized the importance of identity management, having acquired field-tested technology and having experimented with Metabases in IIS 4, as mentioned in Chapter 2. Windows 2000 provides a mature set of identity management solutions based on AD-related interfaces and services:

➤ *Active Directory Services Interfaces (ADSI)*—Offering multidirectory access through a Component Object Model (COM), ADSI provides an API to access and manage Security Accounts Manager in NT 4, Active Directory Services (ADS) in Windows 2000, Novell's Novell Directory Services (NDS), and any LDAP-based directory.

➤ *Active Directory Connector (ADC)*—This connector specifically synchronizes AD with Exchange Server 5.x, Lotus Notes, Novell GroupWise, and LDAP-based directory systems. These connector technologies (as well as Microsoft Directory Synchronization Services—MSDSS—described in the next bulleted item) are based on an LDAP-based control, DirSync, which enables you to efficiently synchronize AD with heterogeneous directory systems. Figure 7.1 shows how the ADC and MSDSS interoperate with these other applications.

➤ *MSDSS*—Like ADC, MSDSS is a component of Services for NetWare version 5 (SFNW5), which provides a method to synchronize identity data changes between AD and Novell NDS.

➤ *Meta-directory technologies*—With its newly acquired Zoomit product, renamed Microsoft Meta-directory Services (MMS), Microsoft has implemented a hub and spoke architecture for building comprehensive identity management solutions. Some application in the center of Figure 7.2 interfaces with the

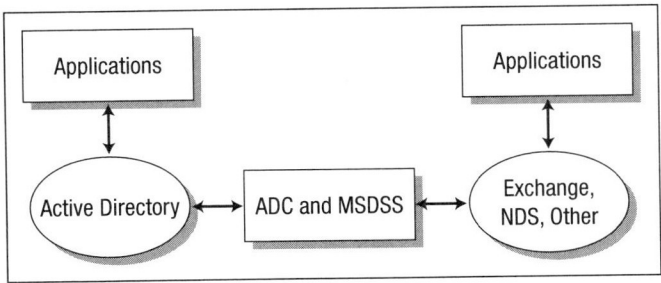

Figure 7.1   The layout of ADCs.

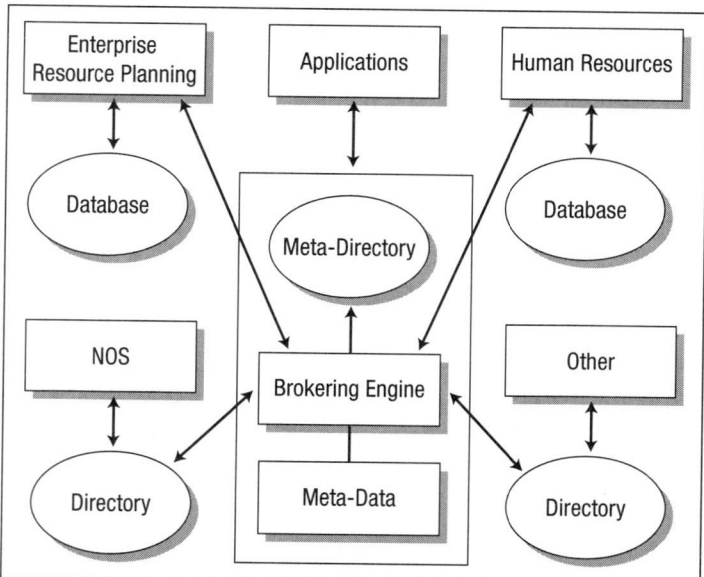

Figure 7.2 Meta-directory hub and spoke architecture.

"hub" meta-directory that represents the aggregate collection of identity data captured from a Human Resources database, some Enterprise Resource Planning (ERP) program, and the network operating system (NOS). Similarly, upon receiving new-hire information from Human Resources, the brokering engine, which follows business rules defined in policy statements, coordinates the creation of mail accounts in the NOS and access rights in the ERP application. All this information is reflected in the aggregate meta-directory repository.

➤ *Directory consolidation opportunities*—The design of, for example, Exchange 2000, has changed; its own internal datastore has been replaced by the AD enterprise datastores.

Security Objectives

Whether you are protecting information in transit during remote access sessions, during persistent branch network connections, or within the confines of an internal network, network security always complements the actual delivery or accessibility of services. In fact, accessibility is one of the primary IT security controls listed in Chapter 2. It is important to remember, though, that you should measure the deployment costs of any security countermeasure in terms relative to corporate security objectives and an organization's TCO. Corporate security objectives, not the consultant, explicitly determine what the organization "needs" and "wants" in its security plan.

 Read every case study carefully. Measure exactly what is said in the documented responses of the participants in each case. Design your responses based on what is written, not what you, as a consultant, consider a "good" design.

As I said in Chapter 2, IT security controls include authentication, authorization, confidentiality, and integrity protection. I include protection against replay attacks under authentication and integrity protection. Similarly, confidentiality in the form of encryption services extends across both distributed and network security subsystems.

TCO and maximized interoperability are important measures of an identity management system's inherent worth. I suggest that the deployment of identity management services requires security subsystems of a similar scope. The strength of these security subsystems directly affects the value of the identity management system. Microsoft emphasizes ease of implementation as a major dimension that measures an identity management system's inherent value. Figure 7.3 shows a diagram of the relationship between ease of implementation and perceived business value. Each service has a different cost versus business benefit ratio because their methods of deployment vary.

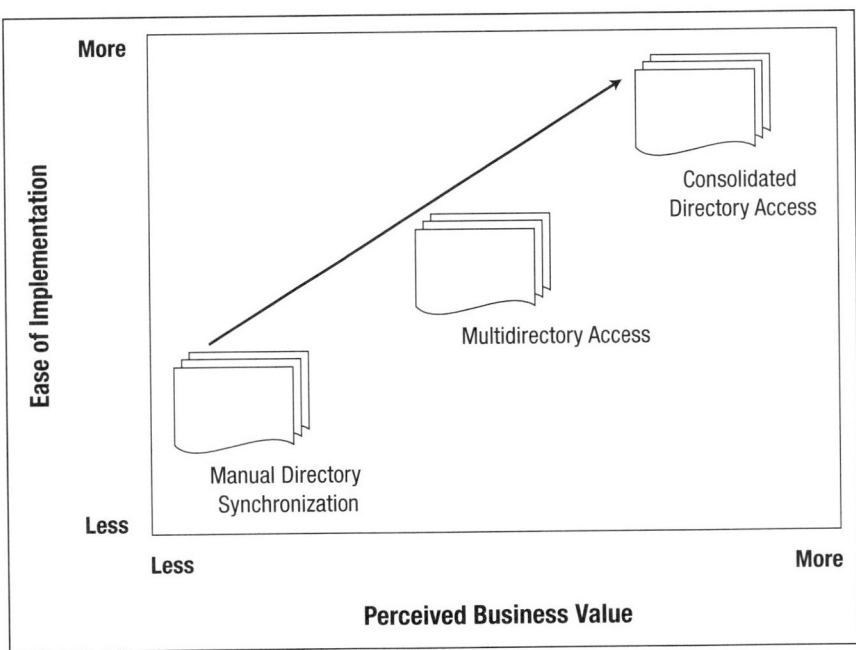

Figure 7.3 Return on investment: identity management and security.

Given the complexity of managing identity data across an enterprise, your deployment plan may involve several technologies applied at the same or different structural layers in terms of an OSI or Microsoft reference model. This affects not only deployment costs but also other TCO variables like maintenance and training. Thus, you can similarly apply the TCO valuation method when you deploy security technologies. As suggested above in the "Requirements for Identity Management" section earlier in this chapter, although theoretically possible and desirable, there is no foreseeable time in the future when all datastores, directory requirements, and support features will be consolidated under one unified service. Similarly, in a security plan, no single system or technology will ever provide all the security controls necessary to protect an enterprise from an intruder assault. Always try to maintain a balance between costs, technologies, and needs.

Practice Questions

Case Study

4Sale, an online bartering company in ThatTherePlace, North Dakota, has merged with Got-a-Deal, and both companies occupy office space in the same office building. They are now running their accounting operation, their bid system, and a knowledge base of their online goods in the same building.

4Sale supports a large Internet audience and many small business brokers around the world. Bids are confidential and must be authenticated. Internet security is important not just for transactions but business reputation. Many of its users, though, are not experienced with the use of secured online services. The Network Manager is considering the addition of a person to support a newly designed Web site and to provide Internet-related help desk support. She is also concerned about securing the IIS server and support for the Proxy Server and certificate services.

Current LAN/Network Structure

4Sale runs native mode Windows 2000 Server in a single domain model with an Exchange 2000 member server, and an IIS 5 and Proxy Server 2 (packet filtering/caching) server. All 100 client machines are running Windows 2000 Professional; Office 2000 is utilized as an applications package. Each system is connected to a 10Mbps hub through 10Mbps local area network (LAN) cards running Category 5 Unshielded Twisted Pair (UTP) cabling in a star topology.

Got-a-Deal is running all 22 client machines in a single child domain under the 4Sale root domain. The client systems are running Windows Professional, with Office 2000 being utilized as an applications package. Each system is connected to a 10Mbps hub through 10Mbps LAN cards running Category 5 UTP cabling in a star topology. These hubs are on the same backbone as 4Sale but have a different subnet.

Proposed LAN/Network Structure

No changes are planned at this time, although management is considering a merger with several business partners running non-Windows environments.

Current WAN Connectivity

4Sale has a T1 connection to an ISP in OverThere, North Dakota. Got-a-Deal has 56Kbps dial-up networking connectivity through the same ISP. The ISP provides simple hosting services and online analysis of traffic.

Directory Design Commentary

No changes are planned at this time.

Current Internet Positioning

4Sale is registered as **4sale.com**. Got-a-Deal has been selling its goods through local companies and through the **4sale.com** Web site.

Company Goal with Windows 2000

Short-term goals are to build enough in-house expertise in handling Web-related issues to bring all online services in-house in six months.

Question 1

> The Network Manager at 4Sale asks you to list the security technologies in typical OSI order for the owners of 4Sale. She assumes that the cost of deploying security at higher OSI layers is greater due to installation, support, maintenance, and training. The three OSI reference layers are:
>
> Application
>
> Transport
>
> Network
>
> Place the following positions under the appropriate OSI layer:
>
> IPSec
>
> S-HTTP
>
> SSL
>
> S/MIME

The correct answer is:

Application

S/MIME

Transport

S-HTTP

SSL

Network

IPSec

Question 2

The Network Manager at 4Sale says, "I often receive a help desk call where the user sees a message in her browser saying the certificate issuer is untrusted. What is happening?" Describe the flow in an SSL (Secure Sockets Layer) exchange by placing the following steps in the proper order.

A certificate is issued to the Web server.

You encounter a security alert message that notifies you that you are about to view pages over a secured connection.

You install a certificate on the browser.

Your browser can now read the server's digital certificate, and the encryption of information will provide secured data.

A certificate is installed on the Web server.

SSL is enabled on a virtual server or directory on that Web server.

You access the SSL-enabled virtual server using a secured Uniform Resource Locator.

The correct answer is:

A certificate is issued to the Web server.

A certificate is installed on the Web server.

SSL is enabled on a virtual server or directory on that Web server.

You access the SSL-enabled virtual server using a secured Uniform Resource Locator.

You encounter a security alert message that notifies you that you are about to view pages over a secured connection.

You install a certificate on the browser.

Your browser can now read the server's digital certificate, and the encryption of information will provide secured data.

Question 3

The Network Manager at 4Sale asks, "What can I do to secure the IIS server?" Choose the security methods that will secure IIS. [Check all correct answers]

☐ a. Disable unnecessary services.

☐ b. Install a dual-homed server.

☐ c. Disable directory browsing.

☐ d. Disable logging and auditing.

☐ e. Disable Server services.

Answers a, b, c, and e are correct. Disabling unnecessary services, installing a second network interface card (a dual-homed server), disabling directory browsing, and disabling Server services are all legitimate security strategies. Another legitimate and highly recommended strategy is to enable (not disable) both logging and auditing on the Web server. Therefore, answer d is incorrect.

Question 4

The Network Manager at 4Sale asks, "Which is the best authentication procedure if 4Sale supports a heterogeneous user population but needs a secured exchange of data?"

○ a. Anonymous access

○ b. Basic authentication

○ c. Digest authentication

○ d. Integrated Windows authentication

○ e. None of the above

Answer e is correct. 4Sale needs to encrypt messages sent over a public network. It also needs to accommodate a heterogeneous population of users. Anonymous access and basic authentication do not support a secure exchange of information. Therefore, answers a and b are incorrect. Digest authentication and integrated Windows authentication are valid only for Windows domain users. Therefore, answers c and d are incorrect. The best answer would have been basic authentication with Secure Sockets Layer, but this is not an option.

Question 5

The Network Manager at 4Sale asks, "What would we be responsible for if we installed our own Certificate Authority?" Answer her question by listing the certificate services.

- ❑ a. Administration
- ❑ b. Logging
- ❑ c. Revocation
- ❑ d. Consolidation
- ❑ e. All of the above

Answers a, b, and c are correct. There are three services: administration (creating certificates), logging (tracking requests for certificates), and revocation (maintaining lists of revoked certificates). Consolidation is not one of the services. Therefore, answers d and e are incorrect.

Question 6

The Network Manager at 4Sale asks, "What identity issues would a directory service provider need to handle?" [Check all correct answers]

- ❑ a. Global address books
- ❑ b. Hire & fire scenarios
- ❑ c. E-commerce applications
- ❑ d. SSL scenarios
- ❑ e. Applications like Exchange Server

Answers a, b, c, and e are correct. A directory services provider would typically use standards-based directory services that provide global address book services (especially for email servers like Exchange Server), hire & fire scenarios that deal with the propagation of information, and e-commerce applications. Secure Sockets Layer has nothing to do with directory services. Therefore, answer d is incorrect.

Question 7

> The CEO at 4Sale asks, "Which service or interface would 4Sale consider if we merged with a company that ran Novell version 5 and Novell Directory Services?" [Choose the best answer]
>
> ○ a. ADSI
>
> ○ b. ADC
>
> ○ c. MSDSS
>
> ○ d. Directory consolidation opportunities
>
> ○ e. MMS

Answer c is correct. Only MSDSS (Microsoft Directory Synchronization Services), a service component of Services for NetWare version 5, provides a method to synchronize identity data changes between Active Directory and Novell Directory Services. ADSI (Active Directory Services Interfaces) offers multidirectory access through a Component Object Model and provides an application programming interface to programmatically access and manage other directory services, including Novell's NDS and any Lightweight Directory Access Protocol-based directory. ADSI is partially correct, but it is not the best answer. Therefore, answer a is incorrect. ADC (Active Directory Connector) specifically synchronizes Active Directory with Exchange Server 5.x, Lotus Notes, Novell GroupWise, and LDAP-based directory systems. Therefore, answer b is incorrect. Directory consolidation opportunities (such as in Exchange 2000) replace their own datastores or repositories with AD. Therefore, answer d is incorrect. Meta-directory technologies like MMS (Microsoft Meta-directory Services) are for building comprehensive identity management solutions. Therefore, answer e is incorrect.

Need to Know More?

 Nichols, Randall K. et. al. *Defending Your Digital Assets against Hackers, Crackers, Spies, and Thieves, First Edition.* McGraw-Hill Professional Publishing, New York, NY, 2000. ISBN 0-07-212285-4. Both Chapter 9 (Digital Signatures and Certificate Authorities) and Chapter 10 (Permissions Management: Identification, Authentication and Authorization) discuss topics from a legislative and business viewpoint without sacrificing technical details. The sections on Web security in Chapter 10 are especially relevant from a nontechnical, managerial viewpoint and are an excellent introductory source of issues for constructing a network policy.

 Santry, Patrick and Mitch Tulloch. *Administering IIS 5.0.* Computing McGraw-Hill, New York, NY, 2000. ISBN 0-07-212328-1. Chapter 4 (Administering Security) and Chapter 11 (Administering SSL with Certificate Services) offer well-documented, procedural instructions regarding the installation of IIS security services, as well as discussions concerning the strategy behind various option settings.

 Stallings, William. *Network Security Essentials: Applications and Standards.* Prentice Hall, Upper Saddle River, NJ, 1999. ISBN 0-13-016093-8. Chapter 7 deals exclusively with Web security and offers a detailed, technical view of the SSL and TLS protocol architectures. Chapter 5 deals specifically with electronic mail security and covers both S/MIME and PGP.

 Search the TechNet CD (or its online version through **www.microsoft.com**) and the *Windows 2000 Server Resource Kit* CD using the keywords "security", "meta-directory", "ICS", and "MSDSS". This is Microsoft's definitive online resource for technical papers and bulletins.

 **www.armadillo.huntsville.al.us/** This site, maintained by members of the Fortezza program office in the Department of Defense, hosts a comprehensive list of technical papers, protocol specifications, product links, cryptographic interface libraries, and other materials related to Fortezza security technologies.

www.ietf.cnri.reston.va.us/rfc/rfc2246.txt?number=2246 This site contains RFC 2246, the TLS Protocol, which is the actual specification for the TLS protocol. TLS provides end-to-end communication privacy over a public network, and it also prevents tampering and message forgery.

 **www.microsoft.com/windows2000/library/howitworks/iis/ iis5techoverview.asp** This Windows 2000 Technical Paper, titled *Internet Information Services 5.0 Technical Overview* and originally posted in September 1999, provides information about reliability and performance, security, and the application environment.

 **www.rsasecurity.com/standards/smime/resources.html** This is the RSA Security-hosted Web page of S/MIME resources and related information, including working drafts of S/MIME version 2 and S/MIME version 3 specifications as well as special topics such as certificate handling.

Constructing a
Security Policy

Terms you'll need to understand:

✓ Network security plan

✓ Disaster recovery plan

✓ Principals

✓ Single Sign-On (SSO)

✓ Two-factor authentication

✓ Smart card technologies

✓ Secure Channel (SChannel) security protocols

✓ Microsoft Directory Synchronization Services (MSDSS)

✓ Meta-directory

✓ Lightweight Directory Access Protocol (LDAP) version 3

✓ Active Directory Connectors (ADCs)

✓ Remote access technologies

✓ Network deployment plan

✓ Security Support Provider Interface (SSPI)

✓ Security Support Provider (SSP)

Techniques you'll need to master:

✓ Developing a network security plan

✓ Developing a physical security plan

✓ Developing strategies for secure network connections

✓ Developing rationales for security policies

✓ Applying a performance-oriented, milestone-based methodology for deploying security systems

✓ Preparing project deliverables and building an action plan

This chapter shows you how to develop a *network security plan*, which is the integration of security techniques and technologies combined under some formal management policy that grows out of the corporate business objectives. This plan is the balance among acceptable levels of protection, acceptable perceived risk, and acceptable expense. The corporate business objectives explicitly define or help you assess what your client perceives to be network security risks. The first step in this assessment is to determine the scope of the enterprise.

As I explain later in this chapter in the context of identity management, the Windows 2000 enterprise goes far beyond what the legacy NT 4 domain model would typically support. The basic dichotomy of distributed and network security services was especially useful in the NT 4 domain model to determine the initial scope of a security plan. *Distributed security* refers to security features applied within the boundaries of the enterprise; *network security* refers to connectivity beyond enterprise boundaries, specifically through the Internet. With the integration of remote access and Virtual Private Networks (VPNs), however, a Windows 2000 enterprise typically includes various forms of network connectivity outside the boundaries of the enterprise. VPNs are discussed in detail in Chapter 6. You will see that the needs of various components of your user population can radically change the scope of your enterprise as well as the security requirements.

Remember that all security planning is a balance between ease of use and a total system lockdown. In a perfect world, granting the Everyone group full control would be wonderful; conversely, powering down a server or using a pair of wire clippers on a connecting network cable will secure it from an outside attack in the most absolute of ways. Although these extremes are all impractical in a corporate environment, they illustrate the balance which must be struck to deliver reliable computer services. I will distinguish a variety of control and responsibility areas for reasons of design, analysis, and deployment; remember each area contributes specific costs and benefits to the total cost of ownership (TCO).

Steps in Planning Network Security

The network security plan is a fundamental component of any corporate deployment of information technology (IT) services. It is either a part of or complementary to the corporate disaster recovery plan. In developing the network security plan, you should follow these specific steps:

1. Determine short-term corporate objectives and long-term goals.

2. Identify user groups and their specific needs.

3. Determine the scope, sizing, and placement requirements of IT resources.

4. Assess network security risks.

5. Create and publish security policies and procedures.

6. Prepare the support staff for maintenance and help desk services.

7. Conduct pilot studies to test strategies.

8. Formalize a methodology to deploy security technologies.

It is noteworthy that although security technologies tend to come in complicated, highly sophisticated packages, the services must be properly deployed, configured, and managed. The best of services will fail unless they are combined with good business practices and a compliant corporate culture. In fact, your enterprise may require more than one security plan based on functional, operational, or regional considerations. Corporate security objectives, which are discussed in Chapter 2, would indicate the need for such divisions in scope. Distributed security involves coordinating many technologies; thus, a Windows 2000 security policy should also cover these specific topics:

➤ *Network logon and authentication procedures*—The administration of users and logon authentication practices have now been extended to cover remote access and smart card technologies. The impact of these methods in terms of new protocols, specialized servers, and identity management is covered in Chapter 9.

➤ *Public key infrastructure (PKI) policies*—The deployment of certificate authorities needs to be planned in advance, especially for use outside the boundaries of the enterprise (such as in e-commerce applications and extranet-based business alliances).

➤ *Administrative policies*—Administration, authorization, and auditing remain the primary responsibilities of IT personnel. Systematic monitoring and strategically deployed audit logs are cost-effective and typically transparent methods of securing network exchanges.

➤ *Group Policy and security group descriptions*—It is especially important in the deployment of Windows 2000 to understand the rationale behind the built-in policy structure (for example, Group Policy, default domain policy, and so on) and the mapping of specific policies to user groups in your enterprise. Microsoft has provided policies and security templates that encompass a broad range of business needs and scenarios; using them properly will profoundly impact your TCO.

➤ *Information security strategies*—The driving forces of e-commerce and Internet connectivity have fostered the need for specific strategies that deal with securing exchanges involving online services such as email and Web-based communications.

Identifying the User Population

Although all business resources and operations are expected to serve the organization's mission statement and corporate objectives, the network infrastructure provides for the functional needs of an organization's members. In general, you can divide employees into three groups: executives, staff, and users, as shown in Figure 8.1.

A relatively new category, business partner, is especially common in organizations that have formed business alliances with different but complementary business concerns that are geographically separated from the primary company. In these situations, network connectivity through an extranet provides the common platform for daily operations. Another category, everyone, includes all principals that access network resources and is critical when you are performing security audits. Although this default built-in group is usually removed from an object's access control list (ACL), the everyone category provides the broadest definition of named objects in a directory namespace. It offers truly comprehensive monitoring of system utilization and intruder activity. Thus, in addition to the classic built-in local groups—administrator, guest, account operator, and so on—I usually categorize members of an organization into the following groups:

➤ *Everyone*—The universe of principals in the Active Directory (AD) namespace is too comprehensive to individually identify, so this group provides a reliable catchall label.

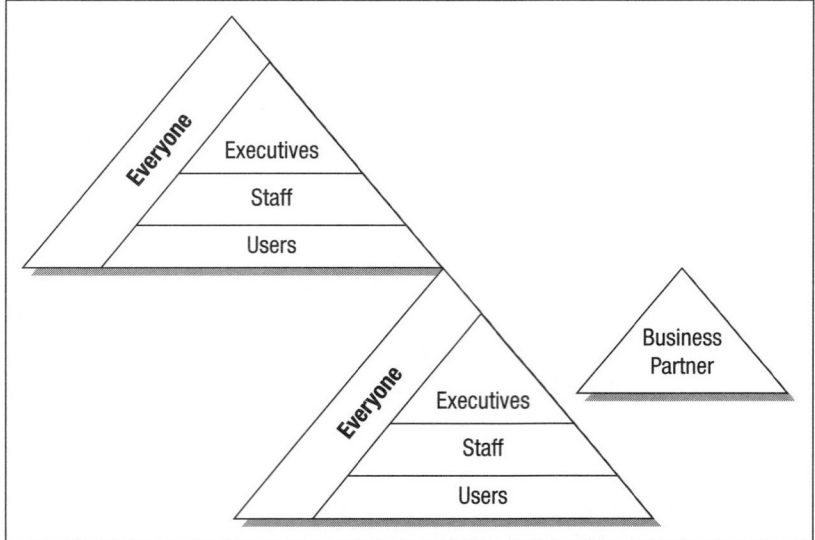

Figure 8.1   Groups in a typical user population.

➤ *Executives*—This group includes principals with all comprehensive rights, permissions, and/or privileges.

➤ *Staff*—This group not only works with most (if not all) system resources but is also expected to comply with standard procedures and policies.

➤ *Users*—This group includes the staff members who access resources and perform their daily functions through software applications.

➤ *Business partners*—This group includes principals who have some special relationship with the organization. They are expected to comply with all standard policies and procedures, as well as utilize resources exactly like the other groups.

Determining the Scope, Sizing, and Placement of IT Resources

Determining the scope, sizing, and placement of IT resources is a function of business objectives and budget. Often, the functional needs of the different groups in the user population (outlined in the "Identifying the User Population" section earlier in this chapter) also influence these determinations. From a security perspective, security scope, in functional terms, determines where control boundaries lie. I define these boundaries in functional terms wherever possible to both reflect the corporate business objectives and map how people perform their work in an organization.

From a practical, financial, or physical view, number (sizing) and placement of hardware rarely follow textbook descriptions. Although it is possible or necessary to run multiple services on one server machine, doing so is typically not recommended. Workload characteristics of services vary not just in functional terms but also over time with respect to network utilization. Concurrent demands by different services for similar resources on the same hardware platform can cause a server to panic and crash. These concurrently running services may also expose security weaknesses that would never appear if they were run separately. Such security weaknesses could expose all services on that server to unexpected security risks. For purposes of this book, sizing and placement issues are generally operational. With regard to Microsoft certification examination questions, I have and will follow the Windows 2000 Competency guidelines and stress rationales supporting design issues; sizing, placement and related topics on optimization and performance tuning are best left for more comprehensive texts.

Scoping Physical Assets

The scope of any physical security plan, as described in Chapter 2, typically relates to secured server room(s) or wire closet(s). The scope is documented in a physical security plan that describes:

➤ An inventory of physical assets, including both data and telephone components, routers, printers, tape backup units, and uninterrupted power supplies (all listed with manufacturer, model number, and serial number)

➤ A diagram of the physical area, including architectural plans that show cabling, power, High Voltage/Air Conditioning (HVAC), and so on

➤ A definition of the security perimeter that separates the secured facilities from the rest of the world and who has rights of access

The plan would typically document perceived security risks, countermeasures, and, if appropriate, costs and benefits. It might also document policies and procedures regarding personnel allowed access to the facility, emergency personnel call lists, and specific vendors responsible for maintenance of, for example, telephone equipment, air conditioning units, and building maintenance. Backup media sets should be stored in a locked storage area inside this locked facility. Wiring diagrams and emergency contact lists (with account numbers where appropriate) should be prominently displayed. Never overlook the possibility of simple theft of physical equipment or the security risk of a member of the janitorial staff splashing soapy water on a patch panel. The simplest countermeasure is a locked door with a restricted number of keys and a strict company policy regarding accessibility. Any employee handbook should explicitly state that noncompliance of policies—especially relating to physical assets—is grounds for immediate dismissal and possible legal recourse.

Scoping Logical Assets

The security scope that encompasses logical assets is at the heart of identity management and security models, which are covered in Chapter 7. *Identity management*, the services that administer the security credentials of named objects or principals, will become increasingly important as enterprises grow and users roam within them. Windows 2000 uses a security model that determines authentication and authorization of principals based on legitimate credentials administered by AD directory services. The access control mechanism implements authorization and is triggered when the resource is requested; an object-specific ACL that defines various categories of permissions is referenced when the consumer requests access or services. Some strategies applicable in securing these network assets are:

➤ Authenticating all consumers, clients, and services

➤ Applying appropriate authorization controls

➤ Establishing uniform security policies across the domain

➤ Applying appropriate trust relationships among domains

➤ Enabling data protection for sensitive data

Determining Scope within the Legacy Domain Model

The domain model in Windows 2000 is a collection of principals or named objects that are stored in a directory repository called the *directory database*. These named objects or principals can be users, machines, or service accounts that log on to remote machines and act as part of the operating system. The domain identifies a security authority that defines internal security policies for this collection and explicit security relationships with other domains.

Determining Scope Regarding Windows 2000 Authentication Services

Windows 2000 authentication services now enable Single Sign-On (SSO) to all network resources using a single password or two-factor authentication using a smart card. Two-factor authentication requires both a physical object and some password to be present when authentication is requested. Smart cards carry integrated circuitry that stores a digital certificate and the holder's private key. The password or personal identification number (PIN) is entered at the keyboard at the same time the data is read from the card.

Both the standards-based Kerberos protocol and the PKI suite have been enhanced to support smart card technologies, which are discussed in greater detail in Chapter 12. Authentication in Windows 2000 is implemented either by the Microsoft Kerberos protocol or NT LAN Manager (NTLM) authentication protocol. Accounts are managed using AD Users And Computers snap-in to Microsoft Management Console (MMC). User accounts can be functionally organized into Organizational Units (OUs) within the AD namespace. Creation of a named account defines that object as a principal and entitles it to access through the enterprise. When domain authentication services are integrated with the enterprise directory namespace, the user account is also a global address book directory entry, thus distributing credentials throughout a domain forest. I further discuss this topic in Chapter 7.

Determining Scope Relating to Trust Management and the Internet

Native Windows 2000 supports SSO for consumers within the domain forest. SSO is transparently supported by several network protocols in providing requested services to some authenticated consumer no matter where they log on to the enterprise. These protocols are the NTLM, Kerberos, and Secure Channel (SChannel) security protocols. NTLM is a legacy authentication protocol used primarily in mixed mode installations where the NT 4 domain model is still operational. Kerberos, the default security protocol in native Windows 2000, makes no assumptions regarding authentication; the identity of both the consumer and service is verified. Trust relationships in the domain forest extend the scope of

Kerberos authentication. Kerberos trusts are bidirectional or transitive by default, so authentication in one domain can be referred or passed-through to service providers in some other domain. With regard to network connectivity, the SSO feature is similarly supported through the SChannel security protocols, such as Secure Sockets Layer (SSL) version 3 and Transport Layer Security (TLS) version 1.

Clients and services are also authenticated when they connect to a domain or when they request services. Computer policies are exchanged during the logon process once authentication is validated. Clients and services in an N-tier architecture need to be "trusted for delegation" where, in the security context of the consumer, one service requests, on behalf of the consumer, additional services from some other client or service. Similarly, you can set the mutual authentication flag so that upon receiving a Kerberos Application Request (KRB_AP_REQ), the service provider authenticates itself to the consumer in the form of a Kerberos Application Reply (KRB_AP_REP).

Assessing Network Security Risks

The concept of a workgroup emphasizes collaboration and communication. With the privilege to share resources comes the ability to intentionally or unintentionally misuse someone else's property. In an enterprise based on collaboration and communication, identity management and security control in the form of authentication, authorization, and auditing (AAA) are critical functions. Although one approach to security controls is to minimize network security risks through isolation ("the best network security control is a pair of wire cutters"), I don't believe this is a realistic way of conducting business operations. Contemporary social and business activities use information technologies; IT is based on network connectivity. Even the most limited access to the Internet exposes an internal network to some form of risk. In my opinion, risks of this nature are a cost of doing business and a fact of contemporary life.

Attack Modalities

The three attack modalities—interference, interception, and impersonation—were discussed in Chapter 2. Acting as a framework, these categories encompass a comprehensive range of possible security assault methods. Chapters 3 through 7 have described various security technologies applied at different structural layers of the Open Systems Interconnection (OSI) model. In the analysis of a security environment, you should systematically work through each network layer to expose possible security risks using samples from each of the three categories. Distributed security systems, working primarily within the boundaries of the enterprise, form a functional core or center security perimeter. To systematically assess network security risks, work outward from that core. Instead of dichotomizing distributed and network security systems, you can think of the various security systems outside the enterprise as a series of concentric rings, each dealing with broader namespaces and more comprehensive identity management. This ring model helps organize the analysis of a case study or a real-life business scenario.

The next section discusses the ring model more in depth. It will help you place several different services in some meaningful perspective. I conceptualize Routing and Remote Access Service (RRAS), Remote Authentication Dial-In User Service (RADIUS), Microsoft's Internet Authentication Service (IAS), and Microsoft Directory Synchronization Services (MSDSS) all on a single dimension that describes greater consolidation of directory services. I believe this concept will help you understand the relationship among these services and how secured boundaries will evolve with increasing interoperability of these meta-directory structures. See Chapter 7 for a discussion of Microsoft's hub-and-spoke meta-directory architecture, where directory services are consolidated under an umbrella directory system of separate directory services.

 It is unlikely that you will encounter a case study that deals directly with the services mentioned in Chapter 7's "Identity Management" section. Microsoft's technical papers on this subject and meta-directories are hard to understand but significant in describing future trends.

Ring Model

At the heart of the enterprise is the AD: in the simplest case, a single domain and single namespace. AD makes credential data stores accessible to all objects requiring authentication and authorization services within this inner ring. The trend in consolidation of directory services fosters this directory-centric view. This is similar to the hub in what Microsoft calls its hub-and-spoke architecture, discussed in Chapter 7's "Identity Management" section. If current trends continue, boundaries between heterogeneous network operating systems will gradually dissolve. The business need for functional interoperability will force identity management and directory services to converge. Different namespaces will be consolidated into some universal namescape much like domains link together to form forests. Surrounding the center ring in Figure 8.2 are two additional rings, representing the Internet and extranet, respectively. Lightweight Directory Access Protocol (LDAP)-based meta-directories will assume a position similar to the LDAP version 3 icon, in Figure 8.2, outside any single network operating system but central to all enterprises that have some functional association. Figure 8.2 shows other protocols and services that support the expansion to larger and larger enterprises; this movement is directed outward from the center ring with its core directory services.

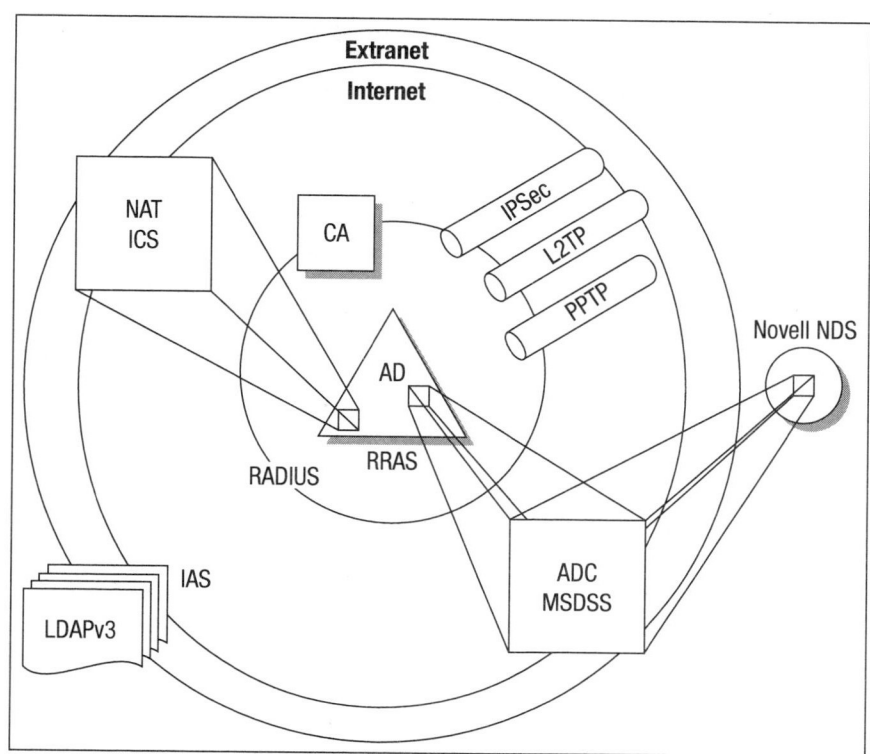

Figure 8.2 Protocols and services in a ring model.

As the enterprise increases in scale, the ability to request and receive services will push its limits beyond its physical boundaries into the Internet. Beyond the capacity to support remote access is the bridging of separate enterprises and the linking of extranets. This shift is toward larger, distributed systems with their greater scalability (meta-directories) and a greater security scope for the credentials they hold. AD and directory services like it, such as Novell Directory Services (NDS), will be at the center of these concentric, logical rings. For example, remote access connectivity on an increasingly large scale is supported by RRAS; on a larger wide area network (WAN), by RADIUS; and finally, between WANs, by IAS. Independent LDAP-based directories either support several IAS servers or eliminate them entirely through consolidation. Similarly, Active Directory Connectors (ADCs), and specifically MSDSS, link the heterogeneous directory services supported by AD and NDS. In the figure, both the Network address translation (NAT) from RRAS and Internet Connection Sharing (ICS) from Dial-Up Connections tool are positioned on the outside physical perimeter of the inner ring, the core enterprise, as features supporting Small Office/Home Office (SOHO) connectivity to the Internet represented by the second ring. The three protocol pipes—Point-To-Point Tunneling Protocol (PPTP), Layer 2 Tunneling Protocol (L2TP), and IP Security (IPSec)—represent VPNs connecting both public networks and extranets. The Certificate Authority (CA) is needed to support the L2TP connections. Some of these services are only meaningful in special heterogeneous or mixed-platform situations. The efforts especially of both Novell through NDS and Microsoft through MSDSS in developing a consolidated directory are very real and significant trends that need to be recognized in today's strategic network planning.

From a case-study perspective, notice the progression of policy management moving outward from the center of the ring, as shown in Figure 8.3. The three different levels are described here:

➤ *The center ring*—Policy management within the physical boundaries of the enterprise

➤ *The middle ring*—Policy management outside the enterprise to support remote access services in unsecured, public spaces

➤ *The outer ring*—Policy management extending session pipes directly out to some extranet

Microsoft is moving toward a consolidation of separate directory services into meta-directory namescapes, as discussed in Chapter 7, which are shared between enterprises. This trend is shown in Figure 8.4. The figure shows that manual directory synchronization requires the most maintenance and is perceived to

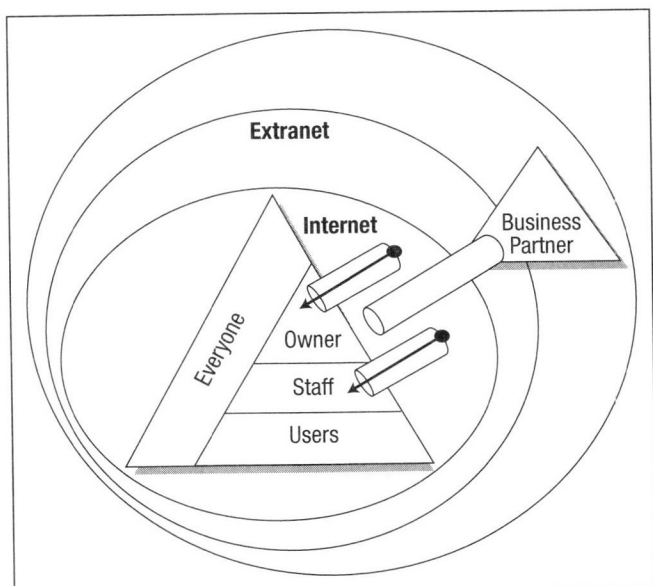

Figure 8.3   A progression of policy management.

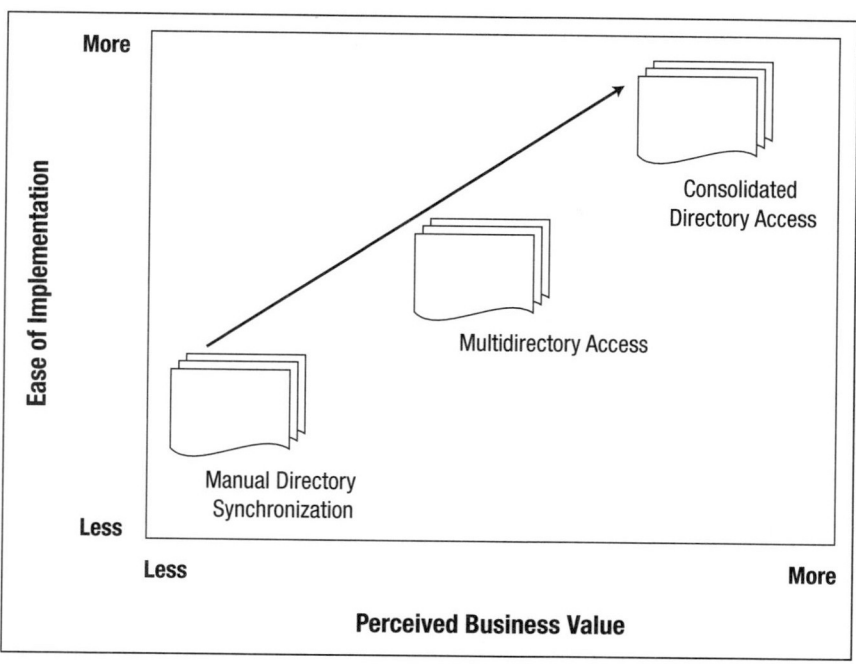

Figure 8.4 Return on investment: identity management and security.

have the least business value, whereas consolidated directory access is superior to both manual directory synchronization and multidirectory access in both ease of implementation and perceived business value. It also suggests that at some point umbrella or meta-directory services will integrate directory services across enterprises in some LDAP-based, "universal" cloud services specializing in identity management.

Creating Secure Boundaries: Physical Scoping

A security perimeter between a more-secured area and a less-secured area depends in general on the way servers running specific services are placed in the network topology. A realistic approach to network security is to isolate specialized and particularly vulnerable servers and services in specially created security zones within your network infrastructure. The classic example of such an area is called a demilitarized zone (DMZ), which uses firewall techniques (discussed in Chapter 6) and technologies that force inbound and outbound traffic to servers and their running services within the zone through restrictive choke points. This approach is said to harden the boundaries around this logical zone to many forms of attack. A DMZ must be secured from physical access and configured to be outside the logical scope of the user population. Similarly, services within the DMZ are both physically and logically scoped in the most restrictive way; only required services, resources, and rights are made available.

Creating Secure Boundaries: Protocol Scoping

Secured boundaries now extend beyond the physical borders of an enterprise; Windows 2000 has integrated services that easily extend secured forms of communication over both private and public networks. These services, now integrated within the operating system, provide transparent security services at the OSI Data Link, Network, and Transport layers, as well as through services at the Application layer. For example, security protocols like L2TP and PPTP operate at the Data Link layer to encrypt messages exchanged through branch network connections as well as remote access sessions. The SChannel security protocols, such as SSL version 3 and TLS, protect Hypertext Transfer Protocol (HTTP) sessions. Finally, the IPSec protocol suite provides client-to-client (end-to-end) security across internal connections.

Creating Secure Boundaries: Application Scoping

Other techniques mentioned in Chapter 6 (besides the DMZ) involve gateways that run as application services. An example is Microsoft Proxy Server 2, which performs both a caching function to improve performance and packet filtering. When this service is installed in a network environment, all client applications must direct their requests for services, such as File Transfer Protocol (FTP) or HTTP, through the Proxy Server. This arrangement restricts the message flow and permits centralized logging, as well as effective monitoring and control of system resources.

Creating Secure Boundaries: Policy Scoping

Distinctions between distributed and network security are blurring because several technologies are now fully integrated into the operating system. Remote access is becoming a necessary business requirement for staff in most enterprises. The management of remote access services is primarily through policy. Windows 2000 policy-based management has been simplified and is now centrally administered primarily because of LDAP version 3 and RADIUS. RRAS provides the remote access services. Microsoft, through the use of the published application programming interface (API) and well-known protocols like LDAP and RADIUS, has extended AD services to include remote access user authentication and to guarantee future interoperability with multivendor directory services. These feature trends are discussed in the "Identity Management" section in Chapter 7.

The call-accounting features of full-featured RADIUS services are incorporated in IAS. Through these features, Windows 2000 can manage large-scale, heterogeneous, remote access environments. Microsoft has integrated IAS with RRAS and AD to build a centrally administered, remote access service that offers policy-based management and detailed call accounting services. The integration of IAS and AD with RADIUS-enforced policy management can control many exchange variables, such as:

➤ Internet Protocol (IP) address

➤ Originating client IP address

➤ Network Access Server (NAS) manufacturer

➤ Type of service requested

➤ Type of protocol used

➤ Transport Control Protocol (TCP)/User Datagram Protocol (UDP) port

➤ User ID telephone number

➤ Originating phone number

➤ User group

➤ Time of day

Integration of the AD directory service provides centrally managed control of both direct-dial and VPN services. Although previous remote access solutions failed to address both client and management issues, this kind of comprehensive policy management and RADIUS-based accounting services in the form of enhanced directory services reduce TCO while improving staff productivity and the overall security and management efficiency. It changes the way enterprises provide services to their staff. If companies can manage remote access services in this manner, there are few reasons not to offer it as a standard business tool. Windows 2000 now offers these kinds of integrated management tools and policy-based services to its users without the company having to incur additional costs in support, maintenance, or training.

Preparing a Support Team

Security technologies require not just expertise but careful and diligent monitoring. Sophisticated security systems—like, for example, firewall technologies installed as a standalone security system—give an organization a false sense of comfort. These systems are usually deployed in concert with other technologies that carefully fortify them. Two key activities associated with the successful installation of any security system are monitoring and auditing. Your support team must not only have sufficient training to deploy these systems, but also experience using instrumentation that measures system usage and daily activity. They should play an active role in all pilot studies where systems are scrutinized and, often, rebuilt and fine-tuned.

When abnormal or unexpected activity is observed, your support team should first formalize and then systematically follow a set of procedures to isolate the problem, determine its nature, and follow through with some corrective action. These standardized procedures are documented in a disaster recovery plan, a security network plan, or a deployment plan. Help desk support thus plays an integral part in testing the system so that, following deployment, the support team can aggressively and confidently support the system users.

Monitoring and Auditing

The best security technology will fail if it is improperly deployed or configured. Pilot testing is necessary to confirm that systems work as planned. Nevertheless, even the most thorough planning cannot anticipate every conceivable plan of attack within any particular attack modality. In fact, environments will change over time, especially in response to the changing needs of a business or a large user population. Companies need to maintain baselines of network activity. Although ongoing system checks are necessary to maintain system integrity, regularly planned (though randomly scheduled) security audits, especially when you are dealing with network security, are important and can minimize risks. Companies should also systematically apply one or two assault methods from each attack modality to locate security weaknesses and prevent a real attack before it happens.

You should use tools that capture details about network flow so that you can observe system utilization, any changes in baseline behavior, or shifts in workloads. Microsoft Proxy Server 2 automatically produces production reports. Logging data to a text file tracks system usage and errors by supported online service. You can easily import these text files to analysis tools. Alternatively, data can be stored as Open Database Connectivity (ODBC)/Structured Query Language (SQL) database files to facilitate automated analysis and fault management through programmed triggers. Windows 2000 automatically logs events and audits specific activities. IAS also has activity reporting functions. It is important, though, to review the accumulated data, not just collect it.

Another increasingly important approach in network management is Simple Network Management Protocol (SNMP). Based on a simple architecture of management agent (information collector), network management protocol (SNMP), management station (some host server), and an extensive management information knowledge base, a network and its servers can be remotely monitored and maintained. The advantages of this important protocol are a single operator interface and minimal separate equipment outside of the agent and the host. SNMPv3, as specified in RFC 2570 through 2575, defines a framework for incorporating network security and access controls into this architecturally simple system.

Help Desk Support

The support function or user help desk is critical to an organization's health as well as to the implementation of its security policy. You should view the help desk as an in-house service business where performance is measured in terms of quality of service. Employee satisfaction and goodwill are important because both foster compliance with security policies and procedures, as well as shape a corporate culture.

Developing a Security Deployment Plan

At this stage of the process, you begin implementing security plans on a small or pilot scale to test assumptions in the real corporate environment in the hands of nontechnical, perhaps hostile users. Some deployment plans are suggested later in this section. Finally, after the support team has had time to monitor, audit, and analyze the efficacy of the security technologies, the final rollout of the formal security systems is performed. At that point in time, the support staff and help desk are fully empowered and confident in resolving any user issues.

Creating and Publishing a Security Policy

There are social and legal implications in publishing a security policy. It is the management's responsibility to formally communicate its goals, objectives, and restrictions to all employees. It is also necessary to distribute this policy in a way that fosters a sense of compliance among employees. Adding some legal text in a dialog box during the logon process plays an important part in providing an employer with the legal grounds to dismiss an employee for misconduct without fear of legal repercussions.

Developing Strategies for Secure Network Connections

Having prepared an overall strategy and identified the specific needs of various segments of your user population, you must then plan or strategize the deployment of services. Wherever possible, you would have replaced specific user needs with built-in groups and security templates. One of the key benefits of writing a deployment plan is to uncover duplication or overlapping in security services at different layers. Several security systems are mutually dependent, like the dependence of L2TP on IPSec for VPN client-gateway security. IPSec seeks machine certification to authorize the client-server connection. Without certification services provided in that domain, this planned exchange will fail. You must set Group Policy features for auto-enrollment so that clients have the necessary credentials for the IPSec exchange to occur. Group Policy in AD can centralize administration on a domain basis. This topic is discussed in greater detail in Chapter 10.

Thus, the deployment plans also indicate strengths and weaknesses in scoping, especially in the complex area of policy management.

Deploying Network Strategies for the Everyone Group

Depending on the structure of the corporate business objectives, use the Everyone group *conceptually* as the lowest common denominator for assigning network services. Although I do not use the group when assigning access to resources, I use it for security reasons to configure auditing of various objects early in a project. Likewise, I design access for Everyone, so I have to protect myself from Everyone. Deployment of, for example, Proxy Server 2 provides an easily installed and maintained choke for network connectivity as well as a central point for packet filtering and maintaining service logs when Everyone tries to attack my installation. Although it requires slightly more maintenance, deploying an Internet Information Server (IIS) also provides security control over network connectivity and various online services such as FTP and HTTP. Thus, in planning my deployment for the Everyone group, I have actually established three security scopes:

➤ The Proxy Server at the Application layer implicitly gave me control over TCP/UDP protocols and ports through its packet filtering capabilities.

➤ IIS gave me similar functionality, except I could control the online services that run at the application level.

➤ Tracking system auditing (e.g., unsuccessful logon activity) represents policy scoping.

Deploying Network Strategies for Staff Members

The primary security concerns regarding staff members are authentication and confidentiality. This group has some degree of privileges, so you must secure the initial logon. This user group would be assigned to a class of services that would typically include Internet access. Given the low administrative overhead involved in remote access services, it is increasingly common for this to also be included in a class of services for this particular group. Within this broad class of services, both IIS and RRAS allow policy definitions at the user level. Whether implemented as local policies or as part of Group Policy, remote access policies can enforce both authentication and encryption. When you are deploying specifically RRAS security, the following issues are relevant:

➤ Which groups or users will have access

➤ What kind of authentication will be used

➤ What kind of data encryption will be used

Deploying Remote Access Policy Using VPN

Another approach to remote access services is to provide the features of a private network except over unsecured namespace such as the Internet. Windows 2000 provides VPNs as part of the standard operating system and at reduced costs compared to other solutions on the market. Although VPN deployment is more complicated than deployment of unsecured public connections, the full features of a private network across a public network such as the Internet offer significant benefits. A VPN can be deployed between any two sites, even when both are within an internal network, using a variety of connections to enhance security. Windows 2000 includes VPN software as part of RRAS.

When deploying a VPN, consider the following issues:

➤ Integration of the VPN in your remote access policy

➤ Choice of either PPTP or L2TP security protocols; if L2TP is used, decide whether to implement IPSec; if you use IPSec, choose what certificate to use

➤ Placement of the VPN server

➤ Centralized management tools like Connection Manager, discussed later in this chapter

Remote access policies specifically deal with users of RRAS. Policies can be based on user group, phone number, hours of usage, and other kinds of information. Profiles can be applied to connections that specify session length; maximum idle time; dialup media; allowed addresses; and security methods such as authentication, encryption, or VPN. You can set these policies for RRAS or IAS. It's important that you carefully plan the creation and application of policies to various groups because it is possible to overlap and unintentionally contradict or disallow one specification with another. For a discussion of the VPN protocol choices, see Chapter 6.

Placing Servers

Placement of, for example, a VPN server, especially in relation to a firewall, is very important and is an example of planning, sizing, and placement of server services before deploying security systems. Both VPN technology and firewall technology offer complementary benefits and thus may be deployed at the same time. Their placement in relation to each other is very important. Although both services could be installed on the same physical machine it is best to distribute services across different servers whenever possible to provide fault tolerance, hardware capacity, and so on. At the very least, given the importance of running both services concurrently, the unavailability or loss of this server jeopardizes the network security of an entire enterprise. Figure 8.5 shows a sample VPN/firewall placement.

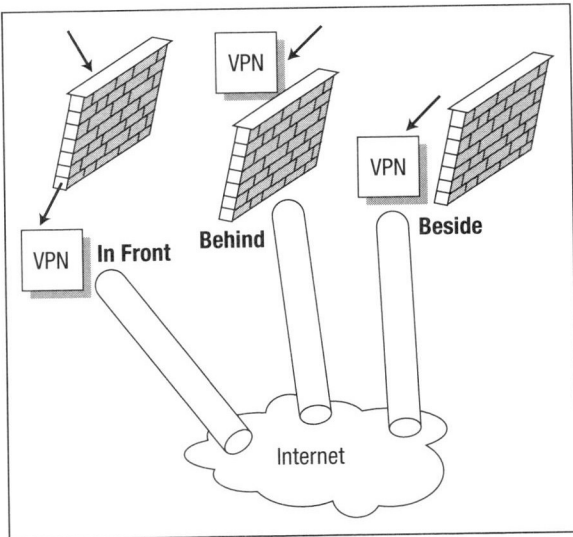

Figure 8.5 An example of VPN/firewall placement.

Figure 8.5 shows three scenarios (I assume that each service is running on a separate server). Each scenario has advantages and disadvantages, as described in Table 8.1.

There is not one single correct relationship between these two security technologies. The final decision is a function of corporate objectives, budget, user population, and in this case, the expertise of the support team responsible for deploying and maintaining the security plan.

An Example of Centralized Administration: Connection Manager

Deploying client software for VPN is labor intensive, especially because the user population is by definition located outside the enterprise's boundaries. Windows

Table 8.1	The advantages and disadvantages of various VPN/firewall configurations.	
Configuration	**Advantages**	**Disadvantages**
VPN in front of firewall	Firewall is secure	Provides only external services
VPN behind firewall	Firewall provides all services to VPN users	You must configure additional TCP/UDP ports to accommodate which security protocols are chosen; these open ports weaken the wall
VPN beside firewall	Fault tolerance, physical layout of services	Double the costs of support, maintenance, auditing; double the security risks of penetration

2000 provides for relatively simple setup through Connection Manager, which runs on both legacy NT 4 and Windows 9x clients. The Connection Manager Administration Kit (CMAK), like other administration tools such as the Internet Explorer Administration Kit and Outlook Deployment Kit, provides an administrator with a tool that cost-effectively creates customized connections for most if not all end users. From a service business perspective, your support team can distribute an installation kit that efficiently "empowers" nontechnical remote users to configure direct dial-up and VPN remote access connections with little or no dependence on technical support. Like the other administration kits, CMAK permits on-demand updating of remote clients from some centralized source. Here again is an example of Microsoft's integrated administrative features that provide enhanced end-user functionality at little or no increase in TCO.

Deploying Network Strategies for Users and Applications

A security approach, common in relational database management systems such as SQL Server, defines access not in terms of users or groups but in terms of applications. This application role provides a security context within which a user can perform a predetermined task in a controlled environment or security sandbox. The application is secured with either its own dedicated directory database of authorized users or, based on recent trends in directory consolidation (as discussed in Chapter 7), in some centralized global directory. Examples of these applications are time management, company benefits registration, and Web-based e-commerce storefronts. The security technologies that support this kind of application development are rapidly increasing, with the trends toward thinner remote clients and fatter distributed hosts. Relevant security technologies here depend on:

➤ Specifications of the application

➤ The sophistication in design with respect to backend integration and security

➤ Application performance issues

➤ Complexity of administration required to support the application

Depending upon how the application is integrated with the network through the Security Support Provider Interface (SSPI), application-oriented security technologies include:

➤ Kerberos, discussed in Chapter 4

➤ SSL3/TLS1, discussed in Chapters 2 and 7

➤ Digital certificates, discussed in Chapter 2

These distributed applications interface with SSPI, which in turn negotiates with installed Security Support Providers (SSPs) to establish a mutually supported secured session pipes through which all subsequent information exchanges will occur. Refer to Chapter 4 for a discussion of SSPI and installable SSPs. Figure 8.6 shows how an application interfaces the various communication and security layers. In brief, some distributed application uses a Distributed Component Object Model (DCOM) interface, an Internet API (WinInet), or the Windows Sockets 2 interface (Winsock) to communicate with some host server. These connections, or others using Remote Procedure Calls (RPCs) or Transmission Control Protocol/Internet Protocol (TCP/IP) directly (the Winsock interface) all interface with the SSPI. This common platform gives Windows 2000 a major architectural advantage because it allows any third-party application to negotiate with any one of several installed security libraries (NTLM, Kerberos, or SChannel security protocols) on some host server.

Deploying Network Strategies for Business Partners

With the expansion of communication and the forces of e-commerce, business alliances not only offer complementary services but directly share data and other enterprise resources. This access from outside the boundaries of the enterprise exposes an internal network to considerable risks. The network and security technologies that support such cross-enterprise access are collectively called an *extranet*. Access technologies include VPN and RRAS. One important characteristic that

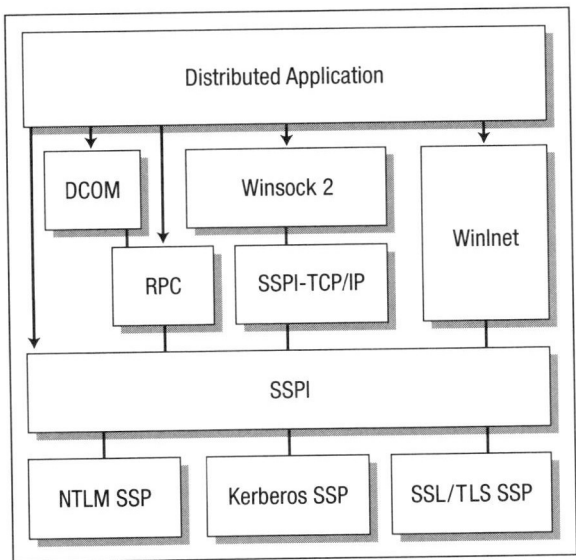

Figure 8.6 Relationships among network application security technologies.

distinguishes the extranet scenario from other remote access situations is that the extranet has location and link specificity. Thus, IP addressing between the two enterprises is predefined.

These predetermined links have both advantages and disadvantages. As with the deployment of all the other population groups, it is critical for daily operation, security, and support that you carefully consider how business units will communicate with each other, their functional relationships, the workflows between units, and the deployment of services. You should carefully monitor traffic patterns across extranet connections because the workloads characteristic among partners are typically several orders of magnitude greater than workloads transferred among staff members. You must carefully consider WAN connection speeds with regard to capacity. Finally, security controls here focus on scalability, availability, accessibility, and timeliness because pipes among partners can be expected to carry mission-critical data. The priorities of these security controls would be detailed in the corporate business objectives.

A Security Policy Case Study

ExamCram Ltd. Reformulates Its Plans

ExamCram Ltd., having merged with MyCompany Inc., located in the same building, has created a new company called ExamCram Company. There is a growing contingent of dissatisfied MyCompany Inc. personnel. At the moment, management is reassessing its financial situation and corporate strategy. There have been some leaks to the press regarding ExamCram Company's plans to increase capitalization through an initial public offering (IPO). This has placed top-level management in an awkward situation. They have hired outside management consultants to evaluate internal policies and procedures, as well as auditors to review the financial data.

MyPartner Inc. still works exclusively for the Sales division of MyCompany Inc. over an extranet.

Company Goal

One immediate objective is to protect the confidentiality of information. Another is to formalize corporate policies and procedures. Outside auditors and consultants agree that ExamCram Company has grown a profitable business from a small, startup company but that it must now develop more sophisticated business policies and procedures before it can take any further strategic steps. A newly formulated Board of Directors wants to plan the growth of the new enterprise carefully.

Exhibit

The original organizational chart for both ExamCram Ltd. and MyCompany Inc. is shown in Exhibit 1.

Current LAN/Network Structure

All 100-client machines are running native mode Windows 2000 in the root domain of a tree. Each workstation is connected to a 10Mbps hub through 10Mbps local area network (LAN) cards, although Category 5 Unshielded Twisted Pair (UTP) cabling connects each system and hub in a star topology. The network protocol is TCP/IP.

MyCompany Inc., composed of 20 users, is in a child domain, **mycompany.examcram.com**, under **examcram.com**. The tree is well connected.

Proposed LAN/Network Structure

The VPN server IP address on the Internet is 201.101.1.1. The HTTP, FTP, and PPTP packet filters are properly configured on the Internet interface.

ExamCram Ltd.				MyCompany Inc.		
VP Fin	VP Sales	VP Ops	CEO	President		
Accnt Mngr	Sales Mngr	Tech Mngr	Project Mngr1	Vice President/Sales Mngr		
			Project Mngr2	Accnt Mngr		SysAdmin
		DBA/Developer	Project Mngr3			
		Webmaster	Project Mngr4			
		Programmer	Project Mngr5			
Bookkeep	Sales1	Tech1		Bookkeep	Sales1	Tech1
Clerk1	Sales2	Tech2		Clerk1	Sales2	Tech2
Clerk2	Sales3	Tech3		Clerk2	Sales3	Tech3
Clerk3	Sales4				Sales4	

Exhibit 1   Original organizational chart.

Current WAN Connectivity

Both companies use Internet access to communicate. ExamCram Company wants MyCompany Inc. to continue to work directly with its business partner, MyPartner Inc.

Proposed WAN Connectivity

No plans are proposed at this time.

Design Commentary

The CEO at ExamCram Company says, "We need a methodology to grow our enterprise that is results oriented and milestone based. In my five-year plan, I want to deliver services as quickly and efficiently as possible. I want to shorten the review process of every project so that ExamCram Company adapts quickly to changing business, financial, and technical events in the world of e-commerce."

The IT Director at ExamCram Company says, "I want to create a security blueprint that will address our business, application, and technical needs. I want the IT department to serve as an internal service organization that supports our staff."

Current Internet Positioning

ExamCram Ltd. is registered as **examcram.com**. Its IP address is 201.101.1.1. MyCompany Inc. is registered as **mycompany.com** at IP address 198.2.4.6. ExamCram Company will continue to use the **examcram.com** domain as ExamCram Ltd. has done in the past.

Future Internet Plans

No changes in the current structure are proposed at this time.

Commentary

Figure 8.7 shows the same organizational chart as Exhibit 1, except that it is deployed as a number of organizational global groups that would typically extend across a flat NT 4 legacy domain structure. Figure 8.8 shows the revised categorization of users, as described in the "Identifying the User Population" section earlier in this chapter. However, to support the enterprise, the company would still need two one-way trusts in Windows 2000 mixed mode.

The organization shown in Figures 8.7 and 8.8 can be improved. You can see the transition from the flat NT 4 domain structure (Figure 8.7) and multiple domains with nontransitive trusts (Figure 8.8) to a hierarchical, single domain model (Figure 8.9) using AD without trusts or, worst case, transitive trusts between regional divisions (namely, **east.examcram.com** and **west. examcram.com**).

ExamCram Company is looking for a vision statement. It has little or no idea how to take a first step. The company doesn't know what corporate business objectives

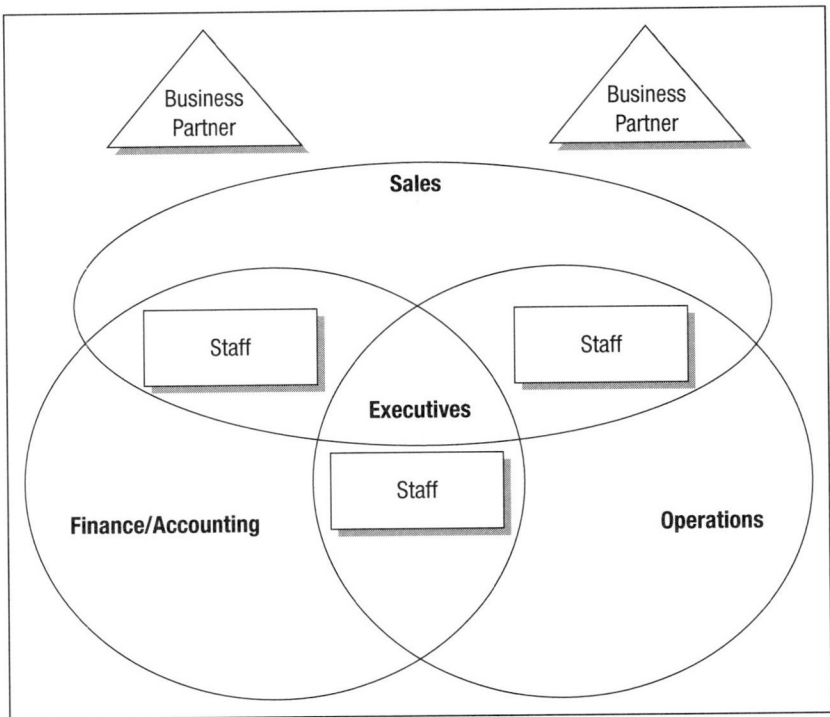

Figure 8.7   Organizational chart: original flat domain structure.

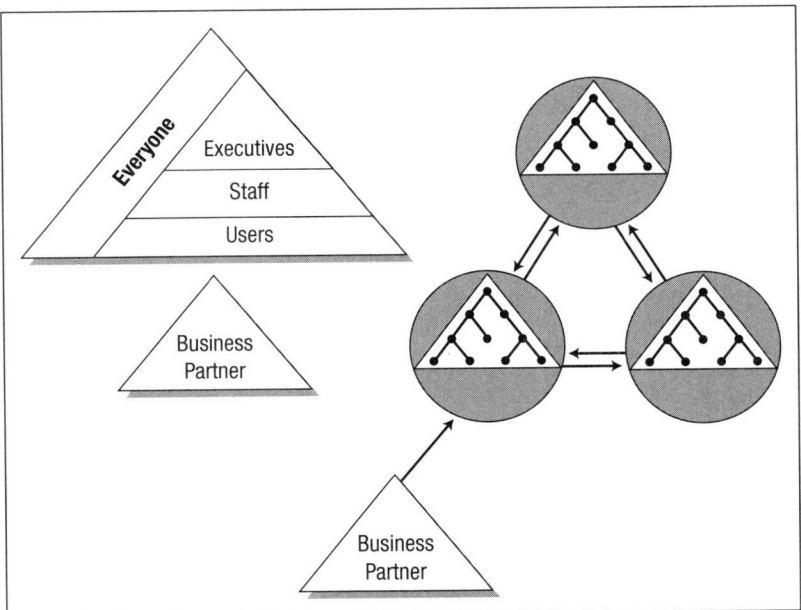

Figure 8.8   Groups in a user population.

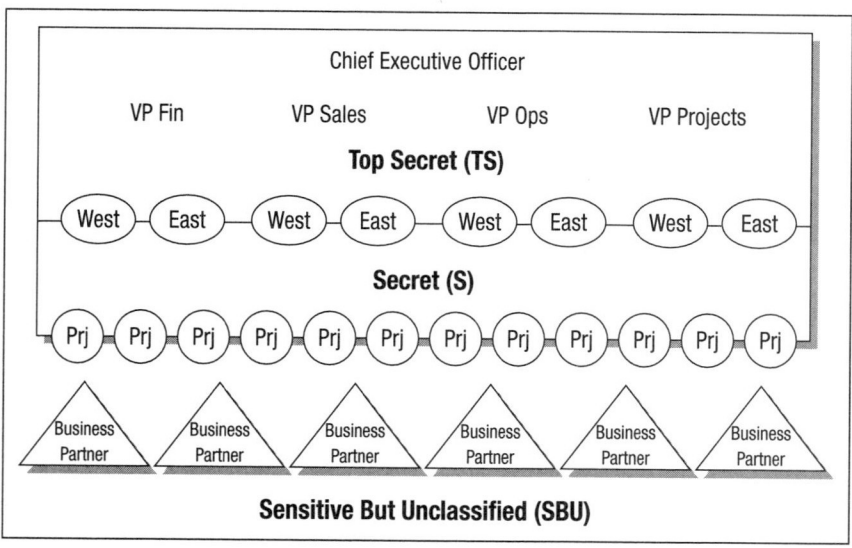

Figure 8.9 Proposed organization after phase 1.

are. However, it does need to evolve into a single corporate structure with unified policies and procedures. The policies and procedures take time to write and will require many revisions and modifications before a final form is achieved.

Note: Always begin with a simple action plan. Approach this task as an iterative process that establishes a specific schedule, a scope of actions to be completed in that timeframe, and a list of required resources. Determine what your deliverables are (scope) and when they are due (schedule), and then determine what you need to complete your action plan (resources).

My action plan is set out in the following sections.

Short-Term Objective 1: Deploy a Technology that Will Correct the Security Leak

The time frame for this objective is as soon as possible. Management believes that future security leaks can be prevented through the deployment of security systems that will limit access to information. The immediate objective is therefore to provide and maintain confidentiality. My initial solution is to establish policies regarding both resource accessibility and user authorization without the need for capital investment. Additional solutions deploying security technologies will typically follow the establishment of policies and procedures based on whether top management wants to allocate financial resources.

I begin by defining four categories of confidentiality. These categories, although arbitrary, would typically be decided by top management and would be based upon perceived damage to the corporation following, for example, full public disclosure. The typical categories are:

➤ *Top secret (TS)*—The highest level of required confidentiality; unauthorized disclosure of this category of information would result in the gravest of consequences to an organization.

➤ *Secret (S)*—Disclosure of this type of material would correspond to serious but not irreparable damage.

➤ *Sensitive but unclassified (SBU)*—This type of material is confidential; disclosure might prove embarrassing.

➤ *Unclassified (U)*—This type of material would have little or no meaning to outsiders.

Categories should be based on the same criterion or dimension to simplify compliance. For example, in the bulleted list, the constant criterion I use is the amount of damage to the corporation would suffer through disclosure. Next, I simplify job categories by assigning different roles to the user population groups identified in the "Identifying the User Population" section earlier in this chapter: executives, staff, user, and everyone. I then rebuild the organizational chart based on this new classification scheme, as shown in Figure 8.10.

I determine groups by applying the principle of least privilege, where access is permitted only to information that is necessary to accomplish any one job. I focus first on confidentiality by classifying documents in very simple ways. I will suggest to the Board of Directors a second phase of security deployment where I would deploy security technologies that reduce accessibility to all information at any one time, thus reducing the capability of an intruder to cause damage.

Notice how levels of confidentiality decrease from Exec to Staff to User. Nevertheless, these three categories correlate fairly well with job function in that data-entry material is sensitive but not classified. Operational reports typically prepared and reviewed by staff are ranked as S. Financial reporting that represents the consolidation of material is for executive decision support and therefore TS.

Short-Term Objective 2: Deliver a First-Draft Action Plan that Describes a Scalable Enterprise Architecture

The time frame for this objective is two weeks. Once I have placed the users and resources into some manageable framework, I will present my proposed organizational plan; information space has been divided into three specific security levels: TS, S, and SBU resources, as shown previously in Figure 8.9. Instead of adopting the flat domain structure of NT 4, I use a hierarchical arrangement, which offers greater degrees of scalability, especially in the context of regional expansion. This is

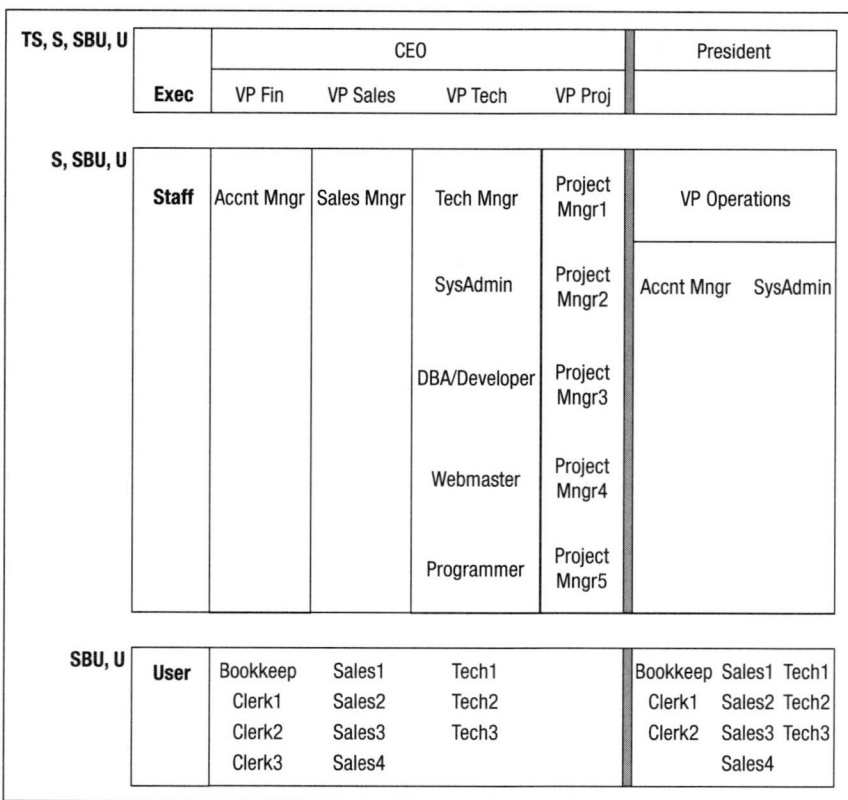

TS, S, SBU, U		CEO				President
	Exec	VP Fin	VP Sales	VP Tech	VP Proj	

S, SBU, U						
	Staff	Accnt Mngr	Sales Mngr	Tech Mngr	Project Mngr1	VP Operations
				SysAdmin	Project Mngr2	Accnt Mngr SysAdmin
				DBA/Developer	Project Mngr3	
				Webmaster	Project Mngr4	
				Programmer	Project Mngr5	

SBU, U					
	User	Bookkeep	Sales1	Tech1	Bookkeep Sales1 Tech1
		Clerk1	Sales2	Tech2	Clerk1 Sales2 Tech2
		Clerk2	Sales3	Tech3	Clerk2 Sales3 Tech3
		Clerk3	Sales4		Sales4

Figure 8.10   Proposed organizational chart of ExamCram Company.

a first draft of the organization that is intended to simplify the flow of information. I will present the Board of Directors with an organizational view that provides a framework within which to develop a more comprehensive policy. The issue of confidentiality needs to be addressed as quickly as possible. By reclassifying users and introducing a conceivably uniform criterion, management can rapidly implement a plan without spending any money.

I will urge the Board of Directors to define policies by creating a security blueprint. I will need to create group policies that begin with account policies, then grow local policies and restricted groups within domains. Figure 8.9 uses a hierarchical domain model with secured, functional boundaries. For example, each project can be isolated from the others. Similarly, as divisions grow, each will join the tree as a child domain under the corporate root domain.

Note: An enterprise is the combination of business, application, information, and technical architectures composed primarily of services. I define a service as a group of related workflows, functions, or outputs that collectively are a named object; the service object has an account in the directory database. Services are implemented through a consistent and documented set of outputs and interfaces composed of these business, application, information, or technical architectures. The value of any service is ultimately determined by the consumer of that service, hence our consumer–service provider relationship. Security controls are based on standards of due care and due diligence, practices that are readily available at a reasonable cost or are in regular use and are applied to reduce risk to that service.

Short-Term Objective 3: What Will My Deliverable Look Like?

It is not appropriate for me to create for ExamCram Company a vision statement that encompasses its business and technical objectives. I can, however, propose a vision statement that includes a framework for a network security plan and recommend some key themes that will help me to eventually create it. I would conceptualize the enterprise as three interdependent areas that provide:

➤ Business services (services inventory, workflow controls, and business rules)

➤ User services (services inventory based on the user population's needs)

➤ Data services (corporate assets)

Note: Create a statement that considers each of the three themes in the context of industry growth trends, frequency of changes, trends in development of competitive businesses, current and future ExamCram Company business needs, and changes in geographic scope associated with sizing issues.

I will create an inventory of business services based on ExamCram Company's business mission and statement. For example, there is a full-charge accounting system that includes Accounts Receivable, Accounts Payable, General Ledger, Payroll, and some kind of purchase order system to take book orders. In addition, a project management system handles book deals..

I create based on the identified user population an inventory of services that includes:

➤ Line-of-business (LOB) applications

➤ Internal/external messaging

➤ Information management (file/print/Web services)

➤ Data storage and archiving

➤ Network support

➤ Service-level guarantees (such as authentication based on a functional WAN link)

I also create a preliminary inventory of internal IT functions, including:

➤ System administration

➤ Configuration management

➤ Problem management

➤ Contingency planning

➤ Help desk

I create a physical equipment inventory and a topology that shows WAN and Domain Name System (DNS) architecture. I then create the appropriate domain architecture; create trees; and create a forest based on the inventory of services, the distribution of my user population, and the actual deployment of equipment. I complete site planning by designing a global catalog and DC placement. I conclude by proposing Organizational Units and group policies that mirror the functional organization of the enterprise where appropriate. These latter structures are discussed in Chapters 9 and 10.

From these inventories and needs list, I begin outlining a deployment plan to determine what components are critical and required during the first phase of deployment. I start with as simple a design as possible (such as Figure 8.9). Where possible, I start with a single tree at a single site; I define site, domain, or OUs in terms of hierarchical, functional workflows (geopolitical, business, and technical). In Figure 8.9, top-level management oversees regional divisions, which in turn manage local projects.

Practice Questions

Case Study

4Sale, an online bartering company in ThatTherePlace, North Dakota, has merged with Got-a-Deal, and both companies occupy office space in the same office building. The companies are now running their accounting operation, their bid system, and a knowledge base of their online goods in the same building.

Current LAN/Network Structure

4Sale is presently running Windows 2000 server in native mode. One member server supports Exchange server, and another is running IIS 5 and Proxy Server 2. All 100 client machines are configured in a single domain model. The client systems are running Windows Professional; Office 97 is utilized as an applications package. Each system is connected to a 10Mbps hub through 10Mbps LAN cards running Category 5 UTP cabling in a star topology.

Got-a-Deal has merged with 4Sale and is running all 22 client machines in a single child domain under the 4Sale root domain. The client systems are running Windows Professional, with Office 97 being utilized as an applications package. Each system is connected to a 10Mbps hub through 10Mbps LAN cards running Category 5 UTP cabling in a star topology. These hubs are on the same backbone as 4Sale but have a different subnet.

Proposed LAN/Network Structure

4Sale is developing its online barter/trading business through business alliances. It is investigating the use of secured private networks for branch offices. It has formed several partnerships with brokers throughout the country. These brokers will connect to the system and place bids for clients.

Current WAN Connectivity

4 Sale has a T1 connection to an Internet Service Provider (ISP) in OverThere, North Dakota. Got-a-Deal has 56Kbps dial-up networking connectivity through the same ISP.

Proposed WAN Connectivity

No changes are planned at this time.

Directory Design Commentary

No changes are planned at this time.

Current Internet Positioning

4Sale is registered as **4sale.com**. Got-a-Deal has been selling its goods through local companies and through the **4sale.com** Web site.

Future Internet Plans

No changes in the current structure are proposed at this time.

Company Goal with Windows 2000

Develop the standards and procedures that the IT department will implement.

Exhibit

See Exhibit 2.

4Sale			Got-a-Deal		
	CEO			President	
VP Fin	VP Sales	VP Ops		Vice President/Sales Mngr	
		Webmaster/ SysAdmin			
		DBA/Developer			
Bookkeep	Sales1	Tech1	Bookkeep	Sales1	Tech1
Clerk1	Sales2	Tech2		Sales2	Tech2
	Sales3	Tech3		Sales3	Tech3
	Sales4			Sales4	

Exhibit 2   Original organizational chart of 4Sale and Got-a-Deal.

Question 1

Considering the case study provided, what issue(s) must you consider when you create the 4Sale network security plan?

○ a. Due care and due diligence

○ b. Information security strategies

○ c. Security group descriptions

○ d. None of the above

○ e. All of the above

Answer b is correct. The network plan is a fundamental part of security deployment. Information security strategies are the specific design and strategic choices that need to be made to secure online exchanges such as email and Web-based communications. This is the best answer to the question. Due care and due diligence describes how procedures are to be carried out and is considered part of the IT security control compliance. It should not be part of the actual security plan itself. Therefore, answer a is incorrect. Similarly, security group descriptions are built into the security policy. These default choices and security templates are critical in deployment but are more administrative in function. Therefore, answer c is incorrect. Only answer b is correct, so answers d and e are incorrect.

Question 2

You have compiled an organizational chart for both 4Sale and Got-A-Deal. You want to categorize the user population into three groups:

Executive

Staff

User

Place the following positions under the appropriate group:

4Sale VP Finance

Got-a-Deal bookkeeper

4Sale DBA/developer

Got-a-Deal Tech1

The correct answer is:

> Executive
>
> Staff
>
>> 4Sale VP of Finance
>>
>> Got-a-Deal bookkeeper
>>
>> 4Sale DBA/developer
>
> User
>
>> Got-a-Deal Tech1

Got-a-Deal is a small company. Often, titles are misleading; never make assumptions about what people do or what responsibilities and security access levels they ought to have. When you assign network access and responsibilities, it is a good practice to have at least one person (preferably, two people) at each functional level to ensure proper workflows. The Got-a-Deal President is in the Executive group. The VP functions more like an office manager in this company than Vice President; this person is in the staff group. The Got-a-Deal bookkeeper, sales staff, and technical staff all report to the VP/Sales Manager. Depending on the "corporate culture," you might recommend that the Vice President could assume the President's role in her absence; there is no backup at the Executive level. Don't be surprised if the President says she doesn't want the Vice President to have an Administrator security role. Remember, the security plan reflects exactly what top-level management wants and needs.

Question 3

> Based on the user population in Question 2 and depicted in Exhibit 2, what kind of internal business services does 4Sale offer? [Check all correct answers]
>
> ❏ a. Line of business (LOB) applications
>
> ❏ b. Messaging
>
> ❏ c. Data storage
>
> ❏ d. Network support

Answers a, b, c, and d are correct. Often, a company (for example, Microsoft) will use its own LOB applications in internal operations, so answer a is correct. 4Sale supports a broad range of business services to its user population in addition to its bidding system. Messaging for communication (answer b), data storage (answer c), and file and print sharing are key to any network environment. In addition, the IT department offers softer services like system and configuration management, contingency planning, and help desk support (answer d). It is important that these business-related functions be included in the inventory of services for a security plan to be complete.

Question 4

VP of Operations for 4Sale says, "What are relevant security issues we need to address when we formulate network strategies for our e-commerce quote and barter applications?" [Check all correct answers]

❑ a. Application specifications

❑ b. Design sophistication

❑ c. Application performance issues

❑ d. Administrative complexity

❑ e. A consolidated directory

Answers a, b, c, d, and e are correct. When you are dealing with, for example, database management systems, the application specification (answer a) and the design sophistication (answer b) are very important especially in terms of its performance issues (answer c) and level of required administrative support (answer d) during and after installation. There is also a trend among some applications, such as Exchange, to substitute a dedicated directory database of users for a consolidated system database (answer e).

Question 5

VP of Operations for 4Sale says, "What issues should we consider if 4Sale offers its business partners a VPN?" [Check all correct answers]

❑ a. Integrating the VPN into a remote access policy

❑ b. Choice of PPTP or L2TP

❑ c. IIS functionality

❑ d. Administrative complexity

❑ e. Using Connection Manager

Answers a, b, d and e are correct. Integrating Virtual Private Networks into a remote access policy, choice of Point-To-Point Tunneling Protocol or Layer 2 Tunneling Protocol, administrative complexity, and using Connection Manager are critical themes that you need to explore when deploying a VPN. Aside from these considerations, security protocol is a major consideration because L2TP also depends on IP Security. Administrative complexity is another issue. Connection Manager, however, greatly helps in the installation of remote users. Internet Information Server is not an issue when you are considering VPNs. Therefore, answer c is incorrect.

Need to Know More?

 Garfinkel, Simson and Gene Spafford. *Practical UNIX and Internet Security, Second Edition*. O'Reilly & Associates, Sebastopol, CA, 1996. ISBN 1-56592-148-8. Chapter 2, Policies and Guidelines, discusses at great length many components of risk assessment, cost-benefits analysis, and general security issues. This introductory chapter is both descriptive and procedural in its approach and is relevant to any IT installation.

 Nichols, Randall K. et al. *Defending Your Digital Assets against Hackers, Crackers, Spies, and Thieves, First Edition*. McGraw-Hill Professional Publishing, New York, NY, 2000. ISBN 0-07-212285-4. Although the entire book is written from a global perspective, discussions in Chapters 3 and 4 are particularly informative about the way the U.S. government and the military handle security issues. Many of the concepts can be applied just as well to a corporate environment.

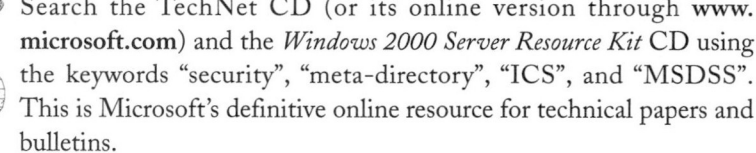 Search the TechNet CD (or its online version through **www. microsoft.com**) and the *Windows 2000 Server Resource Kit* CD using the keywords "security", "meta-directory", "ICS", and "MSDSS". This is Microsoft's definitive online resource for technical papers and bulletins.

 **www.microsoft.com/technet/win2000/dguide/** This link offers the *Windows 2000 Server Deployment and Planning Guide* (from the *Windows 2000 Resource Kit*). This Web site provides the text to the entire *Deployment and Planning Guide*.

 **www.microsoft.com/windows2000/library/howitworks/ activedirectory/identity.asp** This link takes you to the *Active Directory Interoperability and Metadirectory Overview* technical paper, which gives an overview of how identity information among resources is shared yet remains consistent throughout the enterprise. The concept of identity management is presented as a customer situation that has specific requirements (connectivity, brokering, and integrity management) and specific solutions. The adopted Microsoft solution of a hub and spoke meta-directory architecture is discussed.

www.microsoft.com/windows2000/library/resources/reskit/dpg/ default.asp This link takes you to the *Deployment and Planning Guide.* Chapter 7 presents a comprehensive discussion of network connectivity issues, external connectivity from within an organization, and transport and network protocol issues. Chapter 11 provides a detailed guide that outlines sections of a network security plan, administrative policies for a Windows 2000 enterprise, Group Policy issues, and security audit threat detection policies. Chapter 17 describes the network security issues in a security plan, including a discussion of application-oriented network security technologies.

Identity Management Issues

Terms you'll need to understand:

- ✓ Directory services
- ✓ X.500 directory services
- ✓ X.509 recommendations
- ✓ Namespace
- ✓ Simple Authentication and Security Layer (SASL)
- ✓ Microsoft Meta-directory Services (MMS)
- ✓ Microsoft Messaging Application Programming Interface (MAPI)
- ✓ Active Directory Services Interfaces (ADSI)
- ✓ Relative distinguished name (RDN)
- ✓ Distinguished name (DN)
- ✓ Access control list (ACL)
- ✓ Global Catalog (GC)
- ✓ Organizational Unit (OU)
- ✓ Domain controller (DC)
- ✓ Flexible (Floating) Single-Master Operations (FSMO)
- ✓ Encrypting File System (EFS)

Techniques you'll need to master:

- ✓ Identifying the key directory service components
- ✓ Describing the basic components of Windows 2000 architecture
- ✓ Describing the five FSMO roles
- ✓ Describing deployment methods for users
- ✓ Describing deployment methods that control access to resources
- ✓ Understanding how EFS protects data stored on disks

A security threat to a resource depends upon accessibility, a consumer's skills, and consumer motivation. If the built-in Everyone group has access to a file and some authenticated, disgruntled employee with minimal computer skills but malicious intent wants to seek some form of retribution on another company employee or the company itself, that person may attempt to delete a file. If the malicious employee has access and the file provides that person Full Control, he or she will successfully cause damage. If, alternatively, this employee has access to the file but has Read Only object permissions, the malicious attempt will fail. If an administrator has set an account policy to audit such activity, this particular employee's failed attempt is logged for future review, investigation, and possible reprimand.

If you control accessibility, you eliminate most security threats. When someone has access to a resource, however, managing permissions to that object is key to preventing a security incident, no matter what the consumer's skills or motivation. The greater that consumer's skills and motivation to breach security, the more important managing permissions becomes. In fact, permission management is actually a dichotomy: accessibility to resources and management of actions that you can apply to that resource. This chapter begins with a brief discussion of directory services and naming conventions, which provides a foundation for analyzing how systems organize and access directory objects. These objects are primarily users and resources.

This chapter also covers other topics, including a discussion of specific directory services, the X.500 directory standard, and X.509-based directory systems (a subset of X.500) that use public key authentication systems. I then describe Lightweight Directory Access Protocol (LDAP) as an introduction to Active Directory (AD). Having introduced the historical basis for directory services, I briefly discuss each fundamental Windows 2000 logical structure and AD component. I then discuss user and resource topics, as well as how to implement accessibility and permission management in Windows 2000. I conclude this chapter with a discussion of an important Windows 2000 protection technology specifically designed to protect resources themselves—Encrypting File System (EFS).

Basic Directory Services

As you saw in the "A Microsoft Historical Perspective" section in Chapter 2, there is a trend with Windows 2000 toward greater differentiation and specialization of services than earlier versions of the Windows family of operating systems. Windows 2000 provides a greater number of standards-based interfaces than legacy NT. These interfaces provide software hooks for installable extensions to the core system services. As the complexity of information technology expands not only in terms of this specialization but also in terms of distributed objects in and beyond the boundaries of a corporate enterprise, a counterbalancing trend to improve accessibility to these ever-expanding and diversifying services and resources arises. This counterbalancing trend is in a unified directory service that not only catalogs the services and resource objects but also provides access methods to them.

Driving this counterbalancing trend is the need to integrate heterogeneous systems, simplify administration through consolidation and automation, and lower the total cost of ownership (TCO) through easier maintenance, support, and user training. As discussed in Chapter 7, it's a major architectural trend to develop umbrella directory systems that integrate existing directory services across heterogeneous systems called *meta-directories*. A critical maintenance function in identity management systems is synchronizing data across these heterogeneous datastores. It is important that at any given time, changing the credentials of a named object or principal in one datastore is synchronized with copies of credentials or references referring to that principal across all other directory services.

The X.500 Standard

The original idea of directory services is based on a Comité Consultatif International Téléphonique et Télégraphique (CCITT)/International Organization for Standardization (ISO) standard, X.500, which defines a global directory service solution for distributing and retrieving information. Key characteristics of the original specifications as cited in Request for Comments (RFC) 1330 were:

➤ Decentralized management

➤ Powerful searching capabilities

➤ A single global namespace

➤ A structured framework for storing information

The original X.500 standard is described in terms of four service-related models:

➤ *Information model*—Defines information

➤ *Functional model*—Defines how the information is stored and accessed

➤ *Organizational model*—Defines the policy between entities and the information they hold

➤ *Security model*—Defines two types of security for directory data: simple authentication (using passwords) and strong authentication (using cryptographic keys)

X.509 is the International Telecommunications Union (ITU) Telecommunication Standardization Sector (ITU-T) recommendation based on X.500 papers on directory services. It defines a framework for delivering the security model and authentication services. This framework, initially recommended in 1988 and subsequently revised several times, recommends specific message formats like the Public Key Cryptography Standards (PKCS) #7, #10, and #12 referred to in Chapter 3, as well as various authentication protocols. The X.509 specification, based on the idea of using public key cryptography and digital signatures, evolved into these PKCS formats. The directory serves as a repository for public key digital certificates and is discussed in both Chapters 3 and 7.

LDAP v3

The original X.500 specification offered users a unified view or namespace of named objects or principals defined in the universe of the organization. To define objects in an unambiguous way, the concept of a hierarchical, inverted tree structure was used. Due to implementation issues with the original X.500 specification that involved its complexity and protocol support, the IT community has actually adopted a simplified version of another protocol, LDAP (RFC 1777), as the favored platform for directory services. Its data model is based on the original X.500 concepts. In it, named objects have attributes, which, in turn, have a data type and a value. The named objects, just like those originally proposed in the X.500 specification, are stored in a hierarchical tree.

LDAP includes operations to select, add, update, and delete data. Authentication in LDAP version 2 uses unencrypted cleartext or Kerberos version 4 password authentication as cited in RFC 1777. LDAP version 3 uses Simple Authentication and Security Layer (SASL), an extensible security model defined in RFC 2222 that negotiates connection protocols like LDAP with different security providers like Kerberos. LDAP version 3 also supports the Secure Sockets Layer (SSL) protocol. Finally, LDAP version 3 has referral capabilities that allow it to appear as a single directory service to the end user; however, it actually interconnects with independent LDAP servers on a global scale. A major disadvantage of LDAP is its inability to synchronize data across servers.

AD Directory Services

At the core of Windows 2000 is the identity management services called Active Directory directory services, modeled on the X.500 specification. Microsoft's initiative in developing identity management solutions like Microsoft Meta-directory Services (MMS), discussed in Chapter 7, is based on the theme of a unified, global namespace. AD is Microsoft's first step toward this goal. Part of this initiative is already realized in the BackOffice mail product, Exchange 2000. The product uses AD, as opposed to its own separate datastore, to store information about objects. AD thus provides some of the original X.500 features:

➤ A unified catalog of principals

➤ A common repository in which to store an object's data

➤ A single point of administration, brokering features, and rules management

In Chapter 4, I discussed how the Key Distribution Center (KDC) was integrated with AD; KDC offers an authentication mechanism, and AD offers an authorization mechanism through security descriptors in the form of an access token and a centralized repository of security credentials. Thus, Microsoft delivers Single Sign-On (SSO) and authentication services by leveraging the existence of this enterprise-wide datastore with the storage of security credentials. With the addition of Microsoft Certificate Server, public key certificates at the heart of the X.509 recommendation are also incorporated into Windows 2000 through its public key infrastructure enhancements, as discussed in Chapter 3. Thus, Windows 2000 has realized much of the security model of the original X.500 standard.

AD supports the following application programming interface (API) sets:

➤ *LDAP C API (RFC 1823)*—LDAP's de facto C programming standard

➤ *Microsoft Messaging Application Programming Interface (MAPI)*—The Windows Open Services Architecture (WOSA) Messaging API

➤ *Active Directory Services Interfaces (ADSI)*—Microsoft's own directory services API, which is the Component Object Model (COM) interface for X.500-based directory services

I will discuss only the third of these—ADSI—here, because the other two have little if any direct connection with Windows 2000 security. ADSI supports popular applications and directory services such as Exchange, Lotus Notes, and Novell Directory Services (NDS). ADSI, which programmatically allows you to manipulate and query data in any of these three examples, is a part of the Open Directory Services Interface (ODSI), which, in turn, is part of WOSA. ADSI provides a single programming interface regardless of which directory services a developer needs. More significantly, ADSI also provides native support for LDAP. Much like AD added both authorization and auditing to Kerberos, integrating LDAP with AD provides much strength and corrects the one LDAP protocol weakness: synchronization.

Objects and Attributes

An *object* is identified in the directory database as some entity that has a name and a set of attributes or properties. *Attributes* could be purely descriptive or a set of security credentials. A *named object* is also called a *principal*. I refer specifically to a user of services as a *consumer*. Similarly, I refer to a service provider and the client machine that the consumer uses as an object (or principal) in the directory database.

Names/Name Resolution

The purpose of directory services is to represent every object or principal in the directory by a name and a directory database account record. Names must therefore be unique. Objects can have many types of names. AD creates a contextual or relative distinguished name (RDN) and an alias or canonical name for each object created in the directory database. The context of the RDN can be explicitly defined by tracing a reverse path up the hierarchy through each parent container within which that object is found to the most exterior container or root domain. This method guarantees the uniqueness of an object's name based upon its location within concentric containers—that is, an object in a domain tree, in a hierarchical path that describes its logical location in same directory namespace.

Because a forest can consist of multiple domain trees, names do not necessarily have to share the same contiguous namespace in the same domain tree. A *distinguished name (DN)* identifies or distinguishes a specific object by using a name that maps the complete path from the root container or root domain down to its exact location in the domain tree. An analogy is an absolute reference of, for example, a text file named mytext.doc, on a physical or logical hard drive. The DN for mytext.doc located in the **examcram.com** domain is:

```
/O=Internet/DC=Com/DC=Examcram/CN=Text/CN=Mytext.doc
```

An alternative naming scheme is an RDN, which includes only the attribute of the object itself—for example, **CN=mytext.doc.** This is also the default common name for security principals (the SAM account name or security principal name). An analogy is the relative addressing of mytext.doc in your present working directory. When you reference the text file mytext.doc, the context of the present working directory and its parent, grandparent, and root directories are all assumed unless otherwise specified.

Like a Web browser, Windows 2000 supports several other naming conventions. Use the format that is easiest to remember and most efficient to enter in the Logon dialog box. Some examples of naming conventions supported by Windows 2000 are:

➤ *RFC 822 names*—In AD, this is probably the "friendliest" name, the user principal name (UPN), based on RFC 822 and the familiar email syntax—namely, **pschein@examcram.com.** The UPN suffix is the DNS name of the root domain in the domain tree.

➤ *X.500 names*—LDAP uses the X.500 naming convention called *attributed naming.* This is the DN name used in the previous example in this section, specifically:

```
/O=Internet/DC=Com/DC=Examcram/CN=Text/CN=Mytext.doc
```

➤ *LDAP Uniform Resource Locators (URLs)*—You can enter in the Locator box a URL (such as **ldap://mycomputer.examcram.com**), accessible from any LDAP-enabled client or browser.

➤ *Universal Naming Convention (UNC) Names*—You can enter the legacy NT 4 style names to describe resources in Windows 2000-based networks.

 Understanding how principals are named is of critical importance. AD domain names are the full name of the domain according to Domain Name System (DNS) records. User accounts have a logon name, a legacy NT4 (SAM) account name, and a user principal name (UPN) suffix which appears to the right of the "@" character according to specifications in RFC 822. This suffix is the DNS name of the root domain in the domain tree. Each AD computer account has a relative distinguished name, a legacy NT 4 (SAM) account name, a primary DNS suffix, a DNS host name, and a service principal name. The service principal name, based on the DNS host name of the computer, is used during mutual authentication of client machine and service provider.

Terms and Components

Most contemporary directory services are based on X.500, so some terms and components are common if not universal across the services. The future trend among network operating systems is to consolidate these services under some integrated meta-directory infrastructure, so it is likely that the commonality and interoperability among components will increase.

Namespaces

Named objects need to be organized to facilitate their location when corroboration of specific data or retrieval of information is necessary. Just as the directory structure organizes resources in the file system, a hierarchy of named objects can be arranged in a branching tree structure with common branches or paths. The endpoint of a path is called a *leaf node*. Nonleaf nodes are containers. A *container*, much like a folder, contains other named objects. In a directory structure, the endpoint of a path is typically some object like a file or document. The leaf node is a noncontainer; it does not contain other objects. In Windows 2000, a contiguous *subtree* describes a circumscribed group of containers all connected by one or more paths or branches.

Hierarchically speaking, a tree has within it a contiguous group of containers that hold objects with specific attributes. This contiguous group forms a *namespace* or *definable context*. I can trace out a specific object by resolving its context in relation to the series of contiguous containers in which it is found. I begin at some root container and literally walk down the contiguous path of connected subcontainers until I reach my destination endpoint or leaf node. In other network operating system cultures, this is called *walking the tree*. In functional terms, a namespace defines the scope of the directory database; it also defines the collection of objects, their context in the namespace, and their replicated attributes. AD contains one or more naming contexts or partitions; this is the *circumscribed contiguous subtree* of the directory structure. It is also the *unit of replication*.

In database terms, a *data dictionary* is a listing of objects you can create and store in the directory database. Each object can be assigned different attributes. In directory service terms, this data dictionary is part of a *schema*. The schema, like the data dictionary of a table, defines the class or list of possible attributes, as well as the syntax of the data types. It is typically extensible, meaning that it allows you to add new attributes and new data types. It is different from a data dictionary in that it can also describe relationships between objects and rules used to determine how objects handle information. Thus, a schema defines files and folders as leaf objects and containers, respectively. An example of some file, mytext.doc, in some folder, myfolder, is an example of an instance of the *file class*; it has specific characteristics such as a name, creation date, and size. It is defined in the context of its container folder. According to Microsoft, AD is implemented as a set of *object class instances*. A user-naming context is defined as the *contiguous subtrees* off the root container that hold the actual objects in the directory tree. Applications read the schema or data dictionary to learn what objects and properties are available in that particular namespace.

Domains

The *domain* in Windows 2000, like in NT 4, is the core administrative unit in AD. It represents a logical collection of objects and is the boundary for both replication and security. Each domain thus stores information only about the objects located within it. Security policies, administrative rights, and access control lists (ACLs) do not extend beyond the domain boundary. Similarly, a domain administrator's jurisdiction is only within that domain. Just as in the legacy NT 4 model, a domain is a logical structure that can span more than one physical drive.

Trees

In the same way that a *contiguous subtree* describes a group of containers connected by at least one path or branch, a *domain tree* is made up of at least two domains that form a contiguous namespace. Domains in a tree share common schema, a *data dictionary*, and replication (or *configuration*) data collectively stored as assorted system information called *metadata*. The connection between domains is described as a *trust relationship*. I can describe the domain tree as a hierarchical naming structure with the initial domain that forms the root of all subsequently attached subordinate or child domains. This full path to the object can be referred to as a distinguished name (DN, defined earlier in this chapter). The DN is unambiguous and unique. In a domain tree, the domain immediately above another is considered its *parent*. The domain name of the *child* domain added to the beginning of the parent domain name forms the RDN of that child domain. Thus, when the east domain becomes a child of another domain, **examcram.com**, its RDN becomes **east.examcram**.

 In Windows 2000 and AD, a domain is still a collection computers defined for administrative purposes, sharing the same directory database. For DNS, a domain is any tree or subtree found within the DNS namespace of the enterprise forest. Although DNS domain names may correspond to AD domain names, they aren't necessarily describing the same thing in an enterprise or an examination case study.

Forests

Just as a forest in the real world is a collection of separate trees, Windows 2000 can support a forest of noncontiguous domain trees. In other words, each tree has its own root, so the namespace is not contiguous. Two domain trees with different root names are joined as a forest and display disjointed naming schemes. Each tree, however, trusts other trees and shares a common schema and configuration. Forests can be referred to as *noncontiguous* or *disjointed* namespaces. In directory terms, a *forest* is a cross-referenced set of objects (domains) with trust relationships known to all member trees in the namespace. Access to objects within member trees in a forest is through a Global Catalog (GC) that describes that forest namespace. GC is covered in more detail in the "GC" section later in this chapter.

 From a design viewpoint, a domain tree offers the advantage of a contiguous namespace when you are searching for an object. In a forest, a search involves either the local domain tree or the larger GC. When you are providing services, it is always more efficient to establish domain trees rather than forests.

Organizational Units (OUs)

In addition to the domain concept, Windows 2000 provides a second way to partition a logical namespace. *OUs* are containers that can group objects—such as user accounts, groups, clients, printers, and other OUs—into logical administrative units. OUs provide granularity in permission management, such as granting some person the administrative rights for a collection of objects in one OU or in a group of OUs.

GC

AD defines a unified namespace that can consist of partitioned naming contexts such as **east.examcram.com**. A DN provides enough information to allow you to locate that specific object in its partition. In a disjointed namespace or when the DN of some object is not known, the GC provides the location information for objects in the domain tree or the entire forest even when only partial information is known about the object. AD is the repository for all objects in the namespace; GC, a partial index and search engine, stores a replica of each object and a subset of each object's attributes. The subset of object attributes is extensible. The population and synchronization of data is automatic. When a consumer queries the GC for a service provider or resource based on some known attribute, the GC returns the location based on the consumer's access rights. If the consumer doesn't have access rights to that resource, the query for its location fails.

Domain Controllers (DCs)

Although all the terms and components described so far in this section are logical and not bound by physical constraints of equipment, connectivity, or geography, the concepts of site (discussed in the next section) and DCs anchor us in the real world. In native mode Windows 2000, you no longer differentiate primary DCs (PDCs) from secondary or backup DCs (BDCs). All DCs are peers; each contains a writable copy of the domain directory database. Thus, any changes in the directory database of one DC are replicated to all other DCs in the domain.

DC management is further simplified when you are running Windows 2000 Server; the peer controller architecture permits you to promote any standalone or member server to a DC role and vice versa. The AD Installation Wizard (DCPROMO) is an administrative tool that promotes or demotes servers. The act of promoting a standalone or member server to a DC role where one has previously never existed creates a domain. DCs that alternatively join an existing domain receive a copy or replica of the directory database; they are called *replica DCs*. Referential integrity is maintained across databases through directory replication.

 DCs provide many services, so it is best to have several in a domain to balance the service load.

DCs fulfill five Flexible (Floating) Single-Master Operations (FSMO) roles:

➤ *Schema Master (Schema Operations Master)*—Only one per forest; it administers schema updates and changes.

➤ *Domain Naming Master (Domain Naming Operations Master)*—Only one per forest; it administers addition or removal of domains in a forest or cross-references to external directory services.

➤ *Relative ID Master (RID Operations Master)*—Only one per domain; it allocates relative ID (RID) sequences, which are the unique portion of the two components that make up a security identifier (SID); the other component is a common domain security ID.

➤ *PDC Emulator (PDC Advertiser)*—Only one per domain even in native mode; the emulator acts as a PDC for down-level BDCs or clients in mixed mode. In native mode, the emulator assumes a preferential master role over other DCs; it receives replications first and is forwarded logon requests from other DCs before access is denied to the enterprise.

➤ *Infrastructure Master*—Only one per domain; it administers additions and changes in user/group mappings.

Sites

A *site* is a collection of AD servers that are well connected and use Transmission Control Protocol/Internet Protocol (TCP/IP). Whereas trees are logical groupings based on administration or geography, sites are based on the physical network. Site considerations thus deal specifically with physical topology and bandwidth. In the simplest case, the machines at a site typically have the same TCP/IP subnet address and thus are defined by some common physical boundary such as a local area network (LAN) or LAN segment. Sites are analogous to the site concept used in Exchange server architecture.

Note: Microsoft uses the term "well connected" to suggest sufficient bandwidth for transferring system information such as replication data.

Smaller groupings of computers optimize the discovery of the nearest local AD server (DC) at sites, especially when each LAN segment or subnet has at least one DC. Similarly, it may be expedient in a large enterprise to also include at least one GC at each site to facilitate forest-wide searches despite increased demands on bandwidth due to replication exchanges. You need to carefully define sites according to network topology (physical segments and logical subnets) so that you optimize AD access, DC replication, and GC query performance.

Replication

As mentioned in the "Domain Controllers (DCs)" section earlier in this chapter, all replicas of a particular partition of the AD namespace (the DC directory database) are editable. Information is exchanged among DCs automatically through multimaster replication. If the clocks on DCs are synchronized, some directory services can use timestamps to manage database changes. Alternatively, AD uses a 64-bit Update Sequence Number (USN) maintained on each DC to record the property change in the local directory database and to propagate it to the directory databases on other peer DCs.

Access Control

Although Microsoft suggests reverting to a single domain model in Windows 2000, the AD can consist of more than one domain. Domains organize functional areas, partition the directory database, and create security boundaries. These boundaries affect policies and settings such as administrative rights, security policy, and ACLs. Distributed security and permission management rely on many of the terms and components defined earlier in this chapter. Using these constructs, you should deploy several strategies to secure network resources:

➤ Limit authenticated access to system resources.

➤ Manage access controls to available resources.

➤ Manage security administration through deployment of secure applications using role-based access controls and uniform security policies.

➤ Establish trust relationships among domains.

➤ Use protection techniques when storing sensitive or physically exposed data.

Now, I'll discuss each of these in more detail. (Note that protection techniques are covered in the "Resources" section later in this chapter).

Limiting Authenticated Access

The first step in securing resources is limiting access to them. Windows 2000 authenticates users based on user accounts in the AD. Identity management is implemented through the AD Users And Computers snap-in of the Microsoft Management Console (MMC). You can now organize user accounts not only by domain but also by OU, which better reflects the functional needs of your corporation, division, or user population. Creation of an account record is not only integrated with directory services but is added to such items as the global address book as well as other network services. Windows 2000 supports SSO, so the account record is propagated across the forest. In native mode, bidirectional, transitive trust relationships support pass-through or referral authentication to resources and services in other domains in the forest. Any one of the Kerberos, NT LAN Manager (NTLM), or SSL/Transport Layer Security (TLS) security protocols handles the logon process. Windows also supports strong authentication using public key technologies such as smart cards, discussed in greater detail in Chapter 12.

The concept of principals and account records stored in directory service datastores applies to client machines and services as well as consumers. Windows 2000 servers and clients receive policy information from the AD during their startup procedures. Computer policies are applied to the local machine following its authentication but prior to user authentication. In addition to machine authentication during startup and user authentication during logon, Kerberos security provides support for mutual authentication, preventing intruders or rogue users from impersonating a service provider or imposing themselves in the middle of two parties exchanging data (man-in-the-middle attack). You can set policies to permit or deny clients or services to be *trusted for delegation*, where some intermediary creates new network connections on behalf of and in the security context of a consumer. This delegation of authority, discussed in the "Delegation of Authentication" section in Chapter 4, is critical in many applications that use multitier architecture and distributed services.

Deployment

You can harden (strengthen) authentication by using strict account policies that enforce long, complex passwords (which are resistant to dictionary or brute force attacks, discussed in Chapter 2) with reasonable length, lifetime, and constraints on reusability settings. These passive impersonation attacks apply all possible combinations of passwords from a list or dictionary to the authentication mechanism until either the exact combination is found or the list is exhausted. The longer and more complex the character structure of the password, the harder it is to match the exact character combination. However, it is important to balance the need for strong authentication policies (and, for example, strong, long passwords) with concerns for user attitude and compliance (the corporate culture referred to in Chapter 2). A user often will have problems remembering or using too long or complex a password. It is better to have 100 percent compliance with moderate security account policies than compliance of less than 100 percent with especially rigorous security standards. Smart cards and other two-factor authentication methods ("I have something" in addition to "I know something") provide stronger authentication than passwords but also increase TCO. Limit the number of clients and accounts that are trusted for, because their ability to assume an authorized security context of some other party makes them a prime target for an active impersonation attack.

You need to carefully monitor remote access policies, discussed in Chapter 6. Point-To-Point Protocol (PPP) authentication methods offer limited security because they use only username and password. Customized extensions provided by third parties extend the authentication capabilities of Extensible Authentication Protocol (EAP) and provide support for strong two-factor authentication methods. An example of enhancing EAP and providing this two-factor support is EAP-TLS authentication using digital certificates and smart cards. These enhancements harden the dial-up access by basing the authentication process on not just "what you know" but "what you have." Alternatively, using predetermined callback provides another inexpensive countermeasure to impersonation attacks because the system disconnects the caller and calls back a modem-based client located at some prearranged telephone connection. It's always preferable to use Virtual Private Networks (VPNs) as opposed to unsecured remote access despite the increases in overhead that the need for, for example, certificate services creates.

Managing Access Control Lists

After you limit access to resources, the second line of defense is managing accessibility. Access to any resource in the NT File System (NTFS) is based on a collection of permissions or access control entries (ACEs) that specify a user or group and some range of actions they can perform on the specific object. The collection of these ACEs is compiled into a system or discretionary ACL. This topic is discussed in greater detail in the "Managing Security Administration" section later in this chapter.

To simplify administration of ACLs, it is best to use group memberships, not users, when assigning access permissions. Especially when you are creating resources, never assume that default resource permissions are appropriate. Windows 2000 and legacy NT 4 assign the Everyone group Full Control to network shares by default. Make certain you remove this group and replace it with Users or a more appropriate group. Similarly, file system permissions are by default granted to Users. Any authenticated user is part of this built-in group. Always review permissions and minimize access by using Read Only wherever possible.

Individuals and groups are defined in the AD Users And Computers snap-in. Granularity of ACLs has been enhanced in Windows 2000. You must define a group before you can assign it permissions in an ACL. Assign permissions to groups as opposed to users to simplify administration and minimize the need for changes. Although users may change groups often, you should not routinely alter the group assignments at the resource level to minimize errors or misconfigurations. Groups and Group Policies are discussed in greater detail in Chapter 10.

Deployment

Apply the rule of least privilege, where what is not expressly permitted is prohibited. Use the Everyone group for auditing, not for assigning resource permissions.

Managing Security Administration

Three methods for managing the administration of access reflect various approaches to management and security policy. They are:

➤ Discretionary ACLs (DACLs, sometimes referred to as DACs)

➤ Mandatory ACLs (MACLs, sometimes referred to as MACs)

➤ Role-based access controls (RBACs)

The three access schemes typically coexist within a work environment, depending on the kinds of data and job functions people are assigned to perform. There is usually an order of precedence when all three controls are operating; mandatory access control overrides role-based control, which in turn overrides discretionary access. These different forms of access control, as a form of permission management, provide a methodology that helps you manage resources in an environment where all resources are accessible.

DACLs

DACLs require that the owners of the object assume responsibility for the use or misuse of any object they create. The administrator always has the authority to take ownership away from someone. However, of the three approaches, this is the least conservative, exposes resources to the greatest risks, and requires the most monitoring. Aside from internal risks associated with unintentional or malicious acts on the part of authenticated users, DACLs expose resources to manipulation by outside intruders specifically searching for such a target. Intruders can, for example, manipulate read/write access to exploit and further penetrate the operating system. Normally, it's appropriate to use DACLs when you are managing resources in internal workgroup environments where cooperation, collaboration, and sharing are common work themes.

MACLs

MACLs are controlled primarily by the administrator and are typically used in an environment were the principle of least privilege is applied. The administrator assigns only those permissions necessary to complete specific job functions. This form of managing access is appropriate where resources are ranked or categorized—e.g., top secret (TS), secret (S), sensitive but unclassified (SBU), and unclassified (U). The administrator strictly enforces this kind of policy through policy management. Access to all data at any one time is discouraged, and unlikely given the classification scheme. People and processes within a MACL environment are typically in a more secured work environment than a DACL environment because and permissions are administratively controlled.

RBACs

In an RBAC environment, information is categorized in functional terms or by process. Applications can define roles. You—as opposed to the person who accesses the data—could create a specific security context for the application; this technique is used in relational database management systems to simplify permission management. The function of the application determines the scope of permissions; whoever has permission to use the application accesses whatever data is necessary for the application to perform its designed role or function.

Establishing Trust Relationships

Given the scalability of AD, Microsoft recommends migrating even extremely large corporations into a single domain model and eliminating the need for trust relationships. Domains nevertheless remain useful when you are scoping administrative areas and designing enterprises. When migrating to Windows 2000, however, make certain you don't apply old design habits using flat domain models from legacy NT 4 installations. Windows 2000 requires you to re-engineer old design strategies to fully realize the benefits of its hierarchical modeling capability. If you do need to scope administrative or security policies, Kerberos protocol in native mode Windows 2000 has significantly simplified the administration of joining domains. Two-way transitive trusts that are automatically implemented when you add to or create domain trees have replaced legacy nontransitive, one-way trusts. Trust relationships in forests are now implicitly transitive trust relationships; they require little, if any, maintenance. External trusts to either legacy NT 4 domains or across forests, however, still require careful planning because of possible security risks.

Transitive trusts flow up through the domain tree and across the forest, so accounts in any one domain can authenticate in another domain on the other side of the forest. Even though transitive trusts are automatically created between a child and parent domain in Windows 2000, you can still explicitly create one-way nontransitive trusts among, for example, different branches of the same tree or different trees in the same forest. One-way trusts are typically used in one of the following scenarios:

➤ Between Windows 2000 domains in different forests

➤ Between Windows 2000 domains and legacy NT 4 domains

➤ Between Windows 2000 domains and MIT Kerberos 5 realms

Cross-linking domains with transitive relationships shortens trust paths and can facilitate authentication, especially in large, complex forests. Nontransitive trusts, however, are explicitly bound to the two domains; conversely, the nontransitive trust relationship does not flow to neighboring domains.

Deployment

Trust relationships in mixed mode domains continue to function as nontransitive, one-way trusts. Be careful, however, in native mode; trusts are transitive. Any domain administrators can take ownership and modify the Configuration container of any other domain in the forest. Changes are replicated to all other DCs.

The domain administrator of a domain that joins a forest is now immediately trusted and must be considered an equal to other domain administrators. Using explicit one-way (or external) trusts, especially when you are adding new domains, is a good beginning strategy until you have resolved all administrative policies and security issues. An alternative approach is to collapse the domain into an OU, redefine the former domain administrator's administrative scope to that OU, and remove the domain. The administrator continues to have the same scope of responsibilities and authority over resources and users without having administrator-level access to the enterprise.

Resources

In the discussion of attack modalities in the "Scoping Physical Assets" section of Chapter 8, I used the actual theft of equipment as an example of active interception. A CD-ROM burner connected to network drives presents a greater threat to an organization than an intruder roaming your network at will. The CD-ROM can copy organized folders of information; the rogue user or outside hacker typically uncovers data and parts of documents. Another security risk is the road warrior's laptop, which contains perhaps less (but nevertheless well-organized) information, as well as stored passwords; preset, remote access configurations; public and private keys; and internal signatures, such as volume numbers on hard drives. Although many third-party technologies can adequately protect this property, before Windows 2000, no standardized set of tools that specifically addressed these issues was integrated into a Microsoft operating system.

EFS

Encrypting File System (EFS) is a part of Windows 2000 NT File System (NTFS). This enhanced file system is actually different from the NTFS in legacy NT 4 in several ways:

➤ Storage volumes are monitored and can be limited by disk quotas.

➤ Changes are tracked through a change journal.

➤ Data can be protected through an encryption mechanism.

NTFS uses public key technology as the core file encryption technology for securely storing files and folders. EFS is part of the file system, so when the owner of the file or folder works with the object, the owner is actually encrypting or decrypting it in a totally transparent manner. No one except the owner of the files, and an administrator with an EFS Data Recovery certificate, can read the file or folder. Thus, you can configure EFS to encrypt all material saved to specific folders on a local or network drive using NTFS. In the case of a network drive, the data is not encrypted until it is written to the disk. This encryption process would secure material even if someone used a low-level sector editor to read the hard drive directly.

Each file is encrypted with a unique symmetric key. EFS then encrypts the secret, symmetric key using the owner's public key from the EFS certificate. The owner is thus the only person who can decrypt the key used to encrypt the file. There is also a provision for the original encryption key to be encrypted using the public key in an EFS Data Recovery certificate. EFS uses a Data Recovery policy that enables an authorized Data Recovery agent to decrypt the files. In addition, you can use the private key from the EFS Data Recovery certificate to recover the data. It is a good practice for a corporation to establish a recovery agent. Someone can decrypt the file only by first logging on to the network as that original user. The file cannot be read, so it cannot be modified. Thus, EFS supports both confidentiality and integrity.

EFS implementations require that:

➤ Public key infrastructure (PKI) be installed.

➤ At least one administrator has an EFS Data Recovery certificate.

➤ The author of the file has an EFS certificate.

You can encrypt files and folders only on the version of NTFS that is installed with Windows 2000; it does not work with any other file system. To store EFS files on shared drives, EFS "impersonates" the EFS user when making the shared network connection. The servers must be trusted for delegation. You can deploy Certificate Services to issue certificates to EFS recovery agents and EFS users. Cipher.exe is a command-line utility that adds greater functionality to the encryption/decryption process by allowing changes in configuration to be performed from the command line interface.

Practice Questions

Case Study

4Sale, an online bartering company in ThatTherePlace, North Dakota, primarily focuses on selling inexpensive, odd-lot items.

Current LAN/Network Structure

4Sale is presently running Windows 2000 Server in native mode; one member server supports Exchange (Simple Mail Transfer Protocol—SMTP) server, and another is running Internet Information Server (IIS) 4 (Hypertext Transfer Protocol [HTTP] server) and Proxy Server (packet filtering/caching). All 100 client machines are configured in a single domain model. The client systems are running Windows Professional, with Office 97 being utilized as an applications package. Each system is connected to a 10Mbps hub through 10Mbps LAN cards running Category 5 Unshielded Twisted Pair (UTP) cabling in a star topology.

Proposed LAN/Network Structure

4Sale is developing its online barter/trading business through business alliances. It wants secure communications among specific departments. Outside salespeople are using public networks to access the server and office files.

Current WAN Connectivity

No changes in the current structure are proposed at this time.

Proposed WAN Connectivity

No changes in the current structure are proposed at this time.

Directory Design Commentary

No changes in the current structure are proposed at this time.

Current Internet Positioning

No changes in the current structure are proposed at this time.

Future Internet Plans

No changes in the current structure are proposed at this time.

Company Goal with Windows 2000

The Network Manager at 4Sale says, "We are concerned about confidentiality of files, especially among our sales force. A laptop has been stolen, and no one is certain whether valuable customer lists fell into a competitor's hands."

Question 1

The CEO of 4Sale asks, "What is the best interface for future integration with heterogeneous directory services?" [Choose the best answer]

○ a. LDAP C API

○ b. SSPI

○ c. MAPI

○ d. ADSI

○ e. None of the above

Answer d is correct. ADSI (Active Directory Services Interfaces) interfaces natively with Lightweight Directory Access Protocol and with a variety of other directory service products like Lotus Notes, Novell GroupWise, and Exchange Server. LDAP C application programming interface is a de facto C programming standard that allows you to programmatically manipulate directory services structure, but it requires detailed knowledge of each system. Therefore, answer a is incorrect. SSPI (Security Support Provider Interface) does not support directory services; it supports security libraries. Therefore, answer b is incorrect. MAPI (Microsoft Messaging Application Programming Interface) is a Windows API that interfaces with older mail systems and is used primarily for backward compatibility. Therefore, answer c is incorrect.

Question 2

The Network Manager at 4Sale asks, "Are we locked into one naming convention with Windows 2000?" Which of the following are naming conventions you can use with Windows 2000? [Check all correct answers]

❑ a. X.509 names

❑ b. RFC 822 names

❑ c. LDAP names

❑ d. email names

❑ e. Usernames

Answers b, c, d, and e are correct. RFC 822 and email names are the same answer. LDAP names are actual Uniform Resource Locators that use Lightweight Directory Access Protocol. Finally, usernames are the traditional way to log on to a server. X.509 is a recommendation, referring to X.500 directory services, that specifically regards the use of public keys and digital certificates. It does not deal with names. Therefore, answer a is incorrect.

Question 3

> The Network Manager at 4Sale says, "I want to use only one-way trusts. I want to control what administrators can do." Which scenarios support one-way trusts? [Check all correct answers]
>
> ❑ a. Windows 2000 domains in the same forest
>
> ❑ b. Windows 2000 domains in a different forest
>
> ❑ c. Windows NT domains
>
> ❑ d. MIT Kerberos realms
>
> ❑ e. All of the above

Answer e is correct. Answer a, a trick answer, is correct because you can still explicitly establish a one-way trust in a Windows 2000 domain. Answers b, c, and d are correct because the only kind of trust you can establish across forests, within NT domains, or within Kerberos realms is a one-way, nontransitive trust.

Question 4

> The Network Manager at 4Sale asks, "What are the domain controller FSMO roles?" [Check all correct answers]
>
> ❑ a. Schema Master
>
> ❑ b. Domain Naming Master
>
> ❑ c. RID Master
>
> ❑ d. PDC Advertiser
>
> ❑ e. Site Master

Answers a, b, c, and d are correct. The Schema Master administers schema updates and changes. The Domain Naming Master administers the addition or removal of domains in a forest or cross-references to external directory services. The Relative ID Master allocates relative ID (RID) sequences, the unique portion of the two components that make up a security ID. Primary Domain Controller Advertiser acts as a PDC for down-level backup domain controllers or clients in mixed mode. There is no Site Master role. Therefore, answer e is incorrect.

Question 5

> The Network Manager at 4Sale says, "The Kerberos protocol is just as strong as a smart card authentication method." Is the Network Manager correct?
>
> ○ a. Yes
>
> ○ b. No

Answer b, no, is correct. The Network Manager is incorrect. Smart cards and other two-factor security techniques provide stronger authentication than the Kerberos protocol because their method requires both "I have something" and "I know something." Kerberos requires just "I know something" (a password).

Question 6

> The Network Manager at 4Sale says, "I get confused about which logical component goes where among the Windows 2000 structures." Create an ordered list of only the appropriate logical components/subcomponents.
>
> Objects and attributes
>
> Forest
>
> Namespace
>
> Site
>
> Container
>
> Domain controller
>
> Tree

The correct answer is:

Objects and attributes

Container

Tree

Forest

The question asked for logical structures, so domain controller and site are inappropriate. Namespace is not appropriate because it describes the directory database. Only the four objects listed are correct. Forest and Tree are containers.

Question 7

The Network Manager at 4Sale says, "I prefer to assign permissions to individuals because I then have better control over which of our employees can access any one specific resource as compared to using a specific group classification." Is the Network Manager using a good strategy?

○ a. Yes

○ b. No

Answer b, no, is correct. The Network Manager is using a bad strategy. A recommended administrative technique is to assign permissions only to groups. It is more likely that users will change groups than that groups will change their specific resource needs. By assigning permissions to groups, the administrator decreases the possibility of making a mistake.

Question 8

The Network Manager at 4Sale asks, "I want to make certain every salesperson has a secured laptop. What do we have to do?" Which of the following are requirements for deploying EFS on the laptops? [Check all correct answers]

❑ a. PKI must be installed on the laptop.

❑ b. Windows NT must be installed on the laptop.

❑ c. An EFS certificate must be installed on the laptop.

❑ d. All of the above.

Answers a and c are correct. Both public key infrastructure and an EFS (Encrypting File System) certificate must be installed on the laptop. Windows NT does not support EFS, nor is NT File System installed with it. EFS requires you to install Windows 2000 and NTFS. NT is the wrong operating system, so answer b is incorrect, as is answer d.

Need to Know More?

 Nichols, Randall K. et al. *Defending Your Digital Assets against Hackers, Crackers, Spies, and Thieves, First Edition*. McGraw-Hill Professional Publishing, New York, NY, 2000. ISBN 0-07-212285-4. Chapter 8 discusses many concepts that relate to access controls.

 Shinder, Thomas W. and D. Lynn White. *Configuring Windows 2000 Server Security*. Syngress Media, Inc., Rockland, MD, 2000. ISBN 1-928994-02-4. Chapter 4 covers relationships between directory and security services. Chapter 6 discusses Encrypting File System architecture and user operations.

 Stallings, William. *Network Security Essentials*. Prentice Hall, Upper Saddle River, NJ, 1999. ISBN 0-13-016093-8. Subsection 4.2 of Chapter 4 discusses in technical detail the X.509 authentication method, managing certificates and keys, and policies.

 Search the TechNet CD (or its online version through **www.microsoft.com**) and the *Windows 2000 Server Resource Kit* CD using the keywords "OU", "EFS", "ACL", and "FSMO".

 **http://csrc.nist.gov/rbac/** This site offers award-winning RBAC research from the National Institute of Standards and Technology (NIST) and includes technical papers that discuss role-based access control methods.

 **www.faqs.org/rfcs/** The Internet FAQ Consortium provides a variety of archives, including Internet RFCs, Usernet FAQs, and other FAQs. This page of the site is the RFC search page, which provides searches for material using reference numbers and keywords. This particular page also provides links to Internet-related standards organizations such as IETF, IAB, W3C, and so on.

 **www.faqs.org/rfcs/rfc1330.html** This site offers recommendations for the Phase I Deployment of Open Systems Interconnection (OSI) directory services (X.500) and OSI message handling services (X.400) within the ESnet community.

 www.microsoft.com/technet/win2000/win2ksrv/technote/nt5efs.asp At this site, you'll find *Encrypting File System for Windows 2000*, a Windows 2000 Server White Paper that provides an overview of EFS, which is included with Windows 2000.

Group Policy

Terms you'll need to understand:

✓ Universal group

✓ Security groups

✓ Distribution list

✓ Distribution groups

✓ Organizational Unit (OU)

✓ IntelliMirror technology

✓ Group Policy Object (GPO)

✓ Administrative Template

✓ Site

✓ System Policy Editor (poledit.exe)

✓ Group Policy loopback support

Techniques you'll need to master:

✓ Discussing the differences between legacy NT 4 and Windows 2000 policies

✓ Utilizing new features in the Windows 2000 concept of groups

✓ Understanding the Group Policy Microsoft Management Console (MMC) extensions

✓ Outlining Group Policy processing orders

✓ Describing Group Policy loopback support modes

✓ Using tools and utilities for administration of Group Policy

This chapter begins with a comparison of how NT 4 and Windows 2000 implement group management, system policies, and settings. I explore some of the new features in Windows 2000, including the introduction of Organizational Units (OUs) and the ability to nest containers. I then describe how the desktop environment is secured and user management enhanced while reducing total cost of ownership (TCO) using change and configuration management technologies collectively known as IntelliMirror (also discussed in Chapters 11 and 12). Following this broad view of policy-based management of the user's workspace, I focus specifically on Windows 2000 Group Policies. I briefly discuss their architecture and administrative function. In discussing security groups, I describe the default processing order of Group Policy Objects (GPOs) in relation to Group Policy implementation. In my discussion of the Group Policy Microsoft Management Console (MMC) snap-in, I describe the extensions that enhance and extend the software tool.

In an easily maintained yet secure enterprise, order of policy inheritance is a critical design concept. Each account inherits all GPOs for the entire OU path in which they exist. I discuss how you can modify this inheritance flow through the filtering characteristics of security groups. I also discuss the loopback support technique of controlling the exposure to specific policies. Finally, I briefly discuss specific tools and utilities that assist you in building and maintaining Group Policies. This brief selection of tools complements Chapter 11's more detailed discussion of utilities that are potentially useful when you are working with the daily issues of configuring and maintaining Windows 2000.

The Concept of Group

In Chapter 2 and throughout this book, I have used the basic scenario of consumer and service provider to describe the majority of information exchanges that occur in a computerized environment. In fact, the very access to a file on your local machine is an example of this exchange; you request a file object from a file-keeping service (originally called a *file server*). The "file service provider" authenticates who you are and whether you have the authority to request the file. If you have permission to see the file object, you are given access to it.

Based on the discussion of access control in Chapter 9, you should recognize that authentication is performed during the logon process and that you manage permissions through access control entries (ACEs) associated with the target object. Centralized identity management assumes the administrative overhead and complexity of authenticating and authorizing principals in a networking environment. Permission management, on the other hand, is relegated to the object itself; each resource has its own access control list (ACL) that specifies who can do what to the target resource.

Windows 2000, like the legacy NT system, has always been able to deal directly with the rights and permissions of single users. The peer networking traditions of Windows 3.11, however, have fostered a collective management of users, especially as the size of the user population has expanded. Users are administered as collective groups. As workgroups grew into domains, groups of local users evolved into global user groups. These global groups are then assigned to local groups, who, in turn, have permission to access local resources. This system of group assignment not only becomes another layer of centralized identity management but also actually impacts on TCO by simplifying administration and maintenance of principals in an enterprise.

The NT 4 master domain model best illustrates the functional significance of global versus local grouping. According to this model, global groups are organizational and administrative in function and span one or more trusting resource-laden domains; local groups populate these resource domains and possess the permission to use their local resources. For members of a global group to access a local resource, they must first be assigned local group membership.

Enhancements

To handle enterprise scalability, Windows 2000, in native mode, has added several new group features to the directory database schema. *Group nesting*, in particular, adds a hierarchical dimensionality to the group concept by allowing one group to contain one or more groups within its scope of authority. Other features include the following groups new to Windows 2000:

➤ *Universal group*—This collection of named accounts, organized into a security or distribution group, can be used anywhere in the domain tree or forest. In other words, universal groups are to the forest what global groups are to the domain. If you use the Windows 2000 group-nesting enhancement, these groups can contain, or nest, other groups, including other universal groups, global groups, and individual users. Universal groups are defined at the forest level, so these groups and their members have Global Catalog (GC) entries (see Chapter 9 for a discussion of the role the GC plays in the enterprise). Universal groups are visible at the forest level, so they can appear in an ACL anywhere in the enterprise namespace.

➤ *Global groups*—Native mode global groups have the same features as their legacy NT 4 counterparts except that they can now nest other global groups from within their own domain. They are visible from the forest level, so they also appear in the GC; their members, however, do not. In addition, they can appear in an ACL anywhere in the namespace.

➤ *Domain local groups*—These groups act exactly as they did in the legacy NT 4 model except that they can now contain users, global groups, and universal groups from any domain in the forest. Similarly, because of the change in status of domain controllers (DCs) in native mode (see the discussion of domains in the "Terms and Components" section in Chapter 9), domain local groups are visible. Therefore, you can assign them permissions on both member servers and DCs. Local groups are not visible at the forest level, so they do not appear in the GC.

 Universal and global groups, unlike domain local groups, are visible at the forest level and can appear in an ACL anywhere in the enterprise namespace. Local groups act exactly as they did in legacy NT 4 except that they can contain universal groups in addition to global groups and users from any domain in the forest.

In addition, every group in an Active Directory (AD) namespace is a member of one of these groups:

➤ *Security groups*—You can assign these groups as ACEs to some resource. In addition, you can optionally include them in an email distribution list.

➤ *Distribution groups*—You cannot assign these groups as ACEs to some resource, but you can use the membership of these groups for email distribution.

Note that distribution groups are actually an extension of the Microsoft Exchange Server distribution lists that have universal scope in an organization. The universal group is also similar to the distribution list in the Exchange Server schema. Another AD object, called contacts, has no network access; however, you can locate contacts through directory services and add them to distribution lists. The addition of distribution groups in the AD directory schema is a direct result of Microsoft's efforts to consolidate directory services, discussed in Chapter 7.

Policies and Settings

You need to understand how profiles, settings, and Group Policy differ to understand how Windows 2000 has evolved from legacy NT 4 and gained greater centralized control over named accounts and a user's work environment. In addition to a Single Sign-On providing access to network resources anywhere in the enterprise, a user should be reliably provided with her own desktop and work environment from any networked machine. A user profile has historically provided this collection of environmental settings either defined for or changed by a user. Customized working environments were saved as a user profile, a home directory, and sometimes login scripts on the legacy NT 4 platform. A local user profile is available only on a specific machine. When these customized settings "follow" the user to different machines, they are called a roaming profile. When a roaming profile is made read-only by an administrator and automatically imposed on the user during the user's logon sequence, the settings are stored as a mandatory user profile. Different aspects of these environmental settings are stored in different places such as the local Registry, Desktop, Profiles directory, Home directory, and so on. A Group Policy, like a mandatory user profile, is specified administratively. It is stored in a central location and always applied during the user logon.

Group policy not only provides rules-based management of network resources and how the OS generally behaves in relation to both users and computers in the enterprise, but is also the primary tool in Windows 2000 for the change and configuration management technologies collectively called IntelliMirror. Policy-based management is applied to named accounts (users and computers) on the basis of membership in AD domains or organizational units through Administrative Templates, security settings, Software Installation, scripts, and folder redirection. Like the ADM files used in the legacy System Policy Editor, the Administrative Templates are a superset of the older files. They are Unicode-based text files with ADM extensions that hierarchically define options displayed in the administrative interface of the Group Policy Editor. They are stored in the Group Policy Template (GPT) folder in the system volume folder of DCs. Although legacy ADM files can extend the Group Policy interface, the new Administrative Templates are not backward compatible with System Policy Editor. Windows 2000 GPO settings also include the legacy option for Registry-based policy settings.

In fact, the Group Policy model of rules-based management is an extension of the older NT 4 legacy System Policy model. In brief, the legacy System Policy Editor (poledit.exe) created a policy file that configured the work environment and enforced system configuration settings that were stored in (and therefore limited by the scope of the Registry of) that particular machine. These policies characteristically were:

➤ Applied to named accounts in a single domain

➤ Controlled by security group membership

➤ Accessible by the user through regedit.exe and therefore not secure

➤ Persistent in user profiles

➤ Extensible through the use of ADM files

On the other hand, the Group Policy model is a rule-based management system complementing the enterprise-scale identity management system provided by AD. It not only simplifies administering user profiling, OS, and application installation, but also provides the legacy-style Registry-based desktop system lockdowns of the early NT system. In brief, Windows Group Policy characteristically:

➤ Is associated with site, domain, OUs, and OUs nested within OUs

➤ Affects all users and computers in the site, domain, OUs, and OUs nested within OUs

➤ Is controlled by security group membership

➤ Cannot be changed by users and therefore is secure

➤ Is removed and rewritten whenever policy changes

➤ Offers enhanced granularity to control desktop and computing workspace

➤ Is extensible through either ADM files or MMC snap-ins

The scope of this rules-based management system, although broader than the legacy Windows NT System Policy model primarily because of its close association with AD still reflects the fundamental dichotomy of computer configurations (historically system.dat in Windows operating systems) and user configurations (historically user.dat). Each family of configurations is composed of general subareas covering software settings, windows settings, and Administrative Templates. This scope is shown in Figure 10.1, where the sublisting of just security settings is shown.

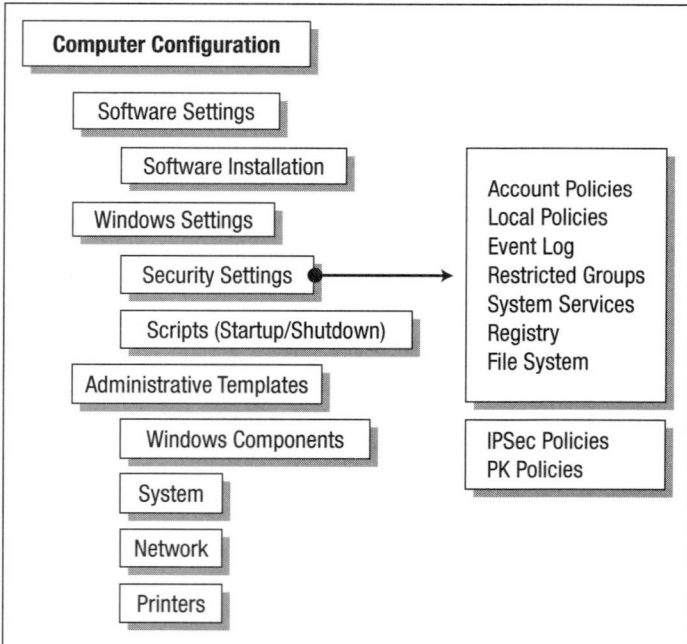

Figure 10.1 Default domain policy: security settings.

Securing the Desktop Environment

A user's working environment is second only to Single Sign-On in importance. Through new management technology, Microsoft provides easy access to your workspace from anywhere in the enterprise. Group Policy simplifies administrative overhead in controlling these environmental settings, and then it relies on Windows 2000 to deliver the policy-managed settings and enforce compliance to corporate security objectives wherever the workspace is used. This theme underlies Windows 2000 change and configuration management services and technologies. One of the IT (information technology) security controls described in Chapter 2 is accessibility to resources and services. Microsoft has developed several desktop management technologies like IntelliMirror, Terminal Services Architecture, and Remote (Operating System) Installation Services (RIS) that provide accessibility to that desktop from anywhere in the enterprise, as well as secure its access from outside interference, intervention, or impersonation without increasing TCO. Both Terminal Services and RIS are discussed in Chapter 12. Windows 2000 change and configuration management services support these security controls and compliance through technologies such as IntelliMirror.

In brief, this Windows 2000 native management technology provides access to a user's computing environment through application management, data protection, and roaming user support based on centralized policy definitions. IntelliMirror centrally manages data resources so that you can replace, restore, or recover users' personal workspace settings, applications, and data anywhere in the Windows 2000 enterprise, whether or not users have permanent network connectivity. An administrator can use the data management, software management, and settings management separately or in combination, depending on the needs of any given situation or working conditions. In concert with AD directory services and Group Policy, IntelliMirror management technology provides policy-based management of users' workspaces in the enterprise. Upon logon authentication, users' desktops are automatically configured according to centrally defined policies based on AD datastores that define their identity, group membership, business role, and location in the enterprise namespace. The ability to roam within an enterprise yet maintain a consistent workspace compliant with the security context within which the user works not only adds to productivity but simplifies the enforcement of security policies and auditing of activities among especially large user populations.

Securing Access and Permissions

Group Policy collectively describes the policy settings that control both user and computer configurations in the Windows 2000 enterprise. The two major themes at the enterprise level are identity management and permission management.

To easily centralize administration of scalable ranges of named accounts, management of users and resources must be applied in both a standardized and systematic way. Especially when applied across a site or organizational unit, policies simplify administration across wide ranges of the user population. You create a GPO and then configure the settings for it. The GPO is a virtual datastore for these settings. By storing settings in separate GPOs, you can describe different configurations for different workspaces. Thus, you define only once the workspaces for a specific group of users or computers; the operating system then automatically delivers the defined workspaces according to the assigned GPO upon network logon. GPO components are stored in the following:

➤ *Group Policy containers (GPCs)*—This is an AD object that contains GPO attributes and subcontainers for user and computer Group Policy information.

➤ *Group Policy templates (GPTs)*—This is a folder hierarchy in the system volume (Sysvol folder) on the DC. The GPT contains all Group Policy information on the Group Policy MMC snap-in extensions: policy templates, security, Software Installation, scripts, and folder redirection. For more information on security settings, see the "Group Policy MMC Extensions" section later in this chapter.

Policy Scoping: Secured Boundaries

GPOs create policy-managed scopes of control, as discussed in Chapter 8. Group Policy settings are stored in GPOs that are linked to hierarchically arranged objects in the AD structure: within the site, the domain, the OU, or OUs within an OU. This hierarchical structure organizes the inheritance of these configurations and thereby simplifies administrative tasks. By default, the scope of a Group Policy is defined by the specific container to which it is assigned and possibly modified by a named account's (user or computer) security group membership. Although security group membership can filter Group Policies, you can't associate a Group Policy directly to a security group.

 You can remember the order or downward flow of Group Policy inheritance through the AD structure as SDOU (site, domain, Organizational Unit, OU within OU). Microsoft uses this mnemonic device to refer collectively to the AD directory containers. Group Policies and IntelliMirror technologies don't support mixed mode Windows 2000 environments, legacy NT 4, or Windows platforms because both are tightly integrated with AD directory services.

You can scope or define a workspace for your employees as broadly (the site) or as narrowly (members of a single workgroup) as you need when you are administering your network, intranet, or enterprise. The effective settings work like file permissions; the most restrictive apply. They are a function of the scope of the AD object to which the GPOs are linked; this level determines the order in which the GPOs are applied. GPOs are typically stored in a specific domain (nonlocal GPOs), also called the *storage domain*. This domain has nothing to do with the domain to which the GPO is linked, but it does impact cross-domain GPO assignments, discussed shortly.

One way you can access these GPOs is to open the Properties page of a given SDOU, select the Group Policy tab, right-click on the GPO in the GPO list, select Properties, and then click on the Security tab. There are two types of Group Policy objects: local and nonlocal. Local GPOs exist on standalone computers and consist of only the GPT portion of a GPO. Only one local GPO is associated with a Windows 2000-based machine, so the typical objects discussed are nonlocal GPOs.

 Local Computer (Group) Policy on a Windows 2000 Professional computer or standalone Windows 2000 Server affects all users who log on locally. In an AD domain, domain group policies, managed by AD, override Local Group Policies.

Types of Policy Management

Centralized or decentralized policy management in conjunction with AD directory services impacts on TCO in the areas of support and maintenance. Although an OU is the smallest scope to which you can apply a Group Policy, different sites, domains, or OUs may use a single GPO, even if it is stored across domains, and thus suffer from slow wide area network (WAN) links and slow performance. Figure 10.2 shows how these cross-domain assignments can cross physical spaces.

Design considerations concerning centralized versus distributed scopes of control impact both performance and maintenance. To simplify administration and enforce corporate security objectives, Group Policy is inherited from upstream GPOs through flows from upper-level directory containers like a site and a domain, to lower-level containers like OUs; everything trickles down. This design optimizes logon times because there are fewer GPOs to process. It also simplifies administering any policy changes because all policies are written at the same level, where they are consolidated as key policy themes; they then trickle downward through the hierarchy. The disadvantage is primarily in the inflexibility of the flow of permissions downstream.

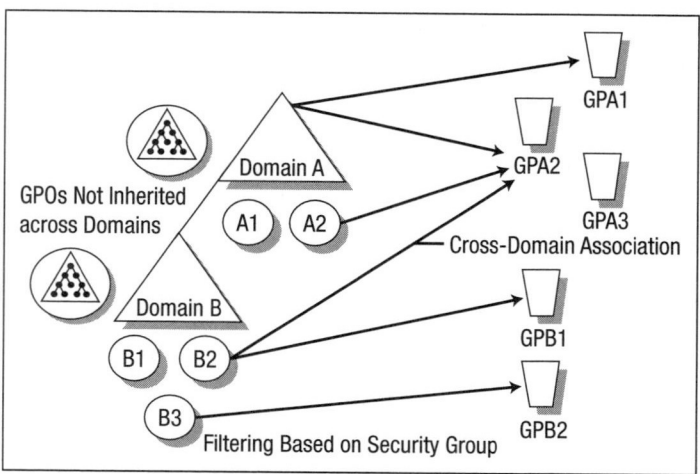

Figure 10.2 How GPOs create secure boundaries through policy management.

Alternatively, a more effective strategy can be to use multiple, decentralized Group Policies in conjunction with OUs that reflect the functional division of labor or authority. The ability to nest OUs within other OUs in a domain adds a dimensionality that was missing in the flat organizational model of legacy NT. Similarly, you can delegate GPO management to different administrative levels. In fact, you can block the setting of policies at various levels, or you can enforce it by object through the use of the No Override option. These features, if you apply them indiscriminately, defeat the effectiveness of a centralized policy management. Finally, once you define policy settings for groups, the operating system automatically and reliably enforces policy settings.

Group Policy Administration

Group Policy handles a wide range of deployment scenarios that scale well in an enterprise environment. The Group Policy MMC snap-in is a familiar tool that integrates with, for example, the AD Users And Computers and AD Site And Services Manager snap-ins, to teach you how to use administrative tools.

In NT 4, System Policy Editor (*poledit.exe*) provided a graphical user interface (GUI) that configured both user and local computer settings stored in the Registry. NT system policies were a list of rules that specified what users saw on their desktops and what they could do at the computer. Thus, you could restrict options in Control Panels, customize desktops, and control network logon and access. Microsoft recommended that the administrator use policy file mode as opposed to Registry mode (directly editing the Registry) to simplify the administration of a uniform domain policy. This mode of operation created or modified the default *ntconfig.pol* file, located in the NETLOGON share on the primary domain controller (PDC). The template ADM files provided policies that appeared in System Policy Editor.

Windows 2000 uses the Group Policy MMC snap-in tool. It not only extends the functionality of System Policy Editor but also provides, in conjunction with AD, enhanced capabilities that go beyond Registry-based policies to include security options, software deployment, scripting, and folder redirection. You set these security settings for a selected SDOU directory container. A Windows 2000 DC must be installed, and you must have Read/Write permission to not only access the system volume on the DC (Sysvol folder), but also permission to change the selected AD object. Group Policy affects all computers and users in a selected AD container by default. However, membership in a security group can filter the effect of a specific policy by overriding the policy and interrupting its inheritance by downstream objects, discussed in the "Security Group Effects" section later in this chapter.

Group Policy MMC Extensions

The Group Policy snap-in includes extensions that can extend either or both the User Configuration and Computer Configuration nodes in Windows Settings or Software Settings. By using the Group Policy MMC snap-in and its extensions, you can specify policy settings using the following extensions:

➤ *Administrative Templates*—This extension, applicable for both users and computers, includes Registry-based policies that affect the Windows 2000 operating system and applications. You manage them through the Administrative Templates node of the Group Policy MMC snap-in. There are over 450 available settings; you can add more using the ADM files.

➤ *Security settings*—This extension defines security configuration for computers within a GPO and for network settings, local machine, and domain. It includes, for example, account policies (password policy, lockout policy, Kerberos policy, and so on), local policies (security settings for audit policy, user rights, security options, and so on), and public key policies. Refer back to Figure 10.1 for a listing of the features as they appear under Computer Configuration|Windows Settings in the Default Domain Policy MMC snap-in.

➤ *Software Installation and maintenance options*—This extension, for users and computers, is for centrally managing software installation as well as removing, repairing, and publishing software (to users) or updates. Utilize this setting on application software that complies with the Microsoft Installer (MSI) technology. Target computers need to have Windows 2000 running as well as the client-side extension for software installation. To install Windows 2000 remotely, use RIS, discussed shortly.

➤ *Script options*—Scripts use Windows Scripting Host (WSH), discussed in Chapter 11. In Windows 2000, five script types are supported: legacy logon scripts, Group Policy logon/logoff scripts, and Group Policy startup/shutdown scripts.

➤ *Folder redirection options*—These options redirect users' special folders from their default user profile locations to the alternative network locations where they can be centrally managed. These special folders include My Documents, Application Data, Desktop, and Start Menu.

➤ *RIS*—Use RIS to manage the Remote Operating System Installation feature as displayed to client computers. Group Policy requires a genuine Windows 2000 client for this operation.

Note: Account policies are set only at the domain level. They are ignored if set at the organizational level.

Security Group Effects

Group Policy leverages the AD hierarchical structure by filtering the scope of GPOs in relation to the associated AD directory containers, SDOU. You create security groups and then assign Apply Group Policy and Read permissions to specific groups within the directory container. Security Groups alter the policy scope of a GPO by filtering Group Policy effects using security group membership and discretionary ACLs (DACLs) (discussed in Chapter 9). You can add named accounts to a group by using the Security tab on the Properties page of the GPO. Filtering affects all settings in the GPO except in the case of folder redirection and Software Installation. These nodes have additional GPO ACLs that can refine scope based on security group membership.

Another refinement in Windows 2000 is the ability to delegate control of these GPOs. Any security group member with both Read and Write permissions can delegate GPO control to other users for administrative reasons. Members of the Enterprise Administrators or Domain Administrators group determine which administrator group can modify GPOs through the Security tab on the GPO Properties page. These network administrators can delegate control of some policy to a specific administrator, who can be defined and provided with Read/Write access to select GPOs. Having Full Control of a GPO does not enable an administrator to link it to some site or other AD object unless the Delegation of Control Wizard grants this ability.

Group Policy Processing

Group Policy is inherited from parent to child containers. Assignment of GPO settings to an upstream container applies to all containers downstream, including the users and computer objects in those containers. Explicitly specifying GPO settings for a child container, however, overrides the parent container's GPO settings. If a parent OU has nonconfigured policy settings, the child OU cannot inherit them. Disabled policies settings are inherited as disabled. If a parent OU has configured settings and a child OU does not, the child inherits the parent's configuration. Policies are inherited as long as they are compatible, so a child inherits the compatible settings of a parent and then overlays its own settings on top. Conversely, when settings are incompatible, the settings aren't inherited, and the child's settings are applied.

When you are considering the ordered sequence with which GPOs are applied to both users and computers, you must consider the local GPO first. The local GPO is the only source of Group Policy for a standalone machine or members in a workgroup, so it is always processed. You cannot block this object.

Although Group Policy settings are processed in the following order, Group Policy settings can alter sequential aspects and behavior:

1. Upon computer startup, Group Policy settings under Computer Configuration from all GPOs associated with the named accounts are processed.

2. Startup scripts are run in sequence.

3. GPOs that affect the computer account are processed before the logon screen is displayed.

4. When the user logs on, all GPOs associated with the user account and associated Group Policy settings under User Configuration are processed simultaneously.

5. Group Policy-applied logon scripts run.

6. The Windows 2000 user interface is loaded.

7. Administrator-defined scripts are run.

Local Group Policy Object Processing

Both the No Override and Block Policy Inheritance options affect the presence or absence of GPOs in the order of GPO processing but do not change the ordering sequence.

Local Group Policy settings are processed in Windows 2000 native mode in the following order:

1. *Local Group Policy Object*—This is the one GPO stored on the local machine.

2. *Site*—GPOs linked to the site are processed synchronously.

3. *Domain*—Multiple domain-linked GPOs are processed synchronously and in a specified order.

4. *OUs*—GPOs linked to the highest upstream OU are processed first, then the rest of the GPOs are processed in order downstream.

At each OU level in the AD hierarchy, you can link one, many, or no GPOs. If several are linked to an OU, they are processed synchronously, and in the order specified. This order means that the local GPO is processed first, and the GPO linked to the OU in which the user and computer are located is processed last, overwriting upstream settings.

Default Order Exceptions

Two options change the inherited flow of Group Policy settings down the AD hierarchy from site to local machine. GPOs that are linked downstream at lower levels of the AD closer to either the specific user or computer cannot override the downward flow of policies when the No Override option is set on a specific upstream GPO link. If you set No Override to a GPO that is linked to a domain, the settings apply to all OUs under that domain. GPOs linked to OUs cannot override that domain-linked GPO. In addition, GPOs linked at the same level are prevented from changing the inheritance flow. If several links are set with No Override at the same AD level, the links higher in the list have priority over the lower ones.

You can alternatively block inheritance of GPO settings from upstream AD objects by checking Block Policy Inheritance on the Group Policy tab of the Properties sheet of the domain or OU. If you set this option at a child object level, the child does not inherit policy settings from its parent-level GPO, on the level above it. This ability to block policies does not exist at the site level. To see what a GPO object is linked to, open the GPO console, right-click on the Root node, click on Properties, and then click on the Links tab. Then, select Domain in the drop-down menu and click on Find Now.

 Permissions for GPOs are analogous to file and folder permissions; the most restrictive permissions apply. Be careful when assigning Deny permissions.

Important facts to remember regarding No Override and Block Policy Inheritance are:

➤ You can set No Override only on a link.

➤ You can set Block Policy Inheritance on a domain or OU. It applies to all GPOs linked at that AD level or higher. You can also override settings.

➤ If a No Override option conflicts with a Block Policy Inheritance option, the No Override option takes precedence.

Changes due to inheritance flows regularly occur throughout the network. By default, Group Policy settings are refreshed on client computers every 90 minutes, with a randomized offset difference (plus or minus) of 30 minutes; DCs refresh every 5 minutes. You can change this refresh default value by modifying the Administrative Templates. However, you can apply Software Installation and folder redirection settings during computer startup or user logon. Finally, the user cannot schedule or control the application of GPO settings to a client computer.

Group Policy Loopback Support

GPO settings affect users and computers based on where they are located in the AD hierarchy. Sometimes, however, you must apply policy settings based on the location of the computer object alone. Group Policy loopback provides a way to apply GPOs specifically to one computer that a specific user might use. This feature is supported only in native mode Windows 2000 with both user and computer accounts stored in AD. Thus, in some cases, where processing order is not appropriate, you can specify two additional ways to process the list of GPOs for any user or computer in a specific OU. These two modes are:

➤ *Merge mode*—In this mode, when the user logs on, the typical list of GPOs is compiled in the typical order. However, a second list of GPOs is then requested, this time with respect to the location of the computer in the AD. This second list is appended to the first, causing the computer's GPOs to be processed after the user's GPO; thus, the computer's GPOs exercise greater control over the user's GPOs because the computer's settings have a higher precedence than the user's settings.

➤ *Replace mode*—The user's GPO list is ignored; the GPO list of the computer is applied.

I will use the scenario in Figure 10.3 to explain the power of Group Policy loopback support. In this scenario, you have been granted full Administrative rights over the **examcram.com** site. You want your user population to have Group Policy settings defined according to where they work. If an accountant whose office is in the Accounting section is working in the Art department, what policy settings will she receive? You want Group Policies there to be based on computer location to optimize the running of all graphics software. On the other hand, the accountant's ability to work on any workstation and access financial reports is a potential security risk. When she logs on at her graphics workstation, you want the order of Group Policy processing to be GPO3, GPO1, GPO4, GPO5, applied upon computer startup. In Figure 10.3, within the (triangular) Domain A1, there are (circular) organizational units that inherit Group Policy from upstream SDOU container objects. How can you secure the flow of inheritance? Normally, the accountant's Group Policy processing order is GPO3, GPO1, GPO4, and, in

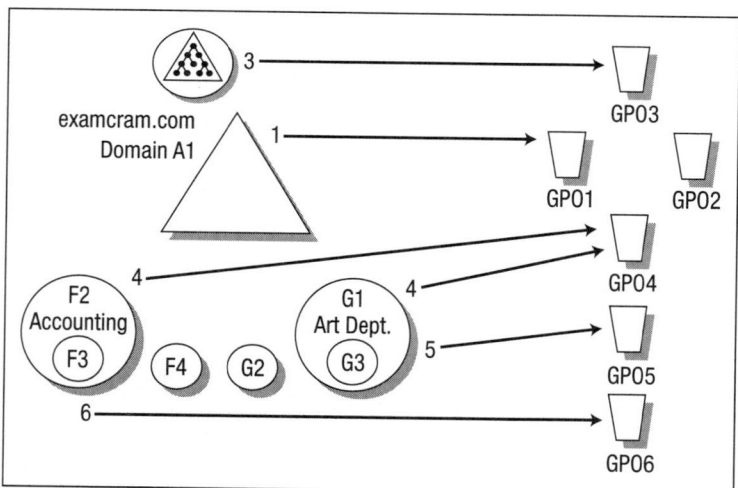

Figure 10.3 How Group Policy loopback support affects policy flow.

the Organizational Unit F3, GPO6, when she logs on to the network. Notice the numbers to the right of each geometric shape indicating these policies.

However, the workstation in question is in the Art department where it's appropriate to manage workspaces based on computer profiles. But what if the accountant attempts to work in the Art department? You can use either Merge or Replace mode to secure the Group Policy processing order. Here's what happens with each mode:

➤ *Merge mode*—When the accountant logs on, her user's list of GPOs is compiled, but then the computer's list of objects is appended at the bottom of her user list. Therefore, the processing order in Merge mode becomes GPO3, GPO1, GPO4, GPO6, GPO3, GPO1, GPO4, and GPO5. The computer GPOs are appended to the user GPO settings, so the computer's GPO list has a higher precedence than the user settings. The workstations will run only graphics applications.

➤ *Replace mode*—The accountant's list of GPOs is not gathered at all. Instead, only the list of GPOs based on the computer object (GPO3, GPO1, GPO4, GPO5) is applied. This is the only list of settings, so the graphics machines in the Art department remain configured exclusively for graphics.

Permission Management Tools

The tools I discuss in this section are especially designed to work with Group Policy. I include not only what they do but also where you can find them. As mentioned in Chapter 11, support tools are part of the installation CD-ROM and therefore must be considered part of the system. The relevant Group Policy command-line interface (CLI) tools are:

➤ *floplock.exe*—This tool, FloppyLock, can lock a microdiskette disk drive so that it is accessible by only Administrators and Power Users. It can be used to prevent the installation of unauthorized software or the copying of confidential information to a diskette. The only way to unlock the diskette drive is to stop the FloppyLock service.

➤ *gpolmig.exe*—This support tool, Group Policy Migration, assists in the migration of NT 4 System Policy settings to Group Policy settings.

➤ *gpresult.exe and gpotool.exe*—These tools, Group Policy Results and Group Policy Verification, are included in the Windows 2000 Resource Kit. Gpresult.exe is a GPO troubleshooting utility that displays system information about GPOs applied to the local computer and user. Gpotool.exe performs command-line operations like creating and deleting GPOs in the directory, checking GPO/Sysvol replication status, and displaying information about a specific Group Policy object.

➤ *ldifde.exe*—This utility, LDIF Directory Exchange, is included with the core server application and is used to import and export AD data. It is located in Windows 2000 Server in %systemdir%\System32. It is not automatically installed in Windows 2000 Professional.

➤ *nltest.exe*—This utility is included with the support tools and is used to test trust relationships between clients and domain controllers as well as to verify relationships between domain controllers. In Windows 2000, nltest.exe accesses information directly from directory services; in legacy NT 4, it queried the browser service for named lists of machines. For more information, see Chapter 11.

➤ *runapp.exe*—This utility, RunApplication, can launch an application or restart one if it is closed. Be careful running this CLI utility from the command prompt.

You need to gain plenty of hands-on experience with these tools. When using any security utility, but especially those listed in this chapter, carefully test the results following execution of the tool. Centralized policy management simplifies administration but also amplifies even a simple change across an Active Directory container and can unintentionally cause widespread disruption in service.

Practice Questions

Case Study

4Sale, an online bartering company in ThatTherePlace, North Dakota, focuses primarily on selling inexpensive, odd-lot items.

The Network Manager says to you, "I need to deploy very standardized workspaces for the majority of our employees. I really don't have time to develop desktops myself. I want the users to have a standard set of desktop applications. Security needs to extend outside our intranet. We are a Web-based, e-commerce company. I want to make certain that security systems are integrated into as many network layers as possible."

Current LAN/Network Structure

4Sale is presently running Windows 2000 Server in native mode; one member server supports Exchange 5.5, whereas another is running Internet Information Server (IIS) 5 and Proxy Server 2. All 100 client machines are configured in a single-domain model. The client systems are all running Windows 2000 Professional, with Office 2000 being utilized as an applications package. Each system is connected to a 10Mbps hub through 10Mbps local area network (LAN) cards running Category 5 Unshielded Twisted Pair (UTP) cabling in a star topology.

Proposed LAN/Network Structure

No changes are planned at this time.

Current WAN Connectivity

No changes are planned at this time.

Proposed WAN Connectivity

No changes are planned at this time.

Directory Design Commentary

No changes are planned at this time.

Current Internet Positioning

No changes are planned at this time.

Future Internet Plans

No changes are planned at this time.

Company Goal with Windows 2000

4Sale wants to establish a policy-management infrastructure that will allow flexibility in the future but that will keep administrative costs to a minimum.

Question 1

> Considering the Network Manager's comments in the case study, which Group Policy extensions are most appropriate? [Check all correct answers]
>
> ❏ a. Security settings
>
> ❏ b. Software specifications
>
> ❏ c. User templates
>
> ❏ d. Administrative Templates

Answers a and d are correct. Of the listed choices, they are the only answers that are extensions. Although the Network Manager mentions software installation, software specifications is not an extension; software installation and maintenance as well as Remote (Operating System) Installation Services are. Therefore, answer b is incorrect. Answer c is incorrect because user templates are not an extension; Administrative Templates are.

Question 2

> The Network Manager at 4Sale says, "I want to delegate responsibility for marketing and sales policies to the supervisors in each department. How can I do this?" [Choose the best answer]
>
> ○ a. Only members of the Enterprise Administrators group can modify GPOs; they cannot delegate that responsibility.
>
> ○ b. Only members of the Enterprise Administrators and Domain Administrators groups can have Full Control over GPOs; they cannot delegate that responsibility.
>
> ○ c. Only members of the Domain Administrators group can have Full Control over GPOs; they cannot delegate that responsibility.
>
> ○ d. None of the above.

Answer d is correct. Answer a is incorrect because members of the Enterprise Administrators and Domain Administrators groups cannot only modify Group Policy Objects, but they can also link them to some Active Directory object. They can also delegate the responsibility of modifying a GPO to any administrator or an administrator group, provided all parties have Read/Write access to the specific GPO. Answers b and c are incorrect because you can grant to any administrator Full Control with the Delegation of Control Wizard.

Question 3

The Network Manager at 4Sale says, "I want a child GPO in our Project OU to inherit policy setting from the parent Marketing OU, but the two policies are exact opposites. The project needs Web services running with basic authentication so that Marketing can use integrated authentication to log in. What do I have to do to the parent OU to solve this problem?" [Choose the best answer]

○ a. Modify the Marketing GPO.

○ b. Modify the Project GPO.

○ c. Do nothing.

○ d. None of the above.

Answer c is correct. The parent OU is incompatible with the child OU, so the parent will not overwrite the child. Answer a is incorrect because modifying the Marketing Group Policy Object is not necessary. Answer b is incorrect because the child's GPO settings will not be affected by inheritance from the parent and will apply as always to objects in its own container.

Question 4

The Network Manager at 4Sale asks, "What is the Group Policy processing order?" Place the following in their proper order. Start with the computer startup.

Upon computer startup, Group Policy settings under Computer Configuration from all GPOs associated with the specific computer account are processed.

Group Policy-applied logon scripts run.

Startup scripts are run in sequence.

Administrator-defined scripts are run.

GPOs that affect the computer account are processed before the logon screen is displayed.

When the user logs on, all GPOs associated with the specific user's account and any associated Group Policy settings under User Configuration are processed simultaneously.

The Windows 2000 user interface is loaded.

The correct order is:

> Upon computer startup, Group Policy settings under Computer Configuration from all GPOs associated with this specific computer account are processed.

Startup scripts are run in sequence.

GPOs that affect the computer account are processed before the logon screen is displayed.

When the user logs on, all GPOs associated with the specific user's account and any associated Group Policy settings under User Configuration are processed simultaneously.

Group Policy-applied logon scripts run.

The Windows 2000 user interface is loaded.

Administrator-defined scripts are run.

Question 5

The Network Manager at 4Sale says, "If the processing order is inappropriate, I can use Merge mode loopback support to apply only the GPO computer settings." Is this statement true or false?

○ a. True

○ b. False

Answer b, false, is correct. The Network Manager is incorrect. Merge mode loopback support appends the computer Group Policy Object settings to the user GPO settings. Replace mode actually replaces the GPO listing because the user GPO list is ignored.

Question 6

The Network Manager at 4Sale says, "Explicit GPO settings of a child container will override a parent containers' settings." Is this statement true or false?

○ a. True

○ b. False

Answer a, true, is correct. The Network Manager is correct. Explicit Group Policy specifications override the Group Policy Objects in a parent's container.

Need to Know More?

 McLean, Ian. *Windows 2000 Security Little Black Book*. The Coriolis Group, Scottsdale, AZ, 2000. ISBN 1-57610-387-0. In Chapter 3, the author discusses Group Policy capabilities and benefits. He also describes immediate solutions for linking GPOs to objects, configuring a Group Policy Management snap-in, accessing GPOs, creating GPOs, and managing policies.

 Nielsen, Morten Strunge. *Windows 2000 Professional Advanced Configuration and Implementation*. The Coriolis Group, Scottsdale, AZ, 2000. ISBN 1-57610-528-8. Chapter 19 not only details the available polices in the Administrative Templates but discusses best practices when you are working in a server environment.

 Nielsen, Morten Strunge. *Windows 2000 Server Architecture and Planning*. The Coriolis Group, Scottsdale, AZ, 1999. ISBN 1-57610-436-2. Chapter 9 discusses the planning of user and group management, introduces the group concept, discusses built-in accounts and groups, and covers Group Policies in detail (including scopes of management and best practices).

 Simanski, Robert E. *Windows 2000 Reducing TCO Little Black Book*. The Coriolis Group, Scottsdale, AZ, 2000. ISBN 1-57610-315-3. The focus of this book is to show you how to use the new Windows 2000 features to lower the TCO of your network. It is primarily intended for experienced administrators who are migrating from legacy NT or non-Windows platforms. Chapter 5 is dedicated to managing groups and OUs. In addition to a brief discussion of group types, scopes, and built-ins, the chapter has an extensive section on immediate solutions that covers most administrative tasks that involve creating and managing GPOs.

  Search the TechNet CD (or its online version through **www. microsoft.com**) and the *Windows 2000 Server Resource Kit* CD using the keywords "Group Policy", "Group Policy Object", "Group Policy template", "OU", and "loopback". This is Microsoft's definitive online resource for technical papers and bulletins.

 www.microsoft.com/windows2000/library/howitworks/management/grouppolicy.asp This is the location of *Using Group Policy Scenarios*, originally posted in February 2000. This Windows 2000 White Paper describes six scenarios using Group Policy in detail: Kiosk, TaskStation, AppStation, Public Computing Environment, low TCO desktop, and laptop.

 www.microsoft.com/windows2000/library/howitworks/management/grouppolicyintro.asp This is the location for *Introduction to Windows 2000 Group Policy*, originally posted in May 1999. This Windows 2000 White Paper provides an overview of Group Policy and explains the major concepts such as change and configuration management, IntelliMirror, Group Policy and TCO, capabilities and benefits of GPOs, Group Policy and AD, and Group Policy and security groups.

 www.microsoft.com/windows2000/library/resources/reskit/samplechapters/dsec/dsec_pol_blsa.asp This is the location for Microsoft's *Windows 2000 Resource Kit* Group Policy chapter. Among the many chapter sections listed here is "Group Policy Processing". Other Group Policy topics you'll find here include an overview, management, storage, object links, loopback, and best practices.

Security and Configuration Tools

Terms you'll need to understand:

- ✓ IntelliMirror
- ✓ Windows Scripting Host (WSH)
- ✓ Terminal Services Architecture (TSA)
- ✓ Remote (Operating System) Installation Services (RIS)
- ✓ Windows Management Instrumentation (WMI)
- ✓ Web-Based Enterprise Management (WBEM)
- ✓ Common Information Model (CIM)
- ✓ Distributed Management Task Force (DMTF)
- ✓ Microsoft Management Console (MMC)
- ✓ Local Computer Policy
- ✓ Security Configuration (SC) Tool Set
- ✓ Security Configuration And Analysis (SCA) snap-in
- ✓ Independent software vendor (ISV)
- ✓ Command-line interface (CLI)
- ✓ Security policy
- ✓ Security templates
- ✓ Microsoft Resource Kit

Techniques you'll need to master:

- ✓ Describing the WBEM initiative
- ✓ Understanding the impact of centralized management on total cost of ownership (TCO)
- ✓ Identifying the security areas of the SCA controls
- ✓ Describing the basic components of the SC Tool Set

This chapter begins with a brief explanation of the many initiatives and technologies that have not only shaped Windows 2000, but which also clearly indicate future trends in how users and resources will be installed and managed. I stress these trends to help put deployment, administration, and maintenance strategies in perspective because the emphasis, especially in security, is changing. As I discussed in Chapter 10, I now rarely have the luxury of dealing with local machines. Instead, the methodology of placing all users in global groups and assigning global groups to local groups now applies to the tools I use in designing, supporting, and troubleshooting security systems. I describe the Microsoft Management Console (MMC) as the framework for tools that are critical in setting baselines, building configuration databases, and conducting security audits. For example, the Security Configuration (SC) Tool Set, and especially the Security Configuration And Analysis (SCA) snap-in, complement but do not replace other legacy NT 4 tools like User Manager For Domains, Server Manager, and Access Control List (ACL) Editor. The SC Tool Set is primarily a wizard that interprets and applies a range of configuration files to standardize security settings.

According to Microsoft, policy management is a scalable approach to system administration, using, for example Group Policy; it is appropriate for a 10-user local area network (LAN) as well as a 10,000-user enterprise. In the legacy domain model, Microsoft urged administrators to assign resource permissions exclusively to groups, never to individual users; now, Microsoft builds on that suggestion by recommending you apply security templates to every workstation, server, and domain controller (DC) to standardize organization, simplify deployment, and lower total cost of ownership (TCO). Having organized users and resources into groups, the application of one central policy simplifies administration and ensures the use of a uniform set of security standards. Nevertheless, there is still a need for command-line interface (CLI) and standalone tools (for example, when automating administrative tasks through the use of batch scripting).

Following a discussion of secedit.exe, one of these CLI utilities, I review a variety of tools: the Microsoft IP Security (IPSec) monitoring tool, Certificate Services CLI tools, security management tools culled from the root directory\Support\Tools directory of the Microsoft Windows 2000 operating system CD-ROM, and tools from the *Windows 2000 Server Resource Kit* CD. The tools in the root directory\Support\Tools directory, which will help you configure the Windows 2000 operating system, are an official part of the operating system. These tools run only on Windows 2000 and it is strongly recommended that both Microsoft support personnel and experienced users should use them. Though Microsoft does not support the tools in the Resource Kits, if information is published in a Resource Kit or online, I assume it will be included somewhere on an exam sometime in the future. Aside from that, the more knowledge technicians accumulate, especially of tools, the more efficiently they will perform their job.

Centralized Administration Tools

This chapter covers a broad range of tools and instrumentation that center on integrated security management and control. The fundamental themes of these various tools are:

➤ *Desktop management*—Features such as Group Policy and IntelliMirror, discussed later in this chapter, facilitate the management of data, software, and local system and user configuration within an organization and a Windows 2000 enterprise.

➤ *Centralized administration and control*—With expanding boundaries and 24/7 scheduling, administration must often be automated and performed remotely. Windows Scripting Host (WSH) and Terminal Services Architecture (TSA) support these automated changes and provide remote management from a central location. Terminal Services are discussed in greater detail in Chapter 12.

➤ *Rapid and inexpensive deployment*—Windows 2000 Professional is easier to deploy than legacy platforms. Aside from using Remote (Operating System) Installation Services (RIS) and creating installation images, you will find that it's fast, efficient, and inexpensive to deploy properly secured local systems. RIS is discussed in greater detail in Chapter 12.

Various security tools, services, and features provide this centralized management and efficient deployment. Security is fundamental in both design and deployment, so it is important that you be at least familiar with these centralized services and features because they provide the foundation for both current and future tools. They include:

➤ Windows Management Instrumentation (WMI)

➤ Windows Scripting Host (WSH)

➤ Terminal Services Architecture (TSA)

➤ Active Directory (AD)

➤ Microsoft Management Console (MMC)

➤ Remote (Operating System) Installation Services (RIS)

WMI

One of the key information technology (IT) initiatives today is Web-Based Enterprise Management (WBEM), which proposes to extend centralized administrative control over software, hardware, networks, and, most significantly, users and security policies. This initiative is based on the Common Information Model (CIM) schema standardized by the Distributed Management Task Force

(DMTF). WMI is WBEM-compliant and provides the basis for many tools that deal with the configuration and operational aspects of Windows 2000. WBEM provides a standardized infrastructure that combines both hardware and software management systems into a unified, common architecture that facilitates easy access from many different networked technologies and platforms. WMI tools are part of this very powerful evolving architecture and will play a future role in remote monitoring and maintenance.

The CIM model catalogs objects that are found in a management environment in an object data dictionary called an *Object Repository*. The CIM Object Manager administers both the collection and manipulation of the objects in this Object Repository. It also collects information from WMI providers, acting as intermediary agents between components that provide operating system services (service providers) and applications that access those components (consumers). These WMI providers collect information by monitoring the session pipes.

You can collect data using the WMI interface for hardware resources installed on the system. WMI can trace data available in AD for core directory service Lightweight Directory Access Protocol (LDAP), Key Distribution Center (KDC), Security Accounts Manager (SAM), Local Security Authority (LSA), and Net Logon service. Trace logging continuously captures events such as network logons, authentication, LDAP operations, and SAM operations.

WSH

WSH is a language-independent, low-memory, scripting platform (host) for 32-bit operating systems. It is a robust and scalable automation engine that supports noninteractive logon, administrative, and maintenance scripting functions. WSH can run from either the desktop as a graphical user interface (GUI)-based host (wscript.exe) or from a command shell-based interface (cscript.exe) as a script file or directly from the command prompt. Microsoft provides Visual Basic Script (VBScript) and JavaScript engines with WSH.

TSA

TSA is now a component of the Windows 2000 operating system rather than a separately purchased legacy NT 4 package. It provides the Windows GUI with remote devices over LANs and wide area networks (WANs), as well as the Internet. Only the data from monitor, keyboard, and mouse is exchanged between the client and host server. Although simultaneous access by multiple remote clients (application server mode) has been the traditional form of deployment, a new feature in Windows 2000 is *remote administration mode*. This operational mode provides remote access to BackOffice server products and DCs. Terminal Services supports up to two remote administration sessions without licenses. Microsoft is apparently encouraging the use of what is intended to be a single-user remote access solution because, at this time, no Terminal Server Client Access License (CAL) is required to use remote administration mode.

RIS

One of the major components of TCO is the initial deployment of new operating systems in the enterprise. RIS for Windows 2000 provides services that install a local copy of the Windows 2000 OS from some central site to remote locations throughout an enterprise. A remote machine would secure an IP address from a Dynamic Host Configuration Protocol (DHCP) server. Using a Client Installation Wizard (CIW) called the Remote Installation Services Setup Wizard, the local machine then receives an RIS image of the operating system and customized file directory structure from a specially designated boot server. This technology will be discussed in greater detail in Chapter 12.

AD

Through centralization of information about named accounts such as users, services and resources, the management of an enterprise is simplified. The arrangement of objects in a hierarchical structure provides AD directory services with a framework to authorize and audit changes and configure users and policies at the physical site level, the domain level, and the organizational unit level within the enterprise. This organizational structure supports enterprise scalability without increasing TCO or compromising the ability to efficiently manage named objects. One way to monitor AD-related activity is to use the NTDS (NT Directory Services) performance object in System Monitor. The NTDS object contains performance counters that provide statistics about AD performance. Counters such as Kerberos Authentications/sec monitor the client authentication rate on a DC, and NT LAN Manager (NTLM) Authentications/sec monitors the DC Service rate of NTLM authentications.

MMC

The MMC is a multiple document interface for an extensible array of administration and management tools. Offering no management functions of its own, the interface hosts a variety of software application components that literally snap into the interface; hence, they are called snap-ins. MMC does not replace any one tool but will over time become an integral part of all other system components. Windows 2000 snap-ins are typically available from the Administrative Tools menu or by typing "mmc" at the Run command line. The collection of tools within the MMC framework is referred to as the *console*.

Performance

Performance, located in the Administrative Tools menu, is an MMC console that displays the performance of many system objects according to selected counters. You can log, print, or view activity according to those counters. It has two tools, both of which can centrally monitor both local and remote computers, periodically collect baseline performance, and summarize data:

➤ *System Monitor*—This collects and displays realtime data about performance objects like Processor, Memory, Logical Disks, Network Interface, and other system activity in graph, histogram, or report format.

➤ *Performance Logs And Alerts*—This provides configured logs to record performance data and create alerts that are triggered by user-defined thresholds and sent to the event log for all recorded baseline exceptions. The Performance And Alert snap-in can also record data continuously in the form of trace logs.

 NT 4 Performance Monitor has been replaced by the Performance MMC with System Monitor and Performance Logs And Alerts. The Computer Management MMC has consolidated Event Viewer, System Information, Performance Logs And Alerts, Shared Folders, Device Manager, Local Users And Groups, Storage-Related Tools, and Services And Applications.

Event Viewer

Either the standalone Event Viewer or the snap-in displays log files and error messages sent by applications and system services running in local or remote computers. Event Viewer monitors a variety of events, including application or system errors, and the start and stop of services. These events are recorded in event logs. Just as in NT 4, when you activate auditing, events are logged in the Security Log. Here are some examples of auditing events:

➤ To activate auditing as a local computer policy, select Local Computer Policy|Computer Configuration|Windows Settings|Security Settings|Local Policies|Audit Policy.

➤ To enable auditing of files and folders, enable Audit Object Access, then select the file or folder and set the access event (successful or failed) in the Auditing Entry dialog box under Properties|Security|Advanced|Auditing. Each entry logs a timestamped successful or failed event as defined in the auditing policy of, for example, object access, logon events, account management, and so on.

Desktop Management with IntelliMirror

Just as WMI provides a key substrate for Windows 2000 tools, the three desktop management components mentioned in the previous section provide the foundation for managing a user's environment. These components are:

➤ *AD directory services*—Supplies enterprise-wide location and policy information.

➤ *WSH*—Provides a robust and scalable automation engine.

➤ *MMC*—Provides a standardized presentation framework for administrative utilities.

These major components will continue to support application deployment and maintenance as much as the need to reduce TCO will drive that deployment and maintenance to greater efficiencies in time and resources. In reality, TCO is greatly affected by issues of deployment and maintenance, and these components all decrease that cost. Another group of technologies, collectively called IntelliMirror, is specifically focused on TCO and desktop management. It offers the following core features:

➤ *Software/application installation and management*—You can install, maintain, repair, and remove software and applications remotely with little user intervention.

➤ *Data protection and management*—By using techniques like folder redirection and synchronization, originally provided by the Windows Briefcase utility, you can save user data on network drives with copies cached on the local machine.

➤ *Roaming user support*—When you centrally manage a user's profile containing his or her desktop preferences, that user's data, applications, and environmental settings follow that user to any client computer connected to the network.

All management is centrally controlled through Group Policies. One significant breach in security will more greatly impact corporate success, goodwill, and reputation in a situation where there is centralized control, than many small deployment and maintenance problems will affect TCO. Network security policy in an enterprise is already as fundamental to the network as its transport protocol. Microsoft and other operating systems like Novell continue to develop initiatives that reduce TCO through consolidating directories, centralizing control, and managing users and resources via policies, and canned scripts, templates, and powerful wizards hide the growing complexity of security infrastructures.

Don't underestimate the ramifications that one poor configuration choice can have on an entire enterprise. Understand not just what the instrumentation can do but also, more importantly, what it doesn't do. Carefully test any policy settings before implementing them on a production platform. Take special care in confirming that all software applications run according to their specifications and intended use. The more tools you know how to use in a variety of situations, the more efficient and versatile your troubleshooting skills will be.

The Security Configuration (SC) Tool Set

Although NT 4 provided adequate tools for maintaining and supporting users and resources, it couldn't analyze security. With security subsystems becoming more complex, companies needed an integrated tools set that could audit security policies of all named objects—namely, users, services, and resources. The SC Tool Set provides a central configuration tool and framework for that analytical functionality. Using MMC provides a multiple document interface for customizable combinations of security-related tools. In addition, the MMC snap-in facilitates task delegation and lower TCO by providing a common, transferable interface with "least privilege features." In other words, an MMC snap-in can be configured with "only the tools needed to get the job done" for some set of specific administrative functions.

The SC Tool Set provides:

➤ Configuration of one or more NT- or Windows 2000-based computers

➤ A standardized security audit on one or more computers

➤ A single, uniform, and integrated point of administration

Security Areas

In providing standardized security functions, the SC Tool Set—specifically in the form of the SCA snap-in—configures and analyzes security configurations or templates, saved as text-based INF files and defined as security attributes, for the following security areas:

➤ *Account policies*—Settings include access policy, password policies, account lockout policy, and, at the domain level, Kerberos policy.

➤ *Local policies*—Settings include audit policy, user rights assignments, and a variety of options, such as control of storage devices like micro-diskettes and CD-ROMs.

➤ *Event log*—Settings include enabling log sizes, access, retention time, and retention methods.

➤ *Restricted groups*—Settings include group membership for user-defined and built-in groups such as Administrators, Server Operators, Backup Operators, Power Users, and so on. The SC Tool Set also tracks and controls reverse membership of each restricted group in the Members Of column—namely, other groups to which this restricted group can belong. You can use this field to manage which other groups can be joined or limit a group of users exclusively to one group.

➤ *System services*—Settings include security and startup policy on services ranging from Net Logon, Alerter, and Messenger to uninterruptible power supply (UPS), fax, Domain Name System (DNS) server, and Internet Authentication Service (IAS).

➤ *Registry*—Settings include the management of system Registry keys by placing a security descriptor on the key object.

➤ *File System*—Settings include the ability to configure NT File System (NTFS) attributes on all local volumes, including assigning permissions, auditing, and ownership at both the file and folder levels.

This architecture, like so many other aspects of Windows 2000, supports new security configuration areas as the system changes over time. You can import a security template into a GPO. Thus, you can either use the predefined configurations or build customized configurations using the Security Configuration Editor. System services similarly accommodate a security configuration attachment that can analyze and configure any third-party–independent software vendor (ISV) service. Thus, you can configure different NT systems to run different services without complicated options. In addition, the functionality of the SC Tool Set is available as a command-line utility, secedit.exe, for script-based configuration and analysis. The secedit.exe tool is discussed later in this chapter.

Security Settings

The phrase *security settings* describes a specific configuration. When it relates to security, it includes account and local policies (passwords and so on), access control (to services, resources, and so on), logging and auditing (event logs), restricted group memberships, IPSec, and public key policies. The security templates described in the "Security Templates" section later in this chapter are the physical collection of security settings having a common dimension (default, compatible, high security, and so on) stored in one file for simplified administration and maintenance. These templates define roles that can be applied to resources in a standardized way. Two additional settings require more customization and are therefore not included in a security template. These two settings are located in the Windows Settings node in the Computer Configuration portion of the Group Policy node. The two additional security policy nodes are:

➤ *Public Key Policies*—These policies include subpolicies that public key infrastructure (PKI) uses: X.509 root certificates, certificate trust lists, and encrypted data recovery agents used in Encrypting File System (EFS).

➤ *IP Security Policies on AD*—These policies point to the IPSec Policy object in the AD, which defines both encryption and signature requirements for IPSec secured information exchanges (discussed in Chapter 5).

Tool Set Components

The SC Tool Set consists of the following components:

➤ *Security Configuration Service*—This parser engine reads security configuration files and analyzes policy settings on the target machine.

➤ *Setup Security*—This component creates an initial security configuration database, called the Local Computer Policy, using predefined configurations.

➤ *Security Templates*—This standalone snap-in manages text-based INF files that define some user-customized security configuration. Templates are covered in more detail in the "Security Templates" section later in this chapter.

➤ *Security Configuration And Analysis Manager*—This standalone snap-in supports the importing of one or more security configuration databases that, when combined with the original Local Computer Policy, become composite configurations.

➤ *secedit.exe*—This full-featured CLI tool is used primarily for security configuration and auditing using script applications.

➤ *Security settings extensions to the Group Policy Editor*—This snap-in tool extends the Group Policy Editor by allowing you to define security configuration as part of a Group Policy Object (GPO), discussed in greater detail in Chapter 10.

The SC Tool Set supports:

➤ Defining a new, or modifying an existing, security database as a baseline configuration.

➤ Analyzing current computer security settings, listed by area, against this baseline configuration. A green checkmark indicates consistency between machine and database settings. A red X indicates a discrepancy between the two configurations. A generic icon indicates that the security attribute was not part of the template.

➤ Configuring the current computer to conform entirely to this baseline or to make individual changes using the Group Policy snap-in. You can define modifications in security policy as part of the GPO at the local machine, domain, or Organizational Unit (OU) in the AD. Thus, GPOs at various levels are imported into the local computer policy database. The composite database configuration, applied to the client computer to ensure compliance, is referred to as its *security policy*.

 Familiarize yourself with the steps involved in using the MMC and in adding and removing standalone snap-ins, such as Security Configuration And Analysis, Group Policy, Security Templates, and so on. The MMC is the fundamental Windows 2000 framework for hosting administrative tools.

Security Templates

When you want to deploy a workstation or server, you install the operating system and use a predefined template to modify the new computer's Local and Group Policies. You can apply settings from a selection of predefined templates or customize one for a specific portion of your user population. You can also export a collection of customized settings to a template file for future use. These templates are not actual settings. Changes made to a predefined or customized template do not alter a machine's policies until that template is actually applied. The templates are text-based INF files that you can use as a baseline to analyze the security configuration of a specific machine or as a collection of settings to configure an existing workstation, server, or DC.

The Security Templates (Configuration Editor) provide editing capabilities for security template files, which describe security attributes in each of the security areas defined in the "Security Areas" section earlier in this chapter. You can import or export these template files to a security database on any specific machine. You can also apply them to domain controller GPOs, which replicate them to local computer policy databases on startup.

Predefined security templates that modify newly installed machines are as follows:

➤ *basicdc.inf*—Basic DC for Windows 2000 Server

➤ *basicsv.inf*—Default server for Windows 2000 Server

➤ *basicwk.inf*—Default workstation for Windows 2000 Professional

➤ *compatws.inf*—Compatible workstation or server

➤ *hisecdc.inf*—Highly secure DC

➤ *hisecws.inf*—Highly secure workstation or server

➤ *securedc.inf*—Secure DC

➤ *securews.inf*—Secure workstation or server

The templates form classes that satisfy five common security needs:

➤ *Basic (basic*.inf)*—These templates reapply default settings to all security areas except user and group rights.

➤ *Compatible (compat*.inf)*—This is not considered a secure environment. These templates implement an ideal Users configuration but a less secure Power Users configuration than a default installation setting. Windows 2000 authenticated users in Windows 2000 Professional (but not Server) are members of the Power Users group by default, so you may need to evaluate their security levels. These templates lower security levels on specific files, folders, and Registry keys that software applications commonly access so that they run successfully under a User security context.

➤ *Secure (secure*.inf)*—These templates implement security settings for all areas except files, folders, and Registry keys because these objects are configured securely by default or by permissions.

➤ *Highly secure (hisec*.inf)*—These templates are for IPSec-enabled network traffic and protocols used between Windows 2000 machines, not down-level NT or Windows clients, which are less secure than Windows 2000 machines. All network communication must be digitally signed and encrypted. Communications between a Windows 2000 secure computer and a down-level client cannot be performed.

➤ *Other INF files*—Special case templates implement specialized configurations. DC security.inf implements ideal file system and Registry permissions settings, especially for local users on Windows 2000 DCs. Microsoft recommends that server-based applications should not be run on DCs, whether under this template or generally. Another file group, ocf*.inf, provides optional component file security for Windows 2000 servers and workstations.

Templates are built on the assumptions that you will apply them to Windows 2000 computers with default configurations, and that these systems will be installed on NTFS volumes. When computers are upgraded from legacy NT, security is not modified. Templates incrementally modify default settings; they do not install default settings and then perform their predefined modifications. Finally, you should not install security templates on production platforms without carefully testing the applications after you apply the templates.

The secedit.exe Tool

When you frequently analyze or configure many machines, you should take advantage of a tool that uses the CLI, which is preferable over the GUI of the SCA tool in terms of both speed and convenience. Command-line operations allow you to configure and analyze security configurations in conjunction with tools like Microsoft System Management Server or the Windows 2000 Task Scheduler. The secedit.exe tool is the CLI version of the SC Tool Set, with which you can view CLI operations. Commands are detailed in the code snippets later in this section only with a usage menu unless details are especially noteworthy; the online help for secedit.exe provides both full command syntax and topical information.

This CLI tool provides five operations:

➤ *Analyze*—This operation corresponds to the same tasks available using the SCA snap-in.

➤ *Configure*—This operation corresponds to the same tasks available using the SCA snap-in.

➤ *Export*—This operation corresponds to the same tasks available using the SCA snap-in.

➤ *RefreshPolicy*—This operation is not included in the SCA snap-in. This operation automatically triggers a Group Policy propagation event when the machine reboots, every 60 to 90 minutes thereafter, and when local security policy is modified. You can enforce refreshes even if no changes have occurred.

➤ *Validate*—This operation forces verification of a template's syntax created using the Security Templates MMC snap-in.

To analyze system security, enter the following at the system prompt of the CLI:

```
SECEDIT /analyze [/DB filename ] [/CFG filename ]
  [/log logpath] [/verbose] [/quiet]
```

To configure system security by applying a stored template, enter the following at the system prompt of the CLI:

```
SECEDIT /configure [/DB filename ] [/CFG filename ] [/overwrite]
  [/areas area1 area2...] [/log logpath] [/verbose] [/quiet]
```

where **/areas** specifies the following security areas to be processed separated by a space:

➤ **filestore**—Security on local file storage

➤ **group_mgmt**—Restricted group settings only on groups specified in the template

➤ **regkeys**—Security on local Registry keys

➤ **securitypolicy**—Local policy and domain policy for the system

➤ **services**—Security for all defined services

➤ **user_rights**—User logon rights and granting of privileges

To refresh system security by reapplying the settings to the GPO, enter the following at the system prompt of the CLI:

```
SECEDIT /refreshpolicy {machine_policy | user_policy}[/enforce]
```

To export a stored template from a security database to a security template file, enter the following at the system prompt of the CLI:

```
SECEDIT /export [/mergedpolicy] [/DB filename ] [/CFG filename ]
   [/areas area1 area 2...] [/log logPath] [/verbose] [/quiet]
```

To validate the syntax of a security template that you want to import, enter the following at the system prompt of the CLI:

```
SECEDIT /validate filename
```

Other System and Security Tools

Although the trend in some aspects of Windows 2000 is toward centralization, the operating system promotes remote management through many system-related tools. Many of these are CLI utilities that use a textual user interface (TUI) to minimize bandwidth consumption during operation. The number and power of these tools in Windows 2000 is greater than those of earlier legacy versions. In fact, many utilities, such as netsh (NetShell), are described as both a command-line and scripting utility. This growing class of tools creates separate and distinct programming environments from the command line that support multiple Windows 2000 components on local and remote machines. This trend is clearly associated with the evolution of network architecture that supports distributed servers and services. One way to manage change and configuration in a cost-effective way is to build an infrastructure that can remotely manage objects with minimal impact on bandwidth—namely, in the form of a CLI utility. Many of the CLI utilities in this section have the same or greater functionality than their GUI counterparts, primarily because a CLI utility can be used in an automated script executed, for example, by WSH.

*Note: Windows 2000, unlike legacy NT 4 with its fundamental **net** command, increasingly resembles Unix and the standards-based Simple Network Management Protocol (SNMP) with regard to remote monitoring and control.*

Assume unless otherwise indicated that the utilities are run on the local computer as well as remotely (if there is a network connection to the remote computer). To execute any one utility, follow these steps:

1. Click on Start|Run.

2. Type "utility + parameter list".

 Following installation of the Windows 2000 Support Tools, a complete, glossary-style listing of support tool syntax and examples is available by typing "w2rksupp.chm" in the Run command dialog box.

IPSec Monitoring Tool

This tool, ipsecmon.exe, though called from the CLI, launches a GUI utility that displays successful, secured communications managed by active security associations on local and remote computers. The refresh rate, updated by default every 15 seconds, is the only option you can configure.

The monitoring tool also:

➤ Determines authentication or security association failures that indicate incompatible security policy settings.

➤ Provides statistics, such as number and type of active security associations, total number of master and session keys, and total number of Encapsulated Security Payload (ESP) or combined ESP and Authentication Header (AH) bytes sent or received.

Certificate Services CLI Tools

Windows 2000 includes three CLI tools to assist you in administering Certificate Services. Although they extend the GUI functionality already provided, they are intended for developers and Certificate Authority (CA) administrators. The tools are:

➤ *CERTREQ*—Used to request certificates from a CA. Here's an example of its usage:

```
CERTREQ -retrieve [-rpc] [-binary] [-config ConfigString]
[RequestId [Certfile [CertChainFile]]]
```

➤ *CERTSRV*—Runs as a standalone application, typically for diagnostic purposes. Here's an example of its usage:

```
CERTSRV -z
```

➤ *CERTUTIL*—Some of the many features supported by certutil.exe are:

➤ Displays Certificate Services configuration information or a file that contains a request, a Public Key Cryptography Standards (PKCS) #7 certificate, or a certification revocation list (CRL).

➤ Gets the CA configuration string, retrieves the CA signing certificate, revokes certificates, and publishes or retrieves a CRL.

➤ Determines if a certificate is valid or if the encoding length is incompatible with old enrollment controls, verifies one or all levels of a certification path, and resubmits or denies pending requests.

➤ Sets attributes or an integer or string value extension for a pending request.

➤ Verifies a public/private key set, shuts down the server, and displays the database schema.

➤ Backs up and restores the CA keys and database, displays certificates in a certificate store, and imports issued certificates that are missing from the database.

Use the following help parameter to display a full listing of features:

```
CERTUTIL [options] -?
```

Support Security Management Tools

You use many of the tools described in this section to troubleshoot change and configuration management issues. These tools were included in previous Windows Resource Kits but are now part of the Windows 2000 Support Tools, located on the Windows 2000 operating system CD-ROM in the root directory\ Support\Tools directory. You must install the Support Tools separately from the Windows 2000 operating system.

➤ *acldiag.exe*—This tool diagnoses and troubleshoots AD objects that have problems with permissions by reading security attributes from ACLs and writing information in either readable or tab-delimited format. This tool displays only the permissions of objects the user has the right to view. You cannot use it on GPOs because they are virtual objects that have no distinguished name.

➤ *ADSI Edit*—This tool is an MMC snap-in that is a low-level editor for AD. It adds, deletes, and moves objects within the directory services using AD Services Interfaces (ADSI). You can view, change, and delete the attributes of each object. It allows you to create a query and scope it to any level in the tree for searching AD.

➤ *dsacls.exe*—This tool provides directory services management of ACLs. Like the Security page on various AD snap-in tools, it can query and manipulate security attributes on AD objects.

➤ *kill.exe*—This tool ends one or more tasks or processes. You can kill processes by entering the process ID number (PID) or by any part of the process name or the name of the window in which it is running (usually the title of the application's main window). You can use either the Resource Kit tool PuList or TList to find the PID.

➤ *ksetup.exe*—This tool configures Windows 2000 clients, either Server or Professional, to use an MIT non-Windows–based Kerberos realm. The Windows 2000 client then uses an MIT-based Kerberos realm instead of a Windows 2000 domain, providing a Single Sign-On (SSO) to the MIT KDC and a local Windows 2000 client account.

➤ *ktpass.exe*—This tool generates Kerberos keytab files as well as sets password and account name mappings for Unix services that will use the Windows 2000 Kerberos KDC. It is part of a group of tools in the Server Resource Kit, including KSetup and Trustdom, which are used to configure Windows 2000 for MIT Kerberos interoperability. With this tool, you can configure a non-Windows 2000 Kerberos service as a security principal in the Windows 2000 AD. It configures the server principal name for the host or service in AD and generates an MIT-style Kerberos keytab file that contains the service's shared secret key. The tool allows Unix-based services that support Kerberos authentication to use the interoperability features that the Windows 2000 Kerberos KDC service provides.

➤ *ldp.exe*—This is a GUI tool that allows you to perform LDAP operations—including connect, bind, search, modify, add, and delete—against any LDAP-compatible directory, such as AD. You can use this tool to view AD objects along with security descriptors and replication metadata, and to search for *tombstones*, which are deleted but not disposed of AD objects.

➤ *movetree.exe*—This tool allows you to move AD objects, such as OUs and users with all of the linked GPOs in the old domain intact, between domains in a single forest. The GPO link is moved and continues to work. Clients, however, receive their Group Policy settings from the GPOs located in the old domain.

➤ *msicuu.exe*—This tool allows you to safely remove Windows Installer settings from a computer. Use this tool to remove Registry entries before reinstalling software applications.

➤ *netdiag.exe*—This tool performs tests that isolate networking and connectivity problems and determine the state of your network client and whether it is functional. This tool does not require you to specify parameters or switches.

➤ *netdom.exe*—This tool manages computer accounts for both workstations and servers through add, remove, and query options that allow specification of the OU for the computer account. It also moves an existing computer account for a member workstation from one domain to another, as well as lists the member workstations or servers in a domain. It manages trust relationships between domains, views all trust relationships, and enumerates direct trust relationships and all (direct and indirect) trust relationships.

➤ *nltest.exe*—This tool checks trust relationships, as well as the connectivity and traffic flow between a network client and a DC. It also checks the secured interprocess communication (IPC) channel between servers to verify that both Windows 2000- and Windows NT 4-based clients connect to DCs. It can also discover domains and sites, list DCs and available Global Catalog (GC) servers, identify which DCs can log on a specific user and provide specific user information to browsers, force shutdowns, and check the status of trust relationships.

➤ *ntdsutil.exe*—This tool maintains the AD database, manages and controls single master operations, and removes metadata left behind by DCs that were removed from the network without being properly uninstalled. Only experienced administrators should use this tool. By default, it is installed in the Winnt\System32 folder.

➤ *PPTP PING*—This tool verifies that Point-To-Point Tunneling Protocol (PPTP) is being routed from a PPTP client to a PPTP server. The pptpclnt.exe and pptpsrv.exe tools work in unison to verify that the required protocol and port for PPTP is being routed from a PPTP client to a PPTP server or vice versa. For a PPTP client to access a remote PPTP server, all routers in between the two hosts *must* allow traffic to pass through Transmission Control Protocol (TCP) port 1723 (PPTP) and must support protocol type 47. Protocol type 47 is the Generic Routing Encapsulation (GRE) protocol. PPTP PING runs on Windows 2000, NT, and 98, but not on 95.

➤ *reg.exe*—This CLI tool manipulates Registry entries on local or remote computers. It enables you to add, change, delete, search, save, restore, and perform other operations on Registry entries from the CLI or a batch file.

➤ *remote.exe*—This tool runs command-line programs on remote computers using named-pipes connections. To use it, you start the server end by running **remote /s** from the CLI on the computer where you want to run the selected program. Connect to the server end from another computer by running **remote /c** from the CLI. This tool neither provides security authorization nor permits anyone with a remote client (**remote /c**) to connect to your remote server (**remote /s**). An alternative to the unsecured communications of remote.exe is rcmd.exe (Remote Command Service), a Resource Kit tool, which authenticates all users with standard Windows 2000 user authentication procedures.

➤ *sdcheck.exe*—This tool displays the security descriptor for any object listed in the ACLs stored in the AD. ACLs define the permissions that users have to manipulate objects. To determine the effective access controls on an object, this tool also displays the object hierarchy and any ACLs that the object has inherited from its parent. It can help determine whether ACLs are being inherited correctly and if ACL changes are being replicated from one DC to another.

➤ *search.vbs*—This VBScript tool, which requires WSH, performs a search against an LDAP server. You can use it to get information from the AD.

➤ *SIDWalker*—These tools—showaccs.exe, sidwalk.exe, and the sidwalk.msc MMC snap-in—manage server resources moved between domains and access control policies.

➤ *snmputilg.exe*—This GUI tool complements the older command prompt SNMP browser tool (snmputil.exe). You can use either tool to obtain information from SNMP-manageable systems on the network.

➤ *tlist.exe*—This tool displays a list of tasks, or processes, that are currently running on the local computer. It also shows the PID, process name, and (if the process has a window) the title of that window for each process. If you locate the running processes, you can selectively stop any executing process by using the task-killing utility, kill.exe.

➤ *wsremote.exe*—This tool can start a server application and connect to it from the client using sockets or named pipes. Compare this tool with Remote Command Line (remote.exe), which allows only named-pipes connections.

 Because support tools are included as part of the operating system, you should understand how and when they are used. Support tools may be mentioned as parts of provided solutions for administration of various aspects of case studies.

Tools from the *Windows 2000 Server Resource Kit* CD

The *Windows 2000 Server Resource Kit* contains more than 300 separate utilities that range in function from AD and security management to job automation. Unlike Windows 2000 support tools that are included on the operating system CD-ROM, Microsoft does not recommend or support the use of these utilities.

Note: Legacy tools are no longer included in the Resource Kits; however, they are available at the Microsoft FTP site: ftp://ftp.microsoft.com/bussys/winnt/ winnt-public/reskit/.

Based on past trends, many of these tools will most likely become either support or integrated system tools in future versions of Windows operating system products.

Familiarity with their specific functions and interaction with other system components may prove useful in a technician's daily work. Never use these tools on a production platform until you are thoroughly familiar with how they operate.

The following are a selection of these Microsoft "as-is" tools that provide support for change and configuration of security-related objects and services:

➤ *addiag.exe*—This tool provides information on the state of software either installed or available for installation on a computer managed by IntelliMirror Software Installation And Maintenance. It provides information about software applications such as current user (including logon credentials and SID) and the platform (processor and locale) that could affect the managed software. It also tells you Windows Installer information, installed or advertised information about software derived from the Registry, advertised information about available software stored in AD directory services, and whether Terminal Server is running on the computer.

➤ *adduser.exe*—This tool creates, writes, and deletes user accounts from a comma-delimited file. Before creating user accounts, execute **addusers /d**, which writes the headings, user accounts, local groups, and global groups to a file and gives a picture of the data structure and headings of the comma-delimited file.

➤ *auditpol.exe*—This tool modifies the audit policy of the local computer or of any remote computer.

➤ *gpotool.exe*—This tool checks the state of GPOs on DCs, checks GPO consistency by reading mandatory and optional directory services properties (version, friendly name, extension Globally Unique Identifiers—GUIDs—and SYSVOL data—gpt.ini), compares directory services and SYSVOL version numbers, and performs other consistency checks. It displays information about a particular GPO, including properties that you can't access through the Group Policy snap-in, such as functionality version and extension GUIDs especially in verbose mode. It browses GPOs by searching policies based on friendly name or GUID. It provides cross-domain support for checking policies in different domains. If all policies are valid, a Policies OK message is displayed; if there are validation errors, information about corrupted policies is printed.

➤ *gpresult.exe*—This tool provides general information about operating system, user information, and computer information. It also provides information about Group Policy (such as the last time policy was applied and the DC that applied policy) for the user and computer and the complete list of applied GPOs and their details (including a summary of the extensions that each GPO contains, applied Registry settings and their details, redirected folders and their details, software management information that details assigned and published applications, disk quota information, IPSec settings, and scripts).

Practice Questions

Case Study

4Sale, an online bartering company in ThatTherePlace, North Dakota, primarily focuses on selling inexpensive, odd-lot items. The Network Manager is preparing to deploy new workstations in the Marketing department and is concerned about setting security policy and configuration.

Current LAN/Network Structure

4Sale is presently running Windows 2000 Server in native mode; one member server supports Exchange (Simple Mail Transfer Protocol—SMTP) server, and another is running Internet Information Server (IIS) (Hypertext Transfer Protocol [HTTP]) and Proxy Server (packet filtering/caching). All 100 client machines are configured in a single domain model. The client systems are running Windows Professional, with Office 2000 being utilized as an applications package. Each system is connected to a 10Mbps hub through 10Mbps LAN cards running Category 5 Unshielded Twisted Pair (UTP) cabling in a star topology.

Got-a-Deal is running all 22 client machines in a single child domain under the 4Sale root domain. The client systems are running Windows Professional, with Office 2000 being utilized as an applications package. Each system is connected to a 10Mbps hub through 10Mbps LAN cards running Category 5 UTP cabling in a star topology. These hubs are on the same backbone as 4Sale but have a different subnet.

Proposed LAN/Network Structure

No changes in the current structure are proposed at this time.

Current WAN Connectivity

No changes in the current structure are proposed at this time.

Proposed WAN Connectivity

No changes in the current structure are proposed at this time.

Directory Design Commentary

No changes in the current structure are proposed at this time.

Current Internet Positioning

No changes in the current structure are proposed at this time.

Future Internet Plans

No changes in the current structure are proposed at this time.

Company Goal with Windows 2000

The 4Sale CEO says, "Make certain our enterprise can operate in a uniform and secure way without increasing TCO given a projected 15 percent growth in sales. I don't want to increase the Technical Services budget line."

The 4Sale Network Manager says, "I need ways to remotely control all machines in the enterprise. I need to have control over what our users can see and do. I want to do this in as transparent a way as possible to nurture our corporate culture of self-reliance. I need tools that will help me troubleshoot system services without concern for slow-link connections or increasing network traffic. I need ways to automate maintenance functions."

Question 1

The CEO of 4Sale asks you, "What sorts of technology help centralize my management services?" [Check all correct answers]

❑ a. WMI

❑ b. WSH

❑ c. TSA

❑ d. AD

❑ e. None of the above

Answers a, b, c, and d are correct. WMI (Windows Management Instrumentation), WSH (Windows Scripting Host), TSA (Terminal Services Architecture), and AD (Active Directory) all contribute to centralizing installation and support services.

Question 2

The Network Manager at 4Sale asks, "How do I measure user authentication activity?" Which of the following performance objects measures Kerberos Authentications/sec activity?

○ a. NTDS

○ b. NTFS

○ c. Processor

○ d. Process

○ e. None of the above

Answer a is correct. The NTDS (NT Directory Services) is one of the listed performance objects in the System Monitor in the Performance MMC; it measures Kerberos Authentications/sec. NTFS (NT File System) is not a performance object; it is the Windows 2000 file system. Therefore, answer b is incorrect. Although most system activities affect Processor, it does not directly measure Kerberos activity. Therefore, answer c is incorrect. Process provides counters of the application components the processor can measure. Therefore, answer d is incorrect.

Question 3

The Network Manager at 4Sale asks, "Which security areas can I standardize whenever we plan a big rollout of computers?" Which of the following are valid security areas? [Check all correct answers]

❏ a. Restricted groups

❏ b. System services

❏ c. Registry

❏ d. DNS server

Answers a, b, c, and d are correct. The restricted groups, system services, Registry, and Domain Name System server (a component of system services) security areas are all correct. Account policies, local policies, event log, and file and folder sharing are missing from the complete list.

Question 4

The Network Manager at 4Sale says, "I don't want to build security profiles myself. What are the default security templates I have to choose from?" [Check all correct answers]

❏ a. Basic (basic*.ini)

❏ b. Compatible (compat*.ini)

❏ c. Highly secure (hisec*.ini)

❏ d. Secure (secure*.ini)

❏ e. None of the above

Answer e is correct. Although all the category names are correct, security templates are text-based files with the .inf extension (not the .ini extension as in answers a, b, c, and d).

Question 5

> The Network Manager at 4Sale says, "I prefer to work with GUI tools. I can use my mouse when I run secedit.exe." Is the Network Manager correct?
>
> ○ a. Yes
>
> ○ b. No

Answer b, no, is correct. The Network Manager is incorrect. The secedit.exe tool is a command-line utility. It does not work with a mouse.

Question 6

> The Network Manager at 4Sale says, "According to my documentation, ntdsutil.exe shows me the security descriptor of any object stored in the AD." Is the Network Manager correct?
>
> ○ a. Yes
>
> ○ b. No

Answer b, no, is correct. As indicated by its name, ntdsutil.exe is a tool that performs database management on the Active Directory. The utility the Network Manager is probably referring to is sdcheck.exe, which displays the security descriptor information stored in the Active Directory.

Question 7

> The Network Manager at 4Sale asks, "What kinds of functions can I perform with secedit.exe?" [Check all correct answers]
>
> ❑ a. Analyze
>
> ❑ b. Configure
>
> ❑ c. Export
>
> ❑ d. Validate

Answers a, b, c, and d are correct. The secedit.exe tool performs all the operations listed—analyzing, configuring, exporting, and validating—that the graphical user interface tool, SCA (Security Configuration And Analysis) MMC (Microsoft Management Console) snap-in, does. It also provides additional features such as template syntax verification (validate) and on-demand Group Policy propagation (RefreshPolicy).

Need to Know More?

 Ivens, Kathy and Kenton Gardinier. *The Complete Reference: Windows 2000*. Osborne McGraw-Hill, Berkeley, CA, 2000. ISBN 0-07-211920-9. Chapter 25 discusses a wide range of configuration tools, including Group Policy management, IntelliMirror, the SCA snap-in, WSH, and WMI. The section on the SCA snap-in gives a concise overview of this MMC snap-in.

 McLean, Ian. *Windows 2000 Security Little Black Book*. The Coriolis Group, Scottsdale, AZ, 2000. ISBN 1-57610-387-0. The author discusses SCA tools in Chapter 12. This chapter covers all key areas in a clear, concise manner and provides immediate solutions for analyzing and configuring Windows 2000 clients. It also discusses the use of secedit.exe.

 Nielsen, Morten Strunge. *Windows 2000 Professional Advanced Configuration and Implementation*. The Coriolis Group, Scottsdale, AZ, 2000. ISBN 1-57610-528-8. Chapter 15 deals with security design and implementation, in terms of both planning and deployment. Although this book deals with Windows 2000 Professional, it covers other Windows 2000 topics clearly and comprehensively. The author takes great pains to explain the rationale behind many of the new features in the Windows 2000 operating system. The book deals with design and planning as well as configuration and deployment; there is an important chapter that discusses Microsoft's project management methodology, Microsoft Solution Framework (MSF).

 Shinder, Thomas. W. and D. Lynn White. *Configuring Windows 2000 Server Security*. Syngress Media, Inc., Rockland, MD, 2000. ISBN 1-928994-02-4. Chapter 5 provides a thorough treatment of the SC Tool Set, including how to create a security tool MMC. This chapter discusses the security areas, how to configure policies, Group Policy integration, and the use of secedit.exe.

 Search the TechNet CD (or its online version through **www. microsoft.com**) and the *Windows 2000 Server Resource Kit* CD using the keywords "Active Directory", "GPO", "ACL", and "secedit".

www.microsoft.com/windows2000/library/howitworks/security/ sctoolset.asp This site provides the *Security Configuration Tool Set* white paper, posted in April 1999. It describes the SC Tool Set, a set of MMC snap-ins that reduces costs associated with security configuration and analysis of Windows NT and Windows 2000 operating system-based networks.

 **www.microsoft.com/windows2000/library/technologies/manage- ment/default.asp** This Web site offers a wide selection of Windows 2000 Server technical papers that cover how to configure and secure Windows 2000-based systems; administer desktop configuration and changes; manage data storage and retrieval; and implement value-added management solutions using technologies such as the AD, IntelliMirror, Group Policy, WMI, MMC, and WSH.

Other Technical Issues

. . . .

Terms you'll need to understand:

✓ Distributed interNet Applications Architecture (DNA)

✓ Enterprise identity management

✓ Active Directory Services Interfaces (ADSI)

✓ Lightweight Directory Access Protocol (LDAP)

✓ Microsoft Messaging Application Programming Interface (MAPI)

✓ Microsoft Directory Synchronization Services (MSDSS)

✓ Remote (Operating System) Installation Services (RIS)

✓ Simple Network Management Protocol (SNMP)

✓ Server Message Block (SMB) signing

✓ Novell Directory Services (NDS)

✓ Services for NetWare version 5 (SFN5)

✓ Services for Unix 2 (SFU2)

Techniques you'll need to master:

✓ Describing the components that support enterprise identity management

✓ Identifying Microsoft's strategic positions in the development of smart card technology

✓ Comparing Kerberos and Secure Sockets Layer

✓ Discussing securing access using SMB signing and the role SMB plays in interoperability

✓ Incorporating both Terminal Services and RIS in the secure deployment of network resources

✓ Describing how to secure the use of SNMP while monitoring system services

✓ Distinguishing parts of the COM+ security model

In this chapter, I discuss enterprise identity management, trends toward network operating system (NOS) consolidation versus coexistence, and securing access to enterprise resources as it relates to the design of Windows 2000, Active Directory (AD), corporate business objectives, and authentication and authorization security controls. I discuss how to standardize user access in a heterogeneous environment. I explore the security aspects of three themes: enterprise consolidation, enterprise enhancement, and enterprise extensibility.

In securing access for users, I discuss two-factor authentication specifically using smart cards as an example of enhancements to the security infrastructure of an enterprise. I then explore other methods of secured access to distributed and network services using Terminal Services and Remote (Operating System) Installation Services (RIS). I discuss how Simple Network Management Protocol (SNMP) can securely monitor subsystems like Dynamic Host Configuration Protocol (DHCP) when providing operating system features like RIS. I also discuss Server Message Block (SMB) signing as an alternative to Kerberos and SChannel security protocols in providing secure exchanges of information at the Open Systems Interconnection (OSI) Application layer. This topic leads to issues of migration and interoperability relating to Novell NetWare and other competitive NOSs.

In my discussion of enterprise consolidation versus coexistence, I examine issues of migration versus interoperability relating to Novell NetWare, Unix, and Macintosh operating systems. I conclude this chapter with a discussion of enterprise extensibility. I discuss the security aspects of COM+ (Component Object Model +), multitier architecture, and Web applications as extensions to the enterprise.

Centralized Identity Management

This book started with corporate business objectives; it also ends with them. Information technology (IT) has evolved into a pantheon of digital technologies that primarily deal with the relationship between consumer and service provider. According to Microsoft, an organization's ability to adapt or evolve depends upon its internal digital processes, or *digital nervous system*. Distributed interNet Applications Architecture (DNA) is a term coined by Microsoft describing multitiered, service-providing software technologies that are location-independent, distributed across the enterprise and the Internet. The digital nervous system, another Microsoft term, is the hypothetical collection of these interdependent services. The digital nervous system of an organization, much like its biological analogy, provides a decision support function in recognizing and reacting to changes in the business environment, competitive challenges, and consumer needs in a systematic and timely fashion. DNA extends that concept beyond physical boundaries of site and local area network (LAN) segments through the use of distributed, asynchronous, self-contained, service-providing software components.

We should assume that from an IT perspective, the consumer is as much the corporate employee as the person who buys merchandise in a store. Fundamental to Microsoft's DNA paradigm is enterprise identity management. As we have learned in this book, where there is a principal, there is some form of access/permission management; where there is access/permission management, there must be security systems.

According to Microsoft, enterprise identity management is composed of the following three functional areas:

➤ *Identity administration*—The data definition function that supports the data of individual entities

➤ *Community management*—The connectivity function that provides relationships among these entities

➤ *Identity integration*—The management of repositories and the business rules that govern their operation and interaction

Identity Administration

The central theme in this area is representing the consumer in relation to business processes. Three functions that provide this service are:

➤ *Existence*—The function that establishes identity

➤ *Context*—The function that maintains an entity's dynamic inventory

➤ *Provisioning*—The function that provides materials that the entity needs to operate in its environment

Existence

This function identifies and automates operations that create the individual entity. Active Directory directory services provide open interfaces in the form of application programming interfaces (APIs), such as Active Directory Services Interfaces (ADSI), Lightweight Directory Access Protocol (LDAP), and Microsoft Messaging Application Programming Interface (MAPI), that can programmatically create, copy, or duplicate entity records across applications and platforms. Synchronization and configurable business logic support the systematic propagation of this information.

Context

Context tracks the working environment of a digital identity based on combinations of data, including physical, functional, and organizational location, in association with level, responsibility, role, and time. Tracking the context of an entity is a dynamic function that changes throughout a work period based on the dynamics of the job function and the role. AD provides context support in the form of hierarchical modeling of organizations, security groups, and Group Policy. Migration from one Organizational Unit (OU) to another can dramatically change individuals' contexts in the organization, their privileges and permissions to use resources, and the rules that govern their activity.

Provisioning

Provisioning calls for dynamically providing materials needed to complete a defined job function or role based on a collection of business roles. Job-related provisions include, but are not limited to, application software, different categories of storage (online, inline, and offline), network resources, different modes of access (local, interactive, and remote), and different quotas that pertain to both storage and network bandwidth. AD supports these functions with hierarchical storage and quotas as well as policy-based management. IntelliMirror management technologies, discussed in Chapter 11, provide this sort of provisioning service with its location-independent application distribution and configuration management. In addition to provisioning resources, AD can supply the rules-based engine to force configuration when an inconsistency from some baseline database template is detected.

Community Management

Digital community management tracks, administers, and (when programmed) creates relationships among entities that the enterprise manages. The following three provide this fostered synergy:

➤ *Authentication*—The function that provides the proof of identity

➤ *Authorization*—The function that grants the rights and privileges to resources

➤ *Rendezvous*—The function that connects the objects targeted for synergy

Authentication and Authorization

Authentication and authorization are exactly where I started with security controls in Chapter 2. Entities are granted access to resources based on security credentials. Authentication here extends beyond username and password to smart cards (discussed in greater detail in the "Enhancement: Smart Cards" section later in this chapter), biometrics, and other two-factor forms of authentication ("what I have" and "what I know"). It is clear that to build and manage a community, you must have technologies that will reliably authenticate its members and invited guests. Windows 2000 has an array of security features, including Kerberos authentication, public key infrastructure (PKI), and X.509 certification working through Secure Sockets Layer (SSL), attribute-level permission management spanning security groups within domain partitions, and highly granular access control lists (ACLs).

Rendezvous

Rendezvous connects the consumers with resources for both collaboration and the exchange of services. Once you have verified authentication and authorization, you need to locate resources and make them available as efficiently as possible. AD supports Internet-based protocols and naming conventions that integrate easily into directory services. Naming conventions as well as the control over exposing specific attributes to facilitate cross-referencing and search functions are critical. Active Directory Connectors (ADCs), discussed in Chapter 7, and DirSync technologies (discussed later in this chapter with regard to directory synchronization) allow you to securely populate and update publicly accessible namespaces.

Identity Integration

Identity integration is the management function that recognizes ownership roles of different systems and establishes the business rules regarding how the datastores are maintained. This topic was discussed in the "Requirements for Identity Management" section in Chapter 7. In the context of that chapter, which describes the trend toward consolidation of directory services, I observe that to make identity data accessible, you need to transparently bridge identity management across disparate directory services. Windows 2000 aims to provide a unified, consistent, and reliable view of identities and their associate relationships across heterogeneous systems within the enterprise namespace. The next step, however, is to consolidate views across enterprise namespaces and thus form one unified namescape. The functions that provide that unified view in Windows 2000 are:

➤ *Connection*—The function that supports cross-system communication within the namespace

➤ *Brokerage*—The function that supports the translation and exchange of datastores

➤ *Ownership*—The function that tracks the primary source for each piece of data in the namespace

Although I discuss the details regarding these functions in Chapter 7, I will briefly describe them again. Here, however, I will discuss this topic in the context of a single enterprise or *one homogeneous namespace*, as opposed to the context in Chapter 7, where I discuss different directory systems or *heterogeneous namespaces*.

Connection

Connection refers to linking within *one enterprise* all heterogeneous systems in a unified namescape. These systems refer to several things, such as internalized directory datastores in Exchange 5.5 and SQL (Structured Query Language) Server 7. They also refer to widely distributed datastores and identity repositories across functionally distinct areas of the enterprise, such as Human Resources and a line-of-business (LOB) project management system. AD provides several APIs (discussed in the "AD Directory Services" section in Chapter 9), such as LDAP C API, MAPI, and its own ADSI, to provide support for other enterprise applications. It is noteworthy that AD provides native support for LDAP, shrewdly incorporating the widely accepted, standards-based protocol into its source code.

Brokerage

Brokerage manages the interchange of identity-related data that is based on business rules coming from business processes but fundamentally from corporate business objectives. Data exchanges refer not only to translations in the entries recorded in disparate and widely distributed datastores within the enterprise, but also in the updating process so that consistency and reliability are always maintained. It is noteworthy that a single move, add, or change in any one normalized piece of data can trigger a disproportionate number of associated changes in foreign tables due to referential constraints found in any typical business application. This complexity increases exponentially when you link datastores across intranets and extranets, the latter most likely subscribing to different identity classes and schema. To help clarify this concept, you can make the analogy of mapping fields in data dictionaries when you are importing database tables from proprietary relational database management systems. AD, especially through Microsoft Directory Synchronization Services (MSDSS) and its Zoomit technology, facilitates these rules-based translations and cross-datastore connections.

Ownership

Ownership refers both to the problem of propagating information across many systems in an enterprise and the necessity of relying on one authority as a definitive source for referential integrity of that piece of data. The hub and spoke architecture that Zoomit technology provides directly addresses the issue of ownership of, for example, Human Resources employee records, and the problems of rapid, reliable propagation of data associated with "hire & fire" scenarios, mentioned in Chapter 7. With this technology, Microsoft's Meta-directory Services (MMS) leverages Windows 2000 AD and provides solutions to this and other common business situations not only within, but more importantly beyond, the enterprise.

Standardizing Access for Users

A shift in business strategy is apparent in Windows 2000 with an effort to provide greater support for coexistence with other competing NOSs like Novell NetWare 5, Apple Macintosh, and Unix. Heretofore, the clear bias was not interoperability among competing NOSs, but support primarily for migration of users and resources from those competitive NOSs to the Microsoft NOS family.

 You should be very familiar with interoperability and migration issues in terms of the following NOSs: Novell NetWare, Unix, and to a lesser extent, Macintosh.

As mentioned previously, AD is clearly marketed as a potential meta-directory or hub around which other non-Microsoft operating systems can interoperate, interfacing through ADSI to access Windows 2000 core directory services. One major theme that is emphasized in documentation is accessibility to network resources and services characterized by a simple logon process: a Single Sign-On (SSO). With this background theme in mind, Microsoft uses two concepts in its integration strategy:

➤ *Strong migration tools*—These tools are typically well designed to encourage the move to Microsoft.

➤ *AD integration as a meta-directory service*—The direction of data sharing remains limited and biased; it is from Microsoft to the other operating systems.

Single Sign-On (SSO)

A key theme in the consolidation of heterogeneous networked environments, and especially in Microsoft and Novell technical and design literature, is the SSO feature, which enables an authenticated consumer to log on and transparently access all authorized resources and services anywhere inside or outside the boundaries of the enterprise. Both Windows 2000 and NetWare NOSs measure their directory services by this feature. Microsoft's evolving strategy with the SSO theme is to have AD provide authentication services no matter from which operating system platform a consumer accesses network resources. This initiative positions Microsoft as the central administrator/manager of security credentials and password account policies. Microsoft has designed Windows 2000 in a truly flexible, scalable manner to encourage the Microsoft meta-directory concept. Not only are the natively implemented security systems like Kerberos, PKI, and SSL/ Transport Layer Security (TLS) standards-based, but the operating system security architecture is actually two APIs: Security Support Provider Interface (SSPI) and Cryptographic Application Programming Interface (CAPI). TLS, one of the SChannel security protocols, is the result of the Internet Engineering Task Force (IETF) standardizing SSL version 3, as cited in Request for Comments (RFC) 2246, which the Microsoft implementation supports. References to SSL are thus sometimes written SSL/TLS.

Note: CAPI is covered in Chapter 3 and in the "Enhancement: Smart Cards" section later in this chapter. SSPI is discussed in Chapter 4, and SSL/TLS is covered in Chapter 7.

Kerberos Protocol

As discussed in Chapter 4, the Microsoft Kerberos, with its tight integration to AD, fully complies with the IETF Kerberos 5 specification. Thus, Windows 2000 native mode domains provide SSO to users and, through trust relationships, support cross-realm referrals (discussed in Chapter 4). Alternatively, an administrator of Windows 2000 enterprise can create AD-named accounts and map non-Windows Kerberized consumers to them, thus managing non-Windows accounts just as if they were native AD consumers. It is significant that non-Windows Kerberized consumers require that you initially create and map accounts to gain the same seamless advantages as native AD consumers who seek services in cross-realm environments. In brief, Windows 2000 manages the Kerberos protocol by running both the Kerberos host protocol and AD on a domain controller (DC), more traditionally referred to as a Key Distribution Center (KDC). The Kerberos client is transparently run on every workstation.

SSL

Although the Kerberos protocol is the default authentication method, it is based on an internal logon procedure and replaces NT LAN Manager (NTLM) in native Windows 2000. Growing use of public networks and the Web-Based Enterprise Management (WBEM) initiative (discussed in Chapter 11), however, calls for alternative forms of access using strong authentication methods.

The old dichotomy of distributed versus network security is particularly applicable here; users log on to the enterprise interactively through workstations compared to remote access from outside physical boundaries of the enterprise. Distributed services are actually server components distributed across the enterprise in a codependent manner (see the "Extensibility: COM+" section later in this chapter). Distributed services require distributed security services. Alternatively, it is common to describe network services and network security services as services provided or requested from sources outside the enterprise namespace. The network security protocols supporting these services cannot provide identity and permission management the same way as distributed services do. The namespace is less defined (supporting, for example, anonymous authentication) and more extensible (for example, requiring the mapping of Kerberized principals from non-Windows environments to NT accounts). The trend showing security systems at different levels of the OSI model "negotiating" the appropriate protocol and level of security between two named principals (a consumer and a service provider) exchanging information is an example of this trend toward interoperability among NOSs.

Microsoft relies on SChannel security protocols like SSL to provide SSO to this growing segment of the user population. Windows 2000 provides a native implementation of a standards-based security protocol suite, PKI, which uses X.509 version 3 public key digital certificates to support its strong authentication methods. SSO is maintained through SSL by managing PKI integrated with AD and either enterprise or standalone certificate services.

A digital certificate is a signed (encrypted) data packet that contains a public key and security credentials of the public key's owner. A Certificate Authority (CA) issues a secured, signed certificate consisting of a public key and the key holder's security credentials bound together . The encryption of this bundle with the CA's private key provides corroborative proof that the public key and associated security credentials are authentic. The Web client uses a copy of the CA's public key to decrypt this signed digital certificate and recover the public key of the targeted key holder. From then on, if the Web client's public key can successfully decrypt a message allegedly sent from the key holder, the receiver can assume with great certainty that the message was encrypted using the secret key complementing the public key authorized by the CA. Similarly, only the holder of the public key can read a message encrypted with the key holder's secret key. Thus, both parties are authenticated.

Securing Access for Users

SSO requests information from the consumer one time. This provided information is matched by an authentication, authorization, and auditing (AAA) server against a list of known accounts stored in some protected database. The information may be provided in the context of a controlled, distributed services environment (like a business enterprise) or in a networked services environment (like that found on the Internet or in some dial-up remote access situation). In either case, the AAA server needs to either corroborate the identity of the consumer requesting services or provide services in a controlled environment.

As discussed in Chapter 9, access to resources can either be defined on the basis of per-user and per-group membership, as in the use of discretionary ACLs (DACLs), or in the security context of the provided service, as in role-based access control (RBAC). This section describes technologies that encompass both extremes in securing access for users to enterprise resources—from a two-factor authentication method that corroborates a consumer's identity with information "I have" in addition to information "I know," to the controlled environment of Terminal Services where the only services accessed are centrally distributed, controlled, and monitored. RIS builds that secure, customized user environment on demand. Finally, the last technology described in this section, SMB signing, returns us to the exchange of security credentials at the OSI Application layer (which is transparent to the consumer). Here, service provider exchanges credentials with service provider or consumer to ensure that the session pipe connecting consumer with service provider is authentic, authorized, and managed in a controlled manner.

Enhancement: Smart Cards

Microsoft has approached the use of two-factor authentication ("what I have" and "what I know") by incorporating smart card logon technology into Windows 2000 as an alternative for domain authentication through username and password keyboard entry. This technology is based on both Personal Computer/Smart Card (PC/SC) Workgroup-compliant smart card infrastructure and Rivest-Shamir-Adleman (RSA)-capable smart card devices that support CAPI cryptographic service providers (CSPs). This workgroup promulgates specifications that can be found in the International Organization for Standardization (ISO) original smart card standards, ISO 7810 and 7816. The PC/SC Workgroup initiative, promoted by a consortium of hardware and software manufacturers in this very critical niche industry, proposes to standardize a specification that ensures interoperability across the smart card, the smart card reader, and the software running on various computer platforms that manage smart card-related operations and business transactions. This initiative has garnered worldwide support across many industries. CSPs are covered in more detail later in this section.

Microsoft's Smart Card Business Strategy

Microsoft's approach to smart card interoperability has been to:

➤ Develop a standard model for interface cards and sensing devices like readers.

➤ Develop device-independent software APIs.

➤ Promote software development kits with appropriate tools.

➤ Integrate the technology into the Windows operating system platform.

This business strategy, a direct extension of the PC/SC Workgroup initiative, has fostered interoperability between the manufacturers of cards and card readers and has especially helped simplify the creation of Win32 software APIs.

The OpenCard Framework (OCF) is an object-oriented software framework for smart card access that complements the PC/SC Workgroup initiative on the hardware interfaces. It also integrates standards such as using Public Key Cryptography Standards (PKCS) #11 formats to standardize the exchange of security credentials and provide extension for inclusion of additional devices like hardware tokens to further harden the digital security schemes. Java Card API 2.1, compliant with the ISO 7816 standard, is another example of an object-oriented software specification where the byte code runs on the card itself.

Device-independent APIs insulate code from future hardware changes and reduce software development costs. By coincidence, the development of these APIs also benefits Microsoft; the Windows 2000 architectural structure is designed much like the MMC. Tomorrow's digital security schemes will "snap in" to either SSPI as security support dynamic link libraries (DLLs) or into CAPI as CSPs.

The Windows 2000 implementation of the smart card technology authentication method uses the Microsoft enhancement to PKI, the Public Key Cryptography for Initial Authentication in Kerberos (PKINIT) protocol, which combines the public key authentication method with the Windows 2000 Kerberos protocol. In brief, an attached card reader or sensing device replaces information retrieved during the Secure Attention Sequence (Ctrl+Alt+Del) on a computer-based system with information stored on the card. Depending on the circumstances, you may need to use a personal identification number (PIN) security code to access the stored information. The smart card may also contain a digital certificate and other security credentials.

Smart Card Types

These credit card sized devices, varying greatly in capability, are typically of two types:

➤ *Stored-value cards*—Stored-value cards are considered smart cards, but they are similar in function to the magnetic stripe cards that you use to access most ATM machines; they just hold data. They do not perform complex operations; they simply hold information that is useful in, for example, key exchanges or digital signatures. Capacity varies as a function of their design. You can protect the information on them; before you can use them and access their information, you may need to know a PIN. You can subdivide these cards into those that require card readers to retrieve the stored information and those that are contactless, requiring only proximity to some sensor device.

➤ *Integrated circuit cards (ICCs)*—ICCs can perform tasks that actually facilitate, for example, key exchanges and digital signatures. In fact, they obviate the need for private keys to even be installed on a local computer. Windows 2000 uses the ICC card format.

Microsoft APIs

From the application perspective, three interfaces support different ways to access smart card services:

➤ *CAPI*—This cryptographic API, for the special, installable CSP, exposes the cryptographic features available in the Windows 2000 operating system. For example, a smart card CSP uses exposed symmetric and asymmetric encryption algorithms already installed in the system as the Microsoft Base Provider CSP while performing its own private key operations.

➤ *SCard COM*—This noncryptographic interface provides a library of generic smart card related services written in a variety of programming languages.

➤ *Win32 APIs*—These APIs are the base-level programming interfaces in Windows operating systems that expose system features as well as the hardware-related operations necessary to interface with the card reader and other devices. These APIs also form the protective wrapper that insulates smart card software applications from changes in hardware devices.

There must be at least one CSP for Windows-based applications to access card-based services. CSPs are exclusively software that resides either in the operating system (like the Microsoft Base Provider CSP) or in the cryptographic engine on the ICC. A CSP that resides on a smart card is called a Smart Card Cryptographic Provider (SCCP) to distinguish it from other CSPs. Both SCCPs and CSPs expose and access services through CAPI. Alternatively, Smart Card Service Providers (SCSPs) expose noncryptographic, predefined services that relate to smart card operations. For these services to be accessible through CAPI, you must register them with the operating system. A resource manager, another specific management function, coordinates these registered services and tracks the operations they perform. It is a trusted service that runs as a single process in the operating system. It allocates available resources exposed through the APIs and supports the transactions that actually deliver information to other processes in the operating system.

Smart Card Logons Using Kerberos

Interactive logon means authentication of a user to a network using some shared credentials, such as a hashed password. Windows 2000 has extended the traditional NTLM logon authentication method requesting the entry of a username and password at the Secure Attention Sequence dialog box (Ctrl+Alt+Delete) to include public key interactive logons and two-factor forms of authentication. For example, a smart card is a separate, physical device that contains an X.509 version 3 digital certificate replacing the username portion of the username/password combination typically used in conjunction with legacy logon methods with authenticated security credentials. A password called an access code or PIN releases the credentials on the smart card to some mechanical card reader interface. The authentication method includes not just "what I know" but also "what I have" as a way to harden the security process. Consumers' security credentials and their secret keys are never passed to the client machine; they remain on the card itself. Follow these steps to log on interactively:

1. The smart card is detected by the card reader device that is attached to the operating system running on the local machine.

2. The operating system, through GINA, a Graphical Identification and Authentication interface, prompts for a PIN that validates use of that specific smart card so that its stored security credentials can be released to the card reader.

3. Depending on the contents of the smart card, typically an X.509 version 3 digital certificate is passed to the Local Security Authority (LSA) that is running in the local machine's operating system.

4. The LSA forwards the logon request to the Kerberos client that is running in the operating system on the local machine.

5. The Kerberos client makes a Kerberos Authentication Service Request (KRB_AS_REQ) to the KDC (as discussed in Chapter 4) on some DC. This KRB_AS_REQ includes the X.509 version 3 digital certificate and an authenticator hash, digitally signed with the private key stored on the smart card in its preauthentication data fields.

6. The KDC verifies the digital certificate by tracing the certification path from the digitally signed X.509 version 3 certificate back to possible intermediate CAs to the root CA. It builds this path by using services that the operating system supplies through CAPI. If the KDC can link digital certificates in a valid certificate chain back to the root CA, it can verify that the CA can be trusted and hence that the named principal can be authenticated within the domain namespace.

7. Through CAPI, the KDC accesses services that verify the authenticator in the KRB_AS_REQ. The KDC does this by decrypting the hash using the public key enclosed in the X.509 version 3 certificate, which is now considered valid. Only the holder with the private key could encrypt this hash. The cardholder could not have accessed that private key without entering the correct PIN number into GINA when swiping the original card (in other words, "what I have" on the smart card can be used to encrypt the hash and authenticate me because of "what I know"—specifically, the PIN); hence, the cardholder must be authentic.

8. Upon validating user authenticity, the KDC validates an accompanying timestamp that is part of the authenticator to prevent replay attacks (this is described in detail in Chapter 4).

9. When the KDC validates the authenticity of the request, security credentials are retrieved from AD directory services based on information, such as User Principal Name (UPN), that is stored in the now-validated X.509 version 3 certificate. You use these credentials, including security ID (SID) and group IDs (GIDs), to create the ticket-granting ticket (TGT).

10. The KDC encrypts the TGT with a random key, which it then signs with the cardholder's public key. It includes this random key in a data field in its Kerberos Authentication Service Reply (KRB_AS_REP).

11. The KDC signs the KRB_AS_REP with its private key so the client can verify the KDC's authenticity.

12. The Kerberos client on the local machine, using CAPI-exposed services, verifies the authenticity of the KDC's digital signature by building its own valid certificate chain back to a trusted root CA. Upon validating the digital signature, it uses the CA's public key to verify the KRB_AS_REP.

13. The client, having validated the KRB_AS_REP, now extracts the encrypted random key and decrypts it with its secret key. It uses this random key to decrypt the actual TGT.

14. Upon decrypting the TGT, the client can request services from domain resources.

Smart Card Logons Using SSL/TLS

Client authentication is required when you establish a secure session pipe between a consumer and a service provider across a public network like the Internet. In Web-based, network scenarios, you use a secure protocol such as SSL or TLS with a trusted X.509 version 3 digital certificate to authenticate the client (for example, Internet Explorer) to a server that supports SSL/TLS (like, for example, Internet Information Server [IIS] 5). Hypertext Transfer Protocol (HTTP) is stateless, so the secure session in this scenario requires both the exchange of authenticated public keys to validate parties and the generation of some unique session key to ensure integrity and confidentiality between those parties during the virtual session.

Another smart card logon scenario involves the use of secure email where cardholders carry security credentials with them. Using SSL/TLS network security authentication, security information is independent of both machine and transport protocols. Cardholders can access mail through a smart card enabled client anywhere, anytime, to receive their mail because the smart card stores the PIN-protected private key. This machine-, platform-, and transport protocol-independence is part of the Microsoft business strategy of accessing information technology anywhere at any time and is critical to the future development of both e-commerce and secure multitier architectural design in a distributed services (and server) environment.

Windows 2000, through AD directory services, relies on information contained in a validated digital certificate with possible account name mappings to local accounts to determine the appropriate account records and access rights to domain resources. The following steps outline the client logon procedure:

1. The service provider authenticates an X.509 version 3 digital certificate that a trusted root CA has validated.

2. The service provider then attempts to locate user information in its directory services based upon credentials, such as UPN, included with the authenticated digital certificate.

3. If an account is located, a security context (based upon ACL authorizations listed in the directory services) is established for the account, and requested services are provided through the contacted service provider. Sometimes in this scenario, it is best for the application that is providing the services to define the security context (RBAC) rather than using a DACL based on a specific user or group security account. An example of a scenario that is less secure than RBAC is using an anonymous user or guest account with limited access to a File Transfer Protocol (FTP) directory. The trend toward RBAC (discussed Chapter 9) plays a significant part in Web application development and the extensibility of the enterprise.

 Two-factor authentication methods, especially using smart cards, apply to both distributed and network services. It is important that you understand the business, technical, and security requirements necessary for successful deployment of this security methodology.

Terminal Services Uses

In Chapter 11, Terminal Service Architecture was mentioned as supporting automated changes and providing remote management of user desktop environments from a central location. IntelliMirror, mentioned in that chapter, lowers total cost of ownership (TCO) through its focus on deployment and maintenance. Terminal Services leverages those featured advantages by providing services even on legacy hardware platforms through robust terminal emulation features. Older, less efficient hardware can now support the running of application software in a session actually run on a more powerful server platform at some remote location. In effect, this session provides a "window" through which services are accessed, but not performed, on the client machine. There is a parallel here with the RBAC discussed in Chapter 9. Where RBAC creates a security context based on the requirements of a software application, Terminal Services provides a controlled server session that can be configured to the specific needs of a user or group.

Prior to Windows 2000, Terminal Services was available but required an additional purchase of software. All versions of Windows 2000 include this service as part of the core operating system. A Terminal Services connection, Remote Desktop Protocol running on TCP (RDP-TCP), is the session pipe (or link) a remote client uses to log on a server and run a session. From Administrative Tools on a server running Terminal Services, you can right-click on the Connections node from within the Terminal Services Configuration console and configure a wide range of connection properties. Using Terminal Services Configuration console, secure default properties can be configured for all sessions running through that link. To secure a server session, you need to set the amount of time active sessions can run, user and group permissions, and levels for protection involving encryption. Security can be set on a per-user basis when the Terminal Services extension to Local Users and Groups is used. You can also configure the Terminal Server settings specifically in the use of temporary folders, default connection security, and licensing for an Internet Connection.

RIS

One of the management features IntelliMirror provides in Windows 2000 is the ability to install the Windows 2000 Professional operating system on any number of remote clients. This technology secures access to enterprise resources by standardizing a user's desktop environment and remotely providing a predetermined, customized configuration from some centralized point of distribution without increasing TCO. However, this powerful feature is demanding in terms of planning, hardware requirements, and procedural steps. RIS depends on several Windows 2000 services, especially AD, but also Windows 2000 Domain Name Service (DNS) and DHCP. RIS will remotely install Windows Professional operating systems configured with customized parameters that are stored in AD. Based on IntelliMirror technology, installation pushes the installation to the client system when triggered by a user logon. An automatic setup feature automates the entire process but can be modified by the AD's default domain account GPO so that additional system options are possible.

Requirements

Because the installation delivers disk images over the network, one limitation to RIS is that the booting installation image can typically be applied only to clients with the same platform hardware and configuration. Exceptions to this rule use a command-line utility called riprep.exe. RIS will currently install only on single partitioned disks, and require that both source and target hardware have the same version of the Windows 2000 hardware abstraction layer (HAL). The clients, in general, need bootable network adapters or a special boot floppy that is scripted to map to the RIS server and launch the installation of the system image. The RIS boot diskette first requests an IP address from some local DHCP server. It then looks for an operating system using preboot execution environment (PXE) remote boot technology, an Intel Specification for remote OS booting that is embedded in the network adapter ROM. This PXE boot ROM needs to be version .99c or higher to support the RIS installation. Furthermore, RIS supports only Windows 2000 Professional; you cannot install Window 2000 Server remotely.

Once the client boots, it accesses an operating system image stored on the RIS Server. According to Microsoft specifications, these RIS servers must be dedicated Windows 2000 Servers with the installation images stored on a volume that is separate from the system volume. Microsoft recommends that because the workload characterization of a RIS server is high, the distribution volume should be a dedicated SCSI (Small Computer System Interface) disk drive. Another design consideration is to dedicate the same physical server to both the RIS and DHCP services.

RIS manages the providing of installation services through the use of one of the following mechanisms:

➤ *Prestaging*—Entries in the AD can specify a certain RIS server for a particular client or group. RIS servers receiving requests for the installation of images validate requests based on a group security ID (GUID) against these AD entries.

➤ *Server referring*—If a RIS server receives an authenticated service request for an image but is not the authorized server to deliver the image, it will forward the service request to the appropriate RIS server.

RIS is an unsecured service vulnerable to both passive interception and impersonation attack modalities like eavesdropping and address spoofing, respectively. Furthermore, the PXE support is available for other operating systems; this support has no way of determining which server to respond to. It is crucial that you use both prestaging and carefully planned network segmentation to manage not only the PXE support but also DHCP and RIS responses to client boot-up requests. You must include other forms of network security to ensure uncompromised software installations, and management systems like SNMP to ensure that support systems are operational.

SNMP

SNMP is a management specification defined by RFCs 1155, 1157, and 1213. The service supports both TCP/IP and IPX protocols and is optionally installed as a service after TCP/IP to provide centralized management of computers through a remotely installed agent. Management software, not included with any version of the Microsoft family of operating systems, must be running on a host machine

for information to be configured or collected. To take advantage of the simplification in network management, third-party software, including simple CLI
utilities like snmputil.exe, is readily available and is, at times, useful. In brief,
management software (also called a management console) exchanges information with an SNMP agent (specialized software running on a client machine).
Communication is restricted to members within a predetermined community for
administrative and security purposes. Each agent and management console has a
community list that requires a minimum of one named community. "Public" is a
universally accepted community name.

The agents can monitor specific services on a remote machine such as DHCP or
Windows Internet Naming Service (WINS). The agent can be configured to
respond to or trap specific data events associated with one of these services occurring on that client machine. Trapped events trigger an alarm message that the
agent sends back to its management host. An SNMP agent can communicate
only when a trap message is triggered and only with a management host in one of
its listed communities. If an agent receives a request from a community not on its
list, SNMP agents will generate an authentication trap and send it to a specific
trap destination.

SNMP provides security through these community names and authentication
traps. Permission levels determine an agent's response to a request by a host in an
authenticated community. Thus, an agent can accept SNMP packets from any
host or only specifically selected hosts. Regarding best practices, Microsoft recommends that the SNMP communities be organized in some functional way
that reflects the pattern of distributed services in that particular enterprise. SNMP
can be used to monitor the operation of support services necessary to keep user
access to enterprise services and resources running in an optimal manner.

SMB Signing

Another method used to secure access across the session pipe involves the Server
Message Block (SMB) file and print protocol. SMB, functioning at the OSI
Application layer, is relevant when integrating legacy NT 4 Workstations or
Windows 2000 Professional with, for example, NetWare Servers (discussed in
the next section). SMB servers, called SAMBA servers, provide similar access to
Unix users.

In brief, SMB protocol historically accessed several types of server services: the
original LAN Manager servers jointly developed by Microsoft and IBM, IBM's
second-generation LAN servers, and legacy NT 4 servers. In Windows 2000,
SMB provides a security substrate for the secure transmission of files between
client and service provider at the Application layer above where SSL/TLS operates. Thus, along with other Application layer security protocols like S-HTTP,

which is used in the exchange of Web-based documents (web pages), SMB signing can complement SChannel security protocols and also provide message authentication and mutual authentication of client and server. When configuring SMB signing, both client and server must be properly configured and have appropriate GPO settings. This form of security is available on both Windows 2000 clients and legacy NT 4 clients (where Service Pack 3 or later has been applied to the operating system). Servers can request SMB signing from Windows clients.

OS Migration vs. Coexistence

Interoperability is a major historical theme driving all IT cultures toward some future point of convergence under the umbrella of a unified directory-based namescape. Microsoft would like the hub of that namescape to be AD directory services. Alternatively, Novell provides Novell Directory Services (NDS). Both network operating system cultures compete for the dominant position. Other cultures, like Macintosh, have through a kind of quasi-selective adaptation found a special niche. Unix, from its inception, has been open, scalable, collaborative, and a technological melting pot. The topic of interoperability is really a business issue and a question of dominance in the IT universe.

Microsoft, on the one hand, does not want to coexist with its desktop competitor Novell. Nevertheless, it must offer IT consumers who use the Novell operating system utilities that bridge the two cultures or, preferably, help migrate them to the Microsoft platform. Macintosh has grown into a niche operating system; it is neither friend nor foe to Microsoft. Hence, Microsoft has provided a means to reliably share resources at no great cost to members of either culture. Finally, Unix, historically uncommon among personal computer users, is nevertheless a giant source of resources, users, and investment capital. Migration paths, though robust and reliable, are only now being considered. In general, Microsoft is still not ready to assert itself in the mini and mainframe computer worlds in which non-Microsoft network operating systems rule and therefore seeks a strategy of growing coexistence, especially with the largest culture, the Unix network operating system.

Interoperability/Migration: NetWare

Microsoft has provided interoperability services—including primarily Client Service for NetWare (CSNW) and Gateway Service for NetWare (GSNW)—that directly interface with its family of NOSs. Both add-ons, especially GSNW, have been designed for occasional and convenient access, not true interoperability and coexistence. These add-ons are designed to function primarily as a segue leading from NetWare-based resources to the Microsoft platform.

Briefly, Microsoft and Novell use different protocols to request services from a server; SMB and NetWare Core Protocol (NCP), respectively. These two protocols are incompatible. To bridge server communications between the two NOSs, you need to either install multiple protocol stacks as client interfaces (CSNW) on all clients, or you need to create one central distribution service provider or gateway (GSNW). CSNW and GSNW automatically install NWLink, the NT/Windows 2000 IPX/SPX/NetBIOS compatible transport protocol necessary to communicate with legacy NetWare platforms (NetWare 2.x to 4.x) as well as NDS and older bindery-based directory information. In a NetWare 5 environment, which, in terms of the two NOS families, is comparable to Windows 2000, the default transport protocol is TCP/IP; CSNW, using exclusively IPX/SPX and NetBEUI, is of little value. CSNW provides the redirector services Windows users need to access NetWare-based file and print resources. This redirection involves the translating from Microsoft's SMB file and print protocol to Novell's NetWare Core Protocol (NCP). From the Novell side, you must install two clients: the NetWare client interface, which understands NCP, and the Microsoft Client interface, which understands the SMB protocol.

Services for NetWare version 5 (SFN5), though similarly designed to encourage users to migrate to Windows 2000, provides a new set of interoperability services and utilities for integrating Windows 2000 platforms into existing NetWare 5 environments. SFN5 also offers older interoperability tools for legacy NT 4 platforms. SFN5 reduces network administration in a mixed platform environment with:

➤ Microsoft Directory Synchronization Services (MSDSS)

➤ File Migration Utility (FMU)

➤ File and Print Services for NetWare version 5 (FPNW5)

Although migration includes conversion of principal and group accounts as well as the access management of resources, specific password assignments, software application configuration, Novell's login scripting, management of Macintosh namespace, and inconsistencies in schema definition and extensions between NDS and AD must be manually modified to conform with Windows 2000 specifications. For a general discussion of issues involving the resolution of inconsistencies in data definitions between directory services, refer to the "Brokerage" section earlier in this chapter. The synchronization of configuration and directory information is stored in the AD service. Access to this AD area is restricted to only authorized administrators in a default MSDSS Admins local security group, specifically responsible for setting up, administering, and monitoring the synchronization process.

MSDSS

MSDSS synchronizes AD datastores with both NDS and NetWare version 3 binderies using Windows 2000 Server. According to Microsoft, MSDSS provides a directory interoperability solution by supporting two-way synchronization with NDS and one-way synchronization with NetWare binderies on a near realtime basis. You can manage principal accounts from either directory service. However, there are differences in how you use the administrative tools and how you deploy directory services. For example, account changes administered through NDS force a two-way synchronization of the entire object between directory services. In comparison, a one-way replication (and a reduction in network traffic) occurs when AD is the point of directory administration because only the object's attribute is changed.

Microsoft suggests that you deploy AD in a NetWare environment without replacing existing directories. MSDSS reduces directory management by:

➤ Providing centralized administration of identity management

➤ Maintaining data integrity across multiple directory services

➤ Synchronizing datastores with different data schema

➤ Providing SSO

FMU

FMU is a migration tool that encourages the migration of resources from NetWare-based servers to Windows 2000. This wizard-based migration-management interface is integrated with MSDSS and preserves file-access control information and security permissions from loss during the migration process.

FPNW5

FPNW5 provides a NetWare interface and SSO to NetWare users by having Windows 2000 servers emulate the Novell file and print services. This particular product greatly impacts TCO because Novell users do not experience any change in their work environment even though the Windows 2000 operating system is providing the actual services. There is no need for training, nor are there issues of noncompliance that result, in part, from user prejudice or frustration.

Interoperability/Migration: Unix

Unlike Novell, which is considered Microsoft's primary competitor in the desktop NOS market, Unix and its dialects has supported mainframe and minicomputer network environments for decades. Microsoft provides many features in legacy NT 4 systems and Windows 2000. Standards-based protocols, as well as new utilities supplied by Interix, foster true interoperability and coexistence specifically between these two operating system cultures. The inclusion of the Portable Operating System Interface (POSIX) in legacy NT 4 and now Interix, a Windows 2000/Unix interoperability product, clearly shows that Microsoft intends for clients of both NOSs to easily and effectively cross-communicate between different file systems without serious performance penalties. Through Interix, Microsoft also provides a cost-effective migration path for Unix-based proprietary software applications.

Services for Unix 2 (SFU2)

SFU2 fosters true interoperability and coexistence between Windows 2000 and Unix, especially through Sun Microsystems' Network File System (NFS) protocol (RFC 1813). The NFS protocol, which is designed to be independent of machine, operating system, and transport protocols, uses remote procedure calls (RPCs). It is also significant that Windows supported POSIX in the legacy NT architecture. POSIX is an Institute of Electrical and Electronic Engineers (IEEE) standard that facilitates the translation or porting of services from one operating system to another. Windows 2000 uses the POSIX.1-compliant subsystem, which supports case sensitivity, multiple file names, and application execution in protected memory space. Unlike the situation with Novell, where available products are primarily for migration, both NFS and POSIX, in combination with SFU2, are the true sources for interoperability between Windows 2000 and Unix.

Network Resources

Enterprise resources on Windows 2000 and Unix can coexist with a variety of client and gateway services, such as:

➤ *Client for NFS*—Provides Windows-based clients access to NFS server resources

➤ *Server for NFS*—Provides NFS clients access to Windows NT and 2000 server resources

➤ *Gateway for NFS*—Provides any Windows-based client access to an NFS resource without SFU2

➤ *Server for PCNFS*—Provides NFS user authentication for NFS resources on Windows NT- or 2000-based servers that act as specially assigned servers (through Server for PCNFS services, accessed through the Services for Unix Microsoft Management Console—MMC)

In addition, Microsoft now offers Interix 2.2 as a migration path for Unix applications and scripts to Windows NT/2000. This operating environment, developed by Softway Systems, Inc. and formerly called OPENNT, provides more than 300 utilities and tools that function like their Unix counterparts. Interix 2.2 is not an emulation product like the Mortice Kern Systems (MKS) Toolkit, another Unix utility suite that runs on the non-Unix operating systems discussed in the "Programming Shells as User Interfaces" section later in this chapter; performance of Unix-based legacy applications and scripts will not suffer. It is a complete replacement for the standard Microsoft POSIX subsystem, which contains enhancements, including scripting languages, sockets, interprocess communication, and other features. Interix functions like a peer to the Win32 subsystem and provides both APIs and services that you need to run the legacy Unix system applications. In fact, its software development kit supports more than 1,900 Unix APIs to facilitate migration. Interix provides these Unix legacy applications a single enterprise operating environment that is fully integrated with Windows 2000 services, security, and file system access.

Identity Management

Although Sun Microsystems' Network Information System (NIS), formerly known as the Yellow Pages, is not an Internet standard, it is a common distributed database system that allows you to share system information in Unix-based environments. It employs a client/server model of database information much like Domain Name System (DNS). SFU2 includes an NIS Migration Wizard, which migrates an existing NIS namespace to the AD on a Windows 2000 server. A DC that runs Server for NIS services emulates an NIS master server and maintains database "maps" of system information, such as passwords and host names. Other SFU2 tools include:

➤ *Password synchronization*—This is a two-way utility that synchronizes password changes across Windows NT/2000 and Unix directory services. SFU2 includes SSO daemons (SSODs) provided in both a precompiled form and as source code and complementary make files that run on Unix servers to support the password changes. In addition, a Password Authentication Mapper (PAM), which passes changes back to the Windows NT/2000 directory services, must run on the Unix server. Password synchronization does not include providing an SSO between Unix and Windows NT/2000, nor does it provide for application passwords. It does not provide for a common authentication scheme between the two systems, though native mode Windows 2000 does default to the Kerberos protocol. The Windows-to-Unix synchronization is provided by default; Unix-to-Windows synchronization is optional. Password changes use both Transmission Control Protocol/Internet Protocol (TCP/IP) sockets and triple Data Encryption Standard (3DES) for encryption and decryption. Password synchronization does not require special installation or additional overhead because it uses standard network and security technologies.

➤ *User name mapping*—This tool bridges differences between the two directory datastores. It can create simple one-to-one maps between principals, as well as bidirectional one-to-many mappings, where you can map a single Unix or Windows NT/2000 principal to multiple accounts in the other directory datastore. For example, you can easily map different Windows NT/2000 administrative accounts to the Unix root account.

Programming Shells as User Interfaces

SFU2 provides a subset of the MKS Toolkit, which has been a very important tool for users of DOS, Windows, and NT operating systems for many years. This toolkit offers a selection of the most common Unix utilities that end users and administrator use, along with a robust implementation of the Korn Shell, a popular Unix programming shell (operating environment). These tools leverage Unix users' knowledge by providing them with the same interface and the same command-line syntax to which they have grown accustomed while working entirely on a Windows-based platform.

Network Administration

Administration tools, which simplify and enhance management, include:

➤ *Telnet server and client*—This client/host combination provides character mode support, which is faster and more robust than the default graphical mode provided in Windows NT. Windows 2000 uses this newer Telnet client. The Telnet server exclusively supports NTLM authentication for client authentication to provide seamless operation without exposing cleartext passwords across the network. However, for authentication to occur, you must support NTLM on both sides of the connection. The Windows 2000 Telnet client supports NTLM. Using this security protocol, however, effectively prevents Kerberized Unix users from accessing Windows NT/2000 servers because they do not have a client that supports this security protocol.

➤ *MMC snap-in*—SFU2 provides a single MMC for all SFU2 services and tools except Gateway for NFS. SFU is compatible with Windows Management Instrumentation (WMI), so you can script management functions from the CLI.

➤ *ActivePerl 5.6*—SFU2 includes ActivePerl 5.6, ActiveState's version of Perl (Practical Extraction and Report Language) 5.6, and Perl Script for Windows NT/2000. This implementation of Perl supports Windows Scripting Host (WSH) for the scripted automation of many administrative system functions.

Interoperability/Migration: Apple Macintosh

Similar to Unix, Macintosh and the Apple OS have not historically been perceived by Microsoft as a true competitor for market share among networked users on the desktop personal computer. The Microsoft strategy with regard to Macintosh is one of mutual coexistence. Besides supporting interoperability with legacy NT operating systems, Windows 2000 continues to support interoperability with Macintosh through File Server for Macintosh (MacFile), an AppleTalk network integration service. AppleTalk network integration (formerly called Services for Macintosh) is a software component of Windows 2000 Server that allows users of both platforms to share enterprise resources. File Services for Macintosh, the Windows 2000 server component that provides Macintosh users with Windows 2000 server access, uses extension-type associations to display Intel-based files with correct icons when viewed through Macintosh Finder. When you install File Services for Macintosh, Windows 2000 creates a directory called the Microsoft User Authentication Module (UAM) volume on an available NT File System (NTFS) partition. Under the Computer Management console tree, you can open Shared Folders to view and manage the properties of the Microsoft UAM volume. Although most applications have cross-platform versions for both Macintosh- and Intel-based clients, both versions can modify the same files stored on this volume. When the UAM volume is mounted on their desktops, Macintosh clients can securely log on and access resources exclusively in this space.

Network Resources

A Windows 2000 server with AppleTalk network integration provides resources to both Intel-based and Macintosh users. Intel-based users see shared files in a shared folder, whereas Macintosh users see the folder as a volume. To use these resources, Macintosh users can mount a Macintosh-accessible volume on their desktop. All Macintosh-accessible volumes must be on an NTFS partition or on a Compact Disc File System (CDFS) volume. Windows 2000 allows you to create and share other Macintosh-accessible volumes in addition to the UAM volume. The four permission levels for a shared volume, as listed in the Create Shared Folder Wizard dialog box, are:

➤ All users have Full Control.

➤ Administrators have Full Control; other users have Read Only access.

➤ Administrators have Full Control; other users have No Access.

➤ Share and folder permissions can be customized to allow Full Control, Change, and Read.

In addition, Print Server for Macintosh (MacPrint) enables Macintosh clients to send and spool documents on Windows 2000 print servers and, similarly, Intel-based clients to send print jobs to any printer on the AppleTalk network. When Print Services for Macintosh is installed, it automatically installs AppleTalk protocol if it is not already present in the protocol stack.

Identity Management

Authentication is an AppleShare extension that provides secure logon sessions to a Windows 2000 server from a Macintosh client. Passwords are encrypted and stored on the Windows 2000 server. Therefore, to ensure correct authentication, Macintosh users must specify the domain when they log on. They optionally log on to the Microsoft UAM version 5 volume, which requires either an AppleShare client 3.8 or greater, or Mac OS 8.5 or greater. AppleTalk network integration provides an level of authentication in addition to Windows 2000 logon authentication within the Microsoft UAM Volume property sheet, with the use of an optional Macintosh-accessible volume password. This case-sensitive password, required when you are accessing the resource as a Macintosh user, is assigned to the volume when you configure it. Intel-based users do not encounter this additional logon restriction.

Access Management

Access control to Macintosh-accessible volumes, the equivalent of a shared folder for an Intel-based user, is the same as it is for Intel-based machines. Macintosh files, however, inherit permissions that are set on their container folders; they do not carry permissions directly.

Extensibility: COM+

If AD develops into a consolidated meta-directory, it rests on top of a NOS, providing the key "primitive" common information management services of configuration, performance, fault management, and auditability. A component-based Windows 2000 NOS using DNA specifications could spawn components throughout some future universal namescape that extends across other NOSs like Novell and UNIX. Each component would call back to the Windows 2000 AD directory services for identity and security information.

Microsoft proposed a software model in 1993 that described this event in terms of a Component Object Model. A server component provides a service to a consumer that is, in fact, distributed throughout the domain namespace as separate, specialized support service components. A transaction server manages all these distributed service components and tells the primary server when all the components are successfully completed; the primary service provider then delivers the service.

The entire Windows 2000 operating system architecture is based upon the inter-dependent software components of the Component Object Model. Consumers and clients at all levels of the OSI model access services provided by COM objects, which are a combination of both data and methods of manipulating that data. The operational methods that a component object possesses are grouped into standardized interfaces that totally encapsulate the data defined within the object itself. These interfaces are independent of any one programming language and thus provide services on theoretically any operating system platform. Distributed COM, first released in 1996 as an extension of COM, did not change the fundamentals of the model, only the distance between calls for service between a consumer and service provider, referred to as remote procedure calls (RPCs).

Windows 2000 enhances COM by integrating the previously separate Transaction Server services and the transaction services security model into each individual component; hence, the current version of the model is called COM+. The service-providing server components are now more feature-laden than the older COM components regarding support for transactions, client authorization, and management of their own state. In addition, Windows 2000 distributed COM+ objects are faster because they use TCP as their transport protocol, as compared to the slower UDP protocol legacy COM components communicated with. The security relating to client authorization and issues of integrity and confidentiality are not dictated by the COM server component; COM applications use either Kerberos or NTLM protocols. Details of the COM+ model pertain more to programming and are outside the scope of this book. However, the way COM+ and Microsoft Message Queue Services (MSMQ) handle these security issues, especially in a distributed services environment, needs to be understood, at least in general terms.

Distributed Services

From online service hosting to high-volume transaction processing, Windows 2000 provides a platform for component-based application development. These components achieve high degrees of reliability and manageability because they are tightly integrated with the many services that the Windows 2000 operating system provides. The layered structure of the NOS protects investments in application development. An example of this protection is in the business strategy involved in the development of smart cards mentioned in the "Enhancement: Smart Cards" section earlier in this chapter. Windows 2000 provides the following key services that provide the foundation for both distributed and networked services on which business scenarios (and examination case studies) will be built in the future:

➤ COM and COM+

➤ IIS 5

➤ MSMQ message queuing

COM

When a consumer requests services from a "primary" service provider, these services sometimes require other support services. The primary server (service provider), through delegation of authority (discussed in Chapter 4), can request additional support services on behalf of the consumer from remote service providers. These requests form a chain of dependencies that determine whether or not the primary server provides the requested service to the consumer. These mutually dependent support service requests are called *transactions*. The success or failure of a transaction depends upon the successful completion of all support service requests. In the simplest case, the primary server provides the requested services and the transaction between the two parties is completed. In the common e-commerce scenario, the consumer makes a request to a Web server that authenticates the client, establishes the session, and presents the consumer with scripted questions. Answers to the questions are processed according to predefined business rules and executed. Processing the information, no matter how many separate service components are involved, is considered one transaction.

IIS 5

Developers can easily build and run Web-based scripts that combine HTML, scripts, and procedure calls to COM+ objects. IIS 5 goes beyond providing the simple Web services of its predecessors by providing developers with an extensible environment that fosters rapid development of these scripts based on powerful technologies like Active Server Pages (ASP). ASP scripts integrate with other component-based software applications because ASP itself is a COM+ application. The real power of this scripting, however, lies in its manageability; developers control how scripts are processed (process isolation), where scripts are processed (through Windows Load Balancing Services—WLBS), and which scripts are processed as single, smart transactional units.

MSMQ

MSMQ fundamentally provides communication services between distributed COM+ server components. Queued components let server components logically participate in transactions whether they are online, unavailable, or offline; messages are stored in queues until you retrieve them. In other words, server components can send asynchronous messages to other COM+ components and continue processing without waiting for a response. MSMQ, when requested, journalizes these messages and automatically notifies components whether messages were received.

MSMQ digitally signs and encrypts messages that are transferred across the network. You can request authentication on a per message basis by including in a message the message sender's X.509 digital certificate and digital signature. Thus,

MSMQ provides authentication and integrity controls by using CAPI and an appropriate CSP. In fact, MSMQ provides the same security services among COM+ server components that are provided to consumers and client machines. MSMQ reduces dependency on synchronization requirements among COM+ server components, so greater interoperability can occur across different software architectures. Finally, all the MSMQ features are independent of network protocols; COM+ server components can send messages based on the name of another application's request queue regardless of the network on which it runs.

Security and RBAC

COM+ server objects, at the component level, provide the same security services as consumer and service provider information exchanges at the intranet, Internet, and extranet levels—namely, authentication, integrity, confidentiality, and authorization. Although authentication, integrity, and confidentiality are functions primarily of PKI, COM+ authorization depends on access controls and permission management. The COM+ runtime engine uses RBAC to provide security within the application (see the discussion of RBAC in Chapter 9). You can set role-based authorization at various application levels, including the server object level.

Practice Questions

Case Study

4Sale, an online bartering company in ThatTherePlace, North Dakota, focuses primarily on selling inexpensive, odd-lot items.

Current LAN/Network Structure

4Sale is presently running Windows 2000 Server in native mode; one member server supports Exchange 5.5, whereas another is running IIS 5 and Proxy Server 2. All 100 client machines are configured in a single-domain model. The client systems are all running Windows 2000 Professional, with Office 2000 being utilized as an applications package. Each system is connected to a 10Mbps hub through 10Mbps local area network (LAN) cards running Category 5 Unshielded Twisted Pair (UTP) cabling in a star topology.

Proposed LAN/Network Structure

No changes are planned at this time.

Current WAN Connectivity

No changes are planned at this time.

Proposed WAN Connectivity

No changes are planned at this time.

Directory Design Commentary

No changes are planned at this time.

Current Internet Positioning

No changes are planned at this time.

Future Internet Plans

No changes are planned at this time.

Company Goal with Windows 2000

4Sale plans to install smart cards at some workstations. The management is also contemplating a merger with another Internet company that has about 45 people on a Novell 5 network.

Question 1

> Considering the case study, what issue might be a major concern when you are installing smart cards? [Check all correct answers]
>
> ❑ a. Device specification
>
> ❑ b. Software specification
>
> ❑ c. User account information
>
> ❑ d. Operating system

Answers a and b are correct. Although Microsoft supports the major specification initiatives, there is still no specific standard among hardware and software manufacturers regarding smart card hardware and software integration. The PC/SC Workgroup is an initiative that is gaining international support but is not a recognized standard. Smart card installation raises no real issues with user account information or operating system because 4Sale is using Windows 2000, which provides PKINIT support. Therefore, answers c and d are incorrect.

Question 2

> The Network Manager at 4Sale asks, "If we were to merge with a company running Novell, what could we use to help keep both directory services talking to each other by having the systems run independently?"
>
> ○ a. MSDSS
>
> ○ b. MDSS
>
> ○ c. FMU
>
> ○ d. FPNW5

Answer a is correct. MSDSS (Microsoft Directory Synchronization Services) synchronizes Active Directory datastores with Novell Directory Services. Answer b is incorrect because there is no Microsoft product called MDSS that relates to Novell NetWare. Answer c is incorrect because FMU (File Migration Utility) is a migration tool. Answer d is incorrect because FPNW5 (File and Print Services for NetWare version 5) provides a NetWare interface and Single Sign-On for Novell users who are running on Windows 2000.

Question 3

> The Network Manager at 4Sale asks, "How can we port Unix applications to our NT system?"
> [Choose the best answer]
>
> ○ a. Interix
>
> ○ b. Enterix
>
> ○ c. Imterix
>
> ○ d. None of the above

Answer a is correct. Interix 2.2 is the preferred migration path from Unix to Windows 2000. Answers b and c are incorrect because there are no such companies that offer Unix-to-Windows migration tools.

Question 4

> The Network Manager at 4Sale asks, "How does Kerberos authenticate using smart cards?" Place the following in the proper order to indicate how authentication occurs. Start with the card reader detecting the smart card.
>
> The card reader device detects the smart card, and then Graphical Identification and Authentication prompts for a personal identification number.
>
> The Key Distribution Center encrypts the ticket-granting ticket with a random key and signs the Kerberos Authentication Service (AS) Reply with its own private key.
>
> The Kerberos client makes a Kerberos Authentication Service (AS) Request.
>
> The Local Security Authority forwards the logon request to the Kerberos client.
>
> The client can request services from domain resources.
>
> The client extracts the encrypted random key and decrypts the ticket-granting ticket.
>
> The Key Distribution Center verifies the digital certificate and authenticator.

The correct order is:

> The card reader device detects the smart card, and then Graphical Identification and Authentication prompts for a personal identification number.
>
> The Local Security Authority forwards the logon request to the Kerberos client.
>
> The Kerberos client makes a Kerberos Authentication Service (AS) Request.

The Key Distribution Center verifies the digital certificate and authenticator.

The Key Distribution Center encrypts the ticket-granting ticket with a random key and signs the Kerberos Authentication Service (AS) Reply with its own private key.

The client extracts the encrypted random key and decrypts the ticket-granting ticket.

The client can request services from domain resources.

Question 5

The Network Manager at 4Sale says, "FMU will keep our Novell people happy." Is the statement true or false?

○ a. True

○ b. False

Answer b, false, is correct. The Network Manager is incorrect. FMU (File Migration Utility) is primarily a migration tool. It is doubtful the Novell people are looking forward to a network migration. The tool that would make the Novell people happy is File and Print Services for NetWare version 5, which provides a NetWare interface and Single Sign-On for NetWare users running on Windows 2000.

Question 6

The Network Manager at 4Sale says, "UAM is the only Macintosh-accessible volume we can configure on a Windows 2000 Server." Is the statement true or false?

○ a. True

○ b. False

Answer b, false, is correct. The Network Manager is incorrect. The UAM (User Authentication Module) is created when you install File Services for Macintosh. You can, however, install additional shares that Macintosh users can access as volumes.

Need to Know More?

 McLean, Ian. *Windows 2000 Security Little Black Book*. The Coriolis Group, Scottsdale, AZ, 2000. ISBN 1-57610-387-0. In Chapter 9, the author discusses smart card installation and how smart cards affect interactive logon and client authentication using SSL/TLS protocols.

 Nielsen, Morten Strunge. *Windows 2000 Professional Advanced Configuration and Implementation*. The Coriolis Group, Scottsdale, AZ, 2000. ISBN 1-57610-528-8. Chapter 19 discusses Microsoft's integration and migration strategy, the importance of providing SSO across platforms, and coexistence issues for Windows and the most popular operating systems—Novell, Macintosh, Unix, and Systems Network Architecture (SNA).

 Nielsen, Morten Strunge. *Windows 2000 Server Architecture and Planning*. The Coriolis Group, Scottsdale, AZ, 1999. ISBN 1-57610-436-2. In Chapter 19, the author clearly and concisely discusses current support for migration to Windows 2000 from Novell and Unix.

 Shinder, Thomas W. and D. Lynn White. *Configuring Windows 2000 Server Security*. Syngress Media, Inc., Rockland, MD, 2000. ISBN 1-928994-02-4. In Chapter 8, the authors describe the history of ISO 7816 and the PC/SC Workgroup initiative. They then discuss various APIs, types of cards, and smart card installation and logon procedures.

 Search the TechNet CD (or its online version through **www.microsoft.com**) and the *Windows 2000 Server Resource Kit* CD using the keywords "MMS", "CAPI", "SFN", "MSDSS", and "SFU". This is Microsoft's definitive online resource for technical papers and bulletins.

 **www.interix.com** The Interix Web site provides details about the company and its Unix migration products.

 **www.iso.ch/search.html** This site offers the ISO search engine, which is provided as part of the ISO's Web site, ISO Online. This is an excellent site to use when you are researching ISO standards.

www.microsoft.com/windows2000/guide/server/solutions/EIM.asp
Here, you will find *Enterprise Identity Management within the Digital Nervous System*, originally posted in July 1999. This Windows 2000 White Paper provides a framework and discussion about managing identity data, the advantages of AD and the digital nervous system, and the functional architecture that supports business relationships and internal business processes.

 **www.microsoft.com/windows2000/library/howitworks/ activedirectory/adinterface.asp** Here, you will find *Active Directory Service Interfaces*, originally posted in April 1999. This Windows 2000 White Paper outlines how Microsoft integrates multiple directory services through ADSI.

 **www.microsoft.com/windows2000/library/resources/reskit/ samplechapters/dsec/dsec_pol_blsa.asp** At this site, you can find topics related to the Group Policy chapter of the *Windows 2000 Resource Kit*. This particular section discusses Group Policy processing orders.

 **www.microsoft.com/windows2000/sfu/sfu2wp.asp** This site offers the *General Services for Unix version 2.0 White Paper*, originally posted in March 2000. This Microsoft White Paper discusses interoperability and management using SFU2.

 **www.pcscworkgroup.com** The PC/SC Workgroup Web site provides technical specifications, including PC/SC Version 1 specifications, compatible products, and other information relating to smart card technologies.

Sample Test

Case Study 1

4Sale, an online bartering and auction company in ThatTherePlace North Dakota, focuses primarily on selling inexpensive, odd-lot items. 4Sale provides customized front-end client application software to its online customers. It uses its Web site to distribute this software. The 4Sale client connects directly with the 4Sale Web site and provides an Internet customer with realtime lists of available items, research material about an item and its history, and a screen with which to bid for the item during online auctions. Due to the nature of this online auction business, all internal and Internet email correspondence is digitally signed.

4Sale has merged forces with a smaller company, Got-a-Deal, which rents space in the same office building. Got-A-Deal is an online association of international brokers of all kinds of retail and wholesale merchandise. This brokers association is looking for an e-commerce company that can provide a centralized marketplace for its odd lot goods. There is no formal set of corporate business objectives or a formal security policy.

Current LAN/Network Structure

4Sale is currently running NT Server 4 on three machines:

➤ A primary domain controller (PDC)

➤ A backup domain controller (BDC) that serves as the Exchange Server 5.5

➤ A member server that is running Internet Information Server 4 and Proxy Server 2

All 100 client machines are configured in a single-domain model. The client systems are running Windows NT Workstation 4, with Office 2000 being utilized as an applications package. Each system is connected to a 10Mbps hub through 10Mbps local area network (LAN) cards running Category 5 Unshielded Twisted Pair (UTP) cabling in a star topology.

The corporate side of the merger between 4Sale and Got-A-Deal has gone well, but the network infrastructure is under construction. Got-a-Deal is undergoing changes to upgrade from its Ethernet bus topology, which uses coaxial cabling, to a more modern configuration. Got-a-Deal is using an NT server in a 22-person workgroup configuration as a file and print server. The network is stable but does not provide scalability.

Proposed LAN/Network Structure

4Sale will use native mode Windows 2000 and develop its online barter/trading business. Some of the security features would help leverage development of its e-commerce plans and future corporate goals. In addition, 4Sale would like to improve the network's speed by implementing newer cards and hubs that support 100Mbps.

Got-a-Deal would also like to upgrade to Windows 2000 under a domain arrangement but has concerns regarding performance, deployment costs, maintenance, and training. The company will be hiring an in-house network engineer to be part of a newly formulated information technology (IT) team that administers the resources of both companies. Got-a-Deal needs a faster network infrastructure in place within the next two months. It will depend on 4Sale for most of its network services.

Current WAN Connectivity

4Sale has a T1 connection to its Internet Service Provider (ISP). Got-A-Deal uses dial-up clients and integrated services digital network (ISDN) to connect to its ISP.

Proposed WAN Connectivity

No changes in the current structure are proposed at this time.

Directory Design Commentary

The CEO of 4Sale says, "My first objective is to integrate Got-a-Deal as seamlessly as possible into our daily operational flow. I will instruct the Human Resources Manager to give you a list of security access levels for both 4Sale and Got-a-Deal personnel. At least for this interim period, I want to defer all internal Got-a-Deal issues to my business associate, the Got-a-Deal president. I want you to talk to other people in our organization and compile a strategic corporate plan, organization layout, and IT program. Remember, though, that 4Sale is the parent company."

The President of Got-a-Deal says, "I don't feel very secure about impending changes in how Got-a-Deal will do business. I want to be the only one who sees top-secret material at Got-a-Deal for the next couple of months!"

The Human Resources Manager at 4Sale says, "The cost of training end users and tech people is rising every month. The CEO wants me to maintain a budgetary range for retraining Got-a-Deal personnel. He also wants me to plan for future changes in the company so that with future mergers, we will not have to go through this same process again."

The Network Manager at 4Sale says, "Software upgrades for applications and operating systems, as well as technical support, cost more than the capital investment in equipment. The CEO is very strict about budget ranges and holds me responsible for making the correct strategic decisions in our short-term purchases and long-term capital investment plans. I am also concerned about security issues like secure email and signed documents. The CEO wants the environment to be as secure as possible."

Current Internet Positioning

4Sale uses virtual hosting services and is registered as **4sale.com**. Got-a-Deal has been selling its goods through local companies, pages on other broker Web sites, and through a Web page on the **4sale.com** Web site.

Future Internet Plans

Got-a-Deal will use the **4sale.com** Web site.

Company Goal with Windows 2000

The CEO of 4Sale says, "4Sale has hired you as an outside consultant to manage the network issues involved in the merger of the two companies. I am giving you strict and confidential instructions. I want all control centralized under the 4Sale Network Manager, no matter what people from 4Sale or Got-A-Deal propose to you on an individual basis. I want the transition to run smoothly. To ensure that employee relations remain upbeat and optimistic, you should not publicize our emphasis on centralized control. Over the next year, I plan to grow 4Sale first by building a scalable base, then by extending lines of communication out to organizations with whom we form business alliances, and finally, by acquiring other mature online service companies. We need our IT infrastructure to support these corporate objectives."

The VP of Finance at 4Sale says, "4Sale is expecting 10 percent quarterly growth in its online catalog. It expects larger growth in online business partners acting as field agents. We will need to assimilate companies and their in-house systems as quickly as possible without interrupting any online services. Depending on the financial markets and our capitalization, you need to prepare the IT department for consolidation of several online businesses, each with its own operating system platform, at the same time."

The 4Sale Network Manager says, "Based on our business, our computer systems need to deliver accessibility, accuracy, and confidentiality 24/7. I want to utilize Windows 2000 Active Directory by using its default schema because I don't have much experience with Windows 2000. I also need you to help develop the standards and procedures that our newly formulated IT team will implement."

Question 1.1

Considering the case study provided, what type of domain structure that allows for all relevant concerns would you recommend? [Choose the best answer]

- O a. Two distinct forests with an extended trust connecting them
- O b. An empty root domain with one domain in place and two Organizational Units (OUs), one at 4Sale and one for Got-a-Deal
- O c. One domain with the root **4sale.com**, with a child domain being **gotadeal.4sale.com**
- O d. One domain called **4sale.com** with two OUs, one at 4Sale and one for Got-a-Deal

Question 1.2

Considering the case study provided, place total cost of ownership (TCO) components in descending order of importance. Choose only the appropriate answers and list the most expensive component first.

Cost of system upgrades

System maintenance

Cost of hardware and software

Cost of disposables

Technical support

User training

Question 1.3

Based on the case study provided, 4Sale provides internal messaging, accounting, data storage, and network support to its client base. These are the only business services you need to provide with primary support.

- ○ a. True
- ○ b. False

Question 1.4

Considering the case study provided and the conclusions you reached in Question 1.3, choose only the appropriate IT security objectives from the list below and order them in descending order of importance.

Confidentiality

Training

Firewall technology

Software authentication

Accessibility

Nonrepudiation

Question 1.5

Considering the case study provided, what primary issue(s) must you consider when you create the 4Sale network security plan? [Choose the best answer]

- ○ a. Due care and due diligence
- ○ b. Information security strategies
- ○ c. Security group descriptions
- ○ d. All of the above
- ○ e. None of the above

Question 1.6

The Network Manager at 4Sale asks, "Which Performance MMC snap-in object do I use to measure Key Distribution Center (KDC) Authentication Service (AS) request activity?" [Choose the best answer]

○ a. NT Directory Services (NTDS)

○ b. Kerberos

○ c. KDC

○ d. None of the above

Question 1.7

The Network Manager at 4Sale asks, "Which security areas can I standardize as we deploy our systems?" [Check all correct answers]

❑ a. Executive, Staff, and User groups

❑ b. Application files

❑ c. A 4Sale proprietary application extension

❑ d. Smart card services

❑ e. All of the above

Question 1.8

The Owner-Network Manager at Got-a-Deal asks, "Which authentication method do you suggest for our staff?" [Choose the best answer]

○ a. PC/smart card technology

○ b. NT LAN Manager (NTLM)

○ c. Kerberos protocol

○ d. SChannel (Secure Channel) protocols

Question 1.9

Considering the case study provided, which security technology would have an optimal effect on TCO? [Choose the best answer]

○ a. Kerberos protocol

○ b. Microsoft IP Security (IPSec) protocol suite

○ c. SChannel protocols

○ d. All of the above

○ e. None of the above

Question 1.10

The Network Manager at 4Sale asks, "From a technical point of view, which security technology would give me confidentiality, data integrity, and flexible security protocols?" [Check all correct answers]

❏ a. Kerberos

❏ b. Secure Sockets Layer (SSL) 3

❏ c. IPSec

❏ d. Transport Layer Security (TLS) 1

❏ e. All of the above

Question 1.11

The Network Manager at 4Sale asks you in what order you would deploy the following security technologies to deliver as many security services as quickly as possible at the cheapest cost:

Secure Multipurpose Internet Mail Extensions (S/MIME)

IPSec

Secure Hypertext Transfer Protocol (S-HTTP)

Secure Sockets Layer (SSL)

Question 1.12

The Network Manager at 4Sale says, "We run an online barter service and our primary business focus is our proprietary front-end client, so we do not have to concern ourselves with directory service issues." Is this statement true or false?

○ a. True

○ b. False

Question 1.13

The Network Manager is a member of the Enterprise Administrators group. She asks, "I want to delegate responsibility for Got-a-Deal administration to the Got-a-Deal Vice President of Operations. How can I do this?" [Choose the best answer]

○ a. She can modify GPOs, but she cannot delegate that responsibility.

○ b. She has Full Control over GPOs, but she cannot delegate that responsibility.

○ c. She has to be added to the Got-a-Deal Domain Administrators group to have Full Control over GPOs, but she cannot delegate that responsibility.

○ d. None of the above.

Question 1.14

The Network Manager at 4Sale says, "Assuming Got-a-Deal is configured as a child domain under 4Sale, I want our 4Sale Corporate News folder to appear on its desktop in addition to whatever the Got-a-Deal Vice President of Operations wants. What is the easiest way to have this automatically happen?" [Choose the best answer]

○ a. Create an OU and assign the appropriate settings.

○ b. Modify the Got-a-Deal domain GPO.

○ c. Do nothing.

○ d. None of the above.

Case Study 2

4Sale, an online bartering company in ThatTherePlace North Dakota, focuses primarily on selling inexpensive, odd-lot items. 4Sale has merged operations with an online brokerage company, Got-a-Deal. Got-a-Deal rents space in the same office building.

As part of the expansion plan proposed by the 4Sale CEO, the online company is now learning how to use its infrastructure and focusing on learning how to leverage the many new Windows 2000 features as they relate to the corporate business objectives.

MyPartner is an antique broker and independent contractor located in Somewhere, New York.

The 4Sale proprietary front end is growing in popularity. This front end provides an interface to the 4Sale online bidding system and online auction services. The back-end application is actually composed of an accounting system, a cataloging system, and an online communication package that supports virtual auction rooms in which Internet customers can participate in realtime bidding. The application is composed of COM+ components that allow third-party developers to rapidly configure their own in-house systems to the 4Sale application.

Current LAN/Network Structure

4Sale is currently running native mode Windows 2000 Server on five Pentium III 600MHz machines:

➤ One member server runs Exchange Server 5.5 with Service Pack (SP) 1

➤ One member server runs Internet Information Server 5 and Proxy Server 2

➤ One member server runs Certificate Server

The client systems are running Windows 2000 Professional, with Office 2000 being utilized as an applications package.

Got-A-Deal is currently running native mode Windows 2000 Server on two Pentium III 600MHz machines.

Got-a-Deal is running 22 client machines on Windows 2000 Professional, with Office 2000 being utilized as an applications package.

The 4Sale system is connected to a 10Mbps hub through 10Mbps LAN cards running Category 5 UTP cabling in a star topology. Got-a-Deal is connected to a 10Mbps hub through 10Mbps LAN cards running Category 5 UTP cabling in a star topology. These hubs are on the same backbone as 4Sale but have a different subnet.

My Partner has no direct connection to the 4Sale domain tree at this time.

Proposed LAN/Network Structure

Network Manager at 4Sale says, "We need My Partner to have a secured connection to Got-a-Deal."

Current WAN Connectivity

4Sale has a T1 connection to its ISP. Got-a-Deal uses dial-up clients and ISDN to connect to its ISP.

Proposed WAN Connectivity

No changes in the current structure are proposed at this time.

Directory Design Commentary

4Sale uses native mode Windows 2000 for its online barter/trading business. All 125 client machines are configured in a single-domain model. Got-a-Deal is a child domain under the root **4sale.com**.

Current Internet Positioning

4Sale is registered as **4sale.com**. Got-a-Deal uses the **4sale.com** Web site.

Future Internet Plans

No changes in the current structure are proposed at this time.

Company Goal with Windows 2000

With the possible extension of communication to online companies that have a business alliance with 4Sale, the immediate goal is to secure 4Sale infrastructure and distributed services. An important theme is to centralize management so that any future expansion does not increase TCO.

Question 2.1

The Network Manager at 4Sale asks, "Based on our needs, what is the best security template to deploy to workstations?"

○ a. Basic (basic*.inf)

○ b. Compatible (compat*.inf)

○ c. Secure (secure*.inf)

○ d. Highly secure (hisec*.inf)

○ e. None of the above

Question 2.2

Considering the case study provided, what component(s) that you need to deploy smart cards is/are missing? [Check all correct answers]

❑ a. Hardware

❑ b. Security Support Provider (SSP)

❑ c. Operating system specifications

❑ d. User account Information

❑ e. All of the above

Question 2.3

The Network Manager at 4Sale says, "I want to automate configuring security policies using secedit.exe." You want to perform the following operations:

Create a verbose log file named sec001215.log.

Use securedb1.sdb as your database file.

Configure the user logon rights only.

You use the following syntax:

```
SECEDIT /configure /db securedb1.sdb /areas user_rights /log
    c:\winnt\security\logs\sec001215.log /verbose
```

The Network Manager at 4Sale says, "This operation will work as intended."

○ a. True

○ b. False

Question 2.4

The Network Manager at 4Sale says, "Got-a-Deal wants to have its own certificate server independent of our root certificate server. I want to be able to validate the certificates from both Certificate Authorities (CAs). How should I install this server?" [Choose the best answer]

○ a. Install an enterprise root CA with a two-way networked trust to the 4Sale root CA.

○ b. Install a standalone root CA with a two-way networked trust to the 4Sale root CA.

○ c. Install a subordinate CA with a two-way networked trust to the 4Sale root CA.

○ d. None of the above.

Question 2.5

The Vice President of Marketing at 4Sale says, "We have received offers from other online services to integrate our front-end client with their software. What protocol would provide 4Sale with the highest levels of security and flexibility?" [Choose the best answer]

○ a. PPP

○ b. DPA

○ c. EAP

○ d. PCT

Question 2.6

The Network Manager at 4Sale asks, " Which is the best authentication procedure if 4Sale supports a heterogeneous user population but needs a secured exchange of data?"

○ a. Anonymous access

○ b. Basic authentication

○ c. Basic authentication with SSL

○ d. Integrated Windows authentication

Question 2.7

The Network Manager at 4Sale says, "I want to install a Virtual Private Network (VPN) using L2TP/PPP for a secured connection with MyPartner. The VPN connection won't have any problems passing through our proxy server."

○ a. True

○ b. False

Question 2.8

The Network Manager at 4Sale gives you the following list and says, "Here are the actions I performed to harden our IIS server. This list is complete and I covered all the major security areas."

1. Disable unnecessary services.

2. Install a dual-homed server.

3. Disable directory browsing.

4. Disable Server services.

Is the Network Manager's statement true or false?

○ a. True

○ b. False

Question 2.9

The Network Manager at 4Sale asks, "Given the heterogeneity of our user population, at which level is it best to apply access controls?"

○ a. User

○ b. Group

○ c. Application

○ d. NT File System (NTFS) level

○ e. None of the above

Question 2.10

The Network Manager at 4Sale says, "I have applied RBACs (role-based access controls) to our barter software but am now having problems running the accounting portion of it in-house. What is the first thing I should do?"

○ a. Modify NTFS permissions.

○ b. Modify user rights.

○ c. Modify domain GPOs.

○ d. Apply a different security template.

○ e. None of the above.

Case Study 3

4Sale, an online bartering company in ThatTherePlace North Dakota, has been building an infrastructure that will support its corporate plans for expansion. Having focused on securing the distributed services within the boundaries of its enterprise network, the company is now extending its virtual boundaries and building both functional and network bridges across public networks to outside online business concerns that share the same or related business interests.

MyPartner is an antique broker and independent contractor located in Somewhere, New York.

Current LAN/Network Structure

4Sale is currently running native mode Windows 2000 Server on six Pentium III 600MHz machines:

➤ One member server runs Exchange Server 2000

➤ One member server runs Internet Information Server 5 and Proxy Server 2

➤ Two member servers manage certificate services: one root Certificate Server and one subordinate Certificate Server

The client systems are running Windows 2000 Professional, with Office 2000 being utilized as an applications package.

Got-a-Deal is currently running native mode Windows 2000 Server on two Pentium III 600MHz machines.

Got-a-Deal is running 22 client machines on Windows 2000 Professional, with Office 2000 being utilized as an applications package.

All 100 client machines at 4Sale are configured in a single domain model. The client systems are running Windows 2000 Professional, with Office 2000 being utilized as an applications package. Each system is connected to a 10Mbps hub through 10Mbps LAN cards running Category 5 UTP cabling in a star topology.

Got-a-Deal has undergone changes. It is running all 22 client machines in a single child domain under the 4Sale root domain. Got-a-Deal client systems are running Windows 2000 Professional, with Office 2000 being utilized as an applications package. Each system is connected to a 10Mbps hub through 10Mbps LAN cards running Category 5 UTP cabling in a star topology. These hubs are on the same backbone as 4Sale but have a different subnet.

Proposed LAN/Network Structure

Network Manager at 4Sale says, "I need to secure all network communications in the most efficient way. I would prefer to do this at the OSI Network layer as opposed to the OSI Application layer."

Current WAN Connectivity

4Sale has a T1 connection to its ISP for its online business.

Proposed WAN Connectivity

The installation of IP Security protocols and the successful deployment of Virtual Private Networks (VPNs) may lead to use of a RADIUS server.

Directory Design Commentary

4Sale is currently running Windows 2000 Server in native mode. No changes in the current structure are proposed at this time. Got-a-Deal is running all 22 client machines in a single child domain under the 4Sale root domain.

Current Internet Positioning

4Sale uses virtual hosting services and is registered as **4sale.com**. Got-a-Deal has been selling its goods through local companies, pages on other broker Web sites, and through a Web page on the **4sale.com** Web site.

Future Internet Plans

No changes in the current structure are proposed at this time.

Company Goal with Windows 2000

Network Manager at 4Sale says, "With the building of business alliances, I need to prepare for the deployment of more persistent VPN connections to extranets all over the country. As we expand our online auction rooms, I will also need to support brokers who will require secure connections when they contact our network."

Question 3.1

Considering the case study provided, for which choice does the IPSec specification not provide countermeasures?

- ○ a. Passive interception like sniffing

- ○ b. Passive impersonation like address spoofing

- ○ c. Active interference like a virus from someone you know

- ○ d. Active interception like man-in-the-middle attacks that reroute a data exchange

- ○ e. None of the above

Question 3.2

For future growth projections, including the probability of new branch offices, what would be the best OU design for the **4sale.com** domain?

○ a. Location then organization

○ b. Organization then location

○ c. Department

○ d. Project

Question 3.3

The Network Manager at 4Sale says, "We need to build a firewall. We have put our Web server behind it. What issues would we face if we put the VPN server in front of the firewall?" [Check all correct answers]

❏ a. User Datagram Protocol (UDP) port number 1701

❏ b. VPN server IP address

❏ c. HTTP packets

❏ d. All of the above

Question 3.4

The Network Manager at 4Sale says, "We need to build a firewall. We have put our Web server behind it. What issues would we face if we put the VPN server behind the firewall?" [Check all correct answers]

❏ a. Transmission Control Protocol/User Datagram Protocol (TCP/UDP) ports for tunnel maintenance

❏ b. VPN server IP address

❏ c. HTTP packets

❏ d. All of the above

Question 3.5

The Network Manager at 4Sale says, "Only MyPartner uses the VPN. My plan is to put the VPN in front of the firewall so that we can use it to restrict MyPartner's access to areas inside our intranet." Who will this plan affect and will it work?

○ a. This plan will affect only MyPartner and will work as planned.

○ b. This plan will affect only MyPartner but will not work as planned.

○ c. This plan will affect others in addition to MyPartner and will work as planned.

○ d. This plan will affect others in addition to MyPartner but will not work as planned.

Question 3.6

The Network Manager at 4Sale asks, "What protocol would I need if I wanted remote access using smart cards?"

○ a. EAP-MD5

○ b. EAP-TLS

○ c. EAP-RADIUS

○ d. TLS

○ e. None of the above

Question 3.7

Considering the case study provided, during the deployment of L2TP over IPSec, the only thing the Network Manager at 4Sale must do is install a computer certificate on the 4Sale VPN server by configuring an auto enrollment Group Policy or manually using the Certificate snap-in.

○ a. True

○ b. False

Question 3.8

The Network Manager at 4Sale asks, "If MyPartner wanted to switch to a non-Microsoft VPN client, what special configurations are necessary for a secure connection?" [Check all correct answers]

❏ a. For PPTP, MPPE must be supported.

❏ b. For L2TP, IPSec encryption must be supported.

❏ c. No configuration is needed; the VPN client will not work.

❏ d. No configuration is needed; the VPN client will negotiate all settings.

Question 3.9

The Network Manager at 4Sale asks, "If we implement IPSec and the VPN server is behind the firewall, what packet filters do I have to set?" [Check all correct answers]

❏ a. Inbound/outbound IP port 50

❏ b. Inbound/outbound IP port 51

❏ c. UDP port 500 for key exchange

❏ d. UDP port 1701 for L2TP

Question 3.10

The Network Manager at 4Sale says, "Even though I use ipsecmon.exe to monitor IP traffic, I am sure I can find similar counters in Performance."

○ a. True

○ b. False

Question 3.11

The Network Manager has asked you to compile a flowchart showing how a company like My Partner will securely connect to Got-a-Deal in a way that minimizes exposure of the firewall to outside attack. The following objects represent the components of the network:

VPN Client | Web Server | Firewall | Domain Controller | VPN Server

Use items from the following list to connect the objects so that they are correct. The diagram should flow from the VPN client on the left side to the 4Sale domain controller on the right. Some items may be used more than once, and some items may not be used at all.

PPP

TCP/IP

RDP/TCP

VPN

Case Study 4

4Sale, an online bartering company in ThatTherePlace North Dakota, focuses primarily on selling inexpensive, odd-lot items. The CEO at 4Sale has slowly implemented a business plan that began with consolidation of the parent company, 4Sale, gradually expanded operations through the use of remote access and Virtual Private Networks (VPNs), and is now concerned primarily with building cost-effective operations with the consolidation of IT resources and the merging of or interoperation with other business platforms such as Macintosh, Novell, and Unix.

Fred Smith, an artist and Web designer, is an independent contractor at 4Sale.

MyPartner is an antique broker and independent contractor located in Somewhere, New York. MyPartner formed a business alliance with 4Sale over one year ago.

Future Inc. is a 15-year old data warehousing service that has developed several proprietary search engines customized for various industries.

Current LAN/Network Structure

4Sale is currently running native mode Windows 2000 Server on six Pentium III 600MHz machines:

➤ One member server runs Exchange Server 2000

➤ One member server runs Internet Information Server 5 and Proxy Server 2

➤ Two member servers manage certificate services: one root Certificate Server and one subordinate Certificate Server

➤ One member server runs RRAS and provides VPN services

All 100 client machines are configured in a single domain model. The client systems are running Windows 2000 Professional, with Office 2000 being utilized as an applications package. Each system is connected to a 10Mbps hub through 10Mbps LAN cards running Category 5 UTP cabling in a star topology.

Fred Smith has 1 iBook laptop and two Power Macintosh G4 workstations running MacOS 8.5 using both MacTCP and AppleTalk.

MyPartner has a 25-user Novell 5.1 network running BorderManager VPN Services, BorderManager FireWALL Services, and Oracle 8i for NetWare 5.1 (8.1.5.0.4c).

Future Inc. has 300 users on an AT&T 6386 System V Unix operating system platform running several proprietary packages and Oracle 8i Release 3.

Proposed LAN/Network Structure

The Network Manager at 4Sale says, "We want Fred to store all his work for us on our system. We will be merging with MyPartner in about three months; I will need a deployment plan from you as soon as possible. Future Inc. will be handling all our data storage. It has proprietary search engine applications that we will need to run on our system to access our data."

Current WAN Connectivity

4Sale has a T1 connection to its ISP for its online business. 4Sale supports remote access through VPN connections provided by its RRAS Server.

Proposed WAN Connectivity

No changes in the current structure are proposed at this time.

Directory Design Commentary

We want the administration of directory services between My Partner and 4Sale to be as simple and efficient as possible.

Current Internet Positioning

4Sale has a registered domain, **www.4sale.com,** and uses virtual hosting services to connect to the Internet. Got-a-Deal has been selling its goods through local companies, pages on other broker Web sites and through a Web page on the **4sale.com** Web site.

Fred Smith has his own registered domain, **www.fredsmith.com,** and uses an Apple AirPort base station to interface with his ISP, which provides him with virtual hosting services. The base station provides NAT services for all his AirPort clients.

MyPartner has its own registered domain, **www.mypartner.com,** and uses an ISP to connect to the Internet.

Future Inc. has its own registered Class B domain, **www.futureinc.com,** and runs its own in-house DNS servers.

Future Internet Plans

No changes in the current structure are proposed at this time.

Company Goal with Windows 2000

The CEO of 4Sale says, "My personal goal over the next three months is to seamlessly incorporate Fred, MyPartner, and Future Inc. into our daily 4Sale operations."

Question 4.1

Considering the case study provided and the proposed merger with MyPartner, what type of domain structure would you recommend allowing for all relevant concerns?

○ a. Two distinct forests (**4sale.com** and **mypartner.com**), with an extended trust connecting them

○ b. One domain with the root **4sale.com**, with a child domain being **mypartner.4sale.com**

○ c. One domain called **4sale.com** with two OUs, one for 4Sale and one for MyPartner

○ d. One domain called **4sale.com** with one OU for MyPartner

Question 4.2

The CEO of 4Sale says, "In terms of migration, rank our three projects in descending order, from the best candidate to the worst candidate."

Fred Smith: Macintosh

MyPartner: Novell

Future Inc.: Unix

Question 4.3

The CEO of 4Sale says, "In terms of interoperability, rank our three projects in descending order, from the best candidate to the worse candidate."

Fred Smith: Macintosh

MyPartner: Novell

Future Inc.: Unix

Question 4.4

The Network Manager at 4Sale asks, "We are not merging for at least six months, so it might be better to run 4Sale and MyPartner as separate entities but allow them to share data. We need to control access to 4Sale resources. What service will handle our security issues?"

○ a. Microsoft Directory Synchronization Services (MSDSS)

○ b. File Migration Utility (FMU)

○ c. File and Print Services for NetWare version 5 (FPNW5)

○ d. Gateway and Client Services for NetWare

Question 4.5

The Network Manager at 4Sale asks, "When we are ready, how do we migrate the Novell user accounts and permissions from Novell Directory Services (NDS) to Windows 2000?" Which of the following is an alternative naming convention you can use with Windows 2000?

○ a. MSDSS

○ b. DSMigrate

○ c. FMU

○ d. None of the above

Question 4.6

The Network Manager at 4Sale says, "Using default settings, we can control Fred Smith's access to our printers." Is this statement true or false?

○ a. True

○ b. False

Question 4.7

The Network Manager at 4Sale asks, "What is the fastest way to port the source code of Future Inc.'s proprietary search engine?" [Choose the best answer]

○ a. Interix

○ b. Portable Operating System Interface for Unix (POSIX)

○ c. Unicode

○ d. Services for Unix 2 (SFU2)

Question 4.8

The Owner-Network Manager at Got-a-Deal says, "I want our people to be as proficient as possible in creating batch scripts to automate many of the administrative functions and dealing with security issues on both the Future Inc. and 4Sale platforms. What is our best strategy?" [Check all correct answers]

❑ a. Interix

❑ b. POSIX

❑ c. Korn Shell programming

❑ d. All of the above

❑ e. None of the above

Question 4.9

The Network Manager has asked you how various acquisition candidates will either merge or fully interoperate over a long term with 4Sale directory services. To answer this question, you must move the labels on the right side of the graphic to their appropriate positions inside the blank connector arrows in the middle of the screen. Some items may be used more than once, and some items may not be used at all.

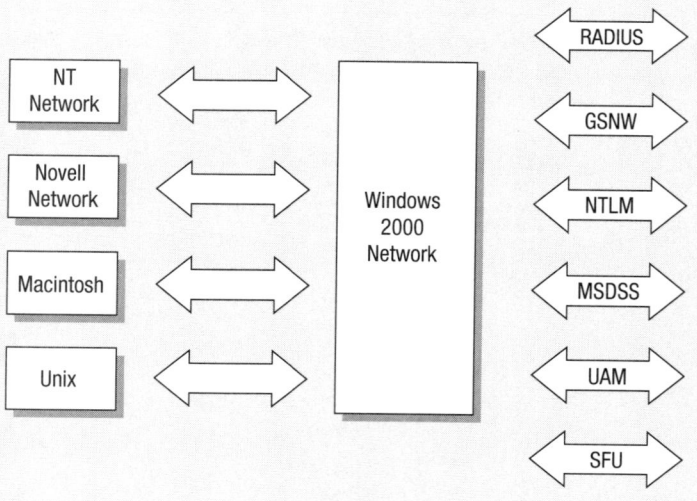

Case Study 5

4Sale, an online bartering company in ThatTherePlace North Dakota, is now a major player in the electronic bidding and online auction business. It has business alliances with major companies in related business such as data warehousing, virtual hosting services, online retail portals, and wholesale dealers. Evidence shows a security breach where a competitor has received copies of interoffice email that details a major business innovation.

Current LAN/Network Structure

4Sale is currently running native mode Windows 2000 Server on 10 Pentium III 600MHz machines:

➤ Two member servers runs Exchange Server 2000

➤ One member server runs Internet Information Server 5 and Proxy Server 2

➤ One member server runs SQL Server 7

➤ Three member servers manage certificate services: one root Certificate Server and two subordinate Certificate Servers

➤ Two member servers run RRAS and provide VPN services

4Sale is currently running Windows 2000 Server in native mode. All 150 client machines are configured in a single domain model. The client systems are running Windows 2000 Professional, with Office 2000 being utilized as an applications package. Each system is connected to a 100Mbps hub through 100Mbps LAN cards running Category 5 UTP cabling in a star topology.

Proposed LAN/Network Structure

No changes in the current structure are proposed at this time.

Current WAN Connectivity

4Sale has a T3 connection to its ISP for its online business. 4Sale supports remote access through VPN connections provided by its several RRAS Servers.

Proposed WAN Connectivity

No changes in the current structure are proposed at this time.

Directory Design Commentary

No changes in the current structure are proposed at this time.

Current Internet Positioning

Although 4Sale has several registered domains, **www.4sale.com** is still the published home page. It runs its Web sites from an affiliated virtual hosting service.

Future Internet Plans

No changes in the current structure are proposed at this time.

Company Goal with Windows 2000

The CEO of 4Sale says, "The Board of Directors is pleased with our substantial increase in market share and our growth in earnings. But the fact that our competitor acquired a copy of an internal memo may cost us a major share of the market. I don't want to just respond to this single incident, however; I want our computer systems to provide a foundation that will support the security needs for the currently planned projects that I have promised will be implemented in the next six months. Over the next six months, I want to deploy persistent branch VPN systems, digital document signing, and two-factor authentication security for our applications within the enterprise."

The Network Manager at 4Sale says, "We must implement both encryption and authentication of email transmissions as soon as possible. I am also worried about the data on laptops that leave our building."

Question 5.1

Considering the case study provided, what is the best security technology that allows for all relevant concerns? [Choose the best answer]

○ a. Kerberos protocol

○ b. SChannel protocols

○ c. PKI technologies

○ d. IPSec protocol suite

Question 5.2

The Network Manager at 4Sale says, "I am concerned about deploying technologies that require the presence of a Certificate Authority infrastructure. Which of the corporate projects and my personal objectives do not require the presence of a CA?" [Choose the best answer]

○ a. EFS

○ b. SSL

○ c. VPN

○ d. None of the above

Question 5.3

The Network Manager at 4Sale asks, "In addition to supporting our other objectives, what do we need to validate a signed document?" [Check all correct answers]

❑ a. A standalone Certificate Authority

❑ b. A root Certificate Authority

❑ c. Active Directory

❑ d. All of the above

❑ e. None of the above

Question 5.4

The Network Manager at 4Sale asks, "What are the key components of a public key infrastructure?" [Check all correct answers]

❑ a. Certificate Authority architecture

❑ b. Public keys and certificates

❑ c. Active Directory integration

❑ d. SSL/TLS protocols

❑ e. None of the above

Question 5.5

The Network Manager of 4Sale asks, "How can we harden the following types of security around the Certificate Server?"

Physical security

Logical security

Place any appropriate answers under the appropriate heading:

Run the root Certificate Authority offline.

Place the Certificate Server in a locked enclosure.

Place the Certificate Server on a machine equipped for two-factor authentication.

Install the Certificate Server inside a demilitarized zone (DMZ) with a Web server.

Place the Certificate Authority private key on a smart card.

Place the Certificate Authority root certificate on a smart card.

Create the longest private key possible.

Regularly run the Security Configuration And Analysis MMC Snap-in using a batch script.

Question 5.6

The Network Manager at 4Sale asks, "What are the key components when you are securing email?" [Check all correct answers]

❑ a. Hash-based signature

❑ b. DSS

❑ c. Fortezza cards

❑ d. MD5

❑ e. All of the above

Question 5.7

The Network Manager at 4Sale asks, "How can I monitor the policy module on a Certificate Authority?"

○ a. Use the **certsvr.exe -z** command.

○ b. Right-click on the appropriate CA node and select Properties on the Certificate Authority MMC snap-in.

○ c. Both of the above.

○ d. None of the above.

Answer Key

For asterisked items, please see textual representation of answer on the appropriate page within this chapter.

1.1.	c	2.4.	b	3.11	*
1.2.	*	2.5.	c	4.1.	d
1.3.	b	2.6.	c	4.2.	*
1.4.	*	2.7.	a	4.3.	*
1.5.	b	2.8.	b	4.4.	a
1.6.	a	2.9.	c	4.5.	b
1.7.	e	2.10.	d	4.6.	b
1.8.	a	3.1.	c	4.7.	a
1.9.	b	3.2.	a	4.8.	d
1.10.	c	3.3.	b, c	4.9	*
1.11.	*	3.4.	d	5.1.	c
1.12.	b	3.5.	c	5.2.	a
1.13.	d	3.6.	b	5.3.	b, c
1.14.	c	3.7.	b	5.4.	a, b, c
2.1.	d	3.8.	a, b	5.5.	*
2.2.	a	3.9.	a, b, c	5.6.	e
2.3.	a	3.10.	b	5.7.	c

Question 1.1

Answer c is correct. One domain with the root **4sale.com**, with a child domain being **gotadeal.4sale.com**, is one of the solutions that would allow for the relevant concerns. For example, the company already has **4sale.com** registered and plans to continue with this naming convention for both companies when they are merged. Having two separate domains allows for distinct password structures, yet having 4Sale as the root still provides a way of implementing strong control. Another solution might have been an empty root with two distinct domains beneath, but this was not an option. Answer a is incorrect because it offers two distinct forests, and this provides a poor solution of unification and control. Answers b and d are incorrect because they offer an empty root but then provide Organizational Units, which will not handle the issue of control over password security between the two locations.

Question 1.2

The correct answer is:

Technical support

System maintenance

Cost of hardware and software

Cost of system upgrades

User training

The prioritized order of total cost of ownership (TCO) components is culled from the discussions with key participants in network deployment. TCO includes cost of system upgrades, system maintenance, and technical support. Cost of disposables is not included in the list because it is not a component of TCO; disposables are typically considered an expense.

Question 1.3

Answer b, false, is correct. 4Sale provides a front-end client to its online customers to facilitate the exchange of bidding information. It also uses its own line-of-business applications in its internal accounting operations. 4Sale supports a broad range of business services to its user population in addition to its bidding system, but messaging and accounting are critical. 4Sale must provide fault-tolerant online transaction processing and storage. Network support is also a business service because its primary information technology security control is accessibility.

Question 1.4

The correct answer is:

   Accessibility

   Software authentication

   Confidentiality

   Nonrepudiation

The most important business corporate objective, though not formally written down, is access to the online services; therefore, accessibility is first. The 4Sale online customers must have confidence in the services. Authenticating the software not only instills that confidence but provides a level of guarantee that both the customer and 4Sale are exchanging data in a predictable way. If the online customer has access and uses the front-end client, the necessary confidentiality will be provided. Finally, from the 4Sale perspective, nonrepudiation is an important business concern because customers bid for product. When bids are placed, they must be considered final and irrefutable. Training and firewall technology are not included in the list because training is not a typical security objective, and firewall technology is not a security objective; it is considered one of many possible solutions.

Question 1.5

Answer b is correct. 4Sale is an online service. Information security strategies are the specific design and strategic choices necessary to secure online exchanges and Web-based communications. Due care and due diligence typically describe those actions that relate to the information technology security control compliance. This IT control is not of primary consideration in this case study. Therefore, answer a is incorrect. Similarly, security group descriptions are built into the security policy. Use of default choices and security templates, as stated in the case study, is critical in deployment and will be automatically carried out assuming proper installation and maintenance. Therefore, answer c is incorrect.

Question 1.6

Answer a is correct. NTDS (NT Directory Services) provides a variety of counters for directory replication, directory services, Lightweight Directory Access Protocol services, Security Accounts Manager (SAM) activity, address book activity, Kerberos activity, and specifically Key Distribution Center activity. Neither Kerberos nor KDC are performance objects. Therefore, answers b and c are incorrect.

Question 1.7

Answer e is correct. You can standardize specific security against some baseline profile in specific areas covered in the security templates supplied with the Security Configuration And Analysis Microsoft Management Console snap-in. The answer options are examples of the following security areas: Executive, Staff, and User groups are restricted groups; application files pertain to the file system; a proprietary application extension is part of machine\software\classes in the Registry; and smart card services are part of system services. Thus, answers a, b, c, and d are all examples of security areas included in security templates.

Question 1.8

Answer a is correct. Smart cards are the best recommendation because 4Sale is running in Windows 2000 native mode, and digitally signed documents are required for exchanges of information. Because 4Sale is running in native mode with the security protocol defaulting to Kerberos and a two-factor authentication method is preferred, NT LAN Manager authentication is not a good answer. Therefore, answer b is incorrect. Although Kerberos is the default authentication protocol, it supports only interactive logons. Therefore, answer c is incorrect. Secure Channel protocols support network logons. Therefore, answer d is incorrect.

Question 1.9

Answer b is correct. Microsoft IP Security adds features like strong encryption, which 4Sale requires, without affecting the total cost of ownership (specifically in terms of software upgrades, training, and hardware). IPSec works at the Open Systems Interconnection Transport layer; 4Sale line-of-business software, system software upgrades, training, and hardware are not directly affected. Kerberos protocol and Secure Channel protocols support public key infrastructure and the use of smart cards. These technologies, however, increase the investment in hardware and software to support the two-factor authentication method. Therefore, answers a and c are incorrect.

Question 1.10

Answer c is correct. The key feature here is flexible security protocols. Only one listed security technology is technically a protocol suite: IPSec. It provides both Authentication Header and Encapsulated Security Payload protocols. Kerberos and Secure Sockets Layer 3/Transport Layer Security 1 provide confidentiality and data integrity but are actual protocol specifications. Therefore, answers a, b, and d are incorrect.

Question 1.11

The correct answer is:

IPSec

Secure Multipurpose Internet Mail Extensions (S/MIME)

Secure Sockets Layer (SSL)

Secure Hypertext Transfer Protocol (S-HTTP)

You should deploy IPSec first because it will have the greatest effect in the shortest period of time at the lowest total cost of ownership. S/MIME is a standard component of most email services, so you should deploy it shortly after IPSec. You can outsource the immediate need for some Certificate Authority to a third party. Both SSL and S-HTTP will most likely require that you modify the 4Sale proprietary front-end software. SSL working at the Open Systems Interconnection Transport layer provides a broader range of support services than the application-specific S-HTTP, so its deployment as a security protocol tends to be more cost-effective when dealing with many HTTP applications. Because S-HTTP works at the OSI Application layer, in comparison to the other four security choices, this choice requires more time to modify specific application software, as well as more money to deploy. You should use S-HTTP on a per-case basis when more broad-based security protocols like SSL/TSL do not provide the necessary support or are not appropriate due to your specific network configuration.

Question 1.12

Answer b, false, is correct. 4Sale uses signed documents and therefore requires public key technologies. It also plans to deploy smart cards, so it will use enterprise certificate services to minimize administrative overhead. Directory services will be a very important part of 4Sale's long-term business strategy to scale its business without incurring additional costs for administration and support.

Question 1.13

Answer d is correct. The Network Manager is a member of the Enterprise Administrators and Domain Administrators group, so she cannot both modify GPOs (Group Policy Objects) and link them to some Active Directory object. Members of either of these administrative groups can also delegate the responsibility of modifying a GPO to any administrator or an administrator group, provided the administrator or group to whom they are delegating this responsibility has Read/Write access to the specific GPO. Answer a is incorrect because the Network Manager specifically wants the Got-a-Deal VP of Operations to have administrative authorization. Remember, the President of Got-a-Deal wants to have exclusive access to top secret information. Under the circumstances, a simpler choice—assigning the VP of Operations membership in the Domain Administrators group—is not an option. Answers b and c are incorrect because the Delegation of Control Wizard can grant Full Control to any administrator.

Question 1.14

Answer c is correct because a child domain will inherit policy settings unless those inherited settings contradict policy about those same settings or are blocked in the child domain. Answer a is incorrect because it is not necessary to create an OU (Organizational Unit) and assign the appropriate settings. Answer b is incorrect because inheritance from the parent domain applies unless incompatibilities exist between the GPO (Group Policy Object) settings across the two domains.

Question 2.1

Answer d is correct. Given the requirement that all correspondence be digitally signed, the only appropriate security configuration template is the hisec*.inf, which is specifically designed for network communications. These machines communicate only with other Windows 2000 workstations. Internet communication is through the proxy server. Answer a is incorrect because basic*.inf is used for reapplying the default security settings of a modified configuration file. Answer b is incorrect because compat*.inf is used for giving the local Users group strict security settings, whereas Power Users receive security levels comparable to legacy NT 4 Users. Compat*.inf templates also lower the security levels on files, folders, and Registry keys commonly used by applications to run. Answer c is incorrect because secure*.inf is used for recommended security settings for all areas except files, folders, and Registry keys. The latter are typically secured by the administrator or by default.

Question 2.2

Answer a is correct. An enterprise mode certificate server is already in place, so the only missing components are the actual card reader hardware and the accompanying software for the appropriate workstations. The Security Support Provider is either Kerberos (Public Key Cryptography for Initial Authentication in Kerberos) or SSL/TLS (Secure Sockets Layer/Transport Layer Security), both of which are provided as part of the operating system. Therefore, answer b is incorrect. There are no issues with operating system or user account information because 4Sale is using native mode Windows 2000. Therefore, answers c and d are incorrect.

Question 2.3

Answer a, true, is correct. This is the correct syntax for using secedit.exe to execute the operations listed.

Question 2.4

Answer b is correct. Got-a-Deal's only choice is to run a standalone Certificate Authority (CA) with a networked trust to the 4Sale root CA. This configuration will permit Got-a-Deal to administer its own certificates for transactions that require Secure Sockets Layer or Secure Multipurpose Internet Mail Extensions and will allow the sharing of certificates between the two CAs. Got-a-Deal is a child domain in the 4Sale enterprise tree. An enterprise root CA already exists, so Got-a-Deal cannot run a second enterprise root certificate server. Therefore, answer a is incorrect. Got-a-Deal wants to have an independent CA, so running a subordinate CA is also not acceptable. Therefore, answer c is incorrect.

Question 2.5

Answer c is correct. EAP (Extensible Authentication Protocol) is an extension to PPP (Point-To-Point Protocol) that works with dial-up, PPP, and Layer 2 Tunneling Protocol clients. EAP provides support for two-factor authentication such as smart cards and public keys. It also plays an important role in Virtual Private Networks. PPP is a communications protocol standard that provides interoperability for remote access protocols and supports a variety of authentication methods so that other authentication protocols run on it. Therefore, answer a is incorrect. DPA (Distributed Password Authentication) is an asymmetric authentication protocol used by online services and part of Microsoft Commercial Internet Systems. Therefore, answer b is incorrect. PCT (Private Communications Technology) is one of the Secure Channel Security Support Providers along Secure Sockets Layer 3 and Transport Layer Security 1. Therefore, answer d is incorrect.

Question 2.6

Answer c is correct. Basic authentication using SSL (Secure Sockets Layer) is supported by most Web browsers and thus supports a heterogeneous population. By using SSL support, which most browsers also support, you make basic authentication more secure. Neither anonymous access nor basic authentication provide for the secure exchange of information. Therefore, answers a and b are incorrect. Integrated Windows authentication is more secure than basic authentication, but it is designed primarily for intranets. Therefore, answer d is incorrect.

Question 2.7

Answer a, true, is correct. L2TP/PPP (Layer 2 Tunneling Protocol/Point-To-Point Protocol) will not have any problems with the Network Address Translation used in Proxy Server because it will not use IPSec for authentication. There are incompatibilities when IPSec components like Internet Key Exchange attempt to exchange session keys and create secured sessions, because internal network IP addresses are translated by NAT and never actually disclosed outside the network. IKE needs the actual destination address to properly encrypt and decrypt packets during a secured exchange of information.

Question 2.8

Answer b, false, is correct. The Network Manager forgot to enable both logging and auditing on the Web server. This one step is the least expensive in terms of overhead and maintenance and is probably the most important action to perform when you are securing an Internet Information Server server.

Question 2.9

Answer c is correct. Role-based (application) access control is the best way to handle 4Sale security. If you assign permissions to the user or group, you have more administrative overhead and more possibilities of a security weakness or conflicts in configuration and permission levels. Therefore, answers a and b are incorrect. Assigning permissions to an applications-based role simplifies administration but also hardens security; the role's security context provides the least privileges for completing that application's specific tasks. Users log on to perform some work function, and then they log out. You should always apply NT File System permissions within an enterprise, but you must carefully test for unpredictable results. Therefore, answer d is incorrect.

Question 2.10

Answer d is correct. The first step should be to apply the compatws.inf template to the appropriate local machines. This security maintains a secure internal environment while possibly allowing all aspects of the software to run successfully. Changing specific NT File System permissions would be a second choice. Therefore, answer a is incorrect. Only part of the software is malfunctioning, so a rights issue pertaining to the application role is unlikely. Therefore, answer b is incorrect. Similarly, Group Policy settings at the domain level are less likely than local permissions to be causing this problem. Therefore, answer c is incorrect.

Question 3.1

Answer c is correct. IP Security does not stop the spread of a virus from a sender you trust primarily because a virus can be incorporated in the message packet. Answers a and b are incorrect because IPSec does provides countermeasures for passive interception and impersonation attack modalities. Answer d is incorrect because IPSec decreases the possibility of active interception attacks (man-in-the-middle) that intercept the data exchanged between the two parties.

Question 3.2

Answer a is correct. The rule is to keep the structure as simple as possible. Even though 4Sale is an e-commerce company, the business infrastructure is still based by location. It's conceivable that an organization subdivided by location schema might help structure 4Sale if it were to specialize in categories of objects. For example, all business functioning and personnel involved in the bartering of automobiles would be assigned to a specific Organizational Unit (OU) separate from other 4Sale operational areas. This OU would then have regions throughout the country. This division of business by organization rather than location, however, would add more complexity at this time without any obvious advantage, so it is not appropriate. Therefore, answer b is incorrect. Answer c is incorrect because separating specific departments would not provide any clear business advantage. Similarly, because 4Sale does not have specific projects requiring a separate organizational structure or special policies, answer d is incorrect. Creating OUs within geographical areas (location) for 4Sale at this time is the simplest and most logical design.

Question 3.3

Answers b and c are correct. Because the VPN (Virtual Private Network) server is in front of the firewall, the firewall must filter traffic to and from the VPN server's designated Internet Protocol address to allow traffic to flow. Therefore, answer b is correct. The Network Manager must also decide whether to force all traffic through the VPN server or allow outbound HTTP packets to pass through the firewall. Therefore, answer c is correct. Answer a is inccorect because the VPN server is in front of the firewall. L2TP encapsulates message packets inside a PPP frame when it creates a tunnel, then puts that package inside a UDP packet assigned to port 1701. If the VPN server were behind the firewall, port 1701 would have to allow UDP packets to pass through it to reach the internally located VPN server. Because the VPN Server is outside the firewall, port 1701 does not have to allow inbound or outbound traffic to pass through the wall. Placing the VPN server in front of the firewall also restricts Internet traffic on the intranet because inbound packets must first pass through the VPN server.

Question 3.4

Answer d is correct. The firewall input and output filters must be able to pass tunnel maintenance traffic, as well as any other server behind it. Answer a is correct because both TCP and UDP packets must be able to pass through ports like 1701 to reach the internally located VPN server. Answer b is correct because the tunneled data must be able to pass to the VPN server where it is then authenticated. Answer c is correct because HTTP (Hypertext Transfer Protocol) packets must cross the wall.

Question 3.5

Answer c is correct. The firewall will restrict access to MyPartner as intended. However, outbound Internet traffic will also have to go through the Virtual Private Network, so the VPN will therefore restrict the use of Internet resources to VPN users. Therefore answers a, b, and d are incorrect.

Question 3.6

Answer b is correct. EAP-TLS (Extensible Authentication Protocol - Transport Layer Security) is used in a certificate-based exchange. You must use this protocol for remote access authentication. EAP-MD5 (Extensible Authentication Protocol - Message Digest 5) is a challenge-handshake protocol that uses EAP messages. This protocol is used in remote access situations when username and password are exchanged. Therefore, answer a is incorrect. EAP-RADIUS (Extensible Authentication Protocol-Remote Authentication Dial-In User Service) passes EAP messages to a RADIUS server for authentication. It does not deal with smart cards. Therefore, answer c is incorrect. TLS (Transport Layer Security) is used in conjunction with EAP packets. Therefore, answer d is incorrect.

Question 3.7

Answer b, false, is correct. The Network Manager must make certain both the Virtual Private Network server and VPN client have computer certificates.

Question 3.8

Answers a and b are correct. For PPTP (Point-To-Point Tunneling Protocol), MPPE (Microsoft Point-To-Point Encryption) must be supported, and for L2TP (Layer 2 Tunneling Protocol), IP Security encryption must be supported. No other configuration is necessary. Therefore answers c and d are incorrect.

Question 3.9

Answers a, b, and c are correct. Ports 50 and 51 support Authentication Header and Encapsulated Security Payload traffic. Port 500 allows Internet Key Exchange traffic. No filters are required for L2TP (Layer 2 Tunneling Protocol) traffic because the tunnel maintenance and tunneled data are encrypted as an ESP payload. Therefore, answer d is incorrect.

Question 3.10

Answer b, false, is correct. There are no relevant performance objects related to IP Security in Performance. The best utility is ipsecmon.exe. Therefore, answer a is incorrect.

Question 3.11

The correct answer is:

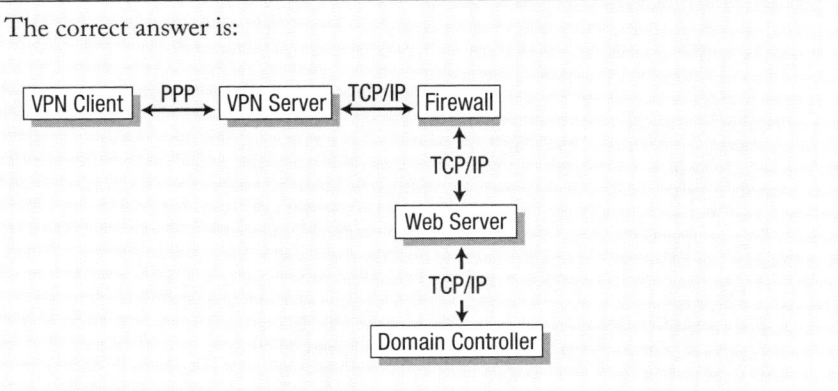

A VPN client connects to a VPN server using a communication protocol like Point-To-Point Protocol (PPP). The VPN server is positioned outside the firewall; only inbound packets with the VPN server's IP address will be permitted through the firewall. 4Sale would typically position its Web server behind the firewall. Between the VPN server, the Web server, and the domain controller, TCP/IP is the protocol of choice.

Question 4.1

Answer d is correct. Creating a separate Organizational Unit within the 4Sale domain is the most cost-effective way to merge the two companies. Answer a is incorrect because MyPartner will be merged with 4Sale, so there is no reason to create a separate namespace by extending a trust across two separate forests. Creating a separate child domain would increase administrative costs as compared to other choices in this question. MyPartner would need a domain administrator. Although the creation of a child domain might be "politically correct," especially in view of how Got-a-Deal is managed in the enterprise, members of a MyPartner Domain Administrators group, because of the transitive trust relationship, would automatically have administrative rights in the 4Sale root domain. Arbitrarily adding a child domain to the domain tree, although administratively easy, can compromise security within the enterprise. A more conservative approach, especially from a security perspective, is to use an organizational unit. Therefore, answer b is incorrect. Answer c is incorrect because the 4Sale CEO has emphasized that 4Sale is the parent company; two OUs under one domain implies more of a sibling relationship between companies. No statement in the case study suggests this kind of relationship.

Question 4.2

The correct answer is:

MyPartner

Fred Smith

Future Inc.

Migration would mean that an entire working environment would change for the user. Employees at MyPartner would see the least amount of change because Novell provides support services; the working interface is typically Windows-based. MyPartner is the best candidate for migration. Fred Smith, on the other hand, uses a Macintosh interface with a different presentation of the workspace, directory services, and access control than a Windows-based interface. Creating a Macintosh-accessible User Authentication Module share would support all of Fred's storage needs and would have little impact on his daily job. Data storage would be under 4Sale's centralized control. Future Inc. is the worst candidate for migration in this case study; not only is it a large company, but its operating system is also well suited to its line-of-business applications and business mission.

Question 4.3

The correct answer is:

Future Inc.

Fred Smith

MyPartner

Windows 2000, like legacy NT, provides several tools that provide a high degree of interoperability. Portable Operating System Interface for Unix remains a native subsystem in the Windows 2000 architecture. Services for Unix 2 provides tools that allow greater levels of interoperability and coexistence than for either Macintosh or Novell. Fred Smith is using the Macintosh operating system, which like Unix, coexisted with legacy NT 4. It can reliably share the same files and, except for slight differences in permission management, coexists well with Windows 2000. Novell is the worst candidate for interoperability because most of the Services for NetWare version 5 are designed for migration.

Question 4.4

Answer a is correct. MSDSS (Microsoft Directory Synchronization Services) synchronizes Active Directory datastores with Novell Directory Services. FMU (File Migration Utility) is a migration tool. Therefore, answer b is incorrect. FPNW5 (File and Print Services for NetWare version 5) provides a NetWare interface and Single Sign-On for Novell users running on Windows 2000. Therefore, answer c is incorrect. Gateway and Client Services for NetWare do not support access to the NWAdmin utility. Administrative control must be handled from the Novell operating system. Therefore, answer d is incorrect.

Question 4.5

Answer b is correct. DSMigrate (Directory Services Migration Tool) migrates user accounts, groups, files, and permissions from MyPartner's Novell Directory Services directory services. MSDSS (Microsoft Directory Synchronization Services) does not migrate accounts. Therefore, answer a is incorrect. FMU (File Migration Utility) migrates only files. Therefore, answer c is incorrect.

Question 4.6

Answer b, false, is correct. Using default settings, you cannot impose user-level access permissions on Macintosh print clients. Macintosh networking provides access control on files but not printers. By default, a Macintosh print client has implicit permission to access a printer because it runs in the security context of a system account.

Question 4.7

Answer a is correct. Interix 2.2 provides a Portable Operating System Interface for Unix-compliant software platform with developer tools and functions that assist in the migration of the source code to the Windows 2000 operating system. POSIX is a set of standards and specifications to facilitate the migration of software. Therefore, answer b is incorrect. Unicode is a character set standard that uses 16 bits; it has nothing to do with Unix. Therefore, answer c is incorrect. Services for Unix 2 is not primarily concerned with the porting of source code. Therefore, answer d is incorrect.

Question 4.8

Answer d is correct. Interix and the Mortice Kern Toolkit working on the POSIX (Portable Operating System Interface for Unix) subsystem on the Windows 2000 platform provide full integration with the Unix-style command line and environment. The Korn Shell is the command-line interpreter used in the Mortice Kern Toolkit.

Question 4.9

The correct answer is:

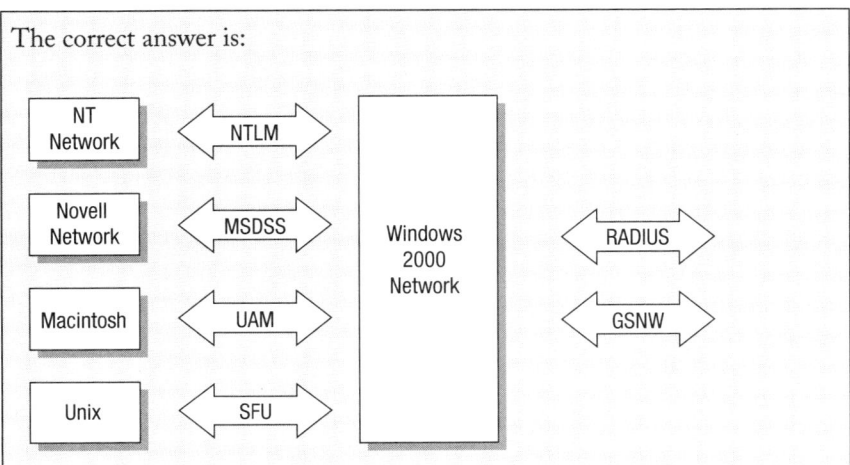

Legacy NT 4 networks will integrate with 4Sale directory services using their default authentication protocol, NTLM, and Novell will use Microsoft Directory Synchronization Services (MSDSS). Although Gateway Service for NetWare (GSNW) provides a method to connect the two operating systems, it does not provide the support for long-term interoperability. The Macintosh OS can use the User Authentication Module (UAM) share to store folders and documents. Unix can use a variety of tools provided by the Services For Unix version 2. The last choice, Remote Authentication Dial-in User Service (RADIUS), is an authentication and auditing system used by many Internet Service Providers; it specifically deals with remote access services.

Question 5.1

Answer c is correct. Public key infrastructure provides the foundation for applications and technologies that require strong authentication. The use of public keys provides support for secure Web transactions (Secure Sockets Layer), secure mail (Secure Multipurpose Internet Mail Extensions), file system encryption (Encrypting File System), IP Security tunneling (Virtual Private Network), smart card logon (Public Key Cryptography for Initial Authentication in Kerberos), and so on. The CEO specifically wants a solution that will also support smart card–based applications, VPN systems, and digital document signing. Kerberos is the default protocol in Windows 2000 for interactive authentication and authorization issues; it does not provide a platform for these other system needs. Therefore, answer a is incorrect. Secure Channel protocols like SSL and Transport Layer Security are the security methods of choice for authentication across a public network and for smart cards, but they do not support VPNs. Therefore, answer b is incorrect. IPSec technologies support encryption and authentication but at the Open Systems Interconnection Network layer; answer d is therefore not the best answer.

Question 5.2

Answer a is correct. EFS (Encrypting File System) on laptops does not require the presence of a Certificate Authority. Secure Sockets Layer and Virtual Private Networks both rely on the authentication of digital certificates issued by some CA to function. Therefore, answers b and c are incorrect.

Question 5.3

Answers b and c are correct. For large enterprise solutions and the 4Sale goals listed in the case study, a hierarchical trust model consisting of a root Certificate Authority (CA) and subordinate CA with Active Directory integration is the best solution because it provides both scalability and administrative flexibility. For security reasons, you can take the root CA offline while keeping the subordinate CA online to handle the authentication process. Through integration with Active Directory, certificates and other security information like certification revocation lists are replicated throughout the domain tree or forest. The standalone CA is an acceptable solution for Secure Sockets Layer and Secure Multipurpose Internet Mail Extensions—that is, issuing certificates to external users—but it is not integrated with the Active Directory. Therefore, answer a is incorrect.

Question 5.4

Answers a, b, and c are correct. The Certificate Authority architecture allows you to administer public keys and digital certificates. Therefore, answers a and b are correct. Active Directory integration is important because it contains the location of Certificate Servers and it supports the publication of digital certificates and certificate revocation lists by automatically replicating this security material as part of the Global Catalog. Therefore, answer c is correct. (Secure Sockets Layer/Transport Layer Security) protocols use public key infrastructure security services but are not critical components. Therefore, answer d is incorrect.

Question 5.5

The correct answer is:

Physical security

Place the Certificate Server in a locked enclosure.

Place the Certificate Server on a machine equipped for two-factor authentication.

Logical security

Run the root Certificate Authority offline.

Place the Certificate Authority private key on a smart card.

Create the longest private key possible.

Several items were not included. You should not install a Certificate Server inside a demilitarized zone with a Web server because you must adjust packet filtering to include all public key infrastructure-related traffic, especially from the internal side of the network. A Web server is also inside the DMZ, so adding a certificate server seriously weakens the DMZ. The root Certificate Server is best installed offline on its own subnet and domain in a separate DMZ. Certificate Authority (CA) root certificate on a smart card is incorrect because the only key that you need to protect is the CA's private key; the public key is distributed throughout the network. Regularly running the Security Configuration And Analysis Microsoft Management Console snap-in using a batch script is incorrect; you cannot run the Security Configuration And Analysis MMC snap-in in a batch mode; the correct tool to accomplish the same function is secedit.exe.

Question 5.6

Answer e is correct. S/MIME (Secure Multipurpose Internet Mail Extensions) uses Secure Hash Algorithm or MD5 (Message Digest 5) for the hash function used to create the digital signature. S/MIME incorporates three public key algorithms, of which DSS (Digital Signature Standard) is preferred. Fortezza cryptocards are smart cards developed by the National Security Agency that securely store public key credentials.

Question 5.7

Answer c is correct. Both methods (using the **certsvr.exe -z** command, or right-clicking on the appropriate CA node and selecting Properties on the Certificate Authority MMC snap-in) will expose policy information such as the identity of the requestor, the state of the request, and so on.

Glossary

access control

The service that manages permissions of an authenticated principal (user or group) to perform an operation or manipulate an object.

access control entry (ACE)

The identifying entry of a principal (user or group) in a list that grants or denies permission to perform an action on an object.

access control list (ACL)

Part of the security descriptor of an object, a list of principals (or trustees) described in individual access control entries (ACEs) that grant or deny permission to perform an operation on an object. The discretionary ACL (DACL) lists the permissions granted or denied to principals listed in separate ACEs. The mandatory ACL (MACL) is a list of permissions centrally controlled by an administrator. The system ACL (SACL) specifies which events the system is to audit per user or group.

Active Directory (AD)

The Windows 2000 directory service that authenticates and authorizes named objects to access network resources based on provided security credentials and other information.

Active Directory Connector (ADC)

The application interface that replicates directory objects between a Microsoft Exchange Server directory (version 5.5 or later) and Active Directory directory services.

Active Directory Services Interfaces (ADSI)

The set of programming interfaces based on the Component Object Model (COM) that enable client applications to access network directory services.

Administrative Template

Special files with the .adm file extension that provide baseline security profiles with access through the Group Policy Microsoft Management Console (MMC) snap-in or the legacy System Policy Editor.

American National Standards Institute (ANSI)

The voluntary organization composed of computer professionals and companies that create standards for the computer industry.

American Standard Code for Information Interchange (ASCII)

A standard (based on an 8-bit character system) for transferring data between systems.

application programming interface (API)

The interface through which you can access program routines, procedures, and functions in an application or operating system component.

architecture

The logical design or schema of a system, such as Windows 2000, or hypothetical construct, such as the Open Systems Interconnection (OSI) Reference Model.

attribute

A single characteristic or property of an object described by a variable within a defined range.

authentication

The process of verifying the identity of a user who is attempting to access computer resources against some trusted credentials. Alternatively, the process of verifying the integrity of a received transmitted message against its content when it is originally sent.

authentication, authorization, and auditing (AAA) server

Taken from the triple A security model, which addresses remote access security, an AAA server performs authentication, authorization, and accounting functions. In this book, I have replaced the more general accounting function with an auditing function to conform to an Open Systems Interconnection (OSI) model of specific functional management areas in a network operating system.

bulk data encryption

A high-speed method of encryption that typically uses a symmetric encryption algorithm. In Encrypting File System (EFS), a unique file encryption key (FEK) is generated for the bulk encryption of data.

Certificate Authority (CA)

A trusted source that issues digital certificates that corroborate the identity of a named principal. This issued certificate contains supporting credentials and a public key of the private key holder authenticated by the CA. With the public key, secured information can be exchanged with the private key holder.

certificate practices statement (CPS)

Defines operational procedures on a Certificate Authority (CA) level based on certificate policies (CPs). These policies include the kinds of policies linked to the CA, method of certificate distribution, how the CA is administered, how revocations are handled, how access to the CA is secured, and so on.

command-line interface (CLI)

A textual user interface, commonly called a command prompt, that enables the communication of instructions to an operating system.

Common Information Model (CIM)

See *Windows Management Instrumentation (WMI)*.

container

An Active Directory (AD) object that is a holder of other objects or other containers.

cross-domain exchange

With regard to Group Policy Objects (GPOs), the linking to Group Policy settings in GPOs stored outside the current domain.

cryptanalysis

Methods and techniques involved in decrypting a message encoded in an unreadable format.

Cryptographic Application Programming Interface (CAPI)

A Microsoft application programming interface (API) that provides programmable support for cryptographic applications through independent modules called cryptographic service providers (CSPs).

data encryption standard (DES)

A symmetric-key encryption method standardized by the American National Standards Institute (ANSI) in 1981 as ANSI X.3.92. This method uses a 56-bit key.

delegation

The transferring of administrative authority or rights from one principal to another.

demilitarized zone (DMZ)

The type of firewall technology that consists of a bastion host sandwiched between two packet-filtering routers that provide the highest level of security among firewall technology configurations. Also called a screened-subnet firewall.

digital certificate

Used for security purposes, an attachment to an electronic message that a Certificate Authority (CA) usually generates. It is used to verify that the message sender is who he or she claims to be; it also provides the receiver with the means to encode a reply to the sender in the form of the sender's public key.

digital envelope

The encryption of a secret key within a message that uses a public key.

digital nervous system

Describes distributed services used to obtain and understand information.

digital signature

An encrypted digital message attached to another message that uniquely identifies the sender.

directory

An Active Directory (AD) container object that stores information about objects on the network.

directory consolidation technology

A technology that substitutes an application's native directory services with the data repositories that the operating system directory services provide.

directory service
Provides services for storing and making accessible object-related information datastores to system services and users.

Directory Services Migration Tool (DSMigrate)
A special tool provided with Windows 2000 that is used to migrate NetWare users and resources to a Windows 2000 enterprise.

disaster recovery plan
Formal documentation outlining policies and procedures that must be followed if an unexpected disaster occurs. This document sometimes includes a network security plan that outlines the information technology (IT) security controls most important to the functioning of the corporation.

discretionary ACL (DACL)
See *access control list (ACL)*.

distinguished name
A unique object description that identifies the domain that holds the object as well as the complete path through the container hierarchy by which the object is reached.

distribution group
A group that is not security enabled, is used exclusively for email distribution, and has no effects on logon times or network traffic.

distribution list
A datastore of contact information for easy retrieval by mail programs.

domain
An administrative and security grouping of Windows NT/2000-based computers that can span more than one physical location and have common user accounts. With regard to the Domain Name System (DNS), a domain consists of a group of domains that share a common DNS namespace.

domain controller (DC)
A Windows NT/2000-based server that holds an Active Directory (AD) partition.

domain local group
An Active Directory (AD) object that contains users and global groups from any domain in the forest, universal groups, and other domain local groups in its own domain.

Domain Name Service
A Windows NT/2000 system service that uses static, hierarchically arranged information for name/address resolution to TCP/IP addressing.

Domain Name System (DNS)
An Internet service that uses a hierarchical, distributed database for name/address resolution to Transmission Control Protocol/Internet Protocol (TCP/IP) addressing.

Encrypting File System (EFS)
A file system that supports the encryption and decryption of files.

enterprise identity management
The management of centralized services that provide authentication and authorization of named objects in

File and Print Services for NetWare version 5 (FPNW5)

An add-on service that NetWare clients use to access Windows 2000-based shared files and printer resources.

firewall technology

A combination of hardware and software solutions that prevent unauthorized access from external sources to an internal network. A screened-host firewall (also called a single-homed bastion) consists of a packet-filtering router and a bastion host with a single network interface card (NIC). A dual-homed bastion is more secure than a single-homed one because the server has two separate network interface cards (NICs) and thus creates an internal router that filters the flow of packets across the two connected networks.

Flexible (Floating) Single-Master Operations (FSMO)

According to the single-master model in an Active Directory (AD) forest, the five operations master roles assigned to at least one domain controller (DC) are, for the entire forest, domain naming and schema master; for the domain, infrastructure, primary DC (PDC), and relative ID (RID).

forest

A group of one or more Active Directory (AD) trees that trust each other and share a common schema, configuration, and Global Catalog (GC).

Fortezza Crypto Card technology

A group of peripheral products, most commonly smart cards, that use security technologies developed by the National Security Agency (NSA) to support public key encryption technologies.

Global Catalog (GC)

Located on domain controllers (DCs) called Global Catalog (GC) servers, a partial replica of every Windows 2000 domain in the directory. It also contains the schema and configuration of directory partitions.

global group

One of the Active Directory (AD) container objects that can appear on access control lists (ACLs) anywhere in the forest and may contain users and other global groups from its own domain.

Group Policy

Refers to applying Registry-based and other types of control settings to groups of computers and/or users within Active Directory (AD) containers. The collections of policies are referred to as Group Policy Objects (GPOs).

Group Policy loopback support

An advanced Group Policy setting that reorders the inheritance sequence in which Group Policy settings for a computer are applied to a user logging on to that specific machine.

Group Policy Object (GPO)

A collection of settings given a unique name stored in either a Group Policy container (GPC) (preferred) or a Group Policy template (GPT) used for file-based data. It stores software policy, script, and deployment information. The GPT is located in the system volume folder of the domain controller (DC).

hash function

A mathematical function that produces hash values for security purposes. A hash value (or simply hash) is a number generated from a string of text.

hash message authentication code (HMAC)

The mechanism for message authentication, which uses cryptographic hash functions.

hierarchical namespace

A hierarchically structured namespace that provides a mechanism that allows the namespace to be partitioned or organized into functional subsections.

Hypertext Transfer Protocol (HTTP)

The stateless protocol on which the World Wide Web is based.

independent software vendor (ISV)

A company that produces software.

IntelliMirror technology

A set of native Windows 2000 features providing desktop change and configuration management technology, which combines centralized computing with the flexibility of distributed computing. Users' data, applications, and settings are centrally managed and controlled anywhere in the enterprise environment. Services include user data management, software installation and maintenance, user settings management, and remote installation services.

Internet Authentication Service (IAS)

Software services specifically designed for wide area network (WAN) deployment that provide centralized remote access authentication, authorization, and auditing for both the remote access server and the Virtual Private Network (VPN) server.

Internet Protocol Security (IPSec) protocol suite

A set of protocols that support secure exchange of packets at the IP layer. The suite consists of two security protocols: Authentication Header (AH) and Encapsulated Security Payload (ESP), two encryption modes (transport and tunnel), and Internet Key Exchange (IKE) security associations for exchanging public keys during secured transmissions.

IP addressing scheme

An identifier for a computer or device on a Transmission Control Protocol/Internet Protocol (TCP/IP) network.

Kerberos Authentication Service (AS) request/reply

Using the Kerberos protocol, the request a client makes to a Key Distribution Center (KDC) for authentication and a ticket-granting ticket (TGT), along with the KDC reply with that TGT.

Kerberos Client/Server (CS) Authentication Service (AS) exchange

Using the Kerberos protocol, the request a client makes to a Key Distribution Center (KDC) for a ticket-granting ticket (TGT).

Kerberos protocol

The default Windows 2000 authentication method, a security protocol that authenticates users but doesn't provide authorization to services or resources.

Kerberos ticket-granting service (TGS) request/reply

Using the Kerberos protocol, the request a client makes to the TGS side of the Key Distribution Center (KDC) for a service-granting ticket, along with the reply.

Key Distribution Center (KDC)

A Kerberos 5 service, run on a domain controller (DC), which issues ticket-granting tickets (TGTs) and service-granting tickets (which Microsoft refers to as service tickets) for obtaining network authentication in a domain.

Knowledge Consistency Checker (KCC)

A built-in service that runs on all domain controllers (DCs) and automatically establishes network connections (or site links) between machines for replicating AD information. These network connections, known as Windows 2000 Active Directory directory services connection objects, are the actual connections through which domain controllers exchange directory

services information within (and outside) their own site.

Lightweight Directory Access Protocol (LDAP)

A simplified version of the Directory Access Protocol (DAP), the native Windows 2000 protocol that provides access to a directory service that is currently being implemented in Web browsers and email programs. It is used to gain access to X.500 directories.

local computer policy

The initial security template applied to a computer.

mandatory ACL (MACL)

See *access control list (ACL)*.

message digest

The process by which a one-way hash function transforms a block of text into a single string of digits. When this transformed block of text is encrypted with a private key, it creates a digital signature, which is used for authentication.

Messaging Application Programming Interface (MAPI)

A Microsoft application programming interface (API) that provides programmable support for messaging applications.

meta-directory

Directory datastores centralized in one location, allowing applications to access them using a single access model and security system instead of having to interact with many different datastores and access methods.

Microsoft four-layer network model

Similar to the Open Systems Inter-connection (OSI) Reference Model except that there are four distinguishing layers: Application Programming Interface (API), Transport Driver Interface (TDI), Network Device Interface Specification, and Physical.

Microsoft Management Console (MMC)

A customizable frame that provides an interface for administrative tools, installable on demand, in the form of snap-ins.

Microsoft Point-To-Point Encryption (MPPE)

An encryption algorithm, especially useful when the IP Security suite is not appropriate or available, providing confidentiality between a remote access client and the remote access or tunnel server. The algorithm uses either 128-bit or 40-bit key encryption and is compatible with Network Address Translation. However, it is only available when either EAP-TLS or MS-CHAP authentication protocols are used.

Microsoft Resource Kit

Subsidiary documentation accompanied by tools and utilities that elaborate on or enhance features and services that are included in the installation CD-ROM for every operating system and BackOffice application.

mixed mode

The mode that allows domain controllers (DCs) that run on both Windows 2000 and Windows NT to coexist in the domain.

multimaster replication

An Active Directory (AD) feature that provides writable copies of the directory database across multiple servers in a domain.

Multipurpose Internet Mail Extensions (MIME)

An Internet mail system specification specifically for non-ASCII (binary or non-ASCII character sets) message packages so that they can be transmitted across a network. These packages typically carry non-HTML information like graphics, audio, and video files that sometimes require add-in applications to enable the browser to properly display their contents.

name resolution

In a defined namespace, the process of resolving a name into an object or information that the name represents.

namespace

Based on a naming convention, a named account (user, computer, group, or service) in a bounded area in which that given name can be resolved.

native mode

The mode in which all the domain controllers (DCs) in a given domain are running on the Windows 2000 operating system and taking full advantage of Active Directory (AD) features.

Network Address Translation (NAT)

An Internet standard that translates one set of Internet Protocol (IP) addresses for internal traffic in a local area network (LAN) to a second set of addresses for external traffic.

network security plan
Formal documentation that describes the security policy based upon corporate business objectives.

network security policy
A formal document that defines the services that will be explicitly allowed or denied on a network, how those services will be used, and special conditions and/or exceptions to rules.

Novell Directory Services (NDS)
Proprietary directory services, provided by Novell NetWare, that offer services similar to Microsoft Active Directory (AD).

object
A distinct, named set of attributes that represent some definable entity, such as a user, a printer, or an application.

Open Systems Interconnection (OSI) Reference Model
An International Organization for Standardization (ISO) standard reference tool for worldwide communications that defines a network in seven protocol layers.

Organizational Unit (OU)
An Active Directory (AD) object that is a container object. It is used to create an administrative partition, which can contain users, groups, resources, and other OUs.

parent-child trust relationship
The two-way, transitive trust relationship that is established in a domain and added to an Active Directory (AD) tree, providing pass-through logon authentication.

policy
The set of rules that govern the interaction between a subject and an object.

primary domain controller (PDC)
In legacy NT 4 or an earlier domain, the computer running Windows NT Server that maintained the directory database for a domain and authenticated domain logons. In Windows 2000, a domain controller still manages user access and shares in authentication through multimaster replication of the Active Directory data stores.

principal
A named object, resolvable in the namespace, that has a database record in the directory datastore.

profile
A collection of settings information that is applied to the interaction between a subject and an object.

public key infrastructure (PKI)
An integrated set of services and administrative tools for creating, deploying, and managing public key-based authentication processes, including the cryptographic methods, the use of digital certificates and Certificate Authorities (CAs), and the system for managing the process.

relative distinguished name (RDN)
The part of the name of an object that is an attribute of the object itself.

remote access technology

The ability to log on to or to connect to a network from a distant location.

Remote Authentication Dial-In User Service (RADIUS)

A distributed security system designed for centrally administering remote access across a wide area network (WAN).

replication

In database management, the service that synchronizes distributed databases by copying the entire database or subsets of the database to other servers in the network.

schema

The definition of the data language used to create an entire database, including the objects that can be stored in that database.

schema master

The domain controller (DC) assigned to control all updates to the schema within a forest.

screened-host architecture

See *firewall technology*.

screened-subnet architecture

See *demilitarized zone (DMZ)*.

Secure Channel (SChannel) security protocols

The protocols—including Secure Sockets Layer 3 (SSL3)/Transport Layer Security 1 (TLS1)—that Security Support Provider Interface (SSPI) provider supports.

Secure Hypertext Transfer Protocol (S-HTTP)

An extension to Hypertext Transfer Protocol (HTTP) that supports sending data securely over the World Wide Web. It sends individual messages, as opposed to data packets, securely.

Secure Multipurpose Internet Mail Extensions (S/MIME)

A version of the Multipurpose Internet Mail Extensions (MIME) protocol that supports encryption of messages based on the public-key encryption technology of RSA (named after Rivest, Shamir, and Adelman).

security association (SA)

In an IP Security (IPSec) exchange, a unidirectional connection between two IPSec systems in either of two modes—tunnel or transport—depending on the protocol involved.

security ID (SID)

A number that uniquely identifies a named principal in the namespace.

Security Parameters Index (SPI)

In IP Security (IPSec) exchanges, a 32-bit value used to identify different security associations with the same destination address and security protocol. See *security association (SA)*.

single-master operations

Active Directory (AD) operations that are not permitted to occur at different places in the network at the same time. See *Flexible (Floating) Single-Master Operations (FSMO)*.

Single Sign-On (SSO)

The process by which an NT/ Windows 2000 domain user or guest can log on to the network once and gain access to all network resources and services within the domain or the enterprise.

site

In a network, a physical location that holds Active Directory (AD) servers and that is defined as one or more well-connected Transmission Control Protocol/Internet Protocol (TCP/IP) subnets. See *well connected*.

store

The physical storage for each Active Directory (AD) replica.

system ACL (SACL)

See *access control list (ACL)*.

transitive trust

The two-way trust relationship between Windows 2000 domains in a domain tree or forest, or between trees in a forest, or between forests. A transitive trust is automatically established, through the Kerberos authentication protocol, when a domain joins an existing forest or domain tree in native mode Windows 2000. In mixed-mode environments, where NTLM is the default authentication protocol, two domains form nontransitive trusts.

Transmission Control Protocol/Internet Protocol (TCP/IP) protocol suite

A suite of networking protocols and utilities used on the Internet that provide an exchange of information in the form of packets across intercon-nected, heterogeneous networks of diverse hardware and operating system architecture.

tree

A set of Windows NT/2000 domains connected through transitive, bidirectional trusts that share a common schema, configuration, and Global Catalog (GC). These domains form a contiguous hierarchical namespace.

tunneling protocol

A protocol that supports a logical connection over which data is exchanged in an encapsulated form. Usually, the data is both encapsulated and encrypted. When this occurs, the tunnel is considered a private, secure link between a consumer and a host.

two-factor authentication

An authentication method that requires two separate sets of security credentials: "what I know" and "what I have."

universal group

The simplest form of group in the enterprise that can appear in access control lists (ACLs) anywhere in the forest and that can contain other universal groups, global groups, and users from anywhere in the forest.

Unix-to-Unix encoding (UUEncoding)

A set of algorithms for converting files into a series of 7-bit American Standard Code for Information Interchange (ASCII) characters that can be transmitted over the Internet; it is especially popular for sending email attachments.

Virtual Private Network (VPN)

A network that is constructed by using public networks to connect private nodes. These systems use encryption and other security mechanisms to ensure that only authorized users can access the network and that the data cannot be intercepted.

Web-Based Enterprise Management (WBEM)

An initiative, using Windows Management Instrumentation (WMI), to establish standards for accessing and sharing management information over an enterprise network.

well connected

Network connectivity that is highly reliable and fast—local area network (LAN) speeds of 10Mbps or greater—to make Windows 2000 and Active Directory (AD) perform in a useful way. The precise meaning of the term is determined by your particular needs.

Windows Management Instrumentation (WMI)

An Web-Based Enterprise Management (WBEM)-compliant initiative that provides integrated support for the Common Information Model (CIM), a data model that describes objects existing in a management environment. It proposes universal access to management information for enterprises by providing a consistent view of the managed environment.

Windows Scripting Host (WSH)

Programming platform or host that enables scripts to be run directly in Windows 2000 through the graphical user interface (GUI) or at the command prompt. It has very low memory requirements and runs in both interactive and noninteractive scripting modes.

X.500

A set of standards that define a distributed directory service developed by the International Organization for Standardization (ISO).

X.509

Used for defining digital certificates, an International Telecommunications Union (ITU) recommendation that has not yet been officially defined or approved.

Index

Bold page numbers indicate sample exam questions.

3DES, 64
64-bit encryption, 64
128-bit encryption, 64

A

AAA, 41, 91–94, **117**
AAA servers, 104
Access, securing
    about, 333–334
    desktop, 339–340
    IntelliMirror, 339–340
    prestaging, 341
    RIS, 340–341
    server referring, 341
    smart cards, 334–339, **355**
    SMB signing, 342–343
    SNMP, 341–342
    terminal services, 339–340
    two-factor authentication, 334
Access, standardizing
    about, 330–331
    Kerberos, 332
    SSL, 332–333
    SSO, 331–333
Access control, **365**
    ACLs, managing, 264
    active interception, 267–268
    authenticated access, limiting,
      262-264
    DACLs, 265
    deploying, 263–264
    EAP, 263–264
    EAP-TLS, 263–264

MACLs, 265
    password length, 263
    PPP, 263
    RBACs, 265–266, 275, **373**
    remote access policies, 263–264
    resources, 267–268, 273
    security administration, managing,
      264–266
    strategies, 262
    trust relationships, establishing,
      266–267
    trusted for delegation, 263
Access control entities. *See* ACEs.
Access control lists. *See* ACLs.
Access management, Apple
    Macintosh, 350
Account database, Microsoft
    Kerberos 5, 101
Account mapping, Microsoft
    Kerberos 5, 103
Account policies, 306
ACEs, 41
acldiag.exe, 314
ACLs, 41–42, 73, 264
Action plan
    for deployment, 34, **56**
    network security, 234–242
Active Directory. *See* AD.
Active Directory Connectors. *See* ADCs.
Active Directory Installation Wizard.
    See DCPROMO.
Active Directory Services. *See* ADS.
Active Directory Services Interfaces.
    See ADSI.

ActivePerl 5.6, 348
AD, **387**. *See also* Access control; Groups.
   about, 38
   APIs, 255
   attributes, 255, **272**
   computer account names, 257
   contacts, 278
   containers, 257, **272**, 282
   DCs, 260–261, **271**
   directory services, 254–255
   domain names, 257
   domains, 258–259, 262
   forests, 39, 259, **272**
   FSMO roles, 260–261, **271**
   GC, 260
   Group Policy, 278–280
   group types, 277–278
   icons, 39
   identity management, 201–202, **210**
   KDC integration, 255
   namespaces, 257–258
   naming conventions, 256–257
   network security plan, 226
   objects, 255, **272**
   OUs, 259
   replication, 261–262
   SDOU, 282
   server collections, 261
   sites, 261
   trees, 258–259, **272**
AD Installation Wizard.
  See DCPROMO.
Adaptive format, 13–14, 17–18
ADCs, 201
addiag.exe, 318
adduser.exe, 318
Administration, Group Policy, 284–286
Administration tools, 301–304
Administrative templates, 279, 285, **293**
ADS
   about, 38–41
   as directory service provider, 40–41
   KDC and, 94
   LDAP and, 40–41
   tools, 303–305
ADSI, 201, 255, **270**
ADSI Edit snap-in, 314
AH, 126, 131–132, 138, 161
AH packet type, 162
Aliases, directory services, 256
American National Standards Institute
  X3.92. *See* ANSI X3.92.

Analyze operation, 311, **322**
Anonymous access, 186–187
ANSI X3.92, 64
Answering routers, 165, **175**
Anti-replay, 131
API layer, 36–37
APIs
   AD, 255
   smart cards, 335–336
Apple Macintosh migration, 349–350, **357**
AppleTalk interoperability, 349–350
Application layer security technologies,
  194–195, **207**
Application programming interfaces.
  See APIs.
Application-level encryption, 128
Application-level gateway, 167
Applications group, 232–233
Application-specific security, 194–196
AS exchange, 90, 94–96
Asymmetric encryption
   PKI, 66–68
   procedural steps (diagram), 67, **82**
   symmetric vs., 67–68, 72, **82**
ATMs, 70
Attack modalities
   categorizing, 45–48
   e-commerce, 48–49
   firewalls, 168
   IIS server, 191–192
   Internet, 49
   IPSec, 126–127
   layered models and, 49–50
   network security plan, 220–221
   RIS, 341
   types of, 28–30, **56–57**
Attributed naming, 256
Auditing
   data flows, 172
   IIS server, 191
   network security plan, 227
auditpol.exe, 318
Authenticated access, limiting, 262–264
Authentication, **366**, **372**.
  See also IPSec; Kerberos.
   client/server Kerberos exchange, 90
   cross-domain, 98–100
   e-commerce, 104–106, **119**
   heterogeneous population with
     secured exchange, 187–189,
     195, **208**
   HTTP, 78, 187–188

identity management, 328
IIS, 186, 191–192
Internet, 105
intranets, 187
IPSec, 138, 162
Microsoft Kerberos 5, 105–106
most secure, 188
network security plan, 219
NTLM vs. Kerberos, 106–107,
   109, **116**
PKI, 68–71
subdirectories, 186
through comparison, 69–70
through proof of possession, 70–71
two-factor authentication, 263,
   271, 334
virtual directories, 186
virtual servers, 186
Web content, 186
Authentication, authorization, and
   auditing. *See* AAA.
Authentication delegation, 93, 100
Authentication Header. *See* AH.
Authentication Service exchange.
   See AS exchange.
Authenticity not assumed, 130, **147**
Authenticode, 77, 196
Authorization. *See also* Kerberos.
   Microsoft Kerberos 5, 105–106
   MIT Kerberos 5, 105
   security controls, 329
Automatic teller machines. *See* ATMs.

B

Backup DCs. *See* BDCs.
Bandwidth Allocation Protocol. *See* BAP.
Banking industry and encryption, 79
BAP, 155
Basic authentication, 186–188, **372**
basic*.inf, 309
Bastion, 126, 166
Bastion hosts, 166
BDCs, 259
Bindings, disabling on IIS server, 190
Blank answers, 17, 19
Block Policy Inheritance, 288–289
Bogies, 49
Bogus nameserver cache loading, 128
Boundaries, secured, 34
Broadcast media, 128
Brokerage function, 330
Brute force attacks, 29
Budgeting your time, 17

Build-list-and-reorder format, 7–8
Bulk data encryption, 64, 68, 71, **82**
Business objectives
   in disaster recovery plan, 30
   e-commerce and, 43
   importance of, 326
   from key personnel, 30, 32, **55**
   from surveys, 28, 30
Business partners
   case studies, 217, 230, **247**
   defined, 217
   network security plan, 233–234
   VPNs and, 217, 230, **247**
Business strategy, smart cards, 334–335

C

CA certificate stores. *See* Certificate stores.
CA hierarchies, 74–75, **84**
Cable TV interception risk level, 128
Calling routers, 165, **175**
Canonical name, 256
CAPI
   overview, 78–79
   supported services, 78, **83**
Carnegie Mellon CERT Coordination
   Center Web site, 21
CAs, **386–387**
   internally managed, 193
   IT security controls provided by, 193
   PKI, 73
   services, list of, 193–194, **209**
   standalone, 75, **371**
   Thawte, 193
   VeriSign, 193
   Web exchanges, verifying parties, 193
Case studies
   access control, 269
   business partners and VPNs, 217,
      230, 247
   confidentiality, 269
   e-commerce security issues,
      220–226, 247
   exam format, 4–5, 13
   exam strategy, 15–16
   Group Policy, 292
   IIS server, 205–206
   internal business services, 241–242,
      244, 246
   IPSec, 141–145
   Kerberos, 110–113
   network issues, 205–206
   network security plan, 234–242
   Novell migration, 354

organizational charts, 216–217,
236–238, 244, 245–246
security decisions, 114–115
security policy, 234–242
sharing resources with other
companies, 110–113
smart cards, 354
tools, 319–320
Case studies, 4Sale
access control, 269
business partners and VPNs, 217,
230, 247
confidentiality, 269
e-commerce security issues,
220–226, 247
Group Policy, 292
IIS server, 205–206
internal business services, 241–242,
244, 246
IPSec, 144–145
network issues, 205–206
Novell migration, 354
organizational charts, 216–217,
236–238, 244, 245–246
remote access, 173–174
security decisions, 114–115
smart cards, 354
tools, 319–320
VPNs, 173–174
Case studies, ExamCram Ltd.
IPSec, 141–143
Kerberos, 110–113
network security plan, 234–242
security policy, 234–242
sharing resources with other
companies, 110–113
VPNs, 154–155
CDFS, 349
Center for Education and Research in
Information Assurance and Security, 21
Center for Education and Research in
Information Assurance and Security
page. See CERIAS Web page.
Center for Information Technology/
National Institutes of Health.
See CIT/NIH Web site.
Centralized administration tools, 301, **320**
CERIAS Web page, 21
CERT Coordination Center, 21
Certificate Authorities. See CAs.
Certificate Authority snap-in, 194
Certificate extensibility, 73

Certificate management services, 78–79
Certificate Revocation List v2.
See CRL v2.
Certificate Server services, 194
Certificate Services CLI tools, 313–314
Certificate stores, 78–79
Certificates, 73–74
Certification exams. See Exams.
Certified for Microsoft Windows logo, 196
CERTREQ, 313
CERTSRV, 313
CERTUTIL, 313–314
Challenge Handshake Authentication
Protocol. See CHAP.
CHAP, 156, **178**
Child domains, 259, **368**
Choke points, 126, 165, 172
Chokes, 166
Ciphertext, 63
Circuit-level gateway, 167
Circumscribed contiguous subtree, 258
CIT/NIH Web site, 21
Cleartext, 63
Cleartext challenge, 70–71
CLI tools
Certificate Services, 313–314
Group Policy, 290–291
SC Tool Set, 310–311
Client configuration, Microsoft Kerberos
5, 103
Client flooding, 128
Client management, VPNs, 165
Client policy, IPSec, 139
Client Service for NetWare. See CSNW.
Client/server authentication exchange.
See CS authentication exchange.
CM, 231–232
COM+, 350–353
COM service, 352
Command-line interface tools.
See CLI tools.
Community management, 328–329
Compact Disc File System. See CDFS.
compatible*.inf, 310, **373**
Competency Model, 27–28, 50–51, **57**
Component Object Model+. See COM+.
Compulsory tunnels, 159
Computer account names, 257
Computer emergency response team
Coordination Center. See CERT
Coordination Center.
Computer profiles, 278–280, 281–282

Confidentiality, **367**. *See also* IPSec; VPNs.
  categories of, 238–239
  EFS, 268
  IPSec, 162
  messages, and key length, 64
  using symmetric encryption, 63–65
Configuration tools, 306–312.
  See also Tools.
Configure operation, 311, **322**
Connection function, 329–330
Connection Manager. *See* CM.
Consumer, defined, 255
Consumer-provider model, 44–48,
  61–62, 103
Consumer-Web server flow, 192, **207**
Contacts, 278
Containers, 257, **272**, 282
Context function, 327–328
Contiguous subtrees, 258
Corporate business objectives.
  See Business objectives.
Corporate culture, 35
Corporate objectives, 61–62
Costs. *See* TCO.
Countermeasures, 61–62
Counters, exam, 3, 17
Crack attacks, 29, 49
Create-a-tree format, 8–10
Credentials cache, 93, 101, **120**
CRL v2, 77
Cross-domain authentication, 98–100
Cryptanalysis, 65–66
Crypto Archive Web site, 21
Cryptographic Application Programming
  Interface. *See* CAPI.
Cryptographic Resources, Inc. Web site, 21
Cryptographic service providers. *See* CSPs.
Cryptography Archives Web site, 21
CS authentication exchange, 90
CSNW, 343
CSPs, 78–79, 105

D

DACLs, 42, 106, 265
Data dictionary, 258
Data Encryption Standard. *See* DES.
Data Encryption Standard-Cipher Block
  Chaining. *See* DES-CBC.
Data protection and management
  tools, 305
Database configuration tools, 308
DCPROMO, 99, 260
DCs, 260–261, **271**

Default deny, 171, 185–186, **383**
Default permit, 171, 185–186
Default protocol, IPSec, 161
Definable context, 257
Delegating Group Policies, 286, **293, 368**
Delegation of authority, 263
Deliverables, security plan, 234–242
Demilitarized zone. *See* DMZ.
Denial of service. *See* DOS attacks.
Deny permissions, 288
Deployment
  access control, 263–264
  Basic authentication, 187–188, **372**
  enterprise security system, 34, **56**
  Group Policy, 284–286
  identity management, 200–202, 204
  IIS permissions, 189–190
  Integrated Windows
    authentication, 188
  IPSec, 128–129
  IPSec strategy, 136–140
  network security plan, 228–234
  SSL, 192
  steps, 34, **56**
  tools, 301
DES, 64
DES-CBC, 131, 134
Desktop
  Group Policy, 281
  management tools, 301, 304–305
  securing, 281, 339–340
DH, 134
Diffie-Hellman. *See* DH.
Digest authentication, 186, 188
Digital certificates, 105, 193
Digital envelopes, 71
Digital nervous system, 326
Digital Signature Standard. *See* DSS.
Digital signatures, 28, 49, 71, 73, 196
Directory browsing, disabling on IIS
  server, 191
Directory consolidation, 232
Directory containers. *See* Containers.
Directory database, defined, 219
Directory service provider, 198–199, **209**
Directory services, **368, 384**
  about, 252–253
  AD, 254–255
  AD server collections, 261
  aliases, 256
  attributes, 255, **272**
  canonical name, 256

child domains, 259, **368**
circumscribed contiguous subtree, 258
components, 257–262
consumers, 255
containers, 257, **272**
contiguous subtrees, 258
data dictionary, 258
DC, 260–261, **271**
definable context, 257
disjointed namespaces, 259
DN, 259
DNs, 256
DNS domains, 259
Domain Naming Master, 261, **271**
domain trees, 258–259
domains, 258
features, 254–255
file class, 258
forests, 259, **272**
FSMOs, 260–261, **271**
GC, 259–260
heterogeneous, 255, **270**
identity management, 199–200
Infrastructure Master, 261, **271**
instances, 258
LDAP v3, 254
leaf nodes, 257
metadata, 258
meta-directories, 201–202,
    223–224, 253
named objects, defined, 255
namespaces, 257–258
naming conventions, 256–257
noncontiguous namespaces, 259
object class instances, 258
objects, 255, **272**
OUs, 259
parent domains, 259
PDC Advertiser, 261, **271**
PDC Emulator, 261
principals, defined, 255
purpose of, 256
RDNs, 256
Relative ID Master, 261, **271**
replica DCs, 260
replication, 260, 261–262
RID Operations Master, 261, **271**
schema, 258
Schema Master, 260, **271**
search engine, 260
sites, 261
subtrees, 257

terms, 257–262
trees, 257–259, **272**
trust relationships, 258
unit of replication, 258
walking the tree, 258
well connected, 261
X.500, 253–254
X.509, 253–254
Disabling directory browsing, 191
Disabling services, protocols, and
    bindings, 190
Disaster recovery plans, 30, 48, 214
Discretionary ACLs. *See* DACLs.
Disjointed namespaces, 259
Distinguished names. *See* DNs.
Distributed interNet Applications
    Architecture. *See* DNA.
Distributed Password Authentication.
    See DPA.
Distributed security
    defined, 214
    risk analysis, 33
Distributed services, COM+, 351–353
Distribution groups, 277–278
DMZ
    firewalls, 170–171
    network security plan, 224
DNA, 326
DNS, 185–186
DNs, 256, 259
DNS domains, 259
DNS servers, 128
DoD four-layer model, 36–37
Domain controllers. *See* DCs.
Domain local groups, 277–278
Domain model features, 42
Domain Name System. *See* DNS.
Domain names, 257
Domain Naming Master, 261, **271**
Domain trees, 39, 258–259
Domains
    AD, 258–259, 262, **364**, **382**
    directory services, 258
    functions of, 262
    single domain model, 41
DOS attacks, 29
Down-level, defined, 93
DPA, 78, 105
Drag-and-connect format, 10–11
dsacls.exe, 314
DSS, 70, 72, **388**
Dual-ported hosts, 169

E

EAP, 105, 155, **178**, 263–264, **372**
EAP-TLS, 263–264
Eavesdropping, 127, 172
E-commerce
    attack modalities, 48–49
    authentication, 104–106, **119**
    business objectives and, 43
    case studies, 220–226, 247
    identification, 197–198
    IPSec and, 129
    permission management, 197–198
    security issues, 220–226, 247
    TCO, 43
EFS, 267–268, 273, 275, **386**
Email, smart cards, 338–339
Encapsulated Security Payload. *See* ESP.
Encapsulation, IPSec, 133
Encrypting File System. *See* EFS.
Encryption and Security Related
    Resources Crypto-farm Web site, 21
Encryption techniques, 133–134
Encryption technologies, 62–63, **80**
Encryption Web sites, 20–22
End-to-end, defined, 154
End-to-end encryption, 127
End-to-end network security, 157
Enterprise CA, 75
Enterprise security system, 34, **56**
ESP, 126, 131–132, 138, 161
ESP packet type, 162
Ethernet interception risk level, 128
Event log, 306
Event Viewer snap-in, 304
Everyone user population, 216, 229
Exams
    adaptive format, 13–14, 17–18
    blank answers, 17, 19
    budgeting your time, 17
    build-list-and-reorder format, 7–8
    case study format, 4–5, 13, 15–16
    counters, 3, 17
    create-a-tree format, 8–10
    drag-and-connect format, 10–11
    exam-readiness, assessing, 2
    exhibits, 4
    fixed-length format, 13, 16–17, 19
    guessing, 18–19
    marking questions for later, 16
    multiple-choice format, 5–6
    number of questions, 15
    partial credit, 6
    practice questions, 19–20
    process of elimination, 18
    question formats, 5
    questions remaining counter, 17
    revisiting questions, 14, 16
    select-and-place format, 11–12
    short-form format, 14, 16–17, 19
    simulations, format, 13
    simulations, practice questions, 13
    test formats, about, 13–14
    test formats, determining, 15
    testing centers, 3–4
    Web sites of interest, 19–22
Exams, strategies
    adaptive format, 17–18
    case study format, 15–16
    fixed-length format, 16–17, 19
    short-form format, 16–17, 19
Exchange 2000, 254
Exchanges. *See* Subprotocols.
Executing utilities, 312
Executive user population, 217, 239–240
Exhibits (exam), 4
Existence function, 327
Expired certificates, 76
Export operation, 311, **322**
Export restrictions on encryption, 79
Extensibility. *See* COM+.
Extensible Authentication Protocol.
    See EAP.
Extensible Authentication Protocol-
    Transport Layer/Level Security.
    See EAP-TLS.
Extensible ticket fields, 92–93
Extranets, 129, **146**, 233.
    See also Business partners; VPNs.

F

FDDI, 128
Federal information processing standard
    180. *See* FIPS PUB 180.
Fiber Distributed Data Interface.
    See FDDI.
File and Print Services for NetWare
    version 5. *See* FPNW5.
File class, 258
File Migration Utility. *See* FMU.
File System tool, 307
Filter actions, IPSec, 139
Filter lists, IPSec, 138, **378**
FIPS PUB 180, 134

Firewalls, **376–377, 379**. *See also* VPNs.
  about, 165–166
  attack modalities, 168
  choke points, positioning at, 172
  components, 166–167
  DMZ, 170–171
  network security plan, 224
  packet filter architecture, 168
  packet filter routers, 166
  packet flow, 167–171, **176**
  policies, 171–172
  proxy servers, 166–167
  screened host architecture, 168–170
  screened-subnet architecture,
    170–171
  topologies, 167–171
  topologies, most secure, 171
Fixed-length format, 13, 16–17, 19
Flags, Microsoft Kerberos 5, 92
Flexible (Floating) Single-Master
  Operations. *See* FSMOs.
FMU, 345, **357**
Folder redirection, 286
Forests, 259, **272**
Fortezza, 21, 197, 211, **388**
Forwarded TGTs, 100
FPNW5, 345
FSMOs, 260–261, **271**

G

Gates, 166
Gateway Service for NetWare.
  See GSNW.
GC, 259–260
General Security Services API.
  See GSS-API.
Generic Routing Encapsulation. *See* GRE.
Global Catalog. *See* GC.
Global encryption policies, 79
Global groups, 277
GPOs, 276, 283, 286, **293, 368**
gpotool.exe, 318
gpresults.exe, 318
GRE, 316
Group Policy
  AD, 278–280
  administration, 284–286
  administrative templates, 279,
    285, **293**
  Block Policy Inheritance, 288–289
  CLI tools, 290–291
  computer profiles, 278–280, 281–282
  delegating, 286, **293, 368**

Deny permissions, 288
deployment, 284–286
desktop, securing, 281
folder redirection, 286
GPOs, 276, 283, 286, **293**
Group Policy MMC extensions,
  285–286, **293**
groups, about, 276–277
groups, nesting, 277
groups, types of, 277–278
identity management, 281–282
inheritance, 282–283, 288, **368**
Local Group Policy processing order,
  287–288
loopback support, 289–290, **295**
Merge mode, 289, **295**
mixed mode environments, 282
MMC extensions, 285–286, **293**
multiple, 284
nesting OUs, 284
No Override, 288–289
permission management, 281–282,
  288, 290–291
policy management, 283–284
processing order, 286–290, **294**
Replace mode, 289
RIS, 286
roaming profiles, 278
rules-based management, 278–280
scope of control, 282–283
scripts, 286
security groups, 282–283, 286
security settings, 285, **293, 368**
security settings extensions, 308
software installation and
  maintenance, 285
storage domains, 283
user profiles, 278–280, 281–282
Web sites, 297
Windows 2000 vs. NT 4, 276–280
Group Policy MMC, 42
Group Policy Objects. *See* GPOs.
Groups
  about, 276–277
  Group Policy, 276–277
  nesting, 277–278, 284
  policies, 278–280
  restricted, 306
  security settings, 278–280
  types of, 277–278
GSNW, 343
GSS-API, 41, 103
Guessing on exam, 18–19

H

Hacker Libraries Web site, 21
HAL, 37
Hardening the boundaries, 34
Hardware Abstraction Layer. *See* HAL.
Hardware compatibility list, 21
Hash function, 28, 67, 69–70
Hash message authentication code.
    See HMAC.
Hash message authentication code-
    Message Digest 5. *See* HMAC-MD5.
Hash signatures, 72
Help Desk support, 228
Heterogeneous directory services, 255, **270**
Heterogeneous environments.
    See also Access, standardizing.
        authentication with secured
            exchange, 187–189, 195, **208**
        Kerberos, 195
        SSL/TLS, 195
Hierarchy of authorities, 74–75
hisec*.inf, 310, **370**
HMAC, 68, 131, 134, **388**
HMAC-MD5, 134
Homogeneous environments
        Kerberos, 195
        SSL/TLS, 195
HTTP, 187–188
HTTP authentication, 78, 187–188
Hypertext Transfer Protocol. *See* HTTP.

I

ICCs, 335
Icons for AD, 39
Identification, 197–198
Identity administration, 327–328
Identity integration, 329–330
Identity management. *See also* AD.
        about, 198–199, 252, 326–327
        AD and, 201–202, **210**
        Apple, 350
        authentication, 328
        community management, 328–329
        context function, 327–328
        deployment, 200–202, 204
        directory service provider,
            198–199, **209**
        directory services and, 199–200
        existence function, 327
        Group Policy, 281–282
        identity administration, 327–328
        interoperability, 203

        LDAP, 199
        NDS, 201, **210**
        provisioning function, 328
        ROI, 203
        security controls, 328
        security objectives, 202–203
        TCO, 203
        Unix, 347–348
IETF Web site, 21
IIS 5
        authentication schemes, 186
        COM+, 352
        DNS, 185–186
        network addressing, 185–186
        security control layers, 185
        security restriction, configuring,
            185–186
IIS permissions
        deploying, 189–190
        with NTFS, 189–190
IIS servers
        attack modalities, 191–192
        auditing, 191
        authentication, 191–192
        disabling directory browsing, 191
        disabling services, protocols, and
            bindings, 190
        logging, 191
        secured end-to-end pipe, 192
        securing, 190–191, **208**, **373**
        SSL3/TLS1, 192
        traffic security, 191–192
IKE, 132, 161–162
Impersonation
        attack techniques, 29–30, 49
        IPSec, 127
        public keys, 72
        thwarting with encryption, 127–128
Import restrictions on encryption, 79
INF files, 306–307, 309–310, **321**
Information exchange steps, 140, **146**
Information technology security controls.
        See Security controls.
InfoSecurity News Web site, 21
Infrastructure Master, 261, **271**
Inheritance, Group Policy, 282–283,
        288, **368**
Inside attacks. *See* IPSec.
Instances, 258
Integrated circuit cards. *See* ICCs.
Integrated Windows authentication,
        186, 188
Integration strategy, 331

Integrity. *See also* IPSec.
    EFS, 268
    IPSec, 162
    PKI, 68–69
Intelligence Briefing Web site, 21
IntelliMirror, 281–282, 304–305, 339–340
Interception
    active, 68, 267–268
    attack techniques, 29
    broadcast media, 128
    cable TV, 128
    Ethernet, 128
    FDDI, 128
    IPSec, 127
    passive, 127–128
    thwarting with encryption, 127–128
Interference attack techniques, 29
Interix 2.2, 346–347, **383–384**
Internal business services, 241–242, 244,
    244, 246, **246**
International Organization for
    Standardization search engine.
    See ISO search engine.
Internet
    about, 22
    architectural weaknesses, 127
    attack modalities, 49
    authentication protocols, 105
    deployment examples, 128–129
    IPSec deployment examples, 128–129
    Microsoft licensing violations and, 190
    passive interception, 127–128
    SMB, 190
    SSPs, 104–106
Internet Engineering Task Force Web site.
    See IETF Web site.
Internet Information Server. *See entries*
    beginning with IIS.
Internet Key Exchange. *See* IKE.
Internet Protocol. *See entries beginning*
    with IP.
Internet Protocol Exchange. *See* IPX.
Internet Protocol Security. *See* IPSec.
Internet Security Association and Key
    Management Protocol. *See* ISAKMP.
Internet sites, blocking access to, 172
Interoperability, **121**, **384**
    about, 102–103
    access management, Apple, 350
    ActivePerl 5.6, 348
    Apple Macintosh migration,
      349–350, **357**

AppleTalk, 349–350
FMU, 345, **357**
FPNW5, 345
identity management, 203
identity management, Apple, 350
identity management, Unix, 347–348
Interix 2.2, 346–347, **383–384**
IPSec, 163
Microsoft Kerberos 5, 94, 102–103
migrations vs. coexistence, 343, **378**
MKS Toolkit, 347–348
MSDSS, 345, **355**
NetWare migration, 343–345, **357**
network administration, 348
OPENNT, 346
password synchronization, 347
SFU2, 346, 348
smart cards, 334–335
Telnet, 348
Unix migration, 345–348, **356**
user name mapping, 348
Intranets authentication, 187
IP 50 packet type, 162, **378**
IP 51 packet type, 162, **378**
IP attack modalities, 126–127
IP and DNS, 128
IP Security. *See* IPSec.
IP Security Policies on AD, 307
IPSec, **367**, **373**
    about, 126
    advantages, 130, **145**
    advantages of, 130
    AH, 126, 131–132, 138, 161
    AH packet type, 162
    architecture, 132–133
    attack modalities, 126–127
    authentication, 138, 162
    authenticity not assumed, 130, **147**
    case study, 4Sale, **144–145**
    case study, ExamCram Ltd., 141–143
    components, 131–132, **147**
    confidentiality, 162
    connection types, 138
    cryptographic key management, 136
    data flow, impact on, 139
    default protocol, 161
    defined, 77
    deployment examples, 128–129
    deployment strategy, 136–140
    DES-CBC, 131, 134
    DH, 134
    disadvantages, 140

encapsulation, 133
encryption techniques, 133–134
ESP, 126, 131–132, 138, 161
ESP packet type, 162
extranet connectivity, 129, **146**
filter actions, 139, **378**
filter lists, 138
HMAC, 131, 134
IKE, 132, 161–162
impersonation, 127
information exchange steps, 140, **146**
integrity, 162
interception, 127
Internet deployment examples,
    128–129
interoperability, 163
IP attack modalities, 126–127
IPX and, 133
ISAKMP, 132, 134–135, 161
key management, 161
key management protocols, 134–135
legacy support, 163–164
methods, 138
NAT incompatibility, 162
NetBIOS and, 133
Oakley, 132, 135, 161
OSI Network layer, 127,
    131–132, **148**
packet encryption, 163
passive interception, 127–128
public networks and, 140
remote access, 129, **146**
rules, 138–139
SA, 132–133
SA bundles, 133
security descriptor, 132–133
security policies, 137–138
security policies, built in, 139
security protocols, 131–132
security services, 132, **149**
software upgrades, 135
TCO, 126, 129, 135–136, **367**
TDI layer, 126
training, 135
transform, defined, 134
transport mode, 162
tunnel mode, 162
tunneling, 133, 138, **148**
VPNs, 161–164
Web sites, 21, 151, 180–181
IPSec monitoring tool, 313, **378**
IPSec Transport, 163–164

IPSec Tunnel, 163–164
IPX, 133
ISAKMP, 132, 134–135, 161
ISO search engine, 22
IT security controls. *See* Security controls.
IT Security Cookbook Web site, 21
IT security objectives.
    See Security objectives.
IUSR_*Servername,* 187

K

KDC, 94, **119**, 255
Kerberos. *See also* Microsoft Kerberos 5;
    MIT Kerberos 5.
    AAA, 41
    AAA servers, 104
    access, standardizing, 332
    authenticity not assumed, 130
    consumer/provider schema, 103
    design of, fictional account, **58**
    in heterogeneous environment, 195
    in homogeneous environment, 195
    as installable SSP, 107–109
    lifetime, 104
    logon, smart cards, 336–338, **356**
    non-Windows 2000 service, 315
    NTLM vs., 106–107, 109, **116**
    policy, 101–102, **120**
    principals, defined, 103
    smart cards, 336–338, **356**
    SSL/TLS vs., 195
    subprotocols, 90, **117**
    trusts, 219–220
    TTL, 104
    user authentication, 78
Key agreements, 71
Key distribution, 66
Key Distribution Center. *See* KDC.
Key length
    message confidentiality and, 64
    PKI, 72, 79
Key management
    IPSec, 134–136, 161
    methods, 63
    PKI, 72–76
Key-escrow systems, 79
kill.exe, 314
ksetup.exe, 315
ktpass.exe, 315

L

L2TP, 155, 160–162, **176, 372, 378**
L2TP/IPSec, 160–161, 163–164, **174, 377**

LAN Rover software, 156
Layer 2 protocols, 155–156, 160, **178**
Layer 2 Tunneling Protocol. *See* L2TP.
Layer 2 Tunneling Protocol/Internet
  Protocol Security. *See* L2TP/IPSec.
Layered models, 36–37. *See also* DoD
  four-layer model; Microsoft four-layer
  model; OSI model.
LDAP, 40–41, 199, 254, 255
ldp.exe, 315
Leaf nodes, 257
Least privilege principle, 135, 239
Legacy domain model, 219
Legacy one-way trusts, 107
Legacy support, IPSec, 163–164
Legacy tools, 317
Lifetime, 104
Lightweight Directory Access Protocol.
  See LDAP.
Link-level encryption, 127
List-and-reorder questions, 7–8
Local Area Network Rover software.
  See LAN Rover software.
Local Group Policy processing order,
  287–288
Local machine, 36, 42
Local policies, 306
Local Security Authority. *See* LSA.
Logging, IIS server, 191
Logical access, defined, 31
Logon, smart cards
  with Kerberos, 336–338, **356**
  with SSL/TLS, 338–339
Long-term keys, 94
Loopback support, 289–290, **295**
LSA, 37

M

MAC, 70–71
Macintosh migration, 349–350, **357**
MACLs, 265
MACs. *See* MACLs.
Management policies, VPNs, 164–165
Mandatory ACLs. *See* MACLs.
Man-in-the-middle attack, 29
MAPI, 255
Marking questions for later, 16
Massachusetts Institute of Technology
  Kerberos 5. *See* MIT Kerberos 5.
MD5, 70, 134, **388**
Merge mode, 289, **295**
Message Authentication Code. *See* MAC.
Message confidentiality and key length, 64

Message digest, 68
Message Digest 5. *See* MD5.
Message Queue Services. *See* MSMQ.
Messaging Application Programming
  Interface. *See* MAPI.
Metabase, 38
Metadata, 258
Meta-directories, 201–202, 223–224, 253
Microsoft Certificate Server, 255
Microsoft Certified Professional
  Web site, 20
Microsoft Cryptographic Application
  Programming Interface. *See* CAPI.
Microsoft Directory Synchronization
  Services. *See* MSDSS.
Microsoft four-layer model
  attack modalities and, 49–50
  compared to others, 36–37
  protocols, 37, 50, **57**
Microsoft Kerberos 5
  account database, 101
  account mapping, 103
  authentication delegation, 93, 100
  authentication services, 105–106
  authorization services, 105–106
  client configuration, 103
  credentials cache, 93, 101
  cross-domain authentication, 98–100
  AS exchange, 94–96
  extensible ticket fields, 92–93
  flags, 92
  forwarded TGTs, 100
  GSS-API, 103
  interoperability, 94, 102–103
  KDC, defined, 94
  Kerberos policy, 101–102
  mutual authentication, 93
  native mode, 102
  Negotiate SSP, 105–106
  non-Microsoft clients, 103
  one-way trust, 103
  PKI, 92
  PKINIT, 92
  proxy tickets, 93
  realms, defined, 99
  service account, 103
  service tickets, 102
  session tickets, 102
  session-granting exchange, 97–98
  smart card support, 92
  system-wide audits, 93
  TGS exchange, 96–97

TGTs, 102
ticket structure, 92
trust management, 93–94
user tickets, 102
Windows 2000 features, 93–94
Microsoft licensing violations, 190
Microsoft Management Console.
See MMC.
Microsoft Message Queue Services.
See MSMQ.
Microsoft Messaging Application
Programming Interface. See MAPI.
Microsoft Meta-directory Services.
See MMS.
Microsoft recommendations, VPNs,
161–162
Microsoft User Authentication Module.
See UAM.
Microsoft Web site, 22
Microwaves interception risk level, 128
Migration, **382**, 382–383
Apple Macintosh, 349–350, **357**
coexistence vs., 343
NetWare, 343–345, **357**
Unix, 345–348, **356**
MIT Kerberos 5
AAA support, 91–94, **117**
assumptions, 89
authorization services, 105
components of, 89–90
goals, 88–89
requirements, 88–89
RFC 1510 enhancements, 90–91
subprotocols, 90
Web site, 21
Mixed mode environments, 282
MKS Toolkit, 347–348
MMC, 42, 303, 305
MMS, 201–202, 223–224, 253
Mnemonic device for AD directory
containers, 282
Mobile IP, 133
Monitoring, 227
Moore's Law, 43
Mortice Kern Systems Toolkit.
See MKS Toolkit.
movetree.exe, 315
MSDSS, 201, **210**, 345, **355**, **378**
msicuu.exe, 315
MSMQ, 352–353
Multiple-choice format, 5–6
Mutual authentication, 93
MY certificate store, 79

N

Named objects, 255
Namespaces, 257–258
Naming conventions, 256–257, **270**, **383**
NAT, 159, 162, **175**
National Institute of Standards and
Technology. See NIST.
National Institute of Standards Web site, 22
National security, 79
National Security Agency. See NSA.
National Security Agency Web site, 22
National Security Institute Web site, 21
Native mode, 102
NDIS layer, 37
NDS identity management, 201, **210**
Negotiate SSP, 105–106
Nesting groups, 277–278, 284
NetBIOS, 133
netdiag.exe, 315
netdom.exe, 315
NetWare migration, 343–345, **357**
Network Address Translation. See NAT.
Network addressing, 185–186
Network administration, 348
Network Basic Input/Output System.
See NetBIOS.
Network Device/Driver Interface
Specification. See NDIS layer.
Network layer security technologies,
194, **207**
Network operating system. See NOS.
Network security, defined, 214
Network security plan
action plan, 234–242
AD integrations, 226
Applications group, 232–233
attack modalities, 220–221
auditing, 227
authentication, 219
business partners, 233–234
case studies, 234–242
CM, 231–232
content, 215
defined, 214
deliverables, security plan, 234–242
deployment, 228–234
disaster recovery plan, 214
DMZ, 224
Everyone user population, 229
ExamCram Ltd. case study, 234–242
firewalls, 224
Help Desk support, 228

Kerberos trusts, 219–220
legacy domain model, 219
Meta-directory, 223–224
monitoring, 227
physical security plan content,
217–218
policy management, 223–224
publishing policy, 228
ring model, 220–224
scope, application, 225
scope, logical assets, 218–219
scope, physical, 217–218, 224
scope, policy, 225–226
scope, protocol, 225
server placement, 230–231
SSO, 219–220
SSPI, 232–233
Staff user population, 229–232
steps for developing, 214–215, **244**
support team, 226–227
trust management, 219–220
user population, identifying, 216–217,
236–238
Users user population, 232–233
VPNs, 230–232, **247**
Network security plan strategies, 215,
228–229, **244**, **365**
New Technology. *See* NT.
NIST, 70
nltest.exe, 316
No Override, 288–289
Nonce, defined, 92
Noncontiguous namespaces, 259
Non-Microsoft clients, 103, **378**
Nonrepudiation, 63, **83**
Nontechnical procedures, documenting, 48
Non-Windows 2000 service, 315
NOS, 326, 331
Novell Directory Services identity
management. *See* NDS identity
management.
Novell migration, 343–345, **355**, **357**
NSA, 70
NT, 37–38
NT File System. *See* NTFS.
NT LAN Manager. *See* NTLM.
NTBugTraq Web site, 21
ntdsutil.exe, 316, **322**
NTFS
ACLs, 263
EFS vs., 267–268
IIS permissions, 189–190

NTLM
authentication service,
limitations of, 41
Kerberos vs., 106–107, 109, **116**
user authentication, 78

O

Oakley, 132, 135, 161
Object class instances, 258
Objectives. *See* Business objectives;
Security objectives.
Objects, 255, **272**
OCF, 334
128-bit encryption, 64
One-way trust, 103, 266–267, **271**
Open Systems Interconnection.
See entries beginning with OSI.
OpenCard Framework. *See* OCF.
OPENNT, 346
Organizational charts, 216–217, 236–238,
244, **244**, 245–246, **245–246**
Organizational data, compiling, 35
Organizational Units. *See* OUs.
OSI layer security technologies,
194–195, **207**
OSI model
attack modalities, 49–50
compared to others, 36–37
mapping protocols to, 49–50
security schema, 44
OSI Network layer, 127, 131–132, **148**
OUs, **376**
AD, 259
defined, 40
directory services, 259
nested, 279–280, 284
Ownership function, 330

P

Packet encryption, 163
Packet filter architecture, 168
Packet filter routers, 166
Packet flow, 167–171, **176**
Packet Internet Groper. *See* Ping.
Packet sniffing, 127
PAP, 156, **178**
Paper trail, need for, 48
Parent domains, 259
Partial credit, 6
Pass-through SSP, 105–106
Password Authentication Protocol.
See PAP.
Password length, 263

Password synchronization, 347
Payload. *See* Tunnels.
PDCs
    PDC Advertiser, 261, **271**
    PDC Emulator, 261
Performance Log And Alerts, 304
Performance snap-in, 303–304, **366**, **378**
Permission management
    e-commerce, 197–198
    Group Policy, 281–282, 288, 290–291
    identification and, 197–198
Permissions, Web server, 189–190
PGP, 22, 197
Physical access, defined, 31
Physical organization, 42–43
Physical security plan, 217–218
PING, 316
Ping, 139
PKCS, 76–77
PKI, **386–387**
    ACLs, 73
    active interception, 68
    asymmetric key encryption, 66–68
    asymmetric vs. symmetric, security, 72
    asymmetric vs. symmetric, speed,
        67–68, **82**
    authentication controls, 68–71
    authentication through comparison,
        69–70
    authentication through proof
        of possession, 70–71
    CA, 73
    CAPI overview, 78–79
    certificate extensibility, 73
    certificate management services,
        78–79
    certificate stores, 78–79
    certificates, 73–74
    cleartext challenge, 70–71
    consumer-provider model, 61–62
    cryptanalysis, 65–66
    CSPs, 78–79
    digital envelopes, 71
    digital signatures, 73
    DSS, 72
    encryption technologies, 62–63, **80**
    expired certificates, 76
    features of, 76–77
    global encryption policies, 79
    hash functions, one-way, 69–70
    hash signatures, 72
    hierarchy of authorities, 74–75

    HMAC generation, 68
    integrity controls, 68–69
    key length, 72, 79
    key management, 72–76
    MD5, 70
    message digest, 68
    Microsoft Kerberos 5, 92
    national security, 79
    public key certificates, 75–76
    public keys and impersonation, 72
    revoked certificates, 76
    RSA, 72
    secret key agreements, 71
    secret key distribution, 66
    security schema, 61–62
    SHA-1, 70
    symmetric key encryption, 63–66
    Web site, 22
PKINIT, 77, 92
PKIX, 77
Point-To-Point Protocol. *See* PPP.
Point-To-Point Tunneling Protocol.
    See PPTP.
Policies, **371**, **388**
    application-specific, 195–196
    built in (IPSec), 139
    case studies, 234–242
    content, 215
    defined, 137
    firewalls, 171–172
    groups, 278–280
    IP Security Policies on AD, 307
    IPSec, 137–138
    Public Key Policies, 307
Policy management
    Group Policy, 283–284
    network security plan, 223–224
Portable Operating System Interface for
    Unix. *See* POSIX.
POSIX, 346, **384**
PPP
    access control, 263
    VPNs, 160, 162–163, **372**
PPTP
    features, 163
    VPNs, 156, 160, 164, **378**
PPTP PING, 316
Practice questions, 19–20
Prestaging, 341
Pretty Good Privacy. *See* PGP.
Pretty Good Privacy Web site, 22
Primary DCs. *See* PDCs.

Principals
  defined, 40, 103, 255
  naming conventions, 256–257
  security schema and, 44–45
Principle of least privilege, 135, 239
Private communication channels.
  See VPNs.
Private network infrastructures, 156–157
Procedural paradigm, 34–35
Process of elimination, 18
Processing order, Group Policy,
  286–290, **294**
Protocols, disabling on IIS server, 190
Provisioning function, 328
Proxy servers, 166–167
Proxy tickets, 93
Public key certificates, 75–76
Public Key Cryptography for Initial
  Authentication in Kerberos.
  See PKINIT.
Public Key Cryptography Standards.
  See PKCS.
Public key infrastructure. *See* PKI.
Public Key Infrastructure X.509.
  See PKIX.
Public Key Policies, 307
Public key-based protocols, 105
Public keys and impersonation, 72
Public networks, 140
Publishing policy, 228

Q

Question formats, 5
Questions-remaining counter, 17

R

Radio interception risk level, 128
RADIUS, 155, 164–165, **178**
Rainbow Series Library, DoD Web site, 22
RBACs, 265–266, 275, 353, **373**
RDNs, 256
Realms, 99
RefreshPolicy operation, 311
reg.exe, 316
Registry, 37–38
Registry tools, 307
Relative distinguished names. *See* RDNs.
Relative ID Master. *See* RID Master.
Remote access, **377**
  application-specific security, 196
  design flow, 164–165, **177**
  incorporated into network operating
    system, 157–158

IPSec, 129, **146**
  policies, 263–264
  policy management, 164–165
  VPNs, 156–157
Remote administration mode, 302–303
Remote Authentication Dial-In User
  Service. *See* RADIUS.
Remote (Operating System) Installation
  Services. *See* RIS.
Remote site connectivity, 129, **146**
remote.exe, 316
Replace mode, 289
Replay attacks, 29
Replica DCs, 260
Replication, 260, 261–262
Request for Comments. *See entries*
  beginning with RFC.
Resources
  access control, 267–268, 273
  Group Policy, 278–280
  rules-based management, 278–280
Restricted groups, 306
Return on investment. *See* ROI.
Revisiting questions, 14, 16
Revoked certificates, 76
RFC 822, 197, 257
RFC 822 names, 256
RFC 1330, 253
RFC 1334, 162
RFC 1510, 90–91, **118**
RFC 1636, 127
RFC 1777, 254
RFC 2003, 133
RFC 2069, 188
RFC 2078, 105
RFC 2222, 254
RFC 2246, 192, 212
RFC 2401, 151
RFC 2402, 151
RFC 2406, 151
RFC 2408, 151
RFC 2411, 131
RFC search page, 275
RFC Web sites, 21
RID Master, 261, **271**
RID Operations Master, 261, **271**
Ring model, 220–224
RIS, 281, 286, 303, 340–341
Risk analysis
  attack modalities, 60
  basic components, 60
  distributed security, 33

Risk management steps, 32–33, 45–48
Roaming profiles, 278
Roaming user support, 305
Rogue attacks, 49, 128
ROI, 203
Role-based access controls. *See* RBACs.
Root CA, 74, 193, **387**
ROOT certificate store, 79
Routers, VPN, 165
Routing and Remote Access Service
    integration. *See* RRAS integration.
RRAS integration, 157–158
RSA, 72
Rules
    Group Policy, 278–280
    IPSec, 138–139

S

S, 239, 265
SA bundles, 133
SACLs, 42
SAs, 132–133
SBU, 197, 239, 265
SC Tool Set, 306–312
    CLI version, 310–311
SCA snap-in, 306–307, **366**
Scalable organization structure, 41
SCard COM, 336
SChannel protocols, 191–194
SChannel services, 105
SChannel SSPs, 78
Schema. *See* Security schema.
Schema Master, 260, **271**
Scope, Group Policy, 282–283
Scope, network security plan
    application, 225
    logical assets, 218–219
    physical, 217–218, 224
    policy, 225–226
    protocol, 225
Screened host architecture, 168–170
Screened-subnet architecture, 170–171
Scripts, 286
sdcheck.exe, 317
SDOU, 282
Search engines, directory services, 260
Search tools, 22
Searching for Web sites, 22
search.vbs, 317
secedit.exe, 308, 310–312, **322**, **371**
Secret. *See* S.
Secret keys. *See entries beginning with* Key.
Secure authentication, 188

Secure Electronic Transaction LLC
    Web site, 22
Secure Hash Algorithm. *See* SHA; SHA-1.
Secure Multipurpose Internet Mail
    Extensions. *See* S/MIME.
Secure Server policy, IPSec, 139
Secure Sockets Layer. *See* SSL.
Secure Sockets Layer/Transport Security
    Layer. *See* SSL/TLS.
Secured end-to-end pipe, 192
secure*.inf, 310
Securing IIS servers, 190–191, **208**, **373**
Security account management, 41–42
Security administration, managing,
    264–266
Security analysis, 60–61
Security areas, list of, 306–307, **321**, **366**
Security Associations. *See* SAs.
Security attack modalities.
    See Attack modalities.
Security attributes, configuring, 306–307
Security component schema, 44–45
Security Configuration And Analysis
    Manager, 308
Security Configuration And Analysis
    snap-in. *See* SCA snap-in.
Security Configuration Service, 308
Security Configuration Tool Set.
    See SC Tool Set.
Security control layers, 185
Security controls
    attack modalities, 28–30
    authorization, 329
    brokerage function, 330
    business objectives and, 28
    categorizing, 46–48
    connection function, 329–330
    examples of, 28
    identity integration, 329–330
    identity management, 328
    matching with corporate objectives,
        61–62
    matching with countermeasures,
        61–62
    ownership function, 330
    VPNs, 164
Security deployment plan, 228–234
Security descriptor, 132–133
Security groups, 278, 282–283, 286
Security Negotiation Mechanism.
    See SNEGO.
Security objectives, 28, **54**, 202–203

Security overview
  AAA, 41
  AD, 38
  ADS, 38–41
  attack modalities, 28–30, 45–48
  boundaries, secured, 34
  business objectives, from key
    personnel, 30, 32, **55**
  business objectives, from surveys,
    28, 30
  business objectives, in disaster
    recovery plan, 30
  Competency Model, 27–28
  consumer/provider schema, 44–48
  corporate culture, 35
  deployment steps, 34
  digital signatures, 28, 49
  disaster recovery plans, 30, 48
  distributed security, risk analysis, 33
  DoD four-layer model, 36–37
  domain model features, 42
  enterprise security system,
    deploying, 34
  group policies, 42
  hash function, 28
  historical trends, 35–38
  impersonation attack modality, 49
  IT security controls, 28–30, 46–48
  layered models, 36–37
  LDAP, 40–41
  logical access, defined, 31
  Microsoft four-layer model, 36–37
  MMC, 42
  nontechnical procedures,
    documenting, 48
  organizational data, compiling, 35
  OSI model, 36–37, 44, 49–50
  OUs, 40
  physical access, defined, 31
  physical organization, 42–43
  procedural paradigm, 34–35
  questions to ask, 26
  risk management steps, 32–33, 45–48
  security account management, 41–42
  security component schema, 44–45
  security policy contents, 30–31
  security protocols and layered
    models, 49–50
  single domain model, 41
  social layer, 35
  system administrator capabilities, 42
  system security audits, 27, 31–32
  system security plan, 27
  TCO, 27
  troubleshooting paradigm, 43–44
  Windows Registry, 37–38
Security plan for Windows 2000
  about, 198–199
  AD, 201–202, **210**
  deployment, 200–202, 204
  directory service provider,
    198–199, **209**
  interoperability, 203
  LDAP, 199
  NDS, 201, **210**
  ROI, 203
  security objectives, 202–203
  TCO, 203
Security plans, 27–28, **53**, **55**
Security policies. *See* Policies.
Security policy categories, 30–31, **54**
Security policy contents, 30–31
Security Portal for Information Security
  Professionals Web site, 21
Security protocols
  IPSec, 131–132
  layered models and, 49–50
  Microsoft four-layer model, 37, 50, **57**
  VPNs, 155–156, 159–164
Security restriction, configuring, 185–186
Security rules. *See* Rules.
Security schema
  about, 44–45
  active vs. passive attacks, 47
  attack modalities, applying security
    controls to, 47–48
  attack modalities, types of, 45–47
  consumer-to-provider model, 44–45
  interception attack modality, 46–47
  interference attack modality, 46
  PKI, 61–62
  principals, defined, 44
  risk analysis, 47–48
  security controls, applying to attack
    modalities, 47–48
  security controls, categorizing, 46–47
  security exposures, targets of, 45
Security services, IPSec, 132, **149**
Security settings
  extensions (Group Policy Editor), 308
  Group Policy, 285, **293**, **368**
  groups, 278–280
  tools, 307
Security support provider interface.
  See SSPI.

Security support providers. *See* SSPs.
Security templates, 308–312, **321**, **370**, **373**
Security tools. *See* Tools.
Security Web sites, 20–22
Select-and-place format, 11–12
Sensitive But Unclassified. *See* SBU.
Server Gateway Cryptography. *See* SGC.
Server Message Block. *See* SMB.
Server placement, 230–231
Server policy, IPSec, 139
Server referring, 341
Service accounts, 103
Service pack Web site, 21
Service principal names, 257
Service tickets, 102
Services, disabling on IIS server, 190
Services for NetWare version 5. *See* SFN5.
Services for Unix 2. *See* SFU2.
Session pipe. *See* Tunnels.
Session tickets, 102
Session-granting exchange, 97–98
Setup Security tool, 308
SFN5, 344
SFU2, 346, 348
SGC, 78
SHA, 134
SHA-1, 70
Shiva LAN Rover software, 156
Shiva Password Authentication Protocol.
    See SPAP.
Short-form format, 14, 16–17, 19
SIDWalker, 317
Simple Network Management Protocol.
    See SNMP.
Simulations, 13
Single domain model, 41, **382**
Single Sign-On. *See* SSO.
Site, domain, Organizational Unit, OU
    within OU. *See* SDOU.
Sites, 261
64-bit encryption, 64
Smart cards, **366**, **371**, **377**
    access, securing, 334–339, **355**
    APIs, 335–336
    authentication, 263
    business strategy, 334–335
    email, 338–339
    ICCs, 335
    interoperability, 334–335
    logon with Kerberos, 336–338, **356**
    logon with SSL/TLS, 338–339
    Microsoft Kerberos 5, 92

SCard COM, 336
    stored-value cards, 335
    two-factor authentication, 334
    types of, 335
    Win32 API, 336
SMB, 190
SMB signing, 342–343
S/MIME, 50, 197, 212, **387**
Snap-ins
    about, 42
    ADSI Edit snap-in, 314
    Certificate Authority snap-in, 194
    Event Viewer snap-in, 304
    Performance snap-in, 303–304, **366**
    SCA snap-in, 306–307, **366**
    where to get, 303
SNEGO, 105
SNMP, 341–342
snmputilg.exe, 317
Social layer, 35
Sockets for Unix compatibility.
    See SOCKS.
SOCKS, 50
Software installation and maintenance
    Group Policy, 285
    tools, 305
SPAP, 156, **178**
Spheres of responsibility, 40
Spoke and hub, 201–202
Spoofing, 29–30, 49
SSL, **372**
    access, standardizing, 332–333
    consumer/Web server flow, 192, **207**
    defined, 77
    deployment, 192
SSL3/TLS1, 192
SSL/TLS, 195, 331–332, 338–339
SSO, 94, 219–220, 255, 331–333
SSPI, 105–106, 108–109, 232–233
SSPs, 104–106, **119**
Staff user population, 217, 229–232, 239
Standalone CA, 75, **371**
Storage domains, 283
Stored-value cards, 335
Strategies
    access control, 262
    network security plan, 215, 228–229,
        244, **365**
Strategies (exam)
    adaptive format, 17–18
    case study format, 15–16
    fixed-length format, 16–17, 19
    short-form format, 16–17, 19

Study guide, Competency Model as, 27–28, 50–51, **57**
Subdirectories, 186
Subordinate CA, 74–75
Subprotocols, 90, **117**
Subtrees, 257
Surveys, 28, 30
Symmetric encryption
    asymmetric encryption vs., 67–68, 72, **82**
    confidentiality, 64–65
    PKI, 63–66
    prerequisites, 64–65
    procedural steps (diagram), 64, **81**
Syntax for tools, 312–313
System ACLs. *See* SACLs.
System administrator capabilities, 42
System Monitor, 304
System Policy Editor, 42
System Policy (NT 4). *See* Group Policy.
System security
    analyzing, 311
    audits, 27, 31–32, **55**, 93
    plan, 27
System services tools, 307

T

TCO, **364**
    application-specific security, 194–196
    defined, 27, **53**
    e-commerce, 43
    identity management, 203
    IPSec, 126, 129, 135–136, **367**
    single domain model, 41
TCP/IP layered model. *See* DoD four-layer model.
TDES, 64
TDI, 36–37, 126
Technical expertise. *See* Competency model.
Telephone, interception risk level, 128
Telnet, 348
Terminal services access, securing, 339–340
Terminal Services Architecture. *See* TSA.
Test. *See* Exams.
Testing centers, 3–4
Testlets. *See* Case studies.
TGS, 96–97
TGS exchange, 90
TGTs, 102
Thawte, 193
3DES, 64
Ticket structure, 92

Ticket-granting service. *See* TGS.
Ticket-granting service exchange. *See* TGS exchange.
Ticket-granting tickets. *See* TGTs.
Time remaining counter, 3
Time to live. *See* TTL.
tlist.exe, 317
TLS, 77, 156, 212
TLS1, 192
Tools. *See also* Group Policy.
    account policies, 306
    acldiag.exe, 314
    AD directory services, 303–305
    addiag.exe, 318
    adduser.exe, 318
    administration tools, 301–304
    ADSI Edit snap-in, 314
    auditpol.exe, 318
    centralized administration, 301, **320**
    Certificate Services CLI tools, 313–314
    CERTREQ, 313
    CERTSRV, 313
    CERTUTIL, 313–314
    CLI, Certificate Services, 313–314
    CLI, Group Policy, 290–291
    CLI, SC Tool Set, 310–311
    configuration tools, 306–312
    data protection and management, 305
    database configuration, 308
    deployment, 301
    desktop management, 301, 304–305
    dsacls.exe, 314
    event log, 306
    Event Viewer snap-in, 304
    executing utilities, 312
    File System, 307
    gpotool.exe, 318
    gpresults.exe, 318
    Group Policy CLI tools, 290–291
    INF files, 306–307, 309–310, **321**
    IntelliMirror, 304–305
    IP Security Policies on AD, 307
    IPSec monitoring tool, 313
    kill.exe, 314
    ksetup.exe, 315
    ktpass.exe, 315
    ldp.exe, 315
    legacy tools, 317
    local policies, 306
    MKS Toolkit, 347–348
    MMC, 303, 305

movetree.exe, 315
msicuu.exe, 315
netdiag.exe, 315
netdom.exe, 315
nltest.exe, 316
ntdsutil.exe, 316, **322**
Performance Log And Alerts, 304
Performance snap-in, 303–304
PPTP PING, 316
Public Key Policies, 307
reg.exe, 316
Registry, 307
remote administration mode,
    302–303
remote.exe, 316
restricted groups, 306
RIS, 303
roaming user support, 305
SC Tool Set, 306–312
SC Tool Set, CLI version, 310–311
SCA snap-in, 306–307, **366**
sdcheck.exe, 317
search.vbs, 317
secedit.exe, 308, 310–312, **322**
security areas, list of, 306–307, **321**
security attributes, configuring,
    306–307
Security Configuration And Analysis
    Manager, 308
Security Configuration Service, 308
security settings, 307, **368**
Security settings extensions (Group
    Policy Editor), 308
security templates, 308–312, **321, 370**
Setup Security, 308
SIDWalker, 317
snap-ins, where to get, 303
snmputilg.exe, 317
software/application installation, 305
syntax, 312–313
System Monitor, 304
system services, 307
tlist.exe, 317
TSA, 302–303
Windows 2000 Server Resource Kit,
    317–318
Windows 2000 Support Tools,
    314–317
WMI, 301–302
WSH, 302, 305
wsremote.exe, 317
Top Secret. *See* TS.
Topologies, firewalls, 167–171

Total cost of ownership. *See* TCO.
Traffic security, 191–192
Training and Certification Web site, 22
Transforms, 134
Transmission Control Protocol/Internet
    Protocol layered model. *See* DoD
    four-layer model.
Transport Driver/Device Interface layer.
    See TDI.
Transport Layer Security. *See* TLS.
Transport layer security technologies,
    194, **207**
Transport mode, 162
Tree format questions, 8–10
Trees, 257–259, **272**
Triple DES. *See* TDES.
Troubleshooting paradigm, 43–44
TRUST certificate store, 79
Trust management
    Microsoft Kerberos 5, 93–94
    network security plan, 219–220
Trust relationships
    CA-based, 75
    deploying, 266–267
    directory services, 258
    establishing, 266–267
    transitive, 266–267
Trusted for delegation, 263
Trusted network infrastructures, 156–157
TS, 239, 265
TSA, 281, 302–303
TTL, 104
Tunnel mode, 162
Tunneling, 133, 138, **148**, 158–159
Tunnels, 158
Two-factor authentication, 263, **271**, 334

U

U, 239, 265
UAM, 349, **357**
UNC, 257
Unclassified. *See* U.
Uniform Resource Locators. *See* URLs.
Unit of replication, 258
Universal groups, 277
Universal Naming Convention. *See* UNC.
Unix migration, 345–348, **356**
Up-level, defined, 93
UPNs, 256–257
URLs, 257
User accounts naming conventions, 257
User Authentication Module. *See* UAM.
User name mapping, 348

User population, identifying, 216–217, 236–238
User principal names. *See* UPNs.
User profiles, 278–280, 281–282
User tickets, 102
UserDS certificate store, 79
Users, deploying access control, 263–264
Users user population, 217, 232–233, 239
UUEncoding, 187

V

Validate operation, 311, **322**
VeriSign, 193
Virtual directories, 186
Virtual Private Network Consortium. *See* VPNC.
Virtual Private Networks. *See entries beginning with* VPN.
Virtual servers, 186
Vision statements, 241–242
Voluntary tunnels, 158
VPN answering routers, 165, **175**
VPN calling routers, 165, **175**
VPN client, 158
VPN Consortium Web site, 22
VPN server, 158
VPN tunneling protocols, list of, 159
VPNC, 180
VPNs, **372, 376–379.** *See also* Firewalls.
    business partners and, 217, 230, **247**
    client management, 165
    defined, 154
    design considerations, 160
    ExamCram Ltd. diagram, 154–155
    IPSec, 161–164
    L2TP, 160–162, **372**
    management policies, 164–165
    Microsoft recommendations, 161–162
    NAT, 159, 162, **175**
    network security plan, 230–232, **247**
    PPP, 160, 162–163, **372**
    PPTP, 156, 160, 164, **378**
    RADIUS, 165
    remote access models, 156–157
    remote access policy management, 164–165
    RRAS integration, 157–158
    security controls required, 164
    security protocols, 155–156, 159–164
    tunneling, 158–159
    Web sites, 180–181

W

Walking the tree, 258
Web content authentication, 186
Web exchanges, verifying parties, 193
Web server. *See* IIS servers.
Web sites
    blocking access to, 172
    finding, 22
    IPSec, 151, 180–181
Web-Based Enterprise Management. *See* WEBM.
WEBM, 301–302
Well connected, 98, 261
Win32 API, smart cards, 336
Windows 2000
    components. *See* AD
    Microsoft Kerberos 5, 93–94
    naming conventions, 256–257, **270**
    NT 4 (Group Policy) vs., 276–280
    remote administration mode, 302–303
    remote installation, 285
Windows 2000 Hardware Compatibility List Web site, 22
Windows 2000 security policy. *See* Network security plan.
Windows 2000 Server Resource Kit, 317–318
Windows 2000 Support Tools, 314–317. *See also* Tools.
Windows for Workgroups, 36
Windows Management Instrumentation. *See* WMI.
Windows Registry, 37–38
Windows Scripting Host. *See* WSH.
WMI, 301–302
World Wide Web, 22. *See also* Internet.
WSH, 302, 305
wsremote.exe, 317

X

X.400 Web site, 275
X.500
    directory services, 253–254
    names, 256
    Web site, 275
X.509
    Authenticode, 196
    directory services, 253–254
    S/MIME, 197

Coriolis introduces

EXAM CRAM INSIDER™

A FREE ONLINE NEWSLETTER

Stay current with the latest certification information. Just email us to receive the latest in certification and training news for Microsoft, Java, Novell, A+, Linux, Cisco, and more! Read e-letters from the Publisher of the Exam Cram and Exam Prep series, Keith Weiskamp, and Exam Cram Series Editor, Ed Tittel, about future trends in IT training and education. Access valuable insider information on exam updates, new testing procedures, sample chapters, and links to other useful, online sites. Take a look at the featured program of the month, and who's in the news today. We pack all this and more into our *Exam Cram Insider* online newsletter to make sure *you* pass your next test!

To sign up for our twice monthly newsletter, go to www.coriolis.com and click on the sign up sheet, or email us at eci@coriolis.com and put "subscribe insider" in the body of the message.

EXAM CRAM INSIDER – Another reason Exam Cram and Exam Prep guides are *The Smartest Way To Get Certified*™. And it's <u>free</u>!

The Coriolis Exam Cram Personal Trainer
An exciting new category in certification training products

The Exam Cram Personal Trainer is the first certification-specific testing product that completely links learning with testing to:

- **Increase your comprehension**
- **Decrease the time it takes you to learn**

No system blends learning content with test questions as effectively as the Exam Cram Personal Trainer.

Only the Exam Cram Personal Trainer offers this much power at this price.

Its unique Personalized Practice Test Engine provides a real-time test environment and an authentic representation of what you will encounter during your actual certification exams.

Much More than Just Another CBT!
Most current CBT learning systems offer simple review questions at the end of a chapter with an overall test at the end of the course, with no links back to the lessons. But Exam Cram Personal Trainer takes learning to a higher level.

Its four main components are:
- The complete text of an Exam Cram study guide in HTML format
- A Personalized Practice Test Engine with multiple test methods
- A database of 150 questions linked directly to an Exam Cram chapter

Plus, additional features include:
- **Hint:** Not sure of your answer? Click Hint and the software goes to the text that covers that topic.
- **Lesson:** Still not enough detail? Click Lesson and the software goes to the beginning of the chapter.
- **Update feature:** Need even more questions? Click Update to download more questions from the Coriolis Web site.
- **Notes:** Create your own memory joggers.

- **Graphic analysis:** How did you do? View your score, the required score to pass, and other information.
- **Personalized Cram Sheet:** Print unique study information just for you.

Windows 2000 Server
Exam Cram Personal Trainer
ISBN: 1-57610-735-3

Windows 2000 Professional
Exam Cram Personal Trainer
ISBN: 1-57610-734-5

Windows 2000 Directory Services
Exam Cram Personal Trainer
ISBN: 1-57610-732-9

Windows 2000 Security Design
Exam Cram Personal Trainer
ISBN: 1-57610-772-8

Windows 2000 Network
Exam Cram Personal Trainer
ISBN: 1-57610-733-7

Windows 2000 Migrating from NT4
Exam Cram Personal Trainer
ISBN: 1-57610-773-6

A+ Exam Cram Personal Trainer
ISBN: 1-57610-658-6

CCNA Routing and Switching
Exam Cram Personal Trainer
ISBN: 1-57610-781-7

$99.99 U.S. • $149.99 Canada

Available: November 2000

CORIOLIS™
Certification Insider Press

The Smartest Way to Get Certified
Just Got Smarter™

Look for All of the Exam Cram Brand Certification Study Systems

ALL NEW! Exam Cram Personal Trainer Systems

The Exam Cram Personal Trainer systems are an exciting new category in certification training products. These CD-ROM based systems offer extensive capabilities at a moderate price and are the first certification-specific testing product to completely link learning with testing.

This Exam Cram study guide turned interactive course lets you customize the way you learn.

Each system includes:

- A Personalized Practice Test engine with multiple test methods
- A database of nearly 300 questions linked directly to the subject matter within the Exam Cram

Exam Cram Audio Review Systems

Written and read by certification instructors, each set contains four cassettes jam-packed with the certification exam information you must have. Designed to be used on their own or as a complement to our Exam Cram study guides, Flash Cards, and Practice Tests.

Each system includes:

- Study preparation tips with an essential last-minute review for the exam
- Hours of lessons highlighting key terms and techniques
- A comprehensive overview of all exam objectives
- 45 minutes of review questions, complete with answers and explanations

Exam Cram Flash Cards

These pocket-sized study tools are 100% focused on exams. Key questions appear on side one of each card and in-depth answers on side two. Each card features either a cross-reference to the appropriate Exam Cram study guide chapter or to another valuable resource. Comes with a CD-ROM featuring electronic versions of the flash cards and a complete practice exam.

Exam Cram Practice Tests

Our readers told us that extra practice exams were vital to certification success, so we created the perfect companion book for certification study material.

Each book contains:

- Several practice exams
- Electronic versions of practice exams on the accompanying CD-ROM presented in an interactive format, enabling practice in an environment similar to that of the actual exam
- Each practice question is followed by the corresponding answer (why the right answers are right and the wrong answers are wrong)
- References to the Exam Cram study guide chapter or other resource for that topic

CORIOLIS™

Certification Insider Press

The Smartest Way to Get Certified™

The MCSE™ Windows® 2000 Network Design Cram Sheet

This Cram Sheet contains the distilled, key facts about the Designing a Windows 2000 Network Infrastructure exam. Review this information immediately before entering the test room, paying special attention to those areas in which you feel you need the most review. Remember, you can transfer any of these facts that you've crammed into your short-term memory onto a blank piece of paper before beginning the exam.

TCP/IP

1. TCP/IP is required with Windows 2000. The Windows 2000 implementation of the TCP/IP suite has been enhanced to support several new features, which include:
   - Increased window size
   - TCP selective acknowledgment (SACK)
   - Internet Control Message Protocol (ICMP)
   - Disabling NetBIOS over IP

2. Along with these new features, Windows TCP/IP includes support for IPSec, which can improve the security of your network. IPSec allows administrators to encrypt TCP/IP communications between hosts. Although Windows 2000 hosts support this feature with no additional software requirements, Windows 9x hosts require third-party software to participate in secured communications. IPSec has three predefined security policies:
   - Client
   - Server
   - Secured Server

3. QoS is a routing mechanism that can guarantee data delivery for a certain application. Paths for traffic flows are determined based on some knowledge of resource availability in the network, as well as the QoS requirements (amount of bandwidth needed) for the flows. QoS-based routing allows the determination of a path that has a good chance of accommodating the requested QoS.

DHCP

4. DHCP is used to assign IP addresses to client computers.

5. DHCP can assign the following items:
   - IP address
   - Subnet mask
   - Default gateway
   - DNS servers
   - WINS server

6. DHCP can specify different configurations for:
   - Hardware vendors
   - Operating system (Windows 98 or Windows 2000)
   - Group of users

7. DHCP Server or Relay Agent is required on each subnet that does not have direct access to a DHCP server.

8. Multicast addressing is used to simultaneously send a multicast session to multiple people.

60. SNA tunneling is encapsulating SNA packets inside TCP/IP packets for transfer over a TCP/IP connection.

61. The Remote Access service can be integrated with:
    - DHCP (to assign IP addresses to remote clients)
    - DNS (to dynamically update the DNS tables with DNS names of remote users)
    - WINS (to dynamically update the WINS tables with WINS names of remote users)
    - Active Directory (for central management of remote policies)

Dfs

62. Dfs acts like a file manager for your network shares. It allows administrators to create a directory tree that appears to be located on one server, when, in actuality, the tree could contain shared folders from several different servers. Common uses for Dfs shares include the following:
    - Centralized network file manager
    - Providing a centralized backup point
    - Increasing availability by creating replicas
    - Load balancing of network traffic

63. Dfs is integrated with the Active Directory (AD) database and replicates between domain controllers. The AD database is used to store the topology information of the Dfs tree. The host domain controller stores the topology information known as the blob (binary large object) and replicates this information to all other Dfs-enabled domain controllers.

64. Two types of Dfs roots can be created:
    - Domain-based
    - Standalone

65. Domain-based roots can be replicated to other servers, which will allow access to the Dfs tree if the server that the root was created on becomes unavailable.

RADIUS

66. RADIUS is used to authenticate remote users on to a network.

67. The Windows 2000 RADIUS can be integrated with other the RADIUS components of other operating systems.

68. The RADIUS server is included in the IAS service in Windows 2000.

69. A RADIUS client is included in the RRAS service in Windows 2000.

COMBINING SERVICES

70. Combine services to use as few servers as possible.

71. Don't compromise security when combining services. Proxy, Web, and authentication services for remote users should be on separate servers.

72. WINS, DNS, and DHCP can be combined onto one server.

73. Large applications such as databases and mail or communication servers should not be combined with other services.

74. Windows Clustering consists of two services:
    - *Network Load Balancing (NLB)*—Spreads incoming TCP/IP service requests across multiple servers. NLB comes with Advanced Server and works with services such as Terminal Services and DNS, and with Web requests coming in through Proxy Server.
    - *Cluster Service*—Combines multiple servers, which act as if they are one. Cluster service provides automatic failover if one of the servers fails. This is more efficient than the primary/secondary method.

36. NLB or DNS round-robin entries serve to load balance incoming Web requests from the Internet to a proxy server.

- Use NLB if the Web server is mission-critical, because NLB automatically adjusts traffic when a server goes down.
- Use DNS round-robin if resources need to be conserved and overhead is an issue.

37. Proxy arrays provide caching and fault tolerance for internal clients. Arrays cannot help when the bandwidth to the Internet is an issue.

38. CARP is the protocol that a Microsoft proxy server array uses for caching.

39. Caching does not help when content is secured with encryption or when it includes active content. These types of pages cannot be cached.

40. Chaining proxy servers allows client requests to be passed upstream to the proxy server with a connection to the Internet. This helps to increase cache hits, which may reduce requests to the Internet.

RRAS

41. Routers are used to isolate LANs from one another.

42. Broadcasts do not travel through a router (by default), but DHCP broadcasts can if BOOTP is enabled.

43. Routers can provide data encryption between routers.

44. Routers can be authenticated to prevent the use of rogue routers.

45. Routing protocols are RIP and OSPF.

46. IGMP is a membership list of users who are participating in a multicast session.

47. If used in an IPX/SPX network, routers will advertise resource servers to other subnets (SAP).

48. IPSec is used for router authentication and data encryption.

49. Filters can be implemented to specify which packets can pass through a router.

50. Packet filters in the RRAS service can control connections by time of day and service type a well as differentiate between blocking incoming and outgoing packets. However, packet filters allow or disallow these functions for *all* users. Remote access policies can control remote connections in the same way, but can apply different controls for different groups of users.

51. VPNs can be established between routers using:

- PPTP
- L2TP
- IPSec

52. L2TP is considered to be a more secure solution than PPTP for a VPN. L2TP provides a stronger encryption protocol, and encryption begins from the client connection. PPTP uses a Microsoft proprietary encryption protocol, MPPE, whereas L2TP uses an open standard encryption protocol, IPSec.

53. For redundancy, RRAS servers should be installed in pairs or clustered.

54. Remote access can be enabled via dial-up clients or through VPNs.

55. Encapsulation is the process of "wrapping" packets of one protocol inside another protocol for transfer over another network, such as the Internet.

56. L2TP allows IP, IPX, or NetBEUI to be encrypted and sent over a PPP connection.

57. PPTP allows IP, IPX, and NetBEUI to be tunneled with TCP/IP.

58. IPX/SPX tunneling is encapsulating IPX/SPX packets in TCP/IP packets for transfer over a TCP/IP network.

59. The different authentication protocols are:

- SPAP
- PAP
- EAP
- CHAP
- MSCHAP
- IPSec

9. DHCP can be integrated with the following:
   - DNS (so DHCP clients are automatically updated in the DNS table).
   - Active Directory (to authorize a DHCP server). Without authorization, a DHCP server cannot start the DHCP services.
   - RRAS servers (to allow automatic IP addressing of remote users).

10. DHCP Relay Agent is not required if all routers are BOOTP enabled.

11. DHCP servers can be clustered for redundancy.

12. Multiple DHCP servers can use a portion of each others' scopes for redundancy.

DNS

13. Place one DNS server per LAN location, unless special circumstances warrant a different arrangement.

14. DNS is a required service when implementing Active Directory.

15. The three types of zones are:
   - Standard primary
   - Standard secondary
   - Active Directory-integrated

16. Use forwarders to control which DNS servers perform iterative queries on the Internet.

17. Use the same namespace for the DNS and Active Directory services. Active Directory services can be implemented as a subdomain of a preexisting DNS namespace.

18. Standard primary and secondary zones are interoperable with other DNS services. Active Directory-integrated zones are not.

19. By default, Windows 2000 DNS clients will update their own A records in the DNS database, and the DHCP server will update the PTR record. For secure dynamic updates, the DHCP server needs to be set to update both the A and PTR records for the clients.

WINS

20. Evaluate the necessity of WINS based on the number of NetBIOS clients.

21. NetBIOS can be turned off, eliminating the need for WINS in an all Windows 2000 environment.

22. It is not necessary to place one WINS server at each LAN location. Use as few WINS servers as possible.

23. Do not build redundancy into the WINS service unless it is specifically requested.

NAT

24. NAT can be used on only a nonrouted network.

25. NAT is used to hide a company's private addressing schemes from public networks.

26. NAT is installed under Routing And Remote Access.

27. NAT changes the IP address in the packet header.

28. NAT has the following requirements:
   - DHCP services are disabled.
   - DNS resolution occurs through the NAT server.
   - NAT supports only TCP/IP.

29. NAT cannot translate the following protocols:
   - SNMP
   - COM/DCOM
   - LDAP

30. The NAT server should be located between the public and private network.

31. NAT can be used over a VPN.

PROXY SERVER

32. All connections from a private network to the Internet or other public network need protection. This protection can be provided by the NAT, Proxy, or RRAS services.

33. The Proxy Server service is designed for larger networks (even routed networks).

34. Web servers need to be isolated in a screened subnet.

35. For security reasons, the proxy server and the server that provides Web services should not be on the same server.

MCSE™
Windows® 2000
Network Design

Kim Simmons
Jarret W. Buse
Todd B. Halpin

MCSE™ Windows® 2000 Network Design Exam Cram

Limits of Liability and Disclaimer of Warranty

The author and publisher of this book have used their best efforts in preparing the book and the programs contained in it. These efforts include the development, research, and testing of the theories and programs to determine their effectiveness. The author and publisher make no warranty of any kind, expressed or implied, with regard to these programs or the documentation contained in this book.

The author and publisher shall not be liable in the event of incidental or consequential damages in connection with, or arising out of, the furnishing, performance, or use of the programs, associated instructions, and/or claims of productivity gains.

Trademarks

Trademarked names appear throughout this book. Rather than list the names and entities that own the trademarks or insert a trademark symbol with each mention of the trademarked name, the publisher states that it is using the names for editorial purposes only and to the benefit of the trademark owner, with no intention of infringing upon that trademark.

The Coriolis Group, LLC
14455 N. Hayden Road
Suite 220
Scottsdale, Arizona 85260

(480)483-0192
FAX (480)483-0193
www.coriolis.com

Library of Congress Cataloging-in-Publication Data
Simmons, Kim.
    MCSE Windows 2000 network design exam cram / by Kim Simmons, Jarret Buse, Todd Halpin.
        p. cm.
    Includes index
    ISBN 1-57610-716-7
    1. Electronic data processing personnel--Certification. 2. Microsoft software--Examinations--Study guides. 3. Computer networks--Examinations--Study guides. I. Buse, Jarret. II. Halpin, Todd. III. Title.
QA76.3 .S56 2000
005.7'13769--dc21

00-060214

Printed in the United States of America
10 9 8 7 6 5 4 3 2 1

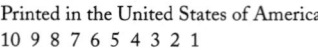

President and CEO
Keith Weiskamp

Publisher
Steve Sayre

Acquisitions Editor
Shari Jo Hehr

Marketing Specialist
Brett Woolley

Project Editor
Karen Swartz

Production Coordinator
Wendy Littley

Cover Designer
Jesse Dunn

Layout Designer
April Nielsen

The Coriolis Group, LLC • 14455 North Hayden Road, Suite 220 • Scottsdale, Arizona 85260

ExamCram.com Connects You to the Ultimate Study Center!

Our goal has always been to provide you with the best study tools on the planet to help you achieve your certification in record time. Time is so valuable these days that none of us can afford to waste a second of it, especially when it comes to exam preparation.

Over the past few years, we've created an extensive line of *Exam Cram* and *Exam Prep* study guides, practice exams, and interactive training. To help you study even better, we have now created an e-learning and certification destination called **ExamCram.com**. (You can access the site at **www.examcram.com**.) Now, with every study product you purchase from us, you'll be connected to a large community of people like yourself who are actively studying for their certifications, developing their careers, seeking advice, and sharing their insights and stories.

I believe that the future is all about collaborative learning. Our **ExamCram.com** destination is our approach to creating a highly interactive, easily accessible collaborative environment, where you can take practice exams and discuss your experiences with others, sign up for features like "Questions of the Day," plan your certifications using our interactive planners, create your own personal study pages, and keep up with all of the latest study tips and techniques.

I hope that whatever study products you purchase from us—*Exam Cram* or *Exam Prep* study guides, *Personal Trainers*, *Personal Test Centers*, or one of our interactive Web courses—will make your studying fun and productive. Our commitment is to build the kind of learning tools that will allow you to study the way you want to, whenever you want to.

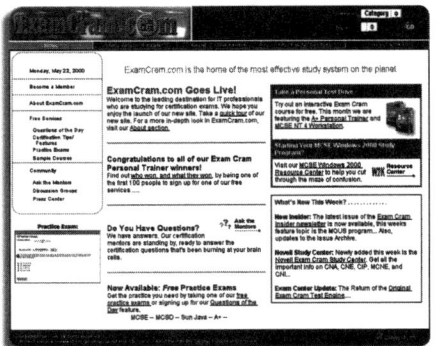

Visit ExamCram.com now to enhance your study program.

Help us continue to provide the very best certification study materials possible. Write us or email us at **learn@examcram.com** and let us know how our study products have helped you study. Tell us about new features that you'd like us to add. Send us a story about how we've helped you. We're listening!

Good luck with your certification exam and your career. Thank you for allowing us to help you achieve your goals.

Keith Weiskamp
President and CEO

Look for these other products from The Coriolis Group:

MCSE Windows 2000 Accelerated
Exam Prep
By Lance Cockcroft, Erik Eckel,
and Ron Kauffman

MCSE Windows 2000 Server Exam Prep
By David Johnson and Dawn Rader

MCSE Windows 2000 Professional
Exam Prep
By Michael D. Stewart, James Bloomingdale,
and Neall Alcott

MCSE Windows 2000 Network Exam Prep
By Tammy Smith and Sandra Smeeton

MCSE Windows 2000 Directory Services
Exam Prep
By David V. Watts, Will Willis, and Tillman
Strahan

MCSE Windows 2000 Security Design
Exam Prep
By Richard Alan McMahon and Glen Bicking

MCSE Windows 2000 Network Design
Exam Prep
By Geoffrey Alexander, Anoop Jalan,
and Joseph Alexander

MCSE Migrating from NT 4
to Windows 2000
Exam Prep
By Glen Bergen, Graham Leach,
and David Baldwin

MCSE Windows 2000
Directory Services Design
Exam Prep
By J. Peter Bruzzese and Wayne Dipchan

MCSE Windows 2000 Core Four
Exam Prep Pack

MCSE Windows 2000 Server
Exam Cram
By Natasha Knight

MCSE Windows 2000 Professional
Exam Cram
By Dan Balter, Dan Holme, Todd Logan,
and Laurie Salmon

MCSE Windows 2000 Network
Exam Cram
By Hank Carbeck, Derek Melber,
and Richard Taylor

MCSE Windows 2000 Directory Services
Exam Cram
By Will Willis, David V. Watts,
and J. Peter Bruzzese

MCSE Windows 2000 Security Design
Exam Cram
By Phillip G. Schein

MCSE Windows 2000
Directory Services Design
Exam Cram
By Dennis Scheil and Diana Bartley

MCSE Windows 2000 Core Four
Exam Cram Pack

and...
MCSE Windows 2000 Foundations
By James Michael Stewart and Lee Scales

About the Authors

Kim Simmons (MCSE, MCP+I, and MCT) includes among her 11 certifications development exams in support of her emphasis in Internet technologies. She is currently a lead instructor at Westwood College of Technology, developing and teaching a postgraduate e-commerce IT professional program. She has worked for MCI Systemhouse and EDS performing network architecture analysis and upgrade recommendations on a per project basis for outside companies. As a technical trainer teaching MCSE certification courses, she received corporate awards for being one of the top 15 and 50 trainers in the ExecuTrain Corporation national system. Before moving into technical training, Kim served in Saudi Arabia in support of the Gulf War, where she used the PATRIOT missile system to do engagement control in search of SCUD missiles.

Kim doesn't have any spare time, but she spends her off-teaching time with her three children and husband. Her goal is to develop a non-computer hobby someday.

Jarret W. Buse (MCT, MCSE+I, CCNA, CNA, A+, Network+, and i-Net+) is a technical trainer and consultant specializing in Microsoft products. He has worked with Microsoft hardware and software for the past eight years and instructs students in the use of various Microsoft products at Micro Computer Solutions in Evansville, Indiana. Now holding an Associate Degree in Programming, he is working toward Microsoft Developer Certification. He can be reached at jbuse@teammcs.com.

Todd B. Halpin (MCSE, MCT, MCP, Network+, and CCNA) has been a Network Support Technician/Engineer since 1995. He is currently employed by Micro Computer Solutions in Evansville, IN, where he is responsible for network design, implementation, and support. He is also a backup trainer for Jarret Buse. Todd provides support services for MCS clients in the Indiana, Kentucky, and Illinois areas, ranging from small mom-and-pop shops to corporate WANs. Along with co-authoring this book and providing training services, his strength is in providing his clients with solutions to challenges they face. The diversity of challenges posed by this wonderful profession cannot be equaled. "I love this game!"

Acknowledgments

· ·

Thanks to Lee Anderson and Karen Akins Swartz for being so supportive. You both made the process much easier. Thanks to Tom Gillen for copyediting and Lydia Bell for tech reviewing our work. Many thanks to the team at The Coriolis Group, including Wendy Littley for production coordination, Jesse Dunn for cover design, April Nielsen for layout design, and Brett Woolley in marketing. Eddie, thanks for understanding while I was locked away during the writing of this book. Jarret and Todd, you are the nicest guys and I wish you the best. Also to SLB, the motivation to write this book came from you.

—*Kim Simmons*

I want to thank my beautiful wife, Cassandra, for her love and support not only during the writing of this book, but also during the wonderful years we have been together. I also cherish our children and appreciate their understanding during the last few months. Devyn, Logan, Caleb, and Eilly, I could not live without you. During the writing of this book, my beautiful daughter, Eilly, was born. During her recovery, my wife dislocated her shoulders and suffered immensely for almost three weeks, and even now is still recovering from the damage done. My family's absence from me, like mine from them, was felt every minute. I will be with all of you soon and forever (especially Eilly, my little princess).

Also during this time I have appreciated the help of my mother-in-law, "Alice", for helping with the family and making me a HOT dinner every night!

I also want to thank my employer and manager for being understanding through the course of this book. Micro Computer Solutions has been a Godsend.

Thanks to my mom and dad for supporting me in all my endeavors and acknowledging my abilities to help me toward a career of my choice.

To my grandmother, this book will be Greek to you, but I think you will love it anyway.

Thanks to my great-aunt for my first computer.

Thanks to my student on Saturdays for his understanding when I cancelled class or hurried through material.

And to anyone I forgot, there is always (hopefully) a next book.

And finally, to save the best for last, thank you God for letting me get this far!

—*Jarret W. Buse*

I have too many to thank to list them all, so I will list the ones that need to be printed. A special thanks to Kim and Jarret for their help and support. With Kim's help in easing my writing burden, this book was completed on time. Jarret is not only a good coworker, but also a good friend, and if his four children take after their father, they will be an awesome force in this industry within a few decades. A big thanks to Kris Miller, co-owner and VP of VirtuCon, for the use of the company name, and for just being Kris.

Last, but not least, a special thanks to my wife Greta, who has the writing skills to make sure that my dyslexia was not apparent to the folks at Coriolis. Without her spelling and grammatical skills, the amount of errors would have driven the editors insane, or at a minimum, given them a nervous tick. If your child has been diagnosed with Attention Deficit Disorder or dyslexia, I encourage you to purchase a copy of *Brilliant Idiot*, by Dr. Abraham Schmitt, as told by Mary Lou Hartzler Clements, ISBN 1-56148-108-4. Don't medicate the child, educate yourself!

—*Todd B. Halpin*

Contents at a Glance

Chapter 1   Microsoft Certification Exams   1

Chapter 2   Overview   23

Chapter 3   TCP/IP Networking Solutions   41

Chapter 4   DHCP Design   65

Chapter 5   DNS   83

Chapter 6   WINS Design   105

Chapter 7   NAT Protocol Design   131

Chapter 8   Microsoft Proxy Server 2.0   149

Chapter 9   Routing in a Windows 2000 Environment   175

Chapter 10   Dfs   197

Chapter 11   Remote Access in a Windows
2000 Environment   219

Chapter 12   Understanding RADIUS   239

Chapter 13   Managing Network Services   263

Chapter 14   Combining Network Services   287

Chapter 15   Putting It All Together   307

Chapter 16   Sample Test   323

Chapter 17   Answer Key   343

Table of Contents

Introduction xxiii

Self-Assessment xxxv

Chapter 1
Microsoft Certification Exams 1
Assessing Exam-Readiness   2
The Exam Situation   3
Exam Layout and Design: New Case Study Format   4
    Multiple-Choice Question Format   5
    Build-List-and-Reorder Question Format   6
    Create-a-Tree Question Format   8
    Drag-and-Connect Question Format   10
    Select-and-Place Question Format   11
Microsoft's Testing Formats   12
Strategies for Different Testing Formats   14
    The Case Study Exam Strategy   15
    The Fixed-Length and Short-Form Exam Strategy   16
    The Adaptive Exam Strategy   17
Question-Handling Strategies   18
Mastering the Inner Game   19
Additional Resources   20

Chapter 2
Overview 23
Changes in Windows 2000   24
    The Way It Was   24
    And Then Came TCP/IP   25
    The Great Name-Resolution Debate   26
Going the Way of the Internet   28
    New Service Requirements   28

Remote Access Connectivity   31
    Routing Improvements   31
    Using the Internet for Connectivity   31
    NAT and Proxy Server   32
Designing Network Services   33
Practice Questions   34
Need to Know More?   39

Chapter 3
TCP/IP Networking Solutions 41
TCP/IP History and Review   42
The OSI Model   42
    Physical Layer   43
    Data Link Layer   43
    Network Layer   44
    Transport Layer   44
    Session Layer   44
    Presentation Layer   44
    Application Layer   44
TCP/IP Addressing   45
Subnet Masks   45
    Variable Length Subnet Mask   45
    Supernetting   45
Addressing Schemes for Private and Public Networks   46
    Public Networks   46
    Private Networks   46
Designing Your TCP/IP Network   46
IP Configuration   48
    DHCP   48
    Automatic Private IP Addressing   49
TCP Performance Enhancements   49
    Increased TCP Window Size   49
    TCP Selective Acknowledgment (SACK)   49
    Internet Control Message Protocol (ICMP)   50
    Disabling NetBIOS over TCP/IP (NetBT)   50
Security   50
    Filtering IP Traffic   50
    Securing TCP/IP Traffic with IPSec   51

Quality of Service (QoS)   54

    QoS Components   54

Practice Questions   56

Need to Know More?   64

Chapter 4
DHCP Design 65

DHCP Overview   66

    Vendor-Specific Option Categories   67

    Multicast Address Dynamic Client Allocation
      Protocol (MADCAP)   68

    Lease Time   70

    DHCP Integration with Windows 2000   70

Designing a LAN DHCP Service   72

Designing WAN DHCP Services   73

    One DHCP Server in a WAN   73

    Multiple DHCP Servers in a WAN   73

Designing DHCP High Availability   74

    Clustered DHCP Server   74

    Multiple DHCP Servers   74

Enhancing DHCP Performance   74

    Hardware Implementation   74

    Software Implementation   75

Practice Questions   76

Need to Know More?   82

Chapter 5
DNS 83

Design Issues for DNS   84

The Importance of a Network Diagram   84

    Documenting Your DNS Server Types   85

    Adding to Your Network Diagram   86

    Documenting Your DNS Client Types   86

Integration of Active Directory and DNS   87

    No DNS or Starting Over   88

    Same Namespace   88

    Different Namespaces   88

    Integration with non-Microsoft DNS Servers   88

Zones   89
    Zone Types   89
    Resource Records   90
Designing a Secure DNS System   91
    Using Access Control Lists (ACLs) in DNS   92
    Screened Subnets   92
    Forwarding, Forwarder, and Slave Servers   93
Increasing DNS Performance   94
    One DNS Server per Location   94
    Zone Delegation   94
    Load Balance Client Requests   95
    Use Caching-Only Servers   95
Practice Questions   96
Need to Know More?   103

Chapter 6
WINS Design **105**
WINS Basics   106
    The NetBIOS Namespace   106
    Broadcasts on a Network   107
    Routers and Broadcasts   107
    WINS-Provided Services   108
Placing and Configuring WINS Servers   108
    WINS Name-Resolution Process   109
    A Network Diagram   110
    Future Plans for the Network   110
    How Many WINS Servers Are Needed?   111
    WINS Traffic   111
    Spoke-and-Hub Design   112
    Understanding WINS Replication   114
Configuring WINS Clients   117
    Support for Non-WINS NetBIOS Clients   118
    Using a WINS Proxy Agent   118
Improving Performance in a WINS Network   118
    Keeping the WINS Database Current   118
    The Importance of Tombstoning   119
    Consistency Checks   119

Security in a WINS Environment   120
WINS over a VPN   120
Using WINS in a Screened Subnet   120
Taking WINS off the Network   121
Disabling NetBIOS on the Network   121
Decommissioning the WINS Servers   121
Practice Questions   122
Need to Know More?   129

Chapter 7
NAT Protocol Design 131

NAT Overview   132
NAT Implementation   132
Installing NAT   133
Configuring NAT   134
NAT in Action   135
Integrating NAT into Existing Networks   136
NAT and DNS   137
Routing and Remote Access Security for NAT   137
NAT Interface Security   137
VPN Security   139
Performance   139
Practice Questions   141
Need to Know More?   148

Chapter 8
Microsoft Proxy Server 2.0 149

What Does a Proxy Server Do?   150
Understanding Internet Connections   150
Protecting the Network   152
A Proxy vs. a Firewall   152
Microsoft Proxy Server   153
Proxy Server Software   153
Microsoft Proxy Server 2.0 and Windows 2000   153
The Local Address Table (LAT)   154
Services Provided by Proxy Server   154
Transparency   155
Improved Performance   155

Optimizing Cache Settings   156

Proxy Arrays   156

Cache Array Routing Protocol (CARP)   157

Security Services Provided by Proxy Server   157

For Outbound Access   157

Controlling Inbound Access   158

Preparing a Network for Proxy Server   159

Private Ranges of IP Addresses   160

The Network Diagram   160

Determining the Number of Proxy Servers   161

Chaining Proxy Server   161

Proxy Server Routes   161

Reverse Proxying   162

Placing Proxy Servers on the Network   163

Joining Disimilar Networks with Proxy Server   163

External Connections   163

Review of Proxy Services   165

Setting up Proxy Clients   165

Web Proxy Clients   165

WinSock and Socks Proxy Clients   165

Practice Questions   167

Need to Know More?   173

Chapter 9
Routing in a Windows 2000 Environment 175

Routing Overview   176

Dynamic vs. Static Routing   177

Enabling Windows 2000 Routing   178

Unicasts, Broadcasts, and Multicasts   179

IGMP   179

Routing Information Protocol (RIP)   180

Comparing RIP versions 1 and 2   180

Routing in a TCP/IP Environment   181

OSPF   181

Routing in a Mixed Environment   182

Routing in a Novell Environment   182

Service Advertising Protocol (SAP)   183

AppleTalk Routing   184
Comparing Routing Protocols   184
Routing in a WAN Environment   184
    Demand-Dial Connections   185
    Leased Line Connections   185
Integration   185
    Internet Protocol Security (IPSec)   185
    Routing and Remote Access   186
    Active Directory   186
Security   186
    Authentication   186
    Virtual Private Network (VPN)   187
Availability   187
Performance   187
Practice Questions   189
Need to Know More?   194

Chapter 10
Dfs **195**
Distributed File System (Dfs) Overview   196
    DfsCapabilities   196
    Common Uses   197
    The Dfs Tree   197
    Active Directory Integration   197
Requirements for Windows 2000 DFS   198
Installing Dfs Host Servers   199
    Windows 2000   199
    Windows NT 4   199
    Client Software   200
Browsing a Dfs Tree   200
Administration Tools   201
    Creating a Dfs Root   203
    Dfs File System Security   204
    Creating a New Link to a Shared Folder   204
    Deleting a Link to a Shared Folder   205
    Creating a Replica   205
    Deleting a Replica   206

Dfs Command Index   206

Optimizing Your Dfs Design   206

Practice Questions   210

Need to Know More?   217

Chapter 11
Remote Access in a Windows 2000 Environment 219

Remote Access Overview   220

Remote Access Implementation   221

Virtual Private Network (VPN)   223

Encapsulation   224

Data Encryption   226

Authentication   226

Features   226

Integration   226

2000 Services   227

LAN Integration   228

WAN Integration   228

Remote Access Placement   228

Security   229

Availability   229

Performance   230

Practice Questions   231

Need to Know More?   238

Chapter 12
Understanding RADIUS 239

What Is RADIUS?   240

Tracking Remote Connections with RADIUS Accounting   240

RADIUS Service Basics   241

Components in a RADIUS Solution   241

Realms   242

RADIUS Servers   243

RADIUS Clients   243

Shared Secret   243

Network Diagram   244

Authentication Protocol   245

Data Encryption   246

Transport Protocols   246

Connection Methods   246

Persistence and Data Rate for Connections   246

Placing RADIUS Components   247

RADIUS Clients   247

Outsourcing RAS Connections   247

Connecting Roaming Users through an ISP   248

Using the Accounting Feature for Billing   249

Ensuring Security in a RADIUS Solution   250

Screened Subnets   250

Remote-Access Policies   251

Increasing RADIUS Availability   251

Configuring Backup IAS Servers   252

Optimizing the Logging Feature   252

Practice Questions   253

Need to Know More?   261

Chapter 13
Managing Network Services 263

Planning Management Strategies   264

Responding to Service Interruptions and Changes   264

Ensuring That the Current Environment Meets the
Design Criteria   265

Planned Expansion to Meet the Future Needs for the
Network Services   266

Implementing Network Status Monitoring   266

Getting Information on the Status of Services   267

Data Collection   267

Generated Events   268

Using Monitoring Tools   271

The System Console   271

Using Logs and Alerts   273

Using the Event Viewer   275

Windows 2000 Support for SNMP   277

Getting Statistics with Scripting and Programming Tools   277

Windows Script Host   277

Custom Applications   277

Windows Management Instrumentation (WMI)   278

Analyzing Collected Data 278
Analysis 278
Response Strategies 279
Proactive Response Strategies 279
Reactive Response 279
Practice Questions 280
Need to Know More? 285

Chapter 14
Combining Network Services 287

Goals of Combining Network Services 288
Combining Network Diagrams 289
Network Diagram Additions 289
Making Service Decisions 291
Hardware Resources 291
Applications on a Server 292
Using Fewer Servers 292
Combinations to Increase Security 293
Adding Screened Subnets to a Network 293
Remote Access Connections 295
Combinations to Increase Performance 295
Reducing Network Traffic 295
Combinations to Increase Availability 295
Windows Clustering 296
Practice Questions 297
Need to Know More? 306

Chapter 15
Putting It All Together 307

Evaluating Existing Network Infrastructure 308
Selecting Appropriate Network Services 308
Selecting Services 309
Selecting Appropriate Service Options 309
Server Placement 309
Creating a Secure Network Design 311
Enhancing Availability 311

Enhancing Performance   311
Identifying Network Services   312
    Including Services in your Design   312
Practice Questions   **317**
Need to Know More?   321

Chapter 16
Sample Test 323

Chapter 17
Answer Key 345

Glossary 357

Index 371

Introduction

Welcome to *MCSE Windows 2000 Network Design Exam Cram*! Whether this is your first or your fifteenth *Exam Cram* book, you'll find information here and in Chapter 1 that will help ensure your success as you pursue knowledge, experience, and certification. This book aims to help you get ready to take—and pass—the Microsoft certification Exam 70-221, titled "Designing a Microsoft Windows 2000 Network Infrastructure." This Introduction explains Microsoft's certification programs in general and talks about how the *Exam Cram* series can help you prepare for Microsoft's Windows 2000 certification exams.

Exam Cram books help you understand and appreciate the subjects and materials you need to pass Microsoft certification exams. *Exam Cram* books are aimed strictly at test preparation and review. They do not teach you everything you need to know about a topic. Instead, we (the authors) present and dissect the questions and problems we've found that you're likely to encounter on a test. We've worked to bring together as much information as possible about Microsoft certification exams.

Nevertheless, to completely prepare yourself for any Microsoft test, we recommend that you begin by taking the Self-Assessment included in this book immediately following this Introduction. This tool will help you evaluate your knowledge base against the requirements for an MCSE under both ideal and real circumstances.

Based on what you learn from that exercise, you might decide to begin your studies with some classroom training or some background reading. On the other hand, you might decide to pick up and read one of the many study guides available from Microsoft or third-party vendors on certain topics, including The Coriolis Group's *Exam Prep* series. We also recommend that you supplement your study program with visits to **ExamCram.com** to receive additional practice questions, get advice, and track the Windows 2000 MCSE program.

We also strongly recommend that you install, configure, and fool around with the software that you'll be tested on, because nothing beats hands-on experience and familiarity when it comes to understanding the questions you're likely to encounter on a certification test. Book learning is essential, but hands-on experience is the best teacher of all!

The Microsoft Certified Professional (MCP) Program

The MCP Program currently includes the following separate tracks, each of which boasts its own special acronym (as a certification candidate, you need to have a high tolerance for alphabet soup of all kinds):

➤ *MCP (Microsoft Certified Professional)*—This is the least prestigious of all the certification tracks from Microsoft. Passing one of the major Microsoft exams qualifies an individual for the MCP credential. Individuals can demonstrate proficiency with additional Microsoft products by passing additional certification exams.

➤ *MCP+SB (Microsoft Certified Professional + Site Building)*—This certification program is designed for individuals who are planning, building, managing, and maintaining Web sites. Individuals with the MCP+SB credential will have demonstrated the ability to develop Web sites that include multimedia and searchable content and Web sites that connect to and communicate with a back-end database. It requires one MCP exam, plus two of these three exams: "70-055: Designing and Implementing Web Sites with Microsoft FrontPage 98," "70-057: Designing and Implementing Commerce Solutions with Microsoft Site Server 3.0, Commerce Edition," and "70-152: Designing and Implementing Web Solutions with Microsoft Visual InterDev 6.0."

➤ *MCSE (Microsoft Certified Systems Engineer)*—Anyone who has a current MCSE is warranted to possess a high level of networking expertise with Microsoft operating systems and products. This credential is designed to prepare individuals to plan, implement, maintain, and support information systems, networks, and internetworks built around Microsoft Windows 2000 and its BackOffice Server 2000 family of products.

To obtain an MCSE, an individual must pass four core operating system exams, one optional core exam, and two elective exams. The operating system exams require individuals to prove their competence with desktop and server operating systems and networking/internetworking components.

For Windows NT 4 MCSEs, the Accelerated exam, "70-240: Microsoft Windows 2000 Accelerated Exam for MCPs Certified on Microsoft Windows NT 4.0," is an option. This free exam covers all of the material tested in the Core Four exams. The hitch in this plan is that you can take the test only once. If you fail, you must take all four core exams to recertify. The Core Four exams are: "70-210: Installing, Configuring and Administering Microsoft Windows 2000 Professional," "70-215: Installing, Configuring and Administering Microsoft

Windows 2000 Server," "70-216: Implementing and Administering a Microsoft Windows 2000 Network Infrastructure," and "70-217: Implementing and Administering a Microsoft Windows 2000 Directory Services Infrastructure."

To fulfill the fifth core exam requirement, you can choose from three design exams: "70-219: Designing a Microsoft Windows 2000 Directory Services Infrastructure," "70-220: Designing Security for a Microsoft Windows 2000 Network," or "70-221: Designing a Microsoft Windows 2000 Network Infrastructure." You are also required to take two elective exams. An elective exam may fall in any number of subject or product areas, primarily BackOffice Server 2000 components. The two design exams that you don't select as your fifth core exam also qualify as electives. If you are on your way to becoming an MCSE and have already taken some exams, visit **www.microsoft.com/trainingandservices** for information about how to complete your MCSE certification.

In September 1999, Microsoft announced its Windows 2000 track for MCSE and also announced retirement of Windows NT 4.0 MCSE core exams on 12/31/2000. Individuals who wish to remain certified MCSEs after 12/31/2001 must "upgrade" their certifications on or before 12/31/2001. For more detailed information than is included here, visit **www.microsoft.com/trainingandservices/**.

New MCSE candidates must pass seven tests to meet the MCSE requirements. It's not uncommon for the entire process to take a year or so, and many individuals find that they must take a test more than once to pass. The primary goal of the *Exam Prep* and *Exam Cram* test preparation books is to make it possible, given proper study and preparation, to pass all Microsoft certification tests on the first try. Table 1 shows the required and elective exams for the Windows 2000 MCSE certification.

➤ *MCSD (Microsoft Certified Solution Developer)*—The MCSD credential reflects the skills required to create multitier, distributed, and COM-based solutions, in addition to desktop and Internet applications, using new technologies. To obtain an MCSD, an individual must demonstrate the ability to analyze and interpret user requirements; select and integrate products, platforms, tools, and technologies; design and implement code, and customize applications; and perform necessary software tests and quality assurance operations.

To become an MCSD, you must pass a total of four exams: three core exams and one elective exam. Each candidate must choose one of these three desktop application exams—"70-016: Designing and Implementing Desktop Applications with Microsoft Visual C++ 6.0," "70-156: Designing and Implementing Desktop Applications with Microsoft Visual FoxPro 6.0," or "70-176: Designing and Implementing Desktop Applications with Microsoft

Table 1   MCSE Windows 2000 Requirements

Core

If you have not passed these 3 Windows NT 4 exams	
Exam 70-067	Implementing and Supporting Microsoft Windows NT Server 4.0
Exam 70-068	Implementing and Supporting Microsoft Windows NT Server 4.0 in the Enterprise
Exam 70-073	Microsoft Windows NT Workstation 4.0
then you must take these 4 exams	
Exam 70-210	Installing, Configuring and Administering Microsoft Windows 2000 Professional
Exam 70-215	Installing, Configuring and Administering Microsoft Windows 2000 Server
Exam 70-216	Implementing and Administering a Microsoft Windows 2000 Network Infrastructure
Exam 70-217	Implementing and Administering a Microsoft Windows 2000 Directory Services Infrastructure
If you have already passed exams 70-067, 70-068, and 70-073, you may take this exam	
Exam 70-240	Microsoft Windows 2000 Accelerated Exam for MCPs Certified on Microsoft Windows NT 4.0

5th Core Option

Choose 1 from this group	
Exam 70-219*	Designing a Microsoft Windows 2000 Directory Services Infrastructure
Exam 70-220*	Designing Security for a Microsoft Windows 2000 Network
➤ Exam 70-221*	Designing a Microsoft Windows 2000 Network Infrastructure

Elective

Choose 2 from this group	
Exam 70-019	Designing and Implementing Data Warehouse with Microsoft SQL Server 7.0
Exam 70-219*	Designing a Microsoft Windows 2000 Directory Services Infrastructure
Exam 70-220*	Designing Security for a Microsoft Windows 2000 Network
➤ Exam 70-221*	Designing a Microsoft Windows 2000 Network Infrastructure
Exam 70-222	Migrating from Microsoft Windows NT 4.0 to Microsoft Windows 2000
Exam 70-028	Administering Microsoft SQL Server 7.0
Exam 70-029	Designing and Implementing Databases on Microsoft SQL Server 7.0
Exam 70-080	Implementing and Supporting Microsoft Internet Explorer 5.0 by Using the Internet Explorer Administration Kit
Exam 70-081	Implementing and Supporting Microsoft Exchange Server 5.5
Exam 70-085	Implementing and Supporting Microsoft SNA Server 4.0
Exam 70-086	Implementing and Supporting Microsoft Systems Management Server 2.0
Exam 70-088	Implementing and Supporting Microsoft Proxy Server 2.0

This is not a complete listing—you can still be tested on some earlier versions of these products. However, we have included mainly the most recent versions so that you may test on these versions and thus be certified longer. We have not included any tests that are scheduled to be retired.

* The 5th Core Option exam does not double as an elective.

Visual Basic 6.0"—*plus* one of these three distributed application exams— "70-015: Designing and Implementing Distributed Applications with Microsoft Visual C++ 6.0," "70-155: Designing and Implementing Distributed Applications with Microsoft Visual FoxPro 6.0," or "70-175: Designing and Implementing Distributed Applications with Microsoft Visual Basic 6.0." The third core exam is "70-100: Analyzing Requirements and Defining Solution Architectures." Elective exams cover specific Microsoft applications and languages, including Visual Basic, C++, the Microsoft Foundation Classes, Access, SQL Server, Excel, and more.

➤ *MCDBA (Microsoft Certified Database Administrator)*—The MCDBA credential reflects the skills required to implement and administer Microsoft SQL Server databases. To obtain an MCDBA, an individual must demonstrate the ability to derive physical database designs, develop logical data models, create physical databases, create data services by using Transact-SQL, manage and maintain databases, configure and manage security, monitor and optimize databases, and install and configure Microsoft SQL Server.

To become an MCDBA, you must pass a total of three core exams and one elective exam. The required core exams are "70-028: Administering Microsoft SQL Server 7.0," "70-029: Designing and Implementing Databases with Microsoft SQL Server 7.0," and "70-215: Installing, Configuring and Administering Microsoft Windows 2000 Server."

The elective exams that you can choose from cover specific uses of SQL Server and include "70-015: Designing and Implementing Distributed Applications with Microsoft Visual C++ 6.0," "70-019: Designing and Implementing Data Warehouses with Microsoft SQL Server 7.0," "70-155: Designing and Implementing Distributed Applications with Microsoft Visual FoxPro 6.0," "70-175: Designing and Implementing Distributed Applications with Microsoft Visual Basic 6.0," and two exams that relate to Windows 2000: "70-216: Implementing and Administering a Microsoft Windows 2000 Network Infrastructure," and "70-087: Implementing and Supporting Microsoft Internet Information Server 4.0."

If you have taken the three core Windows NT 4 exams on your path to becoming an MCSE, you qualify for the Accelerated exam (it replaces the Network Infrastructure exam requirement). The Accelerated exam covers the objectives of all four of the Windows 2000 core exams. In addition to taking the Accelerated exam, you must take only the two SQL exams—Administering and Database Design.

➤ *MCT (Microsoft Certified Trainer)*—Microsoft Certified Trainers are deemed able to deliver elements of the official Microsoft curriculum, based on technical knowledge and instructional ability. Thus, it is necessary for an individual seeking MCT credentials (which are granted on a course-by-course basis) to pass the related certification exam for a course and complete the official Microsoft training in the subject area, and to demonstrate an ability to teach.

This teaching skill criterion may be satisfied by proving that one has already attained training certification from Novell, Banyan, Lotus, the Santa Cruz Operation, or Cisco, or by taking a Microsoft-sanctioned workshop on instruction. Microsoft makes it clear that MCTs are important cogs in the Microsoft training channels. Instructors must be MCTs before Microsoft will allow them to teach in any of its official training channels, including Microsoft's affiliated Certified Technical Education Centers (CTECs) and its online training partner network. As of January 1, 2001, MCT candidates must also possess a current MCSE.

Microsoft has announced that the MCP+I and MCSE+I credentials will not be continued when the MCSE exams for Windows 2000 are in full swing because the skill set for the Internet portion of the program has been included in the new MCSE program. Therefore, details on these tracks are not provided here; go to **www.microsoft.com/trainingandservices/** if you need more information.

Once a Microsoft product becomes obsolete, MCPs typically have to recertify on current versions. (If individuals do not recertify, their certifications become invalid.) Because technology keeps changing and new products continually supplant old ones, this should come as no surprise. This explains why Microsoft has announced that MCSEs have 12 months past the scheduled retirement date for the Windows NT 4 exams to recertify on Windows 2000 topics. (Note that this means taking at least two exams, if not more.)

The best place to keep tabs on the MCP Program and its related certifications is on the Web. The URL for the MCP program is **www.microsoft.com/trainingandservices/**. But Microsoft's Web site changes often, so if this URL doesn't work, try using the Search tool on Microsoft's site with either "MCP" or the quoted phrase "Microsoft Certified Professional" as a search string. This will help you find the latest and most accurate information about Microsoft's certification programs.

Taking a Certification Exam

Once you've prepared for your exam, you need to register with a testing center. Each computer-based MCP exam costs $100, and if you don't pass, you may retest for an additional $100 for each additional try. In the United States and Canada, tests are administered by Prometric and by Virtual University Enterprises (VUE). Here's how you can contact them:

➤ *Prometric*—You can sign up for a test through the company's Web site at **www.prometric.com**. Or, you can register by phone at 800-755-3926 (within the United States or Canada) or at 410-843-8000 (outside the United States and Canada).

➤ *Virtual University Enterprises*—You can sign up for a test or get the phone numbers for local testing centers through the Web page at **www.vue.com/ms/**.

To sign up for a test, you must possess a valid credit card, or contact either company for mailing instructions to send them a check (in the U.S.). Only when payment is verified, or a check has cleared, can you actually register for a test.

To schedule an exam, call the number or visit either of the Web pages at least one day in advance. To cancel or reschedule an exam, you must call before 7 P.M. pacific standard time the day before the scheduled test time (or you may be charged, even if you don't appear to take the test). When you want to schedule a test, have the following information ready:

➤ Your name, organization, and mailing address.

➤ Your Microsoft Test ID. (Inside the United States, this means your Social Security number; citizens of other nations should call ahead to find out what type of identification number is required to register for a test.)

➤ The name and number of the exam you wish to take.

➤ A method of payment. (As we've already mentioned, a credit card is the most convenient method, but alternate means can be arranged in advance, if necessary.)

Once you sign up for a test, you'll be informed as to when and where the test is scheduled. Try to arrive at least 15 minutes early. You must supply two forms of identification—one of which must be a photo ID—to be admitted into the testing room.

All exams are completely closed-book. In fact, you will not be permitted to take anything with you into the testing area, but you will be furnished with a blank sheet of paper and a pen or, in some cases, an erasable plastic sheet and an erasable pen. We suggest that you immediately write down on that sheet of paper all the information you've memorized for the test. In *Exam Cram* books, this information appears on a tear-out sheet inside the front cover of each book. You will have some time to compose yourself, record this information, and take a sample orientation exam before you begin the real thing. We suggest you take the orientation test before taking your first exam, but because they're all more or less identical in layout, behavior, and controls, you probably won't need to do this more than once.

When you complete a Microsoft certification exam, the software will tell you whether you've passed or failed. If you need to retake an exam, you'll have to schedule a new test with Prometric or VUE and pay another $100.

The first time you fail a test, you can retake the test the next day. However, if you fail a second time, you must wait 14 days before retaking that test. The 14-day waiting period remains in effect for all retakes after the second failure.

Tracking MCP Status

As soon as you pass any Microsoft exam (except Networking Essentials), you'll attain Microsoft Certified Professional (MCP) status. Microsoft also generates transcripts that indicate which exams you have passed. You can view a copy of your transcript at any time by going to the MCP secured site and selecting Transcript Tool. This tool will allow you to print a copy of your current transcript and confirm your certification status.

Once you pass the necessary set of exams, you'll be certified. Official certification normally takes anywhere from six to eight weeks, so don't expect to get your credentials overnight. When the package for a qualified certification arrives, it includes a Welcome Kit that contains a number of elements (see Microsoft's Web site for other benefits of specific certifications):

➤ A certificate suitable for framing, along with a wallet card and lapel pin.

➤ A license to use the MCP logo, thereby allowing you to use the logo in advertisements, promotions, and documents, and on letterhead, business cards, and so on. Along with the license comes an MCP logo sheet, which includes camera-ready artwork. (Note: Before using any of the artwork, individuals must sign and return a licensing agreement that indicates they'll abide by its terms and conditions.)

➤ A subscription to *Microsoft Certified Professional Magazine*, which provides ongoing data about testing and certification activities, requirements, and changes to the program.

Many people believe that the benefits of MCP certification go well beyond the perks that Microsoft provides to newly anointed members of this elite group. We're starting to see more job listings that request or require applicants to have an MCP, MCSE, and so on, and many individuals who complete the program can qualify for increases in pay and/or responsibility. As an official recognition of hard work and broad knowledge, one of the MCP credentials is a badge of honor in many IT organizations.

How to Prepare for an Exam

Preparing for any Windows 2000 Server-related test (including "Designing a Microsoft Windows 2000 Network Infrastructure") requires that you obtain and study materials designed to provide comprehensive information about the product and its capabilities that will appear on the specific exam for which you are preparing. The following list of materials will help you study and prepare:

➤ The Windows 2000 Server product CD includes comprehensive online documentation and related materials; it should be a primary resource when you are preparing for the test.

➤ The exam preparation materials, practice tests, and self-assessment exams on the Microsoft Training & Services page at **www.microsoft.com/ trainingandservices/default.asp?PageID=mcp**. The Testing Innovations link offers samples of the new question types found on the Windows 2000 MCSE exams. Find the materials, download them, and use them!

➤ The exam preparation advice, practice tests, questions of the day, and discussion groups on the **ExamCram.com** e-learning and certification destination Web site (**www.examcram.com**).

In addition, you'll probably find any or all of the following materials useful in your quest for Network Infrastructure Design expertise:

➤ *Microsoft training kits*—Microsoft Press offers training kits that specifically target Windows 2000 exams. For more information, visit **http:// mspress.microsoft.com/findabook/list/series_ak.htm**.

➤ *Microsoft TechNet CD*—This monthly CD-based publication delivers numerous electronic titles that include coverage of Directory Services Design and related topics on the Technical Information (TechNet) CD. Its offerings include product facts, technical notes, tools and utilities, and information on how to access the Seminars Online training materials for Network Infrastructure Design. A subscription to TechNet costs $299 per year, but it is well worth the price. Visit **www.microsoft.com/technet/** and check out the information under the "TechNet Subscription" menu entry for more details.

➤ *White papers*—Microsoft Corporation publishes technical papers explaining the design of many of the services in Windows 2000. Often these papers are written by the engineers and designers of the service. White papers are an excellent source of information on the inner workings of a service and are often one of few sources to look at when the service is new. Visit **http://www.microsoft.com/ISN/whitepapers.asp** for a list of currently available technical white papers and links to each of them.

➤ *Study guides*—Several publishers—including The Coriolis Group—offer Windows 2000 titles. The Coriolis Group series includes the following:

➤ *The Exam Cram series*—These books give you information about the material you need to know to pass the tests.

➤ *The Exam Prep series*—These books provide a greater level of detail than the *Exam Cram* books and are designed to teach you everything you need to know from an exam perspective. Each book comes with a CD that contains interactive practice exams in a variety of testing formats.

Together, the two series make a perfect pair.

➤ *Multimedia*—These Coriolis Group materials are designed to support learners of all types—whether you learn best by reading or doing:

➤ *The Exam Cram Personal Trainer*—Offers a unique, personalized self-paced training course based on the exam.

➤ *The Exam Cram Personal Test Center*—Features multiple test options that simulate the actual exam, including Fixed-Length, Random, Review, and Test All. Explanations of correct and incorrect answers reinforce concepts learned.

➤ *Classroom training*—CTECs, online partners, and third-party training companies (like Wave Technologies, Learning Tree, Data-Tech, and others) all offer classroom training on Windows 2000. These companies aim to help you prepare to pass Exam 70-221. Although such training runs upwards of $350 per day in class, most of the individuals lucky enough to partake find it to be quite worthwhile.

➤ *Other publications*—There's no shortage of materials available about Network Infrastructure Design. The resource sections at the end of each chapter should give you an idea of where we think you should look for further discussion.

By far, this set of required and recommended materials represents a nonpareil collection of sources and resources for Network Infrastructure Design and related topics. We anticipate that you'll find that this book belongs in this company

About this Book

Each topical *Exam Cram* chapter follows a regular structure, along with graphical cues about important or useful information. Here's the structure of a typical chapter:

➤ *Opening hotlists*—Each chapter begins with a list of the terms, tools, and techniques that you must learn and understand before you can be fully conversant with that chapter's subject matter. We follow the hotlists with one or two introductory paragraphs to set the stage for the rest of the chapter.

➤ *Topical coverage*—After the opening hotlists, each chapter covers a series of topics related to the chapter's subject title. Throughout this section, we highlight topics or concepts likely to appear on a test using a special Exam Alert layout, like this:

 This is what an Exam Alert looks like. Normally, an Exam Alert stresses concepts, terms, software, or activities that are likely to relate to one or more certification test questions. For that reason, we think any information found offset in Exam Alert format is worthy of unusual attentiveness on your part. Indeed, most of the information that appears on The Cram Sheet appears as Exam Alerts within the text.

Pay close attention to material flagged as an Exam Alert; although all the information in this book pertains to what you need to know to pass the exam, we flag certain items that are really important. You'll find what appears in the meat of each chapter to be worth knowing, too, when preparing for the test. Because this book's material is very condensed, we recommend that you use this book along with other resources to achieve the maximum benefit.

In addition to the Exam Alerts, we have provided tips that will help you build a better foundation for Network Infrastructure Design knowledge. Although the information may not be on the exam, it is certainly related and will help you become a better test-taker.

 This is how tips are formatted. Keep your eyes open for these, and you'll become a Network Infrastructure guru in no time!

➤ *Practice questions*—Although we talk about test questions and topics throughout the book, a section at the end of each chapter presents a series of mock test questions and explanations of both correct and incorrect answers.

➤ *Details and resources*—Every chapter ends with a section titled "Need to Know More?" This section provides direct pointers to Microsoft and third-party resources offering more details on the chapter's subject. In addition, this section tries to rank or at least rate the quality and thoroughness of the topic's coverage by each resource. If you find a resource you like in this collection, use it, but don't feel compelled to use all the resources. On the other hand, we recommend only resources we use on a regular basis, so none of our recommendations will be a waste of your time or money (but purchasing them all at once probably represents an expense that many network administrators and would-be MCPs and MCSEs might find hard to justify).

The bulk of the book follows this chapter structure slavishly, but there are a few other elements that we'd like to point out. Chapter 16 includes a sample test that provides a good review of the material presented throughout the book to ensure you're ready for the exam. Chapter 17 is an answer key to the sample test that appears in Chapter 16. In addition, you'll find a handy glossary and an index.

Finally, the tear-out Cram Sheet attached next to the inside front cover of this *Exam Cram* book represents a condensed and compiled collection of facts and tips that we think you should memorize before taking the test. Because you can dump this information out of your head onto a piece of paper before taking the exam, you can master this information by brute force—you need to remember it only long enough to write it down when you walk into the test room. You might even want to look at it in the car or in the lobby of the testing center just before you walk in to take the test.

How to Use this Book

We've structured the topics in this book to build on one another. Therefore, some topics in later chapters make more sense after you've read earlier chapters. That's why we suggest you read this book from front to back for your initial test preparation. If you need to brush up on a topic or you have to bone up for a second try, use the index or table of contents to go straight to the topics and questions that you need to study. Beyond helping you prepare for the test, we think you'll find this book useful as a tightly focused reference to some of the most important aspects of Network Infrastructure.

Given all the book's elements and its specialized focus, we've tried to create a tool that will help you prepare for—and pass—Microsoft Exam 70-221. Please share your feedback on the book with us, especially if you have ideas about how we can improve it for future test-takers. We'll consider everything you say carefully, and we'll respond to all suggestions.

Send your questions or comments to us at **learn@examcram.com**. Please remember to include the title of the book in your message; otherwise, we'll be forced to guess which book you're writing about. And we don't like to guess—we want to *know*! Also, be sure to check out the Web pages at **www.examcram.com**, where you'll find information updates, commentary, and certification information.

Thanks, and enjoy the book!

Self-Assessment

The reason we included a Self-Assessment in this *Exam Cram* book is to help you evaluate your readiness to tackle MCSE certification. It should also help you understand what you need to know to master the topic of this book—namely, Exam 70-221, "Designing a Microsoft Windows 2000 Network Infrastructure." But before you tackle this Self-Assessment, let's talk about concerns you may face when pursuing an MCSE for Windows 2000, and what an ideal MCSE candidate might look like.

MCSEs in the Real World

In the next section, we describe an ideal MCSE candidate, knowing full well that only a few real candidates will meet this ideal. In fact, our description of that ideal candidate might seem downright scary, especially with the changes that have been made to the program to support Windows 2000. But take heart: Although the requirements to obtain an MCSE may seem formidable, they are by no means impossible to meet. However, be keenly aware that it does take time, involves some expense, and requires real effort to get through the process.

Increasing numbers of people are attaining Microsoft certifications, so the goal is within reach. You can get all the real-world motivation you need from knowing that many others have gone before, so you will be able to follow in their footsteps. If you're willing to tackle the process seriously and do what it takes to obtain the necessary experience and knowledge, you can take—and pass—all the certification tests involved in obtaining an MCSE. In fact, we've designed *Exam Preps*, the companion *Exam Crams*, *Exam Cram Personal Trainers*, and *Exam Cram Personal Test Centers* to make it as easy on you as possible to prepare for these exams. We've also greatly expanded our Web site, **www.examcram.com**, to provide a host of resources to help you prepare for the complexities of Windows 2000.

Besides MCSE, other Microsoft certifications include:

➤ MCSD, which is aimed at software developers and requires one specific exam, two more exams on client and distributed topics, plus a fourth elective exam drawn from a different, but limited, pool of options.

➤ Other Microsoft certifications, whose requirements range from one test (MCP) to several tests (MCP+SB, MCDBA).

The Ideal Windows 2000 MCSE Candidate

Just to give you some idea of what an ideal MCSE candidate is like, here are some relevant statistics about the background and experience such an individual might have. Don't worry if you don't meet these qualifications, or don't come that close—this is a far from ideal world, and where you fall short is simply where you'll have more work to do.

➤ Academic or professional training in network theory, concepts, and operations. This includes everything from networking media and transmission techniques through network operating systems, services, and applications.

➤ Three-plus years of professional networking experience, including experience with Ethernet, token ring, modems, and other networking media. This must include installation, configuration, upgrade, and troubleshooting experience.

Note: The Windows 2000 MCSE program is much more rigorous than the previous NT MCSE program; therefore, you'll really need some hands-on experience. Some of the exams require you to solve real-world case studies and network design issues, so the more hands-on experience you have, the better.

➤ Two-plus years in a networked environment that includes hands-on experience with Windows 2000 Server, Windows 2000 Professional, Windows NT Server, Windows NT Workstation, and Windows 95 or Windows 98. A solid understanding of each system's architecture, installation, configuration, maintenance, and troubleshooting is also essential.

➤ Knowledge of the various methods for installing Windows 2000, including manual and unattended installations.

➤ A thorough understanding of key networking protocols, addressing, and name resolution, including TCP/IP, IPX/SPX, and NetBEUI.

➤ A thorough understanding of NetBIOS naming, browsing, and file and print services.

➤ Familiarity with key Windows 2000-based TCP/IP-based services, including HTTP (Web servers), DHCP, WINS, DNS, plus familiarity with one or more of the following: Internet Information Server (IIS), Index Server, and Proxy Server.

➤ An understanding of how to implement security for key network data in a Windows 2000 environment.

➤ Working knowledge of NetWare 3.x and 4.x, including IPX/SPX frame formats, NetWare file, print, and directory services, and both Novell and Microsoft client software. Working knowledge of Microsoft's Client Service For NetWare (CSNW), Gateway Service For NetWare (GSNW), the NetWare Migration Tool (NWCONV), and the NetWare Client For Windows (NT, 95, and 98) is essential.

➤ A good working understanding of Active Directory. The more you work with Windows 2000, the more you'll realize that this new operating system is quite different than Windows NT. New technologies like Active Directory have really changed the way that Windows is configured and used. We recommend that you find out as much as you can about Active Directory and acquire as much experience using this technology as possible. The time you take learning about Active Directory will be time very well spent!

Fundamentally, this boils down to a bachelor's degree in computer science, plus three years' experience working in a position involving network design, installation, configuration, and maintenance. We believe that well under half of all certification candidates meet these requirements, and that, in fact, most meet less than half of these requirements—at least, when they begin the certification process. But because all the people who already have been certified have survived this ordeal, you can survive it too—especially if you heed what our Self-Assessment can tell you about what you already know and what you need to learn.

Put Yourself to the Test

The following series of questions and observations is designed to help you figure out how much work you must do to pursue Microsoft certification and what kinds of resources you may consult on your quest. Be absolutely honest in your answers, or you'll end up wasting money on exams you're not yet ready to take. There are no right or wrong answers, only steps along the path to certification. Only you can decide where you really belong in the broad spectrum of aspiring candidates.

Two things should be clear from the outset, however:

➤ Even a modest background in computer science will be helpful.

➤ Hands-on experience with Microsoft products and technologies is an essential ingredient to certification success.

Educational Background

1. Have you ever taken any computer-related classes? [Yes or No]

   If Yes, proceed to question 2; if No, proceed to question 4.

2. Have you taken any classes on computer operating systems? [Yes or No]

   If Yes, you will probably be able to handle Microsoft's architecture and system component discussions. If you're rusty, brush up on basic operating system concepts, especially virtual memory, multitasking regimes, user mode versus kernel mode operation, and general computer security topics.

   If No, consider some basic reading in this area. We strongly recommend a good general operating systems book, such as *Operating System Concepts, 5th Edition*, by Abraham Silberschatz and Peter Baer Galvin (John Wiley & Sons, 1998, ISBN 0-471-36414-2). If this title doesn't appeal to you, check out reviews for other, similar titles at your favorite online bookstore.

3. Have you taken any networking concepts or technologies classes? [Yes or No]

   If Yes, you will probably be able to handle Microsoft's networking terminology, concepts, and technologies (brace yourself for frequent departures from normal usage). If you're rusty, brush up on basic networking concepts and terminology, especially networking media, transmission types, the OSI Reference Model, and networking technologies such as Ethernet, token ring, FDDI, and WAN links.

   If No, you might want to read one or two books in this topic area. The two best books that we know of are *Computer Networks, 3rd Edition*, by Andrew S. Tanenbaum (Prentice-Hall, 1996, ISBN 0-13-349945-6) and *Computer Networks and Internets, 2nd Edition*, by Douglas E. Comer (Prentice-Hall, 1998, ISBN 0-130-83617-6).

   Skip to the next section, "Hands-on Experience."

4. Have you done any reading on operating systems or networks? [Yes or No]

   If Yes, review the requirements stated in the first paragraphs after questions 2 and 3. If you meet those requirements, move on to the next section. If No, consult the recommended reading for both topics. A strong background will help you prepare for the Microsoft exams better than just about anything else.

Hands-on Experience

The most important key to success on all of the Microsoft tests is hands-on experience, especially with Windows 2000 Server and Professional, plus the many add-on services and BackOffice components around which so many of the Microsoft certification exams revolve. If we leave you with only one realization after taking this Self-Assessment, it should be that there's no substitute for time spent installing, configuring, and using the various Microsoft products upon which you'll be tested repeatedly and in depth.

5. Have you installed, configured, and worked with:

    ➤ Windows 2000 Server? [Yes or No]

    If Yes, make sure you understand basic concepts as covered in Exam 70-215. You should also study the TCP/IP interfaces, utilities, and services for Exam 70-216, plus implementing security features for Exam 70-220.

 You can download objectives, practice exams, and other data about Microsoft exams from the Training and Certification page at **www.Microsoft. com/trainingandservices/default.asp?PageID=mcp/**. Use the "Exams" link to obtain specific exam information.

If you haven't worked with Windows 2000 Server, you must obtain one or two machines and a copy of Windows 2000 Server. Then, learn the operating system and whatever other software components on which you'll also be tested.

In fact, we recommend that you obtain two computers, each with a network interface, and set up a two-node network on which to practice. With decent Windows 2000-capable computers selling for about $500 to $600 apiece these days, this shouldn't be too much of a financial hardship. You may have to scrounge to come up with the necessary software, but if you scour the Microsoft Web site you can usually find low-cost options to obtain evaluation copies of most of the software that you'll need.

➤ Windows 2000 Professional? [Yes or No]

If Yes, make sure you understand the concepts covered in Exam 70-210.

If No, you will want to obtain a copy of Windows 2000 Professional and learn how to install, configure, and maintain it. You can use *MCSE Windows 2000 Professional Exam Cram* to guide your activities and studies, or work straight from Microsoft's test objectives if you prefer.

For any and all of these Microsoft exams, the Resource Kits for the topics involved are a good study resource. You can purchase softcover Resource Kits from Microsoft Press (search for them at **http://mspress. microsoft.com/**), but they also appear on the TechNet CDs (**www. microsoft.com/technet**). Along with *Exam Crams* and *Exam Preps*, we believe that Resource Kits are among the best tools you can use to prepare for Microsoft exams.

6. For any specific Microsoft product that is not itself an operating system (for example, SQL Server), have you installed, configured, used, and upgraded this software? [Yes or No]

If the answer is Yes, skip to the next section. If it's No, you must get some experience. Read on for suggestions on how to do this.

Experience is a must with any Microsoft product exam, be it something as simple as FrontPage 2000 or as challenging as SQL Server 7.0. For trial copies of other software, search Microsoft's Web site using the name of the product as your search term. Also, search for bundles like "BackOffice" or "Small Business Server."

If you have the funds, or your employer will pay your way, consider taking a class at a Certified Training and Education Center (CTEC) or at an Authorized Academic Training Partner (AATP). In addition to classroom exposure to the topic of your choice, you get a copy of the software that is the focus of your course, along with a trial version of whatever operating system it needs, with the training materials for that class.

Before you even think about taking any Microsoft exam, make sure you've spent enough time with the related software to understand how it may be installed and configured, how to maintain such an installation, and how to troubleshoot that software when things go wrong. This will help you in the exam, and in real life!

Testing Your Exam-Readiness

Whether you attend a formal class on a specific topic to get ready for an exam or use written materials to study on your own, some preparation for the Microsoft certification exams is essential. At $100 a try, pass or fail, you want to do everything you can to pass on your first try. That's where studying comes in.

We have included a practice exam in this book, so if you don't score that well on the test, you can study more and then tackle the test again. We also have exams that you can take online through the **ExamCram.com** Web site at **www. examcram.com**. If you still don't hit a score of at least 75 percent after these tests, you'll want to investigate the other practice test resources we mention in this section.

For any given subject, consider taking a class if you've tackled self-study materials, taken the test, and failed anyway. The opportunity to interact with an instructor and fellow students can make all the difference in the world, if you can afford that privilege. For information about Microsoft classes, visit the Training and Certification page at **www.microsoft.com/education/partners/ctec.asp** for Microsoft Certified Education Centers or **www.microsoft.com/aatp/default.htm** for Microsoft Authorized Training Providers.

If you can't afford to take a class, visit the Training and Certification page anyway, because it also includes pointers to free practice exams and to Microsoft Certified Professional Approved Study Guides and other self-study tools. And even if you can't afford to spend much at all, you should still invest in some low-cost practice exams from commercial vendors.

7. Have you taken a practice exam on your chosen test subject? [Yes or No]

   If Yes, and you scored 75 percent or better, you're probably ready to tackle the real thing. If your score isn't above that threshold, keep at it until you break that barrier.

   If No, obtain all the free and low-budget practice tests you can find and get to work. Keep at it until you can break the passing threshold comfortably.

When it comes to assessing your test readiness, there is no better way than to take a good-quality practice exam and pass with a score of 56 percent or better. When we're preparing ourselves, we shoot for 66-plus percent, just to leave room for the "weirdness factor" that sometimes shows up on Microsoft exams.

Assessing Readiness for Exam 70-221

In addition to the general exam-readiness information in the previous section, there are several things you can do to prepare for the Designing a Microsoft Windows 2000 Network Infrastructure exam. As you're getting ready for Exam 70-221, visit the Exam Cram Windows 2000 Resource Center at **www.examcram.com/ studyresource/w2kresource/**. Another valuable resource is the Exam Cram Insider newsletter. Sign up at **www.examcram.com** or send a blank email message to **subscribe-ec@mars.coriolis.com**. We also suggest that you join an active MCSE mailing list. One of the better ones is managed by Sunbelt Software. Sign up at **www.sunbelt-software.com** (look for the Subscribe button).

You can also cruise the Web looking for "braindumps" (recollections of test topics and experiences recorded by others) to help you anticipate topics you're likely to encounter on the test. The MCSE mailing list is a good place to ask where the useful braindumps are, or you can check Shawn Gamble's list at **www.commandcentral.com**.

You can't be sure that a braindump's author can provide correct answers. Thus, use the questions to guide your studies, but don't rely on the answers in a braindump to lead you to the truth. Double-check everything you find in any braindump.

Microsoft exam mavens also recommend checking the Microsoft Knowledge Base (available on its own CD as part of the TechNet collection, or on the Microsoft Web site at **http://support.microsoft.com/support/**) for "meaningful technical support issues" that relate to your exam's topics. Although we're not sure exactly what the quoted phrase means, we have also noticed some overlap between technical support questions on particular products and troubleshooting questions on the exams for those products.

Onward, through the Fog!

Once you've assessed your readiness, undertaken the right background studies, obtained the hands-on experience that will help you understand the products and technologies at work, and reviewed the many sources of information to help you prepare for a test, you'll be ready to take a round of practice tests. When your scores come back positive enough to get you through the exam, you're ready to go after the real thing. If you follow our assessment regime, you'll not only know what you need to study, but when you're ready to make a test date at Prometric or VUE. Good luck!

Microsoft
Certification Exams

· ·

Terms you'll need to understand:

✓ Case study

✓ Multiple-choice question formats

✓ Build-list-and-reorder question format

✓ Create-a-tree question format

✓ Drag-and-connect question format

✓ Select-and-place question format

✓ Fixed-length tests

✓ Simulations

✓ Adaptive tests

✓ Short-form tests

Techniques you'll need to master:

✓ Assessing your exam-readiness

✓ Answering Microsoft's varying question types

✓ Altering your test strategy depending on the exam format

✓ Practicing (to make perfect)

✓ Making the best use of the testing software

✓ Budgeting your time

✓ Guessing (as a last resort)

1

Exam taking is not something that most people anticipate eagerly, no matter how well prepared they may be. In most cases, familiarity helps offset test anxiety. In plain English, this means you probably won't be as nervous when you take your fourth or fifth Microsoft certification exam as you'll be when you take your first one.

Whether it's your first exam or your tenth, understanding the details of taking the new exams (how much time to spend on questions, the environment you'll be in, and so on) and the new exam software will help you concentrate on the material rather than on the setting. Likewise, mastering a few basic exam-taking skills should help you recognize—and perhaps even outfox—some of the tricks and snares you're bound to find in some exam questions.

This chapter, besides explaining the exam environment and software, describes some proven exam-taking strategies that you should be able to use to your advantage.

Assessing Exam-Readiness

We strongly recommend that you read through and take the Self-Assessment included with this book (it appears just before this chapter, in fact). This will help you compare your knowledge base to the requirements for obtaining an MCSE, and it will also help you identify parts of your background or experience that may be in need of improvement, enhancement, or further learning. If you get the right set of basics under your belt, obtaining Microsoft certification will be that much easier.

Once you've gone through the Self-Assessment, you can remedy those topical areas where your background or experience may not measure up to an ideal certification candidate. But you can also tackle subject matter for individual tests at the same time, so you can continue making progress while you're catching up in some areas.

Once you've worked through an *Exam Cram*, have read the supplementary materials, and have taken the practice test, you'll have a pretty clear idea of when you should be ready to take the real exam. Although we strongly recommend that you keep practicing until your scores top the 75 percent mark, 80 percent would be a good goal to give yourself some margin for error in a real exam situation (where stress will play more of a role than when you practice). Once you hit that point, you should be ready to go. But if you get through the practice exam in this book without attaining that score, you should keep taking practice tests and studying the materials until you get there. You'll find more pointers on how to study and prepare in the Self-Assessment. But now, on to the exam itself!

The Exam Situation

When you arrive at the testing center where you scheduled your exam, you'll need to sign in with an exam coordinator. He or she will ask you to show two forms of identification, one of which must be a photo ID. After you've signed in and your time slot arrives, you'll be asked to deposit any books, bags, or other items you brought with you. Then, you'll be escorted into a closed room.

All exams are completely closed book. In fact, you will not be permitted to take anything with you into the testing area, but you will be furnished with a blank sheet of paper and a pen or, in some cases, an erasable plastic sheet and an erasable pen. Before the exam, you should memorize as much of the important material as you can, so you can write that information on the blank sheet as soon as you are seated in front of the computer. You can refer to this piece of paper anytime you like during the test, but you'll have to surrender the sheet when you leave the room.

You will have some time to compose yourself, to record this information, and to take a sample orientation exam before you begin the real thing. We suggest you take the orientation test before taking your first exam, but because they're all more or less identical in layout, behavior, and controls, you probably won't need to do this more than once.

Typically, the room will be furnished with anywhere from one to half a dozen computers, and each workstation will be separated from the others by dividers designed to keep you from seeing what's happening on someone else's computer. Most test rooms feature a wall with a large picture window. This permits the exam coordinator to monitor the room, to prevent exam-takers from talking to one another, and to observe anything out of the ordinary that might go on. The exam coordinator will have preloaded the appropriate Microsoft certification exam—for this book, that's Exam 70-221—and you'll be permitted to start as soon as you're seated in front of the computer.

All Microsoft certification exams allow a certain maximum amount of time in which to complete your work (this time is indicated on the exam by an on-screen counter/clock, so you can check the time remaining whenever you like). All Microsoft certification exams are computer generated. In addition to multiple choice, you'll encounter select and place (drag and drop), create a tree (categorization and prioritization), drag and connect, and build list and reorder (list prioritization) on most exams. Although this may sound quite simple, the questions are constructed not only to check your mastery of basic facts and figures about designing a Microsoft Windows 2000 network infrastructure, but they also require you to evaluate one or more sets of circumstances or requirements.

Often, you'll be asked to give more than one answer to a question. Likewise, you might be asked to select the best or most effective solution to a problem from a range of choices, all of which technically are correct. Taking the exam is quite an adventure, and it involves real thinking. This book shows you what to expect and how to deal with the potential problems, puzzles, and predicaments.

In the next section, you'll learn more about how Microsoft test questions look and how they must be answered.

Exam Layout and Design: New Case Study Format

The format of Microsoft's Windows 2000 exams is different from that of its previous exams. For the design exams (70-219, 70-220, 70-221), each exam consists entirely of a series of case studies, and the questions can be of six types. For the Core Four exams (70-210, 70-215, 70-216, 70-217), the same six types of questions can appear, but you are not likely to encounter complex multiquestion case studies.

For design exams, each case study or "testlet" presents a detailed problem that you must read and analyze. Figure 1.1 shows an example of what a case study looks like. You must select the different tabs in the case study to view the entire case.

Following each case study is a set of questions related to the case study; these questions can be one of six types (which are discussed next). Careful attention to details provided in the case study is the key to success. Be prepared to toggle frequently between the case study and the questions as you work. Some of the case studies also include diagrams, which are called *exhibits*, that you'll need to examine closely to understand how to answer the questions.

Once you complete a case study, you can review all the questions and your answers. However, once you move on to the next case study, you may not be able to return to the previous case study and make any changes.

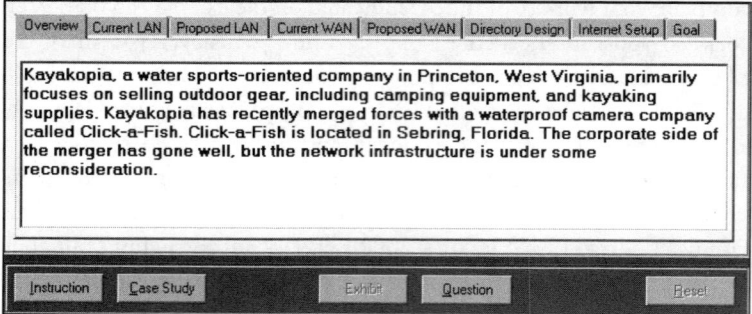

Figure 1.1   This is how case studies appear.

The six types of question formats are:

➤ Multiple choice, single answer

➤ Multiple choice, multiple answers

➤ Build list and reorder (list prioritization)

➤ Create a tree

➤ Drag and connect

➤ Select and place (drag and drop)

Note: Exam formats may vary by test center location. Although most design exams consist entirely of a series of case studies or testlets, a test taker may occasionally encounter a strictly multiple-choice test. You may want to call the test center or visit ExamCram.com to see if you can find out which type of test you'll encounter.

Multiple-Choice Question Format

Some exam questions require you to select a single answer, whereas others ask you to select multiple correct answers. The following multiple-choice question requires you to select a single correct answer. Following the question is a brief summary of each potential answer and why it is either right or wrong.

Question 1

You have three domains connected to an empty root domain under one contiguous domain name: tutu.com. This organization is formed into a forest arrangement with a secondary domain called frog.com. How many Schema Masters exist for this arrangement?

○ a. 1

○ b. 2

○ c. 3

○ d. 4

The correct answer is a because only one Schema Master is necessary for a forest arrangement. The other answers (b, c, d) are misleading because they try to make you believe that Schema Masters might be in each domain, or perhaps that you should have one for each contiguous namespaced domain.

This sample question format corresponds closely to the Microsoft certification exam format—the only difference on the exam is that questions are not followed by answer keys. To select an answer, you would position the cursor over the radio button next to the answer. Then, click the mouse button to select the answer.

Let's examine a question where one or more answers are possible. This type of question provides checkboxes rather than radio buttons for marking all appropriate selections.

Question 2

How can you seize FSMO roles? [Check all correct answers]

❑ a. The ntdsutil.exe utility

❑ b. The Replication Monitor

❑ c. The secedit.exe utility

❑ d. Active Directory Domains and FSMOs

Answers a and b are correct. You can seize roles from a server that is still running through the Replication Monitor or, in the case of a server failure, you can seize roles with the ntdsutil.exe utility. The secedit utility is used to force group policies into play; therefore, answer c is incorrect. Active Directory Domains and Trusts are a combination of truth and fiction; therefore, answer d is incorrect.

For this particular question, two answers are required. Microsoft sometimes gives partial credit for partially correct answers. For Question 2, you have to check the boxes next to items a and b to obtain credit for a correct answer. Notice that picking the right answers also means knowing why the other answers are wrong!

Build-List-and-Reorder Question Format

Questions in the build-list-and-reorder format present two lists of items—one on the left and one on the right. To answer the question, you must move items from the list on the right to the list on the left. The final list must then be reordered into a specific order.

These questions can best be characterized as "From the following list of choices, pick the choices that answer the question. Arrange the list in a certain order." To give you practice with this type of question, some questions of this type are included in this study guide. Here's an example of how they appear in this book; for a sample of how they appear on the test, see Figure 1.2.

Question 3

> From the following list of famous people, pick those that have been elected President of the United States. Arrange the list in the order that they served.
>
> Thomas Jefferson
>
> Ben Franklin
>
> Abe Lincoln
>
> George Washington
>
> Andrew Jackson
>
> Paul Revere

The correct answer is:

George Washington

Thomas Jefferson

Andrew Jackson

Abe Lincoln

On an actual exam, the entire list of famous people would initially appear in the list on the right. You would move the four correct answers to the list on the left, and then reorder the list on the left. Notice that the answer to the question did not include all items from the initial list. However, this may not always be the case.

To move an item from the right list to the left list, first select the item by clicking on it, and then click on the Add button (left arrow). Once you move an item from one list to the other, you can move the item back by first selecting the item and then clicking on the appropriate button (either the Add button or the Remove button). Once items have been moved to the left list, you can reorder an item by selecting the item and clicking on the up or down button.

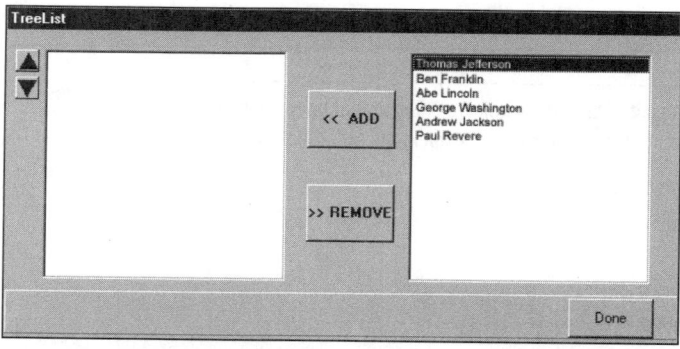

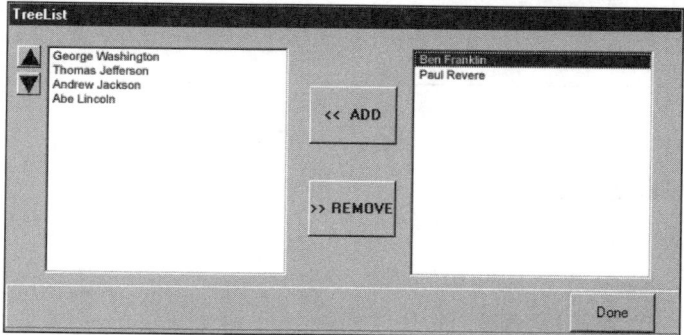

Figure 1.2 This is how build-list-and-reorder questions appear.

Create-a-Tree Question Format

Questions in the create-a-tree format also present two lists—one on the left side of the screen and one on the right side of the screen. The list on the right consists of individual items, and the list on the left consists of nodes in a tree. To answer the question, you must move items from the list on the right to the appropriate node in the tree.

These questions can best be characterized as simply a matching exercise. Items from the list on the right are placed under the appropriate category in the list on the left. Here's an example of how they appear in this book; for a sample of how they appear on the test, see Figure 1.3.

Question 4

The calendar year is divided into four seasons:

Winter

Spring

Summer

Fall

Identify the season when each of the following holidays occurs:

Christmas

Fourth of July

Labor Day

Flag Day

Memorial Day

Washington's Birthday

Thanksgiving

Easter

The correct answer is:

Winter

Christmas

Washington's Birthday

Spring

Flag Day

Memorial Day

Easter

Summer

Fourth of July

Labor Day

Fall

Thanksgiving

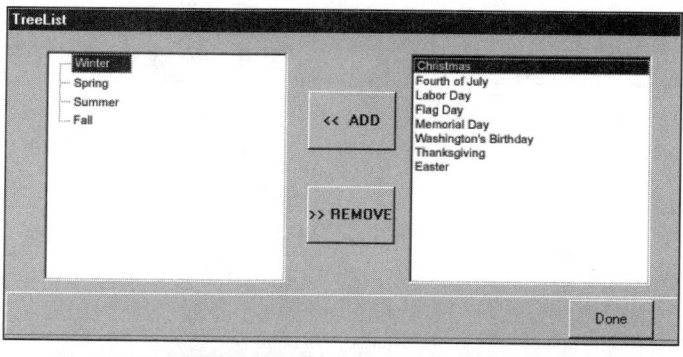

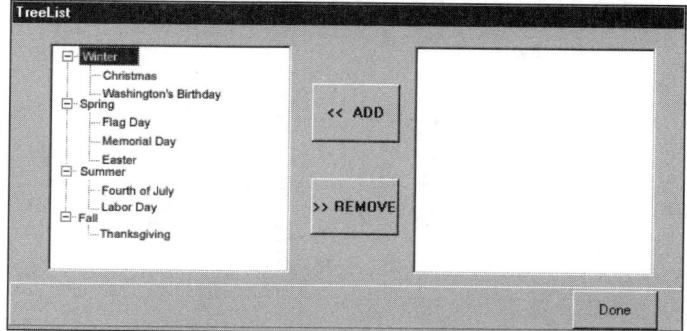

Figure 1.3   This is how create-a-tree questions appear.

In this case, all the items in the list were used. However, this may not always be the case.

To move an item from the right list to its appropriate location in the tree, you must first select the appropriate tree node by clicking on it. Then, you select the item to be moved and click on the Add button. If one or more items have been added to a tree node, the node will be displayed with a "+" icon to the left of the node name. You can click on this icon to expand the node and view the item(s) that have been added. If any item has been added to the wrong tree node, you can remove it by selecting it and clicking on the Remove button.

Drag-and-Connect Question Format

Questions in the drag-and-connect format present a group of objects and a list of "connections." To answer the question, you must move the appropriate connections between the objects.

This type of question is best described using graphics. Here's an example.

Question 5

The following objects represent the different states of water:

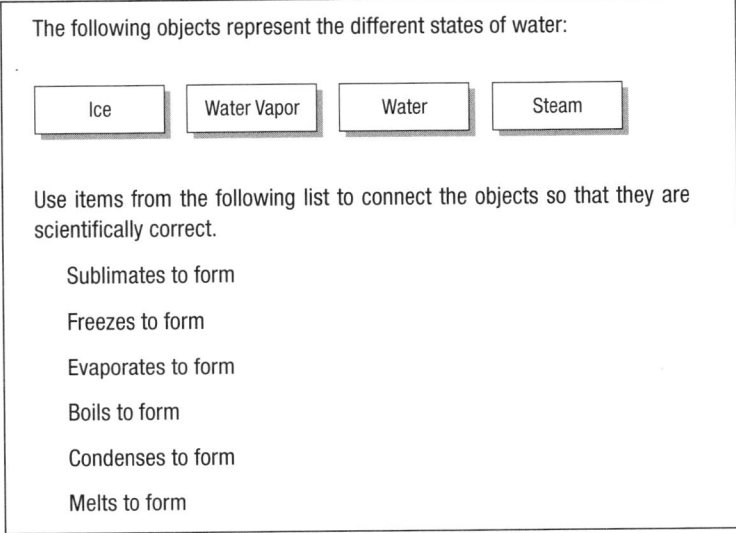

Use items from the following list to connect the objects so that they are scientifically correct.

Sublimates to form

Freezes to form

Evaporates to form

Boils to form

Condenses to form

Melts to form

The correct answer is:

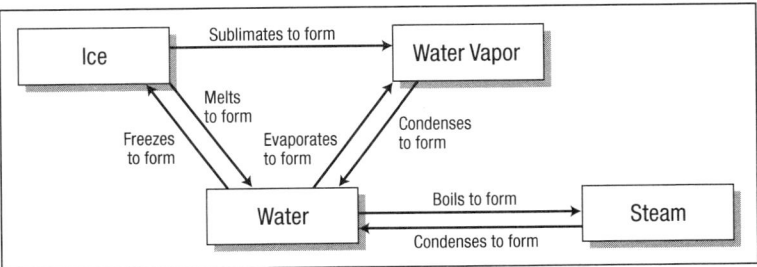

For this type of question, it's not necessary to use every object, and each connection can be used multiple times.

Select-and-Place Question Format

Questions in the select-and-place (drag-and-drop) format present a diagram with blank boxes, and a list of labels that need to be dragged to correctly fill in the blank boxes. To answer the question, you must move the labels to their appropriate positions on the diagram.

This type of question is best described using graphics. Here's an example.

Question 6

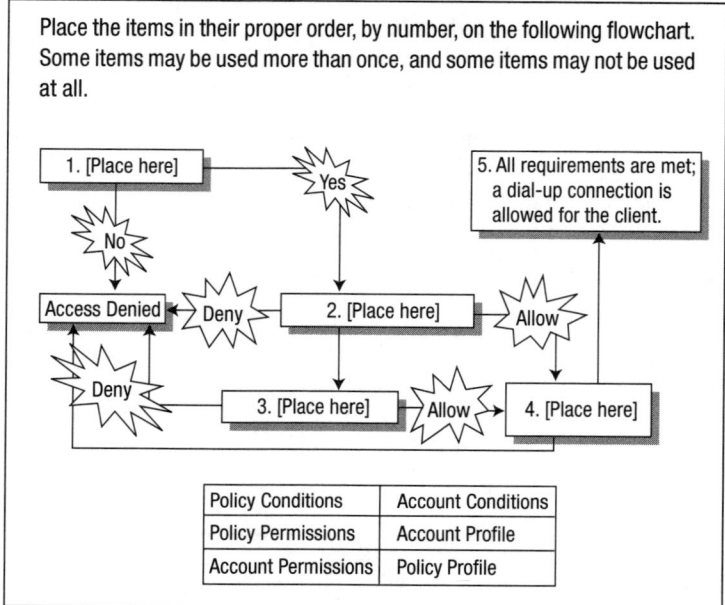

Place the items in their proper order, by number, on the following flowchart. Some items may be used more than once, and some items may not be used at all.

Policy Conditions	Account Conditions
Policy Permissions	Account Profile
Account Permissions	Policy Profile

The correct answer is:

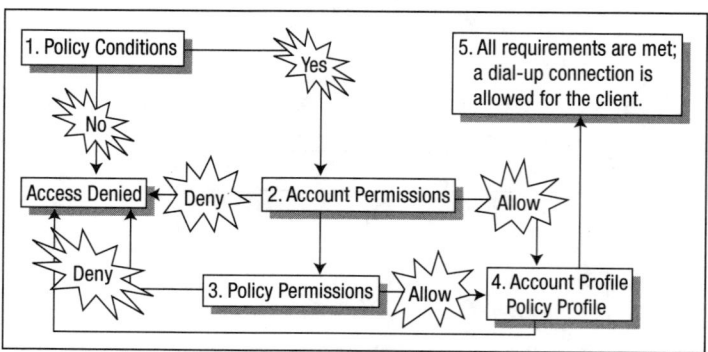

Microsoft's Testing Formats

Currently, Microsoft uses four different testing formats:

➤ Case study

➤ Fixed length

➤ Adaptive

➤ Short form

As we mentioned earlier, the case study approach is used with Microsoft's design exams, such as the one covered by this book. These exams consist of a set of case studies that you must analyze to enable you to answer questions related to the case studies. Such exams include one or more case studies (tabbed topic areas), each of which is followed by 4 to 10 questions. The question types for design exams and for Core Four Windows 2000 exams are multiple choice, build list and reorder, create a tree, drag and connect, and select and place. Depending on the test topic, some exams are totally case-based, whereas others are not.

Other Microsoft exams employ advanced testing capabilities that might not be immediately apparent. Although the questions that appear are primarily multiple choice, the logic that drives them is more complex than older Microsoft tests, which use a fixed sequence of questions, called a *fixed-length test*. Some questions employ a sophisticated user interface, which Microsoft calls a *simulation*, to test your knowledge of the software and systems under consideration in a more or less "live" environment that behaves just like the original. The Testing Innovations link at **www.microsoft.com/trainingandservices/default.asp?PageID=mcp** includes a downloadable practice simulation.

For some exams, Microsoft has turned to a well-known technique, called *adaptive testing*, to establish a test-taker's level of knowledge and product competence. Adaptive exams look the same as fixed-length exams, but they discover the level of difficulty at which an individual test-taker can correctly answer questions. Test-takers with differing levels of knowledge or ability therefore see different sets of questions; individuals with high levels of knowledge or ability are presented with a smaller set of more difficult questions, whereas individuals with lower levels of knowledge are presented with a larger set of easier questions. Two individuals may answer the same percentage of questions correctly, but the test-taker with a higher knowledge or ability level will score higher because his or her questions are worth more.

Also, the lower-level test-taker will probably answer more questions than his or her more-knowledgeable colleague. This explains why adaptive tests use ranges of values to define the number of questions and the amount of time it takes to complete the test.

Adaptive tests work by evaluating the test-taker's most recent answer. A correct answer leads to a more difficult question (and the test software's estimate of the test-taker's knowledge and ability level is raised). An incorrect answer leads to a less difficult question (and the test software's estimate of the test-taker's knowledge and ability level is lowered). This process continues until the test targets the test-taker's true ability level. The exam ends when the test-taker's level of accuracy meets a statistically acceptable value (in other words, when his or her performance demonstrates an acceptable level of knowledge and ability), or when the maximum number of items has been presented (in which case, the test-taker is almost certain to fail).

Microsoft also introduced a short-form test for its most popular tests. This test delivers 25 to 30 questions to its takers, giving them exactly 60 minutes to complete the exam. This type of exam is similar to a fixed-length test, in that it allows readers to jump ahead or return to earlier questions, and to cycle through the questions until the test is done. Microsoft does not use adaptive logic in this test, but claims that statistical analysis of the question pool is such that the 25 to 30 questions delivered during a short-form exam conclusively measure a test-taker's knowledge of the subject matter in much the same way as an adaptive test. You can think of the short-form test as a kind of "greatest hits exam" (that is, the most important questions are covered) version of an adaptive exam on the same topic.

Note: Some of the Microsoft exams can appear as a combination of adaptive and fixed-length questions.

Microsoft tests can come in any one of these forms. Whatever you encounter, you must take the test in whichever form it appears; you can't choose one form over another. If anything, it pays more to prepare thoroughly for an adaptive exam than for a fixed-length or a short-form exam: The penalties for answering incorrectly are built into the test itself on an adaptive exam, whereas the layout remains the same for a fixed-length or short-form test, no matter how many questions you answer incorrectly.

 The biggest difference between an adaptive test and a fixed-length or short-form test is that on a fixed-length or short-form test, you can revisit questions after you've read them over one or more times. On an adaptive test, you must answer the question when it's presented and will have no opportunities to revisit that question thereafter.

Strategies for Different Testing Formats

Before you choose a test-taking strategy, you must know if your test is case study based, fixed length, short form, or adaptive. When you begin your exam, you'll know right away if the test is based on case studies. The interface will consist of a tabbed Window that allows you to easily navigate through the sections of the case.

If you are taking a test that is not based on case studies, the software will tell you that the test is adaptive, if in fact the version you're taking is an adaptive test. If your introductory materials fail to mention this, you're probably taking a fixed-length test (50 to 70 questions). If the total number of questions involved is 25 to 30, you're taking a short-form test. Some tests announce themselves by indicating that they will start with a set of adaptive questions, followed by fixed-length questions.

 You'll be able to tell for sure if you are taking an adaptive, fixed-length, or short-form test by the first question. If it includes a checkbox that lets you mark the question for later review, you're taking a fixed-length or short-form test. If the total number of questions is 25 to 30, it's a short-form test; if more than 30, it's a fixed-length test. Adaptive test questions can be visited (and answered) only once, and they include no such checkbox.

The Case Study Exam Strategy

Most test-takers find that the case study type of test used for the design exams (70-219, 70-220, and 70-221) is the most difficult to master. When it comes to studying for a case study test, your best bet is to approach each case study as a standalone test. The biggest challenge you'll encounter is that you'll feel that you won't have enough time to get through all of the cases that are presented.

 Each case provides a lot of material that you'll need to read and study before you can effectively answer the questions that follow. The trick to taking a case study exam is to first scan the case study to get the highlights. Make sure you read the overview section of the case so that you understand the context of the problem at hand. Then, quickly move on and scan the questions.

As you are scanning the questions, make mental notes to yourself so that you'll remember which sections of the case study you should focus on. Some case studies may provide a fair amount of extra information that you don't really need to answer the questions. The goal with our scanning approach is to avoid having to study and analyze material that is not completely relevant.

When studying a case, carefully read the tabbed information. It is important to answer each and every question. You will be able to toggle back and forth from case to questions, and from question to question within a case testlet. However, once you leave the case and move on, you may not be able to return to it. You may want to take notes while reading useful information so you can refer to them when you tackle the test questions. It's hard to go wrong with this strategy when taking any kind of Microsoft certification test.

The Fixed-Length and Short-Form Exam Strategy

A well-known principle when taking fixed-length or short-form exams is to first read over the entire exam from start to finish while answering only those questions you feel absolutely sure of. On subsequent passes, you can dive into more complex questions more deeply, knowing how many such questions you have left.

Fortunately, the Microsoft exam software for fixed-length and short-form tests makes the multiple-visit approach easy to implement. At the top-left corner of each question is a checkbox that permits you to mark that question for a later visit.

Note: Marking questions makes review easier, but you can return to any question by clicking the Forward or Back button repeatedly.

As you read each question, if you answer only those you're sure of and mark for review those that you're not sure of, you can keep working through a decreasing list of questions as you answer the trickier ones in order.

 There's at least one potential benefit to reading the exam over completely before answering the trickier questions: Sometimes, information supplied in later questions sheds more light on earlier questions. At other times, information you read in later questions might jog your memory about network design facts, figures, or behavior that helps you answer earlier questions. Either way, you'll come out ahead if you defer those questions about which you're not absolutely sure.

Here are some question-handling strategies that apply to fixed-length and short-form tests. Use them if you have the chance:

➤ When returning to a question after your initial read-through, read every word again—otherwise, your mind can fall quickly into a rut. Sometimes, revisiting a question after turning your attention elsewhere lets you see something you missed, but the strong tendency is to see what you've seen before. Try to avoid that tendency at all costs.

➤ If you return to a question more than twice, try to articulate to yourself what you don't understand about the question, why answers don't appear to make sense, or what appears to be missing. If you chew on the subject awhile, your subconscious might provide the details you lack, or you might notice a "trick" that points to the right answer.

As you work your way through the exam, another counter that Microsoft provides will come in handy—the number of questions completed and questions outstanding. For fixed-length and short-form tests, it's wise to budget your time by making sure that you've completed one-quarter of the questions one-quarter of the way through the exam period, and three-quarters of the questions three-quarters of the way through.

If you're not finished when only five minutes remain, use that time to guess your way through any remaining questions. Remember, guessing is potentially more valuable than not answering, because blank answers are always wrong, but a guess may turn out to be right. If you don't have a clue about any of the remaining questions, pick answers at random, or choose all a's, b's, and so on. The important thing is to submit an exam for scoring that has an answer for every question.

 At the very end of your exam period, you're better off guessing than leaving questions unanswered.

The Adaptive Exam Strategy

If there's one principle that applies to taking an adaptive test, it could be summed up as "Get it right the first time." You cannot elect to skip a question and move on to the next one when taking an adaptive test, because the testing software uses your answer to the current question to select whatever question it plans to present next. Nor can you return to a question once you've moved on, because the software gives you only one chance to answer the question. You can, however, take notes, because sometimes information supplied in earlier questions will shed more light on later questions.

Also, when you answer a question correctly, you are presented with a more difficult question next, to help the software gauge your level of skill and ability. When you answer a question incorrectly, you are presented with a less difficult question, and the software lowers its current estimate of your skill and ability. This continues until the program settles into a reasonably accurate estimate of what you know and can do, and takes you on average through somewhere between 15 and 30 questions as you complete the test.

The good news is that if you know your stuff, you'll probably finish most adaptive tests in 30 minutes or so. The bad news is that you must really, really know your stuff to do your best on an adaptive test. That's because some questions are so convoluted, complex, or hard to follow that you're bound to miss one or two, at a minimum, even if you do know your stuff. So the more you know, the better you'll do on an adaptive test, even accounting for the occasionally weird or unfathomable questions that appear on these exams.

 Because you can't always tell in advance if a test is fixed length, short form, or adaptive, you will be best served by preparing for the exam as if it were adaptive. That way, you should be prepared to pass no matter what kind of test you take. But if you do take a fixed-length or short-form test, remember our tips from the preceding section. They should help you improve on what you could do on an adaptive test.

If you encounter a question on an adaptive test that you can't answer, you must guess an answer immediately. Because of how the software works, you may suffer for your guess on the next question if you guess right, because you'll get a more difficult question next!

Question-Handling Strategies

For those questions that take only a single answer, usually two or three of the answers will be obviously incorrect, and two of the answers will be plausible—of course, only one can be correct. Unless the answer leaps out at you (if it does, reread the question to look for a trick; sometimes those are the ones you're most likely to get wrong), begin the process of answering by eliminating those answers that are most obviously wrong.

Almost always, at least one answer out of the possible choices for a question can be eliminated immediately because it matches one of these conditions:

➤ The answer does not apply to the situation.

➤ The answer describes a nonexistent issue, an invalid option, or an imaginary state.

After you eliminate all answers that are obviously wrong, you can apply your retained knowledge to eliminate further answers. Look for items that sound correct but refer to actions, commands, or features that are not present or not available in the situation that the question describes.

If you're still faced with a blind guess among two or more potentially correct answers, reread the question. Try to picture how each of the possible remaining answers would alter the situation. Be especially sensitive to terminology; sometimes the choice of words ("remove" instead of "disable") can make the difference between a right answer and a wrong one.

Only when you've exhausted your ability to eliminate answers, but remain unclear about which of the remaining possibilities is correct, should you guess at an answer. An unanswered question offers you no points, but guessing gives you at least some chance of getting a question right; just don't be too hasty when making a blind guess.

Note: If you're taking a fixed-length or a short-form test, you can wait until the last round of reviewing marked questions (just as you're about to run out of time, or out of unanswered questions) before you start making guesses. You will have the same option within each case study testlet (but once you leave a testlet, you may not be allowed to return to it). If you're taking an adaptive test, you'll have to guess to move on to the next question if you can't figure out an answer some other way. Either way, guessing should be your technique of last resort!

Numerous questions assume that the default behavior of a particular utility is in effect. If you know the defaults and understand what they mean, this knowledge will help you cut through many Gordian knots.

Mastering the Inner Game

In the final analysis, knowledge breeds confidence, and confidence breeds success. If you study the materials in this book carefully and review all the practice questions at the end of each chapter, you should become aware of those areas where additional learning and study are required.

After you've worked your way through the book, take the practice exam in the back of the book. Taking this test will provide a reality check and help you identify areas to study further. Make sure you follow up and review materials related to the questions you miss on the practice exam before scheduling a real exam. Only when you've covered that ground and feel comfortable with the whole scope of the practice exam should you set an exam appointment. Only if you score 80 percent or better should you proceed to the real thing (otherwise, obtain some additional practice tests so you can keep trying until you hit this magic number).

If you take a practice exam and don't score at least 80 to 85 percent correct, you'll want to practice further. Microsoft provides links to practice exam providers and also offers self-assessment exams at **www.microsoft.com/trainingandservices/**. You should also check out **ExamCram.com** for downloadable practice questions.

Armed with the information in this book and with the determination to augment your knowledge, you should be able to pass the certification exam. However, you need to work at it, or you'll spend the exam fee more than once before you finally pass. If you prepare seriously, you should do well. We are confident that you can do it!

The next section covers other sources you can use to prepare for the Microsoft certification exams.

Additional Resources

A good source of information about Microsoft certification exams comes from Microsoft itself. Because its products and technologies—and the exams that go with them—change frequently, the best place to go for exam-related information is online.

If you haven't already visited the Microsoft Certified Professional site, do so right now. The MCP home page resides at **www.microsoft.com/trainingandservices** (see Figure 1.4).

Note: This page might not be there by the time you read this, or may be replaced by something new and different, because things change regularly on the Microsoft site. Should this happen, please read the sidebar titled "Coping with Change on the Web."

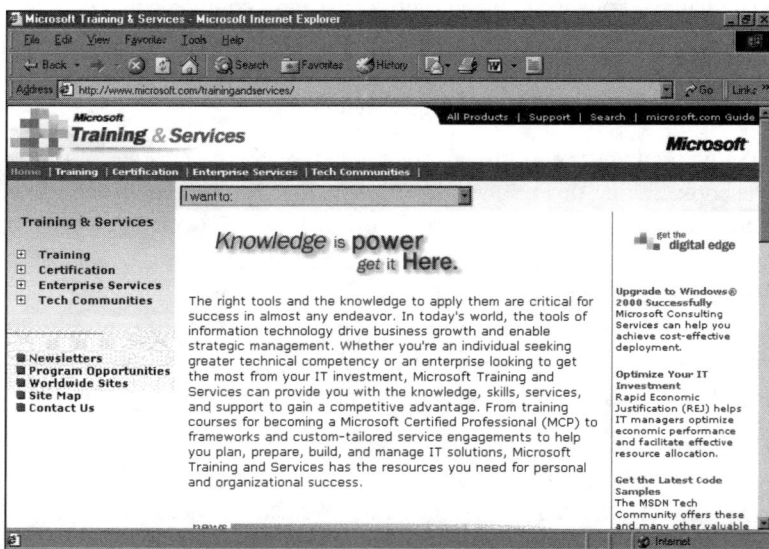

Figure 1.4   The Microsoft Certified Professional home page.

Coping with Change on the Web

Sooner or later, all the information we've shared with you about the Microsoft Certified Professional pages and the other Web-based resources mentioned throughout the rest of this book will go stale or be replaced by newer information. In some cases, the URLs you find here might lead you to their replacements; in other cases, the URLs will go nowhere, leaving you with the dreaded "404 File not found" error message. When that happens, don't give up.

There's always a way to find what you want on the Web if you're willing to invest some time and energy. Most large or complex Web sites—and Microsoft's qualifies on both counts—offer a search engine. On all of Microsoft's Web pages, a Search button appears along the top edge of the page. As long as you can get to Microsoft's site (it should stay at **www.microsoft.com** for a long time), use this tool to help you find what you need.

The more focused you can make a search request, the more likely the results will include information you can use. For example, you can search for the string

```
"training and certification"
```

to produce a lot of data about the subject in general, but if you're looking for the preparation guide for Exam 70-221, "Designing a Microsoft Windows 2000 Network Infrastructure," you'll be more likely to get there quickly if you use a search string similar to the following:

```
"Exam 70-221" AND "preparation guide"
```

Likewise, if you want to find the Training and Certification downloads, try a search string such as this:

```
"training and certification" AND "download page"
```

Finally, feel free to use general search tools—such as **www.search.com**, **www.altavista.com**, and **www.excite.com**—to look for related information. Although Microsoft offers great information about its certification exams online, there are plenty of third-party sources of information and assistance that need not follow Microsoft's party line. Therefore, if you can't find something where the book says it lives, intensify your search.

Overview

Terms you'll need to understand:

- ✓ Open Systems Interconnection (OSI) model
- ✓ Network Basic Input/Output System (NetBIOS)
- ✓ Windows Sockets (WinSock)
- ✓ Network operating system (NOS)
- ✓ Active Directory
- ✓ Domain Name Service (DNS)
- ✓ Dynamic Host Configuraion Protocol (DHCP)
- ✓ Windows Internet Naming Service (WINS)
- ✓ Virtual Private Network (VPN)
- ✓ Point-to-Point Tunneling Protocol (PPTP)
- ✓ Layer 2 Tunneling Protocol (L2TP)
- ✓ Remote Access Service (RAS)

Techniques you'll need to master:

- ✓ Using the OSI model to understand network architecture trends
- ✓ Distributing IP addresses to client computers
- ✓ Tracking the network infrastructure changes to Windows 2000
- ✓ Using encryption to allow private information to travel over the Internet securely

To design a network infrastructure, you must thoroughly understand the network architecture of the operating system. Of the many changes that Microsoft has implemented in Windows 2000, most of them involve the directory services and network architecture. This overview chapter outlines and explains the key differences between the network architectures of Windows 2000 and previous versions of Windows. The reasons for these changes—and what you need to know to understand and master them—will also be explained. Part of this explanation includes an overview of the many networking services that will be covered in later chapters of this book.

Changes in Windows 2000

Not everything has changed in Windows 2000. The operating system architecture and the handling of applications are still essentially the same as they were in Windows NT 4. But why did the directory and network architectures need such major changes? Actually, the answer is simple: Because the nature of networking has changed, vendors of operating systems have had to change—and sometimes entirely transform—their products to keep up. When PCs were first networked, the goal was to connect them only to neighboring computers. Now a desktop computer needs to be able to communicate with local computers as well as those around the world. In Windows 2000, Microsoft made some needed adjustments to support this new requirement.

The Way It Was

To fully understand the changes in the network architecture of Windows 2000, we need to examine decisions that Microsoft made years earlier regarding the networking architecture of the Windows operating system. To do this, we'll compare Microsoft's network architecture to the Open Systems Interconnection (OSI) model for networking (see Figure 2.1). The companies that make operating systems use the OSI model to divide their network architecture into components. When these components and parts are placed into the OSI model, we can compare how different operating systems access the network. Layer 5, the session layer, connects applications and services to the network, allowing two computers to link up and prepare to exchange data. The two main protocols used at this layer—NetBIOS and Sockets—each have a very different assumption of the type of network with which it is working.

Although IBM created NetBIOS, Microsoft gave it a big boost by designing its network structure and services around it. Microsoft wanted its network infrastructure to be simple and as easy to use as possible, and NetBIOS fit nicely into this plan. Computers using NetBIOS will, by default, send broadcast messages to find each other—a feature that allows computers to find and set up sessions with each other with no setup required by a network administrator.

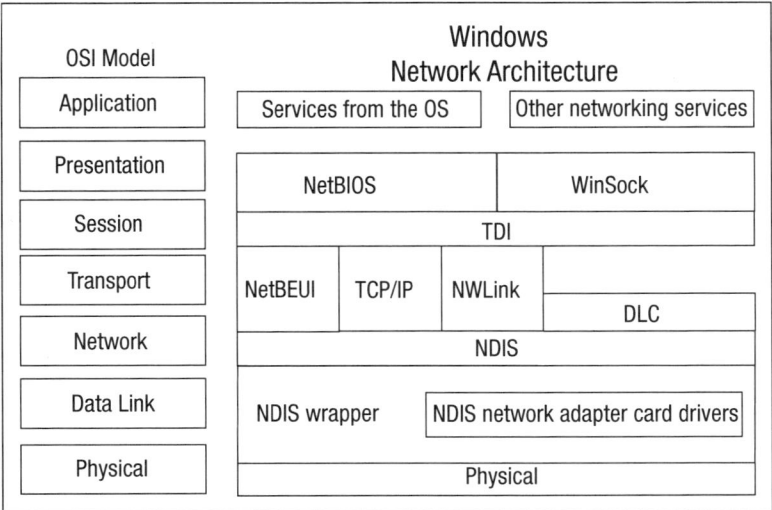

Figure 2.1   The networking structure and services of earlier versions of Windows were designed around NetBIOS at the session layer. NetBIOS works best in a local networking environment.

Previous versions of Windows use NetBIOS as the main interface to the network, and all of their services are dependent on it. If you want to access a file or send a print job, you also have to use NetBIOS, which is loaded during the install of any Windows operating system. NetBIOS is a required service that you cannot delete, except in Windows 2000. This design works best in a small, local networking environment. Broadcasts normally work over only local connections, and this limitation severely affects NetBIOS's performance over WAN connections. As networking became more important to a company's business, scalable network solutions that could grow to include all distant locations became more important. Microsoft had to adjust its strategy.

And Then Came TCP/IP

The creators of the Internet and TCP/IP went with Sockets as the session layer protocol and interface to the network. Instead of emphasizing ease of setup, the emphasis was on long-distance connections and guaranteed delivery. Because NetBIOS isn't the best tool to attain these goals, all TCP/IP and Internet services use Sockets as the interface to the network. (WinSock is short for Windows Sockets and is the implementation of Sockets in a GUI environment.) As TCP/IP and the Internet grew in popularity, Microsoft made adjustments that allowed WinSock to be used in its network architecture if a service called for it, but Microsoft-designed services stayed with NetBIOS as the only interface and session layer protocol.

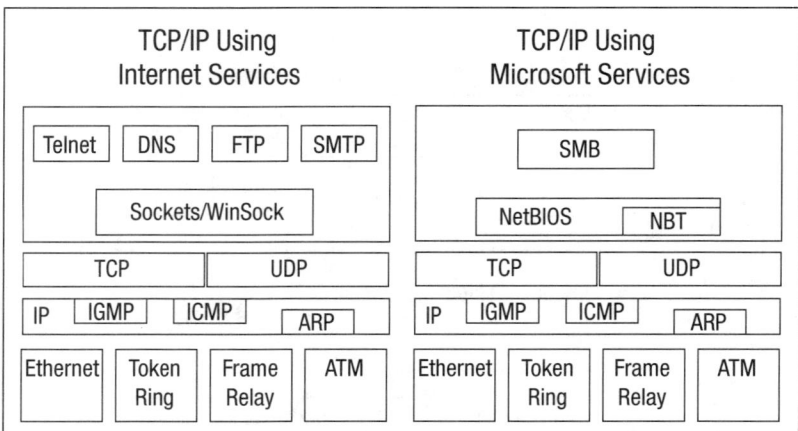

Figure 2.2 TCP/IP using Internet services is designed to use Sockets (or WinSock, in a GUI environment). TCP/IP using Microsoft services must instead use NetBIOS and the NBT protocol to access the network.

Windows' dependence on NetBIOS caused the operating system to have a dual personality in regards to its network architecture. As Figure 2.2 shows, all Internet services use Sockets or WinSock at the session layer as their interface to the network, which means that, when users wants to use an Internet service—by downloading a Web page or an FTP document or even sending email—their computers have to use WinSock. Yet, when using a Microsoft-designed service (such as connecting to a share on the local network or sending a print job through Microsoft printing services), NetBIOS is used as the session layer protocol and interface to the network.

Even TCP/IP has to make adjustments if it is loaded on a Microsoft operating system. TCP/IP normally uses Sockets at the session layer, but, because Microsoft services require NetBIOS, TCP/IP has to use an extra protocol at the session layer. This protocol is called *NetBIOS over TCP/IP* (*NetBT*), and it is needed only when TCP/IP is the transport protocol used to access Microsoft services.

The Great Name-Resolution Debate

Another problem caused by this dual network architecture concerned the naming of computers. Microsoft selected NetBIOS not only for its low administrative overhead, but also for its easy naming scheme for computers. Computer names must be unique among all other computers to which they may connect, and NetBIOS uses a different naming scheme than the Internet does. The NetBIOS namespace demonstrates that it was designed to work in a local network, because computer names can have a maximum of only 15 characters. NetBIOS also uses a flat namespace, which means that names have only one part; in essence, no middle or last names are allowed. These narrow parameters are the equivalent of declaring that all people can have only first names, that no name can have more than 15 characters, and that no name can be used more than once. This might be possible if you stay within your small hometown (a LAN), but these rules can be very limiting if you want to travel the world (a WAN).

The Internet uses the Domain Name Service (DNS) naming convention. Names are hierarchical, which means that you can have two computers named *Sales* so long as each belongs to a different Internet domain, thus making their names unique. Figures 2.3 and 2.4 illustrate the differences between these two naming conventions.

WINS, DNS, or Both?

Although computer names are handy for users, computers don't use them. Instead, they work with numbers in the form of computer addresses. A network

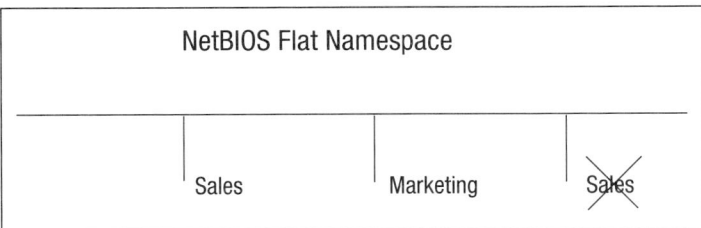

Figure 2.3 The flat namespace of NetBIOS requires that each computer have only one 15-character name to differentiate itself from all other computers. Two computers named *Sales* are not allowed in a NetBIOS environment.

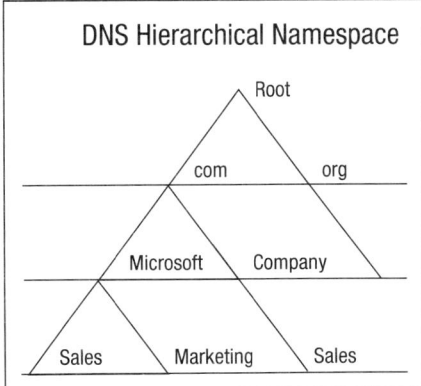

Figure 2.4 DNS uses a hierarchical naming scheme. Both the Microsoft.com and the Company.com domains can have a computer named *Sales*. Because of the hierarchy, Sales.Microsoft.com is a different computer name than Sales.Company. com.

using computer names needs to set up a name-resolution service to handle the translation of computer names to IP addresses. With name-resolution services on a network, people refer to computers by name, and the names are translated into an address. Microsoft's dual network architecture required NetBIOS computer names for its own services and DNS names for the Internet—which meant that, if you wanted to use name-resolution services on your network, you had to set up two different services: a NetBIOS naming service and an Internet name-resolution service. Windows Internet Naming Service (WINS) is Microsoft's NetBIOS naming service. It translates NetBIOS computer names to IP addresses. DNS is used to translate Internet DNS names to IP addresses. With both services on a network, one computer may have to ask WINS to resolve computer names to IP addresses when using any Microsoft service and then have to ask DNS to resolve a computer name to an IP address when using Internet services. The advantages and disadvantages of WINS and DNS should never be debated because they serve different purposes on a network. In Microsoft networking environments, prior to Windows 2000, both DNS and WINS were needed to connect to both networking types.

 You may be asked how many WINS servers are required on a network. If everything has been upgraded to Windows 2000 and no other NetBIOS resources have been mentioned, then no WINS servers are needed.

Going the Way of the Internet

Starting with Windows 2000, Microsoft's dual network architectures are integrated into one. Although the dependence on NetBIOS is gone, Windows 2000 still supports NetBIOS clients, just like previous versions of Windows and Windows NT. NetBIOS support is also needed for backward compatibility with previous versions of Windows operating systems. The change is that Windows 2000 no longer needs NetBIOS for its own services. Breaking the dependence on NetBIOS is just the first of the changes necessary to bring the system into conformance with Internet standards. Windows-provided networking services have also changed.

New Service Requirements

Windows 2000 requires some services and protocols that were optional in previous versions of Windows. The nature of these services—even ones that were often used in Windows NT—have changed: TCP/IP, Dynamic Host Configuration Protocol (DHCP), DNS, and WINS all have new importance and implementations, and these changes have a dramatic impact on how you should design the network infrastructure.

Network Service Changes Required by Active Directory

Network operating systems (NOSs) are different from operating systems in that they don't just provide local control over computer hardware and software. NOSs also allow for the network and its participating computers to be controlled. Directory services refer to the way NOSs manage the network and protect access to the resources on it. Just like Window NT, Windows 2000 is an NOS, but its directory services have undergone a complete transformation—so much so that they hardly resemble the directory services provided by Windows NT. In Windows 2000, the directory services and network infrastructure changes are interrelated to the point that it is not possible to talk about one without at least mentioning the other. Windows NT requires a user account to log on to the network. These user accounts and others are saved in a database called the *Security Access Manager* (*SAM*). This system works fine until an organization wants to centralize security and accounts across WAN connections. Microsoft had many ideas for how to centralize NT's directory services across an enterprise of geographically diverse locations, but all had large drawbacks. The SAM uses NetBIOS to access the network just like all other Microsoft services, which makes it difficult to operate outside of a LAN environment.

Active Directory, the name of the directory services provided by Windows 2000, stores all of the information needed to manage the network. It is much more than the database of accounts that Windows NT used: It changes the nature of your network so that it can support a much larger number of users and a greater number of resources, even if they are spread over many physical locations. If you are going to use Active Directory, be prepared for it to affect even the basic networking services.

TCP/IP

If you're going to take advantage of Active Directory, you should be aware of the many new requirements during the installation of Windows 2000. Installing the TCP/IP suite of protocols changes from an option to a requirement. Other transport protocols can be loaded for compatibility with other systems, but TCP/IP must be loaded during the installation and is the primary transport for a Windows 2000 network.

DNS

Active Directory also requires DNS in order to work correctly. Because NetBIOS names aren't required anymore, the Internet naming convention using the DNS name space is now the primary naming convention in Windows 2000, and DNS is the primary name-resolution service. Unless you disable NetBIOS, your computer will still create a NetBIOS name during installation. Because Microsoft wasn't the only company that used NetBIOS, most networks will still have some need for

NetBIOS names for backward compatibility, either with Microsoft or other systems. If your network is all Windows 2000 and even some Unix, you can turn off NetBIOS and ignore it completely. DNS is covered thoroughly in Chapter 5.

Unix and Macintosh use DNS as their name resolution service. They are not NetBIOS clients and do not use WINS.

WINS

In previous versions of Windows, WINS has an important role in the network infrastructure. NetBIOS computers, by default, broadcast to find another computer on a network. This method is quick and simple on a small network, but it causes too much traffic on the network as it grows in size. Implementing WINS on a network gives NetBIOS clients an alternative to broadcasting. With WINS, the clients make a direct request to the WINS server when they need to translate a computer name to an IP address. The WINS server directly answers the requesting computer, thereby avoiding the broadcast. Also, the direct communication between a WINS server and a client computer can work across routers and help extend the functionality of NetBIOS past a LAN environment. Implementing WINS allows Microsoft operating systems to reduce network traffic and communicate in a larger environment.

The importance of WINS has, of course, changed because NetBIOS no longer has the important role that it held in Windows NT. Nevertheless, the service is still on Microsoft's list of recommended services for the Windows 2000 environment, at least until the need for NetBIOS is completely eliminated from a network. For more information on WINS, refer to Chapter 6.

DHCP and DDNS

When using TCP/IP on a network, you must decide how the IP addresses should be distributed to the clients. The choice is between manually entering the IP address settings on each client and entering a range of addresses on a DHCP server and allowing the server to provide the addresses to the clients via the network. The choice seems simple until you consider the problem of who will update the DNS server to reflect which clients have received which specific IP address from the DHCP server. Until recently, the DNS database was a static database that contained computer names mapped to IP addresses. These database records had to be manually entered. Because DHCP assigned IP addresses in sequential order on a first-come/first-served basis, each computer could end up with a different IP address. Because the nature of DHCP is dynamic and DNS is static, the two systems did not work well together. The time saved entering IP addresses by using DHCP then caused the additional problem of how DNS would get updated.

Although Windows NT provided many suggestions to try to solve this problem, Windows 2000 actually provides a permanent solution by changing DHCP and DNS so that they communicate. Windows 2000 introduces and supports a dynamic version of DNS (DDNS). DHCP and DNS are covered thoroughly in Chapters 4 and 5.

Remote Access Connectivity

Routing and Remote Access Service (RRAS), first offered as a late add-on to Windows NT 4, is greatly expanded and offers many more options in Windows 2000. Large and small networks can select from different services that will allow them to connect with anything from dial-up lines to dedicated digital lines. Companies also have many choices that will allow them to use the Internet as a remote-connection alternative. The best part of all these services is that, regardless of your size and budget, you can find a way to connect all over the world.

Routing Improvements

As in Windows NT 4, Windows 2000 can still act as an IP, IPX, or AppleTalk router. Unlike previous versions of Windows, Windows 2000 supports Routing Information Protocol (RIP) and Open Shortest Path First (OSPF) as dynamic routing protocols (instead of just RIP), which means much larger networks can be supported. Chapter 9 details routing with Windows 2000.

Using the Internet for Connectivity

Dedicated global network connections have always been expensive to set up and maintain. Connections and lines usually have to be leased, at a premium charge, for a high-speed, dedicated, digital connection. The low-cost alternative is to allow remote access to your network through low-speed, analog telephone lines. Even with this alternative, a traveling user has to pay long-distance charges to connect to your network. A low-cost and possibly high-speed alternative is to use the Internet for remote connections. A remote user can make a local call to a nationwide or global ISP, and, whether they are two or 2,000 miles from your network, the connection will have no long-distance charges. The obvious drawback to this solution is that, because the Internet is intended for public use, it is not a secure medium for the transmission of private company information.

For a public network such as the Internet to maintain information security, the information must be altered for transmission. Encryption renders information useless and unreadable to those who may capture and look at the packets. Encryption can be used to change just username and passwords for secure authentication, or it can be used to protect all of the information including the data itself. Internet standards groups are working to make available more encryption solutions to allow the Internet to act as a Virtual Private Network (VPN). Until then, encryption allows users to protect their information so that the Internet acts as if it were a private network solution, but without the considerable cost of actual private dedicated lines.

Changes in VPN Implementation

Windows 2000 has simplified the implementation of VPNs. Now you can set up a VPN with a wizard that walks you through the process. Also, in Windows 2000, you can choose which encryption protocols to use, such as Point-to-Point Tunneling Protocol (PPTP), which is available in Windows NT, and Layer 2 Tunneling Protocol (L2TP). PPTP is the only choice if you must communicate over a VPN with previous versions of Windows, because it's all that clients other than Windows 2000 can use. The major difference between the two protocols is that PPTP uses a Microsoft-proprietary encryption protocol, whereas L2TP is an open Internet standard and uses IPSec (another open Internet standard protocol) as its encryption protocol. When creating a VPN with Windows 2000, L2TP is considered to have greater security, although PPTP has backward compatibility. Having both choices allows for flexibility. For more information on VPN setup, refer to Chapters 9 and 11.

Improved Authentication

Remote Authentication Dial-In User Service (RADIUS) allows your ISP to authenticate your users using their Windows 2000 user account. RADIUS is implemented as part of a larger service, Internet Authentication Service (IAS). Together, IAS and RADIUS allow you to control and manage remote connections coming into your network. In Chapter 12, you will learn to integrate RADIUS into a dial-up or VPN solution.

NAT and Proxy Server

Encrypting your data is not the only way to make an Internet connection secure. Connecting to the Internet is safer when your client computers remain anonymous. Both NAT (Network Address Translation) and Proxy Server allow this anonymity by making all Internet requests for them. A NAT or proxy server usually has at least two network interfaces: one connected to the local network and one connected to the Internet. Client computers make their Internet request to the local NAT or proxy server. The NAT or proxy server protects the internal network by allowing only its own computer and IP address to be exposed to the Internet. The difference between the services is in the size of network that they support. NAT not only provides Internet connections, but it is also a substitute for WINS, DNS, and DHCP. It is somewhat of an all-in-one solution for Internet connectivity on a small network. Proxy Server can be scaled up for much larger networks, but sticks just to protecting and helping Internet connections. NAT and Proxy Server are covered individually in Chapters 7 and 8.

Designing Network Services

This chapter provided an overview of the services included in the Windows 2000 network architecture. It explained what changes you will see in Windows 2000 networking and why those changes were necessary. The most changes occurred to the services that connect and integrate your network with the Internet. Some of these services have been a part of the Microsoft network infrastructure for some time, whereas others are providing new support and connectivity that were not included in previous Microsoft architectures.

Designing a network infrastructure requires a full understanding of each service and how it fits with the rest. Many of the services you will learn about provide the best and most secure solution when implemented together. Also, some services are best suited to networks of a certain size. In this book, each service will be explained in detail so that you gain an understanding of each individually. Then you will learn how to integrate the services so that you will be ready for the exam.

Practice Questions

Question 1

What purpose does the protocol NetBT serve on a network?

○ a. To allow TCP/IP to use NetBIOS

○ b. To allow TCP/IP to use Sockets

○ c. To allow TCP/IP to access the Internet

○ d. To tunnel through the Internet

Answer a is correct. NetBT stands for *NetBIOS over TCP/IP*. Usually, TCP/IP uses Sockets as its interface, but previous versions of Microsoft Windows forced TCP/IP to use NetBIOS to access the network instead. NetBT is a protocol at the session layer of the OSI model and is used when TCP/IP uses NetBIOS to access the network. Because sockets are normally used when accessing the Internet, NetBT is not needed in this case. Tunneling through the Internet requires encryption and does not need NetBT.

Question 2

Which service is not required on a Windows 2000 network when using Active Directory?

○ a. WINS

○ b. DNS

○ c. Sockets

○ d. TCP/IP

Answer a is correct. DNS, Sockets, and TCP/IP are all required when using Active Directory on a Windows 2000 network. WINS is not required because NetBIOS is no longer a requirement, and WINS translates NetBIOS computer names into IP addresses.

Question 3

Which protocols can be used to create a VPN on a Windows 2000 network? [Check all correct answers]

❑ a. L2TP

❑ b. DES

❑ c. PPTP

❑ d. SSL

Answers a and c are correct. Both PPTP and L2TP can be used to create encrypted packets over the Internet and create a Virtual Private Network on a Windows 2000 network. DES is an authentication encryption protocol and encrypts only the username and password. SSL is used to encrypt services over the Internet, but it does not create an end-to-end encrypted connecion for the entire session.

Question 4

Which services can now communicate with and update DNS? [Check all correct answers]

❑ a. VPN

❑ b. NAT

❑ c. RRAS

❑ d. DHCP

Answer d is correct. DHCP can now update the DNS database on behalf of DNS clients. The other services are used to make remote and Internet connections more secure and do not communicate with DNS.

Question 5

> The networking changes in Windows 2000 most affect which layer of the OSI model?
>
> ○ a. Application
>
> ○ b. Presentation
>
> ○ c. Session
>
> ○ d. Transport
>
> ○ e. Network
>
> ○ f. Data link
>
> ○ g. Physical

Answer c is correct. Microsoft ended its dependence on NetBIOS at the session layer, which affected all of its proprietary networking services. WinSock, a version of Sockets, is now the primary, session-layer protocol used in its network infrastructure.

Question 6

> Which VPN protocol uses a proprietary encryption protocol?
>
> ○ a. IPSec
>
> ○ b. PPTP
>
> ○ c. L2TP
>
> ○ d. DES

Answer b is correct. PPTP uses a proprietary encryption protocol while L2TP uses IPSec, a protocol that is an open Internet standard. DES also uses a standard encryption protocol.

Question 7

Why would NAT be used on a network? [Check all correct answers]

❑ a. To provide IP addressing services to client computers

❑ b. To provide remote access to client computers accessing the network

❑ c. To provide name-resolution services to client computers

❑ d. To protect client computers trying to access the Internet

Answers a, c, and d are correct. On a small network, NAT provides all the services needed to access the Internet. NAT can act as a substitute proxy, WINS, DNS, and DHCP server. NAT does not provide remote access services.

Question 8

Which routing protocols does Windows 2000 routing support? [Check all correct answers]

❑ a. EIGRP

❑ b. EGP

❑ c. OSPF

❑ d. RIP

Answers c and d are correct. Windows 2000 routing supports only RIP and OSPF, thus providing routing solutions for both small and large networks.

Question 9

The hierarchical name space used on the Internet is called what?

○ a. DNS

○ b. dotted decimal notation

○ c. WINS

○ d. NAT

Answer a is correct. DNS stands for *Domain Name System* or *Service* and uses a hierarchical naming system that more easily allows unique names. Dotted decimal notation refers to the way IP addresses are written. WINS is a NetBIOS naming service, and NAT is a networking service in Windows 2000.

Question 10

Which services use more than one network interface to protect an internal network from an external one? [Check all correct answers]

❏ a. NAT

❏ b. DNS

❏ c. DHCP

❏ d. WINS

❏ e. Proxy Server

Answers a and e are correct. NAT and Proxy Server make requests directly to the Internet for client computers. When used at the edge of a network, two interfaces allow each service to protect the internal network. They receive client requests from one interface before sending out a separate request to the Internet on the other network interface. DNS, DHCP, and WINS are for use on an internal network and do not provide services that protect clients from Internet connections.

Need to Know More?

 Smith, David. *Managing Windows 2000 Network Services.* Syngress Media, Rockland, MD, 2000. ISBN 1-92899-406-7. This book focuses on network services, including the implementation and overview of the services.

 RFC 2136 Dynamic Updates in the Domain Name Service (DNS UPDATE). **http://ietf.org/rfc/rfc2136.txt?number=2136.** This RFC explains the implementation of DDNS and how the DDNS database is dynamically updated.

 RFC 1631 The IP Network Address Translator (NAT) **http://ietf.org/ rfc/rfc1631.txt?number=1631.** Since NAT is a new service, there isn't much information on how it works. This RFC describes the open Intenet standard for the NAT service.

 Search the TechNet CD (or its online version through **www.microsoft. com/support**) and the Windows 2000 Server Resource Kit CD using the keywords "DDNS", "VPN", "WINS", "RRAS", and "Active Directory".

TCP/IP Networking Solutions

Terms you'll need to understand:

✓ The Open Systems Inteconnections (OSI) model

✓ Transmission Control Protocol/Internet Protocol (TCP/IP) addressing

✓ Private and public networks

✓ IP Filtering

✓ Internet Protocol Security (IPSec)

✓ Bandwidth management using Quality of Service (QoS)

Techniques you'll need to master:

✓ Subnetting

✓ Making a network secure with IPSec

✓ Guaranteeing delivery with QoS

In this chapter, you'll learn about the TCP/IP protocol suite and its many components. You'll become familiar with subnetting a TCP/IP network. We'll discuss the enhancements made to the Windows 2000 implementation of the TCP/IP protocol suite and look at examples of scenerios where these enhancements can be best utilized. We'll also cover security and bandwidth reservations that are available with the Windows 2000 implementation of the TCP/IP protocol suite.

TCP/IP History and Review

The development of the Transmission Control Protocol/Internet Protocol (TCP/IP) was funded by the United States Government's Advanced Research Projects Agency (ARPA) in the 1960s and 1970s. In the mid-1970s, ARPA connected its research sites at universities and research facilities into the world's first packet-switching network, *ARPANET*. Its success drew the interest of other research organizations that combined efforts to transform ARPANET technologies to a standard suite of protocols. In the late 1970s, the Transport Control Protocol (TCP) and the Internet Protocol (IP) were born. Since that time, advancements have been made to the TCP/IP suite, which is also known as the *TCP/IP stack*. These enhancements are developed through a process called the Request for Comments (RFCs) and proposals are approved by the Internet Architecture Board (IAB).

Internet administration is handled by a private organization, the Internet Network Information Center (INTERNIC), which is responsible for the maintenance and distribution of RFCs, as well as top-level administration that makes this network what it is today. The Internet Engineering Task Force (IETF), at **www.ietf.org**, posts the RFCs. With the explosion of the Internet in the mid-1990s, TCP/IP has quickly become the protocol of choice, as well as necessity.

The role of the TCP/IP protocol suite has changed with the release of Windows 2000. With the incorporation of Active Directory and Dynamic DNS (DDNS), TCP/IP is now required. The reason for this change relates to Microsoft's desire to fully integrate Internet functionality into the entire software line. Other protocols, such as IPX/SPX and NetBEUI, are still available for Win9x and Windows for Workgroups connectivity, but have taken a legacy support role. Windows 2000 uses TCP/IP to interoperate with other vendor-based networks (like Unix, Linux, IBM Mainframe, and Novell NetWare) for authentication file and print services, information replication, and connectivity.

The OSI Model

The TCP/IP stack is a suite of protocols that allows the creation of a logical peer network by binding a 32-bit binary address to the physical address (MAC address) of the network interface card (NIC). The Windows 2000 implementation of the TCP/IP stack corresponds to the seven layers of the Open Systems Inter-connections (OSI) model, with the Windows 2000 TCP/IP model spanning several layers of the OSI model (see Figure 3.1). The OSI model was designed to provide a standard for vendors to develop integration with protocol suites that provides easy interoperability with competing networks.

Each layer of the OSI model performs a specific task when receiving data from a host. Lower layers of the OSI model receive data, perform modifications, and pass the modified data to the layer directly above. When the application needs to send data, the process is reversed in the same manner.

Physical Layer

Networks function by sending and receiving binary data streams across a physical medium. Although the physical medium normally consist of wire (such as twisted pair, coaxial cable, and fiber optic), wireless media are not excluded. Wireless technologies can utilize radio waves or infrared and laser light to transmit data. The physical layer describes a set of rules that the transmission of data must abide by to transmit on these different types of physical media.

Data Link Layer

The data link layer assembles the bits into recognizable data called *frames*. Once the physical layer has received the bits, they are passed upward to the data link layer. This layer packages the bits into a frame, which contains the destination

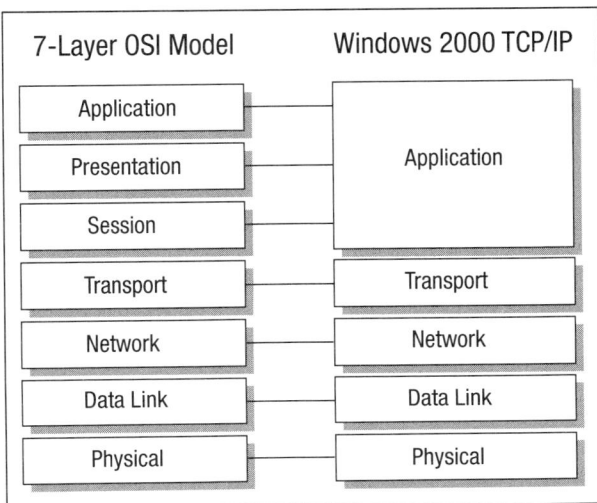

Figure 3.1   The OSI layer and the associated Microsoft implementation of the TCP/IP protocol.

address, the sender's address, the information type, the data itself, and an error-detection checksum. Even though the frame contains a destination address, protocols that reside in this layer are not routable. Although the checksum that is included in the frame will provide error-checking on the received data, it does not guarantee that all of the requested data has been received.

Network Layer

Network-layer protocols provide addressing, routing, and traffic management for transmissions among nodes. The network layer resolves the address forwarded by the data link layer. Traffic management is achieved by prioritization that is now a part of the Quality of Service (QoS). Certain types of data are given priority over others to assure the best possible performance of the message.

Transport Layer

The transport-layer protocols are responsible for making sure that the data was received without errors. It reassembles messages that were subdivided into the intended size by segment sequencing. During this process, an attached sequencing number is used to aid in the regeneration of the original message. This layer also informs the sender that the data has been received.

Session Layer

The session layer defines the management of individual network sessions. It establishes, maintains, and ends sessions between nodes. Basic network services, including login or file transfer, object locking, and data check points are used to create a session. Session-layer protocols are very reliable and can increase throughput.

Presentation Layer

The Presentation layer provides standards for encoding and encryption across a network. This layer acts as a negotiator for the rest of the protocol stack, and it is responsible for making the protocol stack network independent, meaning that communication between competing operating systems is accomplished by utilizing standard encoding.

Application Layer

The application layer is the top layer of the OSI model. However, it does not refer to desktop applications, but rather the connection between services. The Application Program Interface (API) uses this layer to access program utilities such as file and print services.

TCP/IP Addressing

Any device that is connected to a TCP/IP network uses a 32-bit logical address (such as 192.168.2.1) and is called a *host*. The TCP/IP address of the host must be unique in the network. This host address is combined with a subnet mask to separate the host address and the network address. In the above example, the host had a TCP/IP address of 192.168.2.1. If the subnet address were 255.255.0.0, the network address would be 192.168.0.0. Class-based TCP/IP has been reserved for the logical organization of networks, and classes have been defined by the conversion of the TCP/IP address to its 32-bit binary equivalent. Table 3.1 lists examples of class-based IP addresses and their binary 32-bit equivalents.

Subnet Masks

The subnet mask designates which portion of the 32-bit TCP/IP address relates to network identification and which portion relates to the actual host ID. When a host requires information from another host, the destination TCP/IP address is compared to the sender's address and subnet mask through a process called *anding*. If the network addresses (the portion of the IP address that designates the network number) match, the resolution request is sent to the local network. If the network number is not equal, the resolution request is sent to the default gateway.

Variable Length Subnet Mask

The variable length subnet mask (VLSM) is a method to further divide a subnet. An existing subnet mask is subdivided in a hierarchical fashion by using routers that support Routing Information Protocol (RIP) for IP2, or Open Shortest Path First (OSPF). VLSM allows administrators to eliminate unused IP addresses and to create additional network addresses as needed.

Supernetting

Supernetting is used to combine two or more small subnets, thus allowing companies to lease Class C addresses and combine the network addresses to meet the required number of host IDs. Supernetting requires routers that support RIP for IP2, OSPF, or BGP (Border Gateway Protocol). CIDR (Classless Interdomain Routing) supports supernetting and is described in more detail in RFC 1519.

Table 3.1 Class-based addresses and their binary equivalents.			
Address Range	**Binary Equivalent**	**Subnet Mask**	**Class**
1-127	00000001-01111111	255.0.0.0	A
128-191	10000000-10111111	255.255.0.0	B
192-223	11000000-11011111	255.255.255.0	C

Addressing Schemes for Private and Public Networks

In the past, the main reasons for using TCP/IP included the ability to scale the network to better optimize the infrastructure with routing and Internet connectivity. Now with Windows 2000, the reason is simple: It is required. However, effective routing and Internet connectivity should be the design goals. The two major Internet connectivity strategies are *public* and *private*.

Public Networks

If you have a large number of hosts that need to be addressed via the Internet, a public network may be needed. Most companies opt for private networks due to the monetary, administrative, and security overhead.

During your planning, you will need one registered TCP/IP address for each host and two for each router. Additional addresses for future growth will also need to be considered. In most instances, this will become a large and very expensive undertaking. Another important factor will be possible security holes. You can protect your public network from attack with packet-filtering routers and firewalls. Because TCP/IP uses many ports to transmit data between hosts, it will be important to disable any unused ports on the packet-filtering routers to prevent someone from getting to sensitive areas of your network.

Private Networks

If you have a small number of hosts that need to be addressed via the Internet, a private network will be to your advantage. A private network normally uses one Internet connection and registered TCP/IP address to provide its users with full functionality. An IP proxy, such as Microsoft Proxy Server 2.0, is a good way to provide access for your users while reducing the possibility of unauthorized access to your network. In most cases, an IP proxy is also used for caching purposes, which increases the speed with which Web pages are displayed. As with a public network, private networks use packet-filtering routing and firewalls to secure the network from unauthorized access. With a private network, the TCP/IP addresses of your internal network are not limited by the availability of leases through your ISP or InterNic, because they are not directly accessed from the Internet. For a listing of private TCP/IP addresses that are not routed by the Internet, refer to RFC 1918.

Designing Your TCP/IP Network

When you are designing a TCP/IP scheme for your network, you will need to consider the number of hosts needed, the physical groupings of the hosts due to location, logical groupings, redundancy of WAN links, and infrastructure capacity.

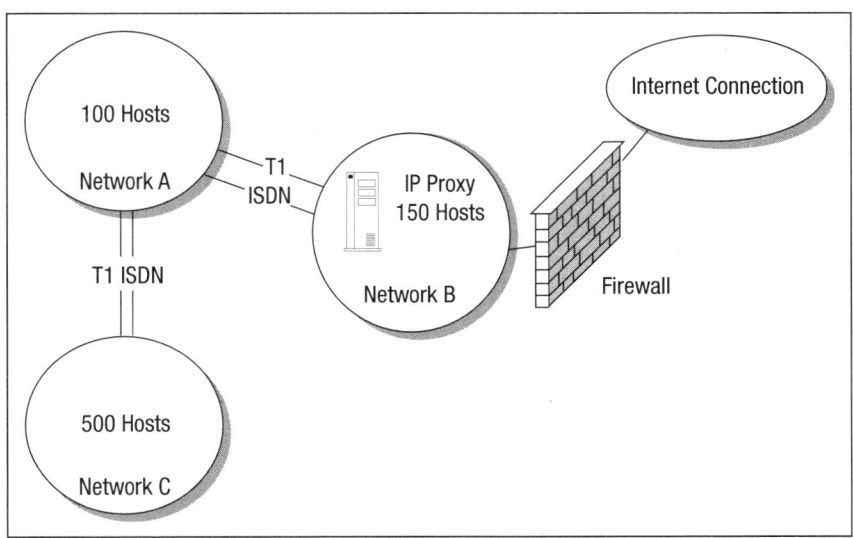

Figure 3.2   The example network scenario.

Let's say that you are a network engineer for a company with three geographical locations connected by T1 links, as illustrated in Figure 3.2.

For redundancy, you also have a dual-channel, ISDN, dial-on-demand connection for each location. The corporate office (Network A) has 100 hosts in a large high-rise office building that houses the marketing department and executive offices. The production plant (Network B) has 150 hosts, and the distribution warehouse (Network C) has 500 hosts. You decide to use a Class B addressing scheme of 192.168.0.0 for your network. This will provide you with one subnet and 65,534 hosts. What you really want is one subnet for Network A and one for Network B. To break up the traffic in Network C, you decide that your current routers and switches should have a maximum of 200 hosts. You do not expect any large increases of hosts in any of your locations, but, to ensure that you are well prepared, an additional subnet is planned at each location. With this in mind, you need to calculate a subnet mask that will allow you to divide your network into eight segments. The easiest way to arrive at a solution is the equation (x^y) equals or exceeds the required subnet amount.

You can use the scientific view on your Windows calculator and the exponent button to calculate this equation. The base, or X, will always equal 2, because a binary number has only two places—0 or 1. The Y is your variable. In this instance, your answer will be 4. This will allow 14 subnets. You will need four binary bits to achieve your appropriate subnet mask as shown in the following calculations:

(2^4)=16-2=14 available subnets

(2^{12})=4096-2=4094 available hosts

These calculations illustrate that, for this subnet mask, you will need a 32-bit binary number of 11111111.11111111.11110000.00000000 or a dotted decimal of 255.255.240.0. This will allow 12 bits for host addresses, or 4,094 hosts per subnet. The first subnet address will be 192.168.32.0 and will continue in increments of 16 until reaching 192.168.240.0.

In Figure 3.2, the Internet connection was installed at Network B, where a proxy server and firewall provides Internet access and security for authorized users. You will need two routers at each location for the WAN links to the other sites. If the WAN link between Network A and Network B goes down, the redundant ISDN connection will be utilized. This is determined by the cost-metric setting for each gateway set from within the advanced properties of the TCP/IP protocol. By setting the cost-metric value higher on the ISDN connection, it will be utilized only when the T1 connection is unavailable.

Due to the amount of users at Network C, three subnets will be implemented— which means that, besides the routers needed for the WAN links, two additional routers will be needed to connect the internal subnets. In most cases, this can be implemented by geographical location within a building. For example, you might separate by different floors of the building, wings, or departments.

IP Configuration

In a Windows 2000 environment, you can automate the TCP/IP configuration in several ways, all of which greatly reduce the overhead of a TCP/IP network. Although manual allocation is not the best way to configure your hosts in most cases, certain pieces do require manual allocation: routers, DHCP servers, WINS servers, and non-Microsoft hosts that do not support DHCP/BOOTP.

DHCP

Dynamic Host Configuration Protocol (DHCP) manager is a database of available TCP/IP addresses that are dynamically assigned to the DHCP client during its boot cycle. The available addresses for the client are created in a scope from within the DHCP manager. By right-clicking on the default scope and choosing properties, you can make changes to the scope, such as reservations or exclusions. The host retains this address for a certain period, which is known as the *lease*.

Note: Automatic Private IP Addressing assigns a unique IP address if no manual or BOOTP/DHCP configuration is available. Some brands of network cards do not support DHCP and require BOOTP for autoconfiguration. If this arises, you will need to configure DHCP to assign addresses to both client types.

Automatic Private IP Addressing

Windows 2000 and Windows 98 support IP autoconfiguration, or Automatic Private IP Addressing, a new feature that uses discovery packets to assign a unique IP address if no manual or BOOTP/DHCP configuration is available. The discovery will assign an unused host address within the Class B network address of 169.254.0.0. You can assign a unique IP address to your NIC using the "LINKLOCAL Network" IP address space. Like 127.0.0.0 and 192.168.0.0, this is a private address and will require a private network with an IP proxy to access the Internet. This new feature has come under criticism for extending the boot time by several seconds. Despite this negative response by some people in the industry, it allows a client to access some resources if a DHCP server becomes disabled in a strictly TCP/IP environment.

TCP Performance Enhancements

The Windows 2000 implimentation of the TCP/IP protocol stack has been ehanced to support several new features. It is important to remember that this is Microsoft's implementation of the stack, and some of these enhancements are not new to the industry as a whole. New enhancements to the TCP/IP stack are made by the IETF, and it is up to the software vendors to incorporate them into their operating systems. Windows 2000 has several enhancements to its TCP/IP stack compared to Windows NT 4.

Increased TCP Window Size

Windows 2000 has a little performance tuning to support network paths, such as fiber-optic or high-capacity packet satellite channels, known as the "long, fat pipe." Networks containing these types of connections are referred as *LFN* or *elephan(t)*. This is explained in detail in RFC 1323. With these large-capacity connections, performance is degraded by the TCP window size. With this larger window size, the host can send more packets without receiving an acknowledgment, which allows administrators to optimize the servers on both sides of this type of WAN connection.

TCP Selective Acknowledgment (SACK)

TCP Selective Acknowledgment (SACK) complements the larger window size by allowing TCP to request a retransmit of only those packets that have not been received within a window. Currently, when a window fills and a bad packet is detected, a retransmit message is sent for all packets to the left of the damaged packet in the TCP window, causing the retransmission of even those packets that have been successfully received. With the implementation of SACK, all packets will be read and only the damaged packets retransmitted. If you have an increased window size, the benefits from this are quite evident. For additional information on SACK, refer to RFC 2018.

Internet Control Message Protocol (ICMP)

Internet Control Message Protocol (ICMP) is another TCP performance enhancement supported by the Windows 2000 TCP/IP stack that will be well received by administrators in a WAN environment. Before a host can send data outside of its subnet, a gateway must be established. In the past, Windows NT 4 used the default gateway address listed in the TCP/IP Properties page for a designated adapter. With ICMP, the gateway can be discovered without an entry using router discovery messages called *router advertisements* and *router solicitations*. Routers will periodically advertise from each interface and announce its IP address. A host can discover the address of the router on its local subnet by listening for this advertisement. When an attached host boots up, it can ask for an advertisement. If it does not receive one, it will retransmit the solicitation. Any router that becomes available will then be designated as the gateway. This enhancement has the opportunity to become one of the most time-saving features in networking. For additional information on ICMP, refer to RFC 1256.

Disabling NetBIOS over TCP/IP (NetBT)

Windows 2000 allows you to disable NetBIOS over TCP/IP (NetBT), although for only those hosts in specialized roles that are accessed by DNS for name resolution and registration. Examples of these hosts are proxy servers and firewalls. See Chapter 6 for an in-depth discussion of this procedure.

Security

With the growing concern over security, it makes sense that Microsoft included several new utilities to help administrators secure their network. Since the beginning of 2000, we have seen an increased interest in Internet security by corporations and the U.S. Government in direct response to denial-of-service attacks and email worm viruses. The U.S. Government has gone so far as to appoint a council to search out new talent for protecting its resources from hackers.

Filtering IP Traffic

In the past, routers and firewalls have been used to keep unwanted and malicious traffic from entering your network. With the Windows 2000 implementation of the TCP/IP protocol, traffic filtering is now possible at the Application layer of the OSI model. The filtering is actually done by specialized portions of the operating system and not at the Network layer of the TCP/IP stack. Figure 3.3 shows the Filtering Properties window.

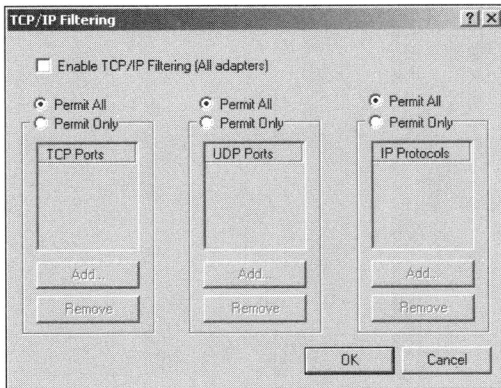

Figure 3.3 The TCP/IP Filtering Properties window.

You can use these filters on a host-by-host basis to block the delivery of any IP packets that do not conform to preset criteria. Exceptions are filtering by the following packet types: TCP, UDP, ICMP, or IGMP. For example, you can set a filter to block inbound FTP packets to port 25 that are not sent from a certain host. However, if the allowed host has forwarded a packet from a host that you would not like to enter your system, the filter cannot be applied. This is because the incoming packet has the source address of the allowed host.

Securing TCP/IP Traffic with IPSec

The Windows 2000 implementation of the TCP/IP stack has been enhanced to include support for the new protocol, IPSec. Windows 9x and other clients will require third-party software to connect with Windows 2000 hosts that require mandatory secure communications. IPSec provides data integrity and data encryption in your Windows 2000 network. IPSec is CPU-intensive, and different security levels of IPSec can degrade system performance. Use your hardware capacity and security needs to decide on an encryption level. Too much encryption and too little hardware can result in long days of monitoring your network resources. Figure 3.4 shows the TCP/IP Security window.

Predefined IPSec Policies

IPSec uses a protocol called ISAKMP/Oakley, which allows the receiver to verify the sender's identity using X.509 digital certificates and then sets up a trusted session after authentication. For two hosts to communicate using IPSec, communication policies must be established to tell the IPSec hosts how they will interface and establish a trust. The process that calculates a security association (SA) between the hosts is called the *Internet Key Exchange*, or *IKE*. The SA controls the encryption between the hosts on a session basis and is recalculated based on the quantity of the data and the session time. The following are predefined policies:

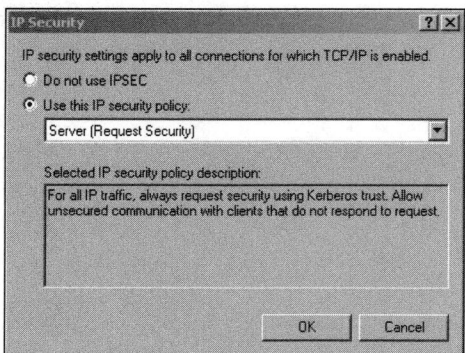

Figure 3.4   The TCP/IP Security window.

➤ *Client policy*—For hosts that use IPSec only when they are requested to by another host. With this setting, the host computer can respond to requests to communicate with IPSec-secured communications.

➤ *Server policy*—For hosts that can accept both secured and unsecured traffic. When a host establishes a session with the sender, a request for secured communications is sent. If the sender responds with an SA, the communications between the hosts will be secured. If the host fails to respond, the communications will continue, but they will not be secured using IPSec.

➤ *Secure Server policy*—For hosts that require secured communication. Any requests to send using unsecured communications are rejected.

IPSec Data Integrity and Data Encryption in Windows 2000 Networks

Data integrity is the ability to allow only certain hosts to communicate. It is attained by using an authentication header (AH) that is inserted after an IP header and before the other information being authenticated.

Data encryption uses encapsulation security and payload (ESP) to provide both data-integrity authentication and data encryption. This means that an AH is not used, or rather, that the ESP provides the same service as the AH, while also providing encryption services to the packet. ESP provides confidentiality and integrity by encrypting data to be protected and placing the encrypted data in the data portion of the IP.

IPSec Authentication Protocols

IPSec uses two protocols to authenticate hosts: Message Digest 5 (MD5) and the Secure Hash Algorithm (SHA).

➤ *MD5*—An authentication algorithm that has been proposed as the default authentication option in IPv6. When enabled, the MD5 protocol operates over the entire data packet, including the header, to provide 128-bit authentication with random keys. For more information, refer to RFC 1321.

➤ *SHA*—A 160-bit authenticator to provide data-origin authentication. The key must ensure that unique keys are allocated and distributed only to the hosts participating in the secured communication. For more information, refer to RFC 2404.

IPSec Encryption Algorithms

IPSec uses the Data Encryption Standard (DES), which describes data encryption from 40-bit DES (needed for secure communication with hosts in France) to 128-bit Triple DES (3DES). Communications scrambled in 56-bit DES (meaning the key to descramble the message has 56 elements) have 70 quadrillion possible keys. Despite this huge number of possible keys, it does not take long to break. In fact, during a contest in February, 1998, a team of programmers broke a 56-bit DES key in 39 days, about a third of the time it took a similar team the year before. Although Triple DES is much more secure, it is a processor-intensive protocol, and, the more bits in the encryption algorithm, the more processor time is used.

Note: The U.S. Government still restricts the export of 128-bit key encryption on the grounds that it could be used by criminals to mask their activities.

Internet Key Exchange Protocol (IKE)

The Internet Key Exchange protocol, formerly known as ISAKMP/Oakley, is a tool for negotiating the terms of the communication before a secure session can begin. These communication security parameters include which encryption algorithms are to be used, the duration of the encryption, and the encryption key. The negotiation process is automatic and secure to allow scaling to the Internet.

When a session between two hosts is established, only those hosts know the security key used. The Internet Security Association and Key Management Protocol (ISAKMP) and the Oakley key-generation protocol create an SA between the hosts. Then Oakley authenticates, and the session can begin. Table 3.2 lists the securtiy peer authentication methods used by IKE to create a session between two IPSec enabled hosts.

Table 3.2	Security peer authentication methods.
Security Association	**Usage**
Kerbose version 5	Default authentication for trusted domain members
Public key certificates	The Internet and remote connections
Preshared keys	Windows 9X and other clients using third-party software

Routing IPSec

IPSec protocols use specific ports and protocol numbers that can be seamlessly routed if they are configured. You will need to enable your routers, firewalls, gateways, and proxy servers to accept the following protocols on these ports:

➤ IPSec Header Traffic Protocol ID 51 (0×33)

➤ IPSec ESP Protocol ID 50 (0×32)

Quality of Service (QoS)

QoS provides a routing mechanism that can guarantee delivery of data for a certain application. Paths for traffic flows are determined based on some knowledge of resource availability in the network, as well as the QoS requirements (needed amount of bandwidth) for the flows. QoS-based routing allows the determination of a path that has a good chance of accommodating the requested QoS. The Windows 2000 implementation of QoS provides bandwidth reservations and priority levels for the data flows based on the user, application, or QoS policies.

Routing deployed in today's Internet is focused on connectivity. The current Internet routing protocols, OSPF and RIP, use shortest-path routing. These opportunistic protocols optimize routing paths based on a hop count. In other words, they choose the best path from point A to point B based on how many routers they will use to get to the destination. They do not allow alternate paths based on available bandwidth. Opportunistic routing will shift from one path to another if a shorter path (one with fewer hops) becomes available. This shifting of paths can produce delays and "jitters" in data-intense applications such as realtime audio and video.

 It is important to remember that for QoS to be fully utilized, all routers between the communication hosts must be QoS aware.

QoS Components

QoS employs several components to set up a data-delivery system for network traffic, which utilizes the available subnet bandwidth. These components each perform a specific role in the creation of the data stream.

➤ *Generic QoS (GQoS)*—An abstract interface that allows application programmers to specify or request bandwidth based on their application or media.

➤ *RSVP SP (Rsvp.dll) (Resource Reservation Protocol Service Provider)*—Accesses the RSVP.exe.

➤ *RSVP (Resource Reservation Protocol)*—A signaling component of QoS. It is not dependent on media, which allows the protocol to facilitate end-to-end communications.

➤ *Traffic Control (Traffic.dll)*—Regulates data by using QoS-defined parameters. Traffic control is called on by the GQoS API.

➤ *Generic Packet Classifier (Msgpc.sys)*—Determines the class of the packet.

➤ *QoS Packet Scheduler (Psched.sys)*—Enforces the parameters of the traffic flow.

➤ *QoS Admission Control Service (QoS ACS)*—Is the central point that allows or denies requests for bandwidth. The QoS ACS service is not required on each network segment; however, high-traffic areas are better served by having a local QoS ACS.

➤ *Local Policy Module (Msidlpm.dll)*—Is responsible for providing a policy-enforcement point and policy-decision point. The QoS ACS uses this module to examine the user's name from the RSVP message and to compare it to the admission control policy located in the Windows 2000 Active Directory.

Putting It All Together

A QoS-enabled client sends a request for service. The QoS-aware application calls the RSVP SP. The RSVP SP calls the RSVP service to request the necessary bandwidth. Then a RSVP message is sent to the QoS ACS server requesting the necessary reservation needed by the application. The QoS ACS verifies the available bandwidth resources and then calls the LPM and compares the user policy with the permissions set in the Windows 2000 Active Directory.

After the permissions have been verified with Active Directory, the QoS ACS grants the request and allocates the available bandwidth. The QoS ACS then passes the message to the receiving host. During this process, QoS-enabled routers are informed of the bandwidth reservation. The routers cache this information and wait for the RSVP message to be returned from the receiving host. The receiving host receives the message and retransmits back to the sender a message that it is ready to receive the data.

When the receiver's message passes through the routers, it is compared to the request sent by the sender and the use of the requested bandwidth is now granted. Throughout this process, the message traffic is sent by best effort until the sender receives its returned request. Now the sender's Traffic Control module classifies, marks, and schedules the packets using the Generic Packet Classifier and QoS Packet Scheduler. For more information, see RFC 2386. It is important to remember that QoS sessions do not begin until the sending host has received its request back from the receiving host. Until the requesting host receives the message, the message is sent by best effort.

Practice Questions

Case Study

VirtuCon is a manufacturer of hi-tech equipment, based in Carson City, Nevada. It has a manufacturing plant in Indianapolis, IN, and a distribution facility in Louisville, KY. The corporate offices in Carson City have 150 hosts. The manufacturing plant in Indianapolis has 300 hosts, and the distribution center has 250 hosts. The network infrastructure was designed in 1995 and needs upgrades. The management staff has assigned you to design the proposed upgrades, utilizing as much of the existing equipment as possible.

Current WAN Structure

VirtuCon is currently using Windows NT 4 servers at all locations. The client workstations are currently running Windows 95 and Windows NT 4 workstation.

The hubs and switches at all locations are autosensing 10/100. The network cards in client and server machines have been replaced in the past year and are also 10/100. The current hub switches and routers will effectively support 200 hosts per subnet.

VirtuCon has doubled in size since its network's installation in 1995. The projected growth over the next 5 years is 20 percent

Proposed WAN Upgrades

VirtuCon's management staff would like to upgrade its network to provide fail over redundancy of its WAN links and to provide better security for sensitive data transferred between locations. It also wants your design to take into consideration a realtime job management database that is located at the Carson City office and is accessed through WAN Links.

Most of the hosts are 166MHz Pentium computers with 16MB of RAM and a 1.6GB hard drive. Management has approved the upgrade of all client machines to PIII class machines with 128MB of RAM and 12GB hard drives. All clients and servers will be upgraded to Windows 2000.

The decisions you make for the upgrades should incorporate the current network state and the expected five-year growth plan with the most economical solutions.

Current WAN Connectivity

The locations have 168Kbps fractional T-1 connections from Carson City to Indianapolis and from Indianapolis to Louisville. The routers have been replaced in the past year and are QoS aware.

Proposed WAN Connetivity

The Carson City site should have a failover 128Kbps ISDN connection with the Indianapolis office. The Indianapolis office should have a failover ISDN connection with the Louisville office. These connections should be dial-on-demand, since the provider bills VirtuCon a monthly carrying fee for the service. If the connection is used, VirtuCon will also be charged for the connection time. Your solution should take this into account and provide automatic connection and disconnection, should the failover link be used.

All clients and servers will be upgraded to Windows 2000.

Directory Design Commentary

VirtuCon's current password policies will be duplicated on the Windows 2000 servers.

Current Internet Positioning

VirtuCon currently accesses the Internet from all locations using a single leased IP address at the Indianapolis location. This location has an IP Proxy and firewall to protect the network and provide access.

A Web-hosting firm hosts the company Web site. The firewall server at the Indianapolis site provides all remote employees with a Web-based email client for remote access to email.

Future Internet Plans

Eventually, VirtuCon would like to host its own site and provide remote users with Web-based access to the job database.

Company Goal with the Proposed Upgrade

VirtuCon has put you in charge of designing and managing the implementation. Your goal is to incorporate all of the previously mentioned requirements and implement the most cost-effective design.

You have a small support staff, so automatic responses to variations in the network infrastructure will provide the best support to the clients.

Question 1

Considering the case study, which subnet mask will provide the proper amount of logical network segments and give the maximum amount of available hosts using a Class C network address?

- ○ a.   255.255.255.0
- ○ b.   255.255.248.0
- ○ c.   255.255.0.0
- ○ d.   None of the above

Answer b is correct. Considering the hosts at each location, the projected growth, and the existing hardware's ability to effectively support 200 hosts, 5 subnets will be needed. This will require a subnet mast of 255.255.248.0. Both answers a and c do not allow you to break down the address range into logical networks.

Question 2

Considering the case study, which of the following options will provide failover redundancy for the WAN connections listed? [Choose all that apply]

- ❑ a.   Third-party software will be needed to manage the links
- ❑ b.   The ISDN router/modem will need to be configured to dial out if it sensed that the fractional T-1 became disabled
- ❑ c.   You need to add the IP address of the router for the fractional T-1 and the ISDN connection as default gateways
- ❑ d.   You need to set the cost metric of the fractional T-1 to 1 and the cost metric of the ISDN router/modem to 40

Answers c and d are correct. The cost metric setting provides additional links that can be utilized if the primary link is not available. When the link is restored, this setting would direct clients to reconnect to the T-1 connection and drop the ISDN connection. Third-party software will provide the connection when needed; however, it will also require an additional purchase.

Question 3

Considering the case study, what could you implement to secure communications between the hosts at all locations?

○ a. IPSec

○ b. QoS

○ c. DHCP

○ d. SNMP

Answer a is correct. With the Windows 2000 implementation of the TCP/IP stack, support for the IPSec protocols has been added. This protocol provides encryption between hosts on a network. QoS provides a routing mechanism that can guarantee delivery of data for a certain application. DHCP is used to automatically assign IP addresses to DHCP and BOOTP clients. SNMP is a component of the TCP/IP suite that allows the remote monitoring and management of network resources.

Question 4

Considering the case study, which predefined security level should you implement on your Windows 2000 hosts?

○ a. Client

○ b. Sever

○ c. Secured Server

○ d. 128-bit triple DES

Answer c is correct. To allow hosts to communicate only with other hosts using IPSec secured connections, Secured Server is the proper predefined security level. All communications from hosts using unsecured communications will be rejected. This will provide the most secure connections between hosts. The Server policy is for hosts that can accept both secured and unsecured traffic, the Client policy is for hosts that use IPSec only when they are requested to by another host. 128-bit triple DES is an encryption standard.

Question 5

Considering the case study, what configurations will need to be made to the routers to allow IPSec to be seamlessly routed through the network? [Choose all that apply]

❏ a. Enable Port 21 to accept SMB packets

❏ b. Enable IPSec ESP Protocol ID 50 (0x32)

❏ c. IPSec Header Traffic Protocol ID 51 (0x33)

❏ d. Do nothing—if routers support RIP for IP, then no configuration is necessary

Answers b and c are correct. To allow IPSec to be seamlessly routed through the network, you must enable IPSec ESP Protocol ID 50 (0×32) and IPSec Header Traffic Protocol ID 51 (0×33). Port 21 is used mainly for FTP communications.

Question 6

Considering the case study, what best describes the type of addressing scheme for the network?

○ a. Public

○ b. Secured

○ c. QoS enabled

○ d. Private

Answer d is correct. Since all of the hosts access the Internet through an IP Proxy at one location, the network would be considered private. Private networks employ IP proxies to provide Internet access by using a single IP address. A public network would require that each host would have a registered IP address. All networks need to be secured from tampering. QoS enabled does not describe the type of addressing scheme for the network.

Question 7

Considering the case study, place the QoS ACS server in the most logical place in the following diagram.

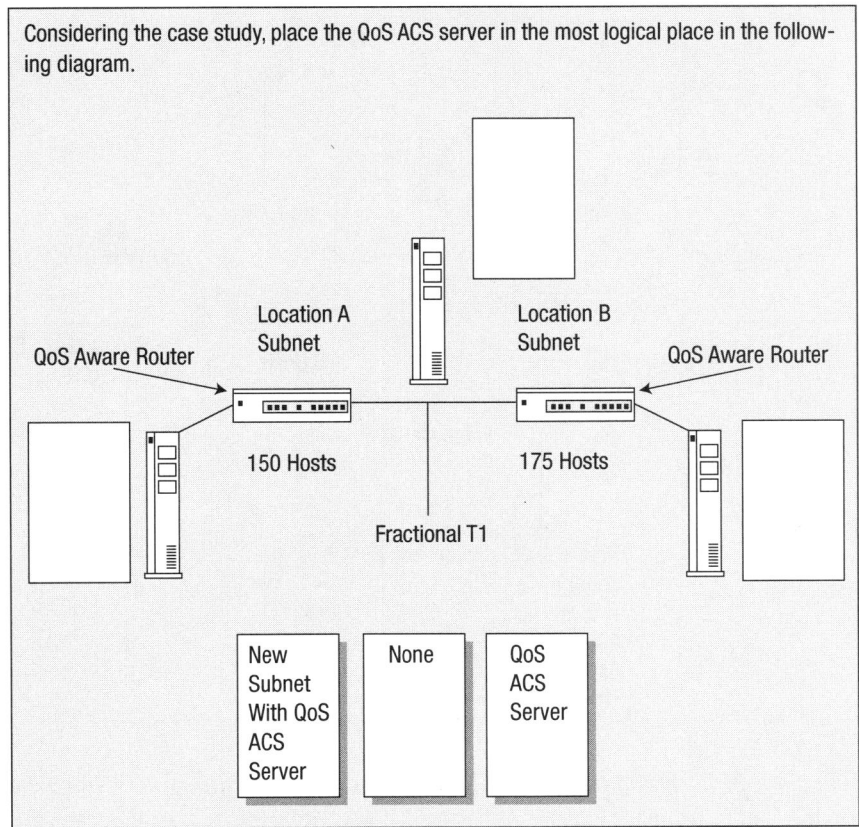

The answer is:

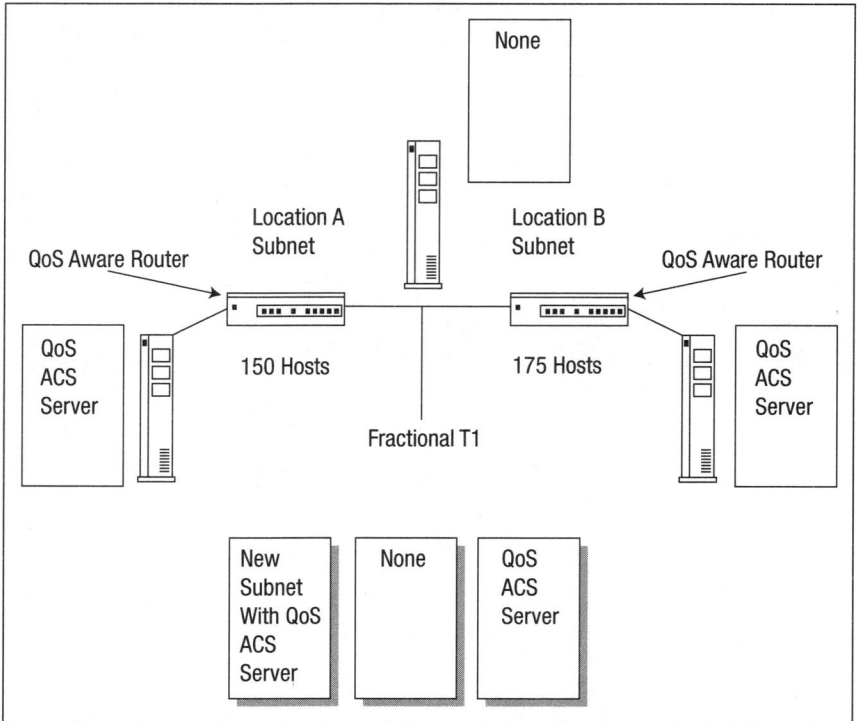

The QoS ACS should be centrally located. Since none of the subnets will be at their maximum capacity, the server should be centrally located. In this case, the QoS ACS server will be placed in the Indianapolis location. If either Carson City or Louisville becomes unavailable or is required to use the redundant ISDN link, the unaffected location will continue to access the QoS ACS server with the best possible bandwidth.

Question 8

Considering the case study, when would a host at the Carson City location be able to establish a QoS session with a host at the Louisville location?

- ○ a. When the router at the Carson City location cached a reservation for bandwidth
- ○ b. When routers at Carson City and Indianapolis had cached a reservation for bandwidth
- ○ c. When routers at Carson City, Indianapolis, and Louisville had cached a reservation for bandwidth
- ○ d. When the request was returned to the sending host at the Carson City location

Answer c is correct. A QoS sender must receive its request message back from the receiving host before a QoS session can begin. A bandwidth allocation is cached at each router alone the path between the two hosts during the session creation.

Question 9

Considering the case study, on which WAN links could the increased TCP/IP window size be employed?

- ○ a. On any T1 connection where the QoS ACS resides
- ○ b. On the T1 connection where the QoS ACS does not reside
- ○ c. On any ISDN connection
- ○ d. None of the above

Answer d is correct. The increased TCP/IP window size is only beneficial with a high-speed connection, such as fiber optic or satellite connections. T1 and ISDN lines are unable to benefit from the window size because the data transfer rates are slow compared to fiber optic and microwave.

Question 10

Considering the case study, on which server should the IPSec Secure Server be located?

- ○ a. At location A
- ○ b. At location B
- ○ c. At location C
- ○ d. None of the above

Answer d is correct. The Secured Server is a predefined security policy that must be set in the advanced properties on each host on the Windows 2000 network. A sever to security is not utilized. QoS uses an ACS or Access Control Server to allocate bandwidth and authenticate users.

Need to Know More?

 Comer, Douglas. *Internetworking with TCP/IP Vol. I: Principles, Protocols, and Architecture.* Prentice Hall. Upper Saddle River, NJ, 2000. ISBN 0-13018-380-6. A great reference for learning about TCP/IP, this book is respected for its clarity and accessibility.

 Microsoft Online Knowledge base, Article ID: Q244910 Description of Reservation State in RSVP.

 RFC 1519. Classless Inter-Domain Routing (CIDR). **www.ietf.org/rfc/rfc1519.txt?number=1519**. This RFC gives detailed information on classless inter-domain routing, or CIDR. It is in-depth but can be tough to follow.

 RFC 1918. Address Allocation for Private Internets. **www.ietf.org/rfc/rfc1918.txt?number=1918**. This RFC outiles public and private adressing, and gives examples of their utilization. An extremely good RFC.

 RFC 2018. TCP Selective Acknowledgment Options. **www.ietf.org/rfc/rfc2018.txt?number=2018**. This RFC deals with the TCP/IP SAC protocol. A very in-depth article that will also explain the benefits of a bigger TCP window size.

 RFC 1256. ICMP Router Discovery Messages. **www.ietf.org/rfc/rfc1256.txt?number=1256**. This RFC outlines the ICMP router discovery message and how it is used by routers to automatically assign a default gateway to hosts on a TCP/IP network.

 RFC 2404. The Use of HMAC-SHA-1-96 within ESP and AH. **www.ietf.org/rfc/rfc2404.txt?number=2404**. This RFC covers the authentication headers and encryption standards used by IPSec.

DHCP Design

. . . .

Terms you'll need to understand:

✓ Dynamic Host Configuration Protocol (DHCP)

✓ DHCP Relay Agent

✓ Scope

✓ Superscope

✓ Boot Protocol (BOOTP)

✓ Vendor options

✓ Multicast

Techniques you'll need to master:

✓ Using vendor options

✓ Securing DHCP

✓ Making DHCP services redundant

✓ Improving DHCP performance

In this chapter, you'll learn how to implement the Dynamic Host Configuration Protocol (DHCP) in a Windows 2000 network infrastructure. You'll learn how to use DHCP services to design a network to enhance Windows 2000 in a networking environment. These designs will decrease your administrative duties for the Windows 2000 TCP/IP while keeping your network secure.

DHCP Overview

The DHCP service is used on TCP/IP networks to automate IP addressing and TCP/IP optional parameters rather than manually assigning IP addresses.

Manually assigning each computer in a TCP/IP network a unique IP address would require an administrator to visit each computer, enter a unique IP address for it, and keep track of the addresses as they are assigned so as to avoid duplicating any of the already used IP addresses. The DHCP service is configured to use a range, or *scope*, of addresses. Once IP addresses are assigned from this range, they are immediately and automatically excluded from being assigned to any other computer by the DHCP server. If you assign a collection of scopes for a network, this is defined as a *superscope*.

 If two computers have the same IP address, the second one that attempts to initialize TCP/IP will not be able to initialize the protocol. If other protocols are bound on the computer, the computer will use those. Until a valid TCP/IP address is used, the two systems will show a conflict and only one system's TCP/IP protocol will initialize at a time.

When a computer is started that has DHCP Client Service enabled, the following occurs:

1. The client sends a broadcast to the network asking for a DHCP server (where the DHCP server services are installed and a scope is assigned).

2. The DHCP server receives the broadcast and returns to the client a broadcast offering an IP address.

3. The client accepts or rejects the offer; if the offer is accepted, an acknowledgment broadcast is sent back.

4. The DHCP server marks the address as being active so that no other computer can have the same one, and then the DHCP server broadcasts a final acknowledgment to give the client final permission to use the assigned IP address.

5. The client starts the TCP/IP service with the newly assigned address.

If multiple DHCP servers are available, they all send an offer for an IP address. The client accepts the first offer, and, when it sends the broadcast back to accept, the other DHCP servers will withdraw their unaccepted offers.

 The DHCP server must be permanently assigned a static IP address that is excluded from the scope so that it cannot be assigned to another computer.

Other optional parameters that can be configured are the default Domain Name Service (DNS) servers, Windows Internet Name Service (WINS) servers, gateways, vendor-specific options, multicast address allocation, and lease time.

 These options are not the only services that DHCP can configure on the client computer, but they are the ones that are most important when designing a network infrastructure. For a more detailed list, search the Windows 2000 help file "DHCP Options Reference".

Vendor-Specific Option Categories

The vendor-specific options are divided into two types: user-specific and vendor-specific. They are defined in RFC 2132.

 You should take note that the vendor-specific options are not all supported on earlier versions of NT DHCP Client and non-Microsoft DHCP clients.

User-Specific Options

The user-specific options are used for clients needing common DHCP configurations, such as IP subnet addresses, WINS server, DNS server, gateways, and so on.

These options can be useful for a group of people in one building who need different DHCP scope options than people in another building who require another set of DHCP scope options. Thus, the two buildings can share a single DHCP server.

This option is used only in Windows 2000 based systems.

Vendor-Specific Options

The vendor-specific options are used for systems that are running Windows 2000 or Windows 98. For instance, one set of DHCP options can be used for everyone running Windows 2000, and another set of DHCP options for those using Windows 98.

This flexibility is useful for a company that requires Windows 2000 on all desktop systems but wants Windows 98 on all laptop systems. The DHCP options will be able to specify that the Windows 98 systems have different options for being able to use Routing and Remote Access Services (RRAS) for mobile users who are dialing into the company's network.

Some of the various vendor-specific options are:

➤ *Release DHCP lease on shutdown*—Allows the IP addresses to be reused when a system is shut down, rather than waiting for the lease to expire. This feature allows a scope to include more available addresses. For example, if someone leaves on vacation for a week and the lease time is set to three days, that IP address is available immediately when the system is shut down rather than after three days.

➤ *Disable NetBIOS over TCP/IP*—Forces the Windows 2000 systems to use DNS rather than WINS and thus reduces some network traffic. Windows 2000 is designed more around DNS than WINS. Address resolution is quicker, because there is no waiting for the WINS request to time out in the absence of a WINS server.

➤ *Default router metric base*—Specifies the default metric for the gateways. The metric determines which gateway is faster than another. For example, if Gateway A has a metric of 100 and Gateway B has a metric of 500, Gateway A will be used before Gateway B (unless it is unavailable).

Multicast Address Dynamic Client Allocation Protocol (MADCAP)

DHCP services also help assign multicast addresses, which are used for the simultaneous transmission of information (such as streaming video) from one PC to multiple PCs. To implement MADCAP on a network, you need a server that is running DHCP services and the Site Server ILS service. Once these are installed and running, a MADCAP scope is set and activated. Any application needing a multicast address can then request one from the DHCP server just as a system requests a standard IP address. The address that is requested by all systems for a multicast broadcast are given the same IP address. (They must already have an existing Class A, B, or C address.) All systems with the same multicast address are listed as a multicast group to receive multicast broadcasts.

Make sure your routers allow the multicast addresses to pass through and not be filtered out when the presentation will span more than one network.

Note: For a DHCP server to offer IP addresses for multicast, it must first be authorized (which is described later in this chapter under "Active Directory Integration").

To set up a Multicast scope, in the DHCP Administrator, right-click on the DHCP server to be used as the multicast server and select New Multicast Scope as shown in Figure 4.1. You then follow the wizard to set up the multicast scopes. The wizard allows you to specify a range of addresses to assign for multicast from 224.0.0.0 to 239.255.255.255 (Class D addresses), as shown in Figure 4.2.

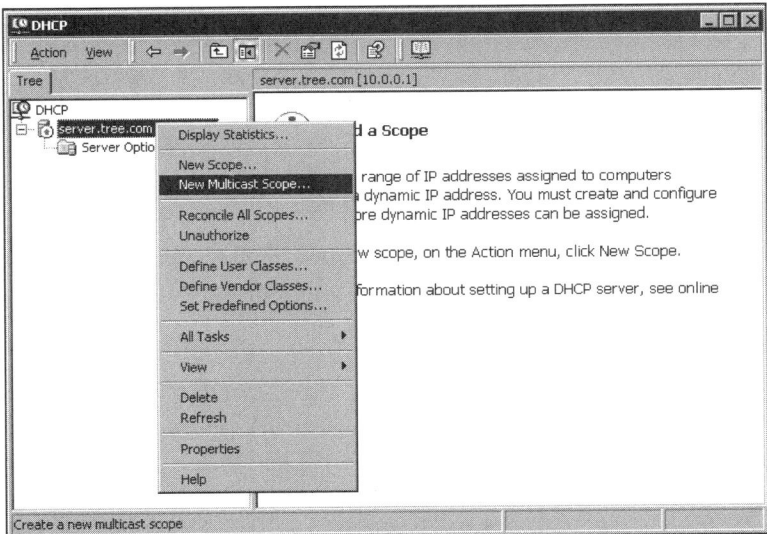

Figure 4.1 Selecting New Multicast Scope.

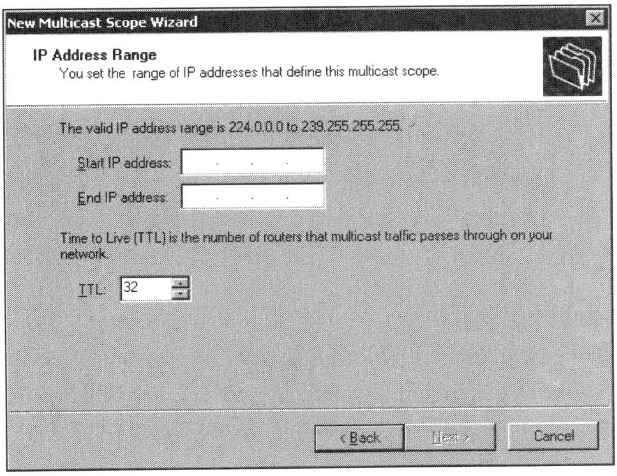

Figure 4.2 Multicast range selection.

Lease Time

The lease time is how long an IP address and options are valid before the DHCP client must request a new IP address or renew the lease on the one it has.

Leases allow a network to retain as much of its scope of IP addresses as possible. For instance, a computer with an assigned IP address is removed from the network. Because the database shows that the absent computer still retains ownership of the IP address, that address cannot be reused. A lease, however, causes this ownership to either be renewed or to expire after a set amount of time (Windows 2000 has a default of eight days).

DHCP Integration with Windows 2000

DHCP integrates well with Windows 2000 because DHCP is used for medium- to large-based networks. (Even though DHCP can be used for small businesses, the full benefits are better realized in larger networks.)

DHCP can integrate with a few different Windows 2000 services to make the network more robust and more secure, with less administrative overhead.

DNS Integration

DHCP in Windows 2000 integrates with DNS to allow DHCP to automatically update the DNS table when DHCP assigns an IP address. This includes non-Microsoft DHCP clients as well as Microsoft DHCP clients. The DHCP service handles the DNS updates, which is set at the DHCP server by selecting the Always Update DNS option located under Properties on the DNS tab and shown in Figure 4.3.

Once this option is enabled, any client receiving an address from the DHCP server will have its address updated in the DNS tables automatically. It will update the Forward (A Record) and Reverse (PTR Record) lookup tables (if they exist). This makes DNS dynamic instead of static, as it was in Windows NT 4 and previous versions.

If the DHCP server is a Windows 2000 server, it can update the records of non-Active Directory DNS servers. This does include non-Windows systems and older Windows DNS servers.

Active Directory Integration

Integrating DHCP in Active Directory allows more security by preventing rogue servers from issuing IP addresses to systems on the network. If a DHCP server is not authorized, the services will not start on a Windows 2000 server.

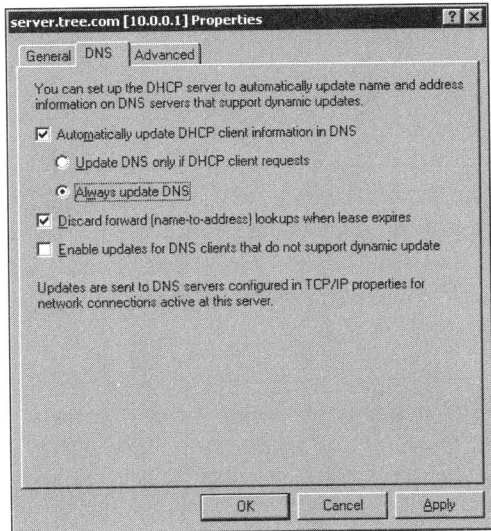

Figure 4.3   DNS update option in DHCP.

 Keep in mind that DHCP services on a Windows 2000 server should be authorized in Active Directory. An authorized DHCP server is one that can answer requests for IP addresses. IP address offers from unauthorized DHCP servers will not be accepted.

Authorizing a DHCP server does require that Active Directory is installed and that you have a domain controller operating. Active Directory will not function in a workgroup.

When using Active Directory, the Windows 2000-based DHCP clients will request a list of DHCP servers that are authorized from the Active Directory. Non-Windows 2000 DHCP clients will request an IP address from authorized and unauthorized DHCP servers.

The built-in group DHCP Administrators has access to DHCP Manager, and the built-in group DHCP Users has read-only permission to access the DHCP Manager. Using built-in groups allows an administrator to assign a specialized administrator to administer DHCP scope and options, thus keeping the DHCP management secure.

In a network using strictly Windows 2000-based DHCP clients and authorized DHCP servers, the issuing of IP addresses can be more secure. To keep it secure, the DHCP services request access to the Active Directory authorized list when starting and every five minutes thereafter, which prevents the DHCP server service from running when it has lost its authority.

Routing and Remote Access Integration

This integration allows remote systems connecting to a RRAS to use DHCP to obtain IP addresses. The number of incoming ports will determine the number of initial IP addresses the RAS server requests from the DHCP server. If a DHCP server has a modem pool with 9 modems set for incoming calls, the RAS server gets 10 addresses from the DHCP server for use: 1 for itself and 9 for the connected users through the 9 modems. If the clients are connecting from the Internet, the RAS server receives an initial 11 addresses: 1 for itself and 10 for the first 10 users to connect. After that, it gets more addresses in blocks of 10, if it needs them.

 When using DHCP with routing and remote access services, decrease the lease expiration time to make the IP addresses available sooner, because most remote access users will not be online for extended periods of time.

If the RAS server also has DHCP Relay Agent, it can get the IP addressing options from the DHCP server. (DHCP Relay Agent is a service that answers the DCHP requests from DHCP clients and forwards the request to the configured DHCP server.) If the DHCP client is on a routed network that is not BOOTP-enabled (that is, connected by a router that does not pass DHCP requests to the other subnet, but instead filters them out), any DHCP client will not be able to communicate with the DHCP server. On the other hand, if the routers are BOOTP-enabled, the requests and offers pass through the router to the other subnets. This basically means that, on a routed network that does not support BOOTP, one must use DHCP Relay Agent.

Designing a LAN DHCP Service

In a single nonrouted network, one DHCP server is sufficient for thousands of DHCP clients. But DHCP can be hard disk-intensive, and Redundant Array of Independent Disks (RAID) implementations should be beneficial. An administrator can use Performance Monitor to watch for bottlenecks when more client systems are added to the network.

Note: Performance Monitor is located in the Administrative Tools under the heading Performance.

Set up one scope on the DHCP server to offer IP addresses to the DHCP clients. If you want to use multiple DHCP servers for redundancy (for example, when one server fails, you will still want DHCP services active on your network), you would divide the scope in two and place half on each DHCP server.

 Just make sure that one-half of the scope is sufficient for your whole network, which may be necessary if one server's downtime is longer than the lease expiration.

In a single LAN, depending on how static the configuration is, the default expiration time should be extended. If the IP addressing options are being changed often for testing, the lease time should be shortened until the testing is completed.

Designing WAN DHCP Services

When dealing with a WAN or a routed network, broadcasts (which are essential to the function of DHCP services) are not allowed to cross the router barrier. If BOOTP is enabled on the routers, then only the DHCP broadcasts are allowed to cross the router barrier (not all broadcasts). If a subnet is joined to a subnet with a DHCP server by a router without BOOTP, that subnet must have DHCP Relay Agent.

In a WAN, DHCP servers must be accessible by all DHCP clients. Depending on whether the routers are configured with BOOTP and if there is enough server hardware to manage DHCP server load will determine whether one or multiple DHCP servers should be implemented.

One DHCP Server in a WAN

Because the DHCP server will need to be accessed by all DHCP clients on every subnet of the WAN, the best performance can be achieved by placing the DHCP server in the subnet with the greatest number of DHCP clients. This will keep the majority of the DHCP requests on the local subnet.

If DHCP Relay Agent is used on other subnets that are not BOOTP-enabled, the majority of the DHCP requests from clients and the relay agents will still be local. The relay agents will direct their requests to the DHCP server directly and not by broadcasts. (This prevents DHCP requests from flooding all of the subnets with requests from other subnets.)

Multiple DHCP Servers in a WAN

If the DHCP client requests overwhelm the hardware capabilities of a DHCP server or bandwidth of a network, multiple DHCP servers should be used. Also, if subnets are connected with unreliable connection paths, the subnet that may or may not be able to contact the other subnet should have its own local DHCP server.

Multiple DHCP servers should also be used to accommodate the growth of the network for more-scalable WAN expansion.

Designing DHCP High Availability

To make sure that DHCP is always available to issue IP addresses to systems on a network, the DHCP service must be functioning somewhere on a network at all times and be accessible by all systems. You can ensure such an availability of DHCP services in two ways: clustered DHCP servers and multiple DHCP servers.

Clustered DHCP Server

DHCP is a cluster-aware service that will function on clustered servers. Setting up a cluster requires two computers of almost identical hardware and configuration. Clusters also require a high-speed connection between the two for fast communications, which allows one system to take over in case the other fails, an event known as a *failover*.

Note: During a failover, all of the cluster-aware services automatically start on the second server in the cluster. The interruption should cause no loss of data or downtime.

Cluster servers support more failover services than just DHCP. Cluster servers can failover such services as Exchange, SQL, IIS, and some third-party software services.

Multiple DHCP Servers

Using multiple DHCP servers can assure that one DHCP server is always online. The problem is that each DHCP server may be issuing addressing for two or more different subnets.

The rule here is 80/20: Assign 80 percent of the IP addresses to a scope for the DHCP server in that subnet, and assign the other 20 percent of the scope to the DHCP server on the other subnet (and vice versa). If one DHCP server fails, the other DHCP server can still issue some IP addresses for the other subnet, plus almost all of its own. The 20 percent for the remote subnet should not be exhausted before an administrator has time to fix the DHCP server that failed (unless the lease time is too small or the server needs major repairs to bring back online).

Enhancing DHCP Performance

Enhancing DHCP performance improves the server's response to DHCP clients. It also reduces the TCP/IP initialization time, which will let the clients start faster.

Hardware Implementation

The hardware can be improved by implementing any of the following options:

➤ Faster CPU (or multiple CPUs)

➤ More memory

➤ Faster network interface cards (NICs) for faster transmissions

➤ Faster disk subsystems

➤ Putting the DHCP server on a subnet of highest system location (the one with most users)

➤ DHCP servers on every side of a WAN link

Software Implementation

The software can be improved by implementing any of the following options:

➤ Share scopes (the 80/20 rule).

➤ Modify lease expiration. (If the expiration is set to a lesser time frame, the DHCP will be contacted more often to renew leases, which causes more overhead. On the other hand, if the expiration time is increased too much, the DHCP server will have less of a load, but some IP addresses will be unavailable until the lease time expires.)

Practice Questions

Case Study

Current LAN/Network Structure

2Market currently has two subnets. One subnet is for the IT department. All servers are located on the IT department subnet so that the servers can be kept in a locked and restricted room, and for backup and restore purposes. The other subnet is composed of the rest of the 2Market network. This subnet has roughly 600 TCP/IP devices (computers, printers, and so on).

Proposed LAN/Network Structure

2Market would like to isolate the sales department on its own subnet.

Current WAN Connectivity

None at the current time.

Proposed WAN Connectivity

2Market would like its traveling sales force to be able to dial in remotely to the sales subnet.

DHCP Design Commentary

The IT department has its own addressing scheme for its subnet. The current DHCP server is a member server that is also hosting an SQL database.

IT Manager

The IT department needs to keep all servers containing data in the locked server room. If a server does not need to be backed up during the daily backup routine, it can be outside the server room.

The IT department's subnet is isolated from the rest of the network by an older router that does not support BOOTP. New equipment will be purchased to isolate the sales department.

Sales Manager

The sales department needs to be accessible to sales reps so that they can enter orders and check on order status when out of town. The department needs to be isolated from the rest of the network to minimize traffic. Any servers it may use for external accessibility will not store any data. The sales department consists of 75 employees, who are currently part of the main subnet.

Current Internet Positioning

2Market is registered as **2Market.com**. 2Market does not currently sell mechandise on its Web site.

Future Internet Plans

No changes are proposed at the current time.

Question 1

> Implementing the least number of servers, how many DHCP servers and relay agents are needed?
>
> ○ a. 1 DHCP server, 1 relay agent
>
> ○ b. 1 DHCP server, 2 relay agents
>
> ○ c. 2 DHCP servers, 1 relay agent
>
> ○ d. 2 DHCP servers, 2 relay agents

The answer is a. Since the IT department is already using a DHCP server that has data on it and cannot be moved and the router is non-BOOTP enabled, a relay agent is needed for the other two subnets, which will be divided by a newer router (with BOOTP).

Question 2

> In the current configuration with all of the required scopes, what is the least number of DHCP servers that can be implemented to support this design?
>
> ○ a. 1
>
> ○ b. 2
>
> ○ c. 3
>
> ○ d. 4

The answer is a. One scope will be created for the IT department and another for the rest of the network. Since multiple scopes can reside on one DHCP server one server is sufficient for company needs. Two or more DHCP servers would just add fault tolerance for the DHCP services.

Question 3

> If there were no specifications on server security, what options would be available for setting up redundancy on the DHCP servers? [Choose all that apply]
>
> ❑ a. Subnet the network.
>
> ❑ b. Install a second DHCP server.
>
> ❑ c. Use the 80/20 rule.
>
> ❑ d. Cluster the DHCP server.

The answers are b, c, and d. Installing a second DHCP server and using the 80/20 rule would allow the network to remain functional if one server failed. The 80/20 rule places 80 percent of a subnet's addresses on one server and the other 20 percent on another. On the IT subnet without BOOTP, clustering the DHCP server would make DHCP redundant on the IT subnet.

Question 4

> 2Market currently uses a Unix server as the DNS server. Without replacing the Unix server, how can you enable a DHCP server to work with the DNS server? [Choose all that apply]
>
> ❑ a. Enable dynamic DNS updates for systems that do not support dynamic updates
>
> ❑ b. Unplug the Unix server
>
> ❑ c. Make the Unix server a secondary DNS server to the Windows 2000 DNS primary server
>
> ❑ d. Do nothing

The answers are a and c. Enabling dynamic updates on a Windows 2000 DHCP server will let it automatically update the DNS services on the Unix server. If the Unix server is a secondary DNS server to the Windows 2000 DNS servers, it will receive a copy of the DNS database from the Windows 2000 DNS servers. Answer b is incorrect because the owners do not want the Unix boxes replaced. Answer d will have no effect because the Unix server will not receive any updates.

Question 5

If all computers in the 2Market network are running Windows 2000, and the laptops (which are not being upgraded) for the sales department are running Windows 98, what can be done to enable different configurations for local and remote users? [Choose all that apply]

- ❏ a. Employ user options
- ❏ b. Employ Multicast scope
- ❏ c. Disable DHCP
- ❏ d. Employ vendor options

The answers are a and d. The Windows 2000 clients can employ user options, and the Windows 98 and 2000 clients can use vendor options. Multicast scopes are used when multicasting. Disabling DHCP would have adverse effects on the current configuration.

Question 6

If, to improve performance, the DHCP server were moved to the non-IT and non-Sales subnets and a DHCP Relay Agent were placed on the IT subnet, would this new design be functional? Yes or no?

- ○ a. Yes
- ○ b. No

The answer is a, yes. DHCP Relay Agent will allow the IT department to receive DHCP addresses. The other router is BOOTP enabled, so the DHCP server will be accessible by all DHCP clients.

Question 7

In the current configuration, how does DHCP Relay Agent contact the DHCP server for a lease?

- ○ a. Through broadcasts
- ○ b. By querying the DHCP server using its IP address
- ○ c. By submitting a specialized packet to the router
- ○ d. By getting an address from its own assigned scope

The answer is b. When DHCP Relay Agent is installed, the IP address of the DHCP server is manually configured. Thus, Relay Agent can send a request packet directly to the DHCP server instead of using a broadcast, which will not cross the non-BOOTP enabled router. Relay Agent sends a standard TCP/IP packet to the router that is addressed with the DHCP server's IP address. No specialized packets are used. Relay Agent has no configured scopes; only the DHCP server has scopes.

Question 8

> The president of 2Market wants to have a monthly or quarterly update sent over the network to all employees at once by video. What option would be used?
>
> ○ a. User options
>
> ○ b. Multicast scopes
>
> ○ c. Gateways
>
> ○ d. Vendor options

The answer is b. Video streaming to computers is called multicasting, and a multicast scope is required to assign multicast addresses.

Question 9

> How would you design the network? Place each label in its appropriate position on the diagram. Options are used only once, and not all options will be used.

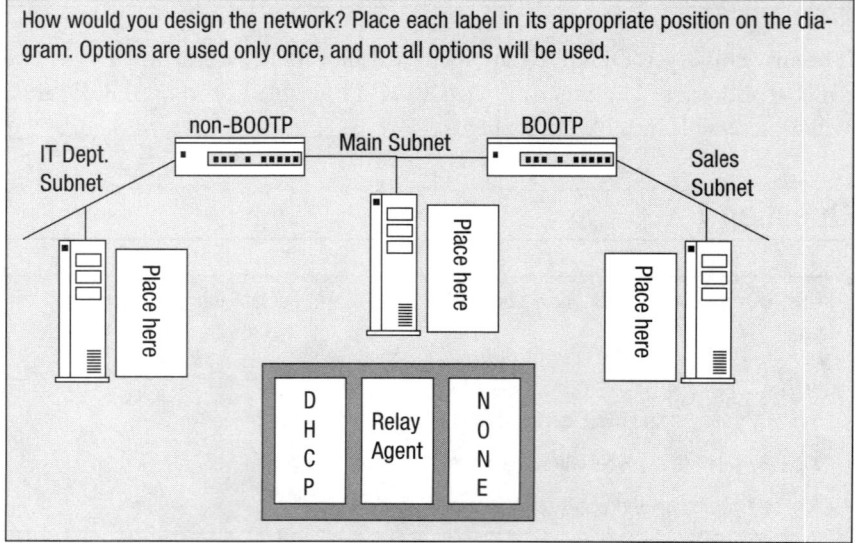

The answer is:

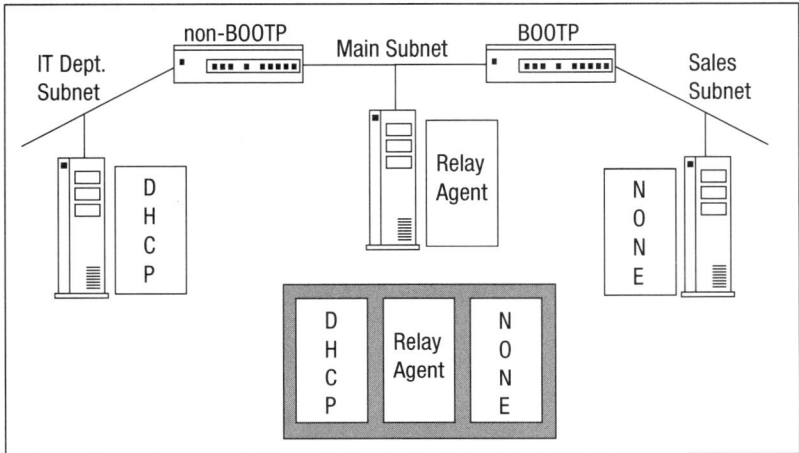

The DHCP server is used on the IT subnet since it has data on it. A relay agent would be used for the remaining subnets (preferably placed on the main subnet since there are more DHCP clients).

Question 10

In the proposed network configuration, the sales department will have a RAS server. It wants to implement 15 dial-in connections from the local phone company. How many total addresses will the RAS server require?

○ a. 11

○ b. 15

○ c. 16

○ d. 18

The answer is c. A RAS server using dial-in connections will request one address for its network interface and one for every dial-in connection, which would equal 16.

Need to Know More?

 Novosel, Gary, Kurt Hudson, and James Michael Stewart. *MCSE TCP/IP Exam Cram 3E*. The Coriolis Group, Scottsdale, AZ, 2000. ISBN 1-57610-677-2. Guide to TCP/IP for Windows NT 4.

 Parker, Timothy. *TCP/IP Unleashed*. Sams Publishing, Indianapolis, IN, 1996. ISBN 0-672-30603-4. Chapter 31, "DHCP and WINS", has extensive information on DHCP, configuration, and options.

 Search the TechNet CD (or its online version through **www.microsoft.com**) and the *Windows NT Server Resource Kit* CD using the keyword "DHCP". Also see the Windows 2000 Server or Advanced Server help.

DNS

. . . .

Terms you'll need to understand:

✓ Domain Name System (DNS) namespace

✓ Berkeley Internet Naming Domain (BIND)

✓ Request for Comment (RFC)

✓ Zone

✓ Screened subnets

✓ Resolver

✓ Forwarder

✓ Slave

✓ Zone delegation

Techniques you'll need to master:

✓ Mapping out your network to view connections

✓ Implementing DNS name resolution with recursion and iteration

✓ Working with different versions of DNS

✓ Integrating DNS with Active Directory in Windows 2000

Designing an effective Domain Name System (DNS) solution can be difficult simply because it has grown so complicated over the past few years. The DNS service now has more than 10 Requests for Comments that define the service. This difficulty is compounded by the fact that different operating systems can have their own version of DNS. Although the basics of the DNS service remain the same, its importance in the network infrastructure has grown: DNS is now the primary name-resolution service in Windows 2000. Also, DNS is a required service for most network configurations in Windows 2000.

Design Issues for DNS

Because of the difference in domains between Windows NT and Windows 2000, many networks may require a redesign of—or at least additions to—the DNS namespace. In Windows 2000, the nature of a Microsoft directory services domain has changed. In Windows NT, the domains used NetBIOS names instead of DNS. Because the NT and DNS domains used separate naming systems, many companies had two unrelated naming conventions: one for NT domains and one for DNS domains. Windows 2000 uses DNS as its primary name-resolution service because its directory services no longer need NetBIOS—and therefore no longer need NetBIOS names.

The Importance of a Network Diagram

Before you start designing a DNS solution for a network, you should have an overview of what the network looks like. Because the features available in DNS have grown more complicated, DNS needs to be designed from a high level to ensure availability, security, and optimized performance. It also must be robust enough to handle the added traffic from Windows 2000 clients. Most networks have a network diagram, even though it may date back to when the network was first installed. You don't need a complicated or professionally designed diagram; in fact, a simple one will be much easier to work from. Figure 5.1 serves as an example.

You will add more to this diagram as your DNS system develops, but, to get started, you need to include only the following elements:

➤ Local area network (LAN) locations

➤ Number of clients at each LAN location

➤ Wide area network (WAN) connections

  ➤ Speed of WAN connections

  ➤ Type of connectivity device (such as router, bridge, or switch)

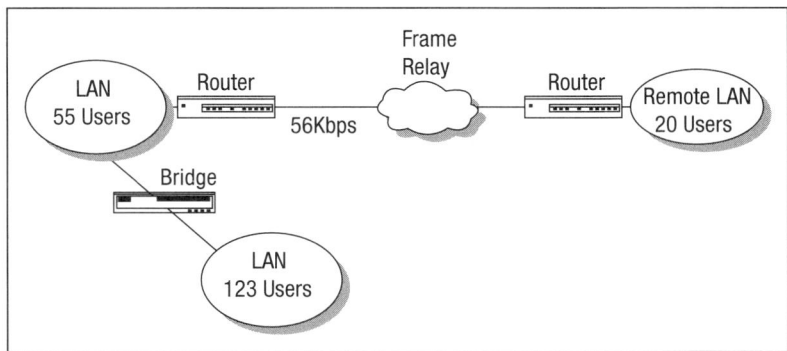

Figure 5.1 A simple drawing of a network and connections, including concentrations of users.

Documenting Your DNS Server Types

Even if a DNS system is currently in place (as is the case in most networks to-day), any updates or modifications to the network infrastructure call for another look at the DNS system currently in place. Keep this in mind because the changes in the directory services for Windows 2000 put a heavier burden on your DNS system. Also, DNS now has features that optimize network usage and add security. So, you must redesign the current system to take advantage of these features.

The Different Faces of DNS

The Windows 2000 DNS Server is capable of implementing DNS in three different ways: a Berkeley Internet Naming Domain (BIND), Windows NT 4, or Windows 2000 DNS Server. This flexibility allows it to more easily integrate with other types of DNS servers and clients. Because it can interact with downlevel clients and servers, Windows 2000 DNS Server does not require that the whole environment be upgraded whenever it is added to an existing DNS system.

A Request for Comment (RFC) is a document that outlines standards for Internet services. Currently, Windows 2000 supports 8 of the 10 RFCs that define the DNS service. (The Windows NT 4 DNS Server supported only two.) Of course, compliance with an RFC does not mean that a DNS server stays within the bounds of the RFC. BIND, Windows NT 4, and Windows 2000 DNS servers all have features outside of the RFCs that they support.

The BIND standard is the most common standard for the implementation of a DNS server. BIND allows DNS servers to communicate and resolve hostnames among themselves even if they are running on different operating systems. Microsoft's DNS servers are automatically BIND-compliant when installed. However, when developing the code for its first DNS server in Windows NT 4, Microsoft decided to write its own code instead of adopting the BIND code. The company had different ideas for extra features that it wanted to include in its own DNS server, and writing its own code was the easiest way to do this. Microsoft's extra features are mainly DNS-to-WINS resolution in Windows NT 4 DNS and Active Directory integration in Windows 2000 DNS.

BIND Compliance

BIND exists in different versions. The DNS service in Windows NT 4 most closely follows the standard for BIND version 4.9.6. This version and Windows NT support only static updates to the DNS database, which means its database does not accept updates from another service. Also, BIND 4.9.6 and Windows NT DNS service use full-zone transfers. Zones and zone transfers will be covered later in this chapter. When a primary DNS server replicates its database to a secondary server, the full database—not just the updates—is copied over.

BIND 8.1.2 has many features in common with Windows 2000 DNS. Both support dynamic updates to the DNS database, and both support incremental instead of full-zone transfers. Although your non-Microsoft DNS servers can be integrated into your DNS structure, you will need to check the version of BIND that they support to find what features will be supported.

Adding to Your Network Diagram

Because different versions of DNS servers support different features, you must overlay the locations and types of DNS servers onto your network diagram. This overlay allows you to see what types of features you can implement, and it also reveals if your current DNS servers need to be upgraded.

Additions to your DNS network diagram include:

➤ Overlay of current DNS infrastructure

    ➤ Locations of current DNS servers

    ➤ Type of DNS server (such as Windows NT 4, non-Windows DNS servers)

    ➤ BIND version of non-Windows DNS servers

Documenting Your DNS Client Types

Now that you have documented your DNS server operating systems, you need to note the operating systems of your DNS clients. You don't need to write each client onto the diagram because DNS servers can provide down-level services. Noting client types will help you to see your administrative overhead for the DNS system that you are designing. All you have to do is to put your clients into one of three categories: non-Microsoft, Windows 2000, and Microsoft clients that are not Windows 2000.

Windows 2000 clients and BIND 8.1.2 clients support dynamic updates to the DNS database, thus eliminating the need for a person to update records in the DNS database (and thus easing a large administrative burden if you are using DHCP on your network). Previous Windows and non-Microsoft clients supporting BIND 4.9.6 will not be able to directly update the DNS database. However, if they are DHCP clients, the Windows 2000 DHCP server can be set to send the updated DNS records to the DNS server instead.

So, the last information for the network diagram is:

➤ Operating system of DNS clients

➤ BIND version of non-Windows DNS clients

➤ Preferred and alternate DNS server for each computer

Marking the preferred and alternate servers for each client will show how the DNS service load is balanced. Ensuring a balanced load will help the performance of the DNS servers on the network. Seeing the preferred and alternate DNS servers will also allow the service designer to better distribute clients to new DNS servers that are added to the design of the DNS system.

Note: Because DNS and Active Directory both use the DNS namespace, you must first decide how to integrate the namespace for the two services. This section of the book refers only to DNS namespace issues, which is not the same as Active Directory-integrated zones. Active Directory integration changes the features that DNS can support in Windows 2000, and this topic is discussed later in the chapter.

Integration of Active Directory and DNS

Now that you have a complete and usable network diagram, you must design DNS to integrate with any DNS or Active Directory services that already exist in the network. A network's previous configuration can affect the DNS design in Windows 2000 because the naming convention for Active Directory has changed. Four categories describe the different possible configurations from which a network can start, and each requires a different approach:

➤ You have no previous DNS configuration (or you are willing to start over).

➤ Active Directory and DNS will use the same namespace.

➤ Active Directory and DNS namespace will not overlap.

➤ Active Directory will integrate with non-Microsoft DNS servers.

Active Directory requires DNS as its name-resolution service and will not install without a DNS server on the network. Because Active Directory uses DNS namespace rules, you must decide when Active Directory is implemented on a network whether DNS and Active Directory will use the same namespace.

No DNS or Starting Over

The ideal situation is to have no previous DNS configuration or to be able to start over and design a new DNS system and namespace. In this case, you could install the first DNS server during the upgrade to Active Directory on your network. Starting over is a possibility for a Windows NT 4 network that implemented Microsoft DNS servers and used DNS-to-WINS resolution. In such a case, the DNS service may not have been greatly developed. However, it is not necessary to start over when implementing Active Directory on a Windows 2000 network. Most networks are more heterogeneous and could have non-Microsoft DNS servers. Keeping the old DNS system in place and integrating with Windows 2000 simply requires more decisions before implementing.

Same Namespace

Another easy answer to Active Directory implementation is to use the same DNS namespace for Active Directory and DNS. In this case, a Windows 2000 server has to be the root DNS server for the domain. This root DNS server would be authoritative for the domain. In this scenario the root server must be a Windows 2000 DNS server, but other DNS servers can be Windows NT 4 and non-Windows, BIND-compliant DNS servers. These other DNS servers can be integrated into the Active Directory DNS system.

Different Namespace

DNS does not have to be redesigned or changed when implementing Active Directory in Windows 2000. Active Directory can be implemented as a subdomain in the current DNS infrastructure. In this configuration, some or even none of the DNS servers need to be on an Active Directory server. If no Active Directory servers are used in the DNS infrastructure, the only restriction is that Windows NT 4 cannot be used as the root DNS server for Active Directory. Active Directory requires DNS servers that support service (SRV) records, and BIND-compliant DNS servers that support versions 4.9.6 and 8.1.2 and up support SRV records. SRV records are used to register network services in DNS. One way that Windows 2000 computers use SRV record queries in DNS is to locate a domain controller for a network logon. DNS record types are covered later in this chapter.

Integration with non-Microsoft DNS Servers

It is important to remember that Active Directory can be integrated with non-Microsoft DNS servers. For test purposes, non-Microsoft DNS servers do not have to be changed to the Microsoft DNS service. In order for this scenario to work, you must install a Windows 2000 standalone server. Then, you need to install DNS on the Windows 2000 server and create a secondary zone to an existing primary zone. Your final step will be to implement Active Directory, which you'll achieve by promoting a Windows 2000 server to a domain controller. You did not change the existing DNS infrastructure or namespace and you still fulfilled the requirements for having DNS in an Active Directory environment.

 In the preceding case, the existing primary DNS server must support SRV records. SRV records are supported by BIND-compliant servers 4.9.6 and above. Active Directory must have DNS servers that support SRV records. Record types are covered later in this chapter.

Zones

The next step in designing a DNS system is to determine which type of zone works best for the network. A DNS database is only authoritative for some records. This authority over records is established by creating a zone. A zone file contains the database of resource records for a DNS server. DNS zones and domains do not have to be equal. In fact, a zone can contain more than one domain as long as the domains are contiguous in the DNS namespace. For example, a zone can contain records from the domain sales.Microsoft.com and east.sales.Microsoft.com. The root domain would be sales.Microsoft.com, and records for east.sales.Microsoft.com could be included in the zone. However, one zone created for records from inside.sales.Microsoft.com as the root could not contain records from outside.sales.Microsoft.com. These two subdomains are not contiguous with each other.

A zone database file is named after its root domain with the addition of the ".dns" extension. So, sales.Microsoft.com would have a zone file named "sales.Microsoft.com.dns" by default.

Configuring a zone is not required for a DNS server to work. A DNS server with no configured zones is referred to as a *caching-only* DNS server. Later in the chapter we will discuss how to improve performance by adding caching-only servers to a DNS design.

Zone Types

When creating a zone, it must be defined as either a standard primary, standard secondary, or Active Directory-integrated zone. A primary zone is said to be authoritative because it is where the records for the zone were created. A secondary zone is simply a copy of a primary zone's database received through a zone transfer. Any zone that is set up to transfer to a secondary zone is considered to be a master zone. Master zones can be primary, secondary, or Active Directory-integrated zones. If the master zone is unavailable or the network connection is down, the secondary will not receive the update. This is referred to as a single point of failure. Active Directory-integrated zones use Windows 2000 Active Directory services to update other DNS servers. How DNS zone information is transferred between DNS servers is the main difference between using standard and Active Directory-integrated zones. Microsoft recommends using Active Directory-integrated zones on Windows 2000 DNS domain controllers, because the transfer of DNS information is included in normal Active Directory updates. This is beneficial to your network for two reasons. First, DNS will not be transferred as a separate service on the network, which can lower network traffic. Second, all Active Directory-integrated DNS servers will accept updates from other domain controller DNS servers. Active Directory-integrated zones eliminate the need for primary and secondary DNS server roles and so eliminate the single point of failure that can occur in a standard DNS zone.

The downside of Active Directory-integrated zones is that they must be Windows 2000 domain controllers. However, Active Directory-integrated zones can work with standard DNS zones. Active Directory-integrated zones can be set up as master zones for standard secondary zones in non-Windows 2000 DNS servers. This means that you can have some Active Directory-integrated zones in your DNS infrastructure mixed in with standard zones in Windows NT 4 and non-Microsoft DNS servers. Also, zones can be changed from standard to Active Directory-integrated and back, which allows a flexible DNS design that can be upgraded to Active Directory-integrated zones in stages.

Resource Records

Zones contain resource records. Although mappings of hostnames to IP addresses is the most common type of DNS resource record, a DNS database can actually contain many types of records. Table 5.1 lists often-used resource records and their purposes.

How to Get Records into Your Zone File

Windows 2000 DNS server supports dynamic and static updates to the DNS database. Until fairly recently, administrators had to update the DNS database manually. (This is called a *static update* because it is performed manually by a person instead of automatically by the system.) Outside of RFC compliance, Windows NT 4 added an extra feature that served as a workaround for static updates. It allowed DNS to ask WINS when it did not have the resource record. Because WINS is a dynamically updated name-resolution service, it gave the DNS database the appearance of being dynamic. This feature is still available in Windows 2000 DNS, but Windows 2000 DNS also allows for true dynamic

Table 5.1 Common resource records and their purposes.	
Resource Record Name	**Purpose of Record**
SOA (Start of Authority)	Identifies the zone as the primary name server and therefore the best source of records for the zone. The first record created in a zone.
NS (Name Server)	Identifies the DNS server as authoritative for the domain. Can be the primary or secondary server.
A (Address)	Host record containing mappings of hostname to IP address.
PTR (Pointer)	Used for reverse lookups in which a client has an IP address and needs to find the domain name.
SRV (Service Location)	Allows a domain controller to register available services in DNS. Clients can then query DNS to locate services like domain controllers on the network. Required record in an Active Directory-integrated zone and in a DNS server supporting Windows 2000 domain controllers.
MX (Mail Exchanger)	Used to locate a mail server on the network.
WINS and WINS-R	Used by DNS to integrate with WINS. The WINS record is for WINS forward lookups, and the WINS-R record is for reverse WINS lookups. Microsoft DNS in versions NT 4 and 2000 are the only DNS servers that support WINS lookup by a DNS server. Other DNS servers do not support the WINS and WINS-R resource records.

updates. DNS can now communicate with the DHCP server and Windows 2000 clients for updates. So, your choices for record additions to your DNS zone file are manual, DNS passing queries to WINS, or dynamic updates from Windows 2000 clients or the DHCP server.

Designing for Dynamic Updates

Dynamic updates are the recommended configuration for DHCP and DNS because of the lowered administrative and query overhead. Even in a mixed environment, Dynamic DNS (DDNS) can still be set up. The default setting for both Windows 2000 DHCP server and DNS clients is for the DNS client to update its own A record. By default, the DHCP server updates the PTR record for even DHCP clients. (Although this is the default setting, the DHCP server can be set up to update both records.)

Designing a Secure DNS System

When implementing changes that are new to DNS, security becomes an issue. In a static DNS environment, only the administrator of the DNS database handled DNS records. Now, because the records can be updated over network connections, impersonation can be a problem. Also, security within a local network isn't a big concern when transferring zones, but DNS works over WAN connections. Zone transfers can even take place over the Internet through Virutal Private Networks (VPNs). Some of the new features in the DNS service help alleviate these security issues.

Using Access Control Lists (ACLs) in DNS

Dynamic updates to the DNS server reduce the administrative overhead of the DNS service. They also allow for DNS and DHCP services to finally work well together on a network. Windows 2000 and BIND-compliant 8.1.2 DNS clients and servers support dynamic updates to DNS, which is referred to as DDNS. As we mentioned, one security problem with dynamic updates is the impersonation of a DNS client, which could reveal IP information or, even worse, change the zone database file.

Windows 2000 DNS server introduces Secure Dynamic Update to make dynamic updates secure. With Secure Dynamic Update, access control lists (ACLs) are used to check the permissions of DNS clients when they update their DNS records. Upon first registration, a permission is set on a DNS record that allows the record to be changed from only the originating client's computer account. Any other client trying to update the record is denied permission to make the change.

Secure Dynamic Update is available only in Active Directory-integrated zones and is enabled by default when an Active Directory-integrated zone is created.

Screened Subnets

Because DNS works as a distributed service, each domain is responsible for providing its own DNS database for the Internet's use. So, users from the Internet may need access to the DNS database on your local network. A screened subnet is created by setting up firewalls between a private network and a public network, such as the Internet. A firewall protects the private network by stopping all incoming connections except those specifically allowed. Any information in your network that needs to be accessed by external clients via the Internet is vulnerable to attack. To protect the internal network, this information needs to be separated from it. A separate DNS server containing only those records that are needed by Internet clients can be separated from the internal network with a screened subnet. As shown in Figure 5.2, a screened subnet protects the DNS server from Internet use by placing it between two firewalls. The second firewall protects the internal network not only from the Internet but also from the users of the DNS server.

However, using firewalls to protect the DNS server and the internal network may not be enough. Because the DNS server in the screened subnet is vulnerable

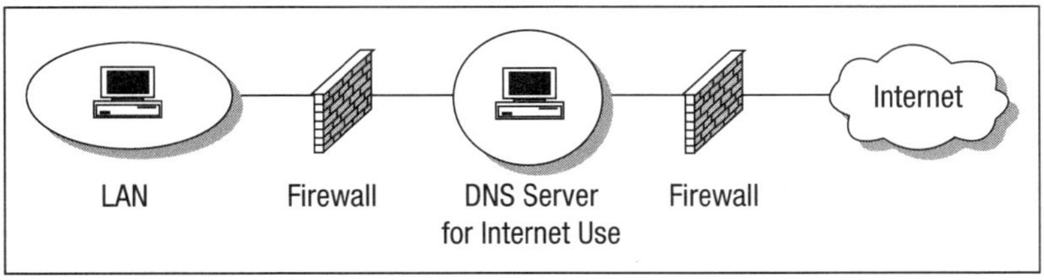

Figure 5.2   Example of a screened subnet.

to attack, more steps need to be taken to protect it. Using a separate namespace from your internal network can help. A DNS server for use on the Internet should contain only that information that is needed on the Internet and should never contain information about internal resources. Also, it is best not to use Active Directory-integrated zones on a screened subnet. Because Active directory-integrated zones can be implemented on only Windows 2000 domain controllers, this leaves valuable information open to attack. Standard secondary servers are best to use in this situation, because they have a read-only zone database file. Secondary servers accept updates from only their master server.

Encrypting Zone Transfers

If the screened subnet DNS server is a secondary, it gets its information from a master server in the internal network. Although the zone transfer is the only data coming from the internal network, even that can present a security risk. A good way to minimize this risk is to encrypt the zone transfer, and this best done by implementing a VPN with IPSec encryption.

Forwarding, Forwarder, and Slave Servers

You can protect the internal network through the use of forwarding, forwarder, and slave servers. The internal DNS server and the DNS server in the screened subnet actually can fill all three roles. The point of using these types of servers is to keep the IP address of the internal DNS server hidden from the Internet. First, have the internal DNS server forward queries that it cannot resolve internally to the DNS server in the screened subnet. At this point, the internal DNS server becomes the forwarding DNS server, and the screened subnet DNS server becomes the forwarder. By default, DNS servers that do not receive a complete response from their forwarder start to perform their own queries to complete the name resolution. Allowing the internal DNS server to make its own queries compromises it. To avoid this, make the internal DNS server a slave to its forwarder, thus forcing it to accept the answer from the forwarder and keeping it from performing its own queries.

Increasing DNS Performance

Security usually degrades performance on a network, but part of the features enhancements in Windows 2000 can increase performance and availability. Even if a DNS infrastructure is already in place, the implementation of Windows 2000 and Active Directory causes not just Internet services but nearly all network services to use DNS as the primary name-resolution service. This places a substantial new burden on the existing DNS system. New and existing DNS infrastructures need to be designed or redesigned to increase client availability and optimize performance.

One DNS Server per Location

One DNS server can support many clients. In earlier Windows environments DNS resolution may have even taken place over a WAN connection because use of the service was only needed for Internet services. Now that the importance of DNS has changed, it is better to place at least one DNS server per LAN location and to avoid DNS resolution over WAN links. DNS resolution will cause a lot more traffic in a Windows 2000 network, and additional DNS servers will be needed to handle the extra load.

Zone Delegation

DNS databases are parsed, read top to bottom, like many reference files on the network. Reducing the file size increases performance for clients making queries. Zone delegation is simply the process of creating more DNS zone files so that they will each have fewer entries and therefore have quicker responses when queried. Creating more domains is one way to increase zone files, but, because zones and domains are not equal, it is not the only way. Four to five subdomains down from a second-level domain are all that is recommended.

In a Windows NT 4 environment, administrators were encouraged to have high-level DNS servers only and then to pass DNS queries to WINS. Zone delegation and the creation of more zone files are ideal for this environment.

Load Balance Client Requests

Increasing zone transfers and copying a database file to secondary zones is another way to create more zones. One primary zone can send a transfer to more than one secondary, and secondary zones can also be master zones performing zone transfers. Increasing the number of secondary zones makes them available on more servers for load balancing. In Figure 5.4, DNS1 is a primary DNS zone. DNS1 does a zone transfer to DNS2 making DNS1 the master server for the zone transfer and making DNS2 a secondary zone. DNS2 then is set up to do a zone transfer to DNS3. For this zone transfer DNS2 is the master. DNS3 is still considered to be a secondary zone because it contains a copy of the zone instead of the original database file.

Creating more DNS servers and zones allows administrators to change the preferred and alternate DNS servers for clients on different parts of the network. Because implementing Windows 2000 and Active Directory results in more DNS requests, DNS client requests should be spread over more DNS servers and zones. The network diagram should be used to see if clients are evenly spread over the available DNS servers. The diagram will also show where another DNS server may be needed to lighten the query load on existing servers.

Use Caching-Only Servers

Although the DNS service has no zones configured when it is first loaded, it can still act as a DNS server. A DNS server with no configured zones is referred to as a *caching-only* DNS server, and such servers can increase performance by working as forwarders. Internal DNS servers can pass their requests on to the caching-only DNS server, which then can pass it out to the Internet and perform the needed queries. The caching-only server will cache the resolved query for, by default, 60 minutes. If it receives another query, it may be able to resolve it through cache instead of having to perform queries.

You can also use caching-only DNS servers in your internal network. The service can be added to an existing server without causing too much of a performance drain on its current services. Adding a caching-only server can increase the number of DNS servers available to the whole network and add to the performance of the DNS system.

Practice Questions

Case Study

The Bongo Drum Company is based in Kalamazoo, MI, and has 300 hosts divided into 2 subnets. The corporate office is located in Kalamazoo and has 45 hosts. The manufacturing plant in Little Rock has 28 hosts.

Current WAN Structure

The network has two locations.

Proposed WAN Structure

The company is growing and the addition of another location is planned in Mobile, AL.

Current WAN Connectivity

Currently, two locations are connected through a 56Kbps modem.

Proposed WAN Connectivity

While planning for the addition of a third location, the company is looking into using the Internet as a connection between its different locations. This seems to be the least expensive alternative for connecting all locations.

Current Internet Usage

The company uses an ISP to provide company employees with connections to the Internet.

Proposed Internet Plans

The company would like to create a Web site and needs to provide a way to allow Internet users to connect to the Web site while keeping the private network secure.

Company Windows 2000 Goal

The client computers have already been upgraded to Windows 2000 Professional. Although the servers are still a mix of Windows NT 4 and Unix, the plan is to upgrade the NT 4 servers to Windows 2000 Server using Active Directory for directory services. Figure 5.3 shows the company's network with the proposed Internet Connection.

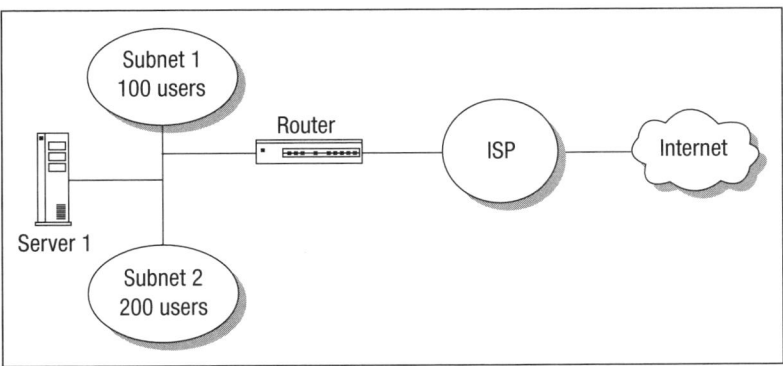

Figure 5.3   A domain with four subdomains.

Question 1

> The company is planning an upgrade to a Windows 2000 network that uses Active Directory services. Active Directory requires a DNS server on the network. Currently, Unix DNS servers are providing DNS services to the network. Since the current DNS infrastructure is working well, many at the company do not want to change it or add any DNS servers to it. What is the easiest way to accommodate their wishes and still upgrade to Active Directory? [Check all correct answers]
>
> ❑ a. This is not possible.
>
> ❑ b. Set up a local DNS server on a Windows 2000 server before promoting to a domain controller.
>
> ❑ c. Install DNS during the promotion of the Windows 2000 server to a domain controller.
>
> ❑ d. Make the DNS a secondary zone to an existing primary zone.
>
> ❑ e. Create a new DNS subdomain for the Active Directory DNS.

Answers b and d are correct. Windows 2000 using Active Directory requires the DNS service. However, since Windows 2000 Active Directory uses an RFC compliant DNS service, it can work with any DNS server that is RFC compliant. It does not have to interact with a Microsoft DNS server. If it is decided that the current DNS structure should not be changed, a secondary zone needs to be created. If DNS is not yet installed on a Windows 2000 server when it is promoted to a domain controller, then the domain controller will install the DNS service locally and automatically create an Active Directory-integrated zone.

Question 2

> While adding Active Directory to the network, an administrator installs a DNS server locally while a Windows 2000 server is upgrading to a domain controller. What type of zone was created by default?
>
> ○ a. Master
>
> ○ b. Primary
>
> ○ c. Secondary
>
> ○ d. Active Directory-integrated

Answer d is correct. When upgrading a Windows 2000 server to a domain controller, Active Directory services require a DNS server. If during the upgrade you elect to install the DNS service locally on the domain controller, it will automatically create an Active Directory-integrated zone.

Question 3

> Now that the network has an Active Directory-integrated zone, what features will that zone support that are not supported by other types of DNS zones and servers? [Check all correct answers]
>
> ❑ a. Dynamic updates
>
> ❑ b. SRV record support
>
> ❑ c. Secure Dynamic Updates
>
> ❑ d. DHCP Server integration

Answer c is correct. All of these services are supported by a Windows 2000 DNS Active Directory-integrated zone, but most of these services are also supported by BIND DNS servers. Dynamic updates and incremental zone transfers are supported starting in BIND version 8.1.2 compliant servers. SRV record support began in BIND version 4.9.6. The only service not yet supported by other DNS servers is Secure Dynamic Updates.

Question 4

After implementing Active Directory, the company wants to set up DNS so that the internal DNS server resolves queries for internal computers, and Internet queries are directed to the ISP's DNS server. How can this set be up?

- ○ a. Make your internal DNS server a slave to the ISP's DNS server.
- ○ b. Set the clients' preferred DNS server to the internal DNS server and the alternate to the ISP's DNS server.
- ○ c. Make the internal DNS server a forwarder for the ISP's DNS server.
- ○ d. Make the internal DNS server a master to the ISP's DNS server.

Answer a is correct. You need to stop the internal DNS server from making queries on the Internet. Making the ISP's DNS server an alternate for the clients will work only if the internal DNS server is not responding to the client request. By default, the internal DNS server will attempt to make queries on the Internet. The only way to block that action is to make the internal DNS server a slave to the ISP's server. First, you will set the internal DNS server to forward queries to the ISP's DNS server. In this case the internal DNS server is the forwarding server, and the ISP's DNS server is the forwarder. This is why c is not the correct answer. To make the internal DNS server a slave to the ISP's DNS server, you would not allow the internal DNS server to make its own queries if the ISP's DNS server returns a "host not found" response to the forwarded query.

Question 5

Users in subnet 2 are complaining of slow connections to internal resources. An administrator finds that the problem is slow name resolution. Without adding another DNS server, what can be done to help resolve this problem?

- ○ a. Use WINS resolution.
- ○ b. Implement dynamic updates to the DNS server.
- ○ c. Create a separate zone for subnet 2.
- ○ d. Use reverse lookups.

Answer c is correct. Without installing a new local DNS server the only answer that will help optimize DNS traffic is to create separate zones in the DNS server for subnets 1 and 2. Each zone file will be smaller and therefore be read more quickly to resolve client requests. WINS resolution will make no difference, because Windows 2000 Professional clients are using DNS instead of WINS. Dynamic updates are implemented by default on a Windows 2000 DNS client, and reverse lookups will slow down the network even more. Also, reverse lookups are used by security services and applications and not by individual DNS clients.

Question 6

The company is ready to add another remote location to the network and wants to use the Internet as the WAN connection. The location will have 10 users, and the decision is made to give them their own DNS server. An administrator wants to set up a zone transfer between locations but is concerned about internal DNS information getting out on the Internet. How can this be set up in a secure manner? [Check all correct answers]

- ❑ a.   Set up SSL for the transfer.
- ❑ b.   Set up a VPN using IPSec for encryption.
- ❑ c.   Set up Secure Dynamic Update.
- ❑ d.   Make the internal DNS server a master to the remote DNS server.

Answers b and d are correct. First, make the internal DNS server a master to the remote DNS server. This will cause a zone transfer from the internal DNS server to the remote DNS server, making the remote DNS server a secondary zone to the internal DNS server. To protect the information sent between the internal and remote networks, you need to set up a VPN using IPSec as the encryption protocol. SSL is used to encrypt Web pages in a Web site, and Secure Dynamic Update deals with dynamic updates to the DNS server from DNS clients. SSL does not deal with zone transfers, and it does not encrypt information.

Question 7

The company is ready to deploy its new Web site and decides to have an ISP host the Web site. However, it also decides to discontinue DNS services with the ISP and provide its own DNS services to incoming Internet client requests. How can this be set up while still protecting the internal network from attack?

- ○ a.   Do nothing. Your VPN with IPSec will protect your internal network.
- ○ b.   Add another DNS server for Internet clients, and make it a slave to the internal DNS server.
- ○ c.   Add another DNS server for Internet clients, and implement Secure Dynamic Updates.
- ○ d.   Create a screened subnet with a separate Internet DNS server between two firewalls.

Answer d is correct. Your VPN encryption is only protecting information transfer between your remote office and your internal network. Adding another DNS server is necessary, but placing the new DNS server in a screened subnet is the best way to protect the internal network. The internal DNS server needs to be a slave to the Internet DNS server instead of the other way around. Secure Dynamic Update is for updates to the DNS database and does not protect against queries.

Question 8

> When implemented, the Internet DNS server was created as an Active Directory-integrated zone. Now the design of the DNS service calls for that zone to be a standard primary zone. Is this possible?
>
> ○ a. Yes
>
> ○ b. No

Answer a is correct. Zones can be changed from Active Directory-integrated to standard and can even be changed back again.

Question 9

> Users are complaining about slow loading Web pages. After troubleshooting, an administrator decides the problem is slow name resolution. The decision is made to add two more DNS servers, which will make one DNS server for each subnet. What other changes need to be made?
>
> ○ a. Configure the new DNS servers as forwarders to each other.
>
> ○ b. Change the preferred DNS server for each client.
>
> ○ c. Configure the Internet DNS server as a forwarder for each new DNS server.
>
> ○ d. Configure each new DNS server as a caching-only server.

Answer b is correct. Changing the preferred DNS server for each subnet will direct traffic to the new DNS servers. Answers a and c will not reduce traffic or speed up query response. Caching-only servers help DNS performance when used in conjunction with DNS servers that are supporting zones.

Question 10

To give DNS performance an added boost, a caching-only DNS server will be added to the network. What is the best location for this new server?

○ a. Inside the screened subnet

○ b. Inside subnet 1

○ c. Inside subnet 2

○ d. Inside subnet 3

Answer a is correct. The original problem was slow loading Web pages, which means the DNS server in the screened subnet needs help handling queries.

Need to Know More?

 Scheil, Dennis and Diana Bartley. *MCSE Windows 2000 Directory Services Design Exam Cram.* The Coriolis Group, Scottsdale, AZ, October 2000. ISBN 1-57610-714-0. A good source for background information on DNS and its implementation.

 Shinder, Debra Littlejohn, Thomas Shinder, and Tony Hinkle. *Managing Windows 2000 Network Services.* Syngress Media, Inc., Rockland, MA, 2000. ISBN 1-92899-406-7. This book provides background on the networking services described in this chapter and shows dialog boxes for implementation hints.

 **www.microsoft.com/windows2000/library/howitworks/ communications/nameadrmgmt/w2kdns.asp**. *Windows 2000 DNS.* Microsoft Corporation, Redmond, WA, 1999. This Microsoft white paper describes the changes to the Windows 2000 implementation of DNS.

 **www.microsoft.com/ntserver/nts/deployment/planguide/dnswp.asp**. *DNS and Microsoft Windows NT 4.0.* Microsoft Corporation, Redmond, WA, 1996. This Microsoft white paper explains its implementation of DNS in Windows NT 4.

 Search the TechNet CD (or its online version through **www.microsoft. com**) and the *Windows NT Server Resource Kit* CD using the keywords "DDNS", "DNS", "Active Directory-integrated zone", and "DNS namespace".

WINS Design

· ·

Terms you'll need to understand:

✓ Network Basic Input/Output System (NetBIOS) namespace

✓ NetBIOS name server (NBNS)

✓ Windows Sockets (WinSock)

✓ Replication partners

✓ Spoke-and-hub design

✓ Convergence time

✓ Persistent connections

✓ Push replication

✓ Pull replication

✓ Tombstoning

Techniques you'll need to master:

✓ Understanding the architecture of Windows Internet Naming Service (WINS)

✓ Working with WINS name registration and resolution

✓ Designing an effective WINS replication strategy

✓ Protecting WINS traffic when using public networks

✓ Removing the WINS service from a network

Windows Internet Naming Service (WINS) translates computer names into IP addresses, just like Domain Name Service (DNS) does. The difference between the two services is the type of names that they translate into IP addresses: DNS translates Internet domain names, and WINS translates Network Basic Input/Output System (NetBIOS) names. (Chapter 2 provides an overview of the OSI model and the session-layer changes in Windows 2000.)

Until Windows 2000, Microsoft built its network infrastructure around NetBIOS, which caused a dual personality in its network architecture: If you wanted to use Internet services, you needed DNS for name resolution; if you wanted to use Microsoft services—such as sending a local print job—you needed WINS.

In Windows 2000, the dependence on NetBIOS is gone. Microsoft redesigned all of its core network services to use Windows Sockets (WinSock)—just like the Internet does—as the interface to the network instead of NetBIOS. In fact, in a purely Windows 2000 environment, NetBIOS and the use of NetBIOS names can be turned off completely. Yet, Microsoft still recommends the use of WINS in the Windows 2000 environment for the sake of backward compatibility. It is a time-consuming task to make a complete transformation to an all Windows 2000 environment. Also, some legacy applications may use NetBIOS instead of WinSock. Although NetBIOS went from a required service to a legacy service in one upgrade, WINS is still needed to support legacy clients and applications. Without WINS, the impact on a network can be severe.

WINS Basics

Until NetBIOS is no longer used in your network, you must understand why WINS is necessary for NetBIOS clients. Basically, NetBIOS just doesn't work as well as WinSock in a large network environment. The NetBIOS default name resolution—combined with the namespace that defines the rules for NetBIOS names—causes problems for networks with many nodes. By default, the design of NetBIOS works best in a small networking environment, and WINS allows NetBIOS clients to work in environments larger than just a LAN.

The NetBIOS Namespace

The NetBIOS namespace limits the size of the network on which it can be used. A namespace sets rules for naming computers. The NetBIOS namespace allows only 15 characters for a computer's name. Because each computer name must be unique from all others with which it communicates, you'll find that the possible permutations of a 15-character set are quickly exhausted in a network with tens of thousands of nodes, particularly if you keep the names friendly so that users can easily remember them.

Broadcasts on a Network

A limited namespace is not all that plagues NetBIOS computers on a large network. NetBIOS computers use broadcasting as the default method for resolving names to IP addresses. The problem is that broadcasts do not work well in a large network environment, because a broadcast is just that: a broadcast of a network packet that is not specifically aimed at one computer. Specifically addressed packets are much easier for a networked computer to see if they are intended for it or a different computer on the network. With a specifically addressed packet, a computer can quickly see if it should ignore or process the packet further to find out what data the packet contains.

If you receive mail addressed to you, you open it. If the mail is addressed to someone else, you don't need to be concerned with it. On the other hand, if you receive junk mail addressed to "occupant," you can be fairly sure it's not important and so you discard it. Broadcasts are like junk mail in that they are addressed to no computer in particular. But, because computers cannot throw away a broadcast without reading it the way you do junk mail, each computer must process the packet to find out if it contains data for that computer. It's easy to see how broadcast traffic clogs each computer's network adapter as it tries to process packets that it would be able to ignore if they were specifically addressed to another computer.

WINS reduces broadcasts by giving NetBIOS clients another method of name resolution. Instead of sending a broadcast when trying to locate another computer's IP address, the WINS client can send a directly addressed packet to the WINS server.

Routers and Broadcasts

The other bonus of using WINS instead of broadcasts for name resolution is that it allows name-resolution packets to pass through routers. Figure 6.1 shows how one network that adds a router—placing nodes on each side of the router—actually creates two separate networks. The router filters traffic by allowing only those packets addressed for the other side to pass through. Routers block broadcast

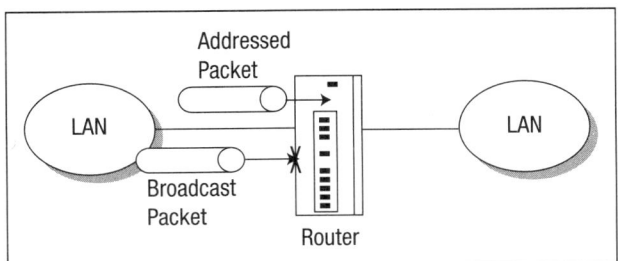

Figure 6.1   A router will allow a packet specifically addressed to a computer in the other part of the network through, but the router will block the NetBIOS broadcast with no specific address.

traffic, by default, by not allowing packets to pass through unless they are specifically addressed for the other side. Because packets sent to and from the WINS server are specifically addressed, the router allows them to pass through.

To fix the broadcast problem for NetBIOS clients, a NetBIOS name server (NBNS) is needed. WINS is Microsoft's version of an NBNS. WINS is still needed until all NetBIOS-dependent clients and applications are replaced on a network. Removing WINS prematurely will cause previous version of Windows and any other NetBIOS clients to resort back to broadcasts for name resolution.

WINS-Provided Services

The design of WINS has always been dynamic and this, of course, has not changed in Windows 2000 WINS. The WINS client software is automatically installed when TCP/IP is installed on a Windows client. The only other setting that is needed for a Microsoft WINS client to work is the IP address of a WINS server. The WINS server IP address can be entered manually or be handed out to the clients by the DHCP server. Once the client has the IP address of the WINS server, it uses the WINS service automatically and broadcasts only if other name-resolution methods (like WINS) fail.

During boot up, a WINS client registers its names with WINS. This registration happens automatically with no intervention from the user or network administrator. A client computer can actually make five or more registrations, not because it has that many computer names but because the WINS service registers more than just generic computer names. WINS registers computer names based on the services that they provide to the network. All Windows 2000 computers will register a computer name for each of the workstation, server, and messenger services as well as the username. Also, a client computer will register as a member of a domain. A domain controller can make 8 to 10 registrations to WINS because it provides more services to the network than a client system does. WINS differentiates between registrations by looking at the 16th character of a NetBIOS name. And this is the reason that NetBIOS computer names can have only 15 characters: The 16th character is reserved to identify the service for which the client is registering. This makes WINS more versatile for the network. A WINS client can query WINS for the IP address of a domain controller or ask for a member of a certain domain or even a username instead of a computer name. All are registered and tracked in the WINS database.

Placing and Configuring WINS Servers

Just like other network services, WINS needs to be designed on paper to create an effective and problem-free WINS solution. Because of the nature of WINS resolution, the placement of servers and the configuration of replication partners can make large differences in the performance of the service.

WINS Name-Resolution Process

Like DNS clients, WINS clients use a query to ask the WINS server for a name-to-IP address translation. The WINS server, like the DNS server, checks its local database of name-to-IP address mappings to resolve the query. But the similarities between the query processes for each end there. DNS servers were designed to work in a WAN environment. To accommodate a large number of computers, the DNS system allows for DNS servers to refer queries to other DNS servers in order to completely resolve them. This procedure is referred to as a *partitioned database*. Figure 6.2 shows an example of a how a partitioned database works in a WAN environment. When referring to the DNS system, it is assumed that different DNS servers will have only a portion of the DNS entries and that no one DNS server will have all of the possible entries throughout the network on which it is working. Partitioning the DNS database is explained in detail in Chapter 5 of this book.

Because NetBIOS names are limited to 15 characters, the service was not designed to assume a partitioned database. A WINS server is expected to resolve the query, and it does not ask other WINS servers for help. This means that one WINS server must have all possible answers for the entire network in its local database that maps names to IP addresses. Figure 6.3 shows that a WINS server needs to contain all possible records to answer any query.

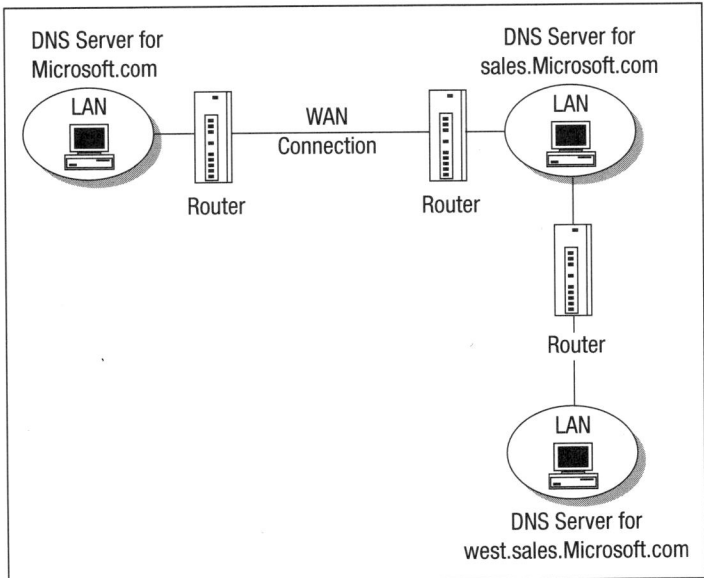

Figure 6.2   The DNS database for Microsoft.com needs to contain records only for its own domain. The DNS servers for sales.Microsoft.com and west.sales.Microsoft.com also need to contain records only for their own domains. Each DNS database can refer queries for records that reside in a different portion of the database—on another server—to that other server.

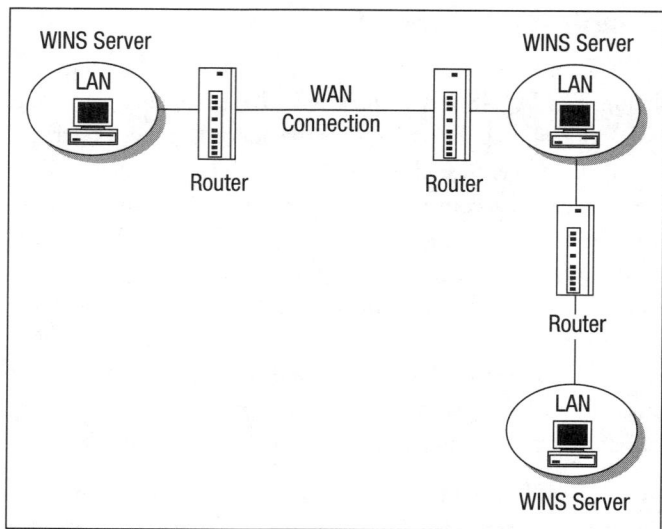

Figure 6.3   In the same network configuration as Figure 6.2, all WINS servers must contain all records possible in the entire network. They cannot contain only those records for the LAN on which they reside.

A Network Diagram

Because good designs start from a high level, a network diagram is essential when designing any network service. You should include the following items in your network diagram when planning for WINS:

➤ LAN locations

➤ WAN connections, including speed of each connection

➤ Number of users at each location

➤ Location of current WINS servers

When designing a service, you must also plan for capacity. You must note concentrations of users so that their queries can be spread out among different WINS servers. Because WINS servers do not refer queries to each other, you'll first need to work out a plan for the replication of WINS records between the servers. This plan will determine the placement of the WINS server as well as the replication relationships.

Future Plans for the Network

Before designing begins, you must ask the question: What will the need for WINS be in six months? A year? If a network is migrating from legacy Windows systems to an all Windows 2000 environment, how long will the migration take?

Are any legacy applications needed that also use NetBIOS? If an analysis of the network shows that a full migration will be completed in one year, then add a plan to disable NetBIOS over TCP/IP on your network and decommission your WINS servers. You can find details for what steps to include in this process at the end of this chapter.

How Many WINS Servers Are Needed?

A frequent mistake of WINS designs is the implementation of too many WINS servers. One WINS server can support 10,000 clients, and this capability should be used as part of your design. Even if one physical location has fewer than 10,000 clients, a backup WINS server should be implemented to provide fault tolerance, in case one goes down or a network connection becomes unavailable. Remember that adding this second WINS server is only for fault tolerance: Only one WINS server is required if there are fewer than 10,000 WINS clients and fault tolerance is not an issue. If WINS resolution is not performing well, then the answer may be to upgrade the hardware of the existing WINS server rather than to add more servers. Adding more WINS servers just adds more replication traffic to the network.

Unlike DNS, WINS does not come with guidelines to place a server at each physical location. The placement decision rests on many different factors such as the bandwidth availability between locations and the number of clients on either side of the connection. The biggest factor is how much the WINS server will be used. Remember that a connection between two Windows 2000 computers does not need WINS. For this connection, DNS is the primary name-resolution service. However, connections between legacy Windows systems and Windows 2000 will need WINS. How much traffic does WINS generate? To calculate how much traffic you can expect, you must first understand the different types of WINS traffic.

WINS Traffic

Although WINS generates very little traffic when compared to other services on the network, even a small amount of traffic can have a big impact when designing a service to use WAN connections. Traffic from the WINS service can be of four different types: registrations, queries, refreshes, and releases. Table 6.1 details the four types.

Even though Windows 2000 clients do not use WINS by default, they will need to use WINS when connecting to a NetBIOS resource. Because all Microsoft client operating systems—even Windows 2000 computers—are WINS clients by default, they will register, renew, and release their NetBIOS names also by default. Until WINS is not needed on the network, this traffic will still be on the network.

Table 6.1	The four types of WINS traffic.	
Type	**When Traffic Occurs**	**Description**
Registration	Boot up	A WINS client registers its records and gets them created and added to the WINS database. This is the most traffic generated by WINS. It generates two packets per service registered.
Query	Connecting to NetBIOS resource	A NetBIOS client connecting to a NetBIOS resource queries the WINS server for a name-to-IP address mapping. Queries can also be made to contact a domain controller or other needed resource on the network. This traffic is just two packets per query.
Refresh	By default, every three days	Because WINS registration is dynamic, WINS clients need to renew their registrations to keep the WINS database from getting out of date. The default renewal interval is six days. WINS clients refresh their registrations by default at 50% of the renewal interval. This traffic is just two packets per refresh.
Release	Shutdown	Part of the shutdown procedure is for a client to release its registered names from the WINS database. If a client loses power suddenly and does not go through shutdown, then the names can remain in the WINS database even though they are no longer valid. This generates as much traffic as a registration with two packets per name released.

Spoke-and-Hub Design

Client-to-server traffic is not the only type of traffic that the WINS service generates. Because WINS servers must have the answer when queried by a client, replication of WINS records is the most important factor in WINS server placement. The servers must replicate their records to each other so that each database contains the records of every WINS client on the network. Server-to-server traffic is generated when WINS servers replicate changes to the database to each other. Because only changes are replicated, each replication event is usually small. The only design that accomplishes this replication without causing unnecessary stress on the network is the spoke and hub. It keeps the WINS database up to date and correct.

One Physical Location

If only one physical location needs to be supported, the WINS design can be kept very simple. Because only one WINS server is needed per 10,000 WINS clients, one physical location may allow for a low number of WINS servers. Even if there are fewer than 10,000 WINS clients, at least one other WINS server will be needed for fault tolerance. Replication is simple to set up with just two WINS servers: The WINS servers will simply replicate to each other.

In a large, single-location environment with more than 10,000 clients, you may need more than two WINS servers. Using an example of 50,000 users, Figure 6.4 shows the spoke-and-hub design needed to set up WINS replication correctly. One WINS server is designated as the hub for replication purposes. In the diagram, WINS1 is the hub. The rest of the WINS servers are configured to replicate to the WINS1 hub. These WINS servers are the spokes, just like spokes in a wheel join at the hub. The spoke-and-hub configuration allows WINS1 (the hub) to gather the changes from the other WINS servers and to replicate these changes out to its replication partners (the spokes) in the least amount of time.

Adjusting for WAN Locations

In a WAN network environment, the spoke-and-hub design still needs to be used. The design is just as simple as it is for a single-location network. Each physical location should be set up as Figure 6.4 shows, with one WINS server chosen as the hub and the rest of the servers serving as spokes. In a multiple-location network, each of the individual hubs will become part of a spoke-and-hub design for the WAN environment. One hub server for a physical location will be chosen as the hub for the WAN. Each of the other local hub servers will then serve as spokes to the WAN hub. Figure 6.5 shows an example of the spoke-and-hub configuration for a WAN environment. WINS1Sea is the hub for the Seattle location as well as for the entire WAN environment. WINS1Den is the hub for the Denver location and a spoke for the WAN environment. WINS1Atl is the

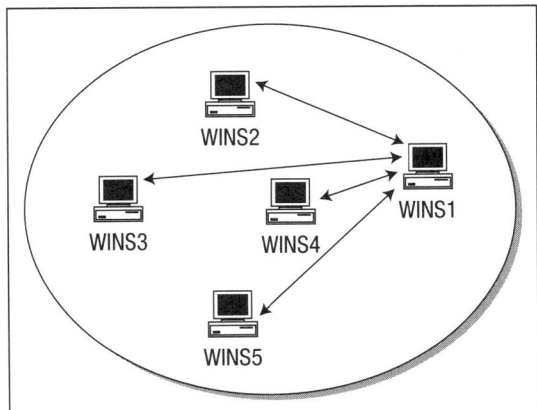

Figure 6.4   Spoke-and-hub design for a single physical location.

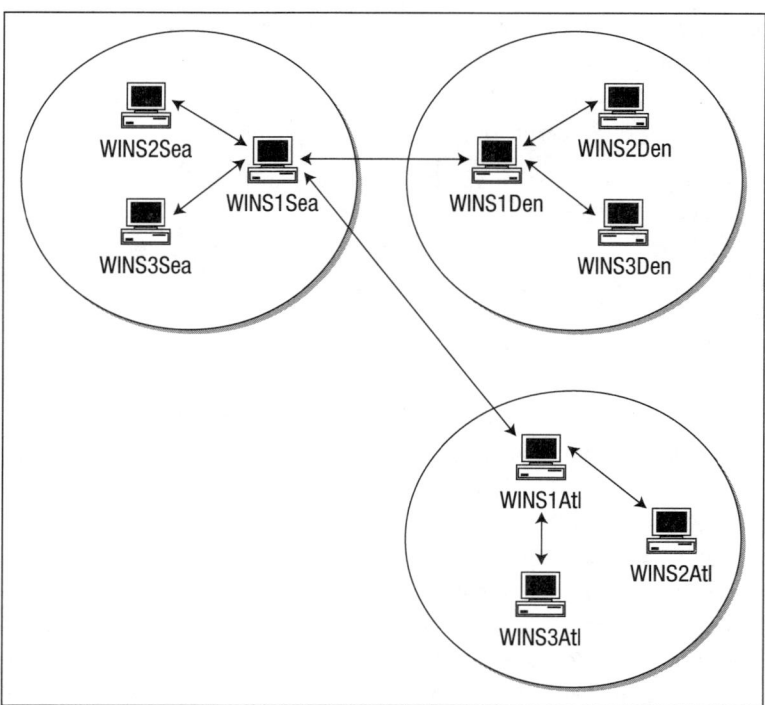

Figure 6.5 Spoke-and-hub design for multiple physical locations.

hub for the Atlanta environment and a spoke for the WAN environment. This design allows for replication of the WINS database throughout the WAN without causing unnecessary traffic or delays getting the changes out.

Understanding WINS Replication

Designing WINS database replication is the biggest factor in determining where to place the WINS server(s). But replication involves more than just placing the servers in the right location. Because WINS replication sends only changes to the database (and only to its configured replication partners), configuring these partners and their relationships also plays an important role in keeping the WINS database current.

Convergence Time

Convergence time is the time it takes to replicate a change to the WINS database throughout the enterprise. How long a designer is willing to wait for convergence has an enormous impact on a WINS design. Part of an effective WINS solution is calculating the convergence time and trying to minimize it. The convergence time is calculated with a worst-case scenario in mind, as if a change just misses a replication interval each time it reaches a new WINS server. But, before you can calculate the convergence time, you need to understand replication times and the types of replications.

Push and Pull Replication

Setting up a spoke-and-hub relationship between WINS servers involves not only the designation of spokes and hubs, but also the configuration of the servers as replication partners. WINS servers replicate their records to each other through a push or pull method. Each partner uses a different method—push or pull—to cause a replication event. A push method uses a certain number of changes as its interval. When configuring a push partner, you can set the number of changes that trigger a replication. A new feature in Windows 2000 WINS is the allowance of persistent connections. This means that the session set up for communication between replication partners does not close when the replication is complete. Maintaining an open session reduces the network overhead of replication. Because of persistent connections, the update count for a push partner can be set to zero, which causes every change to be sent immediately. With persistent connections, the session remains open between replication partners, and the only network traffic is the actual replication information. Microsoft recommends that push partners be configured with zero as the update interval, if persistent connections are being used.

Pull partners use a set amount of time for a replication interval instead of a specified number of changes. This is the recommended setting if WAN servers are separated by a slow or heavily used WAN link. Because WAN connections usually are short on available bandwidth, a pull relationship allows control over when the replication occurs. The amount of time between pull replications should be set based upon two factors: the amount of time that you're willing to wait for convergence and the amount of available bandwidth between WAN connections.

The recommended setting for WINS servers at the same physical location is to configure them as both push and pull partners. Doing so increases the consistency in the WINS database. This relationship is referred to as a push/pull relationship.

 Automatic discovery is a feature that allows WINS servers to automatically discover replication partners. Do not use this feature on a network with more than three WINS servers. Because automatic discovery configures replication partners in a push/pull relationship, it does not configure a spoke-and-hub relationship that would be needed in a large WINS environment. Automatic discovery is best only for small networks with high-speed LAN connections, in which a push/pull relationship among all WINS servers is appropriate.

Calculating Convergence Time

Now that you've placed all the servers and configured all the relationships, you can calculate the convergence time. Figure 6.6 uses the setting in Figure 6.5 with replication relationships configured between servers. Because convergence time is based on a worst-case scenario, you'll use the pull interval to calculate it. The WINS servers within the LANs are using a pull interval of 15 minutes, which sends a change to the hub server in the LAN every 15 minutes. Because of the spoke-and-hub configuration of replication partners, the convergence time within the LAN is kept to 30 minutes: 15 minutes to send the change to the hub server and 15 minutes to send that change out to the other spoke servers.

To calculate convergence time for the WAN, we must add the time it takes to pull a change across the enterprise. Figure 6.7 shows a WAN environment with three locations. Atlanta and Denver are configured as spokes to the Seattle WINS server to keep WAN convergence time to a minimum. Because the WAN pull replication time is set to 60 minutes, a change coming from a WAN server would take two hours to be replicated out to the whole enterprise. The LAN pull time is again 15 minutes. Add 15 minutes for the change to come from a LAN server and 15 minutes for it to be replicated to a local WINS server from its hub. This results in a total of two hours and 30 minutes for the network convergence time.

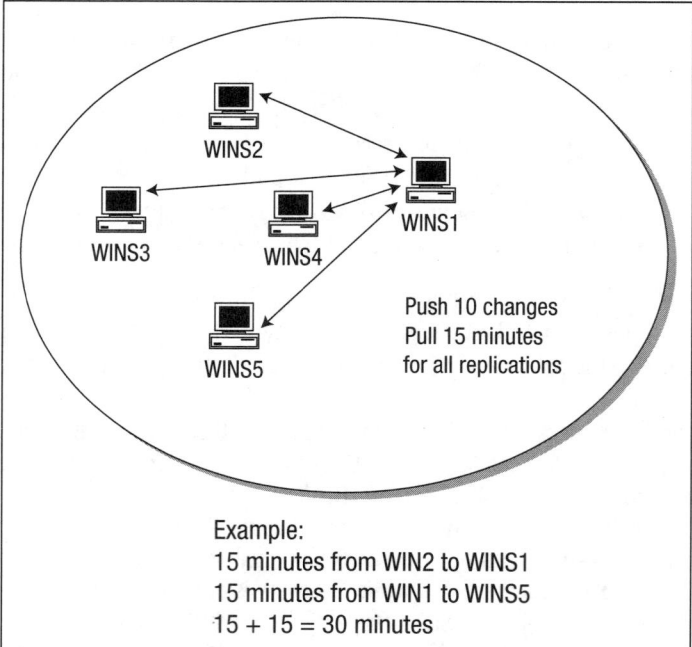

Figure 6.6 Calculating convergence time in a LAN.

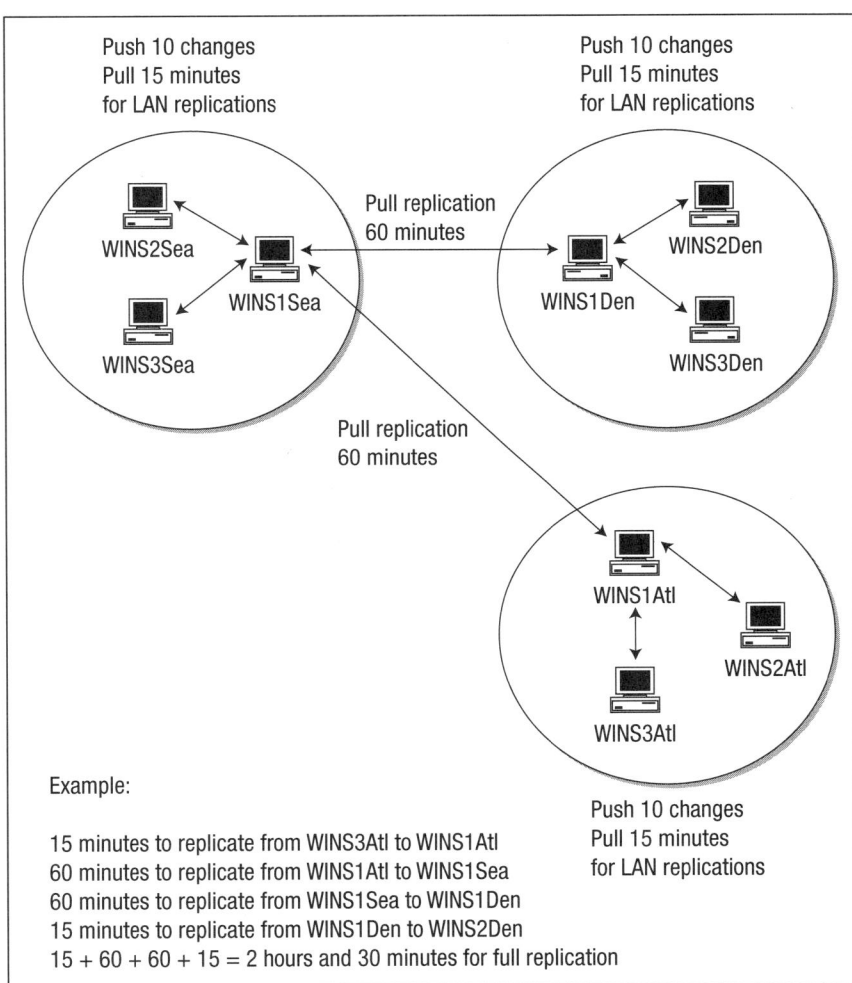

Push 10 changes
Pull 15 minutes
for LAN replications

Push 10 changes
Pull 15 minutes
for LAN replications

WINS2Sea

Pull replication
60 minutes

WINS2Den

WINS1Sea

WINS1Den

WINS3Sea

WINS3Den

Pull replication
60 minutes

WINS1Atl

WINS2Atl

WINS3Atl

Example:

15 minutes to replicate from WINS3Atl to WINS1Atl
60 minutes to replicate from WINS1Atl to WINS1Sea
60 minutes to replicate from WINS1Sea to WINS1Den
15 minutes to replicate from WINS1Den to WINS2Den
15 + 60 + 60 + 15 = 2 hours and 30 minutes for full replication

Push 10 changes
Pull 15 minutes
for LAN replications

Figure 6.7   Calculating convergence time in a WAN.

Configuring WINS Clients

After you've placed and configured the WINS servers, you'll probably find configuring WINS clients simple. WINS clients have settings for a primary and for multiple secondary WINS servers. Previously, Windows 2000 WINS clients could only have one primary and one secondary WINS server. The purpose of a secondary server is to provide an alternative in case the primary WINS server becomes unavailable. This means that, for previous versions of WINS clients, if both WINS servers are unavailable at the time of a query or registration, then the WINS client will have to resort to broadcasts. Windows 2000 WINS clients can accept up to 12 secondary servers. This means that if the primary WINS server is unavailable, then the WINS client can contact each of the secondary servers from the top to the bottom of the list until one responds to its requests, which allows for more fault tolerance if part of the network or servers becomes unavailable. The WINS client has a longer list of WINS servers to try before having to resort to broadcasts to resolve a NetBIOS name.

Support for Non-WINS NetBIOS Clients

Supporting a legacy environment may involve designing a system for NetBIOS clients that are not WINS clients. This could be a Microsoft client that has a really out-of-date operating system or a NetBIOS client that is not a Microsoft operating system. The important thing is to get the client into the WINS database. Because the client can't place itself in the database, the solution is to manually create a static entry in the WINS database. This allows for other clients to get to the non-WINS client through WINS, and thus avoiding the broadcast.

Using a WINS Proxy Agent

To support the non-WINS client fully, WINS proxy agents should be placed in every subnet. A WINS proxy agent helps fill non-WINS client queries. When a non-WINS client broadcasts to find a computer on the network, the computer can't answer if it is not on the same subnet. A WINS proxy agent will hear the non-WINS request and make a request of its own to the WINS server. After receiving the answer from the WINS server, the WINS proxy agent then sends the IP address to the broadcasting non-WINS client. Only one WINS proxy agent is needed per subnet.

Improving Performance in a WINS Network

The spoke-and-hub replication design makes new records available to the network in the least amount of time. Also, client traffic from WINS is only one packet from the client and one packet in response from the WINS server. Because the spoke-and-hub design keeps replication traffic efficient, the best way to help performance is to keep the WINS database free of out-of-date records. Stale records add to replication traffic and cause the database to search through more records than is needed to answer a query. But, before improving this process, it is necessary to understand how records are removed from the WINS database.

Keeping the WINS Database Current

Because WINS uses automatic registration, one possible problem is inconsistencies in the database. If a client loses power and doesn't send a release to the WINS server, then that entry is still in the WINS server, even though it is no longer valid. Out-of-date records cause a performance drain by making the WINS database larger. Microsoft gives a WINS administrator several tools to control stale records and keep the database current and accurate.

The Importance of Tombstoning

Before a record is removed from the WINS database, it goes through a few stages. Immediately after registration from a client, a record is valid for six days. If the client does not refresh the record during that time, it is considered to be released. At this point, it is not removed from the WINS database. Instead, it enters a stage called the *extinction interval*. This interval, by default, lasts for four days. At the end of the extinction interval, the record is considered to be "tombstoned," and it enters a new interval called the *extinction timeout*, which lasts for six more days. At the end of the extinction timeout, the record is deleted from the WINS database. Although it sounds extensive, the design of this system is necessary for a WINS environment in which replication is used.

Tombstoning allows the record to be removed from other WINS servers instead of being replicated back around the system. Remember that WINS servers update each other with records that the other server does not have. The point of tombstoning a record is to get it removed from not only the server from which it originated, but also from all of the servers in which it may exist. If tombstoning was not used, a deleted record would simply be replicated back to its original server from a replication partner. Records would never go away. They would just keep showing up at the next replication interval.

Windows 2000 WINS has a new feature that allows manual tombstoning of a record. When an administrator wants to delete a record, it can be marked for tombstoning to keep it from coming back through replication.

Consistency Checks

To ensure that the WINS database is current with others on the network, the Windows 2000 WINS service allows for a consistency check of the database. A consistency check will take a set of records from one WINS server in the environment and compare it to the same set of records from another WINS server to see if they are identical. You can select whether consistency checks will be performed in the properties of a WINS server and even select how often it will be performed.

 A consistency check is a bandwidth-intensive service. Microsoft recommends that consistency checks be performed only when the administrator believes there is a problem. If you decide a consistency check is needed, it should be performed at a time of light traffic, especially when using WAN connections. It is best to perform consistency checks during the night or whenever bandwidth use is at its lowest.

Security in a WINS Environment

WINS security is an issue if WAN connections are over the Internet. Windows 2000 allows for WAN connections between servers to be public networks, such as the Internet, by allowing for the encryption of sensitive information. Public networks are a less expensive way to implement WAN connections, but sensitive information like IP addresses and computer names sent in a WINS replication needs to be protected. WINS, like other Windows 2000 services, integrates into the security solutions that are used when WAN connections involve public networks.

WINS over a VPN

The safest way to configure sensitive information for transmission over public networks is a Virtual Private Network (VPN). Fortunately, this is made easy with the Windows 2000 WINS service, because it integrates with VPN security and encryption. IPSec is considered to be the strongest VPN encryption protocol and is best to use for sensitive information like WINS replication. For more information on VPN configuration, see Chapter 9 of this book.

Using WINS in a Screened Subnet

WINS can also be used in a screened subnet. External clients can use the Internet to access a company's internal resources using inexpensive lines. If these external clients need NetBIOS resolution, a WINS server may need to be placed in a screened subnet to protect it from Internet exposure. A screened subnet uses firewalls to isolate services that are needed by external clients. Two firewalls are needed to protect the internal network from Internet exposure. Any information that passes the inside firewall (going out from the internal network) should be considered information that can be compromised. If the information is sensitive, it needs to be encrypted. Use encryption for replication traffic between the internal network and the screened subnet. It's best to configure the WINS server inside the screened subnet as a pull partner pulling from the internal WINS server (see Figure 6.8). Screened subnets are explained in detail in Chapter 5 of this book, and firewalls are covered in Chapter 12.

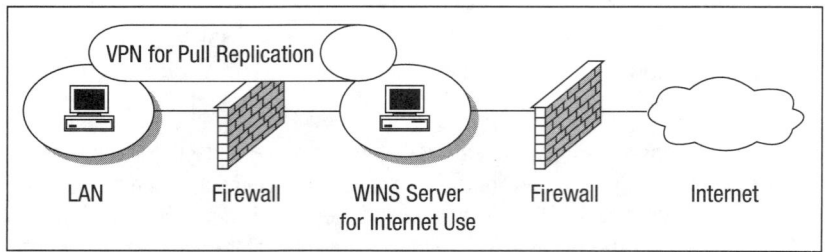

Figure 6.8   Screened subnet with WINS inside.

Taking WINS off the Network

If the plan is to go to an all Windows 2000 environment, a good WINS design should consider the eventual removal of NetBIOS from the network. Once all of the NetBIOS clients are replaced, NetBIOS can be disabled and the WINS servers can be decommissioned.

Disabling NetBIOS on the Network

After all of the NetBIOS dependent clients are removed (or replaced with Windows 2000 clients), NetBIOS needs to be disabled on the network. The Windows 2000 clients were originally configured as WINS clients, and you have two ways to change this: manually and by using DHCP. To make the change manually, you must remove the IP address of the primary and all secondary WINS servers from the network settings of each client. This is a large task if all clients are manually configured for IP addresses and for WINS. Another, much easier method is to use DHCP. First, remove the WINS options 44 and 46 that configure WINS clients to use WINS and to give the IP addresses of the WINS primary and secondary servers. In addition, the Windows 2000 DHCP server has an option number 1 that disables the use of NetBIOS over TCP/IP (NetBT) on the network. Use this option in a Windows 2000 network in which all of the clients have been upgraded and NetBIOS is no longer needed on a network. DHCP is covered thoroughly in Chapter 4 of this book.

Decommissioning the WINS Servers

The last step in removing NetBIOS and all related services from a network is to decommission the WINS servers. It will be much easier on the network and the administrator if this is done correctly. Microsoft recommends using the manual tombstoning feature of Windows 2000 WINS to delete and tombstone the WINS records before removing the WINS service from the server. Doing so lets the other WINS servers know to remove the records from their databases rather than trying to replicate them back.

Practice Questions

Case Study

The Widgets Company is based in Seattle, WA. It has a manufacturing plant in Denver, CO, and a distribution facility in Atlanta, GA. Each facility has its own separate IT department. The corporate offices are located in Seattle and have 210 hosts. The manufacturing plant in Denver has 205 hosts, and the distribution center in Atlanta has 56 hosts. The company is currently upgrading to Windows 2000 but lacks expertise in this operating system.

Current WAN Structure

The company's network has three locations.

Proposed WAN Structure

No additional locations are planned.

Current WAN Connectivity

Currently all locations are connected through a 56Kbps Frame Relay connection.

Proposed WAN Connectivity

No upgrades are planned to increase the bandwidth of the current connections. The company is hoping to design the network services so that they will work with the current available bandwidth.

Current State of Network Administration

The IT department has three separate divisions in each physical location. The network is divided into three Windows NT 4 domains with no trust relationships configured. Each location is separate and distinct from the others.

Future Plans for Network Administration

Since the network is being upgraded to Windows 2000, the decision has been made to create one Active Directory domain with Windows 2000. The IT department will be centralized in Seattle at the corporate headquarters. Individual administrators will provide support at each of the remote locations, but most services will be centralized in Seattle. The centralization of the IT department will take at least eight months to complete.

Company Windows 2000 Goal

The client computers are in the process of being upgraded from Windows NT 4 Workstation to Windows 2000 Professional. Although the servers are still using Windows NT 4, the plan is to upgrade the NT 4 servers to Windows 2000 servers.

Question 1

> A network administrator for the Seattle network decides that he will not need WINS since the network is being upgraded to Windows 2000. He decides to not install the service on the Seattle network. He also decides that now is a good time to disable NetBIOS on his network. What is the quickest way to accomplish this?
>
> ○ a. Use DHCP with option 44, 46, and 1
>
> ○ b. Use DHCP without option 44 or 46
>
> ○ c. Use DHCP without option 44 or 46, but add option 1
>
> ○ d. Do not use DHCP

Answer c is correct. Using DHCP is the quickest way to disable NetBIOS on a network. Because option 44 and 46 are used to set up WINS clients on the network, these options should not be used. Option 1, which is Microsoft specific, disables NBT on the network.

Question 2

> Now that NetBIOS has been disabled on the Seattle network, what problems might occur over the next six months as the clients get upgraded to Windows 2000? [Check all correct answers]
>
> ❑ a. Slow network connections
>
> ❑ b. Increased broadcast traffic on the network
>
> ❑ c. Clients unable to connect to resources on their local subnet
>
> ❑ d. Clients unable to connect to resources outside of their local subnet

Answers a, b, and d are correct. Because the network administrator has upgraded only the servers, all of the clients are still Windows NT 4 workstations and thus dependent on NetBIOS, which they use to access file and print services. Without WINS, the clients will be forced to broadcast to find resources. Although this allows the clients to connect to local resources, it will not work for resources outside of the local subnet.

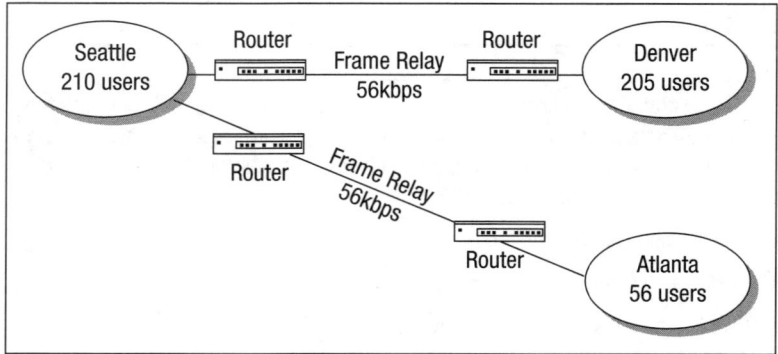

Figure 6.9 Diagram for Questions 3 and 4.

Question 3

It has been decided that a WINS solution is needed for the entire network. Based on Figure 6.9, how many WINS servers are required?

○ a. One

○ b. Two

○ c. Three

○ d. Four

Answer a is correct. This is a tricky question because the focus for WINS design is often on fault tolerance and performance. Because one WINS server can support 10,000 clients, one server is all that is required. A question like this may be asked because designers tend to overdo it when implementing WINS and add too many WINS servers.

Question 4

It is decided that WINS must be available 24 hours a day. Based on the diagram in Figure 6.9, how many WINS servers are required for the network?

○ a. One

○ b. Two

○ c. Three

○ d. Four

Answer b is correct. If WINS must be available at all times, another WINS server is needed. Even though there is a WAN connection, there's no requirement or recommendation for a WINS server to be placed on either side of a WAN link. No more than two WINS servers are needed.

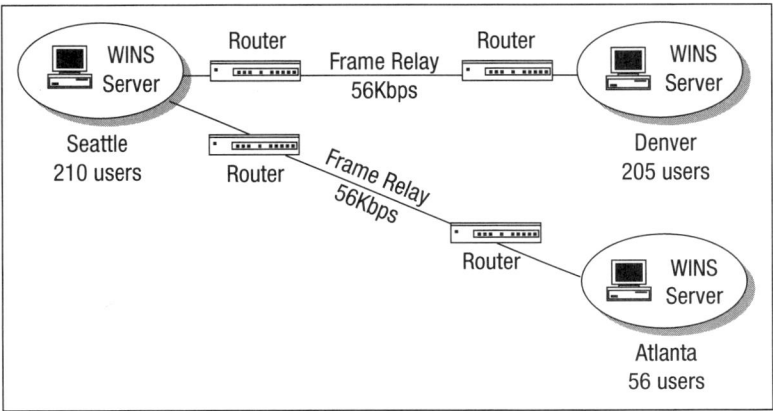

Figure 6.10   Diagram for Questions 5, 6, and 7.

Question 5

As shown in Fiure 6.10, the WINS service is set up by adding WINS servers to each location according to the following diagram. Each client's primary WINS server is configured as the local WINS server on the client's LAN. Replication between the new WINS servers is not configured. How will this affect access to the network? [Check all correct answers]

❑ a. Clients will not be able to access remote resources.

❑ b. Clients will be able access remote resources.

❑ c. Clients will be able to access local resources.

❑ d. Clients will not be able to access local resources.

Answers a and c are correct. Without replication configured between the WINS servers, each WINS server will have only the entries of the local LAN. When a client asks for a remote resource outside of the LAN, the record will not exist in the local WINS server.

Question 6

Replication needs to be configured between the WINS servers on the network. On the diagram in Figure 6.10, draw the best configuration for replication for this network.

The answer is:

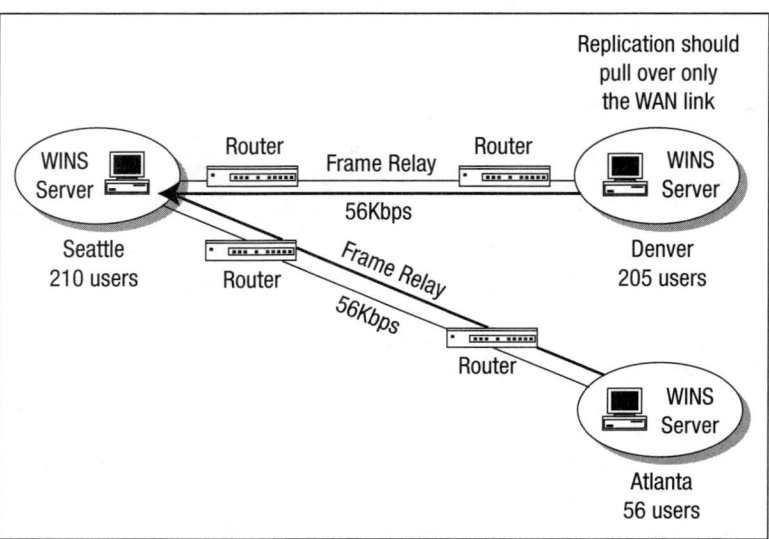

Replication needs to be set up with a spoke-and-hub design. Designate one server as the hub server and the rest of the WINS servers as spoke servers. Set up replication only from spoke to hub.

Question 7

In the diagram in Figure 6.10, which server must be designated as the hub server?

- ○ a. WINS1
- ○ b. WINS2
- ○ c. WINS3
- ○ d. It does not matter
- ○ e. All of the WINS servers

Answer d is correct. Only one WINS server is needed as a hub, and any WINS server can be designated as the hub server.

Question 8

One morning, at the Seattle network an administrator removes a WINS record from the WINS database, but that afternoon, while in the WINS console, she sees that the record is back. Why?

○ a. Replication added the record back to the database.

○ b. Tombstoning brought the record back to the database.

○ c. Restoring from backup brought the record back to the database.

○ d. The WINS server is corrupted.

Answer a is correct. Records that are manually deleted can show back up, because they are replicated back from replication partners. The record will come back if it is not tombstoned before deleting it. A corrupt server and a backup restore did not happen in this scenario.

Question 9

How can the problem from the previous question be fixed? [Check all correct answers]

❏ a. Delete the record again.

❏ b. Turn off replication.

❏ c. Delete WINS database and restore from backup.

❏ d. Manually tombstone the record.

Answers a and d are correct. When a record is manually deleted, it must also be manually tombstoned. Doing so deletes the record from the databases of replication partners, thus preventing the record from being replicated back to the original server. Just deleting the record again will cause the record to come back in the next replication. Replication is a needed service for a WAN location. The same problem will occur if the WINS database is restored from backup.

Question 10

Why is spoke-and-hub the recommended configuration for WINS replication? [Check all correct answers]

□ a. To keep the WINS database from becoming corrupted

□ b. To keep convergence time to minimum

□ c. To keep the WINS replication traffic low

□ d. To keep deleted records from reappearing in the database

Answers a, b, and c are correct. The spoke-and-hub configuration for replication helps to keep the WINS database from becoming corrupted. Also, with spoke-and-hub the replication of a record can be traced and timed to ensure that it is replicated out to other WINS servers in the least amount of time. WINS replication traffic is only from spoke to hub and hub back to spoke which keeps WINS replication traffic low. Deleted records can only be kept from coming back by tombstoning them. WINS replication configuration does not affect the need for tombstoning a record when it needs to be deleted from the system.

Need to Know More?

 www.microsoft.com/NTServer/nts/techdetails/techspecs/WINSwp98. **asp** *Microsoft Windows NT 4.0 Windows Internet Naming Service (WINS) Architecture and Capacity Planning.* Microsoft Corporation, Redmond, WA, 1996. This Microsoft white paper explains its implementation of WINS in Windows NT 4. This paper contains more about convergence time and Windows basics than does the Windows 2000 WINS paper.

 www.microsoft.com/WINDOWS2000/library/howitworks/ communications/nameadrmgmt/wins.asp *Microsoft Windows 2000 Windows Internet Naming Service (WINS) Overview.* Microsoft Corporation, Redmond, WA, 1999. This Microsoft white paper focuses mostly on the changes in the Windows 2000 implementation of WINS.

 Read the WINS help available on a Windows 2000 server that has the WINS service loaded. "Understanding WINS," "Planning WINS networks," and "Migrating from WINS to DNS" contain many hard-to-find hints and advice.

 Search the TechNet CD (or its online version through **support.microsoft. com/directory**) using the keywords "WINS," "WINS convergence," "WINS replication," "tombstoning," and "disabling NetBIOS."

NAT Protocol Design

Terms you'll need to understand:

✓ Network address Translation (NAT)

✓ Public network

✓ Private network

Techniques you'll need to master:

✓ Implementing NAT

✓ Making NAT secure

✓ Improving NAT performance

This chapter introduces you to the implementation of the Network Address Translation (NAT) in a Windows 2000 network infrastructure. You'll learn about the NAT protocol and how to use it to design a network that enhances and makes secure the Windows 2000 operating system.

NAT Overview

Network Address Translation (NAT) is the protocol used to hide the TCP/IP settings of a private network from a public network. A private network is what a company uses internally (with all of its associated hardware such as the cabling, hubs, and routers within the company's buildings). The public network is the Internet, which spans the globe and to which everyone is able to connect.

NAT was originally implemented on routers as a hardware solution to the problem of the dwindling stock of numbers that were available for IP addresses. Now, the NAT service is included with Windows 2000 servers to function as a NAT router.

A problem arises when a private company wants to enable access from its private network to the Internet: The connection allows anyone on the Internet to determine the TCP/IP configuration for the business's internal network. The private network is thus open to persons who may try to illegally access the company's data or equipment.

NAT also allows a company to use unregistered IP addresses within the internal network and to have only a few registered IP addresses for access to the Internet. If private and public IP addresses exist in a one-to-one ratio, IP Routing can be used. However, NAT is used if the IP addresses on the private network outnumber the few registered public addresses—a many-to-few ratio and no enhanced Internet access performance is needed (in this case Proxy should be used, see Chapter 8).

In Windows 2000, NAT can be implemented only under the Routing and Remote Access that is covered in Chapter 9.

NAT Implementation

Implementing NAT is a little more complex than DHCP or DNS. Because NAT handles both DHCP and DNS resolution, it incorporates a little of both services.

Understanding NAT's function is the most important issue in designing a Windows 2000 network infrastructure. Understanding NAT's function will let you determine where to place NAT and how to make it secure. The main issue is when to use NAT or when to use Proxy Server or IP Forwarding for different design issues.

Installing NAT

To install NAT, open Routing And Remote Access under Administrative Tools on the Start menu. Right click on the server name in the left pane:

1. Select Configure And Enable Routing And Remote Access.

2. Select Next from the Configure And Enable Routing And Remote Access Wizard.

3. Select Internet Connection Server from the list as shown in Figure 7.1.

4. Choose Set Up A Router With The Network Address Translation (NAT) Routing Protocol as shown in Figure 7.2.

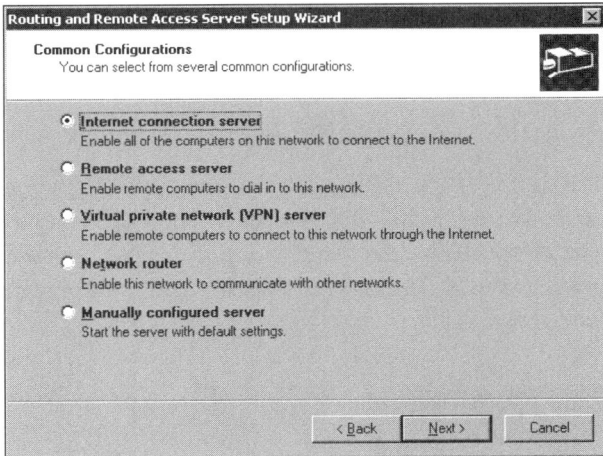

Figure 7.1   Routing and Remote Access configurations.

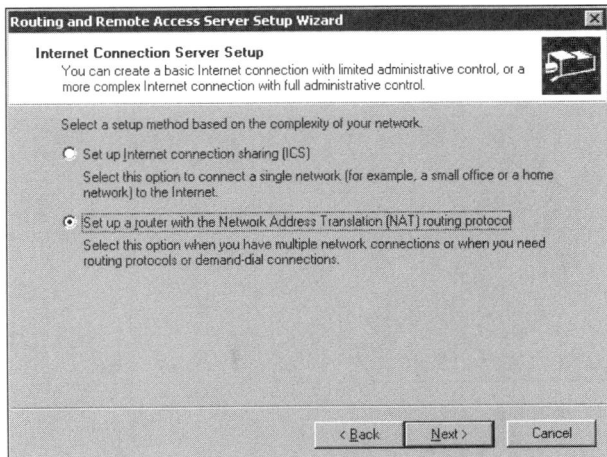

Figure 7.2   Internet server connection setup.

5. Select the type of connection to the Internet such as a modem, in a multi-homed computer, or a device for demand-dial access. (This can also be a Virtual Private Network, or VPN, as discussed later in this chapter.)

Note: Modems and modem banks must be configured for demand-dial connections.

Configuring NAT

Once the wizard finishes the setup, select server name in the left pane and IP Routing in the right pane in the Routing and Remote Access Microsoft Management Console (MMC), and then:

1. Right-click on Network Address Translation.

2. Select Properties.

3. From the dialog box that appears, select the Address Assignment tab, as shown in Figure 7.3.

Here is where you'll assign an IP address scheme for your private network.

The DHCP and DHCP Relay Agent Services cannot be running on the same network. NAT will offer IP addresses to the DHCP clients. The DNS and default gateway address is the IP address for the network card in the NAT system that is connected to the private network. Because NAT doesn't have a relay agent, it doesn't function on a routed network.

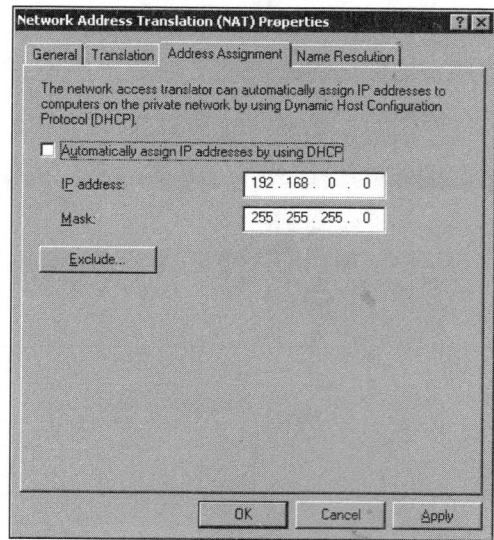

Figure 7.3 The NAT Address Assignment tab.

 Addresses can also be used from the Automatic Private IP Addressing (APIPA). The interface on the private-network side is assigned an APIPA address.

Select the Automatically Assign Ip Addresses By Using DHCP checkbox and configure the IP scope. Select the Exclude button to enter exclusions for the scope. You can also specify to resolve DNS names through the NAT system by forwarding the request to a private or public DNS server. (This is accomplished under the Name Resolution tab.) However, this will not allow a separate DNS to handle name resolution directly; the NAT server must forward it acting as a DNS proxy.

 On a NAT network, the NAT system will replace the DHCP services. The network cannot be routed, so DHCP relay agents cannot be used either. The DNS service is handled differently as noted under "NAT and DNS".

For private networks, one of the following address ranges must be used for NAT.

➤ *Class A*—10.0.0.0 - 10.255.255.255

➤ *Class B*—172.16.0.0 - 172.31.255.255

➤ *Class C*—192.168.0.0 - 192.168.255.255

 NAT does not support multiple or multicast scopes.

NAT in Action

Once all options are configured and in place, a user in your private network should be able to connect to the Internet. The IP address shown to the public should be a NAT public address and not a NAT private address. When a user starts his or her computer, it receives a private IP address that allows it to communicate with other systems in the private (business) network. When using an application to access the Internet (the public network), the computer is assigned a public address from NAT. When a request is sent from the user's system to the default gateway (NAT system), the TCP/IP header information that has the user's source IP address is removed and replaced with the user's assigned NAT address (the public address). When a packet is received from the Internet for the private network, the NAT router table is parsed for the public address and matches it to the private address. The TCP/IP header is then changed once more to put the private address back in the destination address.

Not only does NAT change the header information, it also recalculates the checksum to reset its value if needed so that the packets do not appear to be corrupted.

In most cases, the private network, from NAT's viewpoint, comprises not only IP addresses but also port numbers. Multiple client systems will have the same public address but are kept separate by unique port numbers assigned by NAT. This is how a business can have many private IP addresses to its few Internet addresses. This implementation is different from Proxy Server, in that Proxy Server uses only one public address (and IP Routing uses a one-to-one ratio of IP addresses).

Integrating NAT into Existing Networks

When integrating NAT into an existing network, the following items must be resolved:

➤ DHCP servers must be disabled.

➤ Client computers must be configured to request DHCP-assigned addresses.

➤ NAT supports only the IP protocol. (TCP/IP must be running.)

➤ NAT cannot translate the following protocols:

  ➤ SNMP

  ➤ COM/DCOM

  ➤ LDAP

The NAT server should be placed between the public and private networks to maintain security. NAT can use a standard modem, ISDN, and so on to connect to a public network, or another private network.

Note: To be able to communicate with private systems, the public network interface must have an IP address and a subnet mask that is functional on the private network. The public interface should be assigned the IP address and subnet mask given by the InterNIC or ISP.

NAT can be used to integrate one network into an existing one, and serve as the connection point, for example, between two offices. Let's say both networks have Routing and Remote Access installed and enabled. One system has NAT, and the other is configured to accept incoming connections. The default gateway and DNS server IP address for a network should be configured to the IP address of the private network interface of the local Routing and Remote Access server as shown in Figure 7.4.

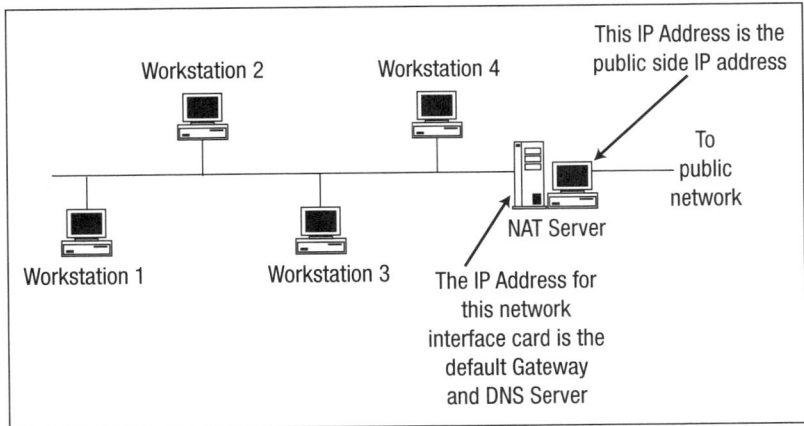

Figure 7.4   NAT network diagram

NAT and DNS

DNS servers cannot be used on the private network. Requests are sent to the NAT server which then resolves the request if it is a private system name. The DNS server IP address option is entered as the IP address of the NAT server on the clients.

If a business's DNS server is not resolved by NAT on the private network, the NAT server will be configured with the address of a DNS server on the public network. These options are shown in Figure 7.5.

NAT has a variety of security features, which can be implemented independently or together for higher security restrictions. A security "fault" in NAT is that all security is set as a whole and not for an individual user; other security options must be used to implement individual security. (See "VPN Security" for individual settings.)

Routing and Remote Access Security for NAT

Security can be implemented by the Routing and Remote Access Service filters to permit or prevent packets coming into any network interface on the NAT server.

NAT Interface Security

Filters can be applied to the private or public interface on the NAT server to allow or disallow packets to pass the specified interface.

A filter on the private network interface will block any packets attempting to pass from the public network to the private network. Also, a filter on the public interface will prevent anyone on the private network from accessing the Internet.

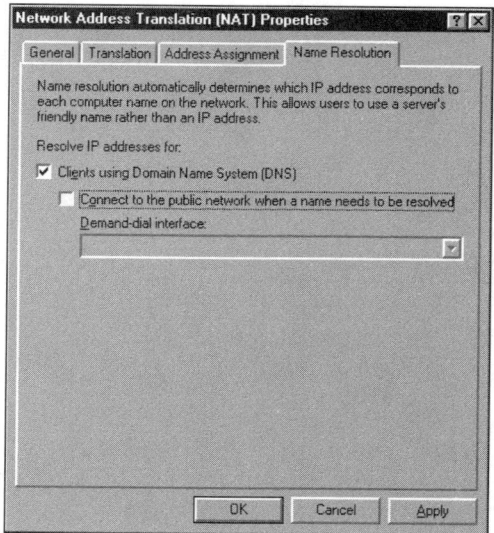

Figure 7.5 DNS configuration in NAT security

 Be careful that the public and private interface filters do not contradict each other. A conflict could prevent IP traffic from exiting or entering the private network through the NAT server.

Filters are basically rules that can be set to allow/disallow packets to pass the interface based on the source IP address, the destination IP address, and the IP port numbers—all of which can be used either independently or together. Combining them makes a more secure filter.

 Filters can also be applied to the demand-dial connections (such as modems and ISDN). But these demand-dial filters cannot be used in conjunction with NAT, as they will be disregarded.

NAT's default security setting is to disallow public network requests to access the private network. Depending upon a business's needs, this default security may have to be changed.

Single IP Address

If the business has only one usable IP address from the InterNIC or ISP, then every computer accessing the Internet will appear to be using the same IP address, but through different ports.

Port mappings must be defined so that ports are available for address translations. An IP address and a port together define a socket. When the NAT server receives a packet from the public network with a certain socket, NAT knows which socket matches to which system, and so retranslates the packet to send it to the proper system. Every resource shared on the private network must have a port mapping for it to be accessed from the public network (if it is to be accessed from the public network).

If the available addresses are in a one-to-many ratio and access performance needs to be enhanced, the solution is to use Proxy Server (as described in Chapter 8).

Multiple IP Addresses

If the business has more than one usable IP address from the InterNIC or ISP, you can make a scope of usable addresses with ports.

Remember to reserve some of the scope if private network resources are to be shared on the public network.

If enough addresses are available, each public address may have one private address (a one-to-one ratio of public to private). Instead of using NAT in this situation, it may be easier to use IP Forwarding. The addresses are not translated back and forth from public to private, and the implementation is simpler (there is no security to hide the TCP/IP configuration of the private network).

VPN Security

Virtual Private Network (VPN) is used when you need to implement security on a user-by-user basis. You can use VPN if you need tighter security for individual users.

VPN on NAT can support Point-to-Point Tunneling Protocol (PPTP) for authentication and encryption. With authentication, access to resources can be allowed or disallowed to a user.

Because of NAT's translations of the TCP/IP header for the addresses, encrypting the packet causes NAT to be unable to do the job it was intended to do. In these cases in which encryption such as L2TP and IPSec must be used, you should use some means other than NAT.

Performance

Performance depends upon a few different factors. To see where you can improve the performance, you should monitor the hardware, the software, and the connections to and from the networks.

Because the NAT system connects to a public network (usually the Internet), the connection between the NAT server and the public network should be able to handle the necessary traffic to and from the private network. Multiple connections to the public network may be required. (Having multiple connections also provides redundancy if one connection fails). The connections can also be upgraded to a faster type, such as replacing modems with an ISDN or T-1 connection.

Connecting to the public network can be slow, and the time that the NAT server takes to connect to the public network can be reduced by having a consistent connection. This way, the connection will be always available when it is needed, thus allowing users immediate access. Users won't have to wait for the NAT server to reconnect to the public network whenever it disconnects or times out.

Another performance boost can be obtained from upgrading the actual server hardware. Monitoring the processor, memory, and hard disk access in a NAT server can reveal bottlenecks that can be remedied with a simple hardware upgrade. Even the network cards can cause such a bottleneck if too much traffic is generated through or to the NAT server. Use Windows 2000's Performance Monitor to monitor specific resources to determine if they are slowing traffic.

Practice Questions

Case Study

Current LAN/Network Structure

2Market currently has 10 servers that are set up for their various data storage and network services, such as SQL, Exchange, SMS, and various application and file servers. Additionally, there are:

➤ 50 Windows 95 workstations

➤ 50 Windows 98 workstations

➤ 20 Windows NT 4 workstations

➤ 75 Windows 2000 Professional workstations

➤ 10 Network printers

The network is not subnetted at all. The network is using a Class A address.

Proposed LAN/Network Structure

2Market proposes no network changes other than a Windows 2000 Server with two interface cards, one connected to the LAN and one connected to the Internet. There are 25 IP addresses that must be reserved on the private network for servers, network printers, and some future additions of servers and network printers.

Current WAN Connectivity

None at the current time.

Proposed WAN Connectivity

None at the current time.

Current Internet Positioning

2Market has leased the following IP address from the InterNIC: 38.187.128.40. The company's domain name is 2Market.com. 2Market will not host its own Web site. Any Internet connections from 2Market will be used strictly for Internet access by the employees.

Future Internet Plans

No new IP addresses will be leased from the InterNIC. All employees need access to the Internet. No company policy is currently in place to specify which browser type is preferred. No individual security settings are required. Sales personnel must be able to access customer Web sites and to send email to customers and perspective clients. Internet access performance is not an issue, although security is a major concern. The private network must remain secure at all times.

Question 1

> What would be the main reason to implement NAT?
>
> ○ a. To confuse the administrator
>
> ○ b. To hide public addresses from the private network
>
> ○ c. To improve Internet performance
>
> ○ d. To hide private addresses from the public network

The answer is d. Answer b is in the wrong order: private addresses are hidden from the public network. Answer c is implemented by Proxy Server. Answer a is obviously incorrect.

Question 2

> In the scenario, which services must be installed on the Windows 2000 Server that will provide NAT? [Check all correct answers]
>
> ❑ a. DHCP
>
> ❑ b. FTP
>
> ❑ c. WINS
>
> ❑ d. DHCP Relay Agent
>
> ❑ e. DNS
>
> ❑ f. Routing and Remote Access
>
> ❑ g. WWW

The correct answer is f. Routing and Remote Access is required for NAT to function. Answers a and d cannot be implemented with NAT at all. Answers b, c, and g are not necessary to the function of NAT. Although answer e could be implemented, it should be a separate system for the sake of performance or to use a DNS server from the public network.

Question 3

In the case study, if a packet's source is the public network and its destination is the private network, what is its route? Place the choices in the correct order. Not all choices will be used.

Private network computer system

Public network interface

Private interface filter

Proxy server

Public network computer system

DNS server

WINS server

Private network interface

DHCP relay agent

IP header translation

Public interface filter

The correct order is:

Public network computer system

Public network interface

Public interface filter

IP header translation

Private interface filter

Private network interface

Private network computer system

Question 4

Click on the appropriate button to install NAT in the Routing And Remote Access Server Setup Wizard:

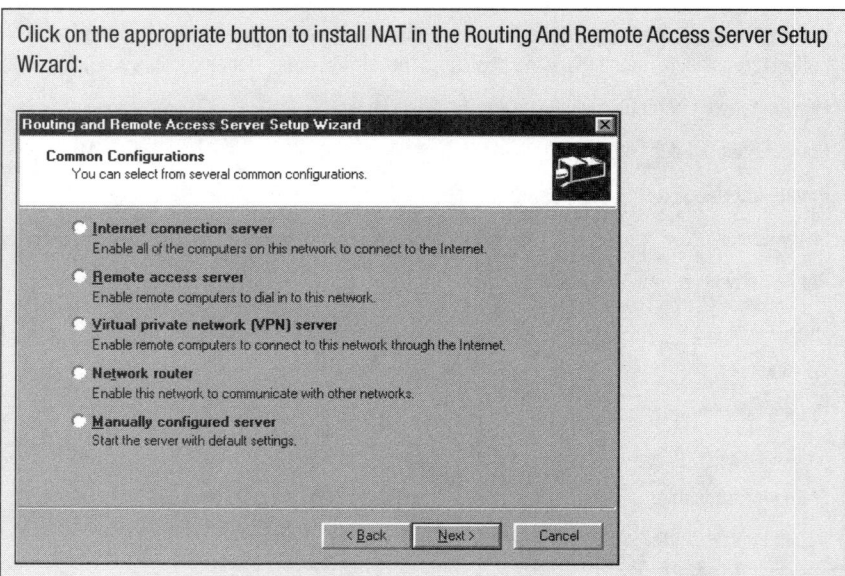

The answer is:

Question 5

In the case study, can the IP address for the private interface be assigned by a DHCP server?

○ a. Yes

○ b. No

The answer is b, No. NAT functions as a DHCP server. DHCP cannot be running on the same network. And, as with a DHCP server, the NAT server must be configured with a static IP address.

Question 6

In the case study, if the NAT server were connecting to a branch office instead of the Internet, which of the following protocols could be used? [Check all correct answers]

❑ a. IPX/SPX

❑ b. NetBEUI

❑ c. TCP/IP

❑ d. AppleTalk

The only correct answer is c. NAT is a service of the Windows 2000 TCP/IP protocol suite, and it functions with only TCP/IP in Windows 2000. None of the other protocols will function with NAT.

Question 7

In the proposed network, NAT can forward DNS requests to which of the following? [Check all correct answers]

❑ a. DNS server on the public network

❑ b. WINS server on the public network

❑ c. Your boss's Windows 98 laptop

❑ d. WINS server on the public network

❑ e. DNS server on the private network

The correct answers are a and e. NAT can forward DNS requests from the client computers to a public or private DNS server. In NAT, DNS requests are forwarded only to DNS servers and not to any other service, such as WINS or

DHCP, nor to any computer unable to run DNS services, such as client computers (which is where the requests are usually initiated).

Question 8

> To implement security features on the Windows 2000 NAT server in the case study, what option can be used?
>
> ○ a. IP addresses
>
> ○ b. Filters
>
> ○ c. Subnet mask
>
> ○ d. A lock with no key

The answer is b. Filters are applied to determine the source addresses, destination addresses, and ports of packets that are allowed or not allowed to pass through the interface. All interfaces on the NAT system that will use TCP/IP must have an IP address and subnet mask to be usable by TCP/IP. Although this allows them to function, it does not work as a security feature. A lock and key has no validity.

Question 9

> In the case study, the design will improve public network performance?
>
> ○ a. True
>
> ○ b. False

The answer is b, false. NAT will not improve Internet access. Its function is to hide the private network from the public network. This scenario should implement Proxy Server, which does improve access

Question 10

In the case study, the IT manager of 2Market wants to implement more security. He has no understanding of NAT and gives you a list of security measures. Which of the following will not work? [Check all correct answers]

❏ a. PPTP

❏ b. IPSec

❏ c. Filters

❏ d. L2TP

The answers are b and d. Answer a is used with NAT for VPNs. Answer c is NAT's main security implementation. Answers b and d use encryption to encrypt the header, and NAT cannot translate the header to replace the IP address.

Need to Know More?

 Microsoft Corporation. *Microsoft Windows 2000 Server Resource Kit.* Microsoft Press, Redmond, WA, 2000. ISBN 1-57231-805-8. The kit consists of seven books and a CD-ROM. Each book contains comprehensive information about the respective area that it covers.

 Search the TechNet CD (or its online version through **www. microsoft.com**) and the *Windows NT Server Resource Kit* CD using the keyword "NAT". Also, see the Windows 2000 Server or Advanced Server help.

 **ftp://ftp.isi.edu/in-notes/rfc1631.txt**. Search for RFC 1597 and 1631 for more information on network address translation.

Microsoft Proxy Server 2.0

Terms you'll need to understand:

- ✓ Proxy
- ✓ Firewall
- ✓ Local Address Table (LAT)
- ✓ Socks
- ✓ Passive caching
- ✓ Active caching
- ✓ Cache Array Routing Protocol (CARP)
- ✓ Domain filtering
- ✓ Demilitarized Zone (DMZ)
- ✓ Packet filtering
- ✓ Chaining
- ✓ Reverse proxying
- ✓ CERN

Techniques you'll need to master:

- ✓ Differentiating a proxy server from a firewall
- ✓ Integrating multiple proxy servers into a network
- ✓ Determining when to set up proxy chains and arrays
- ✓ Learning requirements for proxy client and server setup

An integral part of designing a network infrastructure is the connection of the internal network to external networks, such as the Internet. Because the Internet is designed for public use, connecting an internal network provides an opening that can be exploited by anyone with Internet access. Because each external connection poses a potential security risk, it's difficult to protect a large number of computers on a network when they all have Internet access. Individual Internet access for each networked computer leaves the entire network vulnerable at every connection. Also, client computers that send information over the Internet can become vulnerable by simply making connections to Internet servers.

By acting as a gateway between internal and external networks, Microsoft Proxy Server reduces the risks that are inherent in connecting an internal network to the Internet. In this book, we often discuss screened subnets as part of the design of many of the network services in Windows 2000. Proxy Server allows a network to create screened subnets and to separate their internal network from external, and possibly unsafe, connections.

What Does a Proxy Server Do?

A "proxy" is something that acts as a replacement or stand-in for something else, and a proxy server acts as a gateway for the computers on the network that need to make an Internet connection. A proxy server serves as the single connection to the Internet and, as such, it protects an internal network from the Internet while, at the same time, controlling access to the Internet. This dual function solves both of the major problems associated with computer networks accessing the Internet: the vulnerability of each Internet connection and the difficulty in controlling the Internet access of individual computers.

A proxy server is the only computer actually connected to the Internet, and the computers on the internal network make their Internet requests to it. The proxy server then goes out onto the Internet to fulfill the request and return it to the client. Only the IP address and information of the proxy server is exposed to the Internet, thus protecting the internal network and lessening the risk of external connections.

Understanding Internet Connections

When a client makes a request for information on the Internet, a connection must be made between the client and the Internet server even before the requested data can be sent. This connection works at the session layer of the Open Systems Interconnection (OSI) model. (For more information on the OSI model and the session layer, refer to Chapter 2 of this book.) First, the client needs the

IP address of the Internet server to find the server on the Internet, but this does not complete the connection between the two computers. Because an Internet server can provide many services to the Internet, the client must also have a port number to complete the connection. Ports are better understood if they are thought of as doorways into the server. Just as a building can have many doorways that lead to its different areas, an Internet server can have many ports leading to the different services that it provides. Ports allow Internet servers to simultaneously provide many different services, each of which is assigned to a different port number. The IP address gets you to the server, and the port number gets you inside to the needed information. Just like a building address won't be of any real use if the door is locked, an IP address won't help a client make a connection to the server if the port is closed and not accepting the connection.

Ports

The port number is included in the uniform resource locater (URL) of a Web site. A URL specifies the format of a Web address, as in **http://www.microsoft.com**. Although users don't normally enter the port number nor even realize that it is needed, the port number is supposed to follow the Internet server name or IP address in this way: **http://www.microsoft.com:80**. If a user does not enter a port number in the URL, then the client will default to a port number that is usually used by the protocol in the URL. The protocol used by the Web service, HTTP, defaults to port 80. The Internet actually has more than 65,000 different port numbers, but only the first 1,023 are designated as well-known ports. Many of these are assigned to services on the Internet. The rest are open for any use.

Setting up the Connection

The IP address and the port number together form the socket. If the port is open, the socket is formed and the connection is successful. Once the port is open and the connection is made, the requested data is still not sent to the client until the client and server exchange information. This information is called *header infor-mation* because it is included in the header of the data packets that are sent be-tween clients and servers. Although the header information can vary, it usually includes a client's IP address and other information about the client, such as the type of browser and the Web address from which the client made the new con-nection. This information is intended for the server's use, but it can make the client vulnerable. Providing Internet connections for users also leaves the clients on the network vulnerable. Protecting information such as your internal network's IP addresses is an important security issue. Figure 8.1 shows closed and open ports, one making a connection and the other refusing a connection.

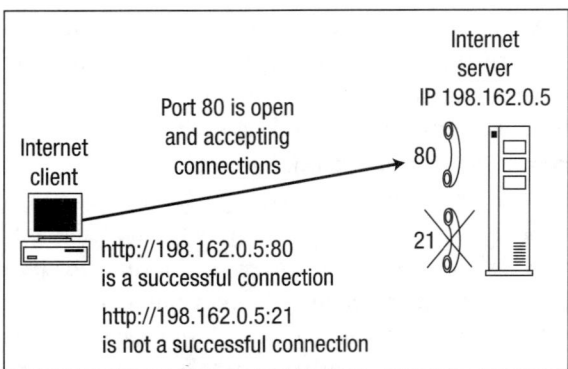

Figure 8.1 Internet connection from client to server using IP address and port number to form socket connection. Port 21 is closed and the connection cannot be made.

Protecting the Network

Although designing a proxy server solution for a network can involve several proxy servers in different roles, the basic role of the proxy server remains the protection of the internal network from the Internet. The proxy server at the edge of the network needs at least two network interfaces: one connected to the internal network and one connected to the Internet. It is important that no IP packets are routed or forwarded between the two interfaces. Instead of the proxy forwarding a client request to the Internet, it reformulates the request so that the origin of the request is not included in packets sent to the Internet. The request is reformulated so that a new request from the proxy server goes out to the Internet. The Internet server returns the requested information to the proxy server, which then sends that information to the original requesting client.

A Proxy vs. a Firewall

Although a proxy server and a firewall are both intended to protect the internal network, they are not the same. A proxy server makes Internet requests for internal computers, and a firewall protects the internal network by blocking packets coming in from the Internet. As explained earlier, Internet computers make connections by using sockets, which are formed with the IP address and the port. A firewall protects the internal network by closing ports and not allowing requests coming from the Internet to make a connection. The request makes it to the server at the IP address, but the port is closed and thus doesn't accept connections. Proxies and firewalls are easily confused, because proxy servers often have firewall capabilities. Microsoft Proxy Server provides both proxy and firewall capabilities. Figure 8.2 shows a proxy server acting as a gateway for outgoing requests and a firewall protecting the internal network by blocking incoming packets.

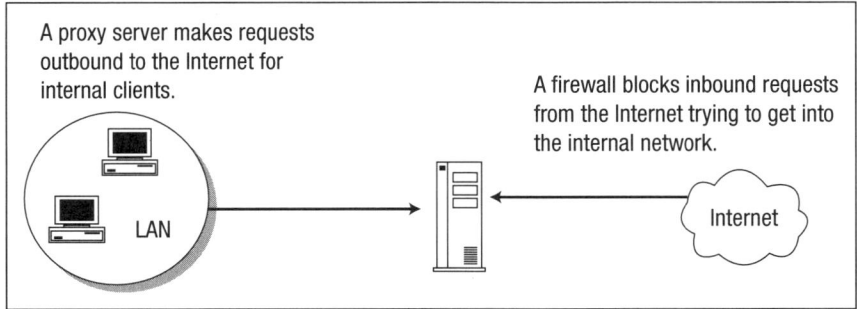

Figure 8.2   Proxy and firewall services serve different purposes on a network.

Microsoft Proxy Server

Proxy Server's current version is 2.0, and has been since 1996. Although the version number has remained the same, Proxy Server has had to adjust as the software on which it runs has changed. For Proxy Server to run, it must be loaded on a Microsoft server operating system, either Windows NT or Windows 2000. Also, Proxy Server runs within Microsoft's Internet Information Server (IIS), and is administered within the IIS administration tool, Internet Services Manager. Internet Services Manger runs within the Microsoft Management Console (MMC). During the time that Proxy Server has been available, IIS has updated from version 3 to version 5. Proxy Server is compatible with all of these versions of IIS.

Proxy Server Software

Proxy Server is a component of BackOffice 4.0 and 4.5, and, although it isn't included on the Windows 2000 Server or Advanced Server CD, it does appear in exam 70-221 Designing a Windows 2000 Networking Infrastructure. It's included on the exam because it is assumed that Internet connections will be included in your network. Microsoft believes that Internet connections are no longer an option, but a necessity in the design of a Windows 2000 network. Because Proxy Server protects your internal network from the vulnerability of Internet connections, it is also considered a necessity for all but the smallest of networks.

Note: Even the smallest of networks need protection from Internet connections. However, proxy services can be provided to small networks with the Network Address Translation (NAT) service. Understanding and implementing NAT is the subject of Chapter 7 of this book.

Microsoft Proxy Server 2.0 and Windows 2000

To install Proxy Server on Windows 2000, IIS must first be loaded. IIS version 5.0 comes with Windows 2000 and can be loaded during or after installation of the operating system. Microsoft has created a special installation file for Proxy Server when it is loaded on Windows 2000. This file can be downloaded from **www.microsoft.com/proxy**. This file does not contain the Proxy Server software: It's simply a program that ensures the correct installation of Proxy Server under Windows 2000. When you run it, you'll be prompted for the BackOffice disk that contains Proxy Server software.

Microsoft's Proxy Server provides both proxy and firewall capabilities. Its default configuration closes all incoming ports so that no connections can be made by incoming requests from the Internet. Packet filters allow some ports to be opened. Configuring packet filters is covered later in this chapter.

The Local Address Table (LAT)

The LAT is very important in the performance of Proxy Server, because the LAT is used to determine whether an IP address is on the internal or external network. The LAT needs to contain all of the IP address ranges from the internal network. When a computer needs to make a connection, it consults the LAT to see if the address is internal or external. If the LAT contains the address, it resides on the internal network and a direct connection can be used. If the address is not on the LAT, then the address is assumed to be external to the network. The packet then needs to be sent to the proxy server to get to its destination. The LAT is created during the installation of Proxy Server, and the server on which Proxy Server is being installed uses its internal routing table to start populating the LAT with IP addresses. An administrator needs to check to make sure that the LAT is correct to prevent packets from being sent to the Internet when they are meant for internal resources.

Services Provided by Proxy Server

There's more to providing proxy services than just retrieving Web pages for internal clients. A proxy server also helps connect Web applications between the client and the Internet server. Often, a Web site provides more than just Web pages for its users. If it provides videos, games, or any other services, these are usually provided by a Web application. A proxy server providing Web pages to internal clients is called a *Web proxy*. A proxy server also needs to provide connections to different types of clients for Web applications. Microsoft Proxy Server is a Web proxy, but it also provides two other proxy services to a network for Web applications: WinSock proxy and Socks proxy. WinSock proxy connects Windows clients to Internet application servers, and Socks does the same for non-Windows clients like Macintosh and Unix.

Note: Although Socks is often written in all uppercase, it is not an acronym and the letters do not stand for anything. The term Socks is derived from sockets. To find out *more about Socks, visit **www.socks.nec.com**. Microsoft Proxy Server supports Socks version 4.3a. This version of Socks does not support UDP connections. Web applications like RealAudio that use UDP as the transport protocol will not work with the Socks proxy service using Microsoft Proxy Server.*

Transparency

Like most proxy servers, Microsoft Proxy Server is not a fully transparent proxy server. It *is* transparent in that the user, when typing in the URL for the Web destination, does not see that the request is being made through a proxy server. It is *not* transparent in that the client computer is aware that it needs to make its request to the proxy server instead of trying to make a direct connection to the Internet.

Improved Performance

A client connecting to the Internet tries to improve performance by caching Web pages on its local hard disk, because it's faster to read Web pages from the local disk than retrieving them from the Internet. Caching for Web pages actually is just storing Web pages on the hard disk. Proxy Server tries to improve Internet performance by allowing all clients to benefit from a centralized Web cache. A client requesting an often-accessed Web page can benefit on the first connection if the page already resides in the Proxy Server cache. Caching is affected by how often Web documents change. Documents that change often require more updates while in cache, and Proxy Server checks how often a Web page is updated to decide how often to update its cache. Proxy Server provides both passive and active caching services for the internal network, and each has a different method for updating cached objects.

Passive caching caches information only when it is requested from client computers. When a Web page is requested, Proxy Server retrieves the page from the Internet and stores it in cache. When another client asks for the same Web page, the request can be filled from the Proxy Server's cache. Because the proxy server cache fulfills the request, instead of reformulating it and forwarding it on to the Internet, internal network performance is improved and traffic on the external connection to the Internet is reduced. To keep the cached information from growing stale, each page is assigned a Time To Live (TTL) when it is cached. If the TTL expires by the time another client requests it, then the proxy server may need to go out to the Internet and refresh the document. However, by default, active instead of passive caching is enabled in Proxy Server.

Active caching does not wait for a document to be requested before it is refreshed in the cache. Active caching automatically refreshes documents that are often used by clients on the internal network or that have frequently updated content.

To ensure that active caching does not create a drag on Proxy performance or the network, it is set to update when Proxy Server is not busy and during times of low network traffic. Active caching adds to performance by updating the cache during times of low Internet traffic, so that it is refreshed and ready for times of high traffic.

Caching Limitations

Caching is only for the Web proxy service. WinSock and Socks are proxy services for only Web application connections and do not cache information. Also, not all Web documents can be cached. Dynamic content contained on Active Server pages and from server-side applications (such as connections to a database or search pages) must receive an update from the server every time the page is accessed. These pages cannot be cached. Also, secure pages encrypted with SSL are not cached by default, because these pages usually contain sensitive information that is meant for only a few individuals. Caching does not help performance for these types of Web pages. Also, caching requires a lot of hard disk space: a minimum of 100MB plus 500K for each client that will be supported by the cache.

Also, information in Web pages can be dated. The header of a Web document can contain information on whether or not the information expires and, if it does expire, how long the information is good before it needs to be updated. Administrators of a Web site can set this information at the Web server, and each page can have a different setting based on its content. Although some information expires immediately (this information cannot be cached), other information can last from 30 minutes to 30 days. The setting depends upon the time sensitivity of the information contained in the page.

Optimizing Cache Settings

Cache settings should be set to provide the highest hit ratio possible. A hit ratio for cache shows what percentage of client requests are serviced from cache rather than forwarded to the Internet to retrieve the page. When trying to increase the cache hit ratio, consider the factors that affect it: active data, users not asking for same pages, and low Web use (information goes stale before it can be used from cache). Also, because secure Web data cannot be cached, users accessing sensitive information can affect cache hits. Regardless of how cache is set up or refreshed, certain Web usage will make it impossible to configure high cache hit ratios.

Proxy Arrays

An array is a set of proxy servers that are designated to work as a single logical unit. Arrays provide fault tolerance and bigger caches for internal clients. If one server in an array goes down, the others can continue. Also, each individual proxy server in an array will add its cache size to the array's cache. The caching protocol used by Microsoft Proxy Server allows the cache on each member of the array to act as if it is one large cache instead of a number of smaller caches. To join proxy servers to the same array, they must belong to the same Active Directory domain and site. Both the fault tolerance and improved cache performance make arrays an important alternative in a proxy design.

Cache Array Routing Protocol (CARP)

A problem in setting up an array of proxy servers is that the cache, although it is supposed to act as if it is a single logical cache, still physically exists on different proxy servers. Originally arrays would query each other for cached objects, but this method degrades performance as the array grows larger. Also, the cache on each member of the array could contain redundant objects. The Cache Array Routing Protocol (CARP) uses an algorithm to spread the cache, without redundancy, across the array. CARP's algorithm calculates a score for each requested URL before placing it in cache, and clients use this same scoring system to determine on which member of the array the requested URL is most likely cached. By default, other members of the array will be checked according to the next highest score for the object before the request is forwarded on to the Internet to be fulfilled. The algorithm adjusts automatically when members are added to or removed from the array. CARP allows arrays to grow more efficient as members are added, although 20 proxy servers are considered to be the maximum in one array.

Security Services Provided by Proxy Server

Even though it works to improve Internet performance, Proxy Server is really set up for security. Most of the services it provides are for the security of the internal network. Because a proxy server acts as a gateway for Internet connections, controls can be placed on these connections, and these controls can be as fine as which services are available, which users can use these services, and which sites users can access.

For Outbound Access

Proxy Server allows administrators to control user access to the Internet. An administrator can set the server so that only certain users or groups of users are allowed access to Internet services. The administrator can even set which Internet sites can and cannot be accessed.

Active Directory Integration

Not everyone on the internal network may need all services provided on the Internet. Proxy Server integrates with Active Directory services provided in Windows 2000 by allowing the administrator to set whom may use Internet services.

For example, the Sales group may need to use the FTP service, but doesn't need to access the Web. Although most users are usually provided access to all Internet services, this control is included in Proxy Server.

Domain Filters

Besides controlling who can use Internet services, Proxy Server can be set to control what Internet sites are accessed. A company may decide that only a company intranet site should be accessed and block access to all other sites, or a company may decide to block access to certain sites while allowing access to all others.

Controlling Inbound Access

By controlling inbound traffic, Proxy Server is, in effect, acting as a firewall for the network. Because Proxy Server is a gateway for all Internet traffic, it can even watch for attacks by evaluating inbound traffic. For example, Proxy Server is aware of such attacks as those that try to overwhelm the network with packets or spoofed packets that have been altered.

When firewalls create a network separate from the internal network and the external (Internet) network, this new network can be called a screened subnet or a demilitarized zone (DMZ). Information is placed in the DMZ when clients coming in from the Internet need the information. By placing the information in the DMZ the internal network is protected from Internet access, yet Internet clients can still get to the needed information.

 A screened subnet and a DMZ are the same thing. Some Microsoft literature refers to screened subnets and some refers to DMZs. It is important to understand that they are the same.

Packet Filters

After installing Proxy Server and connecting it to an external interface, no packets from the Internet are allowed, by default, into the internal network. This is because packet filtering closes all inbound ports to prevent external computers from connecting to internal computers. Packet filters can be implemented on only the external interface to the Internet. Because port access can be outbound or inbound, packet filters actually apply to traffic coming from internal and external sources. Because all ports are closed by default, an administrator needs to create exceptions that will allow some ports to be opened to provide services to the network. Once a packet filter exception is configured, it applies to all three services that Proxy Server provides.

Packet filters can be dynamic or static. A static filter is either open or closed at all times. For example, an outbound request for a Web page would need to use port 80. A static filter would leave port 80 open for outbound connections at all times. A dynamic packet filter would close port 80 until it was needed for an outbound request. It would then open the port for the request, closing it when the request was completed. Dynamic filters are used by default in Proxy Server.

Preparing a Network for Proxy Server

Before Proxy Server can be incorporated into a network, planning must be completed and changes may be needed to prepare the network. One issue that needs to be resolved is IP addressing. Clients that currently have a direct connection to the Internet also must have valid IP addresses for the Internet. Because each IP address used on the Internet must be unique, the use of IP addresses on the Internet must be controlled. An administrator of a network can obtain valid IP addresses directly from the controlling organization or from an Internet Service Provider (ISP). Obtaining a block of IP addresses is not as inexpensive as it once was, and Proxy Server can save a company money. A company that decides to obtain a block of IP addresses directly must contact the American Registry of Internet Numbers (ARIN) at **www.arin.net**. However, this is not a cheap method: The smallest block of IP addresses available to lease is 4,096, and that will cost you $2,500 per year. A smaller block of IP addresses can be obtained from an ISP.

Note: Until the end of 1997, IP addresses for use on the Internet were obtained from Network Solutions, Inc. (InterNIC). Control of IP addressing has now been passed to Regional Internet Registries (RIR). The entire world is divided into three regions for the purpose of contolling the allocation of IP addresses for Internet use. The three RIRs each control the assignment of IP addresses for a large geographical area. ARIN controls the assignment of IP addresses for the Americas and Africa. For more information on the rules of IP addressing, visit www.ARIN.net.

Both methods of obtaining valid IP addresses will cost a company, and paying for an IP address ensures that an individual client on the network is the only one using it. Proxy Server provides an additional benefit in that it doesn't need valid IP addresses for internal clients. Because these addresses will never be used on the Internet, it really doesn't matter what range of IP addresses are used internally. Only the proxy server that sits on the edge of the network and that is connected to the Internet needs an address that is valid for use on the Internet. Clients on the internal network can be assigned a range of what are called *private IP addresses*. Any IP address that is not for use on the Internet needs to be unique for only the local network on which it resides. A company using Proxy Server needs to buy valid IP addresses for only the proxy servers that connect to the Internet.

Private Ranges of IP Addresses

Some ranges of IP addresses are reserved for internal use on networks, which means that these addresses cannot be used on the Internet. Network numbers such as 10.0.0.0 and 192.168.0.0 are examples of private addresses. The recommended setting for Proxy Server is that the internal network use a private range of IP addresses and that only the external connection(s) to the Internet need a valid IP address. This setting adds a measure of safety for the network. If one of the clients tries to connect directly to the Internet instead of through the Proxy Server, the invalid client IP address will prevent the connection.

Because Proxy Server drastically reduces the number of external IP addresses that are needed, you may need to reconsider the use of IP addresses on the network. A private range of addresses needs to be selected for internal use on the network, and you may find that you need only one external IP address. The exact use of IP addresses may be delayed until a network diagram allows a designer to see the needs of the network.

The Network Diagram

Networks are more complicated to design when WAN connections are involved. A network diagram reveals to the designer of network services how users are concentrated and interconnected. A simple network diagram for Proxy Server design should include the following elements:

➤ LANs

➤ WAN connections

➤ Number of users at each LAN

Figure 8.3 shows an example of a simple network diagram.

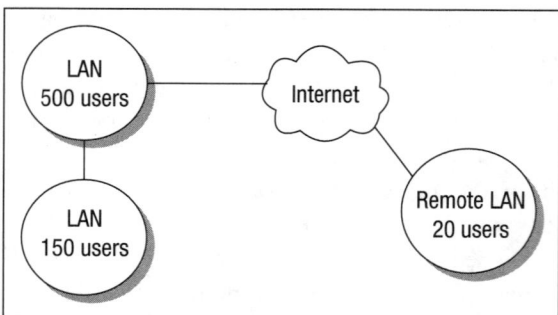

Figure 8.3   Use a network diagram before making decisions with a Proxy Server design.

Determining the Number of Proxy Servers

Depending on its size and geographic distribution, a network can implement one to several proxy servers. In a large network, an overburdened proxy server can act as a bottleneck for Internet traffic, slowing connections when it can't keep up with the demand. Determining the number of proxy servers can be a factor not only of the number of Internet users, but also in the type of Internet traffic and the size of downloaded files. A medium single network location of 500 users may work well with only one proxy server if Internet traffic is light, but that same network—if it uses the Internet heavily to transfer large files—may need a few proxy servers or even an array of proxy servers.

Microsoft recommends that each WAN location have one proxy server. This rule should be followed even if each WAN location does not have its own Internet connection. A proxy server does not necessarily have to be connected to the Internet or even have two network interfaces to be a part of a network design. A proxy server can provide caching services to a network even if it is not providing security services. Proxy servers can fill different roles on the network to help different network situations.

Chaining Proxy Server

Networks that have many locations but only one connection to the Internet can benefit by chaining proxy servers. Chaining proxy servers distributes their load across a network and allows them to check more than one cache before making a request on the Internet. Individual proxy servers or arrays can exist in a chain. Keep chains shallow: Fewer hops are best, because several hops can increase latency.

Upstream vs. Downstream

To design proxy server chains, it is important to understand the terms *upstream* and *downstream*. Going upstream means heading towards the Internet and away from the internal network, and going downstream means heading away from the Internet and towards the internal network. When designing chains, proxy servers will either be upstream or downstream from each other. Downstream proxy servers will pass a request upstream to other proxy servers, and each server will check its cache to try to fulfill the request before passing it upstream. The last upstream proxy server will make a request to the Internet for the requested page.

Proxy Server Routes

Setting up a chain of proxy servers involves configuring routes for the servers to follow when filling client Internet requests. Primary and alternate routes can be configured to provide for fault tolerance. In the event that the upstream proxy server is unavailable, the backup proxy server can be used instead. Proxy arrays work best in a chain of proxy servers. Several proxy servers on the edge of LANs can route to an upstream proxy array. This keeps the chain of proxy servers shallow and increases cache hits by providing a large cache in the array, while keeping the connection to the Internet just a few hops away. Figure 8.4 shows an example of Proxy Server routing. Proxy servers not connected to the Internet can be chained to the proxy servers that do have a connection to the Internet. The downstream proxy server in LAN2 will route Internet requests not fulfilled by cache to the upstream proxy array in LAN1.

Reverse Proxying

Some networks may want to provide Internet users with a Web site. Setting up a proxy server to protect your Web site is called *reverse proxying*. It is "reverse" because proxies normally protect internal clients from being exposed to the Internet. Reverse proxying allows external clients from the Internet to access Web services on an internal network. Proxy Server can be configured to help protect your Web site from this vulnerable situation of being exposed to an Internet connection.

Although Proxy Server must have IIS services loaded on the same server, do not place the Web site on the same server as Proxy Server. Proxy Server is vulnerable because it is on the Internet. Web sites need to be protected from malicious users who may want to break into a Web site and alter the contents of the Web pages. If a Web site and Proxy Server coexist on the same computer, then, when one is

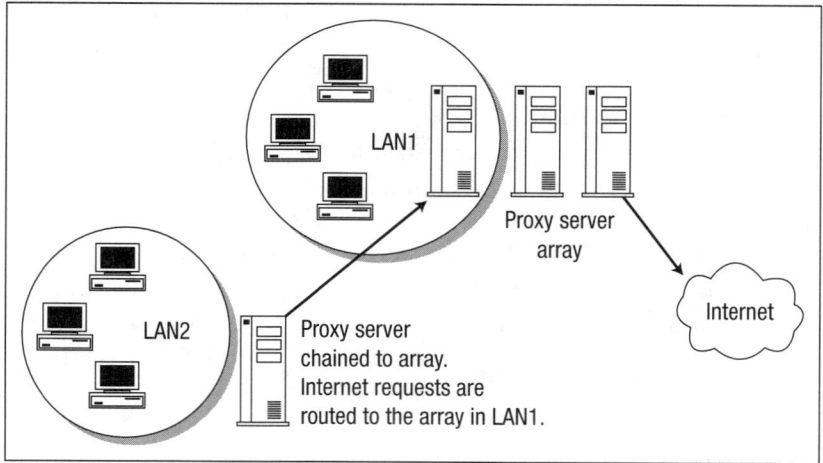

Figure 8.4 Proxy Server is useful for caching services on a network with just one connection to the Internet.

broken into, so is the other. Protect your Web sites by placing them on servers that are downstream of a server providing proxy services.

If security of data is a concern, then the Web server should be placed in a screened subnet that is separated from the rest of the internal network. Remember, any connection from the Internet into an internal network leaves that network vulnerable. An internal network with confidential information should not allow any inbound connections, and moving the Web server to a separate screened subnet with its own proxy server is the most secure solution.

Placing Proxy Servers on the Network

Once the network is diagrammed and Internet use is established, proxy servers can be correctly placed on the network. Proxy Server is not stringent on the types of interfaces with which it will work. Connections can be dial-up, persistent, or a combination of the two. Proxy Server allows for flexibility in selecting protocols from level 2, the data link layer, up to level 4, the transport layer.

Joining Dissimilar Networks with Proxy Server

One proxy server can be connected to networks using different access methods. If one network is using Ethernet and another is using Token Ring or Asynchronous Transfer Mode (ATM), Proxy Server just needs to have an adapter for each of these types of networks. This works because Proxy Server does not forward the requests between the networks. As you'll remember, if Proxy Server cannot fulfill the request from cache, it formulates a new request to pass it upstream to the Internet. No translation for the connections, such as a bridge, is needed.

Proxy Server can also be used on a network that uses IPX/SPX, Novell Netware's proprietary protocol stack, on the internal network. IPX/SPX can be implemented instead of the TCP/IP protocol stack on the internal computers. TCP/IP is required for only the external connection to the Internet.

External Connections

Just using proxy chains and arrays inside a network will not improve performance if there is still a bottleneck at the Internet connection. Proxy Server can allow a company to whittle its Internet connections down to one even if several WAN locations exist within the company. This may save money on the cost of Internet connections, but, if the one Internet connection is saturated, then more may be needed to accommodate the traffic. With this solution, caching throughout the network is maximized because different caches may be checked before sending a request to the Internet. If each WAN location has its own connection to the Internet, caching will be used less. If much of the information from the Internet contains secure or dynamic information, cache would not be as likely to fulfill the requests, and more Internet connections would be needed if a performance improvement is desired.

Ensuring That All Proxies Are Used Evenly

If more than one Internet connection accepts inbound client requests, two different methods may be used to ensure that all proxy servers are used evenly for Internet connections: multiple entries in DNS to create a round-robin effect, and network load balancing (NLB). Both methods ensure the distribution of incoming requests across all available proxy servers.

A DNS server containing records that have the same hostname mapped to different IP addresses will automatically resolve queries in a round-robin fashion. The first query is resolved with the first record in the list, and subsequent queries are resolved with the rest of the records, working down to the last entry then starting back at the top again. The following list shows how round-robin DNS entries work. These entries have the same hostname, but different IP addresses. DNS will start at the top of the list when resolving queries for **www.coriolis.com**. The first query will receive 192.168.0.5 as a response, and the next query will receive 192.168.0.6. DNS will continue to the bottom of the list and start back at the top, automatically load balancing incoming requests.

www.Coriolis.com	192.168.0.5
www.Coriolis.com	192.168.0.6
www.Coriolis.com	192.168.0.7
www.Coriolis.com	192.168.0.8

Installing the NLB service also distributes incoming requests across available proxy servers. Although round-robin DNS entries are a manual way to distribute traffic across available servers, NLB automatically distributes traffic across servers, like clustering. If one server is unavailable, DNS, using round-robin entries, will still send traffic to the unavailable server, whereas NLB will automatically adjust traffic until the unavailable server comes back online. The downside to NLB is that it has more CPU overhead than DNS round-robin entries. NLB is a better service to use if incoming connections must be serviced 24 hours a day with no exceptions.

NLB is not just for Proxy Server use. It is part of the Windows Clustering Service, and it allows incoming TCP/IP services to be distributed across multiple servers.

Review of Proxy Services

Now that you have learned of the services provided by Proxy Server, it is important to remember whether the service protects inbound or outbound connections. Remembering this will help keep the services straight when implementing
them in a network solution. Figure 8.5 shows a list of inbound and outbound
protection services provided by Proxy Server.

Setting up Proxy Clients

Proxy Server provides three different proxy services to the network. Web proxy
has been discussed for most of this chapter, because it has the most features that
can be set. WinSock and Socks proxy clients are used to connect computers using
Web applications. Normally, the connection is made directly from client to server
over the Internet, but, when a proxy server is used, the connection is made through
the proxy server. Proxy clients must be aware of the proxy server and know how
to use it in order for this connection to be successful.

Web Proxy Clients

Browsers making client requests to a Web proxy server need to be compliant with
only the basic Web standards. This standard is from the Swiss Conseil European
pour la Recherche Nucleair (CERN) (which translates as *European Laboratory
for Particle Physics*). CERN is responsible for basic Internet protocol standards
such as HTTP and the original idea for proxy servers. The most recent versions
of Internet Explorer automatically detect a network's Web proxy server and use it
with no configuration changes needed from a network administrator.

WinSock and Socks Proxy Clients

Unlike the Web proxy service, clients needing to connect to Web applications
need some configuration changes in order to use the WinSock or Socks proxy

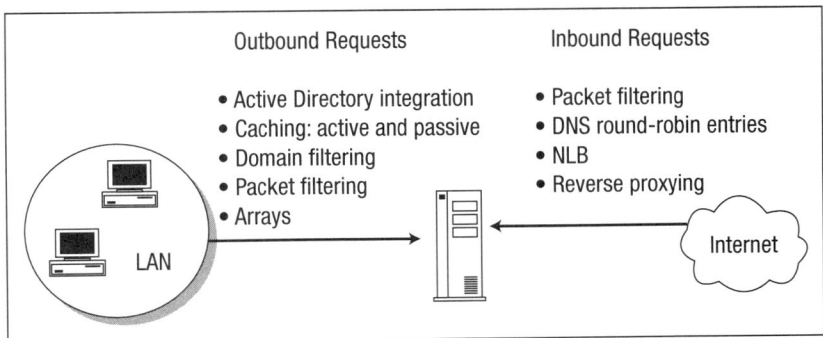

Figure 8.5 Inbound and outbound protection services provided by and used in conjunction
with Proxy Server. Packet filtering is the only overlapping service.

service. Either the WinSock or Socks proxy service is needed, because they are designed for different types of clients. To connect to Web applications through a proxy server, Windows clients using the WinSock interface need the WinSock proxy, and non-Windows clients need the Socks proxy. During the installation of Proxy Server, a script is created that is used to configure WinSock proxy clients. WinSock clients need to connect to the Proxy Server to run the script in order to be configured to use the WinSock proxy service. The script will also configure the proxy clients to update their local LAT from a share on the proxy server. Socks client software does not come with Proxy Server but can be downloaded from **ftp://ftp.nec.com/pub/socks**. Remember to download version 4.3a, which is compatible with the Socks proxy service provided by Microsoft Proxy Server.

Practice Questions

Case Study

Hi-tech Company is located in San Diego, CA, and has 500 users. It would like to expand its presence on the Internet but know that this presents a security risk to its network. The company is looking for ways to secure and improve its Internet connections.

Current WAN Connectivity

Each user has his or her own connection to the Internet through a 56Kbps modem. Each user has a static IP address. The company is having difficulty controlling Internet connections and is wondering if this can be controlled.

Proposed WAN Connectivity

Hi-tech Company decides to simplify and centralize the connection to the Internet. Proxy Server has been suggested as a way to centralize the connection to the Internet and also provide control over the users' connections.

Future Internet Plans

Hi-tech would like to create a Web site for the company and host it from its own network.

Company Goal with Windows 2000

Since the network has been upgraded to Windows 2000 the company would like to take advantage of the new security features for Internet connections. The company would like to know which of these services is best for their network situation.

Question 1

> What changes need to be made to the network to add a proxy server?
>
> ○ a. Load a Web proxy client on the users' computers.
>
> ○ b. Add routers to the network.
>
> ○ c. Assign a private range of IP addresses to the internal network.
>
> ○ d. Do nothing. The network is ready in its current state.

Answer c is correct. The network needs a private range of IP addresses assigned to the internal network. To keep users from making their own connection to the Internet a private range of IP addresses needs to be used for the internal network.

A private range of IP addresses will be a more secure solution for the network. A Web proxy client needs only to be a CERN-compliant browser to use a proxy server. More software is not needed. Routers will have no affect on a proxy server solution.

Question 2

How much hard disk space will be needed on the Proxy Server to adequately provide the clients with caching services?

- ○ a. 100MB
- ○ b. 250MB
- ○ c. 350MB
- ○ d. 500MB

Answer c is correct. Caching requires a lot of hard disk space. This network has 500 users and the recommended setting is 100MB of hard disk space plus 500K (0.5MB) for every supported user. 100 + (500 *0.5) = 350MB.

Question 3

A branch office with 50 users needs to be connected to the main office. The branch office is linked through a 56Kbps frame-relay connection. Without creating another connection to the Internet, how should this branch office be incorporated using a secure proxy server solution? [Check all correct answers]

- ❑ a. Add a proxy server to the branch office.
- ❑ b. Chain the branch office proxy server to the main office server.
- ❑ c. Implement NLB to ensure availability of the main office proxy server.
- ❑ d. Set up a backup route to the Internet for the branch office.

Answers a and b are correct. It is recommended that a proxy server be implemented at every WAN connection, even if it is not connected to the Internet. The proxy server at the branch location will provide a local cache for those users. Creating a proxy server chain will route Internet requests from the branch office to the main office and its connection to the Internet. NLB is for incoming requests from the Internet and not for internal requests. Answer d is a good answer if fault tolerance were an issue or if another connection to the Internet were part of the requirements.

Question 4

> Due to the company's growth and increased Internet usage, performance to the Internet is too slow at the main location and the branch office. What proxy server solutions can help this situation? [Check all correct answers]
>
> ❑ a. Create a proxy array at the main location.
>
> ❑ b. Set up DNS for round-robin entries.
>
> ❑ c. Connect the proxy server at the branch office to the Internet.
>
> ❑ d. Enable packet filtering on the LAN proxy server.

Answers a and c are correct. A proxy array will improve caching of Web pages and improve performance for the large concentration of users at the main location. A separate Internet connection at the branch office will remove the burden off the main office proxy server. DNS round-robin entries work with only incoming packets, and this is not currently enabled for the network. Packet filtering is enabled by default and will not help to improve Internet connection performance.

Question 5

> The company has just won a large contract for a project. Information regarding the project is available on a private Web site that can be accessed from the Internet. The site contains a Web application that users from the company need to use over the Internet. How can this be set up? [Check all correct answers]
>
> ❑ a. Set up a Socks proxy client software on each client.
>
> ❑ b. Run the WinSock proxy client script on each client.
>
> ❑ c. Configure each client as a Web proxy client.
>
> ❑ d. Do nothing. No configuration is needed.

Answer b is correct. During the installation of Proxy Server, a script is created to configure WinSock proxy clients. The script needs to be run on individual clients to configure the use of Web applications over the Internet. Socks proxy is only needed for non-Windows clients, and this network has Internet Explorer running on Windows 2000 Professional. Web proxies are only for Web pages and are not for connecting Web applications.

Question 6

> An array has been set up at the main location. What performance enhancements does an array provide? [Check all correct answers]
>
> ❑ a. Filtering
>
> ❑ b. Caching
>
> ❑ c. Fault tolerance
>
> ❑ d. Chaining

Answers b and c are correct. Proxy arrays improve caching performance by allowing the caches on different proxy servers to act as one logical cache. Fault tolerance is also provided within an array. If one member fails, the others take over. Filtering is not a performance enhancement. It is a security enhancement. Chaining proxy servers is connecting proxy servers linearly and does not combine them logically into one unit.

Question 7

> The company has decided to set up a Web site and host it at the main location. What service needs to be set up to allow this?
>
> ○ a. Packet filtering
>
> ○ b. Domain filtering
>
> ○ c. Reverse proxying
>
> ○ d. Network load balancing

Answer c is correct. Reverse proxying allows for Web publishing inside the screened subnet. It allows inbound requests from the Internet into the network to be serviced by the local Web server. Packet filtering stops incoming packets instead of allowing them in. Domain filtering is for outgoing connections only, and although NLB helps incoming connections, it is not required for these connections to work.

Question 8

Internet performance is still too slow and is causing delays in work performance. Most of the users are connecting to the project site and downloading secure pages. How can performance be improved?

○ a. Add another proxy server with a separate Internet connection.

○ b. Chain a downstream proxy server to the array.

○ c. Use CARP as the caching protocol.

○ d. Change passive caching to active.

Answer a is correct. Because most of the users are accessing secure Web pages, cache improvements will not help improve performance. Secure content cannot be cached. The only performance enhancement that will help the problem is another proxy server with another connection to the Internet. Answers b, c, and d all would improve caching performance, but because most of the pages are secure and therefore not being cached, cache enhancements will not help the problem of slow performance in this situation.

Question 9

The new project is causing security concerns. Information at the main office is confidential and needs to be protected. What security precautions can be taken to protect the information from inbound Internet traffic? [Check all correct answers]

❑ a. Use NLB.

❑ b. Implement domain filtering.

❑ c. Place the Web server in a screened subnet separated from the internal network.

❑ d. Enable dynamic packet filtering.

❑ e. Use packet filtering to close all inbound ports to the internal network.

Answers c, d, and e are correct. Currently, a Web server resides on the internal network, and reverse proxying allows inbound requests from the Internet to access it. The Web server needs to be placed in a screened subnet separated from the internal network. Dynamic filtering will add an extra measure of security by closing ports that are providing services when they are not active. NLB is for load balancing and not for security. Domain filtering blocks internal users from accessing certain Internet domains and does not help inbound traffic. Using packet filtering to close *all* inbound ports will not allow *any* connections to the internal network. Connections made to the Web server in the screened subnet in front of the internal network will be allowed, but traffic will be unable to continue on to the internal network.

Question 10

> Packet filtering is enabled for the Web proxy service. As an added security precaution, the network administrator would also like to set up packet filtering for the WinSock proxy service. What needs to be done to enable this service? [Choose the best answer]
>
> ○ a. Enable packet filtering in Internet Services Manager.
>
> ○ b. Packet filtering is not available for WinSock proxy service.
>
> ○ c. The WinSock proxy service uses domain filters instead.
>
> ○ d. Do nothing. Packet filtering needs to be enabled on only one service.

Answer d is correct. Once packet filtering is enabled for one proxy service, it is enabled for all proxy services. Domain filters are used for outbound traffic to allow certain groups to use the proxy server to gain Internet access. Once packet filtering has been enabled for the Web proxy service, no other configurations are necessary to configure packet filtering for the WinSock proxy service.

Question 11

> A private Web site in support of the project has been established in the company's main office. It is critical that the site be available at all times for external Internet access. What services are needed at the main office to ensure this happens? [Check all correct answers]
>
> ❑ a. Set up a proxy server array.
>
> ❑ b. Implement NLB with additional Web servers.
>
> ❑ c. Use active caching.
>
> ❑ d. Integrate Proxy Server with Active Directory.

Only answer b is correct. NLB with additional Web servers at the main office is the only option that will provide fault tolerance for incoming requests to the Web site. All other choices help fault tolerance or availability for outbound requests only.

Need to Know More?

 Luotonen, Ari. *Web Proxy Servers*. Prentice-Hall, Inc., Upper Saddle River, NJ, 1998. ISBN 0-13-680612-0. Luotonen helped develop the original proxy software, and the book provides an overview of the development and inner workings of proxy servers.

 www.microsoft.com/proxy/Support/win2kwizard.asp? *How to Install Proxy Server on Windows 2000*. Microsoft Corporation, Redmond, WA, 2000. This knowledge base article walks you through the process of installing Proxy Server on Windows 2000. A revised installation file needs to be downloaded from **www.microsoft.com/proxy**. This file does not contain Proxy Server installation files. Those files are included with BackOffice 4.0 and 4.5.

 www.microsoft.com/ISN/whitepapers/network_load_balancing_win2k.asp *Network Load Balancing*. Microsoft Corporation, Redmond, WA, 2000. This Microsoft white paper explains the use of NLB service on a network.

 Search the TechNet CD (or its online version through **http://support.microsoft.com/directory**) and the *Windows 2000 Server Resource Kit* CD. First use the keyword "Proxy Server" and then, from that subset, search on "Windows 2000".

Routing in a Windows 2000 Environment

. . . .

Terms you'll need to understand:

✓ Routing Information Protocol (RIP)

✓ Open Shortest Path First (OSPF)

✓ Unicast

✓ Broadcast

✓ Multicast

✓ Internet Group Management Protocol (IGMP)

✓ Hop

✓ Autonomous system

✓ Service Advertising Protocol (SAP)

✓ AppleTalk

✓ Channel Service Unit/Data Service Unit (CSU/DSU)

Techniques you'll need to master:

✓ Determining when routers are needed

✓ Selecting the right routing protocol

✓ Placing routers within a WAN environment

✓ Improving routing performance

This chapter teaches you how to implement routing in a Windows 2000 network infrastructure. Windows 2000 can work with third-party routers or provide its own routing services through the Routing and Remote Access Service (RRAS). You will need to learn which routing situation is most appropriate for a variety of different network configurations.

Routing Overview

Routing is defined as the procedure of finding a path from a source to a destination. The source and destination points can be any hardware interface on a network, whether a computer, printer, CD-ROM tower, or any similar devices.

Routing plays an important role in the function of wide area networks (WANs), which depend on routing to deliver packets from one local area network (LAN) to another. A *LAN* is defined as a network that covers a small geographical location, such as a single office building, and routing's mission is to deliver a packet of information from one LAN to another. It may help to compare the computers in a LAN to houses in a neighborhood. If you want to deliver a package to a house in your neighborhood, you can just take it yourself. Similarly, a computer that needs to deliver a packet to another computer in its own LAN can send the information directly to that computer. When you need to send a package outside of your own neighborhood, you take it to the post office. The package will be passed through other post offices until it reaches its destination. Computers don't know how to deliver packets outside of their local LAN, and so it simply sends the packet to the router instead. Regardless of whether this delivery is a long or short distance, it is the router's responsibility to start the delivery in the right direction. Because each LAN has a router, the routers simply pass the packet from router to router until it arrives at the correct LAN.

A router can be a physical piece of hardware that is dedicated to routing, or it can be software such as Windows 2000 Server running Routing and Remote Access Service (RRAS) with multiple network interface cards (NICs). A router is called a *gateway* because all packets leaving and entering the LAN must go through the router. When a computer on one LAN generates a packet that is destined for another LAN, the packet is forwarded to the gateway (or the router), which checks a table of available addresses and determines—based on the destination address—the best interface to send the packet out on. The router then forwards the packet to the appropriate LAN, where either one of two things occurs:

➤ The current LAN is the destination, and the packet is delivered to the destination computer; or

➤ The destination of the packet is another LAN, and the packet is sent to the next gateway to be forwarded until it reaches the destination LAN and computer.

Unfortunately, routers need to be told how a network of LANs is arrayed and what the best route is to choose. The best way to configure a router with this information depends on the complexity and size of the network.

Dynamic vs. Static Routing

Because a router's job is to deliver packets to their destinations by forwarding them to other routers, a router must build a table of information that it refers to when sending packets that are bound for different destination networks. This routing table can be built via different methods. A network administrator can enter in the routes manually or pick from different routing protocols to build the table automatically. Whatever method you choose depends on the design and goals of the network. The router refers to the routing table to decide which inter-face to send the packet out on and, if more than one route is available, which route is the best. A routing table determines the best route by comparing the routes' metrics, a value that is assigned to the route. Usually, the route with the lowest metric is the best.

Dynamic routing is implemented when a routing protocol is loaded onto a router. The routing protocol configures the routing table based on the rules of the proto-col. Each routing protocol uses a unique set of rules to build the routing table and, if multiple routes are available, to determine which route is best. Routers using a routing protocol send information to each other that each uses to build the routing table. Windows 2000 RRAS supports some—but not all—of the currently popular routing protocols. Routing Information Protocol (RIP) in ver-sions 1 and 2 and Open Shortest Path First (OSPF) are each supported by the RRAS service in Windows 2000.

 Although the Windows 2000 RRAS service understands RIP version 1, only RIP version 2 can be selected as a routing protocol that can be loaded. RIP version 1 is not listed in the RRAS console.

Note: Interior Gateway Routing Protocol (IGRP) and Extended Interior Gateway Routing Protocol (EIGRP), both of which are popular routing protocols, are not supported by default by the RRAS service and will not be discussed as options in this chapter.

Static routing involves an administrator manually building the routing table. The administrator needs to determine which path, from router to router, that the packets should travel. Each router then needs to be programmed with the correct routing information. Static routers that do not have a routing protocol loaded follow the routes with which they are programmed and do not send information or communicate routing paths to other routers. Although performing these manual entries is difficult and time consuming in a large network, static routing can have advantages over dynamic routing. Because static routers do not communicate with each other, they do not add traffic to a network as dynamic routers do. Also, a static router can be integrated into a network that uses dynamic routing. Knowing the advantages and disadvantages of static and dynamic routing helps in deciding which is best to use when designing a network infrastructure.

Enabling Windows 2000 Routing

Although the routing service on a Windows 2000 server—RRAS—is installed automatically, it still needs to be enabled and configured, and this is done with the RRAS Management Console (MMC). You'll find it by going to Start|Programs|Administrative Tools|Routing And Remote Access.

To configure and enable RRAS, follow these steps:

1. Right-click on Routing and Remote Access in the left pane of the RRAS MMC and select Add Server.

2. Select This Computer and click on OK. In the left pane of the main console screen, highlight Server Status. You should now see other options that include the name of the local server.

3. Right-click on the server name and select Configure And Enable Routing And Remote Access.

4. Allow the wizard to guide you through the RRAS setup process. From the Common Configurations screen, select Network Router.

5. From the Routed Protocols screen, select the protocols that this server will use to communicate with connected LANs. (The protocols used for communication must be installed and bound to the appropriate interfaces.)

6. Specify whether to use demand-dial connections.

7. If you decide not to use demand-dial connections, the setup wizard will end. If you are going to use demand-dial connections, the wizard will ask you how you wish to assign IP addresses for incoming connections: by using DHCP or a newly specified range.

8. If you choose to make a new range of IP addresses, you will be prompted for the scope(s) to use. After entering this information, you'll select either Next or Finish to end the installation.

9. Once RRAS is installed, you need to enable routing on the local server. Click on Properties for the routing server in the RRAS MMC.

10. Under the General tab, check the Router box and select LAN or Demand-Dial Routing.

Unicasts, Broadcasts, and Multicasts

When computers send information to other computers, the information packets can be addressed to one or several computers. These types of transmission are unicasts, broadcasts, and multicasts, and each type has a different overhead and effect on the network. A unicast is a packet that is addressed to only one computer. In most network configurations, all computers see this packet, but, because it is specifically addressed to one computer, they ignore the packet. A broadcast packet, on the other hand, isn't addressed to any one computer in particular. Broadcast transmissions increase the network's workload because each computer must process all broadcast packets to see if the information is intended for them or another computer. Multicasts, however, are different from both unicasts and broadcasts, because they can be addressed to a specific group of computers. This capability helps to reduce network traffic. Unlike a broadcast, computers that do not belong to the multicast group can ignore the multicast just as they would a unicast. Also, instead of sending a separate unicast to each computer, a computer can send one set of packets for all computers in a multicast group.

RIP in versions 1 and 2 and OSPF are unicast routing protocols. By default, routers will pass unicasts that are intended for networks other than the one from which it originated. Routers will not, by default, pass broadcasts. If it is decided that the network needs to pass a certain type of broadcast, then the router can be set up to do so. An example of this is the DHCP service, which uses broadcasts. Loading the DHCP Relay Agent (also called BOOTP relay agent) on an RRAS router allows DHCP broadcasts to pass through that router.

IGMP

Multicasting requires the presence of multicasting protocols on the routers within the network. Although several such protocols are available, Microsoft Windows 2000 routing does not support any of them. However, Internet Group Management Protocol (IGMP) can allow multicast forwarding in a TCP/IP environment using Windows 2000 routing. The flexibility of multicasts is that multicast groups can be any size and that computers can join and leave groups at any time. IGMP keeps track of multicast group memberships. For IGMP to perform multicast forwarding, the network adapter must be able to go into multicast-promiscuous mode. Microsoft supports only one-hop forwarding with IGMP and not hopping through multiple routers in Windows 2000 routing.

Routing Information Protocol (RIP)

RIP uses a distance-vector algorithm that counts the number of hops to select the best route. RIP sends all or part of its routing table to its neighboring routers. It is also a single-path protocol, which means that it will have a preferred path to a destination. If two or more paths to a destination are possible, RIP always chooses the same one, provided the path is available. The type of RIP used depends on the protocol stack that is implemented in the network. TCP/IP uses RIP for IP, and NWLink—IPX/SPX in Novell Netware networks—uses RIP for IPX. Each has different implementation on a network, and the configuration for each will be covered later in this chapter.

RIP is best used in small to medium networks because of the way it builds its routing table and because of its hop limitation. RIP routers build their routing tables by broadcasting the networks and routes that they know about. Other RIP routers listen for these broadcasts and build their routing tables from the information contained within them. Each RIP router sends these broadcasts every 30 seconds by default, which can consume a lot of bandwidth on a large network.

Microsoft recommends that RIP be used only in networks with up to 50 subnets. Even with 50 subnets, the network must be designed so that all routes can be reached in 14 hops. While a packet is being routed, it is passed from one router to the next. Each of these passes is considered a hop. RIP normally has a hop limit of 15, but a Windows 2000 router assumes that all routes that aren't learned through a RIP broadcast have a hop count of two. Because none of a RIP router's own routes were learned from RIP, each RIP router gives its own routes a hop count of two. Thus, in Windows 2000 routing, a packet can travel through 14 routers to get to its destination, but, if it continues to a fifteenth router, it will be discarded.

Another reason why RIP cannot be used in large networks is that RIP uses the hop counts to determine the shortest path to a destination host. This may not always be the best path to the destination. In Figure 9.1, the shortest path (by hop count) is through the satellite connections at a speed of 1Mbps, and the longer path is through a T1 connection (1.544Mbps), which RIP will not use unless the satellite link is down. Other routing protocols (such as OSPF) that use more than just the number of hops to determine the best route may work better.

Comparing RIP Versions 1 and 2

You must understand the distinctions between the different versions of RIP. Because a Windows 2000 router will pass RIP v1 and RIP v2 packets, it can exist in a mixed environment of the two versions. RIP v1 does not accommodate flexibility in subnetting. If a network uses Classless Interdomain Routing (CIDR) with supernetting or variable-length subnet masks (VLSM), then only RIP v2 will

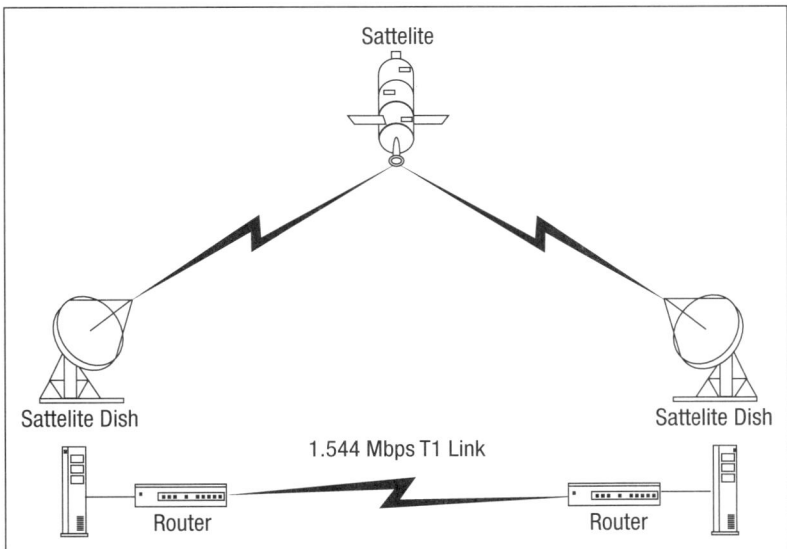

Figure 9.1 RIP hop-count costs.

support these. RIP v1 assumes that all subnet masks are the same across the network and doesn't even include subnet mask information in its routing table, whereas RIP v2 notes this information in the routing table.

In a network with identical network media types of the same speed, RIP is the best choice (provided the network has fewer than 50 subnets with no hop count exceeding 14). If the network media types are different and with differing speeds, OSPF is the best choice for a routing protocol. Although RIP can be used in IP and IPX environments, OSPF can be used only in an IP environment. We'll discuss it in the next section.

Note: Although more than one routing protocol is available, Microsoft recommends that each interface have only one routing protocol for a Windows 2000 router.

Routing in a TCP/IP Environment

In a TCP/IP environment, Windows 2000 RRAS offers two choices: RIP for IP and Open Shortest Path First (OSPF). We've already discussed RIP because it can be used in both a TCP/IP and IPX/SPX environment. The OSPF routing protocol, on the other hand, can be used in only a TCP/IP environment.

OSPF

The OSPF protocol is used in large to very large businesses. Indeed, Microsoft recommends using OSPF when a network has more than 50 subnets. The reason it is not recommended for small to medium networks is because its setup must be carefully planned and tested (which is time consuming). Unlike RIP, which uses a distance-vector algorithm for routing, OSPF uses the more complicated link-state protocol. OSPF routers actually build a map of the network, which is dynamically updated when changes occur. Because OSPF is a multiple-path protocol, it can send packets from the same transmission stream across different routes to the destination.

OSPF requires extensive planning and testing to implement it correctly. OSPF setup involves three levels.

➤ Autonomous system design

➤ Area design (within an autonomous system)

➤ Network design (within an area)

Because multinational companies can be quite large, OSPF designates autonomous systems (AS). Routing tables and maps maintained on the router can handle only so much information, so groups of routers can be designated as belonging to these individual autonomous systems. The routers on the interior of the AS are all a part of the same group and update each other. Border routers join autonomous systems, and all ASes are composed of areas that are connected by a backbone. (Each area that has no connections except to the backbone is called a *stub*.) Figure 9.2 shows four areas joined by a backbone to make one AS. In this diagram, all of the areas are stub networks. If area 4 were connected to area 3 instead of to the backbone, area 4 would be a stub and not area 3.

Routing in a Mixed Environment

Windows 2000 routing with RRAS can be integrated with the other routers. Also, other operating systems that use TCP/IP (such as Unix and Macintosh) can be clients of a Windows 2000 router. Unix uses TCP/IP and can be integrated into a RIP for IP or OSPF environment. AppleTalk routing for Macintosh clients is discussed later in this chapter.

Routing in a Novell Environment

Although new Novell systems use TCP/IP, this section refers to routing in a Novell environment in which IPX/SPX (or NWLink) is being used as the protocol stack for at least a portion of the network. In Windows 2000 routing, only one routing protocol supports this manner of routing: RIP for IPX. The setup for routing in a Novell environment is different than the setup using RIP in a TCP/IP environment.

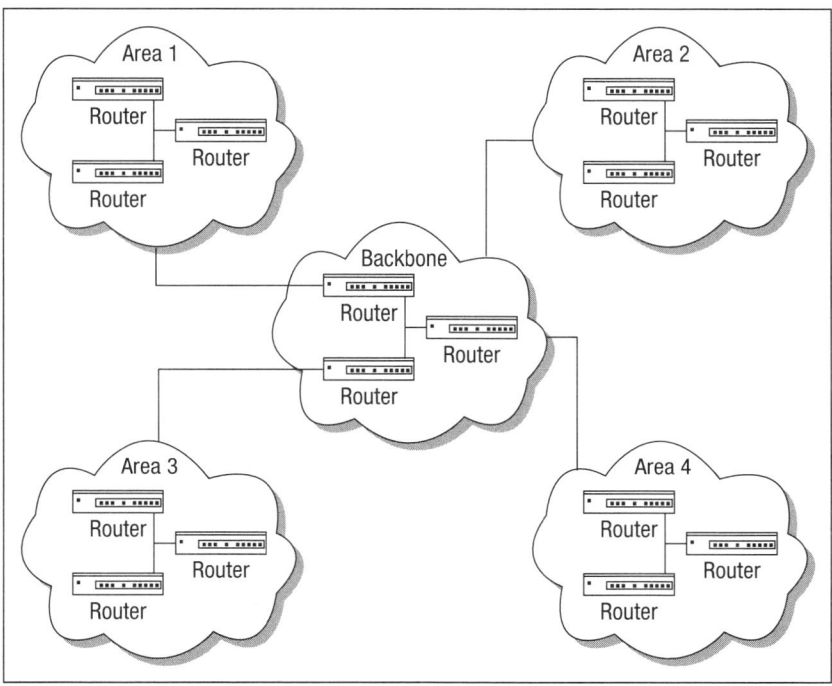

Figure 9.2   Autonomous system network.

Service Advertising Protocol (SAP)

Although it isn't a true routing protocol, SAP is an essential element when set-ting up routing for a Novell environment. Novell Netware servers can advertise services that they provide to the network with SAP. Netware clients can locate needed services by sending SAP requests. SAP allows the Windows 2000 RRAS server to keep a list of the servers and their services so that, when a client requests a service, the server (if on the local network segment) can acknowledge that it has the services requested. If the needed service is on another network segment, the router will acknowledge the server's existence for the client to communicate with the server. All routers that will be acknowledging these requests must have SAP enabled.

When a server comes on line, it broadcasts its service information, and these broadcasts are added to the router's SAP table, which is then broadcast to all networks to which the router is connected. This process continues across the whole network, until all SAP information is eventually propagated throughout the network.

AppleTalk Routing

Besides an IP and IPX router, the Windows 2000 RRAS service also supports AppleTalk routing for Macintosh clients. AppleTalk has two versions of networking: phase 1 and phase 2. Windows 2000 routing supports AppleTalk phase 2. AppleTalk also designates a *seed router* to broadcast routes for a network. (Windows 2000 routing can be a seed or non-seed router.)

Comparing Routing Protocols

As mentioned, each routing protocol has its benefits and drawbacks. Depending on the configuration and size of a given network, one protocol may be preferred—or even required—over another. Table 9.1 compares RIP and OSPF.

Convergence is the time that it takes for all routers in a WAN to update their routing tables with a route change. Although route changes can occur when a LAN is added or removed from the WAN, the main convergence issue is when a router malfunctions and the other routers must route packets around it. RIP updates are timed according to configuration settings, with the default being 30 seconds. When the table is updated, RIP broadcasts it in its entirety. OSPF, on the other hand, updates the routing tables only when a change is detected in the network topology. Further, OSPF broadcasts only the changes. These two features make OSPF's convergence time shorter than RIP's (and reduce the network traffic, also).

Routing in a WAN Environment

A network that contains WAN connections requires more configuration than those without WAN connections. Demand-dial connections and leased lines have required and optional settings for connectivity and security.

Table 9.1   Comparing RIP and OSPF.

Attribute	OSPF	RIP
Convergence	Converges faster	Converges slower
Hop-count limits	Has no limit	Has a hop limit of 15 (14 in Windows 2000)
Path-determination	Uses bandwidth to determine routes	Uses a hop count as its metric
Router table updates	Has optimized updates	Has unwieldy updates

Demand-Dial Connections

Demand-dial connections are controlled by placing routers on either side of the connection. RRAS allows for control of these connections with filters and time restrictions. The filters control which packets will be dropped and which packets are allowed to pass through the router. RRAS allows for packet filters that control which types of traffic are allowed, and these filters are applied to every type of connection including demand-dial connections because they are applied after the connection to the router is made. If you want to restrict just demand-dial connections, you can apply a demand-dial filter. A demand-dial filter is applied before the connection is made, so that the demand-dial connection won't even be used if the criteria are not met. Setting dial-out hours for users can also control demand-dial connections. With this setting, the administrator can set during which hours of the day that dial-in use is permitted. RRAS controls packet types and dial-out hours for the whole connection. If you want to control these settings by groups of users, then a remote-access policy is needed. When you are placing routers at demand-dial connections, Microsoft recommends that you configure static routes to reduce overhead for traffic and administration.

Note: Although demand-dial connections are often pay-per-use, they can also be persistent, as in the case with ISDN.

Leased Line Connections

When using leased lines, extra equipment is needed to adapt the signal. A Channel Service Unit/Data Service Unit (CSU/DSU) connects a T1 or T3 line to a network and is required for both sides of the connection. Routers are used in conjunction with the CSU/DSU to control traffic over the leased line. Figure 9.3 shows a network with a T1 connection that has CSU/DSUs and routers to make the WAN connection.

Integration

The routing features of RRAS integrate well with some Windows 2000 features to enhance the network.

Depending on the needs of the network, the following features may be implemented individually or together.

Internet Protocol Security (IPSec)

When used with RRAS, IPSec enables authentication and encryption between routers. So, not only does IPSec prevent unauthorized routers from being added to the network, it also uses encryption to keep routing information secure. Both of these options are useful when using the Internet as the backbone.

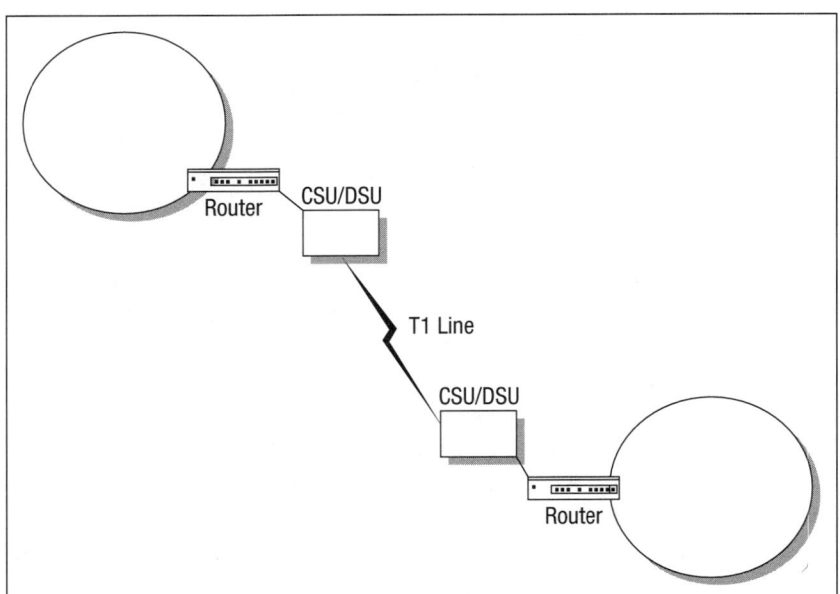

Figure 9.3 Routing with WAN connections (T1 with router).

Routing and Remote Access

Routing and remote access allows connections between routers to be dial-on-demand. This feature can be used with connection devices such as modems and ISDN adapters.

Active Directory

Active Directory allows certificates to be used to authenticate routers. This will be covered in more detail in the following section.

Security

Securing routers in a network is a task crucial to keeping the network safe from other network segments (which may include the Internet).

You have many options in securing routers, and deciding which to implement depends on your network and security needs.

Authentication

Windows can manage access authentication through Active Directory. To be able to communicate with another RRAS server in the group, the remote RRAS server must be a member of the RAS or IAS security group.

Authentication can be set through RADIUS, in which user credentials are used to verify the RRAS server.

Virtual Private Network (VPN)

VPNs can be established between routers to ensure that the transmissions among them are secure.

Through VPNs, security can be set using three possible types of protocols depending on existing architecture:

➤ *Point-to-Point Tunneling Protocol (PPTP)*—Used in networks that already have other Windows 2000 RRAS servers and any third-party routers that can support PPTP. If the network is already using Windows NT 4 RAS servers, then PPTP must be used (if security is needed).

➤ *Layer 2 Tunneling Protocol (L2TP)*—Used in networks that already have other Windows 2000 RRAS servers and any third-party routers that can support L2TP. Windows NT 4 does not support L2TP.

➤ *Internet Protocol Security (IPSec)*—Used in conjunction with L2TP to add authentication to L2TP. Certificates are required with IPSec, and these can be set under Group Policy or by using the Certificate Snap-in. Every RRAS server must have a certificate loaded for IPSec to work properly.

Availability

You can use many strategies to ensure that a RRAS server is available for constant use.

➤ Make sure that one RRAS server is dedicated to routing. Having a dedicated RRAS server prevents you from having to reboot the server whenever you add applications or change a configuration setting.

➤ Have multiple RRAS server connections in a mesh to provide redundant links to all of the network segments. This mesh will prevent any segment from becoming disconnected from the rest of the network.

➤ Have redundant RRAS servers to fill in for a failed RRAS server.

➤ Use persistent connections from the RRAS servers to keep the connections running at all times. This ensures availability between network segments.

Performance

Solutions to performance issues are somewhat the same as the solutions to availability problems.

➤ A RRAS server should be dedicated to its task to prevent its resources from being used by unimportant applications or services. This exclusivity improves routing performance by making sure the resources are available when needed.

➤ Have multiple RRAS server connections in a mesh to allow multiple paths to destinations. This option is extremely important with OSPF, which uses bandwidth as a metric to make path selection. These multiple connections prevent overutilized network segments from being swamped with traffic.

➤ Having multiple RRAS servers to distribute traffic is greatly preferred to having a single, central RRAS server that routes almost all of the traffic. (As stated previously, use multiple connections.)

➤ For better performance between network segments, use persistent connections from the RRAS servers to keep the connections running at all times. Having to establish connections takes time and decreases performance.

Practice Questions

Case Study

Current LAN/Network Structure

2Market currently has 10 branch offices with headquarters in Chicago, Illinois. The branch offices are located in the following cities:

Los Angeles, California

New York City, New York

Houston, Texas

Miami, Florida

Indianapolis, Indiana

Boston, Massachusetts

Salt Lake City, Utah

Nashville, Tennessee

Redmond, Washington

Aspen, Colorado

The branch offices are not currently connected in a network.

Proposed LAN/Network Structure

2Market wants to purchase a Web-based application for the branch managers to place orders and to see upcoming price specials.

Current WAN Connectivity

None at the current time.

Proposed WAN/Internet Connectivity

2Market wants to connect all branches through the Internet while still remaining isolated for security.

All branches will have access to not only resources on the Internet, but also to the Web-based application that is located at the headquarters in Chicago. Access to the Web-based application must be available 24 hours a day, 7 days a week.

Question 1

Which routing protocols could be used? [Check all correct answers]

- ❏ a. NetBEUI
- ❏ b. RIP for IP
- ❏ c. TCP/IP
- ❏ d. RIP for IPX
- ❏ e. OSPF
- ❏ f. IPX/SPX
- ❏ g. IGMP

The answers are b and e. Choices a, c, and f are routed protocols, not routing protocols. Choice d is incorrect because the Internet (which is TCP/IP-based) will be used as the backbone. IGMP is for multicasting purposes, which is not required. This leaves only the choices for RIP for IP and OSPF.

Question 2

If the branch offices had multiple connections to the Internet, with each being a different network media and speed, which routing protocol would be the best choice?

- ○ a. RIP for IP
- ○ b. RIP for IPX
- ○ c. IGMP
- ○ d. OSPF

The correct answer is d. OSPF's metric is based on bandwidth. If there were multiple routes with each a different speed, OSPF would be the best choice for selecting the best route.

Question 3

The Redmond and Salt Lake City offices want to connect to Chicago through a demand-dial connection. In the following diagram, place routers in the correct positions.

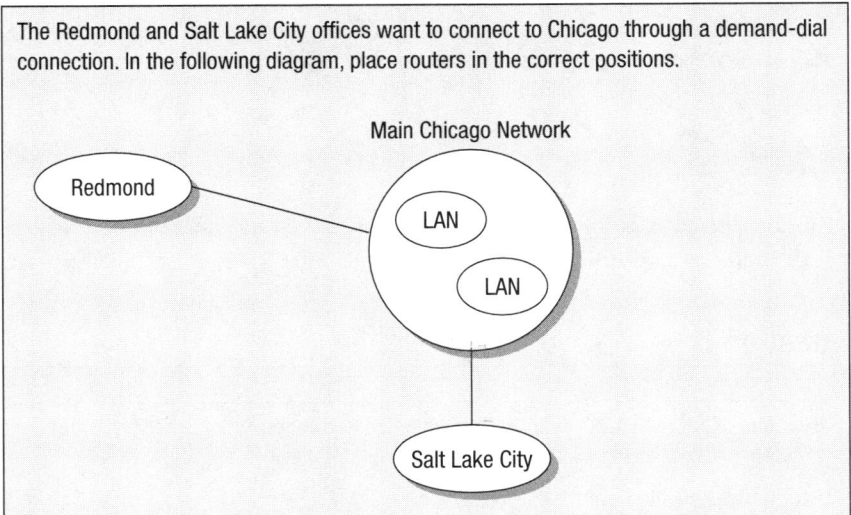

The answer is:

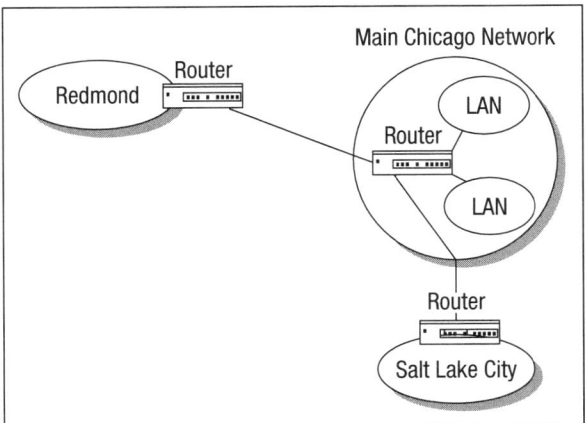

A router needs to be added at each of the remote locations. At least one router is needed at the Chicago office connecting the LANs at Chicago with the remote locations. More than one router can be used at the Chicago location.

Question 4

> If demand-dial connections were used to connect all branch offices and only static routes were used instead of routing protocols, this design would improve performance.
>
> ○ a. True
>
> ○ b. False

The answer is a. Routing protocols will use resources and network bandwidth, which decreases performance. Static routes are preferred for their low overhead.

Question 5

> The Miami office will have T1 connection. What connectivity device(s) is needed with this connection? [Check all correct answers]
>
> ❑ a. A router on either side of the connection.
>
> ❑ b. A router on one side of each connection.
>
> ❑ c. A CSU/DSU on either side of each connection.
>
> ❑ d. A CSU/DSU on one side of the connection.

The correct answers are a and c. A CSU/DSU at the T1 connection is required to connect the network with the T1 line. A router between the CSU/DSU and the network will control traffic over the WAN connection.

Question 6

> Aspen to Chicago is a demand-dial connection. The network administrator wants to allow only TCP port 80 for access into Chicago from this connection and wants to allow users access only between 8 A.M. to 5 P.M. daily. He also wants administrators to be able to use the demand-dial connection 24 hours a day. What will he need to configure to accomplish these goals? [Check all correct answers]
>
> ❑ a. Demand-dial filter
>
> ❑ b. Proxy server
>
> ❑ c. Dial-in hours
>
> ❑ d. Remote access policy

The correct answers are a and d. A demand-dial filter will allow the administrator to close all ports except for port 80. Because this feature is available, the administrator does not need a proxy server. Configuring dial-in hours at the RRAS server will apply to all users including administrators. To apply dial-in hours to selective groups of people will require a remote access policy.

Question 7

If a 2Market branch had four connections to the Internet and OSPF were being used, which would be the chosen route?

○ a. 28.8Kbps link

○ b. 56Kbps link

○ c. 2–56Kbps multilink

○ d. 2–28.8Kbps multilink

The correct answer is c, which gives a total bandwidth of 102Kbps—the most of the available choices.

Question 8

If authentication and encryption were to be used over the VPN, which two options could be used in conjunction? [Choose the two that apply]

❑ a. IPSec

❑ b. PPTP

❑ c. PPP

❑ d. L2TP

The correct answers are a and d. IPSec and L2TP used together provide authentication and encryption. PPTP uses MPPE as its encryption protocol, and MPPE does not need to be selected seprately from PPTP. PPP is used for dial-up connections for remote access (See Chapter 11).

Need to Know More?

 Microsoft Corporation. *Windows 2000 Server Resource Kit.* Microsoft Press, Redmond, WA, 2000. ISBN 1-57231-805-8. The *Internetworking Guide* provides useful information on routing and routing protocols.

 Rees, Matthew, and Jeffrey Coe. *CCNA Routing and Switching Exam Cram.* The Coriolis Group, Scottsdale, AZ, 1999. ISBN 1-57610-434-6. This book covers basic routing concepts in depth.

 Search the TechNet CD (or its online version through **www.microsoft. com**) using the keyword "RRAS", "OSPF", or "RIP". Also, see the Windows 2000 Server or Advanced Server help.

Dfs

Terms you'll need to know:

✓ The Distributed File System (Dfs) tree

✓ Dfs root

✓ Domain-based root

✓ Standalone root

✓ The blob

✓ Dfs link

✓ Root replica

✓ Link replica

Techniques you'll need to master:

✓ Using the Dfs Administration MMC

✓ Creating the Dfs tree

✓ Creating a replica

✓ Ensuring fault tolerance and redundant links

In this chapter, you'll learn what the Distributed File System (Dfs) is and how it can be implemented in your environment. You'll become familiar with the capabilities of Dfs and the requirements for Windows 2000, Windows NT 4, and Windows 9x operating systems. We'll cover Dfs administration and design, along with some practical applications and examples. You'll be introduced to the installation procedure for Windows 2000, as either a Dfs server or client.

Dfs Overview

Microsoft Dfs was first released as an add-on for Microsoft Windows NT 4. In a large-enterprise environment, servers are replaced due to attrition faster than we would like. Moving shared data results in changes to profiles and logon scripts. Another downfall is the transfer sometimes causes mission-critical data to be unavailable for unacceptable lengths of time. Dfs acts like a file manager for your network shares. It allows administrators to create a directory tree that appears to be located on one server when, in actuality, the tree could contain shared folders from several different servers.

Dfs Capabilities

Dfs can make files stored on multiple servers appear to be located on a single server. For example, you have four servers in your LAN. One server is located in the accounting department, one in the sales department, one in the production department, and one in the administration department. All of the departments have shared directories with files that are accessed via drive mappings by all the other departments. With the current design, each client workstation will require four mappings to access the data. With Dfs, you can create a share that will incorporate all of the shared directories on the servers and give the users a single drive mapping. What's more, this can be done seamlessly, during production hours, and with no interruption of the users' access to the files. If you have used logon scripts to create the previous mappings, the process is further simplified. The administrator can simply change the **net use** command within the logon script to point to the new share. After the user reboots, the new share is available.

In addition, let's say that the shipping department has grown and is no longer able to use the production server. After the new server has been placed in the shipping department, you move its data files to the new shipping server. With Dfs, you can change the location of the directories, and the users will not notice the change. Dfs does not display the location of the linked files or rely on UNC (universal naming convention) for user navigation. Dfs can also provide fail-over redundancy for the files at all locations by using root or link replicas, which will be described later in this chapter.

With Dfs, you are no longer limited by the available disk space on a server. When space is needed for Dfs volumes, simply add another server to your Dfs tree. Because the process of adding additional servers is transparent to the clients, it prevents additional mappings or profile changes.

Common Uses

Dfs is most commonly used to provide centralized access to shared files. When creating a Dfs tree in an enterprise environment, the Dfs share becomes a centralized area for managing the shared directories.

By using the Dfs tree, you can add or remove servers or directories without changing the user's environment. For example, you have a tree that includes a directory called Focus on a server called Global. If the server becomes disabled, you can restore the Focus directory from a backup tape to another server and change the Dfs link to refer to the Focus directory on the replacement server. After the directory has been restored, the file is available again in its original context from within the Dfs root. All of these steps can be accomplished without changing the environment for the users. You can then restore the Global server as time allows.

Most enterprise networks use centralized backup, and you can better utilize a backup server by implementing a Dfs file structure in your network. You simply allow Dfs to manage the files. Windows 2000 backup is capable of backing up shared directories on remote servers. Dfs can simplify this process by managing the files and folders for you. Instead of browsing multiple servers and shares during the backup job creation, all you have to do is to select a single shared directory to back up. If you have created replicas of your links and one of the linked files is unavailable at the scheduled backup time, the backup agent will be directed to the replica and the backup will function as if the files were available.

The Dfs Tree

Dfs organizes your network files in a hierarchical structure referred to as the *tree*. The root is the top level of your Dfs tree, and shared folders added to the root are known as *leaf objects*. Leaf objects can be added to the root during or after its creation.

Dfs leaf objects have two limitations: They must reside in the same domain, and they cannot span multiple servers.

Active Directory Integration

Dfs is integrated with the Active Directory (AD) database and replicates between domain controllers. The AD database is used to store the topology information of the Dfs tree. The host domain controller stores the topology information known as the *blob* or Binary Large Object, and replicates this information to all other Dfs-enabled domain controllers. Before the replication is complete (which can take up to five minutes for local DCs), the controller's views of the Dfs tree may not be the same. This is because the blob does not replicate just the changes of the tree design. Instead, the entire blob will be replicated across the domain, which can cause latency and increased network traffic. If the controllers are located across slower WAN links, factor this into your blob replication time. While the replication is taking place, clients local to the DC—which is not synchronized with the hosting server—will also have a copy of the tree that is not current. To force synchronization after changes occur, use the refresh utility from within the Dfs administrator on the hosting DC.

Requirements for Windows 2000 Dfs

Windows 2000 has certain requirements for Dfs root servers to host a domain or standalone Dfs root. Table 10.1 lists the requirements for a Dfs root server in a Windows 2000 domain environment.

Although Windows 2000 can host a Dfs root as either a domain controller or a member server, you are limited to hosting one Dfs root on a server. You can have the root reside on an NTFS or FAT partition, and the advantages of the root residing on an NTFS partition are security and synchronization of shared folders.

Windows NT 4 can host a Dfs root as a member server only. This limitation is because of to the inability of the AD to fully integrate with the older flat-file account database that is incorporated into Windows NT 4.

Windows 2000 has certain requirements for clients to be able to access a Dfs tree or host a linked folder. Table 10.2 lists the requirements for a Dfs client in a Windows 2000 domain environment.

Dfs clients are able to browse the Dfs tree and host a shared file in the tree. Clients are limited to using Dfs from within the domain where they reside. Multiple-domain environments require a Dfs root in each domain that will be used by domain members. The clients cache a referral to a Dfs root or a Dfs link for a

Table 10.1	Requirements for a Dfs root server in a Windows 2000 domain environment.	
Operating System	**Other Requirements**	**Operations**
Windows 2000		Can host Dfs root as DC or member server
Win NT 4	Service Pack 3 or higher	Can host Dfs root as a member server only

Table 10.2	Requirements for a Dfs client in a Windows 2000 domain environment.		
Operating System	**Other Requirements**	**Operations**
Windows 2000 Professional		Able to host shared folders within a Dfs root
Windows NT 4 Server	Service Pack 3 or higher	Able to host shared folders within a Dfs root
Windows NT Workstation	Service Pack 3 or higher	Able to host shared folders within a Dfs root
Windows 98	Client for Dfs 4/5	Able to host shared folders within a Dfs root
Windows 95	Client for Dfs 4/5	Able to host shared folders within a Dfs root
DOS and Windows 3.1	Not supported	

specific time period, which is set by the administrator from within the Dfs administration MMC.

Installing Dfs Host Servers

The following sections detail the installation of the Dfs services that are needed to host the Dfs root.

Windows 2000

With the release of Windows 2000, Dfs is now integrated into the operating system, and you do not need to install any additional software or make any selections during the installation. If the administration tools have been installed on the server, you will find the Dfs administrator in Programs|Administrative Tools. If the administrative tools were either not installed or have been removed, you may install them from the administrative tools setup program located in the I386 directory on the Windows 2000 CD-ROM.

Windows NT 4

Because Windows NT 4 was released before Dfs, a working copy of Dfs was not included with Windows NT 4 Server, Workstation, or BackOffice. The software, however, is free and can be downloaded from Microsoft's Web site. The download file is a self-extracting executable that will expand the files in the appropriate directories when it is launched.

After installing the file, add the Dfs service from the network applet within the control panel. When this has been completed, a Configure Dfs dialog box is displayed. You'll be prompted to enter the name of the share (which will become your root), or you can choose to create a new share.

Client Software

Windows NT 4 requires client software to view Dfs shared trees. With the release of Windows 2000, Windows NT 4 and Windows 98 clients were able to browse and host shared directories without client software. Windows 95 requires a Dfs client 4/5. Windows for Workgroups, DOS, and NetWare servers are not able to either browse or host a Dfs folder.

Browsing a Dfs Tree

You can browse a Dfs tree just like any other shared directory with subdirectories. The root directory of the share is, of course, the Dfs root directory. The subdirectories are shared directories that can be located anywhere with your domain. The example in Figure 10.1 shows the Dfs root "Domain Root". Inside Domain Root, the folders Dfs 1 through 5 are visible. These folders are shares located on servers 2K01 and 2K02 within the domain. The folders Dfs2 and Dfs4 are located on 2K01, and Dfs1, Dfs3, and Dfs5 are located on 2K02. The folder Link On Win98 Client is a shared folder on the Windows 98 workstation Compaq. The Users folder is a subdirectory that resides inside the folder that was designated as the root. This folder is not shared, but, because it is inside the root folder, which is shared, it is also accessible by browsing the root.

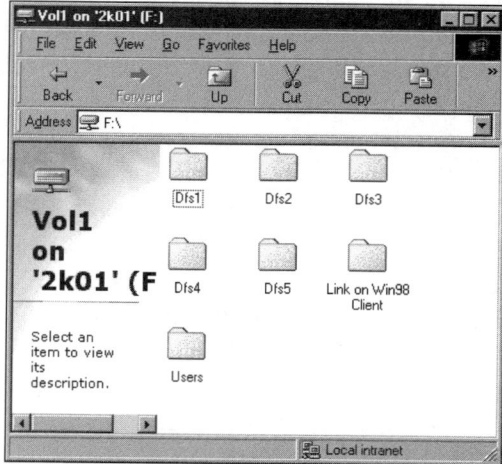

Figure 10.1   The Dfs root "Domain Root".

This example demonstrates the flexibility of the Dfs tree. In this example, you can see the ability to add folders from other servers and clients, and to place folders directly within the Dfs root directory to provide access to the users. The destination or link of the folder is not shown, which gives the users a seamless interface.

Planning is the important key when you build your tree. If you plan correctly, a logical order can be used to prevent users from accessing multiple drive mappings on different servers. Any modifications after the initial implementation will result in different views of the tree until replication has taken place and the workstation's cache has expired.

Administration Tools

Dfs is controlled from a server in your Windows 2000 network. (The server can be a DC or member server.) You can choose to create a Dfs root directory on the server you have accessed, or on another server within your domain, by using the administration tools. Figure 10.2 shows the Dfs administrator and the Dfs domain-based root used in the previous example.

When you launch the Distributed File System MMC from the administrative tools program group, two panes will be displayed. The left pane shows your tree design, and the right pane displays the details of the selected icon. This configuration is very similar to Windows Explorer or WinFile. When the Dfs administration program has been started, the MMC will display the Dfs root on that

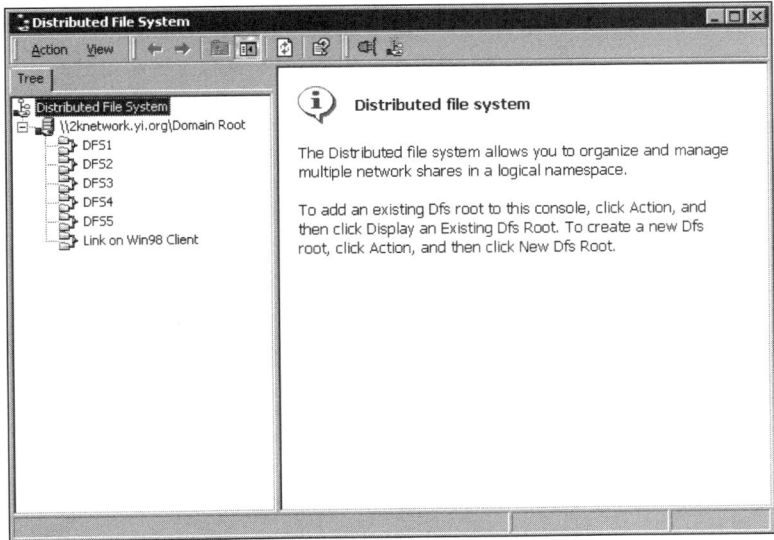

Figure 10.2 The Dfs administrator and the Dfs domain-based root.

server (if one has been created). If you do not have a root on this machine, you can connect and manage any root partition in the domain by right-clicking on the Distributed File System icon in the tree pane and choosing Display An Existing Dfs Root, or by using the action menu.

The toolbar buttons at the top of the MMC allow you to perform functions inside the console. If you click on the Create A New Dfs Root button, a wizard will guide you through the rest of the process.

After you have created the root, Dfs links will be added or deleted from this console. For redundancy, you can create replicas, which allow you to specify an additional directory that the users will be directed to if the primary shared folder becomes unavailable. You can also specify that changes within the replicated directory be duplicated on the replica. This is an extremely powerful tool, but you must be aware that, if you implement this on a large folder that is changed frequently, you will increase the traffic created by the changes. Table 10.3 lists all options available from within the Dfs administration program.

Table 10.3 Dfs administration program options.	
Menu Item	**Action**
New Dfs Link	Creates a link or pointer to a shared directory.
New Root Replica	Replicates a copy of the root share to another server for fault tolerance. Not available on standalone Dfs root shares.
New Replica	Creates a replica of the selected link.
Remove Display Of Dfs Root	Removes the display of the selected Dfs root from the MMC.
Delete Dfs Root	Deletes the Dfs root.
Replication Policy	Allows the administrator to set the replica to automatic replication.
Check Status	Performs a check of the link destination for the specified object.
Open	Opens the selected link or root with Windows Explorer.
New	Another way to create a new link, root, or replica.
All Tasks	Shows the tasks that are available for the selected object.
View	Allows the administrator to customize the detail view.
Refresh	Refreshes the Dfs view or forces a replication of the blob.
Export	Allows the administrator to export the selected item's name and link type to a text file or comma-separated text file.
Properties	Allows the administrator to view the properties of the selected item. Share permissions can be made by selecting the Security tab.
Help	Allows the administrator to view the help files.

Creating a Dfs Root

To create a new Dfs root, first launch the wizard by right clicking on the Distributed File System icon in the tree pane of the Dfs MMC. The first window informs you that you have accessed the wizard and prompts you to click on Next to begin the creation. A dialog box then asks you if you would like to create a standalone or domain-based root. After you have made this decision, continue by clicking on Next. Now you will be prompted to enter the server location, or the server that will host the Dfs root. You can specify this either by typing in the server name, network name, and extension or by simply browsing and selecting it.

After you have entered the root location, you are asked to specify the root share, or the shared directory that will contain the pointers for the Dfs tree. You can use an existing network share or have the wizard create a new one. After you have entered a name for a new directory, the wizard asks you to enter a shared name for the directory and any comments that you would like to include. The next window that appears lists the parameters that you have entered during this process and prompts you to click on Finish to complete the process.

Dfs Fault Tolerance and Load Balancing

In a Windows 2000 environment, Dfs can integrate with Active Directory to provide fault-tolerant root shares. If you have multiple servers in your domain, any or all of the participating hosts can provide fault-tolerant Dfs root shares. Active Directory is used to ensure domain controllers in the domain share of a common Dfs architecture. This is implemented by choosing the domain-based root option during the root creation.

Likewise, you can create a standalone Dfs root, but doing so does not take advantage of Active Directory and does not provide the fault tolerance as with the domain-based option. A standalone Dfs root will, however, allow you to have an unlimited number of Dfs root shares in a domain.

With domain-based Dfs root topology, up to 32 DCs can host a single Dfs root and can have unlimited multiple Dfs root volumes within the domain. Use the new root replica on domain-based Dfs roots by right-clicking on the root and choosing New Root Replica from the drop-down menu.

Additional root or linked folders can provide load balancing by breaking up the shared data to several standalone Dfs root shares. As users request files from the node in the Dfs namespace, they randomly select one of the computers for the accessed node.

By using root and link replicas, you can create a virtual failover cluster for your file structure. If the shared directory is unavailable when a client tries to access it, the user is automatically directed to a replica of that file. This redirection is transparent to the user, occurring without their knowledge or interaction. Mission-critical files located within your Dfs root should be replicated to other servers. At this time, Microsoft's cluster server will not support Dfs topology. Replicas will be explained further in this chapter.

Dfs File System Security

You need to be a member of the administrators group to create a root partition; otherwise, Dfs does not implement any additional security features. For example, if you have created a Dfs link to a shared folder and your account has the appropriate permissions to access the shared directory, accessing through the Dfs root share will be possible.

To assign permissions to a Dfs folder, use My Computer or Windows Explorer. With the exception of the root, all folders will need to be shared before they are added to the tree. After your tree is constructed, you can change permissions using Windows Explorer or My Computer.

To take advantage of file system security, the Dfs root or linked folder must reside on an NTFS partition. FAT partitions provide only share-level security. Also, a Dfs root or shared folders must reside on an NTFS partition to take advantage of automatic replication.

Creating a New Link to a Shared Folder

Now that you have created your Dfs root, it is time to incorporate shared folders to complete your tree design. Like creating a root, pop-up dialog boxes will guide you through the addition of the new Dfs link. To begin the new Dfs link dialog box, right-click on your Dfs root in the left pane of the MMC. From the pop-up menu that appears, select New Dfs Link from the menu, and a Create A New Dfs Link dialog box appears.

Enter the name that you would like to be displayed from within the root share in the Link Name dialog box. Now specify the UNC path to the shared folder in the Send The User To This Shared Folder dialog box. The Comment dialog box allows you to add a comment to the link that will be visible when you right-click on the link and choose Properties.

The Clients Cache This Referral For dialog box allows you to specify the amount of time that the link will appear within the root if it has become unavailable. The default is 1,800 seconds (30 minutes). After you have entered this information and clicked on OK, the link will be added to your root. Figure 10.3 shows the Create A New Dfs Link dialog box.

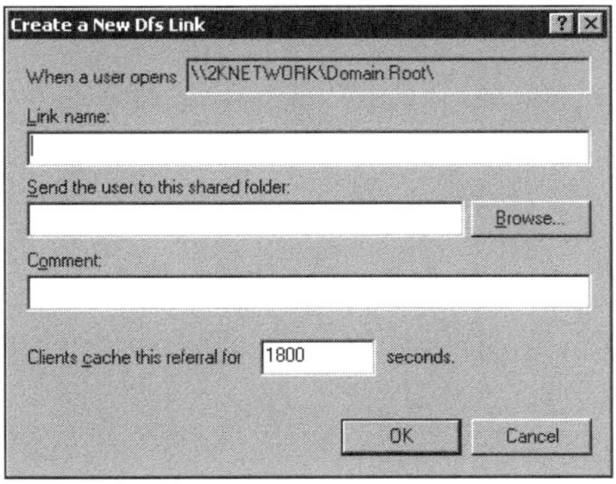

Figure 10.3   The Create A New Dfs Link dialog box.

Deleting a Link to a Shared Folder

Deleting a link is a very simple process. You simply right-click on the link name and choose Remove Dfs Link from the pop-up menu. This immediately deletes the link; however, the link remains visible to the client until the cache has expired.

Creating a Replica

Replicas of a Dfs root or leaf object can be created to provide fault tolerance. Both the primary and the destination of the replicated folder must reside on an NTFS partition to take advantage of automatic replication, which synchronizes the data and files located within these two directories. Doing this, however, increases the amount of traffic on your network. Replicas are better utilized on directories that do not change frequently. A good example is company-related forms that are utilized by departments to complete their daily work.

Banks and insurance companies utilize data normally provided on CD-ROM for value estimation. These files are normally copied from the CD to a network share for company-wide use. If you place this network share inside a Dfs root and use automatic replication, you will not only have redundant copies for fault tolerance, but you will need to update the primary folder with only the new files. The changes will be automatically propagated to replica directories for you.

To create a replica, right-click on the Dfs link or root from within the tree pane of the MMC and choose New Replica from the drop-down menu. This opens the New Replica window. Then send the user to this shared folder dialog box. Specify the destination directory by its UNC path or click the browse button. Now select either the Manual Replication radio button or the Automatic Replication dialog button from the replication policy options group. Manual replication provides no replication service to the destination directory. Any updates will

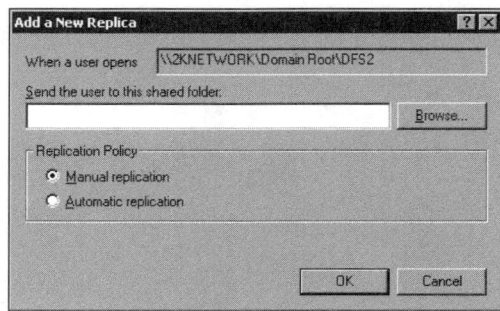

Figure 10.4   The Create New Replica dialog box.

need to be done by the administrator. The automatic replication option will synchronize the primary and destination folders behind the scenes. Figure 10.4 shows the Create New Replica dialog box.

To change the replication policy, right-click on the Dfs link in the tree pane of the MMC and choose Replication Properties from the drop-down menu. This opens the Replication Policy window, where you'll make changes to your configuration. You are also able to change the primary and destination directories.

Root replicas create a copy of the root share on another server for fault tolerance. This feature is available only on domain-based Dfs roots.

Deleting a Replica

Deleting a replica is a simple process. Simply click on the leaf object in the left pane of the MMC. The right pane of the MMC will now display the object and its replica. Now you can right-click on the replica and chose Remove Replica from the drop-down menu.

Dfs Command Index

Dfs supports command-line configuration and management. In most cases, these command-line options will be used in program files or from within a programmer's code. Custom-built applications can utilize the flexibility of the Dfs tree structure in enterprise applications. Table 10.4 lists the available commands and their function.

Optimizing Your Dfs Design

The previous topics of this chapter relate to the requirements and criteria for implementing Dfs in your Windows 2000 environment. This section describes a scenario and the ways to best optimize your Dfs design.

Table 10.4 Available Dfs command index.	
Command	**Function**
NetDfsAdd	Creates a new Dfs link or adds a share to an existing link
NetDfsAddStdRoot	Creates a new standard or standalone Dfs root
NetDfsAddStdRootForced	Creates a new standard or standalone Dfs root in a cluster environment, allowing an offline share to host the standalone Dfs root
NetDfsEnum	Enumerates all Dfs links in a named Dfs root
NetDfsGetClientInfo	Returns the client's cached information regarding a specific Dfs object
NetDfsGetInfo	Returns information about a Dfs link
NetDfsManagerInitialize	Reinitializes the Dfs service on a specified server
NetDfsRemove	Removes a share from a Dfs link; removes the Dfs link if the share is the last associated with the specified link
NetDfsRemoveFtRoot	Removes a server and share from a domain-based Dfs implementation; deletes the Dfs root if there are no more associated shares
NetDfsRemoveFtRootForced	Removes the specified server from a domain-based Dfs implementation even if the server is offline

Let's say that you are designing a Dfs structure for a WAN that consists of three separate locations: A, B, and C, as shown in Figure 10.5.

Location A is the company headquarters, which houses the corporate officers and the IS staff. This location has two DCs, two member servers, and 150 hosts. One of the member servers is a backup server that uses a DLT drive to back up mission critical files. The DCs contain forms that are used in the company's daily operations. DC1 houses shared folders named Employee and Customers that are needed by all locations. DC2 houses a shared folder named Managers that should be available to the management staff at all locations.

Location B is where the marketing and sales headquarters are located. This location has two DCs, no member servers, and 100 hosts. DC3 houses a shared folder called Potential, and DC4 houses a shared folder called Forecast that should be available to all employees at all locations.

Location C is the production facility that has one DC and one member server. The member server contains a shared folder called Production that needs to be accessed by the administrators and sales team at the other locations.

All of the shared folders are located on NTFS partitions. You are responsible for creating a solution for a centralized backup using the standard NT backup, as

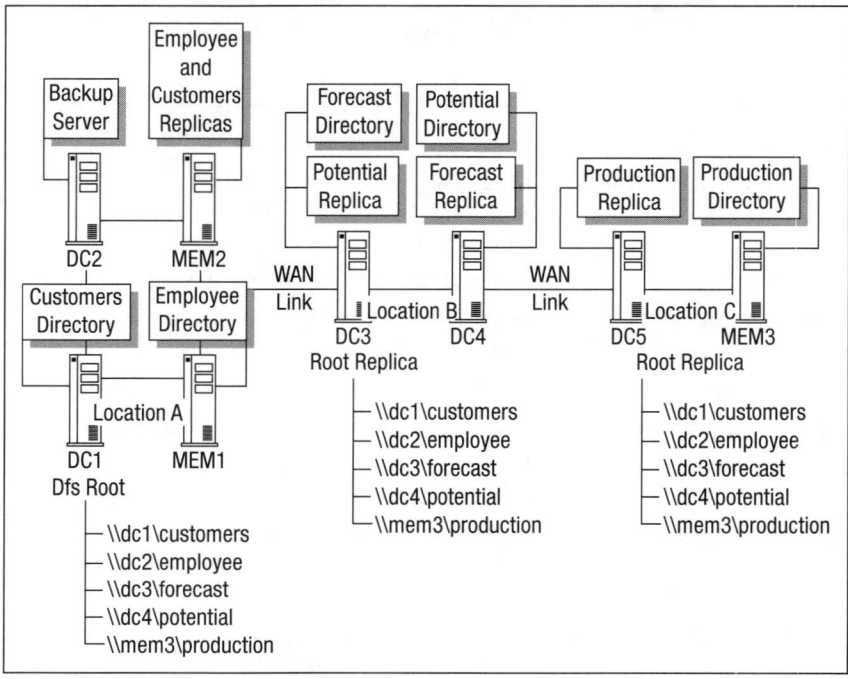

Figure 10.5 The sample Dfs structure for a WAN.

well as a seamless interface to the corporate shared files. Because these files are mission critical, your design should provide redundancy.

You have decided that you will create a domain Dfs root. You will create the root for the shared folders on MEM1 at location A and name it Corpshare. After you have created the root, you add the pointers to the shared folders Customers and Employees at location A. Now, you add the links for the shared folders Forecast and Potential at location B. You then add a link to the shared directory Production at location C.

The folders currently have the correct security permissions, so no changes are needed. Now edit the logon script for the users to point to the DC1 server's Corpshare folder. From the Dfs administrator, right-click on the Dfs root that you created, and choose New Root Replica. Place the replicas on DC3 at location B and MEM3 at location C. This allows the users to access the root if DC1 or a WAN connection becomes disabled.

Now, to provide redundancy of the links, place replicas of the Customers and Employees shared folders on MEM02 at location A. Replicas of the Forecast and Potential shares are located on the servers at locations opposite of which they reside. A replica of the production link is placed on DC05 at location C. All of the root and link replicas have been set to update automatically. This will keep the data in the primary and replicated directories synchronized. Because the locations are geographically separated to minimize the replication traffic, with the exception of the root directories, the replicas have been placed with the subnet. If a WAN link goes down, users will be able to access the shared files local to their subnet and the servers at whichever of the two links has not been disabled.

The backup server is able to access the shared directories from one location provided by the Dfs root. This requires the selection of only one shared directory when the backup job is defined in Windows 2000 Backup.

Practice Questions

Case Study

VirtuCon is a manufacturer of hi-tech equipment, based in Carson City, Nevada. It has a manufacturing plant in Indianapolis, IN, and a distribution facility in Louisville, KY. The corporate offices in Carson City have 150 hosts. The manufacturing plant in Indianapolis has 300 hosts, and the distribution center has 120 hosts. The network infrastructure was recently upgraded. All network cards, hubs, and switches are 10/100. Management has assigned you to design a new file structure that will provide load balancing and failover redundancy.

Current WAN Structure

VirtuCon is currently using Windows 2000 servers at all locations. The client workstations are running Windows 95, Windows 98, Windows NT 4 Workstation, and Windows 2000 Professional.

Carson City has two DCs and one member server. DC1 houses a shared folder named Policies. Mem1 has a DLT drive installed for centralized backup. Indianapolis has one DC and one member server. The DC contains a shared folder named Customers, and the member server contains a realtime job tracking database. Louisville has one DC with a shared folder called Shipping Info. Currently the users have multiple drive mappings to provide access to the files at all locations, and there is no redundancy.

The locations have T1 connections from Carson City to Indianapolis and from Indianapolis to Louisville. The routers have been replaced in the past year and are QoS aware.

The Owners have begun negotiations to purchase a small firm in Evansville, IN. This firm has an existing infrastructure in place that utilizes Windows NT 4 Server. Because this purchase is still in negotiations, further details are not available.

Current WAN Connectivity

The locations have T1 connections from Carson City to Indianapolis and from Indianapolis to Louisville. The routers have been replaced in the past year and are QoS aware.

Proposed WAN Connectivity

There are currently no plans to change your WAN design. However if the ownership purchases the company in Evansville, your design should provide the best integration possible.

Directory Design Commentary

VirtuCon's current password policies will be duplicated on the Windows 2000 servers.

Current Internet Positioning

VirtuCon currently accesses the Internet from all locations using a single leased IP address at the Indianapolis location. This location has an IP Proxy and firewall to protect the network and provide access.

A Web-hosting firm hosts the company Web site. The firewall server at the Indianapolis site provides a Web-based email client for remote access to email to all remote employees.

Future Internet Plans

Eventually, VirtuCon would like to host its own site and provide remote users with Web-based access to its intranet mail.

Company Goal with the Proposed Upgrade

You are a network administrator for VirtuCon. Management has asked you to implement a file management structure that will provide redundancy for mission-critical shared files. The redundancy will need to provide access to all users in the event of a server or WAN link failure. You would also like to provide a more efficient way to utilize the DLT drive on the member server at the Carson City location to back up all of the shared files.

The administrators at all locations would like more efficient access to the CD-ROMs on servers. They use the CD-ROMs to access program installation files and utilities when supporting clients and servers.

Question 1

Considering the case study, which type of Dfs root will provide the appropriate level of redundancy for the shared data files?

○ a. Domain-based Dfs root

○ b. Standalone Dfs root

○ c. Dfs leaf object replicas

○ d. Standalone Dfs root with a root replica

Answer a is correct. A domain-based Dfs root can provide redundancy of the root by using the root replica option. Standalone Dfs roots cannot be replicated to other servers so answers b and d are incorrect. Dfs leaf objects do not provide redundancy to the Dfs root, so answer c is incorrect.

Question 2

Considering the case study, which type of Dfs root will provide the appropriate level of redundancy for the CD-ROM shared folders?

○ a. Domain-based Dfs root

○ b. Standalone Dfs root

○ c. Dfs leaf object replicas

○ d. Standalone Dfs root with a root replica

Answer b is correct. Since redundancy of the tools and utilities was not a requirement of the case study, a standalone root will be sufficient. None of the other options are necessary.

Question 3

Considering the case study, which servers or workstations will be eligible to host the required Dfs root or roots needed? [Check all correct answers]

❑ a. Windows 2000

❑ b. Windows 2000 Professional

❑ c. Windows 98 clients

❑ d. Windows NT Workstation

Answers a, b, and d are correct. With the Windows 2000 implementation of Dfs, Windows 2000, Windows 2000 Professional, Windows NT Server, and Windows NT Workstation can host Dfs roots. Windows 98 clients cannot host Dfs roots.

Question 4

Considering the case study, which clients will require the Dfs client 4/5 to browse the Dfs root or host a Dfs leaf object?

○ a. Windows 95

○ b. Windows 98

○ c. Windows 2000

○ d. Windows 2000 Professional

Answer a is correct. The Windows 2000 implementation of Dfs only requires Windows 95 clients to use Dfs client software.

Question 5

Considering the case study, what should be created to provide redundancy for the shared data files? [Check all correct answers]

❑ a. Two or more identical standalone roots

❑ b. A single domain-based root with replicas at each location

❑ c. Replicas of the Dfs leaf objects at each location

❑ d. None of the above

Answers b and c are correct. In order for the mission-critical files to be redundant, a single domain-based root should be created and a replica placed at each location. The replicas will ensure that the root share will be available if the WAN link is disabled. Replicas of the remote shared files should also be stored on servers at each physical location, since bandwidth is not a limiting factor.

Question 6

Considering the case study, where would you place root and link replicas to provide the proper fault tolerance?

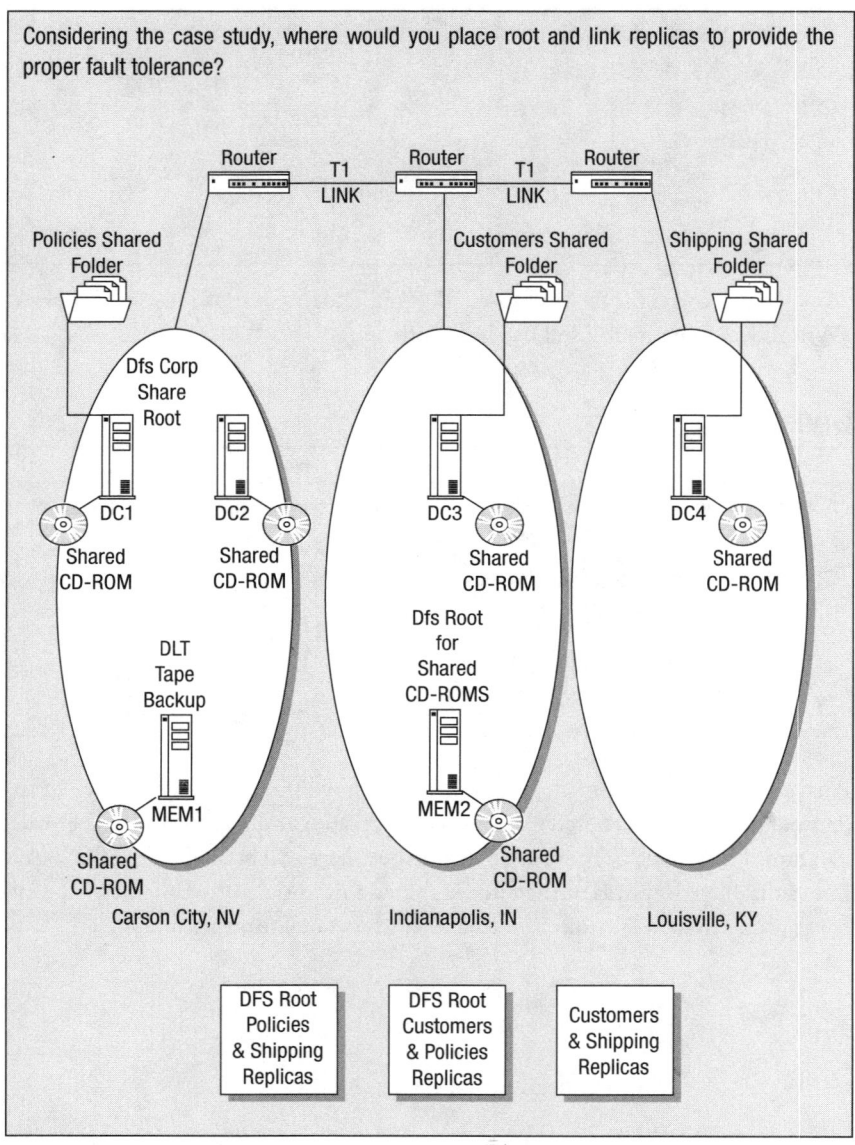

Answer:

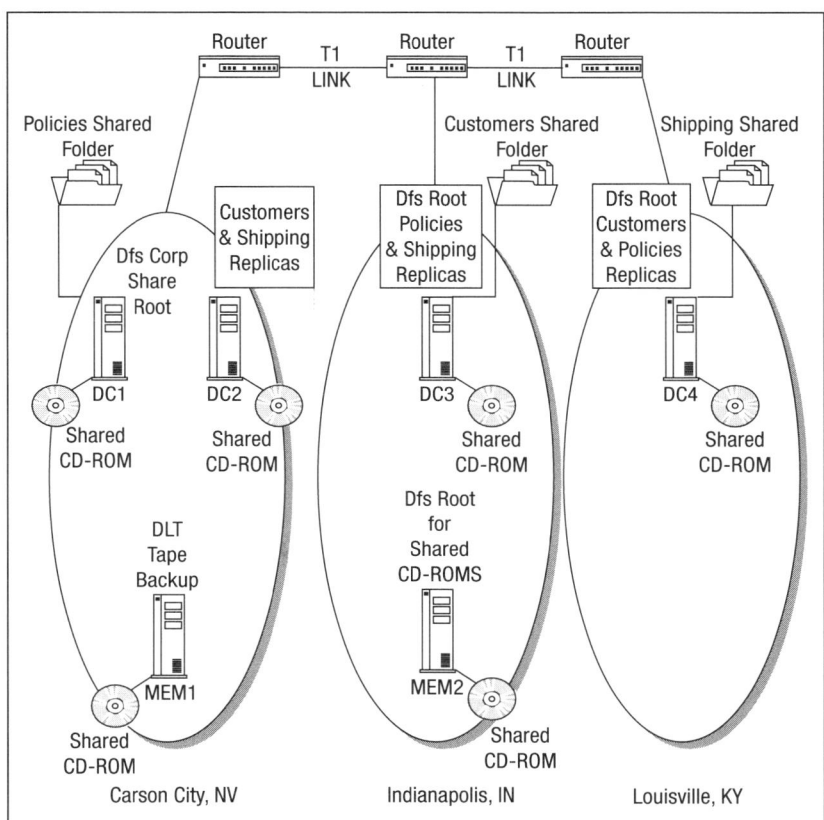

By placing the replicas in this manner, all of the data will be available in the event of a server crash or a temporary interruption of the T1 link. By placing the CD-ROM Dfs root at the Indianapolis location, a WAN link failure will be limited to the failed subnet. For example, if the link between Carson City and Indianapolis fails, both Indianapolis and Louisville will still have access to the CD-ROM Dfs root. If the CD-ROM root was located at the Carson City location and the link failed between Carson City and Indianapolis, only the Carson City location will have access to the CD-ROM Dfs root.

Question 7

> Considering the case study, what additional permissions need to be set to allow the users who currently have access to the shared folders to connect to the same folders though the Dfs root?
>
> ○ a. Security permissions should be set through the Dfs administrator program
>
> ○ b. Security permissions should be set through My Computer
>
> ○ c. Security permissions should be set through the Windows Explorer
>
> ○ d. None

Answer d is correct. The case study mentions that the users are currently accessing the files through multiple drive mappings. This means that the proper security permissions are already set. Dfs does not implement any additional security.

Need to Know More?

 Alexander, Geoffry, Anoop Jalan and Joseph Alexander. *MCSE Windows 2000 Network Design Exam Prep.* The Coriolis Group, Scottsdale, AZ, 2000. ISBN 1-57610-725-6. See chapter 20 for a discussion of Dfs.

 For more information on the subjects covered in this chapter, read the following TechNet article available at **www.microsoft.com**.

TechNet Article Q241452. "How to Install Distributed File System (Dfs) on Windows 2000."

 Search the TechNet CD (or its online version through **www. microsoft. com)** using the keyword "Dfs".

Remote Access in a Windows 2000 Environment

. . . .

Terms you'll need to understand:

✓ Dial-up

✓ Virtual Private Network (VPN)

✓ Remote Access Policy

✓ Point-to-Point Protocol (PPP)

✓ Point-to-Point Tunneling Protocol (PPTP)

✓ Microsoft Point-to-Point Encryption (MPPE)

✓ Layer 2 Tunneling Protocol (L2TP)

✓ Internet Protocol Security (IPSec)

✓ Tunneling

✓ System Network Architecture (SNA)

Techniques you'll need to master:

✓ Determining how to implement remote access

✓ Using remote-access techniques

✓ Implementing remote-access security

✓ Improving remote-access performance

✓ Making remote access available

This chapter teaches you how to implement remote access in a Windows 2000 network infrastructure. You'll learn how to design a network using remote access to enhance and secure the Windows 2000 infrastructure.

Remote Access Overview

Remote access allows users to dial into a Routing and Remote Access Server (RRAS) from a remote location. Using a modem, the user can access the office network as if he or she were sitting in the office (Figure 11.1). Remote access can also be a dial-up connection to the office through the user's Internet Service Provider (ISP) (Figure 11.2). Remote access can also be used to connect multiple remote sites in a WAN, using either direct dial from one site to another or connecting through the Internet (Figure 11.3).

If users connect to the Internet through their ISP, they can use a Virtual Private Network (VPN) to connect to their company's network through the company's

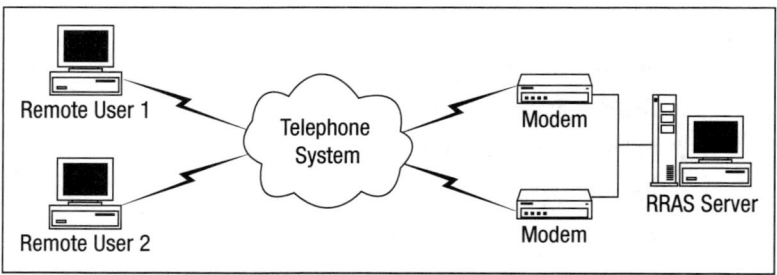

Figure 11.1 Remote telephone dial-up.

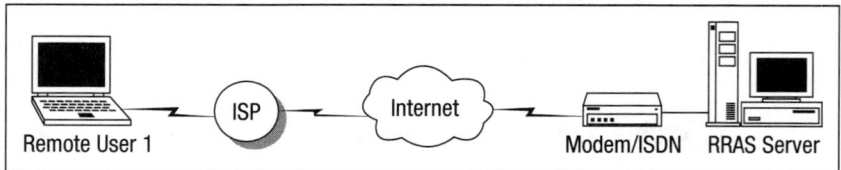

Figure 11.2 Remote ISP dial-up.

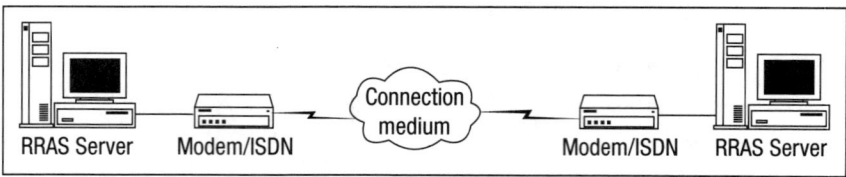

Figure 11.3 Remote site-to-site dial-up.

Internet connection. Remote offices can also use VPNs to connect to one another through the Internet as well.

All of these connections can use various protocols and connection mediums.

Remote Access Implementation

Remote access is enabled when the RRAS service is enabled and configured. By default, remote-access clients have no access unless they are given specific dial-in permissions. These permissions are assigned in the user properties under Active Directory Users And Computers on the Dial-In tab (Figure 11.4).

To specify user dial-in access, change the option under the Remote Access Permission (Dial-in or VPN) section from Deny Access to Allow Access.

Callback options can be set to No Callback, which has no security enforcement. Once a user connects, they are prompted for a username and password, which then allows them access to the network according to their rights and permissions.

When Set By Caller is enabled, the user is prompted to enter a username and password. Once authenticated, the user is then prompted for a phone number, which the RRAS server (after disconnecting) uses to call the user back. This callback allows the remote user to avoid the long-distance charges, which will be billed to the company where the RRAS server is located. The user pays only a

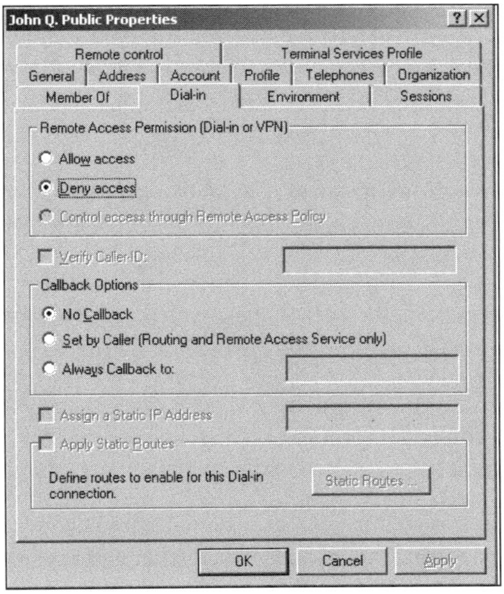

Figure 11.4   Dial-in user properties.

small toll for the initial, brief connection to enter username, password, and call-back phone number.

For a dial-in connection that is more secure, select the option Always Callback To and enter a phone number for the specified user account. By disallowing a user from logging in from locations other than the one specified, this option protects the data from being accessed from an unsecure location. With this option, the user connects from the specified number and is prompted for their username and password. Once the user is authenticated, the RRAS server disconnects and calls the user back at the specified phone number.

Although this type of security is perfectly adequate for a small number of dial-in users, a larger number of users is best handled by implementing policies to assign privileges to groups of users. To implement dial-in policies, select Start|Programs| Administrative Tools|Routing and Remote Access.

Once Routing and Remote Access services are enabled (see Chapter 9), select the local server name in the left pane. In the right pane, double click Remote Access Policies. In the right pane, right-click on an open area and select New Remote Access Policy to start the Remote Access wizard.

To configure the policy, the wizard will go through the following steps:

1. The first screen asks for a policy name. Enter an easily remembered name in the space provided.

2. In the next screen, options can be set to determine whether specifications are to be used for a connection. These are such things as tunnel-type, Windows groups that the user belongs to, protocol type, service being requested, and time and day.

3. The next screen pertains to the previous option selected. For example, on the Time And Day option, you can specify which hours of which day that a group will be permitted or denied access.

4. After all of the conditions are entered, the next screen gives you the option to specify (if the conditions are met) whether the user will be permitted or denied access.

5. The next option is to edit the profile. The profile has the following tabs with the indicated options:

   ➤ *Dial-in constraints*—Set disconnect time, set maximum session connection time, restrict access to specified hours and days, restrict access from a specified phone number, and restrict access by connection media type.

➤ *IP*—Set IP assignment (manual, DHCP, and so forth) and IP filters to and from the RRAS server.

➤ *Multilink*—Specify dial-in client to be permitted to use a specified number of ports; specify to drop a multilink port if bandwidth falls below a certain percentage for a specified amount of time.

➤ *Authentication*—Specify to use the Extensible Authentication Protocol (EAP), for use when using smart-card security. Specify other authentication protocols such as MSCHAP, CHAP, or no authentication. EAP is used for hardware authentication such as smart cards, retina-scan devices, and other hardware security implementations.

➤ *Encryption*—Specify the type of encryption to be used by the remote client. These include None, Basic, and Strong.

➤ *Advanced*—Specify additional options sent to the RRAS server by the client on connection (such as the IP address of the RRAS server that the client wants to log into for authentication).

6. Once you click on the Finish button, the wizard will end and the policy will be listed in the right pane. Once the policies are listed in this pane, you can arrange them in any order—which is important because the policies are applied to the dial-in connections from top to bottom.

Virtual Private Network (VPN)

With the Internet's popularity has come its increasing use as a backbone to connect multiple sites or to connect on a user-by-user basis.

VPNs comprise multiple components (Figure 11.5). These components include:

➤ *Client*—The system that is connecting to the network to use its resources.

➤ *Server*—The RRAS system that is receiving the connection request from the client to connect to the resources on the resource network.

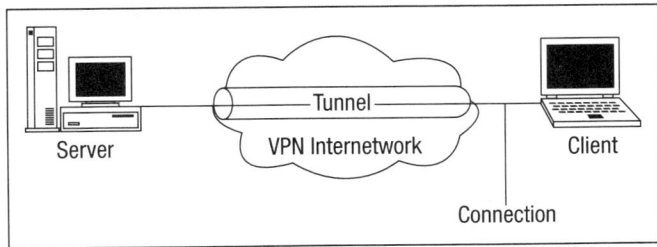

Figure 11.5   VPN component diagram.

➤ *Tunnel*—Where the data is encapsulated through the connection.

➤ *Connection*—Where the data is encrypted through the connection.

➤ *Tunneled data*—Data sent over a point-to-point connection.

➤ *Tunneling protocols*—Used to manage tunnels and data.

➤ *VPN internetwork*—Network media connection between client and server.

Note: For a VPN, data must be tunneled and encrypted.

VPNs can be used between remote connections and also routers (see Chapter 9). VPNs feature three major properties: encapsulation, data encryption, and authentication.

Encapsulation

With a VPN network's encapsulation (or *tunneling*), you can transmit private data over a public network. This is possible because encapsulated frames have a special header that allows them to be routed over the public network.

This special header has the information for routing through the VPN internetwork. Once the packet has reached the endpoint of the VPN, the special header is removed (de-encapsulated), and the packet is then sent to its final destination on the private network. The path that the encapsulated packet takes is the tunnel.

The following sections describe some common types of encapsulation:

Point-to-Point Tunneling Protocol (PPTP)

PPTP allows IP, IPX, or NetBEUI to be tunneled with an IP header for transmission over a TCP/IP network. PPTP uses a Microsoft proprietary encryption protocol called Microsoft Point-to-Point Encryption (MPPE). To encrypt data with PPTP (and MPPE), MSCHAP (version 1 or 2), and EAP are the only user authentication protocols that can be used. When using PPTP for a VPN over an Internet connection, the encryption is only between the ISP and the VPN server at the corporate private server. For example: A user dials in to the ISP and the ISP (acting as the VPN client) connects through the Internet to the corporate VPN server. The encryption works in connection between the ISP VPN client and the VPN corporate server. The connection from the remote client to the ISP is not encrypted.

PPTP encapsulation is created by the following means:

1. The data frame is encrypted with a Point-to-Point Protocol (PPP) header.

2. The PPP frame is then encapsulated with a Generic Routing Encapsulation (GRE) header.

3. The GRE packet is then encapsulated with a header containing the server and client addresses.

4. A final IP header and trailer are added for routing purposes on the VPN network. This is the full PPTP packet.

Layer 2 Tunneling Protocol (L2TP)

L2TP allows IP, IPX, or NetBEUI to be encrypted and sent over a PPP connection. PPP connections are possible over such media types as PSTN, X.25, ISDN, Frame Relay, and ATM using IP, which is the only transport protocol that L2TP currently supports.

L2TP supports not only encryption of frames, but also compression. Each L2TP tunnel can support multiple calls at once.

Unlike PPTP, L2TP works with all user authentication protocols, such as SPAP, PAP, EAP, CHAP, and MSCHAP. Also, L2TP uses IPSec as its authentication protocol, which is an open Internet standard and not proprietary. An L2TP VPN working through an ISP will start encryption from the remote user's computer instead of at the ISP. For these reasons, L2TP is considered to be the stronger protocol for security when compared to PPTP.

IP Security (IPSec) Tunneling Protocol

With IPSec, the data is encrypted and then encapsulated for transmission. The receiving end will de-encapsulate the encrypted data and then decrypt the data for use.

IPX Tunneling

IPX Tunneling is used when the private-network protocol is IPX/SPX, but the IPX/SPX packets will be encapsulated to be sent over a TCP/IP public network.

The encapsulated data is sent as User Datagram Protocol (UDP) packets.

Note: UDP packets are connectionless, which means that they are unreliable as to whether they arrive at the destination.

System Network Architecture (SNA) Tunneling

SNA Tunneling is used to encapsulate SNA packets for transmission over a VPN using TCP/IP.

SNA integrates IBM mainframes with other computer systems such as the PC, Macintosh, Unix, and operating systems such as Windows, OS/2, and DOS.

An SNA server acts as a gateway between the mainframes and the client systems. The SNA server can communicate with the client computers using protocols such as TCP/IP, IPX/SPX, NetBEUI, Banyan VINES IP, AppleTalk, and RRAS. Once requests are received at the SNA server, these packets are converted to SNA packets and sent to the mainframe. The connection between the client and SNA server are physical units (PUs), and the connection from the SNA server to the mainframe are logical units (LUs).

SNA Tunneling allows a private network with a mainframe to be accessed from remote locations over a public network.

Data Encryption

Data encryption is the process by which the encapsulated data is changed by an algorithm (encryption key) to obscure the data content.

Note: The more data that is encrypted, the easier it is to decrypt the data and find the key that decrypts all of the data that uses the same encryption algorithm.

Authentication

The two types of VPN authentication—*user* and *data*—are explained as follows:

➤ *User authentication*—The server authenticates the client when connecting to the server. If mutual user authentication is used, the client and server authenticate each other when connections are initiated.

➤ *Data authentication*—The server verifies that the data is not corrupted and that it is actually being sent from the specified client.

Features

Remote access supports many different connection types, and the protocols and security measures that you use depend upon the connection type.

Dial-in access is used by clients using point-to-point connections using the PPP or MS-RAS protocol.

Dial-in connections allow protocols such as TCP/IP, IPX/SPX (NWLink), NetBEUI, and AppleTalk. Both the server and client must have the same protocol to be able to communicate.

Dial-in connections are not permanent connections, but are initiated on command by using modems, ISDN, and X.25 connections.

Integration

RRAS can be integrated with Windows 2000 network services and be placed in a LAN or WAN. Depending on how a network is or will be set up can determine which options will be integrated with RRAS.

2000 Services

RRAS integrates with other Windows 2000 services to extend capabilities for client use. This integration also helps reduce management overhead for administrators.

Integration with such services as DHCP, DNS, WINS, Active Directory, and RADIUS will help reduce administrative overhead and still allow a remote client full network functionality.

DHCP Integration

Integrating DHCP with remote-access clients allows automatic updates of IP information to the client. These automatic updates eliminate the errors that would result if the IP information were entered manually on the client computers.

DHCP leases 10 IP addresses at a time for client systems. When the addresses are no longer needed, they are returned to the DHCP pool for use by other clients (see Chapter 4). If more than 10 users are connecting to a RRAS server, the RRAS server will lease another 10 addresses. When only 10 clients or fewer are connected to the RRAS server, it will drop the additional 10 addresses and have only 10 addresses at a given time.

DHCP Relay Agent must be configured on the RRAS server to be able to issue more TCP/IP information than just the IP address and subnet mask to the remote clients.

 For performance reasons, DHCP services should not be installed on the RRAS server. Only Relay Agent should be installed for the purposes of the RRAS clients.

DNS Integration

RRAS integration with the DNS server allows dynamic updates of the DNS database by the RRAS clients.

Thus, the remote clients will have their names resolved in the same manner as all of the local clients when using DNS.

When the client disconnects, the client will de-register its DNS account entry.

WINS Integration

Similarly, RRAS integration with the WINS server allows dynamic updates of the WINS database by the RRAS clients.

Thus, the remote clients will have their names resolved in the same manner as all of the local clients when using WINS.

Active Directory Integration

RRAS integration with Active Directory in native mode allows policies to be administered through the Active Directory services for remote clients.

RRAS integration with Active Directory in non-native mode will not allow policies to be administered through the Active Directory services for remote clients.

RADIUS Integration

RADIUS integration allows central management of RRAS servers to manage policies and keep logs of client authentication.

RADIUS can be specified as the authentication provider for remote clients. (See Chapter 12.)

LAN Integration

Using remote access for a LAN provides for centralized connections for the clients. A benefit of this integration is that it allows central management for the administrator.

An administrator can allow access by the usernames and also by creating a policy for groups of users. If more connections are required, more dial-in services can be added to give the required bandwidth needed.

WAN Integration

Because most networks are WANs, this is where more consideration can affect the design. Whether the integration is with a LAN or WAN, identical protocols must be enabled for both the RRAS server and the client.

Clients can access a network (LAN or WAN) in two ways: one uses VPNs (which were discussed earlier in this chapter) and the other uses dial-in access.

Dial-in connections let an administrator specify the maximum number of remote clients that will be supported at one time. This is determined by the number of modems on the RRAS server to accept calls from the clients.

The administrator can also specify which users or groups have access to the network from a remote location. These policies or rights can be set to allow specific times when connections are allowed.

Remote Access Placement

Placement of the remote access server can affect network security when using a VPN.

If the RRAS server is inside the firewall (between the company network and the firewall) and cannot be compromised, confidential data may be stored on it for remote use. In this situation, you need a firewall to protect the RRAS server from illegal access from the Internet.

If the RRAS server does not contain any important data, it can be placed outside the firewall, between the firewall and the Internet. Placing the server here allows only VPN connections from the RRAS server to go through the firewall.

Note: See Chapter 7 for limitations on using VPN protocols with NAT.

Security

We've previously discussed security options for keeping remote access secure—such as setting dial-in permissions for a user in Active Directory Users and Computers. The other options for access will be restricted by a remote-access policy. RADIUS can also be used for remote access authentication (see Chapter 12).

In situations where remote access connections need high security, smart cards offer the strongest type of user authentication that is available with Windows 2000. Each smart card user needs a smart card reader and smart card with a certificate preloaded by an administrator. After smart card logon has been enabled for a domain, a Windows 2000 user can log on with a PIN number instead of username and password. Smart cards can be used across VPNs as long as a certificate has been loaded on the VPN router and the smart card authentication has been enabled for the VPN. For networks needing high security, remote access policies can be set to require remote users to log on only with smart cards.

Availability

For redundancy, you can use more than one RRAS server or VPN connection. Having an extra server or connection allows remote services to be available if a server or connection should fail.

Similarly, each remote client should have multiple phone numbers to dial into the RRAS server if one modem or phone line should fail.

In the case of multiple sites connected in a WAN, multiple RRAS servers and connections should also be available.

With VPNs, each RRAS server should have a round-robin DNS entry to ensure that, when one server goes down, the VPN uses the next server in the list.

Network load balancing can be used if using a cluster. Clusters provide fail-over for the VPN services if one server should fail. All RRAS servers in the cluster need persistent connections for remote users.

Performance

Set specific phone numbers to clients so that a specific node is dedicated to them when they connect to a RRAS server by phone.

RRAS servers should be placed on the network segment that contains the resources that need to be accessed by the remote clients. If needed, add a RRAS server on each network segment or, specifically, each remote site.

Adding multiple VPN servers will increase the resources to handle bandwidth.

Because RRAS services support multiple CPUs in a server, this helps to process the client requests. Multiple modems can be used to increase bandwidth. If connection bandwidth is greater then network bandwidth, upgrade the network cards in the RRAS server to handle the load. With any service on a Windows server, increase memory to reduce the drive swapping that is associated with virtual memory. Also make sure that the disk drives in the RRAS server are fast enough to handle the file access and virtual memory swapping. Use Performance Monitor to check the performance of the memory, CPU, and network card to look for bottlenecks.

RRAS servers should be dedicated to their task of handling remote-access clients.

For VPNs, upgrade the connection to achieve greater bandwidth for the remote clients who use the Internet to tunnel into the company network. Use permanent connections because non-permanent connections take time to dial and connect, which will decrease performance.

Practice Questions

Case Study

Current LAN/Network Structure

2Market currently has 10 branch offices and headquarters in Chicago, Illinois. Its branch offices are located in the following cities:

Los Angeles, California

New York City, New York

Houston, Texas

Miami, Florida

Indianapolis, Indiana

Boston, Massachusetts

Salt Lake City, Utah

Nashville, Tennessee

Redmond, Washington

Aspen, Colorado

The branch offices are not currently connected to headquarters in a WAN.

Proposed LAN/Network Structure

2Market wants to improve communications among branches. All "paperwork" must be approved through headquarters, but sending mail and faxes is too slow and expensive.

2Market is also starting a research-and-development (R&D) department that is considered a highly secure area where only specific employees are allowed. The R&D department will have its own building that will be on the other side of Chicago from the headquarters.

Current WAN Connectivity

2Market has an Internet presence as 2Market.com. The company currently hosts its own Web servers in the IT department at headquarters.

Proposed WAN/Internet Connectivity

2Market wants to connect all offices through the Internet. Sales people at all offices need access to the network not only from home, but also from various remote locations. Some sales personnel have Internet access at home, and some do not.

Question 1

The Windows 2000 network uses Active Directory. The R&D office needs to authenticate users to their accounts in Active Directory. What protocol can be used to implement a retina scanner at the R&D office, but be authenticated at headquarters?

○ a. IP

○ b. IPX

○ c. PPP

○ d. EAP

The correct answer is d. EAP is used for hardware devices connected to the network. IP and IPX are standard protocols, which would encapsulate the EAP protocol; so choices a and b are incorrect. PPP is a dial-in protocol for accessing a network remotely with a modem through a RRAS server, making choice c incorrect.

Question 2

What is the economical way to connect all of the offices?

○ a. Connect the sites directly using multiple links for redundancy.

○ b. Connect all offices through the Internet using VPNs.

○ c. Each site will use a direct-dial connection to the nearest site and create a "linear" link between all of the sites.

○ d. Use a dial-on-demand connection from each site to headquarters.

The correct answer is b. Every site connects to a local ISP for access to the Internet, and VPNs are set up between all sites. This will be the cheapest option. All other connections would require a long-distance connection that would cost a lot.

Question 3

> What is required to allow the sales staff of all of the offices to connect to the network from remote locations or from their homes? [Check all correct answers]
>
> ❑ a. Modems
>
> ❑ b. Connection to ISP
>
> ❑ c. Hub
>
> ❑ d. Switch

The correct answers are a and b. Each sales person will need a modem and (possibly) access to the Internet through an ISP. VPNs can be created from their laptop to the company RRAS server. Or, a sales person could direct dial into the RRAS server if modems were added on the RRAS server to direct dial connections.

A hub and switch would be used in the company network, but not by the sales personnel from their homes or other remote locations. The sales personnel will not need any additional hardware.

Question 4

> With security enabled for dial-in access, would a user dialing in have access if the user had the following allowable times in group policies and the user belonged to all four groups?
>
> Group1 access permitted Monday–Friday 8:00 A.M. to 5:00 P.M.
>
> Group2 access permitted Monday–Friday 8:00 A.M. to 12:00 P.M.
>
> Group3 access permitted Monday–Saturday 8:00 A.M. to 5:00 P.M.
>
> Group4 access denied Saturday–Sunday all hours
>
> The administrator denies dial-in connections on the users properties. Will the user have access on Monday morning at 9:30 A.M.?
>
> ○ a. Yes
>
> ○ b. No

The correct answer is b. If the user properties is set to deny dial-in connections, this setting overrides all policies that could permit the user to dial in at certain times.

Question 5

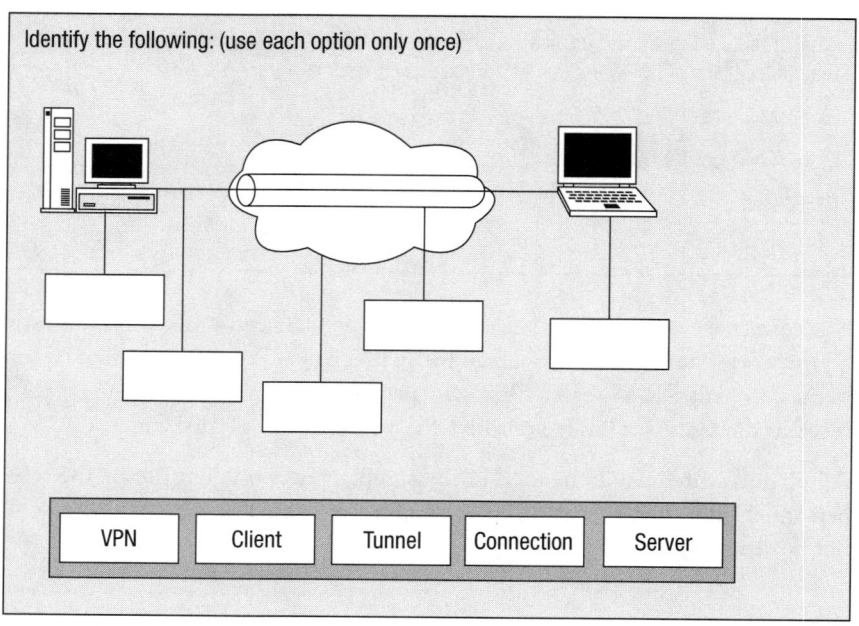

The answer is shown in the following diagram. See Figure 11.5 in this chapter for more information.

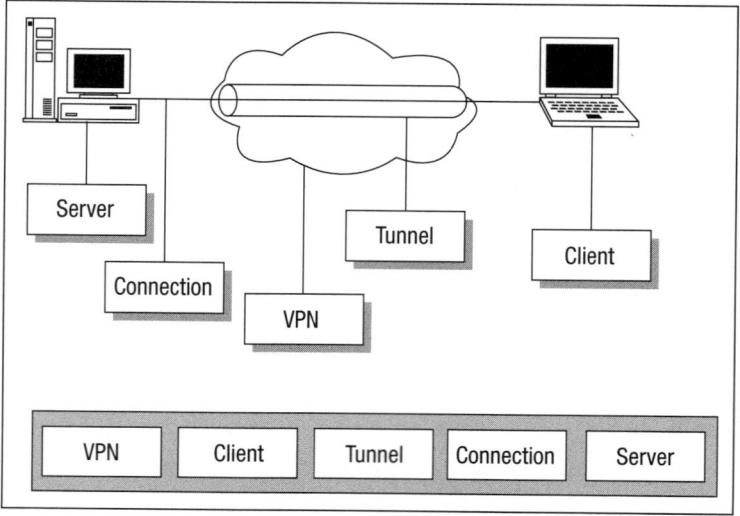

Question 6

Which of the following are connection protocols? [Check all correct answers]

❑ a. PPP

❑ b. L2TP

❑ c. MS-RAS

❑ d. IPSec

The correct answers are a and c. Choices b and d are security encapsulation used in VPNs. PPP and MS-RAS are used as dial-in connection protocols.

Question 7

For best performance and security, which of the following offices should have a RRAS server for remote users to connect to? [Check all correct answers]

❑ a. Headquarters in Chicago, Illinois

❑ b. Los Angeles, California

❑ c. New York City, New York

❑ d. Houston, Texas

❑ e. Miami, Florida

❑ f. Indianapolis, Indiana

❑ g. Boston, Massachusetts

❑ h. Salt Lake City, Utah

❑ i. Nashville, Tennessee

❑ j. Redmond, Washington

❑ k. Aspen, Colorado

❑ l. R&D in Chicago, Illinois

The correct answers are a, b, c, d, e, f, g, h, i, j, and k.

All offices should have their own RRAS server for performance improvements. This will prevent a high load of VPN traffic if all users connect to one office and then tunnel to all of the other offices. If every office has its own RRAS server, then most traffic would be limited to its local network.

For security reasons, the R&D office should not have its own RRAS server to better prevent unauthorized access attempts. The office can also filter out any RRAS connections to pass over the VPN to the R&D network.

Question 8

The IT manager wants to set up the VPN on the RRAS server at headquarters on clustered servers for redundancy. The IT manager also wants this implemented for sharing the VPN traffic to improve performance. This implementation will work for redundancy and performance.

○ a. True

○ b. False

The correct answer is b. Network load balancing must also be enabled to balance the load between the PPTP links.

Question 9

2Market has no important data stored on the RRAS server at the Indianapolis office, but, at the Houston office, the RRAS server doubles as an SQL server. Where should the RRAS servers be placed in the following diagram? [Use each option twice]

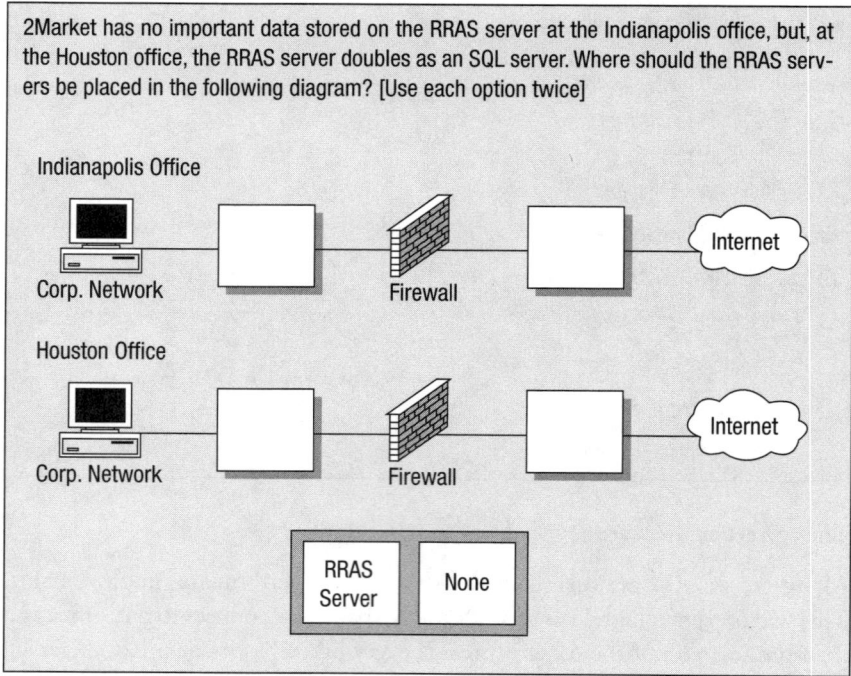

The correct answer is

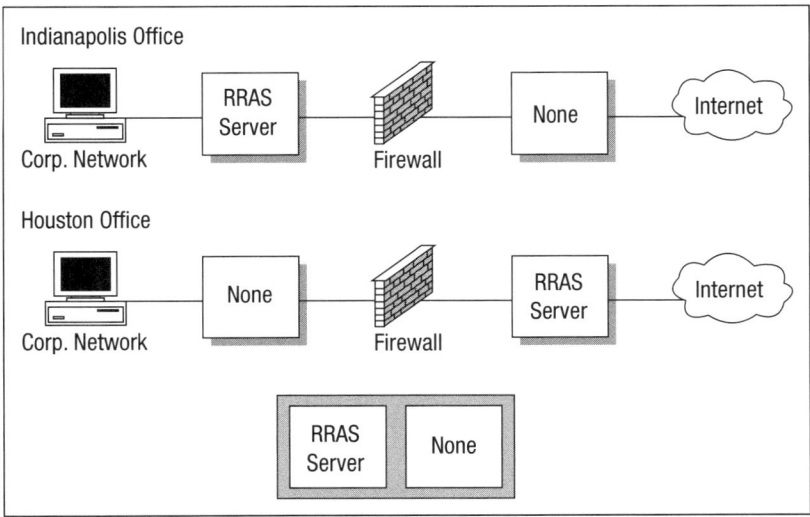

Because the Indianapolis server has important data on it, it needs to be placed behind the firewall for more protection. The Houston office is the opposite.

Question 10

The IT manager wants to increase performance for the remote clients. She wants to implement DHCP on the RRAS server to reduce network traffic on the dial-in clients. This implementation will improve performance.

○ a. True

○ b. False

The correct answer is b. DHCP services should not be run on the RRAS server; it should run only DHCP Relay Agent.

Need to Know More?

 Charles, Kackie. *Windows 2000 Routing and Remote Access Services.* Macmillan Technical Publishing, Indianapolis, IN, 2000. ISBN 0-73570-951-3. This guide to RRAS service offers more in-depth detail about installing and configuring the RRAS service.

 Goncalves, Marcus. *Implementing Remote Access Services with Microsoft Windows 2000.* Que, Indianapolis, IN, 2000. ISBN 0-78972-138-4. This book covers the implementation of remote-access services, with detailed information on configuration and implementation.

 Microsoft Corporation. *Windows 2000 Server Resource Kit.* Microsoft Press, Redmond, WA, 2000. ISBN 1-57231-805-8. Contains chapters dedicated to setting up VPNs and RRAS for remote connectivity.

 Search the TechNet CD (or its online version through **www.microsoft.com**) using the keyword "Remote Access". Also, see the Windows 2000 Server or Advanced Server help.

Understanding RADIUS

Terms you'll need to understand:

✓ Internet Authentication Services (IAS)

✓ Remote Authentication Dial-In Service (RADIUS)

✓ Routing and Remote Access Service (RRAS)

✓ Realm

✓ Network Access Server (NAS)

✓ Point-to-Point Protocol (PPP)

✓ Shared secret

✓ Points of Presence (POP)

✓ Remote access policy

Techniques you'll need to master:

✓ Differentiating between the different components of RADIUS

✓ Understanding how RADIUS fits into a RAS solution

✓ Determining placement of the RADIUS client and server

✓ Improving security and availability in a RADIUS solution

As discussed in previous chapters, Windows 2000 includes many services that allow long-distance connections to a network. As networks grow, so does the need for connections between geographically diverse locations. One problem that has plagued network administrators is how to connect remote users—and especially those who roam among a variety of remote locations—to the network. Remote connections jeopardize the security of a network by their very nature. Yet, in today's network environment, users need access to private network resources regardless of where they are physically located.

What Is RADIUS?

RADIUS (Remote Authentication Dial-In User Service) provides three services to a network: authentication, authorization, and accounting. For a number of reasons, it can be quite difficult to secure a network that has many remote users. Such a network may need to allow remote connections from other locations in the network or from users who are dialing in from home or even while traveling. This last group—roaming users—poses a network's largest security risk. Allowing users to connect from any location makes it difficult to maintain control over incoming connections to the private network. The purpose of RADIUS is to control the actions of remote and roaming users without allowing sensitive network information like usernames and passwords out of the private network. RADIUS does this by using a client/server architecture that is specifically designed for a geographically dispersed environment.

It is important to remember that RADIUS is not a full remote-access solution. It merely adds security and accounting to a remote-access design for a network. RADIUS protects a private network by isolating authentication of remote users from the rest of the data exchange that occurs over lines that are not secure. In a traditional remote-access solution, the RAS server connects users to the network, and all data transfer occurs through the RAS server including authentication and accounting information such as transaction logging. In a RAS solution that uses RADIUS, the RAS server still controls the transfer of data between the remote client and the private network, but it passes to the RADIUS service the responsibility of authenticating the user, authorizing user actions, and tracking remote user actions.

Tracking Remote Connections with RADIUS Accounting

The accounting service provided by RADIUS increases control over remote connections. Because RADIUS can log remote connections to a network, such network usage can be monitored. The accounting service can log the IP address of the computer that requests authentication, the time of the call, the call status (such as success or failure), which RADIUS client sent the request and which RADIUS server accepted the request. This accounting service, which is separate from the authentication and authorization services provided by RADIUS, can also be used for billing or security purposes. Later in this chapter, we'll see how Internet Service Providers (ISPs) can use the accounting feature to charge for RADIUS services that are provided to a network.

RADIUS Service Basics

Although RADIUS is a service supported in Windows 2000, the term *RADIUS* can also refer to a protocol because networking services are often named after the protocol that runs the service. (Just like the FTP service is run by the FTP protocol, the RADIUS service is run by the RADIUS protocol.) Support for RADIUS was first introduced in later versions of the Windows NT 4 Option Pack, and it is integrated into the Routing and Remote Access Service (RRAS) service and the Internet Authentication Service (IAS) in Windows 2000. Before learning about the RADIUS service, it is important to have an overview of the RRAS service, which is provided in Chapter 9.

The standards for implementing RADIUS are currently being determined by the Internet Engineering Task Force (IETF). RFCs 2138 and 2139 describe how the RADIUS service and its accounting features work. Because it is to be an open standard, the Windows 2000 RADIUS service can be integrated into a heterogeneous network with different operating systems such as Unix and Novell Netware.

Instead of using TCP, RADIUS uses UDP as its transport level protocol. UDP provides connectionless, or *not guaranteed*, service—which means that there isn't as much checking to make sure that the information made it to its destination. UDP makes sense because RADIUS is a supporting service on the network. TCP is used when data such as Web pages or files is being transferred. As a transport protocol, UDP requires less traffic and keeps the service lightweight.

When RADIUS was first introduced, the ports used were 1645 for authorization and 1646 for accounting. Because these ports conflicted with another service, the ports have recently been changed to 1812 for authentication and 1813 for accounting. Although either set of ports will still work, all computers involved in the RADIUS process must use the same ports to communicate. If you experience any trouble with connections, check the port settings on each of the machines to ensure that they are the same.

Components in a RADIUS Solution

To design a RADIUS solution, you must understand the different roles that need to be filled. Because RADIUS is designed to be an open standard, it uses generic terms for the different components that are needed to set up the service. So, for a good RADIUS design, you must know the generic terms as well as the specific Windows 2000 service that fills the generic role. The generic terms allow different vendors to supply different RADIUS components, while still ensuring that they operate with each other because the vendors followed the same RADIUS standard.

RADIUS centralizes the authentication process by using a client/server architecture for the service. This architecture allows RADIUS clients to be located in any remote location. These RADIUS clients accept authentication requests from RAS clients and pass them on to a RADIUS server. The RADIUS service does not provide authentication to the client, but instead passes the authentication request in a secure manner from a remote client to the authentication server. Figure 12.1 shows the process that the RADIUS service uses to get the RAS client authenticated onto the private network. In Figure 12.1, a RADIUS client is located at the remote LAN. The RADIUS client accepts authentication requests from RAS clients on the local network. The RADIUS client forwards the requests to the RADIUS server located at the main network location, and the RADIUS server forwards the authentication request to the authentication server on the local network. A successful authentication will be passed back to the RADIUS client and on to the RAS client.

Realms

In a Windows 2000 network, user accounts are authenticated on a domain controller. So, *authentication server* is a generic term in RADIUS, and *domain controller* is the corresponding specific authentication server used in Windows 2000. Similarly, *realm* is another generic term in the RADIUS standard that needs to be mapped to a specific Windows 2000 service. A realm contains the information that is needed to authenticate users onto the network; the RADIUS service uses realms to differentiate between groups of users. The realm used in a Windows 2000 RADIUS service is the Active Directory domain, and the realm in a Novell Netware network would be within Netware Directory Services (NDS). A

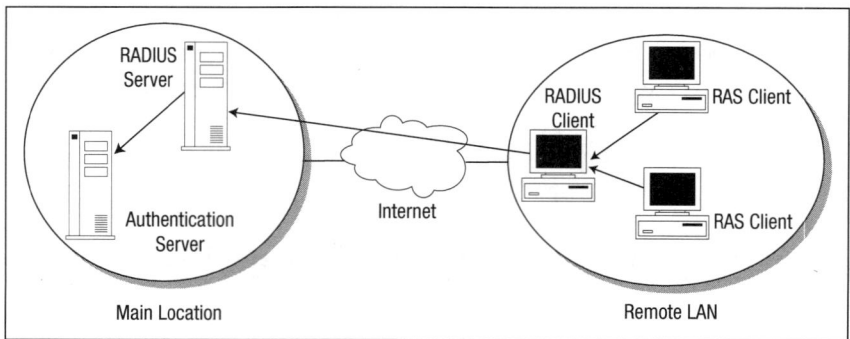

Figure 12.1   A simple RADIUS solution with one remote location.

RADIUS authentication packet specifies the realm for which it is intended. For a Microsoft implementation of RADIUS, Windows NT 4 domains and Windows 2000 Active Directory domains can be used as realms in the RADIUS service.

RADIUS Servers

In Windows 2000, the RADIUS server component is called the Internet Authentication Service (IAS). Installing the IAS service creates a RADIUS server on a Windows 2000 server. Authentication of user accounts between a RADIUS server and an authenticating server within a realm should be within a private network. This means a RADIUS server needs to be located on a local network with the authentication realm. Translating these generic RADIUS terms into terms used by Windows 2000 means that the server with the IAS service loaded (making it a RADIUS server) must be on the same local network as the domain controller that provides authentication for the RADIUS service.

RADIUS Clients

As shown in Figure 12.1, a RADIUS client accepts a request for authentication and passes the request to the RADIUS server. The authentication requests that a RADIUS client receives are from a RAS client, and these clients should be located on the local network with the RADIUS client. The RADIUS service defines a RADIUS client as a Network Access Server (NAS), one that provides a connection to a remote network. In Windows 2000, the RRAS service fulfills the role of an NAS server in the RADIUS standard. This means that a RADIUS client is a RRAS server in the Windows 2000 implementation of RADIUS. The NAS server then, acting as a RADIUS client, passes the authentication request to the RADIUS server.

To centralize and control the remote connections, RADIUS places the local RADIUS client with the RAS clients and the local RADIUS server with the authentication service. This way only the RADIUS client and server are passing sensitive authentication information over WAN connections. The alternative would be for each RAS client to authenticate itself. A RRAS server acting as a RADIUS client centralizes RADIUS requests, which makes the authentication process more secure.

As a review, Table 12.1 lists the generic RADIUS component (as listed in the RADIUS standard) along with the component that fulfills that role in a Windows 2000 RADIUS solution.

Shared Secret

The purpose of having RADIUS clients and servers is to centralize and secure the authentication of remote users. Instead of allowing all remote clients to send

Table 12.1 Generic RADIUS components and their Windows 2000 equivalent.	
Generic RADIUS Component	**Windows 2000 RADIUS Component**
RADIUS client	RRAS server
Network Access Server (NAS)	RRAS server
RADIUS server	Internet Authentication Service (IAS)
Realm	Windows 2000 Active Directory domain

a RADIUS request to a RADIUS server, only a small number of RADIUS clients are authorized. Yet, even this reduced number of RADIUS clients still allows the possibility of someone attempting to impersonate a RADIUS client when communicating with a RADIUS server. To thwart such an attempt, the administrator sets a password—called a *shared secret*—during the configuration of RADIUS. Both the RADIUS client and server know the shared secret, but it is never sent over the network. Instead, the service uses a hashing system to verify the shared secret. Also, the location of each RADIUS client that will be sending authentication packets is specified to the RADIUS server, and only these specified RADIUS clients can forward authentication packets to a RADIUS server.

The shared secret is not used between just the RADIUS client and server. The shared secret is also used during the encryption process for a RAS client's password. This means that a shared secret needs to always be included in a RADIUS solution and that the shared secret needs to be a password that is difficult to guess. Like any password, a shared secret is case-sensitive and must match exactly on RADIUS clients and servers. Microsoft's IAS service allows for the shared secret to be up to 16 characters long, a mixture of upper- and lowercase letters as well as numbers and special characters (such as !, #, %, and so on). Other operating systems' implementation of RADIUS may only allow up to 10 characters and may not allow special characters. Because the shared secret must match exactly between the RADIUS client and server then these differences are important. It's best to use at the maximum characters allowed for a shared-secret password when implementing RADIUS.

Network Diagram

To design an effective RADIUS solution, you'll need a network diagram similar to those used to design other services. To construct such a diagram, use the following steps and add each of the items to the diagram:

1. Draw in the WAN locations.

2. At each WAN location, fill in the number of remote users.

3. Label the type of connection between the WAN locations. Dial-in lines that have a direct connection into the network need a different design than do lines that connect through the Internet.

4. Mark whether the Internet connections are serviced by an ISP or by the local network.

5. Add the locations of domain controllers that can authenticate RADIUS requests.

6. Add the current location of RAS servers that need to be integrated into a RADIUS solution.

7. If users will be roaming and connections to the network are from unknown or several locations that are not marked on the network diagram, then note that a roaming user solution is needed.

8. Note the UDP ports used by the authenticating service and also the accounting service (if it is being used).

Several network services affect the design of a RADIUS solution. Once the basic elements are on the network diagram, you'll need to add some extra information.

Authentication Protocol

When a remote user is authenticated onto a network, the username and password passed between the RADIUS client and server are encrypted. The Windows 2000 RRAS and RADIUS services support six different authentication protocols, each of which is best used with a different type of client operating system. Table 12.2 shows Microsoft's recommendations for which authentication protocol should be used with what remote client operating system. Two authentication protocols are versions of the Microsoft Challenge Handshake Authentication Protocol (MSCHAP), which is Microsoft's version of another accepted authentication protocol (CHAP). Because MSCHAP is a Microsoft-specific protocol, only Microsoft clients can use it. If RAS clients are other than Microsoft operating systems,

Table 12.2 Authentication protocols and recommended client usage.	
Authentication Protocol	**Recommended Client Usage**
MSCHAP version 2	Windows 2000
MSCHAP	Other Windows clients
CHAP	Macintosh, Unix
EAP	Clients using smart cards
Shiva (SPAP)	Shiva LAN Rover
PAP	When the client will accept no other authentication protocol

MSCHAP will not work as the authentication protocol. The network diagram needs to note what authentication protocol is used.

Data Encryption

Authentication is not the only information that needs to be encrypted in a remote-access solution. The data that passes between the user and the private network should also be encrypted by setting up a Virtual Private Network (VPN). Your biggest decision is where the VPN—and therefore the encryption—will begin. Later in the chapter, we will discuss security in a RADIUS solution that includes Internet connections.

Transport Protocols

Both the RRAS and the RADIUS services support more than just TCP/IP as the transport protocol for the networks that they connect. IPX/SPX and AppleTalk are also supported. Because transport protocols are based upon the needs of the clients that RADIUS will connect, you should mark on the network diagram what transport protocols need to be supported at each WAN connection.

Connection Methods

The RRAS service in Windows 2000 allows users to connect to the network using their choice of many different methods. Thus, part of a RADIUS solution involves documenting the types of incoming remote connections.

Of the different ways to connect to the network, dial-in lines have a disadvantage if remote users are outside the local calling area and need to make long-distance connections to the private network. Although connecting to the Internet is a cheaper solution than leasing dial-in lines, the Internet connection causes more concern because private company information is passed over what is essentially a public network. If the Internet is chosen as a connection alternative, then encryption through a VPN is needed.

The next choice to make is whether a network will set up a private connection to the Internet or use an ISP to connect to the Internet. Mark this choice on the diagram, because RADIUS settings are affected. Later in the chapter, we'll cover RADIUS solutions that include ISP connections.

Persistence and Data Rate for Connections

The last thing that needs to be added on the network diagram is whether the connections are persistent and what data rate they can handle. A connection can be either demand-dial, which means that it is used only when a remote connection is in progress, or persistent, which means that it is always available. In Figure 12.2,

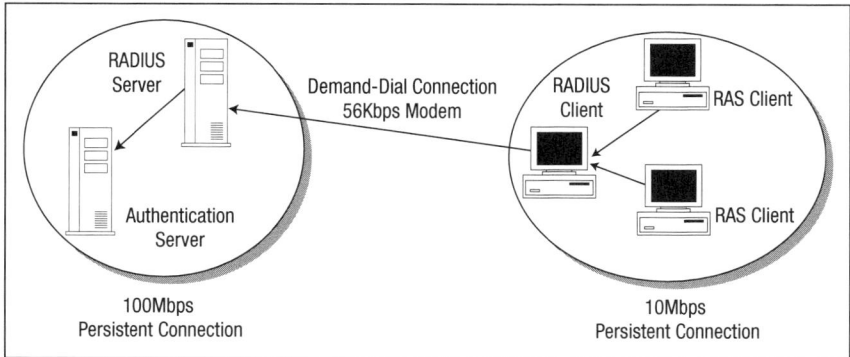

Figure 12.2 A network diagram showing that the persistence of connections can change between different components in a RADIUS solution.

the connection between the RAS client and the RADIUS client is persistent. It is a demand-dial modem connection between the RADIUS client and the RADIUS server, but back to a persistent connection on the private LAN between the RADIUS server and the authentication server. A data rate can be set on a persistent connection to allow the RADIUS service to predict how long a RADIUS component will take to respond.

Placing RADIUS Components

Once the network diagram includes the basic information, the next step is to decide where to place the RADIUS servers. The servers need to be placed on the same network as the domain controllers to which they'll pass authentication requests. This is usually at a central location on the LAN, such as the main office. Locating RADIUS servers with authenticating domain controllers keeps the database of user accounts, and the traffic to and from it, within the protected private network.

RADIUS Clients

The design of RADIUS encourages placing the RADIUS client locally with the RAS clients that need authentication. By placing RADIUS clients on the local network with the RAS clients and placing RADIUS servers on the same local network as the authenticating servers, you'll reduce the amount of sensitive authentication traffic over unsecure connections. The RADIUS service is designed to keep sensitive authentication and authorization traffic just between RADIUS clients and RADIUS servers over WAN connections.

Outsourcing RAS Connections

A company can save money on roaming connections by using a national or global ISP. With an ISP, a roaming user can simply call a local access number, connect to the Internet, and then navigate to the private network. A direct connection to the private network through dial-in lines without going through the Internet involves long-distance telephone charges. Using an ISP adds an additional element to the RADIUS design, because some RADIUS components need to be located at the ISP. This situation points directly to the reason why the RADIUS service was created: A company using an ISP needs the ISP to be a part of the authenticating process, but locating an authentication server at the ISP will make it difficult to maintain control over its security. Using the RADIUS service, an ISP simply needs to install a RADIUS client. A roaming user will connect to the ISP, and the local RADIUS client at the ISP will pass the authentication request to the RADIUS server located on the private network. No authentication information such as user accounts need be given to the ISP, allowing for a secure and a much less expensive connection for roaming users. To ensure the security of the connection, all data needs to be encrypted with the use of a VPN when using Internet connections. This configuration is shown in Figure 12.3.

Connecting Roaming Users through an ISP

Instead of a company maintaining its own connection to the Internet, many choose to go through an ISP. Using an ISP removes the burden of obtaining IP addresses and maintaining an often-expensive connection to the Internet. If a company chooses to use an ISP to connect to the Internet, then the RADIUS service is

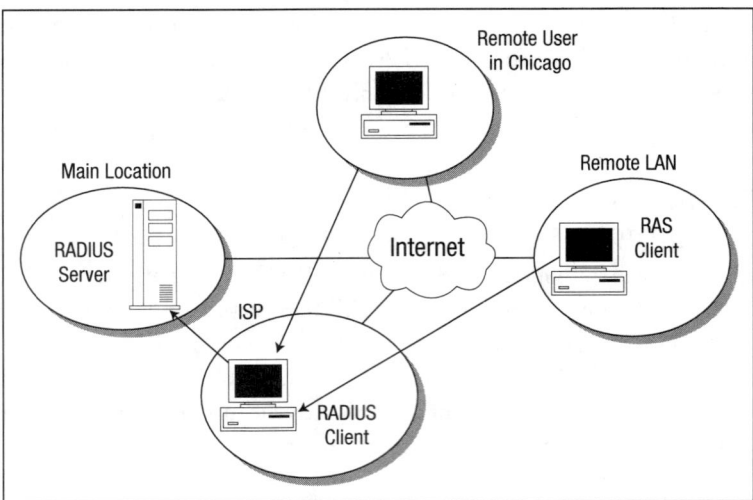

Figure 12.3 A RADIUS client located at the ISP passes authentication requests to the RADIUS server in the private network.

still a secure choice for roaming users and even remote offices to connect to the private network. A national or global ISP uses local Points of Presence (POPs) that let users connect to the Internet with just a local call, wherever they roam. After connecting to a local POP server, the user then needs to access the Internet and, in a RADIUS solution, to connect to a RADIUS client to get to the RADIUS server on the private network. An ISP can locate RADIUS clients configured to pass authentication packets onto a company's RADIUS server at a central location physically near the company that they support. The only problem is that a RADIUS client is normally located in the same physical network as the RAS client. In this case, the roaming RAS client is communicating with the RAS client over the Internet. The secure solution in this case is to implement a VPN between the roaming RAS client and the RADIUS client located at the ISP. Figure 12.4 shows the network configuration when using ISPs to outsource Internet connections.

Using the Accounting Feature for Billing

RADIUS accounting comes with an accounting start and stop feature. An ISP can use this feature to log when remote users place calls and need connections to the RADIUS server in the company network. The ISP can then charge by usage of the service that it provides to the company network. Because the accounting

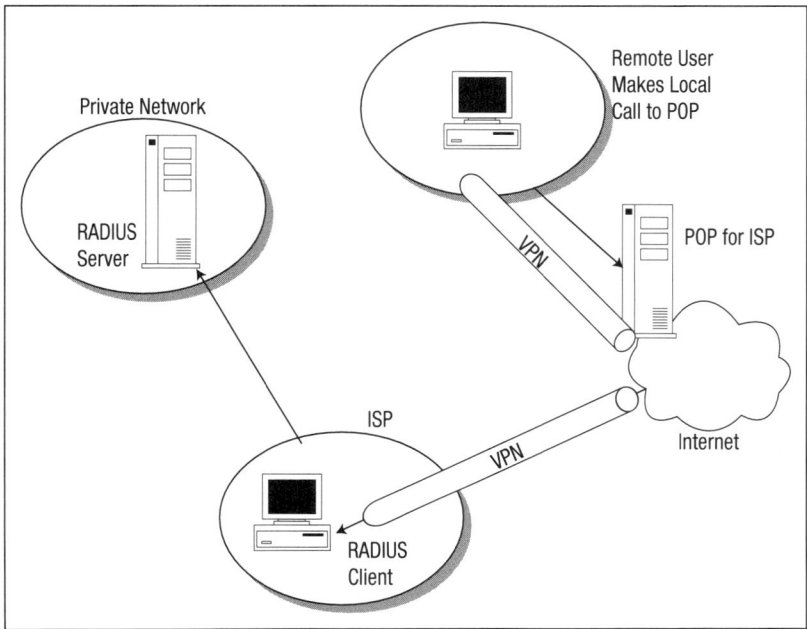

Figure 12.4   RAS client with local connection to POP for ISP using a VPN to securely connect to RADIUS client. RADIUS client at ISP connecting to RADIUS server at company.

feature in the RADIUS server is an open standard, the accounting features need not be provided by the same operating system as the rest of the RADIUS components. The company and ISP can interoperate using the RADIUS service even if only one of them is using Microsoft's implementation of the RADIUS service.

Ensuring Security in a RADIUS Solution

Security can be increased by combining it with other services on a network (just like many of the services in Windows 2000 RADIUS can work in an environment that uses a screened subnet). Also, RADIUS automatically looks to apply remote-access policies to incoming RAS client connections. These policies allow for finer control, such as restricting remote connections by computer name, username, IP address, and/or time of day.

Screened Subnets

RADIUS can work within a network environment that uses screened subnets—also known as DMZs. In such an environment, the RADIUS service needs specific settings on the firewall to allow passage of packets using the RADIUS service. First, make sure that the firewall allows packets that use the correct UDP ports to pass through. As discussed earlier, the UDP ports used by the RADIUS service can vary. Next, to create a secure solution, allow packets to pass through the firewall only to and from specific remote RADIUS clients. The RADIUS servers should be placed inside the screened subnet, and the authenticating domain controller should be inside the private network to protect the user account information. Figure 12.5 shows an example of a RADIUS server inside a screened subnet with only UDP ports 1812 and 1813 open to allow RADIUS authentication and accounting packets to be passed from the outside to the screened subnet.

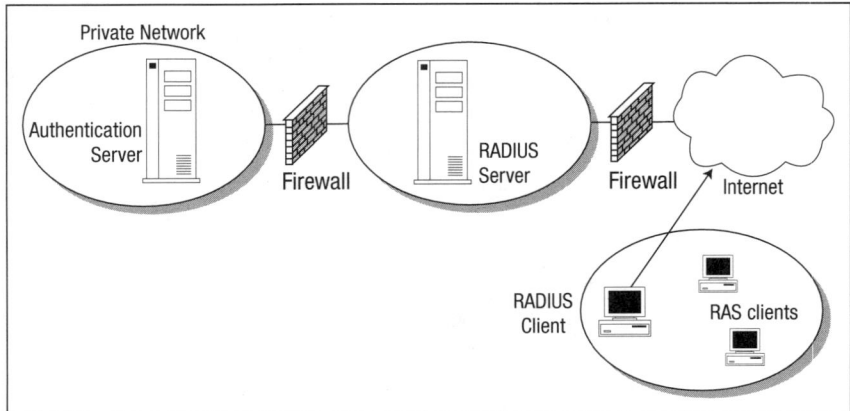

Figure 12.5 Screened subnet with RADIUS server inside and RADIUS client outside.

Remote-Access Policies

In previous versions of Windows, dial-in connections had a simple system of control. The permission to dial in to a network was granted on an all-or-nothing basis. When the user is allowed to enter the network through a remote connection, no extra control is allowed over the connection.

To allow for better control over users who connect from remote locations, Windows 2000 uses remote-access policies. With a remote-access policy, an administrator can set conditions to control what a dial-in user must do to be authenticated to a network. Instead of granting a blanket right to dial in, as in previous versions of Remote Access in Windows, remote-access policies allow a finer level of control. A remote-access policy allows an administrator to assign different permissions to different sets of users. Remote users accessing the network through a VPN can be assigned different conditions than a user accessing the network through a dial-in connection. Conditions can also include the vendor of the RADIUS client, the IP address of the connecting computer, the group to which the user must belong, and the time and day that remote connections can be used. Assigning multiple conditions can better control what connections will be accepted into the network.

The RADIUS service checks for remote-access policies for all incoming users. Every user requesting a remote connection to a network must have at least one remote-access policy that applies to the user's account. If no policy applies to the user (or if the user is not following the guidelines set in a policy that does apply), access will be denied.

 The RRAS service without a remote-access policy can set the same restrictions on a remote connection, such as time of day connection is allowed and types of packets allowed and disallowed, and can even set different settings for traffic entering through a dial-in rather than persistent connection. The difference between remote-access policies and RRAS restrictions is that the latter apply to all connecting users. Remote-access policies can apply restrictions to select groups of users and even to individual user accounts.

Increasing RADIUS Availability

Just as with many other services, fault tolerance can be an issue. Although only one RADIUS server is needed to create a RADIUS solution, backup servers may be needed to ensure that the service is available all of the time. IAS has features that make it easy to add fault tolerance to the RADIUS service.

Configuring Backup IAS Servers

IAS allows the configuration of one RADIUS server to be copied to another. When fault tolerance is included in the design of a RADIUS solution, this feature makes it easy to create backup IAS RADIUS servers. Copying the IAS configuration copies all of the IAS settings also, including registry settings, logging settings, and remote-access policies. Thus, with this feature, you really need to configure only one IAS server, even if more than one IAS server is needed in the RADIUS service design. RADIUS clients can then be configured to try the backup IAS server if the primary RADIUS server is down.

Optimizing the Logging Feature

Because the RADIUS accounting feature involves logging activity, using it may cause a burden on the logging server. Although logging provides the ability to examine remote connection activity (which is useful for checking the security of the service and billing companies or departments for their usage), the overhead of the service needs to be weighed against the needs of the company. For optimized performance, you should log only those settings that are needed. For example, if you are using the logging feature for security, you likely don't need to log successful connections. In this case, you'd be most interested in only those connections that failed, as these may show if someone is trying to break into the network through remote connections.

Practice Questions

Case Study

ABC Company provides telephone customer service support and currently has a main location and a remote location. Due to a large amount of growth and employee requests, the company has decided to allow employees to work from home. However, because of security concerns, company management wants to develop a plan for remote access that makes the connections secure. The decision is to use RADIUS for secure authentication and authorization for remote users.

Current WAN Connectivity

The main LAN and the remote location are connected by a 56Kbps Frame Relay connection.

Proposed WAN Connectivity

Remote users at home will use dial-in lines and locally loaded modems to connect to the main location.

Current Internet Connectivity

This network currently has no Internet connection.

Proposed Internet Connectivity

No Internet connection is planned due to security concerns about private company information on a public network.

Company Goal with Windows 2000

The company is currently upgrading to a Windows 2000 network. The transition is scheduled over the next year.

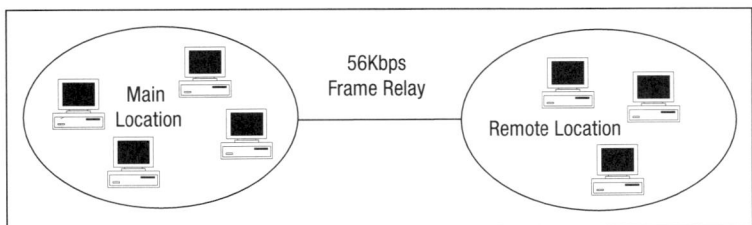

Figure 12.6 The current state of the ABC Company network.

Question 1

> The servers at the main location have been upgraded to Windows 2000 and also upgraded to domain controllers using Active Directory. One Active Directory domain has been created. Based on Figure 12.6, where is the best place to locate the RADIUS server?

The correct answer is:

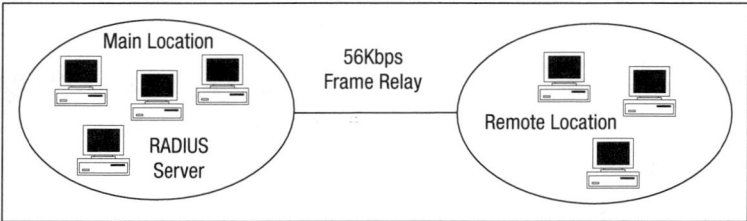

The RADIUS server needs to be placed on the LAN with the authentication server. This allows for the highest amount of security for the authentication information sent between the authentication server and the RADIUS server.

Question 2

> Which service will need to be loaded on the RADIUS server?
>
> ○ a. NAS
>
> ○ b. CHAP
>
> ○ c. IAS
>
> ○ d. POP

Answer c is correct. Internet Authentication Service (IAS) is the service that loads the RADIUS server on a Windows 2000 server. Network Access Server (NAS) is a generic RADIUS term for a RAS server. Challenge Handshake Protocol (CHAP) is used for authentication encryption, and Point of Presence (POP) is a server at an ISP that accepts client connections.

Question 3

> Remote users from home will be using Windows 98, Windows NT 4 Workstation, and Windows 2000 Professional. What authentication encryption protocols are needed for users to securely authenticate with the RADIUS server? [Check all correct answers]
>
> ❑ a. CHAP
>
> ❑ b. MSCHAP
>
> ❑ c. MSCHAP version 2
>
> ❑ d. EAP
>
> ❑ e. SPAP
>
> ❑ f. PAP

Answers b and c are correct. A Microsoft version of CHAP called MSCHAP is designed for encryption of authentication for Microsoft clients. MSCHAP version 2 is for Windows 2000 clients. MSCHAP (before version 2) is used by Microsoft clients other than Windows 2000. CHAP, not in the Microsoft version, is for other clients such as Macintosh and Unix. EAP is used to encrypt authentication for clients using smart cards, and SPAP is used in with clients in a Shiva LAN Rover network. PAP, because of its weak security, is used for clients that accept no other authentication encryption protocol.

Question 4

> How many realms will this network be using?
>
> ○ a. 0
>
> ○ b. 1
>
> ○ c. 2
>
> ○ d. 3

Answer b is correct. *Realm* is the generic RADIUS standard term for a group used for authentication. In a Windows 2000 environment, a domain is a RADIUS realm. The network has only one Active Directory domain and that will be used as the realm for the RADIUS service.

Question 5

> The company is trying to decide on the best way to provide a connection to the main location from the remote users' homes. The two ideas are a modem bank at the main office using dial-in lines or an Internet connection and an ISP. An Internet connection has never been used at the company, and company management would like to know what the advantages are to using an ISP and Internet connection instead of a modem bank. What are the advantages? [Check all correct answers]
>
> ❑ a. If users are outside the local calling area, an Internet connection will be cheaper.
>
> ❑ b. If users are outside the local calling area, an Internet connection will be more costly.
>
> ❑ c. An Internet connection is faster.
>
> ❑ d. An Internet connection is slower.

Answers a and c are correct. An Internet connection is cheaper if the users are outside the local calling area. An Internet connection would allow a local telephone call and connection instead of a long-distance one. An Internet connection is faster than a pure modem connection, because the fastest modems are capable of a maximum connection speed of only 56Kbps. Although a signal would leave the remote user's computer at 56Kbps, it would speed up from the ISP through the Internet. A modem-only connection to the private network would allow only a 56Kbps connection.

Question 6

> The company has decided to go with an Internet connection. Figure 12.6 shows the network in its current state. Where would the RADIUS clients need to be located?

The correct answer is:

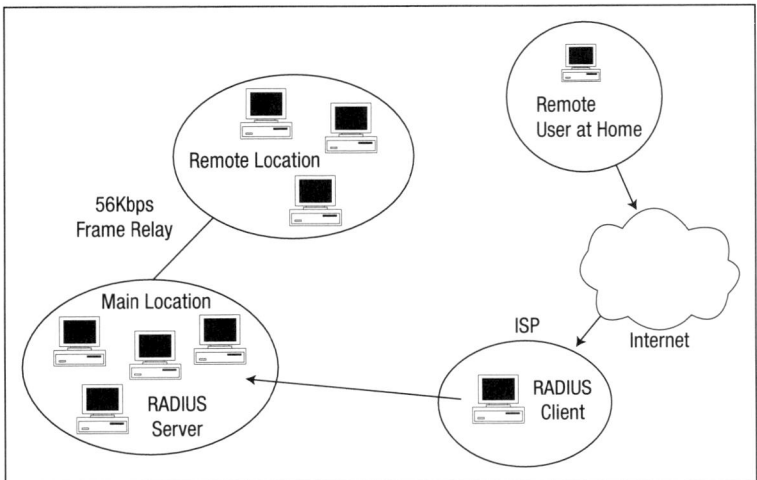

The RADIUS clients need to be placed at the ISP to allow the remote users to connect to the RADIUS client and then be authenticated onto the private network at the main location.

Question 7

How can the connection through the Internet from the remote users to the RADIUS clients be secured?

○ a. Authentication encryption

○ b. A screened subnet

○ c. A firewall

○ d. A VPN

Answer d is correct. A Virtual Private Network (VPN) will encrypt all data from the home user to the RADIUS client. Authentication encryption will encrypt only the username and password information. A firewall would create a screened subnet but would not encrypt the information over the Internet.

Question 8

> Now that a connection to the private network exists, what is the best way to increase security so that only specified users can access the network and only during work hours?
>
> ○ a. A remote-access policy
>
> ○ b. Turn off the service during off peak hours
>
> ○ c. A screened subnet
>
> ○ d. User profiles

Answer a is correct. A remote-access policy allows administrators of the RADIUS service to control which groups of users can use the RADIUS service. The policy can set times that the RADIUS service will accept connections, as well. Turning the service off is unnecessary when a remote-access policy is used. Although a screened subnet protects a private network, it does not turn the RADIUS service off. User profiles set desktop settings and are not related to the RADIUS service.

Question 9

> The ISP needs help deploying the RADIUS service. It has servers that use Windows NT 4, Windows 2000, and Novell Netware 5.x. Which servers can be used as a RADIUS client?
>
> ○ a. None
>
> ○ b. Windows NT 4
>
> ○ c. Windows 2000
>
> ○ d. Novell Netware 5.x
>
> ○ e. Any will work

Answer e is correct because RADIUS is an open standard. Windows NT 4 and Windows 2000 support this standard. Other operating systems like Netware and Unix also support the RADIUS standard and can be used in a Windows 2000 RADIUS solution.

Question 10

The ISP chose to use Windows 2000 for its RADIUS clients. What service needs to be installed in order to set up the RADIUS clients?

○ a. Remote-access policy service

○ b. RRAS

○ c. IAS

○ d. NAS

Answer b is correct. A RADIUS client needs to have the RRAS service loaded. There is no such thing as a "remote-access policy service." The Internet Authentication Service (IAS) is for the RADIUS server service. The Network Access Service (NAS) is a generic RADIUS term for a RAS server, and does not specify a specific service in Windows 2000.

Question 11

The RADIUS servers were set up at the main location of the private network. Now the ISP is setting up the RADIUS clients. How should they set up the shared secret? [Choose the best answer]

○ a. Make it a combination of upper- and lowercase letters as well as numbers and special characters.

○ b. Make it at least 16 characters.

○ c. Make it identical to the shared secret on the RADIUS server.

○ d. Make it difficult to guess.

Answer c is correct. A shared secret needs to be identical on the RADIUS client and server. It is recommended that the shared secret be a combination of upper- and lowercase letters, including numbers and special characters. It is also recommended that the shared secret be at least 16 characters long. A shared-secret password should also be difficult to guess. However, unless the shared secret is identical to the one on the RADIUS server, a connection will not be allowed between the two.

Question 12

> If the company starts to hire people all over the world, what RADIUS and remote-access solution will work best for it? [Check all correct answers]
>
> ❑ a. The ISP will need local POP that remote users can use to connect.
>
> ❑ b. The ISP will need to be global.
>
> ❑ c. An ISP cannot be used in this situation.
>
> ❑ d. The current remote solution will work.

Answers a and b are correct. The current situation will need some adjustment in order for the solution to be a global one for remote users. The ISP will need to have a global presence to be practical. The ISP will need local Points of Presence (POP) that will allow global users to make a local telephone call to get connected to the private network through the Internet.

Need to Know More?

 RFC 2138 Remote Authentication Dial-In User Service (RADIUS), at **http://ietf.org/rfc/rfc2138.txt?number=2138**. Basic information about the RADIUS service and standard.

 RFC 2139 RADIUS Accounting, at **http://ietf.org/rfc/rfc2139.txt? number=2139**. Discusses standards for the RADIUS accounting feature.

 Open Help from the Internet Authentication Service. Because this is a newly supported service, not much documentation is available on it. Help includes explanations of how the IAS service works as well as steps for installation. Troubleshooting information includes specific errors that can occur and fixes for each.

 Search the TechNet CD (or its online version through **support.microsoft. com/directory**) and the *Windows 2000 Server Resource Kit* CD using the keywords "RADIUS", "RRAS", and "IAS".

Managing Network Services

Terms you'll need to know:

✓ Management strategies
✓ Service interruptions
✓ Network status monitoring
✓ Data collection
✓ Distributed data collection
✓ Centralized data collection

Techniques you'll need to master:

✓ Using monitoring tools
✓ Using the system console
✓ Using logs and alerts

In this chapter, you'll learn about managing networking services. You'll become familiar with effective management plans that will incorporate security, availability, and performance into your design.

Planning Management Strategies

A good management plan will use strategies and processes to detect changes in your network and will also incorporate an initial course of action whenever such changes are detected. But a network management plan is not the only management strategy that should be in place by the IT staff and its management. A larger plan should include your network management plan and the applications that your network supports. This plan must outline how all of the other management strategies will work together when the unthinkable happens. Your management plan must contain these actions and the processes and procedures used to detect them, with a list of the responsible people (or groups of people) that it will integrate to resolve any issues when the need arises.

The main goal of the management plan should be to prevent problems and to detect and respond to critical events—such as interruption of service or total network failures—due to any number of internal or external forces. For example, redundancy of communications links and data-loss prevention should be included in your total management plan.

Your management plan should include strategies to:

➤ Respond to service interruptions and changes

➤ Ensure the current environment coincides with the design criteria

➤ Meet the future needs for the network services (planned expansion)

➤ Institute processes and procedures to monitor the network and analyze the collected data

Responding to Service Interruptions and Changes

Before resolving interruptions, you must first detect them. Your resolution strategy should define the process to automatically correct the interruption (such as a redundant link) or to notify responsible personnel of the interruption (if it requires manual correction). If possible, these processes should be initiated before the service becomes disabled so that corrections are made with minimal effect on the network.

Processes should be in place to provide detection and responses for:

➤ Services or server faults

➤ Failure of the network to fill client requests

➤ When predefined service values do not meet the minimum requirements

➤ When calculated values are not within working parameters

When notified of these events, the IS support staff needs to take action, following the steps outlined in the management plan, to minimize the effects of the interruptions on the clients. If you have implemented automated responses to events such as these, the IS staff should be notified to ensure that further action or monitoring is not needed or that services have been returned to their normal operating state.

Ensuring That the Current Environment Meets the Design Criteria

Of course, if your current environment does not meet the design criteria, monitoring for failures is pointless. Also, you will not have a baseline to define the criteria needed to detect failures. If the design goals that were planned are not correctly implemented, the required security, availability, and performance are also not within your design parameters.

A design should allow for fluctuations in the daily operations that are needed to service the clients. A conservative design provides for daily fluctuations and helps your network remain operational when faults occur. You can verify that parameters are within the design criteria either manually or automatically. To ensure that the network is operating within the design criteria, it will be necessary to capture and analyze network data against your predefined baseline. Only then will you be able to tell whether the network is operating within normal parameters. Table 13.1 lists testing methods and brief descriptions.

Table 13.1 Testing methods.	
Testing Method	**Description**
Manual Testing	Certain components of your network may require physical interaction to determine their compliance, such as redundancy links or failover server redundancy.
Schedule Audits	Security and access adjustments are often made. Scheduled audits will help ensure compliance with your intended security and access requirements.
Monitoring	Monitor uptime, service performance, and service to interaction time to ensure compliance.

Planned Expansion to Meet Future Needs for the Network Services

Over time, the requirements of the infrastructure—and the infrastructure itself— can change. For example, the speed at which a server is able to satisfy client's requests degrades with increased client pressure. Day-to-day operations can require changes to the original design that can seem minor at the time, but, when these small changes are compounded by other required changes, redesign can become necessary.

Your management strategies should include provisions for future needs, as well as long-term processes to detect the evolution of the network. These strategies should contain procedures to accumulate data that will track the resource consumption. The data can then be evaluated to plan for future changes.

As an example, with the current popularity of Web-based applications, your IS staff can detect the current Internet information servers that are operating outside the design parameters, because some of your company's applications have been converted to Web-based applications. Monitored data will show a decline in performance of the servers and implement your management policy to facilitate additions or upgrades.

Implementing Network Status Monitoring

Your management plan must have processes in place to detect the status of your network. For example, if a service fails, the responsible parties must be notified immediately to reduce the failure's effects on the clients. Your monitoring process should be able to:

➤ Determine the current state of the network services and infrastructure

➤ Detect trends from collected data

➤ Verify compliance with the network design

➤ Respond to service interruptions and bring performance back within the design parameters

Some companies introduce management software that can provide the network with automated monitoring and management of the network infrastructure. These management applications can significantly reduce the cost of ownership (the total dollars used to purchase and support a network resource). Windows 2000 can be monitored and managed using Microsoft Systems Management Server or other third-party management applications.

Getting Information on the Status of Services

When getting information on the status of services, the status of individual services must be included along with the status of the network as a whole. The detection of parameters outside the design goals can be accomplished by the following:

➤ Data collection

➤ Tools and utilities

➤ Performance logs

➤ Alerts

➤ The simple network management protocol (SNMP)

➤ Event logs

➤ Scripting tools

➤ Programming languages

➤ Management instrumentation

Data Collection

Collecting status information is necessary to the monitoring process. Monitoring a network is an intensive operation that can create large amounts of data. Using an event signal can reduce the amount of stored data, because the event signal notifies the responsible party that a preset threshold has been reached. This notification can also serve as a prompt for action that includes the monitoring of network resources. Notifications can be generated from unprocessed data to determine the status of the network, and events can be generated by tools, utilities, and automated monitors.

The two major data-collection strategies are distributed and centralized. Both methods can employ in-band or out-of-band data collection to generate automated or manual event notification. In-band and out-of-band collection will be explained in detail later in this chapter.

Distributed Data Collection

With a distributed collection strategy, data is monitored and collected from several points within your network infrastructure. With this strategy, responses and the analysis of the collected data can be decentralized to several locations, although, in most instances, the collected data is analyzed and processed at a central management point, such as a call center or help desk.

Centralized Data Collection

With a centralized point for collection and analysis, data is accumulated and analyzed from a single location. In most cases, the central point is also a centralized management station, such as a help desk or a node within a larger management system, such as a technology asset management center. Centralized monitoring can increase traffic on a local segment, and a centralized monitoring center does not provide redundant monitoring points. For instance, if the local network segment or the host(s) responsible for monitoring the network becomes disabled, the current state of the network will not be available.

To design a centralized collection strategy to be available, a path for the collection of data must be available to the monitoring point. There are two strategies for providing a path for the collected data:

➤ *In-band data collection*—With this strategy, the collected monitoring data travels on the same physical infrastructure that provides service to your clients. This means that the monitoring will generate an increase in network traffic. If a failure of the network services occurs and no redundant links are available, no transport service will be available for the collected data.

➤ *Out-of-band data collection*—An alternate path will be used to transmit the monitored data to the centralized management point such as an ISDN or modem connection. If you do not have redundant links built into your network infrastructure, it will be necessary to use an alternate path for monitoring and notification. Otherwise, if a total failure occurs, the centralized management point will not be notified of the failure.

Note: Use the in-band data collection strategy if redundant links are built into your network infrastructure. Use the out-of-band collection strategy if redundant links are not built into your network infrastructure.

Generated Events

Event notification requires that the current state of the network be available to the monitoring-service personnel or software. Software can actively monitor the current status of the network. When predefined thresholds are reached, the software will generate an event that can be used to notify responsible personnel that manual action is needed. In some cases, the event can be used to automatically restart the failed service.

Responsible personnel can use the notifications of service restart to deduce whether further action is needed. If frequent automatic actions are occurring, the design should be reviewed for problems.

Monitoring Tools Used to Generate Events

Many tools and software utilities can generate events when thresholds are reached. The following utilities are some of the more commonly used:

➤ *System Monitor*—Allows events to be logged to a log file when a threshold is exceeded. Notification is displayed as an error that prompts the system administrator to use the event view for further information. Most administrators are familiar with this tool.

➤ *Service Monitor*—Allows events to be available depending on the options that are selected during the installation of Windows 2000. Service recovery and monitoring are a part of the Windows 2000 operating system and is also provided by some BackOffice applications. Microsoft Exchange Server services can provide notification and monitoring of links from within the Exchange Administrator. These notification events can be sent to designated personnel via email or by the message utility built into Windows 2000.

➤ *SNMP (Simple Network Management Protocol)*—An additional TCP/IP utility that can be installed on a Windows 2000 computer. With SNMP, you can create traps that capture data for analysis. SNMP traps may be generated based on the events written to the event log and defined in the Management Information Base (MIB) for a particular service.

Note: To determine whether the SNMP service has been installed, look at the installed services by accessing the services administration tool from within the Windows 2000 administration tools. To add this service, access the network properties by right-clicking on My Network Places and choosing Properties. This opens the Network and Dial-Up Connections window. Now, right-click on the Local Area Network connection that you wish to add the service to and choose Properties. This opens the Local Area Network window. Now click on Install, and the Select Network Component window opens. From within this window, select Service to open the Add Service window. You can now select the SNMP service and click on OK to install the service.

Network Monitor

Network Monitor is used to gather statistics on frames and packets sent through your network. Although Network Monitor will not generate a notification event, it can be used to identify problems and track variations in the quality of service.

Command-Line Monitoring Tools

Command-line monitoring tools can be used to interactively view the current status of the network or to capture data to a file for later review. These tools help administrators to analyze whether the network services are operating within predefined parameters, as well as detect variations in the network's performance.

Following are some of the commonly used command-line monitoring tools and utilities:

➤ *Netdiag*—Performs a series of tests that are local to the host and used to determine the current state of the network client, including the availability of the WINS, DNS, and default gateway. This is a quick way to achieve several tests with one command.

Note: Netdiag is a utility that is added when you install the Windows 2000 Support Tools from the installation disk. The Support Tools installation program is located in the Tools subdirectory of the Support directory. When you install the Support Tools, an icon to launch the command interpreter is placed within the Support Tools folder on the Start menu.

➤ *Ping*—A utility that is used to check connectivity. It sends packets to a host and waits to receive a reply. You can specify the packet size, how many packets to send, whether to record the route used, what Time-to-live (TTL) value to use, or whether to set the "don't fragment" flag. When the response is received from the sending host, the maximum roundtrip time (RTT) is displayed. You can use the results of the RTT to determine whether the path between the two hosts is performing within the network management specifications.

➤ *Tracert*—A utility to discover the route used between two communicating hosts. Tracert uses the IP TTL field in the Internet Control Message Protocol (ICMP) to provide the route information.

➤ *Pathping*—Similar to both ping and tracert. However, pathping is a better diagnostic tool to troubleshoot router congestion, because it tests the path for 125 seconds. The statistics that pathping delivers show the number of packets that have been lost, thus providing the user with the ability to find routers that are not performing within parameters. Pathping is a new tool released with Windows 2000, and it is not supported by Windows 98.

➤ *Nslookup*—Provides an interactive means to check a DNS server resolution. This utility displays the hostname and IP address of the DNS server.

➤ *Netstat*—Displays protocol statistics and current TCP/IP network connections. This utility also displays the currently active ports and their states, such as "listening" or "established".

➤ *Nbtstat*—Displays the NetBIOS of TCP/IP statistics for troubleshooting networks that have clients other than Windows 2000. This tells administrators whether the WINS server or broadcast messages have been used to provide name resolution.

Using Monitoring Tools

Windows 2000 provides several tools to monitor your network. The most widely used monitoring tools are Performance Microsoft Management Console (MMC) and Event Viewer. The monitoring of TCP/IP statistics with Performance MMC requires that the SNMP services be installed on the Windows 2000 host. This section reviews Performance MMC, Event Viewer, and the SNMP protocol. Figure 13.1 shows Performance MMC. The Performance MMC is located in the Administrative tools program group.

The System Console

The system console, which is located within Performance MMC, allows administrators to view graphs of data or collect the data in log files. Graphs are useful for short-term, realtime monitoring of the performance statistics of either local or remote computers. Logs allow you to capture data over a period of time and view the data with graphs and line charts to discover trends. You can also use log alerts to see if the predefined thresholds have been reached. To do this, specify a counter on the local and remote computers. To create log alerts, set triggers on the counter and specify a value to trigger the process.

The counters can monitor system resources and network usage, such as memory and processor usage or network counters like current bandwidth usage. The performance counters can be set to track the local machine or multiple remote machines.

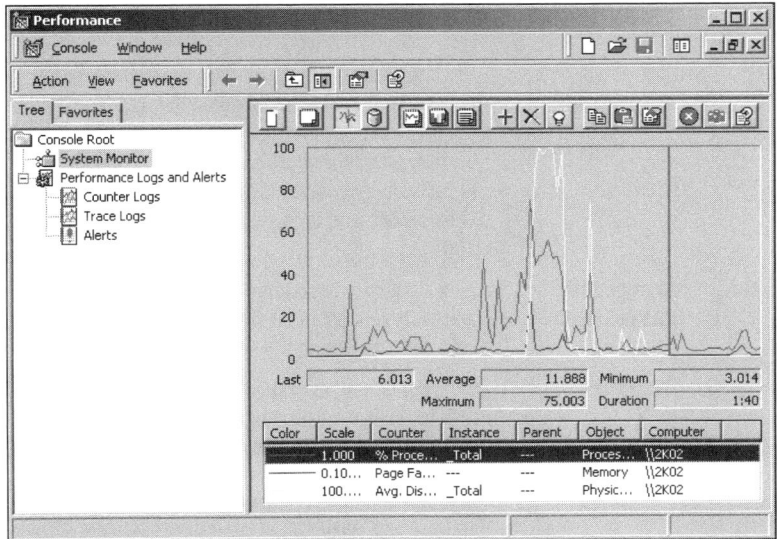

Figure 13.1 Performance MMC.

The counter can also be scheduled to track network or system performance at designated times and for a given period of time.

Using the System Console

The system console monitors performance counters that you designate by adding the counter to the system console. To add a performance counter, open the system console and either right-click in the graph area of the system counter or click on the plus sign on the tool bar. This opens the Add Counters window. To add counters for local system monitoring, click on the Use Local Computer Counters radio button. To monitor a remote system, click on the Select Counter for Computer radio button. If you selected the Use Local Computer Counters button, you can specify the UNC name for the machine you wish to monitor. If you did not select this option, the box will be ghosted.

The performance object is the type of counter that you want to monitor. The processor object allows you to monitor the current status of certain processor counters. After you have selected the type of object, such as processor, memory, or physical disk, that you wish to monitor, add the performance counters to monitor specific types of usage. For example, if you want to evaluate the performance of an application server, select %Processor Time. Microsoft has three counters that are considered important in monitoring server performance. Table 13.2 lists these counters and their descriptions.

Table 13.2 Counters and descriptions.		
Performance Object Type	**Counter Name**	**Application**
Processor	%Processor Time	This counter indicates the percentage of time that the processor is executing a non-idle thread, a primary indicator of processor activity. This statistic is calculated by monitoring the time the service was inactive and then subtracting that value from 100%.
Physical Disk	Average Disk Queue Length	This statistic is the average number of both read and write requests that were queued for the selected disk during the sample interval.
Memory	Pages/Sec	This is the number of pages read from or written to disk to resolve hard-page faults. (Hard-page faults occur when a process requires code or data that is not in its working set nor elsewhere in physical memory and must be retrieved from disk.) This counter was designed as a primary indicator of the kinds of faults that cause system-wide delays.

Windows 2000 Active Directory uses DNS to resolve hostnames to logical IP addresses. To monitor name resolution, use the DNS counters to monitor specific actions that relate to hostname resolution, dynamic DNS updates, and zone transfers. For example, you can monitor counters that relate to query, zone, and secure update failures to indicate a failure of DNS to resolve hostnames.

When you are deciding on the appropriate counters to monitor your network, you can view a description of the counter monitors by clicking the Explain button in the Add Counters window. The explain text window will open to describe the usage of the selected counter.

Using Logs and Alerts

Logs and alerts work in much the same way as the system console. Counters are added to monitor statistics on specific resources and to generate logs or alerts, or to perform an action.

Counter Logs

Counter logs gather data and record the captured statistics to a log file, which is later viewed from the system console. Whereas the system console shows live, realtime status of the selected counters, log files capture data at specific intervals to evaluate long-term trends. For example, you can use a counter log to monitor the %Processor Time counter on an application server for 24 hours to evaluate at what time the server was under the heaviest processing load. With this information, you can decide whether the server is capable of handling the utilization, and then plan for upgrades, if they are needed.

To create a new counter log, expand the Performance Logs and Alerts object by clicking on the "+" sign. After the expansion, you will notice the counter logs icon in the tree pane of Performance MMC. Right-click on the counter logs icon, and choose New Log Settings from the drop-down menu, or select New Log Settings from the action menu. A new log-setting dialog box appears. Enter the name for your new log and clicked on the OK button; the properties box will appear for your new log. The properties box has three tabs, General, Log Files, and Schedule.

The General tab allows you to specify the counters to track, and the interval and units. You now add the counter to capture statistics and set the interval at which the counter is monitored. For example, to monitor the processor utilization every 15 minutes, select the %Processor Time counter and specify "15" in the interval dialog box. Then select "minutes" from the unit's drop-down box.

The Log Files tab allows you to specify the name and location of the log file, the characters that designate uniqueness of the log file names, the type of file that is to be created, a descriptive comment for your counter log, and size limitations. The default name of the log file is the name that was given to the counter log. You can use the end names with the drop-down box to create unique file names, if the counter is scheduled to run at designated times. For example, if you scheduled a counter to run manually (by clicking the counter log icon and designating "nnnnnn" in the End File Names With dialog box, the name file will be "your_log_file_name_000001.blg" the first time it is run. The second time it is run, it will be "your_log_file_name_000002.blg" and will increment by one each time it is run.

Although you can save log files as text or binary files, you should choose binary to reduce the file size. If you choose binary circular file and specify a size limitation of the file, the file will be overwritten when the size limit is reached—which can cause you to lose valuable information. Binary files can be viewed only from within the system console, but text files can be opened with many word processor and spreadsheet applications.

 Microsoft recommends that you always save logs as binary files to reduce the amount of disk space used to store the file.

The Schedule tab allows administrators to schedule the counter log to run at designated times or upon clicking on the counter's icon. Within the schedule, you can also specify a stop time for the counter log and a command to be run. For example, you can use the **net send** command to notify you when the log is completed, or you can use the **copy** command to place a copy of the file at an administrative station, such as the help desk.

Trace Logs

Trace logs record data collected by the operating system provider or one or more nonsystem providers, such as programmers. A new trace log is created in the same manner as a counter log. The Log Properties dialog box has one additional tab, Advanced. The General tab allows you to select the system and nonsystem providers that you wish to monitor. The Log File and Schedule tabs are identical, with exception of the log file type drop-down list in the Log File tab. With a trace log, your log types are sequential and circular. Circular trace logs will overwrite the entries when the specified maximum size has been reached.

Alerts

Alerts prompt an action when a threshold is reached on a counter. The Alert Properties dialog box has three tabs: General, Action, and Schedule. The General tab allows administrators to add a descriptive comment, the counters to be monitored, at what threshold value to trigger the event, and the sample interval and units.

The Alert When Value Is drop-down box allows you to specify whether the trigger will be activated when the threshold value is over or under the value in the Limit Dialog box. For example, you can add the Errors Logon counter from the server object to alert you if the number of failed logon attempts to the server exceeds a certain threshold. This can indicate whether password-guessing programs are being used to crack the security on the server.

The Action tab is where you'll utilize the full power of alerts. You can choose to log an alert in the event viewer, send a network message, start a performance log, and run a program or specify command-line arguments, or any combination of these events, when a threshold is reached. For example, if our Errors Logon counter threshold was reached, we can verify that a message is sent to certain computers, that a performance log is started, that the netlogon service was stopped via the **net stop** command, and that the message contained the variables in the text message and command arguments. Figure 13.2 shows the Action tab of the Alerts utility.

Using the Event Viewer

The Event Viewer server notifies when errors occur in the system, security, application, directory service, DNS server, and file-replication services. This notification is postmortem, meaning that Event Viewer is capable of showing errors only after they occur. Unlike Performance Monitor, Event Viewer does not allow

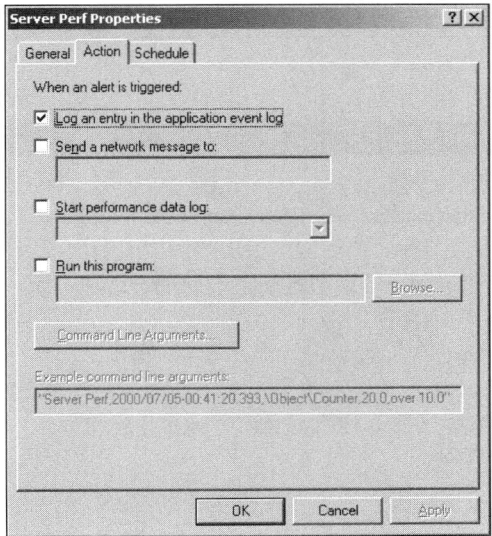

Figure 13.2   The Action tab of the Alerts utility.

the administrator to view the current status of the network or services. It also doesn't provide any ability to capture statistics. However, Event Viewer does keep log files that list all errors, their type, and when they occurred. Figure 13.3 shows Event Viewer.

You can use the filter options inside Event Viewer to filter out log entries that are not needed for your current task. The types of events that are entered into the error log are categorized, and each event type has a descriptive message and a colorful icon to help in quickly locating error messages that indicate possible disruptions of service. Table 13.3 lists the event type and its description.

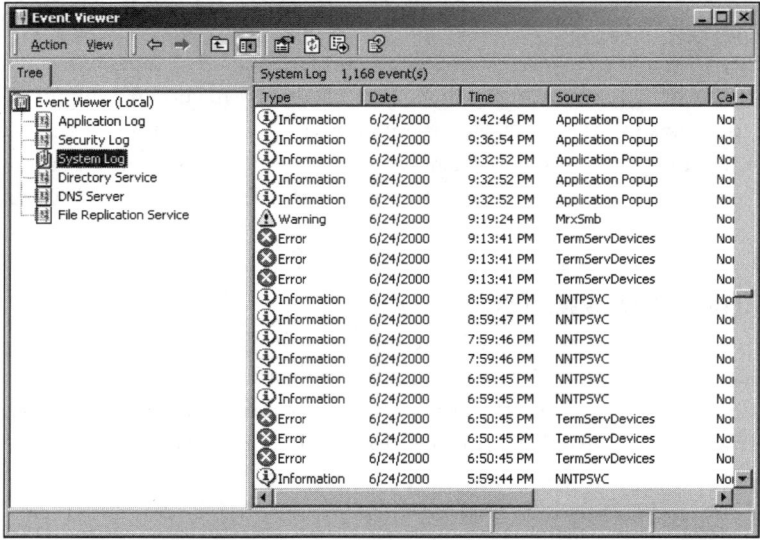

Figure 13.3   Event Viewer.

Table 13.3	Event types and descriptions.
Event Type	**Event Description**
Error	An event has occurred that may cause an interruption of the service that is listed in the log.
Warning	An event has occurred that may cause a future interruption of service, for example, when disk space is getting low.
Information	An event has occurred that indicates that the driver or service has been successfully started.
Success Audit	An event has occurred that indicates that an audited security event has successfully been accessed.
Failure Audit	An event has occurred that indicates that an audited security event has failed to grant access.

Windows 2000 Support for SNMP

The Windows 2000 TCP/IP stack supports the Simple Network Management Protocol (SNMP), and you can use SNMP to monitor the status of the hosts in a TCP/IP network. For TCP/IP counters to be used within the Performance Monitor, the SNMP service must be installed. If you have routers, switches, and hubs that are managed and configured by SNMP, you need SNMP installed to access the support services for these devices.

The SNMP service is used to remotely configure devices and services, monitor network services and performance, and detect network faults. Software components and services using SNMP are referred to as SNMP agents and have a defined management information base (MIB). Reading the MIB can provide status information, and writing to the MIB reconfigures elements of a component service.

Getting Statistics with Scripting and Programming Tools

Windows 2000 allows administrators to gather network statistics using programming and scripting. To provide for the automated running of scripts and programs to collect data and perform other tasks, Windows 2000 administrators can use the **AT** command or the Window Script Host to set automated processes.

Windows Script Host

The Windows Script Host can automatically run script files for logon scripts, and administrative and automated tasks. Scripts can be written in several languages, and the most commonly used are Microsoft Visual Basic Script Editing (VBScript) and Microsoft Jscripts. Windows Script Host also supports other languages, like Perl.

Windows Script Host can be run from within Windows or from the command prompt. To run it from within Windows, use the **Run** command to launch Wscript.exe or, from the command prompt, type "Cscript", followed by the script name and any command-line arguments.

Note: You can type "Cscript" from the command prompt, and the available options will be displayed.

Custom Applications

Applications can be written in languages like Microsoft Visual Basic or Microsoft Visual C++ to gather network statistics and implement a partial or complete solution to the network event. You can create applications that act as separate executable files or that can be accessed from within MMC.

Windows Management Instrumentation (WMI)

WMI is an interface that programmers can use to create custom applications that monitor the status of services. These applications can acquire the status of a service from local and remote Windows 2000 computers using scripts that access a WMI repository or provider.

WMI is started automatically by Windows during its boot process. Windows 9x products also support this programming interface, but the service must be manually started. WMI, which is referred to as the Common Information Model (CIM), is a Microsoft implementation of Web-based Enterprise Management (WBEM). This management architecture was designed by the Distributed Management Interface (DMI) and CIM to provide an extension of management protocols such as SNMP. You can use WMI to provide network statistics automatically using Windows Script Host.

Analyzing Collected Data

You can determine the current status of the network by viewing realtime statistics, logged statistics, and calculated analysis. You must use the collected statistics to create a set of results. The results will be analyzed to look for trends in portions of your network that are not working within the designed parameters. To obtain a result set, you must analyze all of the collected data.

Analysis

Analyzing data involves comparing the collected data to your expected results and the original design parameters to determine the state of the network. You can use any of several techniques to determine the state of the network.

Data can be analyzed manually or by using applications to aid in the process. MS Excel, Access, or SQL Server can be used to not only log the statistics and determine the results, but also to provide recommendations for responses (if they are required). Custom-built applications and third-party software can also be used, and such implementations are often a part of a larger management plan.

Point-in-time analysis of data will alert the administrators to conditions like service or network failures, as well as network operations that are outside the designed parameters. You can use trend analysis to predict possible future variations in your network services, as well as to indicate areas of growth that will require a redesign. You can use one of two types of analysis to determine your network state: manual and automated.

Manual Analysis

Manual analysis is most often used for point-in-time analysis of the network. You use this type of analysis to prompt the pertinent parties to respond to variations in the network. For example, if the disk space on a server is low, the administrators can analyze the current available space, on a daily or weekly database, to predict when the situation will require action.

Automated Analysis

Automated analysis is used when automated responses correct the network variance. Normally, these responses provide an alternate path for the network traffic, such as redundant WAN connections.

Response Strategies

Response strategies are processes that occur when the network service reaches a point at which an action needs to be taken to correct or circumvent a problem. Response strategies fall into two categories: proactive and reactive.

Proactive Response Strategies

Proactive responses to network problems require that trend analysis be used to predict possible failures and growth or variances that will place the network service in a state that does not meet the design requirements. Proactive responses can better serve a network that has requirements of minimal downtime and warnings of capacity limitations. You will find that nearly every network has these expectations and that few ever reach their design goals. With proper monitoring and planning, as well as a conservative design, this is an obtainable goal.

Reactive Response

In the real world, this is the way that variations respond. Even with monitoring, these are the best results you can expect without good trend analysis and planning. With good monitoring, you can minimize the effect of service failures with proper notification and response strategies. For example, if a monitoring tool reports a status failure, it will be resolved much quicker if you have a plan for responding to the failure. In large companies, sometimes the failure of the service is amplified by the time it takes to get approval to restore the service. If your plan was defined before the event and approval for action was already granted, the correction of the service can be accomplished much quicker.

Events that can trigger a reactive response include status logs, email notifications, help desk calls, and monitoring services. The reactive response strategy can be used if some downtime is expected or if redundancy of network services is built into your design. Redundancy of network services can minimize the effect of the failure on the clients and allow the response to be activated promptly.

Practice Questions

Case Study

VirtuCon is a manufacturer of high-tech equipment. Based in Carson City, Nevada, the company has a manufacturing plant in Indianapolis, Indiana, and a distribution facility in Louisville, Kentucky, as shown in Figure 13.4. The corporate offices in Carson City have 150 hosts; the manufacturing plant in Indianapolis has 300 hosts; and the distribution center in Louisville has 120 hosts. The network infrastructure was recently upgraded, and all network cards, hubs, and switches are 10/100. The management staff has assigned you to design a new file structure that will provide load balancing and failover redundancy.

Current WAN Structure

VirtuCon currently uses Windows 2000 servers at all locations. The client workstations currently run Windows 95, Windows 98, Windows NT 4 Workstation, and Windows 2000 Professional.

Carson City has two DCs and one member server. Indianapolis has one DC and one member server. Louisville has one DC. Each location contains a shared folder that needs to be accessible to all users. Currently, the users have multiple drive mappings to provide access to the files at all locations. There is no redundancy.

The locations have redundant T1 connections from Carson City to Indianapolis and from Indianapolis to Louisville. The routers have been replaced in the past year and are QoS aware.

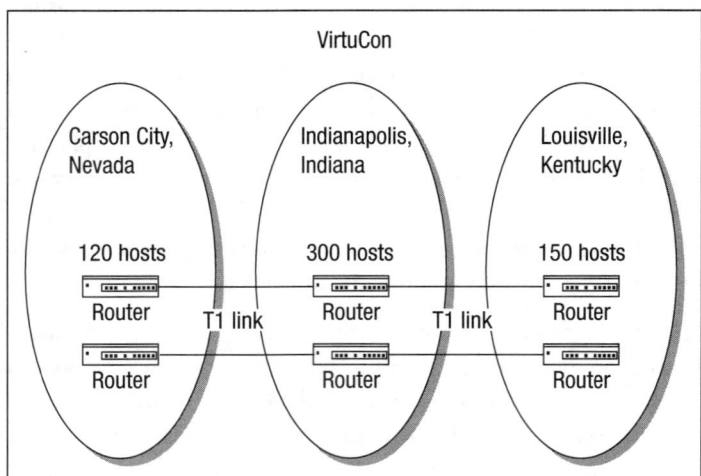

Figure 13.4 VirtuCon WAN.

The owners have begun negotiations to purchase a small firm in Evansville, Indiana. This firm has an existing infrastructure that utilizes Windows NT 4 servers. Because this process is still in negotiations, further details are not available.

Current WAN Connectivity

The locations have redundant T1 connections from Carson City to Indianapolis and from Indianapolis to Louisville. The routers have been replaced in the past year and are QoS aware.

Proposed WAN Connectivity

The company currently has no plans to change its WAN design. However, if the company in Evansville is purchased, your design should provide the best integration possible.

Directory Design Commentary

VirtuCon's current password policies will be duplicated on the Windows 2000 servers.

Current Internet Positioning

VirtuCon currently accesses the Internet from all locations using a single leased IP address at the Indianapolis location. This location has an IP proxy and firewall to protect the network and provide access.

A Web-hosting firm hosts the company Web site. The firewall server at the Indianapolis site provides a Web-based email client for mail access for all employees.

Future Internet Plans

Eventually, VirtuCon would like to host its own site and provide remote users with Web-based access to their intranet mail.

Company Goal for the Network Infrastructure and Responses to Events

Your management plan will use strategies and processes to detect changes in your network, as well as to incorporate an initial course of action, when your network changes.

VirtuCon uses an application that tracks an order from the sales desk to the shipping department. The management staff at your company has placed an emphasis on zero down time to prevent late shipping dates to your customers.

Question 1

Considering the case study, which type of data-collection strategy would best suite your WAN links?

○ a. In-band data collection

○ b. Out-of-band data collection

○ c. Manual data collection

○ d. Automatic data collection

Answer a is correct. Considering that you have redundant WAN links, an in-band collection strategy will provide network statistics, even in the event that one of the WAN links becomes unavailable. Out-of-band collection requires additional connections to the network. Since you have redundant links this would result in unnecessary costs. Manual and Automatic are types of collection that are automatically or manually monitored; they do not require the consideration of WAN links. Both manual and automated data collection can be used in either in-band, or out-of-band collection.

Question 2

Considering the case study, how would you implement a distributed data-collection strategy?

○ a. Configure monitoring on one server.

○ b. Configure monitoring on the Windows 2000 clients only.

○ c. Configure monitoring on the Windows 98 clients only.

○ d. Configure monitoring on several hosts in your domain.

Answer d is correct. To implement distributed data collection, monitoring is done at several hosts on the network. A certain type of host may or may not provide the services needed to gather information.

Question 3

Considering the case study, which of the following would be applicable as tools to monitor your network's status? [Choose all correct answers]

❑ a. System monitor

❑ b. Service monitor

❑ c. SNMP

❑ d. DHCP

Answers a and c are correct. The system monitor and SNMP can be used to monitor the network. To use the service monitor, Microsoft Exchange needs to be installed and service monitors must be defined. In the case study, company mail is accessed via an Internet mail application based in Indianapolis. DHCP provides dynamic IP allocation to TCP/IP hosts and cannot be used to monitor network statistics.

Question 4

Considering the case study, which of the following command-line utilities could be used to evaluate the network status?

○ a. Pathping

○ b. Nslookup

○ c. Netstat

○ d. All of the above

Answer d is correct. Pathping, nslookup, and netstat are command-line utilities that you can use to evaluate the current state of the network.

Question 5

Considering the case study, what graphical utility will be best for viewing a realtime chart of the network services?

○ a. System console

○ b. Network monitor

○ c. Event Viewer

○ d. Windows Script Host

Answer a is correct. The system console can provide a realtime status of your network resources in a line chart format. Network monitor provides network statistics in an information console format. Event Viewer display's post mortem information on failed services in a graphical format. Windows Script Host is used to create custom applications that can monitor or act upon network statistics.

Question 6

Considering the case study, in what format would you save log files to reduce the disk space required by the log files?

○ a.   Binary

○ b.   Text file

○ c.   ASCI

○ d.   None of the above

Answer a is correct. Microsoft recommends that all log files be saved in binary format to limit the space needed by the log files. The other options will not save space.

Question 7

Considering the case study, what interface can programmers utilize to create custom applications that monitor the status of services?

○ a.   Windows Management Interface

○ b.   Windows Script Host

○ c.   Application Programming Interface (API)

○ d.   SMNP

Answer a is correct. WMI is an interface that programmers can use to create custom applications that monitor the status of services. These applications can acquire the status of a service from local and remote Windows 2000 computers using scripts that access a WMI repository or provider. Windows Script Host is used for non-interactive scripting needs, such as logon scripts, administrative scripting, and automated tasks. The API is used by programmers to integrate with Windows 2000 utilities. SMNP is part of the TCP/IP stack and allows the monitoring of network statistics.

Need to Know More?

 Anderson, Duncan, Thomas W. Shinder, Syngress Media. *MCSE Windows 2000 Certification Head Start.* Osborne McGraw-Hill, Berkley, CA, 1999. ISBN 0-07-212250-1. Pages 657-662 overview monitoring tools.

 Microsoft Corporation. *Windows 2000 Server Resource Kit.* Microsoft Press, Redmond, WA, 2000. ISBN 1-57231-805-8. Chapter 8 of the *Development Planning Guide* volume provides some guidelines used for monitoring.

 Spalding, George. *Windows 2000 Administration.* Osborne McGraw-Hill, Berkley, CA, 2000. ISBN 0-07-882582-2. Page 138 provides an overview of the performance console.

Combining Network Services

Terms you'll need to understand:

✓ Routing and Remote Access Service (RRAS)

✓ Proxy server

✓ Network Address Translation (NAT)

✓ Remote Authentication Dail-In User Service (RADIUS)

✓ Virtual Private Network (VPN)

✓ Internet Service Provider (ISP)

✓ Active Directory

✓ Windows Internet Naming Service (WINS)

✓ Domain Name Service (DNS)

✓ Internet Authentication Services (IAS)

✓ Network Basic Input/Output System (NetBIOS)

Techniques you'll need to master:

✓ Determining the resource usage of network services

✓ Combining network services for efficient server use

✓ Determining the sensitivity of data used by network services

✓ Balancing security with performance in network services

Each service in this book is discussed separately to provide an understanding of what the service is and what it adds to the network. After gaining an understanding of each of the services individually, we need to find ways to combine the services. To load each service on a separate server would require an unnecessarily high number of servers on a network—which also would increase the cost and complication of the network design. The best solution is to combine the network services onto one server. Because many of the services also need to communicate with each other, this solution has the added benefit of helping to reduce network traffic by allowing the services to communicate locally instead of over the network. However, the difficulty in combining services is that no one solution fits all networks. Although some services combine well, others work best on their own. In general, the services that are used most often on a network won't combine as well as those services that are used less. Ultimately, the best way to combine network services depends on the needs of each network.

Goals of Combining Network Services

Deciding which network services will work for a network is just the first step in designing a network infrastructure. Determining how to place the services throughout the network requires much more information and effort, because so many factors affect the decision. The goals of combining network services include reducing administration and network traffic to make the network more efficient. Another goal is to increase fault tolerance and security on the network. These goals do not always work well together and oftentimes work against each other. The best way to increase the efficiency of the network is to pare the services down so that the network contains as few servers as possible. However, adding fault tolerance to a service means adding redundancy, and security usually creates extra traffic. This apparent contradiction does not mean that these goals are not attainable. But, when combining services on a network, the designer needs to know which goals are most important—and therefore which should be emphasized when making design decisions.

Design decisions are also affected by other factors, such as hardware resource usage, the number of supported users, and WAN connections. Adding these factors to the goals of combining network services keeps the process from being exact. A network service designer first needs to decide which services are needed on the network. A network overview is then needed so that all of the information is available when making service placement decisions. Network services can be combined to increase the efficiency of the network, even if redundancy and security are needed.

Combining Network Diagrams

A good network overview allows a designer of network services to see what effect placing services in different areas will have. Network diagrams for each network service have some common basic components necessary for design decisions for all network services. These basic components include each network location, concentration of users at each location, bandwidth of WAN connections, and WAN connectivity devices. Some services need extra information, also. Understanding what information is needed to get an accurate picture is important when building a network diagram. Figure 14.1 shows the basic components needed in a network diagram.

Network Diagram Additions

Each service may require additional information on the network diagram, because not every user on the network uses every available service. So, although the basic network diagram shows the total number of users on the network, the number of users of some services may need to be adjusted. Some services such as DNS and DHCP will be needed by nearly all computers in a Windows 2000 network. Services that provide remote connections need information only on the number of users who need a remote connection. Table 14.1 shows additional information needed by each service.

Also, the network may have operating systems other than Windows 2000. The network may be in transition while upgrading to Windows 2000, or it may need to integrate other operating systems into the network. To keep the network diagram

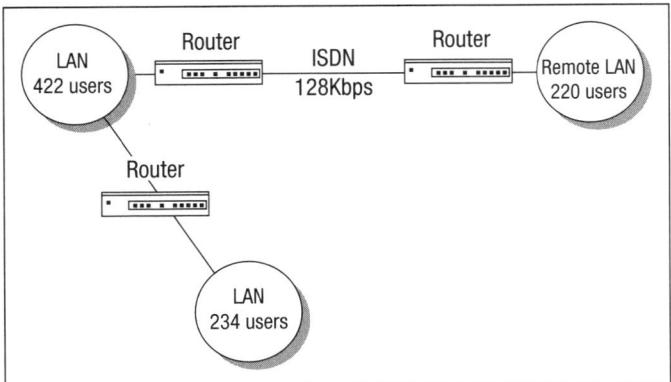

Figure 14.1   Network diagram with basic components, including each of the three network locations, number of users at each location, bandwidth between WAN locations and connectivity devices such as routers, switches, or bridges.

Table 14.1 Network diagram additions.	
Service	**Extra Information Needed on the Network Diagram**
DHCP	Location of DHCP servers
DNS	Location of DNS servers
IAS	Locations of domain controllers
NAT	Location of remote connection into the network
Proxy Server	Location of Internet connection
RRAS (Remote Access)	Number of remote users, connection to ISP (if used)
RRAS (Routing)	Number of users in each subnet
VPN	Location of Internet connection, connection to ISP (if used)
WINS	Location of NetBIOS clients

from becoming too complex, the designer should assume that all computers are Windows 2000 unless otherwise marked. Clients such as Macintosh, Unix, Novell, and Windows operating systems that are other than Windows 2000 need to be marked.

Internet Connections

The biggest change in Windows 2000 is the addition of services that add security to outside connections. We know that the Internet is not a secure connection because it is open to the public, and that connecting a private network to the Internet opens the network up to attack. Services like Routing and Remote Access Service (RRAS), proxy servers, Network Address Translation (NAT), and Remote Authentication Dial-In User Service (RADIUS)—as well as the implementation of virtual private networks (VPNs)—are designed to protect networks from the Internet. With the added security of a combination of these services, a company can choose to use the Internet as a less expensive connection between WAN locations.

The use of an Internet Service Provider (ISP) has a large effect on the placement of Internet-related services. In particular, the inclusion of an ISP in the network design greatly affects NAT, RRAS, and RADIUS designs, and these services may need to be located at the ISP instead of at the remote or private network. Although relocating these servers adds more servers to the network design, it also adds security.

As a last addition to the network diagram, note how many users at each location need the service. Some of the LANs in the whole network may not need the service, or only a few users on a particular LAN may need the service. Services are more easily combined onto one server if they support fewer users. Noting the number of users will help in deciding how many services a single server can support.

Making Service Decisions

Because the goals of combining network services are not often complementary, it's best to try to accomplish them one at a time. First, make the network more efficient by combining the right services onto fewer servers. Then, add fault tolerance and security as needed for your particular network. The servers that are freed up by making the network more efficient can be used to increase fault tolerance and security if these services are needed. To reduce the number of servers, a network designer needs to know what resources each network service uses and how many are needed to support the workload.

Although many services are available in a Windows 2000 network, not every network needs every available service. Designing a network infrastructure involves deciding which services are needed for a network and which services can be left out. Focusing on providing support for the users on your network should help in making your decisions for what services are needed. The number of users that need to be supported for each service can vary. The number of users who need DNS support is probably different than the number of users who need RRAS support. Using only the services needed will reduce the network's administrative overhead and keep the design simple.

Hardware Resources

Services can be loaded onto the same server if the hardware resources on the server can handle the workload. The four main hardware resources are processor, disk, memory, and network. Because most network services do not heavily use all four, one of the tricks to combining network services is to evenly use hardware resources. If one service heavily uses the memory and disk, then it can be combined onto the same server with a service that heavily uses the network or processor. Table 14.2 shows a list of the network services and the hardware resources

Table 14.2 Hardware resources used by network services.	
Service	**Most-Used Hardware Resources**
DHCP	Processor, disk
DNS	Memory, disk
IAS	Memory
NAT	Processor, memory, network
Proxy Server	Processor, memory, disk, network
RRAS (Remote Access)	Processor, memory, network
VPN	Processor
WINS	Disk

that are heavily used by that service. It does not mean that other unlisted hardware resources aren't used. The resources listed are just those the service uses most heavily.

If services that all use the same resource need to be used together, then that resource may need to be increased. If a server's resources are overused, the performance can be enhanced by adding another processor or a more powerful processor, a disk that has better read and write performance, more memory, or more or better-performing network adapters.

Applications on a Server

Network services are not all that gets loaded on a server. Applications that support the network will also use hardware resources when loaded on a server. Application servers on a network can also have network services loaded on them as long as they can still function well. Some applications are so resource intensive that they are best left alone on a server. Applications like SQL Server and Exchange Server work best if they are all that a server supports. Adding a network service on the same server most likely results in poor performance for the network service and the application. However, other applications that are less resource intensive can coexist on one network server with other services.

When loading applications, make sure that they are approved by Microsoft to work with Windows 2000. With Windows 2000, Microsoft differentiates between approved and unapproved software by using digital signatures, which is given to software when it is approved. Windows 2000 checks for this digital signature when software is loaded, and a warning will appear if it is not present. The purpose is to let an administrator loading the software know if it has been tested and is stable on Windows 2000. If a network service that needs to be available as much as possible coexists on a server with unsigned software, then Microsoft warns of the possibility that the unsigned software may crash the server—making the Microsoft network service loaded on the server temporarily unavailable.

Using Fewer Servers

As a general rule, services should be combined onto as few servers as possible. However, this rule is not as simple as it sounds. Separations by WAN connections and limitations of hardware resources will cause the need for services to be spread throughout the network. Even with these obstacles at this stage of design, your emphasis should still be on keeping the network design simple and lowering administrative overhead.

Although some services can be combined, doing so still depends on what is needed for the users of the network. Combinations of services that increase security are different than combinations that increase availability or performance. Now that you've looked at the network diagram for ways to reduce the number of servers, you will need to add more servers for the services based on security and fault tolerance.

Combinations to Increase Security

Some services should be combined, and others—like security when remote and/or Internet connections are used—should remain on separate servers. The creation of screened subnets prompts a need for a separation of services and very often requires the addition of several servers.

Some services contain sensitive information. For example, information contained on a domain controller includes usernames, passwords, and user account information as well as service information if the services are Active Directory-integrated. When combining services, you must evaluate whether the information will be vulnerable when you place it on certain servers. For example, a screened subnet exists outside of the private network and usually allows incoming requests from the Internet. Such a place is a vulnerable place for sensitive information. If the information is of a sensitive nature, it should be kept separate and removed from the Internet connection.

Adding Screened Subnets to a Network

A screened subnet can be created with the Proxy Server or NAT service. Each service protects the internal network by controlling connections from an external network, such as the Internet. Screened subnets are set up between a private network and the (public) Internet to separate the two, because a connection to the Internet is a possible connection to all users—authorized and unauthorized. Companies still set up connections to the Internet, even though it makes their networks more vulnerable, because it is a less expensive and easier way to create a connection for remote users. If set up in a secure manner, a private network can be protected from the Internet and still allow authorized access. Figure 14.2 shows

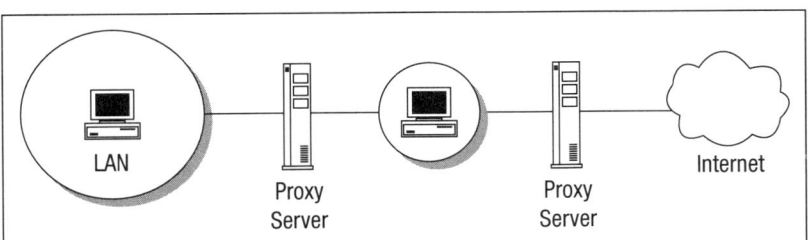

Figure 14.2   A server inside the screened subnet allows access to it from the Internet but also protects the internal network.

a proxy server setup to create a screened subnet and separate the internal network. This effectively separates the public-access network and an internal network for private use.

The service that creates the screened subnet is the most vulnerable. Proxy Server or the NAT service is placed on the Internet to protect the private network, but no service protects the server that creates the screened subnet. Thus, no other service should be placed on a server that is creating the screened subnet, simply because it is the most likely server to have a break-in attempt. When creating a screened subnet, choose a server that will create the screened subnet, and load only the services that are required to create the screened subnet. No other services should be loaded on the server that sits between the public and private network. For Proxy Server, the required services are Internet Information Server and the Proxy Server service. For NAT, the required service is RRAS.

Even services located inside the screened subnet are vulnerable, although less so than the server creating the screened subnet. The service creating the screened subnet must let some traffic in so that Internet users can get to the services inside the screened subnet. Remember that services acting as firewalls close ports so that connections to the services inside the screened subnet are limited. Only the ports that are needed to allow connections to specific services are opened. Connections coming in from the Internet to the private network should all be refused. Allow only connections from the private network out to the screened subnet, so that the information on the servers in the screened subnet can be refreshed from the internal network.

Screened subnets can also be used to isolate services that are needed by remote users coming in over the Internet. Services that are located within the screened subnet should be there only if Internet users need the information. A Web server intended for public access should be in a screened subnet. Internet users will be allowed to access this Web server, but access to other than Web services will be denied to try to protect it. A second proxy server between the Web server and the private network will prevent any incoming connections into the private network, thus protecting it from outside access.

Before placing a service inside a screened subnet, you have to evaluate the sensitivity of the data. A domain controller is a good example of a service that should not be inside a screened subnet nor should WINS and DNS services, which include databases of IP addresses and computer names. If the design of the network must include these services in the screened subnet, then the replication must be tightly controlled. The most secure way to accomplish this replication is a one-way exchange from the private network to the screened subnet. Communication from the screened subnet to the internal network should not be allowed.

Remote Access Connections

A server that creates a screened subnet is not the only type of server that is vulnerable. Any server that is at the edge of a network and open to a public connection is susceptible to attack via that public connection. Even remote access servers with the RRAS service should be isolated because of their connection to an outside network. So, for the sake of security, an RRAS server should have only those services that are needed for the remote clients to connect to the private network.

Combinations to Increase Performance

The ability to increase performance on a network is directly related to individual services being able to complete their tasks in the least amount of time possible. Even though security increases the amount of traffic and the number of servers on a network, this doesn't mean that the service's performance can't be improved. We've already discussed the effect of hardware on a server's performance, which can be measured with monitors and analyzers. These tools can tell you how the server is handling the load placed on it. If the server is overburdened, the solution may be to move services to less-stressed servers or to add more or better-performing hardware to the server.

Reducing Network Traffic

Performance can also be improved by designing the network infrastructure so that it is less burdensome. Some services, such as DNS and DHCP, need to communicate and share information. If services are combined for performance, then it's a good idea to place services that need to share information on the same server. Doing so also reduces network traffic. In general, services do not tend to use as much network bandwidth as application or file traffic. Still, you should try to arrange services around the network so that they can communicate without ever causing any network traffic.

Combinations to Increase Availability

Increasing a service's availability means providing fault tolerance for it. Fault tolerance provides redundancy to a service so that, if a failure occurs on the server on which the service is loaded, the clients have an alternative server. Combining network services onto fewer servers helps make the network perform more efficiently. The goal of adding fault tolerance is not to make the network more efficient, but to keep it working even though a failure has occurred. If some services are deemed to be mission critical or needed 24 hours a day, then that service needs fault tolerance. If such availability is not an issue, then a network will work more efficiently without fault tolerance for the services.

Although fault tolerance can be set up in different ways for different services, it usually means loading the service on a different server and designating a primary and a backup for the client to go to when it needs to use the service. If the designated primary server does not respond to calls from the client, the secondary server (or servers) is contacted. The primary/secondary method is often recommended for services, but other methods are also available, such as using Windows Clustering.

Windows Clustering

Windows Clustering actually comprises two services: Cluster Service and Network Load Balancing. Cluster Service—which is available for use on only Windows 2000 Advance Server and Datacenter Server—can help to provide fault tolerance to services within a network. Cluster Service allows a group of individual servers to act as a larger server, operating as a server cluster. The point of using Cluster Service is to provide fault tolerance for the services loaded in the cluster. It is an alternative to providing fault tolerance for individual services that allows for the use of fewer servers.

Applications loaded on a cluster are either cluster-aware or cluster-unaware. Only large applications like the Enterprise versions of Exchange Server and SQL Server are actually cluster-aware. Network services such as the ones we are planning are often cluster-unaware. This doesn't mean that they can't be used with Cluster Service; it just means that they are not aware that clustering is happening.

Microsoft provides a terminal emulator called Terminal Services. When loaded on a server, Terminal Services allows a client to remotely connect to a server, run services and applications from the server, and receive the Windows 2000 Professional desktop, even though they are running a legacy operating system. Terminal Services should not be loaded on a server that is configured as a domain controller, and it should be installed on a server before loading any of the applications that will use it.

Terminal Services can be loaded onto more than one server and combined with the Windows Clustering service Network Load Balancing to balance incoming requests.

Practice Questions

Case Study

The We Transport company is currently a large operation with one location: Bloomington, Illinois. The company provides delivery services for packages, and, although the industry has experienced much recent growth, the company isn't growing at the same rate. Company management has decided that this lack of growth is due to outdated technology being used to ship and deliver packages. The company needs to expand by adding small remote locations. Also, the company needs to upgrade its network infrastructure to take advantage of new, less expensive connection technologies. Establishing a Web presence is also a top priority. The company would like to learn of connectivity possibilities as well as security solutions. Figure 14.3 shows the current state of the network.

Figure 14.3 The current state of the network includes 1,051 users in a single location. A router divides the network into two subnets of 500 and 551 users each.

Current WAN Connectivity

The company currently has only one main location with no connectivity to the outside world.

Proposed WAN Connectivity

The company has plans for remote locations starting with all major cities. These locations need to be connected in an inexpensive yet secure manner.

Current Internet Connectivity

The network currently has no Internet connection.

Proposed Internet Connectivity

A connection to the Internet will connect the main office to the proposed new remote offices. Also, a new Web site with commerce abilities will be located at the main office.

Company Goal with Windows 2000

The company would like to simplify the network design and lessen administrative overhead. To support the new network infrastructure, Windows 2000 has been chosen as the new operating system. The main office is currently upgrading. Remote offices will be set up with Windows 2000 as the computers are installed.

Question 1

The following diagram shows the network at the main location and the servers in each subnet.

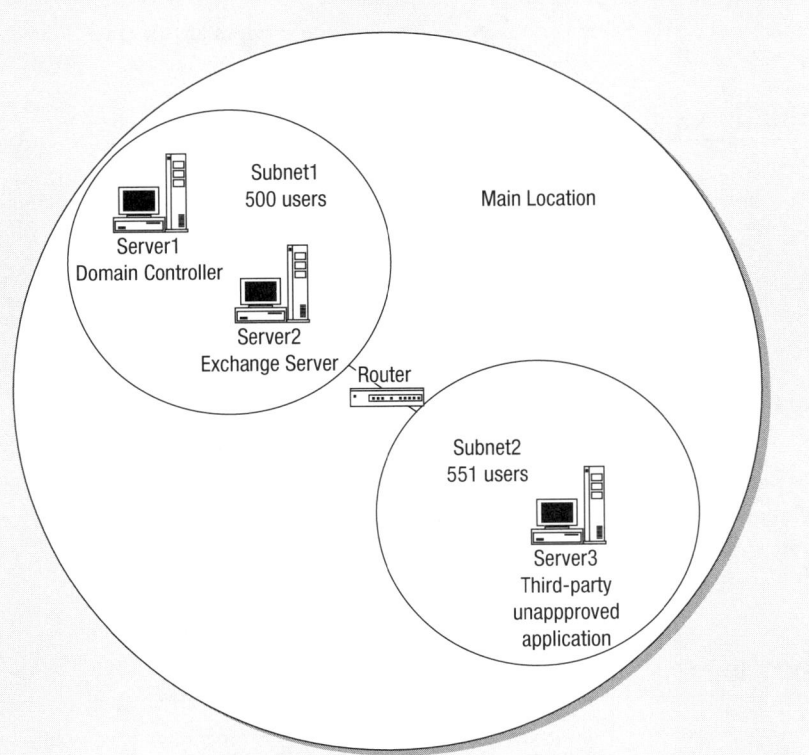

The following list of services has been discussed as possibilities for the main location. Currently, no remote locations are ready to connect to the main network location. Which services are needed for the main location only? [Check all correct answers]

❑ a. WINS

❑ b. DNS

❑ c. DHCP

❑ d. NAT

❑ e. Proxy Server

❑ f. RADIUS

❑ g. RRAS

Answers a, b, and c are correct. With no remote connections and no Internet connection, only WINS, DNS, and DHCP are needed. Because the company has stated that it would like to lessen administrative overhead, each of these services are appropriate for the network. Proxy Server, NAT, RRAS, and RADIUS all provide or protect connectivity to outside networks and, because no outside connection exists, there is no need to install these services at this time.

Question 2

How many servers are needed to provide the users in the main network location with the services selected in the previous question?

○ a. One

○ b. Two

○ c. Three

○ d. Four

Answer a is correct. Fault tolerance is not an issue in this question so only one incidence of each service is needed to support the users in this network. All of the services can be combined onto one server and still support the number of users in this network.

Question 3

Based on the network configuration shown in Figure 14.4, on which of the currently available servers is it best to load the WINS, DNS, and DHCP services?

○ a. Server1

○ b. Server2

○ c. Server3

○ d. No current server will work

Answer a is correct. By process of elimination Server1 is the best choice to load the services on. Server2 is eliminated because it is an Exchange server and should not have any other services loaded on it. Server3 has a third-party unapproved application. Because the WINS, DNS, and DHCP services currently have no fault tolerance, an unapproved application may cause that server to become unstable, making these services unavailable if it crashes.

Question 4

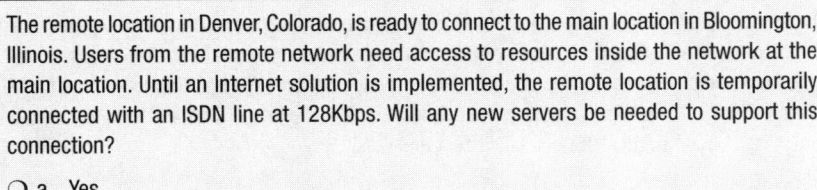

Answer a is correct. A server with the RRAS service loaded is needed to set up remote access from the remote location to the main office. Because the users need access to resources inside the main location, the remote-access service on the RRAS server should be isolated. RRAS should be the only service loaded on the server that accepts remote connections into the network.

Question 5

How many new servers are needed to support the additional service in the preceding question?

- ○ a. One
- ○ b. Two
- ○ c. Three
- ○ d. Four

Answer b is correct. With only one ISDN line, an RRAS server at each end of the connection will centralize and control access to the remote connection. Only one server would have to be at the main location to accept connections. Three and four servers are unnecessary.

Question 6

Two more remote locations are now ready to be added to the network. Now that three remote locations are connected to the main network, company management feels that the use of an ISP would help to more quickly and less expensively connect these and other remote locations to the network. Which services are needed to make the connection to the ISP and main network location secure? [Check all correct answers]

❑ a. WINS

❑ b. DNS

❑ c. DHCP

❑ d. VPN

❑ e. RADIUS

❑ f. RRAS

Answers d, e, and f are correct. RRAS will provide the connection to the main network and RADIUS will provide authentication services. A VPN will provide encryption for the information being passed over the Internet. WINS, DNS, and DHCP are not needed to establish a secure remote connection between the networks.

Question 7

In the following diagram, place on the servers the services that would best provide security and efficiency for the network.

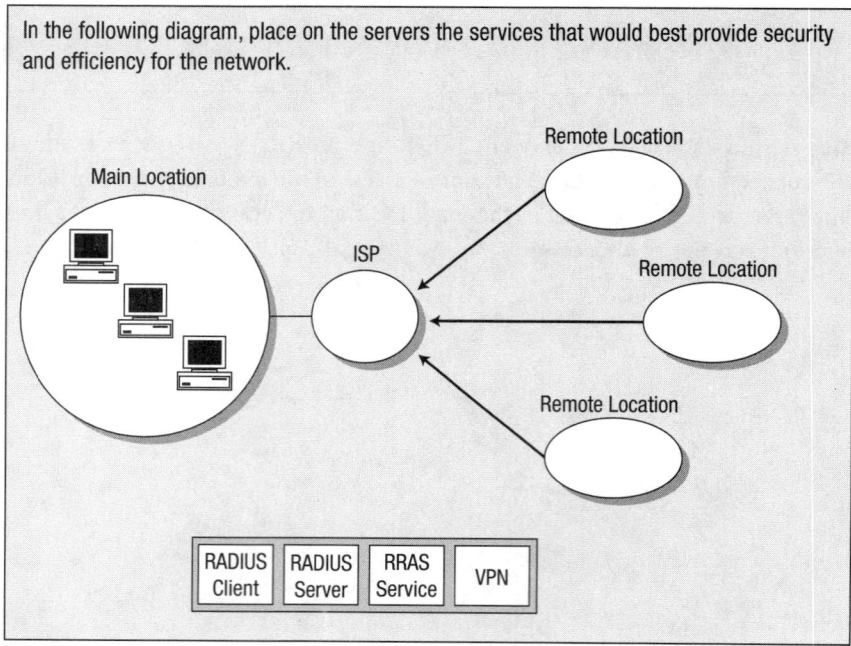

The answer is:

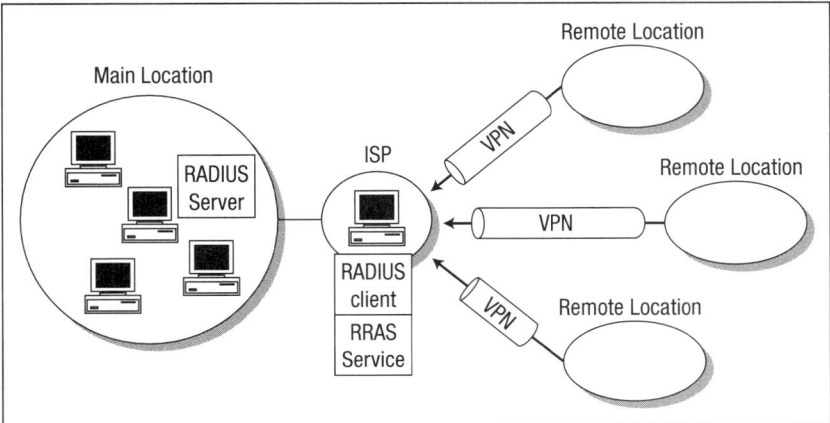

Because the RRAS service is required for the RADIUS client, both services need to be loaded on the same server. These should be located at the ISP. The RRAS service should also be loaded at the remote locations so that the RAS clients can make a centralized connection to the ISP. The RADIUS server needs to be loaded at the main location where the domain controller is located. A VPN needs to be set up between the RAS clients and the RADIUS client.

Question 8

> The company is now ready to add a Web site at its location. What service is needed to keep the Web site separate and secure from the main network?
>
> ○ a. DNS
>
> ○ b. NAT
>
> ○ c. Proxy Server
>
> ○ d. RADIUS

Answer c is correct. The addition of Proxy Server will create a screened subnet to protect the internal network from the incoming Internet requests. Proxy Server can implement reverse proxying to allow incoming requests into the screened subnet. NAT is for smaller networks and does not work with the WINS, DNS, or DHCP services. Because the Web site will be for public use, no authentication service such as RADIUS is needed. DNS is needed to connect to the Web site, but it is not used for the security of a Web site.

Question 9

How many servers will be needed to provide the most security to the main network?

○ a. No additional servers are needed

○ b. One additional server

○ c. Two additional servers

○ d. Three additional servers

Answer d is correct. The most secure solution involves setting up a screened subnet with two proxy servers. The Web server should be placed inside the screened subnet between the two proxy servers. This protects the Web server from most incoming traffic from the Internet. Because the Web server provides Web services, this type of traffic needs to be allowed into the Web server by the proxy server. To protect the internal network, the second proxy server blocks all incoming traffic. Users from inside the main network can update the Web site, because this type of outgoing traffic can be allowed. The following diagram shows the most secure solution for this situation.

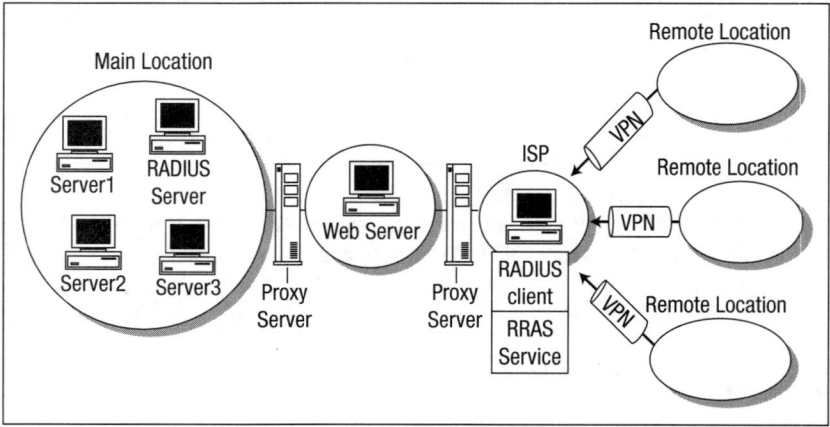

Question 10

The company thinks three servers (as arrived at in the previous question) is too many. Can some or all of the services be combined and still provide a secure solution for the network?

○ a. Yes

○ b. No

Answer b is correct. Each of the three servers is needed for a secure solution. The proxy server cannot protect the Web server if it is located on the server that provides the proxy service. Proxy Server can protect only what is behind it. Also, without the second proxy server, incoming Internet connections will be allowed into the private network, providing an opening into the private main location that jeopardizes the security of the network.

Question 11

The company now wishes to add e-commerce ability to its Web site, so client requests can be processed online. To add these capabilities, an SQL server is added to the network to hold client information. Of the servers currently being used, on which server is it best to load this new service?

○ a. Server1

○ b. Server2

○ c. Server3

○ d. None of the servers listed

Answer d is correct. SQL Server is a resource-intensive application and should not be loaded on any existing servers. All of the existing servers on the network already have services or applications loaded on them. SQL needs to be loaded on a new server.

Need to Know More?

 Smith, David. *Managing Windows 2000 Network Services*. Syngress Media, Rockland, MD, 2000. ISBN 1-928994-06-7. This book focuses on network services, including the implementation and overview of the services.

 www.microsoft.com/windows2000/library/howitworks/cluster/introcluster.asp. *Introducing Windows 2000 Clustering Technologies. Cluster Server Architecture.* Microsoft Corporation, Redmond, WA, 2000. This white paper describes the Clustering Service that is part of Windows Clustering. It serves as an overview of how the service works and provides fault tolerance for services on the network.

 In the Books Online that come with Windows 2000, read the chapters on monitoring and diagnostic tools, networking, and disaster protection. Just click F1 when at the desktop to find Books Online, and then select the "contents" tab.

 Search the TechNet CD (or its online version through **support.Microsoft.com/directory**) and the *Windows 2000 Server Resource Kit* CD using the keywords "Proxy Server", "Windows 2000", "performance", "VPN", "security", and "availability".

Putting It All Together

. . . .

Terms you'll need to understand:

✓ Active Directory

✓ Domain Name Service (DNS)

✓ Windows Internet Naming Service (WINS)

✓ Routing and Remote Access Service (RRAS)

✓ Internet Service Provider (ISP)

✓ Network Address Translation (NAT)

✓ Remote Authentication Dial-In User Service (RADIUS)

✓ Proxy Server

✓ Virtual Private Network (VPN)

Techniques you'll need to master:

✓ Choosing appropriate network services based on a given scenario

✓ Selecting suitable network service options

✓ Improving security in a network design

✓ Improving availability and performance in a network design

✓ Recommending network design changes based on a given scenario

Now that you've learned about the services that are an integral part of a Windows 2000 network, all that remains is putting it all together and designing a network infrastructure. The design process includes evaluating, selecting, placing, and combining services. In the 70-221 exam, case study scenarios provide all of the information you need to make the right design decisions. Each scenario can emphasize different needs for a network that will affect design decisions. For example, if security were a prime concern, this prompts a designer to make different decisions than if performance were the main factor. Searching for and using the right clues in the scenario will lead you to the right design decisions.

 Remember that you are not changing the network based on what you think it needs, but based on what the case study says is important.

Evaluating Existing Network Infrastructure

Network infrastructure design decisions start with an evaluation of the current network infrastructure. Study the current network to see why the infrastructure needs to be upgraded. Will the protocols and current structure need to be changed to support additions to the network? What are the network's limitations that may hinder the upgrade? Also take a look at the applications that are currently in the network. Can these applications stay, or do they need to be expanded throughout the network? If additional locations are being added, will the current main location be able to handle the increased traffic? Even connectivity devices like routers may need to be upgraded to handle the load of more traffic (or of a different type of traffic). Keep in mind which Windows 2000 network services can help to solve some of these problems. Understanding the current state of the network allows a designer to see how changes will affect it and to see what upgrades are needed, but knowing how the company would like to change the network is equally important.

Selecting Appropriate Network Services

Even networks that start in the same configuration can have different issues and goals. To be able to make the correct design decisions, a network designer needs a clear definition of what a company wants. What does the company hope to accomplish with a network infrastructure upgrade? Because some design goals do not work well together, it's important to establish a priority of the company's goals for the network. For instance, security and performance are two goals that work against each other. Because a network designed for security will not have performance as high as one with less security, the company needs to decide which should be more emphasized within the design. A designer needs to establish a balance between performance, connection of remote locations, security, and availability of services. How this balance is found depends on which goals are more important to the company.

Selecting Services

Evaluating the current infrastructure and company goals for the network allows a designer to see problems that need to be addressed. Having done this, the designer can begin to select services that deal with the identified problems and the needed upgrades. Selection of services is only done at this point because evaluation of the current infrastructure and goals of the company provides the designer with a starting point. A designer should try to keep the network design simple by selecting only the services needed on the network. If a service is not specifically needed, it should not be added to the network. Table 15.1 shows network requirements that can be filled with a particular service.

Selecting Appropriate Service Options

Once the services are selected, the next step is to decide which options need to be configured on each service. Options for a service include the different ways that the service can be implemented. The RRAS service can be implemented as a firewall that blocks incoming packets from the Internet or as a RADIUS client that authenticates users onto the network from a remote location. Each setting is a different option that can be set within the RRAS service. Even a DNS server can be set up with different zones and zone types that affect how the service runs. Network services are versatile and have many options that change what they can offer to the network. Selecting the right options puts the services in line with the goals of the company.

Server Placement

The next step is to place the services on servers and in the right location on the network. Too many servers on a network cause a strain on the services and the network as a whole. Careful planning of service placement within the network allows each one to work more effectively. Simply placing more incidences of services on more servers isn't often the best method. When it comes to placing services, a lean design is frequently better. The one exception to this rule is caused

Table 15.1 Network requirements filled by services.	
Network Requirement	Service
All Windows 2000 network	DNS
Mix of Windows operating systems	WINS
Security for remote connections	RRAS
Security for internal Web services	Proxy Server, RRAS
Connecting to external resources	NAT for a small network

by a company's need to emphasize security. Implementing a secure solution—especially for remote or Internet users—will necessitate the placement of servers on the network with just one or a few services loaded on them. RRAS, RADIUS, and Proxy Server are examples of services that may need to be loaded alone or with only supporting services to keep a network secure. Also, the use of an ISP to provide Internet connections may also create a need for more servers, even if they are located at the ISP's location.

The lean approach is best used on services that work internally in a network such as DHCP, DNS, and WINS. Often, one incidence of each of these services is placed per location, even if it is subnetted. A design decision that needs to be made is which subnet to load the service on. Simply put, the service should be loaded on the subnet with the most users. Figure 15.1 shows a network with one physical location that has two subnets. WINS, DNS, and DHCP are all placed on one server on the A subnet, simply because it has more users than subnet B. This method allows for the largest concentration of users to have the shortest distance and time to get to the service.

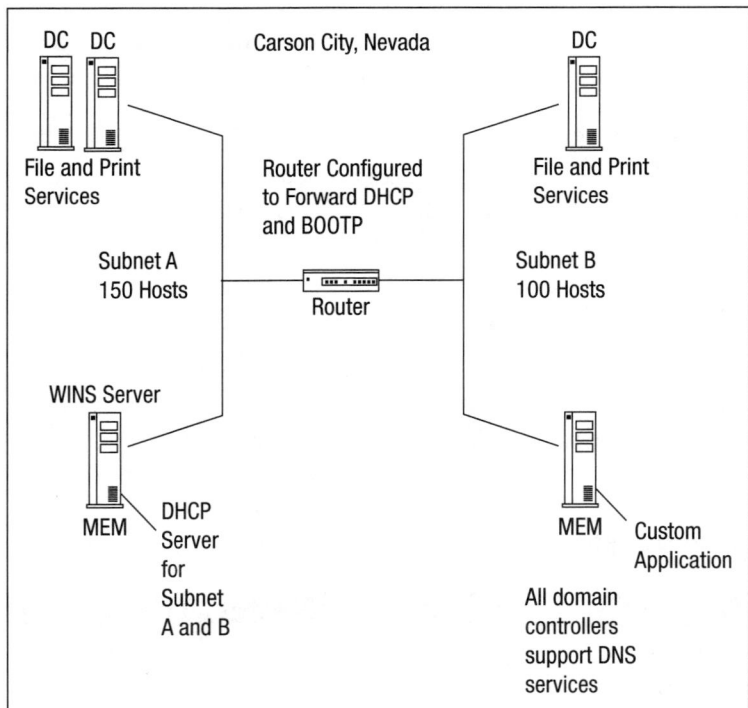

Figure 15.1   Internal network services such as WINS, DNS, and DHCP are best placed with one at each physical location. Within the location, place the services on the subnet with the most users.

Creating a Secure Network Design

Every designer needs to try to identify possible security risks within a network. These risks can vary from unsecured network connections to sensitive data that needs to be protected. Even if security is not considered a primary design objective, the security of the network still needs to be examined. Studying the network design can reveal possible problems. For instance, connections that are open to public networks, such as remote or Internet connections, are not secure. A network can be protected from these connections by separating it from them and adding extra services to ensure that only authorized users are allowed access. Data traveling over a public network is completely exposed unless encryption services such as those used in a VPN are implemented. However, data is not vulnerable only when it is transmitted over a public network. Data of a particularly sensitive nature—such as personal data on employees or customers—may need to be protected even within a private network.

Identifying the possible security risks helps a designer decide what services can help reduce these risks. When choosing services that reduce security risks, a designer needs to balance the benefits of implementing the service with the other goals of the network. Will the security benefit outweigh the decreased performance or other loss?

Enhancing Availability

The availability of a service has to do with how much it is accessible to the user. Services that are deemed to be mission-critical need to be available 24 hours a day, 7 days a week. It is not likely that any service is unimportant, but the designer needs to look into what will happen when a service goes down, even for only a short period. Is the loss of a service a minor inconvenience, or does the business of the company come to a halt? The setup for a mission-critical service is different than the setup for a service that can be unavailable for a short period of time. Microsoft suggests that Cluster Server be used to add fault tolerance to services, so this is a possibility that needs to be understood. Fault tolerance for each service can also be achieved by adding more incidences of a service so that another is available in case one goes down. The use of Cluster Server can reduce the overall number of servers that are needed, and it can also simplify the network design. Microsoft also recommends running multiple instances of services within a cluster.

Enhancing Performance

Designing for performance is different then designing for availability or security. Performance is often not the top priority, because designing for availability and security will usually detract from the network's performance. This does not mean, however, that performance is not a factor when designing a network infrastructure.

Even when security and availability of services is integrated into a design, performance can be improved. The key lies in finding a balance among these goals.

Ensuring that servers have adequate hardware to support the users helps performance. Combining the services so that no hardware resource is overused helps a server better support all of the services that are loaded on it. It may be better to add more or better hardware resources if the number of users or services loaded on it causes any one resource to be overburdened.

Identifying Network Services

To design and implement an effective network infrastructure, you must first identify the correct service for your requirements. Another important point is to make sure that your design has the ability to scale up or down to the changing needs. The layout of the services will be the foundation that allows the network to operate within the design goals. If the services are not planned correctly, not only could the original goals be missed, but the redesign could also prove to be extremely costly, as well as limiting the functionality of the network while the corrections are made.

Windows 2000 services should be included in the design of the physical layout. During the planning, it's important to plan strategic locations for these services to properly serve the clients. A good network schematic outlines and documents the Windows 2000 service and the proposed service to the clients. Table 15.2 lists some of the Windows 2000 services that can be included in your design schematic.

Including Services in Your Design

During your planning stage, your schematic is drawn and the services are placed and outlined. For example, let's say that you have been employed by a company called VirtuCon to design its network infrastructure. VirtuCon is a new startup company, founded in Carson City, Nevada. It currently has a production facility being built in Indianapolis, Indiana, and a distribution center in Louisville, Kentucky. Your assignment is to incorporate the existing infrastructure in Carson City and provide new infrastructure for Indianapolis and Louisville.

Carson City

The Carson City location currently has 250 hosts on two subnets, which are connected by a router. Subnet A has 150 hosts, and subnet B has 100 hosts. The backbone that will connect all of the physical locations will reside on a new subnet that you will implement by adding another router and a T1 connection to the Indianapolis and Louisville sites. Your goal at this location is to use the current

Table 15.2   Windows 2000 services for network design.

Windows 2000 Service	Functionality
TCP/IP	Provides a common transmission protocol suite that will allow seamless Internet connectivity
DHCP	Automatically assigns IP addresses to DHCP or BOOTP clients, as well as other configuration parameters, such as the default gateway, DNS servers search order, and WINS server address
DNS	Provides name resolution of fully qualified domain names to IP addresses
WINS	Provides name resolution of NetBIOS names to IP addresses for clients not running Windows 2000
Microsoft Proxy Server	Provides security by isolating your internal network addresses from the Internet; it requires a single registered IP address to provide connectivity to clients
Routing and Remote Access	Provides connectivity to the different geographical locations of your network and allows you to create Virtual Private Networks by using inexpensive Internet connections

infrastructure, which consists of three domain controllers and two member servers, as illustrated in Figure 15.1. Subnet A contains two domain controllers that provide authentication and file and print services. The member server has DHCP service installed to automatically assign IP addresses to the clients.

Subnet B contains one DC and one member server. The domain controller is used for authentication, file, and print services. The member server has a custom-designed application that tracks daily operations, such as sales, marketing, production, and shipping at all locations.

To minimize network traffic and speed the boot process, you will place one DHCP-enabled server at each physical location. In this case, you will minimize the load on both of the servers on subnet B, while still providing automatic TCP/IP addressing for the hosts on subnet B. To provide this service to the hosts, configure the routers on subnet A and B to forward DHCP requests to the hosts.

Your domain controllers are currently configured to resolve fully qualified domain names for the virtucon.com zone and to automatically update with the DHCP server leases. The hosts at both locations are a mixture of Windows 2000 and Windows 9x clients. To provide NetBIOS name resolution, the member server on subnet A is configured as a WINS server, and all clients on both subnet A and subnet B receive the IP address of the member server from the DHCP server. The DHCP server also specifies the default gateway for the subnets.

You must redesign this existing structure to include connectivity to the backbone for connection to the sites that are currently under construction. Your first order will be to create subnet C. Subnet C will provide a new connection for the WAN link while still allowing subnet A and B to exist in their current states and reduce the interruption of service for its implementation. Subnet C will have three hosts that consist of routers to connect subnet A to subnet C and subnet B to subnet C. By using this model, the change can be made with little interruption of service to the current infrastructure. To accomplish this, two additional routers will be used, as shown in Figure 15.2. The static routing tables will also need to be configured. Router C, which connects the backbone, will not forward DHCP requests, thus preventing clients at the other physical locations from receiving an IP address outside their current scope.

Indianapolis

The Indianapolis, Indiana location production facility will require connection to the backbone and support for 150 hosts. You expect a dramatic increase in the amount of hosts and calculate that with the available resources, an additional subnet will be needed in the next year to provide the required performance. To handle the requirements for the site, your current plan is to implement two subnets. One subnet will connect all of the hosts to the second subnet, while the other subnet will connect to a WAN link. This design will mirror Carson City when the expected growth requires an additional subnet. Your design goal is to incorporate these considerations. As with Carson City, to speed the boot process and

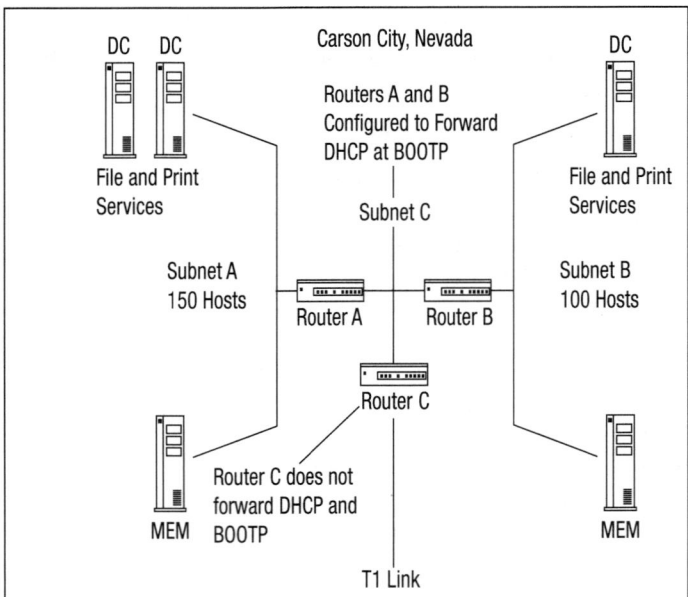

Figure 15.2 The current infrastructure of the Carson City location.

maximize the available bandwidth for intersite communications and the custom application, you will need to provide automatic IP addressing to the initial hosts, as well as plan for the expansion of the additional subnet.

All of the hosts at this location will be Windows 2000 based. This means that NetBIOS name resolution will not be an issue; however, the domain controllers must automatically update the DNS entries and use DHCP to specify the DNS server addresses for the child domain production.virtucon.com. VirtuCon currently has placed orders for two servers, and you will implement these servers to provide the best performance possible. You can configure one server as a domain controller to provide local authentication. This server will also provide DNS services for the production subnet virtucon.com zone. The member server will act as the DHCP servers.

Routing tables will need to be configured on both routers C and D. The routers will not pass DHCP/BOOTP requests, thus preventing clients from receiving IP addresses that are outside of their subnet. Figure 15.3 shows the proposed infrastructure for Indianapolis.

Louisville

The distribution center in Louisville, Kentucky, will support 50 hosts and require connection to Indianapolis and Carson City. Because you do not expect a

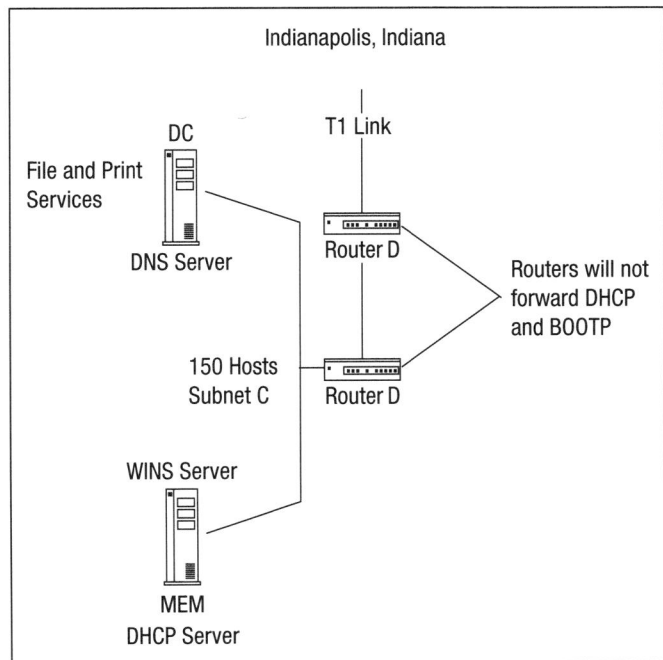

Figure 15.3 The proposed infrastructure for the Indianapolis location

dramatic increase in the amount of hosts, you calculate that, with the available resources, a single subnet will be needed to connect the hosts to the WAN link. Your design goal is to incorporate these considerations. As with Carson City, to speed the boot process and maximize the available bandwidth to intersite communications and the custom application, you will need to provide automatic IP addressing to the hosts.

All of the hosts at this location will be Windows 2000 based. Again, this means that NetBIOS name resolution will not be an issue, but the domain controllers must automatically update the DNS entries and use DHCP to specify the DNS server addresses for the child domain production.virtucon.com. VirtuCon currently has placed orders for one server, which you will implement to provide the best performance possible. You can configure the server as a domain controller to provide local authentication. This server will also provide DNS services for the distribution, virtucon.com zone, and act as the DHCP server.

Routing tables will need to be configured on router E. This router will not pass DHCP/BOOTP requests, and this prevents clients from receiving IP addresses that are outside of their subnet. Figure 15.4 shows the proposed infrastructure for the Louisville location.

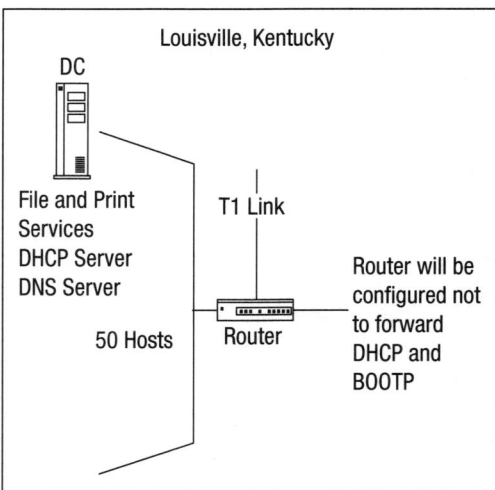

Figure 15.4 The proposed infrastructure for the Louisville location.

Practice Questions

Case Study

VirtuCon, a manufacturer based in Carson City, Nevada, has had significant growth over the past years. The owners have recently acquired an engineering firm in Evansville, Indiana, to reduce the amount of outsourced engineering costs. The engineering firm currently has an outdated network that will need to be incorporated into the VirtuCon infrastructure.

Due to greater competition in the Evansville area, the cost of high-speed Internet connections is significantly less than it is in the other cities, and management would like to provide Internet access to designated users at all locations. The engineers at the Evansville location would like to access the Internet by connecting to a modem pool at the Evansville office. See Figure 15.5.

Current WAN Connectivity

Currently, leased T1 lines connect Carson City, Indianapolis, and Louisville.

Proposed WAN Connectivity

Incorporate Evansville into the VirtuCon infrastructure, using a high speed T1 connection. Incorporate Internet connectivity into the VirtuCon network and provide dial-up connections for the engineers.

Current Internet Connectivity

This network currently has no Internet connection.

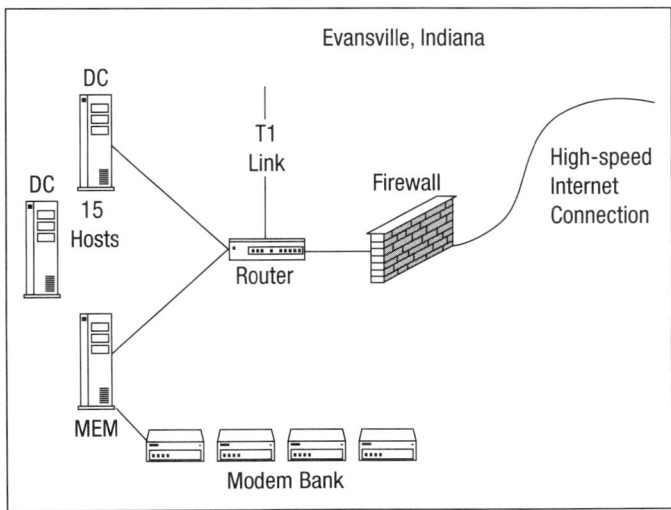

Figure 15.5 Proposed changes to the Evansville site.

Proposed Internet Connectivity

The Evansville location will use a connection to the Internet to provide access to designated users at all locations through the T1 connections.

Company Goal with Windows 2000

The company would like to incorporate the Evansville location into the existing Windows 2000 company network. The Evansville location is currently upgrading from Microsoft Windows NT 3.51.

Question 1

Refer to Figure 15.5 showing the network at the Evansville location and the proposed servers. Which of the following services could be used to automatically configure the clients to resolve fully qualified domain names at the Evansville location?

○ a. WINS

○ b. DNS

○ c. DHCP

○ d. NAT

Answer c is correct. DHCP scope or global options allow administrators to automatically configure BOOTP or DHCP clients to resolve fully qualified domain names to DNS servers.

Question 2

Considering the proposed Internet connectivity, which service could be utilized to control access to the Internet?

○ a. DNS

○ b. DHCP

○ c. WINS

○ d. Proxy Server

Answer d is correct. Proxy Server allows control over Internet connections. DHCP provides IP addressing to clients; DNS and WINS provide name resolution services for clients.

Question 3

> Considering the answer to Question 2, how many registered IP addresses will be required for VirtuCon?
>
> ○ a. 1
>
> ○ b. 2
>
> ○ c. 3
>
> ○ d. 0

Answer a is correct. Microsoft Proxy Server requires one registered IP address for the connection to the Internet. For connections to the internal network, private ranges of IP addresses should be used.

Question 4

> Considering the client type at the Evansville location, what service will be needed for NetBIOS name resolution?
>
> ○ a. WINS
>
> ○ b. DHCP
>
> ○ c. DNS
>
> ○ d. None of the above

Answer d is correct. Because all of the hosts in the Evansville location are Windows 2000 based, NetBIOS name resolution will not be needed.

Question 5

> Considering that the clients will have their IP addresses configured automatically using DHCP, how will you configure DHCP to prevent address resolution problems?
>
> ○ a. Allow dynamic updates
>
> ○ b. Allow secured updates only
>
> ○ c. Automatically update DHCP client information in DNS
>
> ○ d. None of the above

Answer c is correct. DHCP can be configured to automatically update DHCP client information in DNS. Configuring dynamic and secure updates is done in DNS rather that DHCP.

Question 6

> Which options should be set within the Evansville DHCP server to ensure connectivity when the existing infrastructure is achieved? [Check all correct answers]
>
> ❑ a. WINS server address
>
> ❑ b. DNS server address
>
> ❑ c. DHCP servers
>
> ❑ d. Default gateway

Answers b and d are correct. The default gateway allows users to access resources not in the Evansville location. The DNS server resolves the IP address to fully qualified domain names for name resolution. WINS is not needed at the Evansville location, because all the clients are Windows 2000 and a DHCP server option does not exist.

Question 7

> What service should be used to provide the dial-up connections for the engineers at the Evansville location?
>
> ○ a. RADIUS client
>
> ○ b. RADIUS server
>
> ○ c. RRAS service
>
> ○ d. VPN

Answer c is correct. RRAS should be used to provide dial-up connectivity for the Evansville engineering staff. The RADIUS service and VPNs provide security for existing RAS connections.

Need to Know More?

 Smith, David. *Managing Windows 2000 Network Services*. Syngress Media, Rockland, MD, 2000. ISBN 1-928994-06-7. This book focuses on network services, including the implementation and overview of the services.

 **www.microsoft.com/windows2000/library/howitworks/cluster/ introcluster.asp**. *Introducing Windows 2000 Clustering Technologies*. Microsoft Corporation, Redmond, WA, 2000. This white paper describes Cluster Service, which is part of Windows Clustering. It is an overview of how the service works and provides fault tolerance for services on the network.

 In the Online Books that come with Windows 2000, read the chapters "Monitoring And Diagnostic Tools" and "Networking And Disaster Protection".

 Search the TechNet CD (or its online version through **support. Microsoft.com/directory**) and the *Windows 2000 Server Resource Kit* CD using the keywords "Proxy Server", "Windows 2000", "performance", "VPN", "security", and "availability".

Sample Test

Case Study 1

The headquarters of Quick Ride Bus Depot—a small bus company with three bus depots—is located in Los Angeles, California. The company transports passengers between these three sites and also leases a bus and driver for group trips.

Current LAN/Network Structure

Quick Ride Bus Depot currently runs an IBM mainframe with every site running dumb terminals. The other sites are located in:

Las Vegas, Nevada

Redmond, Washington

All of the sites are currently connected using Frame Relay.

Proposed LAN/Network Structure

All current dumb terminals will be replaced with Windows 2000 workstations. The mainframe will be replaced with a Windows 2000 server running SQL.

Current business has improved greatly, and the owner wants to implement a new network with Internet connectivity for a Web site that customers can visit to reserve bus tickets, check on time schedules, and even reserve hotel rooms.

All sites will be connected through the Internet, and the Frame Relay will be removed.

All buildings are to be remodeled and each will include 20 network connections in the lobby of the bus station. Passengers will use these terminals to access the

Internet, so they can check on current time schedules, reserve bus tickets, and reserve hotel rooms at their final destination.

Los Angeles will host the SQL database for all of the information for each depot. No data should be stored locally at any site except Los Angeles.

The network on which the employees connect should be separate from the network that the passengers can use from the lobby of the bus depots.

Current WAN Connectivity

Frame Relay connectivity between Las Vegas, Redmond, and Los Angeles.

Proposed WAN Connectivity

Frame Relay will be removed and replaced with Internet connections. Future plans include the purchase of three new bus depots in the following cities:

Houston, Texas

Phoenix, Arizona

Boise, Idaho

All routers will be BOOTP enabled throughout the entire WAN. (Although the router types have not been determined, they will support BOOTP.)

Current Internet Positioning

Quick Ride Bus Depot is registered as QRBD.COM., with the Web server hosted at headquarters.

Future Internet Plans

No changes in the current structure are proposed at this time.

Future Miscellaneous Plans

Each bus will feature a low-powered device that emits a unique frequency, so that when a bus enters a bus depot it will be registered as arriving and all time schedules will be changed accordingly.

Question 1.1

For redundancy and performance, what should be done with the SQL server in Los Angeles on the proposed network?

- O a. One SQL server
- O b. Two SQL servers with no replication
- O c. Two SQL servers with replication
- O d. Clustered SQL servers

Question 1.2

If Internet private addresses were used on the private network for the employees network (Class A) and a different one for the passengers network (Class B), what scopes would be used for the Los Angeles depot? [Check all correct answers]

- ❏ a. 10.0.1.0/16
- ❏ b. 10.1.0.0/16
- ❏ c. 10.2.0.0/16
- ❏ d. 10.3.0.0/16
- ❏ e. 192.168.1.0/24
- ❏ f. 192.168.2.0/24
- ❏ g. 192.168.3.0/24

Question 1.3

What is required to set up the passenger connections to the Los Angeles depot from the Las Vegas depot? [Check all correct answers]

- ❏ a. Router
- ❏ b. Hub
- ❏ c. WINS
- ❏ d. DNS
- ❏ e. DHCP
- ❏ f. Proxy Server

Question 1.4

Which protocol will be used by the devices that detect the transmissions of the low-powered devices installed on each bus?

- ○ a. BAP
- ○ b. EAP
- ○ c. IPX/SPX
- ○ d. TCP/IP

Question 1.5

How should DHCP servers be implemented for the proposed network?

- ○ a. One DHCP server at Los Angeles with six scopes.
- ○ b. One DHCP server at every depot with two scopes enabled on each.
- ○ c. Two DHCP servers at every site with one scope enabled on each.
- ○ d. One DHCP server at Los Angeles with 20 percent of the scope for all depots and 70 percent of its own scope. One DHCP server at the other depots with 80 percent of its scope and 10 percent of the Los Angeles scope.

Question 1.6

The company buys an existing bus depot in Houston, Texas, that has an existing connection to the Internet that uses an older router that isn't BOOTP compatible. What services would be required in the Houston depot if it were set up like all other sites? [Check all correct answers]

- ❑ a. Router
- ❑ b. Hub
- ❑ c. WINS
- ❑ d. DNS
- ❑ e. DHCP
- ❑ f. Proxy Server
- ❑ g. DHCP Relay Agent

Question 1.7

Considering the scenario in Question 1.6 and the following depots:

Los Angeles

Houston

Redmond

Which of the following should be used in each location? [Some items will be used more than once, and not all items will be used]

DHCP server

NAT server

RRAS server

SQL server

DHCP Relay Agent

Proxy Server

Hub

WINS server

DNS server

Dfs root directory

Question 1.8

If the implementation of the proposed network took months to finish, with the data conversion from the mainframe to the SQL server also taking several weeks, how would the dumb terminals still contact the mainframe if needed?

○ a. Keep the Frame Relay connections as long as needed.

○ b. Install a Windows terminal server at each site.

○ c. Let SNA be encapsulated and sent over the VPN.

○ d. Install a mainframe at each site with data replication.

Question 1.9

If Quick Ride Bus Depot acquired a large number of bus depots and had approximately 5,000 employees and bus drivers, and this growth caused unforeseen network traffic involved in accessing the Internet, what steps could be taken to improve performance? [Check all correct answers]

❑ a. Add a proxy server array at each site with the unacceptable performance.

❑ b. Change the network to Token Ring.

❑ c. Upgrade the Internet browser to a newer version.

❑ d. Upgrade the Internet connections at all sites that have unacceptable performance.

Question 1.10

If the performance has declined for access to the Web server from the Internet, but internal access is still more than acceptable, what could improve the performance?

○ a. Add a proxy server array at Los Angeles.

○ b. Upgrade the Internet connections at all depots.

○ c. Upgrade the Internet browser to a newer version at the Los Angeles depot.

○ d. Upgrade the Internet connection at the Los Angeles depot.

Case Study 2

Fudd Fire Extinguisher Company has three buildings, all located in a three-block area. The company manufactures, repairs, and refurbishes fire extinguishers. The following diagram shows the company's building layout.

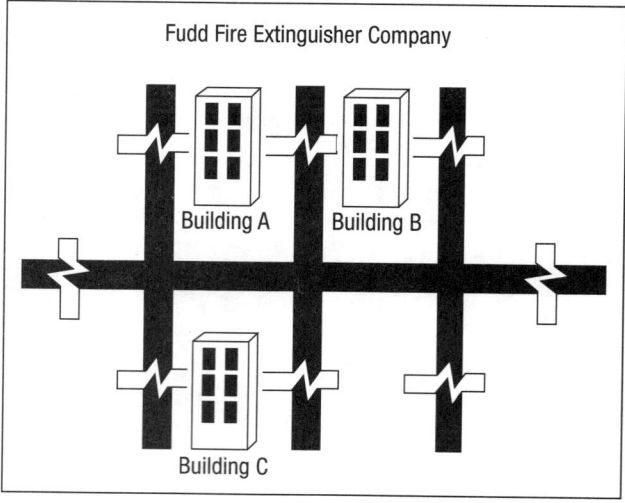

Current LAN/Network Structure

Building A has the administrative, human resource, sales, and accounting departments.

Building B has the marketing, research and development, and IT departments.

Buildings C has the repair and refurbishment department, as well as the storage room for stock.

Buildings A and B have 200 employees, and Building C has 75 employees.

All buildings are connected with bridges: an NT 4 PDC in Building B, and an NT 4 BDC in Building A and C. The PDC runs the Exchange services for the whole company. Building A has SQL running on its BDC to host the customer and sales databases.

All workstations are running Windows 95 or Windows for Workgroups using NetBEUI.

Proposed LAN/Network Structure

All systems will be upgraded to Windows 2000, and 25 dial-up connections will be added for traveling sales people.

Current WAN Connectivity

Each building is connected with fiber-optic cables. Building A is connected to Building B, and Building B is connected to Building C.

Proposed WAN Connectivity

All links will remain, but the bridges will be replaced with routers.

Current Internet Positioning

None at the current time.

Future Internet Plans

An Internet connection will be implemented for remote connectivity for employees to check their mail from home. This implementation will not happen for three to five years. The design must take into account future plans proposed for the WAN.

Question 2.1

How many WINS servers should be implemented at the current time?

○ a. 0

○ b. 1

○ c. 2

○ d. 3

Question 2.2

How many WINS servers should be implemented when the proposed network is completed?

○ a. 0

○ b. 1

○ c. 2

○ d. 3

Question 2.3

Once the proposed network is in place, how should the routers be set up?

○ a. Using RIP version 1

○ b. Using RIP version 2

○ c. Using OSPF

○ d. Using static routes

○ e. Using IGMP

○ f. Using VPNs

○ g. Using IGRP

Question 2.4

Services are needed to be redundant in the proposed network. What option should be implemented for DHCP?

○ a. A DHCP server in Building B

○ b. Three DHCP servers in Building B

○ c. A DHCP server in each building with one scope

○ d. A DHCP server in each building with two scopes

○ e. A DHCP server in each building with three scopes

Question 2.5

For the three buildings:

Building A

Building B

Building C

Match the following services that would be needed at each building in the proposed network. [Some items may be used more than once, and some items may not be used]

DHCP service

WINS service

DNS service

Dial-up service

Proxy service

Dfs service

NAT service

DHCP Relay Agent service

Question 2.6

For complete fault tolerance of the network topology, what should be implemented? (The implementation should also consider cost.)

○ a. Connect Building A and C with a fiber connection

○ b. Extra routers

○ c. VPNs

○ d. Microwave antennae on each building for a backup

Question 2.7

How can a dial-up service in Building A be made secure? Use the following diagram to place objects where they should go. [Options may be used more than once]

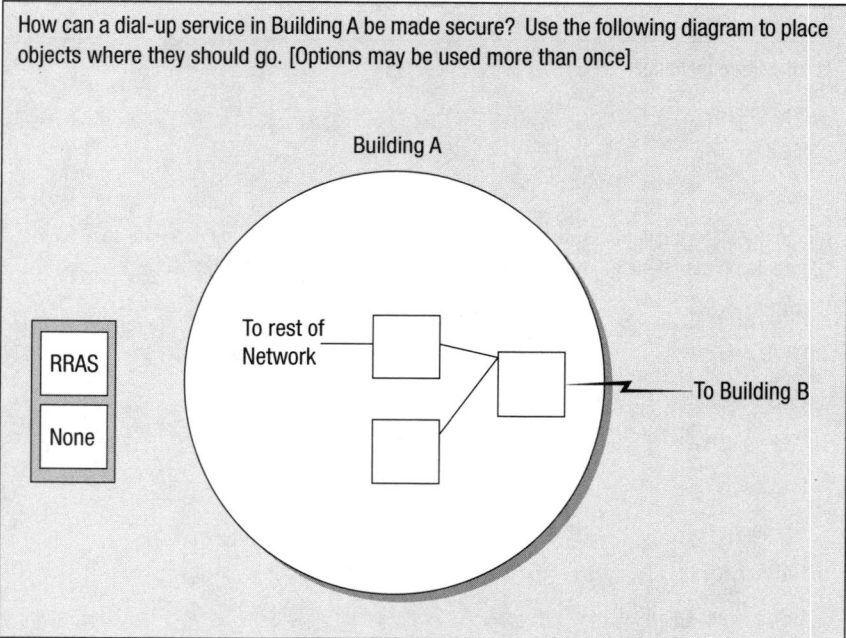

Question 2.8

How could the SQL server and Exchange server be made redundant?

- ○ a. Have each server replicate its services and databases to the other server for the other server to act as a backup if one server should fail.

- ○ b. Have each server replicate its services and databases to the server in Building C for that server to act as a failover if one of the other two servers should fail.

- ○ c. Add a second server to Building A and B, and implement a cluster in each building.

- ○ d. Add a second server to Building A and B, and implement a cluster in each building and have all services and data replicated to the other cluster.

Question 2.9

Arrange the following steps in the recommended order to implement the proposed network:

Upgrade workstations

Upgrade bridges with routers

Add dial-up server in Building A

Change network to TCP/IP

Upgrade servers

Question 2.10

In the next few years, when Internet access is added and a Web site is being hosted onsite, which building should have the Web server and Internet connectivity directly connected?

- ○ a. Building A
- ○ b. Building B
- ○ c. Building C
- ○ d. Buildings A and B

Case Study 3

Mercury Bike Company is a custom bicycle manufacturer located in Nashville, Tennessee. Mercury's management staff has asked you to change the current structure of the network to increase file access and provide load balancing. Your solution should also simplify the logon scripts and reduce the drive mappings needed at the fabrication facility in Nashville and the retail stores in Chattanooga, Tennessee; Denver, Colorado; Bonham, Georgia; and Grand Ledge, Michigan.

Current LAN/Network Structure

The manufacturing and assembly facility in Nashville has recently upgraded to Windows 2000. This location has two DCs, one member server, and 75 client workstations. All of the retail sites currently use Windows NT 4 servers and workstations and access a point-of-sale program from the member server at the fabrication and assembly facility. Each site has a single server and five workstations.

All of the sites share information and have drive mappings for the shared folders at each location. The shared folders contain an employee schedule and a time-clock application that allows the payroll staff at the Nashville location to extract the employee's hours for weekly payroll.

Proposed LAN/Network Structure

The LAN structure will not be modified.

Current WAN Connectivity

Each location is connected with dual-channel ISDN connections.

Proposed WAN Connectivity

No changes will be made at this time.

Current Internet Positioning

All locations have access to the Internet by using a net appliance located in Nashville.

Future Internet Plans

No changes are planned at this time.

Question 3.1

Which location would provide the best placement for the Dfs root?

○ a. Nashville

○ b. Chattanooga

○ c. Grand Ledge

○ d. Bonham

Question 3.2

You would like the Dfs root to be protected in case of failure of the main-office server on which it resides. Where would you place the Dfs root replica to protect file access in the event of a server failure?

○ a. Nashville

○ b. At one of the retail outlets

○ c. At each retail outlets

○ d. None of the above

Question 3.3

Which type of Dfs root will be required at the Nashville location to allow a Dfs root replica to be created?

○ a. Standalone

○ b. Domain-based

○ c. Active Directory

○ d. None of the above

Question 3.4

After the root has been created, what is added to create the Dfs tree?

○ a. Replicas

○ b. Leaf object

○ c. Dfs link

○ d. A binary large object

Question 3.5

You would like to create a redundant copy of the shared directory at each location. How would you accomplish this and not affect the utilization of the WAN links?

○ a. This cannot be done.

○ b. Create replicas on the servers at each location.

○ c. Create replicas at the Nashville site.

○ d. Create a link replica and place it on one of the workstations at each retail site.

Question 3.6

Considering that Service Pack 6a has been installed on all of the Windows NT 4 machines, what additional client software will be needed to browse the Dfs tree?

○ a. Dfs client 4/5

○ b. Third-party software

○ c. No additional software is needed

○ d. Windows NT 4 is not compatible with Windows 2000 Dfs

Question 3.7

What services can the replicas at the retail locations provide? [Check all correct answers]

❏ a. Fault tolerance

❏ b. Load balancing

❏ c. Redundant login

❏ d. Centralized backup point

Question 3.8

What additional security will Dfs provide for the files in the Dfs tree?

○ a. Dfs will require authentication by the Dfs root server.

○ b. You can specify additional file level control.

○ c. To browse the tree, you must have the browse right to the Dfs root.

○ d. None.

Question 3.9

Considering your previous responses, use the provided Dfs services to configure the Mercury Dfs implementation.

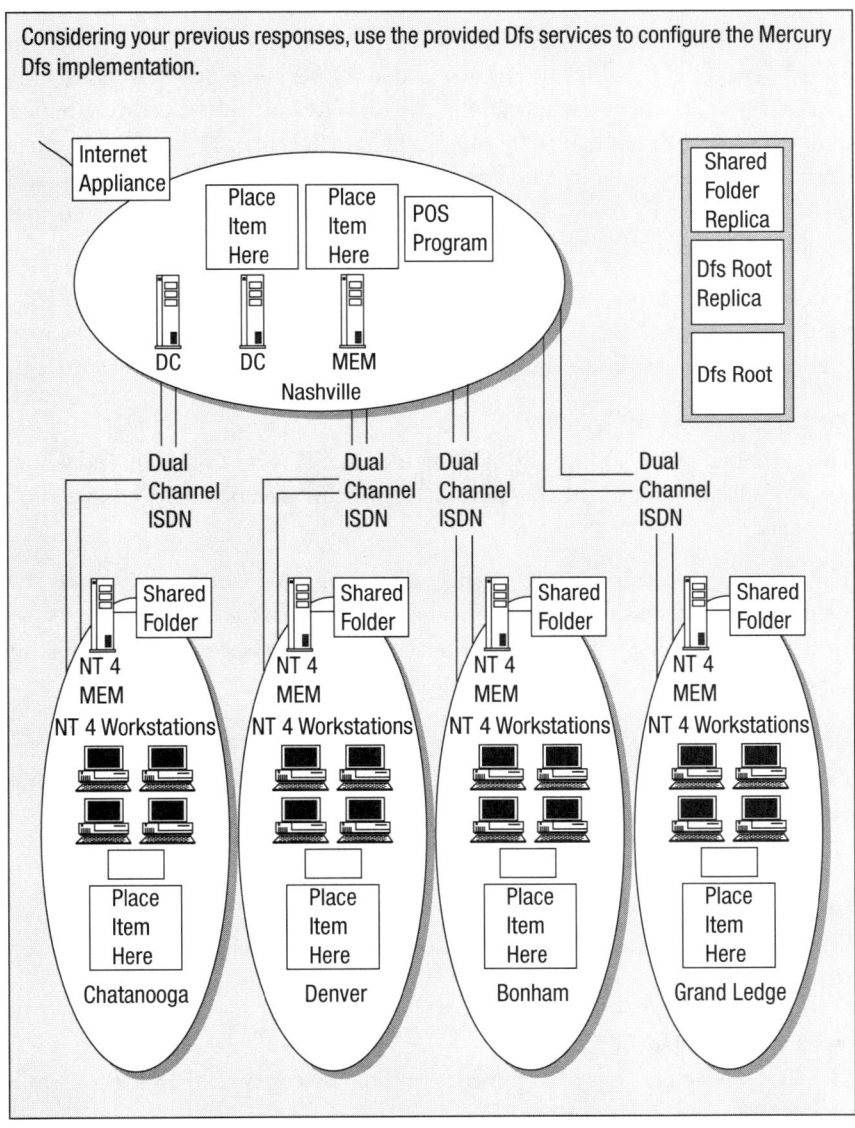

Case Study 4

Fuzzy Fruit is a produce grower in Atlanta, Georgia. Its corporate office is in downtown Atlanta, and the distribution center is on Peachtree Drive just north of the city limits. Fuzzy Fruit recently added 30 new employees to its existing staff of 195 at the downtown location. The corporate office and the distribution center are currently connected by a dedicated 56Kbps line. The corporate office has also purchased an application to track shipments for billing customers, and this application will be located at the corporate office and will be accessed by the employees at the distribution center to enter shipment information.

You are a contract engineer for a local Microsoft solutions provider and have been contracted by Fuzzy Fruit to upgrade its network to accommodate the new employees and to optimize the performance of the shipment-tracking software.

Current LAN/Network Structure

The corporate office is currently using Windows NT 4 on its servers and workstations. The corporate office has purchased two new servers with Windows 2000 preloaded.

The distribution center has 15 client workstations and one server. When the application was tested, the software vendor reported that the application's performance was poor. The cost of a higher-speed connection is significant because of the distribution center's remote location.

Proposed LAN/Network Structure

The IT personnel would like to improve performance of the network by dividing the physical network into two logical networks to improve the performance of the application.

Current WAN Connectivity

The corporate office and the distribution center are connected by a dedicated 56Kbps connection.

Proposed WAN Connectivity

Make any needed changes and provide additional security on the network while maximizing the shipping application.

Current Internet Positioning

Fuzzy Fruit has an Internet connection that is used only by employees to access the Internet (very seldom). The Internet connection is ISDN BRI.

Future Internet Plans

No changes are planned at this time.

Question 4.1

Considering that the current network IP address is 190.65.12.0, what subnet mask could be used to logically separate the network at the corporate office into two subnets and provide the most host IP addresses?

○ a. 255.255.192.0

○ b. 255.255.253.0

○ c. 255.255.248.0

○ d. 255.255.255.248

Question 4.2

What could be implemented to provide security between network hosts?

○ a. QoS

○ b. Packet filtering

○ c. MS CHAP challenge response authentication

○ d. IPSec

Question 4.3

What Windows 2000 TCP/IP enhancement could help prevent the unnecessary retransmission of data over the slow WAN link?

○ a. QoS

○ b. IPSec

○ c. DHCP

○ d. SACK

Question 4.4

Which IPSec predefined policy would prevent nonsecured communications between the network hosts?

○ a. Client

○ b. Server

○ c. Secured Server

○ d. ISAKMP/Oakley

Question 4.5

What configuration would need to be made to the routers to allow seamless routing of IPSec? [Check all correct answers]

❑ a. Header Traffic Protocol ID 51 (0x33)

❑ b. IMAP4 protocol on port 110

❑ c. ESP Protocol ID 50 (0x32)

❑ d. SNMP protocol on port 25

Question 4.6

What could be used to guarantee bandwidth for the shipping application?

○ a. IPSec

○ b. WINS

○ c. DNS

○ d. QoS

Question 4.7

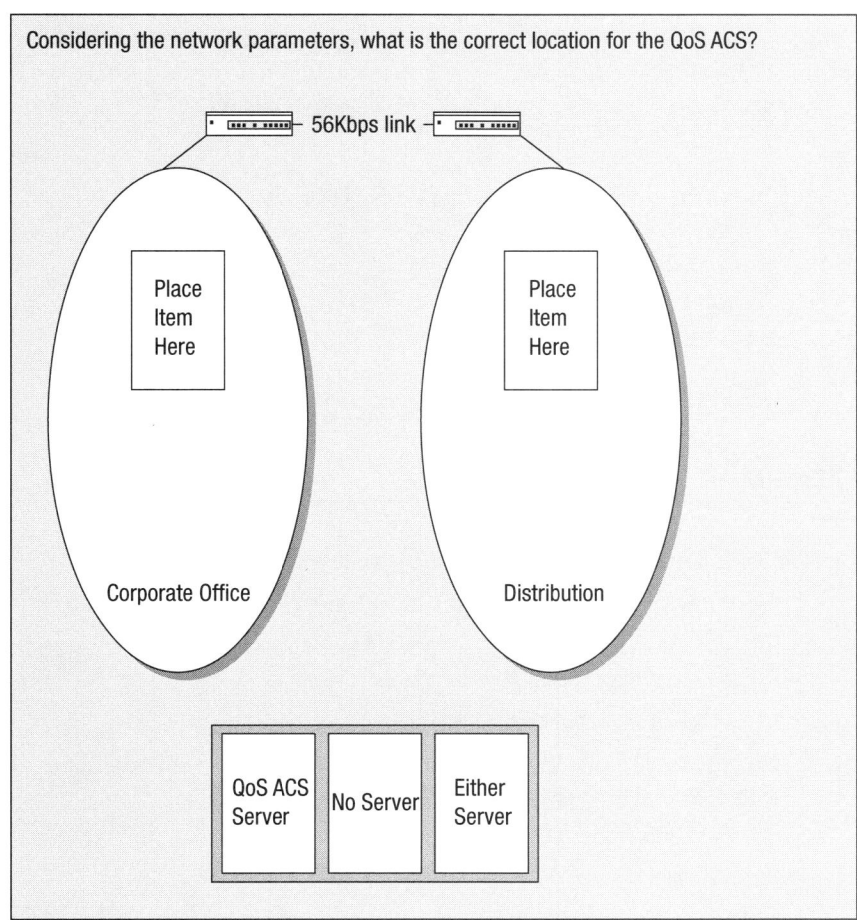

Considering the network parameters, what is the correct location for the QoS ACS?

56Kbps link

Place Item Here

Place Item Here

Corporate Office

Distribution

QoS ACS Server   No Server   Either Server

Question 4.8

The proxy server at the corporate office has an external address of 38.10.74.150 and 190.65.12.5 for its internal address. If an employee at the distribution center were accessing an Internet site, what IP address would the Internet site register the person as having, if the client PC had an address of 190.65.12.250?

○ a. 190.65.12.5

○ b. 38.10.74.150

○ c. 190.65.12.250

○ d. 38.10.74.250

○ e. 192.65.12.150

○ f. 38.10.74.5

Question 4.9

With little network bandwidth, how should DNS be implemented?

○ a. DNS server at corporate integrated with Active Directory.

○ b. DNS server at each site. The DNS server at the corporate office is the primary, while the DNS server at the distribution center is secondary.

○ c. DNS server at both sites integrated into Active Directory.

○ d. Primary DNS server at each site with the distribution center DNS server forwarding to DNS server at the corporate office.

Question 4.10

If all systems except the NT 4 servers were to be upgraded to Windows 2000, what services are required at each location?

Locations

   Corporate office

   Distribution center

Services

   RRAS

   WINS

   DNS

   Dfs

   DHCP

Answer Key

For asterisked items, please see the textual representation of the answer on the appropriate page of this chapter.

1.1	d	2.4	e	3.7	a, b
1.2	b, e	2.5	*	3.8	d
1.3	a, b, d, e, and f	2.6	a	3.9	*
1.4	b	2.7	*	4.1	a
1.5	d	2.8	c	4.2	d
1.6	a, b, d, e, and f	2.9	*	4.3	d
1.7	*	2.10	b	4.4	c
1.8	c	3.1	a	4.5	a, c
1.9	a, d	3.2	a	4.6	d
1.10	d	3.3	b	4.7	*
2.1	b	3.4	c	4.8	b
2.2	a	3.5	d	4.9	c
2.3	d	3.6	c	4.10	*

Question 1.1

The correct answer is d. To cluster the SQL servers would allow both servers to send and receive information at one time and to have the other server available if one server should fail.

One SQL server by itself would provide no performance increase or fault tolerance in case of failure. Having two SQL servers with no replication would provide some performance increase if the database were split into two separate databases, but there would be no redundancy. Two SQL servers with replication would provide a performance increase, because either server could handle information requests from a client, but still no fault tolerance is implemented.

Question 1.2

The correct answers are b and e. Because Los Angeles will be the central connection point for all sites, it should be the first range of addresses (for best practice). So the employees would use the 10.1.0.0/16 subnet, while the passengers would use the 192.168.1.0/24 subnet.

Choice a is incorrect because it is an invalid subnet. Choices c, d, f, and g are not the first subnets. These subnets would make the network functional, but the best practice is to use lower-numbered subnets for the main subnets.

Question 1.3

The correct answers are a, b, d, e, and f. All choices can be implemented for functionality (except WINS). For multiple connections in the lobby for passenger use, a hub is needed to bring all connections together to one point. A proxy server can be implemented to help performance by caching Web pages. The router would be implemented to connect Las Vegas to Los Angeles through a Virtual Private Network (VPN). DNS would be required on the network for Internet name resolution. (For redundancy, a DNS server should be at Las Vegas in case the Internet connection failed between Las Vegas and Los Angeles. This would allow the passengers at Las Vegas to still have name-resolution capabilities.) DHCP would be required for the passengers to receive an IP address for use on the private network (clients must be configured as DHCP clients).

WINS is not required because no NetBIOS name resolution will be required, but WINS will not hinder performance.

Question 1.4

The correct answer is b. EAP is an authentication protocol that is used with hardware devices such as retina scanners and other such devices. The frequency-emitting device could be used as an authentication device to authenticate which bus is arriving at a depot.

BAP is the bandwidth allocation protocol that is used to specify the amount of bandwidth required by an application over dial-up links.

Using the Internet as a backbone, TCP/IP will be used—but only to encapsulate the EAP packets for transmission to Los Angeles from Las Vegas. IPX/SPX is not an option because it does not need to be implemented at all in the scenario.

Question 1.5

The correct answer is d. All options would be functional for the scenario. With each site having two subnets—one for the employees and one for the passengers—each site requires two scopes.

Choice a would have no redundancy, and performance would be based on the bandwidth between a depot and the Los Angeles depot and would have no redundancy if the DHCP server or a connection should fail between a depot and Los Angeles.

Choice b would have excellent performance, but no redundancy if a DHCP server would fail.

Choice c would have excellent performance because it also wouldn't need to send traffic out of the site for DHCP requests. Again, no redundancy is provided if a server failed. This choice also has the cost factor of buying two servers for each depot just to manage DHCP.

Choice d gives excellent performance and is also redundant if a server should fail. If a connection should fail between depots, DHCP requests can still be acknowledged. If a server fails at any depot, another server will be able to answer requests for DHCP (because there are two DHCP servers with a portion of any given scope).

Question 1.6

The correct answers are a, b, d, e, and f. All choices can be implemented for functionality (except WINS). For multiple connections in the lobby for passenger use, a hub is needed to bring all connections together to one point. A proxy server can be implemented to help performance by caching Web pages. The router would be implemented to connect Houston to Los Angeles through a Virtual Private Network (VPN). DNS would be required on the network for Internet name resolution. (For redundancy, a DNS server should be at Houston in case the Internet connection failed between Houston and Los Angeles. This would allow the passengers at Houston to still have name-resolution capabilities.) DHCP would be required for the passengers to receive an IP address for use on the private network (clients must be configured as DHCP clients).

WINS is not required because no NetBIOS name resolution will be required, but WINS will not hinder performance.

DHCP Relay Agent should not be used, because it provides no redundancy. If the network link between Houston and Los Angeles fails, no IP addresses will be assigned to computers. In this scenario, two DHCP servers should be implemented and share a scope, with 50 percent of the scope on each computer. If both DHCP servers should fail, then no addresses would be assigned. These DHCP servers would not be able to provide redundancy for the Los Angeles subnet like the other sites as stated in the answer for Question 1.3. Redundancy could be achieved by having two DHCP relay agents, but, if the link between Houston and Los Angeles were to fail, the DHCP relay agents would be useless.

Question 1.7

The correct answer is:

Los Angeles

> Hub
>
> RRAS
>
> DHCP server
>
> SQL server
>
> DNS server
>
> Proxy server

Houston

> Hub
>
> DHCP server
>
> DNS server
>
> Proxy server

Redmond

 Hub

 RRAS

DHCP server

 DNS server

 Proxy Server

Question 1.8

The correct answer is c. SNA can be encapsulated in TCP/IP packets and sent over a TCP/IP network (in this case, the VPN over the Internet). SNA tunneling must be enabled to encapsulate the SNA packets.

Keeping the Frame Relay connections as long as possible would not be cost effective and would be getting the network closer to the proposed LAN/WAN configuration. Installing a Windows terminal server at each depot would not do anything for the dumb terminals to connect to the mainframe. A terminal server only allows a Windows server to act as a central processor for clients to run applications. Installing a mainframe at each site is not cost effective.

Question 1.9

The correct answers are a and d. Adding proxy arrays will improve performance by caching more sites and helping with some load balancing between the two servers. Upgrading the Internet connection at the depots will increase bandwidth to the Internet at each site and allow better performance.

Changing the network to a Token Ring topology will have little change if going from a 10MB Ethernet network to a 16MB Token Ring network, and would be adversely affected if going from 100MB Ethernet to 16MB Token Ring topology.

Upgrading to newer versions of the Internet browsers used at the depots will have little noticeable effect on performance.

Question 1.10

The correct answer is d. The only area that has access from the Internet to the Web server is the Los Angeles Internet connection. This is the only link that requires an upgrade for increasing performance for access to the Web server.

Question 2.1

The correct answer is b. At the current time, one WINS server is required because there are non-Windows 2000 systems that require a WINS server for better performance. Only one is required because the network has fewer than 10,000 systems.

Question 2.2

The correct answer is a. After the proposed network is in place, no WINS server will be required because all systems will be Windows 2000 based.

Question 2.3

The correct answer is d. In the case of such a small number of sites connected by routers, static routes should be implemented to cut down on overhead of routing protocols. Once the routers are configured, everything should be done. There are no plans for growth in the business (at least for adding sites), and a business can always expect to add a few employees if needed.

Question 2.4

The correct answer is e. Putting a DHCP server in each building with three scopes, using 80 percent of the scope for its subnet and 10 percent of each of the other two building's scopes. This lets a scope manage its own subnet and also a portion of the other two subnets if one of the other DHCP servers should fail. All routers should be BOOTP-enabled to make this work.

Question 2.5

The correct answer is:

Building A

> DHCP service

> DNS service

> Dial-up service

Building B

> DHCP service

> DNS service

Building C

> DHCP service
>
> DNS service

Question 2.6

The correct answer is a. If there were another connection between Building A and C, then there would be another route to each building if a fiber connection should fail. This solution is cheaper than adding microwave antennae for backup. The other options do not provide any fault tolerance.

Question 2.7

The correct answer is:

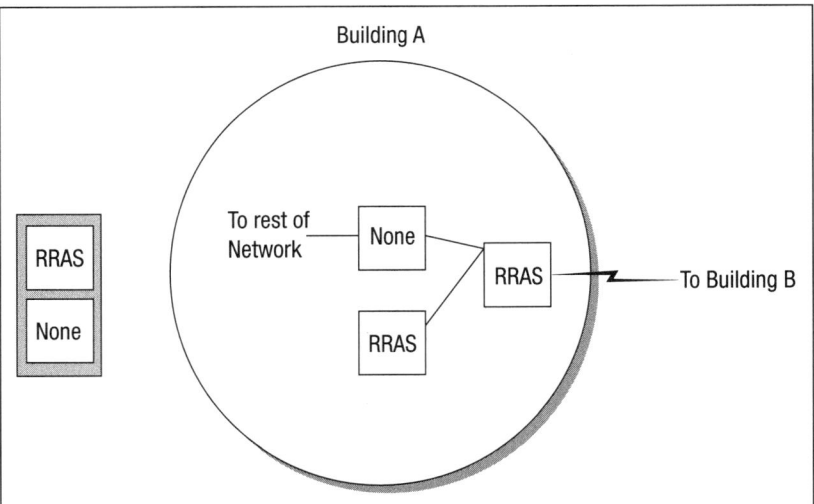

A RRAS server will be used for routing from Building A to Building B with routing services enabled. Another RRAS server will be on its own subnet separate from the rest of the network for better security to provide remote-access services.

Question 2.8

The correct answer is c. The SQL and Exchange server should be clustered for fault tolerance. To replicate databases anywhere would just make a backup of the data.

Question 2.9

The correct answer is:

Change network to TCP/IP

Upgrade bridges with routers

Upgrade servers

Upgrade workstations

Add dial-up server in Building A

Question 2.10

The correct answer is b. The main purpose stated was for employees to access email remotely over the Internet. The Exchange server is located in Building B, so the connections should be placed closest to the service to prevent more network traffic. If remote access were needed to the data on the SQL server, then the SQL server could be moved to Building B, or the Exchange server and Internet connection could go to Building A. (This would be the best choice if Buildings A and C were also connected by a fiber connection.)

Question 3.1

Answer a is correct. By placing the root at the Nashville location, you reduce the impact on all of the retail stores if one of the WAN links becomes disabled. If the root were placed at a retail location, other sites would not have access if the link between the retail store and the Nashville location were disabled.

Question 3.2

Answer a is correct. To protect file access in case of a server failure, a replica should be placed at the Nashville location. This would protect file access if the hosting server fails, and it doesn't increase the network traffic between the Nashville location and the retail stores.

Question 3.3

Answer b is correct. To create a Dfs root replica, a domain-based root must be created. Standalone Dfs roots are not capable of being replicated. Active Directory is not a valid type of Dfs root.

Question 3.4

Answer c is correct. After the root has been created, Dfs links are added that specify the destination of the pointer. After the links are created, they are referred to as Dfs leaf objects. Replicaas re created to rprovide redundancy and load balancing by making a coyp of the shared folder. A binary large object or blob stores the Dfs topology of the Dfs root.

Question 3.5

Answer d is correct. Replicas can be placed on the client workstations. With this design, if the server became disabled, the client could still log on to the domain over the WAN link. The Dfs root is located at the Nashville location, which means it would still be available. If the local Dfs leaf object were replicated to a workstation, the retail store could continue normal operations in the event of a server failure.

Question 3.6

Answer c is correct. Windows NT 4 has the ability to browse the Dfs root and host Dfs leaf objects if Service Pack 3 or higher has been installed.

Question 3.7

Answers a and b are correct. The Dfs link replicas will provide fault tolerance and load balancing at the retail location. The Dfs root would provide a centralized backup point. Dfs does not requite or provide any additional authentication security.

Question 3.8

Answer d is correct. Dfs supplies no additional tools to secure files or directories.

Question 3.9

The correct answer is:

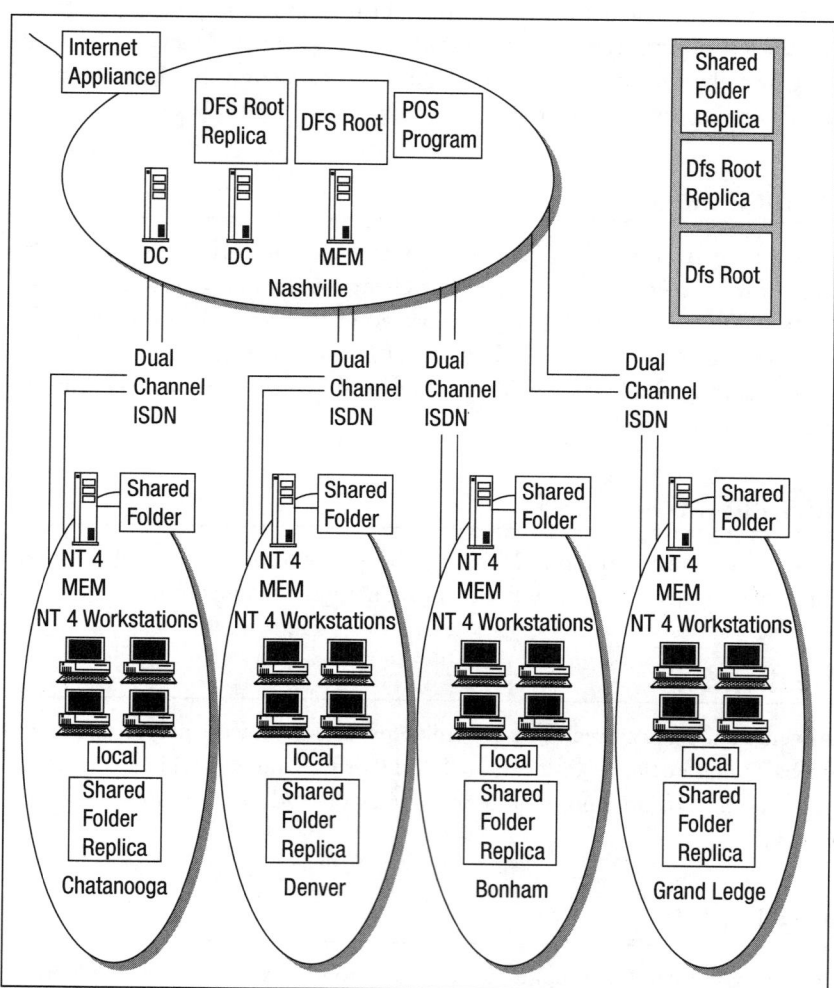

Question 4.1

Answer a is correct. By using 255.255.192.0 as the subnet address, the network could be separated into two logical networks and would provide for 16,382 host IP addresses.

Question 4.2

Answer d is correct. IPSec encrypts TCP/IP communications between hosts. QoS guarantees available bandwidth to QoS applications. Packet filtering can restrict access by a certain type of traffic to a specific TCP/IP port. MSCHAP is a logon challenge authentication protocol that helps prevent unauthorized access but does not provide secure communications between the hosts after the authentication process.

Question 4.3

Answer d is correct. SACK or TCP Selective Acknowledgment reads all data in the TCP window and requests only the retransmission of those packets that have not been correctly received within the TCP window. QoS guarantees the availability of bandwidth for a QoS enabled application. IPSec encrypts communications between hosts. DHCP provides automatic IP addressing for DHCP and BOOTP-enabled clients.

Question 4.4

Answer c is correct. Secured Server requires secured communication. Any requests to send using unsecured communications are rejected. Both client and server will allow unsecured communications. ISAKMP/Oakley is a protocol used for authentication; it does not define the type of communication allowed by either host.

Question 4.5

Answers a and c are correct. IPSec Header Traffic Protocol ID 51 (0x33) and IPSec ESP Protocol ID 50 (0x32) need to be enabled on the router to support IPSec routing. IMAP4 is used by email clients, and ESP headers are used for encryption security.

Question 4.6

Answer d is correct. QoS (Quality of Service) provides a routing mechanism that can guarantee delivery of data for a certain application. Paths for traffic flows are determined based on some knowledge of resource availability in the network. WINS and DNS are used to resolve names to IP addresses. IPSec provides encryption between TCP/IP hosts.

Question 4.7

The correct answer is:

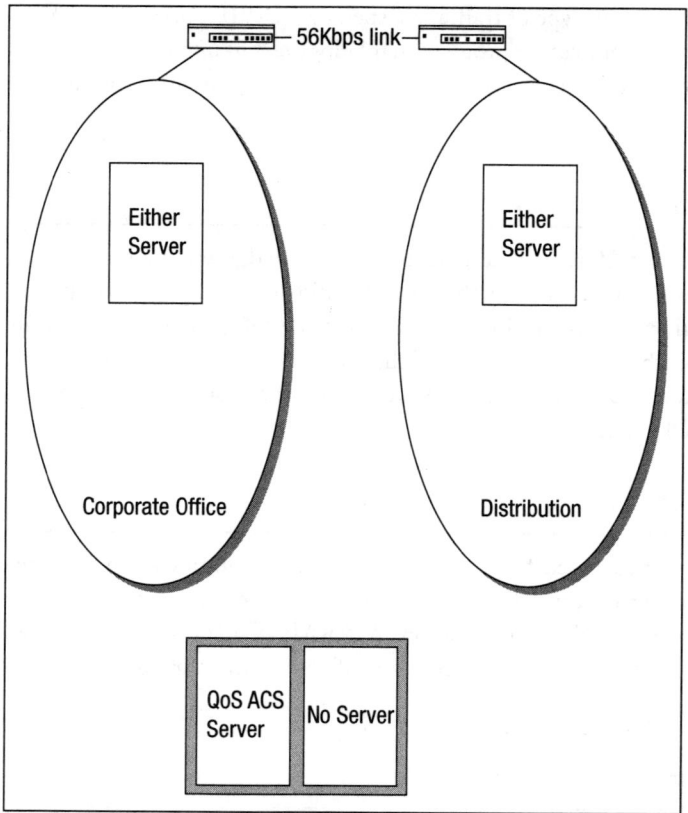

You should place the QoS ACS server on overpopulated segments. Because the 56Kbps link is the limiting factor in this scenario, the ACS server could be placed at either location.

Question 4.8

The correct answer is b. All IP packets will be sent from the proxy server to the Internet. The requests are actually generated by the proxy server with the address of 38.10.74.150.

Question 4.9

The correct answer is c. Because bandwidth is at a minimum, using Active Directory will cause a little less overhead and allow all DNS tables to be synchronized identically. Using forwarders will cause more overhead and consume more bandwidth.

Question 4.10

Corporate office

> RRAS
>
> WINS
>
> DNS
>
> Dfs
>
> DHCP

Distribution center

> RRAS
>
> DNS
>
> Dfs
>
> DHCP

RRAS would be needed at each site if physical routers were not purchased. WINS would be required because an NT 4 system would still be in place. The WINS system should be placed on the same subnet as the location of the most non-Windows 2000 systems, which would be the corporate office. DNS servers are required for Windows 2000 name resolution. Dfs services would be required for the Dfs tree. DHCP services would be required to assign IP addresses. Because the IP addresses are subnetted, it would be best to use DHCP in case the subnet is changed again. For redundancy, a DHCP server should be at each location in case the 56Kbps link were to fail between the sites.

Glossary

Access control list (ACL)
A table listing what actions a user is allowed to perform on network resources.

Active Directory
Windows 2000 directory service to store network object information.

Active Directory-integrated zone
A type of DNS zone that is Microsoft-specific. Integrates with Active Directory.

Alert
Notification of problems on a computer. An alert causes an action to take place when a threshold is reached on a counter.

AppleTalk
Native network architecture used by Macintosh computers.

Application layer
The top or highest layer of the OSI model. The Application Program Interface (API) uses this layer to access program utilities such as file and print services.

ARIN (American Registry of Internet Numbers)
An organization that administers and controls the registration of IP addresses.

ARPANET (Advanced Research Projects Agency Network)
The world's first packet-switching network.

AS (autonomous system)
A group of routers exchanging routing information.

ASP (active server pages)
A set of technologies often used in Web pages for the purpose of creating dynamic content on a Web site.

Authentication
A method to validate log-on information.

Automated Analysis
The use of automated responses to correct the network variance.

Automatic Private Addressing

IP autoconfiguration, or automatic private IP addressing, is a new feature that uses discovery packets to assign a unique IP address if no manual or BOOTP/DHCP configuration is available. Also referred to as Automatic private IP addressing (APIPA).

BackOffice

A suite of server applications designed to provide all the services a company requires for a network.

Bandwidth

The difference between the highest and lowest frequency available over a connection that can be used to transfer information.

BIND (Berkeley Internet Name Domain)

An implementation of DNS server designed by the University of California at Berkeley.

BOOTP (Boot Protocol)

The protocol for a system to obtain boot information. Also defines if a router is BOOTP-enabled to allow DHCP broadcasts to pass through it.

Bottleneck

A situation in which a resource is unable to keep up with required use, such as a hard drive that cannot write data as fast as it needs to be written.

Broadcast

In regards to networking, refers to a packet that is not addressed to any one computer but a group of computers.

Cache

A buffer used to store information for quicker access than without a buffer.

Cache hit ratio

The percentage of Web requests that a proxy server can fulfill from cache instead of having to retrieve the page from the Internet.

CARP (Cache Array Routing Protocol)

A protocol to compute on which single server in a proxy array a Web page should be cached.

Centralized data collection

A process by which there is a centralized point for collection and analysis; data is accumulated and analyzed at a central location.

CERN (Conseil European pour la Reserche Nucleair)

The particle physics lab in Switzerland that created the Web and the first proxy servers.

Chaining

Configuring proxy servers to route their client requests to other upstream proxy servers instead of sending them directly out to the Internet.

CHAP (Challenge Handshake Authentication Protocol)

Protocol used to authenticate usernames and passwords. Encrypts the information for transport over a network.

Client

A device on a network that uses resources from a server to accomplish a task.

Cluster

A combining of two physical hardware computer systems to act as a single logical unit until one fails and the other system will still function for redundancy.

Convergence
Stabilization of routing tables when network topology changes.

Convergence time
When used in reference to the WINS service, convergence time is the time it takes to copy a change to the WINS database to all other WINS replication partners.

Counter logs
Logs used to gather data and record the captured statistics to a log file. The log file is later viewed from the system console.

Data collection
The collecting of statistics to determine the state of a resource or service.

Data link layer
The layer directly above the physical layer. This layer assembles the bits into recognizable data called *frames*.

DES (Data Encryption Standard)
These standards describe data encryption from 40-bit DES to 128-bit Triple DES (3DES).

Dfs (Distributed File System)
A chain of shared folders that can be accessed from one share point to provide a way to centrally manage a group of network shared folders.

Dfs client
A machine that requests Dfs services from a hosting Dfs server.

Dfs leaf object
The name of a link to a shared resource in a Dfs tree.

Dfs replica
Replicas of a Dfs root or leaf object created to provide fault tolerance.

Dfs root server
A server that hosts a Dfs root.

Dfs tree
The hierarchical structure that Dfs uses to organize your network files.

DHCP (Dynamic Host Configuration Protocol)
Protocol used to automate the assignment of IP addresses and other TCP/IP options like IP address, Subnet Mask, Gateway, and others.

DHCP Relay Agent
A service used to act as a "middle man" between clients on a subnet that cannot communicate with a DHCP server on another subnet because the subnets are connected by a non-BOOTP router.

Dial-up
A network connection that is typically open only when in use. When not in use, the connection is closed.

Digital signature
A piece of code that allows someone to sign and therefore authenticate a document electronically for two people to exchange encrypted information.

Directory services
A set of services in a network operating system (NOS) that governs how users can access resources on the network.

Disk subsystem

Any hardware pertaining to hard drives, such as hard drive controllers and hard drives.

Distributed data collection

A strategy that utilizes more than one collection point for network statistics.

DNS (Domain Name System)

A service to resolve a computer host name (or NetBIOS name) to its IP address.

Domain controller

The server that authenticates user logon. Part of Active Directory.

Domain filter

A filter based on the Internet domain to which a packet is connecting.

Downlevel

Refers to earlier versions of a service or operating system.

EAP (Extensible Authentication Protocol)

Extension of PPP allowing user authentication.

Encapsulation

The method used to pass data from one network to another when both networks use different protocols.

Encryption

The method to disguise data and hide its content.

Event Viewer

A service that notifies when errors occur in the system, security, application, directory service, DNS server, and file-replication services.

Exchange Server

Part of the Microsoft BackOffice suite of products. Provides email and communication services to a network.

Failover

The process by which services on one system take over when a cluster fails.

Fault tolerance

The ability of a system to keep working even though a failure has occurred on a clustered system.

Filter

The set of rules that specify whether a packet is permitted to pass from one subnet to another.

Filtering

Allowing only those packets that meet a certain criteria.

Firewall

A system that protects the internal network by closing ports and preventing incoming connections from the public-access network.

Forwarder

A DNS server that directs a query to another DNS server when the query cannot be resolved locally.

Frame Relay

A protocol used in packet-switching networks to provide WAN connections at varying speeds.

Gateway

The service that sends from one subnet the protocols that are destined for another subnet.

GUI (graphical user interface)
A program interface that allows users to click on graphics when they want to perform an action, instead of requiring the user to type in commands.

Hop count
The number of routers that a packet travels through from its source to its destination.

Host
A name that refers to a node on a TCP/IP network.

HTTP (Hypertext Transfer Protocol)
The high-level protocol used by the Web. Part of the TCP/IP suite of protocols.

IAS (Internet Authentication Services)
Service in Windows 2000 that includes the RADIUS server component.

ICMP (Internet Control Message Protocol)
A protocol that allows the gateway to be discovered without an entry using router discovery messages called *router advertisements* and *router solicitations*.

IETF (Internet Engineering Task Force)
Internet Engineering Task Force. The body responsible for posting RFCs.

IGMP (Internet Group Management Protocol)
A list of members that are to receive multicast packets.

IIS (Internet Information Server)
Part of the Microsoft BackOffice suite of products. Provides Web, FTP, and other Web-related services to a network.

In-band data collection
A strategy in which the collected monitoring data travels on the same physical infrastructure that provides service to your clients.

Interface
The device that is used to connect something to a network.

IP addressing
The addressing scheme of four numbers (from 0 to 255) that is a numeric representation of a system on a network.

IPSec (Internet Protocol Security)
A set of protocols that provide data integrity and data encryption in your Windows 2000 network.

IPX/SPX
The transport protocol commonly used by Novell.

ISAKMP/Oakley
A protocol that allows the receiver to verify the sender's identity using X.509 digital certificates.

ISDN (integrated services digital network)
Digital communication for data and voice with speeds of 64 or 128Kbps.

ISP (Internet Service Provider)
A company that provides access to the Internet.

L2TP (Layer 2 Tunneling Protocol)
The method of encapsulating IP, IPX, SNA, or NetBEUI.

LAN (local area network)
The portion of a single network in a small geographical area, such as a building.

Latency
The period of time that one component or computer waits for another to respond.

Lease
The set amount of time that a computer is able to use its assigned IP address before it has to renew the address.

Legacy
Describes an older, usually out-of-date application, hardware, or operating system that is considered necessary to a network that needs to be connected to and integrated into a network.

Lightweight
When used in reference to bandwidth and networking, refers to a protocol or service that is designed to generate little network traffic.

Link state
Router requirement to send routing information from one router to all routers on a network.

Linux
An open-source network operating system.

MAC (media access control) address
The hard-coded physical address that is given to a network interface card by the manufacturer.

Macintosh
A line of Apple computers or their GUI operating system.

MADCAP (Multicast Address Dynamic Client Allocation Protocol)
A protocol that distributes multicast address configuration.

Management strategy
A plan that details the proposed responses to network and application resource variances due to failures and projected growth.

Manual analysis
A technique used for point-in-time analysis of the network.

Manual testing
Testing that requires physical action from the responsible parties.

Master
A server that sends information to another (slave) and which is the only source of that information.

MD5 (Message Digest 5)
Protocol that operates over the entire data packet, including the header, to provide 128-bit authentication with random keys.

Metric
The value of distance through routers from source to destination.

MMC (Microsoft Management Console)
A management tool to control applications and services in Windows 2000.

Modem pool
A set of multiple modems.

MS-CHAP (Microsoft Challenge Handshake Authentication Protocol)
Authentication protocol for dial-up connections to a remote-access server.

Multicast
To send information over a network to multiple systems at once.

Multilink
Using multiple connections to act as one connection.

Namespace
A set of rules that govern the creation of computer names.

NAS (network access server)
A generic RADIUS term referring to the server that acts as the RADIUS client that accepts local RAS client requests and forwards them to the RADIUS server. In Windows 2000, the RRAS service acts as the NAS.

NAT (network address translation)
Translation of IP addresses to other addresses for use on the Internet or other public networks when the original IP addresses need to remain hidden.

NetBT (NetBIOS over TCP/IP)
A protocol, used at the session layer, that is required when protocols in the TCP/IP stack use NetBIOS at the session layer.

Nbtstat
Nbtstat displays the NetBIOS of TCP/IP statistics for troubleshooting networks that have clients other than Windows 2000.

NDS (Novell Directory Services)
The directory services provided by Novell Netware.

NetBIOS (Network Basic Input/Output)
The session layer network designed by API to provide a connection between computers in a LAN environment.

Netdiag
Netdiag performs a series of tests that are local to the host and used to determine the current state of the network client, including the availability of the WINS, DNS, and default gateway.

Netstat
Netstat displays protocol statistics and current TCP/IP network connections.

Network layer
The third layer of the OSI model. This layer provides addressing, routing, and traffic management for transmissions between nodes.

Network Monitor
A monitoring utility to track statistics on network resources and services.

NIC (network interface card)
The hardware peripheral card that allows a computer to be connected to a network.

NLB (network load balancing)
Part of Microsoft's Windows clustering service. Distributes client requests across available servers.

Node
A computer or device connected to a network.

NOS (network operating system)
An operating system that provides services that allow control over a network of users and computers.

Novell Netware
Novell corporation's network operating system (NOS).

Nslookup

Nslookup provides an interactive way to check DNS server resolution. This utility displays the hostname and IP address of the DNS server.

NWLink

Microsoft's version of IPX/SPX.

Option Pack

A set of Web applications and supporting software from Microsoft that are all a part of Internet Information Server. Also called the Windows NT 4.0 Option Pack.

OSI (Open Systems Interconnection) model

A seven-layer model created by the International Standards Organization (ISO) that defines a standard for network communications.

OSPF (Open Shortest Path First)

The protocol used to transmit routing information between routers.

Out-of-band collection

An alternate path will be used to transmit the monitored data to the centralized management point.

Packet filter

A filter based on the protocol and destination port of a packet.

Packets

A collection of data that is transmitted from one computer to another.

PAP (Password Authentication Protocol)

Protocol used to authenticate username and passwords.

Pathping

Does not actually encrypt the username and password over a network. Although similar to both ping and tracert, pathping provides a better diagnostic tool to troubleshoot router congestion by testing the path for 125 seconds.

Performance object

A type of counter associated with a resource that is to be monitored for certain performance values..

Persistent

A network connection that is always open.

Physical layer

The lowest layer of the OSI model. This layer defines architecture standards and is responsible for the transfer of binary data.

Ping (Packet Internet Groper)

A utility that can be used to check connectivity.

POP (point of presence)

A device that will accept a user's connection and allow the user to access an ISP's network.

Ports

The TCP/IP method to determine the program that is sending or receiving data.

PPP (Point-to-Point Protocol)

A protocol used to connect remote clients to a network.

PPTP (Point-to-Point Tunneling Protocol)

The method of encapsulating IP, IPX, SNA, or NetBEUI inside IP packets.

Presentation layer
The sixth layer of the OSI model. This layer provides standards for encoding and encryption across a network. This layer acts as negotiator for the rest of the protocol stack and is responsible for making the protocol stack network independent.

Primary zone
A DNS zone that is authoritative.

Private network
A network to which only certain users have access, such as a corporate LAN.

Proactive response strategies
A strategy requiring that trend analysis be used to predict possible failures and growth or variances that will place the network service in a state such that the service no longer meets the design requirements.

Proxy array
A group of proxy servers that can combine their cache to act as one.

Proxy Server
Part of Microsoft's BackOffice suite. A server used to protect internal network clients by making Internet requests for them and improving performance by caching data.

Public network
A network to which anyone has access, such as the Internet.

Pull replication
A type of WINS replication that uses time as the replication trigger to get the WINS table from replication partners.

Push replication
A type of WINS replication that uses a set number of changes as the replication trigger to send the WINS table to replication partners.

QoS (Quality of Service)
A routing mechanism that can guarantee data delivery for a certain application. Paths for traffic flows are determined based on some knowledge of resource availability in the network.

RADIUS (Remote Authentication Dial-In User Service)
The service used to authenticate remote users onto a network.

Reactive response
This response strategy describes action after the event has occurred.

Realm
A generic RADIUS term that refers to what will authenticate the incoming RADIUS request. In Windows 2000, Active Directory acts as the realm for RADIUS.

Redundancy
The provision of a backup in the event that a service fails.

Replication
When used in reference to the WINS service, replication is the copying of WINS database changes between WINS servers.

Resolver
A client in the DNS system that is trying to resolve a name by querying a DNS server.

Resource record
Individual records in a DNS zone file that map a computer name to an IP address or a computer to some resource type.

Response strategies
Processes that occur when the network service reaches a point at which an action needs to be undertaken to correct or circumvent a problem.

Reverse proxy
A service provided on a proxy server that maps incoming Web requests to an internal Web server.

RFC (Request for Comment)
The documents that specify TCP/IP details.

RIP (Routing Information Protocol)
A protocol used to transmit routing information between routers.

Rogue servers
A DHCP server that is activated on a network but is not authorized to be running.

Router
The device used to forward a packet from one subnet to its destination subnet.

Routing
The process of determining a path over routers for a packet to be sent from one subnet to another.

RRAS (Routing and Remote Access Service)
The service to specify routing and remote-access configuration.

SACK
TCP selective acknowledgment.

SAM (Security Access Manager)
A database of user and computer accounts in Windows NT used as part of directory services.

SAP (Service Advertising Protocol)
The protocol used to advertise resources available on a server.

Scope
A range of IP addresses and options for a DHCP server to assign to DHCP clients.

Screened subnet
A part of a network that is separated from the internal network by a device using packet filtering.

Secondary zone
A DNS zone that is copied from another DNS server.

Server
A device on a network that satisfies the requests of a client.

Session layer
The fifth layer of the OSI model. This layer defines the management of individual network sessions. It establishes, maintains, and ends sessions between nodes.

SHA
A 160-bit authenticator to provide data-origin authentication.

Shared folder
A folder that is shared to allow access by clients.

Shared secret
The password used to authenticate the connection from a RADIUS client to a RADIUS server.

Slave
A DNS server that can send unresolved queries to only a forwarder. It is not allowed to send the query to the Internet.

Smart card
A small device that can be programmed for a range of functions when connected to a computer.

SNMP (Simple Network Management Protocol)
An additional TCP/IP utility that can be installed on a Windows 2000-based computer to allow management of systems and services remotely by using the SNMP protocol.

Socket
A connection between a client and a server that works at the session layer. Created by the combination of an IP address and port, such as 192.168.1.1 port 80.

SOCKS
An IETF standard that allows proxy servers to connect clients to Internet applications.

SOCKS proxy
A service provided on Microsoft Proxy Server that connects non-Windows clients to Web applications.

Spoke and hub
Refers to the way in which WINS servers should be physically set up for replication. One server should be

selected as the center (hub) from which all updates will be replicated to other servers, like the spokes in a wheel.

SQL Server
Part of the Microsoft BackOffice suite of products. A database management product providing database services to a network.

SSL (Secure Socket Layer)
A protocol that works at the Session layer of the OSI model. Used to provide secure Web connections by encrypting Web pages.

Streaming video
Video images that are sent from one system to another or multiple computers over the network.

Subnet
A portion of a TCP/IP network.

Subnet mask
A filter that designates which portion of the 32-bit TCP/IP address relates to network identification and which relates to the actual host ID.

Supernetting
A process by which two or more small subnets are combined.

Superscope
Multiple scopes defined on a DHCP server.

System console
The MMC with the appropriate snap-in to provide management for a specific service.

System Monitor
A utility program that allows the viewing of live or realtime network resource statistics.

T1
A high-speed digital link of 24 64Kbps channels, totaling 1.544Mbps.

T3
A high-speed digital link of 28 T1 lines, totaling 44.736Mbps.

TCP (Transmission Control Protocol)
Transport layer protocol in the TCP/IP stack. Guarantees delivery of packets.

TCP window size
The size of the receiving window determines how many packets can be received before an acknowledgment is sent to the sending host.

TCP/IP (Transmission Control Protocol/Internet Protocol)
The most commonly used suite of protocols in today's networks.

TCP/IP stack
The common term used for the TCP/IP suite of protocols.

Tombstoning
Specifying a record in a WINS database for deletion and allowing it to replicate to all WINS databases. If a simple deletion is done, the record may be replicated back to the database where it was deleted from originally and made active.

Trace logs
Logs that record data collected by the operating system provider or one or more non-system providers, such as programmers.

Tracert
A utility to discover the route used between two communicating hosts.

Transparent
In a network environment, describes a service that works without the user becoming aware of it.

Transport layer
The fourth layer of the OSI model. This layer is responsible for making sure that the data was received without errors.

TTL (Time To Live)
Information used by protocols and services to require that packets be discarded after a set amount of activity on a network.

UDP (User Datagram Protocol)
Transport layer protocol in the TCP/IP stack. Does not guarantee delivery of packets.

UNC (Universal Naming Convention)
A standard used to reference shared resources on a network.

Unix
An operating system that uses a command-line interface and TCP/IP as its networking protocol.

URL (uniform resource locater)
A standard format for specifying an address to a Web page.

Variable length subnet mask (VLSM)
A method to further break down a subnet. An existing subnet mask is subdivided in a hierarchical fashion.

Vendor options
DHCP configuration for specific hardware vendor types.

VPN (Virtual Private Network)
A connection that allows remote access to a private network over a public network.

VPN client
The computer using a VPN to access resources on a VPN server.

VPN connection
The physical link on which a VPN is created.

VPN server
The computer sharing resources through a VPN by VPN clients.

VPN tunnel
The logical connection between VPN server and a VPN client where data transferred is encapsulated and or encrypted.

VPN Tunneled Data
Information transferred between the VPN client and VPN server.

VPN Tunneling Protocols
Protocol used to encapsulate and or encrypt tunneled data.

WAN (wide area network)
Collection of LANs over a wide geographical area.

Web proxy
A service that allows a Web client to connect to a proxy server when requesting a Web page instead of connecting directly to the Internet.

Windows Clustering
A Microsoft service that allows individual servers to act as a group. It includes the Microsoft Cluster Server and Network Load Balancing services.

Windows Management Instrumentation
An interface that programmers can use to create custom applications that monitor the status of services.

Windows Script Host
A service that can automatically run script files for logon scripts, administrative, and automated tasks.

WINS (Windows Internet Naming Service)
A service that resolves a NetBIOS computer's name to IP addresses.

WinSock proxy
A service provided on Microsoft Proxy Server that connects Windows clients to Web applications.

wizard
Setup screen that asks for information to perform the actual configuration for which the wizard is designed.

zone
A portion of the distributed DNS database contained in one file.

Index

80/20 rule, for sharing scopes, 74, 75, **78**

A

A (Address) records, 91
Access control lists, 92
Acknowledgments, selective, **339**
ACLs, in DNS, 92
Active Directory, 29
    with Dfs, 197–198, 203–204
    with DHCP, 70–71
    with DNS, 87–89, **98**, **342**
    with non-Microsoft DNS servers,
      88–89, **97**
    with Proxy Server, 157–158
    router authentication certificates
      from, 186
    RRAS with, 228
    upgrading to, **97**
Active Directory Users and Computers,
    dial-in permissions settings, 221, 229
Active Directory–integrated zones, 90, **98**
    on screened subnets, 93
Adaptive exams, 13–14
    test-taking strategy for, 17–18
Address resolution. *See also* DNS.
    at network layer, 44
Addressing, TCP/IP, 45
Advanced Research Projects
  Agency (ARPA), 42
AH, 52

Alert Properties dialog box, 274–275
Alerts, 274–275
    threshold value setting, 275
American Registry of Internet
  Numbers (ARIN), 159
Anding, 45
API, 44
APIPA addresses, on private networks, 135
AppleTalk
    RADIUS support of, 246
    routing, 184
Application layer, 44
    traffic filtering at, 50
Application Programming Interface.
  See API.
Application servers, 292
Applications
    cluster awareness of, 296
    for network monitoring, 277–278, **284**
ARPANET, 42
Arrays, 156–157, **169**
    performance enhancements from, **170**
    in proxy chains, 161
    spreading cache across, 157
AS, 182
Authentication
    by IPSec, 51
    MD5 for, 52–53
    of remote and roaming users, 240, 242
    of routers, 185
    SHA for, 53
    VPN, 226
Authentication header. *See* AH.

Authentication servers, 242.
> *See also* Domain controllers.
>> RADIUS server placement near, 247, **254**

Authorization, of remote and roaming
> users, 240

Automated data analysis, 278–279

Automatic discovery, 115

Automatic Private IP Addressing, 48, 49

Automatic updates, of IP information, 227

Autonomous systems. *See* AS.

B

Backbone, connecting to, 314

BackOffice, Proxy Server component, 153

Backups, 197, 209

Backward compatibility
> and NetBIOS support, 28
> WINS use for, 106

Bandwidth
> guarantees for, **340**
> increasing, 230, **328**
> requests for, 54, 55
> reservations for, **62**
> routing decisions based on, 54

Berkeley Internet Naming Domain.
> *See* BIND.

BGP, 45

Binary Large Object. *See* Blob.

Binary log files, 274, **284**

BIND, 85
> compliance to, 86

Blob, 198

Boot process, speeding, 313

BOOTP, 48–49

Border Gate Protocol. *See* BGP.

Broadcasts, 24, 30, 179
> as default WINS solution, **123**
> NetBIOS use of, 107
> router blocking of, 107–108

C

Cache Array Routing Protocol. *See* CARP.

Caching, 46
> active, 155–156
> disk space for, 156, **168**
> and number of Internet connections,
>> 163–164
> optimizing performance of, 156–157,
>> **170**
> passive, 155

Caching-only servers, 95, **102**

Callback options, for remote connections,
> 221–222

CARP, 157

Case study exams, 4–5
> test-taking strategy for, 15–16

CERN, 165

Chaining proxy servers, 161

Channel Service Unit/Data Service Unit.
> *See* CSU/DSU.

Checksum, error-checking, 44

CIDR, 45

Class B addresses, 47

Class C addresses, 45, 58

Classless Interdomain Routing. *See* CIDR.

Client authentication, 226

Client computers
> connections between, 154
> determining current state of, 270
> Internet connections of, 150–151
> port numbers of, 151
> serving Web pages to, 154
> vulnerability of, 150

Client requests, failure to fill, 265

Clients
> anonymity of, 32
> IP addressing services for, **37**
> name-resolution services for, **37**
> protection of, **37**
> remote connections for, 296

Cluster Server, 296, 311

Cluster servers, 74, **78**, **325**
> RRAS, 229

Common Information Model (CIM), 278

Computer addresses, 27–28

Computer names, 26–28

Connectivity, checking, 270

Consistency checks, of WINS database, 119

Convergence, 184

Convergence time, 114–115
> calculating, 116–117
> minimizing, **128**

Copy command, 274

Cost metric settings, 48, **58**

Counter logs, 273–274
> creating, 273
> scheduling, 274

Counters, 271–272

CSU/DSU, 185, **192**

D

Data authentication, 226
Data collection, 267–268
  centralized, 268
  distributed, 267, **281**
  in-band, 268, **282**
  out-of-band, 268
Data flows
  bandwidth reservations for, 54
  priority levels, 54
Data integrity, 51
  definition of, 52
Data link layer, 43–44
Date Encryption Standard. *See* DES.
DDNS, 31, 91, 92
Default gateway, **320**
Delivery, guaranteed, 25, 54
Demand-dial connections, 185, 246–247
  filters for, 138, 185, **192–193**
  remote access policy for, 186, **192–193**
  RRAS configuration for, 178, **191–193**
Demilitarized zone (DMZ), 158
DES, 53
Destination address, of frames, 43–44
Devices, remote configuration of, 277
Dfs, 196–198
  with Active Directory, 197–198,
    203–204
  administration tools, 201–206
  command-line options, 206, 207
  file system security, 204
  network diagram of, **337**
  optimizing design of, 206–209
  on Windows 2000 systems, 199
  on Windows NT systems, 199–200
Dfs clients, requirements for, 198–199
Dfs files, security of, **336**
Dfs folders, permissions for, 204
Dfs leaf objects, 197, **335**
Dfs links, **335**
Dfs root
  creating, 202–204
  displaying, 201–202
  domain-based, 203, 208, **211**, **213**
  hosts for, **212**
  placement of, **335**
  placing folders in, 201
  requirements of, 198–199
  standalone, 203, **212**

Dfs root replica
  creation of, **335**
  placement of, **335**
Dfs tree, 197
  adding and removing servers, 197
  adding folders to, 201
  browsing, 200–201, **336**
  creating, **335**
DHCP, **299–300**, 313, **325**, **326**, **342**
  with Active Directory, 70–71
  authorizing for Active Directory, 71
  automatic BOOTP and client
    configuration, **318**
  availability of, 74
  broadcasts use, 179
  disabling NetBIOS with, 121, **123**
  with DNS, 70
  DNS updates by, 30, **35**
  dynamic update configuration, 91
  multicast address assignment
    capabilities, 68–69
  NAT as replacement for, 135, **145**
  overview of, 66–72
  parameters configured by, 67
  performance, enhancing, 74–75
  with RRAS, 72, 227, **237**
  vendor-specific options for, 67–68, **79**
  with Windows 2000, 70–72
DHCP Administrators group, 71
DHCP Client Service, 66–67
DHCP clients
  address scope of, 48
  updating information in DNS, **319**
DHCP manager, 48
DHCP Relay Agent, 72, 73, **77**, **79–80**,
    179, 227
  placement of, **81**
DHCP servers, 66–67, 72
  clustering, 74, **78**
  enabling dynamic updates on, **78**
  IP addresses of, 67, **80**
  multiple, 74, **78**
  number of, **77**, **326**, **331**
  placement of, **81**, **300**, 310, 314,
    326, **331**
  redundancy of, 72, 74, **300**, **331**
  in WANs, 73
DHCP Users group, 71
Dial-in connections, 228, 246.
    See also Remote-access policies.
  settings for, **233**

Dial-in privileges, 222–223
Dial-up connections, 220, 226, **320**
    callback options for, 222
    securing, **332**
Digital certificates, 51
Digital signatures, for approved
    software, 292
Directories, location of, 196
Directory services, 29.
    See also Active Directory.
Discovery messages, router, 50
Discovery packets, 49
Disk space
    for caching, 156, **168**
    for Proxy Server, **168**
Distributed File System. *See* Dfs.
Distributed File System MMC, 201–202
    link creation in, 204
    link deletion in, 205
    replica creation in, 205–206
    replica deletion in, 206
    root creation in, 203–204
Distributed Management
    Interface (DMI), 278
DNS, 27, 28, **37–38**, **299–300**, 313, **325**,
    326, **342**
    design issues, 84
    different namespace from Active
        Directory, 88
    dynamic version. *See* DDNS.
    integration with Active Directory
        services, 87–89, **97**, **342**
    integration with DHCP, 70
    and NAT, 137, **145**
    RFCs of, 85
    round-robin entries, 164
    RRAS with, 227
    same namespace as Active Directory,
        88
    Windows 2000 requirement for, 29–30
    Windows 2000 use of, 68
    zones for, 89–91
DNS clients
    documenting, 86–87
    impersonation of, 92
    preferred servers for, **101**
    Windows 2000 and BIND clients, 87
DNS database
    authority over records, 89
    dynamic updates by RRAS clients, 227
    dynamic updating of, 87, 90–91, **319**
    partitioning, 109

    static updating of, 90
    updating, 30–31, **35**, 70, **78**
DNS servers.
    See also Windows 2000 DNS Server.
    caching-only, 13–14, 89, **102**
    checking resolution, 270
    DHCP configuration of, 67
    documenting, 86
    as forwarding, forwarder, or slave
        servers, 93
    IP address resolution to fully
        qualified domain names, **318**, **320**
    number of, 94
    placement of, **300**, 310, 318
    preferred, **101**
    queries to, referring to other servers, 109
    as slave servers, **99**
DNS system
    optimizing performance of, 94–95,
        99, **101**
    security for, 91–93, **100–101**
Domain controllers, 242
    configuration of, 313, 316
    registration to WINS, 108
    Windows 2000 servers as, **98**
Domain Name Service. *See* DNS.
Domain names, translation to IP
    addresses. *See* DHCP; DNS.
Downstream components, 161
Dynamic content, updating, 156
Dynamic DNS. *See* DDNS.
Dynamic filtering, 158–159, **171**
Dynamic Host Configuration Protocol.
    See DHCP.
Dynamic routing, 177–178

E

EAP, 223, **232**, **326**
    with L2TP, 225
    with PPTP, 224
EIGRP, 177
Elephan(t) connections, 49
Encapsulation
    L2TP, 225
    PPTP, 224–225
    by VPNs, 224–226
Encapsulation security and payload.
    See ESP.
Encoding, 44
Encryption, 31–32, 52, **59**, 226
    DES for, 53
    with IPSec, 51

Microsoft Point-to-Point
Encryption, 224
and NAT, 139
at presentation layer, 44
for remote-access systems, 246
of replication traffic, 120
of routing information, 185
Encryption key, 226
Error-detection checksum, of frames, 44
Errors, displaying, 275–276
ESP, 52
Event generation, tools for, 269
Event signals, 267
Event Viewer, 275–276
Exam, certification
adaptive tests, 13–14
build-list-and-reorder questions, 6–8
case study format, 4–5
create-a-tree questions, 8–10
drag-and-connect questions, 10–11
fixed-length format, 13
multiple-choice questions, 5–6
orientation exams, 3
practice test for, 19
preparation resources, 20–21
preparing for, 2
select-and-place questions, 11–12
short-form tests, 14
simulations, 13
test-taking strategies, 14–19
testing situation, 3–4
Exchange servers, redundancy of, **333**
Extended Interior Gateway Routing
Protocol. *See* EIGRP.
Extensible Authentication Protocol. *See* EAP.
External clients, 92
access to internal services, 162–163

F

Failover, 74. *See also* Redundancy.
Failures, response strategies for, 279
FAT partitions, 204
Fault tolerance, 291, **332**. *See also*
Redundancy.
arrays for, 156
backup WINS servers for, 111
increasing, 288
from proxy arrays, **170**
for proxy server routes, 161–162
replicas for, **214–215**, **336**
for root shares, 203–204

for services, 295–296
for WINS system, **124**
Files, redundancy of, 196–197
Filters
for demand-dial connections, 138
for IP traffic, 50–51
on NAT servers, 137–138
on routers, 185
as security measures for
NAT servers, **146**
Firewalls, 46, 48, 50, 92.
See also Screened subnets.
versus proxy servers, 152
and RADIUS, 250
Fixed-length exams, 13
test-taking strategy for, 16–17
Forwarding servers, 93
Frames, 43–44
compression of, 225
encryption. *See* Encryption.

G

Gateways, 50, 176. *See also* Routers.
cost metric settings of, 48, **58**
default, **58**
default metric of, 68
DHCP configuration of, 67
Generic Packet Classifier, 55
Generic QoS (GQoS), 54
Generic Routing Encapsulation (GRE)
header, 224

H

Hardware resources
balancing use of, 312
services use of, 291–292
Header information, 151
Hit ratios, and cache settings, 156
Hop counts, determining shortest path by,
180
Hops, 180
Hosts, 45
addressing. *See* DHCP.
for Dfs root, **212**
IP address scope of, 66
IPSec policies for, 52
lease of addresses, 48
manual allocation of, 48
monitoring, 277, **282**
security levels on, **59**
TCP/IP addresses of, 45
HTTP, port number of, 151
Hubs, **325**, **326**

I

IAS servers, backup, 252
IAS service, 32, 243, **254**
   shared secrets, 244
ICMP, 50
IGMP, multicasting support, 179
IGRP, 177
IKE, 51, 53
Impersonation of DNS clients, 92
Information security on Internet, 31–32.
   See also Encryption; Security.
Information type, of frames, 44
Interior Gateway Routing Protocol.
   See IGRP.
Internal networks
   caching services for, 155
   connecting to Internet, 150
   firewalls for, 152
   packet filters for, **171**
   private range of addresses for, 160,
     167–168
   protecting from external networks,
     38, 301. *See also* Microsoft Proxy
     Server; NAT.
   proxy servers for, 152.
     See also Microsoft Proxy Server;
     Proxy servers.
   unregistered IP addresses for, 159
Internet
   administration of, 42
   blocking access to, 137
   connecting remote sites through, 220
   DNS for, 27
   inbound requests from, **171**
   for remote connections, 31–32
Internet access
   controlling, 157–159
   through ISP, **233**
Internet Architecture Board (IAB), 42
Internet Authentication Service.
   See IAS service.
Internet Authorization Service.
   See IAS service.
Internet connections, 150–151, 246
   as less-expensive connection option,
     256, 290
   number of, 163–164, **169**
   outsourcing to ISPs, 248–250, **256**
   securing, 32, 150.
     See also Microsoft Proxy Server.

setting up, 151
upgrading, for performance
   optimization, **328**
Internet Control Message Protocol.
   See ICMP.
Internet domain names, translation to
   IP addresses, 106
Internet Engineering Task Force (IETF),
   42, 49
Internet Key Exchange. *See* IKE.
Internet Network Information Center
   (INTERNIC), 42
Internet servers, connection settings,
   133–134
Internet services
   placement of, 290
   Sockets use, 25–26
InterNIC, 159
IP addresses, 27–28
   autoconfiguration of, 48–49.
     See also DHCP.
   binary equivalents of, 45
   class-based, 45
   distribution to clients, 30–31
   duplicate, 66
   internal or external, 154
   leases on, 70
   obtaining blocks of, 159
   one-to-many ratio of public to
     private, 139
   one-to-one ratio of public to private,
     139
   private versus public, 135
   unregistered, 132
IP Forwarding, 139
IP information, automatic updates of, 227
IP proxy, 46
IP Routing, 136. *See also* Routing.
IPSec, 32, 51–54, **59**
   authentication protocols, 52–53
   client policy, 52
   encryption and data integrity
     capabilities, 52, 53
   IKE use, 53
   with L2TP, **193, 225**
   for router security, 187, **339**
   routing of, 54, **60**
   with RRAS, 185
   Secured Server, **340**
   server policy, 52
   as tunneling protocol, 225
   for zone transfer encryption, **100**

IPSec ESP Protocol, 54
    ID 50 (0x32), **60**, **340**
IPSec Header Traffic Protocol, 54, **60**, **340**
IPSec Secure Server, 52
    placement of, **63**
IPX/SPX, 182–183
    and IPX Tunneling, 225
    legacy role of, 42
    Proxy Server support of, 163
    RADIUS support of, 246
IPX Tunneling, 225
ISAKMP/Oakley, 51, 53
ISPs
    global presence of, **260**
    obtaining IP addresses from, 159
    and placement of Internet-related
        services, 290, **302–304**
    RADIUS accounting feature use,
        249–250
    RADIUS client placement at, **256–257**
    and RADIUS settings, 246–248
    for remote and roaming connections,
        247–250

J

Jscripts, 277

L

LANs
    convergence time on, 116
    definition of, 176
    DHCP services for, 72–73
    DNS servers on, 94
    routing packets between, 176
    RRAS for, 228
Large networks
    and broadcasts, 107
    OSPF for, 181
LAT, 154
Layer 5 (session layer), 24–25
Layer 2 Tunneling Protocol. *See* L2TP.
Leaf objects, replicas of, **213**
Leased line connections, 185
Leases, 48, 70, 75
    DHCP configuration of, 67
    releasing on shutdown, 68
LFN connections, 49
Link replicas, 203–204, **336**
LINKLOCAL Network IP address space,
    49

Links
    redundancy for, 208–209
    to shared folders, 204, 205
Load balancing, **328**. *See also* NLB.
    for DNS servers, 87
    by replicas, **336**
    with roots and linked files, 203
    between zones, 94–95
Local address table. *See* LAT.
Local networks, NetBIOS for, 25
Local Policy Module, 55
Log alerts, 271
Log files, 269, 271, 273–274
    error listings, 276
    filtering, 276
    naming, 274
    save formats, 274, **284**
Log-setting properties box
    General tab, 273
    Log Files tab, 273–274
    Schedule tab, 274
Logical addresses, 45
Logical units. *See* LUs.
Long, fat pipe, 49
Long-distance connections, Sockets for,
    25–26
L2TP, 32, 225
    versus PPTP, 32
    for router security, 187
    user authentication protocol support,
        225
    using with IPSec, **193**
    for VPN implementation, **35**
LUs, 226

M

MAC addresses, 42
Macintosh
    NetBIOS use, 30
    routing for, 184
MADCAP, 68–69
Mainframes
    gateways to clients, 225–226
    remote access to, 225–226
Management applications, 266
Management information base. *See* MIB.
Management plan, 264–266
Manual data analysis, 278–279
Master zones, 90
MD5, 52–53
Medium-sized networks, RIP use in, 180
Memory, monitoring, 272

Message Digest 5. *See* MD5.

Messages
  reassembly of, 44
  sequencing number of, 44

MIB, 277

Microsoft certification
  exam format, 12–14
  exam question types, 4–12
  exam-readiness, 2
  exam situation, 3–4
  information resources on, 20–21
  test-taking strategies, 14–19

Microsoft Certified Professional site, 20

Microsoft Challenge Handshake
    Protocol. *See* MSCHAP.

Microsoft Exchange Server, notification
    and monitoring services, 269

Microsoft networking environments,
    DNS and WINS use, 28

Microsoft Point-to-Point Encryption.
    See MPPE.

Microsoft Proxy Server, 32, 136, 139, 150,
    153–154, 313. *See also* Proxy servers.
  caching services, 155–156, **325**
  compatibility with IIS, 153
  disk space for, **168**
  firewall capabilities, 152, 158
  functions of, 150–151
  inbound and outbound protection
    services of, 165
  inbound traffic controls, 158–159
  installing, 153–154
  integration with Active Directory,
    157–158
  Internet access control capabilities,
    318
  IP address requirement, **319**
  IPX/SPX support, 163
  for joining dissimilar networks, 163
  LAT, 154
  network diagram for, 160
  network interfaces, **38**
  outbound traffic controls, 157–158
  packet filtering, 158–159
  placement of, **304**, 310
  preparing network for, 159–160, **167**
  required services for, 294
  reverse proxying, 162–163, **170**, **171**, **303**
  routing scheme, 161–162
  security for, **171**
  security services of, 157–158

  services of, 154–157
  transparency of, 155

Microsoft Proxy Server 2.0, 46

Microsoft Systems Management Server, 266

Microsoft Web pages, searching, 20–21

Mixed environment, routing in, 182

Modems, 226, **233**
  demand-dial connection of, 134

Monitoring
  data collection, 267–268
  network status, 266–270

Monitoring tools, 271–277
  command-line, 269–270
  for event generation, 269

MPPE, 224

MSCHAP, 245–246, **255**
  with L2TP, 225
  with PPTP, 224

MS-RAS, **235**
  for dial-in access, 226

Multicast address allocation, DHCP
    configuration of, 67

Multicast Address Dynamic Client
    Allocation Protocol. *See* MADCAP.

Multicast addresses, 68

Multicast groups, 68, 179

Multicast scopes, **80**
  setting up, 69

Multicasts, 179
  IGMP support of, 179

MX (Mail Exchanger) records, 91

N

Name resolution, 28.
    See also DNS; WINS.
  monitoring, 273

Namespace
  for Active Directory and DNS, 88
  flat, 26–27
  hierarchical, 27, **37–38**
  for Internet-accessible DNS servers,
    92–93
  NetBIOS, 26–27

Naming conventions, NetBIOS versus
    DNS, 26–27

NAS, 243

NAT, 32, **37**, 132
  configuring, 134–135
  and DNS, 137, **145**
  functions of, 135–136
  hiding private network settings with,
    132, **142**

implementation of, 132–136
installing, 133–134, **144**
integration into existing systems,
    136–139
network interfaces, **38**
packet routing by, **143**
performance optimization, 139–140
placement of, 290
as replacement for DHCP, 135, **145**
required service for, **142**, 294
security for, 137, **146**
TCP/IP header translation,
    135–136, 139
NAT servers
filters on, 137–138, **146**
placement of, 136
TCP/IP on, **145**
upgrading, 140
VPN on, 139
NBNS, 108. *See also* WINS.
Nbtstat, 270
net send command, 274
net use command, 196
NetBEUI, legacy role of, 42
NetBIOS, 24–25, **319**
broadcasts from, 107
disabling, 29–30, 121, **123**
discontinued use of, 84, 106
faults of, 106
namespace of, 26–27, 106
naming service for, 28
service identifier in, 108
TCP/IP use, 26, **34**
Windows 2000 support, 28
Windows use of, **36**
NetBIOS name server. *See* NBNS.
NetBIOS names, translation to IP
    addresses, 106
NetBIOS over TCP/IP (NetBT), 26, **34**
disabling, 50, 68
statistics on, 270
Netdiag, 270
Netstat, 270, **283**
Netware servers, service advertisements
    from, 183
Network Access Server. *See* NAS.
Network Address Translation. *See* NAT.
Network addresses, 45
Network administration, minimizing, 288
Network architecture, OSI model for, 24
Network connection, 31

Network design, 46–48
factors affecting, 288
implementation of, 265
of infrastructure, 33
for performance, 311–312
planning for expansion, 266
sample project, 312–316
security of, 311
services for, 312–316
Network diagrams, 84–87
combining, 289–290
DNS clients on, 86–87
DNS servers on, 86
for NAT system, 137
number of users data, 290
for Proxy Server design, 160
RADIUS on, 244–247
services information on, 289
WINS system components on, 110
Network faults
detecting, 277
response strategies, 279
Network infrastructure, designing, 33
Network interface cards. *See* NICs.
Network layer, 44
Network load balancing. *See* NLB.
Network management plan, 264
network status monitoring process,
    266–270
Network Monitor, 269
Network operating systems. *See* NOSs.
Network services. *See* Services.
Network Solutions, Inc., 159
Network statistics
analyzing, 278–279
gathering, with programming and
    scripting, 277–278
gathering, with SNMP, 277
Network status, 278
evaluating, **283–284**. *See also* Data
    collection; Monitoring tools.
realtime view of, 271–273, **283–284**
Network traffic
minimizing, 288, 295, 313, **333**
reducing, with WINS, 30
and replicas, 205
Networking, nature of, 24
Networks
company goals for, 308
current status of, 271–275
evaluating existing infrastructure, 308

functionality of, 43
integrating, with NAT, 7, 136
internal and external, **38**
operation within design criteria, 265
physical medium for, 43
private. *See* Private networks.
public. *See* Public networks.
scalability of, 312, 314
selecting services for, 309.
    See also Services.
testing methods, 265
upgrading, **333**
NICs, 42
NLB, **172, 236,** 296
for balancing proxy server use, 164
NOSs, 29
Notifications, 267, 268–270
of service restarts, 268
Novell environment, routing in, 182–183
NS (Name Server) records, 91
Nslookup, 270, **283**
NTFS partitions
automatic replication on, 205
Dfs root on, 198, 204
linked folders on, 204
NWLink, 182–183

O

Oakley protocol, 53
Open Shortest Path First. *See* OSPF.
Open Systems Interconnection model. *See*
    OSI model.
Operating system architecture, 24
OSI model, 24–25, **36,** 43–45
OSPF, 31, **37,** 45, 54, 181–182, **190, 193**
for differing network media types,
    181, **190**
for large networks, 181
versus RIP, 184
routing table update time, 184
RRAS support for, 177
as unicast routing protocol, 179

P

Packet filters, 154, 158–159, **171, 172,** 185
Packets
retransmission of, 49–50
routing from public to private
    network destinations, **143**
specifically addressed, 107
Partitioned database, 109

Passwords, shared secrets as, 244, **259**
Pathping, 270, **283**
Peer authentication methods, 53
Performance
    and IPSec security levels, 41
    monitoring, with SNMP, 277
Performance counters, 271–272
    adding to System Console, 272–273
Performance MMC, 271
    system console, 271–273
Performance Monitor, 72
Performance optimization, 311–312
    adding proxy servers, **328**
    of DNS system, 94–95, **101–102**
    of NAT system, 139–140
    service combinations for, 295
    upgrading Internet connections, **328**
    of WINS system, 118–119
Perl, 277
Permissions
    for Dfs folders, 204
    for remote users, 221
Persistent connections, between
    replication partners, 115
Physical disk, monitoring, 272
Physical layer, 43
Physical units. *See* PUs.
Ping, 270
Point-in-time data analysis, 278
Point-to-Point Tunneling Protocol.
    See PPTP.
Points of presence (POP) servers, 249, **260**
Port mappings, 139
Port numbers, in URLs, 151
Ports, 151
    state of, 270
PPP, 225, **235**
    for dial-in access, 226
PPP header, 224
PPTP, 32, 224–225
    versus L2TP, 32
    with NAT for VPNs, 139, **147**
    proprietary encryption protocol use, **36**
    for router security, 187
    user authentication protocol support,
    224
    for VPN implementation, **35**
Presentation layer, 44
Primary zones, 89–90
Private IP addresses, 160, **167–168**
    scope order, **325**

Private networks, 46, **60**
    address ranges for NAT, 135
    address scheme settings for, 134
    APIPA addresses on, 135
    filters on interface, 137
    hiding settings of, 132, **142**
    protecting from Internet.
        See Screened subnets.
    security within, 311
    unregistered IP address use, 132
Processor, monitoring, 272
Program utilities, accessing, 44
Proxy clients, 165–166
Proxy servers, 32, 48, 150, **342**.
    See also Microsoft Proxy Server.
    adding, for performance
        optimization, **328**
    arrays of, 156–157, **169, 170, 328**
    balanced use of, 164
    for caching Web pages, **326**
    chaining, 161
    versus firewalls, 152
    functions of, 152
    IP addresses for, 159
    number of, 161–162, **171, 304–305**
    placement of, 163–164, **304–305**
    reverse proxying, 162–163
    at WAN connections, **168**
    Web proxies, 154
PTR (Pointer) records, 91
Public networks, 46. *See also* Internet.
    consistent connections to, 140
    filters on interface, 137
    IP address of, 136
    multiple connections to, 140
    security of, 311
    subnet mask of, 136
    for WAN connections, 120
PUs, 226
Push and pull replication, 115

Q

QoS, 44, 54–55
    for bandwidth guarantees, **340**
    components of, 54–55
QoS Admission Control Service (ACS), 55
    server placement, **61–62, 341**
QoS Packet Scheduler, 55
QoS sessions, **62**
Quality of Service. *See* QoS.
Queries, to WINS servers, 112

R

RADIUS, 32, 240–241, 241
    accounting port number, 241
    accounting service, 240–241, 249–250
    authentication port number, 241
    authentication protocols supported
        by, 245–246
    authentication service, 242, **302**
    domain controllers, 242
    for global access, **260**
    incoming connections, documenting,
        246
    network diagram of, 244–247
    optimizing logging performance, 252
    placement of, 290, **303**, 310
    ports used by, 241
    realms, 242–243, **255**
    RRAS with, 228, **259**
    within screened subnets, 250
    security for, 250–251, **257–258**
    shared secrets, 244, **259**
    transport protocols supported by, 246
    UDP use, 241
RADIUS clients, 242, 243.
    See also RRAS servers.
    operating system support of, **258**
    placement of, 247, **256–257**
RADIUS servers, 243
    availability of, 251–252
    IAS service on, 243, **254**
    placement of, 243, 247, **254**
RAID, for DHCP implementations, 72
RAS, with RADIUS, 240
RAS servers
    address requests to DHCP servers, 72
    addresses for, **81**
Realms, 242, **255**
Records
    manual deletion of, 119, **127**
    tombstoning, 119, 121, **127**
Redundancy, 47, 48, **58**, 279
    of DHCP servers, 72, 74, **78, 331**
    of files, 196–197, **213**. *See also* Dfs.
Redundant Array of Independent Disks.
    See RAID.
Redundant links, and in-band data
    collection strategy, 268, **282**
Refreshes, of WINS client registrations, 112
Regional Internet Registries (RIR), 159
Registrations, 112

Release of names from WINS database, 112
Remote access, 220–221. *See also* RRAS;
  RRAS servers.
    availability of, 229
    callback options, 221–222
    connecting through VPNs, 220–221
    dial-in connections, 220, 226
    dial-in privileges, 222–223
    direct dial site connections, 220
    implementing, 221–223
    placement of servers, 228–229
    security for, 221–222, 229
Remote-access policies, 222–223, 229,
  233, 250–251, **258**
Remote Access wizard, 222–223
Remote Authentication Dial-In User
  Service. *See* RADIUS.
Remote clients, Active Directory services
  for, 228
Remote connections
    centralizing, 243–244.
      See also RADIUS.
    data rate of, 246–247
    managing, 32
    persistent, 246–247
    servers for, **301**
    tracking, 240–241
Remote users.
  See also Remote-access policies.
    authenticating, 221–222, 243
    dial-in permissions, 221
    requirements for remote access, **233**
    RRAS server availability issues, 229
Replicas, 202, **335**
    creating, 205–206
    deleting, 206
    of leaf objects, **213**
    link, 203–204, 208–209
    placement of, **214–215, 336**
    root, 203–204
Replication, **125–126**
    automatic, 205
    convergence time, 114–117
    encryption for, 120
    manual, 205–206
    push and pull, 115
    securing, 294
    setting policy for, 205–206
    spoke-and-hub design for, **128**
    of WINS server records, 112, 114–117

Replication partners
  configuration of, 115
  persistent connection between, 115
Replication traffic, minimizing, **128**
Request for Comments (RFCs), 42
Resource records, 90–91
Resource Reservation Protocol Service
  Provider. *See* RSVP SP.
Resources, hardware, 291–292
Response strategies, 279
Retransmit message, 49
Reverse proxying, 162–163, **170, 171, 303**
RIP, 31, **37**, 45, 54, 180–181
  hop limitation, 180
  versus OSPF, 184
  routing table update time, 184
  RRAS support for, 177
  for small to medium networks, 180
  as unicast routing protocol, 179
RIP for IP, 180, 181, **190**
RIP for IPX, 180, 182–183
RIPv1, 180–181
RIPv2, 180–181
  CIDR support, 180
  VLSM support, 180
Roaming users, 240.
  See also Remote-access policies; Remote
  users.
  connecting through ISPs, 248–250
Root replicas, 203–204, 206
Root share, 203
  fault tolerance for, 203–204
Round trip time. *See* RTT.
Router advertisements, 50
Router solicitations, 50
Routers, 48, 50, 176, **325**
  in AS, 182
  authentication and encryption
    between, 185
  authentication certificates, 186
  bandwidth reservation caching, **62**
  BOOTP-enabled, 72, 73, **79**
  border, 182
  congestion statistics, 270
  convergence time, 184
  default metrics of, 68
  and demand-dial connections, 185,
    186, **191**
  enabling IPSec on, **60**
  IPsec seamless routing on, **340**
  leased line traffic control, 185
  NAT configuration on, 133

packet-filtering, 46
placement of, **191**, **192**, **330**
role of, 176
SAP-enabled, 183
security for, 186–187
seed, 184
traffic filtering by, 107–108
VPNs between, 224, **326**
Routes
discovering, 270
metrics of, 177
Routing, 31, 176–177
AppleTalk, 184
dynamic, 177–178
by IPSec, 54
for large networks, 181–182
in mixed environment, 182
at network layer, 44
in Novell environment, 182–183
opportunistic, 54
protocols for, **37**
QoS-based, 54
for small to medium networks, 180–181
static, 177–178, **192**
in TCP/IP environment, 181–182
in WAN environment, 184–185
Routing And Remote Access
configurations, 133
Routing and Remote Access Service.
See RRAS.
Routing Information Protocol. *See* RIP.
Routing protocols. *See also* OSPF; RIP.
AppleTalk routing, 184
comparing, 184
multiple-path, 182
network bandwidth and resources,
use of, 178, **192**, **193**
single-path, 180
Routing tables, 177, 315
dynamic building of, 177
manual building of, 177–178
updating, 184
RRAS, 31, 221, 313, **320**, **342**
with Active Directory, 228
authentication protocols supported
by, 245
with DHCP, 72, 227, **237**
with DNS, 227
enabling, 178–179
for global access, **260**
with IPSec, 185
for LANs, 228

placement of, 290, **302–303**, 310
with RADIUS, 228, **259**
as requirement for NAT, **142**
restrictions on remote connections, 251
routing protocol support, 177
securing remote connections with, **302**
for WANs, 228
with Windows 2000 services, 227–228
with WINS, 227
RRAS filters, for NAT interfaces, 137–138
RRAS MMC, 178–179
RRAS servers
authentication of, 186–187
availability of, 187, 229
central management of, 228
dedicated to routing, 187, 188
dial-in hours, 185, **193**
isolating, **301**, **303**
multiple connections to, 187, 188
number of, **235–236**
performance of, 187–188
performance of, optimizing, 230,
235–236
persistent connections for, 187, 188
placement of, 228–229, 230, **235–237**
redundant, 187
round-robin DNS entries, 229
security for, **236–237**, **329**
vulnerability of, 295
RSVP, 55
RSVP SP, 54
RTT, 270
Run command, 277

S

SA, 51
SACK, 49–50, **339**
SAM, 29
SAP, 183
Scopes, 66, **77**
sharing among DHCP servers, 74,
75, **78**, **331**
Screened subnets, 92–93, **100–101**, 150, 158
adding, 293–294
caching-only servers in, **102**
for isolating services needed by
remote users, 294, **303–304**
and RADIUS, 250
vulnerability of services in, 294
Web servers in, **171**, **304**
WINS in, 120
Scripts, automatic execution of, 277

Secondary zones, 89–90
Secure content, caching restrictions on, **170**
Secure Dynamic Updates, 92, **98**
Secure Hash Algorithm. *See* SHA.
Secure Web pages, caching restrictions on, 156
Secured Server, **59, 340**
Security, 50–54
    with Active Directory and DHCP, 70–71
    of DNS system, 91–93, **100–101**
    of file system, 204
    implementing, 291
    increasing with service combinations, 293–295, **301, 302–305**
    for Internet connections, 32–33
    IP traffic filtering, 50–51
    IPSec for, 51–54, **59.** *See also* IPSec.
    L2TP and PPTP for, 32
    of Microsoft Proxy Server, **170**
    for NAT system, 137–139, **146**
    negotiation process for, 53
    for network design, 311
    peer authentication methods, 53
    for private networks, 46
    Proxy Server for, 157–158
    for public networks, 46
    for RADIUS implementations, 250–251, **257–258**
    for remote access, 221–222, 229, 240, **257.** *See also* RADIUS.
    of remote users, 240, **257**
    of routers, 186–187
    with screened subnets, **303–304.**
        See also Screened subnets.
    of WINS system, 120
Security Access Manager. *See* SAM.
Security association. *See* SA.
Security risks, identifying, 311
Seed routers, 184
Selective Acknowledgment. *See* SACK.
Sender address, of frames, 44
Sequencing number, 44
Server authentication, 226
Server faults, detecting, 264
Servers
    applications on, 292
    caching-only, 95
    clustering, 296, **325, 333**
    combining services on, 288, **300**
    hardware resources of, 291–292

    monitoring performance of, 272
    number of, **300, 301, 304–305**
    number of, minimizing, 291, 292–293
    placement of, 309–310
    for screened subnet creation, 293–294
    types of, 93
    vulnerability to attack, 295
Service Advertising Protocol. *See* SAP.
Service combinations
    for increasing availability, 295–296
    for increasing performance, 295
    for increasing security, 293–295, **304–305**
Service interruptions, responding to, 264–265
Service Monitor, 269
Service records.
    See SRV (Service Location) records.
Service values, 265
Services
    availability of, 295–296, 311
    combinations of, 288
    monitoring status of, 267, **284**
    for network design, 312–313
    number of users needing, 290, 291
    performance of, 295
    placement on servers, 309–310
    remote configuration of, 277
    required for single sites, **299–300**
    resource usage, 291
    selecting, 312–316
    selecting, based on goals and infrastructure, 309, **327, 331, 342**
    selecting options for, 309
Session layer, 24–25, 44
    Internet connections at, 150
    and Windows 2000, **36**
Sessions
    management of, 44
    security negotiation process for, 53
SHA, 53
Shared directory, redundant copy of, **336**
Shared files. *See also* Dfs.
    centralized access to, 197
    combining, 196
    redundancy for, 196, **213**
Shared folders, 204
Shared secrets, 244, **259**
Short-form exams, 14
    test-taking strategy for, 16–17
Shutdown, lease release upon, 68

Simple Network Management Protocol.
See SNMP.
Site Server ILS system, 68
Slave servers, 93, **99**
Small networks
    NAT versus Proxy Server for, 153
    NetBIOS for, 106
    RIP use in, 180
Smart cards, for user authentication, 229
SNA packets, encapsulating, 225–226, **327**
SNA servers, 225–226
SNA Tunneling, 225–226, **327**
SNMP, 269, **283**
    installing, 269
    Windows 2000 support for, 277
SNMP agents, 277
SNMP traps, 269
SOA (Start of Authority) records, 91
Sockets, 24, 25, 139
    forming, 151
Socks clients, 164–165
Socks proxy, 154–155, 164–165
Software, Microsoft approval of, 292
Spoke-and-hub design, **126**
    for replication, **128**
    for WINS system, 112–114
SQL servers
    clustering, **325**
    placement of, **306**
    redundancy of, **333**
SRV (Service Location) records, 88, 91
Static routing, 177–178, **192**
Stub areas, 182
Subnet masks, 45
    calculating, 47–48, **58**
    variable length, 45
Subnets
    dividing, 45
    number of, **58**
    screened, 92–93, **100–101**
    WINS proxy agents on, 118
Subnetting, 313–314, **339**
    and service placement, 310
Supernetting, 45
Superscopes, 66
Swiss Conseil European pour la
    Recherche Nuclear (CERN), 164
System console, 271–273, **283–284**
    Add Counters window, 272
    adding performance counters to,
      272–273
    Performance Logs and Alerts object,
      273

System Monitor, 269, **283**
System Network Architecture Tunneling.
    See SNA Tunneling.

T

T1 connections, routing over, 185, **192**
TCP/IP, 313
    connection statistics on, 270
    history of, 42
    NetBIOS use, 26, **34**
    role of, 42
    routing, 181
    Sockets use, 25–26
    Windows 2000 requirement for, 29
    windows size, **62**
TCP/IP addresses, 45
    for private networks, 46
    for public networks, 46
    subnet masks of, 45
TCP/IP counters, 277
TCP/IP Filtering Properties window, 51
TCP/IP Security window, 52
TCP/IP stack, 42
    enhancements to, 49–50
TCP Selective Acknowledgment.
    See SACK.
TCP window size, 49
Telephone lines, network connection
    through, 31
Terminal Services, 296
Testing Innovations link, 13
Time to live (TTL), 155
Tombstoning, 119, 121, **127**
    manual, **127**
Trace logs, 274
Tracert, 270
Traffic Control, 55
Traffic filtering, 50–51
Traffic management, at network layer, 44
Transmission Control Protocol/Internet
    Protocol. *See* TCP/IP.
Transport layer, 44
Trend analysis, 278, 279
Triple DES (3DES), 53
Tunneling, 224–226, **234**

U

UDP, RADIUS use of, 241
UDP packets, 225
Unicasts, 179
Unix servers
    for DNS, as secondary servers, **78**
    NetBIOS use, 30

Upstream components, 161
URLs, port numbers in, 151
User accounts, storage of, 29
User authentication, 32, 226, **232**
    MSCHAP for, **255**
    between RADIUS and
        authenticating servers, 243, **255**
    smart cards for, 229
Users
    access to shared files, 204, **216**
    controlling Internet access of, 157–158
    DHCP options for, 67, **79**
    remote access for, 220–221

V

Variable length subnet mask. *See* VLSM.
VBScript, 277
Vendor-specific options
    DHCP configuration of, 67
    user-specific, 67
    vendor-specific, 67–68
Video, multicasting, **80**
Virtual Private Networks. *See* VPNs.
VLSM, 45
VPN security, on NAT, 139
VPN servers, multiple, 230
VPNs, 220–221, 223–226, 246
    authentication, 226
    clients, 223
    and clusters, 229
    components of, 223–224, **234**
    connection, 224
    economy of, **232**
    encapsulation, 224–226
    implementation of, 32, **35**
    Internet as, 31
    internetwork, 224
    IPSec use, **100, 193**
    multiple RRAS servers for, 229
    placement of, **303**
    and placement of RRAS servers,
        228–229
    protocols for. *See* L2TP; PPTP.
    between roaming users and
        RADIUS clients, 249, **257**
    between routers, 187, 224
    RRAS server availability issues, 229
    servers, 223
    smart cards use across, 229
    tunneled data, 224
    tunneling protocols, 224
    WINS over, 120

W

WAN connections
    NetBIOS performance over, 25
    proxy servers at, **168**
    public networks for, 120
WANs
    convergence time on, 116–117
    DHCP services for, 73
    proxy servers for, 161
    pull replication for, 115
    routing between, 176
    routing in, 184–185
    RRAS for, 228
    RRAS server availability issues, 229
    spoke-and-hub WINS design for,
        113–114
WBEM, 278
Web applications, using WinSock and
    Socks proxies to connect, 164–165, **169**
Web-Based Enterprise Management.
    See WBEM.
Web pages
    caching, 155
    dynamic content on, 156
    expiration dates for, 156
    secure pages, 156
Web proxies, 154, 165
Web publishing, in screened subnets, 163,
    170
Web servers
    public access to, 294
    in screened subnets, 163, **171, 304**
Web sites
    controlling access to, 158
    protecting with proxy servers,
        162–163, **303**
Windows 95, Dfs client software for, 200,
    213
Windows 98, RRAS options, 68
Windows 2000
    changes in, 24–28
    Dfs root on, 198, **212**
    NetBIOS support, 28
    service requirements, 28–31
Windows 2000 DNS Server
    BIND compliance, 86
    DNS implementations of, 85
Windows Clustering, 296
Windows Internet Naming Service.
    See WINS.
Windows Management Instrumentation.
    See WMI.

Windows NT
  browsing capabilities, **336**
  Dfs root on, 198, **212**
  SAM, 29
Windows NT DNS Server, 85
  BIND compliance, 86
Windows operating system
  dual network architecture, 26–28
  NetBIOS use, 25–26
  network architecture of, 24–25
Windows Script Host, 277
Windows Sockets. *See* WinSock.
WINS, 28, 30, **34**, **299–300**, 313, **325**, **342**
  addressed packets versus broadcasts, 107
  dynamic updating of DNS, 90
  functions of, 106
  name-resolution process, 109–110
  NetBIOS namespace limitations, 106
  over VPNs, 120
  RRAS with, 227
  in screened subnets, 120
  service provided by, registering, 108
  traffic types, 111–112
WINS clients
  configuration of, 117–118
  multiple primary and secondary
    servers for, 117–118
  name registration, 108
  support for non-WINS clients, 118
WINS database
  consistency checks of, 119
  dynamic updates by RRAS clients, 227
  extinction interval of records, 119
  extinction timeout of records, 119
  out-of-date records on, 118–119
  tombstoning of records, 119
WINS proxy agents, 118
WINS-R resource records, 91
WINS resource records, 91
WINS servers, 28
  automatic discovery capabilities, 115
  backup servers, 111
  comparing records among, 119
  decommissioning, 121

DHCP configuration of, 67
direct communication with clients, 30
hub server, **126**
IP addresses of, 108
network-wide records in local
  database of, 110
number of, 108–117, 111, **124–125**,
  330
at one location, 113
placement of, 108–117, 111, **125**,
  300, 310
push/pull relationships between, 115
replication between, 110, 112,
  114–117, **125–126**
in WANs, 113–114
WINS system
  fault tolerance for, **124**
  future needs for, 111
  network design, **124**
  network diagram of, 110
  performance optimization, 111,
    118–119
  removal from network, 121
  security for, 120
  spoke-and-hub design, 112–114, **126**
  stale records, removing, 118–119
WinSock, 25–26, **36**, 106
WinSock clients, 164–165
WinSock proxy, 154, 164–165, **169**
Wireless technologies, 43
WMI, 278, **284**

Z

Zone transfers, 86
  encrypting, 93, **100**
  increasing, 94–95
Zones, 86, 89–91, **100**
  changing types of, **101**
  delegation of, 94
  file-naming scheme, 89
  primary, 94–95
  resource records in, 90–91
  secondary, 94–95, **97–98**
  types of, 89–90

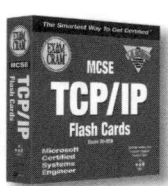

The Coriolis Exam Cram Personal Trainer
An exciting new category in certification training products

The Exam Cram Personal Trainer is the first certification-specific testing product that completely links learning with testing to:

- **Increase your comprehension**
- **Decrease the time it takes you to learn**

No system blends learning content with test questions as effectively as the Exam Cram Personal Trainer.

Only the Exam Cram Personal Trainer offers this much power at this price.

Its unique Personalized Practice Test Engine provides a real-time test environment and an authentic representation of what you will encounter during your actual certification exams.

Much More than Just Another CBT!
Most current CBT learning systems offer simple review questions at the end of a chapter with an overall test at the end of the course, with no links back to the lessons. But Exam Cram Personal Trainer takes learning to a higher level.

Its four main components are:
- The complete text of an Exam Cram study guide in HTML format
- A Personalized Practice Test Engine with multiple test methods
- A database of 150 questions linked directly to an Exam Cram chapter

Plus, additional features include:
- **Hint:** Not sure of your answer? Click Hint and the software goes to the text that covers that topic.
- **Lesson:** Still not enough detail? Click Lesson and the software goes to the beginning of the chapter.
- **Update feature:** Need even more questions? Click Update to download more questions from the Coriolis Web site.
- **Notes:** Create your own memory joggers.

- **Graphic analysis:** How did you do? View your score, the required score to pass, and other information.
- **Personalized Cram Sheet:** Print unique study information just for you.

**Windows 2000 Server
Exam Cram Personal Trainer**
ISBN: 1-57610-735-3

**Windows 2000 Professional
Exam Cram Personal Trainer**
ISBN: 1-57610-734-5

**Windows 2000 Directory Services
Exam Cram Personal Trainer**
ISBN: 1-57610-732-9

**Windows 2000 Security Design
Exam Cram Personal Trainer**
ISBN: 1-57610-772-8

**Windows 2000 Network
Exam Cram Personal Trainer**
ISBN: 1-57610-733-7

**Windows 2000 Migrating from NT4
Exam Cram Personal Trainer**
ISBN: 1-57610-773-6

A+ Exam Cram Personal Trainer
ISBN: 1-57610-658-6

**CCNA Routing and Switching
Exam Cram Personal Trainer**
ISBN: 1-57610-781-7

$99.99 U.S. • $149.99 Canada

Available: November 2000

CORIOLIS™
Certification Insider Press

**The <u>Smartest</u> Way to Get Certified
Just Got Smarter**™

Look for All of the Exam Cram Brand Certification Study Systems

ALL NEW! Exam Cram Personal Trainer Systems

The Exam Cram Personal Trainer systems are an exciting new category in certification training products. These CD-ROM based systems offer extensive capabilities at a moderate price and are the first certification-specific testing product to completely link learning with testing.

This Exam Cram study guide turned interactive course lets you customize the way you learn.

Each system includes:

- A Personalized Practice Test engine with multiple test methods
- A database of nearly 300 questions linked directly to the subject matter within the Exam Cram

Exam Cram Audio Review Systems

Written and read by certification instructors, each set contains four cassettes jam-packed with the certification exam information you must have. Designed to be used on their own or as a complement to our Exam Cram study guides, Flash Cards, and Practice Tests.

Each system includes:

- Study preparation tips with an essential last-minute review for the exam
- Hours of lessons highlighting key terms and techniques
- A comprehensive overview of all exam objectives
- 45 minutes of review questions, complete with answers and explanations

Exam Cram Flash Cards

These pocket-sized study tools are 100% focused on exams. Key questions appear on side one of each card and in-depth answers on side two. Each card features either a cross-reference to the appropriate Exam Cram study guide chapter or to another valuable resource. Comes with a CD-ROM featuring electronic versions of the flash cards and a complete practice exam.

Exam Cram Practice Tests

Our readers told us that extra practice exams were vital to certification success, so we created the perfect companion book for certification study material.

Each book contains:

- Several practice exams
- Electronic versions of practice exams on the accompanying CD-ROM presented in an interactive format, enabling practice in an environment similar to that of the actual exam
- Each practice question is followed by the corresponding answer (why the right answers are right and the wrong answers are wrong)
- References to the Exam Cram study guide chapter or other resource for that topic

CORIOLIS™

Certification Insider Press

The Smartest Way to Get Certified™

MCSE™
Windows® 2000
Professional

Dan Balter
Dan Holme
Todd Logan
Laurie Salmon

MCSE™ Windows® 2000 Professional Exam Cram

Limits of Liability and Disclaimer of Warranty

The author and publisher of this book have used their best efforts in preparing the book and the programs contained in it. These efforts include the development, research, and testing of the theories and programs to determine their effectiveness. The author and publisher make no warranty of any kind, expressed or implied, with regard to these programs or the documentation contained in this book.

The author and publisher shall not be liable in the event of incidental or consequential damages in connection with, or arising out of, the furnishing, performance, or use of the programs, associated instructions, and/or claims of productivity gains.

Trademarks

Trademarked names appear throughout this book. Rather than list the names and entities that own the trademarks or insert a trademark symbol with each mention of the trademarked name, the publisher states that it is using the names for editorial purposes only and to the benefit of the trademark owner, with no intention of infringing upon that trademark.

The Coriolis Group, LLC
14455 N. Hayden Road
Suite 220
Scottsdale, Arizona 85260

(480)483-0192
FAX (480)483-0193
www.coriolis.com

Library of Congress Cataloging-in-Publication Data
Holme, Dan [et al.]
    MCSE Windows 2000 professional exam cram: Microsoft certified systems engineer
        p. cm.
    Includes index.
    ISBN 1-57610-712-4
    1. Electronic data processing personnel--Certification. 2. Microsoft software--Examinations--Study guides. 3. Microsoft Windows (Computer file) I. Holme, Dan II. Series.
QA76.3.M3285 2000
005.4'4769--dc21

00-058960
CIP

President and CEO
Keith Weiskamp

Publisher
Steve Sayre

Acquisitions Editor
Shari Jo Hehr

Marketing Specialist
Brett Woolley

Project Editor
Greg Balas

Technical Reviewer
James Randall

Production Coordinator
Carla J. Schuder

Cover Designer
Jesse Dunn

Layout Designer
April Nielsen

Printed in the United States of America
10 9 8 7 6 5 4 3 2 1

The Coriolis Group, LLC • 14455 North Hayden Road, Suite 220 • Scottsdale, Arizona 85260

ExamCram.com Connects You to the Ultimate Study Center!

Our goal has always been to provide you with the best study tools on the planet to help you achieve your certification in record time. Time is so valuable these days that none of us can afford to waste a second of it, especially when it comes to exam preparation.

Over the past few years, we've created an extensive line of *Exam Cram* and *Exam Prep* study guides, practice exams, and interactive training. To help you study even better, we have now created an e-learning and certification destination called **ExamCram.com**. (You can access the site at **www.examcram.com**.) Now, with every study product you purchase from us, you'll be connected to a large community of people like yourself who are actively studying for their certifications, developing their careers, seeking advice, and sharing their insights and stories.

I believe that the future is all about collaborative learning. Our **ExamCram.com** destination is our approach to creating a highly interactive, easily accessible collaborative environment, where you can take practice exams and discuss your experiences with others, sign up for features like "Questions of the Day," plan your certifications using our interactive planners, create your own personal study pages, and keep up with all of the latest study tips and techniques.

I hope that whatever study products you purchase from us—*Exam Cram* or *Exam Prep* study guides, *Personal Trainers*, *Personal Test Centers*, or one of our interactive Web courses—will make your studying fun and productive. Our commitment is to build the kind of learning tools that will allow you to study the way you want to, whenever you want to.

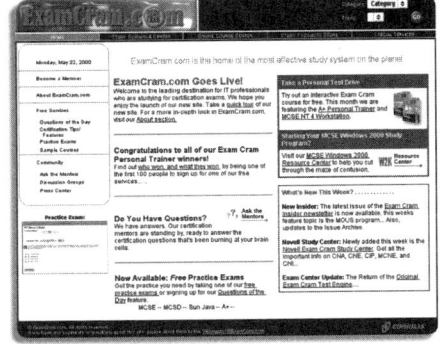

Visit ExamCram.com now to enhance your study program.

Help us continue to provide the very best certification study materials possible. Write us or email us at **learn@examcram.com** and let us know how our study products have helped you study. Tell us about new features that you'd like us to add. Send us a story about how we've helped you. We're listening!

Good luck with your certification exam and your career. Thank you for allowing us to help you achieve your goals.

Keith Weiskamp

Keith Weiskamp
President and CEO

Look for these other products from The Coriolis Group:

MCSE Windows 2000 Accelerated Exam Prep
By Lance Cockcroft, Erik Eckel, and Ron Kauffman

MCSE Windows 2000 Server Exam Prep
By David Johnson and Dawn Rader

MCSE Windows 2000 Professional Exam Prep
By Michael D. Stewart, James Bloomingdale, and Neall Alcott

MCSE Windows 2000 Network Exam Prep
By Tammy Smith and Sandra Smeeton

MCSE Windows 2000 Directory Services Exam Prep
By David V. Watts, Will Willis, and Tillman Strahan

MCSE Windows 2000 Security Design Exam Prep
By Richard Alan McMahon and Glen Bicking

MCSE Windows 2000 Network Design Exam Prep
By Geoffrey Alexander, Anoop Jalan, and Joseph Alexander

MCSE Migrating from NT 4 to Windows 2000 Exam Prep
By Glen Bergen, Graham Leach, and David Baldwin

MCSE Windows 2000 Directory Services Design Exam Prep
By J. Peter Bruzzese and Wayne Dipchan

MCSE Windows 2000 Core Four Exam Prep Pack

MCSE Windows 2000 Server Exam Cram
By Natasha Knight

MCSE Windows 2000 Network Exam Cram
By Hank Carbeck, Derek Melber, and Richard Taylor

MCSE Windows 2000 Directory Services Exam Cram
By Will Willis, David V. Watts, and J. Peter Bruzzese

MCSE Windows 2000 Security Design Exam Cram
By Phillip G. Schein

MCSE Windows 2000 Network Design Exam Cram
By Kim Simmons, Jarret W. Buse, and Todd B. Halpin

MCSE Windows 2000 Directory Services Design Exam Cram
By Dennis Scheil and Diana Bartley

MCSE Windows 2000 Core Four Exam Cram Pack

and...
MCSE Windows 2000 Foundations
By James Michael Stewart and Lee Scales

About the Authors

Dan Balter is a senior partner of *Marina Consulting Group LLC*, a Microsoft Certified Solution Provider firm located in Westlake Village, California. Dan works as an independent consultant and trainer for both corporate and government clients specializing in integrating messaging and scheduling software to improve organizational productivity. MCG provides consulting services, training, and custom application development.

A graduate of U.S.C.'s School of Business in 1983, Dan has authored more than 250 computer training courses on video and CD-ROM for KeyStone Learning Systems Corporation. Throughout his 15-year career, Dan has worked with numerous network operating systems, and achieved a long list of credentials and certifications. He regularly speaks at computer conferences throughout North America on Windows NT, Windows 2000, and other Microsoft BackOffice solutions. In addition, he is a contributing author for three books on the Windows NT 4 network operating system. Dan Balter can be reached at **dan@pcvideos.com**.

Dan Holme is President and CEO of *trainAbility*, a global, integrated IT training company based in Scottsdale, Arizona. The company's independent, solutions-focused curricula, and proprietary technologies allow it to deliver extremely customized solutions that bridge the gap between consulting and training. Dan spearheads the company's efforts to provide advanced, intensive ConsulTraining that meets 21st century clients' needs for cost- and time-efficient knowledge transfer.

Dan comes armed with a Bachelor's degree from Yale, a Master of International Management from Thunderbird, and 12 years of international training, public speaking, and management experience. If he's not buried in work or catching some big air on his snowboard, Dan can be reached at **dan.holme@trainability.com**.

Todd Logan has been training people how to actually use computers instead of throwing them out the window in frustration since 1992, back when the new thing was called "e-mail." Todd's wife took him away from his consulting business and the constant rain of Vancouver, British Columbia to sunny Phoenix, Arizona where he has been a technical trainer for ExecuTrain, Mastering Computers, and now works as a ConsulTrainer at *trainAbility*, where he is known for his penchant for ferreting out extraordinary solutions for clients the likes of Compaq, Hewlett-Packard, Sprint, and Microsoft. In between his never-ending quest for the truth of Windows and the pursuit of the ultimate tofu cookbook, you can reach Todd at **todd.logan@trainability.com**.

Laurie Salmon is a full-time technical consultant with *trainAbility* in Scottsdale, Arizona. Laurie has built a stellar eight-year track record in the computer business providing technical training and consulting services on Windows NT, Microsoft Back Office, Internet Information Server, and Windows 2000. Microsoft asked Laurie to be a keynote speaker for the Windows 95 Launch series touring Texas in April of 1995. Courseware for Windows 95/98, NT, and Windows 2000 that Laurie has written or co-authored is in use at many companies around the world. Laurie has been an MCT and MCSE since 1994, and has taught fast-paced and entertaining technical workshops all over the U.S. Laurie can be reached at **laurie.salmon@trainability.com**.

Acknowledgments

Writing a book is never an easy task; writing a technical book for certification on a new software product is especially daunting and challenging. First of all, I want to express my gratitude to my awe-inspiring wife of more than ten years now, Alison Balter, for teaching me how to really be an effective trainer and author. I also appreciate her putting up with me during the time that I was writing the chapters for this book. I love you, honey—happy tenth anniversary! I also want to acknowledge my two darling kids—Alexis and Brendan, ages 4 and 1 respectively, for just being so loving and fun to be around. Thanks for being so understanding of mom and dad's long hours—I love you both very, very much!

An incredible amount of appreciation also goes to Sonia Aguilar, her husband, Hugo and their children Claudia, Gabby, and little Hugo. Thank you for your incessant love, support, and unparalleled care for our children when we're attending to business matters. Sonia, you're the best.

A big tip of the hat goes to Dan Holme of trainAbility, Inc. (**www.trainability.com**), the finest team leader in the universe and one of the smartest men in the world (at least in my opinion). Congratulations on pulling all of us together and really making this project happen! Thanks for including me in this book and for hanging in there with me when deadlines were looming imminently overhead!

Huge thanks also go out to Greggory Peck and Clint Argyle of KeyStone Learning Systems (**www.keystonetraining.com**). Thank you both for giving me the opportunity to become a trainer using video-based and CD-ROM-based technology. Jeremy Moskowitz and Alan Sugano are also always there whenever I have a burning question—thank you both. Finally, to Charlotte and Bob Roman (my in-laws)—thank you both for everything that you do for us, all the time! To my Mom and Dad—thanks for emphasizing reading and writing, among other things. These skills sure come in handy for the IT industry!

—*Dan Balter*

It was a thrill indeed to contribute to the continued success of the *Exam Cram* series and my thanks go to the whole team at The Coriolis Group, especially Keith Weiskamp, Shari Jo Hehr, Greg Balas, and Carla Schuder for their cooperation, support, and vision. I would also like to thank Bonnie Trenga and Jim

Randall for copyediting and tech reviewing the text. Also, thanks to Andea Stonelook and Jack Lutgen for proofreading, and Christine Karpeles for indexing.

The excellence required was more than met by my stellar colleagues on this project: Dan Balter, thank you, thank you! Todd and Laurie, I cannot begin to express how proud I am to count you as peers and friends at trainAbility—your professionalism, talent, and gusto are indeed the best in the training business! I hope that all of you reading these acknowledgments someday are honored by an opportunity to work with the likes of these folks, Hank, Thom, and the entire extraordinary trainAbility team.

None of *my* work would be possible without the decades of support from my family. Mom, Dad, Bob, Joni, I love you with all my heart and I promise I will *try* to sleep when this page is submitted! Finally, to my beautiful Einstein, for bringing me lunch when I wouldn't have eaten and making the world a fabulous place to return to when the Shut Down command is finally clicked…thank you.

—*Dan Holme*

I would like to thank my coauthor Dan Holme for bringing me on board to help write this book. Dan, you are an inspiration to everyone at trainAbility and a true leader! A thanks also goes to Hank Carbeck for putting up with me while I have been working on this book. Hank, you've been a true friend to my family and me! I would also like to thank my co-authors Dan Balter and Laurie Salmon for their invaluable contributions to this book.

A special thanks goes to my wife Gladys and my son Seth for giving me the time and space to work on this book. I would not have been able to finish this project without your constant love and support. For this I thank you from the bottom of my heart, and I promise we will go on vacation soon!

—*Todd Logan*

Thanks to my loving husband, Scot, who patiently listens to my rants without laughing—I love you, and you are my rock. Chloe, Sasha, and Maggie would pursue certification if they had opposable thumbs—but I love them anyway! I would like to thank my family and friends for their unconditional, unwavering support. Dan—thanks for your constant support and for including me in this project! Hank—thanks for the flowers and for always making me smile! Cindy, Leslie, Gwen, Melany, and Holly—thanks for motivating and inspiring me, and keeping me on track!

—*Laurie Salmon*

Contents at a Glance

Chapter 1   Microsoft Certification Exams   1

Chapter 2   Implementing and
Administering Resources   23

Chapter 3   Implementing, Monitoring, and Troubleshooting
Security Accounts and Policies   75

Chapter 4   Configuring and Troubleshooting the
User Experience   101

Chapter 5   Configuring and Troubleshooting System
Services and Desktop Environment   125

Chapter 6   Installing Windows 2000 Professional   145

Chapter 7   Implementing, Managing, and Troubleshooting
Hardware Devices and Drivers   169

Chapter 8   Implementing, Managing, and Troubleshooting
Disk Drives and Volumes   203

Chapter 9   Implementing, Managing, and Troubleshooting
Network Protocols and Services   233

Chapter 10   Monitoring and Optimizing
Performance Reliability   263

Chapter 11   Sample Test   293

Chapter 12   Answer Key   315

Table of Contents

Introduction xix

Self-Assessment xxxi

Chapter 1
Microsoft Certification Exams 1
Assessing Exam-Readiness   2

The Exam Situation   3

Exam Layout and Design   4

    Multiple-Choice Question Formats   5

    Build-List-and-Reorder Question Format   6

    Create-a-Tree Question Format   8

    Drag-and-Connect Question Format   10

    Select-and-Place Question Format   11

Microsoft's Testing Formats   13

Strategies for Different Testing Formats   14

    The Case Study Exam Strategy   15

    The Fixed-Length and Short-Form Exam Strategy   16

    The Adaptive Exam Strategy   17

Question-Handling Strategies   18

Mastering the Inner Game   19

Additional Resources   20

Chapter 2
Implementing and Administering Resources 23
Managing Access to Shared Folders   24

    Connecting to Shared Resources on a Windows Network   25

    Using Automatically Generated Hidden Shares   26

    Controlling Access to Shared Folders   27

Monitoring, Managing, and Troubleshooting Access
to Shared Files and Folders Under NTFS   29

    NTFS Security: Users and Groups   30

Monitoring, Managing, and Troubleshooting Access
to Files and Folders   42

Configuring, Managing, and Troubleshooting NTFS
File and Folder Compression   42

Controlling Access to Files and Folders by Using Permissions   46

Optimizing Access to Files and Folders   48

Auditing System Access   50

Keeping Data Private with Encrypting File System (EFS)   53

Managing and Troubleshooting Web Server Resources   56

SystemRoot Console Administering the Default
Web and FTP Sites   58

Troubleshooting IIS   58

Managing Local and Network Print Devices   59

Connecting to Local and Network Printers   60

Configuring Printer Properties   63

Managing Printers and Print Jobs   65

Using Internet Printing Protocol (IPP)   66

Practice Questions   67

Need to Know More?   73

Chapter 3
Implementing, Monitoring, and Troubleshooting
Security Accounts and Policies 75

User and Group Accounts   76

Local and Domain Accounts   76

Managing Local User and Group Accounts   77

Managing Domain User Accounts   83

Authentication   85

Understanding Active Directory   86

Understanding and Implementing Policy   89

Local Policy   89

Group Policy   92

Practice Questions   95

Need to Know More?   100

Chapter 4
Configuring and Troubleshooting the User Experience 101

Configuring and Managing User Profiles   102

User Profiles   102

Roaming User Profiles   103

Using Offline Files and Folders   104
  Setting Up Offline Files and Folders   105
  Making Files and Folders Available Offline   106
  Synchronizing Offline Files and Folders   107
  Accessing Offline Files and Folders   108
  Managing Offline Files and Folders   108
Configuring and Troubleshooting
  Desktop Settings   109
  Keyboard Applet   109
  Display Applet   109
  Mouse Applet   110
  Sound Applet   110
  Personalized Start Menu   110
  Quick Launch Pad   111
  Toolbars   111
Windows Installer Service Packages   112
  Installing Packages   113
  Publishing MSI Packages   114
Practice Questions   117
Need to Know More?   124

Chapter 5
Configuring and Troubleshooting System Services
and Desktop Environment **125**
Multiple Location and Language Support   126
  Language Options   126
  Locales   126
  Multilanguage Support   128
  Multilanguage Version of Windows 2000   128
Accessibility Options   129
  Accessibility Options Applet   129
  Accessibility Wizard   131
  Additional Accessibility Features   132
Fax Features   132
  Configuring the Fax Service   132
  Managing the Fax Service Management Console   133
Task Scheduler   134
  Creating a Task   135

Practice Questions 137
Need to Know More? 144

Chapter 6
Installing Windows 2000 Professional..**145**
Performing Attended Installations of Windows 2000 Professional 146
Installation Methods 146
Automating the Installation of Windows 2000 Professional 147
Using Setup Manager to Create an Unattended Installation 148
Using the System Preparation Tool 151
Using Remote Installation Services (RIS) 153
Upgrading to Windows 2000 Professional 157
Pre-Upgrade Checklist 158
Deploying Service Packs (SPs) 159
Slipstreaming SPs 159
Applying SPs after Installing Windows 2000 159
Troubleshooting Failed Installations 159
Practice Questions 161
Need to Know More? 167

Chapter 7
Implementing, Managing, and Troubleshooting
Hardware Devices and Drivers..**169**
Implementing, Managing, and Troubleshooting Hardware 170
Installing, Configuring, and Managing Hardware 170
Driver Updates 172
Updating Individual Drivers 172
Updating Your System Files Using Windows Update 172
Managing and Troubleshooting Device Conflicts 173
Managing and Troubleshooting Driver Signing 173
Managing and Troubleshooting I/O Devices 174
Using Printers 175
Using Keyboards and Mice 176
Using Smart Cards and Smart Card Readers 176
Mobile User 177
Using Cameras and Other Multimedia Hardware 178
Using Modems 179
Supporting Faxes 181

Using Infrared Data Association (IrDA) Devices
and Wireless Devices   181

Using Network Adapters   184

Internet Connection Sharing (ICS)   184

Managing and Troubleshooting
Display Devices   186

Display Settings   186

Configuring Multiple-Display Support   186

Installing, Configuring, and Supporting
a Video Adapter   189

Mobile Computer Hardware   189

Managing Hardware Profiles   189

APM   190

ACPI   190

Managing Battery Power on a Portable Computer   192

Using a Portable Computer on an Airplane   192

Managing Power When Installing a Plug and
Play Device   192

Monitoring and Configuring
Multiple Processors   193

Installing Support for Multiple CPUs   193

Practice Questions   195

Need to Know More?   202

Chapter 8
Implementing, Managing, and Troubleshooting
Disk Drives and Volumes 203

Hard Disk Management   204

Basic Disks   204

Dynamic Disks   204

Comparing Basic Disks to Dynamic Disks   205

Upgrading Disks   206

Moving Disks to Another Computer   207

Reactivating a Missing or Offline Disk   208

Basic Volumes   208

Spanned Volumes on Basic Disks   208

Striped Volumes on Basic Disks   208

Partitions and Logical Drives on Basic Disks   209

Dynamic Volumes   210
   Simple Volumes   210
   Spanned Volumes   210
   Striped Volumes   212
   RAID-5 Volumes   212
   Limitations of Dynamic Disks and Dynamic Volumes   212
Troubleshooting Disks and Volumes   213
   Diagnosing Problems   213
   Monitoring Disk Performance   213
   Detecting and Repairing Disk Errors   214
   Using Disk Defragmenter   215
   Understanding Why Files Are Not Moved to the
     Beginning of NTFS Volumes   215
   Using the Disk Cleanup Wizard   216
File Systems Supported in Windows 2000   216
   FAT and FAT32   216
   The New Flavor of NTFS: Windows 2000's NTFS 5
     File System   216
   Converting from One File System to Another   217
Assigning, Changing, or Removing a Drive Letter   218
Mounted Drives   219
   Creating a Mounted Drive   219
The Logical Drives Tool   220
   Viewing Drive Properties, Changing Drive Labels,
     and Changing Security Settings   220
Disk Quotas   220
NTFS Compression   221
   Moving and Copying Compressed Files and Folders   221
Managing Tape Devices   222
Configuring and Managing DVD Devices   222
Practice Questions   224
Need to Know More?   232

**Chapter 9
Implementing, Managing, and Troubleshooting
Network Protocols and Services 233**
Configuring and Troubleshooting Transmission Control
   Protocol/Internet Protocol (TCP/IP)   234
   Deciphering the TCP/IP Protocol Suite for Windows 2000   234

Understanding TCP/IP Computer Addresses:
It's All about Numbers   237

Configuring TCP/IP   238

Troubleshooting TCP/IP   239

Connecting to Remote Computers Using Dial-up Connections   242

New Authentication Protocols   242

Connecting to Remote Access Servers   245

Setting up and Configuring VPN Connections   248

Connecting to the Internet Using Dial-up Connections   249

Configuring and Troubleshooting ICS   250

Practice Questions   254

Need to Know More?   262

Chapter 10
Monitoring and Optimizing Performance Reliability 263

Backing Up and Restoring Data   264

Using Windows Backup   264

Permissions and Rights   264

Backup Types   265

Configuring File and Folder Backup   266

Backing up the System State   267

Scheduling Backup Jobs   267

Restoring Files and Folders   268

Troubleshooting and Repairing a Windows 2000 System   268

Safe Mode and Other Advanced Startup Options   268

Specifying Windows 2000 Behavior if the System
Stops Unexpectedly   270

The Recovery Console   271

Emergency Repair Disks (ERDs) and the Emergency
Repair Process   274

Optimizing and Troubleshooting Performance   276

System Monitor   276

Performance Logs And Alerts   277

Managing Performance   278

Task Manager   284

Practice Questions   285

Need to Know More?   292

Chapter 11
Sample Test 293

Chapter 12
Answer Key 315

Glossary 327

Index 351

Introduction

Welcome to *MCSE Windows 2000 Professional Exam Cram*! Whether this is your first or your fifteenth *Exam Cram* book, you'll find information here and in Chapter 1 that will help ensure your success as you pursue knowledge, experience, and certification. This book aims to help you get ready to take—and pass—the Microsoft certification Exam 70-210, titled "Installing, Configuring and Administering Microsoft Windows 2000 Professional." This Introduction explains Microsoft's certification programs in general and talks about how the *Exam Cram* series can help you prepare for Microsoft's Windows 2000 certification exams.

Exam Cram books help you understand and appreciate the subjects and materials you need to pass Microsoft certification exams. *Exam Cram* books are aimed strictly at test preparation and review. They do not teach you everything you need to know about a topic. Instead, we (the authors) present and dissect the questions and problems we've found that you're likely to encounter on a test. We've worked to bring together as much information as possible about Microsoft certification exams.

Nevertheless, to completely prepare yourself for any Microsoft test, we recommend that you begin by taking the Self-Assessment included in this book immediately following this Introduction. This tool will help you evaluate your knowledge base against the requirements for an MCSE under both ideal and real circumstances.

Based on what you learn from that exercise, you might decide to begin your studies with some classroom training or some background reading. On the other hand, you might decide to pick up and read one of the many study guides available from Microsoft or third-party vendors on certain topics, including The Coriolis Group's *Exam Prep* series. We also recommend that you supplement your study program with visits to **ExamCram.com** to receive additional practice questions, get advice, and track the Windows 2000 MCSE program.

We also strongly recommend that you install, configure, and fool around with the software that you'll be tested on, because nothing beats hands-on experience and familiarity when it comes to understanding the questions you're likely to encounter on a certification test. Book learning is essential, but hands-on experience is the best teacher of all!

The Microsoft Certified Professional (MCP) Program

The MCP Program currently includes the following separate tracks, each of which boasts its own special acronym (as a certification candidate, you need to have a high tolerance for alphabet soup of all kinds):

➤ *MCP (Microsoft Certified Professional)*—This is the least prestigious of all the certification tracks from Microsoft. Passing one of the major Microsoft exams qualifies an individual for the MCP credential. Individuals can demonstrate proficiency with additional Microsoft products by passing additional certification exams.

➤ *MCP+SB (Microsoft Certified Professional + Site Building)*—This certification program is designed for individuals who are planning, building, managing, and maintaining Web sites. Individuals with the MCP+SB credential will have demonstrated the ability to develop Web sites that include multimedia and searchable content and Web sites that connect to and communicate with a back-end database. It requires one MCP exam, plus two of these three exams: "70-055: Designing and Implementing Web Sites with Microsoft FrontPage 98," "70-057: Designing and Implementing Commerce Solutions with Microsoft Site Server 3.0, Commerce Edition," and "70-152: Designing and Implementing Web Solutions with Microsoft Visual InterDev 6.0."

➤ *MCSE (Microsoft Certified Systems Engineer)*—Anyone who has a current MCSE is warranted to possess a high level of networking expertise with Microsoft operating systems and products. This credential is designed to prepare individuals to plan, implement, maintain, and support information systems, networks, and internetworks built around Microsoft Windows 2000 and its BackOffice Server 2000 family of products.

To obtain an MCSE, an individual must pass four core operating system exams, one optional core exam, and two elective exams. The operating system exams require individuals to prove their competence with desktop and server operating systems and networking/internetworking components.

For Windows NT 4 MCSEs, the Accelerated exam, "70-240: Microsoft Windows 2000 Accelerated Exam for MCPs Certified on Microsoft Windows NT 4.0," is an option. This free exam covers all of the material tested in the Core Four exams. The hitch in this plan is that you can take the test only once. If you fail, you must take all four core exams to recertify. The Core Four exams are: "70-210: Installing, Configuring and Administering Microsoft Windows 2000 Professional," "70-215: Installing, Configuring and Administering Microsoft Windows 2000 Server," "70-216: Implementing and Administering a Microsoft

Windows 2000 Network Infrastructure," and "70-217: Implementing and Administering a Microsoft Windows 2000 Directory Services Infrastructure."

To fulfill the fifth core exam requirement, you can choose from three design exams: "70-219: Designing a Microsoft Windows 2000 Directory Services Infrastructure," "70-220: Designing Security for a Microsoft Windows 2000 Network," or "70-221: Designing a Microsoft Windows 2000 Network Infrastructure." You are also required to take two elective exams. An elective exam can fall in any number of subject or product areas, primarily BackOffice Server 2000 components. The two design exams that you don't select as your fifth core exam also qualify as electives. If you are on your way to becoming an MCSE and have already taken some exams, visit **www.microsoft.com/ trainingandservices/** for information about how to complete your MCSE certification.

In September 1999, Microsoft announced its Windows 2000 track for MCSE and also announced retirement of Windows NT 4.0 MCSE core exams on 12/31/2000. Individuals who wish to remain certified MCSEs after 12/31/2001 must "upgrade" their certifications on or before 12/31/2001. For more detailed information than is included here, visit **www.microsoft.com/ trainingandservices/**.

New MCSE candidates must pass seven tests to meet the MCSE requirements. It's not uncommon for the entire process to take a year or so, and many individuals find that they must take a test more than once to pass. The primary goal of the *Exam Prep* series and the *Exam Cram* series, our test preparation books, is to make it possible, given proper study and preparation, to pass all Microsoft certification tests on the first try. Table 1 shows the required and elective exams for the Windows 2000 MCSE certification.

➤ *MCSD (Microsoft Certified Solution Developer)*—The MCSD credential reflects the skills required to create multitier, distributed, and COM-based solutions, in addition to desktop and Internet applications, using new technologies. To obtain an MCSD, an individual must demonstrate the ability to analyze and interpret user requirements; select and integrate products, platforms, tools, and technologies; design and implement code, and customize applications; and perform necessary software tests and quality assurance operations.

To become an MCSD, you must pass a total of four exams: three core exams and one elective exam. Each candidate must choose one of these three desktop application exams—"70-016: Designing and Implementing Desktop Applications with Microsoft Visual C++ 6.0," "70-156: Designing and Implementing Desktop Applications with Microsoft Visual FoxPro 6.0," or "70-176: Designing and Implementing Desktop Applications with Microsoft

Table 1   MCSE Windows 2000 Requirements

Core

If you have not passed these 3 Windows NT 4 exams	
Exam 70-067	Implementing and Supporting Microsoft Windows NT Server 4.0
Exam 70-068	Implementing and Supporting Microsoft Windows NT Server 4.0 in the Enterprise
Exam 70-073	Microsoft Windows NT Workstation 4.0
then you must take these 4 exams	
Exam 70-210	Installing, Configuring and Administering Microsoft Windows 2000 Professional
Exam 70-215	Installing, Configuring and Administering Microsoft Windows 2000 Server
Exam 70-216	Implementing and Administering a Microsoft Windows 2000 Network Infrastructure
Exam 70-217	Implementing and Administering a Microsoft Windows 2000 Directory Services Infrastructure
If you have already passed exams 70-067, 70-068, and 70-073, you may take this exam	
Exam 70-240	Microsoft Windows 2000 Accelerated Exam for MCPs Certified on Microsoft Windows NT 4.0

5th Core Option

Choose 1 from this group	
Exam 70-219*	Designing a Microsoft Windows 2000 Directory Services Infrastructure
Exam 70-220*	Designing Security for a Microsoft Windows 2000 Network
Exam 70-221*	Designing a Microsoft Windows 2000 Network Infrastructure

Elective

Choose 2 from this group	
Exam 70-019	Designing and Implementing Data Warehouse with Microsoft SQL Server 7.0
Exam 70-219*	Designing a Microsoft Windows 2000 Directory Services Infrastructure
Exam 70-220*	Designing Security for a Microsoft Windows 2000 Network
Exam 70-221*	Designing a Microsoft Windows 2000 Network Infrastructure
Exam 70-222	Migrating from Microsoft Windows NT 4.0 to Microsoft Windows 2000
Exam 70-028	Administering Microsoft SQL Server 7.0
Exam 70-029	Designing and Implementing Databases on Microsoft SQL Server 7.0
Exam 70-080	Implementing and Supporting Microsoft Internet Explorer 5.0 by Using the Internet Explorer Administration Kit
Exam 70-081	Implementing and Supporting Microsoft Exchange Server 5.5
Exam 70-085	Implementing and Supporting Microsoft SNA Server 4.0
Exam 70-086	Implementing and Supporting Microsoft Systems Management Server 2.0
Exam 70-088	Implementing and Supporting Microsoft Proxy Server 2.0

This is not a complete listing—you can still be tested on some earlier versions of these products. However, we have included mainly the most recent versions so that you may test on these versions and thus be certified longer. We have not included any tests that are scheduled to be retired.

* The 5th Core Option exam does not double as an elective.

Visual Basic 6.0"—*plus* one of these three distributed application exams—
"70-015: Designing and Implementing Distributed Applications with
Microsoft Visual C++ 6.0," "70-155: Designing and Implementing Distributed Applications with Microsoft Visual FoxPro 6.0," or "70-175: Designing
and Implementing Distributed Applications with Microsoft Visual Basic 6.0."
The third core exam is "70-100: Analyzing Requirements and Defining Solution Architectures." Elective exams cover specific Microsoft applications
and languages, including Visual Basic, C++, the Microsoft Foundation Classes,
Access, SQL Server, Excel, and more.

➤ *MCDBA (Microsoft Certified Database Administrator)*—The MCDBA credential reflects the skills required to implement and administer Microsoft
SQL Server databases. To obtain an MCDBA, an individual must demonstrate the ability to derive physical database designs, develop logical data
models, create physical databases, create data services by using Transact-SQL,
manage and maintain databases, configure and manage security, monitor and
optimize databases, and install and configure Microsoft SQL Server.

To become an MCDBA, you must pass a total of three core exams and one
elective exam. The required core exams are "70-028: Administering Microsoft
SQL Server 7.0," "70-029: Designing and Implementing Databases with
Microsoft SQL Server 7.0," and "70-215: Installing, Configuring and Administering Microsoft Windows 2000 Server."

The elective exams that you can choose from cover specific uses of SQL
Server and include "70-015: Designing and Implementing Distributed Applications with Microsoft Visual C++ 6.0," "70-019: Designing and Implementing Data Warehouses with Microsoft SQL Server 7.0," "70-155: Designing
and Implementing Distributed Applications with Microsoft Visual FoxPro
6.0," "70-175: Designing and Implementing Distributed Applications with
Microsoft Visual Basic 6.0," and two exams that relate to Windows 2000:
"70-216: Implementing and Administering a Microsoft Windows 2000 Network Infrastructure," and "70-087: Implementing and Supporting Microsoft
Internet Information Server 4.0."

If you have taken the three core Windows NT 4 exams on your path to
becoming an MCSE, you qualify for the Accelerated exam (it replaces the
Network Infrastructure exam requirement). The Accelerated exam covers
the objectives of all four of the Windows 2000 core exams. In addition to
taking the Accelerated exam, you must take only the two SQL exams—
Administering and Database Design.

➤ *MCT (Microsoft Certified Trainer)*—Microsoft Certified Trainers are deemed able to deliver elements of the official Microsoft curriculum, based on technical knowledge and instructional ability. Thus, it is necessary for an individual seeking MCT credentials (which are granted on a course-by-course basis) to pass the related certification exam for a course and complete the official Microsoft training in the subject area, and to demonstrate an ability to teach.

This teaching skill criterion may be satisfied by proving that one has already attained training certification from Novell, Banyan, Lotus, the Santa Cruz Operation, or Cisco, or by taking a Microsoft-sanctioned workshop on instruction. Microsoft makes it clear that MCTs are important cogs in the Microsoft training channels. Instructors must be MCTs before Microsoft will allow them to teach in any of its official training channels, including Microsoft's affiliated Certified Technical Education Centers (CTECs) and its online training partner network. As of January 1, 2001, MCT candidates must also possess a current MCSE.

Microsoft has announced that the MCP+I and MCSE+I credentials will not be continued when the MCSE exams for Windows 2000 are in full swing because the skill set for the Internet portion of the program has been included in the new MCSE program. Therefore, details on these tracks are not provided here; go to **www.microsoft.com/trainingandservices/** if you need more information.

Once a Microsoft product becomes obsolete, MCPs typically have to recertify on current versions. (If individuals do not recertify, their certifications become invalid.) Because technology keeps changing and new products continually supplant old ones, this should come as no surprise. This explains why Microsoft has announced that MCSEs have 12 months past the scheduled retirement date for the Windows NT 4 exams to recertify on Windows 2000 topics. (Note that this means taking at least two exams, if not more.)

The best place to keep tabs on the MCP program and its related certifications is on the Web. The URL for the MCP program is **www.microsoft.com/trainingandservices/**. But Microsoft's Web site changes often, so if this URL doesn't work, try using the Search tool on Microsoft's site with either "MCP" or the quoted phrase "Microsoft Certified Professional" as a search string. This will help you find the latest and most accurate information about Microsoft's certification programs.

Taking a Certification Exam

Once you've prepared for your exam, you need to register with a testing center. Each computer-based MCP exam costs $100, and if you don't pass, you may retest for an additional $100 for each additional try. In the United States and

Canada, tests are administered by Prometric and by Virtual University Enterprises (VUE). Here's how you can contact them:

➤ *Prometric*—You can sign up for a test through the company's Web site at **www.prometric.com**. Or, you can register by phone at 800-755-3926 (within the United States or Canada) or at 410-843-8000 (outside the United States and Canada).

➤ *Virtual University Enterprises*—You can sign up for a test or get the phone numbers for local testing centers through the Web page at **www.vue.com/ms/**.

To sign up for a test, you must possess a valid credit card, or contact either company for mailing instructions to send them a check (in the U.S.). Only when payment is verified, or a check has cleared, can you actually register for a test.

To schedule an exam, call the number or visit either of the Web pages at least one day in advance. To cancel or reschedule an exam, you must call before 7 P.M. pacific standard time the day before the scheduled test time (or you may be charged, even if you don't appear to take the test). When you want to schedule a test, have the following information ready:

➤ Your name, organization, and mailing address.

➤ Your Microsoft Test ID. (Inside the United States, this means your Social Security number; citizens of other nations should call ahead to find out what type of identification number is required to register for a test.)

➤ The name and number of the exam you wish to take.

➤ A method of payment. (As we've already mentioned, a credit card is the most convenient method, but alternate means can be arranged in advance, if necessary.)

Once you sign up for a test, you'll be informed as to when and where the test is scheduled. Try to arrive at least 15 minutes early. You must supply two forms of identification—one of which must be a photo ID—to be admitted into the testing room.

All exams are completely closed-book. In fact, you will not be permitted to take anything with you into the testing area, but you will be furnished with a blank sheet of paper and a pen or, in some cases, an erasable plastic sheet and an erasable pen. We suggest that you immediately write down on that sheet of paper all the information you've memorized for the test. In *Exam Cram* books, this information appears on a tear-out sheet inside the front cover of each book. You will have some time to compose yourself and to record this information.

When you complete a Microsoft certification exam, the software will tell you whether you've passed or failed.

If you need to retake an exam, you'll have to schedule a new test with Prometric or VUE and pay another $100.

 The first time you fail a test, you can retake the test the next day. However, if you fail a second time, you must wait 14 days before retaking that test. The 14-day waiting period remains in effect for all retakes after the second failure.

Tracking MCP Status

As soon as you pass any Microsoft exam (except Networking Essentials), you'll attain Microsoft Certified Professional (MCP) status. Microsoft also generates transcripts that indicate which exams you have passed. You can view a copy of your transcript at any time by going to the MCP secured site and selecting Transcript Tool. This tool will allow you to print a copy of your current transcript and confirm your certification status.

Once you pass the necessary set of exams, you'll be certified. Official certification normally takes anywhere from six to eight weeks, so don't expect to get your credentials overnight. When the package for a qualified certification arrives, it includes a Welcome Kit that contains a number of elements (see Microsoft's Web site for other benefits of specific certifications):

➤ A certificate suitable for framing, along with a wallet card and lapel pin.

➤ A license to use the MCP logo, thereby allowing you to use the logo in advertisements, promotions, and documents, and on letterhead, business cards, and so on. Along with the license comes an MCP logo sheet, which includes camera-ready artwork. (Note: Before using any of the artwork, individuals must sign and return a licensing agreement that indicates they'll abide by its terms and conditions.)

➤ A subscription to *Microsoft Certified Professional Magazine*, which provides ongoing data about testing and certification activities, requirements, and changes to the program.

Many people believe that the benefits of MCP certification go well beyond the perks that Microsoft provides to newly anointed members of this elite group. We're starting to see more job listings that request or require applicants to have an MCP, MCSE, and so on, and many individuals who complete the program can qualify for increases in pay and/or responsibility. As an official recognition of hard work and broad knowledge, one of the MCP credentials is a badge of honor in many IT organizations.

How to Prepare for an Exam

Preparing for any Windows 2000 related test (including "Installing, Configuring and Administering Microsoft® Windows® 2000 Professional") requires that you obtain and study materials designed to provide comprehensive information about the product and its capabilities that will appear on the specific exam for which you are preparing. The following list of materials will help you study and prepare:

➤ The Windows 2000 Professional product CD includes comprehensive online documentation and related materials; it should be a primary resource when you are preparing for the test.

➤ The exam preparation materials, practice tests, and self-assessment exams on the Microsoft Training & Services page at **www.microsoft.com/trainingandservices/ default.asp?PageID=mcp**. The Testing Innovations link offers samples of the new question types found on the Windows 2000 MCSE exams. Find the materials, download them, and use them!

➤ The exam preparation advice, practice tests, questions of the day, and discussion groups on the **ExamCram.com** e-learning and certification destination Web site (**www.examcram.com**).

In addition, you'll probably find any or all of the following materials useful in your quest for Windows 2000 Professional expertise:

➤ *Microsoft training kits*—Microsoft Press offers a training kit that specifically targets Exam 70-210. For more information, visit: **http://mspress. microsoft.com/ prod/books/1963.htm**. This training kit contains information that you will find useful in preparing for the test.

➤ *Microsoft TechNet CD*—This monthly CD-based publication delivers numerous electronic titles that include coverage of Directory Services Design and related topics on the Technical Information (TechNet) CD. Its offerings include product facts, technical notes, tools and utilities, and information on how to access the Seminars Online training materials for Windows 2000 Professional. A subscription to TechNet costs $299 per year, but it is well worth the price. Visit **www.microsoft.com/technet/** and check out the information under the "TechNet Subscription" menu entry for more details.

➤ *Study guides*—Several publishers—including The Coriolis Group—offer Windows 2000 titles. The Coriolis Group series includes the following:

> ➤ *The Exam Cram series*—These books give you information about the material you need to know to pass the tests.

> ➤ *The Exam Prep series*—These books provide a greater level of detail than the *Exam Cram* books and are designed to teach you everything you need to know from an exam perspective. Each book comes with a CD that contains interactive practice exams in a variety of testing formats.

Together, the two series make a perfect pair.

➤ *Multimedia*—These Coriolis Group materials are designed to support learners of all types—whether you learn best by reading or doing:

> ➤ *The Exam Cram Personal Trainer*—Offers a unique, personalized self-paced training course based on the exam.

> ➤ *The Exam Cram Personal Test Center*—Features multiple test options that simulate the actual exam, including Fixed-Length, Random, Review, and Test All. Explanations of correct and incorrect answers reinforce concepts learned.

➤ *Classroom training*—CTECs, online partners, and third-party training companies (like Wave Technologies, Learning Tree, Data-Tech, and others) all offer classroom training on Windows 2000. These companies aim to help you prepare to pass Exam 70-210. Although such training runs upwards of $350 per day in class, most of the individuals lucky enough to partake find it to be quite worthwhile.

➤ *Other publications*—There's no shortage of materials available about Windows 2000 Professional. The resource sections at the end of each chapter should give you an idea of where we think you should look for further discussion.

By far, this set of required and recommended materials represents a nonpareil collection of sources and resources for Windows 2000 Professional and related topics. We anticipate that you'll find that this book belongs in this company

About this Book

Each topical *Exam Cram* chapter follows a regular structure, along with graphical cues about important or useful information. Here's the structure of a typical chapter:

➤ *Opening hotlists*—Each chapter begins with a list of the terms, tools, and techniques that you must learn and understand before you can be fully conversant with that chapter's subject matter. We follow the hotlists with one or two introductory paragraphs to set the stage for the rest of the chapter.

➤ *Topical coverage*—After the opening hotlists, each chapter covers a series of topics related to the chapter's subject title. Throughout this section, we highlight topics or concepts likely to appear on a test using a special Exam Alert layout, like this:

This is what an Exam Alert looks like. Normally, an Exam Alert stresses concepts, terms, software, or activities that are likely to relate to one or more certification test questions. For that reason, we think any information found offset in Exam Alert format is worthy of unusual attentiveness on your part. Indeed, most of the information that appears on The Cram Sheet appears as Exam Alerts within the text.

Pay close attention to material flagged as an Exam Alert; although all the information in this book pertains to what you need to know to pass the exam, we flag certain items that are really important. You'll find what appears in the meat of each chapter to be worth knowing, too, when preparing for the test. Because this book's material is very condensed, we recommend that you use this book along with other resources to achieve the maximum benefit.

In addition to the Exam Alerts, we have provided tips that will help you build a better foundation for Windows 2000 Professional knowledge. Although the information may not be on the exam, it is certainly related and will help you become a better test-taker.

This is how tips are formatted. Keep your eyes open for these, and you'll become a Windows 2000 Professional guru in no time!

➤ *Practice questions*—Although we talk about test questions and topics throughout the book, a section at the end of each chapter presents a series of mock test questions and explanations of both correct and incorrect answers.

➤ *Details and resources*—Every chapter ends with a section titled "Need to Know More?". This section provides direct pointers to Microsoft and third-party resources offering more details on the chapter's subject. In addition, this section tries to rank or at least rate the quality and thoroughness of the topic's coverage by each resource. If you find a resource you like in this collection, use it, but don't feel compelled to use all the resources. On the other hand, we recommend only resources we use on a regular basis, so none of our recommendations will be a waste of your time or money (but purchasing them all at once probably represents an expense that many network administrators and would-be MCPs and MCSEs might find hard to justify).

The bulk of the book follows this chapter structure slavishly, but there are a few other elements that we'd like to point out. Chapter 11 includes a sample test that provides a good review of the material presented throughout the book to ensure you're ready for the exam. Chapter 12 is an answer key to the sample test that appears in Chapter 11. In addition, you'll find a handy glossary and an index.

Finally, the tear-out Cram Sheet attached next to the inside front cover of this *Exam Cram* book represents a condensed and compiled collection of facts and tips that we think you should memorize before taking the test. Because you can dump this information out of your head onto a piece of paper before taking the exam, you can master this information by brute force—you need to remember it only long enough to write it down when you walk into the test room. You might even want to look at it in the car or in the lobby of the testing center just before you walk in to take the test.

How to Use this Book

We've structured the topics in this book to build on one another. Therefore, some topics in later chapters make more sense after you've read earlier chapters. That's why we suggest you read this book from front to back for your initial test preparation. If you need to brush up on a topic or you have to bone up for a second try, use the index or table of contents to go straight to the topics and questions that you need to study. Beyond helping you prepare for the test, we think you'll find this book useful as a tightly focused reference to some of the most important aspects of Windows 2000 Professional.

Given all the book's elements and its specialized focus, we've tried to create a tool that will help you prepare for—and pass—Microsoft Exam 70-210. Please share your feedback on the book with us, especially if you have ideas about how we can improve it for future test-takers. We'll consider everything you say carefully, and we'll respond to all suggestions.

Send your questions or comments to us at **learn@examcram.com**. Please remember to include the title of the book in your message; otherwise, we'll be forced to guess which book you're writing about. And we don't like to guess—we want to *know*! Also, be sure to check out the Web pages at **www.examcram.com**, where you'll find information updates, commentary, and certification information.

Thanks, and enjoy the book!

Self-Assessment

The reason we included a Self-Assessment in this *Exam Cram* book is to help you evaluate your readiness to tackle MCSE certification. It should also help you understand what you need to know to master the topic of this book—namely, Exam 70-210, "Installing, Configuring and Administering Microsoft Windows 2000 Professional." But before you tackle this Self-Assessment, let's talk about concerns you may face when pursuing an MCSE for Windows 2000, and what an ideal MCSE candidate might look like.

MCSEs in the Real World

In the next section, we describe an ideal MCSE candidate, knowing full well that only a few real candidates will meet this ideal. In fact, our description of that ideal candidate might seem downright scary, especially with the changes that have been made to the program to support Windows 2000. But take heart: Although the requirements to obtain an MCSE may seem formidable, they are by no means impossible to meet. However, be keenly aware that it does take time, involves some expense, and requires real effort to get through the process.

Increasing numbers of people are attaining Microsoft certifications, so the goal is within reach. You can get all the real-world motivation you need from knowing that many others have gone before, so you will be able to follow in their footsteps. If you're willing to tackle the process seriously and do what it takes to obtain the necessary experience and knowledge, you can take—and pass—all the certification tests involved in obtaining an MCSE. In fact, we've designed *Exam Preps*, the companion *Exam Crams*, *Exam Cram Personal Trainers*, and *Exam Cram Personal Test Centers* to make it as easy on you as possible to prepare for these exams. We've also greatly expanded our Web site, **www.examcram.com**, to provide a host of resources to help you prepare for the complexities of Windows 2000.

Besides MCSE, other Microsoft certifications include the following:

➤ MCSD, which is aimed at software developers and requires one specific exam, two more exams on client and distributed topics, plus a fourth elective exam drawn from a different, but limited, pool of options.

➤ Other Microsoft certifications, whose requirements range from one test (MCP) to several tests (MCP+SB, MCDBA).

The Ideal Windows 2000 MCSE Candidate

Just to give you some idea of what an ideal MCSE candidate is like, here are some relevant statistics about the background and experience such an individual might have. Don't worry if you don't meet these qualifications, or don't come that close—this is a far from ideal world, and where you fall short is simply where you'll have more work to do.

➤ Academic or professional training in network theory, concepts, and operations. This includes everything from networking media and transmission techniques through network operating systems, services, and applications.

➤ Three-plus years of professional networking experience, including experience with Ethernet, token ring, modems, and other networking media. This must include installation, configuration, upgrade, and troubleshooting experience.

Note: The Windows 2000 MCSE program is much more rigorous than the previous NT MCSE program; therefore, you'll really need some hands-on experience. Some of the exams require you to solve real-world case studies and network design issues, so the more hands-on experience you have, the better.

➤ Two-plus years in a networked environment that includes hands-on experience with Windows 2000 Server, Windows 2000 Professional, Windows NT Server, Windows NT Workstation, and Windows 95 or Windows 98. A solid understanding of each system's architecture, installation, configuration, maintenance, and troubleshooting is also essential.

➤ Knowledge of the various methods for installing Windows 2000, including manual and unattended installations.

➤ A thorough understanding of key networking protocols, addressing, and name resolution, including TCP/IP, IPX/SPX, and NetBEUI.

➤ A thorough understanding of NetBIOS naming, browsing, and file and print services.

➤ Familiarity with key Windows 2000-based TCP/IP-based services, including HTTP (Web servers), DHCP, WINS, DNS, plus familiarity with one or more of the following: Internet Information Server (IIS), Index Server, and Proxy Server.

➤ An understanding of how to implement security for key network data in a Windows 2000 environment.

➤ Working knowledge of NetWare 3.x and 4.x, including IPX/SPX frame formats, NetWare file, print, and directory services, and both Novell and Microsoft client software. Working knowledge of Microsoft's Client Service For NetWare (CSNW), Gateway Service For NetWare (GSNW), the NetWare Migration Tool (NWCONV), and the NetWare Client For Windows (NT, 95, and 98) is essential.

➤ A good working understanding of Active Directory. The more you work with Windows 2000, the more you'll realize that this new operating system is quite different than Windows NT. New technologies like Active Directory have really changed the way that Windows is configured and used. We recommend that you find out as much as you can about Active Directory and acquire as much experience using this technology as possible. The time you take learning about Active Directory will be time very well spent!

Fundamentally, this boils down to a bachelor's degree in computer science, plus three years' experience working in a position involving network design, installation, configuration, and maintenance. We believe that well under half of all certification candidates meet these requirements, and that, in fact, most meet less than half of these requirements—at least, when they begin the certification process. But because all the people who already have been certified have survived this ordeal, you can survive it too—especially if you heed what our Self-Assessment can tell you about what you already know and what you need to learn.

Put Yourself to the Test

The following series of questions and observations is designed to help you figure out how much work you must do to pursue Microsoft certification and what kinds of resources you may consult on your quest. Be absolutely honest in your answers, or you'll end up wasting money on exams you're not yet ready to take. There are no right or wrong answers, only steps along the path to certification. Only you can decide where you really belong in the broad spectrum of aspiring candidates.

Two things should be clear from the outset, however:

➤ Even a modest background in computer science will be helpful.

➤ Hands-on experience with Microsoft products and technologies is an essential ingredient to certification success.

Educational Background

1. Have you ever taken any computer-related classes? [Yes or No]

   If Yes, proceed to question 2; if No, proceed to question 4.

2. Have you taken any classes on computer operating systems? [Yes or No]

   If Yes, you will probably be able to handle Microsoft's architecture and system component discussions. If you're rusty, brush up on basic operating system concepts, especially virtual memory, multitasking regimes, user mode versus kernel mode operation, and general computer security topics.

   If No, consider some basic reading in this area. We strongly recommend a good general operating systems book, such as *Operating System Concepts, 5th Edition*, by Abraham Silberschatz and Peter Baer Galvin (John Wiley & Sons, 1998, ISBN 0-471-36414-2). If this title doesn't appeal to you, check out reviews for other, similar titles at your favorite online bookstore.

3. Have you taken any networking concepts or technologies classes? [Yes or No]

   If Yes, you will probably be able to handle Microsoft's networking terminology, concepts, and technologies (brace yourself for frequent departures from normal usage). If you're rusty, brush up on basic networking concepts and terminology, especially networking media, transmission types, the OSI Reference Model, and networking technologies such as Ethernet, token ring, FDDI, and WAN links.

   If No, you might want to read one or two books in this topic area. The two best books that we know of are *Computer Networks, 3rd Edition*, by Andrew S. Tanenbaum (Prentice-Hall, 1996, ISBN 0-13-349945-6) and *Computer Networks and Internets, 2nd Edition*, by Douglas E. Comer (Prentice-Hall, 1998, ISBN 0-130-83617-6).

   Skip to the next section, "Hands-on Experience."

4. Have you done any reading on operating systems or networks? [Yes or No]

   If Yes, review the requirements stated in the first paragraphs after questions 2 and 3. If you meet those requirements, move on to the next section. If No, consult the recommended reading for both topics. A strong background will help you prepare for the Microsoft exams better than just about anything else.

Hands-on Experience

The most important key to success on all of the Microsoft tests is hands-on experience, especially with Windows 2000 Server and Professional, plus the many add-on services and BackOffice components around which so many of the Microsoft certification exams revolve. If we leave you with only one realization after taking this Self-Assessment, it should be that there's no substitute for time spent installing, configuring, and using the various Microsoft products upon which you'll be tested repeatedly and in depth.

5. Have you installed, configured, and worked with:

➤ Windows 2000 Server? [Yes or No]

If Yes, make sure you understand basic concepts as covered in Exam 70-215. You should also study the TCP/IP interfaces, utilities, and services for Exam 70-216, plus implementing security features for Exam 70-220.

 You can download objectives, practice exams, and other data about Microsoft exams from the Training and Certification page at **www.Microsoft.com/ trainingandservices/default.asp?PageID=mcp/**. Use the "Exams" link to obtain specific exam information.

If you haven't worked with Windows 2000 Server, you must obtain one or two machines and a copy of Windows 2000 Server. Then, learn the operating system and whatever other software components on which you'll also be tested.

In fact, we recommend that you obtain two computers, each with a network interface, and set up a two-node network on which to practice. With decent Windows 2000-capable computers selling for about $500 to $600 apiece these days, this shouldn't be too much of a financial hardship. You may have to scrounge to come up with the necessary software, but if you scour the Microsoft Web site you can usually find low-cost options to obtain evaluation copies of most of the software that you'll need.

➤ Windows 2000 Professional? [Yes or No]

If Yes, make sure you understand the concepts covered in Exam 70-210.

If No, you will want to obtain a copy of Windows 2000 Professional and learn how to install, configure, and maintain it. You can use *MCSE Windows 2000 Professional Exam Cram* to guide your activities and studies, or work straight from Microsoft's test objectives if you prefer.

For any and all of these Microsoft exams, the Resource Kits for the topics involved are a good study resource. You can purchase softcover Resource Kits from Microsoft Press (search for them at **http://mspress.microsoft.com/**), but they also appear on the TechNet CDs (**www.microsoft.com/technet**). Along with *Exam Crams* and *Exam Preps*, we believe that Resource Kits are among the best tools you can use to prepare for Microsoft exams.

6. For any specific Microsoft product that is not itself an operating system (for example, SQL Server), have you installed, configured, used, and upgraded this software? [Yes or No]

If the answer is Yes, skip to the next section. If it's No, you must get some experience. Read on for suggestions on how to do this.

Experience is a must with any Microsoft product exam, be it something as simple as FrontPage 2000 or as challenging as SQL Server 7.0. For trial copies of other software, search Microsoft's Web site using the name of the product as your search term. Also, search for bundles like "BackOffice" or "Small Business Server."

If you have the funds, or your employer will pay your way, consider taking a class at a Certified Training and Education Center (CTEC) or at an Authorized Academic Training Partner (AATP). In addition to classroom exposure to the topic of your choice, you get a copy of the software that is the focus of your course, along with a trial version of whatever operating system it needs, with the training materials for that class.

Before you even think about taking any Microsoft exam, make sure you've spent enough time with the related software to understand how it may be installed and configured, how to maintain such an installation, and how to troubleshoot that software when things go wrong. This will help you in the exam, and in real life!

Testing Your Exam-Readiness

Whether you attend a formal class on a specific topic to get ready for an exam or use written materials to study on your own, some preparation for the Microsoft certification exams is essential. At $100 a try, pass or fail, you want to do everything you can to pass on your first try. That's where studying comes in.

We have included a practice exam in this book, so if you don't score that well on the test, you can study more and then tackle the test again. We also have exams that you can take online through the **ExamCram.com** Web site at **www.examcram.com**. If you still don't hit a score of at least 80 percent after these tests, you'll want to investigate the other practice test resources we mention in this section.

For any given subject, consider taking a class if you've tackled self-study materials, taken the test, and failed anyway. The opportunity to interact with an instructor and fellow students can make all the difference in the world, if you can afford that privilege. For information about Microsoft classes, visit the Training and Certification page at **www.microsoft.com/education/partners/ctec.asp** for Microsoft Certified Education Centers or **www.microsoft.com/aatp/default.htm** for Microsoft Authorized Training Providers.

If you can't afford to take a class, visit the Training and Certification page anyway, because it also includes pointers to free practice exams and to Microsoft Certified Professional Approved Study Guides and other self-study tools. And even if you can't afford to spend much at all, you should still invest in some low-cost practice exams from commercial vendors.

7. Have you taken a practice exam on your chosen test subject? [Yes or No]

If Yes, and you scored 70 percent or better, you're probably ready to tackle the real thing. If your score isn't above that threshold, keep at it until you break that barrier.

If No, obtain all the free and low-budget practice tests you can find and get to work. Keep at it until you can break the passing threshold comfortably.

 When it comes to assessing your test readiness, there is no better way than to take a good-quality practice exam and pass with a score of 80 percent or better. When we're preparing ourselves, we shoot for 85-plus percent, just to leave room for the "weirdness factor" that sometimes shows up on Microsoft exams.

Assessing Readiness for Exam 70-210

In addition to the general exam-readiness information in the previous section, there are several things you can do to prepare for the Installing, Configuring and Administering Microsoft Windows 2000 Professional exam. As you're getting ready for Exam 70-210, visit the Exam Cram Windows 2000 Resource Center at **www.examcram.com/studyresource/w2kresource/**. Another valuable resource is the Exam Cram Insider newsletter. Sign up at **www.examcram.com** or send a blank email message to **subscribe-ec@mars.coriolis.com**. We also suggest that you join an active MCSE mailing list. One of the better ones is managed by Sunbelt Software. Sign up at **www.sunbelt-software.com** (look for the Subscribe button).

You can also cruise the Web looking for "braindumps" (recollections of test topics and experiences recorded by others) to help you anticipate topics you're likely to encounter on the test. The MCSE mailing list is a good place to ask where the useful braindumps are, or you can check Shawn Gamble's list at **www.commandcentral.com**.

 You can't be sure that a braindump's author can provide correct answers. Thus, use the questions to guide your studies, but don't rely on the answers in a braindump to lead you to the truth. Double-check everything you find in any braindump.

Microsoft exam mavens also recommend checking the Microsoft Knowledge Base (available on its own CD as part of the TechNet collection, or on the Microsoft Web site at **http://support.microsoft.com/support/**) for "meaningful technical support issues" that relate to your exam's topics. Although we're not sure exactly what the quoted phrase means, we have also noticed some overlap between technical support questions on particular products and troubleshooting questions on the exams for those products.

Onward, through the Fog!

Once you've assessed your readiness, undertaken the right background studies, obtained the hands-on experience that will help you understand the products and technologies at work, and reviewed the many sources of information to help you prepare for a test, you'll be ready to take a round of practice tests. When your scores come back positive enough to get you through the exam, you're ready to go after the real thing. If you follow our assessment regime, you'll not only know what you need to study, but when you're ready to make a test date at Prometric or VUE. Good luck!

Microsoft
Certification Exams

. . . .

Terms you'll need to understand:

✓ Case study

✓ Multiple-choice question formats

✓ Build-list-and-reorder question format

✓ Create-a-tree question format

✓ Drag-and-connect question format

✓ Select-and-place question format

✓ Fixed-length tests

✓ Simulations

✓ Adaptive tests

✓ Short-form tests

Techniques you'll need to master:

✓ Assessing your exam-readiness

✓ Answering Microsoft's varying question types

✓ Altering your test strategy depending on the exam format

✓ Practicing (to make perfect)

✓ Making the best use of the testing software

✓ Budgeting your time

✓ Guessing (as a last resort)

Exam taking is not something that most people anticipate eagerly, no matter how well prepared they may be. In most cases, familiarity helps offset test anxiety. In plain English, this means you probably won't be as nervous when you take your fourth or fifth Microsoft certification exam, as you'll be when you take your first one.

Whether it's your first exam or your tenth, understanding the details of taking the new exams (how much time to spend on questions, the environment you'll be in, and so on) and the new exam software will help you concentrate on the material rather than on the setting. Likewise, mastering a few basic exam-taking skills should help you recognize—and perhaps even outfox—some of the tricks and snares you're bound to find in some exam questions.

This chapter, besides explaining the exam environment and software, describes some proven exam-taking strategies that you should be able to use to your advantage.

Assessing Exam-Readiness

We strongly recommend that you read through and take the Self-Assessment included with this book (it appears just before this chapter, in fact). This will help you compare your knowledge base to the requirements for obtaining an MCSE, and it will also help you identify parts of your background or experience that may be in need of improvement, enhancement, or further learning. If you get the right set of basics under your belt, obtaining Microsoft certification will be that much easier.

Once you've gone through the Self-Assessment, you can remedy those topical areas where your background or experience may not measure up to an ideal certification candidate. But you can also tackle subject matter for individual tests at the same time, so you can continue making progress while you're catching up in some areas.

Once you've worked through an *Exam Cram*, have read the supplementary materials, and have taken the practice test, you'll have a pretty clear idea of when you should be ready to take the real exam. Although we strongly recommend that you keep practicing until your scores top the 75 percent mark, 80 percent would be a good goal to give yourself some margin for error in a real exam situation (where stress will play more of a role than when you practice). Once you hit that point, you should be ready to go. But if you get through the practice exam in this book without attaining that score, you should keep taking practice tests and studying the materials until you get there. You'll find more pointers on how to study and prepare in the Self-Assessment. But now, on to the exam itself!

The Exam Situation

When you arrive at the testing center where you scheduled your exam, you'll need to sign in with an exam coordinator. He or she will ask you to show two forms of identification, one of which must be a photo ID. After you've signed in and your time slot arrives, you'll be asked to deposit any books, bags, or other items you brought with you. Then, you'll be escorted into a closed room.

All exams are completely closed book. In fact, you will not be permitted to take anything with you into the testing area, but you will be furnished with a blank sheet of paper and a pen or, in some cases, an erasable plastic sheet and an erasable pen. Before the exam, you should memorize as much of the important material as you can, so you can write that information on the blank sheet as soon as you are seated in front of the computer. You can refer to this piece of paper anytime you like during the test, but you'll have to surrender the sheet when you leave the room. You will have some time to compose yourself, and record this information, before you begin the exam.

Typically, the room will be furnished with anywhere from one to half a dozen computers, and each workstation will be separated from the others by dividers designed to keep you from seeing what's happening on someone else's computer. Most test rooms feature a wall with a large picture window. This permits the exam coordinator to monitor the room, to prevent exam-takers from talking to one another, and to observe anything out of the ordinary that might go on. The exam coordinator will have preloaded the appropriate Microsoft certification exam—for this book, that's Exam 70-210—and you'll be permitted to start as soon as you're seated in front of the computer.

All Microsoft certification exams allow a certain maximum amount of time in which to complete your work (this time is indicated on the exam by an on-screen counter/clock, so you can check the time remaining whenever you like). All Microsoft certification exams are computer generated. In addition to multiple choice, you'll encounter select and place (drag and drop), create a tree (categorization and prioritization), drag and connect, and build list and reorder (list prioritization) on most exams. Although this may sound quite simple, the questions are constructed not only to check your mastery of basic facts and figures about Windows 2000 Professional, but they also require you to evaluate one or more sets of circumstances or requirements. Often, you'll be asked to give more than one answer to a question. Likewise, you might be asked to select the best or most effective solution to a problem from a range of choices, all of which technically are correct. Taking the exam is quite an adventure, and it involves real thinking. This book shows you what to expect and how to deal with the potential problems, puzzles, and predicaments.

In the next section, you'll learn more about how Microsoft test questions look and how they must be answered.

Exam Layout and Design

The format of Microsoft's Windows 2000 exams is different from that of its previous exams. For the design exams (70-219, 70-220, 70-221), each exam consists entirely of a series of case studies, and the questions can be of six types. For the Core Four exams (70-210, 70-215, 70-216, 70-217), the same six types of questions can appear, but you are not likely to encounter complex multiquestion case studies.

For design exams, each case study or "testlet" presents a detailed problem that you must read and analyze. Figure 1.1 shows an example of what a case study looks like. You must select the different tabs in the case study to view the entire case.

Following each case study is a set of questions related to the case study; these questions can be one of six types (which are discussed next). Careful attention to details provided in the case study is the key to success. Be prepared to toggle frequently between the case study and the questions as you work. Some of the case studies also include diagrams, which are called *exhibits*, that you'll need to examine closely to understand how to answer the questions.

Once you complete a case study, you can review all the questions and your answers. However, once you move on to the next case study, you may not be able to return to the previous case study and make any changes.

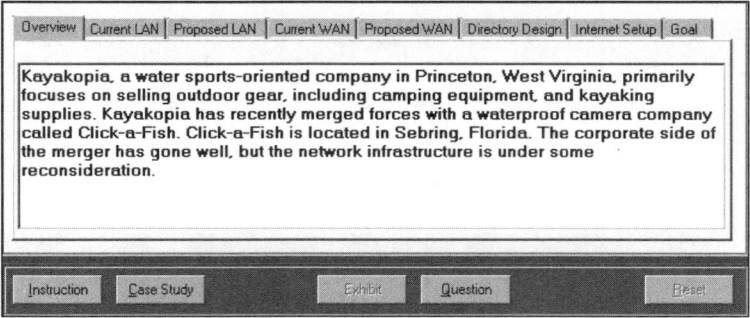

Figure 1.1   This is how case studies appear.

The six types of question formats are:

➤ Multiple choice, single answer

➤ Multiple choice, multiple answers

➤ Build list and reorder (list prioritization)

➤ Create a tree

➤ Drag and connect

➤ Select and place (drag and drop)

Note: Exam formats may vary by test center location. You may want to call the test center or visit ExamCram.com to see if you can find out which type of test you'll encounter.

Multiple-Choice Question Formats

Some exam questions require you to select a single answer, whereas others ask you to select multiple correct answers. The following multiple-choice question requires you to select a single correct answer. Following the question is a brief summary of each potential answer and why it is either right or wrong.

Question 1

You are installing Windows 2000 on a system with a blank hard drive. You boot the system with a DOS bootable floppy containing CD-ROM drivers. What must you do to launch the installation of Windows 2000 Professional?

○ a. Run winnt32 from the i386 directory.

○ b. Run setup.exe.

○ c. Run winnt from the i386 directory.

○ d. Run setup.exe from the i386 directory.

The correct answer is c because that is the only command that runs under DOS and launches an installation of Windows 2000. The other answers (a, b, d) are misleading because they name commands that do not run under DOS (a), or do not exist (b, d), but sound like valid setup commands.

This sample question format corresponds closely to the Microsoft certification exam format—the only difference on the exam is that questions are not followed by answer keys. To select an answer, you would position the cursor over the radio button next to the answer. Then, click the mouse button to select the answer.

Let's examine a question where one or more answers are possible. This type of question provides checkboxes rather than radio buttons for marking all appropriate selections.

Question 2

How can you launch installation of Windows 2000 on a system with a blank hard drive? [Check all correct answers]

❑ a. Boot with the Windows 2000 CD-ROM.

❑ b. Boot using a DOS-bootable floppy and run i386\winnt.

❑ c. Boot using a DOS-bootable floppy then insert the Windows 2000 CD-ROM and wait for AutoRun to launch.

❑ d. Boot using a DOS-bootable floppy and run i386\winnt32.

Answers a and b are correct. Both are options to launch an installation of Windows 2000. AutoRun does not function under DOS, and winnt32 does not work in DOS, therefore answers c and d are incorrect.

For this particular question, two answers are required. Microsoft sometimes gives partial credit for partially correct answers. For Question 2, you have to check the boxes next to items a and b to obtain credit for a correct answer. Notice that picking the right answers also means knowing why the other answers are wrong!

Build-List-and-Reorder Question Format

Questions in the build-list-and-reorder format present two lists of items—one on the left and one on the right. To answer the question, you must move items from the list on the right to the list on the left. The final list must then be reordered into a specific order.

These questions can best be characterized as "From the following list of choices, pick the choices that answer the question. Arrange the list in a certain order." To give you practice with this type of question, some questions of this type are included in this study guide. Here's an example of how they appear in this book; for a sample of how they appear on the test, see Figure 1.2.

Question 3

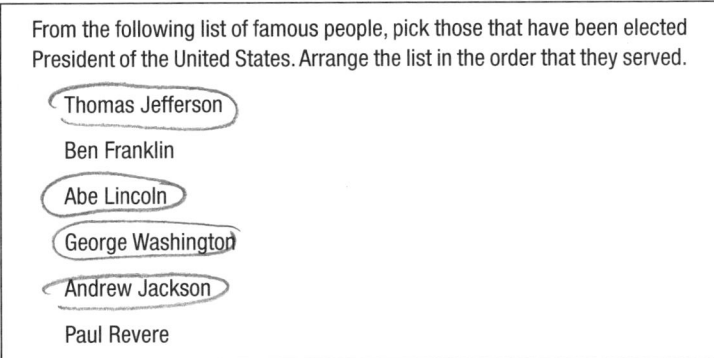

From the following list of famous people, pick those that have been elected President of the United States. Arrange the list in the order that they served.

Thomas Jefferson

Ben Franklin

Abe Lincoln

George Washington

Andrew Jackson

Paul Revere

The correct answer is:

George Washington

Thomas Jefferson

Andrew Jackson

Abe Lincoln

On an actual exam, the entire list of famous people would initially appear in the list on the right. You would move the four correct answers to the list on the left, and then reorder the list on the left. Notice that the answer to the question did not include all items from the initial list. However, this may not always be the case.

To move an item from the right list to the left list, first select the item by clicking on it, and then click on the Add button (left arrow). Once you move an item from one list to the other, you can move the item back by first selecting the item and then clicking on the appropriate button (either the Add button or the Remove button). Once items have been moved to the left list, you can reorder an item by selecting the item and clicking on the up or down button.

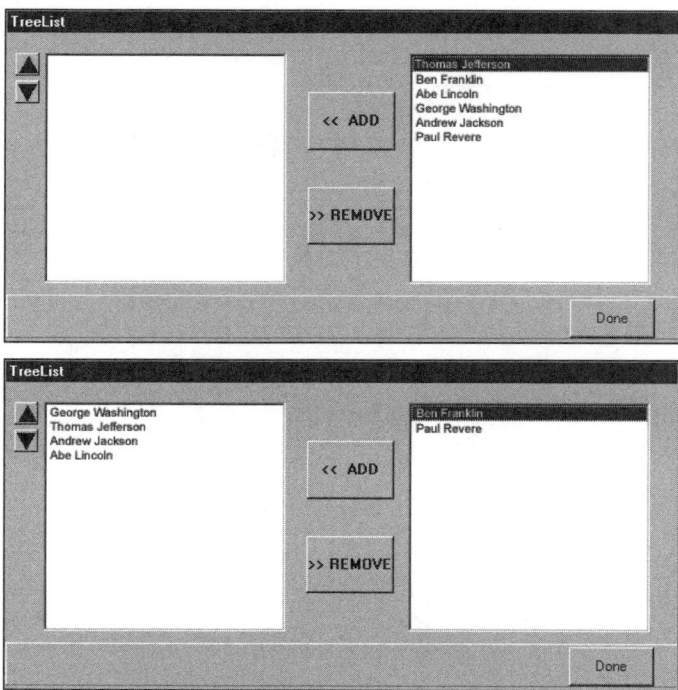

Figure 1.2 This is how build-list-and-reorder questions appear.

Create-a-Tree Question Format

Questions in the create-a-tree format also present two lists—one on the left side of the screen and one on the right side of the screen. The list on the right consists of individual items, and the list on the left consists of nodes in a tree. To answer the question, you must move items from the list on the right to the appropriate node in the tree.

These questions can best be characterized as simply a matching exercise. Items from the list on the right are placed under the appropriate category in the list on the left. Here's an example of how they appear in this book; for a sample of how they appear on the test, see Figure 1.3.

Question 4

The calendar year is divided into four seasons:

Winter

Spring

Summer

Fall

Identify the season when each of the following holidays occurs:

Christmas

Fourth of July

Labor Day

Flag Day

Memorial Day

Washington's Birthday

Thanksgiving

Easter

The correct answer is:

Winter

Christmas

Washington's Birthday

Spring

Flag Day

Memorial Day

Easter

Summer

Fourth of July

Labor Day

Fall

Thanksgiving

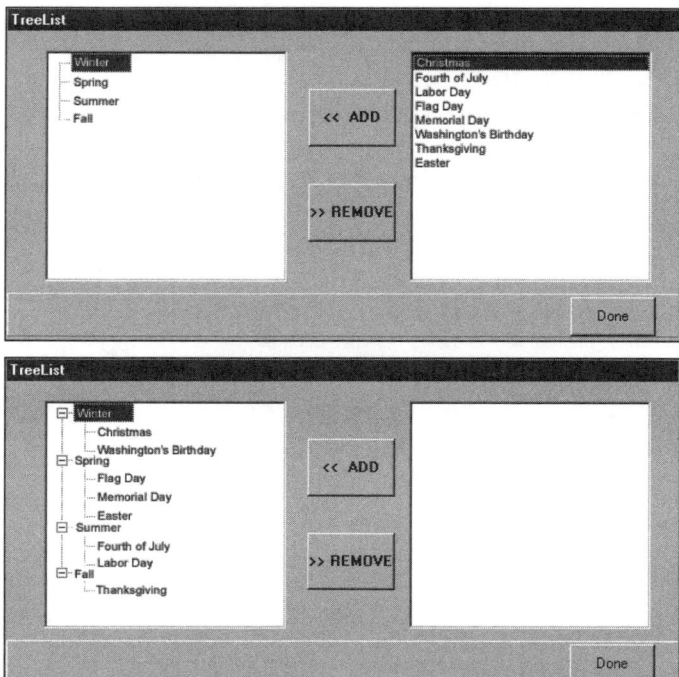

Figure 1.3   This is how create-a-tree questions appear.

In this case, all the items in the list were used. However, this may not always be the case.

To move an item from the right list to its appropriate location in the tree, you must first select the appropriate tree node by clicking on it. Then, you select the item to be moved and click on the Add button. If one or more items have been added to a tree node, the node will be displayed with a "+" icon to the left of the node name. You can click on this icon to expand the node and view the item(s) that have been added. If any item has been added to the wrong tree node, you can remove it by selecting it and clicking on the Remove button.

Drag-and-Connect Question Format

Questions in the drag-and-connect format present a group of objects and a list of "connections." To answer the question, you must move the appropriate connections between the objects.

This type of question is best described using graphics. Here's an example.

Question 5

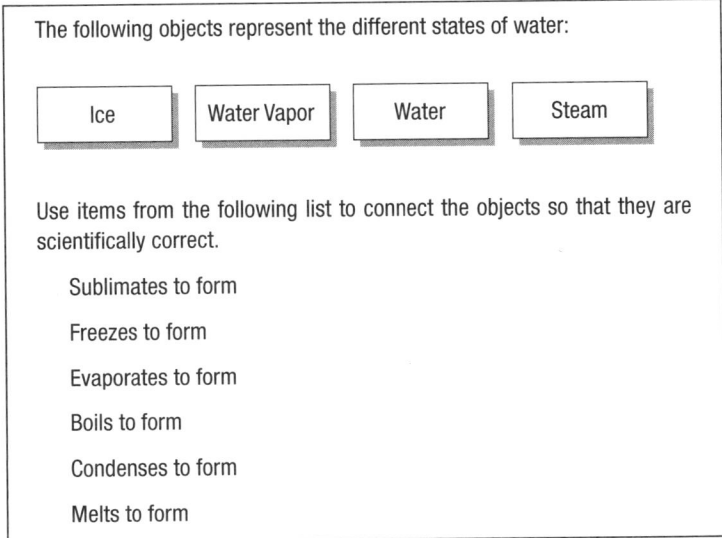

The following objects represent the different states of water:

| Ice | Water Vapor | Water | Steam |

Use items from the following list to connect the objects so that they are scientifically correct.

Sublimates to form

Freezes to form

Evaporates to form

Boils to form

Condenses to form

Melts to form

The correct answer is:

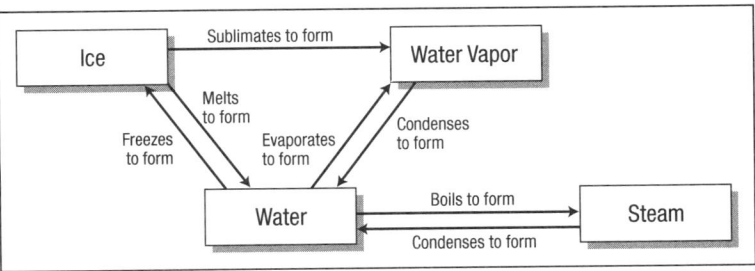

For this type of question, it's not necessary to use every object, and each connection can be used multiple times.

Select-and-Place Question Format

Questions in the select-and-place (drag-and-drop) format present a diagram with blank boxes, and a list of labels that need to be dragged to correctly fill in the blank boxes. To answer the question, you must move the labels to their appropriate positions on the diagram.

This type of question is best described using graphics. Here's an example.

Question 6

Place the items in their proper order, by number, on the following flowchart. Some items may be used more than once, and some items may not be used at all.

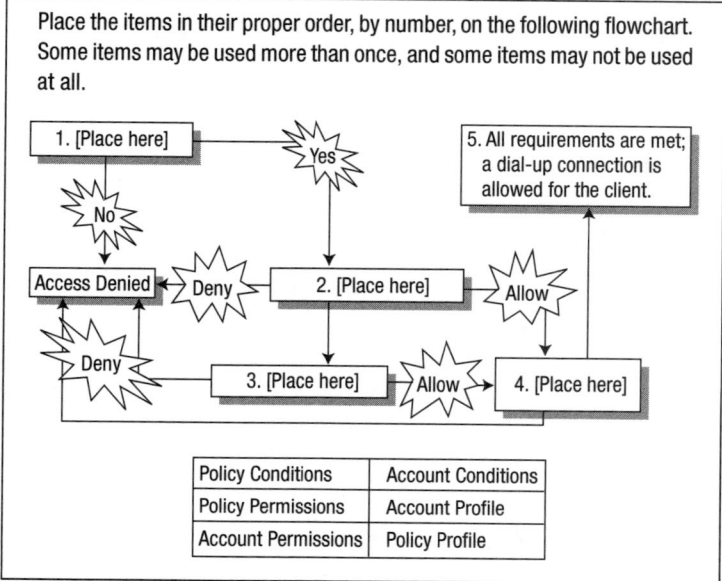

Policy Conditions	Account Conditions
Policy Permissions	Account Profile
Account Permissions	Policy Profile

The correct answer is:

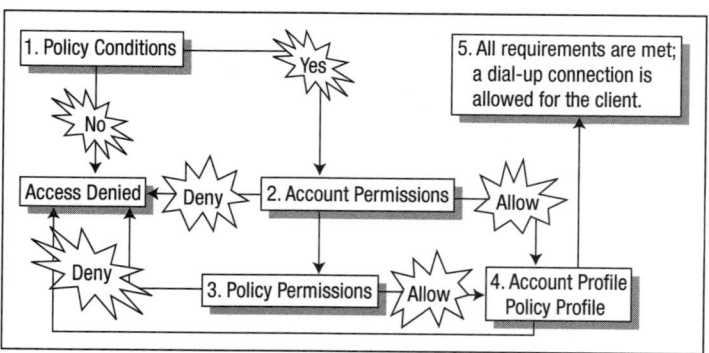

Microsoft's Testing Formats

Currently, Microsoft uses four different testing formats:

➤ Case study

➤ Fixed length

➤ Adaptive

➤ Short form

As we mentioned earlier, the case study approach is used with Microsoft's design exams, 70-219, 70-220, and 70-221. These exams consist of a set of case studies that you must analyze to enable you to answer questions related to the case studies. Such exams include one or more case studies (tabbed topic areas), each of which is followed by 4 to 10 questions. The question types for design exams and for Core Four Windows 2000 exams are multiple choice, build list and reorder, create a tree, drag and connect, and select and place. Depending on the test topic, some exams are totally case-based, whereas others are not.

Other Microsoft exams employ advanced testing capabilities that might not be immediately apparent. Although the questions that appear are primarily multiple choice, the logic that drives them is more complex than older Microsoft tests, which use a fixed sequence of questions, called a *fixed-length test*. Some questions employ a sophisticated user interface, which Microsoft calls a *simulation*, to test your knowledge of the software and systems under consideration in a more or less "live" environment that behaves just like the original. The Testing Innovations link at **www.microsoft.com/trainingandservices/default.asp?PageID=mcp** includes a downloadable practice simulation.

For some exams, Microsoft has turned to a well-known technique, called *adaptive testing*, to establish a test-taker's level of knowledge and product competence. Adaptive exams look the same as fixed-length exams, but they discover the level of difficulty at which an individual test-taker can correctly answer questions. Test-takers with differing levels of knowledge or ability therefore see different sets of questions; individuals with high levels of knowledge or ability are presented with a smaller set of more difficult questions, whereas individuals with lower levels of knowledge are presented with a larger set of easier questions. Two individuals may answer the same percentage of questions correctly, but the test-taker with a higher knowledge or ability level will score higher because his or her questions are worth more.

Also, the lower-level test-taker will probably answer more questions than his or her more-knowledgeable colleague. This explains why adaptive tests use ranges of values to define the number of questions and the amount of time it takes to complete the test.

Adaptive tests work by evaluating the test-taker's most recent answer. A correct answer leads to a more difficult question (and the test software's estimate of the test-taker's knowledge and ability level is raised). An incorrect answer leads to a less difficult question (and the test software's estimate of the test-taker's knowledge and ability level is lowered). This process continues until the test targets the test-taker's true ability level. The exam ends when the test-taker's level of accuracy meets a statistically acceptable value (in other words, when his or her performance demonstrates an acceptable level of knowledge and ability), or when the maximum number of items has been presented (in which case, the test-taker is almost certain to fail).

Microsoft also introduced a short-form test for its most popular tests. This test delivers 25 to 30 questions to its takers, giving them exactly 60 minutes to complete the exam. This type of exam is similar to a fixed-length test, in that it allows readers to jump ahead or return to earlier questions, and to cycle through the questions until the test is done. Microsoft does not use adaptive logic in this test, but claims that statistical analysis of the question pool is such that the 25 to 30 questions delivered during a short-form exam conclusively measure a test-taker's knowledge of the subject matter in much the same way as an adaptive test. You can think of the short-form test as a kind of "greatest hits exam" (that is, the most important questions are covered) version of an adaptive exam on the same topic.

Note: Some of the Microsoft exams can appear as a combination of adaptive and fixed-length questions.

Microsoft tests can come in any one of these forms. Whatever you encounter, you must take the test in whichever form it appears; you can't choose one form over another. If anything, it pays more to prepare thoroughly for an adaptive exam than for a fixed-length or a short-form exam: The penalties for answering incorrectly are built into the test itself on an adaptive exam, whereas the layout remains the same for a fixed-length or short-form test, no matter how many questions you answer incorrectly.

The biggest difference between an adaptive test and a fixed-length or short-form test is that on a fixed-length or short-form test, you can revisit questions after you've read them over one or more times. On an adaptive test, you must answer the question when it's presented and will have no opportunities to revisit that question thereafter.

Strategies for Different Testing Formats

Before you choose a test-taking strategy, you must know if your test is case study based, fixed length, short form, or adaptive. When you begin your exam, you'll know right away if the test is based on case studies. The interface will consist of a tabbed window that allows you to easily navigate through the sections of the case.

If you are taking a test that is not based on case studies, the software will tell you that the test is adaptive, if in fact the version you're taking is an adaptive test. If your introductory materials fail to mention this, you're probably taking a fixed-length test (50 to 70 questions). If the total number of questions involved is 25 to 30, you're taking a short-form test. Some tests announce themselves by indicating that they will start with a set of adaptive questions, followed by fixed-length questions.

 You'll be able to tell for sure if you are taking an adaptive, fixed-length, or short-form test by the first question. If it includes a checkbox that lets you mark the question for later review, you're taking a fixed-length or short-form test. If the total number of questions is 25 to 30, it's a short-form test; if more than 30, it's a fixed-length test. Adaptive test questions can be visited (and answered) only once, and they include no such checkbox.

The Case Study Exam Strategy

Most test-takers find that the case study type of test used for the design exams (70-219, 70-220, and 70-221) is the most difficult to master. When it comes to studying for a case study test, your best bet is to approach each case study as a standalone test. The biggest challenge you'll encounter is that you'll feel that you won't have enough time to get through all of the cases that are presented.

 Each case provides a lot of material that you'll need to read and study before you can effectively answer the questions that follow. The trick to taking a case study exam is to first scan the case study to get the highlights. Make sure you read the overview section of the case so that you understand the context of the problem at hand. Then, quickly move on and scan the questions.

As you are scanning the questions, make mental notes to yourself so that you'll remember which sections of the case study you should focus on. Some case studies may provide a fair amount of extra information that you don't really need to answer the questions. The goal with our scanning approach is to avoid having to study and analyze material that is not completely relevant.

When studying a case, carefully read the tabbed information. It is important to answer each and every question. You will be able to toggle back and forth from case to questions, and from question to question within a case testlet. However, once you leave the case and move on, you may not be able to return to it. You may want to take notes while reading useful information so you can refer to them when you tackle the test questions. It's hard to go wrong with this strategy when taking any kind of Microsoft certification test.

The Fixed-Length and Short-Form Exam Strategy

A well-known principle when taking fixed-length or short-form exams is to first read over the entire exam from start to finish while answering only those questions you feel absolutely sure of. On subsequent passes, you can dive into more complex questions more deeply, knowing how many such questions you have left.

Fortunately, the Microsoft exam software for fixed-length and short-form tests makes the multiple-visit approach easy to implement. At the top-left corner of each question is a checkbox that permits you to mark that question for a later visit.

Note: Marking questions makes review easier, but you can return to any question by clicking the Forward or Back button repeatedly.

As you read each question, if you answer only those you're sure of and mark for review those that you're not sure of, you can keep working through a decreasing list of questions as you answer the trickier ones in order.

 There's at least one potential benefit to reading the exam over completely before answering the trickier questions: Sometimes, information supplied in later questions sheds more light on earlier questions. At other times, information you read in later questions might jog your memory about Windows 2000 Professional facts, figures, or behavior that helps you answer earlier questions. Either way, you'll come out ahead if you defer those questions about which you're not absolutely sure.

Here are some question-handling strategies that apply to fixed-length and short-form tests. Use them if you have the chance:

➤ When returning to a question after your initial read-through, read every word again—otherwise, your mind can fall quickly into a rut. Sometimes, revisiting a question after turning your attention elsewhere lets you see something you missed, but the strong tendency is to see what you've seen before. Try to avoid that tendency at all costs.

➤ If you return to a question more than twice, try to articulate to yourself what you don't understand about the question, why answers don't appear to make sense, or what appears to be missing. If you chew on the subject awhile, your subconscious might provide the details you lack, or you might notice a "trick" that points to the right answer.

As you work your way through the exam, another counter that Microsoft provides will come in handy—the number of questions completed and questions outstanding. For fixed-length and short-form tests, it's wise to budget your time by making sure that you've completed one-quarter of the questions one-quarter of the way through the exam period, and three-quarters of the questions three-quarters of the way through.

If you're not finished when only five minutes remain, use that time to guess your way through any remaining questions. Remember, guessing is potentially more valuable than not answering, because blank answers are always wrong, but a guess may turn out to be right. If you don't have a clue about any of the remaining questions, pick answers at random, or choose all a's, b's, and so on. The important thing is to submit an exam for scoring that has an answer for every question.

 At the very end of your exam period, you're better off guessing than leaving questions unanswered.

The Adaptive Exam Strategy

If there's one principle that applies to taking an adaptive test, it could be summed up as "Get it right the first time." You cannot elect to skip a question and move on to the next one when taking an adaptive test, because the testing software uses your answer to the current question to select whatever question it plans to present next. Nor can you return to a question once you've moved on, because the software gives you only one chance to answer the question. You can, however, take notes, because sometimes information supplied in earlier questions will shed more light on later questions.

Also, when you answer a question correctly, you are presented with a more difficult question next, to help the software gauge your level of skill and ability. When you answer a question incorrectly, you are presented with a less difficult question, and the software lowers its current estimate of your skill and ability. This continues until the program settles into a reasonably accurate estimate of what you know and can do, and takes you on average through somewhere between 15 and 30 questions as you complete the test.

The good news is that if you know your stuff, you'll probably finish most adaptive tests in 30 minutes or so. The bad news is that you must really, really know your stuff to do your best on an adaptive test. That's because some questions are so convoluted, complex, or hard to follow that you're bound to miss one or two, at a minimum, even if you do know your stuff. So the more you know, the better you'll do on an adaptive test, even accounting for the occasionally weird or unfathomable questions that appear on these exams.

> Because you can't always tell in advance if a test is fixed length, short form, or adaptive, you will be best served by preparing for the exam as if it were adaptive. That way, you should be prepared to pass no matter what kind of test you take. But if you do take a fixed-length or short-form test, remember our tips from the preceding section. They should help you improve on what you could do on an adaptive test.

If you encounter a question on an adaptive test that you can't answer, you must guess an answer immediately. Because of how the software works, you may suffer for your guess on the next question if you guess right, because you'll get a more difficult question next!

Question-Handling Strategies

For those questions that take only a single answer, usually two or three of the answers will be obviously incorrect, and two of the answers will be plausible—of course, only one can be correct. Unless the answer leaps out at you (if it does, reread the question to look for a trick; sometimes those are the ones you're most likely to get wrong), begin the process of answering by eliminating those answers that are most obviously wrong.

Almost always, at least one answer out of the possible choices for a question can be eliminated immediately because it matches one of these conditions:

➤ The answer does not apply to the situation.

➤ The answer describes a nonexistent issue, an invalid option, or an imaginary state.

After you eliminate all answers that are obviously wrong, you can apply your retained knowledge to eliminate further answers. Look for items that sound correct but refer to actions, commands, or features that are not present or not available in the situation that the question describes.

If you're still faced with a blind guess among two or more potentially correct answers, reread the question. Try to picture how each of the possible remaining answers would alter the situation. Be especially sensitive to terminology; sometimes the choice of words ("remove" instead of "disable") can make the difference between a right answer and a wrong one.

Only when you've exhausted your ability to eliminate answers, but remain unclear about which of the remaining possibilities is correct, should you guess at an answer. An unanswered question offers you no points, but guessing gives you at least some chance of getting a question right; just don't be too hasty when making a blind guess.

Note: If you're taking a fixed-length or a short-form test, you can wait until the last round of reviewing marked questions (just as you're about to run out of time, or out of unanswered questions) before you start making guesses. You will have the same option within each case study testlet (but once you leave a testlet, you may not be allowed to return to it). If you're taking an adaptive test, you'll have to guess to move on to the next question if you can't figure out an answer some other way. Either way, guessing should be your technique of last resort!

Numerous questions assume that the default behavior of a particular utility is in effect. If you know the defaults and understand what they mean, this knowledge will help you cut through many Gordian knots.

Mastering the Inner Game

In the final analysis, knowledge breeds confidence, and confidence breeds success. If you study the materials in this book carefully and review all the practice questions at the end of each chapter, you should become aware of those areas where additional learning and study are required.

After you've worked your way through the book, take the practice exam in the back of the book. Taking this test will provide a reality check and help you identify areas to study further. Make sure you follow up and review materials related to the questions you miss on the practice exam before scheduling a real exam. Only when you've covered that ground and feel comfortable with the whole scope of the practice exam should you set an exam appointment. Only if you score 80 percent or better should you proceed to the real thing (otherwise, obtain some additional practice tests so you can keep trying until you hit this magic number).

 If you take a practice exam and don't score at least 80 to 85 percent correct, you'll want to practice further. Microsoft provides links to practice exam providers and also offers self-assessment exams at **www.microsoft.com/trainingandservices/**. You should also check out **ExamCram.com** for downloadable practice questions.

Armed with the information in this book and with the determination to augment your knowledge, you should be able to pass the certification exam. However, you need to work at it, or you'll spend the exam fee more than once before you finally pass. If you prepare seriously, you should do well. We are confident that you can do it!

The next section covers the sources you can use to prepare for the Microsoft certification exams.

Additional Resources

A good source of information about Microsoft certification exams comes from Microsoft itself. Because its products and technologies—and the exams that go with them—change frequently, the best place to go for exam-related information is online.

If you haven't already visited the Microsoft Certified Professional site, do so right now. The MCP home page resides at **www.microsoft.com/trainingandservices/** (see Figure 1.4).

Note: This page might not be there by the time you read this, or may be replaced by something new and different, because things change regularly on the Microsoft site. Should this happen, please read the sidebar titled "Coping with Change on the Web."

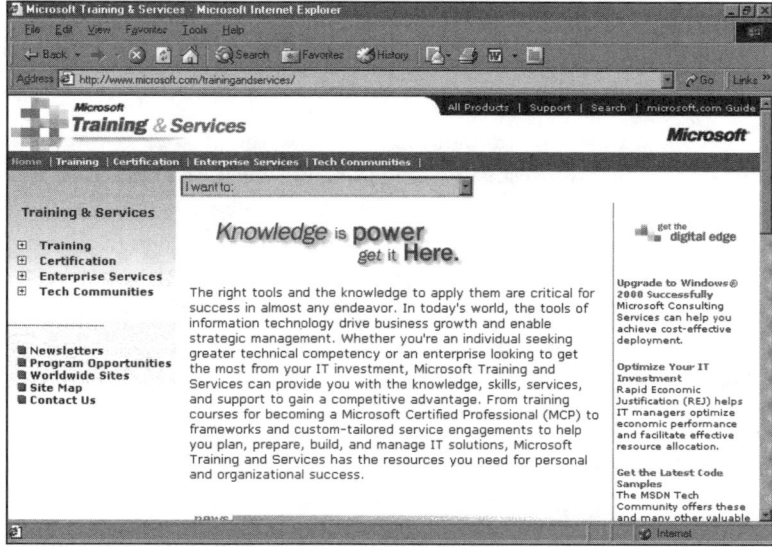

Figure 1.4   The Microsoft Certified Professional home page.

Coping with Change on the Web

Sooner or later, all the information we've shared with you about the Microsoft Certified Professional pages and the other Web-based resources mentioned throughout the rest of this book will go stale or be replaced by newer information. In some cases, the URLs you find here might lead you to their replacements; in other cases, the URLs will go nowhere, leaving you with the dreaded "404 File not found" error message. When that happens, don't give up.

There's always a way to find what you want on the Web if you're willing to invest some time and energy. Most large or complex Web sites—and Microsoft's qualifies on both counts—offer a search engine. On all of Microsoft's Web pages, a Search button appears along the top edge of the page. As long as you can get to Microsoft's site (it should stay at **www.microsoft.com** for a long time), use this tool to help you find what you need.

The more focused you can make a search request, the more likely the results will include information you can use. For example, you can search for the string

```
"training and certification"
```

to produce a lot of data about the subject in general, but if you're looking for the preparation guide for Exam 70-210, "Windows 2000 Professional," you'll be more likely to get there quickly if you use a search string similar to the following:

```
"Exam 70-210" AND "preparation guide"
```

Likewise, if you want to find the Training and Certification downloads, try a search string such as this:

```
"training and certification" AND "download page"
```

Finally, feel free to use general search tools—such as **www.search.com**, **www.altavista.com**, and **www.excite.com**—to look for related information. Although Microsoft offers great information about its certification exams online, there are plenty of third-party sources of information and assistance that need not follow Microsoft's party line. Therefore, if you can't find something where the book says it lives, intensify your search.

Implementing and Administering Resources

Terms you'll need to understand:

✓ Shared folders
✓ Hidden shares
✓ Offline files/client-side caching
✓ Share permissions
✓ NT File System (NTFS)
✓ NTFS permissions
✓ User rights

✓ Access control list (ACL)
✓ NTFS compression
✓ Taking ownership of objects
✓ Auditing
✓ NTFS Encrypting File System (EFS)
✓ Printer ports
✓ Internet Printing Protocol (IPP)

Techniques you'll need to master:

✓ Creating network shares
✓ Configuring share permissions
✓ Configuring options for offline files
✓ Setting basic and advanced NTFS permissions

✓ Enabling/disabling NTFS data compression
✓ Learning how to turn on auditing
✓ Working with EFS
✓ Connecting to printers over the Internet

Why do we have computer networks anyway? Well, they empower us to collaborate on projects and share information with others. If you're working on a Windows 2000 Professional system that is connected to a network, you can share one or more of that system's folders with other computers and users on that network. Drive volumes and folders are not automatically shared for all users in Windows 2000 Professional. Members of the Administrators group and the Power Users group, discussed later in this chapter, retain the rights to create shared network folders.

Managing Access to Shared Folders

To share a folder with the network, follow these steps:

1. Open a window in either My Computer or Windows Explorer.

2. Right-click the folder that you want to share and then select Sharing from the pop-up menu.

3. Click the Share This Folder radio button, as shown in Figure 2.1.

4. Type in a Share Name or accept the default one. Windows 2000 uses the actual folder name as the default Share Name.

5. Type in a Comment, if you desire. Comments appear in the Browse list when users search for network resources. Comments can help them to locate the proper network shares.

6. Specify the User Limit: Maximum Allowed or Allow x number of Users. Windows 2000 Professional permits a maximum of 10 concurrent network connec-

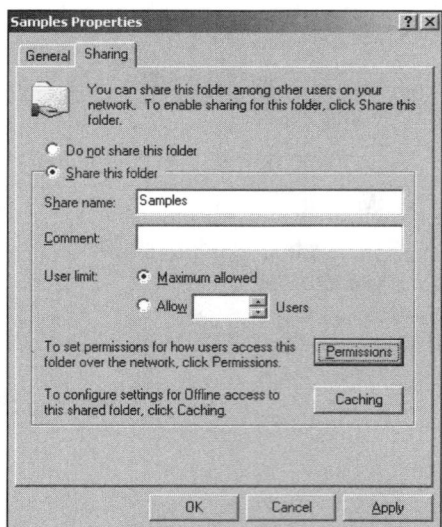

Figure 2.1 You create a network share by accessing the Sharing tab of a folder's Properties sheet.

tions per share. Specify the Allow x number of Users option only if you need to limit the number of concurrent users for this share to fewer than 10 users.

7. Click OK to create the shared folder. The folder now becomes available to others on your network.

Note: To remove a network share, right-click the shared folder and choose the Sharing option. Click the Do Not Share This Folder radio button and click OK. The folder will no longer be shared with the network.

Connecting to Shared Resources on a Windows Network

Users and network administrators have several options available to them for connecting to shared network resources. These options include the following:

➤ Typing in a Universal Naming Convention (UNC) path from the Start⏐Run dialog box in the format **servername\sharename**.

➤ Navigating to the share from the My Network Places window.

➤ Employing the **net use** command from a command prompt window.

If you want to connect to a shared folder named "samples" that resides on a Windows computer named "7800pro", click Start⏐Run. Next, type **7800pro\samples** and click OK. At this point, you are connected to that shared resource, provided you possess the required security permissions needed to access the shared folder.

Connecting to Network Resources with the My Network Places Window

You can connect to a network share from My Network Places. Double-click the My Network Places icon on the Windows 2000 desktop. Double-click the Add Network Place icon, which reveals the Add Network Place Wizard, as shown in Figure 2.2. Enter the location of the network place, or click Browse to locate the

Figure 2.2   You can easily connect to shared network folders with the Add Network Place Wizard.

network share by viewing the available network resources. Click Next to enter a name for the network place or accept the default name. Click Finish to establish the connection to the shared folder, provided that you have the proper permissions. A list of network resources to which you have already connected is then displayed within the My Network Places window.

For Command Line Junkies: The **net use** Command

You also have the option of connecting to network shares via the **net use** command. For help with the various options and syntax of the **net use** command, type **net use /?** at the command prompt. To connect to a remote resource from the command line, follow these steps:

1. Open a command prompt window (Start|Programs|Accessories|Command Prompt).

2. At the command prompt, type **net use X:\\7800pro\samples** and press Enter, where **X:** is a drive letter that you designate. If you possess the appropriate permissions for that network share, you should see the message The Command Completed Successfully displayed in your command prompt window.

Using Automatically Generated Hidden Shares

Windows 2000 Professional automatically creates shared folders by default each and every time the computer is started. These default shares are often referred to as *hidden* or *administrative* because a dollar sign ($) is appended to their share names. The dollar sign at the end of a share name prevents the shared folder from being displayed on the network Browse list; users cannot easily discover that these shares exist. When users browse through the My Network Places window, for example, they cannot see that such hidden shares even exist; Microsoft Windows Networking does not allow hidden shares to be displayed. These hidden network shares include the following:

➤ *C$, D$, E$, and so on*—One share gets created for the root of each available hard drive volume on the system.

➤ *ADMIN$*—This shares the systemroot folder with the network (e.g., C:\WINNT).

➤ *IPC$*—This share is used for InterProcess Communications (IPCs). IPCs support communications between objects on different computers over a network by manipulating the low-level details of network transport protocols. InterProcess Communications enable the use of distributed application programs that combine multiple processes working together to accomplish a single task.

Although you can temporarily disable hidden shares, you cannot delete them without modifying the registry (which is not recommended) because they get re-created on each restart. You can connect to a hidden share, but only if you provide a user account with administrative privileges along with the appropriate password for that user account. Administrators can create their own custom administrative (hidden) shares simply by adding a dollar sign to the share name of any shared folder. Administrators can view all the hidden shares that exist on a Windows 2000 Professional system by accessing the Shares folder within the System Tools/Shared Folders container of the Computer Management console.

Controlling Access to Shared Folders

When you, as a network administrator, grant access to shared resources over the network, the shared data files become very vulnerable to unintentional as well as intentional destruction or deletion by others. This is why network administrators must be vigilant in controlling data access security permissions. If access permissions to shared folders are too lenient, shared data may become compromised. On the other hand, if access permissions are set too stringently, the users who need to access and manipulate the data may not be able to do their jobs. Managing access control for shared resources can be quite challenging.

Revisiting a Shared Folder's Properties

By right-clicking on a shared folder and selecting Sharing, you can modify some of the shared folder's properties. You can specify whether network users can cache shared data files on their local workstations. To configure offline access settings for the shared folder, click the Caching button. If you allow caching of files for a shared folder, you must choose from three options in the Caching Settings dialog box:

➤ *Automatic Caching For Documents*—This option relies on the workstation and server computers to automatically download and make available offline any opened files from the shared folder. Older copies of files are automatically updated.

➤ *Automatic Caching For Programs*—This setting is recommended for folders that contain read-only data or for application programs that have been configured to be run from the network. This option is not designed for sharing data files, and file sharing in this mode is not guaranteed.

➤ *Manual Caching For Documents*—This is the default caching setting. This setting requires network users to manually specify any files they want available when working offline. This setting is recommended for folders that contain user documents.

Click OK on the Caching Settings dialog box after making any configuration changes for offline access to the shared folder.

If you do not want files within the shared folder to be cached locally on workstations, you must deselect the Allow Caching Of Files In This Shared Folder checkbox, as shown in Figure 2.3.

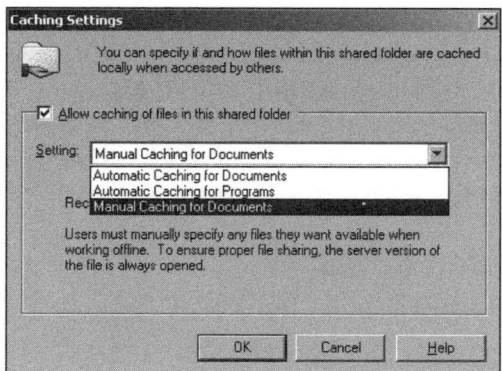

Figure 2.3   The Caching Settings dialog box with Manual Caching For Documents selected.

Note: The default cache size is configured as 10 percent of the client computer's available disk space. You can change this setting by selecting Tools\Folder Options from the menu bar from any My Computer or Windows Explorer window. The Offline Files tab of the Folder Options dialog box displays the system's offline files settings, as shown in Figure 2.4.

*Note: The Offline Files feature is also known as Client-Side Caching (CSC). The default location on Windows 2000 computers for storage of offline files is System-Root\CSC (e.g., C:\WINNT\CSC). You can use the **Cachemov.exe** tool from the Windows 2000 Professional Resource Kit and the Windows 2000 Server Resource*

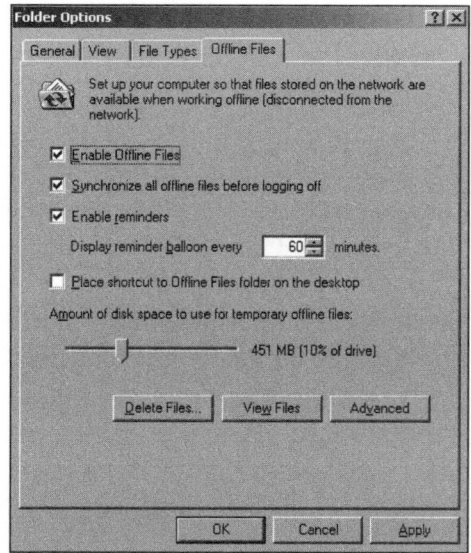

Figure 2.4   The Offline Files tab of the Folder Options dialog box.

Kit to relocate the CSC folder onto a different drive volume. The **Cachemov.exe** *utility moves the CSC folder to the root of the drive volume that is specified. After the CSC folder has been moved from its default location, all subsequent moves place it in the root of the drive volume.* **Cachemov.exe** *never returns the folder to its original default location.*

Network Share Permissions

In addition to the Caching button, located at the bottom of the Sharing tab of a shared folder's Properties sheet, is the Permissions button. The caption next to this button reads To Set Permissions For How Users Access This Folder Over The Network, Click Permissions. However, these "share" permissions are intended solely for backward-compatibility purposes; you should actually avoid such permissions unless a share resides on a file allocation table (FAT) or FAT32 drive volume, which provides no file system security. In most circumstances, you should store all data and applications on NT File System (NTFS) drive volumes. In fact, as a general rule, you should configure all system drive volumes in NTFS. With the availability of third-party tools as well as the native Windows 2000 Recovery Console, which permit command line access to NTFS drives (even if the system won't boot), it's difficult to argue against NTFS for all drives in Windows 2000.

Network share permissions have their roots back in the days of Windows for Workgroups 3.1x, before Windows NT and NTFS. Share permissions provided a way for administrators to control access to files for network users. Only three permissions are available: Full Control, Change, or Read. These three permissions can be explicitly allowed or denied. The default is Allow Full Control for the Everyone group. For shared folders that reside on FAT or FAT32 drives, share permissions do offer some degree of access control for network users. They provide *no security* for *local access*! Share permissions apply only to access over the network; these permissions have absolutely nothing to do with the underlying file system.

Monitoring, Managing, and Troubleshooting Access to Shared Files and Folders Under NTFS

Although you can somewhat control access to shared network folders by managing share permissions, Windows 2000 NTFS provides a very robust access control solution. In addition to offering administrators more granularity of security access control over files and folders than network share permissions, NTFS permissions reside at the file system level, which allows administrators to manage only one set of access control settings for both network users and local users.

NTFS Security: Users and Groups

You can apply NTFS security permissions to resources like files, folders, and printers for specific users or groups of users. Windows 2000 Professional installs two local users by default: Administrator and Guest. The Guest user is disabled by default. The Administrator user account is all powerful on the local machine and cannot be deleted, although it can be renamed. Six local groups are installed automatically: Administrators, Backup Operators, Guests, Power Users, Replicator, and Users. The Power Users group is not present in any edition of Windows 2000 Server; it exists only as a local group in Windows 2000 Professional. The Administrators account is all powerful because it is a member of the Administrators group, and, you cannot remove the Administrator from membership in the Administrators group. Table 2.1 outlines the local groups that are installed by default when you first install Windows 2000 Professional.

Table 2.2 displays the special built-in groups that are present in the Windows 2000 Professional network operating system (NOS). The primary purpose of the

Table 2.1 Local groups installed by default in Windows 2000 Professional.	
Local Group	**Role**
Administrators	Group members possess full administrative control for managing the local system, local users, and local groups.
Backup Operators	Group members have the rights to back up and restore files and folders on the local system.
Guests	Group members can't make permanent alterations to their desktop settings. The default Guest account is automatically a member of this group. By default, group members possess no specific rights or permissions on objects. If the local computer joins a Windows NT Server or Windows 2000 Server domain, the global Domain Guests group automatically becomes a member of the local Guests group.
Power Users	Group members can add new local user accounts and change existing local user accounts. Members can also create shared folders and shared printers on the network.
Replicator	This group supports file replication within a Windows 2000 domain context.
Users	Group members can perform tasks only after an administrator has specifically granted them rights to do so. They can access resources on only those that an administrator has granted them permissions. When user accounts get created, each new user automatically becomes a member of the local Users group. If the local computer becomes a member of a Windows NT Server or Windows 2000 Server domain, the global Domain Users group automatically becomes a member of the local Users group.

Table 2.2	Built-in system groups installed by default in Windows 2000 Professional.
Built-in Group	**Role**
Everyone	Group members include all users who access the computer. The best practice is to avoid using this group. If you enable the Guest account, any user can become authorized to access the system, and the user inherits the rights and permissions assigned to the Everyone group.
Authenticated Users	Group members have valid user accounts on the local system, or they possess a valid user account within the domain of which the system is a member. It is preferable that you use this group over the Everyone group for preventing anonymous access to resources.
Creator Owner	A user becomes a member of this built-in group by creating or taking ownership of a resource. Whenever a member of the Administrators group creates an object, the Administrators group is listed as the owner of that resource in lieu of the actual name of the user who created it.
Network	Group members include any user accounts from a remote computer that access the local computer via a current network connection.
Interactive	This group includes the user account for the locally logged on user.
Anonymous Logon	Group members include any user accounts that Windows 2000 did not validate or authorize.
Dialup	Group members include any user accounts that are currently connected via Dial-up Networking.

groups listed in Tables 2.1 and 2.2 is to facilitate managing access control settings (especially in NTFS) by allowing administrators to assign security permissions to groups of users rather than having to assign and maintain security permissions on resources to *hundreds or thousands* of individual users. Special built-in groups also exist under Windows 2000 Professional. These built-in groups include the groups that appear in Table 2.2.

Setting NTFS Security Permissions

Because share permissions apply to network access only, they can serve only to complicate and possibly confuse access control settings when you apply them on top of NTFS security permissions, which take effect at the file system level. If share permissions and NTFS permissions conflict, the *most restrictive* permissions apply. For example, let's say that you set share permissions on the shared folder named C:\Samples. Suppose you have set the share permissions for the Users group to Read. At the same time, let's suppose that you also have NTFS permissions set on that folder. Let's say that you've applied the Change permission for the Users group on that folder in NTFS. So now, you have conflicting permissions: Read at the share level and Change at the NTFS level. The net result is that members of the Users group are granted only the ability to Read the files within that folder; they cannot make any changes to those files because the most restrictive permissions always win.

As you can see, conflicting permissions may make it difficult to decipher which permissions users are granted when they are accessing files over the network. Therefore, the best practice is to place all shared network data and applications on NTFS drive volumes and set the appropriate security permissions for users and groups at the NTFS level. Do not change the default shared folder permissions; leave them at Full Control for the Everyone group. The most restrictive permissions apply, so all NTFS permissions "flow through" the network share. NTFS security settings can then apply equally to both local users and network users, and administrators have to manage only one set of permissions.

Local Accounts vs. Domain Accounts

In Windows NT and Windows 2000 environments, user accounts and group accounts always participate in one of two security contexts: workgroup security (also known as *peer-to-peer networking*) and domain security. Workgroup security is the default security context for individual and networked Windows NT Workstation 4 and Windows 2000 Professional computers that *are not members* of a Windows NT Server or Windows 2000 Server domain. Workgroups are logical groupings of computers that do *not* share a centrally managed user and group database. Local users and groups are managed from each computer's Local Users And Groups folder within the Computer Management console. You must maintain users and groups separately on each computer. No centralized management scheme exists within a workgroup environment; duplicate user and group accounts must exist on each computer to grant and control access permissions on each workstation's individual resources. User and group accounts are stored within a local database on each Windows 2000 Professional computer.

In a Windows NT Server/Windows 2000 Server domain network environment, on the other hand, the domain acts as a central administration point for managing users, groups, and security permissions. A *domain* is simply a logical grouping of computers that share a centrally managed database. Duplicate user and group accounts are unnecessary and unwarranted within the domain security context. Users simply log on to the domain from any domain member computer and their domain group memberships, along with their user rights, follow them wherever they travel throughout the domain.

A Windows 2000 Server Active Directory domain maintains a domain-wide database of users and groups that is referred to as the *directory*. The Active Directory database is physically stored on domain controller computers. The Active Directory can contain much detailed information about its users. The Active Directory database is *replicated* and *synchronized* with all the other domain controllers within a domain. For Windows NT Server domains, domain group memberships can travel with users across domains, provided that the proper trust relationships have been established among domains. For Windows 2000 Server Active Directory domains, group memberships can travel with users throughout the entire forest.

The Windows 2000 Logon Process

When a Windows 2000 Professional computer initially boots, the boot process ends with the system displaying the Welcome To Windows dialog box. The Ctrl+Alt+Delete keystroke sequence invokes the Winlogon process, which runs as a service in the background on Windows 2000 machines, unless you, as an administrator, have set up an automatic logon procedure, or if you have removed the Windows 2000 Professional requirement for users to press Ctrl+Alt+Delete to log on to the system. This keystroke combination advances you to the Log On To Windows dialog box, where you are prompted for a valid User Name and Password. By clicking on the Options button, you can log on using a Dial-Up Networking connection. Another option, if the computer is a member of a domain, is that you can select to log on to a domain or to log on to the local system by using the Log On To drop-down list.

After you enter your logon credentials and click OK, the Winlogon process passes this information to the Windows 2000 Local Security Authority (LSA) subsystem, which compares the information you entered with the user information stored within the local security database for the system. When you are logging on to a domain, the Winlogon process forwards the user logon information that was entered to the LSA, which then forwards the information to the Netlogon process. The Netlogon process locates a domain controller computer, where the information gets compared to the domain's directory database of valid users and passwords. Once the user and password information gets processed and the results are returned, if the Winlogon process can confirm that the user's logon credentials are valid, an *access token* is generated for the user and the user is permitted to log on.

Once the user has been allowed to log on to the system, the Windows 2000 operating system shell (Windows Explorer) launches to provide the user's desktop. The user's access token that gets generated is like a *passport with various admission tickets* attached. The access token is similar to a passport in that users "carry" it with them wherever they go. The admission tickets that come with the passport consist of a list of objects and resources that users can access. In Windows 2000, users are granted two types of access control settings:

➤ *Rights*—Windows 2000 user rights determine what privileges the user has to interact with the operating system (e.g., shut down the system, install software, log on locally, log on over the network, and so on). Administrators for Windows 2000 Professional computers can modify the default rights for users through the Local Security Settings snap-in of the Microsoft Management Console (MMC), shown in Figure 2.5.

➤ *Permissions*—Windows 2000 permissions pertain to what the user can do to objects (e.g., permissions for reading, creating, modifying, or deleting files, folders, or printers). Windows 2000 objects include a wide variety of items in addition to files, folders, and printers, including processes, threads, ports, and devices.

Access Control Lists (ACLs)

Every object within Windows 2000 Professional has various properties associated with it. One of those properties is the ACL. The ACL for an object delineates the specific users and groups that have been granted access to the object, along with the particular security permissions that have been granted to each one of those listed users and groups. To view the ACL for an object, like a folder or a file, right-click the object, click Properties, and then click the Security tab, shown

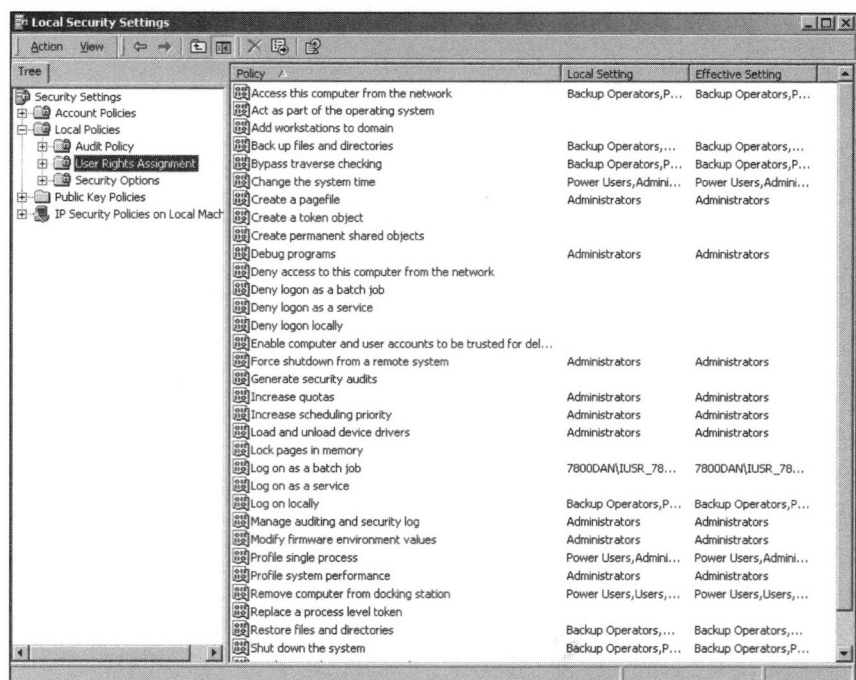

Figure 2.5 User Rights Assignment is highlighted in the Local Security Settings snap-in.

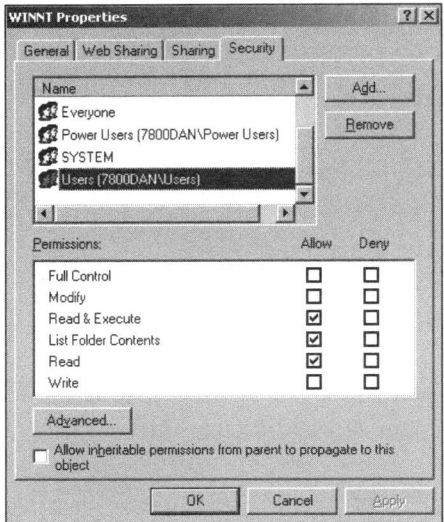

Figure 2.6 The Security tab of WINNT Properties.

in Figure 2.6. NTFS uses the information stored within ACLs to allow or deny access permissions on files and folders to users.

Another way to view and modify the ACL for a file or folder is by employing the command line tool **CACLS.exe**, shown in Figure 2.7.
Here's the **CACLS.exe** command syntax, which is explained in Table 2.3:

```
CACLS filename [/T] [/E] [/C] [/G user:perm] [/R user [...]]
[/P user:perm [...]] [/D user [...]]
```

You can use wildcard characters (* or ?) to specify more than one file or folder for a given command as well as specify more than one user in a command. ACLs are broken down into basic and advanced security permission entries.

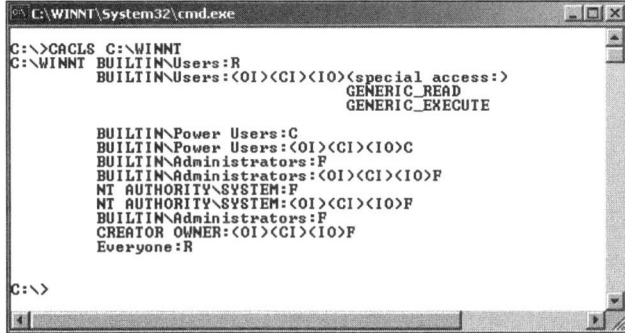

Figure 2.7 Viewing an object's Access Control List using **CACLS.exe**.

Table 2.3	Command line options for the CACLS.exe utility.
Option	**Description**
filename	Displays ACLs for the specified file or folder.
/t	Changes ACLs of specified files in the current directory and all subdirectories.
/e	Edits the ACL instead of replacing it.
/c	Continues to change ACLs and ignores errors.
/g user:perm	Grants specified user access rights. The permission can be Read (R), Write (W), Change (write) (C), and Full Control (F).
/r user	Revokes a specified user's access rights (valid only with **/e**).
/p user:perm	Replaces a specified user's access rights. The permission can be: None (N), Read (R), Write (W), Change (write) (C), and Full Control (F).
/d user	Denies access to the specified user.

Basic Permissions

Basic permissions are actually comprised of predefined advanced NTFS permissions and are applied per user and per group. Individual file permissions differ slightly from the permissions that apply to folders. Table 2.4 highlights the basic permissions available for files, whereas Table 2.5 outlines the basic permissions available for folders.

Note: The List Folder Contents permission is inherited by folders but not files, and it should appear only when you view folder permissions. Read & Execute is inherited by both files and folders and is always present when you view file or folder permissions.

Table 2.4	Basic NTFS security permissions for files for specified users and groups.
Permission	**Description**
Full Control	Allows/denies full access to the file. Includes the ability to read, write, delete, modify, change permissions, and take ownership of the file.
Modify	Allows/denies the ability to read, write, delete, modify, and read permissions for the file.
Read & Execute	Allows/denies specified users and groups the ability to execute the file and read its contents, read the file's attributes and extended attributes, and read the file's permissions.
Read	Allows/denies the same permissions as Read & Execute except for Execute File.
Write	Allows/denies the ability to write data to the file, create files and append data, and write attributes and extended attributes.

Table 2.5	Basic NTFS security permissions for folders for specified users and groups.
Permission	**Description**
Full Control	Allows/denies full access to objects within the folder. Includes the ability to read, write, delete, modify, change permissions, and take ownership of the folder.
Modify	Allows/denies the ability to read, write, delete, modify, and read permissions for the folder.
Read & Execute	Allows/denies specified users and groups the ability to traverse the folder, execute files within the folder, list its contents, read its contents, read the folder's attributes and extended attributes, and read the folder's permissions.
List Folder Contents	Allows/denies essentially the same permissions as Read & Execute. Allows/denies the ability to display files and subfolders, but this permission does not affect a user's ability to run (execute) an application program as the Read & Execute permission does.
Read	Allows/denies the same permissions as List Folder Contents except for Traverse Folder and Execute File.
Write	Allows/denies the ability to create files and write data, create folders and append data, and write attributes and extended attributes.

By default, NTFS security permissions are inherited from an object's parent. An administrator can manually override the default inheritance and can explicitly configure ACL settings. To disable permission inheritance, deselect the Allow Inheritable Permissions From Parent To Propagate To This Object checkbox on the Security tab of the folder's Properties sheet. As soon as you uncheck this box, the Security message box, shown in Figure 2.8, appears. It prompts you to either copy the existing permissions or remove them entirely.

Advanced Permissions

NTFS advanced permissions are the building blocks for basic permissions. In Windows 2000, advanced permissions allow administrators to have very granular

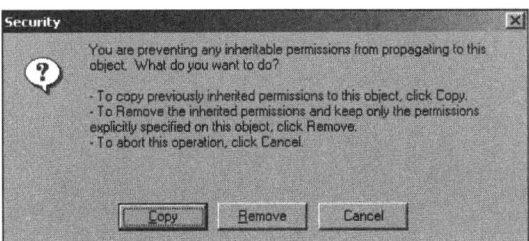

Figure 2.8 The Security message box.

control over exactly what types of access users can have over files and folders. Advanced permissions are somewhat hidden from view. They allow administrators to fine-tune ACL (security) settings. The Security tab in a file or folder's Properties sheet notifies you when advanced permissions are present. Click the Advanced button to view, add, modify, or remove advanced permissions. Figure 2.9 shows you how Windows 2000 notifies you that more than just basic permissions exist for an object. At the bottom of the Security tab, the system displays a text message notification just to the right of the Advanced button that says Additional Permissions Are Present But Not Viewable Here. Press Advanced To See Them.

After you click Advanced, you see the Access Control Settings dialog box, which shows each access control setting that has been applied per user and per group. To view individual advanced permission entries, click one of the users or groups listed and then click the View/Edit button. The Permission Entry dialog box, shown in Figure 2.10, appears. It gives administrators very fine control over individual users' and groups' abilities to manipulate data and program files that are stored on NTFS drive volumes.

From this dialog box, you can:

1. Change the Name so that this permission entry applies to some other user or group.

2. Modify the Apply Onto drop-down list to specify exactly where these advanced permissions should apply.

3. Alter the actual permission entries themselves by marking or clearing the Allow or Deny checkbox for each permission that you want to affect.

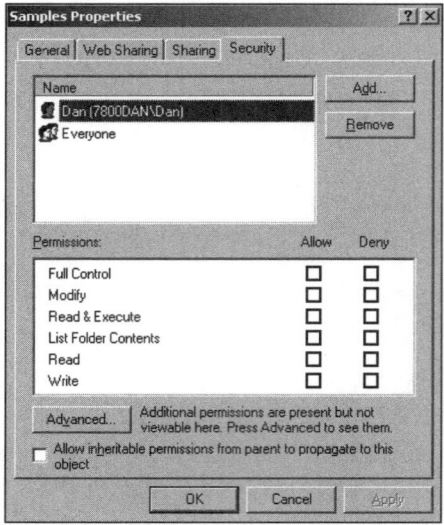

Figure 2.9   The Security tab of Samples Properties.

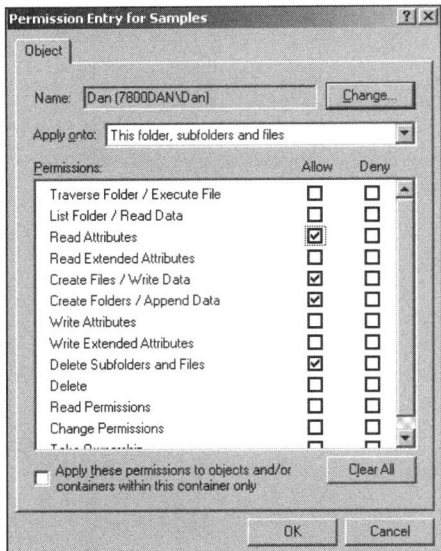

Figure 2.10   The Object tab of Permission Entry For Samples.

To change NTFS security permissions, you must be the owner of the file or folder whose permissions you want to modify, or the owner must grant you permission to make modifications to the object's security settings. Groups or users who are granted Full Control for a folder can delete files and subfolders *within* that folder *regardless* of the permissions protecting those files and subfolders. If the checkboxes for the Security tab under Permissions are *shaded*, the file or folder has *inherited* the permissions from the parent folder. By cleaning the Allow inheritable permissions from parent to propagate to this object checkbox, you can copy those inherited permissions and turn them into explicit permissions, or you can remove them entirely and manually establish new explicit permissions.

Table 2.6 concisely defines Windows 2000 advanced permissions.

NTFS security permissions are *cumulative*. Users obtain permissions by having them assigned directly to their user accounts in addition to attaining permissions via group memberships. Users retain all permissions as they are assigned. If a user named Dan has the Allow Read permission for the Graphics folder and if Dan is a member of the Users group, which has been assigned Allow Write for the same folder, Dan has both the Allow Read and Allow Write permissions. Permissions continue to accumulate. However, Deny entries always override Allow entries for the same permission type (Read, Modify, Write, and so on).

Table 2.6 Advanced NTFS security permission entries for files and folders.

Permission	Description
Traverse Folder/Execute File	Allows or denies moving through folders to reach other files or folders, even if the user has no permissions for the traversed folders (applies to folders only). Traverse Folder takes effect only when the group or user is not granted the *Bypass traverse checking* user right in the Group Policy snap-in. (By default, the Everyone group is given the *Bypass traverse checking* user right.)
Execute File	Allows or denies running application program files. Setting the Traverse Folder permission on a folder does not automatically set the Execute File permission on all files within that folder.
List Folder/Read Data	Allows or denies viewing file names and subfolder names within the folder.
Read Data	Allows or denies viewing data in files.
Read Attributes	Allows or denies viewing the attributes—such as read only, hidden, and archive—of a file or folder.
Read Extended Attributes	Allows or denies viewing the extended attributes of a file or folder. Some extended attributes are defined by application programs and can vary by application. The NTFS compression and encryption attributes are considered extended (or advanced) attributes.
Create Files/Write Data	Allows or denies creating files within a folder (applies to folders only).
Write Data	Allows or denies making changes to a file and overwriting the existing data (applies to files only).
Write Attributes	Allows or denies changing the attributes—such as read-only or hidden—of a file or folder.
Write Extended Attributes	Allows or denies changing the extended attributes of a file or folder. Extended attributes are defined by programs and may vary by program. Some extended attributes are defined by application programs and can vary by application. The NTFS compression and encryption attributes are considered extended (or advanced) attributes.
Delete Subfolders and Files	Allows or denies deleting subfolders and files, even if the Delete permission has not been granted on the subfolder or file.
Delete	Allows or denies deleting the file or folder. If you don't have the Delete permission on a file or folder, you can still delete it if you have been granted Delete Subfolders and Files on the parent folder.

(continued)

Table 2.6 Advanced NTFS security permission entries for files and folders (continued).	
Permission	**Description**
Read Permissions	Allows or denies reading permissions of the file or folder.
Change Permissions	Allows or denies changing permissions—such as Full Control, Read, and Modify—of the file or folder.
Take Ownership	Allows or denies taking ownership of a file or folder. The owner of a file or folder can always change permissions on it, regardless of any other permissions that have been assigned to protect the file or folder.
Create Folders/Append Data	Allows or denies creating folders within a folder.
Append Data	Allows or denies making changes to the end of a file, but not changing, deleting, or overwriting existing data (applies to files only).

Default NTFS Security Permissions

By default, all NTFS-formatted drive volumes are assigned the Allow Full Control permission for the Everyone group for the root of each drive. Folders and subfolders within each drive volume automatically inherit this default permission setting. Unfortunately, this setting leaves your Windows 2000 systems very vulnerable. By default, any user who can log on to the system, either locally or over the network, can modify or delete some or all of the files and folders that reside on the system! As a best practice, you should remove the Everyone group's permissions entry from all drive volumes, except from the systemroot drive, where the Windows 2000 system files are stored. When you install Windows 2000 Professional on an NTFS volume, the systemroot folder (e.g., C:\WINNT) is automatically assigned special default security permissions for the following groups: Administrators, Creator Owner, Everyone, Power Users, System, and Users.

The Everyone group's permissions are assigned *no Allows* and *no Denies* for the systemroot folder by default. Users must be granted permission to access a file or a folder with the type of access specified (Read, Modify, Full Control, and so on). If the user's account, or one of the groups that the user is a member of, is not specifically granted or denied permission, the user cannot access the file or folder. This is known as an *implied* or *implicit* Deny.

 You should not change the default security settings for the systemroot folder and its subfolders. Modifying the default permissions for the Windows 2000 Professional system files can have very adverse effects on the system. In addition to not changing its default permissions, you

should never attempt to compress or encrypt the systemroot folder or any of its subfolders. Compression or encryption placed on the system folders can render Windows 2000 Professional unstable or possibly unbootable.

NTFS Permission Conflicts

Obviously, a user may be a member of several different groups. You can apply NTFS permissions to both users and groups for access control on resources such as files and folders. For security permissions assigned to a user that conflict with other security permissions that have been granted to groups of which the user is also a member, the most *liberal* permissions take precedence for that user. The one *overriding* exception is any explicit Deny permission entry. Deny permissions always take precedence over Allow permissions.

 Just as Deny permissions always take precedence over Allow permissions, explicit permissions always override inherited permissions.

Monitoring, Managing, and Troubleshooting Access to Files and Folders

NTFS for Windows 2000 Professional offers several accessibility features that help administrators maintain and safeguard applications and data. In addition to providing local and network access control permissions, NTFS offers native data compression to save disk space. Folders that do not implement NTFS data compression can take advantage of native data encryption to help protect the confidentiality of data. For troubleshooting resource access, you can enable auditing for folders and files housed on NTFS volumes.

Configuring, Managing, and Troubleshooting NTFS File and Folder Compression

Unlike previous data compression schemes like DoubleSpace or DriveSpace for the Windows 9x platform (where you had to compress entire drive volumes), Windows 2000 NTFS data compression works folder by folder (or even file by file). NTFS compression is simply an advanced (or extended) file system attribute that you can apply to files and folders. NTFS data compression enables you to compress individual files or folders. You can compress individual files within uncompressed folders; compressed files and folders are identified by being displayed in blue.

NTFS Compression for Files

To enable compression for a specific file, follow these steps:

1. Right-click the file from Windows Explorer or My Computer.

2. Click Properties.

3. Click the Advanced button in the Compress Or Encrypt Attributes section of the Advanced Attributes dialog box, shown in Figure 2.11. This dialog box gives you mutually exclusive options to either Compress Contents To Save Disk Space or Encrypt Contents To Secure Data.

4. Click the Compress Contents To Save Disk Space checkbox.

5. Click OK in the Advanced Attributes dialog box.

6. Click OK in the file's Properties sheet.

The file name that gets compressed will be displayed in the color blue, indicating that it is now a compressed file. Figure 2.12 shows uncompressed files.

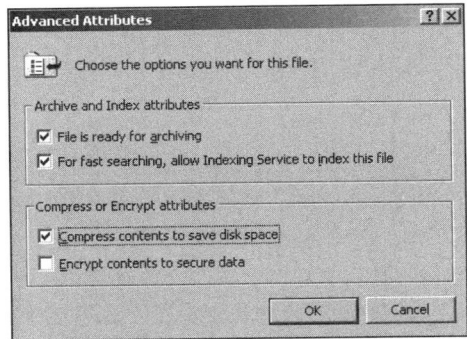

Figure 2.11   The Advanced Attributes dialog box.

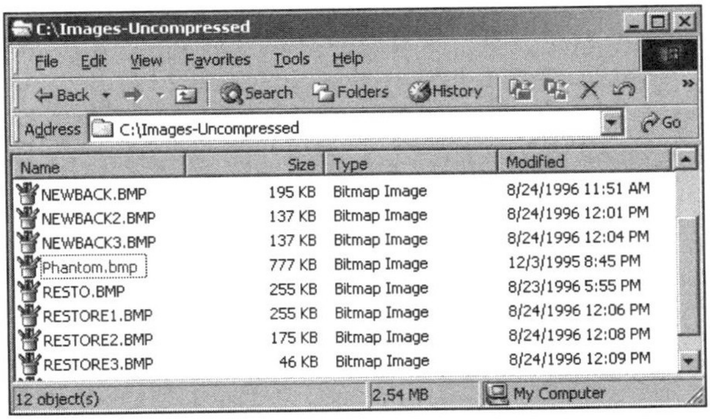

Figure 2.12   Uncompressed files.

To uncompress a specific file, be sure that sufficient disk space exists for the uncompressed size of the file, and then follow these steps:

1. Right-click the file from Windows Explorer or My Computer.

2. Click Properties.

3. Click the Advanced button in the Attributes section.

4. Deselect the Compress Contents To Save Disk Space checkbox.

5. Click OK in the Advanced Attributes dialog box.

6. Click OK in the file's Properties sheet.

NTFS Compression for Folders

You turn on compression for NTFS folders in the same manner as for files:

1. Right-click the folder from Windows Explorer or My Computer.

2. Click Properties.

3. Click the Advanced button in the Attributes section.

4. Select the Compress Contents To Save Disk Space checkbox.

5. Click OK in the Advanced Attributes dialog box.

6. You are attempting to compress an entire folder, not just a single file, so the Confirm Attribute Changes dialog box, shown in Figure 2.13, appears. It prompts the user to specify which files and/or folders compression is applied to. If you click Cancel, you can abort the data compression process. In our case, however, we don't want to do this. Therefore, click one of the two available options—either Apply Changes To This Folder Only or Apply Changes To This Folder, Subfolders And Files.

7. Click OK after you have chosen an option. The Confirm Attribute Changes dialog box closes, and the compression attributes are applied to the files and any subfolders you specified.

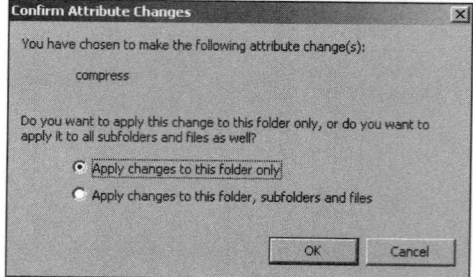

Figure 2.13 The Confirm Attribute Changes dialog box.

Figure 2.14 illustrates the significant difference that compression can make on saving valuable disk storage space. By right-clicking a folder and selecting Properties, you can determine the folder's actual physical size on the disk, as shown under Size On Disk. By comparing folders with identical contents, one compressed and the other uncompressed, you can readily assess the impact that compression can make.

To uncompress a folder, first make sure that enough disk space is available to accommodate the *uncompressed* size of the folder. Next, simply reverse the previously outlined procedure.

Moving and Copying Compressed Files and Folders

Moving or copying compressed files and folders to non-NTFS drive volumes results in those objects being stored in their uncompressed state for the destination drive volume. If you *move* a compressed file or folder into an *uncompressed* folder, the object *retains* its compressed attribute; it remains compressed. If you *copy* a compressed file or folder into an *uncompressed* folder, the object *inherits* its attribute from the destination folder; it loses its compression attribute and becomes uncompressed within the target folder. Of course, the original file or folder that is copied remains unchanged; it stays compressed.

If you *move* an *uncompressed* file or folder into a *compressed* folder located on the same drive volume, the object *retains* its *uncompressed* attribute; it remains *uncompressed*. If you *move* an *uncompressed* file or folder into a *compressed* folder located on a different drive volume, or from a non-NTFS volume, the object

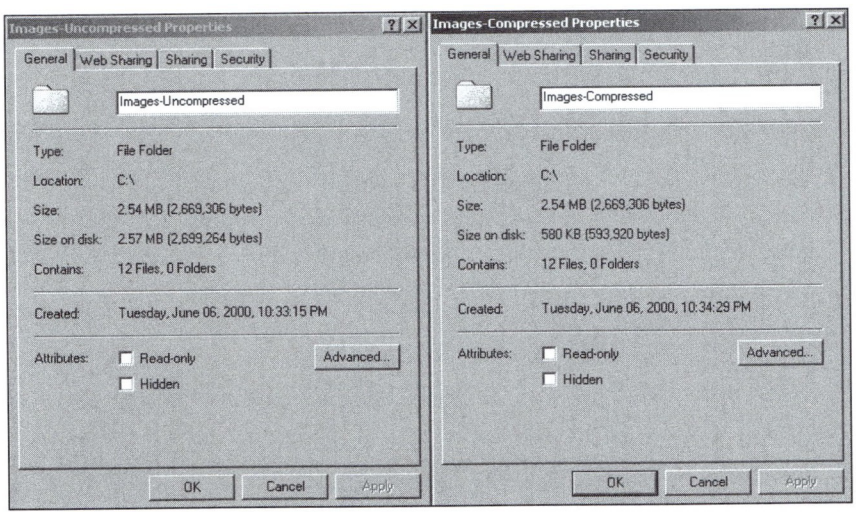

Figure 2.14   Comparing compressed and uncompressed sizes of files and folders.

inherits the compression. If you *copy* an *uncompressed* file or folder into a *compressed* folder, the object *inherits* its attribute from the destination folder; it gains the compression attribute and becomes compressed within the target folder. Of course, the original file or folder that is copied remains unchanged; it stays uncompressed.

 Compressed files and folders still require NTFS security permission settings to ensure data integrity.

Controlling Access to Files and Folders by Using Permissions

Users attain access to NTFS files and folders by virtue of being granted explicit or implicit (inherited) permissions for those resources directly to their user account or through access permissions granted to groups to which the users belong. To assign Read Only security permissions to a user or a group for a specific folder, follow these steps:

1. Right-click the folder on which you wish to apply permissions and select Properties.

2. Click the Security tab.

3. If permissions are being inherited for the user and/or group that you want to work with, deselect the Allow Inheritable Permissions From Parent To Propagate To This Object checkbox.

4. If the user(s) or group(s) to which you want to assign permissions do not currently appear, click the Add button.

5. From the Select Users, Computers, Or Groups dialog box, shown in Figure 2.15, select the group or user to which you want to assign permissions. This dialog box lets you choose from available users and groups for assigning NTFS security permissions onto files and folders.

6. Click the Add button.

7. Click OK to return to the Security tab of the folder's Properties sheet.

8. Verify that the Allow checkboxes are marked for the Read And Execute, List Folder Contents, and Read permissions.

9. Click OK to accept your settings.

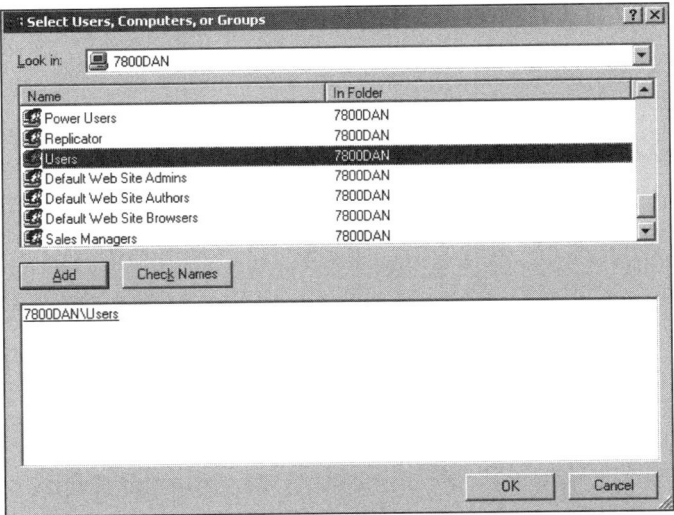

Figure 2.15   The Select Users, Computers, Or Groups dialog box.

Denying Access to a Resource

Deny permissions always override Allow permissions, so you can be assured that once you establish Deny permissions for a particular user or group on a resource, no other combination of Allow permissions through group memberships can circumvent the Deny. To assign Deny security permissions to a user or a group for a specific folder, follow these steps:

1. Right-click the folder on which you wish to apply permissions and select Properties.

2. Click the Security tab.

3. If permissions are being inherited for the user and/or group that you want to work with, deselect the Allow Inheritable Permissions From Parent To Propagate To This Object checkbox.

4. If the user(s) or group(s) to which you want to assign permissions do not currently appear, click the Add button.

5. Select the group or user that you want to assign permissions to from the Select Users, Computers, Or Groups dialog box.

6. Click the Add button.

7. Click OK to be returned to the Security tab of the folder's Properties sheet.

8. Click the Deny checkbox for each permission that you wish to explicitly disallow.

9. Click OK to accept your settings.

If you deny the Read permission for a group on a particular folder, any member of that group is denied the ability to read the contents of that folder. When you assign Deny permissions for a user or a group on a file or folder, as soon as you click OK in the Properties sheet, a Security message box, shown in Figure 2.16, appears. It reminds you that Deny permissions take precedence over Allow permissions.

Click Yes in the Security message box to have the new Deny permissions take effect. When users who are members of the group that was assigned Deny permissions for reading the folder attempt to gain access to that folder, they are greeted by an Access Is Denied message box, shown in Figure 2.17.

Optimizing Access to Files and Folders

The best practice is to always assign NTFS security permissions to groups rather than to individual users. You should place users into appropriate groups and set NTFS permissions on those groups. In this manner, permissions are easier to assign and maintain.

NTFS Permissions: Moving and Copying Files and Folders

Moving or copying files and folders from an NTFS drive volume to network drives or other media that are non-NTFS volumes results in the *loss of all NTFS security permission settings* for the objects moved or copied. The result of moving or copying NTFS files and folders to different NTFS folders varies depending upon whether the objects are being moved or copied, and depending upon the destination drive volume. Table 2.7 shows the different effects on NTFS permissions when copying files and folders versus moving files and folders.

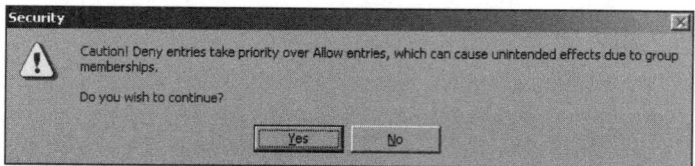

Figure 2.16　A Security message box.

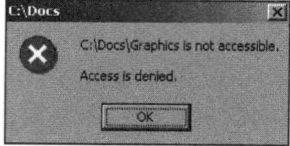

Figure 2.17　The Access Is Denied message.

Table 2.7 NTFS permissions that are retained or inherited when you move and copy files and folders.	
Type of Transfer	**Effective Permissions after Move or Copy**
Moving within the same NTFS volume	Files and folders that are moved retain their permissions from the source folder.
Moving to a different NTFS volume	Files and folders that are moved inherit their permissions from the destination folder.
Copying within the same NTFS volume	Files and folders that are copied inherit their permissions from the destination folder.
Copying to a different NTFS volume	Files and folders that are copied inherit their permissions from the destination folder.

The standard Windows 2000 **xcopy.exe** command line utility offers -O and -X options that retain an object's NTFS permissions in addition to inheriting the destination folder's permissions. The -X switch also retains any auditing settings (which are discussed later in this chapter). To retain only an object's source permissions without inheriting any permissions from the destination folder, use the **scopy.exe** tool or the **robocopy.exe** tool from the *Windows 2000 Professional Resource Kit* or the *Windows 2000 Server Resource Kit*.

Taking Ownership of Files and Folders

A user who has ownership of a file or folder can transfer ownership of it to a different user or to a group. Administrators can grant users the ability to take ownership of specified files and folders. In addition, administrators have the authority to take ownership of any file or folder for themselves. Object ownership cannot be assigned to others; a user must have permission to take ownership of an object.

Changing ownership of files and folders can become necessary when someone who is responsible for certain files and folders leaves an organization without granting any other users permissions to them. To take ownership of a folder as an administrator, follow these steps:

1. Log on to the system as the administrator or an equivalent user.

2. Right-click the folder from Windows Explorer or My Computer and select Properties.

3. Click the Security tab.

4. Click the Advanced button.

5. Click the Owner tab in the Access Control Settings dialog box.

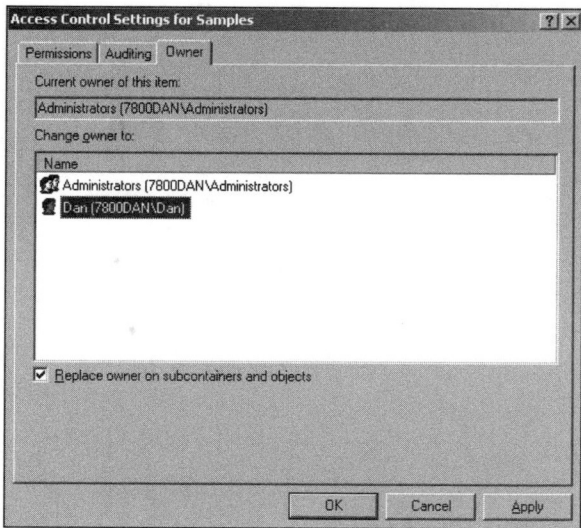

Figure 2.18   Changing the ownership of a file or folder.

6. Click the name of the person in the Change Owner To section to change the folder's ownership, as shown in Figure 2.18.

7. If you also want the ownership to change for the subfolders and files, click the Replace Owner On Subcontainers And Objects checkbox.

8. Click OK in the Access Control Settings dialog box.

9. Click OK in the Properties sheet.

Auditing System Access

Windows 2000 Professional allows administrators to audit both user and system events using the auditing feature. When auditing is enabled for specific events, the occurrence of the events triggers a log entry in the Windows 2000 Professional Security Log. You view the security log with the Event Viewer snap-in of the MMC. By default, auditing is turned off. Before you enable auditing, you should formulate an audit policy to determine which workstations will be audited and which events audited on them. When planning the events to audit, you also need to decide whether you will audit successes and/or failures for each event.

Auditing for the local Windows 2000 system is enabled through the Local Security Settings snap-in of the MMC, shown in Figure 2.19. You must initially turn on auditing from the Local Security Settings console for each type of event that you want to monitor.

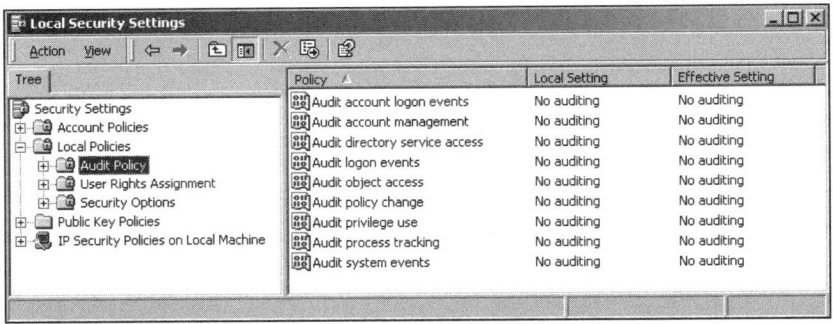

Figure 2.19   The Local Security Settings console.

You can audit several types of events, such as:

➤ File and folder access

➤ Logons and logoffs

➤ System shutdowns and restarts

➤ Changes to user and group accounts

➤ Changes attempted on Active Directory objects if the Windows 2000 Professional computer is a member of a Windows 2000 Server domain

When you track successful events, you can gauge the how often different resources are used. This information can be useful when you are planning for future resource allocation. By tracking failed events, you can become aware of possible security intrusions. Unsuccessful logon attempts, attempts to change security permissions, or efforts to take ownership of files or folders can all point to someone trying to gain unauthorized access to the system or the network. If such attempts occur at odd hours, these events take on an even more suspicious tone. To enable auditing on a Windows 2000 Professional system, follow these steps:

1. Launch the Local Security Policy MMC snap-in from the Start|Programs| Administrative Tools folder.

2. At the Local Security Settings console, expand the Local Policies folder and then click Audit Policy.

3. Double-click the event policy to choose which one you want to enable and to display the Local Security Policy Setting dialog box, shown in Figure 2.20. To enable object access auditing, double-click the Audit Object Access policy (refer back to Figure 2.19).

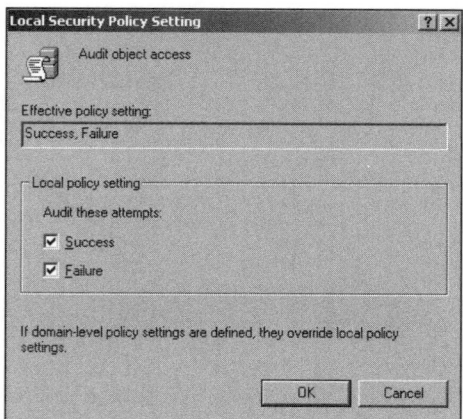

Figure 2.20   The Local Security Policy Setting dialog box for the Audit Object Access event.

4. Click the Success checkbox, the Failure checkbox, or both checkboxes.

5. Click OK.

6. Close the Local Security Settings console and restart the computer.

Once you have turned on audit tracking for object access events, you need to specify which files and folders you want to audit. You should be fairly selective about which ones you choose to audit. If you have enabled auditing for successes as well as failures, the system's Security Event log may become filled very quickly if you are auditing heavily used files and folders. To enable audit logging for specific files and folders, follow these steps:

1. Log on to the system as the administrator or an equivalent user.

2. Right-click the file or folder from Windows Explorer or My Computer and select Properties.

3. Click the Security tab.

4. Click the Advanced button.

5. Click the Auditing tab in the Access Control Settings dialog box.

6. Click the Add button.

7. Click the user or group that you want to track for access to the file or folder and click OK. The Auditing Entry dialog box, shown in Figure 2.21, appears.

8. Select each access event that you want to track by marking each event's associated Successful checkbox, Failed checkbox, or both.

9. By default, audit settings apply to the current folder, subfolders, and files. You can change this behavior by clicking on the Apply Onto drop-down list.

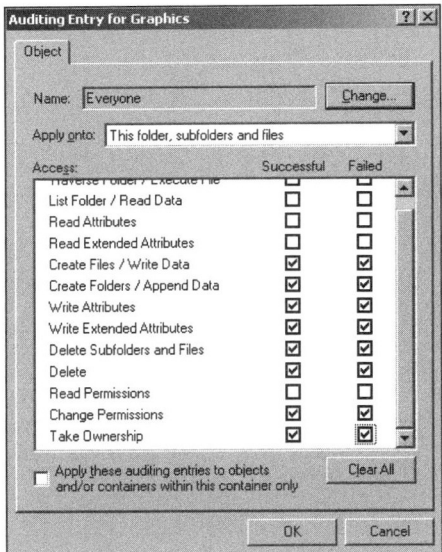

Figure 2.21   The Auditing Entry dialog box.

10. Click OK in the Auditing Entry dialog box.

11. Click OK in the Access Control Settings dialog box.

12. Click OK in the Properties sheet.

After you have properly set up auditing, all events that meet your auditing criteria are logged into the system's Event Viewer Security Log. You access the Event Viewer console from Start|Administrative Tools|Event Viewer or by right-clicking on the My Computer desktop icon and selecting Manage. You'll find the Event Viewer beneath the System Tools folder in the Computer Management console. By selecting the Security Log, you can view all of the auditing events that the system has recorded based on the parameters you have set. If a user deletes an object, for example, that event is listed with all the pertinent information in the security log, shown in Figure 2.22. Double-clicking on an event in the log displays the detailed information.

Keeping Data Private with Encrypting File System (EFS)

Microsoft designed the new EFS for Windows 2000 to ensure the confidentiality of sensitive data. EFS employs public key/private key-based cryptography. EFS works only in the Windows 2000 NTFS 5. Its use is transparent to users. You can either compress or encrypt files and folders, but you can't do both. Files that are encrypted using EFS remain encrypted even if you move or rename them. Encrypted files that are backed up or copied also retain their encryption attributes as long as they reside on NTFS-formatted drive volumes. EFS leaves

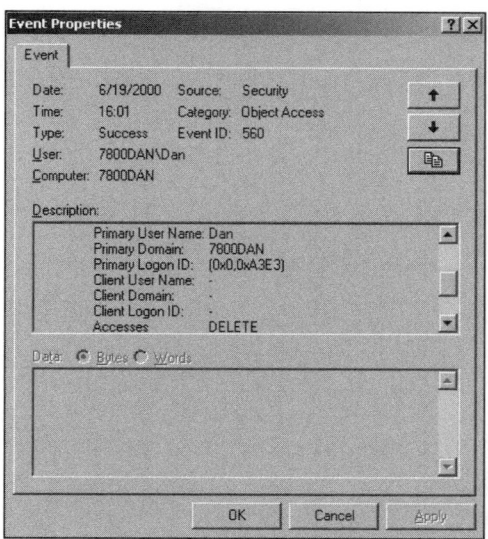

Figure 2.22   An Event Properties window from the Event Viewer security log.

no file remnants behind because it modifies an encrypted file, nor does it leave any traces of decrypted data from encrypted files in temporary files or in the Windows 2000 pagefile. You can encrypt and decrypt files and folders from the graphical user interface (GUI) using Windows Explorer as well as from the command line using the **cipher.exe** tool.

The best practice for using encryption is to first encrypt a folder and then move files into the encrypted folder. Folders do not actually become encrypted; folders get marked with the encryption attribute. The files contained within an encrypted folder are the objects that actually become encrypted. You can also individually encrypt files without their having to reside within a folder that is marked for encryption. To encrypt and decrypt files physically located on a Windows 2000 server over the network, that server must be trusted for delegation. By definition, domain controllers are already trusted for delegation. Member servers require this Trust for Delegation. To encrypt a file or folder from Windows Explorer, follow these steps:

1. Right-click the file or folder and select Properties.

2. Click the Advanced button in the Compress Or Encrypt Attributes section of the General tab of the folder's Properties sheet.

3. Click the Encrypt Contents To Secure Data checkbox in the Advanced Attributes dialog box.

4. Click OK.

5. Click OK in the Properties sheet. An empty folder will then become encrypted, and any files and folders that are placed within it are encrypted. If subfolders or files exist within the folder, the Confirm Attribute Changes dialog box, shown in Figure 2.23, appears.

6. Click either Apply Changes To This Folder Only or Apply Changes To This Folder, Subfolders And Files for the object(s) that you want encryption to affect.

7. Click OK; the encryption attribute is applied to the appropriate objects.

Accessing Encrypted Files and Data Recovery Agents (DRAs)

Encryption is just an extended (or advanced) attribute of a file or folder. If you set NTFS permissions to deny the Write Extended Attributes permission on a file or folder, the users to whom you have assigned this Deny permission cannot use encryption. Once a file has the encryption attribute, only the user who encrypted it or the DRA can access it. DRAs are users who are designated as recovery agents for encrypted files. Only these users have the ability to decrypt *any* encrypted file, no matter who has encrypted it. Other users who attempt to access an encrypted file receive an Access Is Denied message. The default DRAs are:

➤ Local Administrator account for Windows 2000 Professional non-domain member computers

➤ Local Administrator account for Windows 2000 Server non-domain member computers

➤ Domain Administrator account for Windows 2000 Server domain controllers, Windows 2000 domain member servers, and Windows 2000 Professional domain member computers

DRAs can log on to a system and decrypt files and folders so that they are once again accessible to other users. In fact, if you remove the DRA from a standalone Windows 2000 computer or from a Windows 2000 Server domain, no Data Recovery policy is in place and EFS *prohibits* users from encrypting files and folders.

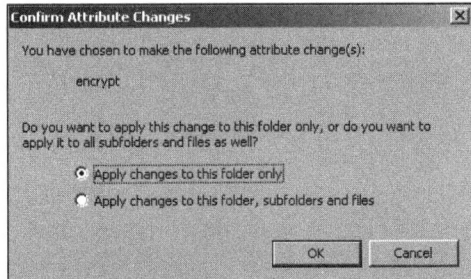

Figure 2.23 The Confirm Attribute Changes dialog box.

Moving and Copying Encrypted Files

Encrypted files that are moved or copied to another NTFS folder remain encrypted. Encrypted files that are moved or copied to a FAT or FAT32 drive volume become decrypted because EFS is supported only on NTFS 5 volumes. Files also become decrypted if they are moved or copied to a floppy disk. Users who did not originally encrypt a file or folder receive an Access Is Denied message if they try to copy an encrypted file or folder. If users other than the one who encrypted the file attempt to move it to a different NTFS volume, or to a FAT or FAT32 drive volume, they receive an Access Is Denied error message. If users other than the one who encrypted the file attempt to move the encrypted file to a different folder located on the *same* NTFS volume, the file is moved.

Managing and Troubleshooting Web Server Resources

Unlike its big brother, Windows 2000 Server, Windows 2000 Professional does not install Internet Information Services (IIS) by default. You must manually install IIS by going to the Control Panel, double-clicking the Add/Remove Programs icon, and clicking the Add/Remove Windows Components button. Mark the checkbox for Internet Information Services (IIS) and click Next to have the Windows Components Wizard install the Web server resources for you. If you *upgrade* your computer from Windows NT 4 Workstation to Windows 2000 Professional, IIS 5 is installed automatically only if you installed Peer Web Services on your previous version of Windows.

Before you can install IIS, your computer must already have the Transmission Control Protocol/Internet Protocol (TCP/IP) network protocol and its related connectivity utilities installed. In addition, Microsoft recommends that you have a Domain Name System (DNS) server available on your network for host name to IP address resolution. For very small networks, you may use a HOSTS file or an LMHOSTS file in lieu of a DNS server. A HOSTS file maps DNS host computer names to IP addresses. An LMHOSTS file maps NetBIOS computer names to IP addresses. Windows 2000 Professional looks for these two text files in the SystemRoot\system32\drivers\etc folder. Sample HOSTS and LMHOSTS files are also installed by default into this folder.

Once you have installed IIS, you manage the services from the Internet Information Services snap-in of the MMC. You can launch the IIS console by clicking on Start|Programs|Administrative Tools|Internet Service Manager. From the IIS console, you can administer the default FTP site, default Web site, and the default Simple Mail Transfer Protocol (SMTP) virtual server for the Windows 2000 Professional computer, as shown in Figure 2.24.

Additional, Web-based documentation on IIS administration is available by pointing to **http://localhost/iisHelp/iis/misc/default.asp** in your Web browser, as shown in Figure 2.25.

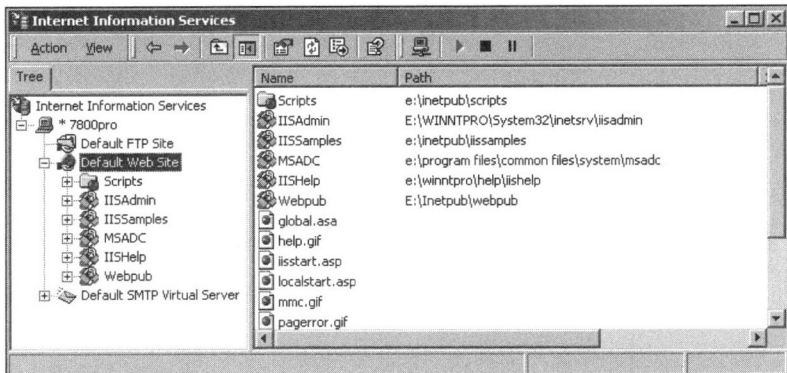

Figure 2.24 The Internet Information Services console.

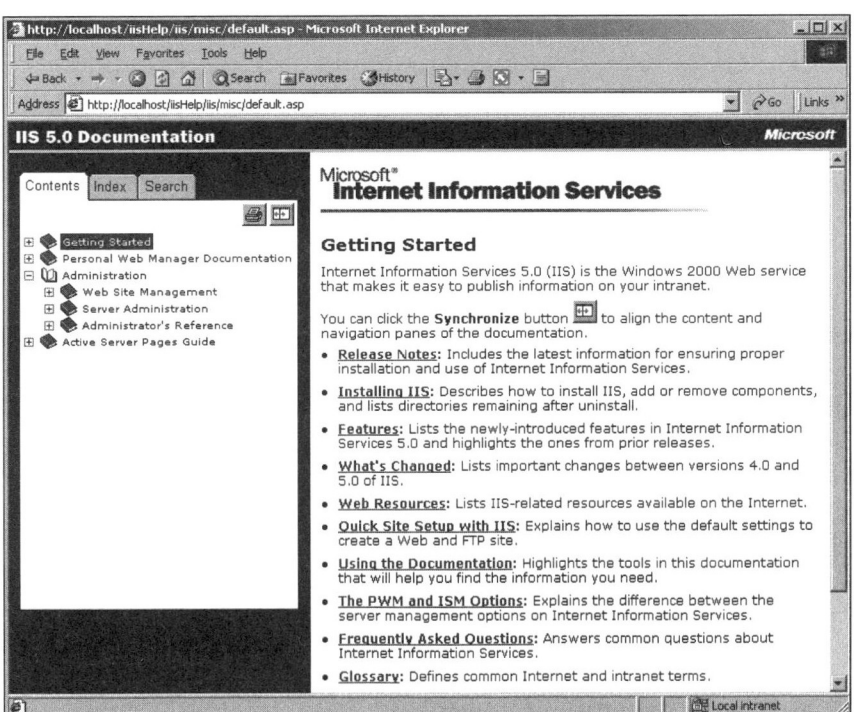

Figure 2.25 The Getting Started Web page for IIS HTML-based help documentation.

SystemRoot Console Administering the Default Web and FTP Sites

You can view and modify the settings for IIS through the IIS console by right-clicking on the computer name container in the left-hand pane of the console window and selecting Properties. From the computer name Properties sheet, you can view the system's overall Master Properties for both the World Wide Web (WWW) Service and the File Transfer Protocol (FTP) Service for all sites created on the computer. The WWW Service Master Properties that you can modify include the following:

➤ Web site identification, connections, and logging settings

➤ Performance tuning settings

➤ Internet Server API (ISAPI) filters

➤ Home directory settings

➤ Default document names

➤ Directory security

➤ Hypertext Transfer Protocol (HTTP) header information

➤ Custom HTTP error messages

➤ IIS 3 administration options

You can work with the properties for the default FTP site by right-clicking on the Default FTP Site folder and selecting Properties. Similarly, you can right-click the Default Web Site folder and choose Properties to configure many of the same settings that apply to the WWW Master Service Properties at the individual Web site level. You can create a new virtual directory for the default Web site by right-clicking on Default Web Site and selecting New|Virtual Directory. When the Virtual Directory Creation Wizard launches, you assign a name to the new virtual directory. You must also designate the path for the physical folder where the Web files are stored for the new virtual directory. After you have entered this information, you can complete the wizard and you will have set up a new virtual directory that users can access via the **http://computer_name/ virtual_directory_name** Uniform Resource Locator (URL), also known simply as a Web address.

Troubleshooting IIS

If users are experiencing problems connecting to the default Web site, to the default FTP site, or to a new virtual directory that you have created, you can follow the steps listed in the next few sections to rectify the problem(s).

Internet Web Site

To isolate problems that may be preventing users from connecting to the Internet Web site:

➤ Check that the Web server contains HTML files in the drive_letter:\ inetpub\wwwroot folder.

➤ Attempt to connect to the Web server's home directory using a browser on a computer that has a live connection to the Internet. Your Web site must have a public IP address that is registered with the InterNIC, and that public IP address must be registered with the Internet's DNS servers. For example, if your registered domain name is **ExamCram.com** and you want to view a virtual directory on that Web site named "aboutus", type in **www.ExamCram.com/ aboutus** in the Address line of your Web browser. The Web page that you requested should appear within your Web browser's window.

Intranet Web Site

To isolate problems that may be preventing users from connecting to an intranet Web site:

➤ Check that the Web server and the client computers have active network connections.

➤ Verify that a Windows Internet Naming Service (WINS) and/or DNS server is available and functioning on your network for computer name to IP address name resolution.

➤ Go to a client computer, launch a Web browser, and type in a valid URL for the Web server computer. Intranet URLs take the **http://computer_name/ home_page_name.htm** or **http://computer_name/virtual_directory_ alias_name** form. Examples of this syntax are **http://computer1/myhome-page.htm** and **http://computer1/myvirtualdirectory**.

Managing Local and Network Print Devices

You manage print devices in Windows 2000 Professional from the Printers folder, which is accessible from the Control Panel or by clicking Start | Settings | Printers. When working with printing in Windows 2000, you need to fully understand the following printing terminology as defined by Microsoft:

➤ *Printer*—A *software* interface between the operating system and a print device. It defines ports through which print jobs get routed. Printer names direct print jobs to one or more print devices.

➤ *Print device*—A piece of equipment (hardware) that physically produces printed documents. A print device may be attached to a local computer or connected via a network interface.

➤ *Printer port*—A software interface through which print jobs get directed to either a locally attached print device or a network-connected print device. Windows 2000 supports local line printer terminal (LPT), COM (serial), and Universal Serial Bus (USB) ports. It also supports network-connected printer port devices such as the Intel NetPort and the Hewlett-Packard (HP) JetDirect.

➤ *Print server*—A computer that serves as the host for printers that are associated with print devices.

➤ *Printer driver*—Software specific to each print device (designed to run in Windows 2000) that translates printing commands into printer language codes for each print device. PCL5 and PostScript are examples of two types of printer languages.

➤ *Print job*—The actual document to be printed along with the necessary print processing command.

➤ *Print resolution*—What determines the quality and smoothness of the text or images that the print device will render. This specification is expressed in dots per inch (DPI). Higher DPI numbers generally result in better print quality.

➤ *Print spooler*—The process (service) that runs in the background of Windows 2000 that initiates, processes, and distributes print jobs. The spooler saves print jobs into a temporary physical file on disk. Print jobs are then de-spooled and transferred to the appropriate print device.

➤ *Print queue*—A logical "waiting area" where print jobs are temporarily stored until the print device is available and ready to process each job according to the job's priority level and according to its order within the queue.

Connecting to Local and Network Printers

Once you add a local printer to a Windows 2000 Professional computer, you have the option of sharing it with other users on the network. To add a local printer to your system, follow these steps:

1. Log on as an administrator.

2. Click Start|Settings|Printers.

3. Double-click the Add Printer icon from the Printers folder. The Add Printer Wizard appears. Click Next to continue.

4. Click the Local printer button. If the printer that you are adding is not Plug and Play compatible, you may clear the Automatically Detect And Install My Plug And Play Printer checkbox. If the printer is Plug and Play compliant, Windows 2000 Professional automatically installs and properly configures it for you.

5. If the printer is not Plug and Play, the Select Printer Port dialog box appear. Click the port you want to use, or click the Create New Port button and choose the type of port to create from the drop-down list.

6. Click Next.

7. Select the printer Manufacturer and Model. Click the Have Disk button if you have a CD-ROM or diskette with the proper printer drivers from the manufacturer.

8. Click Next.

9. Enter a name for the printer. The name should not exceed 31 characters, and best practice dictates that the printer name should not contain any spaces. Specify whether this printer will be designated as the system's default printer.

10. Click Next.

11. In the Printer Sharing dialog box, click the Share As button if you want to share this printer with the network. Enter a share name for the printer; it's good to limit the share name to 14 characters or fewer and to place no spaces within the share name.

12. Click Next.

13. Enter an optional Location and Comment.

14. Click Next.

15. Click Next when prompted to print a test page; it's always a good idea to make sure that the printer has been set up and is working properly.

16. Click Finish to exit the Add Printer Wizard.

To connect to a network printer, you also use the Add Printer Wizard from the Printers folder. Simply follow these steps:

1. Log on as an administrator.

2. Click Start|Settings|Printers.

3. Double-click the Add Printer icon from the Printers folder. The Add Printer Wizard appears. Click Next to continue.

4. Click the Network printer button.

5. Click Next.

6. Type in the network Printer Name, or leave the Name box blank and click Next to browse for the printer on the network.

7. Locate the network printer at the Browse For Printer dialog box, shown in Figure 2.26.

8. Click Next.

9. If the print server for the printer that you are connecting to does not have the correct printer driver installed, you are prompted to install the correct version on the local Windows 2000 computer, as shown in Figure 2.27.

10. Click Yes or No about whether this printer should be the default printer for this computer.

11. Click Next.

12. Click Finish to exit the Add Printer Wizard.

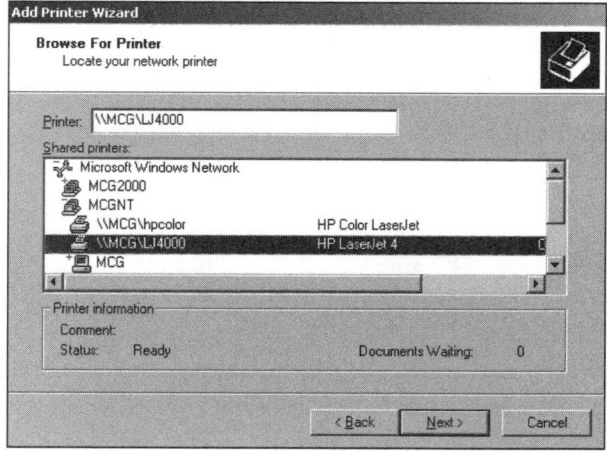

Figure 2.26   The Browse For Printer dialog box helps you locate a network printer.

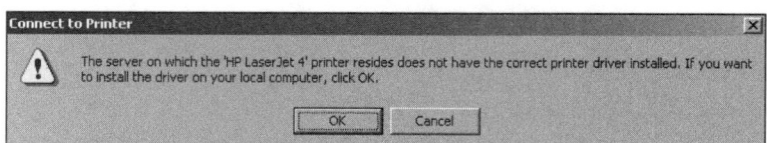

Figure 2.27   The Connect To Printer message box.

Connecting to Network Printers via the Command Line

As mentioned earlier in this chapter, you can use the **net use** command to connect to network drive shares. You can also use this command to connect to remote printers from a command prompt window. The syntax is as follows:

```
net use lptx: \\print_server_name\printer_share_name
```

Printer ports lpt1, lpt2, or lpt3 are represented by **lptx**. The **net use** command is the only way to connect client computers that are running MS-DOS to network printers.

Configuring Printer Properties

You can easily configure many of the properties of your Windows 2000 Professional system as a print server by clicking on the File menu from the Printers window and selecting Properties. You can configure many print server settings—such as changing the location of the Spool Folder—from the Print Server Properties dialog box, shown in Figure 2.28. Using this dialog box means that you don't have to edit the Registry directly.

By right-clicking on one of the available printer icons in the Printers folder and choosing Properties, you can configure that printer's settings and options. The printer Properties sheet contains six tabs: General, Sharing, Ports, Advanced, Security, and Device Settings.

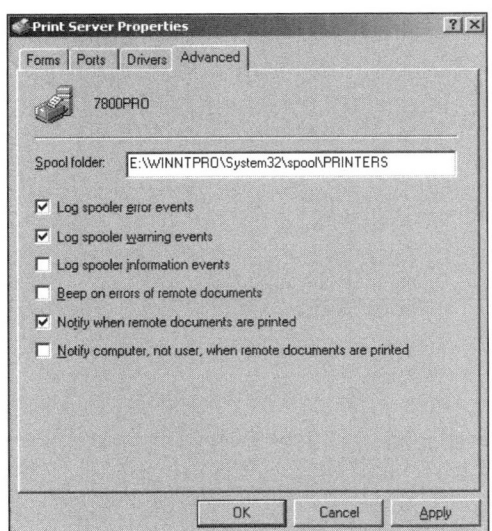

Figure 2.28 The Print Server Properties dialog box.

The General Tab

From the General tab, you can work with the following settings:

➤ Add or modify printer location and comment information

➤ Set printing preferences such as portrait or landscape orientation

➤ Select paper source and quality

➤ Print a test page

The Sharing Tab

The Sharing tab displays the following options:

➤ Share the printer, change the network share name, or stop sharing the printer

➤ Set printing preferences such as portrait or landscape orientation

➤ Install additional printer drivers for client computers that use different operating systems or different Windows NT CPU platforms

 Windows 2000 print server computers automatically download the correct printer drivers for client computers running Windows 95, Windows 98, Windows NT, and Windows 2000 that connect to the print server, as long as the correct drivers have been installed on the print server.

The Ports Tab

On the Ports tab, you have these configuration options:

➤ Select a port to print to

➤ Add, configure, and delete ports

➤ Enable bidirectional printing support

➤ Enable printer pooling, which allows you to select two or more identical print devices that are configured as one logical printer; print jobs are directed to the first available print device

The Advanced Tab

On the Advanced tab, you work with scheduling and spooling settings, like these:

➤ Set time availability limits

➤ Set print job priority

➤ Change the printer driver or add a new driver

➤ Spool print jobs and start printing immediately, or start printing after the last page has spooled

➤ Print directly to the printer; do not spool print jobs

➤ Hold mismatched documents

➤ Print spooled documents first

➤ Retain documents after they have been printed

➤ Enable advanced printing features (such as metafile spooling) and enable advanced options (such as Page Order, Booklet Printing, and Pages Per Sheet); advanced options vary depending upon printer capabilities

➤ Set printing defaults

➤ Select a different print processor: RAW, EMF, or Text

➤ Specify a separator page

The Security Tab

You can configure the following security settings with the Security tab:

➤ Set permissions for users and groups (similar to NTFS file and folder permissions): Allow Print or Deny Print, Manage Printers, and Manage Documents.

➤ Set up printer auditing (similar to NTFS file and folder access auditing) via the Auditing tab by clicking on the Advanced button.

➤ Take ownership of the printer (similar to taking ownership of NTFS files and folders) via the Owner tab by clicking on the Advanced button.

The Device Settings Tab

The Device Settings tab allows you to configure printer-specific settings. The available settings on this tab vary depending on the manufacturer and the model of the printer that you are working with.

Managing Printers and Print Jobs

Members of the Printer Owners, Print Operators, and Print Job Owners groups have permissions to manage print jobs that are listed in the print queue. From the Printers folder, you manage print jobs by double-clicking on the printer icon that you want to work with. Once you have opened the printer's print queue window, you can pause printing or cancel all documents from the Printer menu. You can also take the printer offline from the Printer menu. If you select an individual print job that is listed, you can Pause, Resume, Start, or Cancel that job by selecting one of these options off the Documents menu. The print queue window itself displays the Document Name, the Status, the Document Owner, the number of Pages for each print job, the size of the job, the time and date that the job was Submitted, and the Port used.

Users may manage only their own print jobs unless they are members of the Administrators group, the Power Users group, or the Print Operators group (if the print server is a member of a domain). Users can also manage other users' print jobs if they have been granted the Allow Manage Documents permission.

Using Internet Printing Protocol (IPP)

Windows 2000 Professional computers can connect to printers that are attached to Windows 2000 print servers through a Web browser. IPP works over a corporate intranet or through an Internet connection. IPP gives users the ability to print over an Internet connection. You can enter one of two URLs into your Web browser:

➤ *http://print_server_name/printers*—This address connects you to the Web page for the Printers folder on the Windows 2000 print server computer.

➤ *http://print_server_name/printer_share_name*—This address connects you to the Web page for the print queue folder for the printer that you specify, as shown in Figure 2.29.

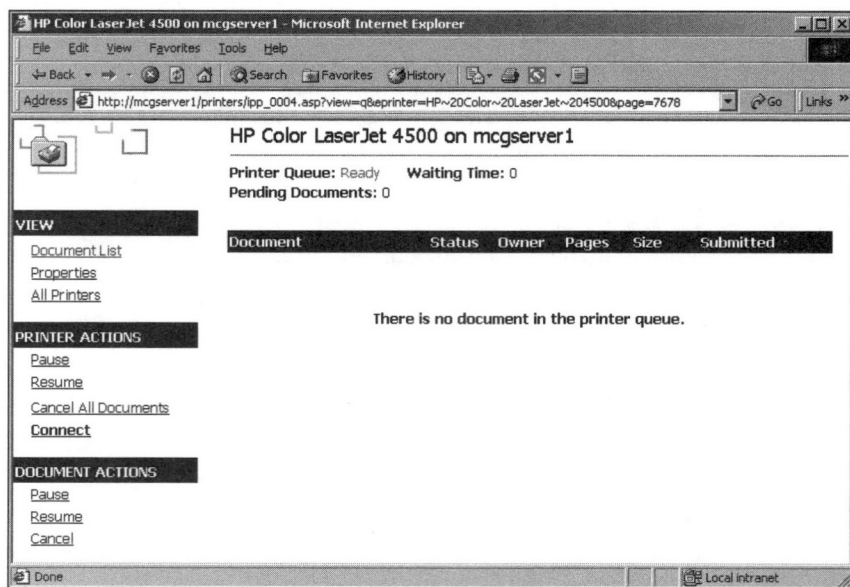

Figure 2.29 The Web browser interface for a network printer that uses IPP.

Practice Questions

Question 1

John Smith of XYZ Corporation has used EFS to encrypt all of the files stored within the \\Server1\Projects\JohnS folder. John subsequently leaves XYZ Corporation. John's boss has permissions to fully access the \\Server1\Projects\JohnS folder; however, he cannot work with any of the files because he receives an Access Is Denied message whenever he attempts to open any of the encrypted files. What does the company's IT department need to do so that John's files can become accessible to other users?

○ a. Log on to the domain as a member of the Backup Operators group and decrypt the files.

○ b. Log on to the domain as the DRA and decrypt the files.

○ c. Restore the files from a recent backup.

○ d. Have John's boss take ownership of the files.

Answer b is correct. Only a DRA can unencrypt files that someone else encrypted.

Question 2

Stuart Scott of ABC Company encrypts a folder named Spreadsheets and applies the encryption attribute to the folder, subfolders, and files. Two days later, Stuart's co-worker, Lisa, attempts to copy one of the encrypted files to a different NTFS folder located on the same drive volume on the same server. Neither Stuart nor Lisa is a member of the Administrators group, and neither user is a DRA. What will happen when Lisa attempts to copy the encrypted file?

○ a. The encrypted file is copied successfully.

○ b. The encrypted file is not copied successfully.

○ c. Lisa is prompted for the password for the DRA before the copy process can be completed.

○ d. The encrypted file is copied successfully, but an entry is logged into the Event Viewer about the encrypted file being copied.

Answer b is correct. Only the person who encrypted the files or the DRA can copy encrypted files.

Question 3

> Where can Administrators view all of the shared folders for a Windows 2000 Professional computer?
>
> ○ a. In the Shared Folders folder within the My Computer window.
>
> ○ b. From the Control Panel Folder Options icon.
>
> ○ c. From the System Tools folder of the Computer Management console.
>
> ○ d. In the **usrmgr.exe** utility.

Answer c is correct. The Computer Management console is an MMC snap-in. Shared folders for the local computer are listed for Administrators within the System Tools|Shared Folders|Shares folder.

Question 4

> Jeff is an Administrator who creates a network share named Docs on Server7. He sets the Share permissions on the shared folder by leaving the default Everyone group, but he clears the Allow checkboxes for Full Control, Change, and Read. Jeff sets NTFS permissions on the folder as well. He sets NTFS permissions to Allow Read for the Everyone group. What will happen when users attempt to connect to the Docs share over the network?
>
> ○ a. Users will inherit the Allow Read permission for the folder.
>
> ○ b. Users will inherit Allow Full Control permissions for the folder.
>
> ○ c. Members of the Administrators group will be allowed access to the folder over the network.
>
> ○ d. Users will be denied access to the shared folder over the network.

Answer d is correct. Whenever share permissions and NTFS permissions conflict, the most restrictive permissions take precedence. Clearing all the Allow checkboxes establishes an implicit Deny for those permissions.

Question 5

Amy moves a file from a FAT32 drive volume over to an NTFS drive volume folder named Compressed. The Compressed folder has been marked for NTFS compression for the folder, subfolders, and files. What happens when the file is moved into the Compressed folder?

○ a. The file remains uncompressed within the "Compressed" folder.

○ b. The file becomes compressed by inheriting the compression attribute from the destination folder.

○ c. Amy receives an error message informing her that encrypted files cannot be compressed.

○ d. Amy receives an error message informing her that files from FAT32 volumes do not support compression.

Answer b is correct. Files that are moved to an NTFS compressed folder from a non-NTFS drive volume inherit the compression attribute from the destination folder.

Question 6

Robert is using the network to print to \\wkstn4\printer11. All of a sudden, the print device for printer11 stops functioning. Fortunately, a similar print device is available on \\wkstn5\printer22. How can you, as an administrator, allow users to continue to print to the same network printer name without having to reconfigure any of the users' computers?

○ a. Add a new port for \\wkstn4\printer11. Have the new port point to \\wkstn5\printer22.

○ b. Modify the share name for printer11 to printer22.

○ c. Change the print server properties for printer11 so that the Print Spool folder points to \\wkstn5\admin$\system32\spool\printers.

○ d. Enable printer pooling on \\wkstn5\printer22.

Answer a is correct. By adding a new port with a UNC path for a similar printer on another computer, you are effectively redirecting the print jobs to another functioning printer.

Question 7

Greggory is member of the Administrators group. Some executives in his company feel that he may be reading or even altering confidential company documents. What can you do as the head of IT for the company to track which users are accessing sensitive files? [Check all correct answers]

❑ a. Enable auditing for success and failure of process tracking in the Local Security Settings console.

❑ b. Enable auditing for failure of object access in the Local Security Settings console.

❑ c. Enable auditing for success of object access in the Local Security Settings console.

❑ d. Enable auditing for the folder that contains the confidential files. Audit activities such as successful List Contents/Read Data and successful Create Files/Write Data.

❑ e. Turn on auditing for privilege use.

Answers c and d are correct. Enable auditing for success, failure, or both for object access from the Local Security Settings console. Then you can audit the success of object access events.

Question 8

As the network Administrator, you are concerned about several encrypted folders that contain very important data on Server A. You want to back up those folders while maintaining all security permission settings and having all the files retain their encryption. What is the best way to accomplish this?

○ a. Copy the files and folders onto a network share on Server B that resides on a FAT32 drive volume using the **scopy.exe** utility from the *Windows 2000 Resource Kit.*

○ b. Copy the files and folders onto a Novell NetWare server.

○ c. Copy the files and folders onto a network share on Server B that is formatted as NTFS.

○ d. Copy the files and folders onto CD-recordable media.

Answer c is correct. Only NTFS-formatted drive volumes in Windows 2000 support NTFS security permissions and EFS.

Question 9

The office administrative personnel are members of a group called Staff. The members of the Staff group are responsible for managing print jobs in the office. The Staff group has been assigned the Allow Manage Documents permission for all the printers in the office. Kimberly joins the company as a new Staff group member, and she is going to be responsible for managing the printers and the print jobs. What is the best way to assign permissions to Kimberly so that she can manage printers and print jobs?

○ a. Create a new group named Printer Admins and add Kimberly to that group. Assign the Allow Manage Printers permission to the Printer Admins group for each printer in the office.

○ b. Place Kimberly into the Print Operators group. Remove her from the Staff group.

○ c. Keep her as a member of the Staff group and add her to the Administrators group.

○ d. Modify the printer permissions for all the printers in the office to Allow Manage Printers for the Staff group. Assign the Deny Manage Printers permission individually for all members of the Staff group, except for Kimberly. Assign the Allow Manage Documents permission to the Everyone group for all the printers in the office.

Answer a is correct. It is best to assign permissions only to groups. The Print Operators group is a domain group. Membership in this group would give Kimberly authority to manage printers within the entire domain, and such a wide scope of authority is unnecessary. Therefore, answer b is incorrect.

Question 10

> IIS is installed and running on your Windows 2000 Professional computer. Your users want to utilize IPP to print from their Web browsers over the corporate intranet. When users type in the URL **http://server1/printers**, they receive a Cannot Find Server message. However, you notice that you can type **http://192.168.1.103/printers** and you get connected to the printer's Web page for that server. What's the most probable cause of this problem?
>
> ○ a. Dynamic Host Configuration Protocol (DHCP) is not functioning.
>
> ○ b. DNS and/or WINS are/is not set up properly on the network.
>
> ○ c. The default gateway IP address information is missing on the computer.
>
> ○ d. Automatic Private IP Addressing is turned on by default. You need to make a change in the Registry to turn this feature off.

Answer b is correct. If you can access a TCP/IP network resource by its IP address but not by its computer name (host name), it is most likely a name resolution problem. You can solve it by installing either a DNS or WINS server, or by manually adding HOSTS or LMHOSTS files on each computer on the network.

Need to Know More?

 Microsoft Corporation. *Microsoft Windows 2000 Professional Resource Kit*. Redmond, Washington: Microsoft Press, 2000. ISBN: 1-57231-808-2. The book provides invaluable information on administering resources and setting NTFS security permissions.

 Stinson, Craig, and Carl Siechert. *Running Microsoft Windows 2000 Professional*. Redmond, Washington: Microsoft Press, 2000. ISBN: 1-57231-838-4. This guidebook to Windows 2000 Professional is a good source for information on administering resources.

 Wood, Adam. *Windows 2000 Active Directory Black Book*. Scottsdale, Arizona: The Coriolis Group, 2000. ISBN: 1-57610-256-4. This book provides comprehensive coverage of Active Directory.

 Search the TechNet CD-ROM (or its online version through **www.microsoft.com**) and/or the *Windows 2000 Professional Resource Kit* CD-ROM using the keywords "NTFS", "offline files", "EFS", "compression", "auditing", "shared folders", and "Internet Printing Protocol".

Implementing, Monitoring, and Troubleshooting Security Accounts and Policies

3

Terms you'll need to understand:

✓ Local users and groups

✓ Workgroup

✓ Domain

✓ Domain users and groups

✓ Active Directory

✓ Organizational Unit (OU)

✓ Policy

✓ Privilege, or user right

Techniques you'll need to master:

✓ Creating local users and groups

✓ Creating domain users and groups

✓ Managing user and group properties

✓ Dealing with changes in your user population: renaming and copying accounts

✓ Securing a system

✓ Creating a local and group policy

Networks' *raison d'être*—their life's purpose—is to allow users to access resources such as files, printers, and applications on computers other than the ones at which they are sitting. In an ideal world, we would trust every user with every file we create, and all we'd have to do is connect our computer to a network and share it all. Unfortunately, we don't. In the real world, certain users need access to resources that others should be restricted from accessing. Therefore, we need user accounts to identify and authenticate users when they attempt to access a resource. But imagine trying to define who can access a resource and at what level if you had to worry about each individual user! Using groups significantly eases the process of defining resource access—you can assign permissions and privileges to groups and thereby define access for their members, which may contain one, dozens, hundreds, or thousands of users.

This chapter highlights critical skills and concepts related to user, group, and computer accounts, and the process of creating security configurations and policies for a Windows 2000 Professional system.

User and Group Accounts

Now we'll discuss user and group accounts.

Local and Domain Accounts

User and group accounts are stored in one of two locations: the *local security database* or the domain's *Active Directory* database. When an account is created in the local security database, that account is called a *local user* or *local group*.

Each Windows 2000 Professional system has two default local user accounts, Administrator and Guest (which is disabled by default), and several built-in group accounts, which are discussed shortly. Local user and group accounts provide privileges and permissions to resources of the system on which they are defined. For example, the Users group has the privilege to log on locally. As you create local user accounts, they are members of the Users group by default; those users are then given the privilege to log on to that system.

Local user and group accounts cannot be given privileges or permissions to resources on any other system because the security database of the system where they are created is truly local—no other system can "see" it. If a user has logged on to a computer with a local account, the only way that user can be given access to resources of a remote system is to create an account for that user on the remote system. That account must be given privileges and permissions or must be placed into appropriate groups on that system. When a duplicate or redundant account is created with the same username and password, the user "seamlessly" accesses resources on the remote system—it is invisible to such users that the remote system is authenticating them. However, if the username or password on the remote system is different, users are prompted with an authentication dialog box when they first attempt to connect to the system.

When two or more systems that use only their own local accounts are on a network, this creates what is called a *workgroup*, a kind of peer-to-peer network. You can imagine how difficult managing redundant accounts for a single user on two different systems might become. If users change their passwords on one machine, they must remember to change it on the other; otherwise, they are prompted for authentication at each connection. Such challenges would become multiplied many times over in a larger workgroup with multiple users and multiple machines.

Thus, networks of any size turn to a *domain* model, in which one or more servers, called *domain controllers*, maintain a centralized database of users and groups. Security accounts in a domain are stored in the domain's Active Directory. When a user is created in a domain, that single user account can be given privileges and permissions to resources and systems throughout the domain, and in other domains within the enterprise's Active Directory. Active Directory is covered in more detail in the "Understanding Active Directory" section later in this chapter.

In a domain, it is unusual (and not a best practice) to create or use local user accounts. Most computers that are members of a domain have only the local Administrator and Guest user accounts in their security databases.

Managing Local User and Group Accounts

The Local Users And Groups snap-in allows you to manage—surprise—local users and groups. You can get to the snap-in by choosing Start|Settings|Control Panel|Administrative Tools|Computer Management and then by expanding the tree pane of the Computer Management console until you see snap-in. In this Snap-in, you can create, modify, duplicate, and delete users (in the Users folder) and groups (in the Groups folder).

Built-in User and Group Accounts

There are two built-in user accounts: Administrator and Guest. The Administrator account:

➤ Cannot be disabled, locked out, or deleted.

➤ Cannot be removed from the Administrators group.

➤ Has, through its membership in the Administrators group, all privileges required to perform system administration duties.

➤ Can be renamed.

The Guest account:

➤ Is disabled by default. Only an Administrator can enable the account. If it is enabled, it should be given a password, and User Cannot Change Password should be set if multiple users will log on with the account.

➤ Cannot be deleted.

➤ Can be locked out.

➤ Can be renamed.

➤ Does not save user preferences or settings.

Built-in local groups have assigned to them specific privileges (also called user rights) that allow them to perform specific sets of tasks on a system. The default local group accounts on a Windows 2000 Professional system are the following:

➤ *Administrators*—Have all built-in system privileges assigned. They can create and modify user and group accounts, manage security policies, create printers, and manage permissions to resources on the system. The local Administrator account is the default member and cannot be removed. Other accounts can be added and removed. When a system joins a domain, the Domain Admins group is added, but it can be removed.

➤ *Backup Operators*—Can back up and restore files and folders regardless of security permissions assigned to those resources. They can log on and shut down a system but cannot change security settings.

➤ *Power Users*—Can share resources and create user and group accounts. They cannot modify user accounts they did not create, nor can they modify the Administrators or Backup Operators Groups. Power Users cannot take ownership of files, back up or restore directories, load or unload device drivers, or manage the security and auditing logs. Power Users can run all Windows 2000-compatible applications as well as legacy applications, some of which members of the Users group cannot execute.

 If you want certain users to have broad system administration capabilities but do not want them to be able to access all system resources, consider putting them in Backup Operators and Power Users rather than Administrators.

➤ *Users*—Can log on, shut down a system, use local and network printers, create local groups, and manage the groups they create. They cannot create a local printer or share a folder. Some down-level applications do not run for members of the Users group because security settings are tighter for the Users group in Windows 2000 than in Windows NT 4. By default, all local user accounts you create are added to the Users group. In addition, when a system joins a domain, the Domain Users group is made a member of that system's local Users group.

➤ *Guests*—Have limited privileges but can log on to a system and shut it down. Members cannot make permanent changes to their desktop or profile. By default, the built-in local Guest account is a member. When a system joins a domain, the Domain Guests group is added to the local Guests group.

➤ *Replicator*—Is used to support file replication services in a domain.

There are also built-in *system* groups, which you do not see in the user interface while managing other group accounts. Membership of system groups changes based on how the computer is accessed, not on who accesses the computer. Built-in system groups include the following:

➤ *Everyone*—Includes all users who access the computer, including the Guest account.

➤ *Authenticated Users*—Includes all users with a valid user account in the local security database or (in the case of domain members) in Active Directory's directory services. You use the Authenticated Users group rather than the Everyone group to assign privileges and group permissions because doing so prevents anonymous access to resources.

➤ *Creator Owner*—Contains the user account that created or took ownership of a resource. If the user is a member of the Administrators group, the group is the owner of the resource.

➤ *Network*—Contains any user with a connection from a remote system.

➤ *Interactive*—Contains the user account for the user logged on locally at the system.

➤ *Anonymous Logon*—Includes any user account that Windows 2000 did not authenticate.

➤ *Dial-up*—Contains all users that currently use a dial-up connection.

Creating Local User and Group Accounts

To create a local user or group account, right-click the appropriate folder (Users or Groups) and choose New User (or New Group), enter the appropriate attributes, and then click Create.

User account names:

➤ Must be unique.

➤ Are recognized only up to their 20th character, although the name itself can be longer.

➤ Cannot contain the following characters: " / \ [ ] ; : | = + * ? < >.

➤ Are not case sensitive, although the user account's name property displays the case as entered.

You should determine a policy for accommodating users with the same name, perhaps by adding a number after the username (JohnD1, JohnD2). Some organizations also identify certain types of users by their username (e.g., JohnDoe-Temp for a temporary employee).

User account passwords:

➤ Are recommended.

➤ Are case sensitive.

➤ Can be up to 127 characters, although down-level operating systems like Windows NT 4 and Windows 9x support only 14-character passwords.

➤ Should be a minimum of seven to eight characters.

➤ Should be difficult to guess and, preferably, should mix uppercase and lowercase letters, numerals, and nonalphanumeric characters (other than those listed above as prohibited).

➤ Can be set by the Administrator (who can then determine whether users must, can, or cannot change their password) or the user (if the Administrator has not specified otherwise).

Select User Must Change Password At Next Logon to ensure that the user is the only one who knows the account's password. Select User Cannot Change Password when more than one person (such as Guest) uses the account.

Note: The User Cannot Change Password option is not available when User Must Change Password At Next Logon is selected.

The Password Never Expires option is helpful when a program or a service uses an account. To avoid having to reconfigure the service with a new password, you can simply set the service's account to retain its password indefinitely.

Configuring Account Properties

The information you can specify when creating an account is limited in Windows 2000. Therefore, after creating an account, you often need to go to the account's properties sheet, which you can access by right-clicking on the account and choosing Properties. Figure 3.1 shows the Properties sheets of two accounts.

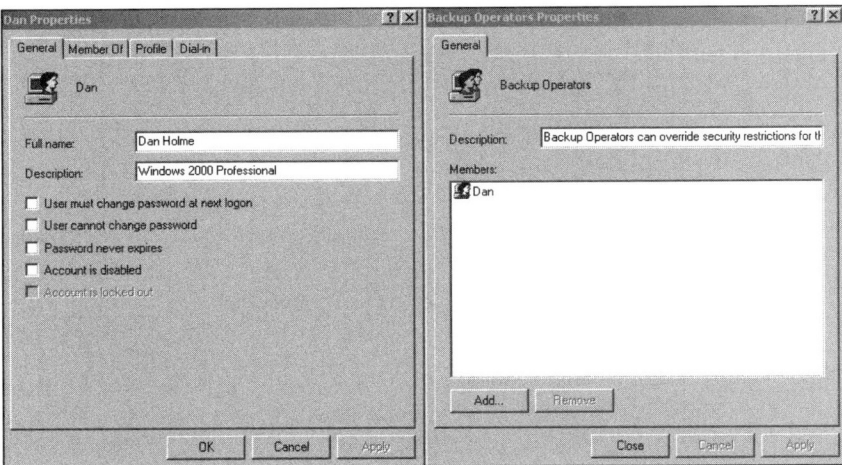

Figure 3.1   The properties sheets of Dan and Backup Operators.

Managing Local Group Membership

To manage the membership of a local group, right-click the group and choose Properties. To remove a member, select the account and click Remove. To add a member, click Add and select or enter the name of the account.

In a workgroup, local groups can contain only accounts defined in the same machine's local security database. When a system belongs to a domain, its local groups can also include domain accounts, including user accounts, universal groups, and global groups from the enterprise's Active Directory, as well as domain Local Groups from within the system's domain.

Note: Universal groups and domain local groups are available to add as members only when the domain is in native mode, meaning that it contains only Windows 2000 domain controllers and no legacy backup domain controllers.

Renaming Accounts

To rename an account, right-click the account and choose Rename. Type the new name and press Enter. Each user and group account is represented in the local security database by a long, unique string called a *security identifier (SID)*, which is generated when the account is created. The SID is what is actually assigned permissions and privileges. The user or group name is just a user-friendly "face" on that process. Therefore, when you rename an account, the account's SID remains the same, so the account retains all of its group memberships, permissions, and privileges.

There are two situations that mandate renaming an account: The first occurs when one user stops using a system and a new user requires the same access as the first.

Rather than creating a new local user account for the new user, simply rename the old user account. The account's SID remains the same, so its group memberships, privileges, and permissions are retained. You should also specify a new password in the account's properties sheet and select the User Must Change Password At Next Logon option.

The easiest way to "replace" a user is to rename the account. Therefore, when one user leaves and another requires the same group memberships, rights, and resource access permissions, simply rename the former user's account. Don't forget to set an initial password because the new user won't otherwise know the old user's password.

The second situation that warrants renaming a user account is the security practice of renaming the built-in Administrator and Guest accounts. You cannot delete these accounts, nor can you disable or remove the Administrator account from the Local Administrators group, so renaming the accounts is a recommended practice for hindering malicious access to a system.

Disabling or Enabling User Accounts

To disable or enable a user account, open its Properties sheet and select or clear the Account Is Disabled checkbox. If an account is disabled, a user cannot log on to the system using that account. The Administrator account cannot be disabled, and only Administrators can enable the Guest account.

Deleting Accounts

You can delete a local user or group account (but not built-in accounts like Administrator, Guest, or Backup Operators) by right-clicking the account and choosing Delete. When you delete a group, you delete the group account only, not the accounts of its members. A group is a membership list, not a container.

Note: When you delete an account, you are deleting its SID. Therefore, if you delete an account by accident and re-create the account, even with the same name, it will not have the same permissions, privileges, or group memberships—you will have to regenerate them. For that reason, and to facilitate auditing, it is recommended that you disable, not delete, any user that leaves an organization.

Using The Users and Passwords Applet

Another tool for administering local user accounts is the Users And Passwords applet in Control Panel. This applet allows you to create and remove user accounts as well as specify group membership for those users. It is wizard driven and is useful for novice administrators and home users. To launch the Local

Users And Groups snap-in, click the Advanced tab and the Advanced button (in the Advanced User Management section).

Note: The Users And Passwords applet provides an opportunity to override the logon requirement for a system. This feature will be discussed below in the "Authentication" section later in this chapter.

Managing Domain User Accounts

Domain user accounts are managed with the Active Directory Users And Computers snap-in. To access it, choose Start|Settings|Control Panel|Administrative Tools|Active Directory Users And Computers. Note that, unlike in Windows NT 4, all domain controllers in Windows 2000 can make changes to the Active Directory database. When you open the tool, you connect to an available domain controller. If you want to specify which domain controller, or which domain you wish to connect to, right-click the Active Directory Users And Computers node and choose Connect To Domain or Connect To Domain Controller.

Unlike the local security database, which is a flat list of users and groups, Active Directory has containers like domains and Organizational Units (OUs), which collect database objects such as users that are administered similarly. Therefore, when you manage domain user accounts in Windows 2000, you need to start in the container or OU that you want to modify.

Creating Domain User Accounts

You create domain user accounts by right-clicking the OU or container in which you want the user account and then choosing New User. A wizard prompts you for basic account properties, including the following:

➤ First name

➤ Initials

➤ Last name

➤ Full name (by default, the combination of the first name and last name)

➤ User logon name and User Principal Name (UPN) suffix

➤ User logon name (pre-Windows 2000)

➤ Password and confirmed password

Windows 2000 user accounts have two logon names. The UPN is used for logon to a Windows 2000 system and consists of a logon name followed by the @ symbol and a suffix, by default the Domain Name System (DNS) name of the domain. Each user must have a unique UPN in the domain. The down-level logon name is used for logging on to pre-Windows 2000 systems such as Windows NT 4, and Windows 95, 98, and ME. Each user's pre-Windows 2000 logon name must be unique in the domain and by default is the same as the logon name portion of the UPN.

Modifying User Account Properties

Once an account is created, Active Directory provides dozens of attributes to further define that user. Right-click a user and choose Properties to open up a multi-tabbed dialog box full of attributes that can be defined for that user. The only properties you can specify when creating the user are those on the Account tab. You must set the remainder of the properties after the account has been instantiated.

Copying User Accounts

A user object in Active Directory may have numerous attributes defined, including work location, group membership, and organizational superiors. Often, a new user object shares many of its attributes with one or more other user objects. In that case, it is faster to copy an existing user object than to create a new object and define each and every property. To copy a user, right-click the object and choose Copy. You are asked to enter some of the basic account properties, such as name and password. You can copy a user only with domain user accounts, not with local user accounts.

Creating Template User Accounts

When you expect to create multiple user objects with highly similar properties, you can create a "template" account that, when copied, initiates the new accounts with its defined attributes. The only trick to working with templates is to *disable the template account*. Then, when copying the account to create a new user with predefined attributes, make sure to enable the new account.

 When you copy a user account—whether a "real" user account or a template—the new copy belongs to all the same groups as the original and therefore has the same resource access that was assigned to the groups of the original account. However, the new copy does *not* have access to resources for which permissions were assigned directly to the original user account.

Disabling and Deleting User Accounts

The process for disabling and deleting domain user accounts is the same as for local user accounts, except that you use the Active Directory Users And Computers snap-in to perform the tasks. The checkbox for disabling an account is on the user's Account property sheet.

Adding Domain User Accounts to Local Groups

In Windows 2000, you can add a user to a group with either the group's Members property sheet or the user's Member Of property sheet, except when adding *domain* user accounts to *local* groups, in which case you must use the group's Members property sheet. A domain user's Member Of property sheet displays only memberships in global, domain, local, and universal groups.

Authentication

When a user wants to access resources on a machine, that user's identity must first be verified through a process called *authentication*. For example, when a user logs on, the security subsystem evaluates the user's username and password. If there is a match, the user is authenticated. The process of logging on to a machine where you are physically sitting is called *interactive logon*. Authentication also happens when you access resources on a remote system. For example, when you open a shared folder on a server, you are being authenticated as well, only this time, the process is called *remote* or *network logon* because you are not *physically* at the server.

The Security Dialog

The *security dialog* allows for interactive logon to a Windows 2000 system. You can access the Security dialog shortly after a system has started, and at any time after logon, by pressing Ctrl+Alt+Delete. If you are not currently logged on, you can enter a username and password. If the system belongs to a domain, you need to be certain that the domain in which your account exists is authenticating you. You can either select the domain from the drop-down list or enter your UPN. The UPN is an attribute of an Active Directory user object and, by default, is of the form **username@dnsdomain.name**. The suffix, following the @ symbol, indicates the domain against which to authenticate the user.

If you are currently logged on to a system, pressing Ctrl+Alt+Delete takes you to the Windows 2000 Security dialog, at which point you can:

➤ Log off the system, which closes all programs and ends the instance of the shell.

➤ Lock the system, which allows programs to continue running but prevents access to the system. When a system is locked, you may unlock it by pressing Ctrl+Alt+Delete and entering the username and password of the user who locked the system, or an administrator's username and password.

To lock a workstation automatically after a period of idle time, use a screensaver password.

> ➤ Shut down the system.

> ➤ Change your password.

> ➤ Open Task Manager.

Automating Logon

You can configure Windows 2000 Professional systems so that you are not re-quired to enter a username and password but rather that the system automatically logs on as a specified user account. From the Users And Passwords applet in the Control Panel, click the Advanced tab and clear the Require Users To Press Ctrl+Alt+Delete Before Logging On checkbox. The same setting is available through Policy, which is discussed later in this chapter.

Understanding Active Directory

Windows 2000's Active Directory goes far beyond what the Security Accounts Manager (SAM) database did for Windows NT 4. Although SAM and Active Directory store security account information for users, groups, computers, and user rights, that's where the similarity ends. Active Directory's database stores *objects* that represent an enterprise resource, including users, groups, computers, printers, folders, applications, connections, security and configuration settings, and network topology. For each of these types, or *classes*, of objects, Active Directory can store numerous properties, or *attributes*. So a user account is far more than a username and password—it is now information about the user's mailbox, the user's address and phone number, the organizational role of the user (including the user's manager and location), and far, far more.

As a central store of information related to the enterprise network, Active Directory allows administrators to create a virtual representation or model of the enterprise—linking various objects together, grouping objects based on how they are administered, and structuring the enterprise information technology (IT) to best support the organization's goals. In addition, Active Directory's database is *extensible*, which means that you can customize and append it with additional attributes and object classes. So, if an organization wants to keep track of salary information for each employee, it can simply extend the information that Active Directory stores about employees to include salary or, better yet, purchase a payroll application that is Active Directory aware and would automatically extend the directory appropriately.

Now, a database is of no use if it simply stores information. One must be able to access and manipulate that information somehow, and Active Directory includes numerous services, most based on Internet standard, that allow you to do just that. To provide the functionality required to search or query the database for a particular enterprise resource, locate that resource out on the network, manage that resource's record in Active Directory, and ensure that the record is consistent throughout the network.

Active Directory's database and services reside on servers that have been designated domain controllers. Unlike with Windows NT 4, Windows 2000 domain controllers are not created while the operating system is installed. Rather, a functioning server is *promoted* to act as a domain controller, at which time it obtains a copy of Active Directory and launches the required services. Also unlike with NT 4, there is no "primary" domain controller. All domain controllers can write to the directory. So, a change to the domain is replicated to all domain controllers, making Active Directory a *multi-master* replication model.

On the Windows 2000 Professional exam, it is important to have a basic understanding of Active Directory's structure, which, like that of Windows NT 4, begins with a domain. The *domain* is the fundamental administrative, security, and replication unit of Active Directory. The domain is specified by two names: its down-level NetBIOS name—such as CONOSCO, which was also used in NT 4—and its DNS name, such as **conosco.com**. DNS is the primary name resolution methodology in Windows 2000.

When an enterprise decides to implement a multidomain model within its Active Directory, it creates what are called domain *trees* or *forests*. Multidomain models, however, fall outside the scope of the Windows 2000 Professional exam, so we will focus on what you need to know in a single-domain environment.

In a single domain, Active Directory can contain millions of objects. To make those objects more manageable, you can place those objects in containers called OUs. OUs can contain other OUs, allowing a nested, hierarchical structure to be created within a domain (see Figure 3.2).

An enterprise uses its OU structure to control the administration and configuration of objects in the enterprise. For example, the organization depicted in Figure 3.2 might give an IT Admins group full control over the OUs, which would allow that group to create, delete, and fully manage all of the objects in those OUs. A Help Desk group might be given permission to reset passwords for user objects in the Finance and Marketing OUs, and to put users in those OUs into groups based on the resource access they require. Workstations in the Finance OU could be configured to limit which users are allowed to log on locally. And users in the Payroll OU might have the payroll application installed on their machines, all through properties of the OU.

The OUs' virtual model of administration and configuration offers enormous flexibility and simplifies the effort it takes to manage large and small networks. As objects are moved between OUs, they are administered and configured differently.

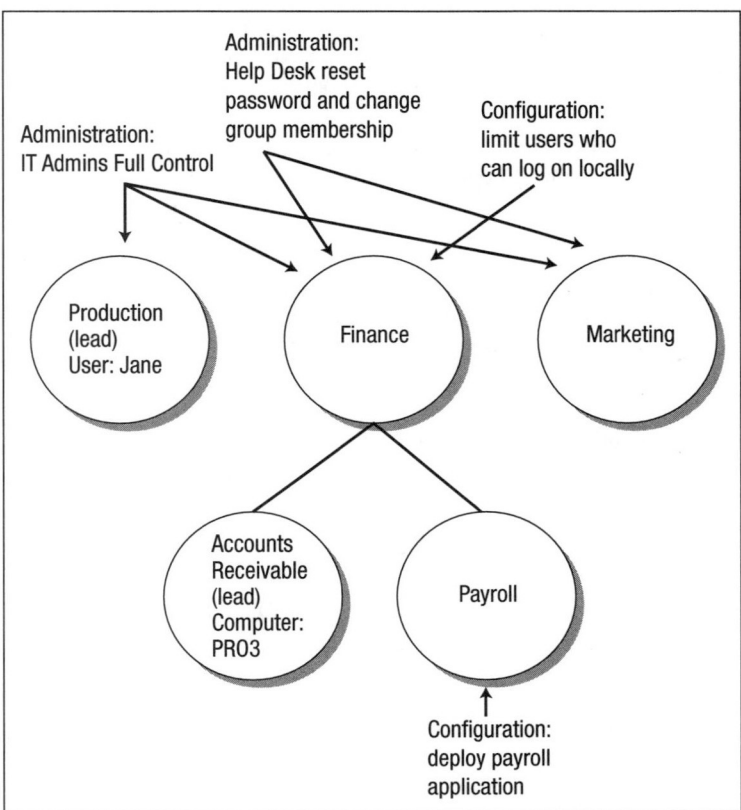

Figure 3.2 A sample Windows 2000 domain that contains several OUs.

For example, referring again to Figure 3.2, if a user named Jane is moved from the Production OU to the Payroll OU, the payroll application is deployed, automatically. In addition, the Help Desk can reset her password because, by default, properties of OUs (including delegated administrative permissions) are *inherited* from their parent OU. If a computer, PRO3, is moved from the Accounts Receivable OU to the Marketing OU, the limitation on which users can log on locally (which it was inheriting from the Finance OU) is removed.

The complexities and mechanics of designing and implementing Active Directory are not among the objectives of the Windows 2000 Professional exam. However, it is important to realize that within a domain, you can use OUs to control administration and configuration of all objects, including users and computers, and that OUs by default inherit the administrative and configuration properties of OUs higher up in the OU structure. We will see these concepts in action in the discussion of Group Policy later in this chapter.

Understanding and Implementing Policy

Configuring a particular system and the environment for a particular user begins with its defaults—the settings determined by Microsoft during the development of Windows 2000. Of course, there are always numerous settings for which Microsoft's defaults are not appropriate for one or more computers or users. Therefore, users and administrators alike often find themselves modifying the defaults.

In the past, if several settings needed to be changed, you often had to use several tools, including User Manager, Server Manager, System Policy Editor, and even the Registry Editor. If those settings needed to be changed on multiple computers, it was often necessary to make those changes on each system, individually. And if a setting you specified was later changed inappropriately, there was often no way to set it back to the desired setting except for manually making the change again.

Managing changes and configuration has been significantly improved in Windows 2000 thanks to the introduction into the Windows environment of *policy-based administration*. Policies provide administrators with a single list of configuration settings in one tool, rather than many tools, and allow administrators to apply those configuration settings to one machine, many machines, or every machine.

Local Policy

On a Windows 2000 Professional system, you can configure security-related settings using the Local Security console, which contains the Security Settings Microsoft Management Console (MMC) snap-in. Simply choose Start| Settings|Control Panel|Administrative Tools|Local Security Settings. Each of the nodes in the Local Security Settings console is a security area or scope, within which you will find dozens of security related settings, or attributes.

The Local Policy column of the details pane displays the settings specified by local policy. The Effective Policy column shows what is currently in effect. The two columns may differ if the local policy has not been implemented—changes to security settings take effect when the system is restarted, or following a refresh interval, which is by default 90 minutes. The columns may also differ as local policy is overridden by group policy, which is discussed later in this chapter.

Account Policies

Account policies control the password requirements and how the system responds to invalid logon attempts. The policies you can specify include the following:

➤ *Maximum password age*—This is the period of time after which a password must be changed.

➤ *Minimum password length*—This is the number of characters in a password. Passwords can contain up to 127 characters; however, most passwords should not exceed 14.

➤ *Passwords must meet complexity requirements*—This policy, if in effect, does not allow a password change unless the new password contains at least three of four character types: uppercase (A through Z), lowercase (a through z), numeric (0 through 9), and nonalphanumeric (such as !).

➤ *Enforce password history*—The system can remember a specified number of previous passwords. When a user attempts to change his or her password, the new password is compared against the history; if the new password is unique, the change is allowed.

➤ *Minimum password age*—This specifies the number of days that a new password must be used before it can be changed again.

➤ *Account lockout threshold*—This is the number of denied logon attempts after which an account is locked out. For example, if this is set to three, a lockout occurs if a user enters the wrong password three times; any further logon attempt will be denied. If this is set to zero, there is no lockout threshold.

➤ *Reset account lockout counter after*—This is the number of minutes after which the counter, which applies to the lockout threshold, is reset. For example, if the counter is reset after five minutes and the account lockout threshold is three, a user can log on twice with the incorrect password. After five minutes, the counter is reset, so the user can log on twice more. A third invalid logon during a five-minute period locks out the account.

➤ *Account lockout duration*—This specifies how long logon attempts are denied after a lockout. During this period, a logon with the locked out username is not authenticated.

Audit Policies

Audit policies specify what types of events are entered into the Security Log. The most important policies to understand are the following:

➤ *Logon events*—Authentication of users logging on or off locally and making connections to the computer from remote systems.

➤ *Account management*—Any change to account properties, including password changes and adding, deleting, or modifying users or groups.

➤ *Object access*—Access to objects on which auditing has been specified. Auditing object access, for example, enables auditing of files and folders on an NT File System (NTFS) volume, but you must also configure auditing on those files and folders. See Chapter 2 for a detailed discussion of auditing.

➤ *Privilege use*—Use of any user right, now called a *privilege*. For example, this policy audits a user who changes the system time because changing system time is a privilege.

For each policy, you can specify to audit successes, failures, or both. As events are logged, they appear in the Security Log, which can be viewed, by default, only by administrators. Other logs can be viewed by anyone.

User Rights Assignment

User rights, also called privileges, allow a user or group to perform system functions such as changing the system time, backing up or restoring files, and formatting a disk volume. Some rights are assigned to built-in groups. For example, the Administrators group can format a disk volume. You cannot deny that right to Administrators, nor can you assign that right to a user or group you create. Other rights are assignable. For example, the right to back up files and folders is given by default to Administrators and Backup Operators, but you can remove the right for those groups or assign the right to other users or groups. You can modify the rights that are visible in the Local Security Policy console. You do not see the "hard wired" rights in this interface.

User rights, because they are system-oriented, override object permissions when the two are in conflict with each other. For example, a user may be denied permission to read a folder on a disk volume. However, if the user has been given the privilege to back up files and folders, a backup of the folder succeeds, even though the user cannot actually read the folder.

Security Options

In the *Security Options* node are a number of useful security settings. This node highlights one of the advantages of policy, because while many of these settings are accessible elsewhere in the user interface (for example, you can specify driver signing in the System applet), policy allows you to compile all those settings, from all those tools and applets, into a unified configuration tool.

Some particularly useful options to be familiar with are the following:

➤ *Disable Ctrl+Alt+Delete requirement for logon*—If this policy is enabled, the logon dialog box does not appear at startup and the system boots directly to the desktop. This policy is enabled by default on standalone systems and disabled by default when a machine joins a domain, due to the obvious security implications of bypassing a secure logon.

➤ *Clear the Virtual Memory Pagefile when the system shuts down*—By default, the pagefile is not cleared and could allow unauthorized access to sensitive information that remains in the pagefile.

➤ *Do not display last username in logon screen*—This option forces users to enter both username and password at logon. By default, the policy is disabled and the name of the previously logged-on user is displayed.

Managing Local Policies

The local policy and the Local Security Policy tool are most helpful on standalone systems. The local policy drives configuration of the computer, and if a setting is changed through tools other than policy, the change is reverted to the policy-specified setting when the system is restarted, or following the policy refresh interval.

It is possible, however, to transfer security policies between systems. Right-click the Security Settings node and you can export and import policies. This allows you to copy a policy you have created on one machine to other machines. However, you can imagine the complexity of trying to maintain consistent local policies across multiple systems. That complexity is addressed by group policy.

The Security Configuration And Analysis snap-in allows you to capture the security configuration of a system as a database, and to use that database as a baseline against which you can gauge changes to security settings. When modifications are made that deviate from the database setting, you can reapply the original setting. You can also save the database as a template, which you can then apply to other systems to duplicate security settings. There are also preconfigured security templates that you can apply to Windows 2000 systems to implement a variety of security environments.

Group Policy

Group policy takes the concept of policy-enforced configuration and applies it to one or more computers with one or more users. Like local policy, group policy provides a centralized enumeration of configuration settings, some of which are also available through other tools in the user interface, some of which are available only through Policy. However, you can apply, or *link*, a group policy to the following:

➤ *A domain*—This causes the configuration specified by the policy to be applied to every user or computer in the domain.

➤ *An OU*—This applies policy to users or computers in the OU.

➤ *A site*—This is an Active Directory object that represents a portion of your network topology with good connectivity—a local area network (LAN), for example.

To access group policy, you must go to the properties of a site, domain, or OU (SDOU), and click the Group Policy tab. Therefore, to work with group policy for a site, you use the Active Directory Sites And Services console, right-click on a site, and choose Properties. To work with group policy for a domain or OU, use Active Directory Users And Computers, right-click on a domain or OU, and choose Properties.

Whereas an individual machine can have only one local policy, a SDOU can have multiple policies. On the Group Policy Properties sheet, you can create a new Group Policy Object (GPO) by clicking New, or link an existing group policy to the SDOU by clicking on Add. If you select a group policy and click on Edit, you expose the GPO in the Group Policy Editor.

Application of Group Policy

GPOs are divided into the Computer Settings and User Settings nodes. The computer settings apply to every computer in the SDOU to which the policy is linked, and, by default, to all child OUs. Computer settings take effect at startup and every refresh interval, by default 90 minutes. User settings affect every user in the SDOU and its children at logon, and after each refresh interval.

When a computer starts up, its current settings are modified first by any configuration specified by the local policy. Then, the configuration in group policies is applied: first, the policies linked to the computer's site, then the policies for its domain, and finally the policies for each OU in the branch that leads to the computer's OU. If there is ever a conflict in a particular configuration setting, the last setting applied takes effect. Therefore, the policies that are "closest" to the computer—the policies linked to its OU, for example—take precedence if a conflict arises. The same application of policies applies to a user at logon: local policy, site policy, domain policy, and OU policy.

 You can remember the order of policy application as LSDOU, or "el-stew." Policies are applied in the order local, site, domain, and OU.

It is a quite intuitive process, at first. But policy application can get extremely complex when multiple policies are applied to a single container (SDOU), when inheritance is blocked or No Override is specified, and when policies are modified by access control lists (ACLs). Luckily, the enterprise scale application of group policy is not an objective of the Windows 2000 Professional exam. Simply understand the basic order of policy application—LSDOU.

Group Policy and OU Design

Group policy is a major factor in determining an enterprise's OU structure. If an OU contains users or computers that require different configurations and settings, the best practice is to subdivide the OU into one or more OUs, each of which contains objects that are configured similarly. By doing so, you can then manage the configuration by applying an appropriate group policy to each OU.

For example, you might remember the organization depicted in Figure 3.2. If within the Marketing OU a group of salespeople needed a sales application, and that sales application was not appropriate for all users in the Marketing OU, the best practice would be to create an OU, perhaps called Sales, within the Marketing OU (see Figure 3.3). By placing the Sales OU within the Marketing OU, it inherits all of the existing administration and configuration of the Marketing OU. But now, you can create a policy linked only to the Sales OU, and you can use that policy to deploy the sales application. As users are moved into the Sales OU, the sales application is deployed to them. See Chapter 4 for more information about deploying applications through group policy.

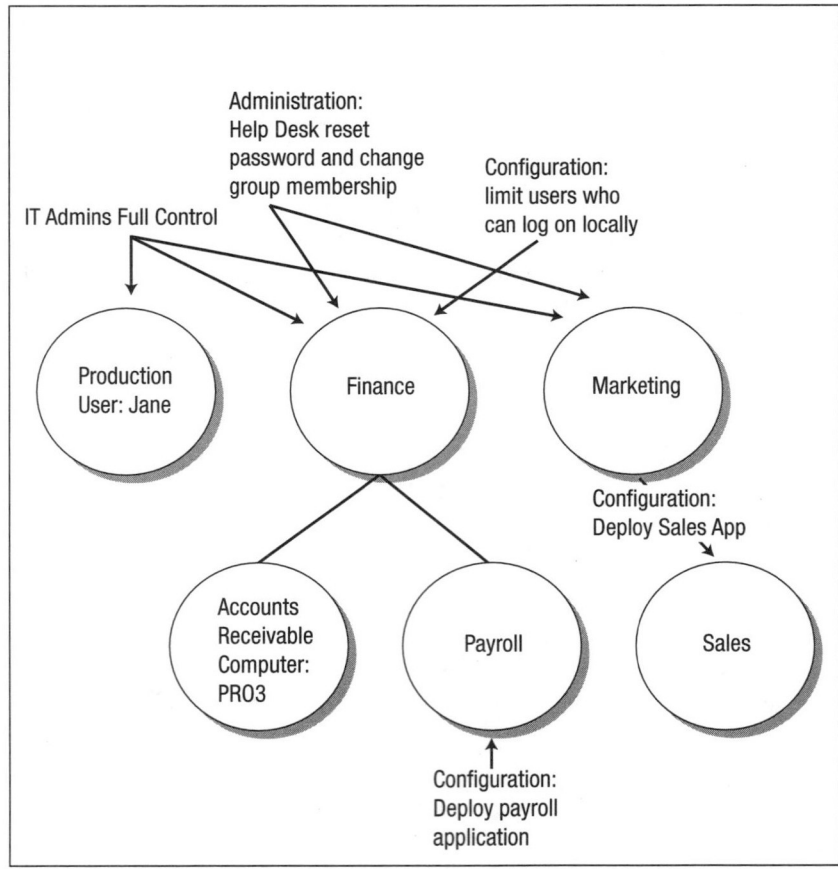

Figure 3.3 The OU Sales within the Marketing OU.

Practice Questions

Question 1

Computer1 is a member of the SAFTA domain. A local user account, John, is in the Administrators group. When John logs on to the domain, he is unable to perform all administrative functions on his system. What should you do to enable John to have full administrative control over his computer?

○ a. Delete the local user account John.

○ b. Add John's domain user account to the Administrators group.

○ c. Add John's domain user account to the Administrators group on the domain.

○ d. Give John Full Control permission to the C:\WINNT directory.

Answer b is correct. John is logging onto the domain, and even if his domain username is John, it is still a different account than the local user account. Therefore, he is not actually a member of the Administrators group when he is logging on to the domain.

Question 2

Susan is an administrator of Computer5. Other users who log on to Computer5 complain that Susan occasionally formats the D: drive to get rid of old files and folders, and that she is destroying their data in the process. You want Susan to be able to manage basic user and group accounts as well as restore files, but you want to prevent her from unnecessarily harming the system. What should you do? [Check all correct answers]

❏ a. Add Susan to the Backup Operators group.

❏ b. Add Susan to the Power Users group.

❏ c. Deny Susan Full Control permission to the System32 folder.

❏ d. Remove Susan from the Administrators group.

Answers a, b, and d are correct. The Backup Operators group can restore files and folders, and the Power Users group can manage basic user and group accounts. By removing Susan from the Administrators group, you are denying her many privileges that are built into that group, including the privilege to format disk volumes.

Question 3

> You want to enable a colleague to access files on your Windows 2000 Professional system from her system, which is part of a Novell network. You have shared the folder in which the files are stored, and both share and NTFS permissions indicate that Everyone has Full Control. However, she calls you and indicates she still cannot access the files. What can you do to grant her access? [Check all correct answers]
>
> ❑ a. Give the Authenticated Users group Full Control of the folder.
>
> ❑ b. Create a user account for her and tell her the password.
>
> ❑ c. Enable the Guest account and tell her the password.
>
> ❑ d. Stop the WINLOGON service.

Answers b and c are correct. In order to access a resource, one must first have a valid user account. The system is part of a Novell network, implying that it is not in a domain and is a standalone or workgroup system. Therefore, all accounts must be created locally. You can either create an account for her or enable the Guest account.

Question 4

> You have just installed Windows 2000 Professional and when it starts up it goes directly to the desktop, without asking for a username and password. You want to improve the security of the system by enforcing logon. What tools could you use? [Check all correct answers]
>
> ❑ a. Local Security Policy
>
> ❑ b. Domain Security Policy
>
> ❑ c. Group Policy
>
> ❑ d. Users And Passwords applet
>
> ❑ e. System applet
>
> ❑ f. Computer Management console

Answers a, c, and d are correct. All three tools expose the security setting to automate logon, or require logon. The System applet and Computer Management consoles do not expose the setting to require logon. Therefore, answers e and f are incorrect.

Question 5

> You are deploying a mobile computer called Laptop3 for Maria. Laptop3 is in the Sales OU. Maria is in the Outside Sales OU, which is contained within the Sales OU. You want to ensure that the sales application is deployed to Maria and all others who take Laptop3 on the road. Which of the following is the best-practice solution for deploying the sales application?
>
> ○ a. Use group policy's User Settings to deploy the application's MSI file to the Outside Sales OU.
>
> ○ b. Use local policy to deploy the application's MSI file to Laptop3.
>
> ○ c. Use group policy's User Settings to deploy the application's MSI file to the Sales OU.
>
> ○ d. Use group policy's Computer Settings to deploy the application's MSI file to the Outside Sales OU.
>
> ○ e. Use group policy's Computer Settings to deploy the application's MSI file to the Sales OU.

Answer e is correct. You want all users to have the application as long as they are on Laptop 3, so you want to use the Computer Settings node of group policy. Laptop3 belongs to the Sales OU. Applying the policy to the Outside Sales OU would not affect Laptop3, which is "above" the Outside Sales OU in the OU structure.

Question 6

> Lou has an account in the domain that is a member of the Sales, Trainers, and Managers groups. You are hiring Beth, who will also be a member of the same groups. You want to create Beth's account with the least administrative effort. What should you do?
>
> ○ a. Create an account for Beth and add the account to the Sales, Trainers, and Managers groups.
>
> ○ b. Rename Lou's account as Beth.
>
> ○ c. Copy Lou's account and call the new account Beth.
>
> ○ d. Rename the Guest account Beth.

Answer c is correct. If you copy Lou's account, the new account will be a member of the same groups as Lou.

Question 7

Lou has a local user account that is a member of the Sales, Trainers, and Managers groups. You are hiring Beth, who will also be a member of the same groups. You want to create Beth's account with the least administrative effort. What should you do?

○ a. Create an account for Beth and add the account to the Sales, Trainers, and Managers groups.

○ b. Rename Lou's account as Beth.

○ c. Copy Lou's account and call the new account Beth.

○ d. Rename the Guest account Beth.

Answer a is correct. You cannot copy a local user account.

Question 8

Lou has an account in the domain that is a member of the Sales, Trainers, and Managers groups. The Sales group has access to the Sales Reports folder, the Trainers group can read the Curricula folder, and the Managers can read the Financials folder. Lou can also modify the Curricula folder. You hire Beth, who will be performing the same job function as Lou. You copy Lou's account and name the new account Beth. Which of the following statements are true? [Check all correct answers]

❑ a. Beth is a member of the Sales, Trainers, and Managers groups.

❑ b. Beth can read the Curricula folder.

❑ c. Beth can modify the Curricula folder.

❑ d. Beth's password is the same as Lou's.

Answers a and b are correct. The access Beth enjoys is because her account is a member of the same groups as Lou's, but access permissions assigned to a user account are not changed when you copy the account. Similarly, user passwords are not copied when an account is copied. Beth cannot modify the Curricula folder because that permission was assigned directly to Lou. Therefore, answer c is incorrect.

Question 9

You bring your system from your home network into the office and connect it to the enterprise network. When you log on, the settings and applications that normally affect you at the office do not apply. What can you do to correct the situation?

○ a. Renew your system's DHCP=address.

○ b. Log on as Administrator.

○ c. Join your system to the domain and log on with your domain account.

○ d. Log on as Guest.

Answer c is correct. The system is not part of the domain, so it does not apply policies that are part of your domain's Active Directory.

Question 10

You have configured the local policy of your domain workstation, a Windows 2000 Professional machine, to disable the requirement to press Ctrl+Alt+Delete and log on. However, when you start the computer, it still requires you to press Ctrl+Alt+Delete. What tool should you use to locate the source of the problem?

○ a. Computer Management

○ b. System Information

○ c. Event Viewer

○ d. Local Security Policy

○ e. Group Policy

Answer e is correct. Your system's local policy is being overridden by a site, domain or OU group policy. Group Policy allows you to examine the policies applied to your system's SDOUs. Although Local Security Policy shows you that there is a discrepancy between the local policy and the effective policy, it does not help you locate the source of the discrepancy. Therefore, answer d is incorrect.

Need to Know More?

 Microsoft Corporation. *Microsoft Windows 2000 Professional Resource Kit.* Redmond, Washington: Microsoft Press, 2000. ISBN: 1-57231-808-2. This book has invaluable information on implementing security accounts and policy.

 Stinson, Craig, and Carl Siechert. *Running Microsoft Windows 2000 Professional.* Redmond, Washington: Microsoft Press, 2000. ISBN: 1-57231-838-4. This guidebook to Windows 2000 Professional is a good source for information on user and group account management.

 Wood, Adam. *Windows 2000 Active Directory Black Book.* Scottsdale, Arizona: The Coriolis Group, 2000. ISBN: 1-57610-256-4. This book provides comprehensive coverage of Active Directory.

 Search the TechNet CD (or its online version through **www.microsoft.com**) and/or the Windows 2000 Professional Resource Kit CD using the keywords "account", "policy", "SAM", "authentication", "group", "user rights", and "group policy."

Configuring and Troubleshooting the User Experience

4

Terms you'll need to understand:

✓ User profiles

✓ Offline Files and Folders

✓ Windows Installer Service

✓ MSI files

✓ ZAP files

Techniques you'll need to master:

✓ Configuring Offline File and Folder options

✓ Implementing Windows Installer Packages

✓ Understanding the functionality of various Control Panel applets

✓ Implementing software Group Policies

With Windows 2000 Professional, Microsoft has answered various complaints that many users had with Windows NT Workstation. Mobile users of Windows NT Workstation had a difficult job of keeping files on a network file server synchronized with copies they kept on their laptop. Windows 2000 Professional goes a long way toward fixing this age-old problem and other problems such as Dynamic Link Library (DLL) conflicts, application repair, and software updates. This chapter discusses how Windows 2000 Professional addresses these problems. Also, the user environment has been configured and enhanced in Windows 2000 Professional by using various control applets.

Configuring and Managing User Profiles

A *user profile* is the look and feel of the user's desktop environment. A profile is a combination of folders, data, shortcuts, application settings, and personal data. For example, users can configure their computer with the screen saver they like and their favorite desktop wallpaper. These settings are independent of other users' settings. When users log on to their computer for the very first time, a new profile is created for those users from a default user profile. So, when Joe logs on, a profile is created just for Joe. This type of profile is known as a *local profile* and is stored on the computer on which it was created. If Joe logged onto a different computer, his profile would not follow him to the computer he just logged onto. However, you can have a user's profile follow a user around the network if you so choose. This type of profile is called a *roaming user profile*. These profiles are stored on a network server. A local copy of the roaming profile is also found on the client computer.

User Profiles

User profiles in Windows 2000 contain a new folder structure compared to Windows NT. A new folder in a profile called Local Settings is local to the machine it resides on and won't roam. Also, a new folder called My Documents is contained in a profile. This folder is the default location where files are saved to. This folder does roam.

Local Profiles

Windows 2000 Professional local profiles are found in a different location than those in Windows NT 4 Workstation—maybe. If you perform a clean install of Windows 2000 Professional, a user profile is stored in a system partition called root\Documents and Settings\user_logon_name. If, however, you upgrade a Windows NT 4 Workstation to Windows 2000 Professional, the local profile is stored in the same location as it always was: %SystemRoot%\Profiles\user_logon_name.

Logon Scripts, Home Folders

When a user logs on, a *logon script* might execute and a *home folder* might be assigned to the user. Logon scripts are often used to map network drives or to execute some type of batch file. To configure a logon script for a user, perform the following steps:

1. Place the logon script in %SystemRoot%\sysvol\domain\scripts (this is a new location in Windows 2000 for logon scripts).

2. Next, open Active Directory Users And Computers and select the User Object Properties. Go to the Profile tab and simply type the name of the logon script in the Logon Script field.

A *home folder* is a central location on a network server where users can store their files. All users have their own home folder to store data. This way, if their computer fails, they don't lose all their data. Home folders also provide one central location in which users can back up all their data. To create a home folder, perform the following steps:

1. Create a share on a network server to enable home folders.

2. Next, open Active Directory Users And Computers and select the User Object Properties. Go to the Profile tab and select the Connect radio button.

3. Select the drop-down arrow and choose an available drive letter.

4. Type in the Uniform Naming Convention (UNC) path to the user's home folder (e.g., "\\server1\homedir\todd").

 Microsoft suggests that users store their data in My Documents instead of home directories. You can then enable a Group Policy to redirect My Documents from the local computer to a network file server. The Group Policy also activates offline caching of My Documents to the user's local computer. Group Policy as well as offline files and folders are covered later in this chapter.

Roaming User Profiles

If you have users who move from computer to computer, you can configure their profiles to move with them. A roaming profile is stored on a network server so that the profile is accessible regardless of which computer a user logs on to in the domain. You can put the profile on the server in two ways. You can copy a profile that is stored locally on a client computer to the profile server the next time the user logs on to the computer. Or, you can create on a client computer a profile that you will use as a company standard and then manually copy it to the profile server.

 Roaming user profiles behave differently in Windows 2000 than in Windows NT 4 Workstation. When a user logs on to a computer for the first time, the roaming profile is copied to the client computer. From that point forward, whenever a user logs on to a computer, the locally cached copy of the profile is compared to the roaming user profile. If the local profile and the roaming profile are the same, the local copy is used. Windows 2000 copies only files that have changed, not the entire profile, as was the case in Windows NT.

Use the following steps to configure a roaming profile:

1. Create a shared folder on a server for the profiles.

2. Open the Control Panel and then open the System Control Panel.

3. Select the User Profile tab.

4. Select the user's profile you wish to roam and select Copy To. Then, type in the UNC path to the shared folder that was created (e.g., "\\server1\profiles\Todd").

5. In Active Directory Users And Computers, select the account properties for the user. Then select the Profile tab and enter the UNC path to the profile server in the Profile Path field.

 In Windows 2000, new permissions are assigned to the Roaming Profile directory. If you create a roaming profile on an NT File System (NTFS) volume by using the **%username%** variable, the user and the built-in local Administrators group are assigned Full Control permission of that directory.

Note: Local or roaming profiles are protected from permanent change by renaming NTUSER.DAT to NTUSER.MAN. By renaming the file, you have effectively made the profile read only, meaning that Windows 2000 does not save any changes made to the profile when the user logs off. NTUSER.DAT is found in the root of a profile and is hidden by default. This file is responsible for the user portion of the Registry and contains all the user settings.

Using Offline Files and Folders

Windows 2000 offers a new feature called *Offline Files*. This feature addresses several file access problems that plagued Windows NT such as the file server is down now and users need to access files on the file server, or users are not connected to the network and cannot get access to the files they may need. By using Offline Files and Folders, users can select files on a network file server and mark them for offline usage. This means that users now have a cached copy of the file on their local computer and can work on the file just as if they were connected to the network. Any offline files that have been changed on a local computer are synchronized with the network file server when the users connect to the network.

Setting Up Offline Files and Folders

There are two steps involved in configuring offline files. The first is to configure the share point for offline usage. The second is to cache the files to the client computer.

Configuring Share Points

Use the following steps to configure the share point:

1. Share the files that you want to make available offline.

2. From the Sharing tab, select the Caching button.

3. Select the Allow Caching Of Files In This Shared Folder option (this option is selected by default).

4. Select one of the following three options from the Settings drop-down list and then click on OK:

   ➤ *Manual Caching For Documents*—This option is the default setting. With this option selected, users must select the files they want available for offline usage.

   ➤ *Automatic Caching For Documents*—This option caches all files that users have opened to their local disk for offline usage. Any older files that are out of synchronization are automatically deleted and replaced by a newer version of the same file.

   ➤ *Automatic Caching For Programs*—This option provides the same capabilities as Automatic Caching For Documents but also caches applications that are run from the network.

5. Click on OK to close the Share Point dialog box and to accept the options that you selected.

 By default, Windows 2000 does not allow you to cache files with the .slm, .ldb, .mdw, .mdb, .pst, and .db extensions. However, you can override this setting through a Group Policy. Create a computer policy for Administrative templates\Network\Offline Files\Files not cached.

> The policy excludes files with specific file extensions from being cached. However, if the policy is enabled and no file extensions are added, all file types can be made available offline. This setting overrides the default configuration; it does not allow files with the .slm, .ldb, .mdw, .mdb, .pst, and .db extensions to be cached.

Making Files and Folders Available Offline

By default, a Windows 2000 Professional computer is configured for offline file and folder usage. Use the following steps to make a file or folder available offline:

1. Connect to a share point on a domain or workgroup file server. Select and right-click on a file that you want.

2. Select Make Available Offline from the flyout menu.

3. A wizard appears if you are using this feature for the first time.

4. The wizard asks if offline files should be synchronized during logon and logoff. Click on the Next button to accept the default. (Additional options are available after the wizard is finished.)

5. If you want the operating system to remind you that you are not connected to the network, click on the Finish button to accept the default option, Enable Reminders. If you accept this option, a computer icon appears in the system tray. Whenever you are disconnected from the network, a balloon appears; it notifies you that offline files are available.

Once you have completed these steps, a little double arrow icon, shown in Figure 4.1, appears on the file or folder that you have selected for offline usage. This is simply a graphic indicator to inform users that the file is located on the network and that a local cached copy of the file is located on their computer.

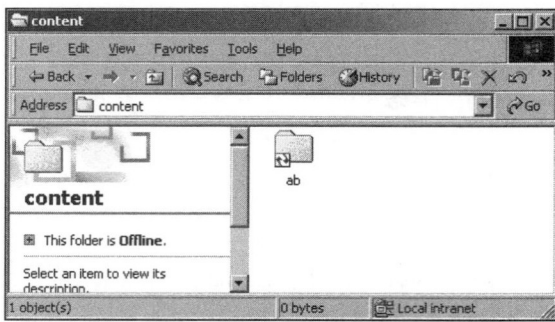

Figure 4.1 The offline file indicator.

Note: A Windows NT 4 client cannot use the offline feature of Windows 2000 servers. However, a Windows 2000 Professional client can make files available for offline usage from a Windows NT 4 server share.

To view offline files once you are disconnected from the network, open My Network Places. Yes, that is correct. Offline files maintain their original location even though the computer is offline. Go to My Network Places and select the file server that contains the files. You can see only the files that you made available while offline. Users don't see the "network" while they are offline.

Synchronizing Offline Files and Folders

Locate the file that you need and continue working. Once you have established a connection and have logged on to the network, any changes you made to the file while you were offline are then synchronized with the original file on the network. However, if you have logged on to the network from a slow dial-up connection, it could take a long time to synchronize offline files while you are logging on.

Several options are available to customize the synchronization process to deal with this type of problem. To customize the process when offline files are synchronized, open a Windows Explorer window, select the Tools menu item, and then choose Synchronize. The first dialog box displays the files and folders that are available offline. To configure synchronization, click on the Setup button. This brings up the Synchronization Settings dialog box, shown in Figure 4.2.

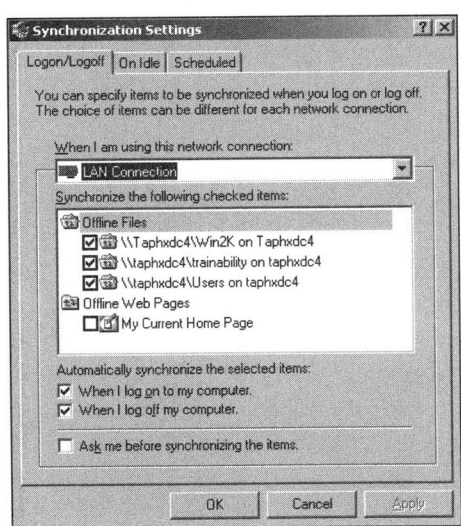

Figure 4.2 The Synchronization Settings dialog box.

This dialog box offers three tabs that help you determine when you should synchronize offline files: Logon/Logoff, On Idle, and Scheduled. However, you can also select over what network connection synchronization takes place. For example, to have synchronization occur only when you are connected to the network (versus when you have a slow dial-up connection), select LAN Connection in the When I Am Using This Network Connection drop-down list.

Synchronization Details

Now that you have configured synchronization, you are probably wondering what actually happens during this process. Well, that depends. Below are several synchronization scenarios:

➤ *An offline file has been deleted and the original network version of the file has not changed*—If this happens, Windows 2000 Professional removes the file from the network file server during synchronization.

➤ *A network file has been deleted and the offline version of the file has not changed*— If this happens, Windows 2000 Professional presents a dialog box of this state and gives you the option to either remove the file from the local computer during synchronization or keep the local version.

➤ *The offline file has changed and the network version has changed*—If this happens, you are presented with a dialog box during the synchronization; it asks you what should be done. The options are: keep the network version, keep the local version, and keep both and rename the local version.

➤ *Only files that have changed are synchronized*—If no changes have occurred, the locally cached copied is used before the network version of the offline file.

Accessing Offline Files and Folders

To access offline files, use My Network Places; however, that is not where the files are actually kept. Offline files are kept in %SystemRoot%\CSC. (CSC is hidden by default.) This directory contains a database of the offline files. You cannot view or edit individual files from this location. However, if the CSC directory gets quite large and if you use offline files frequently, it is advisable to move this directory from the system partition to a different partition or drive. However, you can't move this directory using the Explorer. To move the CSC directory from one partition to another, use the Windows 2000 Resource Kit utility named **Cachemov.exe**.

Managing Offline Files and Folders

To manage offline files, open a Windows Explorer window and select the Tools menu item. Select Folder Options and then select the Offline Files tab. The key options for managing offline folders are: turn off the Offline Files feature, delete

Offline Files, and view all the Offline Files in one window. You can also use a sliding bar to control the amount of disk space made available for files that have been automatically cached to the local drive. The default disk space made available for automatically cached files is 10 percent.

Configuring and Troubleshooting Desktop Settings

The Windows 2000 desktop is a combination of Windows NT options, Windows 98 options, and some new ones. In general, a regular local or domain user account can configure very few changes on a Windows 2000 Professional computer. The options that users can configure to customize their desktop are the following Control Panel applets and customization options:

➤ Keyboard applet

➤ Display applet

➤ Mouse applet

➤ Sound applet

➤ Personalized Start menu

➤ Quick Launch Pad

➤ Toolbars

Keyboard Applet

The Keyboard applet adjusts the cursor blink rate, the speed at which a character repeats when you hold down a key, the time lapse before a character repeats, and the input locale for different language groups of keyboard hardware. For example, you can use several language locales with a U.S. keyboard layout so that you can add foreign accent marks to documents that are written in French, Spanish, Italian, and so on. The Regional applet can also be used to configure Input Locales. Chapter 5 contains more information on this topic.

Display Applet

The Display applet has changed a little in Windows 2000 from Windows NT. You can now choose from six tabs to affect various aspects of the display:

➤ *Background*—Selects and adds a desktop wallpaper or pattern.

➤ *Screen Saver*—Selects a screen saver but is also a shortcut to the Power Options applet. The Power button on the Screen Saver tab allows you to adjust power schemes and configure Standby and Hibernate modes.

➤ *Appearance*—Adjusts the color and font schemes that are displayed in all dialog boxes and windows.

➤ *Web*—Is a new tab. It displays an HTML page on the desktop.

➤ *Effects*—Adjusts how menus fly out, changes the default icons, and makes other visual enhancements.

➤ *Settings*—Is probably the most important of the bunch. If Windows 2000 doesn't detect a Plug and Play monitor, it assigns default color depths and resolutions.

Often, these parameters need to be changed to suit the users' needs.

Mouse Applet

The Mouse applet adjusts for left-handed or right-handed use. It also adjusts the double-click speed and the rate at which the cursor moves across the screen.

Sound Applet

The Sound applet controls the startup and logoff sounds. It also controls what WAV files are used for critical error alerts and general alerts.

Personalized Start Menu

Windows 2000 makes it much easier to arrange and customize the Start menu items than Windows NT did. You can very easily sort menu items by dragging and dropping them. You can drag a menu item from one submenu to another. Also, you can open pop-up menus by right-clicking on them. Windows 2000 automatically adjusts menu items as well. Windows 2000 attempts to clean up the Start menu by displaying only those items that are used most frequently. Items that are not used often are hidden. Windows 2000 Professional displays a Screen Tip to click on a double down arrow so that you can access the infrequently used or hidden items on the Start menu. You can turn off this feature quite easily: Right-click on the taskbar and select the Properties command. Doing so displays the General tab of the Taskbar And Start Menu Properties dialog box. Deselect the option for Use Personalized Menus.

You can find even more options on the Advanced tab of the Taskbar And Start Menu Properties dialog box, as shown in Figure 4.3. You can add flyout menus for typical Start menu items such as the Control Panel. Some Start menu items such as Administrative Tools are hidden by default.

The following is a list of the items that you can configure from the Advanced tab:

➤ Display Administrative Tools

➤ Display Favorites

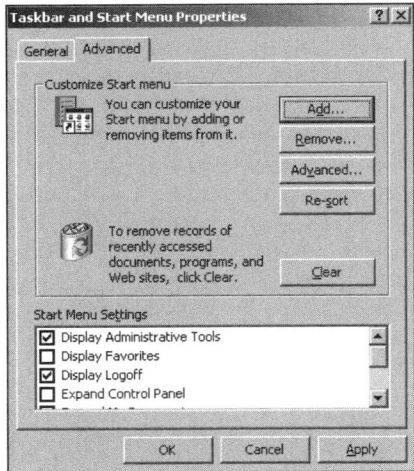

Figure 4.3 Customizing Start menu settings.

➤ Display Logoff

➤ Expand Control Panel

➤ Expand My Documents

➤ Expand Network And Dial-up Connections

➤ Expand Printers

➤ Scroll The Programs Menu

Quick Launch Pad

The taskbar can serve as a multipurpose tool to help make navigating the interface more efficient. The taskbar in Windows 2000, similar to that in Windows 98, contains a Quick Launch Pad, which is a location that contains shortcuts to programs that you use most frequently. By default, Windows 2000 places the Show Desktop (minimizes all windows), Internet Explorer, and Outlook Express shortcuts on the Quick Launch Pad. You can add or remove shortcuts simply by dragging and dropping them on or off the Quick Launch Pad.

Toolbars

The taskbar can also display *toolbars* that allow you to access frequently used files and folders. A default toolbar called the Address toolbar, for example, provides space on the taskbar to allow you to go directly to a Web site or a file path by simply typing the Uniform Resource Locator (URL) or the path to the file that you want to go to. For example, instead of opening a Web browser and then typing the URL, simply type the URL (such as **www.microsoft.com**) in the Address toolbar and press Enter on the keyboard. The Web browser starts automatically and goes to **www.microsoft.com**.

Use the following steps to configure an Address toolbar:

1. Right-click the taskbar and select the Toolbars submenu.

2. Select Address from the submenu. A field called Address is added to the taskbar.

Windows Installer Service Packages

Microsoft has created a new method for installing applications in Windows 2000 called *Windows Installer Service Packages*. The Windows Installer Service actually installs packages on a computer.

The Windows Installer Service has two essential functions:

➤ It is an operating system service that is responsible for installing, removing, and updating software by asking the Windows Installer Service Package for instructions on how the application should be installed, removed, or modified.

➤ To create a standard for installing, removing, or modifying applications, you use an application programming interface (API) to communicate with the Windows Installer Service about how a package should be modified after an application is installed.

Once an application has been installed, the Windows Installer Service checks the state of the application while it is being launched. This service provides "self-healing" capabilities to applications if they were installed as a Windows Installer Service Package. The service is always checking to see if the application needs to be repaired.

The service also helps to resolve DLL conflicts. Windows 2000 has devised a way to allow an application to alter the location from which DLLs are loaded, instead of having all DLLs located in the system32 directory. This helps to protect DLLs from being overwritten and from other conflicts.

Key parts of an application have a protected tag on them. A Windows Installer Service Package lists critical files that you would need to replace if they were deleted or missing. For example, executables are listed as critical files. If, for example, Todd.exe were deleted, the Windows Installer Service would locate Todd.exe from a network server or ask the user to insert the CD-ROM that contains Todd.exe. Once Todd.exe was located, it would be installed and the application would launch.

The Windows Installer Service does a much better job of removing applications compared to previous versions of Windows. During the installation of an application, the Windows Installer Service sits in the background looking at everything that is installed, where everything is installed, and what has been changed during the installation. When it comes time to uninstall an application, the Windows Installer Service knows exactly where every last component of the application is, thereby successfully uninstalling the application.

If during the installation of an application something happens and the install fails, the Windows Installer Service can restart the installation from the point of failure. That may not always be the best solution, though. The Windows Installer Service can also roll back everything that was installed up to the point of failure, allowing the user to start the install from scratch.

Installing Packages

A Windows Installer Package (.msi file) contains all the information necessary to tell the Windows Installer Service how the application should be installed. To take advantage of the features that Windows Installer Service offers, you must install an application as an .msi file. Applications such as Office 2000 have their own .msi files. Software developers must design their applications to use this new service. However, existing applications can still gain some of the functionality that .msi files have to offer.

An application can repackage existing applications using third-party tools such as WinInstall LE. WinInstall is available on the Windows 2000 Professional CD-ROM. This application tracks the installation process and note all the files that were installed, their locations, and modifications they made to the Registry. You can then customize this information and turn it into an .msi file.

You may be wondering what to do if you don't have an .msi file or if you can't repackage the file. Non-Windows Installer-based applications such as setup.exe must use a ZAP file to publish a package. A *ZAP file* is just a text file with a .zap extension. The file provides information about how to install a program and the application properties. The following is a basic example of how to create a ZAP file:

```
[application]
FriendlyName= "WinZip Version 7.0"
SetupCommand= \\server1\apps\winzip\WinZip70.EXE
DisplayVersion = 7.0
[ext]
ZIP =
```

Publishing MSI Packages

You typically install .msi files over the network or locally on the client computer. A common method for installing .msi files in a Windows 2000 domain environment is to publish or assign applications to users through the Active Directory. Users in the Active Directory can be grouped into containers called Organizational Units (OUs). You can create a Group Policy Object (GPO) for an OU that either publishes or assigns Windows Installer Packages (.msi files). Any users in the OU would then receive the software when they log on to their Windows 2000 Professional computer. The software they receive when they log on can be either published to them or assigned to them.

Using Group Policy to Publish or Assign Windows Installer Packages

Windows Installer Packages are published or assigned to users through an Active Directory-based Group Policy. Perform the following steps to create a software Group Policy:

1. Open Active Directory Users And Computers.

2. Select the domain to deploy the software to all users in the domain, or select a specific OU to deploy software to users just in that OU.

3. Right-click the domain or OU and choose Properties from the Context menu.

4. Select the Group Policy tab.

5. Click the New button to create a new Group Policy. Type in a name for the Group Policy and press Enter.

6. Select the policy and then press Edit.

7. Under User Configuration, expand Software Settings. Next, right-click Software Installation and then select New|Package from the Context menu.

8. Type the UNC path to the .MSI package on the network (e.g., "\\server1\office2000\data1..msi").

9. Select either Published or Assigned from the Deploy Software dialog box and then press the OK button.

Note: If you are using a transform, you must select Advanced Published Or Assigned. (You can create a transform to install only specific applications from a Software suite of applications.)

10. Close the Group Policy console and press the Close button for the OU properties.

The software Group Policy will take effect when the users of the domain or OU log on to the network. The users can then install the software.

Publishing Applications

A software package is typically published to users when it is not mandatory that they have a particular application installed on their computer. This is a means to make the applications available for users if they decide they want to use them. Once you have created a Group Policy Object to publish a software package, you can log on to your computer and find any applications that were published from Add/Remove Programs, shown in Figure 4.4.

Select the Add New Programs button to see which applications have been published. Users can install a published application with user credentials. The Windows Installer Service installs the published application with elevated credentials on behalf of users. This method provides a central location for users to install applications. This saves users from having to search for network share points that contain applications they want to install.

Assigning Applications

Assigning an application is very similar to publishing one. When an application has been assigned, you can install it from Add/Remove Programs. Additionally, a shortcut for the application that has been assigned is placed on the Start|Programs menu when users log on to their computer. The software does not get installed until users select the shortcut for the first time.

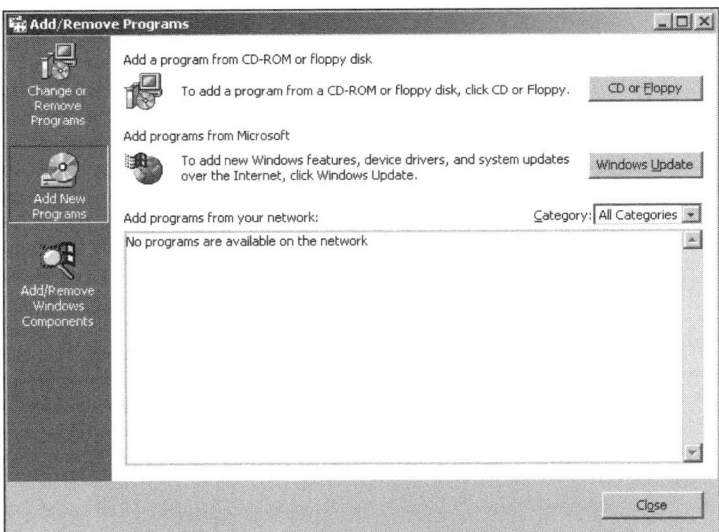

Figure 4.4 Add/Remove Programs.

 Software that has been published or assigned is also installed if users double-click on a file with the extension supported by the published or assigned application.

Practice Questions

Question 1

A salesperson for your company has selected files from the network file server to be made available offline to her laptop computer. She needs access to the files for a sales presentation in another city. When she connects to the corporate office from her hotel room over a dial-up connection, the synchronization process is unacceptably long. What can be done to resolve this problem without disabling offline files?

○ a. Verify that the share point on the network file server is set to Automatic Caching For Documents.

○ b. Use the Synchronization Manager to synchronize files only during a scheduled interval.

○ c. Use the Synchronization Manager to synchronize files only while the computer is connected to the local area network (LAN) connection.

○ d. Select the Never Allow My Computer To Go Offline option from the Offline Files tab in the Folder Options dialog box.

Answer c is correct. When the Synchronization Manager is set to synchronize only while the computer is connected to the LAN, the offline files aren't synchronized via the dial-up connection. Therefore, answer a is incorrect. Automatic Caching has nothing to do with controlling when synchronizing of offline files will occur, but rather to make files available while offline. Scheduling an interval for synchronization while the computer is connected via a dial-up connection may simply delay the process of synchronization but won't prevent synchronizing of files while connected to a modem. Therefore, answer b is incorrect. If the Never Allow My Computer To Go Offline option is selected, the salesperson will not have access to the files she made available offline. Therefore, answer d is incorrect.

Question 2

A user that works for a global organization needs to add foreign accent characters to memos that are sent to its employees in France. How can this be accomplished? [Check all correct answers]

❏ a. Use the Regional Control Panel and select the language the user needs to communicate in.

❏ b. Install the Multilanguage edition of Windows 2000.

❏ c. Use the Keyboard applet and select Input Locales Properties For United States–International.

❏ d. Use the Regional Control Panel and select Input Locales Properties For United States–International.

Answers c and d are correct. Both the Keyboard applet and Regional Control Panel allow users to select a keyboard layout that they can use to add foreign accents to documents. It is not necessary to use the Regional Control Panel to select a separate language, nor is it necessary to install the separate Multilanguage edition of Windows 2000. Therefore, answers a and b are incorrect.

Question 3

While at work, you add data to an Access database that is located on a Windows 2000 network file server. You want to finish adding the data to the database from home. You select the database and make it available offline to your laptop computer. When you log off the network, the synchronization process begins but stops due to an error stating that files with an .mdb extension cannot be made available for offline usage. How do you resolve this problem?

○ a. Verify that Access is installed on the laptop and manually synchronize the database.

○ b. Ensure that the .mdb file extension is associated with the correct application.

○ c. Enable a Group Policy to allow for files with the .mdb extension to be cached offline.

○ d. View the Synchronization Manager options to ensure that the database is selected for offline usage.

Answer c is correct. By default, files with the .mdb extension cannot be cached for offline usage. To override this default, you must configure the Files Not Cached policy by not listing .mdb files for Access databases to be made available for offline usage. The error you received is not related to whether or not Access is installed. Therefore, answer a is incorrect. Synchronization proceeds normally whether or not a file extension is registered correctly to an application. Therefore, answer b is incorrect. An error is not displayed if the file isn't selected to be synchronized via the Synchronization Manager. Therefore, answer d is incorrect.

Question 4

A public library has consulted you to create a common desktop for all Windows 2000 Professional machines that the library patrons use. You need to ensure that if a library patron makes a change to the desktop, the change cannot be saved. Currently the library has a mixed environment of Windows 95, 98, and 2000 computers. The following is a list of user account configurations. Create a list of required settings and configurations to implement a common desktop for all Windows 2000 Professional machines. Place the items in the list in the correct order:

User Account Configurations

Logon Scripts for all clients

Home directories for all clients

Ntuser.man

User.man

UNC path to profile

Common Windows 2000 Profile

Common Windows 95 and 98 Profile

Required Settings

Common Windows 2000 Profile

Ntuser.man

UNC path to profile user Ntuser

User.dat is the profile settings file that Windows 95 and Window 98, not Windows 2000, uses. To lock down the patron's desktop, a mandatory profile is being implemented. You create a mandatory profile for Windows 2000 by renaming ntuser.dat to ntuser.dat and then pointing users to the profile via the UNC path. User.dat is the wrong file.

Question 5

A user at a Windows NT 4 workstation is logged on to a Windows 2000 domain and is accessing a Windows 2000 file server. The user reports that he cannot make files available for offline usage. What is the problem?

○ a. The file server is not configured to allow caching of files in the shared folder.

○ b. The user has not enabled offline files from the Offline tab in the Folder Options dialog box.

○ c. The Offline Files and Folders is not available on the Windows NT 4 operating system.

○ d. The Active Directory client needs to be installed on the Windows NT 4 workstation.

Answer c is correct. Windows NT 4 (Server and Workstation) cannot cache files for offline use therefore answer b is incorrect. Also, a Windows NT server lacks the capability for configuring caching options. Therefore, a is incorrect. However, a Windows 2000 computer can make files available for offline use from a Windows NT 4 server or workstation. Adding the Active Directory client will not enable is functionality on a Windows NT 4 workstation, therefore answer d is incorrect.

Question 6

You create a Group Policy for users at the domain level to publish a Windows Installer Package. When users log on to their computers, they report that the software has not been installed. What needs to be done to install the software?

○ a. Users should select the shortcut for the application from the Programs menu. This will install the application.

○ b. Users should use Add/Remove Programs to install the software.

○ c. Users should configure a logon script to execute the Windows Installer Package when they log on.

○ d. Users should configure the Group Policy to publish the software for computers.

Answer b is correct. When an application has been published to users, you can install the application in two ways. Users can use Add/Remove Programs or they can double-click on a file that is associated with the application that needs to be installed. Answer a is incorrect because the application was published, which does not create a shortcut from the Programs menu. Answers c and d are not related to the problem. The application has been published and is ready to install via the Add/Remove applet.

Question 7

Nurses need to log on to nursing stations equipped with Windows 2000 Professional in a Windows 2000 domain. A nurse may log on to three or four different stations. You need to ensure that each nurse's desktop environment is available no matter which station each nurse logs on to. What do you need to do to implement this?

○ a. Configure the nurses' account profile on each workstation with the UNC path to the nurses' profiles.

○ b. Configure the nurses' domain account with the UNC path to the nurses' home directory.

○ c. Configure the nurses' domain account with the UNC path to the Profile directory.

○ d. Configure a logon script to map the Profile directory.

Answer c is correct. To have the nurses' desktop be available on any workstation, you must create a roaming user profile. The workstations are in a domain environment, so the domain user account must have the UNC path for the Profile configured. Answer a is incorrect because the question states the nurses' are in a domain. Configuring each workstation would be correct for a workgroup environment. Answer b is incorrect because the home directory is not used for roaming profiles. Answer d won't make a user profile roam.

Question 8

You have implemented roaming user profiles and home directories for all users. However, users report that their files are being saved to their local hard disk instead of to the network server. What must be done to ensure that users' files are being saved to the network server? [Check all correct answers]

❑ a. Redirect the My Documents folder to a network file server using a Group Policy.

❑ b. Redirect the My Documents folder to a network file server by providing the UNC path to the user's home directory on the Target tab of the My Documents property sheet.

❑ c. Verify that the UNC path to the home directory is correct.

❑ d. Verify that the UNC path to the Profile directory is correct.

Answers a and b are correct. The default location that applications save their files to is the My Documents directory. The default location for the My Documents directory is in the user's profile. However, this portion of the profile is not included in the roaming user profile. The My Documents directory needs to be redirected via a Group Policy or through the My Documents property sheet. Therefore, answers c and d are incorrect.

Question 9

You create a Group Policy for users at the domain level to assign a Windows Installer Package. When users log on to their computers, they select the shortcut for the assigned application. The installation of the application fails. What needs to be done to ensure the assigned application will install?

○ a. The users must install the application from Add/Remove Programs.

○ b. The users must verify that the correct UNC path to the software distribution point was configured for the Group Policy.

○ c. The users must double-click on a file with a file extension that is supported by the assigned application to trigger the installation process.

○ d. The users must create a logon script that maps the software distribution point for the domain user accounts.

Answer b is correct. You must use a UNC path to point to the location of the Windows Installer Package to assign or publish a Windows Installer Package via a Group Policy. If the UNC path is incorrect or if a local path is used, the Group Policy points to the wrong location for the software distribution point and so the install will fail.

Question 10

You want to deploy a legacy application to all Windows 2000 Professional clients in the Windows 2000 domain via Group Policy. The legacy application is not a Windows Installer Package. What do you need to do to deploy this application by using a Group Policy?

○ a. Non-Windows Installer applications cannot be deployed with a Group Policy.

○ b. Create a .ZAP file for the legacy application.

○ c. Add a transform to the package that executes a batch file to install the legacy application.

○ d. Choose Advanced Published Or Assigned when creating the software package to select the Allow Legacy Application Environment variable.

Answer b is correct. Applications that install using a setup.exe command require a .ZAP file or a third-party utility to use a Group Policy to deploy the application. If a .ZAP file is used, non-Windows applications can be deployed with a Group Policy. Therefore, answer a is incorrect. You cannot use a transform with a setup.exe command to install the application. Therefore, answer c is incorrect. The Advanced Published Or Assigned option doesn't include any options to install legacy applications. Therefore, answer d is incorrect.

Need to Know More?

 Finnel, Lynn. *MCSE Training Kit Microsoft Windows 2000 Server.* Redmond, Washington: Microsoft Press, 2000. ISBN: 1-57231-903-8. Chapter 7 discusses roaming user profiles. Chapter 15 provides information on deploying applications through Group Policy.

 Wallace, Rick. *MCSE Training Kit Microsoft Windows 2000 Professional.* Redmond, Washington: Microsoft Press, 2000. ISBN: 1-57231-901-1. Chapter 4 discusses user account properties. Chapter 15 provides information on Offline Files and Folders.

 **www.microsoft.com/WINDOWS2000/library/planning/management/swinstall.asp**. This Web site contains additional information regarding ZAP.

Configuring and Troubleshooting System Services and Desktop Environment

5

Terms you'll need to understand:

✓ User locales

✓ Input locales

✓ StickyKeys

✓ FilterKeys

✓ ToggleKeys

✓ MouseKeys

✓ Narrator

✓ Utility Manager

✓ Fax Service Management console

✓ Scheduled Task Wizard

Techniques you'll need to master:

✓ Configuring support for multiple languages

✓ Configuring accessibility options

✓ Implementing and configuring the Fax service

✓ Configuring and managing tasks with Task Scheduler

Windows 2000 offers many new services and options that can accommodate people's special needs. You can configure this new operating system very easily to adjust for different locales and languages. Also, you can customize Windows 2000 Accessibility options to adjust the interface and keyboard responses for people with disabilities. We will also learn how to configure and troubleshoot the Fax service and the Scheduled Task Wizard in this chapter.

Multiple Location and Language Support

The Windows 2000 operating system jumps ahead of previous versions of Windows support of multiple languages. It allows you to support people and companies that need to communicate in different languages by using locales. In addition, a Multilanguage version of Windows 2000 allows users to easily switch between different language user interfaces to suit their needs.

Language Options

There are essentially two key areas of language configuration options within Windows 2000 Locale and Language Group options.

Locales

A *locale* is a collection of information that Windows 2000 maintains about a user's language. A locale contains information such as the following:

➤ Currency symbol

➤ Format of date, time, and numbers

➤ Localized calendar settings

➤ Character encoding

➤ Country abbreviation

Applications use the locale information to input the correct symbols and characters. There are two types of locales:

➤ *User locale*—A separate locale is maintained for each user. This locale controls the settings for date, time, and numbers on a per-user basis. When a locale is changed, Windows 2000 adjusts all the regional settings (such as the currency symbol) to reflect the selected locale.

➤ *Input locale*—A language is associated with an input method. For example, you could add the Spanish input locale to combine the Spanish keyboard with the English and French languages. This configuration would allow a user to use the Spanish keyboard layout to input data in both English and French. Input locales allow users who need to converse in multiple languages to use one keyboard layout that can be switched on the fly and that maps to other languages as needed.

Configuring User Locales

You configure all locales and language settings through the Regional Options applet in the Control Panel folder. Perform the following steps to select a different user locale:

1. Open the Regional Options applet.

2. Select the General tab.

3. Select the locale required in the Your Locale (Location) drop-down list.

4. Click OK.

No reboot is required. The change of locale takes effect immediately. In addition, applications that depend on these settings reflect the new locale immediately. When you change the locale, the Numbers, Currency, Time, and Date tabs reflect the new configurations that are related to the new locale. Another way to configure these settings is to type a new entry for the desired option. For example, a user could select the Currency tab and type in a new currency symbol to be used.

Configuring Input Locales

If a keyboard layout needs multiple layouts, you must add input locales. Doing so allows a user to switch between locales when working in different languages. Perform the following steps to add an input locale:

1. Open the Regional Options applet.

2. Select the Input Locales tab.

3. Click Add and choose an input locale from the drop-down list.

4. Click OK.

5. Select a method to switch between input locales:

   ➤ Cycle through input locales by pressing left Alt+Shift.

   ➤ Assign a hot key sequence to specific input locales.

6. Click OK to close the Regional Options applet.

When you have completed these steps, an icon appears in the system tray; it indicates the input locale that is currently being used. Another way to select input locales (besides assigning hot keys) is to click the Input Locale icon and then select the specific input locale that you need.

Note: Additional input locales are available for each new language that is installed. For example, if a user needs an input locale for Estonian, install the Baltic language setting.

Multilanguage Support

Locales are used to adjust keyboard layouts for entering text. However, what if a user needs to read text that is in a different language? In this situation, you can install additional language groups in Windows 2000. For example, if the English-language version of Windows 2000 is installed and a user needs to read documents written in French, you can add the French-language group to Windows 2000. In this instance the application that is being used to read the French text must also support the ability to use Windows 2000 language groups.

Installing Multiple Language Settings

Perform the following steps to install additional language settings:

1. Log on as an administrator (users can't install language settings).

2. Open the Regional Options applet.

3. Select the General tab.

4. Click the checkbox for the language settings to be installed.

5. Insert the Windows 2000 Professional CD-ROM to copy the files. After the files have been copied, reboot the computer for the changes to take effect.

Once the computer has been rebooted, the additional language settings and additional locales are available.

Multilanguage Version of Windows 2000

Companies that have a global presence often need different language versions of an operating system. Previous versions of Windows require that you install a separate version of the operating system for each language that you are using. This goes a step further than input locales and language settings. The separate language edition of Windows 95, 98, or NT displays the user interface of the language edition that was installed. For instance, if the French edition of Windows 98 were installed, the user interface would be displayed in French characters and symbols. This, however, adds a tremendous amount of administrative overhead. These operating systems are distinctly different from the English versions, so they require separate Service Packs (SPs) and hot fixes. In this environment, an administrator might have to support three or four different versions of Windows 98.

Windows 2000 changes all of this. You can install a separate Multilanguage version of Windows 2000, which allows you to install additional languages to the existing English version of the operating system. After you have completed the basic installation of Windows 2000, you can install additional user interfaces that support other languages. The end result is a single version of Windows 2000 that supports multiple languages. The same SPs, hot fixes, and upgrades that you apply to the standard English version of Windows 2000 also apply to the Multilanguage edition of Windows 2000.

After you have installed a language user interface, a user can easily switch between interfaces via the Regional Options applet. A new tab that selects the desired interface is added to the applet. After the interface has been selected, the user must log off and log back on for the change to take effect. The user interface selection is established on a per-user basis. Several people can use the same computer but have completely different interfaces. Each user's profile contains the settings for which user interface should be used. The user interface provides the local language characters and symbols for the operating system and for the installed applications.

Accessibility Options

Windows 2000 provides several options to make navigating and using the operating system easier. You can enhance the interface and keyboard settings for users who have limited vision, hearing, and manual dexterity.

Accessibility Options Applet

The Accessibility Options applet contains several useful tabs: Keyboard, Sound, Display, and Mouse.

Keyboard Tab

Several options are available on the Keyboard tab to control repeat rate and key combinations:

➤ *StickyKeys*—This option allows a user to press multiple keystrokes such as Ctrl+Alt+Delete, by using one key at a time. To enable this feature, select the StickyKeys option in the Accessibility Options applet. You can also enable it by pressing the Shift key five times. At that point, a dialog box appears; it asks the user if this feature should be turned on. Click OK to enable and close the dialog box. In addition, a StickyKeys icon appears in the system tray. Double-clicking this icon opens the Accessibility Options applet.

➤ *FilterKeys*—This option lets you control the keyboard repeat rate, ignore repeated keystrokes, and control the rate at which a key repeats the keystroke if a user holds it down. You can apply granular settings to configure the repeat delay in number of seconds. If, for example, a user presses the L key and holds the key down, the letter L will repeat every x seconds (x represents the number of seconds for the repeat key delay). When you have enabled FilterKeys, an icon in the shape of a stopwatch appears in the system tray. You can also enable FilterKeys by holding down the right Shift key for eight seconds.

 If a user has enabled FilterKeys but finds that the keystrokes repeat with no delay, either someone has selected the No keyboard repeat settings or the repeat time delay has been configured to its lowest setting.

➤ *ToggleKeys*—When enabled, this option causes a high-pitched sound to be played when the Num Lock, Caps Lock, or Scroll Lock key is pressed. This feature is enabled via the Accessibility Options applet or by holding down the Num Lock key for 5 seconds.

Sound Tab

On the Sound tab, you can enable the following two sound features to help notify users of warnings and other events:

➤ *SoundSentry*—When enabled, this option displays visual warnings when Windows 2000 generates audible alerts. This feature is helpful for users with hearing impairments. A user can specify which part of the screen actually flashes when a sound is generated. The options are Flash Active Window, Flash Active Caption Bar, and Flash Desktop. To enable this feature, simply select the SoundSentry checkbox. No shortcut is available for this feature.

➤ *ShowSounds*—If applications use sounds to convey messages and information, this feature displays text captions that represent those sounds. Selecting the ShowSounds checkbox enables this feature. No shortcut is available for ShowSounds.

Display Tab

The Display tab allows you to set color schemes:

➤ *High Contrast*—When enabled it informs applications to change the color scheme to a High Contrast scheme to allow for easier reading. For example, you can enable a white on black scheme, a black on white scheme, or a custom color scheme. Doing so allows users to adjust colors and font sizes for Windows 2000 and all applications. To enable this feature, select the Use High Contrast checkbox; or, press left Alt+left Shift+Print Screen keys as a shortcut. When you press these three keys at the same time, a dialog box that asks if the feature should be turned on appears.

Mouse Tab

The Mouse tab allows you to use the keyboard as a mouse using these two features:

➤ *MouseKeys*—When enabled, this feature allows a user to use the numeric key-pad to move the mouse pointer. The keypad can also perform single-click, double-click, and drag-mouse actions. In addition, you can assign settings that control the pointer speed. To enable this feature, select the MouseKeys checkbox or press left Alt+left Shift+Num Lock. A dialog box will appear asking if the MouseKeys feature should be enabled. If you click the OK button an icon will appear in the system tray to graphically indicate the feature has been enabled.

 You can turn off StickyKeys, FilterKeys, ToggleKeys, SoundSentry, High Contrast, and MouseKeys after a specified idle period has passed. For example, you could assign a five-minute idle period. These six features would then all be turned off if the computer were idle for five or more minutes. To assign an idle period, select the General tab in the Accessibility Options applet and then click the Turn Off Accessibility Features After Idle For option.

➤ *SerialKey*—Enable this option for users who cannot use a standard keyboard and must install an alternative input device into a serial port. This option is located on the General tab.

Accessibility Wizard

You can configure most of the accessibility options quite easily through the Accessibility Wizard. The wizard asks a series of questions to determine if you need to configure keyboard, sound, display, and mouse accessibility features. For example, the wizard displays a sentence in varying font sizes. The user then selects a sentence with the font size that is easy to read. After the user has answered all the questions, the interface immediately changes to reflect large fonts and any other options that were configured.

Note: The Accessibility Wizard allows users to save the settings they have selected. These settings are saved in a file with the .acw file extension. These settings can be used on another computer or can serve as a backup. If many users require the same accessibility configurations, an administrator can save some time by saving the settings and using them on other computers that need the same configuration. However, there is a gotcha here. The default permissions assigned to the .acw file are for the user who is logged on and for the administrator. Before you can share the settings, make sure that you have added to the access control list (ACL) any global groups or individual user accounts that need access to this file.

Additional Accessibility Features

Windows 2000 provides three additional accessibility tools that are not available in the Accessibility Options applet. These tools, which you can locate by navigating to Start|Programs|Accessories|Accessibility, are the following:

➤ *Narrator*—This tool is for people who have low vision or are blind. When enabled, the Narrator uses a synthesized voice to read what is displayed (such as menu options, text, dialog boxes, and alerts).

➤ *Magnifier*—This tool splits the screen into two portions, magnified and non-magnified. The magnified portion of the screen magnifies the size of anything that the mouse pointer is hovering over. The nonmagnified area selects what needs to be magnified. You can increase or decrease the magnification level and the size of the magnification.

➤ *On-Screen Keyboard*—This tool displays a virtual keyboard on the Windows 2000 desktop. Users use the mouse pointer to press the virtual keys. They can also use a joystick with the on-screen keyboard to select keys.

Utility Manager

Utility Manager allows users to access these three tools from one interface. You can also use Utility Manager to check the status, and start or stop the tools. Also, an administrator can configure these tools to start when Windows 2000 starts.

Fax Features

Windows 2000 provides support for sending and receiving faxes via an internal or external modem. The Fax applet appears in the Control Panel folder once a modem has been installed. You use this applet to configure the Fax service and to access the Fax Service Management console. By default, the Fax service is configured to allow users to only send faxes, not receive them.

To fax a document, follow these steps:

1. Select the Print command within the application.

2. Select the fax printer and then click the Print option to submit a fax. The Send Fax Wizard opens. The wizard allows you to enter the recipient's name and fax number, cover page information, and other configurations. Figure 5.1 shows the Send Fax Wizard.

Configuring the Fax Service

The Send Fax Wizard gathers some information such as the sender's name and fax number. This information is gathered from settings contained in the Fax applet.

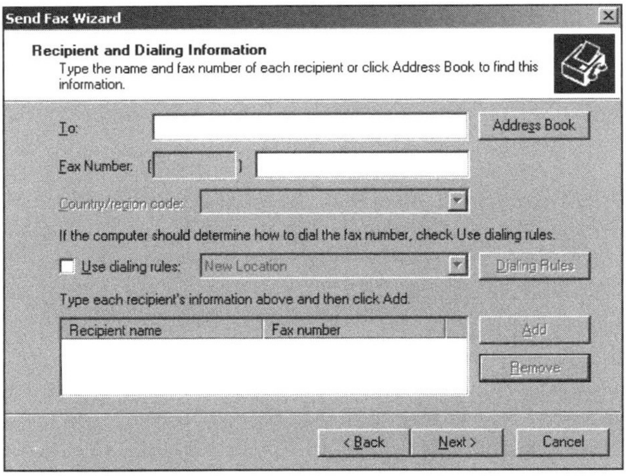

Figure 5.1   Send Fax Wizard.

You can also use this applet to troubleshoot and monitor fax transmissions. Here are the Fax applet tabs:

➤ *User Information*—This tab contains information such as fax number, email address, name, mailing address, and phone numbers. The Send Fax Wizard and the Fax Cover Page Editor use this information.

➤ *Cover Pages*—This tab contains options to add existing cover pages or to create new ones using the Fax Cover Page Editor.

➤ *Status Monitor*—This tab contains options to display the send/receive status monitor, stop fax transmissions, display a status icon on the taskbar, and manually answer incoming fax calls.

➤ *Advanced Options*—Important! This tab is visible only if the user logs on as an administrator. This is a key area of fax administration. You can configure the Fax service and add fax printers via this tab. Of particular importance is the Fax Service Management option. When this option is selected, the Fax Service Management console opens.

Managing the Fax Service Management Console

You can do the following with the Fax Service Management console:

➤ Configure the modem(s) to send or receive faxes. If more than one modem is installed, the first modem is used by default to send or receive faxes.

➤ Change or apply fax-related security permissions for users or groups. By default, the Everyone group can submit faxes and view fax jobs. However, only Administrators and Power Users can manage fax jobs, service, and devices.

➤ Configure the number of rings before a fax device answers a fax call. The default number is two.

➤ Configure the number of retries that are allowed before the fax device aborts sending the fax job.

➤ Choose where to store faxes that have been sent or received. The default location for both options is All User Profile\My Faxes.

➤ Adjust the priority for sending faxes.

➤ Change the detail of the fax logs.

➤ Print faxes upon reception.

➤ Prevent the use of personal cover pages.

➤ Configure the Transmitting Station Identifier (TSID), which is typically the sender's fax number.

➤ Configure the Called Station Identifier (CSID), which is typically the recipient's fax number.

Another way to open the Fax Service Management console (besides checking the Fax Service Management option, described earlier) is to select Start|Programs| Accessories|Communications|Fax|Fax Service Management. Any user can open it using this method. However, a user is denied access to making any configurations in the console. Only Administrators and Power Users can actually configure this service.

One of the main reasons for having a computer network is to share resources. Unfortunately, the Windows 2000 fax printer cannot be shared.

If faxes aren't being sent or received, verify that a user has permission to use the fax device and make sure the fax device is configured to send and receive faxes. If those settings are correct and faxes are still not being sent or received, stop and restart the Fax service.

Task Scheduler

In Windows NT 4 Workstation the **at** command is used to schedule when batch files, scripts, or backups should run. Windows 2000 has a graphical user interface (GUI) utility called Task Scheduler to run these same tasks. This utility is almost a carbon copy of the Windows 98 Task Scheduler.

You can open Task Scheduler from the Scheduled Tasks folder (located in the Control Panel folder) or Start|Programs|Accessories|System Tools|Scheduled Tasks. The Scheduled Tasks folder is shared by default. You can create a task on a computer and then copy it to another one. This is helpful if a similar task needs to run on many computers. By copying the task from one computer to another, you don't have to recreate it multiple times.

Creating a Task

To create a new task, open the Scheduled Tasks folder and double-click the Add Scheduled Task icon to launch the Scheduled Task Wizard. This wizard steps users through the process of selecting a program, batch file, or a script to run automatically at a scheduled time. Perform the following steps to create a task:

1. Select the program to be scheduled and then click Next.

2. Choose how often the task should run and then click Next. The options are as follows:

   ➤ Daily

   ➤ Weekly

   ➤ Monthly

   ➤ One Time Only

   ➤ When My Computer Starts

   ➤ When I Log On

3. Depending on what you chose in Step 2, users may have to set up what time of the day, what days of the week, or what months of the year the task should run. Choose the appropriate options and then click Next.

4. The next step requires you to enter a username and password. The username must have the right to run the selected application. Click Next.

5. The last dialog box of the wizard asks users whether or not to open the Advanced Properties sheet after the task has been created. The Properties sheet allows the user to edit the schedule, delete the task if it is not scheduled to run again, stop the task, start the task during idle periods, and not start the task if the computer is running on batteries. Also, you can assign Security permissions to the task to control which users can modify the task options. Click Finish.

Once you have closed the Scheduled Task Wizard and the Advanced Properties sheet, an icon that represents the task is created. Users can double-click a task to view and configure its advanced properties after they have created the task.

Troubleshooting Tasks

The Scheduled Task Wizard makes it very easy to create tasks. However, sometimes, tasks do fail to run. The most common reason for this is that the wrong username or password was entered for the task. If a task failed, verify that you entered the correct username and password on the task.

Another area where an incorrect account can cause problems is if a task has been created for old 16-bit applications. It may fail to run if the system account is used on the task service. If an error relating to the task service is generated, change the account used to run the service. Open the Task Service, which is located in Start|Programs|Administrative Tools|Services, and select the Log On tab to change the account. Figure 5.2 shows the Task Service Properties sheet. If the task still won't run, stop and restart the Task Service. You can configure it to restart automatically if it fails. To do so, go to the Recovery tab of the Task Service Properties sheet.

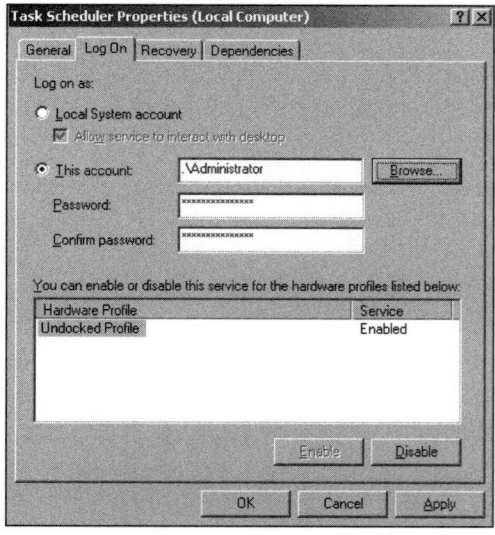

Figure 5.2 Task Service Properties sheet.

Practice Questions

Question 1

A user has the Fax service configured to send faxes, but when a fax is sent to this user, the computer cannot receive any faxes. What must be configured to allow the client computer to receive faxes?

○ a. Install a new fax printer and select receive faxes when installing the printer.

○ b. Reinstall the fax service and select receive faxes during the installation.

○ c. Use the Fax Service Management console to redirect faxes to the My Faxes folder.

○ d. Use the Fax Service Management console to configure the fax modem to receive faxes.

Answer d is correct. You can configure the fax modem to receive faxes after installation. It is not required to reinstall any fax-related services to configure the modem to receive faxes. Therefore, answer b is incorrect. You can configure the fax modem to receive faxes via the Fax Service Management console by selecting Devices, selecting the properties of the device, and choosing Receive.

Question 2

A user has completed a document that needs to be faxed. The user wants to fax the document using the Windows 2000 Fax service but there is no fax printer to print the document to. What needs to be installed or configured so the user can fax the document?

○ a. Restart the Fax service so the user can print to the fax printer.

○ b. Install a modem device.

○ c. Select the Advanced Options tab in the Fax applet to Add A Fax Printer.

○ d. Use the Add Printer Wizard to add a fax printer.

Answer b is correct. The Fax service won't install unless a modem has been detected which is why answer b is correct. Once Windows 2000 detects a modem, the Fax applet is present in the Control Panel folder and a fax printer driver is installed so a client can send and receive faxes. Answers a, c, and d are not viable options until a fax modem has been installed.

Question 3

> A user has limited dexterity. You want to configure his Windows 2000 Professional computer to ignore brief or repeated keystrokes. What must be enabled to configure the computer for this user?
>
> ○ a. FilterKeys
>
> ○ b. StickyKeys
>
> ○ c. ToggleKeys
>
> ○ d. MouseKeys

Answer a is correct. Enable FilterKeys if you want Windows 2000 to ignore repeated keystrokes. StickyKeys allows keystrokes such as Ctrl+Alt+Delete to be selected individually therefore answer b is incorrect. ToggleKeys plays a high-pitched sound when the Num Lock, Caps Lock, or Scroll Lock key is pressed; therefore answer c is incorrect. The MouseKeys Accessibility option is used to control the mouse pointer with the numeric keypad. The other options do not allow for this functionality, therefore answer d is incorrect.

Question 4

> You are the Administrator of a small network of 50 Windows 2000 Professional clients and 4 Windows 2000 servers. You want to use one of the Windows 2000 Professional clients as a fax server. How do you configure this client to function as a fax server?
>
> ○ a. Enable sharing of the fax printer driver.
>
> ○ b. Use the Fax Service Management console to select the properties of the modem and enable sharing.
>
> ○ c. The Windows 2000 fax print driver cannot be shared.
>
> ○ d. Open the Fax applet in Control Panel and enable sharing from the Advanced tab.

Answer c is correct. The current release of Windows 2000 Professional does not support the sharing of the fax printer therefore answer c is correct. Since Windows 2000 doesn't support fax sharing natively, answers a, b, and d are incorrect. Third-party fax software is required to configure Windows 2000 as a fax server.

Question 5

You require users to log on to your Windows 2000 domain to gain access to their computer and network resources. Several users in your organization have limited dexterity. You need to configure computers for these users to allow the Ctrl+Alt+Delete sequence to be pressed one key at a time. What must be enabled to allow for this functionality?

○ a. FilterKeys

○ b. StickyKeys

○ c. ToggleKeys

○ d. MouseKeys

Answer b is correct. Enable StickyKeys to allow multiple keystroke combinations such as Ctrl+Alt+Delete to be pressed one key at a time. Enable FilterKeys if you want Windows 2000 to ignore repeated keystrokes, therefore answer a is incorrect. ToggleKeys plays a high-pitched sound when the Num Lock, Caps Lock, or Scroll Lock key is pressed, therefore answer c is incorrect. The MouseKeys Accessibility option is used to control the mouse pointer with the numeric keypad. The other options do not allow for this functionality, therefore answer d is incorrect.

Question 6

You need to enable Windows 2000 Professional to read text from all dialog boxes and all applications to visually impaired users. What must you configure to allow for this functionality?

○ a. SoundSentry

○ b. ShowSounds

○ c. Narrator

○ d. Windows Media Player Close Caption

Answer c is correct. The Narrator accessibility option is used to read aloud onscreen text, dialog boxes, menus, and buttons that are selected in Windows 2000 Professional. SoundSentry generates visual warnings when the computer generates sound alerts, while ShowSounds tells applications to display captions for sounds the application may make, therefore answers a and b are incorrect. Windows Media Player cannot speak aloud written text, but can display text in Close Caption, therefore answer d is incorrect.

Question 7

> You have been asked to help plan the deployment of Windows 2000 Professional for a company that has offices in New York, France, and Germany. The offices in Europe frequently send documents in their native language to the office in New York. The office in New York sends documents in English to the offices in Europe. Users in all offices need to quickly switch between their native language and the language they need to correspond in. Also, it is required that ongoing administration of this environment be kept to a minimum. How can you deploy Windows 2000 to facilitate this?
>
> ○ a. Deploy the Multilanguage edition of Windows 2000 Professional to the offices in New York, France, and Germany.
>
> ○ b. Include the input locales for each language and create and deploy them using a Remote Installation Service (RIS) image.
>
> ○ c. Deploy the English-language edition and manually add input locales for each language as needed.
>
> ○ d. Add the Keyboard layout/IME for each language.

Answer a is correct. To allow users to regularly work in multiple languages and to reduce the administration of a computer with different language requirements, you should deploy the Multilanguage edition of Windows 2000 Professional as it uses the same Service Packs and hot fixes as the English language edition of Windows 2000. To install a separate edition of Windows 2000 Professional for each language that is used would add to the ongoing administration of the environment as separate Service Packs and hot fixes would be required for these systems. Answers b, c, and d would add to the administrative overhead to maintain the required environment and would not achieve all the goals. Answers b, c, and d don't allow a user to change user interfaces on the fly. Only the Multilanguage edition of Windows 2000 provides this functionality.

Question 8

You have used Task Scheduler to configure a 16-bit application to run every night at 11 P.M. However, when you log on the next day, you see an error that states the application could not run due to a service error. How do you resolve this problem?

- ○ a. Enter the correct password for the domain account on the scheduled task.
- ○ b. Configure the Task Scheduler service to log on with a domain username and password.
- ○ c. Verify that the task is set to run daily.
- ○ d. Verify that the local administrator username and password were used to run the task.

Answer b is correct. By default, the Task Scheduler service runs under the context of the local system account. Some older applications may try to start the service with a different account; thus, a service-related error is displayed. Enter a domain username and password for the service to resolve this problem. The error that was displayed was not related to the user account that was entered for the task to run. Two accounts are used: one for the task and the other for the service. The problem here was the account on the service. Therefore answers a and d are incorrect. These answers are concerned with the account being used to run the task. The problem is with the account used to run the service and not the task. Answer c has nothing to do with the problem. Because the service won't run then the task won't run. Verifying if the task is set to run daily doesn't affect the underlying problem with the service account.

Question 9

You have configured Task Scheduler to run a disk defragmentation tool at 11 P.M. each evening. You want five other Windows 2000 Professional computers to use this same task. How can you configure the five computers to use the same task without recreating the task?

- O a. Configure a Group Policy for the five computers to run a logon script that executes the task.

- O b. Go to each computer and copy the task that was created from its shared Scheduled Tasks folder to each of the five clients' Scheduled Tasks folder.

- O c. Import the scheduled task using the **at** command.

- O d. Import the scheduled task using the Task Scheduler service properties sheet.

Answer b is correct. Tasks are placed in the Scheduled Tasks folder. This folder is shared to everyone by default. Users can access any Scheduled Tasks folder on the network and either move or copy a task that has already been created to their Scheduled Tasks folder. Group Policy is not used to take tasks that were create on one computer and then copy them to another computer, therefore answer a is incorrect. The **at** command is a command line scheduler that does not allow for the importation of tasks that were created using the Scheduled Task Wizard, therefore answer c is incorrect. The Task Scheduler property pages do not provide any options for importing a task; therefore answer d is incorrect.

Question 10

You need to configure a Windows 2000 Professional computer to use Danish configurations (such as Danish usage of numbers and Danish currency) for an employee visiting the head office of your company in the United States. You want to allow the user to quickly switch from one locale to another using a key sequence or the system tray. Currently, the computer is using only the Western Europe and United States settings. How do you configure the computer to also use Danish settings?

- ○ a. Open the Regional Options applet and select the General tab. Add the Danish locale.

- ○ b. Open the Regional Options applet and select the General tab. Add the Danish language group for the system.

- ○ c. Open the Regional Options applet and select the Input Locales tab. Add Danish as a new locale and assign a hot key to this locale.

- ○ d. Open the Regional Options applet and manually enter the Danish configurations on the Numbers, Currency, Time, and Date tabs.

Answer c is correct. The Input Locales tab allows you to assign which input languages are loaded into memory every time the computer is started. It also allows you to assign hot keys that let you switch between input locales, and it places a small icon in the system tray to also allow a user to switch between input locales on the fly. Answer a would change the user locale to Danish and would then be used as the default locale. The goal is to allow users using a English keyboard to switch on-the-fly to Danish when needed which is not achieved by making Danish the default locale, therefore answer a is incorrect. Adding Danish group simply makes the keyboard layout available as an input locale, which it is as a default. This option doesn't add the Danish keyboard layout to the system tray, only input locales provide that functionality, therefore answer b is incorrect. Answer d does simply hard codes these options as default configurations. It does not allow a user to select the Danish keyboard layout from the system tray or via a keystroke; therefore answer d is incorrect.

Need to Know More?

 Microsoft Corporation. *Microsoft Windows 2000 Professional Resource Kit.* Microsoft Press: Redmond, WA, 2000. ISBN: 1-57231-808-2. The book provides invaluable information on Windows 2000 Professional.

 Stinson, Craig, and Carl Siechert. *Running Microsoft Windows 2000 Professional.* Microsoft Press: Redmond, WA, 2000. ISBN: 1-57231-838-4. This guidebook to Windows 2000 Professional is a good source for information on administering and configuring Windows 2000 Professional.

 Search the TechNet CD-ROM (or its online version through **www.microsoft.com**) and/or the *Windows 2000 Professional Resource Kit* CD-ROM using the keywords "Fax", "Accessibility", "Regional Options".

6

Installing Windows 2000 Professional

Terms you'll need to understand:

✓ winnt32.exe

✓ winnt.exe

✓ unattend.txt

✓ sysprep folder

✓ Remote Installation Service (RIS)

✓ winnt32.exe/checkupgradeonly

✓ Migration Dynamic Link Libraries (DLLs)

✓ Slipstreaming

Techniques you'll need to master:

✓ Understanding the different options available for installing Windows Professional

✓ Performing upgrades

✓ Applying service packs (SPs)

✓ Understanding RIS configurations

Microsoft has made available several ways to install Windows 2000 Professional. This chapter looks at the key areas involved in deploying a manual or automated installation of Windows 2000 Professional. In addition, you need to understand how to use all the utilities that are required for installing, upgrading, and verifying compatibility with Windows 2000.

Performing Attended Installations of Windows 2000 Professional

An attended installation of Windows 2000 Professional requires someone to sit in front of the target computer and answer all the installation prompts such as the End User License Agreement (EULA). Before you start the installation process, you need to ensure that the computer meets the minimum hardware requirements of Windows 2000 Professional. Unlike Windows NT, Windows 2000 supports only Intel-based computers. The following are the minimum hardware requirements for installing Windows 2000 Professional:

➤ 133MHz Pentium, or higher, Central Processing Unit (CPU)

➤ 32MB of memory (Microsoft recommends 64MB)

➤ A 2GB hard drive with a minimum of 650MB of free space

➤ VGA, or higher-resolution, monitor

➤ Keyboard

➤ Mouse

➤ 10X CD-ROM for CD-ROM installations

Once you've verified that the computer meets these minimum hardware requirements, you should check to see if devices such as the video adapter and the network adapter are compatible. To do this, check the Hardware Compatibility List (HCL), which every Windows 2000 CD-ROM contains. However, that file is out of date. To view the most current HCL, visit **www.microsoft.com/hcl**.

Installation Methods

You can perform an attended install of Windows 2000 in three ways: using a CD-ROM, the setup disks, or the network.

CD-ROM

One of the easiest methods for installing Windows 2000 Professional is simply to put the Windows 2000 Professional CD-ROM in the computer and boot the computer. The computer boots from the CD-ROM, starts the first phase of the installation, and copies the installation files to the local hard drive. Then, the computer reboots (remember to remove the CD-ROM) and starts the graphical user interface (GUI) phase of the installation. You can install Windows 2000 Professional in this fashion if your computer's BIOS supports the option to boot from a CD-ROM drive and the CD-ROM is El-Torito compatible.

Setup Disks

If you can't configure your computer to boot from a CD-ROM, you can install Windows 2000 Professional by using the four floppy setup disks that came with your Windows 2000 Professional CD-ROM. Simply place setup disk number one in the computer to start the installation.

*Note: If the four setup disks are lost or become corrupted, you can create them using the Windows 2000 Professional CD-ROM. Open the Bootdisk folder on the CD-ROM and execute either makeboot.exe or makebt32.exe. A command prompt window that asks you to insert a floppy disk into drive A opens. Continue the process until you have created all four disks. Use makeboot.exe if you are running in a DOS environment or Windows for Workgroup. Use makebt32.exe if you are running in Windows 95, 98, NT, or 2000. This method of creating a boot disk replaces the Windows NT 4 method of executing the **winnt32.exe /ox** switch, which does not create Windows 2000 setup disks.*

Network

Another installation method is to place the contents of the Windows 2000 Professional CD-ROM in a folder on a network server and then share the folder. This network server is referred to as a *distribution server*. Establish a network connection to the distribution server to start the installation. If Windows 95, 98, or NT is on the target computer, connect to the share point and execute winnt32.exe to start the installation process. If no operating system is on the target computer, use a network boot disk to connect to the source files and use winnt.exe to start the installation. You use winnt32.exe in a 32-bit environment, whereas you use winnt.exe in a 16-bit/DOS environment.

Automating the Installation of Windows 2000 Professional

When you use the three attended installation options, someone must be in front of the computer to answer all the installation prompts. This is a very inefficient means of installing Windows 2000 Professional when you need to install the operating system on many computers. This section discusses how to use Setup Manager, the System Preparation Tool, and Remote Installation Service (RIS) for automating the installation process.

Using Setup Manager to Create an Unattended Installation

The Setup Manager utility answers the installation prompts and saves the answer results in an answer file called unattend.txt. Windows 2000 can then use unattend.txt during the installation to configure the screen resolution and other typical hardware and operating system settings. This tool is much improved in Windows 2000 and adds more options and greater flexibility than its predecessor. Setup Manager can now:

➤ Agree to the EULA

➤ Create a distribution share point

➤ Create a listing of unique computer names for a Uniqueness Database File (UDF)

➤ Add third-party Plug and Play drivers and other resources

➤ Add printers, scripts, batch files, and other commands to the distribution share

You must extract Setup Manager from a cab file on the Windows 2000 Professional CD-ROM to create unattend.txt. To extract Setup Manager, perform the following steps:

1. Insert the Windows 2000 Professional CD-ROM into the computer and select the deploy.cab file, located in the Support\Tools folder.

2. Double-click on the deploy.cab file to view the contents.

3. Right-click on setupmgr.exe and select Extract. Choose a location from the Explorer menu to extract the file. Right-click setupmgx.dll and extract this file to the same location of setupmgr.exe.

You can now create the answer file. Double-click on the setupmgr.exe icon to launch the wizard. The setupmgr.exe utility is a multipurpose tool because you can use it to create answer files for several types of unattended installations. We will concentrate on a Windows 2000 unattended installation. Perform the following steps to create an answer file:

1. Double-click on the setupmgr.exe icon to start the utility.

2. Click on Next to pass the welcome page.

3. Select the Create A New Answer File radio button (it will be selected by default) and click Next.

4. The next page displays which product the answer file installs. There are three choices: Windows 2000 Unattended Installation, Sysprep Install, or RIS. Select the Windows 2000 Unattended Installation radio button and click Next.

5. Choose the Windows 2000 Professional radio button and click Next.

6. The next page displays several options regarding user interaction. Typically, no user interaction is required. If, however, you want the installation to stop so you can enter the computer name, select Hide Pages. This option hides all pages in which answers were provided but stops at any areas that you have left blank. Select the Fully Automated radio button and click Next.

7. Select the checkbox to agree to the EULA and click Next.

8. Type in a name and an organization and click Next.

9. Type in the computer names or import a comma-delimited file that contains all computer names that should be used for the installation of new computers. Optionally, you can select the Automatically Generate Computer Names Based On Organization Name checkbox. Checking this results in a combination of the organization name that you typed in the dialog box and a unique alphanumeric combination (e.g., coriol-1AD2RT). Use either method and click on the Next button.

10. Enter a password that the local administrator of the computer will use.

Note: The password can be up to 127 characters long.

Enter a password and click Next.

11. Select display settings such as Color, Screen area, and Refresh frequency. Unless all computers have identical video cards with identical monitors, you should set these fields to Use Windows Default. Click on Next to continue.

12. This page provides two options for Network Settings—Typical and Custom. If you select Typical, Microsoft Client, File and Print Sharing as well as the Transmission Control Protocol/Internet Protocol (TCP/IP) protocol are installed. Additionally, the client will be configured as a Dynamic Host Configuration Protocol (DHCP) client. If you need to enter a static IP address or add or subtract network services, use the Custom option. Select Typical or Custom and click Next.

13. The Workgroup or a Domain page appears next. If the computer is to join a domain during the installation, you must type in the name of the domain as well as enter a user name and password of a user who has the right to add workstations to a domain. Fill in the appropriate fields and click Next.

14. The Time Zone page appears next. Simply choose the correct time zone the computer is located in and click Next.

15. You've reached the end of creating a basic answer file. If you need to add other drivers or scripts, select the Yes, Edit The Additional Settings radio

button. For the purposes of our discussion, select No, Do Not Edit The Additional Settings and click Next.

16. You can use the next page to create a distribution share for the Windows 2000 Professional files or to simply create an answer file that you will use in conjunction with the CD-ROM distribution.

Note: If you choose to create a distribution share, you must name the answer file winnt.sif and you must place it on a floppy disk. A CD-ROM-based install looks for the presence of this file on a floppy disk and uses it to provide an unattended install via the CD-ROM distribution.

For demonstration purposes, select Yes, Create Or Modify A Distribution Folder and click Next to continue.

17. The next page offers suggested locations and folder names for the distribution share point. If you have already created the distribution share, select Modify An Existing Distribution Folder. If you select this option, just the answer file is created. Accept the default by clicking the Next button.

18. If you need drivers for a hardware Redundant Array of Independent Disks (RAID) controller card, add them here. Click Next to continue.

19. If you need a third-party Hardware Abstraction Layer (HAL) for multiple processor support or other configurations, add that now and click Next.

20. If you need to run a batch file after the installation is done, add those files in the Additional Commands page and click Next.

21. The OEM Branding page appears next. It allows you to replace the default bitmaps that are displayed during the installation process with custom bitmaps and logos. Click Next to continue.

22. The Additional Files Or Folders page appears. Here, you can place files on the computer and install any third-party Plug and Play drivers that don't come with Windows 2000. Click Next.

23. We're almost finished. Enter a name for the answer file and the location of the distribution share. The default name for the answer file is unattend.txt. In a working environment, you should change this name because setupmgr.exe takes a basic answer file from the Windows 2000 CD-ROM that overwrites the one you just created. Click Next.

24. You now have to copy the distribution files from the Windows 2000 Professional CD-ROM to the distribution share. Put the CD-ROM in the computer and click Next.

25. The files are copied to the distribution share; the last page displayed is a summary page of the files that you created. Click Finish.

Putting It All Together

Now that you have created the answer file and the distribution share, let's put it all together to see how to launch an unattended install of Windows 2000 Professional. To master this task, you must understand a few switches that are involved. winnt.exe has multiple switches to control its functionality. Below is a list of switches that relate to unattended installs:

➤ */u:answer file*—This switch is used for an unattended installation. The file contains answers to the installation prompts.

➤ */s:sourcepath*—This switch points to the location of the Windows 2000 installation files.

➤ */udf:id*—This switch is used in conjunction with a UDF file, which overrides the values of the answer file. You typically use this file to provide unique configuration parameters during the installation process. ID designates which settings contained in the UDF file should be used.

➤ */unattend*—This switch is used with winnt32.exe to create an unattended upgrade to Windows 2000.

You use these switches in combination to launch an unattended installation of Windows 2000 Professional using Setup Manager. To launch an unattended install, follow these steps:

1. Use a network boot disk to connect the target computer to the network.

2. Next, use the **net use** command to map to the distribution share point using an available drive letter.

3. Then, switch the command prompt to the mapped drive letter (such as I) and use the following as an example to launch an unattended install for a computer called machine1:

```
I:\WINNT.EXE /s:I:\i386 /u:unattend.txt /
udf:machine1,unattend.udf
```

Practice using the Setup Manager several times while choosing different options each time to see how the results vary. Remember that you can use this Setup Manager utility to also create answer files for System Preparation Tool installs, which is our next topic, and RIS installs, which are discussed a bit later.

Using the System Preparation Tool

The *System Preparation Tool* prepares a master image of a computer that contains Windows 2000 Professional and any software applications that users might need. You can use this tool in conjunction with third-party disk imaging software. Disk imaging software makes an exact mirror image of whatever is on the computer, including all the unique parameters of Windows 2000. Each Windows 2000 computer has its own unique Security Identifier (SID) and its own unique computer name. Other computers can't use these settings. If you applied an image that contained these unique settings to several computers, they would all have the same computer name and the same SID. The System Preparation Tool removes all the unique parameters from a Windows 2000 computer before the computer is imaged. It is a very easy tool to use, but you must follow several specific steps to use it. The first step is to create a folder called sysprep in %SystemRoot% (e.g., c:\sysprep).

To use the System Preparation Tool, you must extract it from the deploy.cab file and place it in the sysprep folder. Perform the following steps to extract sysprep.exe and a helper file called setupcl.exe:

1. Insert the Windows 2000 Professional CD-ROM into the computer and select the deploy.cab file, located in the Support\Tools folder.

2. Double-click the deploy.cab file to view the contents.

3. Right-click on sysprep.exe and select Extract. Use the Explorer menu to extract the file to the sysprep folder that you created. Right-click setupcl.exe and extract it to the sysprep folder.

The next step is to install and configure all applications that must be in the disk image. Once you have accomplished this, run sysprep.exe in the sysprep folder. Sysprep.exe removes all unique parameters from the computer and then shuts down the computer. Reboot the computer with a disk image boot disk and create an image of the computer.

After you have applied an image to a computer, a Mini-Setup Wizard runs. It prompts you to put back the unique parameters that you took out. The SID is generated automatically at this point. However, you'll have to input the following settings:

➤ Computer Name

➤ User Name

➤ Product ID

➤ Regional Settings

➤ Company Name

➤ Network Settings

➤ Time Zone

➤ Place Computer In A Workgroup Or Join A Domain

As you can see, you need to enter a fair amount of information for every computer you apply the image to. You can use Setup Manager, discussed earlier in this chapter, to create an answer file called sysprep.inf. This file provides the above settings to the Mini-Setup Wizard to answer all the installation prompts. The end result is an unattended install of the image.

Note: You must place sysprep.inf in the sysprep folder or on a floppy disk, which are the default locations where the Mini-Setup Wizard looks for the answer file (it checks the sysprep folder first) after you have applied the image. Another point: You should apply the image to computers with similar hardware. When you apply the image, sysprep.exe triggers Plug and Play into action. Plug and Play can resolve some differences in hardware. However, if the hard disk controller and the HAL on the image are different than those on the computer to which you are applying the image, the image installation will fail (e.g., if you create the image on a computer that contains an HAL for a computer with multiple processors but you are applying the image to a uniprocessor computer.)

Using Remote Installation Services (RIS)

You can use RIS to deploy Windows 2000 Professional over a network from a remote installation server. RIS integrates a few of the installation methods we have discussed into one tight bundle. You can use it to install Windows 2000 Professional to a computer with a blank hard drive or to reinstall Windows 2000 Professional to repair a corrupted installation.

The main goal of RIS is to reduce total cost of ownership (TCO) by having one central location for either the end users or administrators to install Windows 2000 Professional. To install Windows 2000 Professional using RIS, a user presses the F12 key during the boot process to find RIS server and start the installation. Three steps are involved in making RIS work: configure the client, configure network servers for RIS, and create a Windows 2000 Professional image. The next few sections uncover the details of these areas.

Configuring Clients

The client computer can connect to an RIS server in two ways. The first method is to install a peripheral connection interface (PCI) network adapter that contains a Preboot Execution boot ROM (PXE). You then have to configure the computer's BIOS to boot from the PXE network adapter. When the computer boots from the PXE network adapter, it attempts to get an IP address from a DHCP server. Once the network adapter has an IP address, the user is prompted to press the F12 key to locate an RIS server.

In the second method if the network adapter is not PXE compliant, you can use an RIS boot disk with some network adapter manufacturers such as 3Com and Intel. Use the rbfg.exe utility to create an RIS boot disk. Once you have installed RIS, you can find the utility in RemoteInstall\Admin\i386\rbfg.exe.

Configuring Network Services and Hard Drive Space Requirements

Before you can install and configure the RIS service, several prerequisites must be in place on the network. The following is a list of the RIS requirements you must meet before you install it:

➤ *DHCP server*—The client needs to obtain an IP address from a DHCP server during the boot process. You cannot configure RIS until a DHCP server is available. A Windows 2000 DHCP server cannot give IP addresses to clients unless it is authorized to do so. Perform the following steps to authorize the DHCP server:

1. Open the DHCP Manager Microsoft Management Console (MMC) by going to Start|Programs|Administrative Tools|DHCP.

2. Select the DHCP node and choose Action from the menu bar.

3. Choose Manage Authorized Servers from the menu.

4. Click on the Authorize button and type the host name or IP address of the DHCP server. Click on OK and close the dialog box.

➤ *Active Directory and Domain Name Service (DNS)*—Once the network adapter has an IP address, it needs to find an RIS server. The client finds RIS by querying a DNS server to find where an Active Directory server (domain controller—DC) is. The Active Directory then tells the client where an RIS server can be found.

➤ *Its own partition*—RIS demands its own partition. You cannot install RIS on a system or boot partition, usually the C partition.

Once you have met the three conditions for an RIS installation, make sure a separate partition is available (or will be created) for RIS. It is recommended to reserve at least 2GB for an RIS partition.

Installing and Configuring the RIS Service

You can install the RIS service on a Windows 2000 DC or on a Windows 2000 member server if you have met all the prerequisites. After you have installed the service, you must configure it. Perform the following steps to install the RIS service:

1. Log on to the server as an Administrator.

2. Open the Control Panel (Start|Settings|Control Panel) and double-click Add/Remove Programs.

3. Click on the Add/Remove Windows Components button and select the Remote Installation Services checkbox.

4. Insert the Windows 2000 Server CD-ROM. The service is copied to the server and you are prompted to reboot the server once the service has been installed.

Now that you have installed the RIS service, you must run risetup.exe to respond to clients' requests for an RIS server and to put the initial image of Windows 2000 Professional on the RIS server. The initial image is simply a copy of the I386 folder found on the Windows 2000 Professional CD-ROM. Perform the following steps to configure the RIS service:

1. Type "risetup.exe" from Start|Run and click the OK button.

2. The Remote Installation Services Setup Wizard presents a welcome page that reminds you of some of the RIS prerequisites. Click the Next button.

3. By default, the Wizard offers to create the RIS folder structure and files on the C partition (even though the wizard itself reminds us that this can't be done). Choose a drive letter for a nonsystem partition to place the files into and click the Next button.

4. The next dialog box asks if the RIS server should respond immediately to client requests before you have even finished the configuration. Leave the checkbox deselected. You can select it after you have configured Active Directory Users And Computers.

5. The next dialog box asks where the system should look for the Windows 2000 Professional installation files. Type the drive letter for the CD-ROM drive and the path to the installation files (e.g., D:\I386). Click Next.

6. The next dialog box suggests a folder name for the initial image. Each image that is created has its own folder. Use the default name provided or type in a different name, and then click Next.

7. The next dialog box asks you to provide a descriptive name for this image. Use the default or type in a different name. Click the Next button to get to the finish line.

8. You're at the end. The final dialog box summarizes the parameters that you selected. Click on the Finish button. Risetup.exe now copies the contents of the I386 folder to the folder structure that you just created and completes the installation process.

When the installation is finished, you need to configure the RIS server to respond to RIS clients. You have to log on as a domain administrator to complete this final step. Launch the Active Directory Users And Computers console by clicking on Start|Programs|Administrative Tools|Active Directory Users And Computers. Next, double-click on the Domain Controllers container if RIS was installed on a DC; otherwise, double-click on the Computers container. Next, right-click on the RIS Server Computer object and select Properties from the Context menu. Click on the Remote Install tab from the Properties page. On this tab, select the Respond To Client Computers Requesting Service option, shown in Figure 6.1.

Creating Additional Images

The risetup.exe Wizard created the first image of Windows 2000 Professional for us. However, that image provides only an attended installation of the operating system. You can create additional images that contain the operating system as well as any necessary applications and configuration. RIS installs a utility called riprep.exe that you can use to create images of the operating system and any installed applications. The functionality of riprep.exe is similar to that of a third-party disk imaging application. However, riprep.exe has some limitations. It can only make an image of the C partition of a computer. If a computer contains a C and D partition, only the C partition will be part of the image. Also, when you apply the image to a computer via RIS, any existing partitions are deleted. The entire hard drive is repartitioned as a single partition and then is

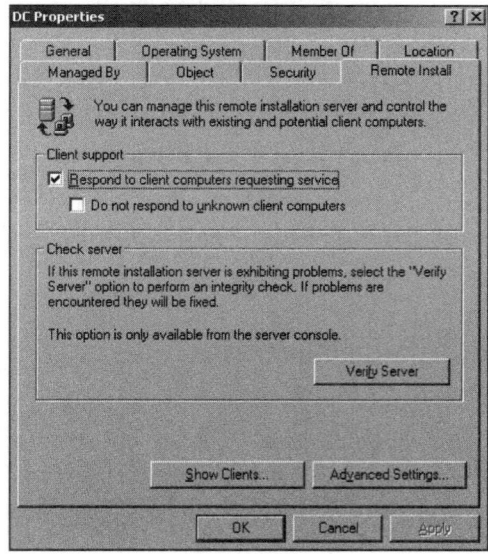

Figure 6.1   The Remote Install tab.

formatted with the NTFS file system. If you can work within those limits, you can easily configure and deploy riprep.exe images. Perform the following steps to create a riprep.exe image:

1. Connect the computer that you are imaging to the network.

2. Install Windows 2000 Professional and any applications that users may need. Connect to the REMINST share point on the RIS server. Run riprep.exe from \RIS Server\REMINST\Admin\I386\riprep.exe.

3. The Remote Installation Preparation Wizard is launched. It asks you on which RIS server the image should be placed and the name of the folder to which the image should be copied.

4. The last task is to provide a user-friendly name for the image (such as the Marketing or the Sales image).

After you complete these steps, riprep.exe copies the image to the designated RIS server. However, riprep.exe acts a lot like sysprep.exe. In addition to creating an image, riprep.exe removes the unique attributes, such as the SIDs and the computer name. When the RIS client downloads the image, a Mini-Setup wizard that asks you to put back what was taken out.

Note: You can use Setup Manager to create answer files for RIS images.

Downloading an Image

After you have configured an RIS server with several images, users can boot their computers from the network adapter and press F12 to find an RIS server. The server then displays a welcome screen; simply press Enter to bypass this screen. Next, users must log on to the domain. Once they are logged on, they see a list of images to choose from. The users select an image from the list, and RIS reformats the entire drive as well as downloads the image to the target computer. After about 30 to 40 minutes, users have a clean install of the operating system and applications.

Upgrading to Windows 2000 Professional

Windows NT 4 supports only upgrades from previous Windows NT operating systems. Windows 2000, on the other hand, allows for many upgrade paths. The following is a list of Windows operating systems that you can directly upgrade to Windows 2000 Professional:

➤ Windows NT 4 and 3.51

➤ Windows 95 (all editions)

➤ Windows 98 (all editions)

Note: You can directly upgrade Windows NT 4 or 3.51 with or without service packs (SPs). Installing a specific SP before installation is not required when you are upgrading. SPs are discussed later in this chapter.

The easiest operating system to upgrade from is Windows NT. This operating system shares a lot of features with Windows 2000, including its Registry. You can upgrade Windows 95 and 98 quite smoothly as well, but you need to take some precautions, which are detailed in the next section.

Pre-Upgrade Checklist

Before you upgrade to Windows 2000 Professional, you need to check the current operating system configuration for any of the following areas that could cause conflicts during and after the upgrade process:

➤ *Hardware and software compatibility*—The Windows 2000 Professional CD-ROM contains a utility called chkupgrd.exe, which scans the current operating system and hardware to see if there are any known items incompatible with Windows 2000 Professional. You can run the utility using various methods. One of the most common methods is to place the Windows 2000 CD-ROM in the computer and click on the Upgrade option. The utility runs before the upgrade to alert you about any incompatibilities. However, if you are not prepared to perform an upgrade on the computer, you can run the utility by placing the Windows 2000 Professional CD-ROM in the computer, selecting Start|Run, and then typing "D:\I386\winnt32.exe /checkupgradeonly" (where D: is the drive letter your CD-ROM drive uses). The utility scans the system and creates a text file of the results, which you can save to the computer or print. Chkupgrd.exe tool is also referred to as the Readiness Analyzer.

➤ *Update packs*—Due to the major differences between the Windows 2000 Registry and those of Windows 95 and 98, some applications may not work after the upgrade. Software vendors may supply an update pack (also called *migration Dynamic Link Libraries—DLLs*) that you can use during the upgrade process. Obtain an upgrade pack and place it on the local hard drive. During the upgrade process, the installer asks if any upgrade packs should be used. Select Yes and then type in the file path to the upgrade pack to continue the installation process.

➤ *Disk utilities*—Windows 2000 Professional uses a new version of NT File System (NTFS) that causes conflicts with antivirus software and disk defragmenting software. You should remove such applications before you upgrade.

➤ *Drive compression*—Before upgrading, you should uncompress any drives that you have compressed with DriveSpace or DoubleSpace. These Windows 95 and 98 drive compression utilities are incompatible with Windows 2000.

Deploying Service Packs (SPs)

Installing SPs in Windows NT is a very time-consuming process. First, you have to install the operating system, and then you must apply the SP. Windows 2000 allows you to incorporate an SP with the installation files. Combining the latest SP with the Windows 2000 installation files allows you to install them as one. In Windows NT, however, if you installed a new service after applying an SP, you had to reapply the SP for the new service to gain any benefits the SP might have to offer. Additionally, you had to reinstall some services after you applied an SP. Thankfully, you don't have to contend with these situations in Windows 2000.

Slipstreaming SPs

The process of combining the Windows 2000 installation files with an SP is called *slipstreaming*. You apply an SP to a distribution share of the installation files by executing **update.exe /s**.

*Note: As of this writing, the switch that is used for slipstreaming is the **/s** switch. Some older references state that the slipstreaming switch is **/slip**. That is no longer the case. However, if you encounter the **/slip** switch on an exam, you should probably select that option (if the **/s** switch is not an available choice).*

If you install Windows 2000 using the slipstreamed distribution, the installations contain the SP. Using this method can save you a ton of time and helps you avoid having to apply an SP after each installation.

Applying SPs after Installing Windows 2000

If you didn't have the opportunity or ability to create a slipstreamed distribution share, you can apply an SP simply by running update.exe on the local machine. If you install any new services after applying the SP, Windows 2000 gets any files it needs for those services from the installation files or the SP. This process updates a service or an application without requiring you to continually reapply the SP whenever you add something new.

Troubleshooting Failed Installations

Windows 2000 Professional should install on most new computers without too much difficulty. However, there are some common reasons why it may not install properly. The following is a list of typical installation problems:

➤ *Media errors*—These are problems you encounter with the distribution CD-ROM. Make sure the problem exists with the media itself, not access to the media. If you place the Windows 2000 Professional CD-ROM in a shared drive for installation, too many people could be using the drive at one time.

This may generate some errors. However, if only one person is connected to the shared drive and errors persist, get a replacement for the distribution CD-ROM. In addition, always restart failed installations due to media errors.

➤ *Noncompatible CD-ROM drive*—There are many specifications for CD-ROM drives. You can install Windows 2000 from most drives, but there are always exceptions. If the CD-ROM drive is not compliant, replace it or place the distribution files on the network. Also, as mentioned earlier in this chapter, the Windows 2000 CD-ROM is bootable and can be installed from El-Torito-compatible drives. If the CD-ROM can't boot, ensure that the drive is compliant and that the boot order in the BIOS has been set to the CD-ROM drive. Also, the controller card for the CD-ROM drive could be failing, or the drive itself could be failing.

➤ *Installation halts or errors*—If a STOP error occurs during the installation, it is typically the result of incorrect or incompatible drivers. Obtain the correct and current drivers and restart the installation process. Also, the installation may stop just after the copy or text phase due to a warning that the master boot record has a virus. This warning typically results when the BIOS has enabled the virus warning option. Turn this option off and restart the installation. As a final measure, ensure that all devices are on the HCL.

➤ *Lack of drive space*—Windows 2000 needs much more free space compared to its predecessors. Ensure that at least 650MB of free space is available.

➤ *Dependency failures*—For the installation to be completed successfully, all services must be able to start when needed. Some services depend upon others to complete a task. For example, if the drivers for the network adapter could not load, that will affect all services that depend on the network adapter's successful installation. As a result, the computer won't be able to join the domain.

➤ *Problems joining the domain*—If the network adapter has initialized but the computer still can't join the domain, verify that the DNS server is online and that you are using the correct IP address of the DNS. Also, verify that you typed the domain name correctly. If problems persist, install the computer to a workgroup to complete the installation.

Practice Questions

Question 1

> You want to use an RIS server to install Windows 2000 Professional on 200 client computers. To use RIS, what other network services must you install and configure? Create a list of network services that must be installed in order to implement an RIS server. The list can be in any order.
>
> Active Directory
>
> Remote Access Services (RAS) server
>
> DHCP server
>
> Windows Internet Naming Service (WINS) server
>
> Proxy server
>
> DNS server

Answer

Active Directory

DHCP server

DNS server

Active Directory contains information about the RIS servers, DHCP gives IP addresses to the RIS clients during the boot process, and DNS locates the RIS server. You cannot configure RIS for use until Active Directory, DHCP, and DNS are installed. RAS, WINS, and Proxy are not used by RIS nor are they used for the installation and configuration of RIS. These servers can be in place, but they do not provide any roles for an RIS Server.

Question 2

You want to install Windows 2000 Professional on 500 client workstations using an RIS server. The workstations do not have a PXE-compliant network card. How can these clients boot to the network to locate an RIS server?

○ a. You can't use RIS without a PXE-compliant network card.

○ b. Boot the client workstation with an rbfg.exe boot floppy.

○ c. Use Network Client Administrator to create a network boot floppy.

○ d. Configure the BIOS to boot from the PC Card.

Answer b is correct. If the computer doesn't have a PXE-compliant network card, use rbfg.exe to create an RIS boot disk. Answer a is false, a remote boot disk can be used. The Network Client Administrator does not create remote boot disk floppies, just network boot disks. Answer d is incorrect because the computers don't have a PXE-compliant network card.

Question 3

You want to use an unattend.txt file to automate the installation of Windows 2000 Professional from a CD-ROM. You place unattend.txt on a floppy disk and boot from the Windows 2000 Professional CD-ROM. However, the installation proceeds without using the unattend.txt file. What do you need to do to automate the installation?

○ a. You can't automate a CD-ROM-based install.

○ b. Rename unattend.txt to winnt.sif.

○ c. During the text phase of the installation, press F3 to locate unattend.txt on a network server.

○ d. During the text phase of the installation, press F3 to locate unattend.txt on the floppy disk.

Answer b is correct. You can automate a CD-ROM-based install if an answer file called winnt.sif is located on a floppy disk during the installation. The default unattended.txt answer file can be renamed to winnt.sif and used for a CD-ROM based installation. Answer a is false. A CD-ROM-based install can be automated with winnt.sif. Answers c and d are incorrect as pressing F3 won't allow a user to locate these files from a network server or from a floppy disk.

Question 4

You used sysprep.exe to prepare a model computer to be imaged using a third-party imaging software. You created the sysprep folder at the root of c:\, and you placed sysprep.exe and setupcl.exe in this directory. You used Setup Manager to create an answer file for the sysprep image. However, once you applied the image to a workstation, the Mini-Setup Wizard prompted you for every installation parameter. Why did this happen?

○ a. You did not place sysprep.sif in the sysprep folder.

○ b. You did not place unattend.txt in the sysprep folder.

○ c. You did not place winnt.inf in the sysprep folder.

○ d. You did not place sysprep.inf in the sysprep folder.

Answer d is correct. For the Mini-Setup Wizard to use the sysprep answer file, sysprep.inf must be located in the sysprep folder. Answer a is incorrect because the wrong file extension was used. Answers b and c are incorrect because the wrong file was used. The correct file is sysprep.inf.

Question 5

You want to upgrade a Windows 95 computer to Windows 2000 Professional. You need to ensure that applications on the Windows 95 computer will run after the upgrade has completed. What do you do?

○ a. You can't upgrade and run applications that run on Windows 95 under Windows 2000.

○ b. Use upgrade packs for the required applications during the upgrade process.

○ c. Use the apcompat.exe utility and select Windows 95 so that applications will run in Windows 2000.

○ d. Import the comptwa.inf security template to allow the applications to run in Windows 2000.

Answer b is correct. You can obtain upgrade packs (migration DLLs) from third-party vendors to ensure that the Windows 95 applications will run in Windows 2000 Professional after the upgrade. Answer a is false, a Windows 95 computer can be upgraded but some applications that run under Windows 95 may not be compatible with Windows 2000. Answer c is incorrect as apcompat.exe doesn't ensure that applications will be compatible. Only upgrade packs can ensure this.

Apcompat.exe can be used as a last resort to try to run a noncompliant application in Windows 2000. Answer d is incorrect, as the security settings found in comptwa.inf do not relate to application compatibility. They relate to security compatibility.

Question 6

Before you upgrade 100 Windows 98 computers to Windows 2000 Professional, you want to see if there are any hardware or software incompatibility issues. What should you run before the upgrade to search for incompatibilities?

○ a. winnt.exe /checkupgradeonly

○ b. apcompat.exe

○ c. winnt32.exe /cmdcons

○ d. winnt32.exe /checkupgradeonly

Answer d is correct. You use winnt32.exe /checkupgradeonly to run the Readiness Analyzer, which searches for any hardware or software incompatibilities with Windows 2000. The Readiness Analyzer is a GUI tool, and you run it only within an operating system. Winnt.exe /checkupgradeonly will not work. Therefore, answer a is incorrect. Answer b is incorrect because this tool is not used to test hardware and software compatibility. Answer c is incorrect as it would install the Recovery Console, which is used after Windows 2000 has been installed.

Question 7

You want to upgrade a Windows 98 computer that has 16MB of memory, a 1GB hard drive with 200MB of free space, and a Pentium 200MHz CPU. The installation of Windows 2000 fails due to insufficient hardware. What hardware do you have to upgrade before the installation can proceed?

○ a. Install an additional 16MB of memory.

○ b. Install an additional 16MB of memory and a 2GB hard drive.

○ c. Install a Pentium II 400MHz CPU.

○ d. Install an additional 32MB of memory.

Answer b is correct. The minimum requirements for Windows 2000 Professional are 32MB of memory, a 2GB drive with 650MB of free space, and a Pentium 133MHz or higher CPU.

Question 8

You've downloaded the most current SP and need to incorporate it into the distribution share. How do you accomplish this?

O a. Run setup.exe /s.

O b. Run update.msi /sl.

O c. Run update.exe.

O d. Run update.exe /s.

Answer d is correct. Slipstreaming, via running update.exe /slip, is a new method to upgrade Windows 2000 to incorporate SPs into the operating system. This method replaces the current files with the files that are contained in the SP. Answer a is incorrect as setup.exe is used to install Windows 2000, not to update it. Answer b is incorrect because service packs don't have a .msi file extension. Answer c will apply the service pack but it won't slipstream the service pack because the slip switch was not used.

Question 9

After the text phase of the installation of Windows 2000 Professional has finished, an error states that the master boot record is corrupted. How do you fix this problem?

O a. Boot with the Windows 2000 CD-ROM, install the Recovery Console, and run the **fixmbr** command.

O b. Turn off virus checking in the BIOS.

O c. Run winnt32.exe /checkupgradeonly.

O d. Run the fixmbr.exe utility from the Windows 2000 CD-ROM.

Answer b is correct. The error occurred because virus checking was enabled in the BIOS, so you need to turn it off. Answer a is incorrect as the Recovery Console is only used after Windows 2000 has been installed. It cannot be used to troubleshoot a failed installation. Winnt32.exe /checkupgradeonly is only just to verify the compatibility of hardware and software with Windows 2000. It cannot be used to troubleshoot failed installations. Therefore answer c is incorrect. Fixmbr.exe is a command that runs inside the Recovery Console. Therefore answer d is incorrect for the same reason answer a was incorrect.

Question 10

> How do you apply an SP after you have installed Windows 2000 Professional?
>
> ○ a. Run setup.exe /s.
>
> ○ b. Run update.msi /s.
>
> ○ c. Run update.exe.
>
> ○ d. Run update.exe /s.

Answer c is correct. You use update.exe to install SPs after you install Windows 2000. You apply update.exe /slip to distribution files. Therefore, answer d is incorrect. Answer a is incorrect as setup.exe is used to install Windows 2000, not to apply a service pack. Answer b is incorrect because service packs don't have a .msi file extension. Answer c will apply the service pack but it won't slipstream the service pack because the slip switch was not used.

Need to Know More?

 Read unattend.doc for more information regarding the unattended installation process. This document is located on every Windows 2000 CD-ROM in Support\Tools\deploy.cab\unattend.doc.

 For more information regarding the installation and configuration of Remote Installation Service download Microsoft's white paper on this topic at: **www.microsoft.com/windows2000/library/planning/management/remoteos.asp**.

Implementing, Managing, and Troubleshooting Hardware Devices and Drivers

Terms you'll need to understand:

- ✓ Universal Serial Bus (USB)
- ✓ Plug and Play versus non Plug and Play
- ✓ Advanced Power Management (APM)
- ✓ Advanced Configuration and Power Interface (ACPI)
- ✓ Add/Remove Hardware Wizard
- ✓ Device Manager
- ✓ Driver signing
- ✓ FireWire, or IEEE (Institute of Electrical and Electronics Engineers) 1394
- ✓ Internet Printing Protocol (IPP)
- ✓ Spooler Service
- ✓ Smart cards and smart card readers
- ✓ Multilink support
- ✓ Infrared Data Association (IrDA) devices
- ✓ Network adapter, or network interface card (NIC)
- ✓ Multiple-display support
- ✓ Video adapter
- ✓ Mobile computer power modes
- ✓ Hardware profiles
- ✓ Multiple-processor support

Techniques you'll need to master:

- ✓ Installing, configuring, and troubleshooting hardware devices and drivers
- ✓ Updating drivers and system files
- ✓ Managing and troubleshooting driver signing
- ✓ Managing and troubleshooting various types of input/output (I/O) devices
- ✓ Configuring and troubleshooting Multilink support for a Dial-up Connection
- ✓ Configuring and troubleshooting multiple-display support, hardware profiles, and multiple-processor support

Implementing, Managing, and Troubleshooting Hardware

Hardware includes any physical device that is connected to your computer and that your computer's processor controls. This includes equipment that was connected to your computer when it was manufactured, as well as equipment that you added later. Modems; disk drives; CD-ROM drives; printers, network cards, keyboards, and display adapter cards and USB cameras, are all examples of devices. Windows 2000 contains full support for Plug and Play devices and partial support for nonPlug and Play devices. "Partial" support means only one thing: Some work; some do not. Sometimes, testing a device may be the only sure way to determine if it will work with Windows 2000. Always consult the latest Windows 2000 Hardware Compatibility List (HCL) before installing a new device.

For a device to work properly with Windows 2000, software (a device driver) must be installed on the computer. Each device has its own unique device driver(s), which the device manufacturer typically supplies. However, many device drivers are included with Windows 2000 and work even *better* with Windows 2000 than the manufacturer's own driver. Look for Microsoft to recommend using its own drivers for a given device rather than those of the manufacturer. Big surprise there.

Because Windows 2000 controls your computer's resources and configuration, you can install Plug and Play hardware devices and many other devices *without* restarting your computer. Windows 2000 automatically identifies the new hardware and installs the drivers it needs. If you are using an older computer that does not support Advanced Power Management (APM) or the "newer APM" called Advanced Configuration and Power Interface (ACPI), you must set up the device manually and restart your computer when installing new hardware devices. For now, you need ACPI-compliant hardware to make your Windows 2000 hardware setup experience smoother. We will discuss APM and ACPI in greater detail later in this chapter.

Installing, Configuring, and Managing Hardware

You configure devices on Windows 2000 machines using the Add/Remove Hardware Wizard in the Control Panel, or the Device Manager. Keep in mind that in most cases, you need to be logged on to the local machine as a member of the Administrators group to add, configure, and remove devices.

You can use the System Information snap-in to view (yes, view *only!*) configuration information about your computer.

Installing Plug and Play Devices

Connect the device to the appropriate port or slot on your computer according to the device manufacturer's instructions. You may need to start or restart your computer, but this happens *much less often* than it did with previous versions of Windows NT and 9x. If you are prompted to restart your computer, do so. Windows 2000 should detect the device and then immediately start the Found New Hardware Wizard.

Installing Non Plug and Play Devices

To install a device that is not Plug and Play, follow these steps:

1. Open Add/Remove Hardware in the Control Panel.

2. Click Next, click Add/Troubleshoot A Device, and then click Next. Windows 2000 attempts to detect new Plug and Play devices.

3. If your device is not in the device list, click Add A New Device.

4. Click Next, and then do one of the following:

   ➤ *Click Yes, Search For New Hardware*—Do this if you want Windows 2000 to try and detect the new non Plug and Play device you want to install.

   ➤ *Click No, I Want To Select The Hardware From A List*—Do this if you know the type and model of the device you are installing and if you want to select it from a list of devices.

5. Click Next, and then follow the instructions on your screen.

6. You may be prompted to restart your computer, depending on the type of non Plug and Play device you just installed.

Tips on Installing Devices

Using a Plug and Play driver to install a *non* Plug and Play device may provide *some* Plug and Play support. (Don't get your hopes up.) Although the system cannot recognize the hardware and load the appropriate drivers on its own, Plug and Play can oversee the installation by allocating resources, interacting with Power Options in the Control Panel, and recording any issues in the Event Log.

If your computer is connected to a network, network policy (Group Policy) settings may prevent you from installing any devices on your computer. To add and set up a *non* Plug and Play device connected directly to your computer, you *must* be logged on as an administrator or a member of the Administrators group.

 If an administrator has already loaded the drivers for the device, you can install the device *without* having administrator privileges.

Driver Updates

Keeping drivers and system files updated ensures that your operating system performs at peak level. Microsoft recommends using *Microsoft* digitally signed drivers whenever possible. The driver.cab cabinet file on the Windows 2000 CD-ROM contains all of the drivers that Windows 2000 ships with. This cabinet file is copied to the %SystemRoot% folder when Windows 2000 is installed. Whenever a driver is updated, Windows 2000 looks in the driver.cab file first. The location of driver.cab is stored in a registry key and can be changed via HKLM\Software\Windows\CurrentVersion\Setup\DriverCachePath.

Updating Individual Drivers

To update individual drivers, follow these steps:

1. You update Drivers using the Device Manager. Right-click the device and choose Properties. A Properties dialog box appears.

2. Choose the Drivers tab and then the Update Driver button.

You use Driver Verifier to troubleshoot and isolate driver problems. It is not enabled by default. To use it, you must enable it by changing a registry setting. The Driver Verifier Manager, verifier.exe, provides a command-line interface for working with Driver Verifier.

 Just know that the Driver Verifier tool does exist—it is not a figment of anyone's imagination. You do not need to learn the various parameters and switches that work with it.

Updating Your System Files Using Windows Update

Windows Update is a Microsoft database of items such as drivers, patches, help files, and Internet products that you can download to keep your Windows 2000 installation up to date. Using the Product Updates section of Windows Update, you can scan your computer for outdated system files, drivers, and help files, and automatically replace them with the most recent versions.

To update your system files using Windows Update, follow these steps:

1. Go to Windows Update at **www.windowsupdate.microsoft.com**. (This Uniform Resource Locator—URL—can change at any time, because Microsoft is prone to shuffling Web page locations frequently.) You can also open Windows Update by clicking on Start|Windows Update.

2. On the Windows Update home page, click Product Updates.

> You must be logged on as an administrator or a member of the Administrators group to complete this procedure. If your computer is connected to a network, network policy settings may prevent you from updating any system files or drivers.

> The first time you go to the Product Updates page, click Yes when prompted to install any required software or controls.

Managing and Troubleshooting Device Conflicts

You configure devices using the Add/Remove Hardware Wizard in the Control Panel, or the Device Manager. Each resource—e.g., a memory address range, Interrupt Request (IRQ), input/output (I/O) port, Direct Memory Access (DMA) channel, and so on—that is assigned to your device must be unique or the device does not function properly. For Plug and Play devices, Windows 2000 attempts to ensure automatically that these resources are configured properly. For devices where there is a resource conflict, or where the device is not working properly, you see next to the device name a yellow circle with an exclamation point inside it.

Occasionally, two devices require the same resources, but keep in mind that this does not always result in a device conflict—especially if the devices are Plug and Play compliant. If a conflict arises, you can manually change the resource settings to be sure that each setting is unique. Sometimes, two or more devices can share resources, such as interrupts on peripheral connection interface (PCI) devices, depending on the drivers and the computer. For example, get accustomed to seeing Windows 2000 share IRQ 9 among multiple devices on many laptops.

When you install a nonPlug and Play device, the resource settings for the device are not automatically configured. Depending on the type of device you are installing, you may have to manually configure these settings, which should be supplied in the instruction manual that came with your device.

 Generally, you should *not* change resource settings manually, because when you do so, the settings become fixed, and Windows 2000 then has less flexibility when allocating resources to other devices. If too many resources become fixed, Windows 2000 may not be able to install new Plug and Play devices.

Managing and Troubleshooting Driver Signing

Microsoft is promoting driver signing for devices as a method to advance the quality of drivers and to reduce support costs for vendors and total cost of ownership (TCO) for customers. Windows 2000 uses a driver signing process to make sure drivers have been certified to work correctly with the Windows Driver Model (WDM) in Windows 2000. If you are having problems, it may be because you are using a driver not correctly written for Windows 2000. To identify such drivers, use the Signature Verification tool. This utility, sigverif.exe, helps you quickly identify unsigned drivers if a device is not working or if you want to ensure that all drivers in use are signed.

Using the Signature Verification Tool

To use the Signature Verification tool, perform the following steps:

1. Start sigverif.exe (Start|Run|sigverif.exe).

2. Click Advanced.

3. Select Look For Other Files That Are Not Digitally Signed.

4. For the folder, select %SystemRoot%\system32\drivers.

Controlling the Use of Signed and Unsigned Drivers Using Group Policy

Windows 2000 can provide a good degree of control over whether or not users can install signed or unsigned drivers, or both, for a chosen device. The selection in the Group Policy Object (GPO) or Local Computer Policy is an object called Driver Signing. The three choices for the Driver Signing piece of policy are:

➤ *Ignore*—Selecting this does just what the name indicates: ignores whether a driver is signed or not, allowing the user to proceed with the driver installation.

➤ *Warn*—This issues a dialog box warning if an unsigned driver is encountered during a device installation, and gives the user the option of continuing with the installation or terminating the device's setup.

➤ *Block*—This is the most important of the three selections. To prevent the installation of any unsigned device drivers, this is the option you should select in Group Policy or the Local Computer Policy.

Managing and Troubleshooting I/O Devices

Windows 2000 supports a wide variety of I/O devices, including printers, scanners, and multimedia devices (such as cameras, keyboards, mice, smart card readers, modems, infrared devices, and network adapters). This is just the beginning of the list! This section covers the specifics you need to know about supporting I/O devices on Windows 2000 Professional for the exam. Think "big picture" when you are studying these hardware sections, and remember you do *not* need to know specifics about certain brands or models of hardware.

Using Printers

Windows 2000 Professional supports the following printer ports: line printer terminal (LPT), Component Object Model (COM), USB, FireWire, or Institute of Electrical and Electronics Engineers (IEEE) 1394, and network attached devices with a Universal Naming Convention (UNC) path. Print services can be provided only for Windows and Unix clients on Windows 2000 Professional. Windows 2000 Professional automatically downloads the printer drivers for clients that are running Windows 2000, NT 4, NT 3.51, and 9x.

 Windows 2000 Server is required to support Apple and Novell clients.

Internet Printing Protocol (IPP)

Internet printing using IPP is a feature in Windows 2000 that is also supported in Windows 98. Clients have the option of entering a URL to connect to network printers and manage their network print jobs. This is proving to be much easier for users than browsing aimlessly within My Network Places or Network Neighborhood to locate network printers. IPP's other advantage is that it can significantly contribute to efforts to cut down browse traffic on your network.

The print server must be either a Windows 2000 Server running Internet Information Server (IIS) 5, or a Windows 2000 Professional system running Personal Web Server (PWS), which is the "junior" version of IIS. You can view all shared IPP printers at **http://servername/printers**, for example **http://Server2/printers**.

Printer Property Settings

The following are some useful printer property settings:

➤ *Print Pooling*—This allows you to install two or more identical printers as one logical printer.

➤ *Print Priority*—You set this by creating multiple logical printers for one physical printer and assigning different priorities to each. Priority ranges from 1, the lowest (the default), through 99, the highest.

➤ *Availability*—Enabling this option allows Administrators to specify the hours the printer is available. This option is good for large print jobs that you want to print in the middle of the night or early morning so they do not interfere with routine business.

➤ *Separator Pages*—These are available to separate print jobs at a shared printer. You can create and save a template for the design and appearance of the separator page in the %SystemRoot%\system32 directory with a .sep file extension.

➤ *Restart*—You can select this in the printer's menu to reprint a document. It is useful when a document is printing and the printer jams. You can select Resume to start printing where you left off.

Advanced Server Properties allows you to change the directory that contains the print spooler for the printer. This feature is new to the Windows operating system with the release of Windows 2000.

Restarting the Spooler Service

You must restart your spooler service if purging a print queue does not resolve your printing problem. To remedy a "stalled spooler," you must stop and restart the Spooler Service in the Services applet in Administrative Tools in the Control Panel. You *do* need to be logged on as an administrator or member of the Administrators local group to successfully restart the Spooler Service.

Using Keyboards and Mice

You install keyboards under Keyboards in the Device Manager. On the other hand, you install mice, graphics tablets, and other pointing devices under Mice And Other Pointing Devices in the Device Manager. See the "USB" section later in this chapter for more information on USB graphics tablets and pointing devices. You troubleshoot I/O resource conflicts using the System Information snap-in. Take a look under Hardware Resources, I/O for a list of memory ranges in use.

Using Smart Cards and Smart Card Readers

Smart cards and smart card readers, which interpret the data on the cards, are fully supported in Windows 2000. Smart cards enable portability of user credentials and other private information among computers in many locations—such as at work, at home, or on the road. Smart card technology eliminates the need for you to transmit sensitive information, such as user authentication tickets and private keys, over networks. Smart cards also support certificate-based authentication. See the "Mobile User" section later in this chapter for more information on certificate-based authentication.

Installing Smart Card Readers

To install a smart card reader on a computer, perform the following steps:

1. Shut down and turn off the computer.

2. Depending on the type of card reader you have purchased, attach your reader to an available serial port or insert the PC card reader into an available PCMCIA Type II slot.

3. Restart your computer and log on as an administrator.

4. One of the following happens next:

➤ If the device driver software for the smart card reader is available in the driver.cab file (installed on the hard drive as part of the Windows 2000 installation), the driver is installed without any prompting. This could take a few minutes.

➤ If the device driver software for the smart card reader is not available in the driver.cab file, the Add/Remove Hardware Wizard starts. Follow the directions for installing the device driver software.

You can confirm that installation has successfully taken place by the appearance of the Unplug Or Eject Hardware icon in the toolbar (if it was not previously present) and by the appearance of the just-installed reader in the list of hardware devices in the Unplug Or Eject Hardware dialog box.

If the smart card reader is not installed automatically or the Add/Remove Hardware Wizard does not start automatically, your smart card reader is probably not Plug and Play compliant. You should contact the smart card reader manufacturer for the device driver and instructions on how to install and configure the device for Windows 2000.

Logging on to a Computer with a Smart Card

To log on to a computer with a smart card, perform the following steps:

1. At the Windows logon screen, insert your smart card in the smart card reader.

2. Type the personal identification number (PIN) for the smart card when your computer prompts you.

If the PIN you enter is recognized as legitimate, you are logged on to the computer and to the Windows domain, based on the permissions that the domain administrator has assigned to your user account. If you enter the incorrect PIN for a smart card several times in a row, you cannot log on to the computer using that smart card. The number of allowable invalid logon attempts before you are locked out varies according to the smart card manufacturer.

Mobile User

If you are a *mobile user*, you need to enable the use of certificates on your computer. Unless your system administrator preconfigures your computer with machine and user certificates before you receive it, you must connect to your corporate network using conventional, password-based authentication methods to get your machine and user certificates. When you connect, you join your computer to the corporate domain, obtain certificates, and set certificates policy. The next time you connect to the corporate network, you can use certificate-based authentication methods such as Extensible Authentication Protocol (EAP), an extension to Point-to-Point Protocol (PPP).

EAP was developed in response to the increasing demand for remote access user authentication that uses other security devices, such as smart cards. EAP provides a standard mechanism for supporting additional authentication methods within PPP. By using EAP, you can add support for a number of authentication schemes, including token cards, one-time passwords, public key authentication using smart cards, certificates, and others. EAP, in conjunction with strong EAP authentication methods, is a critical technology component for secure Virtual Private Network (VPN) connections because it offers more security against brute-force or dictionary attacks and password guessing than other authentication methods, such as Challenge Handshake Authentication Protocol (CHAP).

 A Windows 2000 Professional computer that needs to authenticate to a Remote Access Services (RAS) server using a smart card and a certificate must have EAP, and Microsoft Challenge Handshake Authentication Protocol (MSCHAP) and/or MSCHAP version 2 enabled in the dial-up connection's properties settings.

Enabling the Use of Certificates

To enable the use of a certificate on a computer, perform the following steps:

1. Connect to a network by using a dial-up or Point-to-Point Tunneling Protocol (PPTP) network connection, and authentication protocols such as MSCHAP or MSCHAP version 2. When you connect, your Windows 2000 computer joins the corporate domain and receives machine certificates.

2. Request a user certificate from one of the possible Certificate Authorities.

3. Create another connection that uses *certificate-based authentication*, and then connect again by using certificate-based authentication methods such as EAP or IPSec.

Using Cameras and Other Multimedia Hardware

Cameras and scanners appear in the Control Panel when you install your first digital camera or scanner. If you have a Plug and Play camera or scanner, Windows 2000 detects it and installs it automatically. Then you can use the Scanners And Cameras applet in the Control Panel to install other scanners, digital still cameras, digital video cameras, and image-capturing devices.

After a device is installed, Scanners And Cameras can link it to a program on your computer. For example, when you push Scan on your scanner, you can have the scanned picture automatically open in the program you want.

Installing Scanners or Digital Cameras

To install a scanner or digital camera, perform the following steps:

1. Open Scanners And Cameras in the Control Panel.

2. Click Add, and then follow the instructions on the screen.

Remember that you must be logged on as an administrator or a member of the Administrators group to complete this procedure. If your computer is connected to a network, network policy settings may prevent you from installing devices.

Testing Scanners or Digital Cameras

To test a scanner or digital camera, perform the following steps:

1. Open Scanners And Cameras in the Control Panel.

2. Click the scanner or camera you want to test, and then click Properties.

3. On the General tab, click Test Scanner Or Camera.

An onscreen message tells you if the camera or scanner completed the test successfully. You can also check your Event Log to see if the test was successful.

Using Modems

At one time or another, if you've used a computer, you have probably used a modem to connect to your office or an Internet Service Provider (ISP) using a dial-up connection. This section details what you need to know about modem support and troubleshooting in Windows 2000 Professional.

Installing Modems

If Windows 2000 starts the Install New Modem Wizard as soon as your new modem is physically in your machine, you are in luck! You have nothing more to do than follow the prompts the wizard provides, if any, to complete the setup of your new modem.

If the Install New Modem Wizard does not detect your modem or you cannot find it listed, you are faced with installing an unsupported modem. Good luck on your mission. Windows 2000 *cannot* automatically detect certain internal modems. You must install the modem manually through the Add/Remove Hardware Wizard in the Control Panel, or by following these instructions:

1. Open Phone And Modem Options in the Control Panel.

2. (Optional) If you are prompted for location information, enter dialing information for your location and click OK.

3. On the Modems tab, click Add.

4. Follow the instructions in the Install New Modem Wizard.

Using Multilink Support

Multilinking, or multiple-device dialing, allows you to combine two or more modems or integrated services digital network (ISDN) adapters into one logical link with increased bandwidth. The Network And Dial-up Connections feature performs PPP Multilink dialing over multiple ISDN, X.25, or modem lines. The feature combines multiple physical links into a logical bundle, and the resulting aggregate link increases your connection bandwidth. For example, you could use Multilink to combine the power of two 33.6Kbps modems to achieve approximately a 67.2Kbps dial-up connection. Although you will not see this frequently in the real world, Multilinking is definitely a term to understand for the 70-210 exam.

Configuring Multilink

To configure Multilink, perform the following steps:

1. Select Start|Settings|Network And Dial-up Connections.

2. Right-click the connection where you want Multilink enabled, and then select Properties.

3. On the Options tab, in Multiple Devices, do one of the following:

   ➤ If you want Windows 2000 to dial only the first available device, click Dial Only First Available Device.

   ➤ If you want Windows 2000 to use all of your devices, click Dial All Devices.

   ➤ If you want Windows 2000 to dynamically dial and hang up devices as needed, click Dial Devices Only As Needed, and then click Configure.

4. In Automatic Dialing, click the Activity At Least percentage and Duration At Least time you want to set. Another line is dialed when connection activity reaches this level for the amount of time that you specify.

5. In Automatic Hangup, click the Activity No More Than percentage and Duration At Least time you want to set. A device is hung up when connection activity decreases to this level for at least the amount of time that you specify.

Multilink Tips

If you use multiple devices to dial a server that requires callback, only one of your Multilinked devices is called back. This is because only one phone number is stored in a user account. Therefore, only one device connects, all other devices fail to complete the connection, and your connection loses Multilink functionality. You can avoid this problem if the Multilinked phonebook entry is to an ISDN line or modem with two channels that have the same phone number.

If you select Dial All Devices, links that get dropped in the Multilinked bundle are not automatically reinitialized. You can force links to reinitialize by selecting Dial Devices Only As Needed and then Configure, and then by setting easily achieved Automatic Dialing conditions, which cause another line to be dialed. For example, set Activity At Least to 1 percent and Duration At Least to 3 seconds.

 To dial multiple devices, both your connection and your remote access server must have Multilink enabled.

Troubleshooting Modems

You can verify that your modem is working properly by using the diagnostic tool that is available through the Phone And Modem Options icon in the Control Panel, or the Device Manager. Another choice for troubleshooting a modem problem is use the Hardware Troubleshooter, available in the Add/Remove Hardware Wizard in the Control Panel, but use this as a last resort because it is similar to Windows Help.

Supporting Faxes

If a fax device or fax modem is installed, the Fax applet appears in the Control Panel. It does not appear if no fax device is installed. You use the Fax applet to set up rules for how your device receives faxes, the number of retries when it is sending, where to store retrieved and sent faxes, user security permissions, and so on. If the Advanced Options tab is not available in the Fax applet, you must log off and then log back on as an administrator.

 You *cannot* share the Fax printer in your Printers folder.

Using Infrared Data Association (IrDA) Devices and Wireless Devices

Windows 2000 supports IrDA protocols that enable data transfer over infrared connections. This provides an infrastructure that allows other devices and programs to communicate with Windows 2000 through the IrDA interface. Windows 2000 installs with the Wireless Link program, which transfers files to or from another computer that runs Windows 2000 or 98.

Windows 2000's Plug and Play architecture automatically detects and installs the infrared component for computers with built-in IrDA hardware. For computers without built-in IrDA hardware, a user can attach a serial port IrDA transceiver to a serial COM port and use the Add/Remove Hardware Wizard to install the device in Windows 2000.

After an infrared device is installed, the Wireless Link icon appears in the Control Panel. When another IrDA transceiver comes in range, the Wireless Link icon appears on the desktop and on the taskbar. You can then send a file over the infrared connection with any of the following actions:

➤ Specify a location and one or more files using the Wireless Link dialog box

➤ Use drag-and-drop operations to move files onto the Wireless Link icon on the desktop

➤ Right-click any selection of files on the desktop, in Windows Explorer, or in My Computer, and then click Send To Infrared Recipient

➤ Print to a printer configured to use an infrared port

In addition to sending or printing files, you can create a network connection that connects two computers using the infrared port. You can use this capability to map shared drives on a host computer and work with files and folders in Windows Explorer or My Computer. You can also use an infrared network connection to connect directly to another computer without modems, cables, or network hardware.

Enabling or Preventing Receiving Files

To enable or prevent receiving files, perform the following steps:

1. Open the Wireless Link applet in the Control Panel.

2. On the File Transfer tab, do *one* of the following:

    ➤ *To enable your computer to receive files from others*—Select the Allow Others To Send Files To Your Computer Using Infrared Communications checkbox.

    ➤ Or select the Send Files To Your Computer Using Infrared Communications checkbox.

Viewing Power Allocations for USB Hubs

To view power allocations for USB hubs, perform the following steps:

1. Open the Device Manager.

2. Double-click Universal Serial Bus Controller.

3. Right-click USB Root Hub, and then click Properties.

4. On the Power tab, view the power consumed by each device in the Devices On This Hub list.

Hubs for USB devices are self-powered or bus-powered. Self-powered, or plugging a hub into an electrical outlet, provides maximum power to the device, whereas bus-powered, plugging a device into another USB port, provides minimum power. Devices that require a lot of power, such as cameras, should be plugged into self-powered hubs. Universal Serial Bus Controller appears only if you have a USB port on your computer. The Power tab appears only for USB hubs.

Viewing Bandwidth Allocations for USB Host Controllers

To view bandwidth allocation for a USB host controller, perform the following steps:

1. Open the Device Manager.

2. Double-click Universal Serial Bus Controllers.

3. Right-click Intel PCI To USB Universal Host Controller, and then click Properties.

4. On the Advanced tab, view the bandwidth consumed by each device in the Bandwidth Consuming Devices list.

You can view bandwidth only for a USB controller.

Certain ports are not listed in the Ports tab unless a printer that requires one of them is installed. USB and FireWire printers support Plug and Play, so when you plug a printer into the correct physical port (USB or IEEE 1394), the correct port monitor is installed automatically. Windows 2000 detects the device and displays its settings on the screen, prompting you to approve.

Dealing with USB Controllers That Do Not Install Properly

In the Device Manager, USB controllers are listed under Human Interface Devices (when you are viewing Devices By Type, which is the default view). If the controller does not appear in the Device Manager, USB may not be enabled in the system's BIOS. When prompted during system startup, enter the BIOS setup and enable USB.

If USB is enabled in the BIOS, but the USB host controller does not appear in the Device Manager (under Universal Serial Bus Controllers), or a yellow warning icon appears next to the host controller name, the version of BIOS may be outdated. Contact your computer's maker or vendor and obtain the current version of BIOS.

If the controller appears in the Device Manager, right-click the controller name and select Properties. In Device Status, a message describes any problems and suggests what action to take. USB ports have a separate entry in the Device Manager. To check the device status, select Universal Serial Bus Controllers, right-click USB Root Hub, and then select Properties.

Using Network Adapters

You install network adapters using the Add/Remove Hardware applet in the Control Panel. You can make changes to the binding order of protocols and the network provider order using Advanced Settings under the Advanced menu of the Network And Dial-up Connections window (accessed by right-clicking on the My Network Places icon, or via the Control Panel). Each network adapter has its own separate icon in the Network And Dial-up Connections folder. Right-click a network adapter icon to set its properties, install protocols, change addresses, or perform any other configuration changes for the connection.

Internet Connection Sharing (ICS)

With the ICS feature of Network And Dial-up Connections, you can use Windows 2000 to connect your home or small-office network to the Internet. For example, you might have a home network that connects to the Internet using a dial-up connection. By enabling ICS on the computer that uses the dial-up connection, you are providing network address translation (NAT), addressing, and name resolution services for all computers on your home network. The ICS feature is intended for use in a small office or home office where network configuration and the computer running Windows 2000 where the shared connection resides manages the Internet connection. It is assumed that on your small network, this computer is the *only* Internet connection—the only gateway to the Internet—and that it sets up all internal network addresses.

After you enable ICS and users verify their networking and Internet options, home or small-office network users can use applications such as Internet Explorer and Outlook Express as if they were already connected to the ISP. The ICS computer then dials the ISP and creates the connection so that the user can reach the specified Web address or resource. To use the ICS feature, users on your home-office or small-office network must configure Transmission Control Protocol/Internet Protocol (TCP/IP) on their local area connection to obtain an IP address automatically. Also, home-office or small-office network users must configure Internet options for ICS.

You might need to configure applications and services on the ICS computer to work properly across the Internet. For example, if users on your home network want to play a game such as Doom with other users on the Internet, you must configure Doom on the connection where ICS is enabled. Conversely, you must configure services that you provide so Internet users can access them. For example, if you are hosting a Web server on your home network and want Internet users to be able to connect to it, you must configure the Web server service on the ICS computer. Here are some guidelines for using ICS:

➤ To configure ICS, you must be a member of the Administrators group on the computer where you want to set this up.

➤ You should not use this feature in an existing network with other Windows 2000 Server domain controllers, DNS servers, gateways, Dynamic Host Configuration Protocol (DHCP) servers, or systems configured for static IP addresses. If you are running Windows 2000 Server, and one or more of these components exist, you must use NAT to achieve the same result.

➤ A computer with ICS needs two connections. One connection, typically a local area network (LAN) adapter, connects to the computers on the home network. The other connection connects the home network to the Internet. You need to ensure that ICS is enabled on the connection that connects your home network to the Internet. If you do so, the home network connection appropriately allocates TCP/IP addresses to its own users, the shared connection can connect your home network to the Internet, and users outside your home network are not at risk of receiving inappropriate addresses from your home network. If you enable ICS on a connection, the ICS computer becomes a DHCP allocator for the home network. DHCP distributes TCP/IP addresses to users as they start up.

 If ICS is enabled on the wrong network adapter, the home network DHCP allocator might grant TCP/IP addresses to users outside your own home network, causing problems on their own networks.

➤ When you enable ICS, the adapter connected to the home-office or small-office network is given a new static IP address configuration. Consequently, TCP/IP connections established between any small-office or home-office computer and the ICS computer when ICS is enabled are lost and need to be reestablished.

➤ You cannot modify the default configuration of ICS. This includes items such as disabling the DHCP allocator or modifying the range of private IP addresses that are distributed, disabling the DNS proxy, configuring a range of public IP addresses, or configuring inbound mappings. If you want to modify any of these items, you must use NAT.

➤ If your home-office users need to access a corporate network that is connected to the Internet by a tunnel server from an ICS network, they need to create a VPN connection to tunnel from the computer on the ICS network to the corporate tunnel server on the Internet. The VPN connection is authenticated and secure; creating the tunneled connection allocates proper IP addresses, DNS server addresses, and Windows Internet Naming Service (WINS) server addresses for the corporate network.

Managing and Troubleshooting Display Devices

You manage desktop display properties (software settings) through the Display applet in the Control Panel. You install, remove, and update the drivers of display adapters through Display Adapters under the Device Manager. To do the same for monitors, use Monitors under the Device Manager.

Display Settings

Much of your display settings deal with aesthetics such as wallpaper, screen fonts, and screensavers. The exam will test your knowledge of the technical aspects of display settings, not aesthetics. For example, if you receive an error about an unavailable overlay surface, reduce the display resolution or number of colors. You may also get the—Unable To Create Video Window. Please Try Altering Your Display Settings—error. Troubleshooting these display errors is covered in this section.

Modifying Your Display Settings

To modify your display settings, perform the following steps:

1. Right-click your desktop and select Properties, or open the Display applet in the Control Panel.

2. Select the Settings tab and make the appropriate changes.

Configuring Multiple-Display Support

Windows 2000 has a new multiple-monitor functionality that increases your work productivity by expanding the size of your desktop. Multiple displays do have to use PCI or Accelerated Graphics Port (AGP) port devices to work properly with Windows 2000.

 You can connect up to 10 individual monitors to create a desktop large enough to hold numerous programs or windows.

You can easily work on more than one task at a time by moving items from one monitor to another or by stretching them across numerous monitors. Edit images or text on one monitor while viewing Web activity on another. Or you can open multiple pages of a single, long document and drag them across several monitors to easily view the layout of text and graphics. You could also stretch a spreadsheet across two monitors so you can view numerous columns without scrolling.

One monitor serves as the primary display; you see the Logon dialog box when you start your computer. In addition, most programs display windows on the primary monitor when you initially open them. You can set different resolutions and different color depths for each monitor. You can also connect multiple monitors to individual graphics adapters or to a single adapter that supports multiple outputs.

Arranging Multiple Monitors

To arrange multiple monitors, perform the following steps:

1. Open the Display applet in the Control Panel.

2. On the Settings tab, click Identify to display a large number on each of your monitors, showing which monitor corresponds with each icon.

3. Click the monitor icons and drag them to positions that represent how you want to move items from one monitor to another, and then click OK or Apply to view the changes.

The icon positions determine how you move items from one monitor to another. For example, if you are using two monitors and you want to move items from one monitor to the other by dragging left and right, place the icons side by side. To move items between monitors by dragging up and down, place the icons one above the other. The icon positions do not have to correspond to the physical positions of the monitors. You can place the icons one above the other even though your monitors are side by side.

Changing the Primary Monitor

To change the primary monitor, perform the following steps:

1. Open the Display applet in the Control Panel.

2. On the Settings tab, click the monitor icon that represents the monitor you want to designate as the primary one.

3. Select the Use This Device As The Primary Monitor checkbox. This checkbox is unavailable when you select the monitor icon that is currently set as your primary monitor.

The monitor that is designated as the primary monitor displays the Logon dialog box when you start your computer. Most programs display their window on the primary monitor when you first open them.

Moving Items between Monitors or Viewing the Same Desktop on Multiple Monitors

To move items between monitors, or to view the same desktop on multiple monitors, perform the following steps:

1. Open the Display applet in the Control Panel.

2. On the Settings tab, click the monitor icon that represents the monitor you want to use in addition to your primary monitor.

3. Select the Extend My Windows Desktop Onto This Monitor checkbox. Selecting this checkbox allows you to drag items across your screen onto alternate monitors. You can also resize a window to stretch it across more than one monitor.

Troubleshooting Multiple Displays

The default refresh frequency setting is typically 60Hz, although your monitors may support a higher setting. A higher refresh frequency might reduce flicker on your screens, but choosing a setting that is too high for your monitor can make your display unusable, not to mention damage your hardware.

 If your refresh frequency is set to anything higher than 60Hz and your monitor display(s) go(es) black when you start Windows 2000, restart the system in Safe Mode. Change your refresh frequency for all monitors to 60Hz. You may need to double-check this setting in your Unattended Installation script file, commonly called unattend.txt. Again, set it to 60Hz.

Multiple-display support in Windows 2000 presents some challenges when you are dealing with some older applications and DOS applications. If you start a DOS application on your multidisplay Windows 2000 machine, and then both of your screens flicker and completely go dark, you can fix the problem without much difficulty. Multiple-display support allows you to adjust the display settings so that your application runs and is viewable on both monitors. First, you may need to restart your system; then, you select Safe Mode at the F8 startup menu. Then, once you can see the contents of your desktop, you configure the DOS application to run in a window and change your Display settings from Default to Optimal.

Installing, Configuring, and Supporting a Video Adapter

When Windows 2000 is being installed, your system's BIOS selects the primary video/display adapter based on PCI slot order. You can install and configure any additional video adapters you want to use with your system using the Display applet or the Add/Remove Hardware applet in the Control Panel.

Mobile Computer Hardware

PCMCIA (PC Card) adapters, USB ports, IEEE 1394 (FireWire), and infrared devices are now supported in Windows 2000. You manage these through the Device Manager. Support is provided in Windows 2000 Professional for APM and ACPI, which we discuss shortly.

Hot (computer is fully powered) and warm (computer is in suspend mode) docking and undocking are now fully supported for computers with a Plug and Play BIOS. Hibernation (complete power down while maintaining the state of open programs and connected hardware) and Suspend (deep sleep with some power) modes are also now supported, extending battery life.

When you install a PC Card, USB, or infrared device, Windows 2000 automatically recognizes and configures it (if it meets Plug and Play specifications). If Windows does not have an entry in its driver.cab file for the new hardware, you are prompted to supply one.

Equipping mobile computers with smart cards and NTFS using Encrypting File System decreases the likelihood of confidential data being compromised if the computer is stolen, lost, or simply placed into the wrong hands.

Managing Hardware Profiles

A *hardware profile* stores configuration settings for a collection of devices and services. Windows 2000 can store different hardware profiles so that users' needs can be met even though their computer may frequently require different device and service settings depending on the circumstances. The best example is that of a laptop or portable computer that is used in an office while in a docking station that is then undocked so the user can travel with the laptop. The two situations do require different power management settings, possibly different network settings, and various other configuration changes.

You can enable and disable devices in particular profiles through their properties in the Device Manager snap-in. You manage services using the Services applet in the Control Panel. You create and manage hardware profiles using the System applet in the Control Panel, or by right-clicking on the My Computer icon on the desktop and choosing Properties. Once inside the System applet, go to the Hardware tab and select Hardware Profiles.

At installation, Windows 2000 creates a single hardware profile called Profile 1 (Current). You are prompted to select a hardware profile at system startup only when two or more hardware profiles are stored on your machine. You can create and store as many hardware profiles on your machine as you like. You select the desired hardware profile at Windows 2000 startup to select which device and service configuration settings you need for the current session. If Windows 2000 detects that your computer is a portable (laptop), it tries to determine whether your system is docked or undocked; then it selects the appropriate hardware profile for the current conditions. Do not confuse hardware profiles with *user profiles*—the two are *unrelated*!

APM

Windows 2000 supports the APM 1.2 specification. APM helps to greatly reduce your computer's power consumption, which is particularly helpful for laptop users. You use the Power Options applet in the Control Panel to configure your computer to use APM. Once you are in the Power Options applet, look for a tab labeled APM. On the APM tab, select the Enable Advanced Power Management checkbox to enable APM. You do not need to restart your system.

If your computer does not have an APM-compliant BIOS, Windows 2000 cannot install APM. This means no APM support for your machine, plus no APM tab in the Power Options applet in the Control Panel. Keep in mind, though, that your machine can still function as an ACPI computer if your BIOS is ACPI-compliant. The ACPI-based BIOS will take over your system configuration and power management from the Plug and Play BIOS.

APM is available only in Windows 2000 Professional. It is not available in any of the Windows 2000 Server versions.

ACPI

Many people call ACPI the next-generation replacement for the APM specification. ACPI is an open industry specification that defines a flexible and extensible hardware interface for your system board. Windows 2000 is a fully ACPI-compliant operating system. Software developers and designers use the ACPI specification to integrate power management features throughout a computer system, including hardware, the operating system, and application software. This integration enables Windows 2000 to determine which applications are active and to handle all of the power management resources for computer subsystems and peripherals.

ACPI enables the operating system to direct power management on a wide range of mobile, desktop, and server computers and peripherals. ACPI is the foundation for the OnNow industry initiative, which allows manufacturers to deliver computers that will start at the touch of a key on a keyboard.

ACPI design is *essential* when you want to take full advantage of power management and Plug and Play in Windows 2000. If you are not sure if your computer is ACPI-compliant, check your manufacturer's documentation. To change power settings that take advantage of ACPI, use the Power Options applet in the Control Panel.

Power Options Overview

By using Power Options in the Control Panel, you can reduce the power consumption of any number of your computer devices or of your entire system. You do this by choosing a *power scheme*, which is a collection of settings that manages your computer's power usage. You can create your own power schemes or use the ones provided with Windows 2000.

You can also adjust the individual settings in a power scheme. For example, depending on your hardware, you can:

➤ Turn off your monitor and hard disks automatically to save power.

➤ Put your computer on standby, which puts your entire system in a low-power state, if you plan to be away from your computer for a while. While on standby, your entire computer switches to a low-power state, where devices such as the monitor and hard disks turn off and your computer uses less power. When you want to use the computer again, it comes out of standby quickly, and your desktop is restored exactly as you left it. Standby is useful for conserving battery power in portable computers.

 Standby does not save your desktop state to disk, so if there is a power failure while the computer is on standby, you can lose unsaved information. If there is an interruption in power, information in memory is lost. If this concerns you, hibernation or a complete power down might be better choices to consider.

➤ Put your computer in hibernation mode. When you restart your computer, your desktop is restored exactly as you left it. It takes longer to bring your computer out of hibernation than out of standby. Put your computer in hibernation when you will be away from the computer for an extended time or overnight.

 The hibernation feature saves everything in memory on disk, turns off your monitor and hard disk, and then turns off your computer.

Managing Battery Power on a Portable Computer

Using the Power Options applet in the Control Panel, you can reduce consumption of battery power on your portable computer and still keep the computer available for immediate use. You can view multiple batteries separately or as a whole, and set alarms to warn you of low battery conditions.

Using a Portable Computer on an Airplane

Most airlines request that you turn off portable computers during certain portions of the flight such as takeoff and landing. To comply with this request, you must turn off your computer *completely*. Do not get cute, here, folks. Turn it off.

 When you board an airplane, your mobile computer must be completely powered down or turned off. *None* of the power modes (hibernation, suspend, standby, and so on) are acceptable substitutes. You want to avoid interfering with the aircraft's instrumentation, and completely powering down is the only way to guarantee that.

Your computer may *appear* to be turned off while in either standby or hibernation mode. However, the operating system might automatically reactivate itself to run certain preprogrammed tasks or to conserve battery power. To prevent this from occurring during air travel, be certain to shut down your computer completely when it's not in use. In addition, if your computer is equipped with a cellular modem, you must ensure that this modem is completely turned off during air travel, as required by FCC and FAA regulations.

Managing Power When Installing a Plug and Play Device

Plug and Play works with Power Options in the Control Panel to be sure that your system runs efficiently while you are installing or removing hardware devices. Power Options controls the power supply to the devices attached to your computer, supplying power to those that you are using and conserving power for those you are not. Windows 2000 automatically manages the power for devices. However, some devices may have options you can set in the Device Manager.

To take full advantage of Plug and Play, you need to use Windows 2000 on an ACPI-compliant computer that is running in ACPI mode, and the hardware devices must be Plug and Play and/or ACPI compliant. In an ACPI computer, the operating system, not the hardware, configures and monitors the computer's devices.

Monitoring and Configuring Multiple Processors

Adding an additional processor to your Windows 2000 system to improve performance is called *scaling*. Windows 2000 Professional can support up to two processors. You add a second processor usually due to the demands of Central Processing Unit (CPU)-intensive applications, such as Computer Aided Design (CAD) and graphics rendering. Windows 2000 supports Symmetric Multiprocessing (SMP) as well as processor affinity. Asymmetric Multiprocessing (ASMP) is not supported.

Windows 2000 provides support for single or multiple CPUs. However, if you originally installed Windows 2000 on a computer with a single CPU, you must update the Hardware Abstraction Layer (HAL) on your computer for it to be able to recognize and use multiple CPUs.

Windows 2000 Professional supports a maximum of two CPUs, without Original Equipment Manufacturer (OEM) modifications. If you need more than 2 CPUs, consider using Windows 2000 Server (up to 4 CPUs), Advanced Server (up to 8 CPUs), or Data Center Server (maximum of 32 CPUs).

Keep monitoring performance after you add an additional processor because upgrading to multiple CPUs might increase the load on other system resources.

In NT 4, the uptomp.exe tool added support for multiple CPUs. However, this tool is no longer used in Windows 2000. Instead, you use the Device Manager to make these changes. Before changing the computer type, contact your computer manufacturer to determine if there is a vendor-specific HAL you should use instead of the standard ones included in Windows 2000.

Installing Support for Multiple CPUs

To install support for multiple CPUs, perform the following steps:

1. Click Start|Settings|Control Panel, and then click System.

2. Click the Hardware tab, and then click the Device Manager.

3. Double-click the Computer branch to expand it. Note the type of support you currently have.

4. Double-click the computer type listed under the Computer branch, click the Drivers tab, click Update Driver, and then click Next.

5. Click Display A List Of Known Drivers For This Device, and then click Show All Hardware Of This Device Class.

6. Click the appropriate computer type (one that matches your current type, except for multiple CPUs), click Next, and then click Finish.

Note: You can use this procedure only to upgrade from a single-processor HAL to a multiple-processor HAL. If you use this procedure to change from a standard HAL to an ACPI HAL (for example, after a BIOS upgrade) or vice versa, unexpected results may occur, including an inability to boot the computer.

Practice Questions

Question 1

You have several MPS-compliant machines that you have upgraded from NT 4 Workstation to Windows 2000 Professional. Each machine has dual Pentium III 400MHz processors because the machines are used for high-end AutoCAD and CAD drawing applications. After the upgrade, users tell you that these machines are running their drawing applications much slower than they did in NT 4. What should you do?

○ a. Use the Device Manager to install ACPI-compliant drivers for the second processor in each machine.

○ b. During startup, press F8. Then install the MPS-compliant drivers for the second processor in each machine.

○ c. Use the Device Manager to install the MPS-compliant drivers for the second processor in each machine.

○ d. Double the amount of memory in each machine.

○ e. Use the Device Manager to enable the AGP bridge controller in each of the machines.

Answer c is correct. The MPS-compliant drivers for the second processor in each machine have not been installed. Drivers for a second processor will be MPS-compliant, not necessarily ACPI-compliant, therefore answer a is incorrect. You do not need the F8 startup menu for this scenario, nor does this question have anything to do with adding memory or enabling AGP bridge controllers. Therefore, answers b, d, and e are incorrect.

Question 2

> You have eight Windows 2000 Professional computers in your company's Art department. They all have built-in USB controllers. You install a USB tablet-pointing device on each machine. You also install the manufacturer's 32-bit tablet software on each machine. A tablet icon shows up in the Control Panel, but none of the tablets work. You examine the Device Manager and notice no device conflicts. What do you need to do to get the USB tablets to work?
>
> ○ a. Enable the USB ports in the system BIOS, and then reinstall the USB tablet device drivers.
>
> ○ b. Enable the USB root hub controller, and then reinstall the USB tablet device drivers.
>
> ○ c. Disable USB error detection for the USB root hub controller, and then enable the USB tablet device in each machine's hardware profile.
>
> ○ d. Reinstall the USB tablet device drivers, and then disable the USB error detection.

The correct answer is a. You do not need a USB root hub controller for these devices to work properly. Disabling error detection for a USB root hub controller is also irrelevant to this question. Reinstalling the device drivers and then disabling USB error detection makes no sense because you would always attempt to disable error detection prior to reinstalling the drivers.

Question 3

> You buy a USB-based ISDN terminal adapter for your Windows 2000 Professional laptop. You plug it into the USB port and are surprised when Plug and Play fails to detect the device. You test the adapter on a Windows 2000 desktop machine at your office, and Plug and Play detects the adapter with no difficulty. You have examined the Device Manager on your laptop, and there are no device conflicts. You need this adapter to work with your laptop because you travel frequently. What should you do?
>
> ○ a. Turn off your laptop. Plug in the adapter and restart the machine.
>
> ○ b. Contact the hardware manufacturer to get an upgrade for the Plug and Play BIOS on your laptop.
>
> ○ c. Use the Device Manager to enable the USB root hub in the current hardware profile.
>
> ○ d. Use the Device Manager to enable the USB host controller in the current hardware profile.

Answer b is correct. Answer a is not a good choice because essentially you have already tried this, and it did not work. Answers c and d deal with a USB root hub and USB host controller, neither of which are needed to get this ISDN adapter to work properly. All that is really needed is a BIOS upgrade so that your USB support is current and can accommodate the new ISDN adapter.

Question 4

You have Windows 2000 Professional installed on six machines that are all equipped with network cards and static IP addresses. Setup detected and installed a 10/100Mbps Unshielded Twisted Pair (UTP)-only NIC on Workstation 3 and Workstation 5, and a 10Mbps BNC/UTP combination NIC on the other four machines. You accepted the default settings for the network cards on all six machines. All six machines are connected to a 10/100 switch that uses Category 5 UTP cable. Now, only Workstation 3 and Workstation 5 can talk to each other on your network, but you need all the machines to be able to communicate with each other. What should you do?

- ○ a. Configure the 10/100 NICs to transmit at the 10Mbps rate.
- ○ b. Configure the 10/100 switch to transmit at only the 100Mbps rate.
- ○ c. Change the BNC/UTP combination NICs so that they use the BNC transceiver setting only.
- ○ d. Change the BNC/UTP combination NICs so that they use the UTP transceiver setting only.

Answer d is correct. All devices were detected, and the switch allows for cards at different speeds to communicate. Therefore the issue is most likely a transceiver setting—the BNC cards are using BNC. Changing the transmission rates would not help if the cards were still using different transceiver settings. Therefore answers a, b, and c are incorrect.

Question 5

You install Windows 2000 Professional on your computer at home. You create a new Dial-up Connection to connect to your company's RAS server. You configure the connection to use both of your external modems and to use Multilink to bind the modems together. You start the Dial-up Connection and connect to the RAS server. You notice that only one of the modems is connected to the RAS server. What should you do to get both modems to connect successfully to the RAS server?

○ a. Configure the Dial-up Connection to use a Serial Line Internet Protocol (SLIP) connection instead of a PPP connection.

○ b. Replace your modems with new ones that support Multilink and ACPI.

○ c. Configure the company's RAS server to accept Multilink connections.

○ d. Grant your user account Multilink permission on the company's RAS server.

Answer c is correct. Remember that for Multilink to work, not only must the client have setup Multilink properly, but also the RAS server must allow Multilink connections. Until the RAS server is configured to accept Multilink connections, it allows only one of your modems to connect at a time.

Question 6

Your Windows 2000 Professional computer has a 33.6Kbps built-in modem. You've just installed a new 56Kbps Industry Standard Architecture (ISA) modem. You want your computer to use only the 56Kbps modem. When you start up the computer, you notice in the Device Manager that the two devices are in conflict. What change should you make? (This question could be multiple choice or drag and drop, so be prepared.)

○ a. Disable the 33.6Kbps modem in the Device Manager and reinstall the 56Kbps modem.

○ b. Remove the 33.6Kbps modem in the Device Manager and reinstall the 56Kbps modem.

○ c. No "action" is required; just reboot the computer and Plug and Play will detect the device.

○ d. Remove both modems in the Device Manager. Reboot into Safe Mode, and then reinstall the 56Kbps modem.

Answer a is correct. Disabling the built-in 33.6Kbps modem prevents it from being reenabled upon startup. Removing the 33.6Kbps modem in the Device Manager produces an undesirable result: redetection of the device at system startup. Therefore, answer b is incorrect. You know that some action is required to fix this problem. Therefore, answer c is incorrect. Booting into Safe Mode is not going to help further your cause. Therefore, answer d is incorrect.

Question 7

You attach an IrDA transceiver to a serial port on your Windows 2000 machine. What step should you take to correctly install the device?

- ○ a. Use the Device Manager.
- ○ b. Restart the computer and let Plug and Play detect the device.
- ○ c. Use the Add/Remove Hardware Wizard.
- ○ d. Use the Wireless Link icon in the Control Panel.

Answer c is correct. You must install an external IrDA device attached to a serial port with the Add/Remove Hardware Wizard. You can use the Device Manager to view Port settings, but you must use the Add/Remove Hardware Wizard to add new hardware. Therefore, answer a is incorrect. Only internal IrDA devices are detected during Windows 2000 Setup or at the next system reboot. Therefore, answer b is incorrect. The Wireless Link icon is of use to you only *after* the device is correctly installed. Therefore, answer d is incorrect.

Question 8

You have replaced the network card on a computer running Windows 2000 Professional. The new card uses a different driver than the original network card. What utility should you use to ensure that the device driver for the original card is removed from your system's hard disk?

- ○ a. Device Manager
- ○ b. Add/Remove Programs
- ○ c. Network And Dial-up Connections
- ○ d. Add/Remove Hardware Wizard
- ○ e. Network icon in the Control Panel

Answer d is correct. You must use the Add/Remove Hardware Wizard to make certain that the network card drivers no longer in use are completely removed from your hard disk. The Device Manager would allow you to remove the device, but it would not remove the drivers from disk. Add/Remove Programs is not used to remove devices and their related drivers. Network and Dial-up Connections can be used to disable a network connection, but it has no functionality to allow you to remove a device and its drivers from disk. The Network icon in the Control Panel has the same limitation.

Question 9

> You need to tell your Windows 2000 users how to connect to shared IPP printers on your network, as well as how to manage their own print jobs, using their Web browser. The printers are all shared from a single Windows 2000 server on your network named PrintBoss. What is the correct syntax for users to type in the URL bar within their browsers to make this type of connection?
>
> ○ a. **ftp://PrintBoss/Printers**
>
> ○ b. **ipp://PrintBoss/Printers**
>
> ○ c. **http://PrintBoss/Printers**
>
> ○ d. **http://PrintBoss/Printer_Share_Name**

Answer c is correct. The Windows 2000 Server machine that is your print server has IIS installed and a default virtual directory configured under the name "Printers". Your clients and the print server use the Web service to communicate using IPP, so the correct URL address to type in is **http://servername/Printers**. Your server name is PrintBoss, and the virtual directory name is Printers. This is the default virtual directory configured for shared printers on a Windows 2000 machine running IIS or PWS with the default Web site started.

Question 10

You are deciding on specifications for 50 new computers your company will purchase. These computers will run Windows 2000 Professional for the Engineering department. You want Windows 2000 to be able to use all the hardware that comes in the computers. What is the maximum amount of memory you *could* have in your new Windows 2000 computers?

○ a. 2GB

○ b. 4GB

○ c. 8GB

○ d. 16GB

Answer b is correct. Windows 2000 Professional can address up to a maximum of 4GB of RAM. This is a hard-coded limitation of Windows 2000 Professional, and knowing your RAM maximum is helpful when deciding on machine configurations. Original equipment manufacturers (OEMs) may modify this limitation in versions of Windows 2000 Professional that they ship preinstalled on their hardware.

Need to Know More?

 Microsoft Corporation. *Microsoft Windows 2000 Professional Resource Kit*. Microsoft Press: Redmond, Washington, 2000. ISBN: 1-57231-808-2. This book has invaluable information on installing, managing, and troubleshooting hardware devices.

 Nielsen, Morten Strunge. *Windows 2000 Professional Configuration and Implementation*. The Coriolis Group: Scottsdale, AZ, 2000. ISBN: 1-57610-528-8. This book is a good reference because it has a wealth of information on configuring and troubleshooting hardware on Windows 2000 Professional.

 Stinson, Craig, and Carl Siechert. *Running Microsoft Windows 2000 Professional*. Microsoft Press: Redmond, Washington, 2000. ISBN: 1-57231-838-4. This guidebook to Windows 2000 Professional is a good source for information on configuring devices and managing hardware devices.

 Search the TechNet CD (or its online version through **www.microsoft.com**) and/or the *Windows 2000 Professional Resource Kit* CD using the keywords "devices", "hardware", "driver updates", "driver signing", "APM", "ACPI", and "Device Manager".

Implementing, Managing, and Troubleshooting Disk Drives and Volumes

8

Terms you'll need to understand:

- ✓ Basic versus dynamic disks
- ✓ Partitions and logical drives
- ✓ Simple, spanned, and striped volumes
- ✓ **diskperf.exe**
- ✓ File allocation table (FAT), or FAT16
- ✓ FAT32
- ✓ NT File System (NTFS) version 5
- ✓ **convert.exe**
- ✓ Mounted drives, or mount points
- ✓ Disk quotas
- ✓ NTFS compression

Techniques you'll need to master:

- ✓ Using the Disk Management tool
- ✓ Monitoring and troubleshooting disks using the Performance tool
- ✓ Using the Disk Cleanup Wizard and Disk Defragmenter
- ✓ Selecting a file system for Windows 2000
- ✓ Using **convert.exe** to convert a FAT partition to NTFS version 5
- ✓ Establishing and managing disk quotas
- ✓ Managing NTFS compressed files and folders
- ✓ Using Device Manager to manage tape devices and DVD drives

Hard Disk Management

This chapter discusses how to manage and troubleshoot hard disks in Windows 2000 Professional. We will look at options for creating partitions, formatting partitions, and disk administration available in Windows 2000. In addition, we will uncover features of the new disk storage types. Windows 2000 now supports two new disk configuration types—basic storage and dynamic storage. We will compare the differences between basic and dynamic storage types and learn how to configure and manage disks that have been initialized with either type of storage.

Basic Disks

A Windows 2000 *basic disk*, which is similar to the disk configuration we're used to in NT, is a physical disk with primary and extended partitions. As long as you use the file allocation table (FAT) file system (discussed in detail later in this chapter), Windows 2000, Windows NT, Windows 9x, and DOS can access basic disks. You can create up to three primary partitions and one extended partition on a basic disk, or just four primary partitions. You can create a single extended partition with logical drives on a basic disk. You *cannot* extend a basic disk.

Basic disks store their configuration information in the master boot record (MBR), which is stored on the first sector of the disk. The configuration of a basic disk consists of the partition information on the disk. Basic fault tolerant sets inherited from Windows NT 4 are based on these simple partitions, but they extend the configuration with some extra partition relationship information, which is stored on the first track of the disk.

Basic disks may contain spanned volumes (volume sets), mirrored volumes (mirror sets), striped volumes (stripe sets), and Redundant Array of Independent Disks (RAID)-5 volumes (stripe sets with parity) created using Windows NT 4 or earlier. These kinds of volumes are covered later in this chapter.

Dynamic Disks

A Windows 2000 *dynamic disk* is a physical disk that does not use partitions or logical drives. Instead, a single partition is created that includes the entire disk, which can then be divided into separate volumes. Also, dynamic disks do not have the same constraints of basic disks. For example, a dynamic disk can be resized on-the-fly without requiring a reboot. Dynamic disks are associated with *disk groups*, which are disks managed as a collection, which helps to organize dynamic disks. All dynamic disks in a computer are members of the same disk group. Each disk in a disk group stores replicas of the same configuration data. This configuration data is stored in a 1MB region at the end of each dynamic disk.

Dynamic disks can contain any of the types of volumes discussed later in this chapter. You can extend a volume on a dynamic disk. Dynamic disks can contain an unlimited number of volumes, so you are not restricted to four volumes per disk, as you are with basic disks. Regardless of the type of file system, only Windows 2000 computers can *directly* access dynamic volumes. However, computers that are not running Windows 2000 can access the dynamic volumes remotely when they are connected to shared folders over the network.

Comparing Basic Disks to Dynamic Disks

When you install Windows 2000, the system automatically configures the existing hard disks as basic disks. Windows 2000 does *not* support dynamic disks on laptops, and, if you're using an older (nonlaptop) machine that is not Advanced Configuration and Power Interface (ACPI)-compliant, the Upgrade To Dynamic Disk option (discussed later in this chapter) is not available. Dynamic disks have some additional limitations. You can install Windows 2000 on a dynamic volume that you *converted* from a basic disk, but you can't extend either the system or the boot partition. Volumes and upgrading are covered later in this chapter. Any troubleshooting tools that cannot read the dynamic Disk Management database work only on a basic disk.

Basic and dynamic disks are Windows 2000's way of looking at hard disk configuration. If you're migrating to Windows 2000 from NT, the dynamic disk concept might seem odd in the beginning, but once you understand the differences, working with dynamic disks is not complicated. You can format partitions with FAT16, FAT32, or NT File System (NTFS) on a basic or a dynamic disk. FAT and NTFS are discussed later in this chapter. Table 8.1 compares the terms used with basic and dynamic disks.

Table 8.1 Terms used with basic and dynamic disks.	
Basic Disks	**Dynamic Disks**
Active partition	Active volume
Extended partition	Volume and unallocated space
Logical drive	Simple volume
Mirror set	Mirrored volume (Server only)
Primary partition	Simple volume
Stripe set	Striped volume
Stripe set with parity	RAID-5 volume (Server only)
System and boot partitions	System and boot volumes
Volume set	Spanned volumes

Upgrading Disks

Upgrading Basic Disks to Dynamic Disks

You use Windows 2000's Disk Management tool to upgrade a basic disk to a dynamic disk. To access Disk Management, click Start|Programs|Administrative Tools|Computer Management; or simply right-click the My Computer icon on the desktop and select Manage. You'll find Disk Management under Storage.

For the upgrade to succeed, any disks to be upgraded must contain at least 1MB of unallocated space. Disk Management automatically reserves this space when creating partitions or volumes on a disk, but disks with partitions or volumes created by other operating systems may not have this space available. (This space can exist even if it is not visible in Disk Management.) Before you upgrade disks, close any programs that are running on those disks.

To change or convert a basic disk to a dynamic disk, perform the following steps:

1. Open the Disk Management tool.

2. Right-click the basic disk you want to change to a dynamic disk and then click Upgrade To Dynamic Disk.

When you upgrade a basic disk to a dynamic disk, you do not need to reboot. However, if you do upgrade your startup disk or upgrade a volume or partition, you must restart your computer for the change to take effect. The good news is that you do not need to select a special command like **Commit Changes Now** before restarting your computer or closing the Disk Management tool.

When you upgrade a basic disk to a dynamic disk, any existing partitions on the basic disk become simple volumes on the dynamic disk. Any existing mirrored volumes, striped volumes, RAID-5 volumes, or spanned volumes become dynamic mirrored volumes, dynamic striped volumes, dynamic RAID-5 volumes, or dynamic spanned volumes, respectively.

You *cannot* dual-boot to another operating system if you upgrade a basic disk to a dynamic disk, which typically isn't an issue for servers. However, it's something to consider for Windows 2000 Professional machines. After you upgrade a basic disk to a dynamic disk, you cannot change the dynamic volumes back to partitions. Instead, you must delete all dynamic volumes on the disk and then use the **Revert To Basic Disk** command.

Note: Upgrading to a dynamic disk is a one-way process. Yes, you can convert a dynamic disk with volumes back to a basic disk, but you'll lose all your data. Major downside! If you find yourself needing to do this, though, first save your data, convert the disk to basic, and then restore your data.

Because the upgrade from basic to dynamic is per physical disk, all volumes on a physical disk must be either basic or dynamic. Again, you do not need to restart your computer when you upgrade from a basic to a dynamic disk. The only times you must restart your computer are if you upgrade your startup disk or if you upgrade a volume or partition.

Convert Dynamic Disks to Basic Disks

You must remove all volumes from the dynamic disk before you can change it back to a basic disk. Once you change a dynamic disk back to a basic disk, you can create only partitions and logical drives on that disk. Once upgraded, a dynamic disk cannot contain partitions or logical drives, nor can Microsoft operating systems other than Windows 2000 access it.

To convert a dynamic disk to a basic disk, perform the following steps:

1. Open Disk Management.

2. Right-click the dynamic disk you want to change back to a basic disk and then click Revert To Basic Disk.

Moving Disks to Another Computer

To move disks to another computer, perform the following steps:

1. Before you disconnect the disks, look in Disk Management and make sure the status of the volumes on the disks is healthy. If the status is not healthy, repair the volumes *before* you move the disks.

2. Turn the computer off, remove the physical disks, and then install the physical disks on the other computer. Restart the computer that contains the disks you moved.

3. Open Disk Management.

4. Click Action and then on Rescan Disks.

5. Right-click any disk marked Foreign, click Import Foreign Disks, and then follow the instructions on your screen.

Guidelines for Relocating Disks

Every time you remove or import disks to a computer, you must click Action, click Rescan Disks, and then verify that the disk information is correct. Aside from following Steps 1 through 5 above, you can choose which disks from the group you want to add by clicking on Select Disk—you do not have to import all of the new disks.

Disk Management describes the condition of the volumes on the disks before you import them. Review this information carefully. If there are any problems, you will know what will happen to each volume on these disks once you have imported them. After you import a dynamic disk from another computer, you can see and use any existing volumes on that disk.

Reactivating a Missing or Offline Disk

A dynamic disk may become missing when it is corrupted, powered down, or disconnected. Only dynamic disks can be reactivated—not basic disks. Sorry!

To reactivate a missing or offline disk, perform the following steps:

1. Open Disk Management.

2. Right-click the disk marked Missing or Offline, and then click Reactivate Disk.

3. The disk should be marked Online after the disk is reactivated.

Basic Volumes

Basic volumes include partitions and logical drives, as well as volumes created using Windows NT 4 or earlier, such as volume sets, stripe sets, mirror sets, and stripe sets with parity. In Windows 2000, these volumes have been *renamed* to spanned volumes, striped volumes, mirrored volumes, and RAID-5 volumes, respectively. You can create basic volumes on basic disks only.

Spanned Volumes on Basic Disks

Disk Management offers limited support of spanned volumes on basic disks. You can delete spanned volumes, but you *cannot* create new spanned volumes or extend spanned volumes on basic disks. You can create new spanned volumes only on dynamic disks. Deleting a spanned volume deletes all the data contained in the volume as well as the partitions that make up the spanned volume. You can delete only entire spanned volumes. Disk Management renames all existing volume sets to Spanned Volumes. These spanned volumes reside only on basic disks. In Windows 2000, you can delete spanned volumes created using Windows NT 4 or earlier.

Striped Volumes on Basic Disks

Likewise, Disk Management offers limited support of striped volumes on basic disks. You can delete striped volumes, but you *cannot* create new striped volumes on basic disks. You can create new striped volumes on dynamic disks only. Deleting a striped volume deletes all the data contained in the volume as well as the partitions that make up the volume. You can delete only entire striped volumes. Disk Management renames all stripe sets to Striped Volumes. These striped volumes reside only on basic disks. In Windows 2000, you can delete striped volumes created using Windows NT 4 or earlier.

Partitions and Logical Drives on Basic Disks

You can create primary partitions, extended partitions, and logical drives only on basic disks. You should create partitions instead of dynamic volumes if your computer also runs a down-level Microsoft operating system.

Partitions and logical drives can reside only on basic disks. You can create up to four primary partitions on a basic disk, or up to three primary partitions and one extended partition. You can use the free space in an extended partition to create multiple logical drives.

You should create basic volumes, such as partitions or logical drives, on basic disks if you want computers running Windows NT 4 or earlier, Windows 98 or earlier, or MS-DOS to access these volumes.

Creating or Deleting a Partition or Logical Drive

To create or delete a partition or logical drive, perform the following:

1. Open Disk Management.

2. Right-click an unallocated region of a basic disk and then click Create Partition; alternatively, right-click free space in an extended partition and then click Create Logical Drive. (Delete Partition would be your selection if that were your goal.)

3. Using the Create Partition Wizard, click Next; click Primary Partition, Extended Partition, Or Logical Drive; then follow the instructions on your screen.

If you choose to delete a partition, all data on the deleted partition or logical drive is lost. You cannot recover deleted partitions or logical drives. You cannot delete the system partition, boot partition, or any partition that contains the active paging file.

Windows 2000 requires that all the logical drives or other volumes in an extended partition be deleted before you can delete the extended partition.

Dynamic Volumes

What are called *sets* (like mirrored sets and striped sets) in Windows NT 4, are called *volumes* (now mirrored volumes and striped volumes) in Windows 2000. Dynamic volumes are the only type of volume you can create on dynamic disks. With dynamic disks, you are no longer limited to four volumes per disk (as you were with basic disks). The only dynamic volumes that you can install Windows 2000 on are simple and mirrored volumes, and these volumes must contain the partition table (which means that these volumes must be either basic or upgraded from basic to dynamic). Only computers running Windows 2000 can access dynamic volumes. The five types of dynamic volumes are simple, spanned, mirrored, striped, and RAID-5.

Simple Volumes

A *simple volume* is made up of disk space on a single physical disk. It can consist of a single area on a disk or multiple areas on the same disk that are linked together.

To create a simple volume, perform the following steps:

1. Open Disk Management.

2. Right-click the unallocated space on the dynamic disk where you want to create the simple volume and then click Create Volume.

3. Using the Create Volume Wizard, click Next, click Simple Volume, and then follow the instructions on your screen.

Here are some guidelines about simple volumes:

➤ You can create simple volumes on dynamic disks only.

➤ Simple volumes are not fault tolerant.

➤ Simple volumes cannot contain partitions or logical drives.

➤ Neither MS-DOS nor Windows operating systems other than Windows 2000 can access simple volumes.

Spanned Volumes

A spanned volume is made up of disk space on more than one physical disk. You can add more space to a spanned volume by extending it at any time.

To create a spanned volume, perform the following steps:

1. Open Disk Management.

2. Right-click the unallocated space on one of the dynamic disks where you want to create the spanned volume and then click Create Volume.

3. Using the Create Volume Wizard, click Next, click Spanned Volume, and then follow the instructions on your screen.

Here are some guidelines about spanned volumes:

➤ You can create spanned volumes on dynamic disks only.

➤ You need at least two dynamic disks to create a spanned volume.

➤ You can extend a spanned volume onto a maximum of 32 dynamic disks.

➤ Spanned volumes cannot be mirrored or striped.

➤ Spanned volumes are not fault tolerant.

Extending a Simple or Spanned Volume

To extend a simple or spanned volume, perform the following steps:

1. Open Disk Management.

2. Right-click the simple or spanned volume you want to extend, click Extend Volume, and then follow the instructions on your screen.

Here are some guidelines about extending a simple or a spanned volume:

➤ You can extend a volume only if it contains *no* file system or if it is formatted using NTFS. You cannot extend volumes formatted using FAT or FAT32.

➤ You can extend a simple volume within its original disk or onto additional disks. If you extend a simple volume across multiple disks, it becomes a *spanned volume*.

➤ Once a volume is extended onto multiple disks (spanned), you cannot mirror or stripe it.

➤ Once a spanned volume is extended, no portion of it can be deleted without the entire spanned volume being deleted.

➤ You can extend a simple or extended volume only if the volume was created as a dynamic volume. You cannot extend a simple or extended volume that was upgraded from basic to dynamic.

➤ You can extend simple and spanned volumes on dynamic disks onto a maximum of 32 dynamic disks.

Note: You cannot extend a system volume or boot volume. You cannot extend striped, mirrored, and RAID-5 volumes.

Striped Volumes

A *striped volume* stores data in stripes on two or more physical disks. Data in a striped volume is allocated alternately and evenly (in stripes) to the disks of the striped volume. Striped volumes can substantially improve the speed of access to your data on disk. In addition, you can create striped volumes on both Windows 2000 Professional and Server machines.

To create a striped volume, perform the following steps:

1. Open Disk Management.

2. Right-click unallocated space on one of the dynamic disks where you want to create the striped volume and then click Create Volume.

3. Using the Create Volume Wizard, click Next, click Striped Volume, and then follow the instructions on your screen.

Here are some guidelines about striped volumes:

➤ You need at least two physical, dynamic disks to create a striped volume.

➤ You can create a striped volume onto a maximum of 32 disks.

➤ Striped volumes are not fault tolerant and cannot be extended or mirrored.

RAID-5 Volumes

You can create RAID-5 volumes *only* on Windows 2000 Server machines.

Note: Mirrored and RAID-5 volumes are available only on computers that are running Windows 2000 Server. Windows 2000 Professional computers can use basic and dynamic disks but cannot host software-based fault-tolerant disk configurations such as mirror sets and stripe sets with parity. You can, however, use a computer running Windows 2000 Professional to create mirrored and RAID-5 volumes on a remote computer running Windows 2000 Server.

Limitations of Dynamic Disks and Dynamic Volumes

You can use dynamic disks and dynamic volumes in specific circumstances; you need to be familiar with when you can and cannot utilize them.

When You Are Installing Windows 2000

If you create a dynamic volume from unallocated space on a dynamic disk, you cannot install Windows 2000 on that volume. The setup limitation occurs because Windows 2000 Setup recognizes only dynamic volumes that contain partition tables. Partition tables appear in basic volumes and in dynamic volumes only when they have been upgraded from basic to dynamic. If you create a new dynamic volume on a dynamic disk, that new dynamic volume does not contain a partition table.

When You Are Extending a Volume

If you upgrade a basic volume to dynamic (by upgrading the basic disk to a dynamic one), you can install Windows 2000 on that volume, but you *cannot* extend the volume. The limitation on extending volumes occurs because the boot volume, which contains the Windows 2000 files, cannot be part of a spanned volume. If you extend a simple volume that contains a partition table (that is, a volume that was upgraded from basic to dynamic), Windows 2000 Setup recognizes the spanned volume but cannot install to it because the boot volume cannot be part of a spanned volume.

You can extend volumes that you created only after you convert the disk to a dynamic disk. You can extend volumes and make changes to disk configuration in most cases without rebooting your computer. If you want to take advantage of these features in Windows 2000, especially software fault-tolerant features, you must change or upgrade a disk from basic to dynamic status, covered earlier in this chapter. Use dynamic disks if your computer runs only Windows 2000. If you want to use more than four volumes per disk, create fault-tolerant volumes such as RAID-5 and mirrored volumes, or extend volumes onto one or more dynamic disks.

Troubleshooting Disks and Volumes

If a disk or volume fails, naturally you want to repair it as soon as possible to avoid losing data. The Disk Management snap-in makes it easy to locate problems quickly. In the Status column of the list view, you can view the status of a disk or volume. The status also appears in the graphical view of each disk or volume.

Diagnosing Problems

To diagnose disk and/or volume problems, perform the following steps:

1. Open Add/Remove Hardware in the Control Panel. Click Next.

2. Click Add/Troubleshoot A Device and then click Next. Windows 2000 tries to detect new Plug and Play devices.

3. Choose the device you want to diagnose and fix, and then click Next.

4. Follow the instructions on the screen.

Monitoring Disk Performance

The *Windows 2000 Performance tool* is composed of two parts: System Monitor and Performance Logs And Alerts. On the Start menu, the Performance tool is no longer labeled Performance Monitor; it's just Performance. With *System Monitor*, you can collect and view realtime data about disk performance and activity in graph, histogram, or report form. *Performance Logs And Alerts* allows you to configure logs to record performance data and to set system alerts to notify you when a specified counter's value is above or below a defined threshold.

To open Performance, perform the following steps:

1. Click Start|Settings|Control Panel.

2. In the Control Panel, double-click Administrative Tools, and then double-click Performance. You will use System Monitor within Performance to monitor disk performance.

Diskperf.exe

Diskperf.exe controls the types of counters that you can view using System Monitor. You must enable **diskperf.exe** *before* you can monitor logical disks. By default, the system is set to collect *physical* drive data. Logical drive data is *not* collected by default; you enable it specifically with **diskperf.exe**. Table 8.2 lists the available **diskperf.exe** parameters, or switches.

Detecting and Repairing Disk Errors

In pre-Windows 2000 operating systems, ScanDisk detected and fixed disk errors. In Windows 2000, you can use the Error-Checking tool to check for file system errors and bad sectors on your hard disk.

To run the Error-Checking tool, perform the following steps:

1. Open My Computer and right-click the local disk you want to check.

2. Select Properties.

3. Click the Tools tab.

4. Under Error-Checking, click Check Now.

5. Under Check Disk Options, select the Scan For And Attempt Recovery Of Bad Sectors checkbox.

All files must be closed for the Error-Checking process to run. Your volume is not available to run any other tasks while this process is running. If the volume is currently in use, a message asks if you want to reschedule the disk checking for the next time you restart your system. Then, the next time you restart your system, disk-checking runs. If your volume is formatted as NTFS, Windows 2000 automatically logs all file transactions, replaces bad clusters automatically, and stores copies of key information for all files on the NTFS volume.

Table 8.2 Diskperf.exe parameters.	
Parameter	Description
-y	Sets the system to start both physical and logical disk performance counters when the system is restarted.
-yd	Enables disk performance counters that are used for measuring performance of physical drives when the system is restarted. This is the default setting.
-yv	Enables disk performance counters that are used for measuring performance of logical drives when the system is restarted.
-n	Sets the system to not use any disk performance counters when the system is restarted.
-nd	Disables disk performance counters for physical drives when the system is restarted.
-nv	Disables disk performance counters for logical drives when the system is restarted.
Computername	Specifies the computer on which you want to see or set disk performance counter use. If a computer name is not specified, the local computer is assumed.

Using Disk Defragmenter

Disk Defragmenter rearranges files, programs, and unused space on your computer's hard disk(s), allowing programs to run faster and files to open more quickly. Putting the pieces of files and programs in a more contiguous space on disk reduces the time the operating system needs to open a requested item.

To run Disk Defragmenter, perform the following steps:

1. Click Start|Programs|Accessories|System Tools and then click Disk Defragmenter tool.

2. Select which disk(s) you would like to defragment and any additional options you would like.

Understanding Why Files Are Not Moved to the Beginning of NTFS Volumes

On NTFS volumes, Windows 2000 reserves a portion of the free space for a system file called the *master file table (MFT)*. The MFT is where Windows stores all the information it needs to retrieve files from the volume. Windows stores part of the MFT at the beginning of the volume. Windows reserves the MFT for exclusive use, so Disk Defragmenter cannot and does not move files to the beginning of volumes.

Using the Disk Cleanup Wizard

Disk Cleanup helps free up space on your hard drive by searching your drive(s) and then showing you a list of temporary files, Internet cache files, and unnecessary program files that you can safely delete. You can instruct Disk Cleanup to delete none, some, or all of those files.

To use the Disk Cleanup Wizard, perform the following steps:

1. Click Start|Programs|Accessories|System Tools.

2. Click the Disk Cleanup icon.

File Systems Supported in Windows 2000

The *Compact Disc File System (CDFS)* does have full support for CD-based media in Windows 2000. Although Windows 2000 does not support *High Performance File System (HPFS)*, it fully supports the FAT, FAT32, and NTFS file systems.

FAT and FAT32

Windows 2000 has full FAT (also known as FAT16) and FAT32 file system support with the following conditions or specifications:

➤ Pre-existing FAT32 partitions up to 127GB mount and are supported in Windows 2000.

➤ Windows 2000 allows you to create only new FAT32 volumes of 32GB or less.

➤ You can install Windows 2000 onto a FAT, FAT32, or NTFS partition. Keep in mind that you have *no* local security for Windows 2000 unless you place the operating system on an NTFS partition.

➤ If you initially install Windows 2000 to a FAT or FAT32 partition and then later used the Convert.exe utility to convert the partition to NTFS, default security settings are not applied.

The New Flavor of NTFS: Windows 2000's NTFS 5 File System

Windows 2000 contains a new version of NTFS File System. NTFS 5 is Windows 2000's native file system. This newest version of NTFS includes capabilities such as much more granular file permissions than NTFS 4, such as, disk quotas, an Encrypting File System (EFS), and a number of other useful features. Disk quotas is covered later in this chapter.

 When you install Windows 2000, existing NTFS volumes are automatically upgraded to NTFS 5. No options are presented to choose NTFS 5 during the installation. The existing volumes are simply converted to NTFS 5 whether you want it or not.

When you install Windows 2000 to an NTFS partition, part of the Setup process is to apply default security settings to the system files and folders located on the boot partition (essentially the \WINNT and \Program Files structures).

All local NTFS volumes, including removable media, are upgraded to the new version of NTFS. This occurs after you restart your computer the first time after the graphical portion of Setup. Any NTFS volumes that are removed or powered off during the installation or upgrade process are upgraded automatically when those drives are mounted. If, during the installation, the system detects a version of Windows NT earlier than NT 4 Service Pack 4 (SP4), you see a warning message indicating that an earlier version of Windows NT was found; which states that Windows NT will not be accessible if you continue. Windows NT *can* be upgraded without service packs. However, if you want to create a new installation of Windows 2000 and dual boot with Windows NT 4, then the warning will be seen.

 If you want to configure your computer to run Windows NT 4 and Windows 2000, you need to upgrade your version of Windows NT to SP4 or later. There is an updated NTFS.SYS driver in NT 4 SP4 and later SPs that allows NT 4 to read from and write to NTFS 5 volumes in Windows 2000. If you expect to dual-boot Windows 98 and Windows 2000, remember that Windows 98 can read only FAT and FAT32 file systems.

Converting from One File System to Another

Windows 2000 supports converting from one file system to another, with some special caveats and limitations that you need to be well aware of.

Reality—Converting a FAT Partition to an NTFS Partition

Let's say that you want to convert drive D to NTFS, from either FAT or FAT32. No problem! From the command line (CMD.EXE), enter the command **convert d: /fs:ntfs**. This command is one way and is not reversible. If the FAT or FAT32 partition is the system partition, the conversion takes place when the machine reboots next.

After the conversion, NTFS file permissions are set to Full Control for the Everyone Group. However, if you install Windows 2000 directly to NTFS, the permissions for the \WINNT folder and \Program Files folder structures are best secured.

Myth—Converting an NTFS Partition to a FAT Partition

You *cannot* convert an NTFS partition to a FAT partition. A simple conversion using the **convert.exe** command is not possible. Your only course of action if you want to keep the data is to back up all the data on the drive. Then, use the Disk Management tool to reformat the disk to the flavor of FAT you prefer and restore your data backup to your newly formatted disk.

Reapplying Default NTFS Permissions

You may need or want to reapply the default NTFS permissions to the system boot partition if you changed them or if you never applied them to begin with (because you converted the boot partition to NTFS after installation). To reapply the default NTFS permissions, use the secedit.exe utility, which comes with Windows 2000, from the command prompt. The computer must still be bootable to Windows 2000 for this to work.

Assigning, Changing, or Removing a Drive Letter

To assign, change, or remove a drive letter, perform the following steps:

1. Open Disk Management.

2. Right-click a partition, logical drive, or volume, and then click Change Drive Letter And Path.

3. Do one of the following:

   ➤ *To assign a drive letter*—Right-click target volume and select Add, click the drive letter you want to use, and then click OK.

   ➤ *To change a drive letter*—Right-click target volume and select Edit, click the drive letter you want to use, and then click OK.

   ➤ *To remove a drive letter*— Right-click target volume and then select Remove from the context menu.

An old "gotcha" still applies. Be careful when assigning drive letters because many MS-DOS and Windows applications refer to a specific drive letter, especially at installation. For example, the path environment variable shows specific drive letters in conjunction with program names.

You can use up to 24 drive letters, from C through Z. Drive letters A and B are reserved for floppy disk drives. However, if you do not have a floppy disk drive B, you can use the letter B for a network drive. You cannot change the drive letter of the system volume or boot volume.

An error message may appear when you attempt to assign a letter to a volume, CD-ROM drive, or other removable media device, possibly because a program in the system is using it. If this happens, close the program that is accessing the volume or drive, and then click the Change Drive Letter And Path command again.

Windows 2000 allows you to statically assign drive letters on volumes, partitions, and CD-ROM drives. This means that you permanently assign a drive letter to a specific partition, volume, or CD-ROM drive. When you add a new hard disk to an existing computer system, it does not affect statically assigned drive letters. You can also mount a local drive at an empty folder on an NTFS volume by using a drive path instead of a drive letter. Read on—we'll get to this shortly.

Mounted Drives

Mounted drives, also known as *mount points* or *mounted volumes*, are useful for increasing a drive's "size" without disturbing it. For example, you could create a mount point to drive E as C:\CompanyData, thus seeming to increase the size available on the C partition, which would specifically allow you to store more data in C:\CompanyData than you could otherwise. Drive paths are available only on empty folders on NTFS volumes. The NTFS volumes can be basic or dynamic.

Creating a Mounted Drive

To create a mounted drive, perform the following steps:

1. Open Disk Management.

2. Right-click the partition or volume you want to mount and then click Change Drive Letter And Path.

3. Do one of the following:

   ➤ *To mount a volume*—Select Add. Click Mount In This NTFS Folder and type the path to an empty folder on an NTFS volume, or click Browse to locate it.

   ➤ *To unmount a volume*—Select the volume and then click Remove.

When you mount a local drive at an empty folder on an NTFS volume, Windows 2000 assigns a drive path to the drive rather than a drive letter.

To modify a drive path, remove it and then create a new drive path using the new location. You cannot modify the drive path directly. If you are administering a local computer, you can browse NTFS folders on that computer. If you are administering a remote computer, browsing is disabled and you must type the path to an existing NTFS folder.

The Logical Drives Tool

Logical Drives is a tool within the Computer Management snap-in that lets you manage mapped drives and local drives on a remote computer or local computer. You can change drive properties only on computers for which you are an Administrator.

Viewing Drive Properties, Changing Drive Labels, and Changing Security Settings

To view drive properties, change drive labels, or change security settings, perform the following steps:

1. Open Computer Management (Local). You can view drive properties on a remote computer as well if you want. To access a remote computer, right-click Computer Management (Local), click Connect To Another Computer, and then select the computer you wish to manage.

2. In the console tree, click Logical Drives. Perform the following actions to view the Logical Drives:

   ➤ Expand the Computer Management (Local) item.

   ➤ Expand the Storage item.

   ➤ Expand the Logical Drives item.

3. Right-click the drive for which you want to view the properties and then click Properties.

The General tab shows the drive label, its type, the file system for which the drive is formatted, its total capacity, how much space on the drive is used, and how much space is free (available). The Security tab shows the access permissions, audit entries, and ownership that have been set for the drive. The Security tab appears only on drives formatted to use NTFS.

Disk Quotas

Windows 2000 disk quotas track and control disk usage per user and per volume. You can apply disk quotas only to Windows 2000 NTFS volumes. Quotas are tracked for each volume, even if the volumes reside on the same physical disk. The per-user feature of quotas allows you to track every user's disk space usage regardless of which folder the user stores files in. Disk quotas do not use compression to measure disk space usage, so users cannot obtain or use more space simply by compressing their own data. To enable disk quotas, open the Properties dialog box for a disk, select the Quota tab, and configure the options.

When a user no longer stores data on a volume, you need to delete disk quota entries. The catch to this is that you can delete the user's quota entries only after you have removed from the volume all files that the user owns, or after another user has taken ownership of the files. By default, only members of the Administrators group can view and change quota entries and settings.

 Set identical or individual disk quota limits for all user accounts that access a specific volume. Then, use per-user disk quota entries to allow more (a fairly common scenario) or less (for those disk space hogs!) disk space to individual users when necessary.

NTFS Compression

NTFS in Windows 2000 allows you to compress individual files and folders so that they occupy less space on the NTFS volume. Any Windows- or DOS-based program can read and write to compressed files *without* having to decompress them first. They decompress when opened and recompress when closed. NTFS handles this entire process. You can use Windows Explorer to have compressed items display in a different color than uncompressed items.

Setting the compression state (compressed or uncompressed) on a file or folder is as simple as setting a file or folder attribute. Simply right-click the object you'd like to compress/uncompress and select Properties. On the General tab, select the Advanced button. Check or clear the Compress Contents To Save Disk Space checkbox. Click OK twice to exit both dialog boxes.

Moving and Copying Compressed Files and Folders

There is a simple method to remembering whether the original compression attribute of an object is retained or inherited when you are moving and/or copying files and folders. When you move a compressed or uncompressed file or folder from one location to another within the same NTFS volume, the original compression attribute is retained. That's it. That is the only piece of this puzzle you need to remember because in *all* other scenarios, the compression attribute is inherited from the new, or target, location.

NTFS Compression Guidelines

NTFS allocates disk space based on the *uncompressed* size of a file. If you try to copy a compressed file to an NTFS volume with enough space for the compressed file, but not the uncompressed file, you get an error message telling you there is inadequate disk space to copy the file to the target. Plan ahead.

 If you attempt to copy or move a compressed file to a floppy, be prepared for the Insufficient Disk Space error. If the uncompressed size of the file is larger than the capacity of the floppy, you cannot copy or move the file. Use a third-party compression tool, such as WinZip, for this operation.

Make it a practice to compress only static data rather than data that frequently changes, because applying or removing the compression attribute does incur system overhead. NTFS encryption and compression are mutually exclusive. You can encrypt or compress a file or folder but not both. Windows 2000 does not support NTFS compression for volumes with cluster sizes larger than 4KB because of the performance degradation it would cause.

Managing Tape Devices

Windows 2000 provides comprehensive control of tape devices. You can back up or restore from tape devices, enable or disable specific tapes in your library, insert and eject media, and mount and dismount media. Good news: Tape devices are no longer the exclusive media that the Windows Backup program utilizes. Backing up to tape is still very popular, though.

If the tape device is Plug and Play compliant, you can rely on Windows 2000 to detect the device and install the appropriate drivers, as well as allocate system resources for the device. If you are using a tape device that is not Plug and Play compliant, use the Add/Remove Hardware applet in the Control Panel to install the drivers and assign resources for the device. Use Device Manager to enable, disable, or edit settings for any tape device.

Configuring and Managing DVD Devices

Windows 2000 supports a variety of DVD drives and formats. Check with the most recent Hardware Compatibility List (HCL) or your hardware vendor to see if your DVD device will work with Windows 2000. For more details on managing hardware in Windows 2000, see Chapter 7.

If the DVD device is Plug and Play compliant, you can rely on Windows 2000 to detect the device and install the appropriate drivers, as well as allocate system resources for the device. If you are using a DVD drive that is not Plug and Play compliant, use the Add/Remove Hardware applet in the Control Panel to install the drivers and assign resources for the device.

 You can control whether or not unsigned drivers for DVD drives and other hardware are permitted. You can make this decision in two places. If you are performing unattended installations of Windows 2000, you can add an entry to the Unattend.txt file in the [Unattended] section called DriverSigningPolicy=Ignore. The other location where you can control whether drivers must be signed is within Policy—either a Group Policy Object applied to a site, domain, or OU (SDOU); or simply the Local Computer Policy. Within Policy, you have three choices for how unsigned drivers are handled when they are encountered: Ignore them; Warn about them, but allow their installation; and Block their installation completely.

Your DVD drive needs either a hardware or software decoder to play movies, as well as Windows 2000-compatible sound and video cards with their respective drivers. Your decoder must be Windows 2000 compliant to play movies after you install Windows 2000. Most hardware decoders are Windows 2000 compliant. Most software decoders, however, need an update. You do not need a decoder for reading data DVDs. If no update is available, buy a new decoder that is Windows 2000 compliant.

Practice Questions

Question 1

> You upgrade a computer that is running Windows NT 4 Workstation to Windows 2000 Professional. The computer has a single disk drive with three primary partitions and one extended partition. The extended partition is configured with four logical drives. One of the primary partitions is configured as drive F and is formatted as NTFS. You convert the disk to a dynamic disk. You add a second hard disk, convert it to a dynamic disk, and then attempt to extend drive F to include 2GB of the unallocated space on the new disk. The bad news: You cannot extend drive F. What is the most likely reason for this?
>
> ○ a. Drive F is formatted with a pre-Windows 2000 version of NTFS.
>
> ○ b. You do not have enough free space (at least 1MB) on the original hard disk.
>
> ○ c. A volume can be extended only on its original hard disk.
>
> ○ d. You cannot extend a volume that was originally created on a basic disk.

Answer d is correct. When Windows 2000 is installed on a machine running Windows NT Workstation 4, any existing NTFS partitions and logical drives are updated to the Windows 2000 version of NTFS, also called NTFS 5. If a primary partition or a logical drive is created on a basic disk and the disk is then converted to a dynamic disk, the partitions and logical drives on the disk are converted to simple volumes. You cannot extend these simple volumes that were originally created on a basic disk. It is true that 1MB of free space must be available on a basic disk before it can be converted to a dynamic disk. It is also true that a volume can be extended to include available space on another fixed disk. Once this is done, the extended volume becomes, in Windows 2000 terms, a spanned volume instead of a simple volume.

Question 2

You want to run Windows 98 and Windows 2000 Professional on your computer. Your computer has three disks that are each configured as a single partition. Disk 0 is where you have Windows 98 installed. Disk 1 is where Windows 2000 is installed. You need file security for Windows 2000. Disk 2 is where you are storing Graphics department files and projects. You need to be able to access the data on Disk 2 regardless of which operating system you are using. Drag and drop the best file system choice for each drive next to the appropriate place.

Disk 0 _____   FAT16

Disk 1 _____   FAT32

Disk 2 _____   NTFS

The correct answer should show Disk 0 as FAT32, Disk 1 as NTFS, and Disk 2 as FAT32. FAT32 is needed on Disk 2 so both operating systems can access files stored on this disk, plus it is the most efficient file system. NTFS is needed on Disk 1 as file security is needed.

Question 3

You create two primary partitions and one extended partition on a basic disk of a computer that is running Windows 2000 Professional. The disk has 8GB of unallocated space. You create three logical drives in the extended partition. You format one of the logical drives (let's call it drive G) as NTFS and use it for storing Engineering department data. You decide that you need more space allocated to this logical drive. You have 4GB of unallocated space available on a second disk drive on the same machine. What can you do to increase the amount of storage available in that logical drive?

○ a. Convert both disk drives to dynamic disks. Extend the simple volume that was the original logical drive by using that volume and unallocated space from the second disk drive.

○ b. Extend drive G by creating a volume set using the logical drive and unallocated space from the second disk drive.

○ c. Create a new partition or volume on the second disk drive. Create a new folder on drive G. Mount the new partition or volume to that folder.

○ d. Create a new partition or volume on the second disk drive and mount it to the folder in which the Engineering department data resides.

Answer c is correct. You need to create a new partition (basic disk) or volume (dynamic disk) and mount it to an empty folder on drive G. A partition or folder can be mounted only to an empty folder. Only a volume you initially create on a dynamic disk can be extended. Because the logical drive here was created on a basic disk, it cannot be extended, therefore answers a and b are incorrect. Answer d is incorrect as it makes the problem worse. Mounting the folder in the Engineering department partition is the partition in which we are trying to increase the amount of space. Mounting the folder to this partition would decrease the amount of space available.

Question 4

For a new DVD drive, you have decided to use a vendor-supplied hardware driver that is not digitally signed. You are preparing for the unattended installation of 150 Windows 2000 Professional machines that will have identical hardware, including the new DVD drive. How do you prepare for using non-signed drivers in an unattended installation to avoid interactive warnings?

- ○ a. In the driver subdirectory of the distribution folder, change this vendor-supplied driver's .INF file where it references the driver catalog file.

- ○ b. In the [Unattended] section of the answer file, add an entry with this syntax: "DriverSigningPolicy=Ignore".

- ○ c. On the server where your distribution source resides, go to the System Properties Hardware tab. Select the Driver Signing button and then choose the Ignore radio button. After you complete the unattended installations, change this setting back to the default.

- ○ d. Flag this specific driver in the Txtsetup.oem file specified in the [OEMBootFiles] section of the answer file.

Answer b is correct. You must use the answer file to indicate that there is a non-signed driver so that Setup will continue without requiring user intervention. Any manual settings in this case, other than within the answer file, are incorrect and will cause Setup to halt and require intervention. Therefore, answers a and c are incorrect. The [OEMBootFiles] section is the wrong place to make the setting change in the answer file. Therefore, answer d is incorrect. The txtsetup.oem file cannot be used for assigning an unsigned driver parameter, which makes answer d incorrect.

Question 5

You install Windows 2000 Professional on a computer in your office on which Windows NT 4 Workstation was installed. During the installation, you create a new 3.5GB partition and indicate the partition should be formatted as FAT. You want to be able to boot back to Windows NT 4, so you indicate that the Windows 2000 system files should be installed on this new 3.5GB partition. Once installation is finished and you boot the computer back to Windows NT 4, you discover that you cannot access the new partition from Windows NT 4. What's the most likely reason?

○ a. Setup converted the partition to FAT32.

○ b. Windows NT 4 cannot access a partition that is larger than 2.5GB.

○ c. Setup converted the partition to Windows 2000 NTFS when you indicated that the partition should be used for the system files.

○ d. The Windows NT logon account you are using does not have permission to access the new partition.

Answer a is correct. When you use Setup to create and format a partition, Setup formats a partition larger than 2GB as FAT32, even if you indicate that it is to be formatted as FAT. The FAT file system does not support partitions larger than 2GB. Windows 2000 system files do not have to be on an NTFS partition, so Setup does not convert the partition to NTFS 5. Therefore, answer c is incorrect. If you have at least SP4 for NT 4 installed, you can access NTFS 5 partitions from your Windows NT 4 installations. Windows NT can access partitions larger than 2GB—in fact, it can access partitions as large as 16EB! Therefore, answer b is false. Permissions for your NT account are a potential problem only if you formatted the new partition as NTFS. For both NT 4 and Windows 2000, the default NTFS permissions for a new partition give Full Control to the everyone group. Therefore, answer d is incorrect.

Question 6

You are teaching people in your office how to manage NTFS permissions and compression attributes because they are unfamiliar with NTFS. You want to give them a simple system to help them remember what happens to the original NTFS file and folder permissions and attributes when you move and/or copy data. Drag and drop the correct result on the right to the actions on the left. You may of course use each selection more than once if needed.

Files and folders moved among different NTFS volumes _____	RETAINED
	INHERITED
Files and folders moved within the same NTFS volume _____	
Files and folders copied to a different NTFS volume _____	
Files and folders copied within the same NTFS volume _____	

The correct answer should show INHERITED, RETAINED, INHERITED, INHERITED from top to bottom. There is only one instance when file permissions are retained and that is when a file has been moved to a new location on the same partition. In all other instances file permissions will be inherited.

Question 7

You want to delete a quota entry defined for a user's account on drive E of a computer that is running Windows 2000 Professional. What utility or command should you use to locate the files owned by the user and move the files to a shared folder on another Windows 2000 machine on your network?

○ a. System applet in Control Panel

○ b. Windows Explorer

○ c. Disk Management

○ d. Active Directory Users And Computers

Answer c is correct. You use the Disk Quota Management System within Disk Management. From the dialog box where Quota Entries for drive E are listed, delete the user's quota entry. Doing so yields the Disk Quota dialog box and allows you to move, delete, or take ownership of the files that the user owns on drive E. Therefore, answer a is incorrect as the System applet can be used to open the Disk Management console, but it cannot be used to edit quota entries. Windows Explorer does have a search feature, but a file's owner is not an available search criteria. Therefore, answer b is incorrect. Information about individual files that a user owns is not available in Active Directory Users And Computers, not to mention that Active Directory Users And Computers is not installed by default on Windows 2000 Professional. Therefore, answer d is incorrect.

Question 8

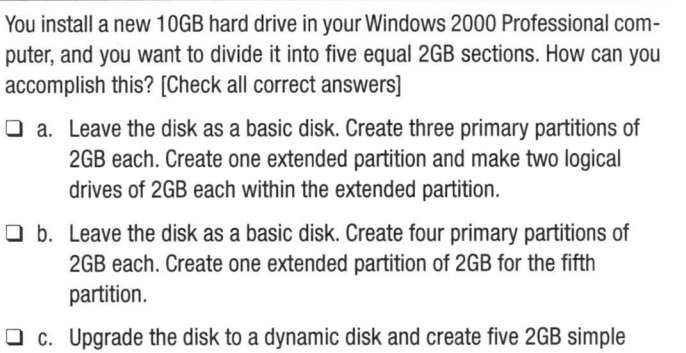

You install a new 10GB hard drive in your Windows 2000 Professional computer, and you want to divide it into five equal 2GB sections. How can you accomplish this? [Check all correct answers]

❑ a. Leave the disk as a basic disk. Create three primary partitions of 2GB each. Create one extended partition and make two logical drives of 2GB each within the extended partition.

❑ b. Leave the disk as a basic disk. Create four primary partitions of 2GB each. Create one extended partition of 2GB for the fifth partition.

❑ c. Upgrade the disk to a dynamic disk and create five 2GB simple volumes on it.

❑ d. Upgrade the disk to a dynamic disk. Create five primary partitions of 2GB each on the disk.

Answers a and c are correct. You cannot have more than four partitions on a basic disk, but you can overcome this limitation by converting a disk from basic to dynamic. Dynamic disks do not contain partitions or logical disks; they contain volumes. Answer d is incorrect as a dynamic disk cannot contain primary partitions. It just contains volumes. A basic disk can have the maximum of four primary partitions or three primary partitions, and one extended partition, therefore answer b is incorrect.

Question 9

> You are trying to create a striped volume on your Windows 2000 Professional computer to improve performance. You confirm that you have plenty of unallocated free space on two disks in your computer. When you right-click an area of free space on a disk, your only option is to create a partition. Explain the problem and the best way to resolve it.
>
> ○ a. You can create striped volumes only when you have at least one dynamic disk. Upgrade one of the disks from basic to dynamic, and then you can create the striped volume.
>
> ○ b. You can create striped volumes only if the disks involved are dynamic, not basic. Upgrade the disks that will be participating in the striped volume from basic to dynamic. After the disks are dynamic, you can create the striped volume.
>
> ○ c. In order to create a striped set, you need a second controller in the computer so that there is a single controller for each disk. Upgrading the disks from basic to dynamic is also required.
>
> ○ d. Windows 2000 Professional does not support striped volumes. To create a striped volume, you need to first install Windows 2000 Server or Advanced Server on your computer.

Answer b is correct. You can create striped volumes only on dynamic disks, but you do not need multiple controllers. The option to create a partition rather than a (striped) volume indicates that the disk you are trying to use is a basic disk. If you upgrade all the disks to dynamic, they can be part of a striped volume. Answer a is incorrect as the minimum of two dynamic disks are required to create a striped volume, not one. Answer c is incorrect because a second controller is not needed. Windows 2000 Professional does support striped volumes but it does not support RAID-5 volumes, therefore answer d is incorrect.

Question 10

You add a new disk to your computer. Next, you try to extend an existing volume to include the unallocated space on the new disk, but the option to extend the volume is not available. What is the most likely cause of the problem?

○ a. The existing volume is part of a striped volume on a dynamic disk.

○ b. The existing volume is part of a spanned volume on a basic disk.

○ c. You cannot extend the volume because the disk is basic instead of dynamic.

○ d. The existing volume is not formatted with NTFS. Only NTFS volumes can be extended.

Answer d is correct. A volume can be extended regardless of whether it is on a basic or dynamic disk therefore answer c is incorrect. The option to extend the disk is only related to the fact the drive had not been formatted with NTFS yet, and therefore answers a and b are incorrect.

Need to Know More?

 Microsoft Corporation. *Microsoft Windows 2000 Professional Resource Kit.* Redmond, Washington: Microsoft Press, 2000. ISBN: 1-57231-808-2. Chapter 1 of this book has invaluable information on file systems and disk concepts. Chapter 6 offers valuable details on file system considerations and multiple boot configurations.

 Nielsen, Morten Strunge. *Windows 2000 Professional Configuration and Implementation.* Scottsdale, Arizona: The Coriolis Group, 2000. ISBN: 1-57610-528-8. This book provides useful information on NTFS 5 and working with Windows 2000 disks, volumes, and file systems.

 Stinson, Craig and Carl Siechert. *Running Microsoft Windows 2000 Professional.* Redmond, Washington: Microsoft Press, 2000. ISBN: 1-57231-838-4. This guidebook to Windows 2000 Professional is a good source for information on NTFS 5 and disk management.

  Search the TechNet CD (or its online version through **www.microsoft.com**) and/or the Windows 2000 Professional Resource Kit CD using the keywords "Disks," "Volumes," "Basic and dynamic," "NTFS 5," "File systems," "Disk quotas," and "Disk management."

Implementing, Managing, and Troubleshooting Network Protocols and Services

9

Terms you'll need to understand:

✓ Transmission Control Protocol/Internet Protocol (TCP/IP)

✓ Dynamic Host Configuration Protocol (DHCP)

✓ Domain Name System (DNS)

✓ Windows Internet Name Service (WINS)

✓ Automatic Private IP Addressing (APIPA)

✓ Serial Line Internet Protocol (SLIP)

✓ Point-to-Point Protocol (PPP)

✓ Point-to-Point Tunneling Protocol (PPTP)

✓ Layer 2 Tunneling Protocol (L2TP)

✓ World Wide Web (WWW)

✓ Hypertext Transfer Protocol (HTTP)

✓ Internet Information Services (IIS) 5

✓ File Transfer Protocol (FTP)

✓ Simple Mail Transfer Protocol (SMTP)

✓ Address Resolution Protocol (ARP)

✓ **hostname**

✓ **ipconfig**

✓ **ping**

✓ **route**

✓ **tracert**

✓ Dial-up Networking (DUN)

✓ Remote Access Services (RAS)

✓ Virtual Private Network (VPN)

✓ Internet Connection Sharing (ICS)

Techniques you'll need to master:

✓ Configuring and troubleshooting TCP/IP

✓ Setting up DUN connections

✓ Establishing VPN connections

✓ Configuring and troubleshooting ICS

You can think of computer networking protocols as languages. Just as two people must speak the same language in order to communicate well, two or more computers on a network must share the same protocol so that they can communicate. Imagine that we could build a bridge to China from the United States—think of the bridge as the physical cabling of a network that allows traffic to pass over it. But even though traffic can be physically transported over the bridge, if the people going across the bridge can't speak a common language (e.g., English or Chinese), very little communication will take place. The popularity of the Internet has made the TCP/IP protocol a *de facto* standard for networking today. Windows 2000 makes extensive use of TCP/IP.

Configuring and Troubleshooting Transmission Control Protocol/Internet Protocol (TCP/IP)

TCP/IP is a time-proven and robust set of computer networking tools and services. Born in the 1960s out of the ARPANET project for the U.S. Department of Defense (DoD), TCP/IP encompasses a vast array of utilities and network services. This suite of services has evolved to become a de facto standard for both the Internet and for local area networks (LANs) using personal computer network operating systems like Novell NetWare 5 and Windows 2000.

TCP/IP is the default protocol when you install Windows 2000 Professional. It provides a means for connecting dissimilar computer systems. TCP/IP scales well—it works well for small, medium-sized, or large organizations. TCP/IP and its name resolution partner, Domain Name System (DNS), are both required components for implementing Active Directory in the Windows 2000 Server family of products.

Deciphering the TCP/IP Protocol Suite for Windows 2000

TCP/IP is more than just a standardized specification for data transport over a network wire. It is a sophisticated toolbox of data transport services, name resolution services, and troubleshooting utilities. Microsoft's implementation of TCP/IP for Windows 2000 includes the following network services and components:

➤ *Dynamic Host Configuration Protocol (DHCP)*—This service is based on an industry-standard specification for automatically assigning (or leasing) IP addresses to computers connected to the network. The addresses are assigned from a pre-defined pool (or *scope*) of IP addresses that an administrator must specify. DHCP makes the chore of assigning and maintaining TCP/IP addresses on hundreds or thousands of computers much easier than having to maintain an exhaustive list of IP addresses and computer names by hand. However, administrators should manually assign static IP addresses for server computers. You can install the DHCP service only in the Windows 2000 Server product line, but DHCP can assign addresses to both servers and workstations. Any operating system that can make DHCP-compliant requests for IP addresses can utilize a DHCP server that is running Windows 2000. DHCP-compatible operating systems include Windows 3.x, 9x, ME, NT, and 2000.

➤ *DNS server*—Computers understand and work well with numbers, but unfortunately, we humans have more of an affinity for names. TCP/IP requires that each network device be assigned a numeric IP address. DNS, in conjunction with DNS servers, maps numeric IP addresses to computer (host) names and vice versa. DNS employs a hierarchical system of domains and subdomains that helps to make this name resolution service very scalable. DNS servers mitigate the need for a manually maintained HOSTS file to be stored on each computer. Windows 2000 DNS servers offer added functionality such as Active Directory Integrated Zones, Incremental Zone Transfers, and Dynamic Updates. DNS is a requirement for implementing Active Directory.

➤ *Windows Internet Name Service (WINS)*—This service is Microsoft's implementation of a name resolution mechanism to match IP addresses to NetBIOS computer names and vice versa. WINS servers can greatly reduce NetBIOS traffic on networks by decreasing the amount of broadcast traffic that occurs when computers attempt to resolve unknown IP addresses to NetBIOS computer names. For an Active Directory-based network in Windows 2000 native mode with no applications that require NetBIOS, WINS becomes unnecessary.

➤ *Auto Private IP Addressing (APIPA)*—Microsoft first introduced this feature in Windows 98. For computers that are configured to obtain an IP address automatically, APIPA kicks in if no DHCP server is available on the network to lease out an IP address. APIPA automatically queries the other computers on the network and then assigns a unique IP address to the local computer using the IP address scheme of 169.254.x.y with the subnet mask of 255.255.0.0. The Internet Assigned Numbers Authority (IANA) has reserved the IP address range of 169.254.0.0 through 169.254.255.255 for APIPA. This ensures that any IP address that APIPA generates does not conflict with any public, routable addresses. This feature is turned on by default in Windows 2000 Professional.

➤ *Serial Line Internet Protocol (SLIP)*—This specification is an older Unix standard for serial communications. Windows 2000 supports SLIP primarily for backward-compatibility purposes. You can use SLIP only for outbound connections on Windows 2000 Professional.

➤ *Point-to-Point Protocol (PPP)*—PPP has effectively replaced SLIP. PPP is a remote access/dial-up protocol that supports industry-standard network protocols such as TCP/IP, NWLink, NetBEUI, and AppleTalk. PPP is optimized for low-bandwidth connections, so it is the preferred remote access protocol for dial-up/modem connections.

➤ *Point-to-Point Tunneling Protocol (PPTP)*—The only Virtual Private Network (VPN) protocol that shipped with Windows NT 4, PPTP encapsulates TCP/IP, Internet Protocol Exchange (IPX), or NetBEUI data packets and encrypts the data being transmitted as it travels (tunnels) through the Internet. PPTP clients can connect to any Microsoft-compatible PPTP servers via the Internet with proper security credentials. This service, shipped with Windows 2000 Professional, allows users to connect to the Internet using local (non-long distance) connections and offers them a way to connect to PPTP computers in remote locations without incurring toll charges or requiring dedicated data lines.

➤ *Layer 2 Tunneling Protocol (L2TP)*—An alternative to PPTP, L2TP is new to Windows 2000 and offers similar functionality. However, L2TP is an industry-standard VPN protocol and is shipped with Windows 2000 Professional. L2TP also encapsulates TCP/IP, IPX, or NetBEUI data packets and encrypts the data being transmitted as it travels (tunnels) through the Internet. You can also use L2TP in conjunction with Microsoft IP Security (IPSec) for enhanced security. L2TP is covered in more detail later in this chapter.

➤ *IPSec*—This is a relatively new Internet security protocol, also referred to as Secure IP. It provides computer-level authentication in addition to data encryption for VPN connections that use the L2TP protocol. IPSec negotiates between the client computer and the remote tunnel server before an L2TP connection is established, which secures both passwords and data. L2TP uses standard PPP-based authentication protocols, such as Extensible Authentication Protocol (EAP), Microsoft Challenge Handshake Authentication Protocol (MSCHAP), CHAP, Shiva Password Authentication Protocol (SPAP), and Password Authentication Protocol (PAP) with IPSec. IPSec and EAP are covered in more detail later in this chapter.

➤ *World Wide Web (WWW) publishing service*—This is a major component of Internet Information Services (IIS) 5, that ships with Windows 2000 Professional. Although not installed by default in Windows 2000 Professional, IIS 5 and the WWW publishing service provide Web page hosting for HTML-based and Active Server Pages (ASP)-based documents.

➤ *File Transfer Protocol (FTP) service*—This is another major component of IIS 5. FTP is an industry standard protocol for transferring files between computers over TCP/IP-based networks, such as the Internet.

➤ *Simple Mail Transfer Protocol (SMTP)*—The Microsoft SMTP service implements the industry-standard SMTP to transport and deliver email messages. The SMTP service for Windows 2000 is also a component of IIS 5.

Understanding TCP/IP Computer Addresses: It's All about Numbers

TCP/IP assigns a unique set of numbers to each computer that is connected to a TCP/IP-based network or internetwork. This set of numbers consists of four separate numbers, each delimited by a period or a dot (.). For example, an IP address of 192.168.1.20 illustrates this concept, known as *dotted decimal notation*. Each device on a TCP/IP-based network must be assigned a *unique* IP address so that it can send and receive data with the other devices on the network. A network device can be a computer, a printer, a router, a firewall, and so on.

We write IP addresses in a dotted decimal format for ease and convenience. However, TCP/IP addresses are actually 32-bit *binary* numbers! By converting these binary numbers into decimal, most of us can work with these addresses much more easily than if we had to work with them in their native binary format. The real binary address of 192.168.1.20, mentioned above, translates into 11000000.10101000.1.10100.

 If you're not sure how to convert decimal numbers into binary or vice versa, just use the Windows Calculator by clicking Start|Run, typing **calc**, and clicking OK. Click View|Scientific from the menu bar and you can easily perform these conversions.

Certain IP addresses are reserved for specific functions:

➤ The address 255.255.255.255 (11111111.11111111.11111111.11111111 in binary) is reserved for network broadcasts.

➤ The IP address 127.0.0.1 (1111111.0.0.1 in binary) is reserved as a loopback address for testing proper configuration of the IP address(es) for the local host computer.

➤ The address schemes 192.168.x.y and 10.0.x.y have been reserved as nonroutable by the bodies that govern the Internet.

Therefore, IP addresses such as 192.168.1.20 and 10.0.0.7 are restricted to being used only for the internal addressing of LANs. By definition, you cannot route these addressing schemes onto the Internet. Routers (devices that route network data packets) do not forward any data packets that originate with a nonroutable addressing scheme.

Configuring TCP/IP

TCP/IP is installed by default when you install Windows 2000 Professional, unless you override this default setting. In addition, the protocol's default configuration is to *obtain an IP address automatically*. This means that the computer automatically requests a unique TCP/IP address for your network from a DHCP server. If no DHCP server is available, the operating system invokes APIPA to query the other computers that are currently powered on and connected to the network so that it can assign itself a unique IP address.

If you work with TCP/IP, you need to become familiar with the following terms:

➤ *Subnet mask*—This is essentially an IP address filter that gets applied to each unique IP address. The subnet mask (or filter) determines which part of the IP address for a computer specifies the network segment where the computer is located versus which part of the IP address specifies the unique node (or host) address for that individual computer. As an example, an IP address of 192.168.1.20 with a subnet mask of 255.255.255.0 is determined to have the network segment address of 192.168.1. The node or host address for the computer, therefore, is 20. This is analogous to the street name of a postal address versus the actual house number of the address. There may be many houses on the same street, but only one house has a house number of 20.

➤ *Default gateway*—This IP address specifies the router for the local network segment (or subnet). If this address is absent, the computer cannot communicate with other computers that are located outside of the local network segment (also known as a *subnet* or *subnetwork*). Default gateway information is often obtained through DHCP if the computer is configured to obtain an IP address automatically.

➤ *Preferred and alternate DNS servers*—Having more than one DNS server on a network helps provide load balancing and fault tolerance for client computers that need to perform IP address to hostname lookups as well as hostname to IP address lookups. Name resolution is a critical issue in TCP/IP. DNS server information is often obtained through DHCP if the computer is configured to obtain an IP address automatically.

➤ *WINS addresses*—WINS provides name resolution between IP addresses and NetBIOS computer names. WINS server addresses are often obtained through DHCP if the computer is configured to obtain an IP address automatically.

To manually set up a Windows 2000 Professional computer with a static IP address for the TCP/IP network protocol, click Start|Settings|Network And Dial-up Connections. Right-click the Local Area Network (LAN) Connection icon that you want to configure and select Properties. If TCP/IP is not currently installed, follow these steps:

1. Click Install from the LAN connection's Properties sheet.

2. Click Protocol and then click Add.

3. Click Internet Protocol (TCP/IP) and then click OK.

4. Restart the computer.

To configure the necessary settings so that TCP/IP can communicate with other computers and devices over the network, follow these steps:

1. Click Internet Protocol (TCP/IP) and then click Properties.

2. Click Use The Following IP Address.

3. Type the IP Address, Subnet Mask, and Default Gateway.

4. Type the proper IP address for a Preferred DNS Server and an Alternate DNS Server (if any).

5. Click the Advanced button to add additional IP addresses and default gateways. You can also add, edit, or remove DNS server address information, and you can change other DNS settings. You can specify IP addresses for any WINS servers on the network, you can enable NetBIOS name resolution using an LMHOSTS file, and you can enable or disable NetBIOS over TCP/IP. You can also set up IPSec and TCP/IP filtering as optional settings from the Advanced TCP/IP Settings Properties sheet.

6. Click OK to close the Advanced TCP/IP Settings Properties dialog box.

7. Click OK to close the Internet Protocol (TCP/IP) Properties dialog box.

8. Click OK to close the Local Area Connection Properties dialog box.

Troubleshooting TCP/IP

Windows 2000 Professional comes with several software tools and utilities to help you isolate and resolve TCP/IP-related issues. You must run all of these utilities from the command line. Connectivity tools include the following:

➤ *Finger*—Displays information about a user for a particular computer. The target computer must be running the Finger service.

➤ *FTP*—Copies files to and from FTP servers over a TCP/IP connection.

➤ *LPR*—Sends one or more files to be printed via a line printer daemon (LPD) printer.

➤ *RCP*—Copies files between a Windows 2000 Professional computer and a computer system running the remote shell daemon (RSHD).

➤ *REXEC*—Executes commands on remote computer systems that are running the REXEC service.

➤ *RSH*—Executes commands on remote computer systems that are running the RSH service.

➤ *Telnet*—Establishes a terminal emulation session for working on remote systems, including environments such as Unix, Mainframe, and Mini computers.

➤ *TFTP (Trivial File Transfer Protocol)*—Copies files to and from remote computers that are running the TFTP service.

Diagnostic tools include the following:

➤ *ARP (Address Resolution Protocol)*—Lists and edits the IP-to-Ethernet (or Token Ring) physical translation tables that ARP uses.

➤ *HOSTNAME*—Lists the name of the local host (computer).

➤ *IPCONFIG*—Shows all of the current TCP/IP configuration settings for the local computer such as its IP address, subnet mask, and any WINS servers and DNS servers assigned to the computer.

➤ *LPQ*—Shows the current status of the print queue on a computer that is running the LPD service.

➤ *NBTSTAT*—Delineates network protocol statistics and lists the current connections that are using NetBIOS over TCP/IP.

➤ *NETSTAT*—Delineates network protocol statistics and lists the current TCP/IP connections.

➤ *PING*—Is used to test TCP/IP-related connectivity to remote computers. This command also verifies the proper TCP/IP configuration of the local host computer by attempting to **ping** the loopback address for the local host (computer). For example: **ping 127.0.0.1**.

➤ *ROUTE*—Edits the local computer's routing tables.

➤ *TRACERT*—Displays the route (path) that data packets follow as they travel from the local computer to a remote destination computer.

Troubleshooting TCP/IP Configuration and Connectivity
Whenever you initially set up TCP/IP, you should always test and verify that the protocol is working properly. Here are the steps you can take to check the computer's TCP/IP configuration and to test its connectivity:

1. Open a command prompt window; **ipconfig** and **ping** are strictly command-line utilities.

2. Run **ipconfig** to display the computer's current IP configuration. Use **ipconfig** /all to display more detailed information (see Figure 9.1).

3. Use the **ping** command to ping the computer's loopback address: **ping** 127.0.0.1. This tests whether TCP/IP is correctly installed and bound to the network adapter card (see Figure 9.2).

4. Ping the IP address of the local computer to verify the uniqueness of the IP address on the network.

5. Ping the IP address of the default gateway for the local subnet to check that the default gateway is up and running. This step also demonstrates whether the computer can successfully communicate over the local network segment.

6. Ping the IP address of a computer that is located on a different network segment (subnet). This step indicates whether the computer can send and receive network data packets through a router.

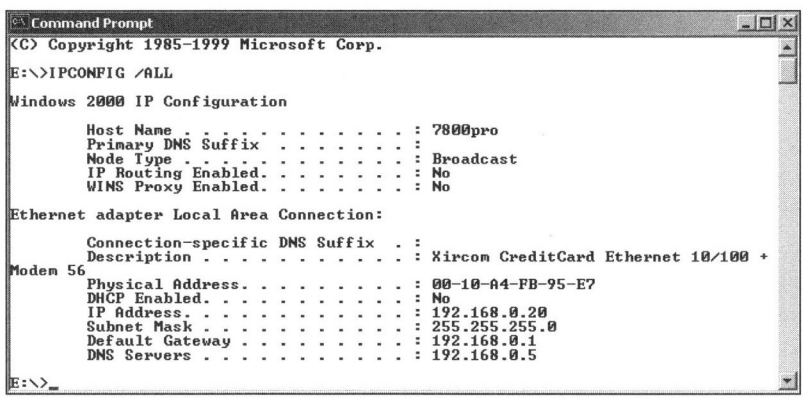

Figure 9.1   An example of running the **ipconfig** command.

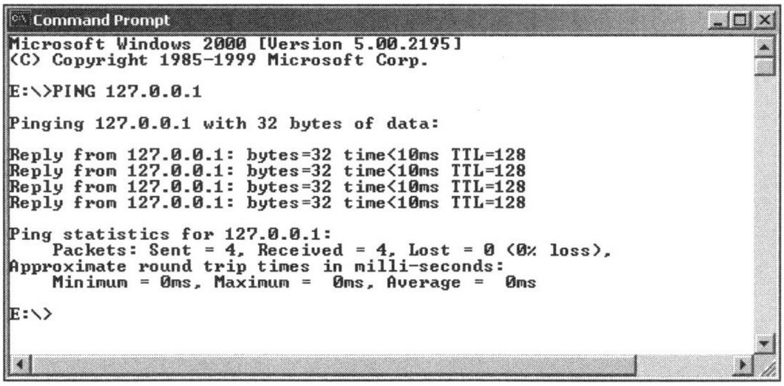

Figure 9.2   An example of pinging a computer's loopback IP address.

Using APIPA

If a computer is set up to obtain an IP address automatically from a DHCP server but no DHCP servers are available, APIPA temporarily assigns an IP address to the local computer while it searches the network to make sure that no other network devices have been assigned the same IP address. By running **ipconfig**, you can view the current TCP/IP information for the local computer. An address such as 169.254.x.y generally indicates that APIPA is currently in effect.

Connecting to Remote Computers Using Dial-up Connections

Dial-up connectivity still maintains an important role for connecting remote computers. In Microsoft terms, *Dial-up Connections* generally refers to client computers dialing out to server computers. Remote Access Services (RAS) generally refers to server computers that accept inbound remote connections from dial-up clients. Dial-up Connections usually involve regular phones using analog modems and/or dial up integrated services digital network (ISDN) lines.

New Authentication Protocols

Windows 2000 Professional provides advanced support for remote access authentication protocols, which offer enhanced security and dynamic bandwidth allocation for remote access. These authentication protocols, some of which have already been mentioned in this chapter, validate the logon credentials for all users who attempt to connect to a Windows 2000-based network. Windows 2000 Professional supports all the authentication protocols that Windows NT 4 offered, including PAP, CHAP, MSCHAP, SPAP, and PPTP (used for VPN support).

Windows 2000 Professional also supports several new authentication protocols that greatly enhance its dial-up and remote access capabilities for data encryption, user authentication, and bandwidth allocation. These newly supported standards include IPSec, L2TP, EAP, Remote Authentication Dial-in User Service (RADIUS), and Bandwidth Allocation Protocol (BAP).

IPSec

IPSec is a suite of security-related protocols and cryptographic functions for establishing and maintaining private and secure IP connections. IPSec is easy to implement and offers vigilant security for potential network attacks. IPSec-enabled clients establish a Security Association (SA) that serves as a private key for encrypting data. IPSec uses policies for configuring its security services. IPSec policies support different gradations of security levels for different types of network traffic. Administrators can set IPSec policies at the User, Group, Application, Domain, Site, or Global Enterprise level. You configure IPSec policies with the IP Security Policy Management snap-in of the Microsoft Management Console (MMC).

L2TP

You can compare L2TP to PPTP in that it provides an encrypted "tunnel" for data to pass through an untrusted (public) network such as the Internet. However, although *L2TP* does provide a tunnel for data to pass through, it does *not* provide encryption for the data. L2TP works in conjunction with other encryption services and security protocols, such as IPSec, to provide a secure VPN connection. Both L2TP and PPTP use PPP to establish initial communications. Some of the major differences between L2TP and PPTP are:

➤ L2TP requires IPSec for encryption services; PPTP uses the encryption functions of PPP.

➤ L2TP provides header compression support. When you enable header compression, L2TP uses only 4 bytes for its overhead. PPTP requires 6 bytes for its overhead and does not support header compression.

➤ L2TP offers support for tunnel authentication; PPTP does not support tunnel authentication. If you implement IPSec with L2TP or PPTP, IPSec provides its own tunnel authentication, rendering L2TP's tunnel authentication unnecessary.

➤ Unlike PPTP, L2TP does not have to run over an IP-based network transport. L2TP needs only a packet-oriented, point-to-point connection. L2TP can function using User Datagram Protocol (UDP), Frame Relay Permanent Virtual Circuits (PVCs), X.25 Virtual Circuits (VCs), or Asynchronous Transfer Mode (ATM) VCs over TCP/IP.

EAP

EAP is an extension of PPP for DUN, L2TP, and PPTP clients. EAP supports a negotiated authentication model where the actual authentication mechanism is determined between the dial-up connection client and the remote access server. EAP provides support for several authentication protocols, including the following:

➤ *Message Digest 5 Challenge Handshake Authentication Protocol (MD5-CHAP)*— This encrypts usernames and passwords using its own MD5 algorithm.

➤ *Generic token cards*—These cards provide passwords for users and can support multiple authentication methods.

➤ *Transport Level Security (TLS)*—The TLS protocol works with smart cards and other types of security certificates. A smart card stores a user's security certificate and private key electronically inside the card. Smart card technology requires physical cards and card readers.

Note: By using EAP application programming interfaces (APIs), software developers can design and implement new authentication methods for smart cards, generic token cards, and even biometric devices like fingerprint identification scanners. In this way, EAP can support authentication technologies that will be developed in the future. To add EAP authentication methods, go to the Security tab of the remote access server's Properties sheet.

RADIUS

RADIUS offers accounting services and authentication functions for distributed dial-up connections. Windows 2000 Professional can take on the role of a RADIUS server or a RADIUS client, or it can assume the roles of both. A RADIUS client is often used as a remote access server for an Internet Service Provider (ISP). The RADIUS client forwards authentication requests to a RADIUS server. A Windows 2000 RADIUS client can also forward remote access accounting information to a RADIUS server. You configure RADIUS client settings from the Security tab of the remote access server's Properties sheet.

RADIUS servers validate requests from RADIUS clients. For authentication, Windows 2000 provides Internet Authentication Services (IAS) as an optional Windows component that you can add during installation or through the Add/Remove Programs icon in the Control Panel. RADIUS servers maintain RADIUS accounting data from RADIUS clients in associated log files.

BAP

BAP works in conjunction with the Bandwidth Allocation Control Protocol (BACP) as an enhancement to the Multilink feature found in Windows NT 4. Multilink enables you to bind together two or more modem or ISDN lines, allowing you to achieve higher throughput (more bandwidth) than you would if you used the lines individually. BAP and BACP work together to dynamically add or drop lines for Multilinked devices on an on-demand basis. Both protocols serve as PPP control protocols. These protocols provide a means for optimizing bandwidth while holding down connection costs by responding to network bandwidth needs on demand. For organizations that incur line-usage charges based on bandwidth use (such as ISDN lines), BAP and BACP can significantly cut costs.

Administrators can turn on the Multilink feature as well as BAP and BACP from the PPP tab of each remote access server's Properties sheet. You configure BAP settings using remote access policies. By implementing a remote access policy using BAP, you can specify that an extra line should be dropped if the connection for that line falls below 65 percent usage, for example, for a particular group. You can additionally specify that an extra line should be dropped only if usage falls below 35 percent for a different group of users.

Connecting to Remote Access Servers

You create new connections to remote access servers from the Network And Dial-Up Connections window. You can make new connections as well as modify or delete existing dial-up connections from this window. To create a new DUN connection for connecting to remote access servers, follow these steps:

1. Click Start|Settings|Network And Dial-up Connections.

2. Click Make New Connection to display the Network Connection Wizard.

3. Click Next.

4. At the Network Connection Type dialog box, you can accept the default choice—Dial-up To Private Network, as shown in Figure 9.3.

5. Click Next.

6. Mark the checkbox for the device(s) that you want to use for this connection.

7. Click Next.

8. Specify the phone number for the remote access server to which you want to connect. Mark the Use Dialing Rules checkbox if you want your system's dialing rules to automatically determine how to dial from different locations.

9. Click Next.

10. Specify the Connection Availability For This Dial-up entry. Click For All Users or Only For Myself.

11. Click Next.

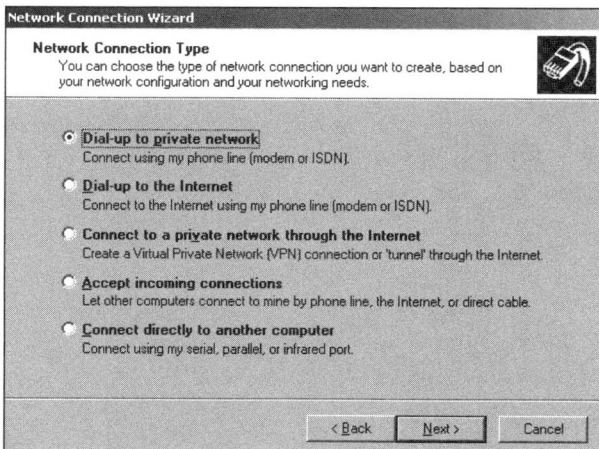

Figure 9.3 The Network Connection Type dialog box of the Network Connection Wizard.

12. Complete the Network Connection Wizard by typing the name that you want to assign to this connection. Mark the Add A Shortcut To My Desktop checkbox if you would like a shortcut added.

13. Click Finish.

As soon as you complete the Network Connection Wizard, a Connect dialog box appears. It prompts you for a User Name and a Password and offers a Dial drop-down list for the phone number to be dialed (see Figure 9.4). You can type the proper User Name and Password as well as verify the phone number to be dialed for connecting to the remote access server. Click the Dial button to initiate the connection. Click the Properties button to modify some of the dial-up connection's properties.

You can modify the properties of any Dial-up Connection or network connection listed in the Network And Dial-up Connections window by right-clicking on the connection's icon and selecting Properties, as shown in Figure 9. 5. From the Dial-up Connection's Properties sheet, you can configure connection devices (modems and so on), list alternate phone numbers, and configure dialing options and redialing options. You can specify security options, configure dial-up server settings, and modify network connection components. You can also set up Internet Connection Sharing (ICS) from the Sharing tab, if this connection connects to the Internet. ICS is covered in more detail later in this chapter.

The Networking tab of a Dial-up Connection's Properties sheet allows you to configure several essential components for successful connections (see Figure 9.6). Be sure to specify the proper dial-up server type to which you will be connecting (either PPP or SLIP). You can change PPP settings by clicking on the Settings button (as shown in Figure 9.7). Be sure that your connection has at least one

Figure 9.4   The Connect dialog box for connecting to remote access servers.

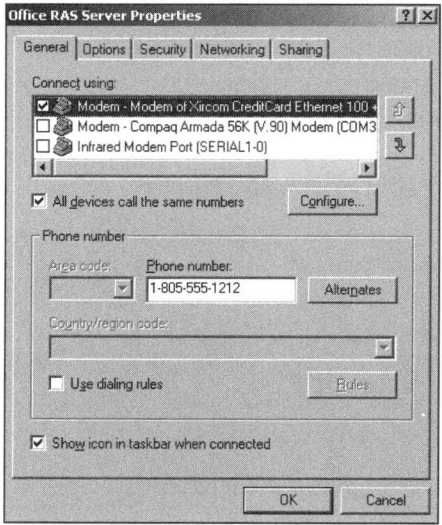

Figure 9.5   The Properties sheet for a Dial-up Connection.

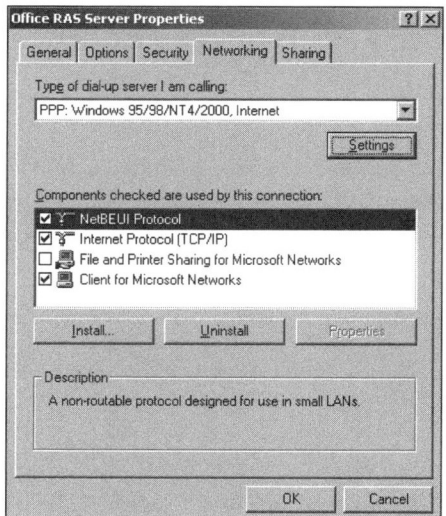

Figure 9.6   The Networking tab of a Dial-up Connection's Properties sheet.

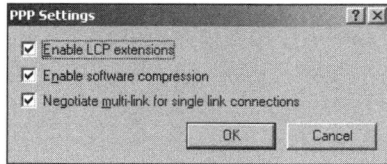

Figure 9.7   The PPP Settings dialog box.

dial-up network protocol in common with the remote access server to which it will be attempting to connect. You can install and uninstall networking components, such as protocols, from the Networking tab. You can also enable or disable any listed component by marking or clearing its checkbox.

Setting up and Configuring VPN Connections

Setting up and configuring VPN connections is similar to establishing dial-up connections. VPN connections allow you to connect to remote computers anywhere in the world by tunneling through the Internet using a VPN protocol such as PPTP or L2TP. VPN protocols encapsulate TCP/IP, NetBEUI, or NWLink data packets for transport over TCP/IP via the Internet. PPTP and L2TP utilize encryption to secure all the data that they encapsulate as it travels to the destination VPN server. To create a new VPN connection, follow these steps:

1. Click Start|Settings|Network And Dial-up Connections.

2. Click Make New Connection to display the Network Connection Wizard.

3. Click Next.

4. At the Network Connection Type dialog box, click Connect To A Private Network Through The Internet.

5. Click Next.

6. At the Public Network dialog box, select Do Not Dial The Initial Connection If This Computer Does Not Need To Dial Up To Connect With The Internet. Click the Automatically Dial This Initial Connection drop-down list to select an existing Dial-up Connection for connecting to the Internet.

7. Click Next.

8. Type the host name or IP address of the computer or network to which you will be connecting.

9. Click Next.

10. Specify the Connection Availability for this dial-up entry. Click For All Users or Only For Myself.

11. Click Next.

12. Complete the Network Connection Wizard by typing the name that you want to assign to this connection. Mark the Add A Shortcut To My Desktop checkbox if you would like a shortcut added.

13. Click Finish.

When you double-click the Virtual Private Connection icon to access a VPN server, you are prompted to connect to the Internet using the Dial-up Connection you specified. Once you have established a connection to the Internet, Windows 2000 Professional attempts to connect to the remote VPN server.

Connecting to the Internet Using Dial-up Connections

Creating dial-up connections to the Internet is similar to adding a connection for a remote access server. To set up a new Dial-up Connection to connect to an ISP, perform the following:

1. Click Start|Settings|Network And Dial-up Connections.

2. Click Make New Connection to display the Network Connection Wizard.

3. Click Next.

4. At the Network Connection Type dialog box, click Dial-up To The Internet.

5. Click Next. The Internet Connection Wizard appears.

6. Select the type of Internet connection that you want to use. Unless you want to establish a new Internet access account with an ISP through the Microsoft Internet Referral Service, you can select the one of the other two options: I Want To Set Up My Internet Connection Manually or I Want To Connect Through A Local Area Network .

7. Click Next.

8. Specify how this computer will connect to the Internet: I Connect Through A Phone Line And A Modem or I Connect Through A Local Area Network. To use a Dial-up Connection, choose the first option.

9. Click Next.

10. Specify the communications device (modem) to use for this dial-up connection to the Internet from the drop-down list.

11. Click Next.

12. Type the area code and telephone number for the ISP connection that you will be using. Clear the Use Area Code And Dialing Rules checkbox if you do not wish to use those features.

13. Click the Advanced button to specify settings for your ISP's connection. You can modify the Connection Type and Logon Procedure settings from the Connection tab, if necessary.

14. Click the Addresses tab for the Advanced Connection Properties dialog box. From this page, you can click Always Use The Following and type An

IP Address Required By The ISP if the ISP requires that you use a static IP address.

15. In the DNS Server Address section, click Always Use The Following and type a Primary IP Address and Alternate IP Address for the ISP's DNS servers (unless the ISP provides this information automatically).

16. Click OK to close the Advanced Connection Properties dialog box.

17. Click Next.

18. Type the User Name and Password for the ISP account to which you will be connecting.

19. Click Next.

20. Type a Connection Name for this dial-up Internet connection.

21. Click Next.

22. Click No when you are prompted to set up an Internet mail account. You can always set up Internet email accounts later.

23. Click Next.

24. Complete the Network Connection Wizard by clearing the To Connect To The Internet Immediately, Select This Box checkbox.

25. Click Finish.

26. Right-click the Internet connection you just created and select Properties. Click the Security tab. Verify that Typical is selected and that The Validate My Identity As Follows drop-down list has Allow Unsecured Password selected.

27. Click OK.

After completing the preceding steps, you should be able to connect to the Internet via a dial-up connection. By double-clicking the icon for the Internet connection that you just configured, you will see a Connect dialog box that displays the username and password that you specified. Clear the Save Password checkbox if you do not want the password saved for future connection attempts. Click the Dial button to have the connection established.

Configuring and Troubleshooting ICS

Windows 2000 Professional allows you to have one IP address from an ISP and share that connection (through the Windows 2000 Professional computer) with other computers on the net vork. This feature is known as Internet Connection Sharing (ICS). Microsoft accomplishes this feat by enabling a new feature of Windows 2000, network address translation (NAT). NAT translates (or maps) a set of nonroutable IP addresses (such as 192.168.x.y) to an external (public) IP address that exists on the Internet. Computers on the LAN can then access external resources on the Internet, like Web sites and FTP sites, but they are somewhat sheltered from outside intrusions because the LAN computers are using nonroutable IP addresses.

 Although turning on NAT can be a good idea, you should never use it as a substitute for a quality firewall product that can provide a much higher level of security between the LAN and the public Internet. Generally speaking, you should always place a firewall product between your internal local network and the external public network. With more and more people gaining access to the Internet, you need to keep security concerns at the forefront to ensure the integrity of all your internal systems and your users' valuable, private, and confidential data.

Configuring ICS

To set up ICS, follow these steps:

1. Click Start|Settings|Network And Dial-up Connections.

2. Right-click a connection icon for an Internet connection and select Properties.

3. Click the Sharing tab.

4. Click the Enable Internet Connection Sharing For This Connection checkbox. Once you have marked this checkbox, the other settings for ICS become available.

5. Select the Enable On-Demand Dialing checkbox if you want this Internet connection to automatically dial and establish a connection to the Internet when another computer on the LAN attempts to access Internet resources through this computer.

6. Click the Settings button. From the Applications tab, you can specify individual application programs that you want to enable for other computers that will be sharing this connection over the LAN.

7. Click the Services tab. Mark the checkboxes for each Internet-related service you want to enable for this shared connection. You can also add services that are not currently listed by clicking on the Add button.

8. Click OK to close the Internet Connection Sharing Settings dialog box.

9. Click OK to close the Properties sheet for the Internet connection. As soon as you close the Properties sheet, you see a message box, as shown in Figure 9.8.

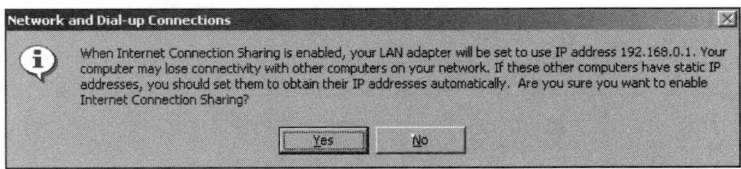

Figure 9.8 Internet Connection Sharing message box.

10. Click Yes in this message box if you are sure that you want to enable this feature.

After you have set up ICS, you should verify that the computer's IP address is now set to 192.168.0.1 with a subnet mask of 255.255.255.0. Test the local Internet connection to verify that the computer can connect to the Internet successfully. For each computer on the LAN that wants to take advantage of the shared Internet connection, perform the following steps:

1. Click Start|Settings|Network And Dial-up Connections.

2. Right-click the LAN connection and select Properties.

3. Click Internet Protocol and then click Properties.

4. Configure TCP/IP to obtain an IP address automatically. This is the preferred method to use with ICS (as opposed to obtaining the address manually, covered shortly). When you enable ICS, the Windows 2000 Professional DHCP Allocator uses the default IP addressing range of 192.168.0.1 through 192.168.0.254 and the DNS Proxy service becomes enabled so that clients on the network can connect to the shared Internet resource.

As an alternative, you can manually set up workstations to work with ICS; however, this is not the recommended method according to Microsoft. To do this, follow these steps:

1. Click Start|Settings|Network And Dial-up Connections.

2. Right-click the LAN connection and select Properties.

3. Click Internet Protocol and click on Properties.

4. Click Use The Following IP Address and type a unique IP address in the range from 192.168.0.2 through 192.168.0.254.

5. Type **255.255.255.0** for the Subnet Mask.

6. Type **192.168.0.1** for the Default Gateway (the IP address for the Windows 2000 Professional computer that is hosting the shared Internet connection).

7. Type the Preferred DNS Server according to your ISP's documentation (if your ISP does not provide this information automatically).

8. Type the Alternate DNS Server according to your ISP's documentation (if your ISP does not provide this information automatically).

9. Click OK in the Internet Protocol (TCP/IP) Properties sheet.

10. Click OK in the LAN connection Properties window.

Troubleshooting ICS

Here are some tips for troubleshooting ICS:

➤ If you encounter problems with computers on the network not being able to connect to Web sites through the shared Internet connection, verify the DNS server IP addresses with your ISP.

➤ To verify that the new IP settings have taken effect, type **ipconfig** at a command prompt; sometimes you may need to restart the computer for all the settings to become active.

➤ Check the subnet mask; it must read 255.255.255.0 or else the computer that is attempting to connect to the ICS computer cannot connect.

➤ Make sure that each IP address that you assign to the other computers on the network falls within the range of 192.168.0.2 through 192.168.0.254, with no duplicate addresses on any computer.

➤ If computers on the network can connect to the Internet only after you manually initiate the Internet connection from the ICS host computer, check that Enable On-Demand Dialing is checked on the Sharing tab of the Internet connection's Properties sheet.

Practice Questions

Question 1

A computer named Station01 is configured with TCP/IP and is set up to obtain an IP address automatically. There is a DHCP server on the network. When Mary turns on the workstation, she cannot access any network resources. As the administrator, you run **ipconfig** on the workstation and discover that the computer has an IP address of 169.254.0.2. What is the most likely cause of this problem?

- ○ a. Someone has entered a static IP address for the workstation for a different subnet.

- ○ b. The DHCP server is currently down, or the network cable for the workstation has become disconnected.

- ○ c. DHCP has been configured with an incorrect scope.

- ○ d. The WINS server is currently unavailable.

Answer b is correct. If a computer that is configured with TCP/IP to obtain an IP address automatically cannot contact a DHCP server, Windows 2000 Professional invokes APIPA to assign a unique, nonroutable IP address in the range of 169.254.0.1 through 169.254.255.254. The computer's IP address of 169.254.0.2 would indicate that it obtained its IP address from APIPA.

Question 2

As the Administrator, you need to set up a Dial-up Connection using TCP/IP on a Windows 2000 remote access server computer. Which settings do you need to configure for the Windows 2000 Professional dial-up client to create the dial-up connection and enable it to connect to the remote access server?

- ○ a. The type of connection, the server's phone number, and which EAP the server is using.

- ○ b. The DNS IP addresses for the server and whether DHCP is enabled.

- ○ c. The phone number for the server, how IP addresses are allocated to dial-up clients, and which authentication options have been enabled on the server.

- ○ d. The phone number for the server, whether to use PPTP or L2TP, and the scope of IP addresses for the subnet.

Answer c is correct. A Dial-up Connection must know the server's phone number. In addition, the connection must either have a static IP address that is compatible with the remote access server's addressing scheme or it must obtain a dynamic IP address from the remote access server when it connects. The dial-up client must also be compatible with at least one of authentication methods for which the server is configured.

Question 3

What additional settings must you configure to enable smart card support with custom settings for Dial-up Connections?

○ a. From the Dial-up Connection's Properties sheet, go to the Advanced Security Settings dialog box, select Use Extensible Authentication Protocol (EAP), and choose Smart Card Or Other Certificate (encryption enabled) from the drop-down list.

○ b. From the Dial-up Connection's Properties sheet, go to the Advanced Security Settings dialog box, select Use Extensible Authentication Protocol (EAP), and choose MD5-Challenge from the drop-down list.

○ c. From the Dial-up Connection's Properties sheet, go to the Advanced Security Settings dialog box, select Allow These Protocols, and choose Shiva Password Authentication Protocol (SPAP) from the drop-down list.

○ d. From the Dial-up Connection's Properties sheet, go to the Advanced Security Settings dialog box, select Allow These Protocols, and choose Challenge Handshake Authentication Protocol (CHAP) from the drop-down list.

Answer a is correct. EAP provides smart card support. The Advanced Security Settings dialog box allows you to specify custom settings for smart card support.

Question 4

You are the Administrator for a LAN with four different subnets. TCP/IP is the only network protocol used. The network has 110 Windows 2000 Professional workstations, 4 Windows 2000 servers, and 3 Windows NT 4 servers. Currently, the network uses NetBIOS computer names for name resolution on the network. The workstations are all set up using static IP addresses. What do you need to configure on a new Windows 2000 Professional computer to get it up and running on the network?

○ a. A unique IP address, the subnet mask, and DNS server address.

○ b. A unique IP address, the subnet mask, the DHCP server address, and the default gateway address.

○ c. A unique IP address, the subnet mask, the default gateway address, and a properly configured HOSTS file.

○ d. A unique IP address, the subnet mask, the default gateway address, and a WINS server address.

Answer d is correct. WINS resolves NetBIOS computer names to IP addresses and vice versa.

Question 5

One Windows 2000 Professional computer is going to share its Internet connection with three other computers over a LAN. The computer will use a 56Kbps modem and a dial-up phone line account with an ISP to connect to the Internet. What components must you configure on the Windows 2000 Professional computer to enable ICS? [Check all correct answers]

❑ a. Right-click the dial-up connection and select Sharing. Click the Sharing option.

❑ b. Mark the Enable On-Demand Dialing checkbox from the Sharing tab of the dial-up connection's Properties sheet.

❑ c. Mark the Enable Internet Connection Sharing For This Connection checkbox from the Sharing tab of the dial-up connection's Properties sheet.

❑ d. Physically connect the modem to the computer. Go to the Control Panel, double-click Phone And Modem Options. Click Modems, select the modem you want to share, and click Properties. Click the Advanced tab and then click the Share This Device option.

❑ e. Physically connect the modem to the computer. Open the Network And Dial-Up Connections window and double-click Make New Connection to create a dial-up connection to the Internet.

❑ f. Go to Start|Programs|Administrative Tools and select Routing And Remote Access. Configure the shared Internet connection from the Routing And Remote Access Service (RRAS) MMC snap-in.

Answers b, c, and e are correct. To enable ICS, you need a LAN connection or a dial-up connection to the Internet. You also need to mark Enable Internet Connection Sharing checkbox for this connection. For a dial-up Internet connection, you should mark the Enable On-Demand Dialing checkbox.

Question 6

> Robert wants to be able to use a VPN connection via dial-up to connect to his company's headquarters in New York. He already uses a dial-up connection to access the Internet from his notebook PC. At times, he wants to have the option of logging onto the corporate Windows 2000 network domain from the Log On To Windows dialog box by selecting the Log On Using Dial-Up Connection checkbox. He wants to use the corporate VPN connection for this purpose. What must Robert configure to accomplish this?
>
> ○ a. When creating the VPN connection, he must select For All Users in the Connection Availability dialog box of the Network Connection Wizard.
>
> ○ b. He must mark the Include Windows Logon Domain checkbox from the Options tab of the VPN connection's Properties sheet.
>
> ○ c. He must make sure that the Net Logon service Startup Type is set to Automatic. Use the Services console in the MMC.
>
> ○ d. No special settings are necessary after the VPN connection has been created.

Answer a is correct. To display the VPN option for logging on to a Windows 2000 Professional computer, you cannot select the Only For Myself option in the Connection Availability dialog box of the Network Connection Wizard.

Question 7

Heidi uses a Windows 2000 Professional computer at her company's branch office in San Mateo, California. Her computer is connected to the LAN for the branch office. Heidi's computer uses a public IP address for Internet access over the LAN. What is the best method for her to connect to a remote access server computer in Toronto, Canada (the company's headquarters), which has a public Internet IP address of 197.41.146.12?

○ a. Heidi can use a dial-up connection to the Internet to use a VPN connection to the remote access server.

○ b. Heidi can use a dial-up connection to connect directly to the remote access server using a modem and a phone line.

○ c. Heidi can use her computer's public IP address for Internet access to establish a VPN connection to the remote access server over the existing LAN.

○ d. Heidi can take advantage of an infrared connection to the remote access server.

○ e. Heidi can connect directly to the remote access server by using SLIP and the remote access server's IP address of 197.41.146.12.

Answer c is correct. A VPN connection works well over a LAN connection to the Internet. VPN connections via LANs are always preferable to VPN connections over dial-up links.

Question 8

Alexis is the Administrator for a LAN with 2 Windows 2000 servers and 17 Windows 2000 Professional computers. TCP/IP is the only network protocol that is used on the LAN. One of the server computers is also a DHCP server for the network, and all 17 workstations are configured to obtain their IP addresses automatically. Alexis decides to give her users access to the Internet by connecting a 56Kbps modem with a phone line to one of the Windows 2000 Professional computers and enabling ICS. After Alexis sets up the computer to dial up to the Internet successfully, she turns on ICS. However, none of the other computers on the LAN can access the shared connection. What is the most likely cause of this problem?

O a. Alexis needs to add the ISP's DNS server addresses as DHCP options.

O b. Alexis must remove the DHCP server service from the network.

O c. Alexis must assign all the computers on the LAN static IP addresses.

O d. Alexis needs to configure ICS for the LAN connection instead of the dial-up connection to the Internet.

Answer b is correct. When ICS is enabled, it becomes the DHCP Allocator as long as no active DHCP server is on the network. A DHCP server on the same network inhibits ICS from operating as the DHCP allocator. DNS server settings are by proxy in ICS as long as the ISP is acting as the external DNS host.

Question 9

What is APIPA?

O a. It's DHCP for Windows 2000 Professional.

O b. It's used only in conjunction with ICS to assign IP addresses to other computers on the network so that they can share the Internet connection.

O c. It's a scope of IP addresses assigned to Windows 2000 Professional computers by default.

O d. It's a feature of Windows 2000 Professional for computers using the TCP/IP protocol that are configured to obtain an IP address automatically. APIPA becomes active only if no DHCP server is available on the network. APIPA assigns nonroutable IP addresses to computers on a LAN.

Answer d is correct. APIPA becomes active only if the Windows 2000 Professional computers connected to the LAN cannot contact any DHCP servers. APIPA uses a reserved IP address range of 169.254.0.0 through 169.254.255.254, which is nonroutable, with a subnet mask of 255.255.0.0.

Question 10

You are the Administrator for a Windows 2000 Server network, complete with DNS servers, WINS servers, and DHCP servers, that is installed as well as up and running. You will be installing 30 new Windows 2000 Professional computers with all the default installation settings. You want to ensure that all these new workstations will obtain their IP addresses automatically. What do you need to do?

○ a. Open the Network And Dial-Up Connections window. Right-click the LAN and select Properties. Click Client For Microsoft Networks and then click Properties to configure automatic IP addressing.

○ b. Open a command prompt window and run the command **ipconfig /configure** to allow the computer to obtain an IP address automatically.

○ c. Open the Network And Dial-Up Connections window. Right-click the LAN and select Properties. Select Internet Protocol (TCP/IP) and click Properties. Click the Advanced button and enable automatic IP addressing from the IP Settings tab.

○ d. Nothing. Life is good.

Answer d is correct. The TCP/IP network protocol is the default protocol when you install Windows 2000 Professional. Obtaining an IP address automatically is the default selection for TCP/IP. Therefore, the Administrator does not need to make any adjustments for the new computers to be automatically assigned IP addresses from the DHCP server(s) on the existing LAN.

Need to Know More?

 Microsoft Corporation. *Microsoft Windows 2000 Professional Resource Kit.* Redmond, Washington: Microsoft Press, 2000. ISBN: 1-57610-808-2. This book has invaluable information on setting up LANs, working with dial-up connections, and troubleshooting TCP/IP issues.

 Stinson, Craig, and Carl Siechert. *Running Microsoft Windows 2000 Professional.* Redmond, Washington: Microsoft Press, 2000. ISBN: 1-57231-838-4. This guidebook to Windows 2000 Professional contains good information on administering and troubleshooting LAN configurations and dial-up connections.

 Wood, Adam. *Windows 2000 Active Directory Black Book.* Scottsdale, Arizona: The Coriolis Group, 2000. ISBN: 1-57610-256-4. This book provides comprehensive coverage of Active Directory.

 Search the TechNet CD-ROM (or its online version through **www.microsoft.com**) and/or the *Windows 2000 Professional Resource Kit* CD-ROM using the keywords "APIPA", "Dial-Up Connection", "TCP/IP", "PPTP", "L2TP", "DNS", and "ICS."

Monitoring and Optimizing Performance Reliability

Terms you'll need to understand:

✓ Windows 2000 Backup

✓ Normal backup

✓ Differential backup

✓ Incremental backup

✓ System state

✓ Safe Mode startup options

✓ Last Known Good Configuration

✓ Recovery Console

✓ Emergency Repair Disk (ERD)

✓ makeboot.exe and makebt32.exe

✓ Optimization

✓ Counters

✓ Objects

✓ Sample (or update) interval

✓ Baselining

✓ Paging file

Techniques you'll need to master:

✓ Backing up and restoring data

✓ Backing up and restoring the system state

✓ Starting a Windows 2000 system in the appropriate Safe Mode

✓ Using the Last Known Good Configuration

✓ Installing and using the Recovery Console

✓ Creating an ERD

✓ Using the emergency repair process

✓ Creating a set of Windows 2000 setup boot disks

✓ Using System Monitor

✓ Creating a log with Performance Logs And Alerts

✓ Setting performance alerts

✓ Establishing a baseline

✓ Configuring the paging file

✓ Changing process priorities

✓ Viewing performance with Task Manager

Once a Windows 2000 system has been installed, configured, and secured, an administrator's goal is to ensure reliable and optimal performance. This chapter will explore the skills required to prepare for, and recover from, system failures, and will provide a foundation for performance monitoring and optimization.

Backing Up and Restoring Data

In Windows 2000, Windows Backup helps you plan for and recover from data loss by allowing you to back up and restore files, folders, and system state data (which includes the registry) manually, or on a schedule. The new-and-improved backup tool supports all kinds of storage devices and media, including tape drives, logical drives, removable disks, and recordable CD-ROMs. The tool also has wizards to help administrators new to Windows 2000 to implement backup and recovery processes.

Using Windows Backup

To open Windows Backup, perform the following:

1. Click Start|Run and then enter "ntbackup". Click OK.

2. Open Backup from System Tools in the Programs folder on the Start menu.

You can also open Windows Backup from within Administrative Tools on the Start menu, or from within the Control Panel. Windows Backup provides a Backup Wizard that steps you through the choices and configurations related to the backup, or you can manually configure the backup by clicking on the Backup tab of the Windows Backup tool.

Permissions and Rights

To successfully back up or restore data on a Windows 2000 system, users must have appropriate *permissions* and *user rights*. Users can back up all of their own files and folders, plus files for which they have the Read permission. To restore files and folders, users must have the Write permission.

Each system has two user rights: Backup Files And Directories and Restore Files And Directories. Users with these rights can back up or restore all files, regardless of the permissions assigned to them. By default, administrators, backup operators, and (on a server) Server Operators groups have these two user rights. You can assign one or both of these rights to any other security principal (user, group, or computer), although the best practice is to assign rights to a domain local group in a Windows 2000 native mode domain.

Backup Types

There are several different kinds of backup jobs that allow you to create a backup procedure that maximizes efficiency, minimizes media utilized, and minimizes performance impact. Each file has an archive attribute, also called a *backup marker*. When a file is changed, the archive attribute or marker is set, indicating that the file has been modified since the last backup. This marker is the focus of the different backup types because some types look for the marker; others do not. Some types clear the marker; others do not. Table 10.1 clarifies the different backup types.

Table 10.1 The different backup types.			
Backup Type	**Looks for Marker**	**Clears Marker**	**Resulting Backup Set**
Normal	No	Yes	Backup of all selected files and folders. The most complete backup and the most straight-forward to recover, but also the lengthiest to create.
Copy	No	No	Copies all selected files and folders.
Differential	Yes	No	Backup of selected files that have changed since the last normal backup. If you create a normal backup, then one week later a differential backup, and then another week later another differential backup, you could restore all data using the normal backup and the second differential backup, which contains all files that have changed since the normal backup. You could, in this example, discard the first differential backup.
Incremental	Yes	Yes	Backup of all data that has changed since the most recent (normal or incremental) backup. If you create a normal backup, then one week later an incremental backup, and then another week later a second incremental backup, you would need all three backups to recover data.
Daily	Yes	No	Backup of all files and folders that have changed during the day.

Backup Strategies

Backup strategies generally combine different backup types. Some backup types require more time to create the backup. A normal backup takes the most time to create because it is backing up all selected files; however, it creates a "baseline" or complete backup. The second backup could be incremental or differential—the result would be the same. The third and subsequent backups are where the difference starts to be significant. If the second and third backups are differential, the third backup includes all files changed since the normal backup. If the second and third backups are incremental, the third backup includes only files changed since the second, incremental, backup.

So why wouldn't you just do a normal backup and then do incremental backups until the end of time? Because incremental backups take longer than a differential backup to *recover*. Imagine recovering a machine that had a normal backup one year ago, and an incremental backup every week since. To recover that system after a catastrophe, you would have to restore the normal backup and then restore 51 incremental backups. If you had used differential backups, you would have to restore only the normal backup and the most recent differential backup.

Therefore, you should balance the "cost" of backup time against the "cost" of recovery time. Also factor in the media required to support your backup plan. You must save incremental backups until the next normal backup. You need keep only the most recent differential backup, along with the most recent normal backup.

Configuring File and Folder Backup

When you create a backup job using the Backup Wizard or the Backup tab of the Windows Backup utility, you can specify:

➤ Drives, files, or folders to back up. Select the checkmark next to a drive, file, or folder. Selected items are backed up according to the backup type. Cleared items are not backed up. A grayed-out checkmark indicates a container (disk or folder) in which some, but not all, contents are selected.

➤ A backup destination. You can back up to a file or to any other storage device configured on your system.

➤ A path and file name for the backup file, or a tape to use.

➤ Backup options such as backup type and log file type.

➤ A description of the job, to help you identify the job.

➤ Whether the backup medium already contains existing backup jobs.

➤ Advanced backup options, including compression and data verification.

Backing Up the System State

The Backup utility can back up what is called *system state* data, which includes critical files that you can use to rebuild the system. You can reinstall a failed system with the Windows 2000 CD-ROM. Then, you can restore the system state data, bringing the system back to its original condition as of the system state backup.

 Be familiar with backing up the system state! Know that the backup program *can* provide you with a backup of the system's registry as a whole, but it cannot back up individual components of system state data.

System state data includes the following:

➤ The registry

➤ The component services class registration database—Component Object Model + (COM+) objects

➤ System startup files

➤ Certificate Services database—domain controllers (DCs) and member servers running Certificate Services only

➤ Active Directory—DCs only

➤ Sysvol folder—DCs only

Configuring System State Backup

To configure system state backup, perform the following steps:

1. In the Backup Wizard, on the What To Back Up page, select Only Back Up The System State Data.

2. In the Backup Wizard, on the Items To Back Up page, expand My Computer and select the System State Data checkbox.

Scheduling Backup Jobs

You can use the Backup utility in conjunction with Task Scheduler to schedule backups to occur at regular intervals or during periods of relative inactivity on a network.

Scheduling a Backup When Using the Backup Wizard

To schedule a backup when using the Backup Wizard, perform the following steps:

1. In the Backup Wizard, on the Completing The Backup Wizard page, click Advanced.

2. On the When To Back Up page, click Later.

3. Enter a Job Name.

4. Click Set Schedule.

5. In the Schedule Job dialog box, you can configure start time and frequency.

6. Click OK.

Configuring a Job Using the Scheduled Jobs Tab

To configure a job using the Scheduled Jobs tab, perform the following steps:

1. In the Backup utility, click the Scheduled Jobs tab.

2. Double-click the day you wish to start scheduled backups.

3. Complete the information in the Backup Wizard.

Restoring Files and Folders

You can restore files and folders by using the Backup utility, using the Restore Wizard, or manually restoring them (without the wizard). When you restore files and folders, you specify which ones to restore, a restore location (original location, alternate location, or a single folder), and options (such as replace existing files with backup files).

If you backed up data from an NT File System (NTFS) volume, you must restore data to an NTFS volume to avoid data loss and preserve permissions, Encrypting File System (EFS) settings (encryption), disk quota settings, mounted drive configuration, and remote storage information.

Troubleshooting and Repairing a Windows 2000 System

Windows 2000 has several features that allow you to repair a system that will not start or will not load Windows 2000: Safe Mode (and other advanced startup options), the Recovery Console, and the Emergency Repair Disk (ERD). These features are useful if some of your system files become corrupted or are accidentally erased, or if you have installed software or device drivers that cause your system to not work properly.

Safe Mode and Other Advanced Startup Options

Safe Mode lets you start your system with a minimal set of device drivers and services. For example, if newly installed device drivers or software are preventing your computer from starting, you may be able to start your computer in Safe Mode and then remove the software or device drivers from your system. Safe Mode does not work in all situations, especially if your system files are corrupted or missing, or if your hard disk is damaged or has failed. All Safe Modes start using standard VGA and create a boot log, which is useful when you are determining the exact cause of system startup problems.

In Safe Mode, Windows 2000 uses default settings, including the VGA monitor, Microsoft mouse driver, no network connections, and the minimum device drivers required to start Windows. If your computer does not start successfully using Safe Mode, you may need to use the Recovery Console feature or ERD, covered later in this chapter, to repair your system.

Windows 2000 also provides several startup modes to help you troubleshoot and repair Windows 2000 systems, as well as recover from various types of disaster. Understanding each mode allows you to make informed decisions about the best startup method to use in a particular crisis situation. To select an advanced startup option, press F8 during the operating system selection phase of the Windows 2000 startup process. These startup options definitely provide extra troubleshooting capabilities for your Windows 2000 machines.

Safe Mode with Networking

This starts Windows 2000 using only safe mode drivers and services and drivers required to enable network connections. If you are confident that network issues are not the cause of your problem, it can be useful to boot to a mode that allows you to connect to a remote system, access installation files and service packs, or back up data.

Safe Mode with the Command Prompt

This option uses the Safe Mode configuration but displays the command prompt instead of the Windows graphical user interface (GUI) after you log on successfully. This is useful if you believe a process spawned by the Explorer shell is causing your problem.

Advanced Startup Option: Enable Boot Logging

This starts Windows 2000 and logs all drivers and services that the system loads (or fails to load) to a log file called ntbtlog.txt, located in the %SystemRoot% directory. Safe Mode, Safe Mode with Networking, and Safe Mode with Command Prompt also create a boot log file. The boot log is useful when you are determining the exact cause of system startup problems.

Advanced Startup Option: Enable VGA Mode

This option employs the extremely stable and well-debugged standard VGA driver for Windows 2000. This mode is useful when you have installed a new video card or have configured the wrong or faulty driver. Video is a common troubleshooting issue in the Windows environment. This driver is used in the various Safe Modes.

Advanced Startup Option: Last Known Good Configuration

Windows 2000 starts using the registry configuration (ControlSet) that was saved at the last successful logon to Windows 2000. Last Known Good Configuration helps you recover from incorrect configuration of hardware device drivers and services. However, it does not solve problems caused by corrupted or missing drivers or files. Any changes made to the ControlSet key of the registry since the last successful startup and logon are lost when you select to start up with the Last Known Good Configuration. You should try this option before resorting to the emergency repair process, discussed later in this chapter.

Advanced Startup Option: Directory Services Restore Mode

This option applies only to Windows 2000 DCs and is used to restore Active Directory and the sysvol folder.

Advanced Startup Option: Debugging Mode

In this mode, Windows 2000 starts and sends debugging information through a serial cable to another computer.

Advanced Startup Option: Remote Installation Options

If you are using or have used Remote Installation Service (RIS) to install Windows 2000 on your computer, you may see additional options related to restoring or recovering your system using RIS. RIS is covered in detail in Chapter 4.

Specifying Windows 2000 Behavior if the System Stops Unexpectedly

To specify Windows 2000 behavior if the system stops unexpectedly, follow these steps:

1. Right-click My Computer and then select Properties.

2. On the Advanced tab, click Startup And Recovery, and under Recovery, select the actions that Windows 2000 should perform if a Stop error occurs.

Available Recovery Actions

The following are the available recovery actions:

➤ If you select Write An Event To The System Log or Send An Administrative Alert, you must have a paging file that is at least 2MB on the computer's boot volume.

➤ The Write An Event To The System Log option is available only on Windows 2000 Professional. On Windows 2000 Server, this action occurs by default every time a Stop error occurs.

➤ The Write Debugging Information To option requires a paging file on the boot volume large enough to hold all of the computer's physical RAM, plus 1MB. If you also select the Write Kernel Information Only checkbox, Windows 2000 writes only kernel information to the listed file instead of the entire contents of system memory.

➤ You can save some memory if you clear the Write Debugging Information To, Write An Event To The System Log, or Send An Administrative Alert options. The memory saved depends on the computer, but the drivers that enable these features typically require about 60KB through 70KB.

➤ If you contact Microsoft Product Support Services about a Stop error, it may ask for the system-memory dump file generated by the Write Debugging Information To option. For each dump file generated, Windows always writes to the same file name. To save successive dump files, change the file name after each Stop error.

Setting Up Recovery Actions to Take Place When a Service Fails

To set up recovery actions to take place when a service fails, perform the following steps:

1. Open Services.

2. Right-click the service for which you want to set recovery actions and then click Properties.

3. On the Recovery tab, click the actions you want in First Attempt, Second Attempt, and Subsequent Attempts.

If you select Run A File, do not specify programs or scripts that require user input. If you select Reboot The Computer, you can specify how long to wait before restarting the computer by clicking on Reboot Computer Information. You can also create a message to display to remote users before the computer restarts.

The Recovery Console

The *Recovery Console* is a startup option that provides you with a command-line interface that lets you repair system problems using a limited set of command-line commands. Using the Recovery Console, you can start and stop services, read and write data on a local drive (including drives formatted to use NTFS), format drives, repair a corrupted master boot record, and perform many other administrative tasks. This feature gives you maximum control over the repair process; only advanced users and administrators should use it.

The Recovery Console is particularly useful if you need to repair your system by copying a file from a floppy or CD-ROM to your hard drive. It can also help you when you need to reconfigure a service that is preventing your computer from starting properly. You should try this option before resorting to the emergency repair process, discussed later in this chapter.

Running the Recovery Console on a System that Will Not Start

To run the Recovery Console on a system that will not start, perform the following steps:

1. Insert the Windows 2000 Professional Setup Disk 1 (3.5-inch floppy) into your disk drive; or, if you have a bootable CD-ROM drive, insert the Windows 2000 Professional CD-ROM into your CD-ROM drive.

2. Restart your computer.

3. Follow the directions on the screen. If you are using the Setup Disks, you are prompted to insert the others into the disk drive. It may take several minutes to load files. Choose the options to repair your Windows 2000 installation and, finally, to start the Recovery Console.

Before a system fails, open a command prompt in Windows 2000, and, from the i386 folder on the Windows 2000 CD-ROM or an equivalent distribution, enter the command **winnt32/cmdcons**. Doing so installs the command console on the local hard drive (this requires 7MB of disk space) and configures it as a valid startup option. Then, if you wish to start the system to the Recovery Console, you do not require the Windows 2000 CD-ROM or Setup Disks. Simply boot the machine and press F8 for startup options.

Launching the Recovery Console

The Recovery Console is quite powerful, so only advanced users who have a thorough knowledge of Windows 2000 should use it. Also, it is recommended that you install the Recovery Console on each Windows 2000 machine so it is always an available startup option.

After you start the Recovery Console, you must choose which drive you want to log on to (if you have a dual-boot or multiboot system), and you must log on with a local administrator account and password. The design of Recovery Console grants the administrator access to the root of the hard drives, the **\cmdcons** directory if it exists, and the **\winnt directory** and all directories below it. You will have full access to the CD-ROM and to floppy drives. These limitations are in place for security concerns, and access to other devices or systems is functionally beyond the scope and purpose of the Recovery Console. You use the Recovery Console only to allow you to repair the existing installation and to successfully boot Windows 2000.

Recovery Console Commands

The easiest way to work in the Recovery Console—as in any unfamiliar environment—is to type "help" at the command prompt and then press the Enter key. The commands available in the Recovery Console are listed in Table 10.2.

Table 10.2 Recovery Console commands.	
Command	**Description**
chdir (cd)	Displays the name of the current folder or changes the current folder.
chkdsk	Checks a disk and displays a status report.
cls	Clears the screen.
copy	Copies a single file to another location.
delete (del)	Deletes one or more files.
dir	Displays a list of files and subfolders in a folder.
disable	Disables a system service or a device driver.
enable	Starts or enables a system service or a device driver.
exit	Exits the Recovery Console and restarts your computer.
fdisk	Manages partitions on your hard disks.
fixboot	Writes a new partition boot sector onto the system partition.
fixmbr	Repairs the master boot record of the partition boot sector.
format	Formats a disk.
help	Displays a list of the commands that you use in the Recovery Console.
logon	Logs on to a Windows 2000 installation.
map	Displays the drive letter mappings.
mkdir (md)	Creates a folder.
more	Displays a text file.
rename (ren)	Renames a single file.
rmdir (rd)	Deletes a folder.
systemroot	Sets the current folder to the SystemRoot folder of the system that you are currently logged on to.
type	Displays a text file.

Emergency Repair Disks (ERDs) and the Emergency Repair Process

The *ERD* feature helps you repair problems with system files, your startup environment (if you have a dual-boot or multiboot system), and the partition boot sector on your boot volume. Before you use the emergency repair process feature to repair your system, you must create an ERD. Without a recent ERD, you may not be able to leverage the full functionality of the repair process.

The ERD is quite different in Windows 2000 than it was in Windows NT 4, and you create the ERD using a different method than in NT 4. It does not contain a complete, or even partial, copy of the registry—it simply contains system and disk configuration information. But the ERD remains a very important tool.

 The rdisk.exe tool, which in Windows NT allowed you to create the ERD, *does not exist* in Windows 2000.

To create an ERD, perform the following steps:

1. Open the Backup utility.

2. Click Emergency Repair Disk on the Welcome tab.

3. Insert a blank, 1.44MB floppy into the floppy disk drive and click OK.

You can also specify to back up the registry to the repair directory to help recover from a damaged registry. When the process is complete, click OK, and then remove and label the floppy.

 *No*, you cannot boot a Windows 2000 machine with the ERD. The ERD never has been, and *is not* a bootable disk. Read your exam questions and answers closely!

Using the Emergency Repair Process

The *emergency repair process* will enable you to restore corrupted system files and configuration. Even if you have not created an ERD, you can still try to use the emergency repair process; however, you may lose any changes you have made to your system, such as service packs and updates, and you may need to reinstall them.

You can also use the emergency repair process to reinstall Windows 2000 over a damaged Windows 2000 system. This may be time-consuming but is useful if the emergency repair process does not solve your problem. To have a chance at making the emergency repair process work properly, you must follow five steps closely.

Step 1: Starting with the Windows 2000 Setup Disks or CD-ROM

Boot the computer using the Windows 2000 CD-ROM (you may need to configure your system's BIOS to enable booting to the CD-ROM if your system supports bootable CDs). You can, alternatively, boot with the first of the four Windows 2000 Setup Disks (the process will prompt you for subsequent disks). If you don't have a bootable CD-ROM and don't have the boot disks handy, run the batch file in the CD-ROM's bootdisk folder.

 **makeboot.exe** and **makebt32.exe** in Windows 2000 replace the **winnt /ox** or **winnt32 /ox** commands from NT. You can produce the boot disks on any system—it does not have to be a Windows 2000 system. Simply execute **makeboot.exe** on 16-bit operating systems and **makebt32.exe** on 32-bit platforms.

Step 2: Choosing the Repair Options during Setup

As the computer starts, Windows 2000 Setup launches. During Setup, you are prompted whether you wish to continue installing Windows 2000. Press Enter to confirm and start the process. You are then asked whether you want to install a new installation of Windows 2000 or repair an existing installation. To repair a damaged or corrupt system, press R. You are then prompted as to whether you wish to use the Recovery Console or the emergency repair process. To select the emergency repair process, press R again.

Step 3: Choosing the Type of Repair

There are only two types of repair to choose from. You are asked to select either of the following:

➤ *Fast Repair*—This requires no further interaction or choices. It checks your system and attempts to repair any problems related to the registry, system files, partition boot sector on the boot volume, and startup environment (in a multiboot environment). The Fast Repair option restores the registry from the repair directory, so it is important to have updated that directory recently. You can back up the registry to the repair directory as part of the ERD creation procedure. If your repair directory is quite outdated, Fast Repair is not the best choice because you may lose any recent changes to hardware, software, drivers, services, or other settings.

➤ *Manual Repair*—This requires user interaction and prompts you to select whether to repair system files, boot sector problems, or startup environment problems.

Note: Manual Repair does not allow you to repair the registry. To have that option, you must perform a Fast Repair.

Step 4: Starting the Repair Process

To start the repair process, you should have the ERD for the system. It is *not* advised to repair a system with another system's repair disk because each system is unique; as such, each system's ERD is also unique. You should also have the Windows 2000 installation CD handy. If you do not have the ERD, the emergency repair process attempts to locate the Windows 2000 installation on the system and begin the repair process, but it may fail.

Step 5: Restarting the Computer

Assuming the repair was successful, you should be able to restart into a functional Windows 2000 system. If not, you should consider other recovery options or, perhaps, the option of recovering by re-installing the system and restoring data from backup sets.

Optimizing and Troubleshooting Performance

Although Windows 2000 Professional performs extremely well as a general workstation platform, with the right tools, techniques, and knowledge, you can further optimize the operating system for particular roles as well as troubleshoot performance challenges. This section looks at System Monitor, Performance Logs And Alerts, Task Manager, and other tools you can use to improve Windows 2000's performance.

System Monitor

The *System Monitor snap-in* is a node of the Performance console (Start|Settings| Control Panel|Administrative Tools|Performance) and available for inclusion in custom MMC consoles. This tool allows you to visually inspect the activity of system components such as the memory, processor, disk subsystem, network cards, paging file, and applications. The plethora of performance metrics, or *counters*, available for monitoring can make the task a daunting one, indeed. We will examine the most useful counters after a tour of the Performance console's snap-ins.

Using System Monitor

System Monitor, like all MMC snap-ins, is best controlled by right-clicking. If you right-click the main portion of the Details pane, you can select Add Counters. Counters are the granular statistics related to a specific aspect of system performance. The thousands of available counters are organized hierarchically:

➤ *Computer*—You can monitor performance on the local (default) or a remote system.

➤ *Object*—Is a system component, such as processor, memory, disk, or network protocol.

➤ *Counter*—This is a performance metric related to the object on the computer selected above. There can literally be thousands of counters available for monitoring, so take advantage of the Explain button in the Add Counters dialog box—clicking on it produces a description of the selected counter.

➤ *Instance*—When an object occurs more than once on a computer, you see instances. For example, a multiprocessor machine has instances for each processor when you select the processor object. When you select the logical disk object, you see instances for each drive volume on a system. Often, instances are numbered, with the first instance being 0, the second instance 1, and so on. Often, an additional instance provides the total for all instances. For example, a dual processor system has a _Total, which reflects the combination of processors 0 and 1.

After you select a computer, object, counter, and (if necessary) instance, click Add to add the counter to your System Monitor view. By right-clicking the view and choosing Properties, you can alter all properties of the monitor, including the display color of counters, the scale and sample rate, and the format of the monitor's display—which can be in graph (default), histogram (bar chart), or report (numeric display) format.

Performance Logs And Alerts

The *Performance Logs And Alerts snap-in*, also part of the Performance console, allows you to collect and save performance data as well as proactively configure a system to generate a notification based on a performance threshold.

Configuring Alerts

Alerts allow you to generate actions based on a counter reaching a particular threshold. For example, you might want to be notified when a disk's capacity reaches 90 percent so that you might work to increase the disk's capacity before it fills up. By specifying a counter (such as %Free Space for a logical disk) and a threshold (under 10 percent), you can cause an event to be logged, a program to be run, a log to be started, or a network message to be sent.

To configure alerts, select the Alerts node in the Performance Logs And Alerts snap-in. Then, right-click in the Details pane and choose New Alert Settings. Enter a name for your alert settings—the name is for your use only. Then in the Properties dialog box, add the counter(s) appropriate for the alert you are configuring. For each counter, you must specify a threshold (over or under a particular amount) on the General tab. You can then configure, on the Action tab, what will happen when those alerts are generated. On the Schedule tab, you can specify when the selected counters should be scanned. If you specify no schedule, scanning will begin as soon as you click OK. The alert settings you have specified will appear in the Alerts node of the snap-in. Right-click an alert setting to change its configuration, delete it, or stop or start scanning.

Configuring Logs

Logs collect and store performance counters. You can view them using System Monitor, retrieve them in a spreadsheet like Excel, or import them into a database. There are two types of logs:

➤ *Counter logs*—These record data captured over a span of time and are useful for detecting trends, setting baselines of performance, and spotting performance bottlenecks. Baselines are discussed later in this chapter.

➤ *Trace logs*—These collect performance data when an event such as a process creation, disk input/output (I/O), or page fault occurs. Trace logs are useful for debugging.

To create a counter log, select the Counter Logs node of the snap-in and then right-click the Details pane and choose New Log Settings. Give the log a name that will help you identify it in the future and then click OK. In the Log dialog box, add one or more counters to be recorded and then specify the sample rate—the interval at which counter data will be collected. Obviously, a shorter sample rate provides more data but also fills up the log more quickly.

Logs are stored, by default, in the %SystemDrive%\Perflogs folder. The default format is binary (.blg extension). You can stop and start logs as desired and view them in System Monitor. To view a log with System Monitor, right-click the Display and choose Properties. Then, on the Source tab, click Log File and enter or browse to the log file name.

To analyze a log with Excel, Access, or other database and reporting tools, save the log as a comma- or tab-delimited file (.csv or .tsv extensions). Once you stop these logs, you cannot restart or append them as you can with binary logs.

Managing Performance

Monitoring, troubleshooting, and optimizing performance are some of the most important tasks you will perform as an administrator of Windows 2000 Professional systems. Managing performance involves several steps:

1. Creating a baseline

2. Proactively monitoring

3. Evaluating performance

4. Identifying potential bottlenecks

5. Taking corrective action

6. Monitoring the effectiveness and stability of the change

7. Returning to Step 2

Creating a Baseline

One of the most important, and most often overlooked, steps of managing performance is creating a baseline. A *baseline* is a range of acceptable performance of a system component under normal working conditions. Baselining, or establishing a baseline, requires that you capture key counters while a system performs with normal loads and all services running. Then, you can compare future performance against the baseline to identify potential bottlenecks, troubleshoot sudden changes in performance, and justify system improvements.

 A baseline should cover a relatively large timeframe so that it captures a range of data reflecting acceptable performance. The sample interval for the log should be somewhat large as well, so the baseline log does not become enormous. You should generate baselines regularly—perhaps even once a month—so that you can identify performance trends and evaluate bottlenecks to system and network performance. If you follow these guidelines, you will produce a baseline that gives an accurate overview of system performance.

The most useful objects to understand and monitor are the following:

➤ *Cache*—Physical memory used to store recently accessed disk data.

➤ *Memory*—RAM used to store code and data.

➤ *Paging file*—The file used to extend physical RAM and create virtual memory.

➤ *Physical disk*—The disk drive or Redundant Array of Independent Disks (RAID) device. A physical disk may contain multiple logical disks.

➤ *Logical disk*—The disk volume, including simple, logical, spanned, striped, mirrored, or RAID-5 volumes. A logical disk may span multiple physical disks.

➤ *Process*—Executable code that represents a running program.

➤ *Processor*—The Central Processing Unit (CPU).

➤ *Server*—The server service, which offers data and print services, even on a Windows 2000 Professional system.

➤ *System*—Counters that apply to all system hardware and software.

➤ *Thread*—Code that the processor is processing.

Baselines should include these critical objects as well as the other counters discussed in this chapter.

Managing Memory Performance

The counters in the Memory object represent the memory available through the system's physical RAM and virtual memory or paging file. The most important counters in the memory object are the Pages/sec counters and the Available Bytes counter:

➤ *Memory:Pages/sec, threshold over 20 pages/sec*—This counter, and all related counters (including Page Reads/sec, Page Writes/sec, Page Faults/sec, Page Inputs/sec, and Page Outputs/sec) reflect the transfer of data and code from physical RAM to the virtual paging file, and paging-related events. When any one of these counters is high, it indicates a potential memory shortage, because when a system does not have enough RAM to satisfy its needs, inactive data and code are moved from physical RAM to the virtual paging file to make room for active data and code.

➤ *Memory:Available Bytes, threshold under 4MB*—Available Bytes reflects the amount of physical RAM available after the working sets of applications and the cache have been served. Windows 2000 Professional trims working sets and page memory to the disk to maintain at least 4MB of available RAM. If this counter is consistently lower than 4MB, it generally indicates a memory shortage.

 Memory is often the first performance bottleneck in the "real world." The counters related to processor and hard drive utilization might be well beyond their thresholds simply because inadequate memory is causing paging, which impacts those two components. So always check the memory counters to make sure that they are not the "root" performance bottleneck.

To correct a memory shortage, your first reaction might be to add more RAM, which is certainly one solution. However, it is often equally valid to optimize memory usage by stopping unnecessary services, drivers, and background applications, or moving services or applications to systems with excess capacity.

Managing the Paging File

When physical RAM is not sufficient to support active processes, the *Virtual Memory Manager (VMM)* moves less active data or code from physical RAM to virtual memory stored in the paging file. When a process later attempts to address data or code currently in the paging file, the VMM transfers that memory space into physical RAM. The paging file thus provides for efficient utilization of a system's physical RAM and allows a system to support more activity than its physical RAM alone would allow. Transfer of pages, 4KB blocks of memory, to and from the paging file is normal on any system, but excessive paging or *thrashing* indicates a memory shortage. In addition, the paging file itself can impede performance if it is not properly optimized.

You configure the paging file using the System applet in Control Panel. Click the Advanced tab, the Performance Options button, and then, in the Virtual Memory section, click Change. The paging file, called pagefile.sys, is created on the %SystemRoot% volume by default, and its default initial size is 1.5 times physical RAM. You can configure the paging file to be placed on other volumes or to be split across multiple volumes, in which case there will be a pagefile.sys on selected volumes, and the total size of the paging file is the sum of all paging files. You can also configure the Initial Size, the space created initially by the VMM and reserved for paging activity, and the Maximum Size, a setting that can permit the VMM to expand the paging file to a size greater than the Initial Size.

You can optimize paging by doing the following:

➤ *Remove the paging file from the system and boot partitions.* The system partition is technically the partition that is used to start the system—it contains NTLDR and the boot sector. To make things confusing, the boot partition contains the operating system and is indicated by the variable %SystemRoot%. Luckily, most computers are configured with Windows 2000 on the C: drive (the first partition), making the boot partition, the system partition, and %SystemRoot% all equal to C:. To remove the paging file from a partition, set its Initial Size and Maximum Size to 0 and click the Set button.

➤ *Configure the paging file to reside on multiple physical disks, and configure the Initial Size and Maximum Size identically on all drives.* The paging subsystem then spreads written pages evenly across all available pagefile.sys files.

➤ *Configure the paging file to reside on fast, less active drives.* If you have drives of various speeds, put the paging file on the fastest one. If you have drives that are less active, put the paging file on those so the paging system doesn't have to compete as often with other read or write requests.

➤ *Before moving the paging file, defragment the volumes on which you will put the paging file.* Doing so helps prevent a fragmented paging file.

➤ *Set the Initial Size to be sufficient for the system's paging requirements, and then set the Maximum Size to the same size.* When the Maximum Size is greater than the Initial Size, and the system must expand the paging file, the expansion puts an additional burden on both the processor and disk subsystems. In addition, the paging file is likely to become fragmented, further hitting the performance of paging.

 The ideal paging file configuration is to split it evenly over multiple *physical* disks except for the disk with the system and boot partitions.

Managing Disk Performance

The PhysicalDisk and LogicalDisk performance objects collect metrics related to individual disk drives and logical disk volumes, respectively. PhysicalDisk counters focus on a storage device, so you should use them to analyze hardware performance. Use LogicalDisk counters, which focus on a specific volume, analyze read and write performance.

In Windows 2000, PhysicalDisk counters are available in System Monitor and Performance Logs And Alerts, but LogicalDisk counters are not gathered until you run the **diskperf–yv** (**v** for "volume") command. The switches for the **diskperf** command include **–yd** (enables PhysicalDisk counters, which is the default), **-y** (enables both PhysicalDisk and LogicalDisk counters), **-nv, -nd**, and **–n** (disable LogicalDisk, PhysicalDisk, and both sets of counters, respectively).

 Until you enable the counters with the appropriate **diskperf** switch, the counters are not visible in System Monitor or Performance Logs And Alerts.

The following disk counters will help you to monitor and manage disk performance:

➤ *PhysicalDisk/LogicalDisk: %DiskTime, threshold close to 100%*—This reports the amount of time that a disk is busy servicing read or write requests.

➤ *PhysicalDisk/LogicalDisk: Disk Queue Length, threshold 2*—The Average and Current disk queue length counters reflect the read/write requests that are pending and being serviced. If the queue is long, processes are being delayed.

When disk performance is a bottleneck, you can add capacity; replace disks with faster hardware; move applications, services, or data to underutilized disks; or implement spanned, striped, or RAID-5 volumes.

Managing Network Performance

Although Windows 2000 Server can support Network Monitor for relatively sophisticated network traffic analysis, Windows 2000 Professional has limited network performance tools. Counters are available for the number of bytes and packets received and sent over a particular network interface. However, you cannot analyze the contents or properties of packets using Windows 2000 Professional tools alone.

To conduct detailed network analysis for a Windows 2000 Professional system, install the Network Monitor Driver. From the Network And Dialup Connections folder, right-click a connection, choose Properties, and then click Install|Protocol|Network Monitor Driver. Network Monitor Driver can collect packets that the Windows 2000 Professional's network interfaces send or receive. You can then analyze those packets using the version of Network Monitor that ships with Systems Management Server (SMS) 2, SP1, or later.

Managing Processor Performance

A system's processor is one of the more difficult components to optimize because every other component impacts it. Low memory leads to paging, which increases processor usage; fragmented disk drives increase processor usage; hardware interrupts keep the processor busy; and, of course, applications and services are placing demands on the processor. Therefore, to optimize a processor, you need to look at Processor counters, as well as counters for other objects. Some of the most useful Processor counters are the following:

➤ *Processor:%ProcessorTime, threshold near 100%*—A processor being fully used (100 percent) is not necessarily a sign of a performance bottleneck—in fact, one would hope that you would be utilizing this expensive system component at its full capacity. Therefore, although %ProcessorTime is a flag that indicates a potential bottleneck, it is not in itself enough to prescribe a solution. Check Memory:Pages/sec to examine paging and determine whether low memory is causing excessive paging.

➤ *Processor:Interrupts/sec, threshold varies*—A malfunctioning hardware device may send excessive interrupts to the processor. Compare this counter to a baseline; a significant rise in this counter without a corresponding increase in system activity may indicate a bad device. Network cards are particularly infamous for generating bogus interrupts.

➤ *System:Processor Queue Length, threshold 2*—A queue length that is regularly above 2 indicates that threads are backing up as they wait for processor attention.

➤ *Process:%ProcessorTime (Instance—each service or application)*—This counter enumerates the activity of individual applications and services, allowing you to identify processes that are placing demands on the processor.

If Processor Queue Length is low and %ProcessorTime is averaging above 85 percent for extended periods of time, these settings indicate that a single threaded application or service is keeping the processor busy. A faster processor may improve performance of such a system. However, if Processor Queue Length is high, a second processor would be a better solution, or you might consider moving processes to underutilized systems.

Task Manager

Task Manager enables you to view applications and processes and a number of other common performance counters. To open Task Manager, right-click the taskbar and choose Task Manager, or press Ctrl+Shift+Esc. The Applications tab enumerates active applications. The Performance tab displays useful performance metrics beginning when Task Manager is opened. The Processes tab can display a number of process-related counters. Click View|Select Columns to indicate which counters you wish to view.

Managing Application Performance

Windows 2000 preemptively multitasks active processes, ensuring that all threads gain access to the processor. Processes do run at different priorities, however. Priority levels of 0 to 31 are assigned to a process, and higher-level processes are executed before lower-level processes. As a user, you can specify process priority using Task Manager. Right-clicking a process on the Processes tab enables you to set a process' priority. Processes are assigned a priority of Normal by default. Choosing Above Normal or High will increase the priority of a process and thereby increase the frequency with which its threads are serviced. Choosing Below Normal or Low will diminish the servicing of a process.

Do not use the Realtime priority. This priority should be reserved for real-time data gathering applications and operating system functions. Setting an application to Realtime priority can cause instability and can be difficult to reverse without restarting the system.

Process priority can also be controlled when an application is launched, using the **start** command with the **/low, /belownormal, /normal, /abovenormal, /high,** and **/realtime** switches.

Practice Questions

Question 1

You have just installed a new tape drive in your Windows 2000 Professional computer. You want to create a reliable backup of your machine's entire registry, all system settings, and your COM+ objects. How would you accomplish this?

○ a. Use Windows Backup to back up the system state to tape.

○ b. Use Windows Backup to perform an incremental backup of the system to tape.

○ c. Use Windows Backup to perform a full backup of the system to tape.

○ d. Copy the contents of \WINNT\SYSTEM32\CONFIG to a secure network share on a server.

Answer a is correct. Remember that backing up the system state is how Windows 2000 provides a method for you to obtain a backup of the registry and system settings, as well as COM+ objects. Backing up data does not back up these settings, so answers b and c are incorrect. The **config** directory's files are locked during operation, so they cannot be copied therefore answer d is incorrect.

Question 2

> You are attempting to install a Plug and Play modem in a Windows 2000 Professional computer. The modem appears to be working when you install it, but later it stops working entirely. You try several more times to reinstall the modem, but it keeps failing. What should you do?
>
> ○ a. Use the Add/Remove Hardware Wizard to remove the modem driver. Power down the computer. Let Windows 2000 locate the device driver of its choice.
>
> ○ b. Start the computer in Safe Mode. Remove the device driver for the modem. Restart the computer normally and let Windows 2000 find the device driver of its choice.
>
> ○ c. Use the Add/Remove Hardware program to troubleshoot the device. Select the modem from the list that appears. The Hardware Troubleshooter starts.
>
> ○ d. Install the modem in another computer to see if it fails there as well. If not, reinstall it in the first computer and use the manufacturer's most current driver when Windows 2000 prompts for the file location of the driver files.

Answer b is correct. To fix a device installation "gone wrong" (when reinstallation doesn't work), use Safe Mode to remove the device driver and then let Windows 2000 select a device driver. Remember that the manufacturer's driver may not work as well as a driver from Windows 2000, which is similar. Answers a, c, and d will not enable the modem to function.

Question 3

> You have been editing the Windows 2000 registry with regedt32.exe to try to get a device to work. Now, as punishment for your attempted good deed, your Windows 2000 computer will not boot. What should you try first for a quick system restoration?
>
> ○ a. Power on the computer and hit the F8 key to get into Safe Mode.
>
> ○ b. Power on the computer and hit the F8 key to select Last Known Good Configuration.
>
> ○ c. Use the Emergency Recovery Disk to boot and restore system files.
>
> ○ d. In the Recovery Console, set the path to a floppy drive or a CD where you have a backup of the system files. Copy the files from the floppy or CD to the hard drive.

Answer b is correct. Powering on the computer and hitting the F8 key to select Last Known Good Configuration is your first choice because you know that the registry was just changed—by you! Safe Mode is better for situations where a new device or software was just added and now your system won't start up. Therefore, answer a is incorrect. You cannot boot using the ERD. Therefore, answer c is incorrect. The Recovery Console is an option, but you would resort to it if selecting Last Known Good Configuration did not work. Therefore, answer d is incorrect.

Question 4

You performed a normal backup of your Windows 2000 Professional computer on Sunday. For the remaining days of the week, you want to back up only the files and folders that have changed since the previous day. What is the best backup type for you to select?

○ a. Daily

○ b. Differential

○ c. Incremental

○ d. Normal

Answer c is correct. An incremental backup backs up the changes since the last markers were set and then clears the markers. So, for Monday through Saturday, you back up only the changes since the previous day. Differential, normal, and daily backups do not perform the same function, and therefore answers a, b, and d are incorrect.

Question 5

You install a new device driver for a SCSI adapter in your Windows 2000 machine. When your restart the computer, though, trouble is on the horizon. Windows 2000 stops responding after the kernel load phase. How can you get Windows 2000 to restart successfully?

○ a. Boot your computer with the Emergency Repair Disk, and then remove the new device driver.

○ b. Boot your computer with the Windows 2000 CD-ROM and then select Restore to restore the system state.

○ c. Restore the system from the most recent backup.

○ d. Select the Last Known Good Configuration option to start Windows 2000.

Answer d is correct. The Last Known Good Configuration option is the best, and quickest, choice because it does not contain any reference to the new (and possibly noncompliant) device driver for your SCSI adapter. The Emergency Repair Disk is not bootable, and there is no "Restore" startup option, therefore answers a and b are incorrect. Answer c may produce something like the desired result, but is not the *best* answer.

Question 6

You want to monitor PhysicalDisk performance counters of a logical drive. With a standard installation of Windows 2000 Professional, what additional operation must you perform to enable the monitoring of the PhysicalDisk counters?

- ○ a. Install the Network Monitor Driver.
- ○ b. Run the **diskperf** command with the **–y** switch.
- ○ c. Install the Network Monitor Driver and run **diskperf –yv**.
- ○ d. No additional operations are required. The PhysicalDisk counters are accessible by default.

Answer d is correct. PhysicalDisk counters are enabled in Windows 2000 Professional, unlike in Windows NT 4. Network Monitor Driver is used for collecting network traffic counters and for capturing packets. It is not used for any physical disk monitoring. Therefore, answers a and c are incorrect. The **diskperf –y** command *does* enable the PhysicalDisk counters if they have been disabled, as will **diskperf –yd** in answer c, but it is not *necessary* to run these commands because the counters are enabled by default. Therefore, answer b is incorrect.

Question 7

A user runs the CADDraw application several times a day to produce renderings of technical drawings. While CADDraw is running, the user catches up on email and writes memos and reports. You want to teach the user how to maximize the responsiveness of CADDraw so that the renderings don't take as long to complete. What do you teach the user?

○ a. Configure Performance Options in the System applet to optimize for applications.

○ b. Use Task Manager to change the priority of all applications to Above Normal.

○ c. Use Task Manager to set the CADDraw process priority to Realtime.

○ d. Use Task Manager to set the CADDraw process priority to High.

Answer d is correct. By setting the CADDraw process priority to High, CADDraw will be relatively higher than all other applications, including email and word processors, which launch at a default priority of Normal. Using Task Manager to set the CADDraw process priority to High increases the amount of attention CADDraw receives from the processor and improves its performance. Answer a is incorrect because Performance Options changes the performance for *all* applications, not just CADDraw—this does not maximize CADDraw. Answer b is incorrect because raising all applications to Above Normal does not maximize CADDraw—it will still be at the same priority level as the other applications. Answer c, although it might maximize CADDraw, would likely cause system instability and would not be the best choice. Therefore, answer c is incorrect.

Question 8

Your Windows 2000 Professional system is experiencing decreased performance, and you suspect excessive paging. Which counter provides you with the best measure with which to confirm your suspicion?

○ a. Paging File:%Usage

○ b. Paging File:%Usage Peak

○ c. Memory: Pages/sec

○ d. PhysicalDisk: Disk Writes/sec

Answer c is correct. The Pages/sec counters (and there are many of them) all relate to paging activity—the transfer of memory from physical RAM to the virtual memory of the paging file. The paging file counters are useful to determine if you need a larger paging file but do not really tell you what is excessive. For example, you might have a %Usage counter of 90 percent, but if your paging file is only 20MB, there might not be too much paging—you might just have too small a paging file. Therefore, answers a and b are incorrect. PhysicalDisk counters increase when there is paging, but they do not tell you specifically that paging is causing the disk activity. Therefore, answer d is incorrect.

Question 9

> A Windows 2000 Professional system is not performing to specifications. You want to determine what course of action to take, and you examine a performance log, which reveals the following:
>
> Processor: %ProcessorTime: 95
>
> System: Processor Queue Length: 3
>
> Memory: Pages/sec: 10
>
> PhysicalDisk: Avg Disk Queue Length: 1
>
> Paging File: %Usage: 25
>
> What should you do to improve performance?
>
> ○ a. Add a second processor.
>
> ○ b. Add memory.
>
> ○ c. Replace the hard disk with a faster disk drive.
>
> ○ d. Enlarge the paging file.

Answer a is correct. The processor is overworked, and the processor queue indicates that threads are backed up and are not being serviced. Answer b would often be correct, because memory is often the primary bottleneck, but in this instance, paging is well within the acceptable range. Therefore, answer b is incorrect. The disk subsystem and paging file are not beyond thresholds either. Therefore, answers c and d are incorrect.

Question 10

Which of the following tools is best suited for creating a baseline of system performance?

○ a. System Monitor

○ b. Performance Logs And Alerts

○ c. Task Manager

○ d. System Information

○ e. NTBackup

Answer b is correct. Performance Logs And Alerts captures counters during a representative period of normal activity to create the baseline. You can use System Monitor to *view* the baseline, but it is not appropriate for creating the baseline in the first place. Therefore, answer a is incorrect. Task Manager, System Information, and NTBackup are not suited for baselining either. Therefore, answers c, d, and e are incorrect.

Need to Know More?

 Microsoft Corporation. *Microsoft Windows 2000 Professional Resource Kit.* Redmon, Washington: Microsoft Press, 2000. ISBN: 1-57231-808-2. This has invaluable information on backing up and recovering data, as well as on using the Recovery Console and the emergency repair process.

 Nielsen, Morten Strunge. *Windows 2000 Professional Configuration and Implementation.* Scottsdale, Arizona: The Coriolis Group, 2000. ISBN: 1-57610-528-8. This book offers comprehensive coverage of configuration and implementation with Windows 2000 Professional.

 Stinson, Craig and Carl Siechert. *Running Microsoft Windows 2000 Professional.* Redmon, Washington: Microsoft Press, 2000. ISBN: 1-57231-838-4. This guidebook to Windows 2000 Professional is a good source for information on optimizing and troubleshooting Windows 2000 systems, and on using the Recovery Console.

 Search the TechNet CD (or its online version through **www.microsoft.com**) and/or the Windows 2000 Professional Resource Kit CD using the keywords "backup," "restore," "Recovery Console," "emergency repair," "system state," "taskman," "performance," "optimizing," "counters," and "last known good."

Sample Test

Question 1

You wish to secure a Windows 2000 Professional system beyond the default security level, with as little guesswork as possible. Which tool do you use?

○ a. Local Policy

○ b. Group Policy

○ c. Security Configuration And Analysis

○ d. Domain Security Policy

Question 2

You have a domain policy that clears the name of the last user who logged on from the logon dialog box. You want your Windows 2000 laptop to display your name each time you log on, to save time logging on. What must you do to achieve this?

○ a. Change the DontDisplayLastUser registry entry.

○ b. Configure a local security policy that disables the Do Not Display Last User Name In Logon Screen policy.

○ c. Configure a security database with the Do Not Display Last User Name In Logon Screen option cleared.

○ d. Configure a Group Policy for the OU of your laptop that disables the Do Not Display Last User Name In Logon Screen policy.

Question 3

What can you use to configure user rights in Windows 2000? [Check all correct answers]

❏ a. Local Security Policy

❏ b. Group Policy

❏ c. User Manager

❏ d. Users and Passwords applet

Question 4

You want Cory to be able to format partitions on the hard drive of her Windows 2000 Professional system. Which tool will you use to give her this privilege?

○ a. The Users And Passwords applet

○ b. Disk Management snap-in

○ c. Local Security Policy

○ d. Registry Editor

Question 5

You have a template account created for all new salespeople. It specifies group membership, logon script, profile location, dial-up permission, and other attributes common to sales users. Immediately after you create individual user accounts based on the template, users report that they cannot log on. Which setting is causing the problem?

○ a. Account Is locked out.

○ b. Account Is disabled.

○ c. User Must Change Password At Next Logon.

○ d. Enforce Password Complexity.

Question 6

You back up PRO1 each morning using the following backup strategy:

Monday: Incremental

Tuesday: Incremental

Wednesday: Incremental

Thursday: Incremental

Friday: Normal

On Wednesday afternoon, PRO1 crashes and you must recover the hard drive. Which backup sets must you restore, and in which order?

Monday

Tuesday

Wednesday

Thursday

Friday

Question 7

You want to back up service and software settings on a Windows 2000 Professional system. What must you do?

○ a. Create an ERD.

○ b. Back up the system state.

○ c. Copy the WINNT folder to a server.

○ d. Back up the user profile folder.

Question 8

You are monitoring performance of a Windows 2000 Professional system that seems to be performing below expectations. You note the following counters:

Memory: Pages/sec—80

Processor: % Utilization—90

Physical Disk: % Disk Time—85

System: Processor Queue Length—3

Which of the following would be most likely to overcome the performance bottleneck on this system?

○ a. Additional memory

○ b. A faster processor

○ c. A second processor

○ d. A faster hard drive

○ e. A larger hard drive

Question 9

You are monitoring performance of a Windows 2000 Professional system that seems to be performing below expectations. You note the following counters:

Memory: Pages/sec—10

Processor: % Utilization—99

Physical Disk: % Disk Time—20

System: Processor Queue Length—2.5

Which of the following would be most likely to overcome the performance bottleneck on this system?

○ a. Additional memory

○ b. A faster processor

○ c. A second processor

○ d. A faster hard drive

○ e. A larger hard drive

○ f. A larger paging file

Question 10

You have noticed steadily decreasing performance of your system and suspect drive fragmentation. From what tool can you initiate a disk defragmentation?

○ a. The Properties sheet of a drive volume

○ b. The Disk Management snap-in

○ c. The Add/Remove Hardware Wizard

○ d. The System applet in Control Panel

Question 11

Which of the following tools allows you to monitor an application's priority?

○ a. Computer Management

○ b. System applet in Control Panel

○ c. Task Manager

○ d. Add/Remove Programs

Question 12

What folder contains local profiles on a clean installation of a Windows 2000 Professional computer?

○ a. %SystemRoot%\Winnt\system32\profiles

○ b. %SystemRoot%\Winnt\profiles

○ c. %SystemRoot%\Winnt\documents and settings

○ d. %SystemRoot%\documents and settings

Question 13

Your sales staff needs to keep a locally cached copied of the presentations share on server1, which is a Windows 2000 server. When the sales staff selects the presentations share on \\server1, they report there is no option to make files available offline. How do you resolve this problem?

○ a   Configure the caching properties to allow caching of files for the presentation share on the sales staff's computers.

○ b.   Configure the caching properties to allow caching of files for the presentation share on \\server1.

○ c.   Configure the caching properties to manual caching for documents for the presentation share on the sales staff's computers.

○ d.   Configure the caching properties to manual caching for documents for the presentation share on \\server1.

Question 14

As the administrator for your Windows 2000 domain called **corp.com**, you create a Group Policy to deploy a Windows Installer Package service release to update the clients' word processing application. The update applied successfully to all but one client computer. What should you do to apply the service pack to the remaining client?

○ a.   Redeploy the service package with a zap file.

○ b.   Redeploy the service package with a mst file.

○ c.   Restart the Windows Installer service on the domain controller.

○ d.   Restart the Windows Installer service on the failed client computer.

Question 15

A user, Jerry, has enabled files located on the network to be available for offline usage. Jerry has configured synchronization to occur every day at 4:30 P.M. and has disabled synchronization during logon or logoff. Today, Jerry needs to leave at 3:00 P.M. and must synchronize the changes that have been made before logging off. How can he synchronize the offline files before logging off from the network?

- ○ a. Configure Synchronization Manager to synchronize during an idle period.
- ○ b. Use Synchronization Manager to force synchronization before leaving.
- ○ c. Configure Synchronization Manager to synchronize during logon.
- ○ d. Copy the files that have been changed to the network file server share point.

Question 16

You need to enable Windows 2000 Professional to read text from all dialog boxes and all applications to visually impaired users. What must you configure to allow for this functionality?

- ○ a. SoundSentry
- ○ b. ShowSounds
- ○ c. Narrator
- ○ d. Windows Media Player captioning

Question 17

What is the function of the sysprep.inf file?

- ○ a. It is used for remote installations.
- ○ b. It is the answer file for **Sysprep** installations.
- ○ c. It is used to configure custom parameters for **sysprep.exe**.
- ○ d. It is the settings file for custom keyboard layouts.

Question 18

You want to deploy Windows 2000 Professional to network clients by using a remote installation server. However, when the clients attempt to boot their computer from their network adapter, the client cannot connect to the remote installation server. How else can the client connect to it?

- ○ a. Use the Network Client Administrator to create a network boot disk to connect to the remote installation server.
- ○ b. Use **rbfg.exe** to create a network boot disk to connect to the remote installation server.
- ○ c. Use **dcpromo.exe** to create a network boot disk to connect to the remote installation server.
- ○ d. Use Recovery Console to create a network boot disk to connect to the remote installation server.

Question 19

A computer on which you want to install Windows 2000 Professional has 96MB of memory, a Pentium II 400MHz CPU, and a 4GB hard drive with 500MB of free space. You attempt the installation but it fails before the graphic phase of the process. What must you do to install Windows 2000 Professional on this computer?

- ○ a. Install a Pentium III 500MHz CPU.
- ○ b. Install 128MB of memory.
- ○ c. Configure the hard drive with at least 650MB of free space.
- ○ d. Install an AGP video adapter.

Question 20

You have eight Windows 2000 Professional computers in your company's Art department. They all have built-in USB controllers. You install a USB tablet-pointing device, as well as the manufacturer's 32-bit tablet software on each machine. A Tablet icon shows up in the Control Panel, but none of the tablets works. You examine the Device Manager and notice no device conflicts. What should you do to get the USB tablets to work?

○ a. Enable the USB ports in the system BIOS, and then reinstall the USB tablet device drivers.

○ b. Enable the USB root hub controller, and then reinstall the USB tablet device drivers.

○ c. Disable USB error detection for the USB root hub controller, and then enable the USB tablet device in each machine's hardware profile.

○ d. Reinstall the USB tablet device drivers, and then disable the USB error detection.

Question 21

You plan to install Windows 2000 Professional on a new computer with two monitors. All of the hardware is Windows 2000 compatible. You want to accomplish the following:

- Provide the user to place items on either monitor.

- Configure the display adapter built into the motherboard as the secondary display.

- Provide the user with the ability to start applications from the primary display.

- Allow the resolution for each display to be configured separately.

You perform the following tasks:

1. Install the additional display adapter in an available slot.

2. Attach the cable from each monitor to the appropriate display adapter.

3. Run Setup to install Windows 2000 and allow Setup to detect and configure the display adapters.

Which result or results do these actions produce? [Check all correct answers]

❑ a. Provides the user with the ability to start applications from the primary display.

❑ b. Provides the user with the ability to place items on either monitor.

❑ c. Configures the display adapter built into the motherboard as the secondary display.

❑ d. Allows the resolution for each display to be configured separately.

Question 22

> You back up PRO1 each morning using the following backup strategy:
>
> Monday: Incremental
>
> Tuesday: Differential
>
> Wednesday: Differential
>
> Thursday: Incremental
>
> Friday: Normal
>
> On Wednesday afternoon, PRO1 crashes and you must recover the hard drive. Which backup sets must you restore, and in which order?
>
> Monday
>
> Tuesday
>
> Wednesday
>
> Thursday
>
> Friday

Question 23

> You are deciding on specifications for 50 new computers your company will purchase for the Engineering department. They will run Windows 2000 Professional. You want Windows 2000 to be able to use all the hardware that comes in the computers. What is the maximum amount of memory you could have in your new Windows 2000 computers?
>
> ○ a. 2GB
>
> ○ b. 4GB
>
> ○ c. 8GB
>
> ○ d. 16GB

Question 24

Your original network adapter card fails. You replace the network adapter card on your computer, which is running Windows 2000 Professional. What utility should you use to make sure that the device driver for the original network card is removed from your machine?

○ a. Device Manager

○ b. Add/Remove Programs

○ c. Network and Dial-up Connections

○ d. System applet in Control Panel

○ e. Add/Remove Hardware Wizard

Question 25

You are dual-booting Windows 98 and Windows 2000 Professional on your computer. You upgraded the second hard drive in the machine from basic to dynamic, and you are using it to store business records. The next time you boot the machine to Windows 98 and try to access your business records, you cannot read the files at all. What is most likely to be the cause of this problem?

○ a. You formatted the partition(s) on the second drive to NTFS 5, so now Windows 98 cannot read the data on that drive.

○ b. You forgot to convert the second disk from dynamic back to basic before booting to Windows 98.

○ c. The data on the second drive is either encrypted or corrupt.

○ d. Only Windows 2000 can read data stored on dynamic disks.

Question 26

Your Windows 2000 Professional machine has a shared compressed folder on drive D called Sales. The D: drive is formatted as NTFS. You move the Sales folder into an uncompressed folder called CompanyData on drive D. Which of the following statements most accurately describe the Sales folder now?

○ a. The Sales folder is uncompressed because it resides in an uncompressed folder.

○ b. The Sales folder is uncompressed because it was removed from its original location.

○ c. The Sales folder is still compressed because it was moved within the same NTFS volume.

○ d. The Sales folder is still compressed because it was moved between two NTFS volumes.

Question 27

You want to dual-boot your computer using Windows 98 and Windows 2000 Professional. You are going to be using resource-intensive CAD applications while booted to both of the operating systems, and you need to be able to access all files on the machine regardless of which operating system you are using. What file system should you select for this single partition, single disk, machine?

○ a. FAT16

○ b. FAT32

○ c. NTFS

○ d. HPFS

Question 28

You are viewing the status of all disks and volumes using Disk Management on your Windows 2000 machine. You notice that all the disks and respective volumes have their status listed as Healthy, except for one. One disk shows each of its volumes status listed as Healthy (At Risk). What does this mean, and what step(s) should you take, if any?

○ a. The volume is initializing and is displayed as Healthy once initialization is finished. You do not need to take any action.

○ b. The volume is accessible but errors have been detected on this disk. You can return the disk to Healthy and Online status by reactivating the disk. Right-click the disk and select Reactivate Disk. Make sure you have a recent backup of the data on the disk.

○ c. This status indicator has appeared because this disk is on the verge of failure. Make sure you have a recent backup of the data on the disk, and replace the disk before failure occurs.

○ d. This status indicator appears when the underlying disk is no longer online. Right-click the disk and select Bring Online.

Question 29

On a Windows 2000 Professional computer, which type of volume includes areas of equal size on multiple physical disks to which data is written at the same time?

○ a. Mirrored volume

○ b. Spanned volume

○ c. Simple volume

○ d. Striped volume

○ e. RAID-5 volume

Question 30

In Windows 2000, how do you change or convert a hard disk from dynamic to basic?

○ a. Use Disk Management to right-click the disk and select Revert To Basic Disk.

○ b. Use the Storage snap-in to right-click the disk and select Revert To Basic Disk After Rescan.

○ c. Remove all the volumes from the disk. Then use Disk Management to right-click the disk and select Revert To Basic Disk.

○ d. You cannot do this in Windows 2000—you can convert only from basic to dynamic.

Question 31

You need to delete a quota entry defined for a user's account on drive F of a computer running Windows 2000. What utility should you use to locate the files owned by the user and move the files to a shard folder on another server?

○ a. **ntdsutil**

○ b. Windows Explorer

○ c. Active Directory Users And Computers

○ d. Disk Management

Question 32

What happens to encrypted files that are made available offline?

○ a. Nothing happens; the files are available and are still encrypted.

○ b. Encrypted files can't be made available offline.

○ c. The user who encrypted the file must decrypt the file for offline usage.

○ d. Encrypted files are not encrypted in the offline cache.

Question 33

Users report that when they access the Presentations share on a Windows 2000 server named \\server1, they can select files from this share to be available while offline. However, when users select files located in the Finance share on \\server1 the Make Available Offline option does not appear. What do you need to configure to allow files in the Finance share to be available while users are offline?

○ a. Configure the caching properties for the Finance share to allow caching of files.

○ b. Ensure that the users have the share permission to the Finance share on \\server1.

○ c. Enable Offline Files on the users' computers.

○ d. Create a logon script that maps \\server1\finance for all users.

Question 34

Users in the **corp.com** domain require that the settings and configurations that have been established on their computer to be available on any computer they may log on to. How do you accomplish this task? [Check all correct answers]

❑ a. Configure the local user account to use the local profile on every client computer.

❑ b. Rename ntuser.dat to ntuser.man.

❑ c. Create a profile share point.

❑ d. Configure the users' Profile option with the UNC path for their profile.

Question 35

You have created a Group Policy software package to assign an office suite package to all domain users. You want to prevent the office suite from appearing in the Add/Remove Programs applet. How do you configure this?

○ a. Configure a Group Policy to hide the Add/Remove Programs applet.

○ b. Configure the properties of Software installation Group Policy to display the office suite in a Category.

○ c. Enable the Uninstall This Application When It Falls Out Of The Scope Of Management feature.

○ d. Configure the properties of the office package in Group Policy.

Question 36

Alice has enabled files located on the network to be available for offline usage. She wants to configure synchronization to occur every day at 4:30 P.M. How should Alice configure synchronization to occur each day at a specific time?

○ a. Configure Synchronization Manager to synchronize during an idle period.

○ b. Use Synchronization Manager to force synchronization before leaving.

○ c. Use the Scheduled Task Wizard to configure when synchronization will occur.

○ d. Use Scheduled Synchronization Manager to configure when synchronization will occur.

Question 37

A user requires that the Narrator Accessibility tool be launched automatically when Windows 2000 starts. How do you configure this option?

○ a. Use the Accessibility Options applet to configure the Narrator Settings to start when Windows starts.

○ b. Select the Start Narrator Minimized option.

○ c. Add a registry entry to enable the Narrator to run when Windows starts.

○ d. Use Accessibility Utility Manager to enable the option to start automatically when Windows starts.

Question 38

A user needs to move the mouse pointer by using the numeric keypad on her keyboard. What feature of Windows 2000 Professional do you need to enable to provide this functionality?

○ a. ToggleKeys

○ b. FilterKeys

○ c. MouseKeys

○ d. StickyKeys

Question 39

You need to configure a user's Windows 2000 Professional computer to display a virtual keyboard. This will allow the user to type data using the mouse pointer. What utility must you enable?

○ a. ToggleKeys

○ b. FilterKeys

○ c. StickyKeys

○ d. On-Screen Keyboard

Question 40

You are using a 32-bit Windows word processing application. You have added the French input locale. You have been typing documents in English and now want to start typing in French. How do you do this?

○ a. Change to the French input locale within the word processor.

○ b. Close the application and select the French user locale from the Regional Options applet and restart the application.

○ c. Close the application and log off the computer and then log on and choose the French input locale.

○ d. Select the French input locale using the Language icon in the system tray.

Question 41

You work for a large multinational company with offices in Europe and the United States. Users in Europe regularly need to read and write documents in several different languages and work with the interface of the required language. You need to deploy Windows 2000 to support a Multilanguage configuration while keeping to a minimum the administrative overhead of the deployment and ongoing administration of these computers. How should you deploy Windows 2000 to achieve these goals?

○ a. Deploy a separate version of Windows 2000 for each needed language.

○ b. Deploy the Multilanguage edition of Windows 2000 and install language User Interfaces as needed.

○ c. Deploy Windows 2000 with all required language groups.

○ d. Deploy Windows 2000 with all the required input locales.

Question 42

A user accidentally pressed the Shift key five times. The computer made a high-pitched sound when this occurred. Why did the computer make this sound?

○ a. MouseKeys was enabled.

○ b. FilterKeys was enabled.

○ c. StickyKeys was enabled.

○ d. ToggleKeys was enabled.

Question 43

You have lost the Setup Disks that come with Windows 2000 Professional and you need to recreate them. You boot a Windows 2000 Professional computer and put the Windows 2000 Professional installation CD-ROM in the computer. What command do you use to create the Setup Disks?

○ a. **winnt32.exe /ox**

○ b. **makebt32.exe**

○ c. **makeboot.exe**

○ d. **winnt.exe /ox**

Question 44

You want to create a remote installation image of a Windows 2000 Professional computer and its installed applications. What utility is required for this task?

○ a. **risetup.exe**

○ b. **rbfg.exe**

○ c. **sysprep.exe**

○ d. **riprep.exe**

Question 45

A computer on which you want to install Windows 2000 Professional has 28MB of memory, a Pentium II 400MHz CPU, and a 500MB hard drive with 50MB of free space. You attempt the installation but it fails. What must you do to install Windows 2000 Professional on this computer? [Check all correct answers]

❏ a. Install a Pentium III 500MHz CPU.

❏ b. Install 32MB or more of memory.

❏ c. Configure the hard drive with at least 650MB of free space.

❏ d. Install a 2GB hard drive or greater.

Question 46

You want to deploy Windows 2000 Professional with an RIS server. The client computers have a PXE-compliant network adapter. You have installed a Windows 2000 domain controller as well as Domain Name System (DNS) and Dynamic Host Configuration Protocol (DHCP) on a Windows 2000 server. You have installed and configured RIS. However, when clients boot from their network adapter, they fail to connect to the RIS server. What is the problem?

○ a. Verify that DHCP has been authorized in Active Directory.

○ b. Create reserved TCP/IP addresses for all RIS clients in the RIS scope.

○ c. Configure the clients with a static TCP/IP address.

○ d. Create a host record in DNS for the RIS server.

Question 47

Which of the following operating systems can you directly upgrade to Windows 2000 Professional? [Check all correct answers]

❏ a. Windows 95

❏ b. Windows 98

❏ c. Windows 3

❏ d. Windows NT 4

❏ e. Windows NT 3.51

❏ f. Windows 3.11

Question 48

Which two protocols work with the Multilink feature to dynamically add or remove Dial-up Connections as needed? [Check all correct answers]

❑ a. Bandwidth Allocation Control Protocol (BACP)

❑ b. EAP

❑ c. Bandwidth Allocation Protocol (BAP)

❑ d. Remote Authentication Dial-In User Service (RADIUS)

Question 49

Where do you configure encryption settings for both passwords and data for a Dial-up Connection?

○ a. Open the Network And Dial-up Connections window. Right-click the Dial-up Connection and choose Properties. Click the Networking tab. Select Client For Microsoft Networks and choose Properties.

○ b. Configure a remote access policy.

○ c. Open the Network And Dial-up Connections window. Right-click the dial-up connection and choose Properties. Click the Options tab.

○ d. Open the Network And Dial-up Connections window. Right-click the dial-up connection and choose Properties. Click the Security tab.

Question 50

What IP address range does ICS use by default?

○ a. 10.0.0.2 through 10.0.0.254

○ b. 169.254.0.1 through 169.254.255.254

○ c. 192.168.1.2 through 192.168.1.254

○ d. 192.168.0.2 through 192.168.0.254

Answer Key

1. c	18. b	35. d
2. d	19. c	36. d
3. a, b	20. a	37. d
4. a	21. a, d	38. c
5. b	22. *	39. d
6. *	23. b	40. d
7. b	24. e	41. b
8. a	25. d	42. c
9. c	26. c	43. b
10. a	27. b	44. d
11. c	28. b	45. b, d
12. d	29. d	46. a
13. b	30. c	47. a, b, d, e
14. d	31. d	48. a, c
15. b	32. d	49. d
16. c	33. a	50. d
17. b	34. c, d	

This is the answer key to the sample test presented in Chapter 11.

Question 1

Answer c is correct. Security Configuration And Analysis allows you to apply security templates, including the High Security Workstation template created by Microsoft. Local Policy and Group Policy would require more "guesswork" and Domain Security Policy applies only to domain controllers, making answers a, b, and d incorrect.

Question 2

Answer d is correct. A Group Policy for the OU of your laptop overrides a domain policy. The registry entry and local security policy are overridden by the domain policy, so answers a and b are incorrect. A security database is used to evaluate security settings, so answer c is incorrect.

Question 3

Answers a and b are correct. You can use Local Security Policy to configure user rights on any Windows 2000 Professional system. You can use Group Policy to configure user rights for Windows 2000 Professional systems that are members of a domain. You cannot use User Manager (a Windows NT 4 tool) or the Users and Passwords applet to manage user rights. Therefore, answers c and d are incorrect.

Question 4

Answer a is correct. The right to format a hard drive partition is given to administrators only. Therefore, you would have to put Cory into the Administrators group, which you can do with the Users And Passwords applet. The other tools do not let you manage the Administrators group. Therefore, answers b, c, and d are incorrect.

Question 5

Answer b is correct. Template accounts are generally disabled so that they are not active accounts. When you copy the account, you should ensure that the Disabled attribute is cleared for the new user. Answer a is not a setting of a template account, and answers c and d would not be causing the logon problem. Therefore, these answers are incorrect.

Question 6

The correct order is Friday, Monday, Tuesday, and Wednesday. Normal backups are "complete," so you can begin with Friday's backup. Incremental backups back up only what has changed since the last incremental or normal backup, so you must restore each incremental backup since the normal backup.

Question 7

Answer b is correct. You must back up the system state so that you can back up the registry in Windows 2000. The ERD no longer contains a backup of the registry. Therefore, answer a is incorrect. You cannot "copy" the registry while the system is running, and the user profile does not contain machine-specific registry settings. Therefore, answers a, c, and d are incorrect.

Question 8

Answer a is correct. Memory: Pages/sec over 20 indicates too much paging activity, which itself contributes to processor and disk usage. Lack of memory is therefore the bottleneck on this system. Enhancing the processor or disk subsystem would not address this bottleneck, so answers b, c, d, and e are incorrect.

Question 9

Answer c is correct. This system's processor is at capacity, and the queue length is above 2, indicating that threads are waiting to be processed and a second processor could alleviate the bottleneck. Answers a, b, d, e, and f would not be the best solutions to address this bottleneck.

Question 10

Answer a is correct. From the Properties sheet of a drive volume, you can launch defragmentation from the Tools tab. You cannot perform defragmentation using the tools in answers b, c, and d.

Question 11

Answer c is correct. Task Manager allows you to monitor at what priority an application is running. Computer Management, System, and Add/Remove Programs will not allow you to change an application's priority, so answers a, b, and d are incorrect.

Question 12

Answer d is correct. The local profiles on a Windows 2000 Professional computer are found in %SystemRoot%\Documents and settings. However, if the computer had been upgraded from Windows NT to Windows 2000 then the profiles would be found in %SystemRoot%\Winnt\profiles.

Question 13

Answer b is correct. If a share point is not configured to allow caching of files, then you cannot cache files from that share point. Also, the option to make files available offline is not available until this option is selected, so answer a is incorrect. Answer d is not an available option until the share point has been configured to allow for caching of files; therefore answer d is incorrect. Answer c is incorrect because it is the wrong computer. The problem is on \\server1 not of the sales staff's computers.

Question 14

Answer d is correct. If you restart the Windows Installer service, the service release is installed the next time the client logs on to his or her computer. If there had been a problem with the service release msi file, it would not have installed on any computers. However, it did install on all but one of the client computers. This indicates that the failed install of the service package is an issue with the client computer. Therefore, answers a and b incorrect. Restarting the Windows Installer service would only be an appropriate answer if the application couldn't be installed on the domain controller. The domain controller is simply being used to deploy applications; therefore answer c is incorrect.

Question 15

Answer b is correct. Jerry can use Synchronization Manager to synchronize on the fly by clicking the Synchronize button. Doing so forces a synchronization of all files that have been changed. Copying the file to the share point could potentially overwrite the existing files. Therefore, answer d is incorrect. Answer a would require the user to wait until an idle period before the files were synchronized. The user must disconnect the computer from the network before the idle period sets in, therefore answer a is incorrect. If answer c were chosen the user may not have synchronized files before removing the computer from the network. The user must synchronize files before logging off the network. Answer c doesn't synchronize files until the users logs back on to the network, which is too late; therefore answer c is incorrect.

Question 16

Answer c is correct. You use the Narrator accessibility option to read aloud on-screen text, dialog boxes, menus, and buttons that are selected in Windows 2000 Professional. SoundSentry generates visual warnings when the computer generates sound alerts, whereas ShowSounds tells applications to display captions for sounds the application may make. Therefore, answers a and b are incorrect. Windows Media Player cannot speak aloud written text, but it can display text in Close Caption. Therefore, answer d is incorrect.

Question 17

Answer b is correct. The sysprep.inf file is the answer file for **Sysprep** installations of Windows 2000. It is not used for remote installations. It could be if it were renamed and placed in the correct location. Therefore, answer a is incorrect. This file is not used to configure **sysprep.exe**, nor could it ever be used to adjust settings for keyboard layouts. Therefore, answers c and d are incorrect.

Question 18

Answer b is correct. The only utility that you can use to create network boot disks to connect to a remote installation server is **rbfg.exe**. The Network Client Administrator is a Windows NT 4 server utility that creates generic network boot disks; you can't use it to find and connect to a remote installation server. Therefore, answer a is incorrect. You use **dcpromo.exe** to promote a member server to a domain controller, and the Recovery Console is a Windows 2000 troubleshooting tool. Therefore, answers c and d are incorrect.

Question 19

Answer c is correct. Windows 2000 Professional requires at least 650MB of free hard disk space to complete a successful installation. You can install Windows 2000 Professional on a computer with only 32MB of memory and a Pentium 166MHz CPU, so this system meets minimum requirements, which makes answers a and b incorrect The installation fails before Plug and Play would attempt find the video adapter, so that is not the issue. By process of elimination, an incorrect configuration of the hard drive is the best answer.

Question 20

Answer a is correct. The operating system is recognizing the tablets, but they do not work. You need to enable the USB ports in the system's BIOS, and then reinstall the drivers for the tablets. Having the single USB tablet device on each machine does not necessitate having a USB root hub controller, nor would answers b and c solve the problem unless the USB ports were enabled in the BIOS. Therefore, answers b and c are incorrect. Answer d is a distracter, so it is incorrect.

Question 21

The correct answers are a and d. You have to install Windows 2000 before you install a display adapter other than the one that is built-in. Otherwise, Setup will disable the built-in adapter when it detects another one present. The order that you completed the tasks results in only one display adapter and monitor being enabled. So, the user can start apps from the primary display and configure each display's settings separately—but that's it. Answers b and c are incorrect.

Question 22

The correct order is Friday, Monday, and Wednesday. Normal backups are "complete," so you can begin with Friday's backup. Incremental backups back up only what has changed since the last incremental or normal backup, so you must restore each incremental backup since the normal backup (Monday). Differential backups back up all files that have changed since the last normal or incremental backup, so Wednesday's backup includes all files that have changed since Monday morning.

Question 23

Answer b is correct. Windows 2000 Professional can address up to 4GB of RAM.

Question 24

Answer e is correct. You must use the Add/Remove Hardware Wizard to ensure that drivers are removed from your hard disk. You can use Device Manager to uninstall drivers, but it does not remove the driver from your machine—it just makes sure the driver is not loaded during system's startup. Therefore, answer a is incorrect. From Network and Dial-up Connections, you can disable a Local Area Connection for a network adapter card, but the drivers are not removed from the hard disk. Therefore, answer c is incorrect.

Question 25

Answer d is correct. Down-level operating systems (Windows versions before Windows 2000) cannot read the Windows 2000 dynamic disks. Answer a is incorrect because you have no information about the file systems in use in this scenario. You do not convert dynamic disks back to basic solely for the purpose of reading them once you've rebooted to a down-level operating system. Therefore, answer b is incorrect. You have no evidence to support the assertion that data on the second drive is missing or corrupt, so you cannot select answer c.

Question 26

Answer c is correct. When you move an object within the same NTFS volume, it retains its compression attribute. This is a golden rule to remember.

Question 27

Answer b is correct. Windows 98 cannot read NTFS or HPFS. FAT32 uses smaller cluster sizes and is more efficient than FAT16, plus both Windows 98 and Windows 2000 can use FAT32. FAT16 would work, but it is not the best choice because it uses larger cluster sizes and less efficient use of disk space. Therefore, answer a is incorrect. Answers c and d are incorrect because Windows 98 cannot read them.

Question 28

Answer b is correct. When the disk is Healthy (At Risk), it is not simply offline. "At Risk" means errors have been detected on the disk. Healthy (At Risk) does not display when a volume is initializing, so answer a is incorrect. There is not enough information to conclude this disk is on the verge of failure, so answer c is incorrect.

Question 29

Answer d is correct. This questions deals with the straight definition of a striped volume. A striped volume has areas of equal size on multiple disks to which data is written at the same time. Just as a side note and something to keep in mind—Windows 2000 Professional does not support mirrored volumes or RAID-5 volumes. Therefore, answers a and e are incorrect.

Question 30

Answer c is correct. You *must* remove all the volumes from the disk before you convert or revert a dynamic disk back to basic. You do not use the Storage snap-in for this. Therefore, answer b is incorrect. Answer d is preposterous—of course you can convert a disk from dynamic back to basic. Therefore, answer d is incorrect.

Question 31

Answer d is correct. You use the disk quota management system within Disk Management. When you delete the user's quota entry, a dialog box that allows you to move, delete, or take ownership of files owned by the user on drive F appears. **ntdsutil** is a command-line utility that manages the Active Directory database, so answer a is incorrect. Windows Explorer has no feature to expose files owned by a specific user. Therefore, answer b is incorrect. Information about individual files owned by a user is not available in Active Directory Users And Computers. Therefore, answer c is incorrect.

Question 32

Answer d is correct. Files that have been encrypted can be made available while a user is offline, so answer b is incorrect. However, the encrypted files are not encrypted in the offline cache, so answer d is correct. Answer c is not a required action. Files are encrypted and decrypted in the same manner whether or not they are tagged for offline usage. No, user action is necessary to decrypt a file that has been encrypted. This action is performed automatically by the security subsystem.

Question 33

Answer a is correct. The caching properties for the Finance share have been disabled, and you need to enable them before the clients can cache files contained in this share. Because the users can get to the files in the Finance share, we know that there is nothing wrong with the permissions. Therefore, answer b is incorrect. We know that the users' computers have enabled the Offline Files option because they can make files in the presentations share available for offline usage; therefore answer c is incorrect. Answer d wouldn't correct the problem. A drive mapping would be created but the files would not be cached, therefore answer d is incorrect.

Question 34

Answers c and d are correct. To allow a user profile that has been created on a user's computer to be available on any computer the user logs on to, there must be a central profile share that the user's profile is uploaded to. In addition, you must then enter the UNC path to the share for each user account that needs roaming profiles. Answer a would not use a central profile that would be available on every computer a user might log on to. Instead the local profile would be used, thus answer a is incorrect. Answer b would simply make a profile mandatory, but it does not enable a profile to roam, therefore answer b is incorrect.

Question 35

Answer d is correct. You can configure assigned applications not to appear in the Add/Remove Programs applet. This configuration is simply a software policy option that you can use for either assigned or published applications. However, you should use it just for assigned applications. You don't want to hide the entire Add/Remove Programs applet, just the presence of the office suite within the applet, therefore answer a is incorrect. Answer b doesn't solve anything as the Category option is found within the Add/Remove Programs applet. The policy had instructed the package not to appear in the Add/Remove Programs applet so placing the software within a Category won't make the application appear, therefore answer b is incorrect. Answer c does not control whether or not a software package will appear in the Add/Remove Programs applet. It is used to remove the entire application from a computer when a user account is moved from on Organization Unit (OU) to another.

Question 36

Answer d is correct. The Synchronization Manager can be used to control synchronization to occur during an idle period, or at a scheduled interval. In this case the user Alice needed to schedule synchronization to occur at 4:30 each day. Answer d provides this capability. You can use Synchronization Manager to synchronize on the fly by clicking the Synchronize button. Doing so forces a synchronization of all files that have been changed, but requires the users to be present to manually push a button. This option doesn't allow for synchronization to be configuration at a specific time, therefore answer b is incorrect. The Scheduled Task Wizard doesn't control when offline files can be synchronized, therefore answer c is incorrect.

Question 37

Answer d is correct. You can use Accessibility Utility Manager to configure the Narrator to start automatically when Windows starts. The other options do not provide this capability. Therefore, answers a, b, and c are incorrect.

Question 38

Answer c is correct. You use the MouseKeys accessibility option to control the mouse pointer with the numeric keypad. The other options do not allow for this functionality. Therefore, answers a, b, and d are incorrect.

Question 39

Answer d is correct. The On-Screen Keyboard is a virtual keyboard that is displayed on a user's desktop. Users can use a pointing device such as a mouse to enter data with this keyboard. ToggleKeys plays a high-pitched sound when the Caps key is pressed. Therefore, answer a is incorrect. FilterKeys adjusts the keyboard repeat delay. Therefore, answer b is incorrect. StickyKeys allows users to select keystrokes such as Ctrl+Alt+Delete individually. Therefore, answer c is incorrect.

Question 40

Answer d is correct. You can select an input locale by using a keyboard shortcut or by selecting the Language icon in the system tray. Changing the user locale to French would not affect the input locale. French characters do not appear until the input locale is selected. Therefore, answer b is incorrect. Answer a is not even possible. The input locale has to be switched either by using hot keys or the system tray. At that point an application could then type characters from different languages. Therefore answer a is incorrect. It is not necessary to log off the computer to invoke different input locales. They can be changed on the fly, therefore answer c is incorrect.

Question 41

Answer b is correct. If you use the Multilanguage edition of Windows 2000, you don't need to use separate SPs, hot fixes, and upgrades. If you deploy a separate version of Windows, you increase the administrative burden because these computers do require separate SPs, hot fixes, and upgrades. Therefore, answer a is incorrect. While the Multilanguage edition can use the same service packs, answers c and d do not provide enough options for the user.

Question 42

Answer c is correct. By default, pressing the Shift key five times enables StickyKeys Pressing Left Alt+Left Shift+Num Lock enables MouseKeys, thus answer a is incorrect. Holding down the Right Shift key for eight seconds enables FilterKeys, thus answer b is incorrect. ToggleKeys can be invoked by holding down the Num lock key for five seconds, which makes answer d incorrect.

Question 43

Answer b is correct. The user booted into a Windows 2000 computer, so **makebt32.exe** is the correct executable. Therefore, answer a is incorrect. **Winnt32.exe /ox** is not a viable command. This switch provides no functionally at all with this executable, therefore answer a is incorrect. If the user had booted to a DOS prompt, **makeboot.exe** would have been the right executable to use. Therefore, answer c is incorrect. **winnt.exe /ox** is the method to create setup floppy disks for Windows NT 4. The **/ox** switch does not create the Setup Disks for Windows 2000. Therefore, answer d is incorrect.

Question 44

Answer d is correct. **riprep.exe** creates remote installation images of Windows 2000 Professional computers. These images are automatically placed on a RIS server. In contrast **risetup.exe** is used to configure a server to be a remote installation server, thus answer a is incorrect. The **rbfg.exe** utility is used to create remote boot disks for RIS clients to connect to a RIS server, thus answer b is incorrect. **Sysprep.exe** is used to prepare a computer to be imaged with third party imaging software by removing unique parameters from the computer. Therefore answer c is incorrect.

Question 45

Answers b and d are correct. The minimum requirements for Windows 2000 Professional are 32MB of memory, a 2GB drive with 650MB of free space, and a Pentium 133MHz or higher CPU.

Question 46

Answer a is correct. Active Directory needs to authorize a Windows 2000 DHCP server to give TCP/IP addresses. If the server has not been authorized, it does not give out IP addresses and the RIS clients cannot connect to the RIS. Unless the DHCP server has been authorized created reserved TCP/IP addresses for the RIS clients still won't obtain a TCP/IP address, thus answer b is incorrect. Answer c is incorrect as the client must obtain a TCP/IP address from a DHCP server. A static TCP/IP address can't be used; therefore answer c is incorrect. Answer d is not related to the problem. Unless the DHCP server has been activated clients won't get a TCP/IP address and cannot connect to the RIS server. RIS could be completely configured unless there was a host record for the RIS server in DNS. Therefore answer d is incorrect.

Question 47

Answers a, b, d, and e are correct. You can upgrade only Window 95, 98, NT 4, and NT 3.51 to Windows 2000 Professional. You cannot upgrade Windows 3 or 3.11. Therefore, answers c and f are incorrect.

Question 48

Answers a and c are correct. BAP and BACP work together in conjunction with Multilink to combine multiple communications devices (modems and ISDN terminal adapters) for achieving higher throughput. BAP and BACP can dynamically drop or add lines based on pre-determined usage rates as specified in remote access policies. EAP is the Extensible Authentication Protocol, which is an authentication protocol, not a bandwidth protocol. RADIUS is a set of remote access accounting services, which do not concern bandwidth.

Question 49

Answer d is correct. The Security tab displays the settings necessary for configuring password and data encryption. Encryption settings are not configured from the Networking tab, the Options tab, nor from remote access policies.

Question 50

Answer d is correct. By default, ICS uses the IP address range of 192.168.0.2 through 192.168.0.254 for clients, with 192.168.0.1 reserved for the Windows 2000 computer sharing its Internet connection. Although the IP scheme 10.x.y.z is a private nonroutable set of addresses; ICS does not use it, so answer a is incorrect. The range of 169.254.x.y is used by APIPA, not ICS. Therefore, answer b is incorrect. The range of 192.168.1.x is also private and nonroutable; it is not the default IP scheme that ICS uses. Therefore, answer c is incorrect.

Glossary

A (address) resource record

A resource record used to map a Domain Name System (DNS) domain name to a host Internet Protocol (IP) address on the network.

Accelerated Graphics Port (AGP)

A new interface specification (released in August 1997) developed by Intel. AGP is based on peripheral connection interface (PCI) but is designed especially for the throughput demands of 3D graphics. Rather than using the PCI bus for graphics data, AGP introduces a dedicated point-to-point channel so that the graphics controller can directly access main memory. The AGP channel is 32 bits wide and runs at 66MHz. This translates into a total bandwidth of 266Mbps, as opposed to the PCI bandwidth of 133Mbps. AGP also supports two optional faster modes, with throughputs of 533Mbps and 1.07Gbps. In addition, AGP allows 3D textures to be stored in main memory rather than in video memory. AGP has a couple important system requirements: The chipset must support AGP, and the motherboard must be equipped with an AGP bus slot or must have an integrated AGP graphics system.

access control entry (ACE)

An element in an object's discretionary access control list (DACL). Each ACE controls or monitors access to an object by a specified trustee. An ACE is also an entry in an object's system access control list (SACL) that specifies the security events to be audited for a user or group.

account lockout

A Windows 2000 security feature that locks a user account if a certain number of failed logon attempts occur within a specified amount of time, based on security policy lockout settings. Locked accounts cannot log on.

Active Directory

The directory service included with Windows 2000 Server. It is based on the X.500 standards and those of its predecessor, Lightweight Directory Access Protocol (LDAP). It stores information about objects on a network and makes this information available to users and network administrators. Active Directory gives network users access to permitted resources anywhere on the network using a single logon process. It provides network administrators with a hierarchical view of the network and a single point of administration for all network objects.

Active Directory Users And Computers snap-in

An administrative tool designed to perform daily Active Directory administration tasks. These tasks include creating, deleting, modifying, moving, and setting permissions on objects stored in the directory. These objects include Organizational Units (OUs), users, contacts, groups, computers, printers, and shared file objects.

Address Resolution Protocol (ARP)

A Transmission Control Protocol/Internet Protocol (TCP/IP) protocol that translates an Internet Protocol (IP) address into a physical address, such as a MAC address (hardware address). A computer that wants to obtain a physical address sends an ARP broadcast request onto the TCP/IP network. The computer on the network that has the IP address in the request then replies with its physical hardware address.

Advanced Configuration and Power Interface (ACPI)

A power management specification developed by Intel, Microsoft, and Toshiba. ACPI enables Windows 2000 to control the amount of power given to each device attached to the computer. With ACPI, the operating system can turn off peripheral devices, such as CD-ROM players, when they are not in use. As another example, ACPI enables manufacturers to produce computers that automatically power up as soon as you touch the keyboard.

Advanced Power Management (APM)

An application programming interface (API) developed by Intel and Microsoft that allows developers to include power management in Basic Input/Output Systems (BIOSes). APM defines a layer between the hardware and the operating system that effectively shields programmers from hardware details. Advanced Configuration and Power Interface (ACPI) will gradually replace APM.

ARPANET

A large wide area network (WAN) created in the 1960s by the U.S. Department of Defense (DoD) Advanced Research Projects Agency for the free exchange of information between universities and research organizations.

Asynchronous Transfer Mode (ATM)

A networking technology that transfers data in cells (data packets of a fixed size). Cells used with ATM are relatively small compared to packets used with older technologies. The small, constant cell size allows ATM hardware to transmit video images, audio, and computer data over the same network as well as ensures that no single type of data consumes all of the connection's available bandwidth. Current implementations of ATM support data transfer rates from 25 to 622Mbps. Most Ethernet-based networks run at 100Mbps or below.

attribute

A single property that describes an object; e.g., the make, model, or color that describes a car. In the context of directories, an attribute is the main component of an entry in a directory, such as an email address.

auditing

The process that tracks the activities of users by recording selected types of events in the security log of a server or workstation.

authentication ticket

A permission to access resources indirectly that a Kerberos Key Distribution Center (KDC) grants to clients and applications.

authorize

To register the Remote Installation Services (RIS) server or the Dynamic Host Configuration Protocol (DHCP) server with Active Directory.

Auto Private IP Addressing (APIPA)

A client-side feature of Windows 98 and 2000 Dynamic Host Configuration Protocol (DHCP) clients. If the client's attempt to negotiate with a DHCP server fails, the client automatically receives an Internet Protocol (IP) address from the 169.254.0.0 Class B range.

backup domain controller (BDC)

In Windows NT Server 4, a server that receives a copy of the domain's directory database (which contains all of the account and security policy information for the domain). BDCs can continue to participate in a Windows 2000 domain when the domain is configured in mixed mode.

Bandwidth Allocation Protocol (BAP)

A protocol that dynamically controls the use of Multilinked lines. BAP eliminates excess bandwidth by allocating lines only when they are required. You can control dynamic links with remote access policies, which are based on the percent of line utilization and the length of time the bandwidth is reduced.

baselining

The process of measuring system performance so that you can ascertain a standard or expected level of performance.

basic disk

A Windows 2000 term that indicates a physical disk, which can have primary and extended partitions. A basic disk can contain up to three primary partitions and one extended partition, or four primary partitions. A basic disk can also have a single extended partition with logical drives. You *cannot* extend a basic disk.

Basic Input/Output System (BIOS)

Built-in software that determines what a computer can do without accessing programs from a disk. On PCs, the BIOS contains all the code required to control the keyboard, display screen, disk drives, serial communications, and a number of miscellaneous functions. A BIOS that can handle Plug and Play devices is known as a Plug and Play BIOS. A Plug and Play BIOS is always implemented with flash memory rather than read-only memory (ROM). Windows 2000 benefits if your machine has the latest Advanced Configuration and Power Interface (ACPI)-compliant BIOS.

boot partition

The partition that contains the Windows 2000 operating system and its support files.

Challenge Handshake Authentication Protocol (CHAP)

An authentication protocol used by Microsoft remote access as well as network and dial-up connections. Using CHAP, a remote access client can send its authentication credentials to a remote access server in a secure form. Microsoft has created several variations of CHAP that are Windows specific, such as Microsoft Challenge Handshake Authentication Protocol (MSCHAP) and MSCHAP 2.

Client-Side Caching (CSC)

See *offline file*.

compression

The process of making individual files and folders occupy less disk space with the NT File System (NTFS) 5 file system in Windows 2000. Compressed files can be read and written to by any Windows- or DOS-based program *without* having to be decompressed first. They decompress when opened, and recompress when closed. The NTFS 5 file system handles this entire process. Compression is simply a file attribute that you can apply to any file or folder stored on an NTFS 5 partition.

computer account

An account that a domain administrator creates and that uniquely identifies the computer on the domain. The Windows 2000 computer account matches the name of the computer that joins the domain.

container

An object in the directory that contains other objects.

counter

A metric that provides information about particular aspects of system performance.

daily backup

A backup of files that have changed today but that does not mark them as backed up.

Data Recovery Agents (DRA)

A Windows 2000 administrator who has been issued a public key certificate for the express purpose of recovering user-encrypted data files that have been encrypted with Encrypting File System (EFS). Data recovery refers to the process of decrypting a file without having the private key of the user who encrypted the file. A DRA may become necessary if a user loses his or her private key for decrypting files, or if a user leaves an organization without decrypting important files that other users need.

default gateway

An address that serves an important role in Transmission Control Protocol/Internet Protocol (TCP/IP) networking by providing a default route for TCP/IP hosts to use when communicating with other hosts on remote networks. A router (either a dedicated router or a computer that connects two or more network segments) generally acts as the default gateway for TCP/IP hosts. The router maintains its own routing table of other networks within an internetwork. The routing table maps the routes required to reach the remote hosts that reside on those other networks.

Device Manager

The primary tool in Windows 2000 used to configure and manage hardware devices and their settings.

dial-up access

When a remote client uses the public telephone line or integrated services digital network (ISDN) line to create a connection to a Windows 2000 remote access server.

differential backup

A backup that copies files created or changed since the last normal or incremental backup. It does *not* mark files as having been backed up (in other words, the archive attribute is not cleared). If you are performing a combination of normal and differential backups, restoring files and folders requires that you have the last normal backup as well as the last differential backup.

digital signature

The use of public key cryptography to authenticate the integrity and originator of a communication.

digital versatile disc or digital video disc (DVD)

A type of CD-ROM that holds a minimum of 4.7GB, enough for a full-length movie. The DVD specification supports disks with capacities from 4.7 to 17GB and access rates of 600Kbps to 1.3Mbps. One of the best features of DVD drives is that they are backward compatible with CD-ROMs. This means that DVD players can play old CD-ROMs, CD-I disks, video CDs, and new DVD-ROMs. Newer DVD players can also read CD-R disks. DVD uses Moving Picture Experts Group (MPEG)-2 to compress video data.

Direct Memory Access (DMA)

A technique for transferring data from main memory to a device without passing it through the CPU. Computers that have DMA channels can transfer data to and from devices much more quickly than can computers without a DMA channel. This is useful for making quick backups and for realtime applications. Some expansion boards, such as CD-ROM cards, can access the computer's DMA channel. When you install the board, you must specify the DMA channel to be used, which sometimes involves setting a jumper or dual in-line package (DIP) switch.

discretionary access control list (DACL)

A list of access control entries (ACEs) that lets administrators set permissions for users and groups at the object and attribute levels. This list represents part of an object's security descriptor that allows or denies permissions to specific users and groups.

disk group

A Windows 2000 term for multiple dynamic disks that are managed as a collection. All dynamic disks in a computer are members of the same disk group. Each disk in a disk group stores replicas of the same configuration data. This configuration data is stored in a 1MB region at the end of each dynamic disk.

Disk Management

A Windows 2000 MMC snap-in that you use to perform all disk maintenance tasks, such as formatting, creating partitions, deleting partitions, and converting a basic disk to a dynamic disk.

disk quota

A control used in Windows 2000 to limit the amount of hard disk space available for all users or an individual user. You can apply a quota on a per-user, per-volume basis only.

domain

The fundamental administrative unit of Active Directory. A domain stores information about objects in the domain's partition of Active Directory. You can give user and group accounts in a domain privileges and permissions to resources on any system that belongs to the domain.

domain controller

A computer running Windows 2000 Server that hosts Active Directory and manages user access to a network, which includes logging on, authentication, and access to the directory and shared resources.

domain forest

A collection of one or more Windows 2000 domains in a non-contiguous DNS namespace that share a common schema, configuration, and Global Catalog and that are linked with two-way transitive trusts.

Domain Name System (DNS)

The standard by which hosts on the Internet have both domain name addresses (for example, **rapport.com**) and numerical Internet Protocol (IP) addresses (for example, 192.33.2.8). DNS is a service that you use primarily for resolving fully qualified domain names (FQDN) to IP addresses.

domain tree

A set of domains that form a contiguous DNS namespace through a set of hierarchical relationships.

driver signing

A method for marking or identifying driver files that meet certain specifications or standards. Windows 2000 uses a driver signing process to make sure drivers have been certified to work correctly with the Windows Driver Model (WDM) in Windows 2000.

dynamic disk

A physical disk in a Windows 2000 computer that does not use partitions or logical drives. It has dynamic volumes that you create using the Disk Management console. A dynamic disk can contain any of five types of volumes. In addition, you can extend a volume on a dynamic disk. Dynamic disks can contain an unlimited number of volumes, so you are not restricted to four volumes per disk as you are with a basic disk.

Dynamic Host Configuration Protocol (DHCP) server

A Windows 2000 server that dynamically assigns Internet Protocol (IP) addresses to clients. Along with the assignment of IP addresses, it can provide direction towards routers, Windows Internet Naming Service (WINS) servers, and Domain Name System (DNS) servers.

dynamic volume

The only type of volume you can create on dynamic disks. There are five types of dynamic volumes: simple, spanned, mirrored, striped, and RAID-5. Only computers running Windows 2000 can directly access dynamic volumes. Windows 2000 Professional machines *cannot* host, but *can* access, mirrored and RAID-5 dynamic volumes that are on remote Windows 2000 servers.

Emergency Repair Disk (ERD)

A disk created by the Backup utility that contains information about your current Windows system settings. You can use this disk to attempt to repair your computer if it will not start or if your system files are damaged or erased.

emergency repair process (or repair process)

A feature that helps you repair problems with system files, your startup environment (if you have a dual-boot or multiple-boot system), and the partition boot sector on your boot volume. Before you use the emergency repair process to repair your system, you must create an Emergency Repair Disk (ERD). You can do this using the Backup utility. Even if you have not created an ERD, you can still try to use the emergency repair process; however, any changes you have made to your system, for example service pack updates, may be lost and might need to be reinstalled.

Encrypting File System (EFS)

A subsystem of NT File System (NTFS) that uses public keys and private keys to provide encryption for files and folders on computers using Windows 2000. Only the user who initially encrypted the file and a recovery agent can decrypt encrypted files and folders.

Extensible Authentication Protocol (EAP)

An extension of Point-to-Point Protocol (PPP) that provides remote access user authentication by means of other security devices. You may add support for a number of authentication schemes, including token cards; dial-up; the Kerberos v5 protocol; one-time passwords; and public key authentication using smart cards, certificates, and others. EAP works with dial-up, Point-to-Point Tunneling Protocol (PPTP), and Layer 2 Tunneling Protocol (L2TP) clients. EAP is a critical technology component for secure Virtual Private Networks (VPNs) because it offers more security against brute force or dictionary attacks (where all possible combinations of characters are attempted), and password guessing than other authentication methods, such as Challenge Handshake Authentication Protocol (CHAP).

fault tolerance

The ability of a computer or operating system to ensure data integrity when hardware failures occur. Within Windows 2000 Server, Advanced Server, and Datacenter Server, mirrored volumes and Redundant Array of Independent Disks (RAID)-5 volumes are fault tolerant.

file allocation table (FAT) or FAT16

A 16-bit table that many operating systems use to locate files on disk. The FAT keeps track of all the pieces of a file. The FAT file system for older versions of Windows 95 is called virtual file allocation table (VFAT); the one for Windows 95 (OEM Service Release—OSR—2) and 98 is called FAT32. Windows 2000 can use the FAT file system; however, it is often not used on Windows 2000 and NT machines because of its larger cluster sizes and inability to scale to larger volume sizes. The FAT file system has no local security.

file allocation table (FAT)32

A newer, 32-bit version of FAT available in Windows 95 OEM Service Release (OSR) 2 and 98. FAT32 increases the number of bits used to address clusters and reduces the size of each cluster. The result is that it can support larger disks (up to 2 terabytes) and better storage efficiency (less slack space) than the earlier version of FAT. The FAT32 file system has no local security. Windows 2000 can use and format partitions as FAT, FAT32, or NT File System (NTFS).

FireWire or Institute of Electrical and Electronics Engineers (IEEE) 1394

A new, very fast external bus standard that supports data transfer rates of up to 400Mbps. Products that support the 1394 standard go under different names, depending on the company.

Apple originally developed the technology and uses the trademarked name FireWire. Other companies use other names, such as i.link and Lynx, to describe their 1394 products. You can use a single 1394 port to connect up to 63 external devices. In addition to its high speed, 1394 supports time-dependent data, delivering data at a guaranteed rate. This makes it ideal for devices that need to transfer high levels of data in realtime, such as video devices. Although extremely fast and flexible, 1394 is expensive. Like Universal Serial Bus (USB), 1394 supports both Plug and Play and hot plugging as well as provides power to peripheral devices. The main difference between 1394 and USB is that 1394 supports faster data transfer rates and is more expensive. For these reasons, it is used mostly for devices that require large through-puts, such as video cameras, whereas USB is used to connect most other peripheral devices.

forward lookup

In Domain Name System (DNS), a query process in which the friendly DNS domain name of a host computer is searched to find its Internet Protocol (IP) address.

forward lookup zone

A Domain Name System (DNS) zone that provides host name to Transmission Control Protocol/Internet Protocol (TCP/IP) address resolution. In DNS Manager, forward lookup zones are based on DNS domain names and typically hold host (A) address resource records.

Frame Relay Permanent Virtual Circuit (PVC)

A protocol where messages are divided into packets before they are sent. Each packet is then transmitted individually and can even follow different routes to its destination. Once all the packets that form a message arrive at the destination, they are recompiled into the original message. Several wide area network (WAN) protocols, including Frame Relay, are based on packet-switching technologies. Ordinary telephone service is based on a circuit-switching technology where a dedicated line is allocated for transmission between two parties. Circuit switching is best suited for data that must be transmitted quickly and must arrive in the same order in which it is sent. Most realtime data, such as live audio and video, require circuit-switching technology. Packet switching is more efficient and robust for data that can withstand some delays (latency) in transmission, such as email messages and Web content.

global group

A group that can be granted rights and permissions and can become a member of local groups in its own domain and trusting domains. However, a global group can contain user accounts from its own domain only. Global groups provide a way to create sets of users from inside the domain that are available for use both in and out of the domain.

Group Policy

The mechanism for managing change and configuration of systems, security, applications, and user environments in an Active Directory domain.

Group Policy Editor (GPE)

A Windows 2000 snap-in that allows customers to create custom profiles for groups of users and computers.

Group Policy Object (GPO)

An object created by the Group Policy Editor (GPE) snap-in to hold information about a specific group's association with selected directory objects, such as sites, domains, or Organizational Units (OUs).

Hardware Abstraction Layer (HAL)

A component of an operating system that functions something like an application programming interface (API). In strict technical architecture, HALs reside at the device level, a layer below the standard API level. HAL allows programmers to write applications and game titles with all the device-independent advantages of writing to an API, but without the large processing overhead that APIs normally demand.

hardware profile

A profile that stores configuration settings for a collection of devices and services. Windows 2000 can store different hardware profiles so that users' needs can be met even though their computer may frequently require different device and service settings depending on circumstances. The best example is a laptop or portable computer used in an office while in a docking station and then undocked so that the user can travel with it. The two environments do require different power management settings, possibly different network settings, and various other configuration changes.

Hash message authentication code (HMAC) Message Digest 5 (MD5)

A hash algorithm that produces a 128-bit hash of the authenticated payload.

hibernation

A power option in Windows 2000 Professional portable computers that helps to conserve battery power. Hibernation is a complete power down while maintaining the state of open programs and connected hardware. When you bring your computer out of hibernation, your desktop is restored exactly as you left it, in less time than it takes for a complete system restart. However, it does take longer to bring your computer out of hibernation than out of standby. Put your computer in hibernation when you will be away from the computer for an extended time or overnight.

home directory

A location for a user or group of users to store files on a network server. This provides a central location for files that users can access and back up.

HOSTS file

A local text file in the same format as the 4.3 Berkeley Software Distribution (BSD) Unix /etc/hosts file. This file maps host names to Internet Protocol (IP) addresses. In Windows

2000, this file is stored in the \%SystemRoot%\System32\Drivers\Etc folder.

incremental backup
A backup that backs up only those files created or changed since the last normal or incremental backup. It marks files as having been backed up (in other words, the archive attribute is cleared). If you use a combination of normal and incremental backups, you need to have the last normal backup set as well as all incremental backup sets to restore your data.

Infrared Data Association (IrDA) device
A device that exchanges data over infrared waves. Infrared technology lets devices "beam" information to each other in the same way that your remote control tells the TV to change the channel. You could, for example, beam a document to a printer or another computer instead of having to connect a cable. The IrDA standard has been widely adopted by PC and consumer electronics manufacturers. Windows 2000 supports the IrDA standard.

input locale
The specification of the language you want to type in.

input/output (I/O) port
Any socket in the back, front, or side of a computer that you use to connect to another piece of hardware.

integrated services digital network (ISDN)
An international communications standard for sending voice, video, and data over digital telephone lines or normal telephone wires. ISDN supports data transfer rates of 64Kbps. Most ISDN lines offered by telephone companies give you two lines at once, called B channels. You can use one line for voice and the other for data, or you can use both lines for data, giving you data rates of 128Kbps.

integrated zone storage
Storage of zone information in an Active Directory database rather than in a text file.

Internet Connection Sharing (ICS)
A feature that is intended for use in a small office or home office where the network configuration and the Internet connection are managed by the computer running Windows 2000 where the shared connection resides. ICS can use a dial-up connection, such as modem or integrated services digital network (ISDN) connection to the Internet, or it can use a dedicated connection such as a cable modem or digital subscriber line (DSL). It is assumed that the ICS computer is the only Internet connection, the only gateway to the Internet, and that it sets up all internal network addresses.

Internet Printing Protocol (IPP)
A standard that allows network clients the option of entering a Uniform Resource Locator (URL) to connect to network printers and manage their network print jobs using a Hypertext Transfer Protocol (HTTP) connection in a Web browser. In Windows 2000, IPP is

fully supported. The print server is either a Windows 2000 server running Internet Information Services (IIS) 5, or a Windows 2000 Professional system running Personal Web Server (PWS). PWS is the "junior" version of IIS. All shared IPP printers can be viewed at **http://servername/printers** (e.g., **http://Server2/printers**).

Internet Protocol (IP)

One of the protocols of the Transmission Control Protocol/Internet Protocol (TCP/IP) suite. IP is responsible for determining if a packet is for the local network or a remote network. If the packet is for a remote network, IP finds a route for it.

Internet Protocol (IP) address

A 32-bit binary address used to identify a host's network and host ID. The network portion can contain either a network ID or a network ID and a subnet ID.

Interrupt Request (IRQ)

A hardware line over which a device or devices can send interrupt signals to the microprocessor. When you add a new device to a PC, you sometimes need to set its IRQ number. IRQ conflicts used to be a common problem when you were adding expansion boards, but the Plug and Play and Advanced Configuration and Power Interface (ACPI) specifications have helped to remove this headache in many cases.

Internet Protocol Security (IPSec)

A Transmission Control Protocol/Internet Protocol (TCP/IP) security mechanism. IPSec provides machine-level authentication, as well as data encryption, for Virtual Private Network (VPN) connections that use Layer 2 Tunneling Protocol (L2TP). IPSec negotiates between your computer and its remote tunnel server before an L2TP connection is established, which secures both passwords and data.

ipconfig

A command that allows you to view, renegotiate, and configure Internet Protocol (IP) address information for a Windows NT or 2000 computer.

Kerberos v5

A distributed authentication and privacy protocol that protects information on a network between devices and enables Single Sign-On (SSO). Kerberos v5 is used in the Windows 2000 security model.

language group

A Regional Options configuration that allows you to type and read documents composed in languages of that group (e.g., Western Europe and United States, Japanese, and Hebrew).

Last Known Good Configuration

Starts Windows 2000 using the registry information that Windows saved at the last shutdown. Use this only in cases when you have incorrectly configured a device or driver. Last Known Good Configuration does not solve problems caused by corrupted or missing drivers or files. Also, you will lose any changes you made since the last successful startup.

Layer 2 Tunneling Protocol (L2TP)

An industry-standard Internet tunneling protocol. Unlike Point-to-Point Tunneling Protocol (PPTP), L2TP does not require Internet Protocol (IP) connectivity between the client workstation and the server. L2TP requires only that the tunnel medium provide packet-oriented point-to-point connectivity. You can use the protocol over media such as Asynchronous Transfer Mode (ATM), Frame Relay, and X.25. L2TP provides the same functionality as PPTP.

local group

A group account that is stored in the Security Access Manager (SAM) of a single system. You can give a local group access to resources only on that system.

local user

A user account that is stored in the Security Access Manager (SAM) of a single system. A local user can belong only to local groups on the same system and can be given access to resources only on that system.

logical drive

A simple volume or partition indicated by a drive letter that resides on a Windows 2000 basic disk.

logon script

A file that you can assign to user accounts. Typically a batch file, a logon script runs automatically every time the user logs on. You can use it to configure a user's working environment at every logon, and it allows an administrator to influence a user's environment without managing all aspects of it. You can assign a logon script to one or more user accounts.

makeboot.exe or makebt32.exe

The command that you use to create a set of four setup boot disks for Windows 2000. You use **makeboot.exe** on 16-bit operating systems and **makebt32.exe** on 32-bit operating systems. To create the setup disks, you'll need four 3.5-inch floppy disks; the disks will be formatted before they are created.

Microsoft Challenge Handshake Authentication Protocol (MSCHAP) 1

A special version of Challenge Handshake Authentication Protocol) (CHAP) that Microsoft uses. The encryption is still two-way and consists of a challenge from the server to the client that is made up of a session ID. The client uses a Message Digest 4 (MD4) hash to return the username to the server.

Microsoft Management Console (MMC)

A set of Windows 2000 utilities that allow authorized administrators to manage the directory remotely. The MMC provides a framework for hosting administrative tools, called consoles.

mirrored volume

A fault-tolerant set of two physical disks that contain an exact replica of each other's data within the mirrored portion of each disk. It is supported only on Windows 2000 Server versions.

mixed mode domain

A migration concept that provides maximum backward compatibility with earlier versions of Windows NT. In mixed mode domain, domain controllers that have been upgraded to Active Directory services allow servers running Windows NT versions 4 and earlier to exist within the domain.

mounted drive, mount point, or mounted volume

A pointer from one partition to another. Mounted drives are useful for increasing a drive's "size" without disturbing it. For example, you could create a mount point to drive E: as C:\CompanyData. Doing so makes it seem that you have increased the size available on the C: partition, specifically allowing you to store more data in C:\CompanyData than you would otherwise be able to.

Moving Picture Experts Group (MPEG)

A family of digital video compression standards and file formats. MPEG generally produces better-quality video than competing formats. MPEG files can be decoded by special hardware or by software. MPEG achieves a high compression rate by storing only the changes from one frame to another, instead of each entire frame. There are two major MPEG standards: MPEG-1 and MPEG-2. The MPEG-1 standard provides a video resolution of 352x240 at 30 frames per second (fps), which is video quality slightly below that of conventional VCR

videos. A newer standard, MPEG-2, offers resolutions of 720x480 and 1,280x720 at 60 fps, with full CD-quality audio. This is sufficient for all the major TV standards, including NTSC and even HDTV. DVD-ROMs use MPEG-2. MPEG-2 can compress a two-hour video into a few gigabytes. Currently, work is being done on a new version of MPEG called MPEG-4 (there is no MPEG-3). MPEG-4 will be based on the QuickTime file format.

Multilink

An extension to Point-to-Point Protocol (PPP), that allows you to combine multiple physical connections between two points into a single logical connection. For example, you can combine two 33.6Kbps modems into one logical 67.2Kbps connection. The combined connections, called *bundles,* provide greater bandwidth than a single connection.

Multiple Processor Support (MPS)-compliant

Windows 2000 provides support for single or multiple CPUs. If you originally installed Windows 2000 on a computer with a single CPU, you must update the Hardware Abstraction Layer (HAL) on your computer so that it can recognize and use multiple CPUs.

name resolution

The process of translating a name into an Internet Protocol (IP) address. This could be either a fully qualified domain name (FQDN) or a NetBIOS name.

namespace

The method or conventions by which objects in a group of cooperating directories or databases are hierarchically structured and named.

native mode domain

A migration concept in which all domain controllers are running Windows 2000. The domain uses only Active Directory services multimaster replication between domain controllers, and no Windows NT domain controllers can participate in the domain through single-master replication.

network directory

A file or database where users or applications can get reference information about objects on the network.

network interface card (NIC) or network adapter

A piece of computer hardware called an adapter card that physically connects a computer to a network cable.

normal backup

A backup that copies all files and marks those files as having been backed up (in other words, clears the archive attribute). It is the most complete form of backup.

NT File System (NTFS) 5

An advanced file system designed for use specifically within the Windows 2000 operating system. It supports file system recovery, extremely large storage media, and long file names.

NT File System (NTFS) permission

A rule associated with a folder, file, or printer to regulate which users can gain access to the object and in what manner. The object's owner allows or denies permissions. The most restrictive permissions take effect between share permissions and NTFS permissions on an object.

object

In the context of performance monitoring and optimization, a system component that has numerous counters associated with it. Objects include Processor, Memory, System, Logical Disk, and Pagefile.

offline file

A new feature of Windows 2000 that allows users to continue to work with network files and programs even when they are not connected to the network. When a network connection is restored or when users dock their mobile computers, any changes that were made while users were working offline are updated to the network. When more than one user on the network has made changes to the same file, users are given the option of saving their specific version of the file to the network, keeping the other version, or saving both.

Open Systems Interconnect (OSI) model

A layer architecture developed by the International Organization for Standardization (ISO) that standardizes levels of service and types of interaction for computers that are exchanging information through a communications network. The OSI model separates computer-to-computer communications into seven layers or levels, each building upon the standards contained in the levels below it.

optimization
The process of tuning performance for a particular system component.

Organizational Unit (OU)
A type of container object used within the Lightweight Directory Access Protocol (LDAP)/X.500 information model to group other objects and classes together for easier administration.

Packet Internet Groper (Ping) utility
A utility that determines whether a specific Internet Protocol (IP) address for a network device is reachable from an individual computer. It works by sending a data packet to the specified address and waiting for a reply. You use it to troubleshoot network connections in the Transmission Control Protocol/Internet Protocol (TCP/IP) network protocol.

paging file
Formerly called the swap file or virtual memory file, an extension of memory space stored on the disk drive as a kind of virtual memory.

partition
The information area beginning at a branch of a directory tree and continuing to the bottom of that tree and/or to the edges of new partitions controlled by subordinate Directory System Agents (DSAs).

Password Authentication Protocol (PAP)
The protocol that allows clear-text authentication.

peripheral connection interface (PCI)
A local bus standard developed by Intel. Most modern PCs include a PCI bus in addition to a more general Industry Standard Architecture (ISA) expansion bus. Many analysts, however, believe that PCI will eventually replace ISA entirely. PCI is a 64-bit bus, though it is usually implemented as a 32-bit bus. It can run at clock speeds of 33 or 66MHz. Although Intel developed it, PCI is not tied to any particular family of microprocessors.

Personal Computer Memory Card International Association (PCMCIA)
An organization of some 500 companies that developed a standard for small, credit card-sized devices called PC Cards. Originally designed for adding memory to portable computers, the PCMCIA standard has been expanded several times and is suitable for many types of devices. There are in fact three types of PCMCIA cards, along with three types of PC slots the cards fit into: Type I, II, and III, respectively.

Plug and Play
A standard developed by Microsoft, Intel, and other industry leaders to simplify the process of adding hardware to PCs by having the operating system automatically detect devices. The standard's intention is to conceal unpleasant details, such as

Interrupt Requests (IRQs) and Direct Memory Access (DMA) channels, from people who want to add a new hardware device to their system. A Plug and Play monitor, for example, can communicate with both Windows 2000 and the graphics adapter to automatically set itself at the maximum refresh rate supported for a chosen resolution. Plug and Play compliance also ensures that devices will not be driven beyond their capabilities.

Point-to-Point Protocol (PPP)

A method of connecting a computer to a network or to the Internet. PPP is more stable than the older Serial Line Internet Protocol (SLIP) and provides error-checking features. Windows 2000 Professional is a PPP client when dialing into any network.

Point-to-Point Tunneling Protocol (PPTP)

A communication protocol that tunnels through another connection, encapsulating PPP packets. The encapsulated packets are Internet Protocol (IP) datagrams that can be transmitted over IP-based networks, such as the Internet.

policy

A configuration or setting that is specified for one or more systems or users. Policies are refreshed at startup, logon, and after a refresh interval, so if a setting is manually changed, the policy refreshes the setting automatically. Policies provide for centralized management of change and configuration.

primary domain controller (PDC)

In a Windows NT Server 4 or earlier domain, the computer running Windows NT Server that authenticates domain logons and maintains the directory database for a domain. The PDC tracks changes made to accounts of all computers on a domain. It is the only computer to receive these changes directly. A domain has only one PDC.

primary master

An authoritative Domain Name System (DNS) server for a zone that you can use as a point of update for the zone. Only primary masters can be updated directly to process zone updates, which include adding, removing, or modifying resource records that are stored as zone data. Primary masters are also used as the first sources for replicating the zone to other DNS servers.

primary monitor

The monitor designated as the one that displays the logon dialog box when you start your computer. Most programs display their window on the primary monitor when you first open them. A Windows 2000 computer can support multiple monitors or displays.

privilege

The capability to perform a system behavior, such as changing the system time, backing up or restoring files, or formatting the hard drive. A privilege used to be, and often still is, referred to as a user right.

public key cryptography

An asymmetric encryption scheme that uses a pair of keys to code data. The public key encrypts data, and a corresponding secret key decrypts it. For digital signatures, the sender uses the private key to create a unique electronic number that can be read by anyone who has the corresponding public key, thus verifying that the message is truly from the sender.

Recovery Console

A command-line interface (CLI) that provides a limited set of administrative commands that are useful for repairing a computer. For example, you can use the Recovery Console to start and stop services, read and write data on a local drive (including drives formatted to use NT File System— NTFS), repair a master boot record (MBR), and format drives. You can start the Recovery Console from the Windows 2000 Setup disks or by using the **winnt32.exe** command with the **/cmdcons** switch.

Redundant Array of Independent Disks (RAID)-5 (or striped set with parity) volume

A fault-tolerant collection of equal-sized partitions on at least three physical disks, where the data is striped and includes parity data. The parity data is used to help recover a member of the striped set if one of its members fails. Windows 2000 Professional cannot host a RAID-5 volume but Windows 2000 Server versions can.

Remote Authentication Dial-In User Service (RADIUS)

A protocol used by Internet Authentication Services (IAS) to enable the communication of authentication, authorization, and accounting to the homogeneous and heterogeneous dial-up or Virtual Private Network (VPN) equipment in the enterprise.

Remote Installation Service (RIS)

A RIS server provides Windows 2000 Professional operating system image(s) that can be downloaded and installed by network clients using network adapter that comply with the Pre-boot eXecution Environment (PXE) boot read-only memory (ROM) specifications. RIS requires Active Directory, Dynamic Host Configuration Protocol (DHCP), and Domain Name System (DNS) to serve clients.

reverse lookup zone

A Domain Name System (DNS) zone that provides Transmission Control Protocol/Internet Protocol (TCP/IP) address to host name resolution.

route

A Windows 2000 command-line utility that manipulates Transmission Control Protocol/Internet Protocol (TCP/IP) routing tables for the local computer.

Safe Mode startup options

The options you get at startup when you press the F8 function key. Safe Mode helps you diagnose problems. When started in Safe Mode, Windows

2000 uses only basic files and drivers (mouse, monitor, keyboard, mass storage, base video, and default system services, but no network connections). You can choose the Safe Mode With Networking option, which loads all of the above files and drivers plus the essential services and drivers to start networking. Or, you can choose the Safe Mode With Command Prompt option, which is exactly the same as Safe Mode except that a command prompt is started instead of Windows 2000. You can also choose Last Known Good Configuration, which starts your computer using the registry information that Windows 2000 saved at the last shutdown. If a symptom does not reappear when you start in Safe Mode, you can eliminate the default settings and minimum device drivers as possible causes. If a newly added device or a changed driver is causing problems, you can use Safe Mode to remove the device or reverse the change. In some circumstances, such as when Windows system files required to start the system are corrupted or damaged, Safe Mode cannot help you. In this case, the Emergency Repair Disk (ERD) may be of use.

sampling (or update) interval
The frequency with which a performance counter is logged. A shorter interval provides more detailed information but generates a larger log.

scalability
A measure of how well a computer, service, or application can grow to meet increasing performance demands.

Security Account Manager (SAM)
The database of local user and local group accounts on a Windows 2000 member server or Windows 2000 Professional system.

Security Identifier (SID)
A unique number that represents a security principal such as a user or group. You can change the name of a user or group account without affecting the account's permissions and privileges, because the SID is what is granted user rights and resource access.

Serial Line Internet Protocol (SLIP)
An older remote access communication protocol used in Windows 2000 for outbound communication only.

service (SRV) record
A resource record used in a zone to register and locate well-known Transmission Control Protocol/Internet Protocol (TCP/IP) services. The SRV resource record is specified in Request for Comments (RFC) 2052 and is used in Windows 2000 or later to locate domain controllers for Active Directory Service.

Setup Manager
Used to create answer files for Windows 2000 unattended installations. Setup Manager can create answer files for an unattended, Sysprep or RIS installations.

share permission
A rule associated with a folder, to regulate which users can gain access to the object over the network and in what manner.

Shiva Password Authentication Protocol (SPAP)

A protocol that third-party clients and server typically use. The encryption for the protocol is two-way, but it is not as good as that for Challenge Handshake Authentication Protocol (CHAP).

simple volume

In Windows 2000, the disk space on a single physical disk. It can consist of a single area on a disk or multiple areas on the same disk that are linked together. You can extend a simple volume within the same disk or among multiple disks. If you extend a simple volume across multiple disks, it becomes a spanned volume.

slipstreaming

The process of integrating a Windows 2000 Service Pack into an existing Windows 2000 installation share. Subsequent installations of Windows 2000 will then include the service pack that you have slipstreamed into the installation share.

smart card

A credit card-sized device used to securely store public and private keys, passwords, and other types of personal information. To use a smart card, you need a smart card reader attached to the computer and a personal identification number (PIN) for the smart card. In Windows 2000, you can use smart cards to enable certificate-based authentication and Single Sign-On (SSO) to the enterprise.

smart card reader

A small external or internal device, or even a built-in slot, into which you insert a smart card so that it can be read.

spanned volume

In Windows 2000, the disk space on more than one physical disk. You can add more space to a spanned volume by extending it at any time. In NT 4 and earlier, a spanned volume was called a volume set.

spooler service

The primary Windows 2000 service that controls printing functionality.

standard zone storage

Storage of zone information in a text file rather than in an Active Directory database.

standby mode

A power-saving option in Windows 2000. Your computer switches to a low-power state where devices, such as the monitor and hard disks, turn off and your computer uses less power. When you want to use the computer again, it comes out of standby quickly, and your desktop is restored exactly as you left it. Standby is useful for conserving battery power in portable computers. Standby does not save your desktop state to disk; if you experience a power failure while on Standby, you can lose unsaved information. If there is an interruption in power, information in memory is lost.

static pool

A range of Internet Protocol (IP) addresses configured on the remote access server that allows the server to allocate IP addresses to the remote access clients.

striped volume

A volume that stores data in stripes on two or more physical disks. Data in a striped volume is allocated alternately and evenly (in stripes) to the disks of the striped volume. Striped volumes are *not* fault tolerant. Striped volumes can substantially improve the speed of access to your data on disk. You can create them on both Windows 2000 Professional and Server machines. Striped volumes with parity, also known as RAID-5 volumes, can be created *only* on Windows 2000 Server machines. In NT 4 and earlier, a striped volume was called a striped set.

subnet mask

A filter used to determine which network segment, or subnet, an Internet Protocol (IP) address belongs to. An IP address has two components: the network address and the host (computer name) address. For example, if the IP address 209.15.17.8 is part of a Class C network; the first three numbers (209.15.17) represent the Class C network address, and the last number (8) identifies a specific host (computer) on this network. By implementing subnetting, network administrators can further divide the host part of the address into two or more subnets.

suspend mode

A deep-sleep power-saving option that still uses some power.

Symmetric Multiprocessing (SMP)

A computer architecture that provides fast performance by making multiple CPUs available to complete individual processes simultaneously (multiprocessing). Unlike with asymmetric processing, you can assign any idle processor any task as well as add additional CPUs to improve performance and handle increased loads. A variety of specialized operating systems and hardware arrangements support SMP. Specific applications can benefit from SMP if their code allows multithreading. SMP uses a single operating system and shares common memory and disk input/output (I/O) resources. Windows 2000 supports SMP.

Sysprep

A tool that prepares a Windows 2000 computer to be imaged using third-party disk image software. It does this by removing unique identifiers such as computer name and Security Identifiers (SIDs). **Sysprep** adds a service to the image that generates a unique local domain SID after the image has been applied.

system state

In Backup, a collection of system-specific data that you can back up and restore. For all Windows 2000 operating systems, the system state data includes the registry, the Component Object Model (COM)+ Class Registration database, and the system boot files. For Windows 2000 Server, the system state data also includes the Certificate Services database (if the server is operating as a certificate server). If the server is a domain controller, the system state data also includes the Active Directory directory services database and the Sysvol directory.

Sysvol

A shared directory that stores the server copy of the domain's public files, which are replicated among all domain controllers in the domain.

ticket

A feature of the Kerberos security model by which clients are granted access to objects and resources only indirectly, through services. Application servers use the service ticket to impersonate the client and look up its user or group Security Identifiers (SIDs).

tracert

A Windows 2000 command-line utility that follows that path of a data packet from a local computer to a host (computer) somewhere on the network (or internetwork). It shows how many hops the packet requires to reach the host and how long each hop takes. You can use **tracert** to figure out where the longest delays are occurring for connecting to various computers.

universal group

A security or distribution group that you can use anywhere in the domain tree or forest. A universal group can have members from any Windows

2000 domain in the domain tree or forest. It can also include other universal groups, global groups, and accounts from any domain in the domain tree or forest. Universal groups can be members of domain local groups and other universal groups but cannot be members of global groups. Universal groups appear in the Global Catalog and should contain primarily global groups.

Universal Serial Bus (USB)

An external bus standard (released in 1996) that supports data transfer rates of 12Mbps. You can use a single USB port to connect up to 127 peripheral devices, such as mice, modems, and keyboards. USB also supports Plug and Play installation and hot plugging. It is expected to completely replace serial and parallel ports.

User Datagram Protocol (UDP)

A connectionless protocol that runs on top of Internet Protocol (IP) networks. Unlike Transmission Control Protocol/Internet Protocol (TCP/IP), UDP/IP provides very few error recovery services and does not guarantee delivery of data. UDP is a direct way to send and receive datagrams over an IP network. It's used primarily for sending broadcast messages over an IP network.

user locale

Controls the date, time, currency, and numbers on a per-user basis. These settings are used by all applications and can be configured via the Regional Options applet in the Control Panel folder.

user profile
The collection of desktop and environmental settings that define the work area of a local computer.

user right
See *privilege*.

video adapter
The electronic component that generates the video signal sent through a cable to a video display. The video adapter is usually located on the computer's main system board or on an expansion board.

Virtual Private Network (VPN)
A private network of computers that is at least partially connected using public channels or lines, such as the Internet. A good example would be a private-office local area network (LAN) that allows users to log in remotely over the Internet (an open, public system). VPNs use encryption and secure protocols like Point-to-Point Tunneling Protocol (PPTP) and Layer 2 Tunneling Protocol (L2TP) to ensure that unauthorized parties do not intercept data transmissions.

Windows Backup
A Windows 2000 utility that helps you plan for and recover from data loss by allowing you to create backup copies of data as well as restore files, folders, and system state data (which includes the registry) manually or on a schedule. The Windows 2000 Backup program allows you to back up data to a variety of media types, not just tape.

Windows Installer Packages
Files with the .msi extension that install applications. These files contain summary and installation instructions as well as the actual installation files. You can install Windows Installer Packages locally or remotely through Windows 2000 Group Policies.

Windows Internet Naming Service (WINS)
A service that dynamically maps NetBIOS names to Internet Protocol (IP) addresses.

Windows Management Instrumentation (WMI)
An initiative supported in Windows 2000 that establishes architecture to support the management of an enterprise across the Internet. WMI offers universal access to management information for enterprises by providing a consistent view of the managed environment. This management uniformity allows you to manage your entire business rather than just its components. You can obtain more detailed information regarding the WMI Software Development Kit (SDK) from the Microsoft Developer Network (MSDN).

Windows or Win32 Driver Model (WDM)
A 32-bit layered architecture for device drivers; it allows for drivers that Windows 2000, NT, and 98 can use. It provides common input/output (I/O) services that all operating systems understand. It also supports

Plug and Play; Universal Serial Bus (USB); Institute of Electrical and Electronics Engineers (IEEE) 1394 bus; and various devices, including input, communication, imaging, and digital versatile disc or digital video disc (DVD).

winnt32 /cmdcons

The command and switch used to install the Recovery Console onto a Windows 2000 computer. This command uses **winnt32** on the installation media, or in the distribution source.

workgroup

A peer-to-peer network in which user accounts are decentralized and stored on each individual system.

X.25 Virtual Circuit (VC)

A connection between two devices that acts as though it's a direct connection although it may physically take different routes. X.25 connections involve at least two hosts in a packet switching network. With X.25 VCs, two hosts can communicate as though they have a dedicated connection, although the data packets might actually travel very different routes before arriving at their destinations. VCs can be either permanent or temporary.

ZAP

A file that you use to allow applications without an .msi file to be deployed via Windows 2000 Group Policy.

zone

In Domain Name System (DNS) standards, the namespace partition formed by each domain within the global namespace or within an enterprise namespace. Each zone is controlled by an authoritative DNS server, or in the case of Active Directory services, by a group of domain controllers.

zone transfer

Copying of Domain Name System (DNS) database information from one DNS server to another.

Index

Bold page numbers indicate sample exam questions.

A

Access permissions, 46-48, **98**
Accessibility options
Accessibility Options applet,
129-131
Accessibility Wizard, 131-132
Display tab, 130
FilterKeys, 129-130
High Contrast, 130
Keyboard tab, 129-130
Magnifier, 132
Mouse tab, 131
MouseKeys, 131
Narrator, 132
On-Screen Keyboard, 132
SerialKey, 131
ShowSounds, 130
Sound Tab, 130
SoundSentry, 130
StickyKeys, 129
ToggleKeys, 130
Utility Manager, 132, **324**
Accessibility Options applet, 129-131
Accessibility Wizard, 131-132
Account policies, 89-90
ACLs, 34-36
Active Directory, 86-88, **161**
Add/Remove Hardware Wizard, 170,
173, **199-200, 320**
Add/Remove Programs, 115, **120-121**

Administrators group, 30, 78, **95**
Advanced permissions, 37-41
Append Data permission, 41
Change Permissions permission, 41
Create Files/Write Data
permission, 40
Create Folders/Append Data
permission, 41
Delete permission, 40
Delete Subfolders and Files
permission, 40
Execute File permission, 40
Read Attributes permission, 40
Read Data permission, 40
Read Extended Attributes
permission, 40
Read Permissions permission, 41
Take Ownership permission, 41
Traverse Folder/Execute File
permission, 40
Write Attributes permission, 40
Write Data permission, 40
Write Extended Attributes
permission, 40
Anonymous Logon built-in group, 31
APIPA, 235, 242, **260-261**
Application performance, managing, 284
ARP, 240
Attended installation
CD-ROM installation, 146-147
hardware requirements, 146
installation methods, 146-147
network installation, 147

overview, 146
setup disks, installation with, 147
Audit policies, 90-91
Auditing, 50-51, **70**
enabling, 51-52
specific files and folders, enabling
auditing for, 52-53
Authenticated Users built-in group, 31
Authentication
automating logon, 86
overview, 85
security dialog, 85-86
Authentication protocols
BAP, 244, **326**
EAP, 243-244
IPSec, 242-243
L2TP, 243
RADIUS, 244
Automated installation
launching, 151
RIS, 153-157
Setup Manager utility, 148-151
switches, 151
System Preparation Tool, 151-153

B

Backing up and restoring data
backup marker, 265
backup strategies, 266
backup types, 265
Backup Wizard, scheduling
backups with, 267-268
configuring file and folder
backup, 266
copy backups, 265
daily backups, 265
differential backups, 265
incremental backups, 265
normal backups, 265
permissions, 264
restoring files and folders, 268
Scheduled Jobs tab, configuring
jobs with, 268
scheduling backups, 267-268
system state data, backing up, 267
user rights, 264
Windows Backup, 264
Backup marker, 265
Backup Operators group, 30, 78, **95**
Backup strategies, 266, **317**
Backup types, 265

Backup Wizard, scheduling backups with,
267-268
BACP, 244, **326**
Bandwidth Allocation Protocol. *See* BAP.
BAP, 244, **326**
Baseline, creating, 279-280
Basic disks, 204, **224, 229.**
See also basic volumes.
detecting disk errors, 214
diagnosing problems, 213
Disk Cleanup Wizard, 216
Disk Defragmenter, 215
diskperf.exe, 214-215
dynamic disks compared, 205
monitoring disk performance,
213-214
repairing disk errors, 214
troubleshooting, 213-216
upgrading to dynamic disks, 206-207
Basic permissions
files, 36
folders, 37
Basic volumes
extending, 213
logical drives, 209
overview, 208
partitions, 209
spanned volumes on basic disks, 208
striped volumes on basic disks,
208-209
troubleshooting, 213-216
BIOS, **165**, 183, **196-197**
Boot disk, 154, **319**
Built-in groups, 30-31
Administrators group, 78
Backup Operators group, 78
Guests group, 79
Power Users group, 78
Replicator group, 79
Users group, 78-79
Built-in system groups
Anonymous Logon group, 79
Authenticated Users group, 79
Creator Owner group, 79
Dial-up group, 79
Everyone group, 79
Interactive group, 79
Network group, 79
Built-in user accounts
Administrator account, 77
Guest account, 78

C

Caching files, 27-29, **318**, **322**
CACLS.exe utility, 36
Cameras
  installing, 179
  overview, 178
  testing, 179
CD-ROM installation, **162**
Certificates, 178
Chdir command, 273
Chkdsk command, 273
Cls command, 273
Copy backups, 265
Copy command, 273
Counter logs, 278
Creator Owner built-in group, 31

D

Daily backups, 265
Debugging Mode, 270
Default gateway, 238
Default permissions, 41-42
Delete command, 273
Desktop settings
  Display applet, 109-110
  Keyboard applet, 109
  Mouse applet, 110
  overview, 109
  Quick Launch Pad, 111
  Sound applet, 110
  Start menu, customizing, 110-111
  toolbars, 111-112
Device conflicts, 173
Device Manager, 170, 172–173, **195**
DHCP, 234-235, **325-326**
DHCP servers, **161**, 235, **254**, **260**
Dial-up built-in group, 31
Dial-up Connections, 242, **326**
  BACP, 244
  BAP, 244
  EAP, 243-244
  Internet connections, creating, 249-
    250
  IPSec, 242-243
  L2TP, 243
  RADIUS, 244
  RAS servers, connecting to, 245-248
  VPN connections, 248-249
Differential backups, 265, **320**
Dir command, 273

Directory Services Restore Mode, 270
Disable command, 273
Disk Cleanup Wizard, 216
Disk Defragmenter, 215
Disk Management, **228-229**, **322**
  accessing, 206
  basic volumes. *See* basic volumes.
  dynamic volumes. *See* dynamic
    volumes.
  moving disks, 207-208
  offline disks, reactivating, 208
  troubleshooting disks and volumes,
    213-216
  upgrading disks, 206-207
Disk performance, managing, 282
Disk quotas, 220-221
Diskperf.exe, 214-215
Display applet, 109-110
Display settings, 186, **320**
Display tab, 130
DNS server, 56, **72**, **161**, 235, 238
Domain accounts, 76-77, **99**, **121**
Domain controllers, 77
Domain security, 31-32
Domain user accounts
  copying, 84
  creating, 83-84
  deleting, 84
  disabling, 84
  local groups, adding to, 85
  managing, 83-85
  modifying, 84
  template user accounts, creating, 84
DRAs, 55, **67**
Drive letters
  assigning, 218-219
  changing, 218
  removing, 218
Driver signing, 173-174
Driver updates
  device conflicts, 173
  driver signing, 173-174
  Group Policy Object (GPO), 174
  overview, 172
  Signature Verification tool, 174
  system files, Windows Update used
    for updating, 172-173
  updating individual drivers, 172
DVD devices, managing, 222-223
DVD drives, 223, **226**

Dynamic disks, 204-205, **229**, **321**.
  See also dynamic volumes.
    basic disks compared, 205
    conversion to basic disks, 207, **322**
    detecting disk errors, 214
    diagnosing problems, 213
    Disk Cleanup Wizard, 216
    Disk Defragmenter, 215
    Diskperf.exe, 214-215
    limitations of, 212-213
    monitoring disk performance,
      213-214
    troubleshooting, 213-216
Dynamic volumes
    extending, 211, 213
    limitations of, 212-213
    overview, 210
    RAID-5 volumes, 212
    simple volumes, 210
    spanned volumes, 210-211
    striped volumes, 212
    troubleshooting, 213-216

E

EAP, 178
EFS
    accessing encrypted files, 55
    copying encrypted files, 56
    moving encrypted files, 56
    overview, 53-54
    Windows Explorer, encrypting file or
      folders from, 54-55
Emergency Repair Disks. *See* ERDs.
Enable Boot Logging, 269
Enable command, 273
Enable VGA Mode, 269-270
Encrypted files, 54-56, **67**, **70**, **322**
ERDs
    emergency repair process, 274-276
    Fast Repair option, 275
    Manual Repair option, 275
    overview, 274
    repair process, starting, 276
    restarting computer, 276
    Setup, choosing repair options
      during, 275
    type of repair, choosing, 275
Everyone built-in group, 31
Exit command, 273
Extensible Authentication Protocol.
  See EAP.

F

FAT, 216
FAT32, 216, **225**, **227**, **321**
Fax service
    configuring, 132-133, **138**
    Fax Service Management console,
      133-134
    sending faxes, 132
    support for, 181
Fax Service Management console,
  133-134, **137**
Fdisk command, 273
File compression, 42-44
File systems
    conversion between systems,
      217-218
    default NTFS permissions,
      reapplying, 218
    FAT, 216
    FAT32, 216
    NTFS 5, 216-217
    NTFS partition, converting from
      FAT partition to, 217
Files
    basic permissions, 36
    copying compressed, 45-46
    moving compressed, 45-46
    offline files. *See* offline files.
    optimizing access to, 48-50
    ownership of, 49-50
    permissions and copying, 48-49
    permissions and moving, 48-49
    permissions used to control access to,
      46-48
FilterKeys, 129-130, **138**
Finger, 239
Fixboot command, 273
Fixmbr command, 273
Folder compression, 44-45
Folders
    basic permissions, 36–37
    copying compressed, 45-46
    moving compressed, 45-46
    offline folders. *See* offline folders.
    optimizing access to, 48-50
    ownership of, 49-50
    permissions and copying, 48-49
    permissions and moving, 48-49
    permissions used to control access to,
      46-48
    shared folders. *See* shared folders.

Format command, 273
FTP service, 58, 236, 239

G

Group accounts, local.
   See local group accounts.
Group Policy, 92-93, **96–97, 99, 118-119,**
   122-123, 316, 323
   application of, 93
   OU design and, 93-94
Group Policy Object (GPO), 174
Guests group, 30, 79

H

Hard disk management
   basic disks. *See* basic disks.
   dynamic disks. *See* dynamic disks.
   guidelines for relocating disks,
      207-208
   missing disks, reactivating, 208
   moving disk to another computer,
      207-208
   offline disks, reactivating, 208
   troubleshooting, 213-216
Hardware
   configuring, 170
   driver updates, 172-174
   I/O devices, 174-184
   IrDA devices. *See* IrDA devices.
   keyboards, 176
   mice, 176
   mobile computer hardware.
      See mobile computer hardware.
   mobile users, 177-178
   modems, 179-181
   monitors. *See* monitors.
   network adapters, 184
   non Plug and Play devices,
      installing, 171
   overview, 170, 174
   Plug and Play devices, installing, 171
   printers. *See* printers.
   scanners, 178-179
   smart card readers, 176-177
   smart cards, 176-177
   tips on installing devices, 171
   wireless devices. *See* wireless devices.
Help command, 273
Hidden network shares, 26-27
High Contrast, 130
Home folders, 103
HOSTNAME, 240

I

ICS, 184-186, **257, 326**
   configuring, 251-253
   overview, 250-251
   troubleshooting, 253
IIS
   administration, 56-57
   installing, 56
   Internet Web sites, problems
      connecting to, 59
   intranet Web sites, problems
      connecting to, 59
   settings, viewing and modifying, 57
   troubleshooting, 58-59
Incremental backups, 265, **287, 320**
Input locale, 126-127, **142**
Installation
   attended installation, 146-147
   automated installation.
      See automated installation.
   dependency failures, 160
   domains, problems joining, 160
   drive space, lack of, 160
   errors, 160
   halts, 160
   hardware requirements, 146
   media errors, 159-160
   memory requirements, 146, **319**
   noncompatibile CD-ROM
      drive, 160
   troubleshooting, 159-160
Interactive built-in group, 31
Internet Connection Sharing. *See* ICS.
Internet Printing Protocol. *See* IPP.
I/O devices
   IrDA devices. *See* IrDA devices.
   keyboards, 176
   mice, 176
   mobile users, 177-178
   modems, 179-181
   network adapters, 184
   overview, 174
   printers. *See* printers.
   scanners, 178-179
   smart card readers, 176-177
   smart cards, 176-177
   wireless devices. *See* wireless devices.
IP addresses, 237, **256, 261**
IPCONFIG, 240
IPP, 66, **200**
IPSec, 236

IrDA devices
   bandwidth allocations for USB host
      controllers, viewing, 183
   described, 181-182
   enabling receiving files, 182
   preventing receiving files, 182
   USB controllers, improper
      installation of, 183-184
   USB hubs, viewing power allocations
      for, 182-183

K

Keyboard applet, 109, **118**
Keyboard tab, 129-130
Keyboards, 176

L

Languages, multiple.
   See multiple language support.
Last Known Good Configuration, 270,
   286-287, 287-288
Local group accounts
   built-in local groups, 78-79
   built-in system groups, 79
   configuring account properties,
      80-81
   creating, 79-80
   deleting, 82
   managing, 77-79
   membership, 81
   overview, 76-77
   passwords, 80
   renaming, 81-82
Local groups, 30-31
Local Policy, 89, 92
Local profiles, 102, **318**
Local Security Policy, 92, **96, 316**
Local user accounts, 76-77, **98**
   built-in user accounts, 77-79
   configuring account properties,
      80-81
   creating, 79-80
   deleting, 82
   disabling, 82
   enabling, 82
   managing, 77-79
   passwords, 80
   renaming, 81-82
   Users and Passwords applet, 82-83
Logical Drives, 209, 220
LogicalDisk counters, 282
Logon command, 273

Logon scripts, 103
LPQ, 240
LPR, 239
L2TP, 236

M

Magnifier, 132
Map command, 273
Memory, 146, **201**, 280, **319–320**
Memory:Available Bytes, 280
Memory:Pages/sec, 280, **289-290**
MFT, 215
Mice, 176
Microsoft Certification exams
   adaptive exam strategy, 17-18
   adaptive testing format, 13-14
   build-list-and-recorder question
      format, 6-8
   case study exam strategy, 15-16
   case study testing format, 13
   create-a-tree question format, 8-10
   drag-and-connect question format,
      10-11
   exam situation, 3-4
   exam-readiness, assessing, 2
   fixed-length exam strategy, 16-17
   fixed-length testing format, 13
   layout and design of exam, 4-12
   multiple-choice question format, 5-6
   practice exams, 19
   preparing for, 19-20
   question formats, 5-12
   question-handling strategies, 18-19
   select-and-place question format,
      11-12
   short-form exam strategy, 16-17
   short-form testing format, 14
   testing formats, 13-14
   test-taking strategies, 14-18
   Web sites, 20-21
Microsoft Certified Professional
   Web site, 20
Mkdir command, 273
Mobile computer hardware
   ACPI, 190-191
   airplanes, using portable computers
      on, 192
   APM, 190
   battery power, managing, 192
   hardware profiles, managing,
      189-190

hibernation mode, 191-192
overview, 189
Plug and Play devices, managing
   power when installing, 192
power options, 191-192
standby mode, 191
Mobile users, 177-178
Modems, **137-138**, 179-181, **198-199**
installing, 179
multilinking, 180-181
troubleshooting, 181
Monitors
arranging multiple monitors, 187
configuring, 186-188
display settings, 186, **320**
moving items between monitors, 188
multiple-display support, 186-188
primary monitor, changing, 187-188
troubleshooting multiple
   displays, 188
viewing same desktop on multiple
   monitors, 188
More command, 273
Mounted drives, 219
Mouse applet, 110
Mouse tab, 131
MouseKeys, 131, **324**
Multilanguage edition, 128-129, **140, 324**
Multilink
configuring, 180
overview, 180
tips for, 180-181
Multiple language support
input locale, 126-127, **142, 324**
installing multiple language
   settings, 128
language options, 126
locales, 126-127
Multilanguage version of
   Windows 2000, 128-129
user locale, 126-127
Multiple processors, 193-194
Multiple-display support
arranging multiple monitors, 187
configuring, 186-188
moving items between monitors, 188
primary monitor, changing, 187-188
troubleshooting multiple
   displays, 188
viewing same desktop on multiple
   monitors, 188

My Documents folder, 103, **122**
My Network Places, 25-26, 107

N

Narrator, 132, **139, 319**
NBSTAT, 240
Net use command, 26
NETSTAT, 240
Network adapters, 184
Network built-in group, 31
Network cards, **197**
Network performance, managing, 283
Network protocols. *See* TCP/IP.
Normal backups, 265, **320**
NTFS, 5, 29, 216-217, **225, 321**
copying compressed files and folders,
   45-46
denying access to a resource, 47-48
file compression, 42-44
folder compression, 44-45
moving compressed files and folders,
   45-46
optimizing access to files and folders,
   48-50
ownership of files and folders, 49-50
permissions, 46-48, 48-49, **228**
security. *See* NTFS security.
NTFS compression, **69**, 221, **228**
copying compressed files and
   folders, 221
guidelines, 221-222
moving compressed files and
   folders, 221
NTFS security
ACLs, 34-36
Administrators local group, 30
advanced permissions, 37-41
Anonymous Logon built-in
   group, 31
Authenticated Users built-in
   group, 31
Backup Operators local group, 30
basic permissions, 36-37
built-in groups, 30-31
CACLS.exe utility, 36
Creator Owner built-in group, 31
default permissions, 41-42
Dial-up built-in group, 31
domain security, 31-32
Everyone built-in group, 31
Guests local group, 30

Interactive built-in group, 31
local groups, 30-31
Network built-in group, 31
permission conflicts, 42
permissions, setting, 31-32
Power Users local group, 30
Replicator local group, 30
Users local group, 30
Windows 2000 logon process, 33-34
workgroup security, 31

O

Offline files
accessing, 108
managing, 108-109
overview, 104-105
setting up, 105-106
share points, configuring, 105-106
steps for making files available
offline, 106-107
synchronizing, 107-108
Offline Files and Folders, 104-105, **120**
Offline folders
accessing, 108
managing, 108-109
overview, 104-105
setting up, 105-106
share points, configuring, 105-106
steps for making files available
offline, 106-107
synchronizing, 107-108
On-Screen Keyboard, 132, **324**

P

Paging file, managing, 280-282
Partitions, 209, **225-226**
Passwords, 80, **96, 98**
Performance
application performance,
managing, 284
baseline, creating, 279-280
configuring alerts, 277-278
configuring logs, 278
counter logs, 278
disk performance, managing, 282
LogicalDisk counters, 282
managing, 278-284
memory performance, managing, 280
network performance, managing, 283
paging file, managing, 280-282
Performance Logs And Alerts,
277-278

PhysicalDisk counters, 282
processor performance, managing,
283-284
System Monitor, 276-277
Task Manager, 284
trace logs, 278
VMM, 280-281
Performance bottleneck, 280, **317**
Performance Logs And Alerts,
277-278, **291**
Permission conflicts, 42
Permissions, 264
access to files and folders, 46-48
copying files and folders, 48-49
moving files and folders, 48-49
setting, 31-32
shared folders, 29
PhysicalDisk counters, 282, **288**
PING, 240
Point-to-Point Protocol. *See* PPP.
Policies
account policies, 89-90
audit policies, 90-91
group policy. *See* Group Policy.
Local Policy, 89
local policy, 92
overview, 89
Security Options node, 91-92
user rights, 91
Power Users group, 30, 78, **95**
PPP, 178, 236
PPTP, 236
Preferred and alternate DNS servers, 238
Print device, 60, **69**
Print jobs, 60, **71**
managing, 65-66
Print queue, 60
Print resolution, 60
Print server, 60
Print spooler, 60
Printer driver, 60
Printer port, 60
Printer Properties sheet
Advanced tab, 64-65
Device Settings tab, 65
General tab, 64
Ports tab, 64
Security tab, 65
Sharing tab, 64
Printers, 59, **71**
Availability setting, 175

command line, connecting to
network printer via, 63
IPP, 66, 175
local printer, adding, 60-61
managing, 65-66
network printer, connecting to,
61-63
Print Pooling setting, 175
Print Priority setting, 175
printer ports, 175
printer property settings, 175-176
properties, configuring, 63-65
Restart setting, 176
Separator Pages setting, 175
Spooler Service, 176
Processor performance, managing,
283-284, **290**
Processors, multiple, 193-194

Q

Quick Launch Pad, 111

R

RAID-5 volumes, 212, **321**
RAS, 242
RAS servers, **198,** 245-248
Rbfg.exe, 154
RCP, 239
Recovery Console
chdir command, 273
chkdsk command, 273
cls command, 273
commands, 273
copy command, 273
delete command, 273
dir command, 273
disable command, 273
enable command, 273
exit command, 273
fdisk command, 273
fixboot command, 273
fixmbr command, 273
format command, 273
help command, 273
launching, 272-273
logon command, 273
map command, 273
mkdir command, 273
more command, 273
overview, 271-272
rename command, 273

rmdir command, 273
system that won't start, running
Recovery Console on, 272
systemroot command, 273
type command, 273
Remote Installation Options, 270
Rename command, 273
Repairing Windows 2000 system
Debugging Mode, 270
Directory Services Restore Mode, 270
Enable Boot Logging, 269
Enable VGA Mode, 269-270
Last Known Good
Configuration, 270
Remote Installation Options, 270
Safe Mode, 268-269
Safe Mode with Command
Prompt, 269
Safe Mode with Networking, 269
Replicator group, 30, 79
Restoring files and folders, 268
REXEC, 240
Riprep.exe, 156-157, **325**
RIS
clients, configuring, 153-154
configuring, 154-156
downloading images, 157
images, creating additional, 156-157
installing, 154-156
overview, 153
requirements for, 154
RIS server, 153-157, **162**
Rmdir command, 273
Roaming user profiles, 103-104
ROUTE, 240
RSH, 240

S

Safe Mode, 268-269, **286**
Safe Mode with Command Prompt, 269
Safe Mode with Networking, 269
Scanners
installing, 179
overview, 178
testing, 179
Scheduled Jobs tab, configuring jobs
with, 268
Scheduling backups, 267-268
Security
auditing. *See* auditing.
authentication. *See* authentication.

encrypted files. *See* encrypted files.
NTFS security. *See* NTFS security.
Security Options node, 91-92
SerialKey, 131
Service packs. *See* SPs.
Setup disks, 147, **325**
Shared folders. *See also* NTFS.
    access, 24-25, **68**
    automatically generated hidden
      shares, 26-27
    caching of files, 27-29
    controlling access to, 27-29
    permissions, 29
    properties, modifying, 27-29
Shared network resources
    connecting to, 25-26
    My Network Places, 25-26
    net use command, 26
ShowSounds, 130
Signature Verification tool, 174
SLIP, 235
Slipstreaming, 159, **165**
Smart card readers, 176-177
Smart cards, 176-177, **255**
SMTP, 237
Sound applet, 110
Sound Tab, 130
SoundSentry, 130
Spanned volumes, 208, 210-211
SPs, **318**
    applying, 159, **166**
    deploying, 159
    slipstreaming, 159
Start menu, customizing, 110-111
StickyKeys, 129, **139**, **325**
Striped volumes, 208-209, 212, **230**
Subnet mask, 238
Synchronizing offline files and folders,
    107-108, **117**, **318**, **323**
Sysprep.inf, 153, **163**, **319**
System files, Windows Update used for
    updating, 172-173
System Monitor, 276-277
System Preparation Tool, 151-153
System state data, backing up, 267, **317**
Systemroot command, 273

T

Tape devices, managing, 222
Task Manager, 284, **289**, **317**

Task Scheduler, 134-135, **141**
    creating a task, 135
    opening, 135
    troubleshooting tasks, 136
TCP/IP, 234, **254-255**
    APIPA, 235, 242
    ARP, 240
    configuring, 238-239
    default gateway, 238
    DHCP, 234-235
    DNS server, 235
    Finger, 239
    FTP, 239
    FTP service, 236
    HOSTNAME, 240
    IP addresses, 237
    IPCONFIG, 240
    IPSec, 236
    LPQ, 240
    LPR, 239
    L2TP, 236
    NBSTAT, 240
    NETSTAT, 240
    PING, 240
    PPP, 236
    PPTP, 236
    preferred and alternate DNS
      servers, 238
    RCP, 239
    REXEC, 240
    ROUTE, 240
    RSH, 240
    SLIP, 235
    SMTP, 237
    subnet mask, 238
    Telnet, 240
    TFTP, 240
    TRACERT, 240
    troubleshooting, 239-241
    WINS, 235
    WINS addresses, 238
    WWW publishing service, 236
Telnet, 240
Template account, 84, **316**
TFTP, 240
ToggleKeys, 130
Toolbars, 111-112
Trace logs, 278
TRACERT, 240
Transmission Control Protocol/Internet
    Protocol. *See* TCP/IP.

Troubleshooting
    basic disks, 213-216
    basic volumes, 213-216
    dynamic disks, 213-216
    dynamic volumes, 213-216
    hard disk management, 213-216
    ICS, 253
    IIS, 58-59
    installation, 159-160
    modems, 181
    service fails, recovery actions for
        when a, 271
    system stopping unexpectedly,
        270-271
    tasks, 136
    TCP/IP, 239-241
Type command, 273

U

Update packs, 158, **163**
Updating individual drivers, 172
Upgrades, **326**
    disk utilities, 158
    drive compression, 158
    hardware compatibility, 158, **164**
    operating systems, supported,
        157-158
    pre-upgrade checklist, 158
    software compatibility, 158, **164**
    update packs, 158, **163**
USB, 182-184, **196, 320**
User accounts, local.
    See local user accounts.
User profiles, 102, **119, 323**
    home folders, 103
    local profiles, 102
    logon scripts, 103
    roaming user profiles, 103-104
User rights, 91, 264
Users and Passwords applet, 82-83,
    96, 316
Users local group, 30
Utility Manager, 132, **324**

V

Video adapters, 189
VMM, 280-281
VPN, 248-249, **258–259**

W

Web sites
    Microsoft, 21
    Microsoft Certified Professional, 20
    search tools, 21
Windows 2000 logon process, 33-34
Windows Backup, 264, **285**
Windows Installer Service Packages
    assigning applications, 115
    Group Policy, creating, 114-115
    installing packages, 113
    .msi files, 114
    overview, 112-113
    publishing applications, 115
    ZAP files, 113, **123**
WINS, **72,** 235, 238
Wireless devices
    bandwidth allocations for USB host
        controllers, viewing, 183
    described, 181-182
    enabling receiving files, 182
    preventing receiving files, 182
    USB controllers, improper
        installation of, 183-184
    USB hubs, viewing power allocations
        for, 182-183
Workgroup security, 31
Workgroups, 77
WWW Master Service Properties, 58
WWW publishing service, 236

Z

ZAP files, 113, **123**

Look for All of the Exam Cram Brand Certification Study Systems

ALL NEW! Exam Cram Personal Trainer Systems

The Exam Cram Personal Trainer systems are an exciting new category in certification training products. These CD-ROM based systems offer extensive capabilities at a moderate price and are the first certification-specific testing product to completely link learning with testing.

This Exam Cram study guide turned interactive course lets you customize the way you learn.

Each system includes:
- A Personalized Practice Test engine with multiple test methods
- A database of nearly 300 questions linked directly to the subject matter within the Exam Cram

Exam Cram Audio Review Systems

Written and read by certification instructors, each set contains four cassettes jam-packed with the certification exam information you must have. Designed to be used on their own or as a complement to our Exam Cram study guides, Flash Cards, and Practice Tests.

Each system includes:
- Study preparation tips with an essential last-minute review for the exam
- Hours of lessons highlighting key terms and techniques
- A comprehensive overview of all exam objectives
- 45 minutes of review questions, complete with answers and explanations

Exam Cram Flash Cards

These pocket-sized study tools are 100% focused on exams. Key questions appear on side one of each card and in-depth answers on side two. Each card features either a cross-reference to the appropriate Exam Cram study guide chapter or to another valuable resource. Comes with a CD-ROM featuring electronic versions of the flash cards and a complete practice exam.

Exam Cram Practice Tests

Our readers told us that extra practice exams were vital to certification success, so we created the perfect companion book for certification study material.

Each book contains:
- Several practice exams
- Electronic versions of practice exams on the accompanying CD-ROM presented in an interactive format, enabling practice in an environment similar to that of the actual exam
- Each practice question is followed by the corresponding answer (why the right answers are right and the wrong answers are wrong)
- References to the Exam Cram study guide chapter or other resource for that topic

CORIOLIS™
Certification Insider Press

The Smartest Way to Get Certified™

15. Use the Windows 2000 Backup utility to back up the AD system state data.

16. Use authoritative restore when you want your restored settings to overwrite existing AD settings on other domain controllers, such as if an object (OU, user account, and so on) is accidentally deleted from the database.

17. Use nonauthoritative restore when you are restoring out-of-date information and want the restored data to be overwritten by newer data stored in Active Directory on other domain controllers. For example, you would do this if you were recovering a DC from a failed hard drive and restored the server.

18. All domains in a tree automatically establish two-way trust relationships called Kerberos trusts.

19. Trust relationships between Windows 2000 domains and NT 4 domains must be config-ured manually, just as you would configure a trust relationship between two NT 4 domains.

INSTALLING, CONFIGURING, MANAGING, MONITORING, AND TROUBLESHOOTING DNS FOR ACTIVE DIRECTORY

20. Caching servers do not store an editable copy of the zone database.

21. Active Directory integrated zones can reside only on domain controllers, not member servers or non-Windows 2000 servers of any kind (NT 4, Unix, and so on).

22. If a user who is trying to log on gets an error that a domain controller cannot be found, check for the presence of SRV records in the DNS database for domain controllers.

23. Secure dynamic updates allow only computers and users who have been given permission to update their records into the DNS database.

24. Secure dynamic update is supported only for Active Directory integrated zones.

25. DNS replication is accomplished through Active Directory replication for AD integrated zones and zone transfer for standard zones.

26. A reverse lookup zone must be configured in order to perform reverse lookup queries.

27. Installing AD through Configure Your Server does *not* create a reverse lookup zone in DNS.

28. Windows 2000 DHCP can act as a proxy for non-Windows 2000 clients to support dynamic updates into the DNS database.

29. DHCP is required to support dynamic updates

INSTALLING, CONFIGURING, MANAGING, MONITORING, OPTIMIZING, AND TROUBLESHOOTING CHANGE AND CONFIGURATION MANAGEMENT

30. The No Override setting takes precedence over Block Policy Inheritance.

31. Group Policy settings are applied in the following order:
   • Local
   • Site
   • Domain
   • OU

32. Local policy will always override global policy settings.

33. Unless modified through Block Policy Inherit-ance or No Override, OU policies overwrite domain policies and domain policies overwrite site policies.

34. Group Policy Objects are linked to sites, domains, and OUs, never directly to security groups.

35. The policies configured in a GPO cannot be selectively applied—it's all or nothing.

36. Create GPOs through Active Directory Users and Computers; edit GPOs with the Group Policy Editor (MMC snap-in).

37. Apply Group Policy and Read are the required permissions to receive the effects of a GPO.

38. Scripts are processed in the following order:
   • Startup
   • Logon
   • Logoff
   • Shutdown

39. Create a RIS boot disk for supported network adapters through the rbfg.exe utility.

40. RIPrep is used to create custom installation images. Run it on a Windows 2000 Profes-sional system from a Windows 2000 RIS server (that is, \\server\riprep.exe from the Run line on a workstation).

41. An active DHCP server must exist on the same subnet as a RIS client for RIS to work.

42. Running RISetup after installing the RIS service creates a CD-based RIS installation image.

43. If you need to support a few Windows 2000 systems that have hardware not contained by the majority of RIS clients, simply use a CD-based image in the appropriate language.

44. RIS clients must either have a network adapter that supports PXE or be directly supported by the RIS boot disk.

45. Deploy software through the Software Installation extension in the Group Policy Editor.

46. Published applications are available for the user to install through Add/Remove Programs.

47. Published applications by default are not configured to auto-install, though they can be configured to auto-install through the package properties.

48. Assigned applications appear in the user's Start menu and/or desktop and automatically install when launched.

49. Assigned applications can be uninstalled by the user but will reinstall themselves after the user logs off and logs back in. Assigned applications are said to be "sticky" applications.

50. Published applications can be uninstalled by the user if so desired.

51. Software deployment problems are almost always attributable to permissions or missing, corrupt, or unavailable source files.

52. Delegate authority for nonadministrators to create GPOs through the Active Directory Users and Computers administrative tool.

53. The following are facts about system policies:
- They are applied only to domains.
- They are limited to Registry-based settings an administrator configures.
- They are not written to a secure location of the Registry; hence, any user with the ability to edit the Registry can disable the policy settings.
- They often last beyond their useful life spans. System policies remain in effect until another policy explicitly reverses an existing policy or a user edits the Registry to remove a policy.
- They can be applied through NT domain security groups.

54. The following are facts about Group Policy:
- It can be applied to sites, domains, or OUs.
- It can be applied through domain security groups and can apply to all or some of the computers and users in a site, domain, or OU.
- It is written to a secure section of the Registry, thereby preventing users from being able to remove the policy through the regedit.exe or regedt32.exe utility.
- It is removed and rewritten whenever a policy change takes place. Administrators can set the length of time between policy refreshes, ensuring that only the current policies are in place.
- It provides a more granular level of administrative control over a user's environment.

55. Active Directory log files should be stored on a separate physical disk from the database for best performance.

MANAGING, MONITORING, AND OPTIMIZING THE COMPONENTS OF ACTIVE DIRECTORY

56. Delegate administrative control of AD objects through the Active Directory Users and Computers snap-in. Right-click on the object and choose Delegate Control to start the Delegation of Control Wizard.

57. ACLs are used to control access to AD resources. These are configured on the Security tab of an object's property sheet.

58. For AD replication, there can be IP or SMTP transports. SMTP is used for unreliable WAN links between sites. IP is used when a LAN or WAN connection is considered reliable.

59. SMTP replication works only intersite. IP replication can be interstie or intrasite.

60. When replicating among multiple sites, there must be a schedule overlap so that replication can complete. Otherwise, replication will either fail completely or changes will not appear in other sites until the next scheduled replication period.

61. Offline defragmentation of the Active Directory database can be performed only while the computer is booted in Directory Service Repair Mode (run ntdsutil). It is also the only way to reduce the size (compact) the database.

CONFIGURING, MANAGING, MONITORING, AND TROUBLESHOOTING ACTIVE DIRECTORY SECURITY SOLUTIONS

62. Security templates can be used to provide a default security level on a Windows 2000 system. They are applied through Group Policy, and the important ones to know are:
- *basicdc.inf*—Default security settings for a domain controller
- *basicsv.inf*—Default security settings for a standalone (or member) server
- *basicwk.inf*—Default security settings for a Windows 2000 Professional system
- *compatws.inf*—Security settings that make Server or Professional backwardly compatible with Microsoft Windows NT 4
- *hisecdc.inf*—High security settings for a domain controller
- *hisecws.inf*—High security settings for a Windows 2000 Professional system
- *securedc.inf*—Secure domain controller settings
- *securews.inf*—Secure Windows 2000 Professional settings

63. The Security Configuration and Analysis tool is used to configure security on *local* systems only. Group Policy is used to configure security in Active Directory.

64. Auditing is not enabled by default. To enable it, use the Group Policy Editor.

65. Select object to audit through the advanced security settings in the object's property sheet (click on the Advanced button on the Security tab, then select the Audit tab).

66. Audited events appear in the Security log in the event viewer.

67. Universal groups are available only when a domain is in native mode.

68. The recommended order of applying permissions to access resources is:
- Place user accounts into global groups.
- Place global groups into universal groups (if in native mode).
- Place universal groups into local groups.
- Apply access permissions to the local groups.

The MCSE
Windows® 2000 Directory Services
Cram Sheet

This Cram Sheet contains the distilled, key facts about the Directory Services Infrastructure exam. Review this information last thing before entering the testing center, paying special attention to those areas where you feel you need the most review. You can transfer any of the facts onto a blank piece of paper before beginning the exam.

INSTALLING, CONFIGURING, AND TROUBLESHOOTING ACTIVE DIRECTORY

1. Active Directory can be installed in one of two ways:
   - With the **dcpromo.exe** command
   - By using the Configure Your Server administrative tool
2. Verify Active Directory installation by checking for SRV and A records on the DNS server for the new domain controller.
3. Active Directory initially installs in mixed mode; if you want to change it to native mode, you must do so manually.
4. Once converted to native mode, a domain cannot revert to mixed mode to support NT 4 domain controllers.
5. Perform an authoritative restore by booting the computer in Directory Services Repair Mode and running ntdsutil.exe.
6. New sites are configured through Active Directory Sites and Services.
7. After creating a new site, the following tasks must be completed:
   - Add appropriate IP subnets to the site.
   - Install or move a domain controller or controllers into the site. Although a domain controller is not required for a site, it is strongly recommended.
   - Connect the site to other sites with the appropriate site link.
   - Select a server to control and monitor licensing within the site.
8. All site links are bridged by default.
9. Site link bridges can be explicitly defined if a network is not fully routed.
10. Inbound replication can be configured through connection objects.
11. The KCC (Knowledge Consistency Checker) maintains schedules and settings for default site links and bridges. Administrator-configured connection objects require manual configuration and maintenance.
12. Cost is used to determine which path to take between sites when multiple links exist.
13. Global Catalog (GC) servers maintain a read-only subset of information in the complete Active Directory database.
14. To configure a server as a GC server, use Active Directory Sites and Services. Select the desired domain controller, then right-click on NTDS settings and choose properties. Check the box for Global Catalog.

MCSE™
Windows® 2000
Directory
Services

Will Willis
David V. Watts
J. Peter Bruzzese

MCSE™ Windows® 2000 Directory Services Exam Cram

Limits of Liability and Disclaimer of Warranty
The author and publisher of this book have used their best efforts in preparing the book and the programs contained in it. These efforts include the development, research, and testing of the theories and programs to determine their effectiveness. The author and publisher make no warranty of any kind, expressed or implied, with regard to these programs or the documentation contained in this book.

The author and publisher shall not be liable in the event of incidental or consequential damages in connection with, or arising out of, the furnishing, performance, or use of the programs, associated instructions, and/or claims of productivity gains.

Trademarks
Trademarked names appear throughout this book. Rather than list the names and entities that own the trademarks or insert a trademark symbol with each mention of the trademarked name, the publisher states that it is using the names for editorial purposes only and to the benefit of the trademark owner, with no intention of infringing upon that trademark.

The Coriolis Group, LLC
14455 N. Hayden Road
Suite 220
Scottsdale, Arizona 85260

(480)483-0192
FAX (480)483-0193
www.coriolis.com

Library of Congress Cataloging-in-Publication Data
Willis, Will, 1971-.
    MCSE Windows 2000 directory services exam cram /by Will Willis, David V. Watts, and J. Peter Bruzzese.
        p. cm.
    Includes index.
    ISBN 1-57610-688-8
    1. Electronic data processing personnel--Certification. 2. Microsoft software--Examinations--Study guides. 3. Directory Services (Computer network technology)--Examinations--Study guides. I. Watts, David V. II. Buzzese, J. Peter. III. Title.
QA76.3.W36 2000
005.4'4769--dc21
                                                    00-058993
                                                        CIP

President and CEO
Keith Weiskamp

Publisher
Steve Sayre

Acquisitions Editor
Shari Jo Hehr

Marketing Specialist
Brett Woolley

Project Editor
Meredith Brittain

Technical Reviewers
Michael D. Stewart
Lance Cockcroft

Production Coordinator
Wendy Littley

Cover Designer
Jesse Dunn

Layout Designer
April Nielsen

Printed in the United States of America
10 9 8 7 6 5 4 3 2 1

The Coriolis Group, LLC • 14455 North Hayden Road, Suite 220 • Scottsdale, Arizona 85260

ExamCram.com Connects You to the Ultimate Study Center!

Our goal has always been to provide you with the best study tools on the planet to help you achieve your certification in record time. Time is so valuable these days that none of us can afford to waste a second of it, especially when it comes to exam preparation.

Over the past few years, we've created an extensive line of *Exam Cram* and *Exam Prep* study guides, practice exams, and interactive training. To help you study even better, we have now created an e-learning and certification destination called **ExamCram.com**. (You can access the site at **www.examcram.com**.) Now, with every study product you purchase from us, you'll be connected to a large community of people like yourself who are actively studying for their certifications, developing their careers, seeking advice, and sharing their insights and stories.

I believe that the future is all about collaborative learning. Our **ExamCram.com** destination is our approach to creating a highly interactive, easily accessible collaborative environment, where you can take practice exams and discuss your experiences with others, sign up for features like "Questions of the Day," plan your certifications using our interactive planners, create your own personal study pages, and keep up with all of the latest study tips and techniques.

I hope that whatever study products you purchase from us—*Exam Cram* or *Exam Prep* study guides, *Personal Trainers*, *Personal Test Centers*, or one of our interactive Web courses—will make your studying fun and productive. Our commitment is to build the kind of learning tools that will allow you to study the way you want to, whenever you want to.

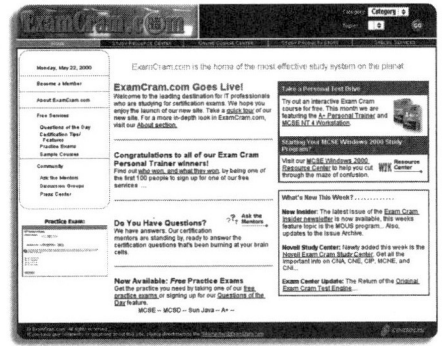

Visit ExamCram.com now to enhance your study program.

Help us continue to provide the very best certification study materials possible. Write us or email us at **learn@examcram.com** and let us know how our study products have helped you study. Tell us about new features that you'd like us to add. Send us a story about how we've helped you. We're listening!

Good luck with your certification exam and your career. Thank you for allowing us to help you achieve your goals.

Keith Weiskamp
President and CEO

Look for these other products from The Coriolis Group:

MCSE Windows 2000 Accelerated Exam Prep
By Lance Cockcroft, Erik Eckel, and Ron Kauffman

MCSE Windows 2000 Server Exam Prep
By David Johnson and Dawn Rader

MCSE Windows 2000 Professional Exam Prep
By Michael D. Stewart, James Bloomingdale, and Neall Alcott

MCSE Windows 2000 Network Exam Prep
By Tammy Smith and Sandra Smeeton

MCSE Windows 2000 Directory Services Exam Prep
By David V. Watts, Will Willis, and Tillman Strahan

MCSE Windows 2000 Security Design Exam Prep
By Richard Alan McMahon and Glen Bicking

MCSE Windows 2000 Network Design Exam Prep
By Geoffrey Alexander, Anoop Jalan, and Joseph Alexander

MCSE Migrating from NT 4 to Windows 2000 Exam Prep
By Glen Bergen, Graham Leach, and David Baldwin

MCSE Windows 2000 Directory Services Design Exam Prep
By J. Peter Bruzzese and Wayne Dipchan

MCSE Windows 2000 Core Four Exam Prep Pack

MCSE Windows 2000 Server Exam Cram
By Natasha Knight

MCSE Windows 2000 Professional Exam Cram
By Dan Balter, Dan Holme, Todd Logan, and Laurie Salmon

MCSE Windows 2000 Network Exam Cram
By Hank Carbeck, Derek Melber, and Richard Taylor

MCSE Windows 2000 Security Design Exam Cram
By Phillip G. Schein

MCSE Windows 2000 Network Design Exam Cram
By Kim Simmons, Jarret W. Buse, and Todd Halpin

MCSE Windows 2000 Directory Services Design Exam Cram
By Dennis Scheil and Diana Bartley

MCSE Windows 2000 Core Four Exam Cram Pack

and...
MCSE Windows 2000 Foundations
By James Michael Stewart and Lee Scales

About the Authors

. . . .

Will Willis (MCSE, A+, Network+) is an MIS responsible for a switched/routed 10/100MB Ethernet and Frame Relay TCP/IP LAN/WAN that connects multiple sites in Texas. His duties include department management, vendor relations (negotiating and securing goods and services as needed), and administering/managing the entire network. Administration includes responsibility for documentation, establishing corporate standard operating procedures, maintaining disaster recovery preparedness, developing antivirus strategies, maintaining firewalls and network security, ensuring server maintenance and upgrades, and ensuring the reliability and availability of network resources.

Will started out as a help desk technician, providing technical support over the phone for PC hardware and software, and later moved up to a desktop/LAN support specialist position at another company, working on an 8-person team that supported a 3,000+ user multiple-site network. Will then moved to his current position, in which he administers NT 4 servers running BackOffice applications Exchange Server 5.5, IIS 3 and 4, SQL Server 6.5, and SMS 1.2. Will also shares ownership in **InsideIS.com**, a Web site devoted to the IT profession. When not busy being a techie, he enjoys spending time with his family and writing and recording original music. You can reach Will at **WWillis@Inside-Corner.com**.

David V. Watts (MCSE, MCSD, CNE, Network+) is currently employed by Hilton Computer Strategies in Houston, TX. David is from Basildon, Essex, in England. He has worked in the United States since 1988, as both a consultant and a project lead on enterprise-level deployments of Microsoft technologies.

David has been working with Windows 2000 since the first betas. He has specific expertise in Microsoft BackOffice products, including Systems Management Server, Microsoft SQL Server, and Microsoft Exchange. David can currently be found teaching these technologies to students at all levels. When he is not teaching, he spends most of his time mentoring fellow professionals in the workplace and online at **InsideIS.com** and **2000tutor.com**. When David is not working on technology, he can be found listening to music. You can reach David at **dwatts@wt.net**.

J. Peter Bruzzese (MCSE+I, MCT, CNA, Network+, A+, i-Net+) has been in the IT training and support field for eight years, working for companies like Goldman, Sachs & Co., Merrill Lynch, and Solomon Smith Barney. Peter is highly regarded by his peers as an expert in public speaking and technical training. He is currently teaching Windows 2000 courses for New Horizons Computer Learning Center of Princeton, New Jersey, which is part of the largest independent IT training company in the world.

Acknowledgments

I'd like to take a moment to acknowledge some of the people that have made an impact on my life and the person I've turned out to be, in no particular order.

Ozzie Smith and Larry Bird—for showing me that excellence on the playing field of life requires countless hours of hard work behind the scenes that no one ever sees or appreciates. Success on "game day" is usually determined by your advance preparation.

Yngwie J. Malmsteen, Fates Warning, and Dream Theater—musical influences that have really lit my creative fire over the years and taught me to bring passion and inspiration to everything I do, and to not always follow the status quo.

Grover Cleveland—the great President who fought the intense resistance to leave the gold standard, forever changing the U.S. economy and making a huge world impact. To stand by your vision when everyone says you're wrong takes tremendous confidence and determination.

Herb Kelleher—Southwest Airlines CEO who has recognized that people are his company's greatest asset. Loyalty and commitment from him has bred loyalty and commitment from his employees, an example that more companies should follow and one I hope to foster as a leader in my own company.

Andrew Carnegie—the richest man in the world during his life, for the conviction that the "surplus wealth that a man accumulates in a community is only a sacred trust to be administered for the good of the community in which it was accumulated." An admirable philosophy of using one's own good fortune for the benefit of others.

Jesus Christ—the light in an increasingly darkening world. Through him hope never fades and life is eternal.

"Let's stare the problem right in the eye … racing the clock to please everyone, all but the one who matters the most"—a favorite quote (of unknown origin) that reminds me not to overcommit myself and lose focus on the person that matters the most to me, Melissa.
—*Will Willis*

I would like to thank my wife, Siobhan Chamberlin, for our years together. They have been wonderful times. I would like to thank my parents for always being there and for understanding that I am sometimes too busy to get to the telephone. To my family overseas, John and Catherine—and to their families—I miss you all! I want to acknowledge others who have affected me through the years. To Siobhan's mother and brother—Moira and Peter—you are forever on our minds. To Siobhan's father whom I never got to meet, I know your family thinks of you always.

As well as family, there have been many others who have in so many ways helped me learn, laugh through troubled times, or have had confidence in me. To Zevi Mehlman, who makes me laugh at the end of the day. To Michael Cook, lifelong friend keeping the bar tab at Basildon, Essex. To David Aldridge, who worries about all the things that keep the wheels oiled at Hilton Computer Strategies in Houston.

I would like to thank all those who currently form part of my team, and others at Hilton. To Jaime, Darrel, Nancy, Boyd, Heidi and Kathy. Together we have created the best damn CTEC in the country. We all share equal credit for what has been achieved. To Jeff Hilton, who has reaffirmed his confidence in what has been created—I am grateful for the opportunity. To Mona Reed, who works tirelessly (if only I had half the energy). To Mike Stewart and his staff, Donna, Alora, Richard, Darrel and Melissa. Not forgetting all the wonderful support from Sandy, Jeannie and Tara. We should all be very proud.

I would like to thank all the musicians who will never read this book but have helped me during the long hours. To Tim Berne, Jacky Terrasson, Richard Thompson, Tom Verlaine, Karlheinz Stockhausen, Phillip Glass, Steve Reich, Earthworks, Gavin Bryars, Joe Lovano, Paul Bley, Gary Peacock, Gary Thomas, Dave Holland, Greg Osby, Keith Jarrett, Kronos Quartet, Brad Mehldau, to name a few! Music is the purest of escapes. Whenever I find time to simply sit and listen, I am never less than enthralled. To all the musicians who help me through both good times and bad—thank you!

As I get older, I realize that I must take time to cherish all the things I have and all the people who are part of who I am. Sometimes people can touch you in the briefest space of time, but their influence can be lifelong. So many people have helped me along the way that there is no space to thank them all. Some were teachers, some colleagues, but none have been disposable. To my grandparents who are no longer with us, I wish I could have known you better—but I still think of you. To lost family friends, thank you for contributing in any small way to helping me be what I am today. Writing acknowledgments is a humbling experience, because you realize there are so many people to reach out to. Sadly, some are no longer here to thank. But you live on in those you taught, mentored, or touched. And that is the greatest legacy any of us can hope for. Never gone, never forgotten.

—*David V. Watts*

First and foremost, I would like to thank Will Willis and David Watts for allowing me the privilege of working with them on this book. You guys are absolute working machines, and it really felt good to work with a team that produced so powerfully. I hope we can work together again.

I would also like to thank the team at Coriolis. I've enjoyed working with everyone there and look forward to further projects. I would specifically like to thank Shari Jo Hehr for bringing this book to my attention and Meredith Brittain for handling the book's project editing. Also included in my thanks is the copyeditor, Joanne Slike, and the technical editors, Michael D. Stewart and Lance Cockcroft. In addition, I would like to thank proofreader Holly Caldwell, production coordinator Wendy Littley, marketing specialist Brett Woolley, layout designer April Nielsen, and cover designer Jesse Dunn.

I would like to thank Ronald Barrett for his encouragement and assistance with this book, and Wayne Dipchan for his work with me on *MCSE Windows 2000 Directory Services Design Exam Prep*, which helped me prepare for writing this book.

Finally, I would like to thank my associates at New Horizons for understanding my obligations when writing this book. I especially thank Ken Foxton, the President of New Horizons of Princeton, New Jersey, and Brenda Martin, Supervisor for Training (and a billion other things), for working around my schedule and for encouraging me in these projects.

—*J. Peter Bruzzese*

Contents at a Glance

Chapter 1   Microsoft Certification Exams   1

Chapter 2   Introduction to Active Directory   23

Chapter 3   Implementing and Administering DNS   45

Chapter 4   Planning and Installing Domains   71

Chapter 5   User and Group Administration   101

Chapter 6   Active Directory Delegation of
Administrative Control   129

Chapter 7   Understanding Group Policy
Implementation   153

Chapter 8   Using Group Policy in Security and
Environment Control   181

Chapter 9   Using Group Policy in Software Deployment
and Management   209

Chapter 10   Publishing Resources within the
Active Directory   231

Chapter 11   Implementing Multiple Tree and
Forest Structures   243

Chapter 12   Active Directory Replication   271

Chapter 13   Operations Masters   297

Chapter 14   Active Directory Database Maintenance   319

Chapter 15   Remote Installation Services (RIS)   343

Chapter 16   Sample Test   371

Chapter 17   Answer Key   389

Table of Contents

Introduction xxiii

Self-Assessment xxxv

Chapter 1
Microsoft Certification Exams 1

Assessing Exam-Readiness   2

The Exam Situation   3

Exam Layout and Design   4

    Multiple-Choice Question Format   5

    Build-List-and-Reorder Question Format   6

    Create-a-Tree Question Format   8

    Drag-and-Connect Question Format   10

    Select-and-Place Question Format   11

Microsoft's Testing Formats   12

Strategies for Different Testing Formats   14

    The Case Study Exam Strategy   15

    The Fixed-Length and Short-Form Exam Strategy   15

    The Adaptive Exam Strategy   17

    Question-Handling Strategies   18

Mastering the Inner Game   19

Additional Resources   20

Chapter 2
Introduction to Active Directory 23

Overview of AD   24

    Objects in AD   25

    The Schema   25

    Directory Service Protocol   25

The Structure of AD   27
  The Logical Structure   27
  The Physical Structure   30
Administering Windows 2000   31
  Centralized Management   32
  Group Policy   32
  Delegation of Control   32
Practice Questions   34
Need to Know More?   43

Chapter 3
Implementing and Administering DNS 45
A Brief History of DNS   46
  Fully Qualified Domain Names (FQDNs)   47
  Relative Distinguished Names (RDNs)   47
Dynamic DNS and AD in Windows 2000   47
DNS Planning Considerations   48
  Site Structure   48
  Types of Name Servers   49
  Types of Network Clients   52
  Naming Hosts and Domains   52
  Static IP Addresses   52
DNS Zones   53
Zone Transfer   53
  Full Zone Transfer   54
  Incremental Transfer   54
  AD Replication   55
Installing DNS   55
Configuring DNS   55
  Root Servers   56
  Forward Lookup Zones   56
  Reverse Lookup Zones   57
  Resource Records   57
  Dynamic DNS (DDNS)   59
Monitoring and Troubleshooting DNS for AD   61
  DNS Logging   62
  NSLOOKUP   62
Practice Questions   65
Need to Know More?   70

Chapter 4
Planning and Installing Domains **71**

The Windows 2000 Domain   72

Requirements for AD   73

The AD Installation Wizard   74

Running the Wizard   74

Installing Your First Domain   74

Deciding which Type of DNS to Use   79

The Lesser-Known Roles of the Wizard   80

Fault-Tolerant Replicas   81

Troubleshooting Your AD Installation   82

Verifying Your AD Installation   83

File Verification   83

SYSVOL   84

Final Checkpoints   84

AD Removal   84

What Removing AD Entails   85

Troubleshooting AD Removal   85

Unattended Installation of AD   86

The GuiRunOnce Section   86

The DCInstall Section   88

Post-AD Installation Options   89

Integrated Zones   89

Domain Mode Options   90

Organizational Units   91

Practice Questions   **93**

Need to Know More?   100

Chapter 5
User and Group Administration **101**

Introducing Users and Groups   102

User Logon Names   103

Types of Logon Names   103

Rules for Logon Names   104

Creating User Accounts   105

The Csvde Utility   106

The Ldifde Utility   108

User Accounts 109

    Resetting Passwords 111

    Unlocking User Accounts 111

    Deleting User Accounts 112

    Renaming User Accounts 112

    Copying User Accounts 113

    Disabling and Enabling User Accounts 113

Finding User Accounts 113

    Using the Find Users, Contacts, And Groups Dialog Box to Administer User Accounts 114

The Use of Groups 115

    Defining Group Types 116

    How to Use Groups 116

User and Group Recommendations 119

Practice Questions 120

Need to Know More? 128

Chapter 6
Active Directory Delegation of Administrative Control 129

Object Security 130

    Terminology for AD Security 130

    From Logon to Object Access 131

Access Permissions on AD Objects 132

    Viewing AD Permissions 133

    To Allow or to Deny 135

Theoretical Delegation of Authority 135

Setting AD Permissions 136

    The Delegation of Control Wizard 137

    The Flow of Permissions 138

    Redirecting the Flow of Permissions 140

Ownership of AD Objects 141

    Viewing Ownership 141

    Taking Ownership 141

Delegation of Administrative Tools 142

    Creating MMC Consoles 142

    Distributing MMC Consoles 143

    Taskpads 144

Practice Questions 146

Need to Know More? 152

Chapter 7
Understanding Group Policy Implementation 153

Change and Configuration Basics   154

Group Policy Overview   155

Group Policy Objects   155

Group Policy vs. System Policies   157

Creating a Group Policy Object   158

Modifying a Group Policy Object   160

Group Policy Editor as a Standalone Console   160

Accessing the Group Policy Editor through Editing a Group Policy Object   163

Working Inside the Group Policy Editor   163

Linking a GPO   164

Linking Multiple GPOs   165

Cross-Domain GPO Links   167

Delegating Administrative Control of Group Policy   167

Managing Group Policy Links   168

Creating GPOs   168

Editing GPOs   169

Group Policy Inheritance   170

Block Policy Inheritance   170

No Override   171

Disabling a GPO   172

Filtering Group Policy   172

Disabling Unused Portions of a GPO   173

Practice Questions   174

Need to Know More?   180

Chapter 8
Using Group Policy in Security and Environment Control 181

Controlling User Environments with Administrative Templates   182

ADM Files and Their Structure   182

Applying Computer and User Templates   188

Managing Security Configurations   191

Security Templates   193

Assigning Script Policies to Users and Computers   195

Windows Script Host   195

Assigning Scripts through Group Policy   197

Use of Folder Redirection   200
Practice Questions   202
Need to Know More?   208

Chapter 9
Using Group Policy in Software Deployment and Management 209

IntelliMirror Concepts   210
Software Installation and Maintenance Overview   212
  Requirements for Software Installation   213
Deploying Software with Group Policy and Software Installation   214
  Configuring Software Installation Properties   214
  Deploying a New Package   216
  Configuring Package Properties   217
Assigned vs. Published Applications   218
Phases of Software Deployment   219
Troubleshooting Software Deployment Problems   220
  Deployment Error Messages   220
  Installation Error Messages   221
  Shortcuts Still Appear for Removed Applications   222
  Installed Application Is Uninstalled from a
    User Workstation   222
Practice Questions   223
Need to Know More?   229

Chapter 10
Publishing Resources within the Active Directory 231

Introduction to Published Resources   232
Publishing Printers   232
  Steps for Publishing Printers   233
  Viewing Published Printers   234
  Searching for Printers   235
Publishing Folders   236
  Steps for Publishing Folders   236
  Additional Search Descriptions   236
Practice Questions   238
Need to Know More?   241

Chapter 11
Implementing Multiple Tree and Forest Structures 243

Adding to a Tree   244

What Is a Domain Tree?   245

   Transitive Trusts   246

Creating a Child Domain   247

   Forest Root Domains   247

   Steps for Creating a Child Domain   248

   Setting up Empty Root Domains   249

Forests   250

   The Design Decision to Create a Forest   250

   Steps for Creating a Forest   251

   Creating Shortcut Trusts   252

Multiple Forests   253

   Why Create a Multiple Forest?   253

   External Trusts   254

Kerberos v5   256

   A Kerberos Transaction   256

   Kerberos and Transitive Trusts   258

GC Servers   260

   GC and Logon Validation   260

   User Principal Names and Logon Validation   260

   Adding GC Servers   261

   Universal Group Strategy   262

   Review of Universal Nesting   262

Practice Questions   264

Need to Know More?   270

Chapter 12
Active Directory Replication 271

The Replication Process   273

   Latency and the Notification Process   274

   Types of AD Conflicts   275

   Conflict Resolution   276

Preventing Replication Loops   277

   USNs   278

Topology for Replication   278
  Directory Partitions   279
  Global Catalog Servers   280
  Knowledge Consistency Checker   280
  Optimizing AD Replication with Sites   280
  Replication within a Site and between Sites   281
  Bridgehead Servers   282
  Protocols that Support Replication   282
  Site Links and Their Default Settings   283
  Site Link Bridge   283
Examining Replication Traffic   284
  Replication Monitor   285
  Repadmin   285
  Modifying the Replication Topology   286
Troubleshooting Replication   287
Practice Questions   289
Need to Know More?   295

Chapter 13
Operations Masters 297

Introducing Operations Masters   298
  The Five Operations Master Roles   299
Managing Operations Master Roles   303
  Determining Operations Masters   303
  Permissions for Changing an Operations Master Server   306
  Seizing a Role   307
Recommendations for Operations Masters   309
Practice Questions   310
Need to Know More?   318

Chapter 14
Active Directory Database Maintenance 319

Introducing AD Maintenance   320
Modifying AD Data   321
  Ntds.dit   321
  Edb*.log   321

Edb.chk   322

Res1.log and Res2.log   322

Garbage Collection   322

Performing Backups   323

Recommendations for Backing up Data   324

Restoring AD   325

Nonauthoritative Restore   326

Authoritative Restore   327

Moving the AD Database   327

Defragmenting the AD Database   328

Online Defragmentation   329

Offline Defragmentation   329

Recommendations for AD Database Maintenance   330

Practice Questions   332

Need to Know More?   341

Chapter 15
Remote Installation Services (RIS) 343

An Overview of RIS   344

A RIS Scenario   344

RIS Functionality   345

RIS Network Requirements   345

RIS Service   345

Domain Name System (DNS) Service   346

Dynamic Host Configuration Protocol (DHCP) Server   346

Active Directory   346

RIS Client and Server Components   346

Client Requirements of RIS   346

Server Components of RIS   348

Setting up and Configuring RIS   349

Installing RIS   349

Configuring RIS with RISetup   350

Creating RIS Images   353

RIPrep   353

Creating Images with RIPrep   354

Creating RIS Boot Disks   357
Managing RIS Security   358
Authorizing a RIS Server   358
Managing RIS Client Options with Group Policy   359
Managing RIS Settings with the AD Users and
Computers Tool   360
Practice Questions   364
Need to Know More?   370

Chapter 16
Sample Test 371

Chapter 17
Answer Key 389

Glossary 401

Index 415

Introduction

Welcome to *MCSE Windows 2000 Directory Services Exam Cram*! Whether this is your first or your fifteenth *Exam Cram* book, you'll find information here and in Chapter 1 that will help ensure your success as you pursue knowledge, experience, and certification. This book aims to help you get ready to take—and pass—Microsoft certification Exam 70-217, titled "Implementing and Administering a Microsoft Windows 2000 Directory Services Infrastructure." This Introduction explains Microsoft's certification programs in general and talks about how the *Exam Cram* series can help you prepare for Microsoft's Windows 2000 certification exams.

Exam Cram books help you understand and appreciate the subjects and materials you need to pass Microsoft certification exams. *Exam Cram* books are aimed strictly at test preparation and review. They do not teach you everything you need to know about a topic. Instead, we (the authors) present and dissect the questions and problems we've found that you're likely to encounter on a test. We've worked to bring together as much information as possible about Microsoft certification exams.

Nevertheless, to completely prepare yourself for any Microsoft test, we recommend that you begin by taking the Self-Assessment included in this book immediately following this Introduction. This tool will help you evaluate your knowledge base against the requirements for an MCSE under both ideal and real circumstances.

Based on what you learn from that exercise, you might decide to begin your studies with some classroom training or some background reading. On the other hand, you might decide to pick up and read one of the many study guides available from Microsoft or third-party vendors on certain topics, including The Coriolis Group's *Exam Prep* series. We also recommend that you supplement your study program with visits to **ExamCram.com** to receive additional practice questions, get advice, and track the Windows 2000 MCSE program.

We also strongly recommend that you install, configure, and fool around with the software that you'll be tested on, because nothing beats hands-on experience and familiarity when it comes to understanding the questions you're likely to encounter on a certification test. Book learning is essential, but hands-on experience is the best teacher of all!

The Microsoft Certified Professional (MCP) Program

The MCP Program currently includes the following separate tracks, each of which boasts its own special acronym (as a certification candidate, you need to have a high tolerance for alphabet soup of all kinds):

➤ *MCP (Microsoft Certified Professional)*—This is the least prestigious of all the certification tracks from Microsoft. Passing one of the major Microsoft exams qualifies an individual for the MCP credential. Individuals can demonstrate proficiency with additional Microsoft products by passing additional certification exams.

➤ *MCP+SB (Microsoft Certified Professional + Site Building)*—This certification program is designed for individuals who are planning, building, managing, and maintaining Web sites. Individuals with the MCP+SB credential will have demonstrated the ability to develop Web sites that include multimedia and searchable content and Web sites that connect to and communicate with a back-end database. It requires one MCP exam, plus two of these three exams: "70-055: Designing and Implementing Web Sites with Microsoft FrontPage 98," "70-057: Designing and Implementing Commerce Solutions with Microsoft Site Server 3.0, Commerce Edition," and "70-152: Designing and Implementing Web Solutions with Microsoft Visual InterDev 6.0."

➤ *MCSE (Microsoft Certified Systems Engineer)*—Anyone who has a current MCSE is warranted to possess a high level of networking expertise with Microsoft operating systems and products. This credential is designed to prepare individuals to plan, implement, maintain, and support information systems, networks, and internetworks built around Microsoft Windows 2000 and its BackOffice Server 2000 family of products.

To obtain an MCSE, an individual must pass four core operating system exams, one optional core exam, and two elective exams. The operating system exams require individuals to prove their competence with desktop and server operating systems and networking/internetworking components.

For Windows NT 4 MCSEs, the Accelerated exam, "70-240: Microsoft Windows 2000 Accelerated Exam for MCPs Certified on Microsoft Windows NT 4.0," is an option. This free exam covers all of the material tested in the Core Four exams. The hitch in this plan is that you can take the test only once. If you fail, you must take all four core exams to recertify. The Core Four exams are: "70-210: Installing, Configuring and Administering Microsoft Windows 2000 Professional," "70-215: Installing, Configuring and Administering Microsoft

Windows 2000 Server," "70-216: Implementing and Administering a Microsoft Windows 2000 Network Infrastructure," and "70-217: Implementing and Administering a Microsoft Windows 2000 Directory Services Infrastructure."

To fulfill the fifth core exam requirement, you can choose from three design exams: "70-219: Designing a Microsoft Windows 2000 Directory Services Infrastructure," "70-220: Designing Security for a Microsoft Windows 2000 Network," or "70-221: Designing a Microsoft Windows 2000 Network Infrastructure." You are also required to take two elective exams. An elective exam can fall in any number of subject or product areas, primarily BackOffice Server 2000 components. The two design exams that you don't select as your fifth core exam also qualify as electives. If you are on your way to becoming an MCSE and have already taken some exams, visit **www.microsoft.com/trainingandservices/** for information about how to complete your MCSE certification.

In September 1999, Microsoft announced its Windows 2000 track for MCSE and also announced retirement of Windows NT 4.0 MCSE core exams on 12/31/2000. Individuals who wish to remain certified MCSEs after 12/31/2001 must "upgrade" their certifications on or before 12/31/2001. For more detailed information than is included here, visit **www.microsoft.com/trainingandservices/**.

New MCSE candidates must pass seven tests to meet the MCSE requirements. It's not uncommon for the entire process to take a year or so, and many individuals find that they must take a test more than once to pass. The primary goal of the *Exam Prep* and *Exam Cram* test preparation books is to make it possible, given proper study and preparation, to pass all Microsoft certification tests on the first try. Table 1 shows the required and elective exams for the Windows 2000 MCSE certification.

➤ *MCSD (Microsoft Certified Solution Developer)*—The MCSD credential reflects the skills required to create multitier, distributed, and COM-based solutions, in addition to desktop and Internet applications, using new technologies. To obtain an MCSD, an individual must demonstrate the ability to analyze and interpret user requirements; select and integrate products, platforms, tools, and technologies; design and implement code, and customize applications; and perform necessary software tests and quality assurance operations.

To become an MCSD, you must pass a total of four exams: three core exams and one elective exam. Each candidate must choose one of these three desktop application exams—"70-016: Designing and Implementing Desktop Applications with Microsoft Visual C++ 6.0," "70-156: Designing and Implementing Desktop Applications with Microsoft Visual FoxPro 6.0," or "70-176: Designing and Implementing Desktop Applications with Microsoft Visual Basic 6.0"—*plus* one of these

Table 1   MCSE Windows 2000 Requirements

Core

If you have not passed these 3 Windows NT 4 exams	
Exam 70-067	Implementing and Supporting Microsoft Windows NT Server 4.0
Exam 70-068	Implementing and Supporting Microsoft Windows NT Server 4.0 in the Enterprise
Exam 70-073	Microsoft Windows NT Workstation 4.0
then you must take these 4 exams	
Exam 70-210	Installing, Configuring and Administering Microsoft Windows 2000 Professional
Exam 70-215	Installing, Configuring and Administering Microsoft Windows 2000 Server
Exam 70-216	Implementing and Administering a Microsoft Windows 2000 Network Infrastructure
Exam 70-217	Implementing and Administering a Microsoft Windows 2000 Directory Services Infrastructure
If you have already passed exams 70-067, 70-068, and 70-073, you may take this exam	
Exam 70-240	Microsoft Windows 2000 Accelerated Exam for MCPs Certified on Microsoft Windows NT 4.0

5th Core Option

Choose 1 from this group	
Exam 70-219*	Designing a Microsoft Windows 2000 Directory Services Infrastructure
Exam 70-220*	Designing Security for a Microsoft Windows 2000 Network
Exam 70-221*	Designing a Microsoft Windows 2000 Network Infrastructure

Elective

Choose 2 from this group	
Exam 70-019	Designing and Implementing Data Warehouse with Microsoft SQL Server 7.0
Exam 70-219*	Designing a Microsoft Windows 2000 Directory Services Infrastructure
Exam 70-220*	Designing Security for a Microsoft Windows 2000 Network
Exam 70-221*	Designing a Microsoft Windows 2000 Network Infrastructure
Exam 70-222	Migrating from Microsoft Windows NT 4.0 to Microsoft Windows 2000
Exam 70-028	Administering Microsoft SQL Server 7.0
Exam 70-029	Designing and Implementing Databases on Microsoft SQL Server 7.0
Exam 70-080	Implementing and Supporting Microsoft Internet Explorer 5.0 by Using the Internet Explorer Administration Kit
Exam 70-081	Implementing and Supporting Microsoft Exchange Server 5.5
Exam 70-085	Implementing and Supporting Microsoft SNA Server 4.0
Exam 70-086	Implementing and Supporting Microsoft Systems Management Server 2.0
Exam 70-088	Implementing and Supporting Microsoft Proxy Server 2.0

This is not a complete listing—you can still be tested on some earlier versions of these products. However, we have included mainly the most recent versions so that you may test on these versions and thus be certified longer. We have not included any tests that are scheduled to be retired.

* The 5th Core Option exam does not double as an elective.

three distributed application exams—"70-015: Designing and Implementing Distributed Applications with Microsoft Visual C++ 6.0," "70-155: Designing and Implementing Distributed Applications with Microsoft Visual FoxPro 6.0," or "70-175: Designing and Implementing Distributed Applications with Microsoft Visual Basic 6.0." The third core exam is "70-100: Analyzing Requirements and Defining Solution Architectures." Elective exams cover specific Microsoft applications and languages, including Visual Basic, C++, the Microsoft Foundation Classes, Access, SQL Server, Excel, and more.

➤ *MCDBA (Microsoft Certified Database Administrator)*—The MCDBA credential reflects the skills required to implement and administer Microsoft SQL Server databases. To obtain an MCDBA, an individual must demonstrate the ability to derive physical database designs, develop logical data models, create physical databases, create data services by using Transact-SQL, manage and maintain databases, configure and manage security, monitor and optimize databases, and install and configure Microsoft SQL Server.

To become an MCDBA, you must pass a total of four exams and one elective exam. The required core exams are "70-028: Administering Microsoft SQL Server 7.0," "70-029: Designing and Implementing Databases with Microsoft SQL Server 7.0," and "70-215: Installing, Configuring and Administering Microsoft Windows 2000 Server."

The elective exams that you can choose from cover specific uses of SQL Server and include "70-015: Designing and Implementing Distributed Applications with Microsoft Visual C++ 6.0," "70-019: Designing and Implementing Data Warehouses with Microsoft SQL Server 7.0," "70-155: Designing and Implementing Distributed Applications with Microsoft Visual FoxPro 6.0," "70-175: Designing and Implementing Distributed Applications with MicrosoftVisual Basic 6.0," and two exams that relate to Windows 2000: "70-216: Implementing and Administering a Microsoft Windows 2000 Network Infrastructure," and "70-087: Implementing and Supporting Microsoft Internet Information Server 4.0."

If you have taken the three core Windows NT 4 exams on your path to becoming an MCSE, you qualify for the Accelerated exam (it replaces the Network Infrastructure exam requirement). The Accelerated exam covers the objectives of all four of the Windows 2000 core exams. In addition to taking the Accelerated exam, you must take only the two SQL exams—Administering and Database Design.

➤ *MCT (Microsoft Certified Trainer)*—Microsoft Certified Trainers are deemed able to deliver elements of the official Microsoft curriculum, based on technical knowledge and instructional ability. Thus, it is necessary for an individual seeking MCT credentials (which are granted on a course-by-course basis) to pass the related certification exam for a course and complete the official Microsoft training in the subject area, and to demonstrate an ability to teach.

This teaching skill criterion may be satisfied by proving that one has already attained training certification from Novell, Banyan, Lotus, the Santa Cruz Operation, or Cisco, or by taking a Microsoft-sanctioned workshop on instruction. Microsoft makes it clear that MCTs are important cogs in the Microsoft training channels. Instructors must be MCTs before Microsoft will allow them to teach in any of its official training channels, including Microsoft's affiliated Certified Technical Education Centers (CTECs) and its online training partner network. As of January 1, 2001, MCT candidates must also possess a current MCSE.

Microsoft has announced that the MCP+I and MCSE+I credentials will not be continued when the MCSE exams for Windows 2000 are in full swing because the skill set for the Internet portion of the program has been included in the new MCSE program. Therefore, details on these tracks are not provided here; go to **www.microsoft.com/trainingandservices/** if you need more information.

Once a Microsoft product becomes obsolete, MCPs typically have to recertify on current versions. (If individuals do not recertify, their certifications become invalid.) Because technology keeps changing and new products continually supplant old ones, this should come as no surprise. This explains why Microsoft has announced that MCSEs have 12 months past the scheduled retirement date for the Windows NT 4 exams to recertify on Windows 2000 topics. (Note that this means taking at least two exams, if not more.)

The best place to keep tabs on the MCP Program and its related certifications is on the Web. The URL for the MCP program is **www.microsoft.com/ trainingandservices/**. But Microsoft's Web site changes often, so if this URL doesn't work, try using the Search tool on Microsoft's site with either "MCP" or the quoted phrase "Microsoft Certified Professional" as a search string. This will help you find the latest and most accurate information about Microsoft's certification programs.

Taking a Certification Exam

Once you've prepared for your exam, you need to register with a testing center. Each computer-based MCP exam costs $100, and if you don't pass, you may retest for an additional $100 for each additional try. In the United States and Canada, tests are administered by Prometric and by Virtual University Enterprises (VUE). Here's how you can contact them:

➤ *Prometric*—You can sign up for a test through the company's Web site at **www.prometric.com**. Or, you can register by phone at 800-755-3926 (within the United States or Canada) or at 410-843-8000 (outside the United States and Canada).

➤ *Virtual University Enterprises*—You can sign up for a test or get the phone numbers for local testing centers through the Web page at **www.vue.com/ms/**.

To sign up for a test, you must possess a valid credit card, or contact either company for mailing instructions to send them a check (in the U.S.). Only when payment is verified, or a check has cleared, can you actually register for a test.

To schedule an exam, call the number or visit either of the Web pages at least one day in advance. To cancel or reschedule an exam, you must call before 7 P.M. pacific standard time the day before the scheduled test time (or you may be charged, even if you don't appear to take the test). When you want to schedule a test, have the following information ready:

➤ Your name, organization, and mailing address.

➤ Your Microsoft Test ID. (Inside the United States, this means your Social Security number; citizens of other nations should call ahead to find out what type of identification number is required to register for a test.)

➤ The name and number of the exam you wish to take.

➤ A method of payment. (As we've already mentioned, a credit card is the most convenient method, but alternate means can be arranged in advance, if necessary.)

Once you sign up for a test, you'll be informed as to when and where the test is scheduled. Try to arrive at least 15 minutes early. You must supply two forms of identification—one of which must be a photo ID—to be admitted into the testing room.

All exams are completely closed-book. In fact, you will not be permitted to take anything with you into the testing area, but you will be furnished with a blank sheet of paper and a pen or, in some cases, an erasable plastic sheet and an erasable pen. We suggest that you immediately write down on that sheet of paper all the information you've memorized for the test. In *Exam Cram* books, this information appears on a tear-out sheet inside the front cover of each book. You will have some time to compose yourself and record this information before you begin the exam.

When you complete a Microsoft certification exam, the software will tell you whether you've passed or failed. If you need to retake an exam, you'll have to schedule a new test with Prometric or VUE and pay another $100.

 The first time you fail a test, you can retake the test the next day. However, if you fail a second time, you must wait 14 days before retaking that test. The 14-day waiting period remains in effect for all retakes after the second failure.

Tracking MCP Status

As soon as you pass any Microsoft exam (except Networking Essentials), you'll attain Microsoft Certified Professional (MCP) status. Microsoft also generates transcripts that indicate which exams you have passed. You can view a copy of your transcript at any time by going to the MCP secured site and selecting Transcript Tool. This tool will allow you to print a copy of your current transcript and confirm your certification status.

Once you pass the necessary set of exams, you'll be certified. Official certification normally takes anywhere from six to eight weeks, so don't expect to get your credentials overnight. When the package for a qualified certification arrives, it includes a Welcome Kit that contains a number of elements (see Microsoft's Web site for other benefits of specific certifications):

➤ A certificate suitable for framing, along with a wallet card and lapel pin.

➤ A license to use the MCP logo, thereby allowing you to use the logo in advertisements, promotions, and documents, and on letterhead, business cards, and so on. Along with the license comes an MCP logo sheet, which includes camera-ready artwork. (Note: Before using any of the artwork, individuals must sign and return a licensing agreement that indicates they'll abide by its terms and conditions.)

➤ A subscription to *Microsoft Certified Professional Magazine*, which provides ongoing data about testing and certification activities, requirements, and changes to the program.

Many people believe that the benefits of MCP certification go well beyond the perks that Microsoft provides to newly anointed members of this elite group. We're starting to see more job listings that request or require applicants to have an MCP, MCSE, and so on, and many individuals who complete the program can qualify for increases in pay and/or responsibility. As an official recognition of hard work and broad knowledge, one of the MCP credentials is a badge of honor in many IT organizations.

How to Prepare for an Exam

Preparing for any Windows 2000 Server-related test (including "Implementing and Administering a Microsoft Windows 2000 Directory Services Infrastructure") requires that you obtain and study materials designed to provide comprehensive information about the product and its capabilities that will appear on the specific exam for which you are preparing. The following list of materials will help you study and prepare:

➤ The Windows 2000 Server product CD includes comprehensive online documentation and related materials; it should be a primary resource when you are preparing for the test.

➤ The exam preparation materials, practice tests, and self-assessment exams on the Microsoft Training & Services page at **www.microsoft.com/trainingandservices/default.asp?PageID=mcp.** The Testing Innovations link offers samples of the new question types found on the Windows 2000 MCSE exams. Find the materials, download them, and use them!

➤ The exam preparation advice, practice tests, questions of the day, and discussion groups on the **ExamCram.com** e-learning and certification destination Web site (**www.examcram.com**).

In addition, you'll probably find any or all of the following materials useful in your quest for Directory Services Infrastructure expertise:

➤ *Microsoft training kits*—Microsoft Press offers a training kit that specifically targets Exam 70-217. For more information, visit: **http://mspress.microsoft.com/findabook/list/series_ak.htm.** This training kit contains information that you will find useful in preparing for the test.

➤ *Microsoft TechNet CD*—This monthly CD-based publication delivers numerous electronic titles that include coverage of Directory Services Infrastructure and related topics on the Technical Information (TechNet) CD. Its offerings include product facts, technical notes, tools and utilities, and information on how to access the Seminars Online training materials for Directory Services Infrastructure. A subscription to TechNet costs $299 per year, but it is well worth the price. Visit **www.microsoft.com/technet/** and check out the information under the "TechNet Subscription" menu entry for more details.

➤ *Study guides*—Several publishers—including The Coriolis Group—offer Windows 2000 titles. The Coriolis Group series includes the following:

➤ *The Exam Cram series*—These books give you information about the material you need to know to pass the tests.

➤ *The Exam Prep series*—These books provide a greater level of detail than the *Exam Cram* books and are designed to teach you everything you need to know from an exam perspective. Each book comes with a CD that contains interactive practice exams in a variety of testing formats.

Together, the two series make a perfect pair.

➤ *Multimedia*—These Coriolis Group materials are designed to support learners of all types—whether you learn best by reading or doing:

➤ *The Exam Cram Personal Trainer*—Offers a unique, personalized self-paced training course based on the exam.

➤ *The Exam Cram Personal Test Center*—Features multiple test options that simulate the actual exam, including Fixed-Length, Random, Review, and Test All. Explanations of correct and incorrect answers reinforce concepts learned.

➤ *Classroom training*—CTECs, online partners, and third-party training companies (like Wave Technologies, Learning Tree, Data-Tech, and others) all offer classroom training on Windows 2000. These companies aim to help you prepare to pass Exam 70-217. Although such training runs upwards of $350 per day in class, most of the individuals lucky enough to partake find it to be quite worthwhile.

➤ *Other publications*—There's no shortage of materials available about Directory Services Infrastructure. The resource sections at the end of each chapter should give you an idea of where we think you should look for further discussion.

By far, this set of required and recommended materials represents a nonpareil collection of sources and resources for Directory Services Infrastructure and related topics. We anticipate that you'll find that this book belongs in this company

About this Book

Each topical *Exam Cram* chapter follows a regular structure, along with graphical cues about important or useful information. Here's the structure of a typical chapter:

➤ *Opening hotlists*—Each chapter begins with a list of the terms, tools, and techniques that you must learn and understand before you can be fully conversant with that chapter's subject matter. We follow the hotlists with one or two introductory paragraphs to set the stage for the rest of the chapter.

➤ *Topical coverage*—After the opening hotlists, each chapter covers a series of topics related to the chapter's subject title. Throughout this section, we highlight topics or concepts likely to appear on a test using a special Exam Alert layout, like this:

> This is what an Exam Alert looks like. Normally, an Exam Alert stresses concepts, terms, software, or activities that are likely to relate to one or more certification test questions. For that reason, we think any information found offset in Exam Alert format is worthy of unusual attentiveness on your part. Indeed, most of the information that appears on The Cram Sheet appears as Exam Alerts within the text.

Pay close attention to material flagged as an Exam Alert; although all the information in this book pertains to what you need to know to pass the exam, we flag certain items that are really important. You'll find what appears in the meat of each chapter to be worth knowing, too, when preparing for the test. Because this book's material is very condensed, we recommend that you use this book along with other resources to achieve the maximum benefit.

In addition to the Exam Alerts, we have provided tips that will help you build a better foundation for Directory Services Infrastructure knowledge. Although the information may not be on the exam, it is certainly related and will help you become a better test-taker.

> This is how tips are formatted. Keep your eyes open for these, and you'll become a Directory Services Infrastructure guru in no time!

➤ *Practice questions*—Although we talk about test questions and topics throughout the book, a section at the end of each chapter presents a series of mock test questions and explanations of both correct and incorrect answers.

➤ *Details and resources*—Every chapter ends with a section titled "Need to Know More?". This section provides direct pointers to Microsoft and third-party resources offering more details on the chapter's subject. In addition, this section tries to rank or at least rate the quality and thoroughness of the topic's coverage by each resource. If you find a resource you like in this collection, use it, but don't feel compelled to use all the resources. On the other hand, we recommend only resources we use on a regular basis, so none of our recommendations will be a waste of your time or money (but purchasing them all at once probably represents an expense that many network administrators and would-be MCPs and MCSEs might find hard to justify).

The bulk of the book follows this chapter structure slavishly, but there are a few other elements that we'd like to point out. Chapter 16 includes a sample test that provides a good review of the material presented throughout the book to ensure you're ready for the exam. Chapter 17 is an answer key to the sample test that appears in Chapter 16. In addition, you'll find a handy glossary and an index.

Finally, the tear-out Cram Sheet attached next to the inside front cover of this *Exam Cram* book represents a condensed and compiled collection of facts and tips that we think you should memorize before taking the test. Because you can dump this information out of your head onto a piece of paper before taking the exam, you can master this information by brute force—you need to remember it only long enough to write it down when you walk into the test room. You might even want to look at it in the car or in the lobby of the testing center just before you walk in to take the test.

How to Use this Book

We've structured the topics in this book to build on one another. Therefore, some topics in later chapters make more sense after you've read earlier chapters. That's why we suggest you read this book from front to back for your initial test preparation. If you need to brush up on a topic or you have to bone up for a second try, use the index or table of contents to go straight to the topics and questions that you need to study. Beyond helping you prepare for the test, we think you'll find this book useful as a tightly focused reference to some of the most important aspects of Directory Services Infrastructure.

Given all the book's elements and its specialized focus, we've tried to create a tool that will help you prepare for—and pass—Microsoft Exam 70-217. Please share your feedback on the book with us, especially if you have ideas about how we can improve it for future test-takers.

Send your questions or comments to us at **learn@examcram.com**. Please remember to include the title of the book in your message; otherwise, we'll be forced to guess which book you're writing about. And we don't like to guess—we want to *know*! Also, be sure to check out the Web pages at **www.examcram.com**, where you'll find information updates, commentary, and certification information.

Thanks, and enjoy the book!

Self-Assessment

The reason we included a Self-Assessment in this *Exam Cram* book is to help you evaluate your readiness to tackle MCSE certification. It should also help you understand what you need to know to master the topic of this book—namely, Exam 70-217, "Implementing and Administering a Microsoft Windows 2000 Directory Services Infrastructure." But before you tackle this Self-Assessment, let's talk about concerns you may face when pursuing an MCSE for Windows 2000, and what an ideal MCSE candidate might look like.

MCSEs in the Real World

In the next section, we describe an ideal MCSE candidate, knowing full well that only a few real candidates will meet this ideal. In fact, our description of that ideal candidate might seem downright scary, especially with the changes that have been made to the program to support Windows 2000. But take heart: Although the requirements to obtain an MCSE may seem formidable, they are by no means impossible to meet. However, be keenly aware that it does take time, involves some expense, and requires real effort to get through the process.

Increasing numbers of people are attaining Microsoft certifications, so the goal is within reach. You can get all the real-world motivation you need from knowing that many others have gone before, so you will be able to follow in their footsteps. If you're willing to tackle the process seriously and do what it takes to obtain the necessary experience and knowledge, you can take—and pass—all the certification tests involved in obtaining an MCSE. In fact, we've designed *Exam Preps*, the companion *Exam Crams*, *Exam Cram Personal Trainers*, and *Exam Cram Personal Test Centers* to make it as easy on you as possible to prepare for these exams. We've also greatly expanded our Web site, **www.examcram.com**, to provide a host of resources to help you prepare for the complexities of Windows 2000.

Besides MCSE, other Microsoft certifications include:

➤ MCSD, which is aimed at software developers and requires one specific exam, two more exams on client and distributed topics, plus a fourth elective exam drawn from a different, but limited, pool of options.

➤ Other Microsoft certifications, whose requirements range from one test (MCP) to several tests (MCP+SB, MCDBA).

The Ideal Windows 2000 MCSE Candidate

Just to give you some idea of what an ideal MCSE candidate is like, here are some relevant statistics about the background and experience such an individual might have. Don't worry if you don't meet these qualifications, or don't come that close—this is a far from ideal world, and where you fall short is simply where you'll have more work to do.

➤ Academic or professional training in network theory, concepts, and operations. This includes everything from networking media and transmission techniques through network operating systems, services, and applications.

➤ Three-plus years of professional networking experience, including experience with Ethernet, token ring, modems, and other networking media. This must include installation, configuration, upgrade, and troubleshooting experience.

Note: The Windows 2000 MCSE program is much more rigorous than the previous NT MCSE program; therefore, you'll really need some hands-on experience. Some of the exams require you to solve real-world case studies and network design issues, so the more hands-on experience you have, the better.

➤ Two-plus years in a networked environment that includes hands-on experience with Windows 2000 Server, Windows 2000 Professional, Windows NT Server, Windows NT Workstation, and Windows 95 or Windows 98. A solid understanding of each system's architecture, installation, configuration, maintenance, and troubleshooting is also essential.

➤ Knowledge of the various methods for installing Windows 2000, including manual and unattended installations.

➤ A thorough understanding of key networking protocols, addressing, and name resolution, including TCP/IP, IPX/SPX, and NetBEUI.

➤ A thorough understanding of NetBIOS naming, browsing, and file and print services.

➤ Familiarity with key Windows 2000-based TCP/IP-based services, including HTTP (Web servers), DHCP, WINS, DNS, plus familiarity with one or more of the following: Internet Information Server (IIS), Index Server, and Proxy Server.

➤ An understanding of how to implement security for key network data in a Windows 2000 environment.

➤ Working knowledge of NetWare 3.x and 4.x, including IPX/SPX frame formats, NetWare file, print, and directory services, and both Novell and Microsoft client software. Working knowledge of Microsoft's Client Service For NetWare (CSNW), Gateway Service For NetWare (GSNW), the NetWare Migration Tool (NWCONV), and the NetWare Client For Windows (NT, 95, and 98) is essential.

➤ A good working understanding of Active Directory. The more you work with Windows 2000, the more you'll realize that this new operating system is quite different than Windows NT. New technologies like Active Directory have really changed the way that Windows is configured and used. We recommend that you find out as much as you can about Active Directory and acquire as much experience using this technology as possible. The time you take learning about Active Directory will be time very well spent!

Fundamentally, this boils down to a bachelor's degree in computer science, plus three years' experience working in a position involving network design, installation, configuration, and maintenance. We believe that well under half of all certification candidates meet these requirements, and that, in fact, most meet less than half of these requirements—at least, when they begin the certification process. But because all the people who already have been certified have survived this ordeal, you can survive it too—especially if you heed what our Self-Assessment can tell you about what you already know and what you need to learn.

Put Yourself to the Test

The following series of questions and observations is designed to help you figure out how much work you must do to pursue Microsoft certification and what kinds of resources you may consult on your quest. Be absolutely honest in your answers, or you'll end up wasting money on exams you're not yet ready to take. There are no right or wrong answers, only steps along the path to certification. Only you can decide where you really belong in the broad spectrum of aspiring candidates.

Two things should be clear from the outset, however:

➤ Even a modest background in computer science will be helpful.

➤ Hands-on experience with Microsoft products and technologies is an essential ingredient to certification success.

Educational Background

1. Have you ever taken any computer-related classes? [Yes or No]

   If Yes, proceed to question 2; if No, proceed to question 4.

2. Have you taken any classes on computer operating systems? [Yes or No]

   If Yes, you will probably be able to handle Microsoft's architecture and system component discussions. If you're rusty, brush up on basic operating system concepts, especially virtual memory, multitasking regimes, user mode versus kernel mode operation, and general computer security topics.

   If No, consider some basic reading in this area. We strongly recommend a good general operating systems book, such as *Operating System Concepts, 5th Edition*, by Abraham Silberschatz and Peter Baer Galvin (John Wiley & Sons, 1998, ISBN 0-471-36414-2). If this title doesn't appeal to you, check out reviews for other, similar titles at your favorite online bookstore.

3. Have you taken any networking concepts or technologies classes? [Yes or No]

   If Yes, you will probably be able to handle Microsoft's networking terminology, concepts, and technologies (brace yourself for frequent departures from normal usage). If you're rusty, brush up on basic networking concepts and terminology, especially networking media, transmission types, the OSI Reference Model, and networking technologies such as Ethernet, token ring, FDDI, and WAN links.

   If No, you might want to read one or two books in this topic area. The two best books that we know of are *Computer Networks, 3rd Edition*, by Andrew S. Tanenbaum (Prentice-Hall, 1996, ISBN 0-13-349945-6) and *Computer Networks and Internets, 2nd Edition*, by Douglas E. Comer (Prentice-Hall, 1998, ISBN 0-130-83617-6).

   Skip to the next section, "Hands-on Experience."

4. Have you done any reading on operating systems or networks? [Yes or No]

   If Yes, review the requirements stated in the first paragraphs after questions 2 and 3. If you meet those requirements, move on to the next section. If No, consult the recommended reading for both topics. A strong background will help you prepare for the Microsoft exams better than just about anything else.

· ·

Hands-on Experience

The most important key to success on all of the Microsoft tests is hands-on experience, especially with Windows 2000 Server and Professional, plus the many add-on services and BackOffice components around which so many of the Microsoft certification exams revolve. If we leave you with only one realization after taking this Self-Assessment, it should be that there's no substitute for time spent installing, configuring, and using the various Microsoft products upon which you'll be tested repeatedly and in depth.

5. Have you installed, configured, and worked with:

   ➤ Windows 2000 Server? [Yes or No]

   If Yes, make sure you understand basic concepts as covered in Exam 70-215. You should also study the TCP/IP interfaces, utilities, and services for Exam 70-216, plus implementing security features for Exam 70-220.

 You can download objectives, practice exams, and other data about Microsoft exams from the Training and Certification page at **www.Microsoft.com/ trainingandservices/default.asp?PageID=mcp/**. Use the " Exams" link to obtain specific exam information.

   If you haven't worked with Windows 2000 Server, you must obtain one or two machines and a copy of Windows 2000 Server. Then, learn the operating system and whatever other software components on which you'll also be tested.

   In fact, we recommend that you obtain two computers, each with a network interface, and set up a two-node network on which to practice. With decent Windows 2000-capable computers selling for about $500 to $600 apiece these days, this shouldn't be too much of a financial hardship. You may have to scrounge to come up with the necessary software, but if you scour the Microsoft Web site you can usually find low-cost options to obtain evaluation copies of most of the software that you'll need.

   ➤ Windows 2000 Professional? [Yes or No]

   If Yes, make sure you understand the concepts covered in Exam 70-210.

   If No, you will want to obtain a copy of Windows 2000 Professional and learn how to install, configure, and maintain it. You can use *MCSE Windows 2000 Professional Exam Cram* to guide your activities and studies, or work straight from Microsoft's test objectives if you prefer.

For any and all of these Microsoft exams, the Resource Kits for the topics involved are a good study resource. You can purchase softcover Resource Kits from Microsoft Press (search for them at **http://mspress.microsoft.com/**), but they also appear on the TechNet CDs (**www.microsoft.com/technet**). Along with *Exam Crams* and *Exam Preps*, we believe that Resource Kits are among the best tools you can use to prepare for Microsoft exams.

6. For any specific Microsoft product that is not itself an operating system (for example, SQL Server), have you installed, configured, used, and upgraded this software? [Yes or No]

If the answer is Yes, skip to the next section. If it's No, you must get some experience. Read on for suggestions on how to do this.

Experience is a must with any Microsoft product exam, be it something as simple as FrontPage 2000 or as challenging as SQL Server 7.0. For trial copies of other software, search Microsoft's Web site using the name of the product as your search term. Also, search for bundles like "BackOffice" or "Small Business Server."

If you have the funds, or your employer will pay your way, consider taking a class at a Certified Training and Education Center (CTEC) or at an Authorized Academic Training Partner (AATP). In addition to classroom exposure to the topic of your choice, you get a copy of the software that is the focus of your course, along with a trial version of whatever operating system it needs, with the training materials for that class.

Before you even think about taking any Microsoft exam, make sure you've spent enough time with the related software to understand how it may be installed and configured, how to maintain such an installation, and how to troubleshoot that software when things go wrong. This will help you in the exam, and in real life!

Testing Your Exam-Readiness

Whether you attend a formal class on a specific topic to get ready for an exam or use written materials to study on your own, some preparation for the Microsoft certification exams is essential. At $100 a try, pass or fail, you want to do everything you can to pass on your first try. That's where studying comes in.

We have included a practice exam in this book, so if you don't score that well on the test, you can study more and then tackle the test again. We also have exams that you can take online through the **ExamCram.com** Web site at www.examcram.com. If you still don't hit a score of at least 70 percent after these tests, you'll want to investigate the other practice test resources we mention in this section.

For any given subject, consider taking a class if you've tackled self-study materials, taken the test, and failed anyway. The opportunity to interact with an instructor and fellow students can make all the difference in the world, if you can afford that privilege. For information about Microsoft classes, visit the Training and Certification page at **www.microsoft.com/education/partners/ctec.asp** for Microsoft Certified Education Centers or **www.microsoft.com/aatp/default.htm** for Microsoft Authorized Training Providers.

If you can't afford to take a class, visit the Training and Certification page anyway, because it also includes pointers to free practice exams and to Microsoft Certified Professional Approved Study Guides and other self-study tools. And even if you can't afford to spend much at all, you should still invest in some low-cost practice exams from commercial vendors.

7. Have you taken a practice exam on your chosen test subject? [Yes or No]

If Yes, and you scored 70 percent or better, you're probably ready to tackle the real thing. If your score isn't above that threshold, keep at it until you break that barrier.

If No, obtain all the free and low-budget practice tests you can find and get to work. Keep at it until you can break the passing threshold comfortably.

 When it comes to assessing your test readiness, there is no better way than to take a good-quality practice exam and pass with a score of 70 percent or better. When we're preparing ourselves, we shoot for 80-plus percent, just to leave room for the "weirdness factor" that sometimes shows up on Microsoft exams.

Assessing Readiness for Exam 70-217

In addition to the general exam-readiness information in the previous section, there are several things you can do to prepare for the Implementing and Administering a Microsoft Windows 2000 Directory Services Infrastructure exam. As you're getting ready for Exam 70-217, visit the Exam Cram Windows 2000 Resource Center at **www.examcram.com/studyresource/w2kresource/**. Another valuable resource is the Exam Cram Insider newsletter. Sign up at **www.examcram.com** or send a blank email message to **subscribe-ec@mars.coriolis.com**. We also suggest that you join an active MCSE mailing list. One of the better ones is managed by Sunbelt Software. Sign up at **www.sunbelt-software.com** (look for the Subscribe button).

Microsoft exam mavens also recommend checking the Microsoft Knowledge Base (available on its own CD as part of the TechNet collection, or on the Microsoft Web site at **http://support.microsoft.com/support/**) for "meaningful technical support issues" that relate to your exam's topics. Although we're not sure exactly what the quoted phrase means, we have also noticed some overlap between technical support questions on particular products and troubleshooting questions on the exams for those products.

Onward, through the Fog!

Once you've assessed your readiness, undertaken the right background studies, obtained the hands-on experience that will help you understand the products and technologies at work, and reviewed the many sources of information to help you prepare for a test, you'll be ready to take a round of practice tests. When your scores come back positive enough to get you through the exam, you're ready to go after the real thing. If you follow our assessment regime, you'll not only know what you need to study, but when you're ready to make a test date at Prometric or VUE. Good luck!

Microsoft
Certification Exams

. . . .

Terms you'll need to understand:

✓ Case study
✓ Multiple-choice question formats
✓ Build-list-and-reorder question format
✓ Create-a-tree question format
✓ Drag-and-connect question format
✓ Select-and-place question format
✓ Fixed-length tests
✓ Simulations
✓ Adaptive tests
✓ Short-form tests

Techniques you'll need to master:

✓ Assessing your exam-readiness
✓ Answering Microsoft's varying question types
✓ Altering your test strategy depending on the exam format
✓ Practicing (to make perfect)
✓ Making the best use of the testing software
✓ Budgeting your time
✓ Guessing (as a last resort)

Exam taking is not something that most people anticipate eagerly, no matter how well prepared they may be. In most cases, familiarity helps offset test anxiety. In plain English, this means you probably won't be as nervous when you take your fourth or fifth Microsoft certification exam as you'll be when you take your first one.

Whether it's your first exam or your tenth, understanding the details of taking the new exams (how much time to spend on questions, the environment you'll be in, and so on) and the new exam software will help you concentrate on the material rather than on the setting. Likewise, mastering a few basic exam-taking skills should help you recognize—and perhaps even outfox—some of the tricks and snares you're bound to find in some exam questions.

This chapter, besides explaining the exam environment and software, describes some proven exam-taking strategies that you should be able to use to your advantage.

Assessing Exam-Readiness

We strongly recommend that you read through and take the Self-Assessment included with this book (it appears just before this chapter, in fact). This will help you compare your knowledge base to the requirements for obtaining an MCSE, and it will also help you identify parts of your background or experience that may be in need of improvement, enhancement, or further learning. If you get the right set of basics under your belt, obtaining Microsoft certification will be that much easier.

Once you've gone through the Self-Assessment, you can remedy those topical areas where your background or experience may not measure up to an ideal certification candidate. But you can also tackle subject matter for individual tests at the same time, so you can continue making progress while you're catching up in some areas.

Once you've worked through an *Exam Cram*, have read the supplementary materials, and have taken the practice test, you'll have a pretty clear idea of when you should be ready to take the real exam. Although we strongly recommend that you keep practicing until your scores top the 75 percent mark, 80 percent would be a good goal to give yourself some margin for error in a real exam situation (where stress will play more of a role than when you practice). Once you hit that point, you should be ready to go. But if you get through the practice exam in this book without attaining that score, you should keep taking practice tests and studying the materials until you get there. You'll find more pointers on how to study and prepare in the Self-Assessment. But now, on to the exam itself!

The Exam Situation

When you arrive at the testing center where you scheduled your exam, you'll need to sign in with an exam coordinator. He or she will ask you to show two forms of identification, one of which must be a photo ID. After you've signed in and your time slot arrives, you'll be asked to deposit any books, bags, or other items you brought with you. Then, you'll be escorted into a closed room.

All exams are completely closed book. In fact, you will not be permitted to take anything with you into the testing area, but you will be furnished with a blank sheet of paper and a pen or, in some cases, an erasable plastic sheet and an erasable pen. Before the exam, you should memorize as much of the important material as you can, so you can write that information on the blank sheet as soon as you are seated in front of the computer. You can refer to this piece of paper anytime you like during the test, but you'll have to surrender the sheet when you leave the room. You will have some time to compose yourself and record this information before you begin the exam.

Typically, the room will be furnished with anywhere from one to half a dozen computers, and each workstation will be separated from the others by dividers designed to keep you from seeing what's happening on someone else's computer. Most test rooms feature a wall with a large picture window. This permits the exam coordinator to monitor the room, to prevent exam-takers from talking to one another, and to observe anything out of the ordinary that might go on. The exam coordinator will have preloaded the appropriate Microsoft certification exam—for this book, that's Exam 70-217—and you'll be permitted to start as soon as you're seated in front of the computer.

All Microsoft certification exams allow a certain maximum amount of time in which to complete your work (this time is indicated on the exam by an on-screen counter/clock, so you can check the time remaining whenever you like). All Microsoft certification exams are computer generated. In addition to multiple choice, you'll encounter select and place (drag and drop), create a tree (categorization and prioritization), drag and connect, and build list and reorder (list prioritization) on most exams. Although this may sound quite simple, the questions are constructed not only to check your mastery of basic facts and figures about Directory Services Infrastructure, but they also require you to evaluate one or more sets of circumstances or requirements. Often, you'll be asked to give more than one answer to a question. Likewise, you might be asked to select the best or most effective solution to a problem from a range of choices, all of which technically are correct. Taking the exam is quite an adventure, and it involves real thinking. This book shows you what to expect and how to deal with the potential problems, puzzles, and predicaments.

In the next section, you'll learn more about how Microsoft test questions look and how they must be answered.

Exam Layout and Design

The format of Microsoft's Windows 2000 exams is different from that of its previous exams. For the design exams (70-219, 70-220, 70-221), each exam consists entirely of a series of case studies, and the questions can be of six types. For the Core Four exams (70-210, 70-215, 70-216, 70-217), the same six types of questions can appear, but you are not likely to encounter complex multiquestion case studies.

For design exams, each case study or "testlet" presents a detailed problem that you must read and analyze. Figure 1.1 shows an example of what a case study looks like. You must select the different tabs in the case study to view the entire case.

Following each case study is a set of questions related to the case study; these questions can be one of six types (which are discussed next). Careful attention to details provided in the case study is the key to success. Be prepared to toggle frequently between the case study and the questions as you work. Some of the case studies also include diagrams, which are called *exhibits*, that you'll need to examine closely to understand how to answer the questions.

Once you complete a case study, you can review all the questions and your answers. However, once you move on to the next case study, you may not be able to return to the previous case study and make any changes.

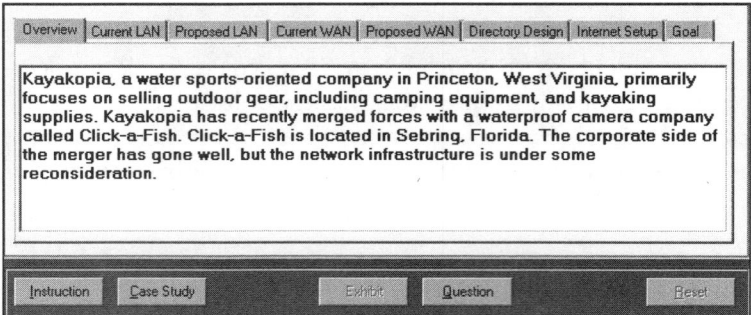

| Overview | Current LAN | Proposed LAN | Current WAN | Proposed WAN | Directory Design | Internet Setup | Goal |

Kayakopia, a water sports-oriented company in Princeton, West Virginia, primarily focuses on selling outdoor gear, including camping equipment, and kayaking supplies. Kayakopia has recently merged forces with a waterproof camera company called Click-a-Fish. Click-a-Fish is located in Sebring, Florida. The corporate side of the merger has gone well, but the network infrastructure is under some reconsideration.

| Instruction | Case Study | | Exhibit | Question | | Reset |

Figure 1.1   This is how case studies appear.

The six types of question formats are:

➤ Multiple choice, single answer

➤ Multiple choice, multiple answers

➤ Build list and reorder (list prioritization)

➤ Create a tree

➤ Drag and connect

➤ Select and place (drag and drop)

*Note: Exam formats may vary by test center location. You may want to call the test center or visit **ExamCram.com** to see if you can find out which type of test you'll encounter.*

Multiple-Choice Question Format

Some exam questions require you to select a single answer, whereas others ask you to select multiple correct answers. The following multiple-choice question requires you to select a single correct answer. Following the question is a brief summary of each potential answer and why it is either right or wrong.

Question 1

Which of the following elements is required to successfully install and configure DNS? [Choose the best answer]

○ a. DHCP

○ b. Static IP address

○ c. Active Directory

○ d. Windows 2000 clients

Answer b is correct. To install and configure a working DNS server, the server running DNS must have a static IP address. Answer a is incorrect because DHCP is not required to use DNS, though it is necessary if you want to enable dynamic update. Answer c is incorrect because Active Directory is not required. Answer d is incorrect because DNS works with legacy clients as well as Windows 2000 clients.

This sample question format corresponds closely to the Microsoft certification exam format—the only difference on the exam is that questions are not followed by answer keys. To select an answer, you would position the cursor over the radio button next to the answer. Then, click the mouse button to select the answer.

Let's examine a question where one or more answers are possible. This type of question provides checkboxes rather than radio buttons for marking all appropriate selections.

Question 2

Kayla is a domain admininstrator who has placed permissions on a parent OU, and through inheritance, those permissions have flowed down toward the child OUs beneath. What can Kayla do to prevent the flow of inheritance while retaining the permissions that already exist on the objects? [Check all correct answers]

❑ a. Go into the properties of the OU and deselect the Allow Inheritable Permissions From Parent To Propagate To This Object checkbox.

❑ b. Go into the properties of the OU and select the Allow Inheritable Permissions From Parent To Propagate To This Object checkbox.

❑ c. Select Copy at the Security screen.

❑ d. Select Remove at the Security screen.

Answers a and c are correct. To remove inheritance, you must deselect the checkbox on the OU that allows inheritance. To retain the preexisting permissions, you must select Copy from the corresponding warning box that appears. Answer b is incorrect because it would apply inheritance from above to the object. Answer d is incorrect because it would remove all permissions that existed prior to the change.

For this particular question, two answers are required. Microsoft sometimes gives partial credit for partially correct answers. For Question 2, you have to check the boxes next to items a and c to obtain credit for a correct answer. Notice that picking the right answers also means knowing why the other answers are wrong!

Build-List-and-Reorder Question Format

Questions in the build-list-and-reorder format present two lists of items—one on the left and one on the right. To answer the question, you must move items from the list on the right to the list on the left. The final list must then be reordered into a specific order.

These questions can best be characterized as "From the following list of choices, pick the choices that answer the question. Arrange the list in a certain order." To give you practice with this type of question, some questions of this type are included in this study guide. Here's an example of how they appear in this book; for a sample of how they appear on the test, see Figure 1.2.

Question 3

From the following list of famous people, pick those that have been elected President of the United States. Arrange the list in the order that they served.

Thomas Jefferson

Ben Franklin

Abe Lincoln

George Washington

Andrew Jackson

Paul Revere

The correct answer is:

George Washington

Thomas Jefferson

Andrew Jackson

Abe Lincoln

On an actual exam, the entire list of famous people would initially appear in the list on the right. You would move the four correct answers to the list on the left, and then reorder the list on the left. Notice that the answer to the question did not include all items from the initial list. However, this may not always be the case.

To move an item from the right list to the left list, first select the item by clicking on it, and then click on the Add button (left arrow). Once you move an item from one list to the other, you can move the item back by first selecting the item and then clicking on the appropriate button (either the Add button or the Remove button). Once items have been moved to the left list, you can reorder an item by selecting the item and clicking on the up or down button.

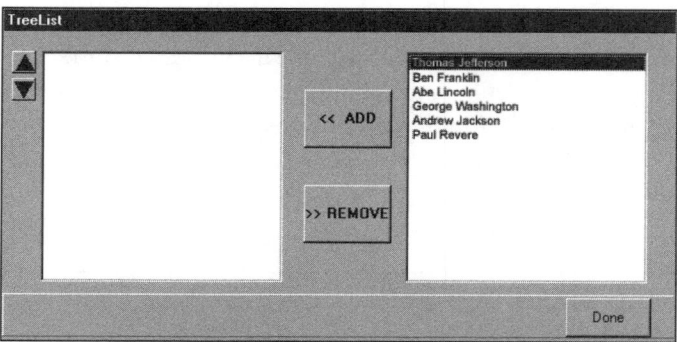

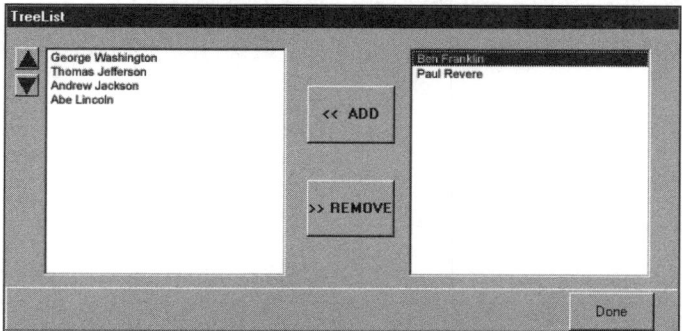

Figure 1.2 This is how build-list-and-reorder questions appear.

Create-a-Tree Question Format

Questions in the create-a-tree format also present two lists—one on the left side of the screen and one on the right side of the screen. The list on the right consists of individual items, and the list on the left consists of nodes in a tree. To answer the question, you must move items from the list on the right to the appropriate node in the tree.

These questions can best be characterized as simply a matching exercise. Items from the list on the right are placed under the appropriate category in the list on the left. Here's an example of how they appear in this book; for a sample of how they appear on the test, see Figure 1.3.

Question 4

The calendar year is divided into four seasons:

    Winter

    Spring

    Summer

    Fall

Identify the season when each of the following holidays occurs:

    Christmas

    Fourth of July

    Labor Day

    Flag Day

    Memorial Day

    Washington's Birthday

    Thanksgiving

    Easter

The correct answer is:

    Winter

        Christmas

        Washington's Birthday

    Spring

        Flag Day

        Memorial Day

        Easter

    Summer

        Fourth of July

        Labor Day

    Fall

        Thanksgiving

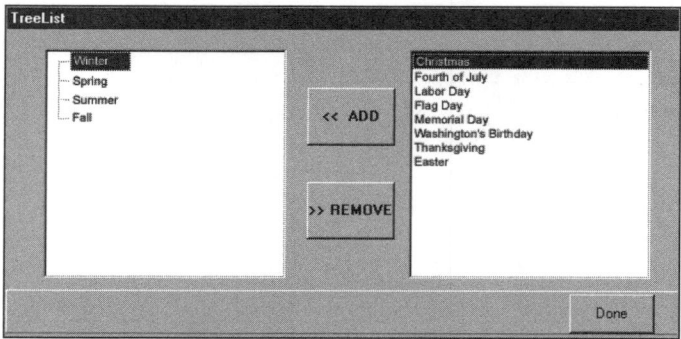

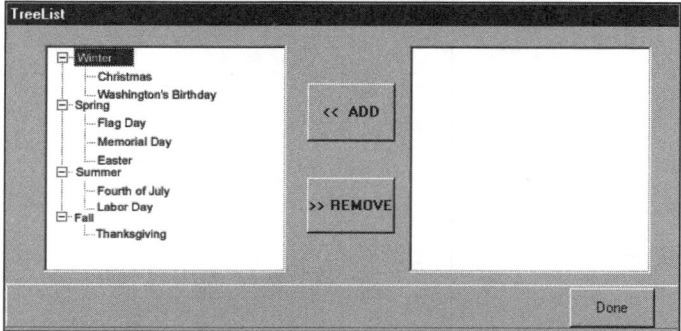

Figure 1.3 This is how create-a-tree questions appear.

In this case, all the items in the list were used. However, this may not always be the case.

To move an item from the right list to its appropriate location in the tree, you must first select the appropriate tree node by clicking on it. Then, you select the item to be moved and click on the Add button. If one or more items have been added to a tree node, the node will be displayed with a "+" icon to the left of the node name. You can click on this icon to expand the node and view the item(s) that have been added. If any item has been added to the wrong tree node, you can remove it by selecting it and clicking on the Remove button.

Drag-and-Connect Question Format

Questions in the drag-and-connect format present a group of objects and a list of "connections." To answer the question, you must move the appropriate connections between the objects.

This type of question is best described using graphics. Here's an example.

Question 5

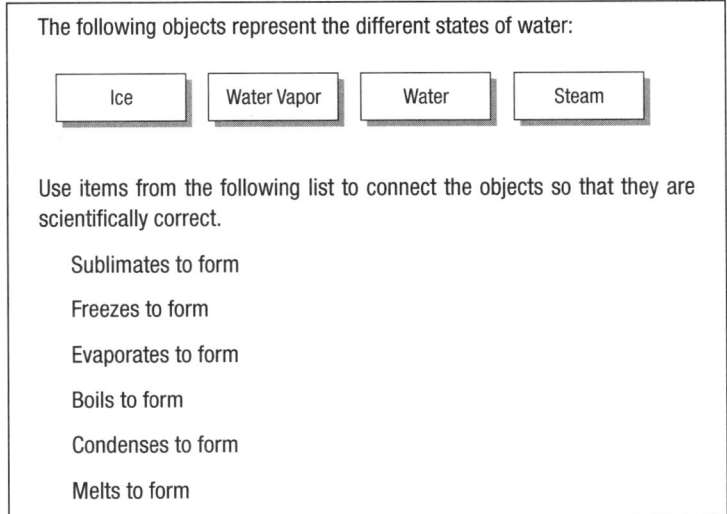

The following objects represent the different states of water:

| Ice | Water Vapor | Water | Steam |

Use items from the following list to connect the objects so that they are scientifically correct.

Sublimates to form

Freezes to form

Evaporates to form

Boils to form

Condenses to form

Melts to form

The correct answer is:

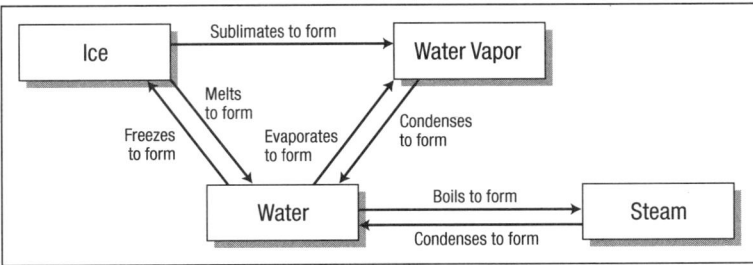

For this type of question, it's not necessary to use every object, and each connection can be used multiple times.

Select-and-Place Question Format

Questions in the select-and-place (drag-and-drop) format present a diagram with blank boxes, and a list of labels that need to be dragged to correctly fill in the blank boxes. To answer the question, you must move the labels to their appropriate positions on the diagram.

This type of question is best described using graphics. Here's an example.

Question 6

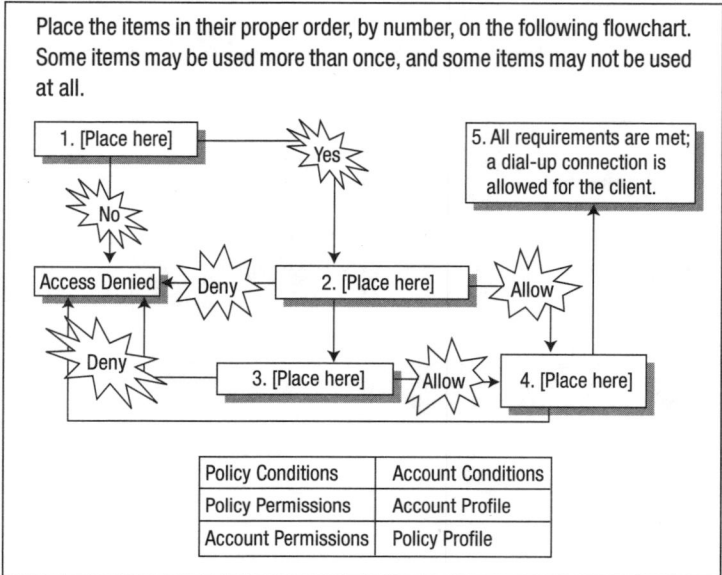

The correct answer is:

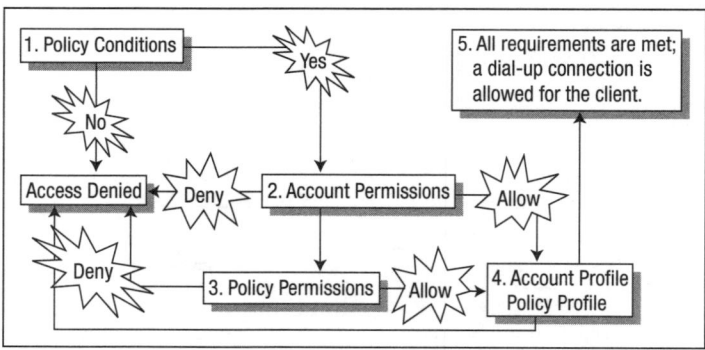

Microsoft's Testing Formats

Currently, Microsoft uses four different testing formats:

➤ Case study

➤ Fixed length

➤ Adaptive

➤ Short form

As we mentioned earlier, the case study approach is used with Microsoft's design exams. These exams consist of a set of case studies that you must analyze to enable you to answer questions related to the case studies. Such exams include one or more case studies (tabbed topic areas), each of which is followed by 4 to 10 questions. The question types for design exams and for Core Four Windows 2000 exams are multiple choice, build list and reorder, create a tree, drag and connect, and select and place. Depending on the test topic, some exams are totally case-based, whereas others are not.

Other Microsoft exams employ advanced testing capabilities that might not be immediately apparent. Although the questions that appear are primarily multiple choice, the logic that drives them is more complex than older Microsoft tests, which use a fixed sequence of questions, called a *fixed-length test*. Some questions employ a sophisticated user interface, which Microsoft calls a *simulation*, to test your knowledge of the software and systems under consideration in a more or less "live" environment that behaves just like the original. The Testing Innovations link at **www.microsoft.com/trainingandservices/default.asp?PageID=mcp** includes a downloadable practice simulation.

For some exams, Microsoft has turned to a well-known technique, called *adaptive testing*, to establish a test-taker's level of knowledge and product competence. Adaptive exams look the same as fixed-length exams, but they discover the level of difficulty at which an individual test-taker can correctly answer questions. Test-takers with differing levels of knowledge or ability therefore see different sets of questions; individuals with high levels of knowledge or ability are presented with a smaller set of more difficult questions, whereas individuals with lower levels of knowledge are presented with a larger set of easier questions. Two individuals may answer the same percentage of questions correctly, but the test-taker with a higher knowledge or ability level will score higher because his or her questions are worth more.

Also, the lower-level test-taker will probably answer more questions than his or her more-knowledgeable colleague. This explains why adaptive tests use ranges of values to define the number of questions and the amount of time it takes to complete the test.

Adaptive tests work by evaluating the test-taker's most recent answer. A correct answer leads to a more difficult question (and the test software's estimate of the test-taker's knowledge and ability level is raised). An incorrect answer leads to a less difficult question (and the test software's estimate of the test-taker's knowledge and ability level is lowered). This process continues until the test targets the test-taker's true ability level. The exam ends when the test-taker's level of accuracy meets a statistically acceptable value (in other words, when his or her performance demonstrates an acceptable level of knowledge and ability), or when the maximum number of items has been presented (in which case, the test-taker is almost certain to fail).

Microsoft also introduced a short-form test for its most popular tests. This test delivers 25 to 30 questions to its takers, giving them exactly 60 minutes to complete the exam. This type of exam is similar to a fixed-length test, in that it allows readers to jump ahead or return to earlier questions, and to cycle through the questions until the test is done. Microsoft does not use adaptive logic in this test, but claims that statistical analysis of the question pool is such that the 25 to 30 questions delivered during a short-form exam conclusively measure a test-taker's knowledge of the subject matter in much the same way as an adaptive test. You can think of the short-form test as a kind of "greatest hits exam" (that is, the most important questions are covered) version of an adaptive exam on the same topic.

Note: Some of the Microsoft exams can appear as a combination of adaptive and fixed-length questions.

Microsoft tests can come in any one of these forms. Whatever you encounter, you must take the test in whichever form it appears; you can't choose one form over another. If anything, it pays more to prepare thoroughly for an adaptive exam than for a fixed-length or a short-form exam: The penalties for answering incorrectly are built into the test itself on an adaptive exam, whereas the layout remains the same for a fixed-length or short-form test, no matter how many questions you answer incorrectly.

The biggest difference between an adaptive test and a fixed-length or short-form test is that on a fixed-length or short-form test, you can revisit questions after you've read them over one or more times. On an adaptive test, you must answer the question when it's presented and will have no opportunities to revisit that question thereafter.

Strategies for Different Testing Formats

Before you choose a test-taking strategy, you must know if your test is case study based, fixed length, short form, or adaptive. When you begin your exam, you'll know right away if the test is based on case studies. The interface will consist of a tabbed Window that allows you to easily navigate through the sections of the case.

If you are taking a test that is not based on case studies, the software will tell you that the test is adaptive, if in fact the version you're taking is an adaptive test. If your introductory materials fail to mention this, you're probably taking a fixed-length test (50 to 70 questions). If the total number of questions involved is 25 to 30, you're taking a short-form test. Some tests announce themselves by indicating that they will start with a set of adaptive questions, followed by fixed-length questions.

 You'll be able to tell for sure if you are taking an adaptive, fixed-length, or short-form test by the first question. If it includes a checkbox that lets you mark the question for later review, you're taking a fixed-length or short-form test. If the total number of questions is 25 to 30, it's a short-form test; if more than 30, it's a fixed-length test. Adaptive test questions can be visited (and answered) only once, and they include no such checkbox.

The Case Study Exam Strategy

Most test-takers find that the case study type of test used for the design exams (70-219, 70-220, and 70-221) is the most difficult to master. When it comes to studying for a case study test, your best bet is to approach each case study as a standalone test. The biggest challenge you'll encounter is that you'll feel that you won't have enough time to get through all of the cases that are presented.

 Each case provides a lot of material that you'll need to read and study before you can effectively answer the questions that follow. The trick to taking a case study exam is to first scan the case study to get the highlights. Make sure you read the overview section of the case so that you understand the context of the problem at hand. Then, quickly move on and scan the questions.

As you are scanning the questions, make mental notes to yourself so that you'll remember which sections of the case study you should focus on. Some case studies may provide a fair amount of extra information that you don't really need to answer the questions. The goal with this scanning approach is to avoid having to study and analyze material that is not completely relevant.

When studying a case, carefully read the tabbed information. It is important to answer each and every question. You will be able to toggle back and forth from case to questions, and from question to question within a case testlet. However, once you leave the case and move on, you may not be able to return to it. You may want to take notes while reading useful information so you can refer to them when you tackle the test questions. It's hard to go wrong with this strategy when taking any kind of Microsoft certification test.

The Fixed-Length and Short-Form Exam Strategy

A well-known principle when taking fixed-length or short-form exams is to first read over the entire exam from start to finish while answering only those questions you feel absolutely sure of. On subsequent passes, you can dive into more complex questions more deeply, knowing how many such questions you have left.

Fortunately, the Microsoft exam software for fixed-length and short-form tests makes the multiple-visit approach easy to implement. At the top-left corner of each question is a checkbox that permits you to mark that question for a later visit.

Note: Marking questions makes review easier, but you can return to any question by clicking the Forward or Back button repeatedly.

As you read each question, if you answer only those you're sure of and mark for review those that you're not sure of, you can keep working through a decreasing list of questions as you answer the trickier ones in order.

 There's at least one potential benefit to reading the exam over completely before answering the trickier questions: Sometimes, information supplied in later questions sheds more light on earlier questions. At other times, information you read in later questions might jog your memory about Directory Services Infrastructure facts, figures, or behavior that helps you answer earlier questions. Either way, you'll come out ahead if you defer those questions about which you're not absolutely sure.

Here are some question-handling strategies that apply to fixed-length and short-form tests. Use them if you have the chance:

➤ When returning to a question after your initial read-through, read every word again—otherwise, your mind can fall quickly into a rut. Sometimes, revisiting a question after turning your attention elsewhere lets you see something you missed, but the strong tendency is to see what you've seen before. Try to avoid that tendency at all costs.

➤ If you return to a question more than twice, try to articulate to yourself what you don't understand about the question, why answers don't appear to make sense, or what appears to be missing. If you chew on the subject awhile, your subconscious might provide the details you lack, or you might notice a "trick" that points to the right answer.

As you work your way through the exam, another counter that Microsoft provides will come in handy—the number of questions completed and questions outstanding. For fixed-length and short-form tests, it's wise to budget your time by making sure that you've completed one-quarter of the questions one-quarter of the way through the exam period, and three-quarters of the questions three-quarters of the way through.

If you're not finished when only five minutes remain, use that time to guess your way through any remaining questions. Remember, guessing is potentially more valuable than not answering, because blank answers are always wrong, but a guess may turn out to be right. If you don't have a clue about any of the remaining questions, pick answers at random, or choose all a's, b's, and so on. The important thing is to submit an exam for scoring that has an answer for every question.

At the very end of your exam period, you're better off guessing than leaving questions unanswered.

The Adaptive Exam Strategy

If there's one principle that applies to taking an adaptive test, it could be summed up as "Get it right the first time." You cannot elect to skip a question and move on to the next one when taking an adaptive test, because the testing software uses your answer to the current question to select whatever question it plans to present next. Nor can you return to a question once you've moved on, because the software gives you only one chance to answer the question. You can, however, take notes, because sometimes information supplied in earlier questions will shed more light on later questions.

Also, when you answer a question correctly, you are presented with a more difficult question next, to help the software gauge your level of skill and ability. When you answer a question incorrectly, you are presented with a less difficult question, and the software lowers its current estimate of your skill and ability. This continues until the program settles into a reasonably accurate estimate of what you know and can do, and takes you on average through somewhere between 15 and 30 questions as you complete the test.

The good news is that if you know your stuff, you'll probably finish most adaptive tests in 30 minutes or so. The bad news is that you must really, really know your stuff to do your best on an adaptive test. That's because some questions are so convoluted, complex, or hard to follow that you're bound to miss one or two, at a minimum, even if you do know your stuff. So the more you know, the better you'll do on an adaptive test, even accounting for the occasionally weird or unfathomable questions that appear on these exams.

 Because you can't always tell in advance if a test is fixed length, short form, or adaptive, you will be best served by preparing for the exam as if it were adaptive. That way, you should be prepared to pass no matter what kind of test you take. But if you do take a fixed-length or short-form test, remember the tips from the preceding section. They should help you improve on what you could do on an adaptive test.

If you encounter a question on an adaptive test that you can't answer, you must guess an answer immediately. Because of how the software works, you may suffer for your guess on the next question if you guess right, because you'll get a more difficult question next!

Question-Handling Strategies

For those questions that take only a single answer, usually two or three of the answers will be obviously incorrect, and two of the answers will be plausible—of course, only one can be correct. Unless the answer leaps out at you (if it does, reread the question to look for a trick; sometimes those are the ones you're most likely to get wrong), begin the process of answering by eliminating those answers that are most obviously wrong.

Almost always, at least one answer out of the possible choices for a question can be eliminated immediately because it matches one of these conditions:

➤ The answer does not apply to the situation.

➤ The answer describes a nonexistent issue, an invalid option, or an imaginary state.

After you eliminate all answers that are obviously wrong, you can apply your retained knowledge to eliminate further answers. Look for items that sound correct but refer to actions, commands, or features that are not present or not available in the situation that the question describes.

If you're still faced with a blind guess among two or more potentially correct answers, reread the question. Try to picture how each of the possible remaining answers would alter the situation. Be especially sensitive to terminology; sometimes the choice of words ("remove" instead of "disable") can make the difference between a right answer and a wrong one.

Only when you've exhausted your ability to eliminate answers, but remain unclear about which of the remaining possibilities is correct, should you guess at an answer. An unanswered question offers you no points, but guessing gives you at least some chance of getting a question right; just don't be too hasty when making a blind guess.

Note: If you're taking a fixed-length or a short-form test, you can wait until the last round of reviewing marked questions (just as you're about to run out of time, or out of unanswered questions) before you start making guesses. You will have the same option within each case study testlet (but once you leave a testlet, you may not be allowed to return to it). If you're taking an adaptive test, you'll have to guess to move on to the next question if you can't figure out an answer some other way. Either way, guessing should be your technique of last resort!

Numerous questions assume that the default behavior of a particular utility is in effect. If you know the defaults and understand what they mean, this knowledge will help you cut through many Gordian knots.

Mastering the Inner Game

In the final analysis, knowledge breeds confidence, and confidence breeds success. If you study the materials in this book carefully and review all the practice questions at the end of each chapter, you should become aware of those areas where additional learning and study are required.

After you've worked your way through the book, take the practice exam in the back of the book. Taking this test will provide a reality check and help you identify areas to study further. Make sure you follow up and review materials related to the questions you miss on the practice exam before scheduling a real exam. Only when you've covered that ground and feel comfortable with the whole scope of the practice exam should you set an exam appointment. Only if you score 80 percent or better should you proceed to the real thing (otherwise, obtain some additional practice tests so you can keep trying until you hit this magic number).

 If you take a practice exam and don't score at least 80 to 85 percent correct, you'll want to practice further. Microsoft provides links to practice exam providers and also offers self-assessment exams at **www.microsoft.com/trainingandservices/**. You should also check out **ExamCram.com** for downloadable practice questions.

Armed with the information in this book and with the determination to augment your knowledge, you should be able to pass the certification exam. However, you need to work at it, or you'll spend the exam fee more than once before you finally pass. If you prepare seriously, you should do well. We are confident that you can do it!

The next section covers other sources you can use to prepare for the Microsoft certification exams.

Additional Resources

A good source of information about Microsoft certification exams comes from Microsoft itself. Because its products and technologies—and the exams that go with them—change frequently, the best place to go for exam-related information is online.

If you haven't already visited the Microsoft Certified Professional site, do so right now. The MCP home page resides at **www.microsoft.com/trainingandservices** (see Figure 1.4).

Note: This page might not be there by the time you read this, or may be replaced by something new and different, because things change regularly on the Microsoft site. Should this happen, please read the sidebar titled "Coping with Change on the Web."

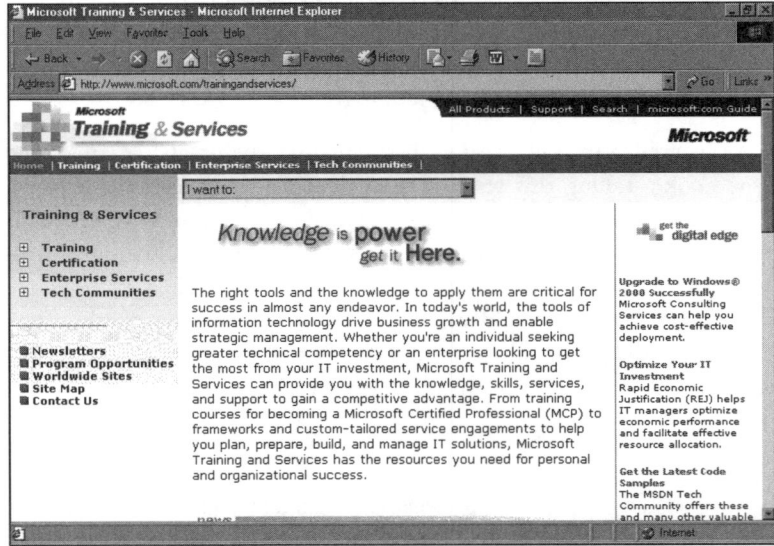

Figure 1.4   The Microsoft Certified Professional home page.

Coping with Change on the Web

Sooner or later, all the information we've shared with you about the Microsoft Certified Professional pages and the other Web-based resources mentioned throughout the rest of this book will go stale or be replaced by newer information. In some cases, the URLs you find here might lead you to their replacements; in other cases, the URLs will go nowhere, leaving you with the dreaded "404 File not found" error message. When that happens, don't give up.

There's always a way to find what you want on the Web if you're willing to invest some time and energy. Most large or complex Web sites—and Microsoft's qualifies on both counts—offer a search engine. On all of Microsoft's Web pages, a Search button appears along the top edge of the page. As long as you can get to Microsoft's site (it should stay at **www.microsoft.com** for a long time), use this tool to help you find what you need.

The more focused you can make a search request, the more likely the results will include information you can use. For example, you can search for the string

```
"training and certification"
```

to produce a lot of data about the subject in general, but if you're looking for the preparation guide for Exam 70-217, "Implementing and Administering a Microsoft Windows 2000 Directory Services Infrastructure," you'll be more likely to get there quickly if you use a search string similar to the following:

```
"Exam 70-217" AND "preparation guide"
```

Likewise, if you want to find the Training and Certification downloads, try a search string such as this:

```
"training and certification" AND "download page"
```

Finally, feel free to use general search tools—such as **www.search.com**, **www.altavista.com**, and **www.excite.com**—to look for related information. Although Microsoft offers great information about its certification exams online, there are plenty of third-party sources of information and assistance that need not follow Microsoft's party line. Therefore, if you can't find something where the book says it lives, intensify your search.

Introduction to
Active Directory

Terms you'll need to understand:

✓ Active Directory (AD)

✓ Object class

✓ Attributes

✓ Lightweight Directory Access Protocol (LDAP)

✓ Domain

✓ Organizational Unit (OU)

✓ Tree

✓ Forest

✓ Site

✓ Delegation of control

Techniques you'll need to master:

✓ Explaining the difference between the logical and physical aspects of AD

✓ Defining trees and forests

✓ Describing how the centralized nature of AD aids in system administration

Windows 2000 is a major step forward for enterprise computing using Microsoft software. It has been designed to achieve improved performance and scalability. Scalability is the ability to support organizations that range from smaller companies with a few hundred users to enterprises with hundreds of thousands of users.

At the heart of Windows 2000 is Active Directory (AD). AD is a directory service that stores data about users and groups, shared folders, and other network resources. This book discusses many facets of AD and how you use it to simplify system administration.

AD lets you centrally manage your network. This means that administrative tasks can be performed from a single location. When necessary, administrators can use the delegation of control tools to assign specific tasks to individuals outside of this central location. Because AD provides a fine level of granularity, you can assign administrative tasks safely, without giving too much power to your users.

This chapter briefly discusses topics that will be important to you when using AD, as well as for Microsoft's MCSE Exam 70-217, "Implementing and Administering a Microsoft Windows 2000 Directory Services Infrastructure." This introductory chapter also lays the foundation for your comprehension of upcoming chapters. The topics discussed here are covered in more detail later in the book.

Overview of AD

AD is the single component that enables many of the new features of Windows 2000. AD is a directory service, which means that it both stores data about your network resources and provides methods for accessing and distributing that data. It does this by adopting several key industry standards. This provides AD with interoperability out of the box.

Although your users need fast and efficient access to the resources on your network, they should not have to know the specifics of where the resources physically reside or how the data is being retrieved. One of the primary functions of AD is to hide the physical elements of your network from your users. This includes all protocols and hardware, such as servers, routers, and hubs. From a user perspective, these are invisible.

AD is the central repository for many different types of data. Some of this data might detail the existence of a particular user object; other data might detail the look and feel of the user's workstation environment. AD can then make sure that this look and feel is applied to all workstations on the network. This is achieved through Group Policy. When Group Policy is applied, AD makes sure that copies of the policies are stored as close to the user as possible, making the application efficient and fast.

AD also allows for a centralized method of authentication. This means that a user can log on to a Windows 2000 network and be authenticated a single time. This feature simplifies the user's ability to access resources no matter where they reside on the network.

Objects in AD

AD must store a great deal of data. Each piece of data stored within AD is an *object*. Each object has a set of attributes associated with it. These attributes are used to describe the object and make it unique.

Objects within AD include users, groups, computers, servers, domains, and sites, among others. As you can see, the list is extensive and far-reaching. Because data is stored as objects, users can search through the directory for objects they wish to access based on object names. Because objects have attributes, you can also search for an object based on its attributes. For a user object, the attributes might include the user's telephone number, job title, and first and last names. This provides a flexible environment where users are empowered in ways we have not seen before.

The Schema

To understand how data is defined within AD, you must be aware of the schema. The *schema* is a definition of all object types and their attributes. Because there is a single schema for an entire Windows 2000 forest, you can achieve consistency no matter how large your enterprise grows.

Two types of definitions are stored in the schema: object classes and attributes. Object classes define the types of objects that can be stored within AD. Each class consists of a class name and a set of attributes that are associated with the object. Attributes are stored separately within the schema. This allows further consistency within the database, because a single definition for the "last name" attribute can be used over and over again.

The schema can be searched by user applications and modified to allow custom object classes and attributes. To prevent it from being modified without permissions, each object is secured using discretionary access control lists (DACLs). These DACLs ensure that only authorized users are able to access the schema.

Directory Service Protocol

We mentioned that Microsoft had adopted some key industry standards to ensure interoperability. One of the key standards that enables AD is the Lightweight Directory Access Protocol (LDAP). This protocol is used to query and update data within the directory. Active Directory supports LDAP versions 2 and 3.

Part of the LDAP standard defines naming standards. It states that objects must be represented by a series of components (such as domain and Organizational Unit), and that these components be represented as a unique path to the object. There are two LDAP naming paths: distinguished names and relative distinguished names.

Distinguished Names

You can think of the *distinguished name* as the complete path from the root domain all the way down to the object. Every object in AD must have a unique distinguished name. Here is an example:

```
CN=Donna George,OU=Sales,DC=HCSNET,DC=COM
```

Table 2.1 defines each of the components of the distinguished name.

Relative Distinguished Names

A *relative distinguished name* is a truncated distinguished name. It identifies the part of the distinguished name that uniquely identifies the object within its container. For instance, in the example given previously, the relative distinguished name would be "CN=Donna George", because Donna George is the name of the unique name within the Sales OU.

Depending upon the details you know about an object, the relative distinguished name may be different. For instance, in this example, we do not know the name of a user object:

```
OU=Sales,DC=HCSNET,DC=COM
```

In this case, the relative distinguished name would simply be "OU=Sales", because Sales is the name that uniquely identifies the OU within the domain.

Table 2.1	Distinguished name elements.	
Key	**Attribute**	**Meaning**
CN	Common Name	Any object stored within the directory, with the exception of domain components and Organizational Units
OU	Organizational Unit	An Organizational Unit that can contain other objects
DC	Domain Component	Defines the DNS name, such as COM

The Structure of AD

AD is made up of two distinct structures: the logical structure and the physical structure. When designing your AD implementation, you are dealing with the logical aspects of what AD offers. When deciding precisely where each component will be on your network, you are dealing with the physical limitations of your infrastructure.

Let's take a brief look at the major elements that make up both the logical and physical pieces of a Windows 2000 network. From a design perspective, you need to know what each element is and how the elements work together to build an enterprise-level system.

The Logical Structure

When designing your Windows 2000 network, you will be using the various logical components. These components are useful for both administrators and users. For administrators, they allow for the logical design of your AD infrastructure. From a user's perspective, they allow for efficient searching of the AD database.

There are five logical components in AD:

➤ Domains

➤ Organization Units (OUs)

➤ Trees

➤ Forests

➤ Global Catalogs (GCs)

Understanding what each of these components does helps you understand how to design and administer AD. They also provide the foundation for your comprehension of the material that follows.

Domains

The *domain* is one of the core elements that make up a Windows 2000 network. A domain is a *security boundary*. This means that each domain has its own administrators that can be assigned full control over the domain—and only the domain (unless specified otherwise).

A domain is an entity with its own users and groups. These users can be granted permissions in other domains if necessary. Some group types can be assigned permissions outside of the domain in which they were created, whereas others cannot.

Domains are also used for replication purposes. Although AD is a single database containing data about all elements of your network, it does not replicate all data across the entire network. Domain data is replicated only within a single domain. A subset of data from a domain can be replicated; this is the function of a GC server, which we will define in a moment.

Domain controllers (DCs) within a domain replicate with each other and share domain information. Controlling this replication is a key part of the design process. A domain can also run in one of two modes: native or mixed. Full functionality cannot be achieved until a domain is running in native mode.

Organizational Units (OUs)

Organizational Units are container objects that are used to organize objects within the directory. Remember that we are talking about the logical layer. Objects are not physically stored within this structure, even if Windows 2000 represents them this way. OUs commonly contain user and group objects. They can also contain computers and other OUs.

OUs are used to simplify administration. Permissions can be assigned at the OU level both to grant container objects access to other network resources (or to deny them) and to assign specific users administrative privileges.

Commonly, the OU structure is built around the administrative model for your organization. Because administrative tasks such as adding user objects or applying policies is done at the OU level, it makes sense to organize network resources and other objects within them. Objects that will be administered by a single administrator or administrative group, or objects that will have policies and permissions assigned to them in a uniform fashion should be grouped within OUs.

Less commonly, OUs are designed around the organizational structure, such as by department or geographic location. A geographic hierarchy of OUs allows you to organize users by country or region.

Administration of objects within an OU can be delegated. This means that once objects have been stored within the OU container, you can assign permissions to manage these objects to groups other than domain administrators. This can reduce the amount of day-to-day administrative tasks that are performed by domain administrators.

Trees

Domains are combined to produce a *tree*, which is a hierarchical representation of your Windows 2000 network. The first domain that is installed in a Windows 2000 network is known as the *root domain*. All subsequent domains are installed beneath this root domain All domains in a tree share a common schema and a common GC.

 You cannot uninstall the root domain. Doing so would effectively force you to uninstall all domains in your environment. Also, you cannot rename a Windows 2000 domain.

If you have more than one domain, each domain forms part of a tree. When you have several domains forming a tree, it is said that they share a *contiguous namespace*. As domains are added to the tree, they become child domains to the domain above them in the hierarchy. For instance, the second domain you install becomes a child of the root domain. It derives part of its name from its position within the hierarchy.

An example of this hierarchical structure can be illustrated in the following way. An AD designer installs a root domain called "chamberlin.local". Once this is complete, she installs a second domain, which becomes a child domain to the root domain. This domain's name is "Houston"; therefore, the full name in Windows 2000 is houston.chamberlin.local. As you can see, the domain inherited part of its name from the root domain. This maintains the hierarchical nature of AD.

This naming scheme echoes the DNS (Domain Name System) naming scheme from which it is derived. DNS is a key part of a Windows 2000 network. Domain names are based on DNS standards.

Note: You might be familiar with trusts from previous versions of Windows NT. Trusts allow objects in one domain to gain access to objects in another domain. In previous versions, these trusts were created manually as needed. In Windows 2000, they are created automatically. In addition, they are transitive. A transitive trust means that a trust between two domains can be used by every other domain. These trusts are always two-way.

Forests

A *forest* is a collection of trees. Trees in a forest do not have to share a contiguous namespace. However, they *must* share a common schema and GC. For instance, say you have two trees, one called chamberlin.local and another with a root domain of watts.local. These trees can be joined together to join a forest via a two-way trust relationship.

Forests allow users in two different trees to access resources in a different namespace, thereby easing administration. Because trees in a forest must share a common schema, they share all object and attribute types.

Global Catalogs (GCs)

Because DCs within a domain only store data about objects contained within the domain, another mechanism must be in place to allow users to gain transparent access to resources outside of the domain in which they are contained. This is the job of a GC.

A GC server is also a DC. It contains data about all objects within a forest. Because this data is stored locally on a DC, a user can quickly search for network resources stored anywhere in the forest. In addition, because the GC contains the permissions list for all objects, it can also grant access. This prevents the user from having to contact a DC in the remote domain, thereby reducing network traffic.

The GC does not contain every attribute for an object. Instead, it contains a subset of attributes defined as those that are most commonly searched. For the user object, this might be the first name or last name. The attributes that are replicated to the GC server are controlled by an attribute of the object. By editing the schema, you can force or prevent attributes from appearing in the GC.

One of the key benefits of the GC is that it makes the logical structure of your Windows 2000 network invisible to your users. Along with a reduction of network traffic, GCs are an essential part of your Windows 2000 implementation.

The Physical Structure

The physical structure of AD is used to manage network traffic on your network. The two elements that make up the physical structure are:

➤ Domain controllers (DCs)

➤ Sites

These elements are involved in the underlying infrastructure that makes up your network. You should consider such issues as the amount of network bandwidth you have available and how your TCP/IP (Transmission Control Protocol / Internet Protocol) network has been segmented.

The physical design of your network is distinct and separate from the logical layer. When designing either one, you do not have to take the other into account. Whichever logical design you come up with, the physical implications will never force you to change it.

Let's look briefly at each of these components. By combining both the logical and physical elements of your network, you can optimize your Windows 2000 network.

Domain Controllers (DCs)

A *domain controller* (DC) is a server on a Windows 2000 network that stores a replica of the AD database. Its job is to manage access to this data via searches and also to accept and make changes to the data as necessary. The DC must then replicate any changes it has accepted to all other DCs in the domain. A small network might require only two controllers (but for fault-tolerance reasons, never less than two), whereas a large network could require hundreds of DCs.

Along with these tasks, the DC also manages the authentication of users as they log on to the network. This authentication includes assigning a security token that contains a list of group memberships and permissions to each user.

Each replica of AD is read/write enabled. This means that any DC has the ability to accept changes. The process of AD replication ensures that all DCs receive copies of these changes. Because this cannot happen in realtime, there will be short periods when one replica may hold slightly different information than other replicas.

AD replication works well for most network operations. However, there are times when the latency involved with moving changes to AD can cause problems. To resolve this issue, some operations on the network do not strictly follow the peer nature of DCs and AD replication. These special servers are called *operations masters*.

Operations masters ensure that security remains intact on your network and that changes made to the schema of your network do not conflict. Operations masters exist at both the domain and forest level.

Sites

Sites can be defined as a group of one or more IP subnets connected by high-speed access links. Sites are used on your network to optimize AD replication traffic and user authentication.

IP subnets within a site are considered to have fast connectivity. By creating a site that contains a group of subnets, you are telling Windows 2000 that communication between these subnets is both fast and efficient. The inverse is also true: By putting two IP subnets into different sites, you are telling Windows 2000 that the IP subnets are separated by a slow or inefficient link. AD uses this information to build its replication topology. Replication among sites can be scheduled to occur during certain times of day. Replication traffic among sites is also compressed (however, replication traffic within a site is not).

Sites are also used for several other Windows 2000 features, including allowing users to find a DC that is local to them (in the same IP subnet) during the logon process. This minimizes logon traffic across the WAN.

Administering Windows 2000

Windows 2000 leverages AD to provide several methods to administer the network. These methods work together to provide an efficient and safe networking environment. The three methods are as follows:

➤ Centralized management

➤ Group Policy

➤ Delegation of control

Let's briefly look at each method.

Centralized Management

AD centrally stores data. This eases administration, because having all data about the domain stored in a central location (on each DC) allows administrators to manage objects easily. It also allows users to locate any object in a single search.

The structure of AD allows objects to be grouped logically into OUs. This structure allows for multiple levels and inheritance. Through the use of Group Policy, you can apply a group of settings at one level of the hierarchy and have it flow down and affect all objects—or a subset of objects—within the domain.

Because all site, domain, and OU data is stored centrally, group policies can be applied at any of these levels. Being able to affect as much or as little of your network as you want further simplifies management.

Group Policy

Group Policy allows you to centrally manage your user environment through the creation and application of policies throughout your domain or domains. When you apply a Group Policy a single time, you can rely on Windows 2000 to continually apply it, even if the user's attributes and permissions change.

Group Policy leverages containers, including sites, domains, and OUs, within AD. Using this information is efficient, because it has already been defined within AD.

Group Policies are applied when a user logs on. If applied to user objects, Group Policies follow the user around the network—regardless of which computer the user logs in to. The ability of group policies to follow the user means your user community will enjoy a consistent interface and experience, reducing help desk calls and total cost of ownership (TCO).

Delegation of Control

When combined with the granular nature of the AD security model, the delegation of control allows administrators of a Windows 2000 network to give unprecedented freedom to groups of users. By delegating control, administrators can allow users to administer their own environment.

You can delegate control at several different levels. For a wide range of control, you can delegate at the OU level. For instance, if you assigned Full Control permission to a user at the OU level, that user would be able to create new user objects within that OU and also delete them. This offloads day-to-day tasks from the central administrative team.

Control can also be delegated at the attribute level. It is entirely possible to assign a group of users the ability to edit a subset of attributes at the OU level. For instance, you might decide that personal information such as first name, last name, or telephone number should be controlled by the user community. You could do this by delegating control of these attributes to the users.

Delegating control relies on the creation of an effective logical structure. You should always design your logical structure before concerning yourself with the physical aspects of your network.

Practice Questions

Question 1

Jeannie Griswold has been asked to give a brief presentation to describe the new features of Windows 2000. One of the most significant new features is the inclusion of Active Directory. Which of the following best describes Active Directory?

○ a. Active Directory is a database that contains a list of all users and their passwords.

○ b. Each domain has its own Active Directory. By creating trusts between domains, each Active Directory can communicate with another. Because trusts are transitive, once you have connected all domains with trusts, a user can go anywhere on the network.

○ c. Active Directory is a database of information regarding users, groups, and computers on a Windows 2000 network.

○ d. Active Directory is a directory service. Not only does it contain data about all network resources, it also provides mechanisms for searching for data.

Answer d is correct. Active Directory is a set of data and services that allows you to manipulate and access information from any location on the network. Answers a and c are incorrect because Active Directory is much more than simply a database. Answer b is incorrect because each domain does not have its own Active Directory.

Question 2

Brad Finch is a system administrator for a video company. The network is widely dispersed. Brad's manager told Brad that he wants all of their video equipment data to be stored within Active Directory. Brad has looked through all of the property sheets but cannot find any way to enter data about these devices. Brad tells his boss that this cannot be done. However, his boss tells him that it can be done and that Brad should do more research. What should Brad do to store this data?

○ a. Brad should store the data as a user object. Because he doesn't have to fill out all of the attributes of an object, he should use just enough attributes to describe each piece of equipment.

○ b. Brad must create a new object class within the schema of Active Directory.

○ c. An object class for video equipment already exists within Active Directory. Brad should use it to store data about his equipment.

○ d. Brad should tell his boss that despite what his boss may have heard, this is not possible. Active Directory does not allow for the storage of objects that represent items such as video equipment.

Answer b is correct. Although it is not often necessary to alter the schema for Active Directory, it would be necessary in this situation. By creating a new object type, Brad would be able to create entries for the equipment. Answer a is incorrect because user objects will not have the properties Brad will need to store data about the video equipment. Answer c is incorrect because Microsoft has not provided an object class for video equipment. Answer d is incorrect because Active Directory can be extended to include information about any kind of device or piece of equipment.

Question 3

Siobhan has suggested to her management team that they migrate their old network to a Windows 2000-based system. However, she is meeting resistance because her bosses do not want to support a proprietary system. What should Siobhan tell her management team?

○ a. Active Directory supports many industry standards. Three key standards are TCP/IP, DNS, and LDAP. These standards allow for interoperability out of the box.

○ b. Although Windows 2000 is a proprietary system, Microsoft has a large market share. Therefore, using Windows 2000 is a good idea.

○ c. Siobhan should come up with an alternative network operating system.

○ d. Although Windows 2000 is proprietary, it does provide access to APIs that allow you to write integration tools.

Answer a is correct. Active Directory supports many industry standards. Answer b is incorrect because, although there are some aspects of Windows 2000 that are indeed proprietary, it does support all key Internet standards. Answer c is incorrect because an alternative operating system would not be necessary. Answer d is incorrect because Active Directory is based upon standards, and therefore is not a proprietary directory service.

Question 4

Gene Simmons is a system administrator who has hired a consultant to help him integrate two trees and make them a forest. Gene knows that this involves creating a trust and thinks it will only be a short period of time before they are done. However, the consultant tells him that the consolidation cannot happen because one company has customized the schema to include data about video equipment. Gene doesn't see why this is a problem. Who is correct?

○ a. Gene is correct. Because he effectively is only setting up a trust between two trees, it does not matter that one tree has a different schema.

○ b. Gene is correct. When the trust is created, the schemas will merge.

○ c. The consultant is correct. Because the schemas are currently different, creating a forest is not possible.

○ d. The consultant is correct. When the trust is created, the schemas will merge. However, before they can proceed, they need to determine which schema will be adopted for the forest.

Answer c is correct. Before the merge can take place, the two schemas must be identical. Answer a is incorrect because trees in a forest must share a common schema. Answers b and d are incorrect because there is no mechanism built into the trust process to merge schemas. All trees in a forest share both a schema and a Global Catalog.

Question 5

Which of the following is a distinguished name?

○ a   CN=Donna George,OU=Sales,DC=HCSNET,DC=COM

○ b. CN=Donna George

○ c. OU=Donna George,CN=Sales,DC=HCSNET,DC=COM

○ d. DC=Donna George,DC=Sales,OU=HCSNET,CN=COM

Answer a is correct. Distinguished names are read from right to left, becoming increasingly more unique. A distinguished name uniquely identifies an object within the directory. Answer b is incorrect because a distinguished name must list the entire path to the object. Answer c is incorrect because the container (CN) must always be listed first. Answer d is incorrect because you must not list DCs first.

Question 6

> John Watts is in the process of designing his Windows 2000 network. He has two sets of users—one in London and another in Houston. Although they share many items, they do have different security requirements, help desks, and administrative teams. John decides to incorporate two domains in his network design. However, the review committee in his organization tells him that it wants a single domain. It tells John that he should use OUs to create the security requirements. John considers this request and then resolves to attend the next committee meeting to justify his position and to insist that he be allowed to create two domains. Why did John decide to do this?
>
> ○ a. John does not understand the scalability of Windows 2000. Because Windows 2000 scales better than previous versions of Windows NT, it is a good idea to make things as simple as possible. One domain is simpler than two.
>
> ○ b. John knows that domains are security boundaries. He knows that in the case of two regions that must have their own security settings and control, creating two domains is far easier.
>
> ○ c. John does not understand OUs. John should create a single domain and use OUs to create the security model he wants.
>
> ○ d. John understands that multiple domains are a good idea when data needs to cross slow links. Active Directory works well when there are fast connections, but slow connections cause problems.

Answer b is correct. There are times when you are forced into creating multiple domains. A domain acts as a security boundary. By giving each geographic area its own domain, they can be totally autonomous. John can be a member of the Enterprise Admins group to maintain control over both domains. Answer a is incorrect because it addresses scalability without meeting the security requirements. Answer c is incorrect because OUs allow for control over objects contained within the OU, but will not help with dividing Domain Admins on his network. Answer d is incorrect because Active Directory traffic can be controlled with sites; it is not necessary to create multiple domains to deal with slow links.

Question 7

Peter Chamberlin is designing a Windows 2000 network with two domains, one in London and the other in Houston. His design calls for 50 DCs in each domain. He then decides to add another DC in each domain. The additional DC in London will be placed in Houston and vice versa to enable users in each domain to search for data in the other's network. When Peter presents this idea to a consultant, the consultant tells him that he does not need these additional DCs. Peter concludes that the consultant probably has never worked in an enterprisewide network before, and he forges ahead with his plan. Who is right?

○ a. Peter is right. If users will be performing searches across domains, they need access to a DC in all domains.

○ b. Peter is right. Because each domain will contain a DC from the other domain, they will be able to replicate data between them.

○ c. The consultant is right. Even if the DCs are moved, it will not solve the problem. Peter needs to set up a directory connector between the domains.

○ d. The consultant is right. It is not the job of a DC to allow searches across domains. To achieve this, the DC must be designated as a Global Catalog server.

Answer d is correct. A Global Catalog server allows searches to be performed across domains. Although a Global Catalog server is indeed a DC, it is not necessary that the DC belong to a specific domain. No additional DCs are needed in this instance. Answer a is incorrect because DCs cannot perform searches across domains. Answer b is incorrect because the issue at hand is not replication, it is searches across domains. Answer c is incorrect because it is not necessary to create a directory connector between the domains; directory connectors are used to connect different types of directory services, such as Active Directory and Novell Directory Services.

Question 8

Jason inherited a Windows 2000 network. When the network was installed, the root domain was misnamed. Instead of reading Basildon.local, it was named Absildon.local. Jason's manager has told him that this must be corrected as soon as possible because it is confusing users. Jason's network is made up of several child domains. All user accounts exist in these child domains (there are a few accounts in the root domain). Because the root domain has been created incorrectly, the names of the other domains have inherited the problem. Jason assures his manager that he will uninstall the root domain the next weekend. Once this is done, he will reinstall it with the correct spelling. He will then go ahead and rename the child domains. What will happen if Jason uninstalls the root domain?

○ a. Jason will lose his entire network. If the root domain goes away, all other domains will be orphaned and fail.

○ b. Jason will lose all user accounts. Although the user accounts appear to exist in the child domains, they are, in fact, first created in the root domain. Jason will need to re-create the user accounts.

○ c. Jason will finish more quickly than he thought. Because the domain names are inherited, once he reinstalls the root domain, the corrected name will flow down through the domain hierarchy.

○ d. Jason can simply rename the child domains. There is no need to uninstall the root domain.

Answer a is correct. The root domain should not be uninstalled. If you uninstall a root domain, you have essentially destroyed the tree. Jason would have to start again and re-create all objects and network resources. Answer b is incorrect because accounts are not created in the root domain first. Also, Jason will lose his tree once he has uninstalled the root domain. Answer c is incorrect because uninstalling the root domain means Jason will have to re-create all domains, and this will not save him time. Answer d is incorrect because child domains cannot simply be renamed.

Question 9

> Natasha is a system designer who is new to Windows 2000. She has just finished her first Windows 2000 network design for a pharmaceutical company. This company will have three domains. Natasha is just putting the finishing touches on a list of tasks that must be done. One of the items reads: "Create two-way trusts between each of the domains." When Natasha shows this plan to a friend, he tells her that this step is not necessary. Natasha, who has worked extensively with Windows NT 4, does not believe him. Who is correct?
>
> ○ a. Natasha is correct. Without specific trusts, users won't be able to access resources in other domains.
>
> ○ b. Natasha is correct. Although trusts are set up automatically in Windows 2000, they are one-way trusts, and they only travel up the hierarchy.
>
> ○ c. The friend is correct. This step is not necessary. Windows 2000 creates two-way transitive trusts.
>
> ○ d. The friend is correct. However, because the trusts automatically created are not transitive, Natasha will have to create some trusts manually. They will be far fewer in number than anticipated, though.

Answer c is correct. Although it is possible to create trusts between domains in Windows 2000, this is not generally necessary. All trusts created by Windows 2000 are two-way transitive. Answer a is incorrect because Windows 2000 automatically creates two-way transitive trusts. Answer b is incorrect because the trusts automatically created by Windows 2000 are not one-way—they are two-way. Answer d is incorrect because trusts are indeed transitive.

Question 10

Zevi Mehlman is working with a single Windows 2000 domain. Zevi's company has offices around the country with 128Kbps links between them. They have their own DCs and IP subnets. No office has more than 500 users. Zevi has a problem with the slow links on his network. During the day, these links are getting swamped with traffic. When he analyzes the traffic, he finds it is all related to Active Directory. Zevi decides to fix this problem. Fortunately, it did not take long. What did Zevi do to resolve this issue?

- ○ a. Zevi created multiple domains, one for each office. This reduced the amount of Active Directory traffic.

- ○ b. Zevi ordered faster connections between each office. The extra bandwidth will solve the problem.

- ○ c. Zevi changed his work hours. Because he will now only be in the office in the evenings, the amount of traffic generated by his administrative tasks should not inconvenience anyone.

- ○ d. Zevi created sites within his domain. Each remote office was given its own site. Zevi then scheduled replication to occur on a schedule in the evening.

Answer d is correct. Sites are used to facilitate management of replication traffic. By creating sites, Zevi will enjoy the benefits of compressed replication data, and he'll be able to schedule when replication occurs. Answer a is incorrect because creating multiple domains would increase the administrative burden on his network. Answer b is incorrect because although faster connections would help with the problem, a more reasonable alternative is available. Keep in mind that faster connections do not always solve bandwidth issues. Answer c is incorrect because Zevi is doing nothing to control when replication takes place on his network.

Need to Know More?

 Blum, Daniel J. *Understanding Active Directory Services*. Microsoft Press, Redmond, WA, 1999. ISBN 1572317213. This book includes details of AD design.

 Iseminger, David. *Active Directory Services for Microsoft Windows 2000*. Microsoft Press, Redmond, WA, 2000. ISBN 0735606242. This book includes design tips for AD and introduces you to new terminology.

 Minasi, Mark. *Mastering Windows 2000 Server, Second Edition*. Sybex Computer Books, Berkeley, CA, 2000. ISBN 0782127746. This book does a good job of aiming content at all levels of readers.

 Northrup, Anthony. *Introducing Microsoft Windows 2000 Server*. Microsoft Press, Redmond, WA, 1999. ISBN 1572318759. This book acts as a high-level introduction to AD and its features.

 Willis, Will, David Watts, and Tillman Strahan. *Windows 2000 System Administration Handbook*. Prentice-Hall, Upper Saddle River, NJ, 2000. ISBN 0130270105. This book examines a day in the life of an administrator and gives examples of day-to-day tasks you will need to perform.

Implementing and Administering DNS

Terms you'll need to understand:

✓ Domain Name System (DNS)

✓ HOSTS

✓ Fully qualified domain name (FQDN)

✓ Relative distinguished name

✓ Windows Internet Naming Service (WINS)

✓ Zone

✓ Active Directory (AD) integrated zone

✓ Primary zone

✓ Secondary zone

✓ Dynamic update

✓ Forward lookup

✓ Reverse lookup

✓ Root server

✓ Resource records (RR)

✓ NSLOOKUP

Techniques you'll need to master:

✓ Installing and configuring DNS for AD

✓ Integrating AD DNS zones with non-AD DNS zones

✓ Configuring zones for dynamic update

✓ Managing replication of DNS data

✓ Troubleshooting DNS

The Domain Name System (DNS) is a name resolution database most commonly associated with the Internet. It was first defined as a way to replace the aging HOSTS file system, which is explained in the next section. With Windows 2000, Microsoft has made DNS the primary method of name resolution for Active Directory (AD) networks. In fact, DNS is a required element for installing AD—so much so that the process of upgrading a member or standalone server to an AD domain controller (DC) automatically installs the DNS server service if you do not have a valid DNS server for AD to use.

We'll briefly touch on how and why DNS was created because without that background, troubleshooting DNS by testing with alternate name resolution methods won't fully make sense.

 You will need to know how to install, configure, and troubleshoot the DNS server service.

A Brief History of DNS

As we mentioned previously, DNS has its origins in the Internet. When the Internet was small, every single TCP/IP (Transmission Control Protocol/Internet Protocol) host on the Internet had a file called HOSTS, which contained mappings of every other host on the Internet and its IP address (hence, the name). Whenever a new host (such as a workstation or server) was added to the Internet, a new master HOSTS file was created and posted, and everyone on the Internet would download the updated file. This was fine when the Internet was small and changes were infrequent. However, as the Internet grew, the process of updating HOSTS files on every system became increasingly unmanageable. Enter DNS. DNS was conceived as a hierarchical namespace that allowed the management of the Internet namespace to be partitioned and distributed. As such, not every system needed to know the name and IP address of every other system on the Internet. Conceptually, the DNS hierarchy looks like a tree. At the very top is what is known as the *root domain*, which is represented by a period (.). Below the root domain are the *top-level domains*, which are the com, net, edu, org, and so on that we are all familiar with.

Below the top-level domains are the *second-level domains*, which are what we work with every day when sending email or visiting a Web site. Microsoft.com is a second-level domain, as is Army.mil, Harvard.edu, and Coriolis.com. When you visit **www.InsideIS.com**, you are accessing a host computer called *www* in the *InsideIS.com* second-level domain.

Fully Qualified Domain Names (FQDNs)

With DNS, another important term to understand is the *fully qualified domain name (FQDN)*. This refers to the complete, unambiguous name of a host. The FQDN contains everything from the hostname through the root domain. An example is the **www.microsoft.com.** FQDN. In that example, *www* is the host, *microsoft.com* is the second-level domain, *com* is the top-level domain, and the trailing period represents the root domain. This FQDN is said to be unambiguous because it uniquely defines a single host on the Internet.

Relative Distinguished Names (RDNs)

Unlike an FQDN, a *relative distinguished name (RDN)* is just the part of the hostname that represents the host system. In the previous example, *www* would be the RDN. These types of names are not used on the Internet because of the likelihood the name would be ambiguous and unable to be resolved to an IP address. However, RDNs are common on internal networks, because corporate DNS servers check their local zones first to resolve a name (more on zones later).

Now that we have explored some background information, let's examine DNS as it relates to Windows 2000 and AD.

Dynamic DNS and AD in Windows 2000

Windows 2000 runs on TCP/IP, and to utilize AD, you must forsake the older WINS (Windows Internet Naming Service) technology in favor of DNS. The biggest downside to DNS has been that although distributed, it was still designed as a system that requires manual updates. Whenever a new host was added to a domain, an administrator needed to manually update the zone database on the primary DNS server to reference the new host. If there were secondary name servers on the network, the changes were replicated in a zone transfer.

However, a dynamic updating feature proposed in RFC 2136 provides the means for updating a zone's primary server automatically. Windows 2000 supports this new dynamic DNS, or simply DDNS. The caveat is that it works only with Windows 2000 clients, and older Windows NT, Windows 9x, and non-Windows clients still require manual updates, or at minimum, a Windows 2000 DHCP proxy to act on their behalf during the dynamic registration process. When DDNS is enabled and Windows 2000 boots up and contacts a DHCP for IP addressing information, it automatically sends an update to the name server it has been configured to use, adding its A (Address) resource record. This greatly simplifies the administration of DNS on a Windows 2000 network. In addition, DDNS simplifies the administration of AD by allowing DCs to automatically register their service (SRV) resource records into DNS without administrator intervention.

Note: WINS is a proprietary Microsoft name resolution scheme for resolving NetBIOS names to IP addresses on Microsoft networks. WINS is a dynamic database that allows clients to register themselves automatically and, as with DNS, was a replacement for an older manually updated system. On Microsoft networks, LMHOSTS was the equivalent of the HOSTS files used on the Internet.

Throughout this chapter, we discuss many of the terms used in this section, including zones, zone transfer, and resource records. Also, before installing DNS, we need to take into account some planning considerations. We examine those next.

DNS Planning Considerations

Before you actually install DNS, you must first analyze your current network and determine your name resolution requirements. The areas of planning include the following:

➤ Site structure

➤ Types of name servers

➤ Types of network clients

➤ Naming hosts and domains

➤ Static IP addresses

Site Structure

The structure of your physical network plays an important role in the design of your DNS infrastructure. How you choose to implement DNS will be different depending on your setup. For example, you wouldn't have the same configuration for a single site with a couple of DCs as you would where you had multiple sites connected by WAN links with multiple DCs in each location.

The concept of sites is discussed in Chapter 12, but for our purposes here, we will define a site to be an IP subnet that is well connected (all hosts in the site have at least a 10Mbps Ethernet connection between them). A common problem with enterprise network environments with many sites connected by WAN links is bandwidth utilization. The DNS name resolution process involves queries against a DNS database, and at times of high network utilization, this traffic can place an extra burden across the WAN links. In this type of situation, it is recommended to place DNS servers at each site so that name resolution traffic does not have to cross the lower bandwidth links.

 When presented with exhibits of existing networks, you need to be able to determine how to set up DNS for those various environments.

Types of Name Servers

There are different types of name servers to consider. In this section, we cover the following:

➤ Primary DNS servers

➤ Secondary DNS servers

➤ Caching-only DNS servers

➤ Forwarding DNS servers

➤ AD integrated servers

Primary DNS Servers

There are really two main types of non-AD DNS servers: primary servers and secondary servers. As we briefly mentioned, the DNS namespace is partitioned into what are known as *zones*. We discuss zones in detail in the "DNS zones" section later in this chapter, but for now just understand that a zone is the part of the overall DNS namespace that is controlled by a primary server. There can only be one primary server in a zone, and that primary server is said to be *authoritative* for the zone. It is the master, and any changes to the DNS domain must be made on the primary server.

Secondary DNS Servers

A secondary server is essentially a backup server for the primary server. Note that during the name resolution process, if a primary server cannot resolve a hostname, the query is *not* submitted to a secondary server (if one exists in the zone). The secondary server is used as a failover if the primary server fails. If a client is unable to contact the primary DNS server, it attempts to use the secondary server if one has been configured. Another potential use of a secondary server is load balancing. If you have 1,000 network clients, for example, you could configure half of them to use the primary server first and half of them to use the secondary server first. This would reduce the load on the primary server.

Changes are never made directly to a secondary server, which receives a copy of the master zone file from the primary name server in a zone. This process is called *zone transfer* and is covered in more detail in the "Zone Transfer" section later in this chapter. Unlike with primary servers, a zone can have multiple secondary servers.

Caching-Only DNS Servers

This type of name server does pretty much what the name implies; it functions only to cache queries. The caching-only name server does not maintain a zone database file, nor does it receive updates from a primary server. It simply performs queries, caches the results, and returns results to querying clients. You can use caching-only name servers to deploy DNS services to sites that you do not wish to have an editable copy of the DNS zone.

The advantage to using a caching-only name server is the reduction in network traffic. The reduction is twofold. First, there is no replication traffic being generated between the primary name server and the caching-only server as there is between a primary and secondary server. Second, a caching-only server reduces name resolution traffic by reducing the need for subsequent queries to go through the entire name resolution process.

The disadvantage of caching-only servers, however, is that if a server is rebooted, the cache is flushed; the server must build its cache back up again from scratch.

Caching-only servers can also perform what is called *negative caching*, which caches failed results. This reduces the timeout process when a client queries for a site that does not exist or is unavailable.

Forwarding DNS Servers

Forwarding DNS servers exist solely to communicate with DNS servers outside the local zone. By default, any DNS server that receives a query it cannot resolve will contact an outside DNS server to resolve the name for the client making the query. A DNS forwarder functions like a proxy, becoming the only DNS server in a zone that can communicate outside the zone. This is similar in concept to a bridgehead server, which improves the utilization of network bandwidth by designating a single server as the contact point to other sites. If the primary name server, for example, cannot resolve a name, it sends the query to the forwarding DNS server for resolution. Figures 3.1 and 3.2 show a DNS infrastructure not using a forwarder and using a forwarder, respectively.

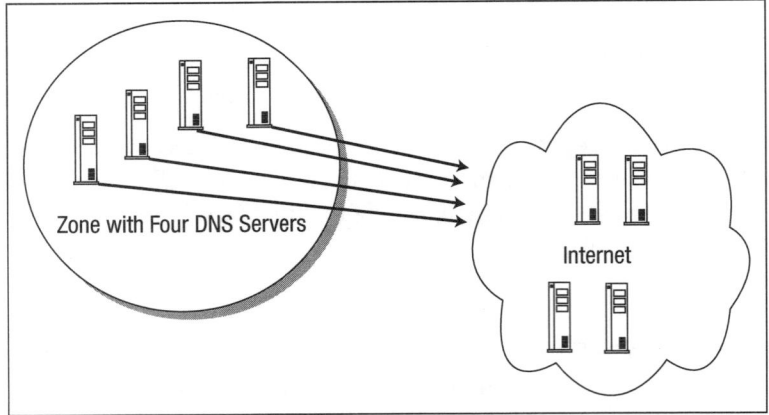

Figure 3.1   A DNS zone where all name servers communicate outside of the local zone.

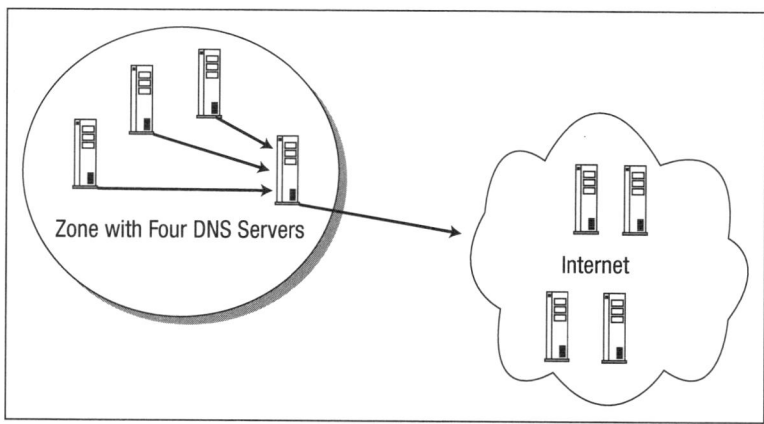

Figure 3.2 A DNS zone that uses a forwarding name server to communicate outside of the local zone.

Forwarding servers can be configured to use either nonexclusive or exclusive mode. In nonexclusive mode, a name server can attempt to resolve a query through its own zone database files if a forwarder cannot resolve the query. In exclusive mode, if a forwarder cannot resolve a query, the server that sent the query to the forwarder does not attempt to resolve the name itself and simply returns a failure notice to the client that originated the request.

AD Integrated Servers

Although the previous types of name servers are what are known as "standard" name server types, Windows 2000 introduces the ability to integrate DNS zones into AD. With AD integrated zones, each DC functions as a primary server and contains an editable copy of the zone. Through multimaster replication, discussed in Chapter 12, AD ensures that each copy of the zone is kept current across all DCs.

AD integrated zones provide the following benefits:

➤ *Fault tolerance*—Standard zones rely on *zone transfer* for replication, a process that requires the primary server to send updates to the secondary servers. If a primary server goes offline, there is no way to promote a secondary server to become a primary, and updates do not occur again until the primary server is brought online. With AD integrated zones, there is not the same single point of failure.

➤ *Security*—AD integrated zones do not store zone information in a text file as standard primary and secondary zones do, and in addition, zone updates can be set so that only secure updates are allowed.

> *Integrated replication*—Because the DNS zone is integrated into AD, it is replicated through the normal AD replication process. Standard zones would require creating an additional replication topology for DNS.

Types of Network Clients

The types of network clients that you have on your network impact your DNS strategy. If you have all Windows 2000 clients, for example, you can utilize all of the features of Windows 2000 DNS, such as dynamic updates and secure updates. Legacy Windows NT and Windows 9x clients can't register their resource records automatically through the dynamic update process. However, Windows 2000 can accommodate these clients if they are DHCP (Dynamic Host Configuration Protocol) clients.

A Windows 2000 DHCP server can register legacy clients on their behalf in DNS by enabling the Enable Updates For DNS Clients That Do Not Support Dynamic Updates option in the DHCP management console.

Naming Hosts and Domains

It is easy to get spoiled by the ability to create DNS domain names that are lengthy. However, if legacy clients exist or you are operating in mixed mode with NT 4 DCs, you must be aware of the limitations on NetBIOS-created names. Windows 2000 attempts to create a default NetBIOS name at the time you create the DNS domain name; however, you might run into problems with existing domains. NetBIOS names are limited to 14 characters, so if you have an existing NT 4 domain called WINDOWSNETWORK and you attempt to create a new domain called windowsnetwork1.com, the default NetBIOS name will be the same as the aforementioned Windows NT domain, and creation will fail.

 You should be comfortable with situations where you have to manage both NetBIOS and DNS domain names.

Static IP Addresses

For obvious reasons, DNS servers must have static IP addresses. If the server you are planning to use for DNS is currently configured as a DHCP client, be sure to assign it a unique static IP address for its subnet before installing the DNS server service. IP addresses are configured through TCP/IP properties within the properties of My Network Places.

Before we get to installing and configuring DNS for AD, we first need to take a moment to expand on the concept of DNS zones.

DNS Zones

We've mentioned zones previously in this chapter, but we haven't really taken the time to talk about them in much depth. As we've said, a zone is a partitioned portion of the overall DNS namespace. Zones make the manageability of the namespace much easier than the flat namespace of HOSTS files did. A zone must encompass contiguous namespace, however. For example, a single zone could not be authoritative for both InsideIS.com and Coriolis.com, because those two domains are not part of the same namespace. *Contiguous namespace* encompasses a single second-level domain name. For example, the domains Inside-Corner.com, Studio.Inside-Corner.com, GuitarShop.Studio.Inside-Corner.com, and Production.Inside-Corner.com are all part of the same namespace.

Multiple zones within a contiguous namespace are used primarily to distribute administrative responsibilities. In many corporations, there are political boundaries that must be managed, with different divisions/departments having their own administrators. Multiple zones allow multiple administrators to be responsible for their individual pieces of the namespace.

Another reason to partition the namespace into zones is to reduce the load on a DNS infrastructure. Consider a megacorporation such as Microsoft, with more than 100,000 nodes on the network spread out across the globe. A single zone would place a tremendous burden on the primary DNS server (remember, there can be only one primary server in a zone), and the replication traffic to secondary DNS servers would make a significant impact on network performance. Dividing the Microsoft.com namespace into multiple zones distributes the load, increasing performance and easing administration. Even using AD integrated zones would require that updates with the zone be replicated to every other DNS server in the zone. Again, the bandwidth usage for this type of traffic would potentially have a detrimental effect on network performance, particularly if changes were being made frequently.

Windows 2000 supports two types of zones: forward lookup and reverse lookup. These zones are associated with the types of name resolution queries they enable. We discuss these zones in greater detail when we look at installing and configuring Windows 2000 DNS later in this chapter.

Zone Transfer

Zone transfer is the process by which changes made on the primary server are replicated to all of the secondary servers in the zone. There are three types of zone transfer to consider:

➤ Full zone transfer

➤ Incremental zone transfer

➤ AD replication

Full Zone Transfer

Originally, the only method of replication between primary and secondary servers was the *full zone transfer*. With this method, the entire zone database file is transferred whenever an update is made. Zone transfer is performed through a "pull" mechanism rather than a "push." This means that the secondary servers initiate a zone transfer. The process is as follows:

1. The secondary server waits a predetermined amount of time before contacting the primary server. When it does establish contact, it requests the primary server's SOA (Start of Authority) record. (Record types are discussed in depth in the "Resource Records" section later in this chapter.)

2. The primary server responds to the secondary server with its SOA record.

3. Whenever a change is made to the primary name server, the serial number held in the SOA record is incremented. When the secondary server receives the SOA record from the primary server, it compares the serial number to its own. If the serial number in the SOA record sent by the primary server is higher than the serial number in the SOA record currently on the secondary server, the secondary server knows its zone database is out of date. It then sends a request back to the primary server for a full zone transfer. This full transfer is done through an AXFR request.

4. The primary server then sends its full zone database file back to the secondary server. After the update is complete, the process begins again with the waiting period.

Incremental Transfer

As you can probably imagine, performing a full zone transfer every time a single change is made to the primary server is inefficient. It also can generate a lot of network traffic if the primary server receives frequent updates and there are multiple secondary servers. To get around this problem, RFC 1995 allows for *incremental zone transfers*. As the name implies, with an incremental transfer, only the portion of the database that has been changed is replicated.

The process with an incremental transfer is the same as a full transfer, except with an incremental transfer, the secondary server sends an IXFR request signifying an incremental transfer, rather than the AXFR request, which signifies a full zone transfer.

If you think of AXFR as A (all) XFR (transfer), it is easy to remember that AXFR is a full transfer. Likewise, you can think of IXFR, as I (incremental) XFR (transfer).

For incremental transfer to work, a version history must be kept so that name servers will know what changes have already been applied. The primary server maintains a version history, which keeps track of all changes that have been made since the last version update was transferred to a secondary server. When a secondary server requests an IXFR transfer, the primary server starts sending the recent updates, beginning with the oldest updates and progressing to the most recent updates.

When the secondary server begins receiving the updates, it creates a new version of the zone and begins applying the updates to that copy. When all of the updates are committed to the copy of the zone database, the original database is replaced with the copy.

If the primary server does not support incremental transfers, it simply ignores the incremental request of the secondary server and performs a full zone transfer.

AD Replication

AD integrated zones are able to piggyback off of the standard AD replication scheme already in place on the network. Therefore, you do not have to manage a separate replication scheme for DNS data as you would if you used standard primary and secondary servers. AD replication is covered in Chapter 12.

Installing DNS

Installing DNS is quite easy. With Windows 2000 already installed, follow these steps:

1. Select Control Panel|Add/Remove Programs|Add/Remove Windows Components.

2. When the Windows Components Wizard launches, navigate to Networking Services.

3. Highlight Networking Services and click on Details.

4. Select the Domain Name System (DNS) checkbox and click on OK.

After you've installed DNS, the real work comes in configuring it for use on your Windows 2000 network.

Configuring DNS

There are a several configuration issues to consider when setting up DNS, such as:

➤ Root servers

➤ Forward lookup zones

➤ Reverse lookup zones

➤ Resource records

➤ Dynamic DNS (DDNS)

Root Servers

When you initially launch the DNS Microsoft Management Console (MMC) snap-in after installing the DNS service, a configuration wizard opens. You initially have the option of configuring your server as a root server. Root servers on the Internet are authoritative for the entire DNS namespace. Obviously, you would not be able to create a root server that is authoritative for the entire Internet, so you should only create a root server if your network is not connected to the Internet. If your LAN is not connected to the Internet and you create a root server, the root server is authoritative for any namespace you create in the AD forest.

Forward Lookup Zones

For DNS services to work, at least one forward lookup zone must be configured on your server. The reason is that forward lookup zones are what enable forward lookup queries, the standard method of name resolution in DNS, to work. Forward lookup zones allow computers to resolve hostnames to IP addresses.

To create a forward lookup zone, right-click on Forward Lookup Zones in the DNS MMC console and click on New Zone. A configuration wizard launches.

The first choice you have to make when configuring a new zone is what type of zone it will be. The choices are as follows:

➤ Active Directory Integrated

➤ Standard Primary

➤ Standard Secondary

The zones correspond with the types of name servers discussed previously in this chapter. If you have not installed AD yet (which isn't required for DNS), the AD integrated option will be grayed out. In many cases, it is easier to configure DNS before installing AD, then create the zones as primary and secondary zones, and finally convert them to AD integrated zones after installing AD. The reason is that installing both at the same time requires configuring two major services and significant network changes simultaneously. Instead, you should take on one task at a time, which makes troubleshooting much easier in the event of problems.

Unless you have a need to communicate with non-Windows 2000 DNS servers, you should use AD integrated zones whenever possible.

 You need to know when to use one type of AD integrated zone versus another.

Reverse Lookup Zones

A reverse lookup zone is not required for DNS services to function; however, you will want to create a reverse lookup zone to allow reverse lookup queries to function. Without a reverse lookup zone, troubleshooting tools such as NSLOOKUP that can resolve hostnames from IP addresses cannot work. Whereas forward lookup zones allow computers to resolve hostnames to IP addresses, reverse lookup zones allow computers to resolve IP addresses to hostnames. As with forward lookup zones, you have the option of creating AD integrated, standard primary, or standard secondary zones.

Unlike naming a forward lookup zone, you name a reverse lookup zone by its IP address. You can either type your network ID into the first field and watch the reverse lookup zone name automatically be created for you, or you can choose to type in the reverse lookup zone name into the second field following RFC conventions. The information text between the network ID and reverse lookup zone name fields describes how to name a reverse lookup zone.

As with forward lookup zones, if you are creating an AD integrated zone, you are done after supplying the zone name. With standard primary and standard secondary zones, you have to also supply the zone file name, which defaults to adding a .dns extension onto the end of your zone name. With a standard secondary zone, you have to list the IP addresses of the primary DNS servers with which the secondary zone should communicate.

With your zones configured and DNS services functioning, let's look at the entries, known as resource records, you'll find within the server.

Resource Records

Resource records (RRs) are the basic units of information within DNS that are used to resolve all DNS queries. When the Windows 2000 DNS service starts up, a number of records are registered at the server.

Several common RRs are used with Windows 2000 DNS:

➤ Start of Authority (SOA)

➤ Name Server (NS)

➤ Address (A)

➤ Pointer (PTR)

➤ Mail Exchanger (MX)

➤ Service (SRV)

➤ Canonical Name (CNAME)

Start of Authority (SOA)

The SOA record is contained at the beginning of every zone, both forward lookup and reverse lookup. It defines a number of details for the zone, such as:

➤ *Time-to-live (TTL)*—The amount of time that a record is considered valid in the DNS database. Higher values reduce network bandwidth utilization but increase the possibility of outdated information existing.

➤ *Authoritative server*—Shows the primary DNS server that is authoritative for the zone.

➤ *Responsible person*—Shows the email address of the person who administers the zone.

➤ *Serial number*—Shows the serial number of the zone. Remember that the serial number is incremented whenever an update is made and that secondary servers use serial numbers to determine whether their copy of the zone database is out of date.

➤ *Refresh*—Shows how often secondary servers check to see if their zone database files need updating.

➤ *Retry*—Shows how long a secondary server will wait after sending an AXFR (full zone transfer for standard zones) or IXFR (incremental zone transfer for standard zones) request before resending the request.

➤ *Expire*—Shows how long after a zone transfer that a secondary server will respond to zone queries before discarding the zone as invalid because of no communication with the primary server.

➤ *Minimum TTL*—Shows the minimum TTL a resource record will use if it does not explicitly state a TTL value.

Name Server (NS)

NS records show all servers that are authoritative for a zone, both primary and secondary servers for the zone specified in the SOA record, and primary name servers for any delegated zones.

Address (A)

The most basic entry in DNS, the A record maps the FQDN of a host to its IP address. When a client sends a standard forward lookup name resolution query, the server uses A records to resolve the name.

Pointer (PTR)

The opposite of A records, PTR records provide reverse lookup services for DNS. That is, a PTR record maps an IP address to an FQDN. When a reverse lookup query is sent to a DNS server, such as through the NSLOOKUP utility, PTR records are consulted to resolve the address. PTR records are mapped in reverse lookup zones, which are in the in-addr.arpa zone.

Mail Exchanger (MX)

MX records designate a mail exchanging server for a DNS zone, which is a host that processes or forwards email. In addition to the standard Owner, Class, and Type fields, MX records also support a fourth field: Mail Server Priority. This field is used when you have multiple mail servers in your domain, and mail exchangers with lower values are "preferred" over mail exchangers with higher values when determining which server to use to process an email message.

Service (SRV)

SRV records allow you to specify the location of servers providing a particular service, such as Web servers. You can create SRV records to identify hosts in the zone that provide a service, and then a resolver can find the A record of a service to resolve the name.

If you are having trouble with name resolution services where clients cannot successfully contact DCs, ensure that the appropriate SRV records exist for the DCs on the network.

Canonical Name (CNAME)

A *CNAME record* creates an alias for a specified host. This type of record is used most commonly to hide implementation details of your network. For example, say you have a Web server running at **www.mycorp.com**. The server that the Web site is running on might really be server1.mycorp.com. You don't want users to have to use the real server name, and you want the flexibility of being able to move the Web site to a newer, faster server in the future as traffic grows, without having to change the address of your Web site from server1.mycorp.com to server2.mycorp.com. CNAME provides the ability to alias the hostname so problems like that do not occur.

Dynamic DNS (DDNS)

DDNS, defined in RFC 2136, is used in Windows 2000 in conjunction with DHCP. When a Windows 2000 client boots up and receives addressing information from DHCP, it can register itself with DNS, automatically adding the requisite resource records.

Dynamic Updates

DDNS is enabled/disabled through zone properties. To do so, open the DNS MMC console from the Start menu, right-click on your forward or reverse lookup zone, and click on Properties. On the General property sheet is the Allow Dynamic Updates? option. Choices are Yes, No, and Only Secure Updates. When DDNS is enabled, DHCP manages the resource records for DHCP clients. When a DHCP lease expires, the DHCP service cleans up the A and PTR records from DNS. By default, dynamic update is performed from Windows 2000 clients every 24 hours, or immediately when one of the following occurs:

➤ A DHCP-obtained IP address is renewed or a new lease is obtained.

➤ A static IP address is added or removed from a computer.

➤ The TCP/IP configuration of a client changes.

➤ A Plug and Play event occurs on a client, such as the installation of a new network adapter.

Secure Updates

In addition to enabling dynamic updates, you can configure Windows 2000 DNS to perform only secure updates. As we just said, this is enabled by selecting Only Secure Updates on the General property sheet of the desired zone. So what do secure updates do?

Once you have enabled secure updates, you can control which users and computers can register themselves into DNS. By default, all members of the Authenticated Users security group are granted permission, although this can be changed as necessary through access control lists (ACLs) by clicking on the Security tab on a zone's property sheet.

Dynamic update in general requires that the client computers be capable of registering an FQDN. Windows 2000 clients are capable of this; Windows NT and 9x clients are not. As we've previously discussed, Windows 2000 DHCP can act as a proxy for these legacy clients, because DHCP can register them in DNS on their behalf. The reason the FQDN consideration is important is that once you've enabled secure updates, you can reserve FQDNs in DNS so that only certain users can use them. To do this, create a new host record in the DNS console with the desired FQDN. Then, on the Security tab, configure the ACL so that only the desired user can update the resource records associated with the particular FQDN.

Note that all resource records for a single FQDN share a single ACL. In other words, if you create an A record for workstation1.inside-corner.com and then create an MX record for the same host, there is only one ACL for the two records. This would be true even if you added additional records for the same host.

Monitoring and Troubleshooting DNS for AD

As with any network service, most likely there will be times when some sort of problem occurs. Windows 2000 provides some tools to monitor and troubleshoot DNS, so there are steps you can take when the DNS service is not behaving as expected.

Figure 3.3 shows the monitoring options in Windows 2000. To reach this window:

1. Right-click on the DNS server you want to monitor in the DNS MMC snap-in and click on Properties.

2. Once there, click on the Monitoring tab. The options and their descriptions are as follows:

   ➤ *Simple query*—As the name implies, a simple forward lookup query is passed to the server for resolution. The results are either pass or fail, and time and date are stamped in the Test Results box at the bottom of the window.

   ➤ *Recursive query*—This is a more complex query where the server queries other servers until it can resolve the query or until it runs out of options and fails. With a recursive query, the name server cannot simply refer the client query to another name server.

   ➤ *Perform automatic testing*—This option tells the server to run the tests you choose at the interval you specify. This is helpful in troubleshooting intermittent server problems.

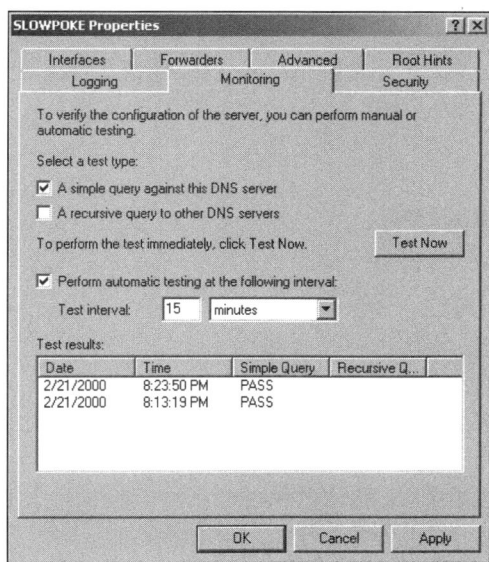

Figure 3.3   Windows 2000 enables an administrator to monitor the DNS service.

DNS Logging

In addition to monitoring, you can also enable logging of selected DNS events. When you install the DNS server service, Windows 2000 adds a log for DNS into the Event Viewer. If you enable logging, you can view the results there.

You configure logging through the Logging property sheet in the DNS server's properties, which is right next to the Monitoring tab previously discussed. Enable logging only for debugging/troubleshooting purposes, because the act of logging will have a negative impact on server performance and hard disk space. The Logging property sheet is shown in Figure 3.4. DNS log files are stored as dns.log in the \winnt\system32\dns folder.

NSLOOKUP

NSLOOKUP is the primary command-line tool for troubleshooting DNS. In addition, it makes a handy security tool for tracing hackers back to their source. If you have the TCP/IP protocol installed, this basic TCP/IP tool is already on your system.

Resolving Hostnames from IP Addresses

Remember that if you want NSLOOKUP to be able to resolve hostnames from IP addresses, you must have already configured a reverse lookup zone. NSLOOKUP

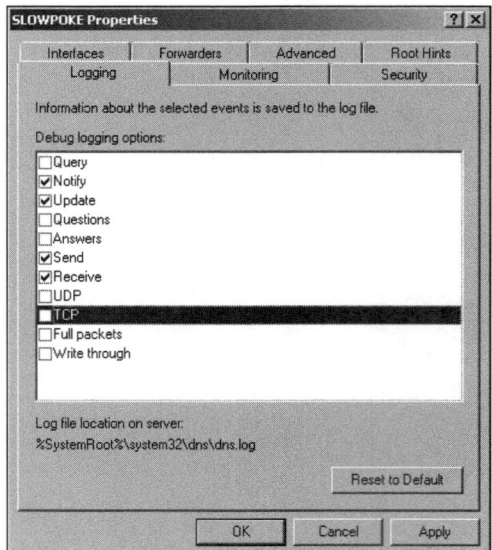

Figure 3.4   Logging is a useful troubleshooting tool when a DNS server is not responding as expected.

has two modes: noninteractive and interactive. In noninteractive, you simply enter a command such as:

```
C:\> nslookup 192.168.0.1 <enter>
```

If NSLOOKUP is successful, it returns the hostname associated with the IP address in question. There are a number of options for NSLOOKUP in noninteractive mode, accessible by typing "nslookup /?" at a command prompt. One of the more common options is -**server**, which allows you to specify a name server to test other than the current primary DNS server configured on the client.

You enter interactive mode just by typing "nslookup" at a command prompt and pressing Enter. To leave interactive mode, type "exit" at a prompt. Typically, you'll use interactive mode when you want more than a single piece of information returned or are running multiple queries one after another.

Verifying Resource Records

You can also use NSLOOKUP to verify the existence of resource records for troubleshooting purposes. For instance, if when workstations log in to a domain you get errors saying that a DC cannot be found, you could use NSLOOKUP to verify that the SRV and A records exist in DNS for the domain controllers. Figure 3.5 shows an example of using NSLOOKUP for this purpose.

Figure 3.5   You can troubleshoot DNS by verifying resource records with NSLOOKUP.

To view the registered SRV records for the inside-corner.com domain, enter NSLOOKUP interactive mode by typing "nslookup" from a command prompt and pressing enter. Then type the following:

```
ls -t SRV inside-corner.com
```

Note: *The syntax for this command is found on the NSLOOKUP help screen, which is accessed by typing "?" and pressing Enter from the NSLOOKUP console.*

This command as written lists all records (**ls**) of type (**-t**) **SRV** (service) for inside-corner.com (the domain in question). The output shows you if the domain controllers are properly registered.

 You should understand how to troubleshoot name resolution scenarios.

Practice Questions

Question 1

> Reorder the following events in setting up an AD network into their
> proper order:
>
> Run dcpromo.exe.
>
> Configure static IP address on DNS server.
>
> Install DNS.
>
> Configure forward lookup zone.

The correct answer is:

Configure static IP address on DNS server.

Install DNS.

Configure forward lookup zone.

Run dcpromo.exe.

Question 2

> Which of the following is not a reason to use AD integrated zones rather
> than standard zones?
>
> ○ a. Fault tolerance
>
> ○ b. Security
>
> ○ c. Simplicity of management
>
> ○ d. Database is stored in easy-to-edit text files

Answer d is correct. AD integrated zones store zone information within the AD
database. Answer d refers to standard zones, which store the DNS database in
text files that carry a .dns extension. Answers a, b, and c are incorrect because
fault tolerance, security, and simplicity of management are all legitimate reasons
to use AD integrated zones.

Question 3

Which of the following DC resource record types would you look for if trying to troubleshoot workstations not being able to log on to a domain? [Check all correct answers]

❑ a. A

❑ b. CNAME

❑ c. SRV

❑ d. MX

Answers a and c are correct. You would check for the proper registration of address and service records. Answer b is incorrect because CNAME records are aliases. Answer d is incorrect because MX records are for mail servers.

Question 4

The following are types of name servers:

Active Directory integrated

Standard primary and secondary

Match the following features with the name server type they are most associated with:

Single point of failure

Zone transfer

Fault tolerant

Replication

Text database

Secure

The correct answer is:

Active Directory integrated

Fault tolerant

Replication

Secure

Standard primary and secondary

Single point of failure

Zone transfer

Text database

Question 5

> Under which of the following circumstances could you use Windows 98
> clients in a dynamic update situation? [Choose the best answer]
>
> ○ a. When the Only Secure Updates option is enabled on the DNS
>   server.
>
> ○ b. When the Allow Dynamic Updates? option is set to Yes on the DNS
>   server.
>
> ○ c. When enabling the Enable Updates For DNS Clients That Do Not
>   Support Dynamic Updates option on the DHCP server.
>
> ○ d. Legacy clients cannot be supported by dynamic update.

Answer c is correct. By default, dynamic update is not supported by legacy clients; however, DHCP can be configured to act as a proxy on their behalf. Answers a and c are incorrect because simply enabling dynamic updating or secure
updates will not allow Windows 98 clients to register with DNS. Answer d is
incorrect because they can be supported.

Question 6

> Which of the following types of name servers store copies of a zone data-
> base? [Check all correct answers]
>
> ❑ a. AD integrated
>
> ❑ b. Caching
>
> ❑ c. Primary
>
> ❑ d. Secondary

Answers a, c, and d are correct. AD integrated, primary, and secondary name
servers all store copies of a zone database. Answer b is incorrect because caching
is the only type in the list that does not store an editable copy of a zone database.

Question 7

Which of the following name resolution methods use manually updated text files to record name mappings? [Check all correct answers]

❑ a. DNS

❑ b. HOSTS

❑ c. WINS

❑ d. LMHOSTS

Answers b and d are correct. HOSTS was a name-to-IP-address mapping system used prior to the advent of DNS on the Internet. LMHOSTS resolved NetBIOS names on Windows networks before WINS and later DNS. Answers a and c are incorrect because DNS and WINS are both dynamically updated databases, whereas HOSTS and LMHOSTS use text files to store their mappings.

Question 8

Which of the following elements is required to successfully install and configure DNS? [Choose the best answer]

○ a. DHCP

○ b. Static IP address

○ c. Active Directory

○ d. Windows 2000 clients

Answer b is correct. To install and configure a working DNS server, the server running DNS must have a static IP address. Answer a is incorrect because DHCP is not required to use DNS, though it is necessary if you want to enable dynamic update. Answer c is incorrect because Active Directory is not required. Answer d is incorrect because DNS works with legacy clients as well as Windows 2000 clients.

Question 9

When monitoring a DNS server, which type of test sends a query to other name servers for resolution? [Choose the best answer]

- ○ a. Simple query
- ○ b. Recursive query
- ○ c. Forward lookup query
- ○ d. Iterative query

Answer b is correct. A recursive query sends a resolution query to other servers when monitoring the server. Answer a is incorrect because a simple query resolves the name against only the server being tested. Answers c and d are incorrect because these are not valid choices for DNS monitoring.

Question 10

In a standard primary zone, what name server(s) can an administrator update the zone database on? [Choose the best answer]

- ○ a. Secondary
- ○ b. Active Directory integrated
- ○ c. Primary
- ○ d. Any server

Answer c is correct. In a standard primary zone, only the primary server can be updated directly. Answer a is incorrect because secondary servers receive updates through zone transfer. Answer b is incorrect because Active Directory integrated servers don't exist in a standard primary zone. Answer d is incorrect because only the primary server can be updated in this way.

Need to Know More?

 Iseminger, David. *Active Directory Services for Windows 2000 Technical Reference.* Microsoft Press, Redmond, WA, 2000. ISBN 0735606242. A solid reference for planning and deploying AD networks, this book has good coverage of DNS as it relates to AD.

 Microsoft Corporation. *Microsoft Windows 2000 Server Resource Kit.* Microsoft Press, Redmond, WA, 2000. ISBN 1572318058. The quintessential resource for Windows 2000 Server and AD, this kit has extensive coverage of AD and DNS in particular.

 Norris-Lowe, Alistair. *Windows 2000 Active Directory Service.* O'Reilly & Associates, Sebastopol, CA, 2000. ISBN 1565926382. Another good AD resource, this book contains good information on DNS planning and infrastructure issues.

 Willis, Will, David Watts, and Tillman Strahan. *Windows 2000 System Administration Handbook.* Prentice-Hall, Upper Saddle River, NJ, 2000. ISBN 0130270105. This handbook explains Windows 2000 systems administration concepts in detail, including building an AD network on a DNS foundation. This is a solid all-around Windows 2000 reference with good coverage of AD.

Planning and Installing Domains

Terms you'll need to understand:

✓ Workgroup

✓ Domain

✓ Member server

✓ Domain controller

✓ Scalability

✓ Forest root

✓ SYSVOL

✓ dcpromo

✓ Organizational Unit

✓ Active Directory (AD) integrated zones

Techniques you'll need to master:

✓ Planning for your AD install

✓ Installing your first AD domain

✓ Making installation decisions based upon your corporate needs

✓ Verifying and troubleshooting your AD installation

✓ Performing an unattended installation of AD

✓ Performing post-installation procedures

After the installation of Windows 2000 Server, Advanced Server, or DataCenter Server, the system will exist in one of two settings. The server will be a member server (or standalone server) of a workgroup, or it will be a member server of an existing domain. In either state, the server will have the capability of holding several roles. For example, a standalone server would be able to handle the sharing of folders and files, Web and media services, database services, print services—the list of functional uses is long. However, directory services are not part of a member server's functionality. For that reason, you may need to consider implementing a "domain" environment.

What are some of the immediate advantages of a domain environment? Perhaps your company requires a single point of logon, centralized management of resources, and scalability, or the ability of your network and directory infrastructure to grow with your company over time. Making that first move toward a domain begins with establishing your first domain controller (DC). To accomplish this with Windows 2000, you need to install the Windows 2000 Active Directory (AD) service and configure it properly to suit your company's needs. This endeavor requires some forethought and planning to allow for a smooth domain deployment.

The Windows 2000 Domain

Domains are not new to the networking vernacular. The way Windows 2000 utilizes the concept, however, is quite advanced. The Windows 2000 domain is defined as being a boundary for security that provides an organized means of structuring users, resources, and directory information. It also provides a method for replicating that information, and it provides the core administrative services in a Windows 2000 network. In Windows 2000, only one directory database, called the AD, stores all of the user accounts and other resources for the domain. This centralized structure means that users need only have one account that will provide access to all resources for which they are given permission.

In the actual creation of a domain, you identify a Domain Name System (DNS) name for the domain. This requires some planning, in harmony with the material in Chapter 3, to choose a name that is appropriate from both a corporate and legal standpoint. Windows 2000 domains utilize the DNS naming convention to maintain an organized structure. Because the first domain created will be the top-level domain in your directories' infrastructure, this domain is the most crucial, especially if you will be implementing additional domains in the network. Another term for the first domain is the *root domain,* so named because it is the root of the entire domain tree and, by extension, the entire forest.

Even though it is small, a single domain without child domains is still considered its own domain tree. In addition, this single domain is called the *forest root* because it becomes the first tree of a possible new forest. The forest root can be likened to the foundation of a building, which holds up the rest of the structure. The foundation of a domain must be solid, and it begins by the promotion of a member server to be a domain controller. You accomplish this promotion by installing AD. Before installation can proceed, however, you must ensure that certain requirements have been met on the server that will be your DC.

Requirements for AD

Whenever you implement a new feature within a Windows product, there are minimum hardware and software requirements so that the features will work adequately. The first requirement is fairly obvious: You must have a computer running Windows 2000 Server, Advanced Server, or DataCenter Server. Meeting this AD requirement ensures that your system meets the minimum hardware for your operating system.

The following list identifies the requirements for the installation of Windows 2000 Server:

➤ *CPU*—Pentium 133MHz or higher

➤ *Memory*—256MB recommended (128MB supported)

➤ *Hard disk space*—2GB with 1GB of free space

➤ *Display*—VGA resolution or higher

➤ *CD-ROM or network installation*—Supported

 Windows 2000 Server will install with 64MB of RAM, but it won't perform well with less than 128MB, so the preceding requirements have been provided by Microsoft.

Once the operating system is installed, the following requirements are necessary to install AD:

➤ Depending on the partition of the hard disk where you plan to install your AD database and transaction log files, you will need 200MB for the database and 50MB for the transaction log. The files can reside on a partition that is formatted with the FAT (file allocation table), FAT32, and NTFS (NT File System) file systems. These files will grow over time and as more objects are added, so you need to ensure the space is sufficient. Additional space is required if your DC is also configured to be a Global Catalog server.

➤ Along with the database and transaction logs, a special folder structure is installed during the installation, and the root folder is called SYSVOL. This folder must reside on an NTFS partition. If your system doesn't have an NTFS partition, then the AD installation will fail.

*Note: If you would like to install your SYSVOL folder on a partition that you already have allocated as FAT, and you cannot reformat the partition without losing critical data (as in the case of your boot and system partition), then you need to use the **convert** command. Go to a command prompt and type "convert.exe c: /fs:ntfs".*

➤ Another requirement is that your system is functioning under TCP/IP and utilizing a Domain Name System (DNS) server. If you've forgotten to establish a DNS server, this will be provided as an option during AD installation.

Once you've established that your server meets the requirements to install AD and you have invested the necessary time in planning your first DC, it's time to kick off the installation.

The AD Installation Wizard

The actual creation of the first domain of your network is not a difficult task. You are simply promoting a Windows 2000 Server to be a domain controller by using the AD Installation Wizard. You are creating your forest root as the first DC of your new domain.

Running the Wizard

The AD Installation Wizard, unlike some wizards, does not have an icon or shortcut to execute; it requires that you select Start|Run. In the box, type "dcpromo.exe" (or just "dcpromo" for short), and hit Enter.

This wizard offers the following directory service installation options:

➤ Create a domain controller for a new domain.

➤ Create a new domain tree or join an existing domain as a child domain.

➤ Create a new forest of domain trees or join an existing forest.

Let's consider the different areas of the wizard.

Installing Your First Domain

To install the first DC by promoting a member server, follow these steps:

Note: If you install Windows 2000 on a server that is a primary or backup domain controller for an NT 4 domain, upgrading the server will automatically upgrade to a Windows 2000 DC and will include the user and group accounts and configurations, unless you specify that the install is not an upgrade of the NT 4 domain controller.

1. Begin the promotion by selecting Start|Run and typing "dcpromo.exe". Hit Enter.

2. Once your AD Installation Wizard has initialized, you will see a screen that welcomes you to the wizard. Select Next.

3. As shown in Figure 4.1, you are presented with two options: creating a DC of a new domain (either a child domain, new domain tree, or new forest), or creating an additional DC for an existing domain (which will take on the account information of the domain joined). Because this is the first domain of a new forest, select the first radio button and hit the Next button.

4. You are now asked if you want to create a new domain tree or create a new child domain in an existing domain tree, as shown in Figure 4.2. In the case of creating a new tree, you select the first radio button and hit the Next button.

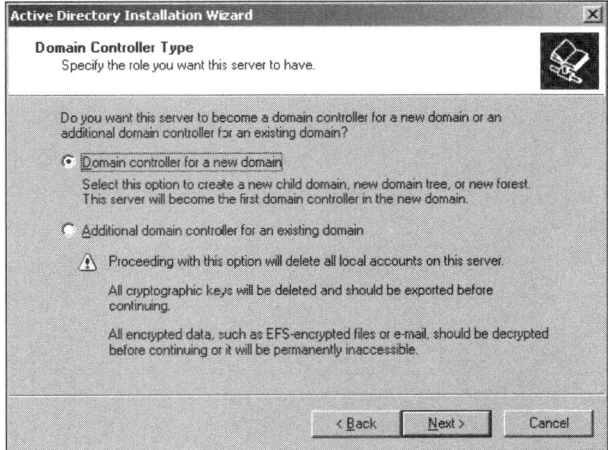

Figure 4.1 Domain Controller Type screen.

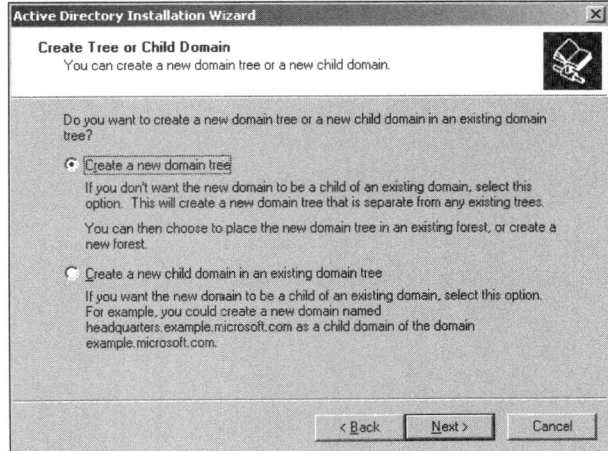

Figure 4.2 Create a new tree or a child domain.

5. The next screen in the wizard asks if you want to create a new forest of domain trees or place the new domain tree in an existing forest, as shown in Figure 4.3. Again, to create the first domain (also considered the forest root domain), select the first radio button and hit the Next button.

6. This next screen is short, as shown in Figure 4.4. You are asked to supply the full DNS name of your domain. If you've planned your naming strategy and registered a name for your company's domain, use that name. If you are implementing your directory structure in a test environment without a registered domain name, use a fictitious DNS name. Hit the Next button.

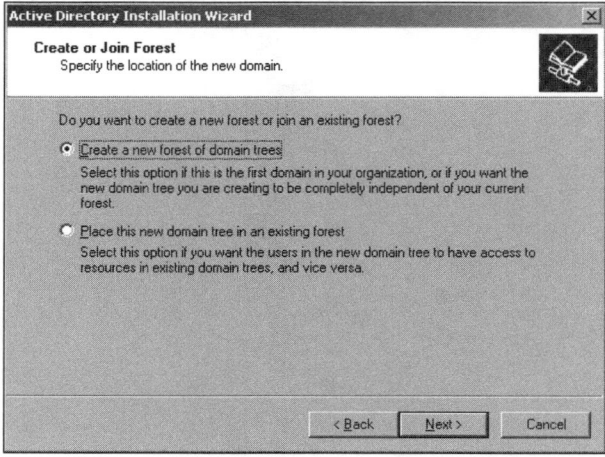

Figure 4.3 Create a new forest or join an existing forest.

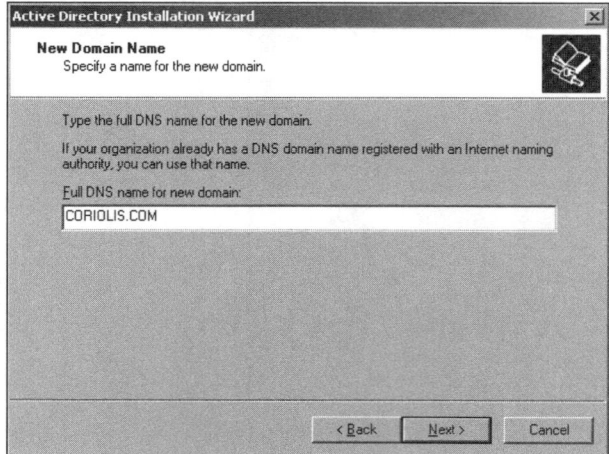

Figure 4.4 Your forest root domain name.

7. Your next screen requests your NetBIOS name. This name is used for clients running earlier versions of Windows or NT that utilize NetBIOS for their location of DCs. It is usually the same as the first part of your domain name. Enter the name and hit the Next button.

8. The next screen, shown in Figure 4.5, specifies the location of the AD database and log files. These files can exist on any of the supported files systems for Windows 2000. Remember, the minimum requirement for AD is 200MB for the database and 50MB for the log files. Also, remember that minimum requirements should usually be exceeded to allow for flexibility and growth. Choose your location, and then hit the Next button.

Note: Placing your database files and your log files on separate hard drives is recommended. Your database holds your directory, whereas your log file holds your temporary database changes before they are written to the actual database. This creates a conflict of interest for your hard drive as information is written back and forth. Placing the files on different drives (not partitions) will ensure equal time to both files.

9. The next screen, shown in Figure 4.6, is quite important and necessary to your AD installation. Here you specify the location for the SYSVOL folder. This folder, which will be shared, allows the DCs to receive replicas of the information within. Therefore, it must be on an NTFS partition. Indicate the location of this folder, and then hit the Next button.

10. The next screen allows you to specify the password for the administrative account that is used during Directory Services Restore Mode. Because the AD service is not started when entering this mode, it will be necessary for

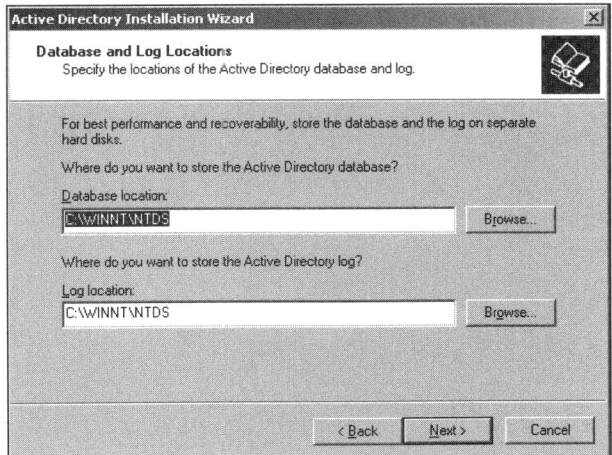

Figure 4.5 Database and log files.

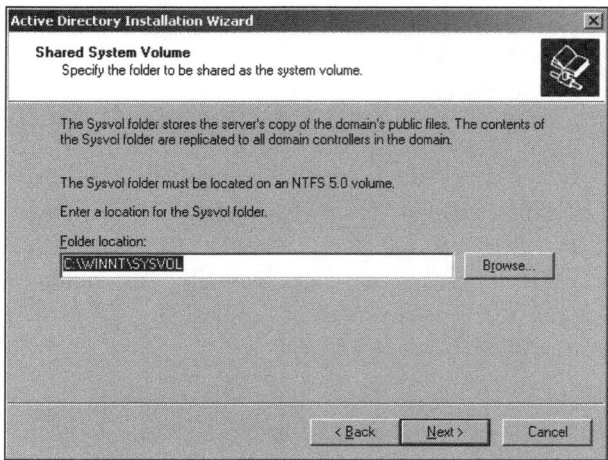

Figure 4.6   The placement of the SYSVOL folder.

you to be authenticated by the server through another means. A non-AD database containing the administrator's name and password allows authentication under these circumstances. Specify your administrative password, and then hit the Next button.

11. This final question screen, shown in Figure 4.7, asks whether you want to allow permissions to be compatible with pre-Windows 2000 servers or if you want to allow Windows 2000-compatible permissions only. The first selection comes with a warning. If you enable this option, anonymous users will be able to read information on the domain. This can be beneficial in some cases—for example, if you are migrating toward Windows 2000 from

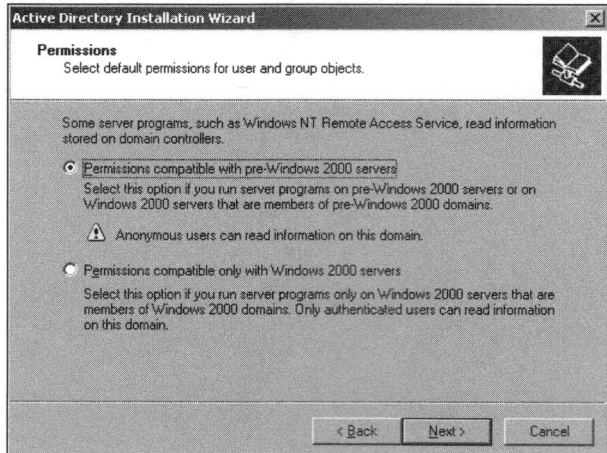

Figure 4.7   Permissions compatibility screen.

an NT 4 platform and will have a mixed environment of remote access servers. With this type of situation, your users dialing in from home will have difficulty logging in to the domain if they contact a Windows 2000 DC, unless the permissions are oriented toward a pre-Windows 2000 system. Select your choice, and then hit the Next button.

12. When all of your information is complete, you get the final screen, shown in Figure 4.8, which is customized to your choices. Look them over before hitting the Next button. Then the installation will follow through until you see a final screen of completion, where you should hit Finish.

Your installation will now proceed by establishing your system as the first DC for your new domain tree under a new forest root.

Deciding which Type of DNS to Use

As already mentioned, having a DNS server for your AD installation is a prerequisite. However, you may determine which type of DNS server you will use. Although your choices are limited, they do exist, as discussed in Chapter 3. Let's assume that you haven't made your decision by the time you install AD. Not a problem—Windows 2000 will make the decision for you.

After you've indicated the location of the SYSVOL folder, the wizard will begin a search for the DNS in the IP stack to see if it exists and if it supports dynamic updates. In our scenario, a DNS server doesn't exist, and you will therefore receive an informative prompt that it will be created for you. Hit OK at this point.

The screen that follows asks whether you want the DNS configured and installed on this computer or if you want to install it yourself, as shown in Figure 4.9.

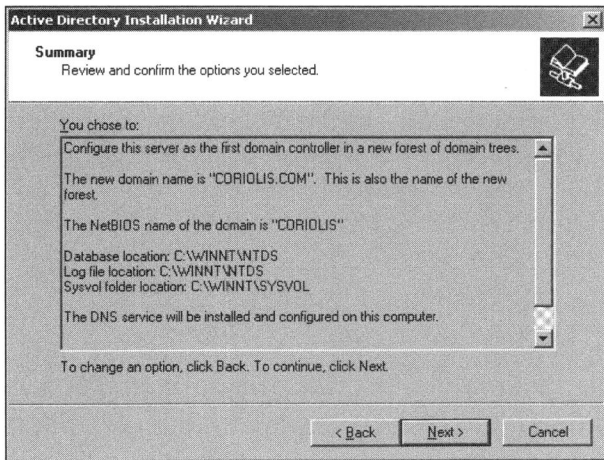

Figure 4.8 The final promotion screen.

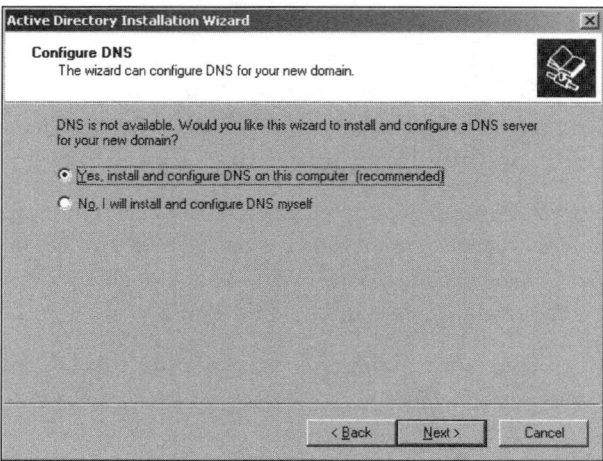

Figure 4.9 The Configure DNS screen.

Once the DNS is configured and it supports the dynamic updates (which would be automatically done during the installation), the rest of your installation proceeds.

Note: AD Installation does not automatically set the DNS to allow automatic updates unless you tell the wizard to do so. Microsoft recommends that you set this or allow the AD Installation Wizard set it for you if the wizard is also installing DNS as part of AD installation. However, AD will work without enabling dynamic updates. If you do not allow dynamic updates, you have to manually synchronize the SRV resource records when you add or remove additional domain controllers.

The Lesser-Known Roles of the Wizard

On the surface, the AD Installation Wizard appears merely to handle the various screens that require user input. However, this understates its full role. Prior to an installation, the wizard performs the following checks:

1. Before the wizard even opens, it makes sure that the user is a member of the local Administrators group and is on a Windows 2000 Server. It also checks that the server is ready to move forward without needing to reboot or complete some previously begun procedure. If the User Interface portion clears, the wizard moves on.

2. The wizard verifies that the NetBIOS and server name are unique.

3. The wizard checks TCP/IP configuration to ensure that the system is fully functional and capable of reaching the DNS server. That DNS server must be able to provide dynamic updates or have manually provided a server (SRV) resource record within your DNS; otherwise, the AD Installation Wizard will prompt you later to create a DNS server.

4. The wizard checks to ensure uniqueness, then validates DNS and NetBIOS domain names.

5. The final stages of verification involve checking the user's credentials to ensure that the user has the correct security permissions, and finally, that the files can be located where you've specified.

In configuring the directory service, the AD Installation Wizard handles the following tasks:

➤ Registry changes for the AD

➤ Setting up Kerberos

➤ Setting the Local Security Authority (LSA) policy

➤ Placing the new tools into Administrative Tools (accessed through Start| Programs|Administrative Tools).

➤ Establishing performance counters for AD

➤ Setting up X.509 certificate acceptance

In addition, depending on the installation, the wizard might create the schema directory partition, the configuration directory partition, and the domain directory partition, which are portions of the directory that are held in a hierarchical fashion and replicated out to other DCs.

Fault-Tolerant Replicas

The concept of fault-tolerant replicas is simple: It refers to creating additional DCs within a single domain tree. Additional DCs in a domain help share the load and improve performance. They also provide fault tolerance, because if one DC goes down, the other DCs can authenticate the users and provide normal operations while the damaged DC is repaired.

When adding more DCs to a domain, keep the following factors in mind:

➤ The more DCs that you have in a domain, the greater the logon authenticity, because when users log on to the domain, they can gain authentication from any one of the DCs.

➤ Each of the DCs will replicate or share its copy of the AD database with the other DCs in the domain. Adding more DCs to a domain also increases the following, thereby degrading network performance:

> ➤ The amount of replication that takes place within the domain

> ➤ The amount of bandwidth that is used on the network

When deciding how many DCs are going to be on the domain, you must consider both of these factors. You need to balance increased speed of logon authenticity against bandwidth usage due to directory replication.

Adding DCs to a domain is not a difficult task. Starting with a Windows 2000 Server, you promote it using the **dcpromo.exe** command, which executes the AD Installation Wizard. Instead of selecting Domain Controller For A New Domain, you select Additional Domain Controller For An Existing Domain (refer back to Figure 4.1).

Once you have created the first domain, you are in a position to create Organizational Units (OUs) within the domain. But how do you know that your installation was a successful one? This topic is discussed in the next section.

Troubleshooting Your AD Installation

Any number of things can cause your AD installation to fail. Here are a few scenarios:

➤ *You get an Access Denied error message when creating or adding DCs.* These types of error messages usually indicate an incorrect user account. Perhaps you have logged on with an account that doesn't have permissions in the Local Administrators group of the server on which you are trying to create a new domain. Or, as in the case of adding a DC to a pre-existing domain, it's possible that you are not a member of the Domain Administrators group.

 Be conscious of situations where you are not a member of the Domain Administrators group, especially if you are asked about the accounts needed to install AD on a system.

➤ *Your DNS and NetBIOS names are not unique.* Not much of a choice here; you must have unique names, so you need to change them to names that are unique. The only exception to this rule would be in the case of a testing/training situation (where you are testing the various options for domain structure in a lab environment—not a production environment, we hope) where you've added systems to the domain and then failed to remove them correctly, perhaps by merely formatting the drive. Now your AD domain tree might still see these nonexistent names as being present. To resolve this problem, you need to edit AD with some additional tools that Microsoft provides, such as ADSI Edit, a snap-in for the Microsoft Management Console (MMC) that acts as a low-level AD Editor.

➤ *The DC cannot be contacted, and you are sure that there is a DC up and running.* This situation might indicate that DNS is not set up correctly. Several areas of concern with DNS have already been discussed, but you should ensure that SRV resource records are present for the domain being contacted. Check your DNS server first to make certain that these records exist. If they do exist, then use the NSLOOKUP tool to determine if you can resolve DNS names on the computer where you are installing AD.

➤ Y*ou have an insufficient amount of disk space or you don't have an NTFS partition.* You must have a minimum disk space of 250MB for the database and transaction logs. You must also have an NTFS partition for the SYSVOL folder. If you can't free enough space, consider using another volume or partition to store these files. If you do not have an NTFS partition and cannot create one, you need to convert your existing partition. If you are running Windows 2000 Server in a dual-boot situation with Windows 98 on a FAT32 partition, you will not be able to make the move toward a DC and retain your Windows 98 operating system under FAT32; you must convert your partition or remain a member server with FAT32.

Note: *Microsoft does not recommend having a Windows 2000 Server in a dual-boot configuration.*

Verifying Your AD Installation

Once your installation is complete and the system has rebooted, you may want to verify your installation. Verification can be accomplished in a number of ways, the easiest being a check of your newly acquired Administrative Tools. However, you have a few other options to ensure a valid install.

File Verification

One way to verify that your installation is complete is to ensure that the AD files are located where you've specified. The following is a list of files that are necessary for AD:

➤ *nts.dit*—The directory database file.

➤ *edb.log and edb.chk*—The EDB files are the transaction logs and the checkpoint files. Transaction logs temporarily hold transactions before they are written to the directory. The checkpoint file is a pointer file that tracks transaction logs once they have been committed to the database. These files work in harmony to ensure an accurate database with multiple points of strength.

➤ *res1.log and res2.log*—The RES files are reserved files that are used for low disk-space situations. These two files are 10MB in size, as are all transaction logs.

Because these are permanent, there is always a way to write to a file, even when disk space is low.

SYSVOL

Another way to make sure you've had a successful install is to make sure that the SYSVOL folder structure is on an NTFS partition and contains a server copy of all shared files, including Group Policy and scripts. The SYSVOL folder should include several subfolders, including:

➤ Domain

➤ Staging

➤ Staging Areas

➤ Sysvol

The Sysvol folder within should be shared out as, you guessed it, SYSVOL. Another necessary folder that should be shared is the Scripts folder under the Domain folder, which is under the SYSVOL folder. The Scripts folder is shared out as NETLOGON and is used for backward compatibility with NT systems that search for scripts during logon in the NETLOGON share.

Final Checkpoints

There are many avenues you can investigate to ensure that an AD install was successful, but the most direct method is to check within the event logs. Event logs retain several different types of logs that help you quickly pinpoint a failure, whether on the system itself or with one of the services, like DNS.

If DNS doesn't seem to be functioning properly, refer to Chapter 3, which focuses on several tools to troubleshoot your DNS installation (such as verifying records with the NSLOOKUP tool and monitoring your DNS forward and recursive queries within the DNS properties on the Monitoring tab).

AD Removal

At times, you might want to remove your AD, especially if you've done some restructuring of your accounts and find that some domains are causing unnecessary strains or if certain DCs are simply not required and are creating a strain on the network because of an overabundance of replication. You remove AD with the same tool that you used to install it—the AD Installation Wizard. Logically, not just any user can remove AD from the DC. If you are the last DC in the forest, then you must be logged on as a member of the Domain Administrators group. If you are not removing the last DC in the forest, then you must be a member of either the Domain Administrators group or the Enterprise Administrators group.

What Removing AD Entails

When you remove AD, the following actions occur (which are reversals of what took place when you installed AD):

➤ Group Policy security settings are removed, and Local Security is reenabled for local security settings.

➤ Any Flexible Single Master Operations (FSMO) roles are transferred over to other DCs, if any exist.

➤ The SYSVOL folder hierarchy is removed, along with any related items within, including the NETLOGON share.

➤ The DNS is updated to remove DC Locator service records.

➤ The local Security Accounts Manager (SAM) is now used for user authentication.

➤ Services that are related to AD are stopped and configured not to start automatically.

➤ If there is another DC, final changes are replicated to that controller before AD is shut down. The system that is removing AD will notify the remaining DCs to remove it from the DC's OU.

Troubleshooting AD Removal

Follow these hints if you run into problems during AD removal:

➤ If your DC cannot verify that there are no child domains existing and you believe that there aren't any, then you probably had these child domains at one time and failed to remove them the correct way from the domain. Your AD database still holds records for these domains, whereas they have been physically taken offline. Now your DC won't allow you to uninstall without cleaning these out with some effort and searching.

➤ If you cannot connect to a DC in the parent domain to replicate changes, your removal may not proceed smoothly or any final changes may not replicate. In either case, your parent DC would not be notified properly of the removal, and a similar dilemma to the preceding one would exist.

Now that we've covered the usual procedures for installation and removal of AD, let's go back and explore some other types of installation, such as unattended installation of AD.

Unattended Installation of AD

An unattended installation is not a new idea, although the AD portion of it is completely new. The concept is simple: Instead of manually answering the questions posed in dialog boxes during installation, an unattended installation of Windows 2000 provides all of the answers to the installation questions automatically. These questions are answered through the use of an answer file and usually a UDF file so that both the standard questions and the unique ones are given responses without human intervention.

Because the installation of Windows 2000 Server only completes to the point where the server is assigned as either a member server of a workgroup or a member server of a domain, the final portion of the installation, the promotion, is still manually handled. Microsoft, however, has established a method of directory services installation that can be either completely automated from start to finish or can at least automate the promotion to AD.

The installation of Windows 2000 Server is not our primary concern at this point, although you should have a thorough understanding of the two executable programs that begin the installation (namely, winnt.exe and winnt32.exe) and the various switches that allow for the selection of an answer file and a UDF (uniqueness database file) file for an unattended installation. You should also know that the Setup Manager program (which can be found in the *Windows 2000 Resource Kit*, officially titled setupmgr.exe) is used to create these important files. Finally, you should be aware that you can automate the installation of AD in one of these ways:

➤ You can provide additional information within the answer file that is used to automate the installation of Windows 2000.

➤ You can create a separate answer file to be run in conjunction with the dcpromo.exe program.

Regardless of the option you choose, the command executed is the same:

```
dcpromo /answer:<answer file>
```

The GuiRunOnce Section

To automate complete installation of both the operating system and AD, you will need to make some configuration changes to the answer file under a section called [GuiRunOnce]. This section contains a list of commands to be executed the first time a user logs on to the computer after GUI (graphical user interface) mode Setup has completed. Each line specifies a command to be executed by the GuiRunOnce entry. One of those entries could include the command to begin the AD Installation Wizard with dcpromo.exe. In addition, the command could include the request to reach out for another answer file (named by the administrator who created it) so that the installation creates a complete DC under Windows 2000.

A side point to keep in mind when running commands using the **GuiRunOnce** key is that they will run in the context of the user that is currently logged in. Therefore, the user must have the permissions to run such a command. However, this is usually not an issue in establishing a complete unattended installation of Windows 2000 Server with AD.

Here is a sample of an unattended installation file that uses the **GuiRunOnce** key to search for the AD answer file:

```
[Unattended]
  OemSkipEula = Yes

[GuiUnattended]
  AutoLogon = Yes
  AdminPassword = *
  OEMSkipRegional = 1
  OemSkipWelcome = 1
  TimeZone = 33

[UserData]
  FullName = "Polo DC Servers"
  OrgName = "Polo Fuzzball Suppliers, Inc."
  ComputerName = DC-Polo1

[LicenseFilePrintData]
  AutoMode = PerSeat

[GuiRunOnce]
  Command0 = "dcpromo /answer:dcanswer.txt"

[Identification]
  DomainAdmin = "CORPDOM\InstallAcct"
  DomainAdminPassword = 12345678A
  JoinDomain = "POLODOM"
```

Logically, if the unattended file can contain a line that utilizes **dcpromo** with an answer file for AD, two things must be true. First, you must create that AD answer file, or the command won't work. Second, you can utilize that answer file at any time by typing in the command and path from the Run option in the Start menu.

The DCInstall Section

This section of the answer file is necessary for the AD Installation Wizard to have its questions answered automatically. Below this section are many keys that hold values that allow for the questions to be answered without human intervention. If a key doesn't have a value specified, a default value will be used. Here are descriptions of a few of the keys; their values and defaults are listed in Table 4.1:

Note: The keys are listed alphabetically, not according to the order in which they are used in the answer file. This is an abbreviated list of important keys. To learn a great deal more about unattended installation files and the keys involved, refer to the \Support\Tools folder on the Windows 2000 installation CD. When executed, the deploy.cab file allows you to view a document called unattend.doc. This document contains about 150 pages of information on unattended installs.

➤ **AutoConfigDNS**—Answers the question as to whether or not DNS should be configured automatically, if dynamic DNS updates aren't available.

➤ **ChildName**—Indicates the name of the child domain. This name would be added to the portion of the domain name that is the parent domain. For example, if the domain you are joining is coriolis.com and the name specified here is sales, then the total domain would be sales.coriolis.com.

➤ **CreateOrJoin**—Indicates whether the new domain that is created is part of an existing forest or would become a separate forest of domains.

➤ **DatabasePath**—Specifies the location of the database files. Logically, enough disk space should be available on the disk that you specify. As mentioned in the "Deciding Which Type of DNS to Use" section earlier in this chapter, for

Table 4.1   Values and defaults of keys.

Key	Value	Default
AutoConfigDNS	Yes | No	Yes
ChildName	*<child domain name>*	—
CreateOrJoin	Create | Join	Join
DatabasePath	*<path to database files>*	"*%systemroot%*\NTDS"
DomainNetBiosName	*<domain NetBIOS name>*	—
LogPath	*<path to log files>*	"*%systemroot%*\NTDS"
NewDomainDNSName	*<DNS name of domain>*	—
ReplicaDomainDNSName	*<DNS name of domain>*	—
ReplicaOrNewDomain	Replica | Domain	Replica
SysVolPath	*<path to database file>*	"*%systemroot%*\sysvol"
TreeOrChild	Tree | Child	Child

performance purposes, placing the database files on a separate disk than the log files is best.

➤ **DomainNetBiosName**—Indicates the NetBIOS name within the domain. Must be a unique name.

➤ **LogPath**—Specifies the location of the log files. Logically, enough disk space should be available on the disk that you specify. As mentioned in the "Deciding Which Type of DNS to Use" section earlier in this chapter, for performance purposes, placing the database files on a separate disk than the database files is best.

➤ **NewDomainDNSName**—Specifies the full name of a new tree within a preexisting domain, or it could also specify the full name when a new forest is being created.

➤ **ReplicaDomainDNSName**—Indicates the DNS name of the domain that will be replicated from. This name must be accurate because the installation will search for the DC that is considered its replication point of contact. That DC must be up and running to handle the request for the replication.

➤ **ReplicaOrNewDomain**—Indicates whether a new DC will be the first DC of a new domain or if it will be a replica of a preexisting domain.

➤ **SysVolPath**—Provides the path for the Sysvol folder structure. By extension, the path must lead toward an NTFS version 5 partition for the install to be functional.

➤ **TreeOrChild**—Indicates whether the new domain will be a root domain of a new tree or if it will become a child domain beneath a preexisting parent domain.

You may be wondering if remembering all of these options is absolutely necessary. That is not the reason they are listed. These are only a portion of the entire list of options that you can research when and if you plan on creating your unattended installation file for AD. They are provided to help you realize the amount of work that can go into setting up the file correctly so that it deploys smoothly.

Post-AD Installation Options

Once AD is installed and running correctly, there are several different options that you might want to investigate.

Integrated Zones

Now that AD is installed, perhaps you would like to implement AD integrated zones within your DNS structure. Integrated zones allow the DNS zone files to be replicated by the AD replication engine, as opposed to being replicated through

DNS zone transfers, because the zone database files will be included within AD rather than stored in their usual systemroot/System32/DNS folder.

Once your server is supporting AD integrated zones, you will be able to configure your zones for secure dynamic updates with the DNS Secure Update Protocol. This will allow a greater level of security on your DNS updates.

Domain Mode Options

Windows 2000 supports two different types of domain modes: mixed mode and native mode. Upon first installing or upgrading your domain to Windows 2000, you will be running in mixed mode. You may decide to change over to native mode, however, to take advantage of added functionality that becomes available. The differences between the two modes are described in the following sections.

Mixed Mode

Mixed mode is used for supporting DCs that are NT 4 controllers. While moving your current structure toward Windows 2000, there may be a period of time where you will continue to use NT 4 backup domain controllers (BDCs), and by running in mixed mode, the Windows 2000 DCs will be able to synchronize information. Although there is no timetable for how long you must run in mixed mode, Microsoft recommends that you switch to native mode when you no longer have NT 4 DCs in your domain so that you can take advantage of native mode's additional functionality.

Note: You can continue to run in mixed mode even if there are no NT 4 DCs in the domain. Also, you can make the move toward native mode even if you still have remaining NT 4 member servers present in your domain because they do not require the synchronization between the servers.

Native Mode

If you are installing Windows 2000 in a fresh environment with no preexisting NT 4 DCs, you should consider native mode. Native mode provides several enhancements, including:

➤ *Group nesting*—Allows you to place groups within other groups to allow for permissions to flow through.

➤ *Universal groups*—Enables another level of group possibilities, allowing for forest-wide group implementations.

➤ *Security ID (SID) history*—Used during migrations to retain the original SID of the objects that are moved.

Keep in mind that although you can change from mixed mode to native mode, you cannot change back. So, if you are going to make the move, ensure your readiness. You can change modes in one of two ways:

➤ Through AD Users and Computers

➤ Through AD Domains and Trusts

In either tool the options will be the same. Open the AD Users and Computers, or AD Domains and Trusts and select the domain, and go into the properties of the domain. On the General tab, you should see a button toward the bottom called Change Mode, as shown in Figure 4.10. Click on the button, and you are eternally committed.

You are still in the early stages of the installation at this point. Now, you move on to thinking about the next stage: Organizational Units.

Organizational Units

Within the domain in Windows 2000, you can implement OUs that will further segment the domain for organization of the objects in the network. Also, OUs have the ability to contain other OUs. This feature enables you to create a hierarchy within a single domain, as opposed to creating additional domains to establish delegation of network authority.

When planning the structure of OUs within a domain, you must first understand the purpose of OUs. To dispel a common misconception: Organizational Units *are not* primarily used to help the end user find resources in the AD database. In

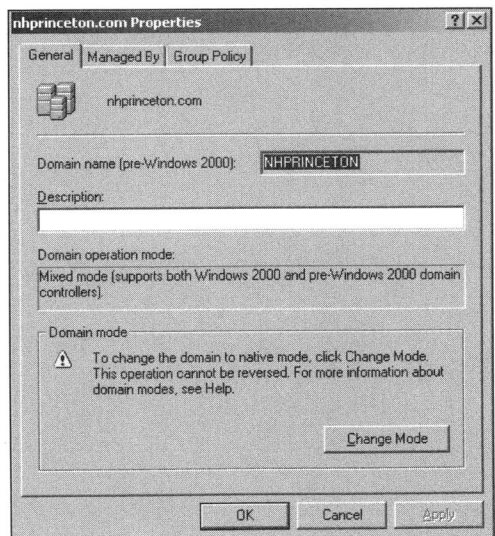

Figure 4.10 Changing domain modes with the click of a button.

fact, the end users will probably not even have to know that OUs exist within the domain. OUs *are* used for the following reasons:

➤ To help administrators manage network resources in an orderly fashion and enable them to keep track of all the objects within a domain. This is accomplished by forming a hierarchy of containers within the domain and assigning permissions directly to the OU at various levels to users or groups of users.

➤ To provide identical security requirements to network resources that require the same levels.

➤ To control Group Policy implementation, which is covered in Chapters 7 through 9.

You can create OUs if you've been delegated permissions to do so by your administrators. By default, members of the Domain Admins and Enterprise Admins groups have permissions to create OUs. If you are not a member of either of these groups, you will have to be assigned the following permissions on a parent OU:

➤ Read

➤ List Contents

➤ Create Child (OU)

Creating OUs is done through the AD Users and Computers tool by selecting the domain or OU that you wish to create the OU in. Then right-click and choose New, and then choose Organizational Unit. Finally, type the name of the OU and hit OK.

You're ready now to understand the next facet of implementing a directory service infrastructure—administration of users and groups—which is covered in Chapter 5.

Practice Questions

Question 1

You install Active Directory on a server, and you want it to be a separate domain that is part of an existing tree structure with a forest root containing a contiguous namespace. What is this type of domain called?

○ a. A replica

○ b. A backup domain controller

○ c. A child domain

○ d. A forest root

Answer c is correct. A child domain is one that exists below a parent domain and continues to use a contiguous namespace. Answer a is incorrect because a secondary domain controller, as a replica, would not be a "separate domain." Answer b is incorrect because Active Directory doesn't have primary and backup domain controllers. Answer d is incorrect because the forest root would have been established first in order to add a child domain.

Question 2

You want to begin an installation of Active Directory. You would like for that installation to be handled automatically and run by an administrator with no background knowledge of Active Directory installation. Which of the following would assist you in this goal? [Check all correct answers]

❑ a. dcpromo.exe

❑ b. udf.txt

❑ c. adpromo.txt

❑ d. ntdsutil.exe

Answers a and c are correct. You need dcpromo to begin the Active Directory Installation Wizard and you need adpromo.txt to be your answer file. The correct syntax for the commands for the administrator running the installation would be **dcpromo /answer:adpromo.txt**. Answer b is incorrect because udf.txt is a UDF that is used for unattended installations of the operating system itself. Answer d is incorrect because ntdsutil.exe is a tool that handles the seizing of FSMO roles and can handle movement of the directory database and log files.

Question 3

You're attempting to install Active Directory within a network infrastructure that already has a DNS server in place. The DNS server is running on a Unix box and, until now, functioned quite well. What could be causing a problem that pushes the installation to request that an additional DNS server be established on the new domain controller?

- ○ a. Unix DNS is not compatible with Active Directory.
- ○ b. The BIND version needs to be updated.
- ○ c. Active Directory requires only Windows 2000 DNS.
- ○ d. Unix uses a different protocol suite than Windows 2000.

Answer b is correct. Most likely, you are using an older version of BIND and need to upgrade to at least 8.1.2. Answer a is incorrect because Unix DNS can be compatible with an upgrade. Answer c is incorrect because Windows 2000 works with DNS servers that support RFCs (SRV records) and (dynamic updates). Answer d is incorrect because both Unix and Windows 2000 use TCP/IP as their protocol suite of choice.

Question 4

Your installation of Active Directory halts because the SYSVOL folder cannot be placed where you've specified. What is the most likely cause of the problem?

- ○ a. You've requested that it go on a partition that doesn't have enough space.
- ○ b. You've formatted the partition with NTFS.
- ○ c. The drive letter you've specified doesn't exist.
- ○ d. The partition you are specifying is FAT or FAT32.

Answer d is correct. The SYSVOL folder structure must be on an NTFS partition. Answers a and c are incorrect because, although they are possible causes, the question asks for "most likely." Answer b is incorrect because putting the SYSVOL folder on an NTFS partition would have actually been the correct thing to do.

Question 5

In selecting the locations of your database and log files, which two of the following options would enhance the performance of these files?

❏ a. Placing them on the same NTFS partition.

❏ b. Ensuring plenty of hard disk space for these files to expand.

❏ c. Placing them in separate physical disks.

❏ d. Restricting them to small-sized partitions for additional control over their size.

Answers b and c are correct. Plenty of room and separate physical disks will make for a healthy database and log file configuration. Answer a is incorrect because, although placing the files on an NTFS partition isn't a bad idea, it doesn't enhance performance. Answer d is incorrect because you don't want to prevent your database and log files from growing. This is a normal part of the directory service.

Question 6

To allow for backward compatibility with NT 4 domain controllers, what mode should your domains be running in?

○ a. Mixed mode

○ b. Native mode

○ c. RIS mode

○ d. FLIP mode

Answer a is correct. Mixed mode allows for backward compatibility and synchronization with the accounts manager. Answer b is incorrect because native mode would ensure incompatibility with NT 4 domain controllers. Answers c and d are invalid modes.

Question 7

Handles Corp. creates handles for various products from broomsticks to briefcases. Its network administration team is planning its AD directory services infrastructure and would like to delegate administrative control over various locations and departments throughout the organization. What should the team use in Active Directory to delegate administrative control over users, groups, and computers within an organization?

○ a. Organizational Units

○ b. Global Catalog servers

○ c. Additional domain controllers

○ d. Additional domains as child domains

Answer a is correct. OUs are used in Windows 2000 to allow for delegation of authority. Answer b is incorrect because Global Catalog servers provide additional searching functionality and logon authentication features within the domain. Answer c is incorrect because, although additional domain controllers will add fault tolerance, they will not delegate authority. Answer d is incorrect; although under NT 4 resource domains would be established, this is no longer necessary under Windows 2000.

Question 8

What utilities would you use to change domain modes from mixed to native mode? [Check all correct answers]

❑ a. Group Policy Editor

❑ b. Active Directory Users and Computers

❑ c. Delegation of Control Wizard

❑ d. Active Directory Domains and Trusts

Answers b and d are correct. AD Users and Computers and AD Domains and Trusts allow for changes in the domain mode. Answer a is incorrect because Group Policy Editor allows you to specify the settings for a user or computer that relate to desktop views or software and security policy. Answer c is incorrect because Delegation of Control Wizard provides a graphical way to assign Active Directory access permissions to individuals with trusted administrative control.

Question 9

> If you want to provide secure DNS updates for Active Directory, what should you implement?
>
> ○ a. A Kerberos server
>
> ○ b. A certificate server
>
> ○ c. Active Directory integrated zones
>
> ○ d. Native mode

Answer c is correct. Active Directory integrated zones allow for the DNS zone files to be replicated with the directory information and also allow for secure updates to be configured. Answers a and b are incorrect because they have nothing to do with secure zones; a Kerberos server is one that issues and verifies tickets for validation, and a certificate server is used in software security systems that employ public key technologies. Answer d is incorrect because you can have secure updates with mixed or native mode domains.

Question 10

> Under which part of the answer file for an unattended installation of both Windows 2000 and Active Directory combined would you specify the command to install Active Directory?
>
> ○ a. GuiRunPromo
>
> ○ b. GuiRunOnce
>
> ○ c. DCInstall
>
> ○ d. ADInstall

Answer b is correct. The GuiRunOnce section within the answer file would specify the command **dcpromo** and then specify an additional answer file that is specific to the Active Directory install. Answer c is incorrect because, although DCInstall is a section of the Active Directory answer file, it is not the section that installs the operating system. Answers a and d are invalid answers.

Question 11

Select from the following list the minimum requirements for installing Active Directory.

120MB of RAM

An NTFS partition

A FAT32 partition

250MB of free hard disk space

TCP/IP

256MB of RAM

Windows 2000 Server

Windows 2000 Professional

Windows 2000 Advanced Server

The correct answer is:

An NTFS partition

250MB of free hard disk space

TCP/IP

256MB of RAM

Windows 2000 Server

Windows 2000 Advanced Server

Question 12

> These three items occur only under a native mode domain:
>
> Group Nesting
>
> Universal Groups
>
> SID History
>
> Match each of these items with the appropriate definition listed here (all definitions will not be used):
>
> Used during migrations to retain the original SID of the objects that are moved.
>
> Allows you to place groups within other groups to allow for permissions to flow through.
>
> Makes it possible to work with pre-existing Windows domains.
>
> Enables another level of group possibilities allowing for forest-wide group implementations.
>
> Starts off the installation of Active Directory.

The correct answer is:

Group Nesting

> Allows you to place groups within other groups to allow for permissions to flow through.

Universal Groups

> Enables another level of group possibilities allowing for forest-wide group implementations.

SID History

> Used during migrations to retain the original SID of the objects that are moved.

Need to Know More?

 Boswell, William. *Inside Windows 2000 Server*. New Riders, Indianapolis, IN, 2000. ISBN 1562059297. This is a great resource for in-depth information on the directory configuration process.

 Bruzzese, J. Peter and Wayne Dipchan. *MCSE Windows 2000 Directory Services Design Exam Prep*. The Coriolis Group, Scottsdale, AZ, 2000. ISBN: 1576106683. Chapter 7 provides a great deal of information on the necessary design considerations when forming extensive domain trees and forest infrastructures.

 Nielsen, Morton Strunge. *Windows 2000 Server Architecture and Planning*. The Coriolis Group, Scottsdale, AZ, 1999. ISBN 1576104362. Although it was written during Windows 2000 beta period, this book is an excellent resource for AD planning and deployment.

 Watts, David V., Will Willis, and Tillman Strahan. *MCSE Windows 2000 Directory Services Exam Prep*. The Coriolis Group, Scottsdale, AZ, 2000. ISBN 1576106241. This book provides tons of additional information on implementation.

 Search the TechNet CD (or its online version through **www.microsoft.com**) using keywords "Unattended Installation" and "Active Directory", along with related query items.

User and Group Administration

Terms you'll need to understand:

✓ Single sign-on
✓ Domain user account
✓ Local user account
✓ Built-in user account
✓ User logon name
✓ User principal name
✓ User principal name prefix
✓ User principal name suffix
✓ Csvde
✓ Ldifde
✓ Attribute line
✓ Universal groups
✓ AGDLP

Techniques you'll need to master:

✓ Bulk-importing user accounts
✓ Using groups to organize user accounts
✓ Deciding on a user logon name strategy
✓ Performing a search of Active Directory

Active Directory (AD) is essentially a database that stores data about network resources and other objects. Two of the most common types of objects stored within AD are users and groups. Having these objects stored within AD allows people to log on to the network and gain access to a range of network resources. Because all objects are stored within AD along with access permissions, you can achieve a single sign-on. *Single sign-on* is a feature in Windows 2000 that allows users to log in to the network with a single username and password and receive access to a host of network resources. The user does not need to enter any additional usernames or passwords to gain access to network shares, printers, or other network resources.

Generally, *groups* are collections of user accounts (although they can also include computers) that are used to ease administration. Because you can create a group and assign permissions for a resource to this single entity, using groups is far easier than assigning permissions to individual user accounts. In Windows 2000, you can also nest groups, which allows groups themselves to contain other groups, further simplifying network administration. In this chapter, we examine users and groups and how they can be used in a Windows 2000 environment.

Introducing Users and Groups

Obviously, if a user cannot log on to a Windows 2000 network, he or she cannot gain access to the data and resources—such as files and folders, email accounts, and printers—that are stored there. User accounts are the fundamental building block of your network. Because they are so important, you will likely spend a lot of time working with user accounts in your environment.

A Windows 2000 network has three different types of user accounts:

➤ *Domain user account*—This account is used to gain access to a Windows 2000 domain and all its associated resources. This is the most common type of logon you will experience on a Windows 2000 network. A logon that exists on one domain can be given permissions in other Windows 2000 domains.

➤ *Local user account*—This account exists on a standalone server or a Windows 2000 Professional system. It enables a user to log on to a specific computer and gain access to the local resources that it offers. By definition, a standalone computer is not acting as part of a Windows 2000 network. Therefore, a local user account cannot grant access to resources in a domain.

➤ *Built-in user accounts*—These accounts have been created for specific administrative tasks to ease the administrative burden. They define special accounts up front that have permissions to both resources and AD itself.

Because your enterprise network might have a few hundred user accounts—perhaps even hundreds of thousands—creating accounts can be an arduous process.

To ease this burden, you can bulk-import accounts using tools provided with Windows 2000. In this chapter, we take a closer look at these tools. Creating user accounts in bulk fashion saves the administrator a great deal of time.

The most commonly used network resources include files, folders, and printers. Given that you might have to deal with several hundred or thousand user accounts, granting access to resources based solely on user accounts would be time-consuming and hugely repetitive. So, instead, we use groups. The concept of groups is very simple: You create a single object within AD and grant access permissions (or deny access) to this single entity. User accounts are then added as members of the group. By being a member of a group, the user accounts inherit the permissions assigned to the group. If these permissions must be changed, you can then simply modify them on the group object a single time. Any changes to the group permissions are applied to the user accounts that are members of the group.

In addition, Windows 2000 allows you to build a hierarchy of groups and assign different permissions to each level of the hierarchy. This is achieved through the nesting of groups. Nesting groups further simplifies your security model.

User Logon Names

User logon names are also known as user account names. However, be careful with your use of terminology in Windows 2000; a user can have more than one type of account, because Microsoft has provided the ability to use older-style usernames in a Windows 2000 network along with a new type of logon name.

Types of Logon Names

When logging in to a Windows 2000 network, users can use either one of the two types of names they have been assigned: their user principal name or their user logon name. The end result will be the same, although the older-style logon names should slowly be phased out. Domain controllers (DCs) are able to authenticate the user regardless of what method they use. Let's look at these two types of usernames.

User Principal Name

The *user principal name* is the new-style logon name on Windows 2000 networks. A user principal name is made up of two parts. One part uniquely identifies the user object in AD; the second part identifies the domain where the user object was created. A user principal name looks like this: **kit@basildon.local**.

As you can see, the two parts of the user principal name are divided by the @ sign. This tells Windows 2000 which part of the name is the user object name and which is the domain name. These two parts can further be defined as the following:

➤ *User principal name prefix*—In the preceding example, this is **kit**.

➤ *User principal name suffix*—By default, the suffix is derived from the root domain name on your Windows 2000 network. You can also create additional user principal names by using other domains on your network, though doing so increases the administrative overhead of your network. Windows 2000 administrators that have deployed Exchange 2000 commonly use the email address as the user principal name. In the preceding example, the user principal name suffix would be **basildon.local**.

Because user principal names are by default tied to the root domain's name, moving a user object from one domain to another on a Windows 2000 network does not require a username change. This effectively makes the change invisible for the user. They need not be concerned that their user account has been moved from one domain to another. Also, because the user principal name can be the same as the user's email account, the name is easy to remember.

User Logon Name

User logon name is used to describe backward-compatible usernames. It is used by clients that are logging on to a Windows 2000 network from an older client, such as Windows 9x or Microsoft Windows NT 4.0.

Logging on to a Windows 2000 domain using the user logon name means that users must provide two distinct pieces of information. First, they must enter their username, and second, they must enter the name of the domain where their account exists. This can be confusing to users who sometimes have trouble remembering all the details of the logon process. In addition, because the user account is unique within a domain only (see the next section on rules for logon names), gaining access to resources outside of that domain can also be unnecessarily difficult. In this case, the user may have to enter an additional username and password. In our example, the user logon name would simply be **kit**.

Rules for Logon Names

Because user accounts are used to gain access to a Windows 2000 network, a username must be unique. The scope of this uniqueness varies depending on the type of logon name you intend to use. This enables single sign-on. The administrator must ensure that user accounts follow a set of rules so that they are unique within a Windows 2000 forest.

User principal names must be unique within a forest. This can make coming up with a naming strategy more difficult, especially when you have tens of thousands of users. The benefits outweigh the difficulties; however, you should come up with a naming strategy that allows for usernames that are easy to remember yet at the same time are easily distinguishable.

User logon names must be unique within the domain in which they are created. If you think you will use these account types exclusively, you have a little more flexibility in naming conventions, because in effect, you can share a single username across multiple domains. However, using a single name exclusively is discouraged. Over time, this will undoubtedly cause a higher administrative overhead.

The username suffix (in our case, **basildon.local**) is derived from the root domain by default. However, this can be changed. By adding additional suffixes, you ensure that users have a standard and easy-to-understand user principal name. Before an additional suffix can be used, it must be added to AD. This is done through the AD Domains and Trusts tool. The dialog box for adding additional suffixes is shown in Figure 5.1.

Creating User Accounts

Creating user accounts in an enterprise environment can be time-consuming. In addition, if you are creating the accounts one at a time, you will find that a lot of repetitive information needs to be entered. To alleviate this, Microsoft has provided two utilities that can be used to import user account information in bulk.

These utilities work by using a text file as the source for new account information. This text file can be in one of two formats—comma-delimited and line-separated—which are supported by the tools that ship with Windows 2000. The format of the source file dictates which utility you use. You can create these files in any database application that supports exporting to either of these formats

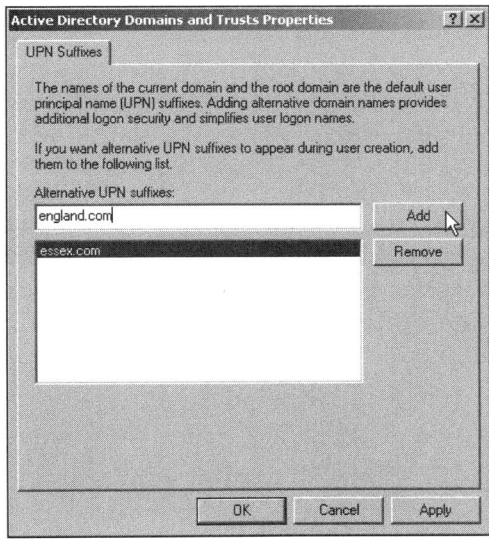

Figure 5.1   Adding additional suffixes.

(almost all database applications on the market today are able to do this) or with a spreadsheet such as Microsoft Excel.

These files can be used to bulk-import user accounts, groups, and even attributes. The two utilities are as follows:

➤ *Csvde*—The Comma-Separated Value Directory Exchange utility can perform a bulk import based on comma-delimited source files.

➤ *Ldifde*—The Lightweight Directory Access Protocol Interchange Format Directory Exchange utility allows you to perform a bulk import based on line-separated values.

Keep the following in mind when you are considering using these bulk import tools:

➤ You must ensure that the user object you are about to create is unique. You achieve this by giving the full path for the user object within the directory, including the Organizational Unit (OU) that will contain the object. You must also specify the object type and the user logon name.

➤ You should set a value to define whether the user accounts you are creating are enabled or disabled. By default, any user accounts you create are disabled. This helps ensure security when objects are created in bulk.

➤ The user principal name is optional; however, because this is the recommended method of logging on to a Windows 2000 domain from a native Windows 2000 system, it is strongly suggested that you provide a user principal name.

➤ You cannot include passwords with the bulk import. When user objects are created with this process, the passwords are blank. The users will be prompted the first time they log on to change their password. Because this could be a significant security breach, it is suggested that you allow the default option of having the new accounts disabled to take effect.

➤ You can also include other properties or attributes, such as a telephone number, of the object to be imported at the same time. The more data you can enter automatically, the less data you have to worry about later. Also, the more data that is included as part of the user object, the more data users will have to search against when they are looking for a particular user in AD.

The Csvde Utility

If you plan to use a source file that is a comma-delimited format, you must use the csvde command-line utility. For help with this utility, type "csvde /?" at the command prompt. Some of the switches are shown in Figure 5.2.

The csvde utility can be used to import data into AD; it cannot be used to delete or modify data. Whenever using command-line bulk import tools, you must make

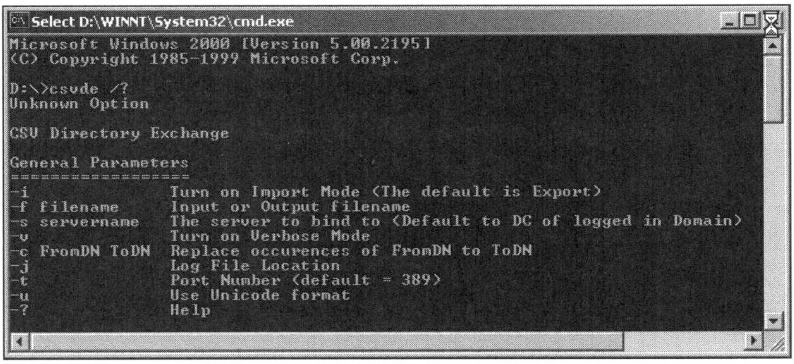

Figure 5.2   Getting help with the csvde utility.

sure that your source file is correctly formatted. An incorrectly formatted file will cause the process to fail. Because the format for this utility is a comma-delimited file, you can use just about any text-editing program to create the source, including all major word processors and spreadsheet applications, and even Notepad.

The format of the source file is fairly simple and is briefly discussed here with some points highlighted. It's not possible to include every parameter that can be added for a user object using this utility. Don't forget that in the real world, you should add as much data as possible to help identify the new user object.

The first line of the source file should contain the *attribute line*. This line defines the format of the data lines to follow. Fields are included on this line separated by commas. Each field entered must be subsequently included in each user record. Windows 2000 does not care what order these fields are in as long as the lines in the file that contain the user data follow the same order. Here's an example of an attribute line:

DN, objectClass,sAMAccountname,userPrincipalName,displayName

Once you have defined which fields exist in your source file, you can enter the user data you want to include in your bulk import. This data must comply with the following set of rules:

➤ The sequence of the source values must be in the same order as those specified in the attribute line.

➤ If a value contains commas, you must contain the value in quotation marks.

➤ If you have a user object that will not have entries for all the values specified in the attribute line, you can leave the field blank; however, you must include the commas.

Here's an example of a code line that conforms to these rules:

```
"cn=michael cook, ou=art department, dc=england, dc=basildon,
  dc=local"user,mikec, mikec@london.local, Michael Cook
```

In this case, the following attributes have been defined:

➤ *DN* (distinguished name)—**cn=michael cook, ou=art department, dc=england, dc=basildon, dc=local**

➤ *objectClass*—user

➤ *sAMAccountName*—mikec

➤ *userPrincipalName*—mikec@london.local

➤ *displayName*—Michael Cook

To include more parameters, simply add them to the attribute line. Make sure you follow the rules outlined in this chapter, paying particular attention to the rules when a particular field is going to be skipped.

Once you have a text file that has been correctly formatted, you can run csvde to perform a bulk import. Two switches that you should pay particular attention to are –i and –f (refer back to Figure 5.2). The –i switch indicates that an import is being performed. The –f switch specifies the name of the source file.

Note: The csvde utility can only be used to add users to AD; it cannot be used to delete objects.

You should always use AD Users and Computers to check the user accounts that you have imported. The csvde utility also provides you with a status message and log file, but regardless, you should double-check to make sure that the accounts were created and that the optional parameters you have specified have been entered correctly.

The Ldifde Utility

The ldifde utility is in some ways similar to csvde. However, it offers additional functionality. Unlike csvde, the ldifde utility can be used to add objects, delete objects, and modify objects in the directory.

To import, delete, or modify data with this utility, you must create a source file. This source file is a text file, but its format differs from that of the csvde utility. The ldifde utility uses a line-separated format, which is a list of records, with each separated by a blank line. A *record* is a distinct collection of data that will either be added to AD or will be used to modify data within the directory. Each entry is considered a record.

The format of the file required by this utility is also known as the Lightweight Directory Access Protocol Interchange Format (LDIF). The format of the file is the attribute name followed by a colon and the attribute value. The names of the attributes are defined within the Schema partition of AD. In the following example of LDIF format, we have used the text from the comma-delimited file data we saw earlier in this chapter. This should make it easier for you to compare the two formats:

```
# create Michael Cook
DN:  cn=michael cook, ou=art department,dc=local
ObjectClass:  user
SAMAccountName:  mikec
UserPrincipalName:  mikec@london.local
DisplayName:  Michael Cook
```

Note that any line that starts with the # sign is a comment line and is ignored when the file is being used to import data into AD. Some significant command-line switches for this utility are shown in Figure 5.3 (you can view this on your own computer by typing "ldifde /?" at the command prompt). Note again the −i and -f switches. These offer the same functionality as mentioned for the csvde utility.

User Accounts

Many of the ongoing administrative tasks performed on a Windows 2000 network are based around user accounts. This includes the creation and maintenance of these accounts. In this section, we look at the common administrative tools you will use, and how to search AD for specific data.

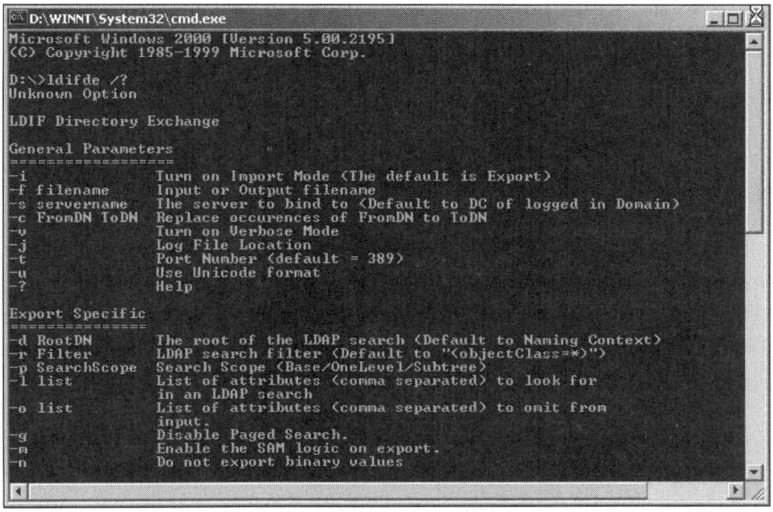

Figure 5.3 Getting help with the ldifde utility.

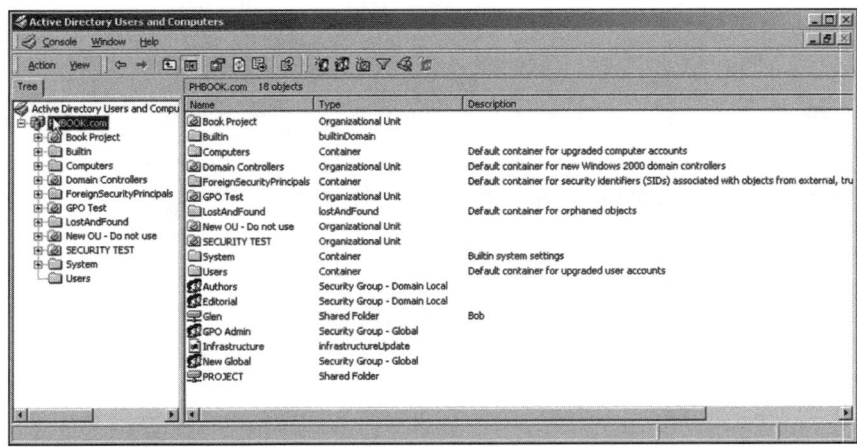

Figure 5.4 AD Users and Computers.

The most common administrative tool, shown in Figure 5.4, is AD Users and Computers. To access this utility, select Start|Programs|Administrative Tools| Active Directory Users and Computers.

AD Users and Computers provides you with all the day-to-day functionality you need. In this section, we look at some of the most common functions you are likely to perform. Being familiar with the interface of AD Users and Computers helps you be more efficient at administering user accounts in your environment. The common administrative tasks we will look at include:

➤ Resetting passwords

➤ Unlocking user accounts

➤ Deleting user accounts

➤ Renaming user accounts

➤ Copying user accounts

➤ Disabling and enabling user accounts

Because these are common tasks, Microsoft has provided an easy method to access them. To access each of these tasks, simply select the Users container in the left-hand panel of AD Users and Computers, and then right-click on the user object you want to change in the right-hand panel. When you do this, you are presented with the context-sensitive menu shown in Figure 5.5.

As you can see, this menu offers you a wealth of functionality. Note that it is possible to perform some tasks on multiple user accounts. For instance, if you highlight five user accounts and then right-click on them, you will see a context-

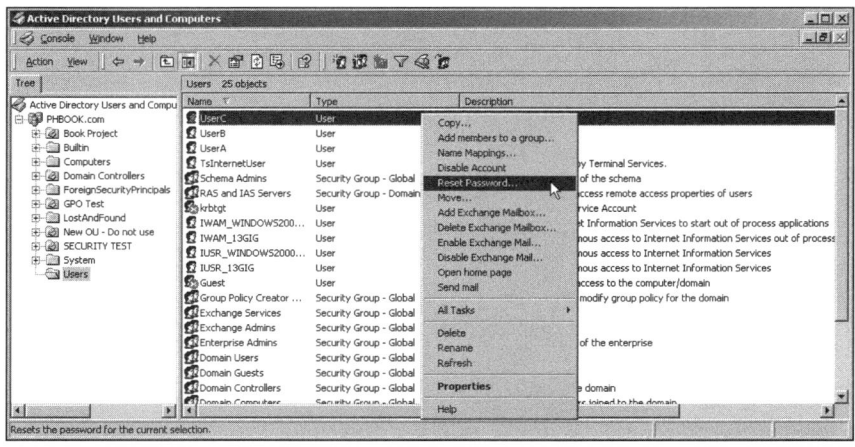

Figure 5.5   AD Users and Computers context-sensitive menu.

sensitive menu with a subset of functions. One of these functions is the ability to disable an account, which lets you disable several accounts simultaneously.

Resetting Passwords

Passwords are at the heart of the security of your network. They should be secure, changed often, and hard to crack (for instance, you should not use the name of your spouse or family pet).

You may also find that users sometimes forget their password and request that you change it for them. As an administrator, you do not need to know the user's old password to change it. If you do make a change to a user's password, don't forget to check the User Must Change Password At Next Logon checkbox.

You access this function by selecting Reset Password from the context-sensitive menu.

Unlocking User Accounts

User accounts are subject to the security settings that have been defined in Group Policy. One of the most common settings is for an account to be locked out after three failed login attempts. This occurs when a user has forgotten his or her password and makes several consecutive attempts, guessing wrong each time.

To unlock an account, click on Properties on the context-sensitive menu. You are then presented with the User Properties dialog box. Click on the Account tab and uncheck the Account Is Locked Out checkbox, as shown in Figure 5.6.

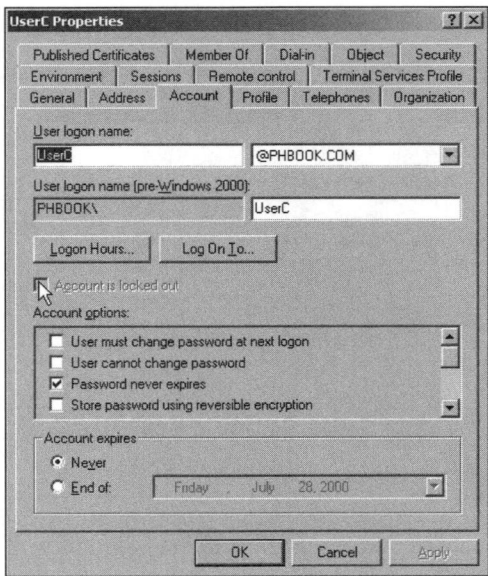

Figure 5.6 The User Properties dialog box.

Deleting User Accounts

If a user leaves your organization, you have two choices. If the user is being re-placed, you can simply rename the account for use by someone else, or you can delete it. The choice here should be based on security, not just convenience. If the user is being replaced immediately, it is easier to rename the account. Other-wise, you should delete the account to maintain the integrity of security on your network.

To delete a user account, select Delete from the context-sensitive menu. When prompted with the message "Are you sure you want to delete this object?", click on Yes to delete the object or No to abort the deletion.

Renaming User Accounts

Renaming a user account is convenient when a user's function is being taken over by someone else. A user account is not simply a name and password; it is also a set of permissions and group memberships. Sometimes it is easier to rename a user account so this data is maintained than re-creating it from scratch.

When renaming a user account, remember to take every object property into account. As a minimum, you should change the first name, last name, and logon name fields. However, several optional attributes will likely need to be changed, such as telephone number and description.

To rename an account, select Rename from the context-sensitive menu. Simply type the new name and press Enter when you are done.

Copying User Accounts

You can also create an account and use it as a template for other accounts. For instance, you might have a standard set of permissions and group memberships that all users are assigned upon creation of the account. Say, for example, you have a member of the Finance group who has already been configured with all necessary group memberships. When a new employee joins the finance department, you can just copy a current account rather than create one from scratch.

When copying an account, you are prompted to enter a new first name, last name, and user logon name. You are also prompted to assign a new password. To copy a user account, simply select Copy from the context-sensitive menu. You are then presented with the Copy Object-User Wizard.

Disabling and Enabling User Accounts

A variation on locking out an account, disabling an account temporarily prevents a user from logging in to the network. This is commonly performed when the user is going on an extended absence. For the account to become active again, you must then enable the account.

To disable an account, select Disable Account from the context-sensitive menu. The account is immediately disabled, and the username is displayed with a red X through it. To enable the account, select Enable Account from the context-sensitive menu (the Disable Account option will be grayed out).

Finding User Accounts

Finding the user accounts you want to administer is a simple task on a relatively small network. However, Windows 2000 is designed to scale to large enterprises, and locating user accounts in AD Users and Computers can take quite some time.

Because AD is a database, it stands to reason that searching for the specific data you want is easily done. In this case, we are interested in user accounts, but you can also search for any AD object, such as a computer or group. Once you have found the user account you are looking for, you can administer the account from within the Search dialog box.

To access the Find option within AD Users and Computers, right-click on the domain name in the left-hand panel and select Find. The Find Users, Contacts, And Groups dialog box appears, as shown in Figure 5.7.

Note the Find and In drop-down boxes in the dialog box. These options allow you to narrow your search to a particular object type and to restrict the search to a particular domain (as opposed to searching the entire directory, which can be time-consuming and resource-intensive).

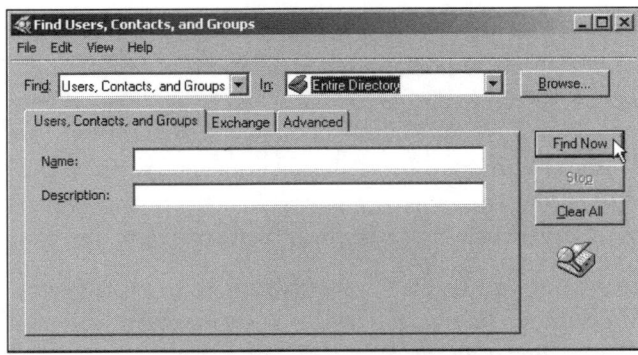

Figure 5.7   The Find Users, Contacts, And Groups dialog box.

Note: If you choose to perform a search against the entire directory, you must contact a Global Catalog server. This can cause heavy network traffic.

The options available on the Find drop-down box include:

➤ Users, Contacts, and Groups

➤ Computers

➤ Printers

➤ Shared Folders

➤ Organizational Units

➤ Custom Search

Most of these options are self-explanatory. They allow you to search for a particular object type and help decrease the amount of time it takes for a search to complete. The Custom Search option is used when you want to make complex searches using additional attributes. You can also access these options when searching for any of the other object types by clicking on the Advanced tab, shown in Figure 5.8.

The Field drop-down box in the Advanced tab allows you to search for a specific attribute of an object. The options you see in this drop-down menu vary depending on the object type you are searching for.

Using the Find Users, Contacts, And Groups Dialog Box to Administer User Accounts

Once you have performed a search for an object, you are presented with an additional pane of information—the Results pane—in the Find Users, Contacts, And Groups dialog box. The Results pane displays all of the objects that have been returned based on your search criteria. By right-clicking on the objects that are

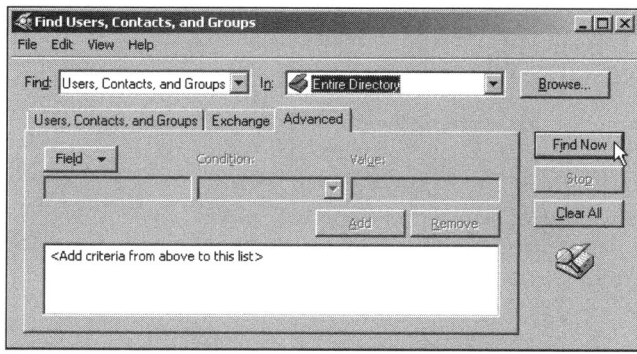

Figure 5.8   The Advanced tab.

listed in the pane, you can access the same context-sensitive menu we saw displayed in AD Users and Computers (refer back to Figure 5.5). This enables you to administer the accounts directly without switching between tools.

The Use of Groups

Groups exist to ease the administrative burden of the system administrator. Groups are used to collect users together and either assign them permissions to a set of files, folders, or network resources, or for the purposes of distribution in email applications. There are two types of groups:

➤ Security groups

➤ Distribution groups

In addition, three different scopes define where the group can be used on the network; groups can be one of the following types:

➤ Local groups

➤ Global groups

➤ Universal groups

Combining the group type and scope determines how a group can be used (in a single domain or in multiple domains within a forest).

Note: Microsoft has published some conflicting documents regarding universal groups. A Windows 2000 domain can be in two modes: mixed mode or native mode. Mixed mode generally means you are still using Windows NT 4 computers as DCs alongside your Windows 2000 DCs. You might read that universal groups are only available if the domain is in native mode. This is only partially correct. In fact, you can create universal groups in mixed mode—but only for distribution lists. Distribution lists cannot be used for security purposes.

Security groups differ from distribution groups in that they can be used to assign security rights—that is, if you want to collect a group of user accounts together so you can more easily assign them access to a shared folder, you must create a security group. You cannot use distribution groups for this purpose.

A new feature of Windows 2000 is the ability to *nest* groups. Nesting groups is used to further simplify the management of users when assigning security permissions. When a group is nested within another group, it inherits all of the security permissions from its parent.

 Group nesting is not available in mixed-mode domains.

A user can be a member of many different groups, thereby inheriting all of the security permissions that have been assigned to them. This is far simpler than assigning permissions on a user basis one by one.

Defining Group Types

All group types are used to gather together a set of users who are going to share a particular set of permissions to a file, folder, or network resource. However, the scope of each group and the possible membership list differs. Table 5.1 lists the differences among the three group types.

How to Use Groups

For groups to be effective, you must use them in a structured way. This helps ensure that you get the maximum benefit from using them. The group scope determines when the best time to use a particular group type is. For instance, if you have a resource that will be available across an entire forest, you will likely start by adding users to global groups and then nesting them within a universal group.

 The mere mention of universal groups implies that you are in native mode (because you cannot use universal groups for security purposes in mixed mode). Be sure to remember what can and cannot be achieved in both modes. If a scenario mentions a single domain, there is no use for universal groups.

The method of assigning permissions within a single domain has been used for a long time, and it still holds true for a Windows 2000 network. Let's now look at using groups in both a single domain and in a forest.

Table 5.1	Group comparison table.		
	Global	**Local**	**Universal**
Member list	Mixed mode: Accounts from same domain	Mixed mode: User accounts and global groups from any domain in the forest	Mixed mode: Distribution lists only
	Native mode: Accounts and other global groups	Native mode: User accounts, local groups from the same domain, global groups and universal groups from any domain in the forest	Native mode: User accounts, global groups, and other universal groups in any domain in the forest
Nesting	Mixed mode: Local groups	Mixed mode: Cannot be a member of another group	Mixed mode: None
	Native mode: Universal and local groups in any domain and global groups in the same domain	Native mode: Local groups in the same domain	Native mode: Local and universal groups in any domain
Scope	Can be used in its own domain and any trusted domains	Can be used only in its own domain	Can be used in any domain in the forest
Permissions to	All domains in a forest	Resources in the domain in which the local group exists only	Resources in any domain in the forest

Groups in a Single Domain

As mentioned previously, in a single domain, there is no need to be concerned about universal groups. With a single domain, you can achieve all the simplification you need using only local and global groups. In this section, we'll use Microsoft's acronym AGDLP to describe the use of both local and global groups. This acronym stands for the following:

➤ *A*—Accounts (user)

➤ *G*—Global group

➤ *DL*—Domain local group

➤ *P*—Permissions

By using this acronym, you can easily recall the order in which permissions should be granted. Although this is only a suggested method, it's designed to make sure you enjoy maximum flexibility and ease of use when assigning permissions to resources.

In the following example, we use this strategy to organize access to a network resource (in this case, a folder share). This illustrates how the AGDLP strategy can work for you. This example assumes a single domain.

A publishing company has an author team. Members of this team need access to files in a folder on the network that contains the text of a book the authors are writing. To achieve this, the system administrator creates a global group called Author Team. The names of the authors are added as members to this global group.

Note: The practical limit on the number of users a group can contain in a Windows 2000 network is 5,000 members.

Next, the administrator creates a local group called Windows 2000 Cram. The Author Team global group is then nested within the Windows 2000 Cram local group. Permissions to the file share are granted to the local group. This offers the flexibility and manageability we are looking for. If additional authors need access to the folder, the administrator simply has to add them to the global group.

Let's take this example one step further. Once the book is halfway complete, the publishing company needs to give access to the editorial team. The system administrator simply creates a second global group called Editors and adds the editorial team as members of the group. This group is then nested within the Windows 2000 Cram local group. This task is now complete. As you can see, because we used our AGDLP strategy, it was very simple to grant permissions to an additional set of users. If the Windows 2000 network had included multiple domains, the method of applying permissions would have changed slightly. In this case, the administrator would use the acronym AGUDLP (where *U* stands for *universal*), creating global groups first and then nesting them within universal groups. The universal group is then nested within the local group.

 Universal groups are unique because AD treats them slightly differently. Although all group names are listed in a Global Catalog server, their membership list is generally not. The exception to this rule is the universal group. Both the universal group name and the membership list are replicated to every Global Catalog server. If you add a single user to a universal group, the *entire* membership list must be replicated. Therefore, it is a good idea to keep your universal group usage to a minimum, and when you do use this type of group, keep the membership lists fairly static. Nesting universal groups is far better than adding members to a single group.

User and Group Recommendations

Users can log on to a Windows 2000 domain using either their principal names or their down-level logon names. From a user perspective, this might not seem to make any difference. However, from an administrative point of view, it is better for users to use principal names. Because using a principal name means users don't have to enter domain names for their accounts, using this type of name exclusively gives administrators the ability to move user objects from one domain to another without any user education. It is always best to use the principal name.

Because you can create a suffix for the principal name, you should consider making it as easy on the user community as possible by making the suffix match their email accounts. This will make remembering their logon names easier.

You will likely be creating a lot of global groups in your domains. It is best to come up with a naming scheme for your groups so they are easily recognizable. In addition, you should create them based on job function. Doing this makes it easy to add users based on their responsibilities within the organization.

Universal groups cause additional replication on your network. Because the group name and the group membership have to be replicated to each Global Catalog server, be careful when using universal groups. Try to make them static. It is far better to nest universal groups than to create a lot of them.

When performing bulk import of user accounts, don't forget two very important defaults:

➤ The password is blank.

➤ The account is disabled.

Do not enable accounts until they are ready to be used. Doing so prematurely can open your network to hackers.

Practice Questions

Question 1

> Active Directory offers Windows 2000 users many advantages, including the ability to search for users, groups, and other network resources. Along with this, logon has been simplified. What is the term used to describe the feature of Windows 2000 that simplifies access to resources for the users?
>
> ○ a. Single-access
>
> ○ b. Single sign-on
>
> ○ c. Domain sign-on
>
> ○ d. Forest sign-on

Answer b is correct. Single sign-on is a feature that allows users to log on a single time and to be granted access to many different resources on the network. When users want to use a network resource, they do not have to log on additional times. Answers a, c, and d are incorrect because they are invalid answers.

Question 2

> Meredith Brittain has been asked to deploy a Windows 2000 network. One of the largest tasks is going to be creating 10,000 user accounts. Her customer has provided her with a text file containing the usernames from their previous network system, along with information such as telephone numbers and first name and last name. This file was exported from Microsoft Excel as a comma-delimited format. What is the best way for Meredith to enter these names into AD?
>
> ○ a. To make sure these accounts are accurate, Meredith should type each account in manually.
>
> ○ b. Meredith should use the ldifde command-line utility.
>
> ○ c. Meredith should use the csvde command-line utility.
>
> ○ d. Meredith should use the Import function on AD Users and Computers.

Answer c is correct. Only csvde will work. Answer b is incorrect because ldifde uses a line-separated format and will not work. Answer d is incorrect because Active Directory User and Computers does not have a bulk-import function. Answer a would work, but it is much more likely that Meredith will make a typo when entering 10,000 user accounts, not to mention it would take a lot more time.

Question 3

> Samantha is in the process of putting together a network security plan.
> Because she will be granting users access to shared folders and printers,
> she wants to use groups extensively. Samantha's company also has several
> kiosks in the foyer of company headquarters that visitors can use to browse
> the Web and access email. Samantha is not sure how she is going to limit
> the access of users. What method would be the easiest from an administra-
> tive standpoint? [Choose the best answer]
>
> ○ a. Because groups can only contain user accounts, Samantha should
>   create groups for her user community and put a firewall between
>   the kiosk machines and her network.
>
> ○ b. Samantha should create groups for the employees of her
>   company. For the kiosk machines, Samantha can create a single
>   logon and apply permissions to this group so users can access the
>   resources they need. Because this can be a single group, this task
>   would not involve a lot of work.
>
> ○ c. Because groups can contain both user accounts and computer
>   accounts, Samantha can go ahead and create a single group that
>   includes both users from her company and the computers that
>   operate as kiosks.
>
> ○ d. Samantha should create a single logon for the kiosk machines.
>   She should create a group for her employees and assign them
>   permissions, and she should grant the user that is going to be
>   used in the kiosks specific permissions to network resources.

Answer c is correct. Groups can contain both user accounts and computer accounts. Although answers a, b, and d are all feasible, they increase the administrative burden for the administrator. Specifically, answer a is incorrect because a
firewall can be difficult to administer. Answers b and d are incorrect because
adding specific user accounts to permissions lists is also administratively intensive.

Question 4

Samantha has been called to troubleshoot a problem on a member server in her domain. A user called BradMehldau says he is logging in to the domain, and although he is being granted access (he is able to get to the desktop of the server), he is not able to access any network resources. Samantha checks BradMehldau's account and finds everything is normal. He has been granted access to resources and is a member of several groups that should enable him to access file shares. No one else has reported a problem with the network. Samantha goes to visit BradMehldau's office. What is a possible cause for this problem?

- O a. The user is typing the wrong password. He is being granted access to the network, but because he used the wrong password, he is being denied access to network resources.

- O b. The user is logging in to the member server using a local user account. This means he has not yet been validated by the domain and is therefore not allowed access to network resources.

- O c. The user's password must be changed. The system is giving him sufficient access to do this, but it will not let him access network resources until the change is confirmed.

- O d. The user has to wait for the logon process to complete. AD is complex, and it can take a long time for the security token to be created for a user the first time he or she logs on.

Answer b is correct. There are three types of user accounts: domain user accounts, local user accounts, and built-in user accounts. Domain accounts are designed to allow users to log in to a network and gain access to resources. Local user accounts are used on member server and Windows 2000 Professional systems to allow users to log on to the local computer without network access. Built-in user accounts are created by default for administrative purposes. Answer a is incorrect because typing an incorrect password would prevent the user from accessing the network. Answer c is incorrect because if the user's password had changed, he would not be allowed any level of access to the network. Answer d is incorrect because the question implies that the user has indeed logged on. Therefore, the security token will already have been created.

Question 5

Keith Jarrett is a system administrator for a Windows 2000 network. He is trying to make a decision about which method users should use to log on to his network. There are four domains in his forest, and he wants to make the logon method as simple for the users as possible. The company is owned by the Smith family. Three generations of Smiths work in his organization, and he has 25 members of the Smith family working in one context or another. Family members include David Smith, David Smith II, Darrell Smith, John Smith, John Smith II, and John Smith III. After careful consideration, Keith decides to stick with using the logon method that requires users to know which domains they belong to. Why did Keith make this decision?

- ○ a. Keith knows that he has some duplicate names on his network. Because a principal name must be unique in a forest, he cannot guarantee he won't run into problems. To avoid this, he is stuck with forcing the users to enter their domain name.

- ○ b. Keith has decided that user education is going to be a problem. His user community has been migrated from a Windows NT 4 environment and is used to entering the domain name. Also, the benefits of using principal names is not great.

- ○ c. Keith eventually wants to collapse two of his domains. By forcing the users to use a domain name, he can more easily identify those that are going to be affected by such a move and perform a smoother transition.

- ○ d. It really doesn't make much difference to Keith which method is used. Because, administratively, it does not gain him anything, he decides to make sure users enter the domain name.

Answer a is correct. Because Keith has a lot of duplicate names, using principal names won't work. Keith would need to come up with a new user naming strategy to use principal names. Answer b is incorrect because principal names are generally the same as a user's email address. This in fact is far simpler for a user to remember. Answer c is incorrect because Keith would do better to use the Active Directory Users and Computers tool to find out who belongs to a specific domain than forcing users to remember which domain they belong to. Answer d is incorrect because the user experience is better when using principal names.

Question 6

> Peter Chamberlin has been asked to secure some shared folders. He knows he should not grant access to network resources at the user level, because this increases the amount of system administration the network requires. He decides to use groups. Rather than having to manage different kinds of groups and worry about their scope, he decides to use universal groups extensively. He creates a lot of groups early Monday morning, but before he can finish, users call in and complain that the network is slow. What would cause this?
>
> ○ a. Adding large amounts of data to AD causes a lot of network traffic, and this traffic has caused the network to be slow. Administration of AD should be performed after hours.
>
> ○ b. Creating groups is processor-intensive because the DC has to gather data about all user accounts in the domain. This should be done after hours.
>
> ○ c. As Peter is adding users to groups, the users are being informed by their local DCs of their new permissions. This is causing the traffic.
>
> ○ d. Universal groups cause more network traffic than other group types because both the group name and membership list is replicated to all Global Catalog servers. If Peter had used another group type, he would not have had this problem.

Answer d is correct. Because the membership of a universal group is replicated to Global Catalog servers, more network traffic is generated. Peter should be careful about creating a large number of universal groups. Answer a is incorrect because although adding new groups does cause data to be replicated, there is no need to perform these tasks after hours. Replication can be managed with sites and site links. Answer b is incorrect because copies of AD are stored on every DC. Because this data is available locally, you should not see a huge increase in processor use. Answer c is incorrect because users are not automatically informed of their new memberships.

Question 7

Jeff Hilton has been migrating his Windows NT 4 network to Windows 2000. He is currently running in mixed mode. Because Jeff has multiple domains, he wants to use local groups, global groups, and universal groups. A consultant tells Jeff that he must be running Windows 2000 in native mode to create universal groups. However, Jeff has already created a universal group, and he doubts the consultant knows what he is doing. Who is right?

○ a. Jeff is correct. Universal groups can be used in either mixed mode or native mode.

○ b. Both are correct. Universal groups can be created in either mode, but they can only be used as distribution groups in mixed mode.

○ c. Both are correct. Universal groups can be created in either mode, but they can only be used as security groups in mixed mode.

○ d. The consultant is correct. Universal groups can only be used in native mode.

Answer b is correct. Although universal groups can be used in mixed mode, their function is limited to distribution groups. You must be in native mode to use them to grant access to network resources. Answer a is incorrect because it is only partially correct. Although universal groups can be created in either mode, there are severe restrictions when they are created in mixed mode—namely, they cannot be used for security purposes. Answer c is incorrect because universal groups cannot be used for security purposes in mixed mode. Answer d is incorrect because universal groups can be used in either mode.

Question 8

Gus is a system administrator of a Windows 2000 network that has a single domain. Gus needs to come up with a group strategy. He decides to use domain local groups and global groups. His manager asks him to go back to the drawing board and come up with a strategy that uses universal groups, unless Gus has good reason not to. Why did Gus choose not to use universal groups?

- ○ a. Gus wants to minimize the replication traffic on his network.

- ○ b. Universal groups simply add another layer of global groups. Gus has a "keep it simple" philosophy.

- ○ c. Universal groups cannot be used for security purposes. They are used for distribution groups. Using universal groups would not help in assigning permissions to network resources.

- ○ d. Universal groups could be used, but in a single-domain environment, they simply add an extra level of complexity. Universal groups are really only useful in multidomain environments.

Answer d is correct. Don't forget, in a single domain, there is no need to use universal groups. They cause additional replication, and in a single-domain environment, you gain nothing by using them. Answer a is incorrect because although universal groups do indeed create increased traffic, it will be controlled by sites and site links (see Chapter 12 for details). Therefore, this is not a valid reason to avoid using universal groups. Answer b is incorrect because universal groups should not be considered as simply another layer. Their scope differentiates them from other group types. Answer c is incorrect; depending on the domain mode type, universal groups can indeed be used for security purposes.

Question 9

Zevi Mehlman has been asked to change the password for a user account. Zevi is a domain administrator. However, Zevi has tried to contact the user to get her current password but has been unable to. His boss is worried that someone might have the password for this account. What is the best course of action for Zevi to take?

○ a. Zevi should delete the user account and re-create it with the new password. The user will call as soon as she is unable to log on.

○ b. Because Zevi is a domain administrator, he does not need the user's current password to make the change.

○ c. Zevi should disable the account. This will force the user to call in with the information Zevi needs.

○ d. Zevi should lock the account out. This will force the user to call in with the information Zevi needs.

Answer b is correct. Zevi does not need the user's password. It is not advisable to change users' passwords without them knowing, but there might be times when it is necessary. Answer a is incorrect because deleting the account will increase his administrative tasks later. He would have to re-create the account and reassign all permissions to it. Answer c is incorrect because disabling the account prevents the user from accessing the network. Answer d is technically correct, however, it also prevents the user from accessing the network.

Question 10

What are the names given to the types of logon names that will be accepted by a Windows 2000 network? [Check all correct answers]

❏ a. User logon name

❏ b. User account name

❏ c. Principal name

❏ d. Domain username

Answers a and c are correct. The user logon name requires the user to enter the name of the domain that contains his or her account. The principal name resembles an email address. The user does not have to specify the domain name when using principal names. Answers b and d are other names commonly used to describe the user logon name. However, you should not use these terms, because they can have more than one meaning on a Windows 2000 network.

Need to Know More?

 Boswell, William. *Inside Windows 2000 Server.* New Riders, Indianapolis, IN, 1999. ISBN 1562059297. This book is a highly technical read that explains the details of all facets of a Windows 2000 Server, including replication.

 Iseminger, David. *Active Directory Services for Microsoft Windows 2000.* Microsoft Press, Redmond, WA, 2000. ISBN 0735606242. This book introduces you to all aspects of working with a Windows 2000 domain, specifically dealing with AD administration.

 Minasi, Mark. *Mastering Windows 2000 Server, Second Edition.* Sybex Computer Books, Alameda, CA, 2000. ISBN 0782127746. This easy-to-read guide to administration offers a wealth of tips and practical ideas.

 Nielsen, Morten Strunge. *Windows 2000 Server Architecture and Planning.* The Coriolis Group, Scottsdale, AZ, 1999. ISBN 1576104362. This book provides assistance with design and migration issues.

Active Directory Delegation of Administrative Control

Terms you'll need to understand:

✓ Security principal

✓ Security ID (SID)

✓ Discretionary access control list (DACL)

✓ System access control list (SACL)

✓ Access control entry (ACE)

✓ Access tokens

✓ Permissions

✓ Child objects

✓ Inheritance

✓ Ownership

✓ Microsoft Management Console (MMC)

✓ Taskpads

Techniques you'll need to master:

✓ Viewing Active Directory object permissions

✓ Assigning delegation of authority with the wizard

✓ Designing administrative control with inheritance and blocking in mind

✓ Viewing and taking ownership of objects

✓ Creating specialized management consoles and taskpads

If you understand that placing permissions on various objects determines who has access to objects like printers, folders, files, and so on, you will easily understand the concept of the delegation of administrative authority. Delegating administrative control defines which trusted individuals will have access to Active Directory (AD) objects (either to create, delete, or modify) for distributing the administrative workload and maintaining control in the process. There are several other ways to maintain control, such as the use of customized Microsoft Management Consoles (MMCs) and taskpads. The implementation of these functions is discussed in the sections "Creating MMC Consoles" and "Taskpads" toward the end of the chapter.

Object Security

AD security involves many abstract technical terms that are often used without being properly defined. Let's look at the terminology behind the security components.

Terminology for AD Security

Often, words are misused in the computer field. Here is a list of important security terms and how each relates to the authentication process.

➤ *Security principal*—This is an account to which permissions can be assigned—for example, a user, a group, or a computer account. If you are Bob, a member of the Accounting group on a computer with a domain computer account named System01, several security principals are involved that permissions could be applied toward—namely, the user "Bob," the group "Accounting," or the computer account "System01."

➤ *Security ID (SID)*—Every security principal is issued a unique SID that is assigned once to an account and is never reused, even if the object is removed. The SID is a numeric value that is assigned automatically when an object is added to the directory.

➤ *Security descriptor*—This becomes part of created objects and defines access control information for that object. When a user attempts to access an object, the descriptor checks its information against the user's SID and then compares the SID against its access control list (ACL). There are two types of ACLs: DACLs and SACLs.

➤ *Discretionary access control list (DACL)*—This is a list of access control entries (ACEs) that indicates security levels of Allow Access or Deny Access permissions and to what degree these permissions apply. One key point in a DACL is that the Deny Access entries are placed first in the ACE. A user could have plenty of access permissions for an object but may belong to one group that has Deny for all permissions. The Deny will prove stronger than all of the other options. By placing the Deny Access entries first in the list, you save a lot of time because the user may not have the permissions for the object he or she was hoping to access.

➤ *System access control list (SACL)*—This is a list used for auditing object access based upon ACEs that indicates to the object when an account has accessed an object or has attempted to access an object. In the event that access is attempted or achieved, a record of the access is placed in the object security list.

➤ *Access control entries (ACEs)*—ACEs are used by DACLs and SACLs. When used with a DACL, the ACE determines the level of security access upon an object by breaking it down into four types: Access Denied, Access Allowed, Access Denied Object Specify, and Access Allowed Object Specify. When used with an SACL, the ACE determines the level of security access based upon two remaining types of ACEs: System Audit and System Audit Object Specific. These six different entry types assist in determining the permissions to be applied.

➤ *Access tokens*—All of the items in this list would be ineffective without an access token. When a user logs on, an access token is created and sent by the DC to the user's machine. This token is necessary for a user to access any network resource. The access token is attached to that user and is needed to access any object, to run any application, and to use system resources. The access token is what literally holds the SID and the group IDs, which indicate what groups the user belongs to. These group IDs are really SIDs that are given to the groups upon their creation. If a user belongs to a group, that group's SID is added to the user's access token.

Note: Only global and domain local groups are added to the token from the DC to which the user logs on. The DC will contact a Global Catalog (GC) for SIDs of universal group membership.

User rights are also included in the access token—for example, the right to log on locally to a computer or a domain controller (DC), if that right is assigned to a specific user.

From Logon to Object Access

To fully understand all of the terms in the preceding list, we need to put them in a context that brings them to life. Say a domain administrator sits down at a DC and creates a user account named "Lamar." This is a security principal, which can now be assigned permissions. Lamar's account is automatically assigned a unique SID, never again to be used. This identifies the Lamar object. Lamar may be assigned to the Sales and Managers groups during creation as well. The account may also be given certain user rights specific to the account.

At the same time, in another part of the building, a physical print device is attached to a print server. The printer object is shared out on the network. Certain permissions are applied to the object, and as a result, the object has a security description. Auditing is also enabled on this printer.

When user Lamar logs on, he receives his access token (a token provided by the DC that contains the SID, group SIDs, and user rights) and then attempts to access the printer object. The object checks its security description for permissions. Specifically, it checks its DACL for ACEs for which the user has either Allow or Deny permissions, and it checks Allow or Deny permissions for any groups to which the user belongs. Then, because auditing is enabled, the object checks its SACL for ACEs that determine if an entry should be made in the log for this attempt at access.

As you can see, accessing a resource requires a rather involved process. This concept is also the key to understanding how AD objects like Organizational Units (OUs) can be structured to allow access from selected individuals.

Access Permissions on AD Objects

Although file/folder permissions and AD object permissions are similar in access theoretics, their purposes are dissimilar. You apply permissions on AD objects (for example, an OU unit, a hierarchical group of OU units, or even an individual object such as a user, group, or computer account) for the purpose of delegating authority, whereas you apply file/folder permissions to control access to those specific resources for the users and groups within your organization.

The actual permissions that you can apply to objects are also different from those of files and folders. The five standard permissions that can be applied to an object are:

➤ *Full Control*—Allows the user the ability to view objects and attributes, the owner of the object, and the AD permissions, along with the ability to change any of those settings. In addition, a user with Full Control can literally change permissions on the object and take ownership of an object.

➤ *Write*—Enables the user to view objects and attributes, the owner of the object, and the AD permissions. Also allows the user to change any of those settings.

➤ *Read*—Enables the user to view objects and attributes, the owner of the object, and the AD permissions.

➤ *Create All Child Objects*—Enables the user to create additional child objects to an OU.

➤ *Delete All Child Objects*—Enables the user to delete existing objects from an OU.

All objects within the AD have an owner. Similar to the owners that exist in files and folders, the owner of an object can change permissions on the object and how those permissions are handed out. Logically, the initial owner of any object is the one who created it. So, if Tim creates an OU named "Sales," Tim's account would be registered as the owner—unless he provides permissions for another individual to have Full Control, in which case that person would be able to take ownership of that object.

Viewing AD Permissions

To view permissions that exist on an AD object (an OU is the embodiment of a perfect-example AD object, so we will consider that as the standard object for this section), you must perform the following tasks:

1. Open AD Users and Computers by selecting Start|Programs|Administrative Tools|Active Directory Users And Computers.

2. On the View menu, make sure that Advanced Features is selected.

3. Expand your domain structure and select an OU that you can use as an example.

4. Right-click on the OU and select Properties.

5. Select the Security tab. From here, you can see the standard permissions for your OU, as shown in Figure 6.1 and mentioned in the previous section.

To see additional permissions options called "special permissions," select the Advanced button. Here you can select one of three tabs: Permissions, Auditing, and

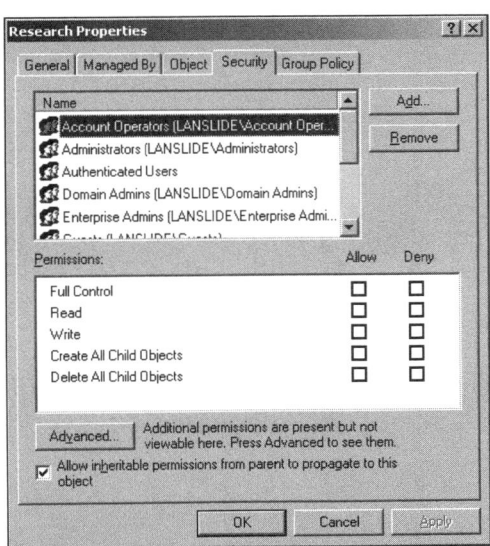

Figure 6.1   Viewing object permissions through the Security tab.

Owner. On the Permissions tab, shown in Figure 6.2, you can see all of the permissions entries that have already been applied. From here you can add or remove user or group permissions, or you can select View/Edit to see the special permissions options shown in Figure 6.3.

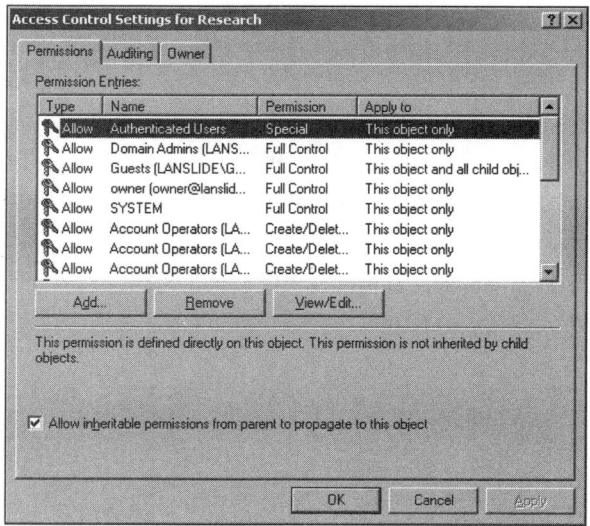

Figure 6.2 The advanced permissions options.

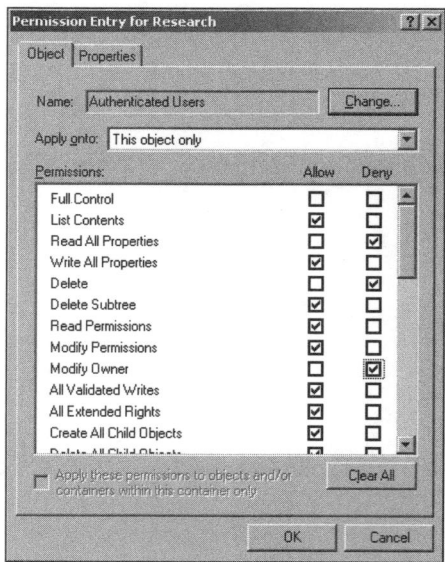

Figure 6.3 The special permissions options.

Also notice the Allow Inheritable Permissions From Parent To Propagate To This Object checkbox at the bottom of Figures 6.1 and 6.2. This option is part of the inheritance concepts that we will discuss shortly.

To Allow or to Deny

Permissions under Windows 2000 are what we call "granular," because of the miniscule ways that permissions can be applied to objects. Allow permissions are always easy to conceptualize, but with AD object permissions, Deny permissions are also available. These Deny permissions have a stronger effect on an individual that attempts certain functions.

For example, if Jeremy is a member of the Research Admins security group and that group has Full Control Allow permissions over the Research OU, then logically, Jeremy also has Allow permissions by extension. However, if it has been determined that Jeremy, as a new employee, should not be given Delete All Child Object permissions, rather than pulling Jeremy out of his security group or changing the permissions for the entire group, you can place specific Deny permissions on Jeremy's user account that will deny him access to the Delete All Child Object permissions. When the DACL for the Research OU sees a Deny permissions setting for Delete All Child Object permissions in its ACE for Jeremy, that permission applies above and beyond the Full Control permissions of his group.

Theoretical Delegation of Authority

After the deployment of a domain, quite a bit of administrative work still needs to be performed. In a small environment, the work would be easy—just put all of your administrators in the Domain Admins group and leave it at that. However, in an enterprise network infrastructure, you need to *delegate* your administration and mold it in your company's best interests.

So, where do you begin? As with many tasks, you begin by documenting your existing structure. A planning team should be put together to examine the current infrastructure of the administrative team, along with the responsibilities that the administrators hold. Keep in mind that the changes made to the network structure in the future will greatly alter some of those administrative responsibilities.

The planning team can take this knowledge and start posing the following types of questions:

➤ Can we combine some of the current administrative teams into a more decisive administrative structure?

➤ Are there employees who might assist to some degree in administration without having the technical background to do so (or the request for a tech's salary)?

➤ What should each administrative group or individual be allowed to control and to what degree?

Once the planning team has a basic understanding of the task at hand, the members can use the following points to help delegate administrative control properly:

➤ *Assign control at the OU level for easier administration.* This allows you to track permissions in a simpler manner. Try to assign administrative control at the highest OU levels as well, and allow inheritance to control the flow of administration. This will be an easier and more efficient way of managing permissions. Remember, the domain and OU levels of the hierarchy are designed to meet the administrative needs of the organization. Design and build it in such a way that it simplifies delegating administrative authority.

➤ *Try to avoid assigning control at the property or task level as much as possible.* To handle permissions more efficiently, try to place objects in OUs based upon management rather than have OUs with multiple objects inside and different access permissions for each object. You can see how this would become messy if you needed to track down a permissions problem. It will also make it difficult for your administrators to know what objects they have control over. On the one hand, they've been told they can control permissions under a certain OU, but perhaps the objects within have permissions all their own.

➤ *Utilize a small Domain Administrators group.* The Domain Admins group contains the all-powerful rulers of the network. They can take ownership of any object, define policies, change passwords at the senior management level, and so on. That makes any member of the Domain Admins group a highly trusted individual. Limit the membership to this group, and allow other administrators to handle administrative tasks throughout the domain at the OU level. Members of the Domain Admins group should also be under strict instruction not to give out their network authentication method, whether it's a password or a smart card (a smart card is a good idea if you need high levels of security).

➤ *Finally, document everything.* Tracking down problems with administrative delegation will be much easier if you've documented your procedures.

Setting AD Permissions

You can establish permissions on AD objects in two ways. The first is by directly adding users and their corresponding permissions. You simply follow the same procedure for the viewing of permissions, noted earlier in the "Viewing AD Permissions" section, and add new users or groups with permissions that will ease your administrative concerns. Microsoft's preferred method is through the Delegation of Control Wizard because it involves a simpler sequence of steps.

The Delegation of Control Wizard

You can use the Delegation of Control Wizard to delegate common tasks, or you can create a customized task to delegate. This section explains how to do both.

Delegating Common Tasks

The standard procedural steps for using the Delegation of Control Wizard are as follows:

1. In the AD Users and Computers administrative tool, find the OU to which you wish to delegate control.

2. To start the wizard, you can select Action|Delegate Control, or you can right-click on the OU and select Delegate Control.

3. The wizard presents an opening screen and dialog box. Click on Next.

4. On the Users And Groups page, you are prompted to select a user, several users, a group, or several groups (the choice depends on your needs). After highlighting your selections, click on Add, and then click on OK.

5. The Tasks To Delegate screen, shown in Figure 6.4, appears. From the list of common tasks, select the tasks you want and then click on Next.

6. Click on Finish.

Creating a Custom Task

The steps for creating a customized task in the Delegation of Control Wizard are as follows:

1. Follow the five steps in the previous section, with the following change: In Step 5, select Create A Custom Task To Delegate instead of choosing from the list of common tasks. Click on Next.

2. The screen in Figure 6.5 appears. Notice that you can set permissions on This Folder, Existing Objects In This Folder, And Creation Of New Objects In This Folder as one option. You can also select the Only The Following Objects In The Folder option, which displays a long list of different types of objects to choose from. Notice the granularity of control that can be implemented on an OU. Make your selections, then click on Next.

3. The next screen shows three options of permissions detail: General, Property-Specific, and Creation/Deletion Of Specific Child Objects, as shown in Figure 6.6. Each selection provides additional checkbox options. By selecting the type of permissions and their corresponding checkboxes, you complete your creation of a customized set of delegation options. Click on Next to move to the final screen.

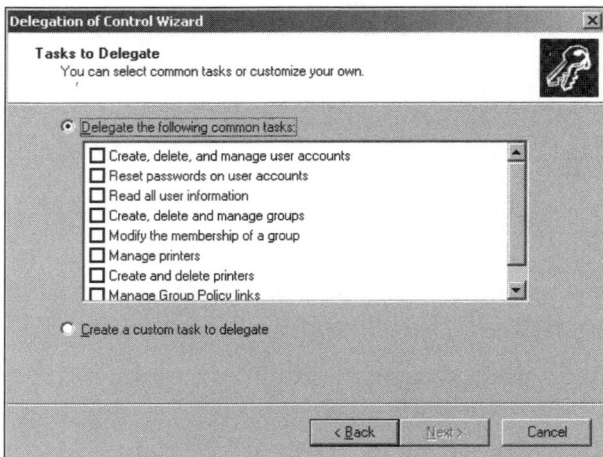

Figure 6.4 Delegating common tasks over an object.

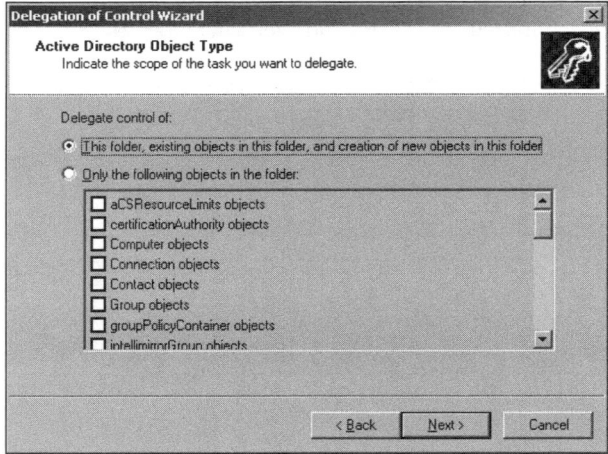

Figure 6.5 Setting customized permissions options.

4. The final screen displays a listing of your choices. Review your selections and click on Finish.

Once you've used the wizard to delegate authority, your next concern is how permissions should flow between parent and child objects.

The Flow of Permissions

To simplify the setting of permissions, the implementation of inheritance is utilized by Windows 2000. Inheritance is automatic for child objects within parent containers. Put simply, if a parent object—an OU, for example—has permissions implemented upon it, the child objects beneath will automatically inherit the

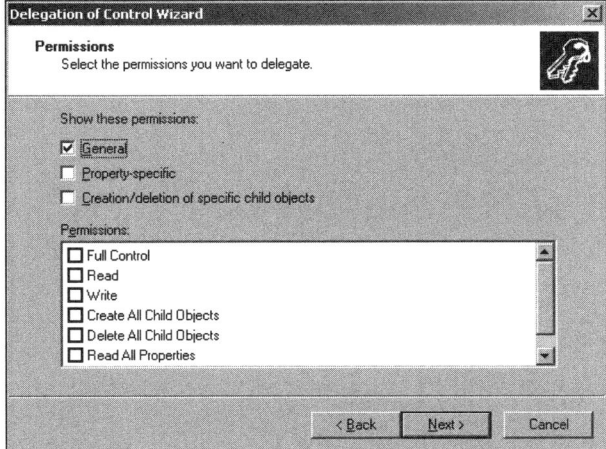

Figure 6.6 The specific permissions that you choose to delegate.

permissions from above. The benefit of inheritance is that permissions need to be applied only at high-level containers, and they will flow down throughout child containers that are already in existence. This makes the administrative task of delegating authority much easier for the following reasons:

➤ When you create a child object within a parent container that holds certain permissions, the child object automatically contains the permissions of its parent, as shown in Figure 6.7.

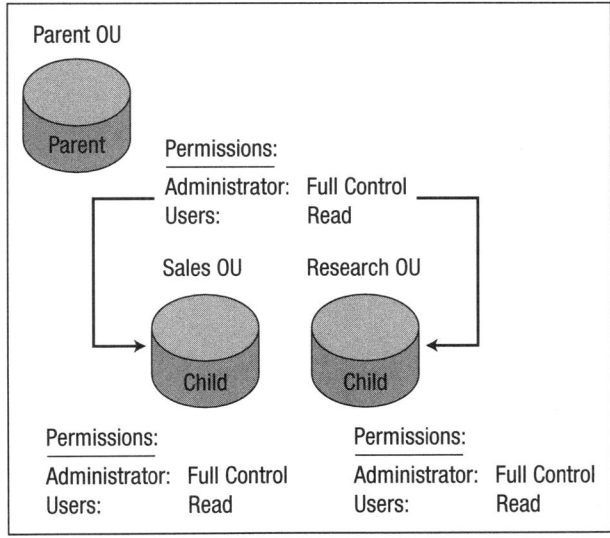

Figure 6.7 The flow of inheritance.

➤ When you set permissions at higher levels, those permissions are applied consistently through the lower child objects.

➤ Any changes made to permissions above automatically apply to the child objects below.

Redirecting the Flow of Permissions

There are times when the flow from above will not logically work for your lower containers. For example, say you have an OU called "Ontario" for your branch location in Ontario. Most tasks and OUs within the Ontario parent container are cared for through the Ontario Admins security group. A special OU has been added to the parent container called "SR" for special secretive research projects concerning cold fusion. The standard admin team cannot handle this container or any administrative tasks in conjunction with it. Permissions flow through inheritance, and so the SR OU has automatically inherited from above. What can be done?

1. First, note the Allow Inheritable Permissions From Parent To Propagate To This Object checkbox at the bottom of Figure 6.2. When this box is selected, permissions are inherited. Remove the check in this box to remove the permissions inheritance.

2. As shown in Figure 6.8, prior to the removal of all permissions from above, you'll see a Security screen that presents two options: Copy and Remove. Choose Copy to retain permissions that were already in place on the OU. With this option, you can then make revisions. Choose Remove to remove all pre-existing permissions. With this option, you must assign permissions from scratch.

 It is important to remember that you have the ability to copy permissions from pre-existing permissions from above, or the ability to remove all permissions from above.

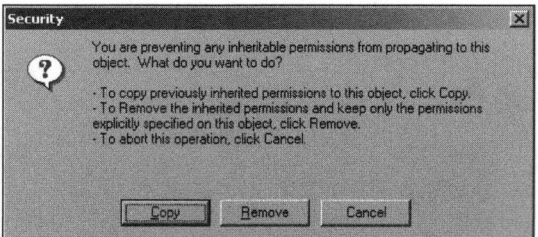

Figure 6.8 The options for removal of inheritance from above.

Ownership of AD Objects

Just as all print jobs, files, and folders have owners, each object within the AD has an owner that is responsible for the existence of the object. The owner is usually the one that created the object and the one that holds full control over that object.

At times, the ownership of an object needs to change hands. If an individual with permissions creates several objects within the AD and that individual is no longer with the company or has changed departments, it may be necessary for another assigned individual to take ownership of those objects. Note the word *take*. Ownership cannot be given away; users with the correct permissions must take it.

Viewing Ownership

As with an OU, to view the owner of a particular object, follow these steps:

1. Go into the Properties of the object by right-clicking on the object itself.

2. At the top of the object's properties, select the Security tab.

3. Select the Advanced button.

4. This takes you to a familiar place—the Access Control Settings tabs. At the top, select the Owner tab, as shown in Figure 6.9. The current owner is displayed.

Taking Ownership

Ownership changes hands in one of two ways. First, the current owner or a user with Full Control over an object specifies that another user can take ownership

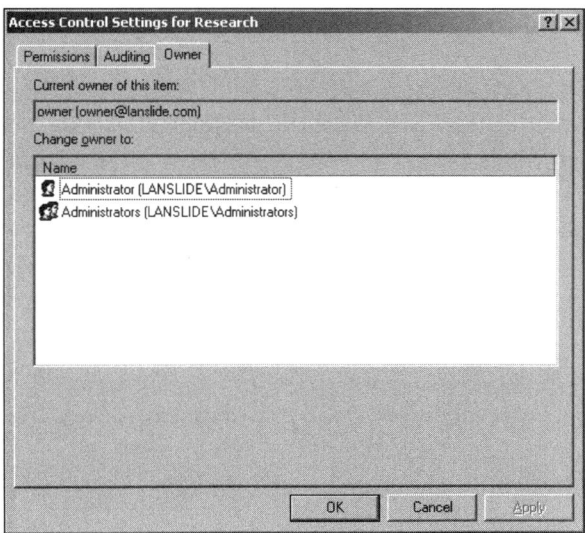

Figure 6.9   The Owner tab shows the current owner of the object you are viewing.

and that user then officially takes ownership of the object. Second, an administrator or a domain administrator takes ownership of an object, regardless of whom the owner currently is or whether the admin was given specific permissions for an object.

If an administrator takes ownership of an object, the Domain Admins group is also listed as an owner for an object. The logic is that if one administrator needs to have ownership control over an object, the entire Domain Admins group should hold ownership.

To take ownership of an object, follow the same steps as for viewing an object's owner:

1. Go into the Properties of the object by right-clicking on the object itself.

2. At the top of the object's properties, select the Security tab.

3. Select the Advanced button.

4. This takes you to the Access Control Settings tabs. At the top, find and select the Owner tab. The current owner is displayed.

5. If you have permissions to be owner, your name will appear in the options below (or if you are an administrator, your name and the Domain Admins group will appear). Select your name and click on Apply. You have taken ownership of the object.

Delegation of Administrative Tools

Although delegating authority is a great way to distribute administrative responsibilities, another way to delegate is to allow individuals to use certain administrative tools that are necessary.

Windows 2000 uses the Microsoft Management Console (MMC) as a one-stop tool for all of the administrative tools within the suite. Although various predefined consoles are already in place when you install Windows 2000, it is important that ordinary users not have access to such tools. However, you may need to allow users access to some of the tools so that they can use the authority that you've delegated. For example, if you've delegated authority over an OU to a user, it is a good idea to provide the user with an MMC that holds the AD Users and Computers tool.

Another benefit of customizable MMC consoles is that they allow you, as an administrator, to create your own consoles with tools that you use most frequently.

Creating MMC Consoles

Before creating a specialized console, you must determine which mode to use to create your console. Two modes are available: Author mode and User mode. The Author mode is for administrative consoles that are specially designed for easy control by other administrators that receive these consoles. Author mode is used to create new consoles and modify existing consoles. User mode is more tailored toward limiting the user from customizing the console any further than what you've already determined. User mode is for working with existing consoles. There are three levels of user mode:

➤ Full access

➤ Limited access, multiple windows

➤ Limited access, single window

Once the mode is determined, you can proceed with the creation. To create a console:

1. Select Start|Run. Type "mmc" in the textbox and hit Enter. An empty console appears.

2. At the top, select Console and choose Add/Remove Snap-In. This takes you to an empty list of snap-ins. (Notice under Console that the Options selection is also available. This is where you would specify the mode.)

3. Select Add. A list of the many available tools appears. Select a few snap-ins, click on Add for each snap-in selected, and select whether it will manage a local computer or another computer. Then click on Finish. Select Close when you are finished adding snap-ins. Click on OK, and you are brought to your newly created MMC console.

4. Once the console is created, you must now save it. Select Console and then Save As. Give the console a name and location, and the console will be saved with an .msc extension.

After creating the console, your next concern is distributing it.

Distributing MMC Consoles

There are a few recommended ways to send consoles:

➤ If small enough, they can be distributed via floppy or email.

➤ They can be placed in a shared folder for administrators to access. This would allow for NTFS (NT File System) permissions to provide a lockdown of Write permissions, preventing changes to your consoles. (Make sure your administrators have Read permissions, though.)

➤ You can package them and distribute them through Group Policy.

How you distribute your saved console is up to you; however, one key point to remember is that any administrator that receives the console also needs to install the tools on his or her system. These tools are not installed on the Windows 2000 Professional workstations. You must install them manually.

Installing Administrative Tools

Microsoft provides these tools on the Windows 2000 Advanced Server CD or off of a server running Windows 2000 Advanced Server in the systemroot/system32 folder. The file is an MSI file called adminpak. Because it is an MSI file, it is part of the Windows Installer team and can be distributed through Group Policy or installed manually. On the system running Windows 2000 Professional, you need to execute and install the adminpak.msi file. Now the consoles you've created will have tools to draw upon.

Taskpads

After you assign permissions to an AD object and create specific MMC consoles, taskpads are the next level of administrative delegation. A *taskpad* is a simplified version of an MMC. It is used when administrators want to delegate administrative control to people who are not yet comfortable using these types of tools.

Creating a Taskpad

Once you've created your customized MMC console, the steps to create a taskpad are simple. You use the Taskpad Creation Wizard as follows:

1. Select Snap-In from within the console that you've created.

2. To start the wizard, then highlight the snap-in and select Action|New Taskpad View.

3. The first screen requires you to determine the taskpad display, as shown in Figure 6.10. From here, you can determine the look of your taskpad and the amount of detail.

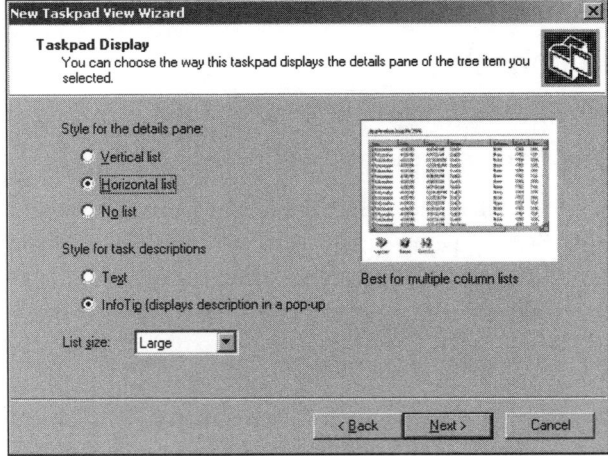

Figure 6.10 The Taskpad Display screen.

The wizard takes you through the steps of configuration. The end result is a simplified presentation to users that are not as comfortable with the true console. The options that users select actually point toward shortcuts of the real MMC console. All of the same rules apply for taskpad distribution that applied for MMC console distribution.

Customizing a Taskpad

Once your taskpad is officially created, you can customize it for your users and simplify it even further. You can establish large buttons that correlate with actual tasks that an individual might perform. For example, Figure 6.11 shows a taskpad view of the AD Users and Computers tool. From there, a specific taskpad was created of the Users folder of the snap-in. Finally, a large shortcut button was added to the taskpad to allow the creation of a new user. Using this taskpad, the user can create users easily; all he or she has to do is hit the shortcut button. By making these types of customizations and distributing the taskpads to others, you will make administration very easy for those to whom you've delegated control.

Note: You can customize your taskpads even further than shortcut buttons by specifying batch files or scripts to be run off of a simple button selection.

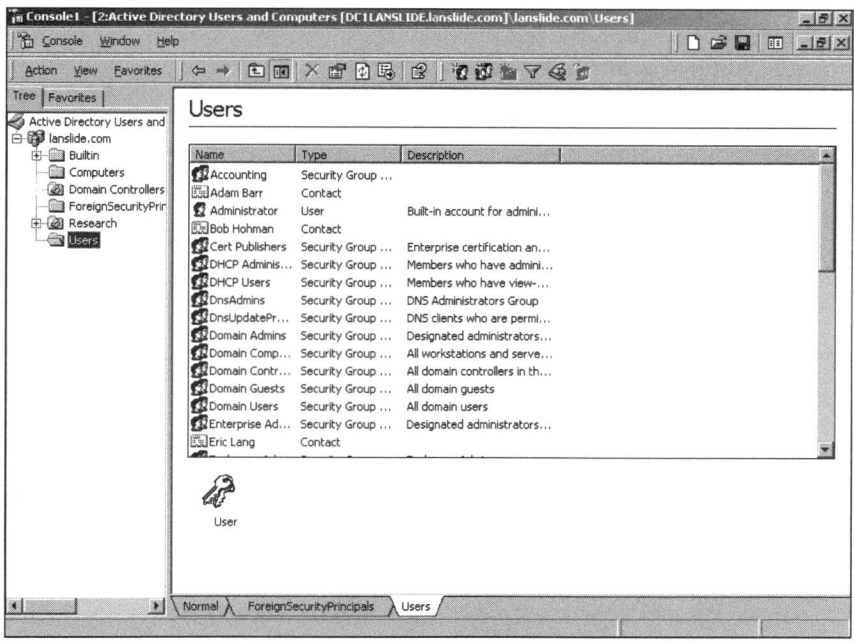

Figure 6.11   A customized taskpad for the creation of users.

Practice Questions

Question 1

To simplify administrative tasks, you've decided to apply permissions of object control to your Active Directory. Where should you assign control to qualified users in your organization?

○ a. Folders

○ b. Files

○ c. OUs

○ d. You should add the users to the Domain Admins group

Answer c is correct. Assigning control at the OU level is the best way to administer control over objects within Active Directory, although it is possible to assign permissions directly to objects, like a user or a printer. Answers a and b are incorrect because they relate to file/folder access permissions and not to Active Directory objects. Answer d is incorrect because, although this will give control over Active Directory objects, it is not a recommended way of delegating responsibility; rather, it is a way of sharing responsibility with peers, not users.

Question 2

In establishing a more granular control over permissions, Windows 2000 provides what permissions options over Active Directory objects? [Check all correct answers]

❑ a. Allow

❑ b. Permission

❑ c. Access

❑ d. Deny

Answers a and d are correct. Through the use of Allow and Deny permissions, administrators can provide a more granular control over the depth of permissions that an individual user might have. Answer b is incorrect because it is not a permissions option. Answer c is incorrect because it, too, is not a permissions option; rather, it is more of a diversion from the correct answer.

Question 3

From the following list, select the permissions options that can be placed upon objects within the Active Directory:

Full Control

Modify

Write

Change

Read

No Access

Create All Child Objects

Access AD Object

Delete All Child Objects

The correct answer is:

Full Control

Write

Read

Create All Child Objects

Delete All Child Objects

Question 4

Which of the following tools would you use to view Active Directory object permissions?

○ a. AD Domains and Trusts

○ b. AD Users and Computers

○ c. AD Sites and Services

○ d. AD Object Permissions

Answer b is correct. You go to AD Users and Computers to view object permissions. Remember to select View and then Advanced Features before going into the properties of an OU to see the permissions on the Security tab. Answers a and c are incorrect because these tools handle site and domain issues, not Active Directory object creation or permissions. Answer d is incorrect because it is not valid.

Question 5

> Kayla is a domain admininstrator who has placed permissions on a parent OU, and through inheritance, those permissions have flowed down toward the child OUs beneath. What can Kayla do to prevent the flow of inheritance while retaining the permissions that already exist on the objects? [Check all correct answers]
>
> ❑ a. Go into the properties of the OU and deselect the Allow Inheritable Permissions From Parent To Propagate To This Object checkbox.
>
> ❑ b. Go into the properties of the OU and select the Allow Inheritable Permissions From Parent To Propagate To This Object checkbox.
>
> ❑ c. Select Copy at the Security screen.
>
> ❑ d. Select Remove at the Security screen.

Answers a and c are correct. To remove inheritance, you must deselect the checkbox on the OU that allows inheritance. To retain the preexisting permissions, you must select Copy from the corresponding warning box that appears. Answer b is incorrect because it would apply inheritance from above to the object. Answer d is incorrect because it would remove all permissions that existed prior to the change.

Question 6

> If an administrator takes ownership of an object, who else is listed as an owner of that object?
>
> ○ a. The object's creator
>
> ○ b. Previous owners
>
> ○ c. The Domain Admins group
>
> ○ d. The Enterprise Admins group

Answer c is correct. The Domain Admins group is also listed as an owner for an object. The logic is that if one administrator needs to have ownership control over an object, the entire Domain Admins group should hold ownership. Answer a is incorrect because the creator isn't always listed under the ownership section, although the creator is always the original owner of an object. Answer b is incorrect because the ownership is tracked from one person to the next. Answer d is incorrect for obvious reasons.

Question 7

> Here is a list of five security terms:
>
> Security principal
>
> Security ID (SID)
>
> Security descriptor
>
> Discretionary access control list (DACL)
>
> Access token
>
> Match the following definitions with the correct terms.
>
> This is a list of ACEs that indicate security levels of Allow or Deny access permissions and to what degree these permissions apply.
>
> This is an account to which permissions can be assigned—for example, a user, a group, or a computer account.
>
> Provided at logon, this item is necessary for a user to access any network resource.
>
> This becomes part of created objects and defines access control information for that object.
>
> This is a numeric value that is assigned automatically when an object is added to the directory.

The correct answer is:

Security principal

> This is an account to which permissions can be assigned—for example, a user, a group, or a computer account.

Security ID (SID)

> This is a numeric value that is assigned automatically when an object is added to the directory.

Security descriptor

> This becomes part of created objects and defines access control information for that object.

Discretionary access control list (DACL)

> This is a list of access control entries (ACE) that indicate security levels of Allow or Deny access permissions and to what degree these permissions apply.

Access token

Provided at logon, this item is necessary for a user to access any network resource.

Question 8

After you create a specialized console and save it in a place for distribution, what will the extension be on that saved console?

○ a. .doc

○ b. .mmc

○ c. .msi

○ d. .msc

Answer d is correct. The console will be saved with an .msc extension. Answer a is incorrect because this is a Word document extension. Answer b is incorrect because "mmc" is typed in the Run box to open an empty console. Answer c is incorrect because an .msi extension indicates a file for the Windows Installer.

Question 9

Quinn has created a console for certain users that are new to their departments. He has assigned them correct permissions and emailed them the console. They attempt to use the console from their Windows 2000 Professional desktops and yet are having difficulty. What is a logical cause of such a problem?

○ a. They are missing the correct permissions.

○ b. They are not in the Domain Admins group.

○ c. They do not have the Administrative Tools installed on their stations.

○ d. They are too new to the company and need more time before all utilities will work.

Answer c is correct. Individuals that attempt to use consoles off of their workstations need to install those tools, either from the server or from the server CD. Answer a is incorrect because permissions were already mentioned as being provided. Answer b is incorrect because the whole point of delegating control is so they don't have to be in a specific group with total control. Answer d is incorrect because utilities aren't judgmental based upon time with the company.

Question 10

Individuals that have been assigned delegation of control are in need of a simpler console because they do not yet understand how to use the customized consoles you've provided. What can you do provide the shortest learning curve for those individuals? [Choose the best answer]

○ a. Create taskpads.

○ b. Delegate less authority.

○ c. Give them a class on using consoles.

○ d. Allow them time to learn.

Answer a is correct. A taskpad makes performing their jobs much easier until they become more comfortable with their tasks. Answer b is incorrect because it defeats the purpose of delegation. Answer c is incorrect, although a good idea for any new administrator. Answer d is incorrect, although again, it is a good idea to be patient with people in new positions.

Need to Know More?

 Boswell, William. *Inside Windows 2000 Server*. New Riders, Indianapolis, IN, 2000. ISBN 1562059297. Delegation of authority is an integral part of Windows 2000, and the functional implementation is logically presented within this necessary resource for Windows 2000 administrators.

 Bruzzese, J. Peter and Wayne Dipchan. *MCSE Windows 2000 Directory Services Design Exam Prep*. The Coriolis Group, Scottsdale, AZ, 2000. ISBN 1576106683. Chapter 15 handles the design and implementation issues for the Delegation of Control Wizard, as well as the manual steps to assign OU permissions.

 Nielsen, Morton Strunge. *Windows 2000 Server Architecture and Planning*. The Coriolis Group, Scottsdale, AZ, 1999. ISBN 1576104362. This book is an excellent resource for AD planning and deployment.

 Watts, David V., Will Willis, and Tillman Strahan. *MCSE Windows 2000 Directory Services Exam Prep*. The Coriolis Group, Scottsdale, AZ, 1999. ISBN 1576106241. This book provides more detailed instruction on the implementation of customized MMC consoles and the development of taskpads.

 Search the TechNet CD (or its online version through **www. microsoft.com**) using keywords "Microsoft Management Console" and "distributed security", along with related query items.

Understanding Group Policy Implementation

- -

Terms you'll need to understand:

✓ IntelliMirror

✓ Security groups

✓ Policy

✓ Group Policy Object (GPO)

✓ Site

✓ Domain

✓ Organizational Unit (OU)

✓ Linking

✓ Storage domain

✓ Delegation of control

✓ Inheritance

✓ No Override

✓ Change and configuration management

✓ Filtering

Techniques you'll need to master:

✓ Creating a Group Policy Object (GPO)

✓ Linking an existing GPO

✓ Modifying Group Policy

✓ Delegating administrative control of Group Policy

✓ Modifying Group Policy inheritance

✓ Filtering Group Policy settings by associating security groups to GPOs

Change and configuration management is a strong area of emphasis for Microsoft with Windows 2000, as the company seeks to enable IT professionals and corporations to reduce the total cost of ownership (TCO) of IT resources. Likewise, change and configuration management topics are emphasized on the exam. In this chapter, we will examine Group Policy as it fits into a change and configuration management strategy, and then show the implementation details you should know.

Change and Configuration Basics

Understanding Microsoft's underlying philosophies with Windows 2000 is important, because these basic philosophies permeate everything Microsoft has done with the operating system and will play a role in how well you do on the exam. Primarily, Windows 2000 and Active Directory (AD) seek to reduce the TCO and increase the return on investment (ROI) for business systems. IT professionals must become increasingly familiar with business terms such as TCO and ROI in today's changing economy, where IT is expected to function more as a business unit than as a traditional cost center.

Change and configuration management concerns the developing of processes within an organization to manage ongoing day-to-day issues that typically arise with computers and information technology. The goal is to maximize a user's ability to be productive while reducing the costs associated with support and downtime. Microsoft includes several technologies in Windows 2000 that are dependent on AD and make up Microsoft's change and configuration management initiative. This collection of technologies is commonly referred to as *IntelliMirror*. Here is a quick summary of IntelliMirror's benefits:

➤ Enables administrators to define environment settings for users, groups, and computers. Windows 2000 then enforces the settings.

➤ Allows the Windows 2000 Professional operating system to be installed remotely onto compatible computers.

➤ Enables users' local folders to be redirected to a shared server location and files to be synchronized automatically between the server and local hard drive for working offline. This is a boon for laptop users.

➤ Enables users' desktop settings and applications to roam with them no matter what computer users log on from.

➤ Enables administrators to centrally manage software installation, updating, and removal. Self-healing applications replace missing or corrupted files automatically, without user intervention.

➤ Makes the computer a commodity. A system can simply be replaced with a new one, and settings, applications, and policies are quickly regenerated on the new system with a minimum amount of downtime.

One of the key features of a Windows 2000 change and configuration management strategy involves Group Policy, which is the focus of this chapter and the following two chapters. After a quick overview of Group Policy, we will show you the skills you need to be successful on the exam.

Group Policy Overview

Group Policy is one cog in the Windows 2000 change and configuration management wheel, but it is arguably one of the most critical features of an AD-based network. In fact, Group Policy relies on AD and its dependencies to function.

The goals of Group Policy are for an administrator to have to define settings only once for a user, group, or computer, and to ensure that those settings are enforced by Windows 2000 until the administrator specifies otherwise. It is extremely important to understand that Group Policy is not the same as system profiles, which were used in Windows NT 4 to specify desktop settings. System policies still exist for backward compatibility; however, in Windows 2000-only environments, using only Group Policy is recommended.

Group Policy is also used to enhance the end-user computing experience by providing customized environments to meet the user's work requirements. That might involve something like putting specialized application icons on the desktop or Start menu, or redirecting the My Documents folder to a network drive so the user's files are available no matter what computer he or she has logged on to. In addition, an administrator can execute tasks such as startup, logon, logoff, or shutdown to meet the user's needs. Group Policy can therefore create a positive working environment for users.

Group Policy supports only Windows 2000 clients, so Windows 9x and NT 4 and earlier systems cannot realize the benefits of a Group Policy implementation. As we've mentioned, system policies are available to use with these legacy clients.

Group Policy Objects

The basic unit of Group Policy is the Group Policy Object (GPO). A GPO is a collection of policies that can be applied at the site, domain, Organizational Unit (OU), or local level. Additionally, GPO settings are passed along from a parent object to all child objects, a process known as *inheritance*.

Group Policy is processed by Windows 2000 in the following order:

➤ Local

➤ Site

➤ Domain

➤ OU

The first level—local—is covered in the "Local GPOs" section later in this chapter. The other three levels are known as *global* GPOs and are stored within the AD database. These policies are applied based on user, group, or computer membership.

In the "Filtering Group Policy" section later in this chapter, we will look at filtering the effects of Group Policy through security groups, but for now, we will consider a GPO that has not been filtered. The following is true of unfiltered GPOs:

➤ A GPO that is linked to a site will apply to all objects in the site.

➤ A GPO that is linked to a domain will apply to all objects in the domain.

➤ A GPO that is linked to an OU will apply to all objects in the OU.

Although the preceding points sound fairly obvious, they are essential in understanding the scope that Group Policy has. As an organizational structure becomes more complex and the number of GPOs grows, keeping track of the effects of individual GPOs and the combined effects multiple GPOs might have becomes more difficult. By default, GPO settings applied later will override settings applied earlier. Therefore, a domain GPO will override settings made by a site GPO. This provides an administrator with highly granular control over the policy behavior on a network. As you will see in the "Group Policy Inheritance" section later in this chapter, this default behavior can be modified if so desired.

Nonlocal GPOs

Nonlocal GPOs are stored within AD. Two locations within the AD database are used to store nonlocal GPOs: a Group Policy container and a Group Policy template. A Globally Unique Identifier (GUID) is used in naming the GPOs to keep the two locations synchronized.

A *Group Policy container* is an AD storage area for GPO settings for both computer and user Group Policy information. In addition to the Group Policy container, AD stores information in a Group Policy template, which is contained in a folder structure in the System Volume (SYSVOL) folder of domain controllers, located under \winnt\SYSVOL\sysvol*domain_name*\Policies.

When a GPO is created, the Group Policy template is created, and the folder name given to the Group Policy template is the GUID of the GPO. Supplied by the manufacturer of a product, a *GUID* is a hexadecimal number that uniquely identifies the hardware or software. The GUID includes the braces that surround the number. A GUID is in the form of:

{*8 characters-4 characters-4 characters-4 characters-12 characters*}

For example,

{15DEF489-AE24-10BF-C11A-00BB844CE637}

is a valid format for a GUID.

Data that is small in size and changes infrequently is stored in Group Policy containers, whereas data that is either large in size or changes frequently is stored in Group Policy templates.

Local GPOs

So far, we've mentioned local GPOs but have not defined them. A local GPO applies only to the local Windows 2000 computer and is *not* a global object, because the GPO is not stored within the AD database. Local GPOs are stored on the local hard drive of the Windows 2000 system, in the \winnt\system32\ GroupPolicy directory. Local GPO settings will override any nonlocal GPO setting applied from the site, domain, or OU level, and are only recommended for use on standalone Windows 2000 Professional systems that are not part of an AD domain.

Because the local GPO does not utilize AD, some AD features that are normally configurable in the Group Policy Editor, such as Folder Redirection and Software Installation, are unavailable. Also keep in mind that a Windows 2000 computer can have only one local GPO.

Group Policy vs. System Policies

As previously mentioned, Group Policy is not the same as NT 4's system policies. The following is a summary of the differences. Keep in mind that for the exam you will need to know under which circumstances you would use one or the other.

Windows NT 4 and Windows 9x System Policies

The following are true of system policies:

➤ They are applied only to domains.

➤ They are limited to Registry-based settings an administrator configures.

➤ They are not written to a secure location of the Registry; hence, any user with the ability to edit the Registry can disable the policy settings.

➤ They often last beyond their useful life spans. System policies remain in effect until another policy explicitly reverses an existing policy or a user edits the Registry to remove a policy.

➤ They can be applied through NT domain security groups.

Windows 2000 Group Policy

The following are true of Group Policy:

➤ It can be applied to sites, domains, or OUs.

➤ It cannot be applied directly to security groups, and settings apply to all users and computers in sites, domains, and OUs linked to the Group Policy object.

➤ It is written to a secure section of the Registry, thereby preventing users from being able to remove the policy through the regedit.exe or regedt32.exe utilities.

➤ It is removed and rewritten whenever a policy change takes place. Administrators can set the length of time between policy refreshes, ensuring that only the current policies are in place.

➤ It provides a more granular level of administrative control over a user's environment.

This overview of Group Policy theory sets the stage for the rest of this chapter. Although you may not think that the theory will be directly applicable to the exam, without the understanding of what Group Policy is and what it is used for, answering scenario questions involving Group Policy implementation would be very difficult. However, because you do need to know how to perform Group Policy tasks, let's end our theory discussion and examine the hands-on skills you will need to have for the Directory Services exam.

Creating a Group Policy Object

The first step when implementing Group Policy is to create a GPO. In fact, without any GPOs created, you cannot even access the Group Policy Editor. Fortunately, Windows 2000 creates a GPO—the Default Domain Policy—by default when you install AD.

Creating a GPO is done primarily through the AD Users and Computers Management Console. To create a GPO, follow these steps:

1. Select Start|Programs|Administrative Tools to access the AD Users and Computers Management Console.

2. From within the console, right-click on the domain name and click on Properties. Next, click on the Group Policy tab, which will bring up the screen shown in Figure 7.1. You will notice the options Add, New, Edit, and Delete. These are the major commands, and they perform the following functions:

   ➤ *Add*—Add a Group Policy Object link.

   ➤ *New*—Create a new GPO.

➤ *Edit*—Modify an existing GPO.

➤ *Delete*—Remove a GPO, a GPO link, or both.

3. To create a new GPO, simply click on the New button. As shown in Figure 7.2, clicking on New will create a new GPO with a generic name, *New Group Policy Object*. You will probably want to rename it something more descriptive.

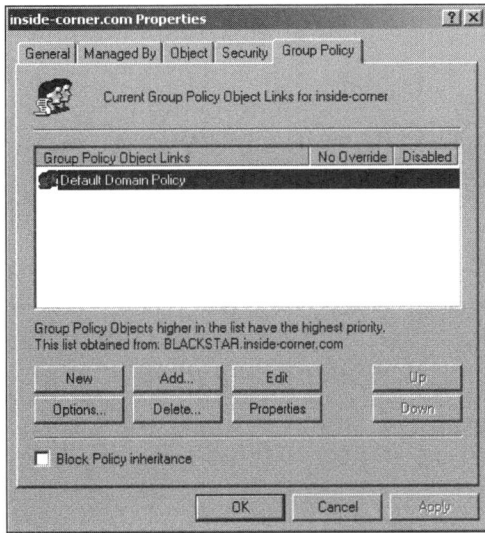

Figure 7.1   The Group Policy tab of a site, domain, or OU's property sheet supplies the options for creating, linking, and modifying GPOs.

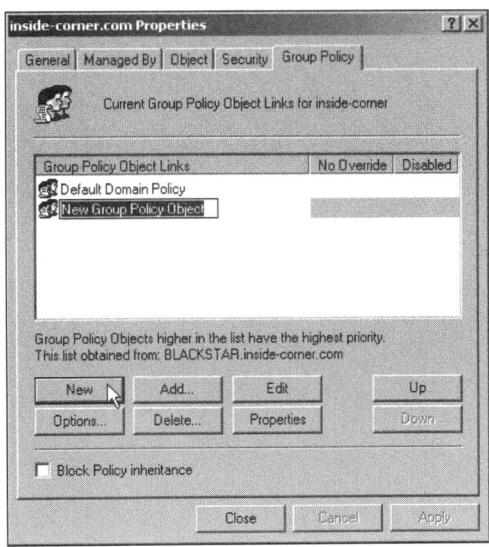

Figure 7.2   Creating a new GPO is as simple as clicking on the New button.

Modifying a Group Policy Object

When you create a GPO, the default settings that are automatically created do not really accomplish anything. You need to edit the GPO to define the settings that will affect the behavior of objects linked to the GPO. To edit a Group Policy Object, you use the Group Policy Editor. Although there is no administrative utility for the Group Policy Editor, it can be invoked in one of two ways:

➤ Via a standalone console

➤ By editing a GPO

Group Policy Editor as a Standalone Console

The first method of accessing the Group Policy Editor is through a standalone console. Follow these steps:

1. To open a new, empty Microsoft Management Console (MMC), select Start|Run and type the following:

   ```
   MMC /A
   ```

2. From the Console menu at the top left, select Add/Remove Snap-in. The dialog shown in Figure 7.3 appears.

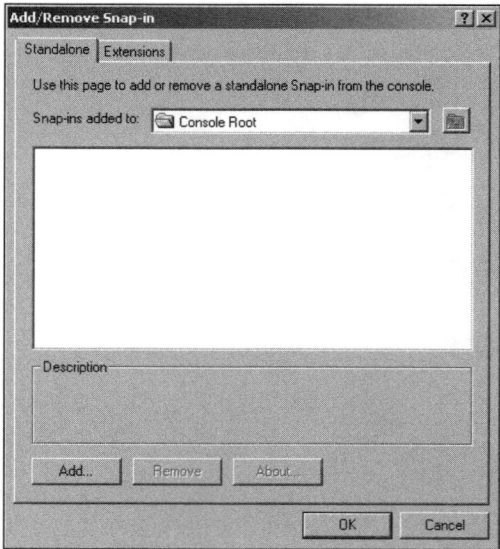

Figure 7.3   The first step in adding a snap-in is to select the Add/Remove Snap-in Console menu option.

3. Select Group Policy from the list of available snap-ins, as shown in Figure 7.4. Click on Add.

4. Now, you must define the scope of the Group Policy Editor, which equates to what GPO you will be editing. Figure 7.5 illustrates that the Group Policy Editor defaults to the *Local Computer* Group Policy Object. Most likely you will want to edit a nonlocal GPO, so click on Browse to look for the desired GPO.

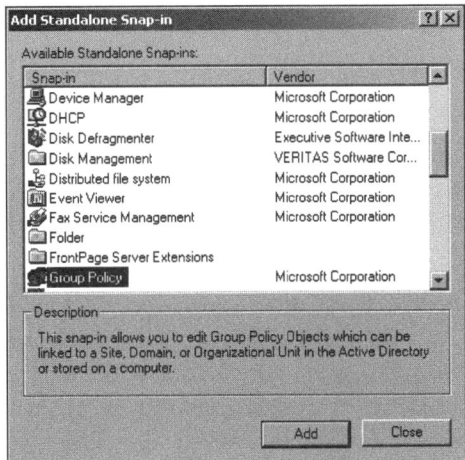

Figure 7.4 The list of snap-ins shows the available standalone snap-ins that can be added to the console.

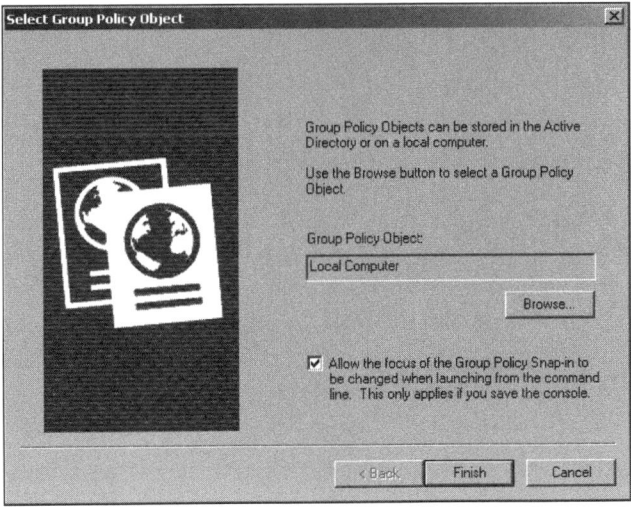

Figure 7.5 You must determine the focus of the Group Policy Editor when you add the snap-in to the console.

Note: Step 4 is the most important and the reason we are stepping through this process in the first place.

As you can see in Figure 7.6, you have a number of browsing options. You can browse by Domains/OUs, Sites, or Computers, or you can browse all GPOs. Windows 2000 defaults to the current storage domain that you are logged in to, but that could be changed by dropping down the list next to Look In.

5. Click on OK. The screen shown previously in Figure 7.5 appears.

6. By default, a checkbox appears that reads Allow The Focus Of The Group Policy Snap-In To Be Changed When Launched From The Command Line. This Applies Only If You Save The Console checkbox is not selected; however, if you plan on saving your console, you might choose to enable this option. The option simply allows you to specify a different GPO to be the focus of the console when entering the command line.

7. If you plan on editing a particular GPO frequently, saving the console after you have opened the snap-in and returned to the console screen makes sense. Windows 2000 will prompt you for a file name, and it will save the file with an .msc extension to your Administrative Tools folder, located in the \Documents and Settings*username*\Start Menu\Programs folder. The name you assign to the console will be what appears as the console name when you browse the Administrative Tools folder in the Start menu, so you should choose something descriptive.

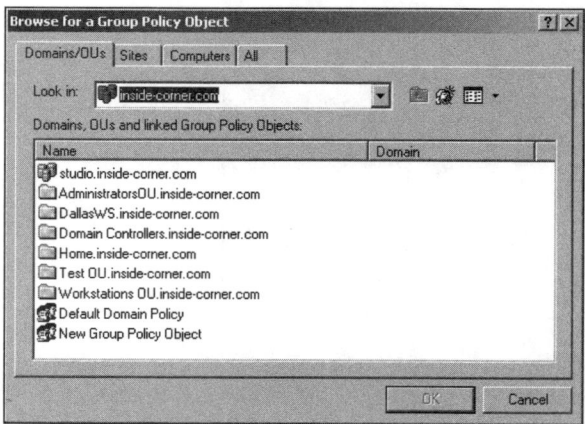

Figure 7.6 You can browse for nonlocal GPOs in the current storage domain, as well as other available domains.

Accessing the Group Policy Editor through Editing a Group Policy Object

The other method of accessing the Group Policy Editor is to simply edit the GPO from the Group Policy tab of a site, domain, or OU's property sheet. This can be accessed from the AD Users and Computers administrative utility. For example, if you want to edit the Default Domain Policy GPO, follow these steps:

1. From AD Users and Computers, right-click on the desired domain (if you have more than one domain) and click on Properties.

2. Select the Group Policy tab.

3. Click on the Edit button, which will launch the Group Policy Editor with the Default Domain Policy GPO as the focus. This is illustrated in Figure 7.7.

In the following two chapters, we will work with the Group Policy Editor to manage the user environment and to manage and deploy software. For now, let's just briefly discuss the Group Policy Editor environment.

Working Inside the Group Policy Editor

No matter whether you open the Group Policy Editor as a standalone console or by editing a GPO in AD Users and Computers, the appearance of the console will be the same. The example console in Figure 7.7 shows the following structure:

➤ *Root container*—Defines the focus of the Group Policy Editor by showing the GPO that is being edited as well as the fully qualified domain name (FQDN) of the domain controller from which you are editing the GPO. In the figure, the GPO *New Group Policy Object* is being edited by blackstar.inside-corner.com. If you were to open the GPO for editing on a domain controller named pulsar.inside-corner.com, the root of the Group Policy Editor would reflect that.

➤ *Computer Configuration*—A container that contains settings specifically covering computer policies. Computer policies are processed before user policies by default.

➤ *User Configuration*—A container that contains settings specifically covering user policies. User policies are processed after computer policies by default.

➤ *Software Settings*—Subcontainer under both Computer Configuration and User Configuration containers that contains Software Installation settings for computers and users.

➤ *Windows Settings*—Subcontainer under both Computer Configuration and User Configuration containers that contains script and security settings, as well as other policy settings that affect the behavior of the Windows environment.

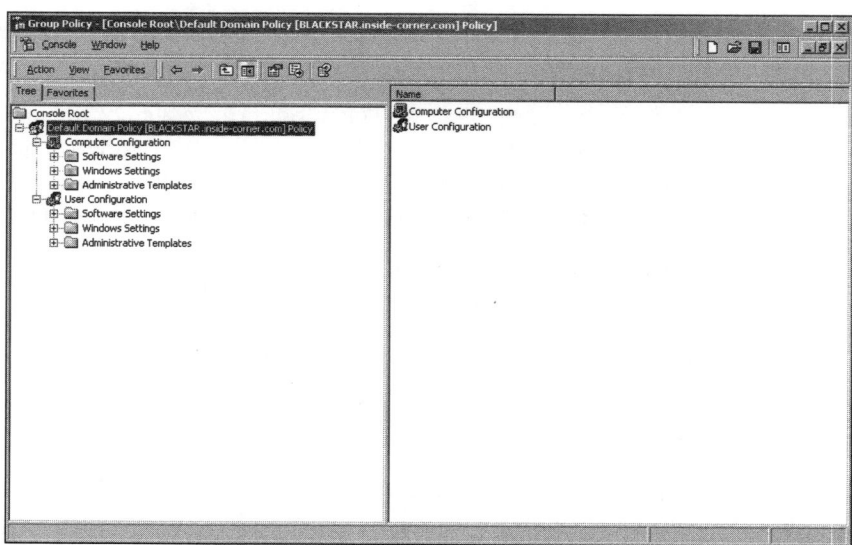

Figure 7.7 Editing a GPO through the Group Policy properties of an AD object launches the Group Policy Editor with the selected GPO as the focus.

➤ *Administrative Templates*—Subcontainer under both Computer Configuration and User Configuration containers that provides the majority of settings for controlling the desktop environment and restricting access to applications, applets, and the appearance of the desktop. Administrative templates are discussed at length in the next chapter.

Linking a GPO

Because nonlocal GPOs are stored within the AD database, they must be linked to an object to apply the desired settings. As you have learned, the object of a GPO link can be a site, domain, or OU. The effects of a GPO are applied to the object(s) that they are linked to.

As previously mentioned, by default, the effects of GPOs are inherited by all child objects of a parent object. Put another way, a GPO linked to a site will apply to all domains and all OUs within the site. A GPO linked to a domain will apply to all OUs within the domain. A GPO applied to an OU will apply to all users, computers, groups, printers, shared folders, contacts, and other Organizational Units within the OU. Because of the effects of inheritance and the overriding effects of policies applied later in the processing order, you should be careful with GPO links. Failure to account for the interaction between different sets of polices can have an adverse impact on your network by introducing undesired behavior of policy recipients.

Before you can link a GPO, you must have at least the permissions necessary to edit it—that is, Read/Write or Full Control permissions. By default, administrators have this capability. As you will see later in this chapter, administrators can delegate the authority to perform certain Group Policy functions such as linking GPOs to nonadministrators.

To link a GPO, follow these steps:

1. Open AD Users and Computers (or AD Sites and Services if you wish to link a GPO at the site level) and right-click on the domain or OU to which you want to link a GPO.

2. Choose Properties, and then choose the Group Policy tab.

3. Click on the Add button and navigate to select the GPO that you want to link to the particular domain or OU. In Figure 7.8, we have selected an OU called *Test OU*. As you can see, there are currently no linked GPOs within Test OU.inside-corner.com. However, if we click on the All tab, as shown in Figure 7.9, we see all of the GPOs that have been created.

4. Click on OK when you are done selecting a GPO to link to. The GPO is now successfully linked to this domain or OU.

Note that GPOs *cannot* be linked to the generic AD containers. Those containers are as follows:

➤ Builtin

➤ Computers

➤ ForeignSecurityPrincipals

➤ LostAndFound

➤ System

➤ Users

Linking Multiple GPOs

Nonlocal GPOs are stored in the AD database and are in theory available to all members of an AD forest. We say *in theory* because in reality there are some limitations on GPO linking. First, let's look at how GPOs can and can't be linked.

Multiple GPOs can be linked to a single site, domain, or OU. As you saw in Figure 7.1, a second GPO was added to the inside-corner.com domain. The converse is also true—that is, multiple sites, domains, and OUs can be linked to a single GPO. Every GPO is stored within AD in the domain in which it was created, which is called its *storage domain*. The storage domain is not necessarily the domain in which

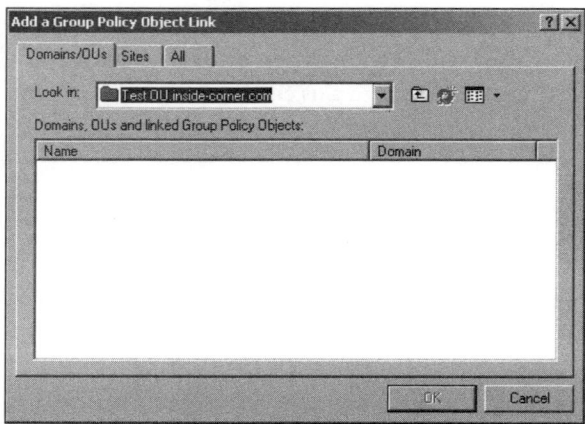

Figure 7.8 When adding a GPO link, you first see the domains, OUs, and linked GPOs within the object selected.

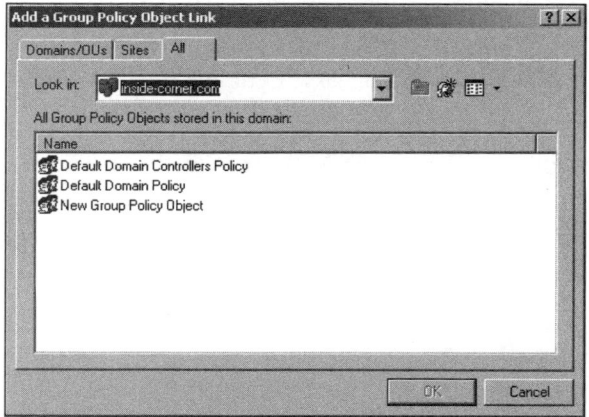

Figure 7.9 Clicking on the All tab brings up the entire list of GPOs stored in the AD database.

the GPO is linked, though that is usually the case. The reason is that linking GPOs across domains causes a significant performance hit; therefore, Microsoft recommends that you avoid linking a GPO to an object in a different domain.

A GPO does not have to be linked to its storage domain, although it usually would be. Linking across domains brings up a security condition as well as the performance issue. To edit a GPO (editing is discussed in the "Modifying Group Policy Objects" section later in this chapter) in another domain, you have to be logged in to the storage domain of the GPO or to a domain that is trusted by the storage domain.

One last note on linking: It is *not* possible to link to only a subset of a GPO's settings. Group Policy Objects are the most basic unit of Group Policy, so you can link to only an entire GPO.

Cross-Domain GPO Links

Creating GPOs in one domain and having them apply to users and computers in another domain is possible. However, as stated in the previous section, this is not recommended in most cases because computer startup and user logon is slowed, sometimes dramatically, if authentication must be processed by a domain controller (DC) from another domain. To apply a GPO, the target of the policy must be able to read the GPO and have the permission to apply Group Policy for the GPO.

There are additional authentication mechanisms to validate the computer or user account in the remote domain, so processing is not as fast as when reading a GPO in the same domain. Because of this, normally it is better to create duplicate GPOs in multiple domains rather than attempting to cross-link GPOs to other domains.

Other than the performance issue, there's no real reason not to cross-link domain GPOs rather than create multiple duplicate GPOs. In fact, cross-linking a single GPO is actually easier to manage, because if you make a modification to the GPO, the change automatically applies to all users and computers in the sites and domains that link to the GPO. Otherwise, you would have to make the same change on every GPO that you had created to perform the same functions in other domains.

Delegating Administrative Control of Group Policy

In larger enterprises, network administration is usually distributed among multiple individuals, often at multiple locations in multiple cities. It becomes necessary for more than one person to be able to complete a given task, and in some instances, you might need to allow a nonadministrator to have a subset of administrative authority to complete a task. Such would be the case at a small, remote branch office that does not have enough staff to warrant having a full-time systems administrator on site to manage the servers. To accommodate this, Windows 2000 provides the ability for administrators to delegate authority of certain Group Policy tasks.

Three Group Policy tasks can be delegated individually:

➤ Managing Group Policy links for a site, domain, or OU

➤ Creating GPOs

➤ Editing GPOs

Keep in mind that the delegation applies to only nonlocal GPOs. Local Group Policy applies to standalone computers only, whereas nonlocal Group Policy requires a Windows 2000 domain controller.

Managing Group Policy Links

The Delegation of Control Wizard is used to delegate control to users or groups that will manage GPO links. To use the wizard, follow these steps:

1. Right-click on the desired domain or OU in AD Users and Computers and select Delegate Control.

2. When the wizard starts, select users or groups to which you want to delegate control. Once the appropriate users and/or groups are selected, click on Next.

3. The window shown in Figure 7.10 appears, displaying a list of tasks to be delegated. As you can see, the Delegation of Control Wizard can delegate tasks other than Manage Group Policy Links. For Group Policy, though, only the last task is applicable. Select your settings and click on Next.

4. Click on Finish; the wizard requires no other settings.

Note: When you delegate control, you are allowing the individuals or groups to perform those functions as if they were an administrator. Therefore, you must be careful not to delegate control wantonly.

Creating GPOs

Delegating the ability to create GPOs is accomplished through AD Users and Computers as well. To create a GPO, a user account must belong to the Group Policy Creator Owners administrators group. Double-click on the Group Policy Creator Owners group in the Users container and click on the Members tab, as shown in Figure 7.11. Add the users who should be able to create GPOs.

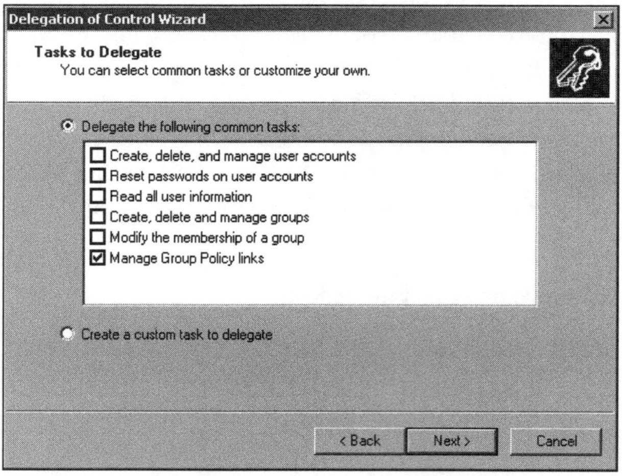

Figure 7.10   The Delegation of Control Wizard is used to delegate control of managing Group Policy links to users and groups.

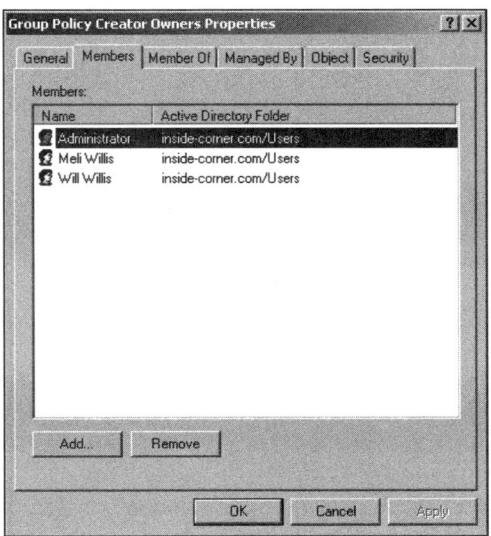

Figure 7.11   To create a GPO, a user or group must belong to the Group Policy Creator Owners group.

Editing GPOs

You might also want a nonadministrator to be able to edit a specific GPO in the domain. The ability to edit a GPO comes from an administrator having delegated administrative control of a specific GPO. To delegate this control:

1. Open the GPO in the Group Policy Editor.

2. Right-click on the GPO name and choose Properties.

3. Click on the Security tab.

4. Add the user(s) you want to have administrative control, and set the appropriate permissions levels. At minimum, a user or group would need Read/Write permissions to edit a GPO, though you could go so far as to grant Full Control if necessary.

You need to know how the following Group Policy tasks are delegated:

➤ *Managing Group Policy links*—Delegated through the Delegation of Control Wizard

➤ *Creating GPOs*—Delegated through the Group Policy Creator Owners membership

➤ *Editing GPOs*—Delegated through security properties of the specific GPO (Group Policy Editor)

Group Policy Inheritance

As mentioned previously in this chapter, Group Policy is processed in the following order:

➤ Local

➤ Site

➤ Domain

➤ Organizational Unit

Inheritance is enabled by default and is the process where a policy applied at one level is passed down to lower levels. Objects have parent-child relationships, and parent objects pass their settings down to child objects. The child objects can override parent settings by explicitly defining different policy settings; however, in the absence of a specifically defined setting, the settings from the parent object apply.

To look at it from the perspective of the preceding list, an OU would automatically inherit all of the settings from the domain it belonged to, which had automatically inherited settings from the site.

In many cases, it is not desirable for inheritance to take effect. An administrator might want a setting to remain unconfigured if it isn't specifically defined. Because of this, Windows 2000 allows for two methods of changing the default behavior of setting inheritance:

➤ Block Policy Inheritance

➤ No Override

Local policy is an exception to the rules of Block Policy Inheritance and No Override. If local policy is used, it will override these policy settings.

Block Policy Inheritance

Block Policy Inheritance prevents policies from higher up in the AD structure from being automatically applied at lower levels. This setting cannot be applied to the site level, because it is the top level and does not inherit policies from anywhere else. However, it can be applied at the domain, OU, and local levels.

You would use Block Policy Inheritance to protect settings from higher-level objects from applying later in the processing order. For example, you can block a domain policy from applying settings to an OU Group Policy Object by selecting the Block Policy Inheritance checkbox.

To enable Block Policy Inheritance, open the Group Policy tab of an object's properties as discussed earlier and select the checkbox in the lower left corner of the Group Policy property sheet.

No Override

Like Block Policy Inheritance, *No Override* is a method of altering the default behavior of policy inheritance in Windows 2000. Unlike Block Policy Inheritance, which is applied at the domain, OU, or local level, No Override is applied to a GPO link. Table 7.1 summarizes these differences.

No Override is used to prevent policies at lower levels in the AD tree from overwriting policies applied from a higher level. For example, say you had linked a GPO to a domain and set the GPO link to No Override, and then you configured Group Policy settings within the GPO to apply to OUs within the domain. GPOs linked to OUs would not be able to override the domain-linked GPO. This is a way to minimize the effects of multiple GPOs interacting and creating undesirable policy settings. If you want to ensure that a default domain policy is applied regardless of OU polices, use No Override.

If you want to view what objects a GPO is linked to in order to determine the effects of setting No Override, follow these steps:

1. Open the Group Policy property sheet for an object in AD Users and Computers.

2. Select the desired GPO and click on Properties.

3. Click on the Links tab.

4. Click on Find Now to search the default domain, or select a different domain from the drop-down list.

 Make sure you know that No Override will take precedence over Block Policy Inheritance when the two are in conflict.

To configure No Override:

1. Open the Group Policy property sheet for an object in AD Users and Computers.

2. Select the GPO in question and click on the Options button. The window shown in Figure 7.12 appears.

Table 7.1 Block Policy Inheritance vs. No Override.		
Method	**Applied To**	**Conflict Resolution**
Block Policy Inheritance	Domains, OUs, local computers	Defers to No Override
No Override	GPO links	Takes precedence

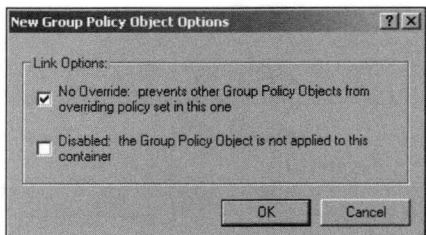

Figure 7.12   You can configure No Override through the Group Policy Object's options.

Block Policy Inheritance and No Override can make troubleshooting policy-related problems on a network extremely complex, especially as the size of the network and the number of GPOs grows. For that reason, avoiding these options whenever possible is recommended.

Disabling a GPO

Although not exactly the same as the previous methods of preventing policy inheritance, Figure 7.12 shows another option that prevents the effects of a GPO from being applied to an object. By selecting the Disabled checkbox, an administrator can prevent this from happening within the selected container, such as a domain or an OU.

Filtering Group Policy

We previously mentioned security groups when we delegated control over editing Group Policy Objects. The other time you use security groups in relation to Group Policy is for the purpose of filtering the scope of a GPO. For example, you might have a GPO that applies to an entire OU, yet there are specific objects within the OU that you do not want to be affected by the policies. Through security groups, you can filter out the desired object from the OU so that the policy won't be applied to it.

When filtering the effects of a GPO by security group, you are essentially editing the discretionary access control list (DACL) on that GPO. Using the DACL, you allow or deny access for users and computers to the GPO based on their memberships in security groups. In addition to DACLs, you also have access control entries (ACEs), which are the permission entries within a DACL. ACEs are permissions such as Full Control, Read, Write, and Apply Group Policy.

All authenticated users have two required default permissions that enable objects to receive policy settings from a GPO. These permissions are as follows:

➤ Read

➤ Apply Group Policy

The easiest way to prevent Group Policy from applying to an object is to remove that object's Read permission. If the Read permission is taken away, an object cannot access the GPO, and therefore policy settings will not be applied. Microsoft strongly recommends removing the Apply Group Policy permission as well, however, because it will speed up the time it takes to process Group Policy for an object if unused permissions are not having to be processed.

To reiterate, the security settings for a GPO are selected by going into the property sheet for a specific GPO and choosing the Security tab.

Filtering affects the entire Group Policy Object. You cannot filter only specific settings within a GPO from applying to a security group. However, if you are not using a portion of a GPO, you can disable it so that it won't apply.

Disabling Unused Portions of a GPO

Windows 2000 Group Policy gives you the option of disabling either the Computer Configuration or User Configuration container (or both, but that would be pointless) within a GPO if you are not using it. Doing so will speed up Group Policy processing and can be beneficial if you have targeted GPOs that apply only to computers or only to users.

To disable an unused portion, open the Group Policy property sheet for an object such as a domain, as was done in the "Creating a Group Policy Object" section earlier in this chapter. Select the desired GPO and click on Properties. As shown in Figure 7.13, at the bottom of the page are options to disable Computer Configuration and User Configuration settings to speed up performance.

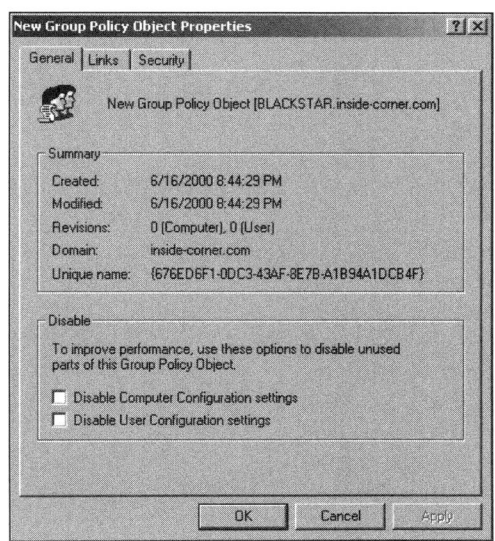

Figure 7.13 Disabling the Computer Configuration or User Configuration settings for a GPO can speed up processing if you have GPOs that apply only to computers or only to users.

Practice Questions

Question 1

> Which of the following levels of GPO processing are nonlocal? [Check all correct answers]
>
> ❑ a. LocalComputer
>
> ❑ b. Site
>
> ❑ c. Domain
>
> ❑ d. User

Answers b and c are correct. GPOs applied at the site, domain, or OU level are considered nonlocal, because they are stored in the Active Directory database. By its name, you can tell that LocalComputer is obviously a local policy and not a nonlocal one, so answer a is incorrect. User is not a level in which GPOs can be applied, so answer d is incorrect.

Question 2

> The following are containers or nodes within a Group Policy Object:
>
> Windows Settings
>
> Computer Configuration
>
> Software Settings
>
> Root
>
> User Configuration
>
> Administrative Templates
>
> Reorder them into their hierarchical structure as would appear in the Group Policy Editor.

The correct answer is:

Root

Computer Configuration

Software Settings

Windows Settings

Administrative Templates

User Configuration

Software Settings

Windows Settings

Administrative Templates

In the Group Policy Editor, the Software Settings, Windows Settings, and Administrative Templates nodes exist under both the Computer Configuration and User Configuration containers, which are under the Root container.

Question 3

Which permissions are required for an object so that the effects of a GPO can be applied? [Check all correct answers]

❑ a. Read

❑ b. Write

❑ c. Full Control

❑ d. Apply Group Policy

Answers a and d are correct. Read and Apply Group Policy are the required permissions to accomplish this objective. Answer b is incorrect because Write permission is not required in order for a GPO's settings to be applied. Although Full Control would accomplish the task of allowing Group Policy settings to be applied, it is not required, so answer c is incorrect.

Question 4

Put the following items in order to show the correct processing sequence for Group Policy.

Domain

Local

OU

Site

The correct answer is:

Local

Site

Domain

OU

Local policies are processed first, followed by nonlocal policies, which are applied starting at the highest level in the Active Directory tree.

Question 5

Which of the following methods are used to change the default behavior for policy inheritance? [Check all correct answers]

❏ a. Disabled

❏ b. Block Policy Inheritance

❏ c. Override

❏ d. No Override

Answers a, b, and d are correct. Block Policy Inheritance and No Override are different means to change inheritance, and Disabled prevents any of the GPO's settings from being applied to the selected container. Answer c is incorrect because Override is actually the default behavior; by default, policy settings are inherited from parent objects to child objects.

Question 6

Choose all of the generic Active Directory containers in the list that Group Policy Objects *cannot* be linked to. [Check all correct answers]

❑ a. Computers

❑ b. Users

❑ c. ForeignSecurityPrincipals

❑ d. LostAndFound

❑ e. Domain Controllers

❑ f. System

❑ g. Builtin

❑ h. Domain

Answers a, b, c, d, f, and g are correct. Computers, Users, ForeignSecurityPrincipals, LostAndFound, System, and Builtin cannot be linked to Group Policy Objects. Answer e is incorrect because Domain Controllers is an OU created when Active Directory is installed and can have GPOs linked to it. Likewise, answer h is incorrect because each domain has a Default Domain Policy GPO created for it when Active Directory is installed.

Question 7

If you want to disable unused portions of a GPO to improve processing times, which portions could you disable? [Check all correct answers]

❑ a. Specific settings within a GPO

❑ b. Windows Settings subcontainer

❑ c. Computer Configuration container

❑ d. User Configuration container

❑ e. Software Settings subcontainer

❑ f. Administrative Templates subcontainer

Answers c and d are correct. Windows 2000 Group Policy allows an administrator to disable the Computer Configuration and User Configuration containers from being processed. Answer a is incorrect because you cannot filter specific settings within a GPO. Answers b, e, and f are incorrect because if either the Computer Configuration or User Configuration container is disabled, the Windows Settings, Software Settings, and Administrative Templates subcontainers for that container would be disabled along with it.

Question 8

What utility would you use to create a new Group Policy Object?

- ○ a. Group Policy Editor
- ○ b. Active Directory Users and Computers
- ○ c. Delegation of Control Wizard
- ○ d. Group Policy MMC Console

Answer b is correct. Active Directory Users and Computers is used to create new GPOs. Answer a is incorrect because the Group Policy Editor cannot be invoked for a GPO that does not exist yet. Answer c is incorrect because the Delegation of Control Wizard only gives permission to manage Group Policy links. Answer d is incorrect because the Group Policy MMC Console is the same thing as the Group Policy Editor.

Question 9

Which of the following Group Policy tasks can be delegated through the Delegation of Control Wizard?

- ○ a. Managing Group Policy Links
- ○ b. Creating GPOs
- ○ c. Modifying/Editing GPOs
- ○ d. Filtering GPOs

Answer a is correct. The Delegation of Control Wizard is used to delegate control of managing Group Policy links. Answers b and c are incorrect because the Active Directory Users and Computers administrative utility is used to delegate control of creating GPOs by editing membership of the Group Policy Creator Owners security group, and the permission to edit a GPO is granted through the GPO's security sheet within its properties, accessible through the Group Policy Editor. Answer d is incorrect because filtering GPOs is not a task that can be delegated; rather, it falls under the category of editing GPOs.

Question 10

> When would you use system policies rather than Group Policy? [Choose the best answer]
>
> ○ a. When you have only Windows 2000 systems on your network
>
> ○ b. When you have a mix of Windows 2000, Windows NT, and Windows 98 systems on your network
>
> ○ c. When you want to have policy settings refresh periodically
>
> ○ d. You would never use system policies above Group Policy

Answer b is correct. Group Policy is supported only on Windows 2000, so you would need to use system policies if you had to support legacy Windows NT and 98 clients. Answer a is incorrect because it refers to Windows 2000 systems. Answer c is incorrect because system policies do not support periodic refresh as Group Policy does. System policies also do not support a host of other features that Group Policy supports; however, they do provide the ability to manage the user environment for legacy systems.

Need to Know More?

 Iseminger, David. *Active Directory Services for Windows 2000 Technical Reference*. Microsoft Press, Redmond, WA, 2000. ISBN 0735606242. A solid reference book for planning and deploying AD networks. Although coverage of Group Policy is minor, there is an extensive change and configuration management section.

 Microsoft Corporation. *Microsoft Windows 2000 Server Resource Kit*. Microsoft Press, Redmond, WA, 2000. ISBN 1572318058. The quintessential resource for Windows 2000 Server and AD, this kit has extensive coverage of AD and Group Policy in particular. If you can have only one Windows 2000 reference, this is the one to have.

 Nielsen, Morton Strunge. *Windows 2000 Server Architecture and Planning*. The Coriolis Group, Scottsdale, AZ, 1999. ISBN 1576104362. Although it was written during the Windows 2000 beta period, this book is an excellent resource for AD planning and deployment.

 Norris-Lowe, Alistair. *Windows 2000 Active Directory Service*. O'Reilly & Associates, Sebastopol, CA, 2000. ISBN 1565926382. A great complement to the *Windows 2000 System Administration Handbook*, this book is another good AD resource. This reference is more of a high-level technical book rather than a hands-on "how to" type of book, and is an excellent way to learn the theory behind the technology.

 Watts, David V., Will Willis, and Tillman Strahan. *MCSE Windows 2000 Directory Services Exam Prep*. The Coriolis Group, Scottsdale, AZ, 2000. ISBN 1576106241. See Chapters 10 through 12 for more detailed coverage of Group Policy.

 Willis, Will, David Watts, and Tillman Strahan. *Windows 2000 System Administration Handbook*. Prentice-Hall, Upper Saddle River, NJ, 2000. ISBN 0130270105. This book explains Windows 2000 systems administration concepts in detail and is a solid all-around Windows 2000 reference with good coverage of AD.

Using Group Policy in Security and Environment Control

8

Terms you'll need to understand:

✓ Administrative templates

✓ Scripts

✓ WScript.exe

✓ CScript.exe

✓ Security templates

✓ Windows Script Host

✓ Folder Redirection

✓ Roaming profiles

Techniques you'll need to master:

✓ Controlling user environments by using administrative templates

✓ Managing security configurations

✓ Assigning script policies to users and computers

✓ Using Folder Redirection

Arguably the most common use of Group Policy is to manipulate the user environment in order to meet specific needs of an organization. Some companies seek to have a consistent desktop appearance across all desktop systems, with the same set of applications. Environments like these often have users who float among multiple systems or seek to reduce customization as a way of keeping down information technology (IT) support costs for desktop systems.

In environments where security is an issue, or where nonemployees are accessing company computers (such as in a mall kiosk or an applicant entry terminal), Group Policy can be used to lock down specific configurations that cannot be modified by the user. These scenarios would use highly restrictive policies that prevented access to certain operating system functions and threw out any configuration changes at system shutdown.

In this chapter, we examine using Group Policy as both a security device for the purpose of locking down system configurations and as a means of supplying consistent user computing environments that will be available no matter what computer a user logs in to on your network.

Controlling User Environments with Administrative Templates

Administrative templates provide the primary means of administering the user environment and defining the end-user computing experience. As an administrator, you can use administrative templates to deny access to certain operating system functionality—for example, the ability to add or remove programs. Additionally, you can define settings such as the wallpaper and screen saver to use on a system, and rely on Windows 2000 to enforce those settings.

You need to know the following about the use of administrative templates:

➤ ADM files and their structure

➤ Computer and User template application

ADM Files and Their Structure

Administrative templates are stored in Windows 2000 as text files in the \winnt\SYSVOL\Sysvol*domain*\Policies*GUID*\Adm folder. These files carry an .adm file extension. A real-world example of this directory structure is the following directory structure on a Windows 2000 domain controller (DC) in the inside-corner.com domain: E:\winnt\SYSVOL\Sysvol\inside-corner.com\ Policies\{31B2F340-016D-11D2-945F-00C04FB984F9}\Adm.

Windows 2000 includes five administrative templates, though not all are installed by default. These files are as follows:

➤ *System.adm*—Installed by default in Group Policy, system.adm is used for Windows 2000 clients.

➤ *Inetres.adm*—Installed by default in Group Policy, inetres.adm contains Internet Explorer policies for Windows 2000 systems.

➤ *Windows.adm*—This template contains user interface options for Windows 9x systems and is used with the System Policy Editor (poledit.exe).

➤ *Winnt.adm*—This template contains user interface options for Windows NT 4 systems and is used with the System Policy Editor.

➤ *Common.adm*—This template contains user interface options common to both Windows NT 4 and Windows 9x systems and is used with the System Policy Editor.

You might have other administrative templates on your system as well, depending on what you have installed on your system. For example, an administrative template called conf.adm is installed with NetMeeting and contains policy settings related to that specific program.

ADM Structure

An ADM file is a text file, so it can be edited with a text editor such as Notepad. You can open any of the ADM files listed previously to view the settings, and you can even modify them if you desire. However, modifying the default administrative templates is not recommended. If necessary, you can create new administrative templates, because Windows 2000 is flexible enough to let you tailor Group Policy to your specific network environment.

The following example is an edited sample from the conf.adm administrative template. Following the sample is a description of the file's structure and a definition of the variables you can use when creating an administrative template.

```
; NetMeeting policy settings
#if version <= 2
;;;;;;;;;;;;;;;;;;;;;;;;;;;;;;;;;
 CLASS USER   ;;;;;;;;;;;;;;;;;
;;;;;;;;;;;;;;;;;;;;;;;;;;;;;;;;;
CATEGORY !!WindowsComponents
CATEGORY !!NetMeeting
        ; App Sharing
           CATEGORY !!AppSharing
           POLICY !!DisableAppSharing
           KEYNAME "Software\Policies\Microsoft\Conferencing"
           EXPLAIN !!DisableAppSharing_Help
           VALUENAME "NoAppSharing"
           END POLICY
```

```
                      POLICY !!PreventSharing
                      KEYNAME "Software\Policies\Microsoft\Conferencing"
                      EXPLAIN !!PreventSharing_Help
                      VALUENAME "NoSharing"
                      END POLICY
                      POLICY !!PreventGrantingControl
                      KEYNAME "Software\Policies\Microsoft\Conferencing"
                      EXPLAIN !!PreventGrantingControl_Help
                      VALUENAME "NoAllowControl"
                      END POLICY
                      POLICY !!PreventSharingTrueColor
                      KEYNAME "Software\Policies\Microsoft\Conferencing"
                      EXPLAIN !!PreventSharingTrueColor_Help
                      VALUENAME "NoTrueColorSharing"
                      END POLICY
END CATEGORY ; AppSharing
[strings]
WindowsComponents="Windows Components"
NetMeeting="NetMeeting"
AppSharing="Application Sharing"
DisableAppSharing="Disable application Sharing"
DisableAppSharing_Help="Disables the application sharing feature of
NetMeeting completely.  Users will not be able to host or view
shared applications."
PreventSharing="Prevent Sharing"
PreventSharing_Help="Prevents users from sharing anything them-
selves.
They will still be able to view shared applications/desktops from
others."
PreventGrantingControl="Prevent Control"
PreventGrantingControl_Help="Prevents users from allowing others
in a conference to control what they have shared.  This enforces a
read-only mode; the other participants cannot change the data in
the shared application."
PreventSharingTrueColor="Prevent Application Sharing in true
color"
PreventSharingTrueColor_Help="Prevents users from sharing applica-
tions in true color. True color sharing uses more bandwidth in a
conference."
```

The structure of this sample is fairly simple. The header at the top defines the purpose of the file. It is a comment, which is denoted by the semicolon at the beginning of the line. The semicolon tells Windows not to process the line when parsing the file. Following the description are sections and variables defined by keywords. Those keywords are as follows:

➤ CLASS—The first entry in the administrative template file, the **CLASS** keyword can either be **MACHINE** or **USER**, which defines whether the section includes entries in the Computer Configuration or User Configuration containers in Group Policy.

➤ CATEGORY—The **CATEGORY** keyword is what is displayed in the Group Policy Editor as a node under Computer Configuration or User Configuration. Whether the category is located under the **MACHINE** or **USER** class determines which node it is located under. In the preceding example, the categories under the user class define the Windows Components, NetMeeting, and Application Sharing subnodes under User Configuration.

➤ POLICY—The **POLICY** keyword defines the policies that are available for modification in the Group Policy Editor. In the administrative template, the **POLICY** keyword specifies a variable that is defined in the **STRINGS** section at the bottom of the file.

➤ KEYNAME—The **KEYNAME** keyword defines the Registry location for the policy the keyname is associated with.

➤ EXPLAIN—The **EXPLAIN** keyword is used to supply help text for a policy setting. When you view the properties of a policy in the Group Policy Editor, note the Explain tab, which contains the help text specified here. Actually, in the administrative template, the **EXPLAIN** keyword specifies a variable that is defined with the help text in the **STRINGS** section at the bottom of the file.

➤ VALUENAME—The **VALUENAME** keyword is also associated with the **POLICY** keyword, and it defines the options available within a policy. It defines the values that are located within the Registry key, specified by the **KEYNAME** keyword.

➤ STRINGS—The **STRINGS** section defines the variables used earlier in the file for the keywords **POLICY** and **EXPLAIN**.

Putting it all together, you see the results in Figure 8.1. This figure shows the Group Policy Editor with the previous administrative template as the focus of the editor. The User Configuration container is expanded to the Windows Components/NetMeeting/Application Sharing nodes, which were defined by the **CATEGORY** keyword. There you find the policies defined by the **POLICY** keywords in the right-side window pane, such as Disable Application Sharing and Prevent Sharing.

If you double-click on the first policy, Disable Application Sharing, and click on the Explain tab, you see the help text defined by the **EXPLAIN** keyword in the administrative template. This is illustrated in Figure 8.2.

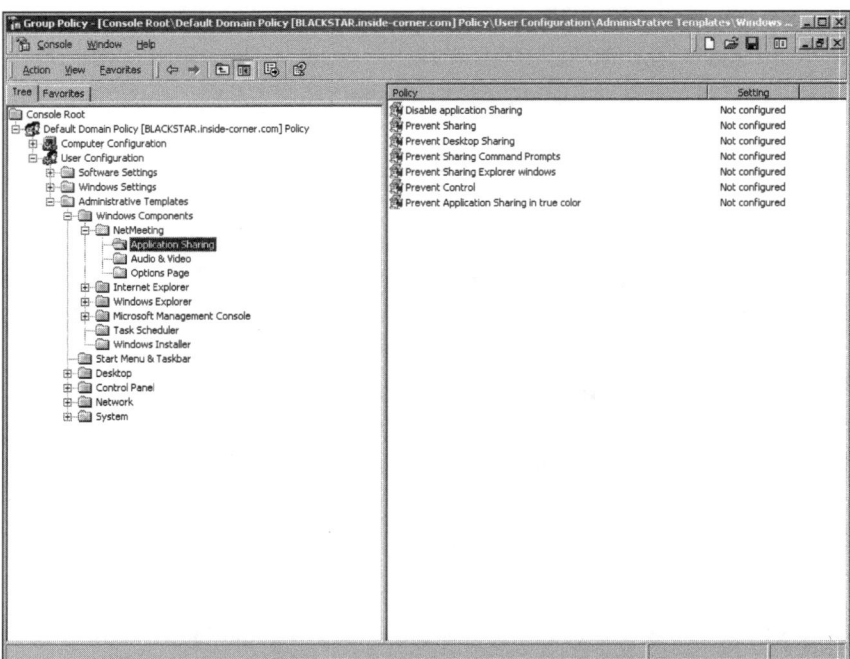

Figure 8.1 The available entries in the Group Policy Editor reflect the contents of the administrative template.

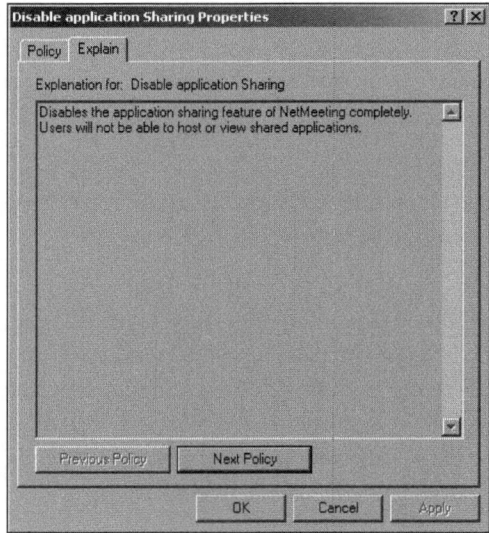

Figure 8.2 The **EXPLAIN** keyword in the administrative template provides the text that appears on the Explain tab in the policy's properties.

Creating administrative templates on your own allows you to define custom settings for your network for situations where the built-in policies are not enough. This is an easier solution than having a developer write a custom Group Policy extension with a software development kit (SDK). Windows 2000 includes everything you need to write an administrative template, which can then be added (or later removed) from a Group Policy Object (GPO), as you will see in the following section.

Adding and Removing Administrative Templates

After you've created a custom administrative template, you need to add it to the GPO in order to be used. Note that your custom administrative templates must be added to *each GPO* that you want them to apply to.

To add or remove an administrative template, right-click on the appropriate administrative templates folder in the Group Policy Editor (either under Computer Configuration or User Configuration) and select Add/Remove Templates. Figure 8.3 shows the dialog box that is presented, which displays the currently installed administrative templates. You can remove an existing one by selecting it and clicking on Remove, or you can add an administrative template by clicking on the Add button. If you click on Add, the dialog box shown in Figure 8.4 appears.

Once you add an administrative template, the additional nodes and policies appear under the administrative templates node you added the template to. It is important to note that the template itself determines whether to install under the Computer or User Configuration container. In our example, conf.adm is a user template containing NetMeeting settings, so it will naturally install under the User Configuration container. Although understanding how administrative templates are constructed and how to add and remove templates is important, the majority of your experience with administrative templates will be in using them to apply policy settings.

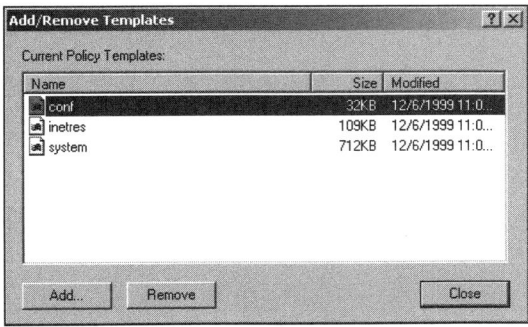

Figure 8.3 When you choose Add/Remove Templates, you first see a listing of currently installed administrative templates.

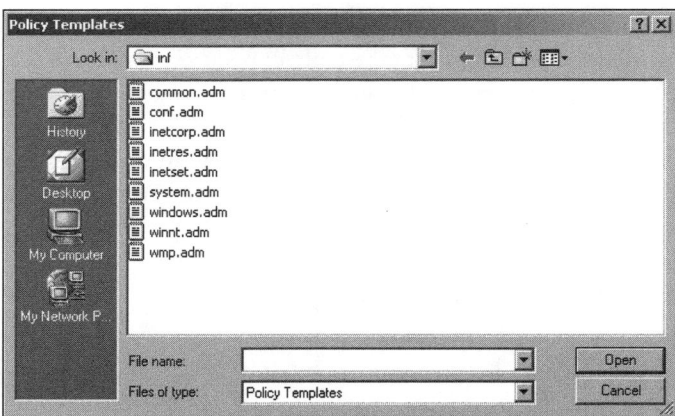

Figure 8.4   Choosing to add an administrative template allows you to browse for an ADM file to add to the current GPO.

Applying Computer and User Templates

Administrative templates allow an administrator to exert a measure of control over the user environment.

There are two different administrative templates sections within a GPO: One is under the Computer Configuration container, and the other is under the User Configuration container. As you would expect, these separate nodes determine whether policies apply to computer accounts or user accounts. Let's look at the similarities between the two, followed by the differences, and then examine a couple of scenarios where you would use administrative templates to manage a Windows 2000 network.

Common Administrative Templates Categories

Whether the Administrative Templates container is under the Computer Configuration or User Configuration containers, the following common categories create nodes:

➤ *Windows Components*—Contains configuration settings for common Windows components such as Internet Explorer, Task Scheduler, NetMeeting, Windows Explorer, Windows Installer, and Microsoft Management Console (MMC). The policies that exist for these categories control the behavior of the programs, from what functionality is available to the user to configuring the features of an application.

➤ *Network*—Contains configuration settings for network options such as Offline Folders and Network and Dial-up Connections. Different policy options are available, depending on whether you are under the Computer or User Configuration container.

➤ *System*—Contains configuration settings that do not really fall neatly under any other category within the administrative templates. Here, policies exist for logon/logoff, disk quotas, Windows File Protection, Group Policy, DNS (Domain Name System) client, and general settings such as whether Registry editing is allowed or certain applications should not be allowed to run.

Differing Administrative Templates Categories

The differences between Administrative Templates under the Computer Configuration and User Configuration containers are outlined here:

➤ *Computer Configuration administrative templates*—User templates are stored under the HKEY_LOCAL_MACHINE hive in the Registry. The administrative template that exists only under the Computer Configuration container is as follows:

> ➤ *Printers*—The Printers category contains configuration settings for printers and their properties. Through these policies, you can control the publication of printers into Active Directory (AD), allow printer browsing, and allow Web-based printing, among other policy settings.

➤ *User Configuration administrative templates*—User templates are stored under the HKEY_CURRENT_USER hive in the Registry. Administrative templates that exist only under the User Configuration container are as follows:

> ➤ *Start Menu & Taskbar*—This template controls the appearance and behavior of the Start menu and the taskbar. Through this administrative template, you can remove functionality (such as the ability to search) or remove the Run line from the Start menu. Additionally, you can alter the default behavior of the Start menu, such as clearing the Documents folder upon exit or not allowing users to change the configuration of the Start menu.

> ➤ *Desktop*—The Desktop policy settings complement the policy settings under the Start Menu & Taskbar category. You can configure the behavior of the Active Desktop, such as choosing the wallpaper, using filtering in AD searches, controlling the appearance of desktop icons, and indicating whether any changes specified by users are saved upon exiting Windows.

> ➤ *Control Panel*—This template contains settings that determine what level of functionality is available to users in the Control Panel. These policies can include Add/Remove Programs, Display, Printers, Regional Options, and even whether the Control Panel is available to Windows users.

Policy Application Scenario #1

As an administrator, you will run into various circumstances that require different applications of Group Policy. To create an effective usage policy, you must first analyze your environment and determine your requirements. With that strategy in mind, let's look at a couple of scenarios and how you might approach them.

In the first scenario, you are the network administrator for a retail chain of computer superstores. Specifically, you are in charge of a customer ordering system where customers can access Windows systems to create custom computer configurations for "build-to-order" systems right in the store. These orders are fed into a database, and credit cards can be processed.

In this type of environment, you would have users who are nonemployees accessing your network. You would not want them to be able to alter the operating system or the user environment in any way. To reach that goal, you would want to use the Start Menu & Taskbar, Desktop, and Control Panel nodes in the User Configuration container to prevent changes to be made. These policies would include disabling the Control Panel, removing the Run line from the Start menu, hiding all icons on the desktop, and preventing changes from being saved on exit. Additionally, you would use settings under the System node in both Computer and User Configuration to disable Registry editing. This would prevent a savvy customer with malicious intent from getting around your policy settings; by disabling them in the Registry and by disabling the command prompt, the administrator can ensure that programs could not be executed there.

These settings essentially lock down the user environment, which is what you would want in this type of scenario. In the following scenario, however, that type of network policy would be counterproductive and inappropriate.

Policy Application Scenario #2

Consider a scenario where you are the network administrator of a medium-sized company that has a Windows 2000 network. The environment is not highly secure, nor is there a real need to limit functionality. However, three shifts of workers use the company computers. Therefore, you have three people using each computer in the company each day.

In this scenario, you would want to use Group Policy to define a common desktop for corporate use and to discard any user changes upon exit. You could approach this goal in one of a couple ways. One way would be to create roaming profiles that followed each user wherever he or she went. With the high number of users accessing the computers, however, simply creating a "corporate standard" and defining the desktop appearance across all computers would be preferable.

To reach this goal, you would use the Control Panel/Display policies under the User Configuration container to disable changing the wallpaper and to specify a screen saver. With the Desktop/Active Desktop policies, you would specify the wallpaper to be used. With the Start Menu & Taskbar policies, you would disable changes to the Start menu and the taskbar, disable personalized menus, and remove users' folders from the Start menu. These settings create a computing environment that has a consistent look and feel across all corporate systems, while still allowing full operating system and application functionality to the users.

With Group Policy, you can also manage security configurations for Windows 2000, as we will see next.

Managing Security Configurations

Group Policy can also be used to manage security settings on a Windows 2000 network. Under the Windows Settings node in both the Computer and User Configuration containers is a node for Security Settings. The vast majority of the settings apply to computer policies, because the only user security settings are related to Public Key Policies (which also exists under Computer Configuration). The security categories available and their purposes are as follows:

➤ *Account Policies*—Contains settings related to user accounts and applies them at the domain level. You can configure the password policy for a domain (minimum length, uniqueness, minimum password age, and so on), account lockout policy (if accounts should be locked out, how many bad password attempts are allowed before lockout, and the length of time after lockout before the counter is reset), and Kerberos policy (maximum lifetime for tickets, ticket renewal threshold, and so on).

➤ *Local Policies*—Contains settings for local system policies, including audit policies, user rights assignment, and security options. Auditing can be used to log the success or failure of common events, such as logging on and logging off, accessing objects, using permissions, and directory service access, among other events. User Rights Assignment allows you to control user rights for users and groups, such as the ability to log on locally, log on as a service, change the system time, shut down the system, and take ownership of objects, among other settings. Security options are numerous; as you can see from Figure 8.5, there is a wealth of policy settings you can configure for local security.

➤ *Event Log*—Contains policy settings that control the behavior of the application, system, and security logs on the local system. Among other settings, you can define maximum log file sizes, the retention period for log files, and whether the system should be shut down automatically when the security log is full.

➤ *Restricted Groups*—Allows you to add restricted groups through Group Policy, which lets you control membership in security groups. You can define who belongs in a particular group and prevent users from being added or removed from the restricted group.

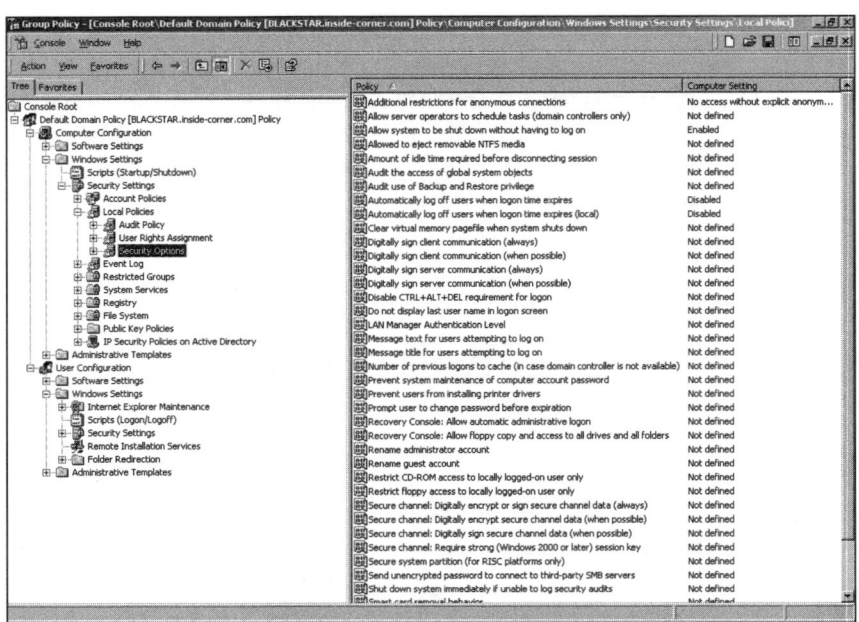

Figure 8.5 Numerous local security policy settings can be configured with Group Policy on a Windows 2000 system.

➤ *System Services*—Contains a list of the installed Windows 2000 services on the local computer and allows you to control the behavior of these services. You can define their startup mode (disabled, manual, automatic) and specify the level of permissions the service will have on the system. Limiting the level of permissions can prevent a hacker from exploiting a system service in an attempt to compromise system security.

➤ *Registry*—Allows you to audit specific Registry keys and their subkeys. You can also restrict editing of certain keys to administrators while making the same keys read-only to general users.

➤ *File System*—Allows you to define security settings for files and folders on the system. One use would be to ensure that only administrators could modify system files, making system files read-only to general users.

➤ *Public Key Policies*—Enables you to add policy settings to manage public-key–related security items, such as trusted certificate authorities (CAs). You can also add additional Encrypted Data Recovery Agents if desired.

➤ *IP Security Policies on Active Directory*—Contains policy settings for the IPSec security protocol. These allow you to tell your server how to respond to IPSec communication requests.

As an administrator, the use of the preceding security settings allows you to provide a much tighter level of security than what is configured by default when you install Windows 2000. However, if configuring security manually seems like a daunting task, you can use one of the security templates that Windows 2000 provides.

Security Templates

Security templates in Windows 2000 are a set of profiles that can be imported into a GPO, and they provide a specific level of security for Windows 2000 DCs, servers, and clients. The types of security templates available in Windows 2000 are as follows:

➤ *Basic*—Applies the default settings that Windows 2000 is configured with during a clean installation. This policy is useful for bringing upgraded Windows NT systems into line with Windows 2000 security, because Windows 2000 has a much higher default level of security than previous versions of NT.

➤ *Compatible*—Increases security over the basic template to allow members of the local Users group to be able to run non–Windows 2000-compliant applications with elevated Power Users privileges. This is useful for environments where administrators do not want to require standard users to be members of the Power Users group (which grants substantial additional privileges over the Users group) to be able to run legacy applications that will not run without Power Users permissions.

➤ *Secure*—Removes all members from the Power Users group and modifies security settings that pertain to the behavior of the operating system and network protocols rather than application functionality. Settings of this type include password and audit policies and Registry settings.

➤ *High Secure*—Goes beyond the secure template to extreme security measures. In doing so, it has no regard for functionality, performance, connectivity with non-Windows 2000 clients, or ease of use. As an example, the Secure template might warn you if you attempt to install an assigned driver. The High Secure template would simply block the installation of the unsigned driver without giving you the opportunity to override it.

To implement security templates, right-click on the Security Settings folder under the Computer Configuration container (this will *not* work under the User Configuration container) and click on Import Policy. The dialog box shown in Figure 8.6 appears.

Note the Clear This Database Before Importing checkbox. If you check the box, any templates currently stored in the GPO are removed. If you leave it blank (the default), any policy settings from the imported template are simply merged into the existing templates, creating a composite security policy. Table 8.1 defines the available security templates.

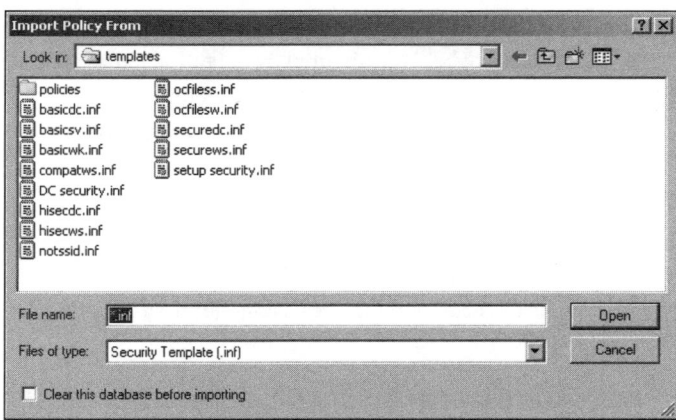

Figure 8.6 You can import Windows 2000 security templates into a GPO through the Computer Configuration container's Import Policy option.

Table 8.1 Windows 2000 security templates.	
Template Name	**Definition**
basicdc.inf	Default security settings for a DC
basicsv.inf	Default security settings for a standalone (or member) server
basicwk.inf	Default security settings for a Windows 2000 Professional system
compatws.inf	Security settings that make server or Professional backward-compatible with Microsoft Windows NT 4
dc security.inf	Default settings (updated) for DCs
hisecdc.inf	High-security settings for a DC
hisecws.inf	High-security settings for a Windows 2000 Professional system
notssid.inf	Removes the Terminal Server SID (security ID) assigned to a Windows 2000 Server
ocfiless.inf	For optional component file settings on servers
ocfilesw.inf	For optional component file settings on Windows 2000 Professional
securedc.inf	Secure DC settings
securews.inf	Secure Windows 2000 Professional settings
setup security.inf	Default settings applied after installation (installation defaults)

Another way to use Group Policy to manage the user environment is through script policies, as we will see next.

Be sure to know how to implement security templates.

Assigning Script Policies to Users and Computers

Windows 2000 has greatly expanded the role of scripts in managing the user environment. In previous versions of Windows NT, scripts were limited to batch files that could only be run at startup. With Windows 2000, however, any or all of the following scripts can be run:

➤ *Startup*—Computer scripts that run under the Local System account and apply settings during computer startup, before the User Logon dialog box is presented.

➤ *Logon*—Traditional user login scripts that run when the user logs on to the system. The scripts run under the user account with which they are associated. Logon scripts are executed only after computer Startup scripts have been processed by Windows 2000.

➤ *Logoff*—User scripts that run when the user either chooses Start|Log Off or chooses to shut down or restart the computer. Logoff scripts are executed before computer shutdown scripts.

➤ *Shutdown*—Computer scripts that run when the computer is shut down. As with Startup scripts, Shutdown scripts run under the Local System account to apply settings at the computer level.

Additionally, Windows 2000 allows you to go beyond the limitations of DOS-based batch files into ActiveX scripting using the VBScript and JavaScript (also known as JScript) engines. To support these ActiveX scripting engines, Windows 2000 provides the Windows Script Host.

Windows Script Host

Windows Script Host (WSH) is a scripting host that allows you to run VBScript scripts (which have a .vbs extension) and JavaScript scripts (which have a .js extension) natively on 32-bit Windows platforms. That means that you can execute VBScript or JScript scripts just as you would DOS batch files. WSH is extensible, so in the future, you might be able to run third-party scripts natively as well, such as Perl or Python.

Windows 2000 ships with WSH 2. WSH 2 replaces Windows Scripting Host 1.0, which shipped with Windows 98 and was available for download as part of the NT 4 Option Pack for use on NT systems. With version 2, Microsoft changed *Scripting* to *Script* in the name. WSH 2 is fully backward-compatible and is able to run any version 1 scripts. It is beyond the scope of this book to point out the differences between versions 1 and 2 other than to note that WSH 2 is XML-based and supports many new features.

WSH comes with two executable files:

➤ WScript.exe

➤ CScript.exe

WScript

WScript.exe is the graphical version of WSH and allows you to run VBScript and JScript scripts inside of Windows by double-clicking on the file name. You can also execute WScript.exe from the Run line in the Start menu. The syntax is as follows:

```
wscript <script name>
```

If the script is not located in a directory included in the environment variable **PATH** statement, you must specify the path to the script in *<script name>* for it to execute properly. WScript provides the following properties that can be configured:

➤ *Stop Script After Specified Number Of Seconds*—This setting specifies the maximum length of time a script can run. By default, there is not a time limit placed on script execution.

➤ *Display Logo When Script Is Executed In A Command Console*—This setting displays a WSH banner while running the script. This setting is turned on by default.

CScript

CScript.exe is the command-line version of WSH and is useful when you need to specify parameters at runtime. CScript is great for the computer and user scripts that are executed during startup, logon, logoff, and shutdown. The syntax of CScript.exe is as follows:

```
cscript <script name> <script options and parameters>
```

The definitions for the options after CScript are as follows:

➤ *<script name>*—The full path and file name of the script to be executed by CScript.exe.

➤ *<script options and parameters>*—Enable or disable various WSH features. Options are preceded by two forward slashes, as in **//logo**. Table 8.2 summarizes the host options.

Table 8.2	WSH options and their meanings.
Option	**Definition**
//b	Batch mode; suppresses script errors for any user prompts that might display. Computer and User scripts that we discuss in this chapter typically have this option specified.
//i	Interactive mode; the opposite of Batch Mode; Interactive Mode is the default if neither is specified.
//logo	Displays a logo banner during script execution; this is the default setting if not explicitly specified.
//nologo	Disables the logo banner from displaying during script execution.
//h:WScript	Changes the default script host to WScript; this is the default setting if none is explicitly specified.
//h:CScript	Changes the default script to CScript.
//e:engine	Specifies which engine to use in executing the script; either the VBScript or JScript engines can be specified.
//t:nn	Time out in seconds; the maximum amount of time the script is allowed to run before it is terminated by the script host.
//d	Debugger; this setting enables Active Debugging.
//x	Executes the script in the debugger.
//s	Save; saves the current command-line options for this user.
//job:<jobID>	Runs the specified *jobID* from a Windows Script Host 2 WSF (Windows script file) file.
//u	Tells WSH to use Unicode for redirected I/O from the console.
//?	Displays the help file for syntax and options.

Assigning Scripts through Group Policy

The hardest part about implementing scripts on a Windows 2000 network is the actual writing of the scripts. Assigning scripts through Group Policy, however, is easily accomplished.

Startup and shutdown scripts apply to computers, and logon and logoff scripts apply to users. As you know, the Group Policy Editor divides the GPO into two main nodes: Computer Configuration and User Configuration. The Scripts node is located under the Windows Settings node in each container, and parentheses indicate the type of scripts that the node supports.

To apply a script, simply click on the Scripts node under the appropriate container. Double-click on the desired script, such as the startup script, which brings up the dialog box shown in Figure 8.7.

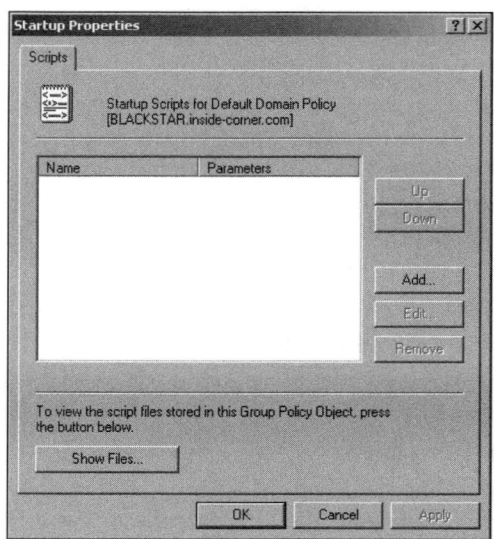

Figure 8.7 Double-clicking on a script brings up a settings dialog box.

In the script's properties dialog box, click on the Add button to add a new script. This brings up the dialog box shown in Figure 8.8.

If you know it, you can type in the name (and path if applicable) of the script you want to use; otherwise, just click on Browse. Select the script you want to use, as in Figure 8.9, and click on Open. This returns you to the dialog box shown in the previous figure. Enter any parameters, such as **//Nologo**, and click on OK.

Although it is not recommended to use other locations for the storage of scripts other than the default directories, shown in Table 8.3, note that when assigning scripts through Group Policy, the script can be located on any drive and folder the system can read. This is in contrast to Windows NT 4, which required login scripts to be located in the NETLOGON share, located at \winnt\system32\ repl\import\scripts.

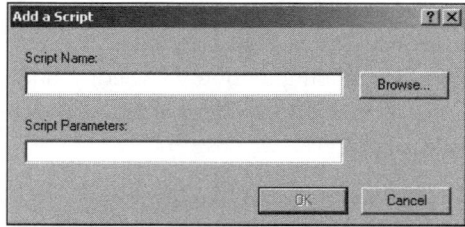

Figure 8.8 The Add A Script dialog box allows you to specify a script name and script parameters.

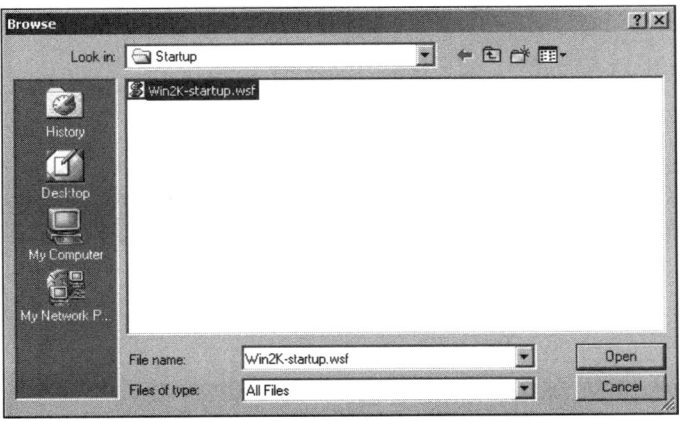

Figure 8.9   After selecting the script that you want to assign, click on Open.

Table 8.3	The default directories for Windows 2000 scripts.
Script	**Directory**
Startup	\winnt\SYSVOL\Sysvol*domain*\Policies*GUID*\MACHINE\Scripts\Startup
Shutdown	\winnt\SYSVOL\Sysvol*domain*\Policies*GUID*\MACHINE\Scripts\Shutdown
Logon	\winnt\SYSVOLSysvol*domain*\Policies*GUID*\USER\Scripts\Logon
Logoff	\winnt\SYSVOL\Sysvol*domain*\Policies*GUID*\USER\Scripts\Logoff

In Windows NT, scripts and other files placed in the \winnt\system32\ repl\export\scripts directory were replicated to the NETLOGON shares on DCs configured for replication. The File Replication Service (FRS) in Windows 2000 has replaced the NT 4 and earlier Directory Replication Service, and now replicates the entire SYSVOL directory tree across all DCs.

The exception to the recommendation about not changing the default location for scripts is if you are supporting legacy clients (Windows 9x, Windows NT 4) on your network. For these clients, you should copy the relevant logon scripts to the NETLOGON share, which in Windows 2000 is located under the \winnt\SYSVOL\Sysvol*domain*\scripts directory. Legacy clients cannot use the Windows 2000 features of startup, shutdown, and logoff scripts, so the NETLOGON share exists for backward-compatibility with their logon script capabilities.

In addition to being able to apply settings through scripts, Windows 2000 provides a Group Policy feature called *Folder Redirection* to help administrators more effectively manage the desktop environment. We discuss this feature next.

Use of Folder Redirection

Folder Redirection is the process where Windows 2000 changes the location of certain user folders from the local hard drive to a specified network share. Only the following folders can be redirected:

➤ Application Data

➤ Desktop

➤ My Documents

➤ My Pictures

➤ Start Menu

Folder Redirection is useful from an administrative standpoint for backups. In most environments, user workstations are not automatically backed up. By having folders redirected to a server share, the files are usually backed up. That provides an extra measure of protection against potential data loss.

When you right-click on one of the special folders in the Group Policy Editor and choose Properties, the first dialog box you see contains the target setting. This dialog box is shown in Figure 8.10. By default, this setting is No Administrative Policy Set, but you can change this to either of the following:

➤ *Basic - Redirect Everyone's Folder To The Same Location*—This policy redirects all folders to the same network share. You can individualize the path by

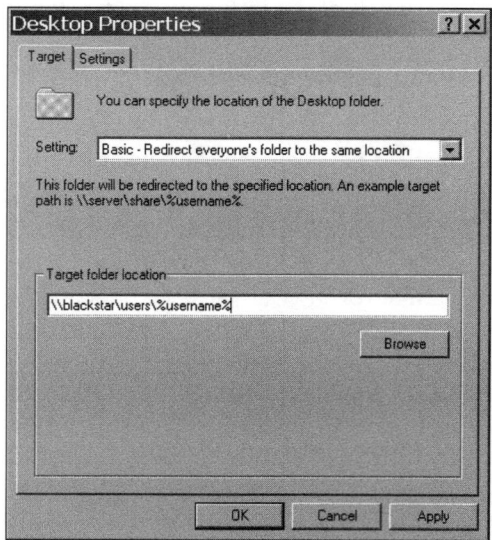

Figure 8.10 You configure Folder Redirection policies within the properties of a special folder.

incorporating the **%username%** variable, such as specifying **\\server\share\ %username%\My Documents**.

➤ *Advanced - Specify Locations For Various Groups*—The Advanced policy allows you to redirect folders based on security-group memberships. Members of one group can have folders directed to one share, and members of another group can be redirected to a different share. Again, you can use the **%username%** variable in your path to establish individual folders for each user.

Whether configuring a basic or advanced policy, you can configure the following additional settings for the Folder Redirection, as shown in Figure 8.11:

➤ *Grant The User Exclusive Rights To <special folder>*—By default, this setting is enabled, and it gives the user and the local system account full control, and no permissions to anyone else (even administrators).

➤ *Move The Contents Of <special folder> To The New Location*—Enabled by default, *<special folder>* is the name of the folder being redirected.

➤ *Policy Removal*—You have the option to either leave the files in the new location when the policy is removed (the default option) or have the files redirected back to their original location.

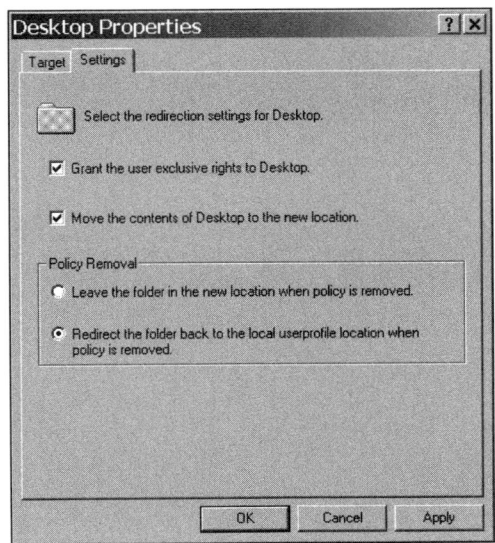

Figure 8.11   Group Policy provides additional settings for greater control over the behavior of redirected folders.

Practice Questions

Question 1

From the following list, choose the keywords that can be used in creating administrative templates, and arrange the keywords in the order that you would use them:

HELP

CATEGORY

EXPLAIN

VARIABLE

POLICY

CLASS

HEADER

STRINGS

REGISTRYKEY

END POLICY

NODE

The correct answer is:

CLASS

CATEGORY

POLICY

EXPLAIN

END POLICY

STRINGS

Question 2

What is the name of the executable for the command-line version of the Windows Script Host?

○ a. WScript.exe

○ b. CScript.exe

○ c. WSH.exe

○ d. CMD.exe

Answer b is correct. CScript.exe is the executable file for the command-line version of WSH. Answer a is incorrect because WScript is the Windows GUI version of Windows Script Host. Answer c is incorrect because WSH is merely the abbreviation for Windows Script Host, not the name of the executable. Answer d is incorrect because CMD.exe is the command interpreter for Windows 2000.

Question 3

Which of the following are administrative templates that are installed by default with Windows 2000? [Check all correct answers]

❑ a. System.adm

❑ b. Windows.adm

❑ c. Inetres.adm

❑ d. Default.adm

❑ e. Common.adm

❑ f. Winnt.adm

❑ g. GPO.adm

Answers a, b, c, e, and f are correct. Windows 2000 installs these five administrative templates by default. Answers d and g are incorrect because these templates would have to be created and installed by the user.

Question 4

There are two Group Policy configuration containers:

Computer Configuration

User Configuration

Identify how each of the following administrative template categories fits into these containers:

Desktop

Printers

Control Panel

Start Menu & Taskbar

The correct answer is:

Computer Configuration

Printers

User Configuration

Desktop

Control Panel

Start Menu & Taskbar

Question 5

Of the following, which are not categories of security settings that can be configured through the Group Policy Editor? [Check all correct answers]

❑ a. Account Policies

❑ b. Event Log

❑ c. Password Policies

❑ d. Registry

❑ e. File System

❑ f. Account Lockout

❑ g. Auditing

Answers c, f, and g are correct. Password Policies and Account Lockout are configured through Account Policies, and Auditing settings are configured through Local Policies. Answers a, b, d, and e are incorrect because they are security categories under Security Settings in the Computer Configuration container.

Question 6

Which of the following types of scripts are applied to computer accounts?
[Check all correct answers]

❑ a. Startup

❑ b. Logon

❑ c. Logoff

❑ d. Shutdown

Answers a and d are correct. Startup and shutdown scripts are applied to computer accounts. Answers b and c are incorrect because logon and logoff scripts are applied to user accounts.

Question 7

Which of the following user folders cannot be redirected to a server location using Folder Redirection?

○ a. My Documents

○ b. Favorites

○ c. Application Data

○ d. Desktop

○ e. Start Menu

Answer b is correct. Windows 2000 Folder Redirection cannot be used to redirect the Favorites folder. Answers a, c, d, and e are incorrect because these files can be used.

Question 8

Windows 2000 includes four default security templates that can be installed. Which template would provide a security configuration that would warn a user if he or she were about to install an unsigned driver?

○ a. Basic

○ b. Compatible

○ c. Secure

○ d. High Secure

Answer c is correct. The Secure template provides a higher level of security than answers a and b, the Basic and Compatible templates, and it would not install an unsigned driver without prompting the user first with a warning. Answer d is incorrect because the High Secure template simply would not allow an unsigned driver to be installed.

Question 9

Which security template would be used to bring a system upgraded from Windows NT to Windows 2000 up to the level of security of a new Windows 2000 installation?

○ a. Basic

○ b. Compatible

○ c. Secure

○ d. High Secure

Answer a is correct. Applying the Basic template to a GPO is a great way to bring upgraded NT systems up to the Windows 2000 default security level. Answer b is incorrect because, although the Compatible template sounds like the likely answer, that security template exists to allow legacy applications to run correctly in a Windows 2000 environment. Answers c and d are incorrect because Secure and High Secure templates are used to provide a higher level of security than what is initially set up when installing Windows 2000.

Question 10

Which Windows 2000 service has replaced the older Windows NT Directory Replication service? [Choose the best answer]

○ a. NETLOGON

○ b. Active Directory replication

○ c. SYSVOL

○ d. FRS

Answer d is correct. FRS (File Replication Service) is a new Windows 2000 service that expands on the capabilities of the older Directory Replication service. FRS replicates the entire SYSVOL tree between DCs (making answer c incorrect). Answer a is incorrect because NETLOGON is the share name for the directory that logon scripts are stored in on a DC for legacy clients. Answer b is incorrect because Active Directory replication is not the mechanism used to replicate directories.

Need to Know More?

 Iseminger, David. *Active Directory Services for Windows 2000 Technical Reference.* Microsoft Press, Redmond, WA, 2000. ISBN 0735606242. This book is a solid reference for planning and deploying AD networks. Although coverage of Group Policy is minor, there is a strong change and configuration management section.

 Microsoft Corporation. *Microsoft Windows 2000 Server Resource Kit.* Microsoft Press, Redmond, WA, 2000. ISBN 1572318058. The quintessential resource for Windows 2000 Server and AD, this kit has extensive coverage of AD and Group Policy in particular.

 Norris-Lowe, Alistair. *Windows 2000 Active Directory Service.* O'Reilly & Associates, Sebastopol, CA, 2000. ISBN 1565926382. Another good AD resource, this is more of a high-level technical book rather than a hands-on "how to" type of book. This is an excellent resource for learning the theory behind the technology and a great complement to the *Windows 2000 System Administration Handbook*, listed next.

 Willis, Will, David Watts, and Tillman Strahan. *Windows 2000 System Administration Handbook.* Prentice-Hall, Upper Saddle River, NJ, 2000. ISBN 0130270105. This book explains Windows 2000 systems administration concepts in detail, including managing user environments using Group Policy. This is a solid all-around Windows 2000 reference with good coverage of AD.

Using Group Policy in Software Deployment and Management

9

. . . .

Terms you'll need to understand:

✓ IntelliMirror

✓ Software Installation feature

✓ Windows Installer

✓ Assigned applications

✓ Published applications

✓ Pilot program

✓ Package

Techniques you'll need to master:

✓ Configuring deployment options

✓ Deploying software by using Group Policy

✓ Maintaining software by using Group Policy

✓ Troubleshooting common problems that occur during software deployment

In Chapters 7 and 8, we discussed how to implement Group Policy and how to use it to manage the desktop computing environment. In this chapter, we discuss another powerful use of Group Policy: software deployment and management. Using Group Policy, you can control what applications a user has on his or her computer. Under certain circumstances, you can even have applications repair themselves if they are missing files or settings. As we will see in a moment, software management is one of the three core functions of Microsoft's IntelliMirror initiative, which relies on Active Directory (AD) and Group Policy for implementation.

 You need to have a solid understanding of how to use Group Policy to assign and publish software and how to troubleshoot when things aren't working as expected.

IntelliMirror Concepts

Many of the Group Policy concepts we discussed in Chapters 7 and 8 are related to *IntelliMirror*, a collection of technologies that work together in Windows 2000 to reduce the total cost of ownership (TCO) by simplifying the management of Windows 2000 computers.

The features of IntelliMirror are as follows:

➤ *Data Management*—This feature, used to manage user data, is implemented in Windows 2000, as we have seen, through Folder Redirection. When Folder Redirection and Offline Folders are used, user data can be synchronized between a server copy and a local copy, ensuring that data files are accessible no matter where the user is and what computer he or she logs on from. Additionally, disk quotas can help track and restrict the usage of server disk space by user files.

➤ *Desktop Settings Management*—Desktop settings can be stored in profiles that roam with a user so that they are applied whenever a user logs in to a networked computer. Group Policy is used to control what settings should be stored and can control a user's ability to make changes to desktop settings. As we discussed in Chapter 8, Group Policy can be used to lock down desktop configurations and define a standard level of security for Windows 2000 computers.

➤ *Software Installation and Maintenance*—The focus of this chapter, this feature of IntelliMirror allows applications to be published by an administrator for use by defined users, computers, and groups, and Windows Installer applications can even be set up to automatically replace corrupt or missing files. This reduces downtime associated with broken applications that would ordinarily require an IT staff member to go out to a workstation and manually reinstall the application.

➤ *Remote Installation Services (RIS)*—RIS allows for the Windows 2000 Professional operating system to be installed remotely through preconfigured images. RIS is the focus of Chapter 15.

Specifically, the following are the available Windows 2000 IntelliMirror technologies and their interdependencies:

➤ *AD*—This is the cornerstone of IntelliMirror, because without AD, none of the rest would be possible. AD stores the Group Policy Objects (GPOs) and other user, group, and computer information, and it provides centralized management for Windows 2000 networks.

➤ *Group Policy*—Through Group Policy, we can manage desktop settings and determine what to apply and where. Group Policy is dependent on AD, because it stores global policy information in the AD database. Group Policy is the primary method of managing the IntelliMirror features in the preceding list.

➤ *Roaming user profiles*—Roaming profiles are used to enable user settings such as desktop wallpaper and customized Start menu settings to follow a user to whichever computer he or she logs on from. Any changes that are made to the user environment while the user is logged on are saved in the profile ntuser.dat and stored in AD. Roaming profiles existed in Windows NT 4 and have largely been superseded by Group Policy.

➤ *Folder Redirection*—Folder Redirection is one of the primary components of the Data Management IntelliMirror feature discussed previously. As you learned in Chapter 8, Folder Redirection can be used to move the contents of certain local user folders seamlessly to a network location. Combined with Offline Folders, you can have much greater data protection and availability than by having files stored only on local hard drives.

➤ *Offline Folders*—Offline Folders is an IntelliMirror capability that allows for the synchronization of files and folders between the local hard drive and a network location. This is particularly useful for users with laptops, because you can use Offline Folders in conjunction with Folder Redirection to ensure they have full access to their files regardless of whether they are in the office on the LAN or working offline on an airplane.

The focus of this chapter is software deployment and management, so let's discuss how the technologies in the preceding list work in this context.

Software Installation and Maintenance Overview

Through IntelliMirror and specifically the Group Policy component, Microsoft has provided the Software Installation and Maintenance feature, which provides a way for administrators to deploy software so that it is always available to users, and so that it repairs itself if necessary. Software Installation and Maintenance is implemented as a Group Policy extension called Software Installation. As shown in Figure 9.1, it is located under both the Computer Configuration and User Configuration containers in a GPO, beneath the Software Settings nodes.

Through Software Installation, you can centrally manage each of the following:

➤ *Deployment of applications*—You can deploy shrink-wrapped applications or custom-built, in-house applications. Almost any type of application can be deployed through Software Installation.

➤ *Upgrades and patches*—Through Software Installation, you can update existing software or even replace it, in the case of a product upgrade. Deploying service packs for operating systems becomes much easier as well.

➤ *Uninstall software*—When a product is no longer in use or supported by the IT department, you can easily remove it from users' computers without their

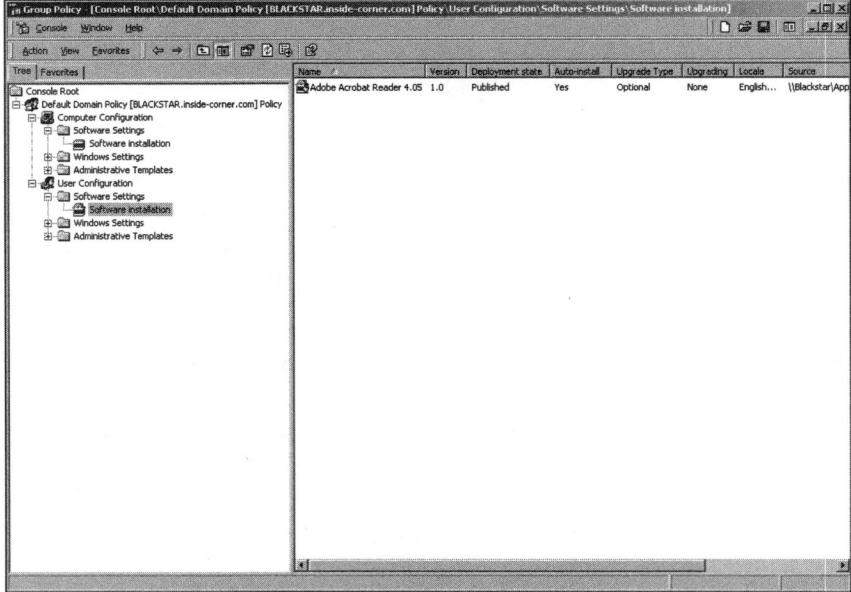

Figure 9.1 The Software Installation extension to Group Policy is located under the Software Settings node in the Computer Configuration and User Configuration containers.

intervention or without physically working on each computer containing the installed software.

The goal of Software Installation is to deploy applications in a way that whenever a user logs on to a computer, no matter where that user is, the user always has his or her applications available. This technology is often referred to as just-in-time (JIT), because deployment occurs either during user logon or when the user goes to launch a particular application. For example, say you have assigned Microsoft Excel to Mark, a particular user. Even though Mark has not explicitly installed Microsoft Excel himself, he sees the icon for it on his desktop or in his Start menu. The first time he attempts to use the program, the system installs the application automatically, with no user intervention, and launches the program.

Likewise, if the same user attempts to use a feature of the program that is not installed by default, the application will be smart enough to automatically install the missing feature on the fly from the network and allow the user to use it. In the past, installing a missing feature has invariably meant manually running the program's setup utility and either reinstalling the entire product to add the missing feature or simply selecting the missing feature and choosing to update the installation. Either case would be an interruption to the workflow of the user and very likely would require a desk-side trip from a desktop support technician.

Requirements for Software Installation

To use the Software Installation extension, two prerequisites must first be met:

➤ *AD dependency*—Because Group Policy is dependent on AD, it makes sense that you cannot use the Software Installation extension unless you have deployed AD on your network. Software Installation relies on GPOs, which are stored in AD, to determine who can access managed software. As with Group Policy, Windows 9x and NT 4 computers cannot participate in AD. At this time, Microsoft has not determined whether it will include AD support in its upcoming Windows Millennium operating system.

➤ *Group Policy dependency*—To use the Software Installation extension, you must be using Group Policy on your network. Because Group Policy is limited to Windows 2000 computers, you can only manage software for your Windows 2000 environment. Any legacy Windows 9x or NT 4 clients won't be able to receive applications through Group Policy and Software Installation.

The primary function of Software Installation is to deploy software, so let's discuss that next.

Deploying Software with Group Policy and Software Installation

In this section, we explore the Software Installation extension—specifically, the following:

➤ Configuring Software Installation properties

➤ Deploying a new package

➤ Configuring package properties

 You need to know how to deploy software using the Software Installation extension and how to configure deployment options.

These topics will allow you to deploy software, from setting up the Software Installation extension's global properties to deploying a new package, and then to configure additional properties for a deployed software package.

Configuring Software Installation Properties

To configure the global properties of the Software Installation extension, simply right-click on the extension and click on Properties. Keep in mind that computer and user settings are independent of each other, so making changes to the computer policy for Software Installation has no effect on the user policy, and vice versa.

The first dialog box you are presented with when you enter Software Installation properties is the General tab, shown in Figure 9.2.

The first section on this property sheet allows the administrator to define the default package location for new packages. This should be a network share rather than a local hard drive path (e.g., \\blackstar\apps rather than E:\apps) and is used if you use a centralized distribution location for your software.

The General property sheet also contains settings that define the behavior of the extension with regard to new package creation. By default, the Deploy Software dialog box is displayed when you choose to create a new package. This dialog box contains the choice to assign or publish a package, allowing you to choose how you want Software Installation to handle a package on a package-by-package basis. Unless you strictly publish or assign applications, there is probably no need to change this default setting.

Additionally, the General tab contains the option to define how much information is presented to the user during package installation. By default, only basic

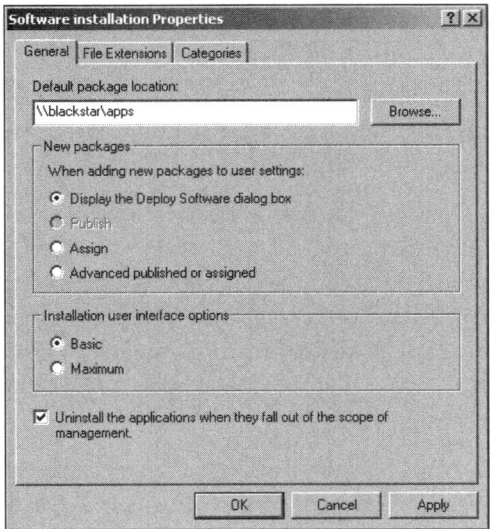

Figure 9.2 The General tab contains information about the default behavior of the Software Installation extension.

information about the software installation is supplied, such as the installation progress meter. Optionally, you can specify that a maximum amount of information and options be shown to the user during installation, which includes all installation messages and dialog boxes.

Finally, the General tab has the optional setting to define whether software should automatically be uninstalled when it falls outside the scope of management. That is, if Software Installation no longer manages the software, it should no longer be available to users. By default, this option is not enabled.

After the General tab is the File Extensions tab. In many cases, you will have more than one application installed on your computer that is capable of opening a given type of file. This property sheet allows you to pick a file type and set the order of precedence for applications that are capable of opening the application. If the first application listed isn't available for some reason—for instance, because it was uninstalled—the second application listed attempts to open it.

The last tab is Categories, which is an organizational option. You can create categories to help keep track of where software is deployed. By default, no categories are listed, so you must create them if you want to use this feature. You might choose to create categories for your software based on department or location or some other naming convention that makes sense for your organization.

Deploying a New Package

To deploy a new package, you must have first copied the installation files to a *distribution point*, which is simply a network share that you designate as a repository for software. Right-click on the Software Installation extension, and select New|Package. The dialog box in Figure 9.3 appears.

In the example, a Windows Installer package for Adobe Acrobat Reader is selected, which is located in the Apps share on the server Blackstar. This is the distribution point. When you select the file and click on Open, you see the dialog box shown in Figure 9.4. You get this dialog box because the default settings in the Software Installation Properties dialog box (refer back to Figure 9.2) were not changed. If you had selected the Assign or Publish option, the action would simply be taken and you would not see this dialog box.

Note that the Published option is available only if the package is being deployed under the User Configuration container. Software deployed to computers does not

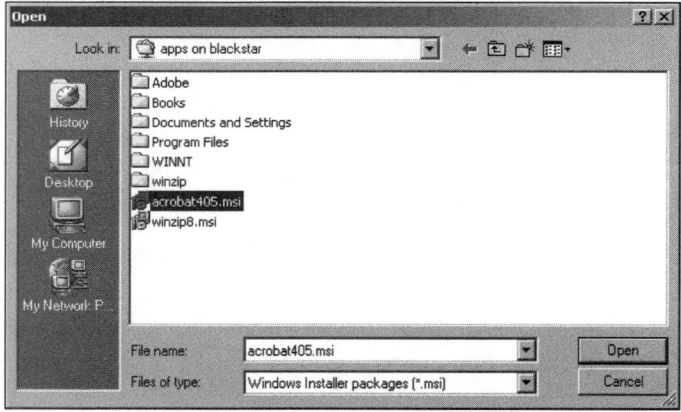

Figure 9.3   The first step in deploying a new package is to select the package that is to be deployed.

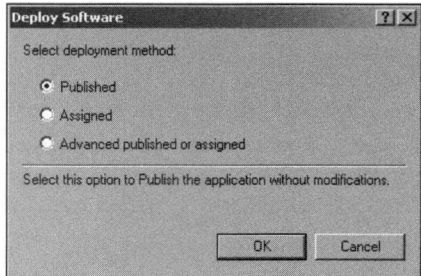

Figure 9.4   After choosing the software package to deploy, you must decide whether to publish or assign it.

support publishing, and therefore, those packages can only be assigned. When you get to the dialog box shown in Figure 9.4 and you've deployed the package under the Computer Configuration container, the Published option will be grayed out.

If you select either Published or Assigned and click on OK, the package is deployed without any further prompting. If you select Advanced Published Or Assigned, the package will still be deployed, but you will be prompted with a dialog box similar to that shown in Figure 9.5. This is the same dialog box you can access later by going into the properties of a package, which is discussed next.

Configuring Package Properties

To access the properties of a package once you've deployed it, simply right-click on the package and click on Properties. You will see the same dialog box as you did previously if you selected Advanced Published Or Assigned during the new package deployment. A number of property sheets contain settings for the package. Here is an overview:

➤ *General*—Contains product information such as the name and version number, as well as contact information.

➤ *Deployment*—Defines the deployment type (assigned or published), which can also be changed here. In addition, this property sheet contains settings for deployment options, including whether the package should be uninstalled if it falls outside the scope of management and if it should be displayed in the

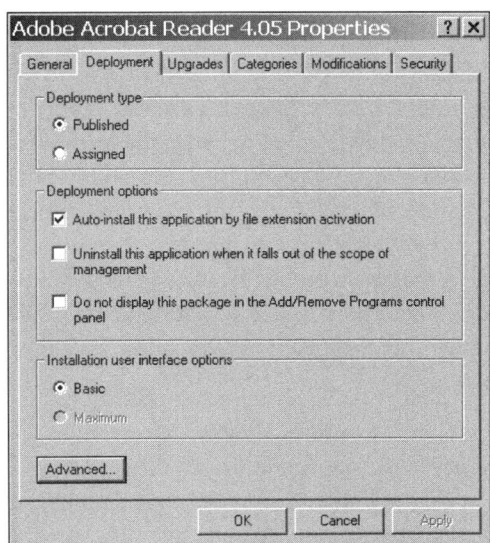

Figure 9.5   You can configure a number of advanced settings for an application once it has been deployed.

Add/Remove Programs applet. Advanced deployment options determine whether the language setting should be ignored when software is installed and whether previous installations of the product should be uninstalled if the software wasn't installed through Group Policy.

➤ *Upgrades*—Defines the applications that are to be upgraded by this package and which packages can upgrade this package.

➤ *Categories*—Determines the categories that the software will be displayed under in the Add/Remove Programs applet.

➤ *Modifications*—Allows you to apply modifications or transforms to the package to customize the deployment.

➤ *Security*—Determines who has what level of access to the package. Through the Security property sheet, you control the deployment of the software to computers, users, and groups.

These are the basics of the Software Installation extension. At this point, we should take a moment to discuss assigned applications versus published applications and when to use one over the other.

Assigned vs. Published Applications

A key aspect to consider when deploying software is whether the application will be assigned directly to users or published into AD. When an application is assigned, its icons appear in the Start menu or on the desktop of the user's computer according to criteria defined by the administrator. The first time a user attempts to launch an assigned application, the software is automatically installed without user or administrator intervention. If a user later uninstalls the application through the Add/Remove Programs applet in Control Panel, the software is still available to the user the next time he or she logs on. If a user attempts to launch a program he or she thought was uninstalled, the software simply reinstalls itself and opens. Because the software has been assigned to the user, the user cannot remove it. The advantage is that users cannot break assigned applications; rather, the software is self-healing and therefore does not require a traditional desk-side trip from an IT staff member to repair it by manually reinstalling.

On the other hand, administrators can choose to simply publish applications into the AD rather than assigning them directly to users. Assigned applications are typically used when a user needs a particular application to do his or her job. Published applications are not necessarily required by users to do their jobs but are beneficial applications that the administrator wants to make available. A published application shows up in Add/Remove Programs but must be explicitly installed by the user. No icons appear in the Start menu or on the desktop in advance to inform the user of the application's availability, and if a user uninstalls the application, it is removed from the computer just as in a traditional uninstall procedure.

Phases of Software Deployment

To ensure success, software deployment is best done through a systematic method. Managing a documented process removes many of the variables associated with deploying new software, thus reducing support costs related to troubleshooting problems.

Microsoft recommends a software deployment strategy similar to the following:

1. *Preparation phase*—The preparation phase of software deployment includes analyzing the requirements of your organization to determine the needs to be filled. Some of the tasks include determining licensing requirements, whether applications will be run from a network server or local hard drives, and if the current network infrastructure will support the deployment or if you need to make modifications before deploying the new application to your users. You must also decide whether you will publish or assign applications in this phase.

2. *Distribution phase*—The distribution phase includes setting up network distribution points for the new software package and copying the source installation files to your distribution points.

3. *Targeting phase*—In the targeting phase, you use Group Policy to create and/ or modify GPOs to effectively manage the software for users, groups, and computers. In addition, you use the Software Installation extension in Group Policy to configure deployment options for the new software package.

4. *Pilot program phase*—The pilot program phase is perhaps the most important. In this phase, you deploy your software package to a select group of users, groups, and computers that is representative of the whole. By deploying to a select group and not everyone who will ultimately receive the package, you can put the application through all possible scenarios without impacting everyone if there are problems to be worked out. Once you have thoroughly tested the application under a pilot program, you are ready to deploy it to everyone.

5. *Installation phase*—The installation phase is where the software is actually deployed to the desktops of all of the users included in the target phase. The installation phase can involve installing new applications, installing modifications or updates to existing applications, repairing existing applications, and removing applications entirely.

Following the phases of this process gives you the best chance for a successful software deployment; however, there will probably be times when you run into difficulties. Therefore, you should know how to troubleshoot some of the common problems.

Troubleshooting Software Deployment Problems

In a perfect world, you would follow the software deployment process outlined in the previous section and roll out an application with no difficulties whatsoever. Unfortunately, things don't always work out in the real world the way they do in a textbook. Because of this hard reality, let's discuss some of the more common problems you might run into with software deployment and what steps you might take to resolve them.

Some general guidelines to follow in troubleshooting are discussed in this section. In many cases, problems can be traced to a lack of necessary permissions. One of the first troubleshooting steps should be to ensure that an appropriate level of permissions exists to access the needed resource. Missing source files or corrupted Windows Installer packages is another potential source of trouble. As part of your troubleshooting steps, you should check to make sure the necessary files are available.

The following subsections detail some common problems and how to resolve them.

Deployment Error Messages

Unfortunately, when working with any technology in the real world, things don't seem to always work quite like they do in a textbook. Any number of variables can come into play, and troubleshooting problems often becomes the most frustrating part of being a systems engineer. With that in mind, here are some common problems related to software deployment and what to look for to fix them.

"Active Directory will not allow the package to be deployed" Error Message

This error is usually a result of a corrupt Windows Installer package or the inability of the Software Installation Group Policy extension to communicate properly with AD.

To resolve this problem, test for connectivity with the DNS server and DCs containing the AD database. You can use the **ping** command to establish basic connectivity and browse through My Network Places to the servers to see if you can access the required share directories. To test for a corrupted Windows Installer package, check whether you can open the package on another similarly configured computer.

"Cannot prepare the package for deployment" Error Message

This error is similar to the preceding AD error in that it can be the result of a corrupt package. However, rather than the Software Installation extension not being able to communicate with AD, in this case it cannot communicate with the SYSVOL share.

The troubleshooting steps are the same as with the previous error. Test for connectivity between the workstation and the SYSVOL share on the DCs, try from another computer if communication fails, and attempt to install the package on another system if connectivity is fine.

Installation Error Messages

A number of different error messages can appear when you install an application on a workstation. There could be a problem with the Windows Installer packages, or there could be a permissions problem where the user or computer account attempting to install the application doesn't have the necessary level of permissions to complete the installation. The permissions problem could relate to not being able to execute the particular package, not being able to access the distribution point, or not being able to install the application to the target directory on the local hard drive as defined by the package.

To troubleshoot, first determine if you have the permission to access the distribution point. If you do, copy the package to the local hard drive and attempt to execute it from there. If the package begins installing and fails, ensure that the user account being used has Write permissions to the target directory. If the package gives an error before attempting to install, make sure the user account has Execute permissions for the package and test the package on another system to ensure its integrity (that is, make sure it is not corrupted).

"The feature you are trying to install cannot be found in the source directory" Error Message

This type of error is most likely related to permissions or connectivity. Either the user doesn't have the necessary permissions level to access the distribution point, or the distribution point is unavailable over the network. Additionally, you should check to ensure that the source files were not accidentally deleted or moved to another location on the network.

To troubleshoot this error, first make sure the required source files exist at the distribution point. If they do, make sure the user attempting to install the feature has connectivity to the server containing the distribution point. If this checks out, check the permissions on the distribution point to see if the user has the required permissions. Most likely, one of these three sources is the cause of the error.

Shortcuts Still Appear for Removed Applications

This isn't an error message, but rather a condition that might exist after uninstalling a managed application. After either the user uninstalls an application or the Software Installation extension removes the software when an administrator removes it from the applications list, the shortcuts for the applications still appear on the Start menu and/or the desktop.

To troubleshoot, determine if the shortcuts were user-created or program-created. In many cases, users copy shortcuts from the Start menu to the desktop for convenience. The application's installation program would not be aware of this type of user-created shortcut and therefore would not be able to remove it during the application's uninstallation process.

Another cause might be that the shortcuts point to another installation of the same program. Perhaps the user belongs to multiple GPOs, and the application has been removed from only one of them. Another possibility is that there was a locally installed copy prior to the installation of the assigned or published application, and those files were not removed.

You should check to see if the shortcuts point to valid programs. If they do, determine why the programs are installed (local install, another GPO, and so on) and if it is appropriate. If the shortcuts do not point to valid applications, simply delete them.

Installed Application Is Uninstalled from a User Workstation

This condition almost always occurs when the software deployment option Uninstall This Application When It Falls Outside The Scope Of Management is selected. However, it could result if a computer account was moved outside of the influence of the GPO managing the software.

If the computer account was not moved, determine if a GPO that the user or computer belongs to is still managing the application.

Troubleshooting is often more of an art than a science, but if you remember to check connectivity, permissions, and the existence of source files, you'll be a long way toward troubleshooting software deployment.

Practice Questions

Question 1

> From the following list, choose the correct phases of software deployment and arrange them in order.
>
> Distribution
>
> Installation
>
> Preparation
>
> Deployment
>
> Targeting
>
> Publishing
>
> Pilot

The correct answer is:

Preparation

Distribution

Targeting

Pilot

Installation

Question 2

> Which of the following Windows 2000 features is not considered an IntelliMirror technology?
>
> ○ a. Group Policy
>
> ○ b. Folder Redirection
>
> ○ c. Terminal Services
>
> ○ d. Offline Folders

Answer c is correct. Terminal Services is a Windows 2000 component that can provide for "thin client" solutions that can reduce total cost of ownership (TCO) for desktop systems, but it is not a part of IntelliMirror. Answers a, b, and d are incorrect because Group Policy, Folder Redirection, and Offline Folders are all IntelliMirror technologies.

Question 3

Which of the following are prerequisites to use Software Installation? [Check all correct answers]

❑ a. Active Directory

❑ b. Published applications

❑ c. Group Policy

❑ d. Roaming profiles

Answers a and c are correct. Software Installation is an extension to Group Policy, which automatically makes Group Policy a prerequisite. Because Group Policy is dependent on Active Directory, that is also a correct answer. Answer b is incorrect because applications can be either published or assigned through Software Installation, and answer d is incorrect because roaming profiles are not required to use Software Installation.

Question 4

Windows 2000 supports the following two features (among others):

IntelliMirror

Software Installation

Identify which feature each of the following components falls into:

Upgrades and patches

Software Installation and Maintenance

Desktop Settings Management

Uninstall software

Data Management

Deployment of applications

The correct answer is:

IntelliMirror

Software Installation and Maintenance

Desktop Settings Management

Data Management

Software Installation

Upgrades and patches

Deployment of applications

Uninstall software

Question 5

Which of the following behaviors is not characteristic of assigned applications? [Choose the best answer]

○ a. Installs automatically the first time a user attempts to launch a program through its shortcut.

○ b. Reappears after the user logs off and logs back in, even if the user uninstalled the application through Add/Remove Programs.

○ c. Is installed by the user through the Add/Remove Programs applet.

○ d. Appears the next time Group Policy is refreshed.

Answer c is correct. Installing a managed application through Add/Remove Programs is characteristic of a published application, not an assigned one. Answer a is incorrect because assigned applications install themselves automatically the first time a user attempts to open them. Answers b and d are incorrect because the shortcuts appear whenever the user logs off and logs back on or whenever Group Policy refreshes. Additionally, users can remove assigned applications; however, they will reappear the next time the user logs on to the computer.

Question 6

Which of the following would most likely be the cause of software deployment problems? [Check all correct answers]

❑ a. Permissions

❑ b. User not logged on to network

❑ c. Missing or corrupt source files

❑ d. Network connectivity between workstation and distribution point down

Answers a, c, and d are correct. Permissions, missing/corrupted source files, and connectivity account for the majority of software deployment problems. Answer b is incorrect because, although it is possible to have Windows 2000 workstation configured to not log on to a network automatically, this is not a setting that typically would be changed if it had been previously configured to log on to a domain.

Question 7

Which of the following would you check if a user complained that a formerly managed application that was uninstalled still left icons on her desktop? [Check all correct answers]

❑ a. If the shortcut pointed to a valid program

❑ b. If the user created the shortcut or if it had been created by the installation program

❑ c. If the program had been reinstalled because of membership in another GPO

❑ d. If another nonmanaged copy of the program had been installed locally on the system to a different directory

Answers a, b, c, and d are correct. All of these choices are valid troubleshooting steps to determine the cause of a formerly managed application still existing on a system after it has been uninstalled.

Question 8

> Which Windows 2000 IntelliMirror feature synchronizes user files and folders between a network share and the local hard drive? [Choose the best answer]
>
> ○ a. Offline Folders
>
> ○ b. Folder Redirection
>
> ○ c. My Briefcase
>
> ○ d. Roaming profiles

Answer a is correct. Offline Folders provides the ability to have files and folders synchronized between server copies and local hard drive copies. This feature is used primarily by mobile users who work offline (off the network) frequently. Answer b is incorrect because Folder Redirection redirects certain local folders to a server share without any kind of synchronization. Answer c is incorrect because My Briefcase was a primitive Windows 95 attempt to synchronize files and folders. Answer d is incorrect because the roaming profiles feature does not synchronize files and folders, but rather stores user environment settings (wallpaper, color schemes, and so on) on the network.

Question 9

> How would you determine if a user had an appropriate level of permissions to execute a managed application? [Choose the best answer]
>
> ○ a. Through the Security tab in the package's properties in Software Installation
>
> ○ b. Through the Deployment tab in the package's properties in Software Installation
>
> ○ c. Through OU membership in Active Directory Users and Computers
>
> ○ d. Through GPO membership in Active Directory Users and Computers

Answer a is correct. The key to this question is the permission to execute a *managed application*. Permissions for managed applications are set through the Security tab in the package's properties in the Software Installation extension. Answer b is incorrect because the Deployment tab is used to configure other package properties, such as whether it is assigned or published. Answers c and d are incorrect because Active Directory Users and Computers is used to control security group membership as a whole rather than setting permissions on a particular resource.

Question 10

In which software deployment phase would you create and/or modify GPOs?
[Choose the best answer]

○ a. Preparation

○ b. Distribution

○ c. Targeting

○ d. Pilot

○ e. Installation

Answer c is correct. The targeting phase is used to create and/or modify GPOs that will be the target of the software package. Answer a is incorrect because in the preparation phase, you determine who the target will be, but you do not actually create GPOs at that point. Answer b is incorrect because the distribution phase involves setting up the source files and on distribution points that you have created. Answer d is incorrect because the pilot phase involves testing the software on a limited number of users, and answer e is incorrect because the installation phase is the actual deployment.

Need to Know More?

Iseminger, David. *Active Directory Services for Windows 2000 Technical Reference*. Microsoft Press, Redmond, WA, 2000. ISBN 0735606242. This is a solid reference for planning and deploying AD networks. Although coverage of Group Policy is minor, there is a strong change and configuration management section.

Microsoft Corporation. *Microsoft Windows 2000 Server Resource Kit*. Microsoft Press, Redmond, WA, 2000. ISBN 1572318058. The quintessential resource for Windows 2000 Server and AD, this kit has extensive coverage of AD and Group Policy in particular.

Norris-Lowe, Alistair. *Windows 2000 Active Directory Service*. O'Reilly & Associates, Sebastopol, CA, 2000. ISBN 1565926382. Another good AD resource, this is more of a high-level technical book than a hands-on how-to type of book. This book discusses software deployment from a strategic perspective, which is a great help in the planning phases.

Willis, Will, David Watts, and Tillman Strahan. *Windows 2000 System Administration Handbook*. Prentice-Hall, Upper Saddle River, NJ, 2000. ISBN 0130270105. A solid all-around Windows 2000 reference with good coverage of AD, this handbook explains Windows 2000 systems administration concepts in detail, including managing user environments using Group Policy.

Publishing Resources within the Active Directory

. . . .

Terms you'll need to understand:

✓ Publish

✓ Active Directory (AD) Users and Computers

✓ Sharing

✓ Universal Naming Convention (UNC)

✓ Pubprn.vbs

✓ Keywords

Techniques you'll need to master:

✓ Publishing non-Windows 2000 printers through AD Users and Computers

✓ Publishing non-Windows 2000 printers through the pubprn.vbs script

✓ Viewing published printers in AD Users and Computers

✓ Searching for a printer by name or location

✓ Publishing a folder within AD

✓ Establishing a description and keyword for a published folder

One of the primary purposes of a directory service is to "publish" objects so they can be easily located by users. The idea is similar to using a telephone directory service, where you call directory assistance and request a phone number. If that number is listed (published), it will be returned to you. If the number is not listed (unpublished), you will get a negative response.

Introduction to Published Resources

Within Active Directory (AD), some resources are automatically published—for example, user accounts. These are created within the AD and are immediately published. Additional objects that are published within AD are computers and printers that are added to the AD database.

There are times, however, when resources are not automatically published to the AD—for example, printers that are available from non-Windows 2000 servers. In such cases, the administrator may need to publish these resources to the AD to help users find them. Another example is folders that are shared on the network.

Note: Remember that printers installed on non-Windows 2000 servers and folders that have been shared on the network are not automatically published and are therefore not included within AD searches. The systems administrator must publish these on an individual basis as necessary.

Before we discuss how to publish resources, here are several important points to remember:

➤ You do not have to publish resources that are published automatically through the AD.

➤ Published information should not change frequently because this causes extensive network traffic.

➤ Published resources enable users to find objects even if they've been moved physically, as long as you update the shortcut within the AD.

Now, let's focus on the two primary objects for publishing: non-Windows 2000 printers and shared folders.

Publishing Printers

Printers are published automatically to the AD if they have been established on a machine running Windows 2000. This makes it possible to search within a domain for printers that exist in diverse physical locations.

Imagine a global corporation with offices in every major city. On the 23rd floor of an office in the Manhattan headquarters, a document-processing member has received a job by fax from Hong Kong. The fax specifies specific edits to a document. Once the edits are completed, the document must be printed to a printer named "Apple," which is located off a server in Hong Kong. The user can know the name of the printer and still not be able to connect to that printer; however, if the printer is published to the AD, the user can search for the printer and find it. If the user has the permission to print to Apple, the job will run smoothly. If the user doesn't know where Apple is, the task becomes a lot more administrator-intensive because the administrator would need to establish a connection to Apple.

When printers are created on a Windows 2000 machine, the printer is integrated with AD by default. When printers are published, the print queue is published, and hence, the AD object that is created is called a *printQueue*. When properties of the printer are modified, these modifications to the object become part of the replication procedure that automatically takes place.

Printers can be published two ways:

➤ By using AD Users and Computers

➤ By using the pubprn.vbs script located within the system32 folder on the system

Let's explore each step of both of these methods.

Steps for Publishing Printers

A printer that is installed and shared on a system that is not Windows 2000—an NT 4 server, for example—will not be published automatically within the AD. To accomplish this task, you must use the UNC (Universal Naming Convention) path.

You establish a UNC path by indicating the location of the printer (or other shared resource). First, you include the name of the server and then the official name of the shared resource. The syntax for a UNC path is *server_name**share_name*. So if you had a non-Windows 2000 server called "PrintServ" and a printer shared off of that server called "HP1," the UNC path for that printer would be \\\\PrintServ\\HP1.

Publishing with AD Users and Computers

To publish a printer with AD Users and Computers, follow these steps:

1. Open AD Users and Computers.

2. Find the OU to which you would like to publish the printer.

3. Right-click on the OU. Click on New, then on Printer.

4. Enter the UNC path of the printer that you wish to publish, as shown in Figure 10.1, and click on OK.

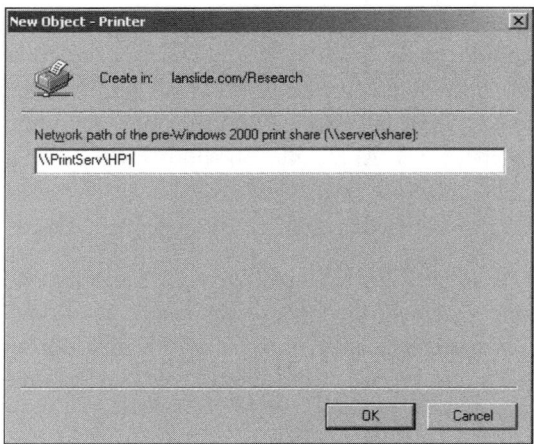

Figure 10.1 Publishing a printer with AD Users and Computers.

Publishing with the Pubprn.vbs Script

The system32 folder in Windows 2000 contains a script called pubprn.vbs. You can use this script to publish all printers shared off of a non-Windows 2000 server, or you can use it to publish only one printer off of a non-Windows 2000 server.

To run the script, type the following at a command prompt:

```
Cscript %systemroot%\system32\pubprn.vbs <additional options>
```

For example, let's say you have a Windows NT 4 Server hosting five shared printers that you would like published within your AD. The server's name is SalesPrint, and you would like to publish it into an OU called Sales off of a domain called coriolis.com. To accomplish this with the script, you would type the following at a command prompt:

```
Cscript %systemroot%\system32\pubprn.vbs SalesPrint
  "LDAP://OU=Sales, DC=coriolis, DC=com"
```

In this example, **%systemroot%** indicates the location of the system32 partition. The name of the server can be changed to the UNC path of one specific printer, rather than publishing all printers off of the server. The LDAP path indicates the place in AD that the printers should be published to.

Viewing Published Printers

Whether you have a printer that exists on a Windows 2000 Server and is published automatically, or a printer that you've manually published, it is certainly important to view the corresponding printer objects. To view the printer objects, you first need to enable a specific option within AD Users and Computers. You need to select View and then choose Users, Groups, And Computers As Containers. By enabling this option, you can view the published printers in the details pane after you select the computer on which the printer is located.

Once you can view the printer, you can also perform specific administrative tasks for that printer. By right-clicking on the printer, you can perform the following:

➤ Move the printer.

➤ Connect to and install a printer.

➤ Open the print queue and perform document maintenance, such as deleting print jobs or pausing them.

➤ Change printer properties or print queue properties.

Searching for Printers

To search for a printer, select Start|Search and then select For Printers. The dialog box in Figure 10.2 appears.

You can search for a printer by providing a name, a location, or a model type. In addition, through the various tabs, such as Advanced, you can narrow your search further.

Printer Locations

One of the nice features of publishing a printer within the AD is the ability to use location definitions to assist users in their searches. When a user indicates a location, the AD search returns a list of printers at that location.

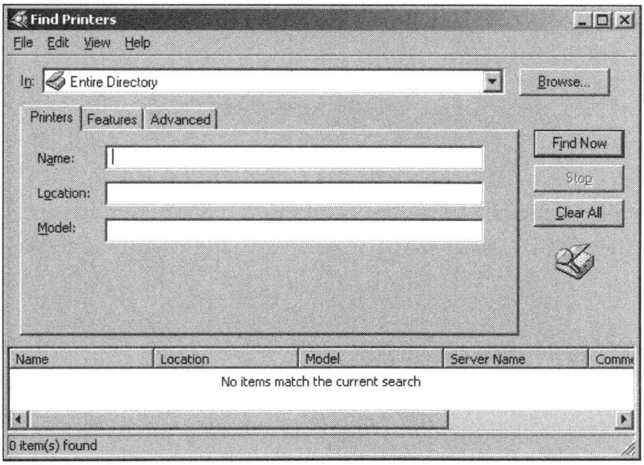

Figure 10.2 The Find Printers dialog box.

In addition, the AD search feature uses IP subnets to determine if printers are within the local proximity. If you have a network with only one subnet, the search operation will assume that all printers are in the same location. An administrator would then relate that subnet with a location naming convention. Establishing this convention would involve a certain amount of planning; for example, you can determine location based upon the floor itself, or based upon the known department.

Note: For additional information on this subject, select Start\Help. Then select the Index tab. In the Type In The Keyword To Find textbox, type "printer location tracking". Here you are offered several helpful topics, such as Enabling Location Tracking, Naming Conventions, and Troubleshooting.

Publishing Folders

Folder sharing allows individuals with the correct permissions to use a UNC path to connect to a shared folder and explore, add to, delete, or modify its contents. Although this operation is not difficult for experienced administrators, users may not be able to comprehend UNC path mapping, or they may not know the servers' names or the share name. The solution is to publish the shared folder in the AD as an object. Once the folder is published, you can define keywords and a description to make searches easier for your users.

Steps for Publishing Folders

Publishing folders through the AD Users and Computers tool is similar to publishing printers. Before publishing the folder, you must share the folder on the network.

Once the folder is shared, perform the following steps:

1. Open AD Users and Computers.

2. Find the OU to which you want to publish the shared folder.

3. Right-click on the OU. Select New, then Shared Folder.

4. Enter a name for the shared folder in the Name dialog box and indicate the UNC path for the shared folder that you are publishing within the AD. Then click on OK.

Additional Search Descriptions

Once the folder is published, you can add descriptions and keywords to the folder to simplify the search process for users. The descriptions and keywords can be likened to the types of words you might include for a Web search. For instance, if you are searching the Web for some information on a Microsoft exam, you might enter "70-217" to indicate the exam covered in this book. In this case, various sites would have specified the keyword "70-217", because this would be a likely request from users.

To add search descriptions and keywords, follow these steps:

1. Open AD Users and Computers.

2. Find the OU and the published folder.

3. Right-click on the published folder and select Properties.

4. In the Shared Properties dialog box that appears, shown in Figure 10.3, enter a description and keywords. When complete, click on OK.

Note: If a printer or folder is ever physically moved, users would not need to be aware of it; the systems administrator would just switch the UNC path. If the printer or folder remains in its physical location, but you need to switch the published resource to a different OU, you can move the object from within AD Users and Computers by right-clicking on the object, selecting Move, and then supplying the destination.

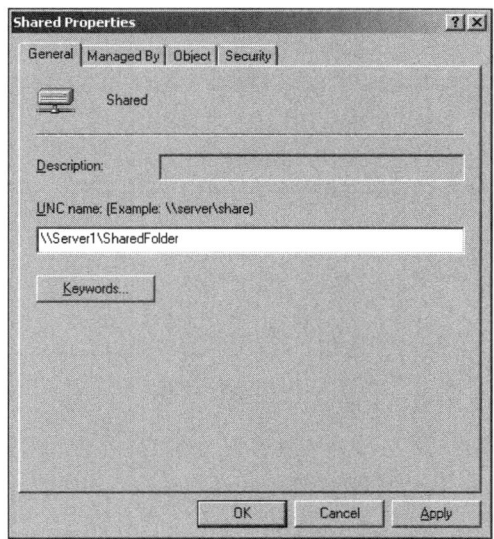

Figure 10.3   Adding search descriptions and keywords to a published folder with the AD.

Practice Questions

Question 1

> You need to ensure that an Active Directory search for a non-Windows 2000
> print server for the marketing department of a company called AfterShock
> will be successful for users within the department. As the systems adminis-
> trator, what best-practice procedure should you perform?
>
> ○ a. Share out the printers to members of the marketing department.
>
> ○ b. Publish the printers to the AD.
>
> ○ c. Upgrade the server to a Windows 2000 machine.
>
> ○ d. Nothing. The search will be successful.

Answer b is correct. You must publish printers to the AD that are located off of
non-Windows 2000 machines. Answer a is incorrect because this won't ensure a
search; it will only ensure the possibility of connecting with those printers. Answer c is incorrect because, although this is possible, it is not considered best practice. Answer d is incorrect because the search will, in fact, fail if you do nothing.

Question 2

> Which of the following options allows you to publish printers to the Active
> Directory? [Check all correct answers]
>
> ❑ a. AD Users and Computers
>
> ❑ b. AD Sites and Services
>
> ❑ c. Pubprn.vbs
>
> ❑ d. Prnpub.vbs

Answers a and c are correct. You can use either the AD Users and Computers
tool or the pubprn.vbs script to publish printers within Active Directory. Answer
b is incorrect because this tool is used to allocate subnets into sites. Answer d is
incorrect because it is an invalid script name.

Question 3

Two departments, Research and Development, are merging into one called Futures. The OUs are being deleted, and all objects are being moved into the new Futures OU. What must you do to ensure that users can still connect to published printers and folders?

○ a. Change the UNC path of the published objects.

○ b. Disconnect the users through Group Policy and force a reconnection.

○ c. Reboot the server.

○ d. Nothing.

Answer d is correct. You don't need to do anything. The users will still be able to connect. Answer a is incorrect because a UNC path change is not necessary if the physical location remains the same. Answer b is incorrect because it's an invalid solution. Answer c will only make people angry and have no effect on their connection to published resources; therefore, it is incorrect.

Question 4

Your company has a Hong Kong branch on the 15th, the 21st, and the 31st floors of a building. You want to find a printer in Hong Kong on the 15th floor that you can print to. You search for it and find several to choose from. What has your network administrator done to allow this type of search?

○ a. The administrator has enabled searching.

○ b. The administrator has enabled location tracking.

○ c. The administrator has established a Hong Kong printer base.

○ d. Nothing, the printer will automatically be indexed this way.

Answer b is correct. Location tracking allows searches to be made within an individual's local site or within other locations through the use of subnet and site allocation of printers within your AD. Answers a and c are incorrect because they are invalid choices. Answer d is incorrect because an administrator has to do much more than nothing to accomplish location tracking.

Question 5

> When you publish folders, which of the following will make locating them easier for users?
>
> ○ a. Keywords and a description.
>
> ○ b. Keywords and location tracking.
>
> ○ c. Location tracking and a description.
>
> ○ d. Nothing. Locating folders is automatic.

Answer a is correct. Keywords and a description can be defined. Answers b and c are incorrect because these are just invalid variations of the actual answer. Answer d is incorrect because locating folders is not automatic.

Need to Know More?

 Boswell, William. *Inside Windows 2000 Server.* New Riders, Indianapolis, IN, 2000. ISBN 1562059297. This is a great resource for clear and in-depth information to strengthen your knowledge of Windows 2000 technology.

 Iseminger, David. *Active Directory Services for Microsoft Windows 2000 Technical Reference.* Microsoft Press, Redmond, WA, 2000. ISBN 0735606242. A strong resource for the structuring of AD implementation, configuration, and troubleshooting.

 Scrimger, Rob, et al. *Microsoft Windows 2000 Server Unleashed.* Sams, Indianapolis, IN, 2000. ISBN 0672317397. This is an in-depth description of Windows 2000 Server and Advanced Server.

 Search the TechNet CD (or its online version through **www.microsoft. com**) using the keywords "publishing" and "location tracking", along with related query items.

Implementing Multiple Tree and Forest Structures

Terms you'll need to understand:

✓ Tree

✓ Child domain

✓ Forest

✓ Tree root domain

✓ Parent domain

✓ Transitive trusts

✓ Shortcut trusts

✓ External trusts

✓ Kerberos

✓ Global Catalog servers

Techniques you'll need to master:

✓ Designing multiple tree structures

✓ Implementing a child domain under the tree root domain

✓ Implementing a new domain within an existing forest structure

✓ Planning and creating shortcut trusts

✓ Creating, verifying, and removing trust relationships

✓ Implementing correct group configurations

The single domain tree is the recommended direction for administering an Active Directory (AD) structure. Organizational Units (OUs) remove the need to create resource domains, because you can now delegate administrative authority. However, at times, circumstances may require additional domains within a domain (called *child domains*) or additional domains that retain a separate namespace (called *forests*). Before implementing these domain structures, you should determine your organization's need for them. Doing so requires a clear understanding of what options are available to you and when you might choose to implement them.

Adding to a Tree

At times, you may need to add domain controllers (DCs) to your specific domain. These will become replica DCs for the same domain. At other times, you may need to add domains below your existing root and form trees with greater fullness. Let's consider the possible reasons for adding to your tree, keeping in mind that you should first make sure that your needs cannot be met by a single domain structure:

➤ *Domain security settings*—Domain-level security settings are enforced throughout the entire domain. To allow for multiple domain-level security settings, it would be necessary to create additional domains that would be connected to the parent domain. For example, say the root domain (coriolis.com) holds to a domain-level security policy that specifies that passwords be complex, yet a branch office in Paris would like to specify a more lax policy. The only way to accomplish this distinction is to have Paris become a separate domain within the tree (perhaps paris.coriolis.com) and establish a domain security policy for that child domain.

➤ *Administrative control*—You may need to create multiple domains if your company has branches in different geographic locations with a qualified information technology (IT) staff that wants full administrative control over the domain. Or, you may need to separate portions of your company because of issues of sensitivity; all objects within a domain come under the supervision of the administrators of that domain, and there may be portions of your company that cannot allow for supervision from above.

➤ *Replication*—DCs are quite chatty. They share every little change with one another. By breaking up your organization into more than one domain under a common root, you limit replication issues to changes made in the Global Catalog (GC), the configuration, and the schema. If you've designed your structure well, you won't be making excessive changes to these facets and your replication will be minimal between the domains.

➤ *Upgrading*—If you are upgrading from an NT 4 structure that contained multiple domains, you may find it easier to work with the domains and upgrade them according to the existing structure. After a migration toward Windows 2000, you may decide to continue with your domain structure, or you might decide to restructure your domains into one domain, which is the method recommended by Microsoft.

Warning: Never under any circumstances should you allow corporate politics to determine the structure of your domain. The politics within a business are a daily issue that has no place in proper domain design.

What Is a Domain Tree?

In theory, you can consider one DC as an entire tree, albeit a small one. In graphical representation, it would be a solitary triangle with any number of OUs inside. The tree holds one contiguous namespace with a common root. If you need to expand the tree in the future, you can create child domains, because they reside beneath a parent domain. These child domains continue to utilize the same contiguous name while branching out with additional naming for organizational purposes. For example, the domains coriolis.com and sales.coriolis.com share the same coriolis.com contiguous namespace. Even corporate.sales.coriolis.com, although a child further down the line, is considered part of the same tree, as shown in Figure 11.1.

A single domain tree obviously has all of the features that you would expect it to. It contains unity of the AD database and a unified relationship among all DCs. When you add a child domain, you may wonder what changes in the structure and what remains the same. When you add additional domains to the tree, you

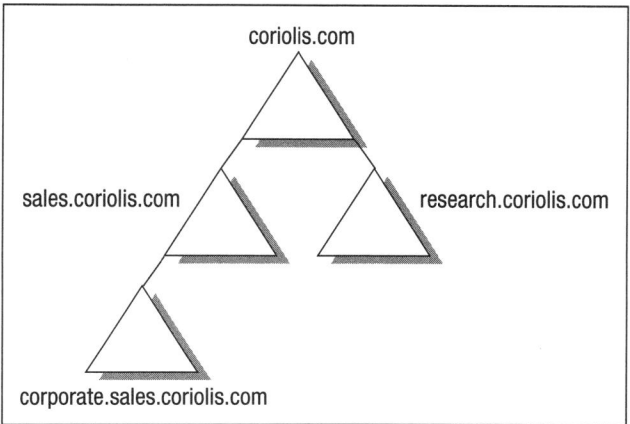

Figure 11.1 A domain tree can include child domains under a contiguous hierarchy.

continue to have a unified relationship; however, these are established through trust relationships. These relationships are automatic when the domains bond under the same name. They also must share a common schema (which means they need to utilize the same class objects and object attributes throughout the domains). In addition, they share the same site and service configuration information, as well as the GC information.

If a child domain joins a pre-existing domain using the contiguous namespace, two-way transitive trusts form. *Trusts* may be a familiar concept to you if you are coming from an NT 4 background. A trust allows for one domain (the trusting domain) to utilize the user and group accounts of another domain (the trusted domain) in the establishing of permissions over resources. Trusts were originally established as one-way. A two-way trust means that both domains trust each other. The concept of *automatic two-way*, however, is definitely new. We'll discuss transitive trusts now, but keep in mind that Windows 2000 allows for other types of trusts—including shortcut trusts and external trusts, which we'll cover later in this chapter.

Transitive Trusts

Trusts allow the domains to work with the user accounts from other domains in such a way that people in one domain (which is a child domain of another domain) can share resources with others and benefit from their resources immediately, as long as the administrator provides permissions to such resources. The transitive concept enables smoother functionality. Conceptually, *transitive* means "by extension." For example, say you have two friends whom you trust, and they both trust you. Transitively, or "by extension," they might trust each other as well. Yet human relationships are complicated, whereas transitive trusts are consistent in Windows 2000.

Under Windows 2000, the trust is automatic between parents and children, and it is transitive between every other domain in the tree. In Figure 11.2, if child domain a.corp.com trusts corp.com and corp.com trusts b.corp.com, then a.corp.com automatically trusts b.corp.com.

Transitive trusts allow users in all connected domains to be validated as domain users. Again, this trust doesn't mean unlimited access to resources for users that are part of the domain tree. In fact, one of the reasons to establish additional domains is to enhance security. Permissions are not transitive (with the exception of the Enterprise Admins group that has administrative permissions within all domains of the forest), nor do domain administrators from various connected domains control them. This safety precaution adds an extra level of security between corporate domains.

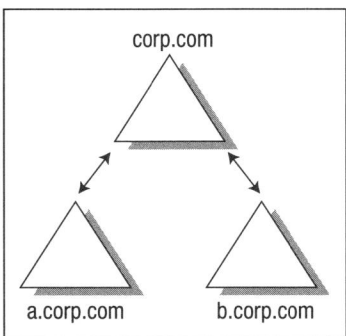

Figure 11.2   Two-way transitive trusts exist between parent and child DCs.

Following are a few points to keep in mind about transitive trusts:

➤ They are two-way agreements that are automatically created.

➤ They exist between child domains and parents or the root domains of a forest.

➤ The trusts are transitive because the trees and forests with connecting trusts make information available with no further trust configuration issues.

➤ After trusts are established, permissions must be granted to an individual or group to allow them to access resources.

Creating a Child Domain

Chapter 4 covered the complete concept of installing a DC by implementing AD. All of the necessities for AD remain true for the creation of a child domain. To create a child domain, you must start, of course, with a parent domain. Perhaps this parent domain is the forest root domain, although it could by any domain in the forest where you would choose to add child domains, as needed.

Forest Root Domains

As mentioned in Chapter 4, the forest root domain is the first domain created in the forest. As a result, it receives certain features that are implemented only once (during the creation of the first domain in the forest), and those features add unique qualities to the forest root. Some of the special features include the following:

➤ Holding the configuration, schema information, and GC.

➤ Holding two forestwide FSMO (Flexible Single Master Operation) roles—the Schema Master and the Domain Naming Master—while the RID (relative ID) Master, PDC (Primary Domain Controller) Emulator, and the Infrastructure Master continue to be implemented in each domain in the tree or forest.

> Holding two forestwide groups: Enterprise Admins and Schema Admins. These groups are initially created under mixed mode as global groups and then switch to universal groups when the domain is changed to native mode.

 The Enterprise Admins group is authorized to make changes to the entire forest, as in the case of adding child domains. The Schema Admins group can make changes that affect the entire forest as well. Changes to the schema are forestwide. The default for both groups is that the administrator of the forest root is the only account added to these two forestwide groups.

Steps for Creating a Child Domain

You begin the AD Installation Wizard from the Run box under the Start menu and type "dcpromo.exe", just as you did in Chapter 4 to create the first domain. The options are similar, with some mild changes to indicate the connection to a parent domain. Once the wizard is activated, perform the following steps:

1. Select the Domain Controller For A New Domain radio button and hit Next.

2. Select Create A New Child Domain In An Existing Domain Tree, rather than starting a completely separate tree (which would lead down the path to creating a forest; see the "Steps for Creating a Forest" section later in this chapter). Then hit Next.

3. Supply the username, password, and domain name (as shown in Figure 11.3) of a user account that is a member of the Enterprise Admins group. Remember, only members of this group can create child domains. Hit Next.

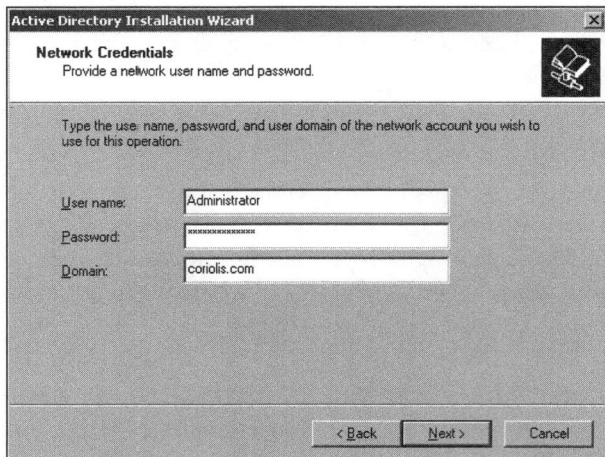

Figure 11.3 Provide an Enterprise Admins user account and the name of the domain.

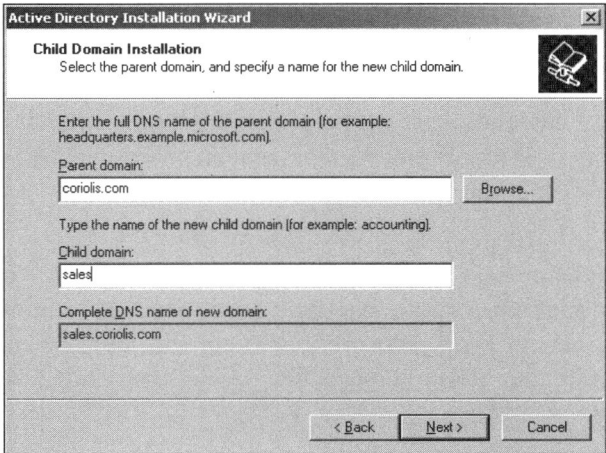

Figure 11.4   The child domain is appended to the parent DNS namespace.

4. Provide the DNS name of the parent and the name of the child domain. The wizard automatically places the two names together, as shown in Figure 11.4. Hit Next.

5. The next wizard pages are familiar. They include the selection of database and transaction logs and then the selection of where to place your SYSVOL folder structure. Remember, for best performance, the database and transaction logs should be on separate physical disks and the SYSVOL folder must reside on an NTFS partition. Complete these pages and press Next twice to move forward.

6. The Permissions page asks whether you need pre-Windows 2000 compatibility. Select your choice and hit Next.

7. Specify a password for restoration of your AD, and then hit Next.

8. Finally, check over your settings and complete the installation of your child domain.

Once your child domain is created, you can see the clear distinctions between your two domains. Each domain can have multiple DC replicas for fault tolerance and authentication speed, and each domain can have distinct security settings and policy. Administrative control would be somewhat segmented. There are other theories of segmented administrative control (for example, the creation of an empty root domain, discussed next).

Setting up Empty Root Domains

You may need to decentralize the administration in an organization without creating separate root domains and forming forests (which we will discuss next).

To keep security policies distinct and keep administrators to a minimum, you can set up an empty root domain. The *empty root domain* does not hold OUs of its own. Unlike a normal root that may be a headquarters for a company, it is a way of segmenting the two child domains for the purpose of administration. Each child domain can hold its own security policy and its own set of administrators, whereas the root administrator, which is called the *Enterprise Admins group,* can be kept small in number.

One possible benefit of this setup is a true lockdown of administrative capability. Enterprise Admins, as a small group, can be requested to use smart card technology to verify themselves and can even require that a user from each child domain is necessary for the authentication to go through. One administrator holds the card; the other has the password.

If these are scenarios that still come under the tree heading, then what is a forest? We'll cover forests in the next section.

Forests

We've already discussed in Chapter 3 that a tree can be made up of one single domain, although it would be considered a small tree. Similarly, a forest has a minimum size of one single domain tree. (Granted, this would be a very small forest.) A true forest, however, contains two or more root domains that are linked by a transitive trust, as shown in Figure 11.5. In using a forest arrangement, you have two distinct domains that do not share a common namespace. For example, coriolis.com and ExamCram.com do not share a contiguous namespace, but they can be joined in a forest arrangement to allow sharing of resources.

The Design Decision to Create a Forest

Understanding what a forest is and what it means to your hierarchal namespace design structure is imperative. Before deciding that you must create a forest, you should establish a clear, nonpolitical reason for doing so. Following are a few reasons why you might need to establish forests:

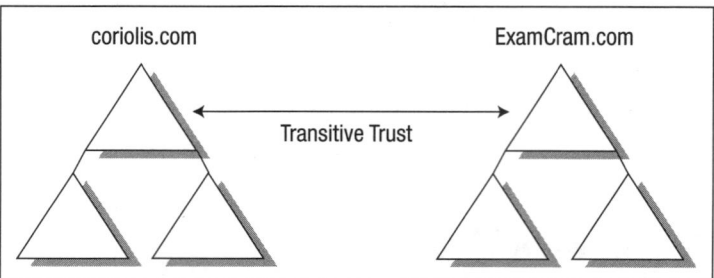

Figure 11.5 A forest contains two or more domains that are linked by a transitive trust.

➤ You establish a forest when two companies have a pre-existing domain namespace that must be retained. The companies will probably be better left within their own spheres.

➤ Your company has subsidiary companies that need to have their own namespaces. For example, say your company has a namespace like junkcars.com, but a subsidiary company has just been acquired that is a seller of baby clothes. Wouldn't babyclothes.junkcars.com be a bit silly?

Note: Currently, Windows 2000 doesn't support the literal merging of two preexisting forests into one forest. These need to be established upon the installation of AD. In addition, one of the two domains must be pre-existing, whereas the other would join the forest under its separate namespace.

Steps for Creating a Forest

As you did in Chapter 4 to create the first domain and to create child domains, to begin the AD Installation Wizard, select Start|Run, and in the Run box, type "dcpromo.exe". The options are similar, with some minor changes to indicate the connection to a pre-existing domain tree. Once the wizard is activated, follow these steps:

1. Select the Domain Controller For A New Domain radio button and hit Next.

2. Select Create A New Domain Tree, then hit Next.

3. Select Join An Existing Forest, then hit Next.

4. Supply the username, password, and domain name of a user account that is a member of the Enterprise Admins group. Remember, only members of this group can join a pre-existing forest. Hit Next.

5. The next wizard pages are familiar. They concern the selection of database and transaction logs, as well as the selection of where you will place your SYSVOL folder structure. Remember, for best performance, the database and transaction logs should be on separate physical disks and the SYSVOL folder must reside on an NTFS partition. Complete these pages and press Next twice to move forward.

6. The Permissions page asks whether you need pre-Windows 2000 compatibility. Select your choice and hit Next.

7. Specify a password for restoration of your AD and then hit Next.

8. Finally, check over your settings and complete the installation of your child domain.

The trusts created between two domains of a forest are two-way transitive, which means, by extension, that the subsequent child domains underneath the roots that are joined are part of the trust relationships of the parent. This transitive trust relationship allows users of one domain tree to be authenticated by the other domain tree in order to share resources. The target domain—that is, the one with the resource that the user is trying to access—must verify that an account is located in the source domain, or the one in which the user resides. Keep in mind that although the transitive trust allows for authentication, this process can be a long one, depending on the levels of domains and forests that the request for authentication goes through. However, you can shorten the path for authentication by creating a shortcut trust.

Creating Shortcut Trusts

Shortcut trusts are two-way transitive trusts, but they shorten the trust path (the length of time and the number of domains that need to be pushed through for verification) that is taken for authentication, as shown in Figure 11.6. Another term used in conjunction with this type of trust is *explicit*, which can include shortcut trusts and external trusts (external trusts are covered in the "External Trusts" section later in the chapter). An *explicit trust* is defined as a trust that you create manually, as opposed to the trusts that are automatically created in Windows 2000.

 Remember, that explicit trusts are manually created. They include shortcut and external trusts. Shortcut trusts are used within a forest to shorten paths of verification. External trusts are used to connect with domains outside the forest to allow for sharing of resources.

You manually create a shortcut trust from within the AD Domains and Trusts tool. Select the domain that you want to involve, access the properties of that

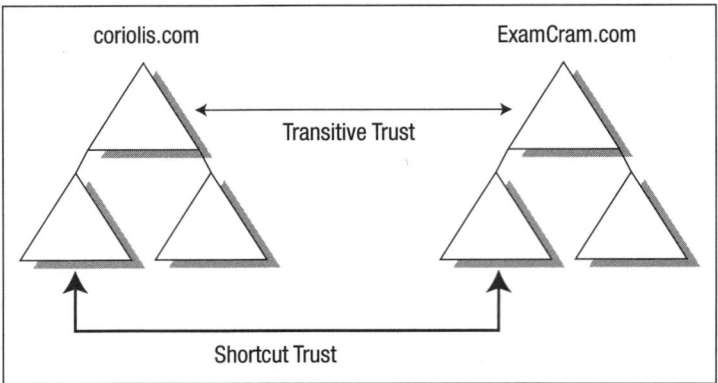

Figure 11.6   A shortcut trust shortens the trust path.

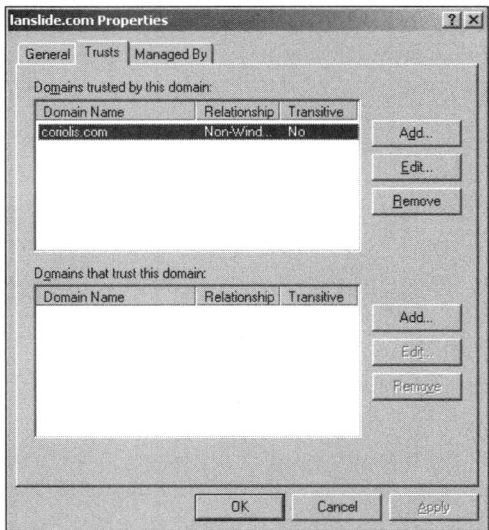

Figure 11.7   The Trusts tab is used to create additional trust possibilities.

domain, and select the Trusts tab, as shown in Figure 11.7. You can specify a trust relationship in the same manner that NT 4 allowed you to create a manual trust. You can add a trusting domain or a trusted domain. You start the relationship from the trusted domain and include a password so that the trust cannot be stolen. Then, on the trusting domain, you perform the same procedure and use the password that was already specified.

There are times, however, when a forest arrangement with transitive trusts will not completely fit the needs of the organizations involved. In that case, a forest arrangement needs to be expanded.

Multiple Forests

You may not officially start out creating multiple forests; in fact, you shouldn't even consider this a corporate plan. However, suppose that you have Forest A and you have a business partnership with another company that has Forest B. You may have no intention of combining these two companies into one, but you may want to allow some authentication privileges. To accomplish this goal, you can create separate forests combined with an external trust relationship.

Why Create a Multiple Forest?

Forests hold a common schema and global directory. But what if you don't want this commonality? You know that you will need certain schema changes with additional classes and attributes in one forest that aren't necessary under the other;

therefore, you might create a separate forest. Although you can synchronize the directories of two forests with the global directory, the general default rule is that there will not be a global directory.

Another reason for setting up multiple forests involves partnerships, as already stated. You may not want to mix too much business together. By using separate forests, you can separate resources between the companies and increase security by forming additional boundaries of verification before users can access certain resources that are available between forests.

External Trusts

Because the two forests have no reason to trust each other, they don't. Therefore, a manual trust relationship is needed, which would again be implemented by the AD Domains and Trusts tool. The resulting trust relationship allows users to be authenticated for the purpose of accessing resources. Permissions determine final access to a resource. This external trust relationship is one-way and nontransitive, as shown in Figure 11.8. It is possible, however, to create a second one-way trust that would make the appearance of a two-way trust (although these don't exist here).

You can see in the figure that Forest A has an arrow pointing to Forest B. This arrow indicates the direction of the trust relationship. Forest A has the actual resource—in this case, a printer. In essence, Forest A is holding out its hand to B and saying, "Here, you can use my printer if you want." That means Forest B has access to A. Forest A is the *trusting* domain (forest), and Forest B is the *trusted*

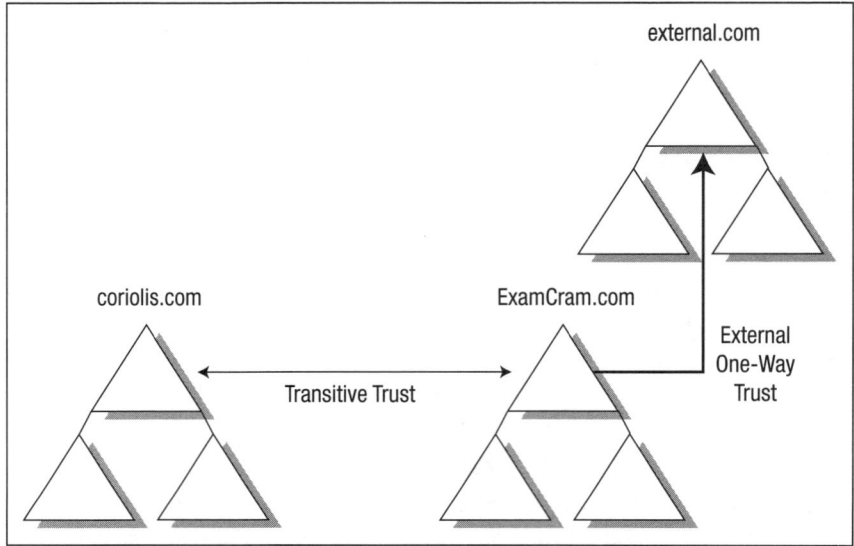

Figure 11.8 An external trust with multiple forests is often used to allow access to resources.

domain (forest). Because the arrow is only one-way, Forest A cannot access anything in Forest B.

To further illustrate this concept, imagine you are loaning your car to someone. You may hold out the keys and say, "You can borrow my car." The person you're lending it to doesn't have to say, "Okay, and you can take mine for a spin, too." The person just has to take your keys.

Once this trust is established, permissions are involved. It is up to the administrators in Forest A to determine to what level that trust is going to be extended to users in Forest B. Not all users will be allowed to access resources, and even selected users will be given only so much leeway. Setting permissions allows each forest to maintain control over their forests and domains.

Creating and Verifying External Trusts

An external trust (also called a nontransitive trust) is a one-way trust relationship that can connect a Windows 2000 domain and one of the following:

➤ A Windows NT account domain

➤ A Windows 2000 domain under a separate forest

➤ A Kerberos v5 security realm

To create this nontransitive trust, you would use the AD Domains and Trusts tool and go to the properties of the domain with which you would like to establish the trust. Select Add and proceed with the steps to create the trust. The trust would, of course, need to be verified on the other end. In addition, you can use the same AD Domains and Trusts tool to verify your trust relationships by selecting the Verify/Reset option to ensure that the trust is still functional. You can also revoke the trust with the same tool by selecting the Remove button for the trust involved. Keep in mind that only nontransitive trusts are revocable. Transitive trusts that are created automatically are retained until the last DC in the domain that is trusted removes the trust.

Using Netdom

Available within the *Windows 2000 Resource Kit*, Netdom is a great command-line tool that you can use to manage domains and trust relationships. The kit includes all of the various options and instructions for utilizing Netdom's many features, including the adding of trust relationships or the dissolving of trusts, the adding of workstations to a domain, and other command-line options.

Use NetDom to perform the following tasks:

➤ Join a Windows 2000 computer to a domain (NT 4 or Windows 2000 domains).

➤ Establish (one or two-way) trust relationships between domains, including trust for the following domain types: NT 4 domains, Windows 2000 domains, or Windows 2000 portions of a trust link to a Kerberos realm.

➤ Manage trust relationships among domains.

➤ View all trust relationships.

To use Netdom, you need to open a command prompt. Then you can perform one of several options:

➤ To see your syntax options with Netdom, type the following:

```
Netdom /?
```

➤ To verify a trust with Netdom, type the following:

```
NETDOM TRUST trusting_domain /domain:trusted_domain /verify
```

➤ To revoke a trust with Netdom, type the following:

```
NETDOM TRUST trusting_domain /domain:trusted_domain /remove
```

Kerberos v5

Developed by the a team at MIT, Kerberos is an open standard named after the three-headed dog in Greek mythology that guarded the gates of Hades. Like its mythological namesake, Kerberos has the ability to see in three directions, allowing you to view the fitting connection to a network authentication protocol. If you are interested, MIT offers a free implementation of this protocol, although Windows 2000 contains a commercial version.

Like its Greek counterpart, there are three sides to Kerberos authentication:

➤ *User*—A client that has a need to access resources off a server.

➤ *Server*—Offers a service, but only to those that can prove their identity. That proven identity doesn't guarantee access to the service; it just proves that they even have a right to request a service.

➤ *Key Distribution Center (KDC)*—An intermediary between the client and the server that provides a way of vouching that the client is really who it says it is.

A Kerberos Transaction

You can read hundreds of different scenarios to explain how a Kerberos transaction works and still never absorb every last detail of it. The vocabulary is unique, and although there are many ways for the transaction to go astray, there is only one way for it to go through.

Under what circumstances is Kerberos necessary? Kerberos is needed when an individual is initially trying to log on to the network and receive an access token, as well as when an authorized user within a domain tries to access a specific resource or service on a server in the domain or forest. Several steps are involved in the process, depending on the domain levels that an individual needs to flow through on his or her way to a resource.

Following is a typical Kerberos transaction. These steps correspond with Figure 11.9.

1. A user logs on to the domain by supplying a username, a password, and a domain choice. Kerberos steps in and checks the information against the DC's KDC database to verify that it knows the user.

2. If the user is valid, the user is provided a ticket-granting ticket (TGT). This means the user is preauthorized to access other resources on the domain. In future transactions, the client doesn't have to reauthenticate; rather, it presents the TGT to the KDC. This speeds up the process.

3. If you want to access a server—for example, the internal email server in order to obtain your email—you can now present that TGT to the KDC

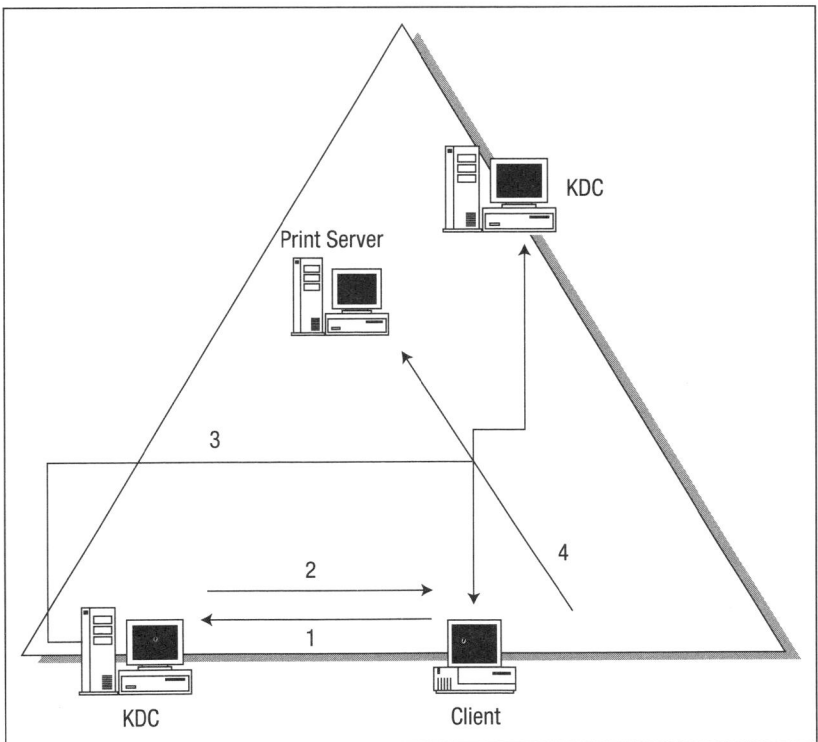

Figure 11.9 The four steps of Kerberos.

ticket-granting server (TGS). This server will give you another ticket (although it doesn't take your first one because that was given to you at logon to validate you to other KDC servers in the domain). This other ticket does not grant permission to access the mail server; rather, it authenticates the client to the mail server.

4. The email server checks to see if you have permissions to read the email. If so, you will receive the mail.

These steps provide a simple look into Kerberos under a single domain structure. Certainly, as additional domains are added to a tree and then as trees are combined into forests, the transactions become more complex.

Kerberos and Transitive Trusts

Now you understand how the Kerberos transaction works within a domain, but what happens when there are multiple domains under the same tree? By now you know that transitive trusts are established to allow authentication; however, we haven't discussed exactly how these trusts are established.

Establishing Transitive Trusts across Multiple Domains

Let's take a look at the steps involved in establishing transitive trusts across multiple domains:

1. A user logs on to the domain (Domain a.company.com) by supplying a username, a password, and a domain choice. Kerberos steps in and checks the information against the DC's KDC database to verify that it knows the user.

2. If the user is valid, the user is given a TGT. This means the user is preauthorized to access other resources on the domain. In future transactions, the client doesn't have to reauthenticate, but rather, it presents the TGT to the KDC. This speeds up the process.

3. If the user wants to access a server in the root domain—for example, a print server that is sharing a printer—the user presents the TGT to the KDC within its domain and receives a session ticket that the user's client machine presents to company.com's KDC.

4. The KDC in company.com takes the session ticket and provides another ticket that validates the user on the member server that is sharing the printer. The member server validates the request, and permissions then come into play. If the user has permissions, he or she will be able to print.

Note: In the preceding scenario, the member server becomes what is called the validation server.

Establishing Transitive Trusts across a Forest

Let's take the authentication to the next level: across a forest. Referring to Figure 11.10, notice a similar path to the path in Figure 11.9 that occurs with the Kerberos transaction. Let's take a look at the process of establishing transitive trusts across a forest step by step:

1. A user logs on to the domain (Domain a.company.com) by supplying a username, a password, and a domain choice. Kerberos steps in and checks the information against the DC's KDC database to verify that it knows the user.

2. If the user is valid, the user is provided a TGT. This means the user is preauthorized to access other resources on the domain. In future transactions, the client doesn't have to reauthenticate; instead, it presents the TGT to the KDC.

3. If the user wants to access a server in another domain in the forest—for example, a file server that is sharing folders with files—the user presents the TGT to the KDC within its domain and receives a session ticket that it presents to company.com's KDC.

4. The KDC in company.com takes the session ticket and provides another ticket that validates the user on corporation.com.

5. The KDC in corporation.com provides the client with a ticket for the KDC of a.corporation.com.

6. The KDC in a.corporation.com issues a ticket that is then presented by the client to the file server. The member server that is sharing those folders

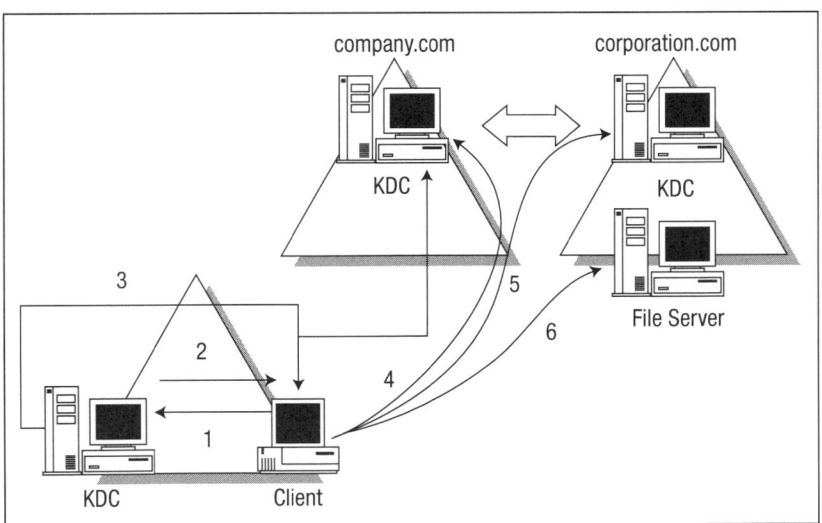

Figure 11.10   Kerberos transactions across a forest.

accepts the ticket (if it is valid) and validates the client on that server. Then permissions determine if the client can access the files.

GC Servers

A GC contains location information for every object created, whether it was created by default upon installation or manually with the AD. It is also responsible for several other important features, such as the following:

➤ Logon validation of universal group membership

➤ User principal name logon validation through DC location

➤ Search capabilities for every object within an entire forest

Note: The GC retains only frequently-searched-for attributes of an object. There is no need, nor would it be very practical from a replication standpoint, for the GC to retain every single detail of every single object. Then the GC would be, in fact, a DC.

There are several factors to consider with regard to the GC and how it functions to enhance logon validation under a native mode situation.

GC and Logon Validation

Universal groups (discussed in Chapter 5) are centrally located within the GC. Which universal groups a user belongs to is quite important to the creation of an access token (discussed in Chapter 6). Those access tokens are necessary for logon validation as well as resource access, so each token must include a user's universal group membership.

When a user logs on to a native mode domain (these are the only ones to include universal groups), the GC updates the DC as to the universal group information for that particular user's access token. But what if the GC is unavailable for some reason? Then the DC will use "cached credentials" to log the user on. However, those credentials would exist only if the user had logged on prior to this point. What if the user had never logged on and the GC is not available for the first logon? Then the user would not be able to log on to the domain and could either log on locally to the machine itself or wait for a GC to become available again.

 Pay keen attention to the functionality of a GC. Your knowledge of GCs will enable you to determine if possible solutions will resolve defined problems.

User Principal Names and Logon Validation

Normally, an individual might log on to a domain with his or her common name and password. For example, suppose the user's common name is DonnaP and her password is bittb356. Now suppose Donna attempts to log on to the system using her principal name—for example, donna@globx.com. If Donna is attempting to log on from a system that is in the accounting domain, the DC in acct.globx.com will not know her account. However, the DC will check with the GC according to the default behavior for a DC that is unsure of an account being used. That will, in turn, lead to the DC for the globx.com domain, which will verify the account. The user will then be validated.

Adding GC Servers

Not all DCs are GC servers. Following are several thoughts to keep in mind:

➤ The first DC in a forest is a GC server.

➤ Any DC can be a GC server if set up to assume that function by the system administrator.

➤ Usually one GC is helpful in each site.

➤ You can create additional GCs if necessary.

To add another GC, perform the following tasks from AD Sites and Services:

1. Within the tree structure on the left pane, expand the DC that will be the new GC.

2. Right-click on NTDS Settings, and select Properties.

3. In the NTDS Settings Properties dialog, under the General tab, select the Global Catalog checkbox, as shown in Figure 11.11.

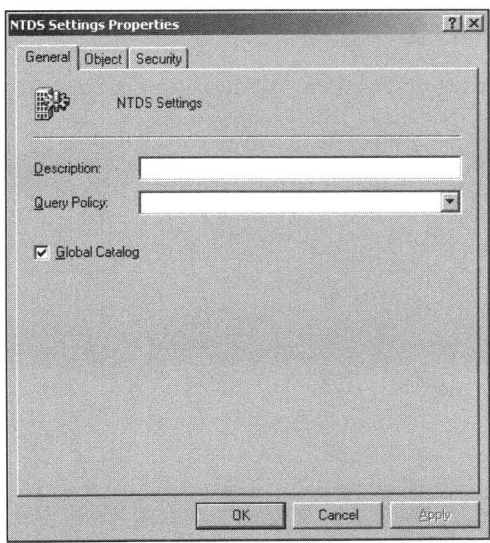

Figure 11.11   Adding a GC.

Universal Group Strategy

Chapter 5 gives a full explanation of the types of groups that Windows 2000 supports; however, we will review certain features in this chapter because Windows 2000 uses the GC to maintain universal group memberships. Because universal groups are replicated to all GCs in the entire forest, replication issues may arise. To minimize these issues, remember the following:

➤ Do not use universal groups unless they are necessary.

➤ Avoid placing individual users within a universal group. Membership information is replicated along with the group. It would be better to place members inside of another group, like a global group, and then add the global group to the universal group. For example, if 100 users need to be part of a universal group, you should add them to a global group and then add that to the universal group. If any user information changes, that information will not affect replication of the GC.

➤ Make only the necessary changes to the membership of a universal group, because any change will initiate a replication of data. The entire membership list is re-replicated, rather than just a changed entry. This could cause quite a bit of traffic.

Review of Universal Nesting

Chapter 5 provides an overview of group nesting. We'll review the information here, however, in case you have to determine the best way to implement a nesting of accounts within a universal group and then use that group to assign permissions to an object. Following is the procedure, in harmony with Figure 11.12:

1. Take user accounts and place them into a global group.

2. Take global groups and, if necessary, place them in other global groups.

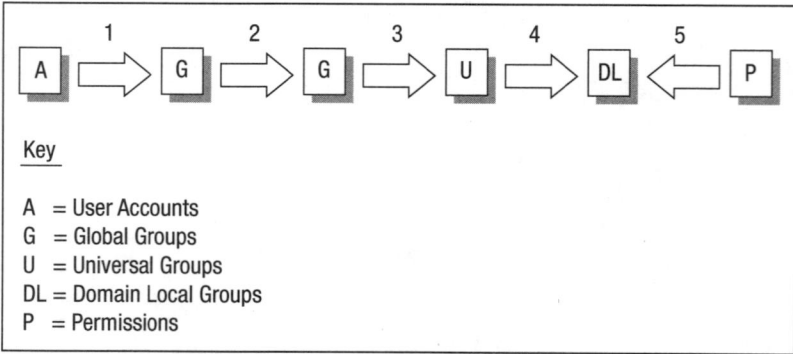

Figure 11.12 Nesting accounts within groups.

3. Take global groups and nest them into universal groups.

4. Take universal groups and place them into domain local groups.

5. Finally, assign permissions for an object directory to a domain local group (DL).

Microsoft recommends this nesting method, because it prevents an unnecessary amount of replication between the GCs of universal group membership.

Practice Questions

Question 1

> You are having some difficulties with a manually created trust relationship.
> You would like to verify that the trust exists. What tools can you use to verify
> the trust relationship's existence? [Check all correct answers]
>
> ❑ a. Active Directory Users and Computers
>
> ❑ b. Active Directory Domains and Trusts
>
> ❑ c. Secedit
>
> ❑ d. Netdom

Answers b and d are correct. The graphical tool used to verify trust relationships
is Active Directory Domains and Trusts, whereas the command-line utility is
Netdom. Answer a is incorrect because Active Directory Users and Computers is
a graphical tool that performs other tasks, including adding OUs, users, computers, and groups (security or distribution). Answer c is incorrect because Secedit is
a command-line tool that provides various functions, such as the enforcement of
security policy.

Question 2

> You are attempting to create a universal group in a child domain. There are
> several child domains under a single parent domain that all have the ability
> to create universal groups with the exception of this one. What would be a
> valid reason for such a dilemma?
>
> ○ a. The domain is still residing in mixed mode.
>
> ○ b. The domain is not connected by means of a shortcut trust to
>   another child domain.
>
> ○ c. The domain is still in native mode and needs to be converted.
>
> ○ d. You are attempting to create the group on a backup domain
>   controller (BDC).

Answer a is correct. If you are still residing in a mixed-mode scenario, your groups
will be only domain local and global. Universal groups exist only in native mode.
Answer b is incorrect because shortcut trusts speed up authentication toward
resources and do not affect security groups. Answer c is incorrect because native

mode is preferable to any other mode, so you would not want to convert from native mode to some other mode. Answer d is incorrect because domains in Windows 2000 do not use BDCs, nor would it matter which DC you tried to implement a security group on if the domain was not in native mode.

Question 3

You are attempting to provide correct access to a printer for individuals that are spread throughout a multiple forest structure. Place the following options in their proper order for correct placement of accounts, groups, and permissions upon the Printer object. Arrows may be used more than once.

Universal group

Right arrow

Global group

Domain local group

Permissions

User accounts

Left arrow

The correct answer is as follows:

User accounts

Right arrow

Global group

Right arrow

Universal group

Right arrow

Domain local group

Left arrow

Permissions

Question 4

You have a parent domain called parent.com with three child domains: a.parent.com, b.parent.com, and c.parent.com. Domain a shares resources in Domain c quite frequently. What would speed up access to those resources for Domain a?

- ○ a. A shortcut trust from a to c
- ○ b. A private Kerberos KDC server
- ○ c. A shortcut trust from c to a
- ○ d. A two-way transitive trust by making a.parent.com a child domain of c.parent.com

Answer c is correct. A shortcut trust where c trusts a allows a to access c more efficiently. The Kerberos authentication still remains in effect through this new trust relationship. Answer a is incorrect because the trust is going in the wrong direction to be effective. Answer b is incorrect because Kerberos servers are functionally hidden and not above domain trust relationship boundaries without shortcut trusts. Answer d is incorrect because a child domain cannot be a child of two domains at the same time.

Question 5

What type of two-way trust relationship is created when a child domain attaches itself to a parent domain?

- ○ a. Multimaster trust
- ○ b. Transitive trust
- ○ c. Shortcut trust
- ○ d. External or nontransitive trust

Answer b is correct. Two-way transitive trusts are created in the joining of child domains or two domain trees into a forest. Answer a is incorrect because multimaster is a form of replication in Windows 2000, not a trust relationship. Answer c is incorrect because a shortcut trust is not automatically created between child/parent domains. Answer d is incorrect because these trusts are used between separate forests.

Question 6

> Two companies have merged into one structure and are required by senior management to be under one contiguous namespace that retains a common schema. The network administrative departments, however, don't want one to be head over the other. What can be formed to allow for segmentation of administrative strength between each domain?
>
> ○ a. Separate forests
>
> ○ b. GC servers
>
> ○ c. KDC servers
>
> ○ d. An empty root domain

Answer d is correct. An empty root domain would allow for unique administrative control while still retaining a common schema and contiguous namespace. Answer a is incorrect because separate forests do not hold either a common schema or namespace. Answer b is incorrect because GC servers are useful for searches and logon validation but not for administrative segregation. Answer c is incorrect because KDC servers are part of the Kerberos authentication procedure, not the administrative control procedures.

Question 7

> Billy is attempting to log on to a domain called research.corp.com, although his user account is located in corp.com. Billy is using his user principal name, billy@corp.com. What will assist Billy in logging on to the system?
>
> ○ a. Organizational Units
>
> ○ b. Global Catalog servers
>
> ○ c. Additional domain controllers
>
> ○ d. Kerberos v5

Answer b is correct. Global Catalog servers search for the domain information necessary during logon when an individual uses his or her user principal name. Answer a is incorrect because Organizational Units assist with delegation of administrative control. Answer c is incorrect because, although this will add fault tolerance, this will not assist in logon validation. Answer d is incorrect because, although Kerberos is used to verify authentication to the resources, it doesn't assist in the location of the domain controller that will validate a user.

Question 8

> If an employee for coriolis.com needs to access a resource in the ExamCram.com domain tree that is connected as a forest, what would be the logical pattern of events based upon the following statements, starting with the initial logon and ending with the actual resource being accessed? Place the following in their proper order according to Kerberos security.
>
> The user presents the TGT to the KDC to receive a session ticket.
>
> The KDC takes the session ticket to obtain a ticket for the other domain.
>
> The user receives a TGT from the KDC.
>
> The KDC in ExamCram.com provides a ticket for the resource itself, and it is accessed.
>
> The user logs on to the local workstation running Windows 2000 Professional.
>
> A ticket is issued by the ExamCram.com domain that allows the client to obtain a ticket for the resource.

The correct answer is:

The user logs on to the local workstation running Windows 2000 Professional.

The user receives a TGT from the KDC.

The user presents the TGT to the KDC to receive a session ticket.

The KDC takes the session ticket to obtain a ticket for the other domain.

A ticket is issued by the ExamCram.com domain that will allow the client to obtain a ticket for the resource.

The KDC in ExamCram.com provides a ticket for the resource itself, and it is accessed.

Question 9

> You want to reduce the replication between Global Catal servers caused by universal group membership. Which of the following methods of group placement would assist in this?
>
> ○ a. Place universal groups into local groups.
>
> ○ b. Place global groups into universal groups.
>
> ○ c. Place global groups into other global groups.
>
> ○ d. Place universal groups into global groups.

Answer b is correct. By placing global groups into universal groups, you reduce the need for replication because changes made to individual users within a global group will not force replication of those changes between the GC servers. Answer a is incorrect because placing universal groups into local groups, although providing a decent method of permissions allocation, would not assist with replication. Answer c is incorrect because placing global groups into other global groups will not assist in reducing replication. Answer d is incorrect because placing universal groups into global groups doesn't eliminate replication issues.

Question 10

> You are dealing with two companies that need to maintain separate security boundaries as well as separate namespace domains. What type of configuration would you implement?
>
> ○ a. Single domain
>
> ○ b. Domain tree
>
> ○ c. Empty root domain tree
>
> ○ d. Forest

Answer d is correct. A forest arrangement is the only way to maintain not only separate security boundaries but separate namespace domains. Answer a is incorrect because a single domain would reside under both the same security and the same namespace. Answer b is incorrect because a single domain tree, although providing security distinction between domains, would still be under a contiguous namespace. Answer c is incorrect because an empty root domain would, again, be under a contiguous namespace.

Need to Know More?

 Boswell, William. *Inside Windows 2000 Server*. New Riders, Indianapolis, IN, 2000. ISBN 1562059297. This is a great resource for the Kerberos transaction process, with an excellent walk-through of this extremely technical topic.

 Bruzzese, J. Peter and Wayne Dipchan. *MCSE Windows 2000 Directory Services Exam Prep*. The Coriolis Group, Scottsdale, AZ, 2000. ISBN 1576106683. Chapter 7 provides a great deal of information on the necessary design issues involved in forming extensive domain trees and forest infrastructures.

 Iseminger, David. *Active Directory Services for Microsoft Windows 2000 Technical Reference*. Microsoft Press, Redmond, WA, 2000. ISBN 0735606242. This book is a great reference for AD design issues, specifically the creation of forests and the various trusts that become a part of the verification process.

 Nielsen, Morton Strunge. *Windows 2000 Server Architecture and Planning*. The Coriolis Group, Scottsdale, AZ, 1999. ISBN 1576104362. This book offers valuable material on forest creation and design and the many planning issues that are involved.

 Search the TechNet CD (or its online version through **www.microsoft.com**) using keywords "Kerberos" and "Authentication", along with related query items.

Active Directory Replication

Terms you'll need to understand:

✓ Multiple-master replication

✓ Loose consistency

✓ Sites

✓ Originating update

✓ Replicated update

✓ Change notification process

✓ Globally unique stamp

✓ Property version number

✓ Propagation dampening

✓ Update sequence number (USN)

✓ Connection object

✓ Direct replication partner

✓ Directory partitions

✓ Global Catalog server

✓ Knowledge Consistency Checker (KCC)

✓ Site link bridge

Techniques you'll need to master:

✓ Understanding Active Directory replication

✓ Understanding how replication conflicts are resolved

✓ Knowing how to examine replication traffic

✓ Understanding the difference between intersite and intrasite replication

When a change, such as the creation of a group or the addition of a new user, is made on a Windows 2000 network, that change is recorded in a copy of the Active Directory (AD). A copy of AD exists on every domain controller (DC) in the domain (with a subset of data stored on every Global Catalog server in the forest). Because each copy of AD must contain the same data, a process known as *replication* takes place. Replication ensures that data recorded in one copy is disseminated to all other copies in the domain.

Because any DC in Windows can accept a change, we can say that DCs on a Windows 2000 network are *peers*. Windows 2000 uses *multiple-master*, or *multimaster*, *replication* to do its work. That is, each DC is a master for its copy of AD. The DC can accept changes and will then propagate them out to other DCs with which it is partnered. We examine this process in some detail in this chapter.

To design and control AD data, you must fully understand the process of replication. Without this knowledge, you won't be able to troubleshoot problems you may encounter or understand how to maintain your replication topology. Consistency of data is a key requirement for AD to work properly in your environment, and it should therefore be one of your prime concerns.

In simple terms, when we talk about replication, we are referring to updating information from one DC to another. This process can also be thought of as copying changed AD data. When a change is made on one DC, all DCs in the domain must be synchronized with this change. In the context of two or three DCs, this concept is easy to envision. However, when considering an enterprise network where there are hundreds of DCs dispersed throughout geographical locations that possibly cross different continents, you begin to see why knowledge of this process is so important.

Administrators do not choose which DC is updated when they make changes to AD. The process of selecting a DC to accept a change is transparent. It is then up to the replication process to replicate this event to other DCs.

Of course, replication takes time. If a change is made at a single DC in, say, Houston, it will take time for the change to appear on a DC in London. This is known as *loose* consistency. A network is not considered to be fully converged until all changes have been copied to all other DCs. In a busy network spread across the globe, it might appear that your network is never fully converged. This is to be expected.

Because no DC maintains control over the AD data, Windows 2000 is able to scale better than older network operating systems. This is because administrators can make changes to AD data on the DC that is closest to them on the network. Replication makes sure everyone else knows about the change.

Note: There are exceptions to this rule. For instance, a set of DCs called operations masters have a unique task to perform in Windows 2000. We discuss operations masters in Chapter 13.

AD replication takes your network into consideration in order to optimize performance. It does this by using sites. *Sites* in Windows 2000 are groups of IP (Internet Protocol) subnets that have fast connectivity between them. IP subnets that are divided by a WAN connection (slower than 10Mbps) should be divided into multiple sites. Replication within a site (and therefore with fast connectivity) takes place automatically and assumes a fast, reliable link. Replication between different sites takes place on a schedule and is designed specifically to reduce network bandwidth usage. We'll look more closely at how sites optimize AD later in this chapter.

The Replication Process

Replication occurs when an update is made to a copy of AD. An update is not only the addition of a piece of data, such as a new user or group. It can also be the deletion of an object, the moving of an object, or a modification to a single property of an object.

Each DC must be able to accept changes from both administrators and other copies of the AD. Although replication takes place throughout an enterprise, note that at any given time, a DC can replicate its changes to only one other server. This means that AD replication occurs between two DCs at a time. Because the data is copied this way, replication conflicts may occur. All conflicts are dealt with automatically following a well-defined process. We discuss this issue in greater detail in the "Conflict Resolution" section later in this chapter.

Because the data in the AD is so important, mechanisms are required to ensure that any change it accepts is either completely committed (recorded in its entirety) or completely rejected (rejected in its entirety). For instance, if a name is changed for a user object, the AD needs to commit either the entire name change or none of it. This prevents a DC from recording a partial change.

AD performs two types of updates:

➤ *Originating update*—Occurs only the first time a change is made to an AD replica.

➤ *Replicated update*—Occurs as a result of this change.

Examining a simple change to AD data allows you to easily see how these two terms are used. Imagine you have three DCs. An administrator logs on to the network and makes a change to a user object's properties. A DC is contacted, and the change is made. This change is *committed* to the AD replica at this DC.

Because this is the first time this change has been made within AD, it is considered an originating update. The change must then be copied from this DC to the other DCs on the network. Replication takes care of this task. When the change is made at the other DCs, it is considered a replicated update, simply because the change did not originate at either of these DCs.

Latency and the Notification Process

Recognize that AD replication takes time, and a delay will occur before the originating update is made to every DC on the network. This delay is known as *latency*. Because of how the notification process works, some level of latency will always occur.

AD uses a system, the *change notification process*, which takes care of replicating data from one DC to another. Here's how it works: When a change is committed at a DC, the replication engine kicks in and waits for a configurable period of time. By default, this period is five minutes. During this time, the replication engine collects all changes made to the replica. This is more efficient because all changes within the configurable period are replicated—rather than AD having to replicate each change as it occurs.

Once this period has expired, the DC sends a *change notification*. This notification is sent to one of the DC's replication partners. Remember what we said earlier: Each DC replicates, one at a time, with its direct partners only. AD replication does not use broadcasting to replicate data; the entire process is controlled and systematic.

A DC can have more than one direct partner. After the first partner is contacted, the DC waits a configurable period of time before letting another replication partner know about the change. By default, this is 30 seconds. After this time, the partner *pulls* the changes.

Note: Data is never pushed from one DC to another; it is always pulled. This occurs after the DC with the change has been through the notification process.

A single DC never has a replication partner that is more than three hops away. A *hop* is a trip across a router (each router is one hop). Given this fact, you can calculate the maximum amount of time for a change to propagate from a single DC to each replication partner. Say, for example, there are three hops (or steps) from the DC with the change to a replication partner three hops away. The maximum time for a change to replicate is 15 minutes (the 5-minute configurable time lapse per DC). This may or may not include the 30-second delay.

If a DC does not receive a change for a period of time (by default, in an hour), it will automatically begin the replication process. This ensures that the DC gathers data even if it missed the notification.

Note: In addition, for security-conscious data, an event called urgent replication occurs. For instance, an account lockout is an urgent replication, and it takes place without waiting for the configurable period. Most replication, however, takes place through the normal method.

Types of AD Conflicts

Because enterprise networks are large, busy entities where administrators are widely dispersed, replication conflicts are bound to occur. Conflict resolution takes care of this issue and maintains the integrity of the data stored within AD.

Conflicts can occur under several different circumstances. Understanding the processes that AD employs to deal with this issue helps you understand why conflicts occur.

Let's look at several types of conflicts. Then, in the next section, we'll discuss how to solve them.

Conflicting Attribute Changes

This type of conflict occurs when an attribute of an object is changed by different administrators. For instance, say your organization has a help desk ticketing system. A user calls in this morning and wants her last name attribute changed. The help desk operator enters this request into the ticketing system.

An administrator in Houston opens the help desk system and sees that a change has been requested. He pulls up the AD User and Computer snap-in and makes the change. At the same time, an administrator in London also sees the ticket. The London administrator also makes the change but accidentally mistypes the new name, transposing two characters.

Because these administrators have changed this attribute, replication will eventually cause a conflict. This conflict must be resolved.

Adding/Moving Objects

Adding or moving objects can also cause a conflict to occur. In this case, an object is added to a container—for instance, a user object being added to an Organizational Unit (OU)—while the parent object is simultaneously being deleted on another DC.

When replication takes place, a conflict inevitably occurs when the user object is unable to be added to the OU on an AD replica because the parent object no longer exists. In effect, the user object is orphaned.

Duplicate Names

Because objects can be easily moved from one location in AD to another, naming conflicts may occur. Say, for example, an administrator moves an object from one parent object to another, and at the same time, another administrator moves a different object to the same location. If both objects have the same relative distinguished name, a conflict will occur.

Note that AD works differently from previous schemes Microsoft has devised for this type of replication (as seen in Microsoft Exchange 5.5). Previous models have replicated at the object level. This meant that if you changed the Description attribute of an object, every attribute of that object had to be replicated. This is far more likely to cause conflicts within the database. AD, on the other hand, replicates at the *attribute level*. This means that in the example given, only the description of the object would be replicated, thereby conserving bandwidth and reducing conflicts.

Conflict Resolution

Conflicts are easily resolved through the use of *globally unique stamps*. These stamps are recorded as part of a change to AD data. This stamp then travels with the AD data as it is replicated throughout the enterprise. If needed, the stamp can be used to resolve any conflicts in a logical and predetermined fashion.

The stamp consists of three pieces of key data, which are used one piece at a time to resolve conflicts. If the first piece of data fails to resolve the conflict, AD uses the second piece of data. If that also fails, the third piece is used. The third piece is effectively a tiebreaker, and it will always resolve a conflict.

The three pieces of data that make up the globally unique stamp are as follows:

➤ *Property version number (PVN)*—The PVN is stored by every attribute. All attributes start with PVN=1. Each time an originating update takes place, this number increments by one. During replication, the property with the highest PVN prevails. For example, a PVN of 2 always overwrites a PVN of 1. Conflicts can still occur when an attribute with a PVN of 1 is changed in two different locations. In this case, the PVN of each would be 2, and a conflict would occur. If this attribute does not resolve a conflict, the second piece of data is used.

➤ *Timestamp*—This attribute records both the time and date the change was made. It is based on the system clock of the DC recording the originating update. In this case, the latest time prevails. So, a change made to an object's attribute at 2:15 P.M. would beat a change made at 2:05 P.M. In the unlikely event of changes being made at the same time, a third tiebreaker is employed.

➤ *Server GUID*—Every DC has a GUID (Globally Unique Identifier) that allows it to differentiate itself from every other DC in the enterprise. This value is stored in the *Invocation ID* property of the server object. The highest server GUID always prevails.

In the case of an object's attributes being changed at two different DCs, the aforementioned globally unique stamp will resolve conflicts. In the vast majority of cases, this takes care of potential problems.

 Making sure that the DCs in your enterprise are time-synced is vital. Although AD is not dependent upon the time set at each server, the tie-breaking mechanism can sometimes rely upon it. It is common for time on a server to drift a little, or for WAN links to go down and for a time problem to occur without your knowing it. Make certain you take this into account when designing your Windows 2000 network.

One case where the globally unique stamp does not help is when objects are moved between containers. For example, say an administrator in London moves an object from the "Sales" Organizational Unit to the "Sales US" Organizational Unit. At the same time, in Houston, Texas, another administrator deletes the "Sales US" Organizational Unit. Of course, now we have a problem, because by the time the originating update made in London replicates to Houston, the Organizational Unit is not going to exist!

In this case, the object is moved to the LostAndFound container. This container is a catchall for all objects that have been orphaned. You should review this container periodically and move objects to their rightful homes or delete them as necessary. The globally unique stamp is not used in this situation.

Another instance in which the globally unique stamp alone does not remedy the situation is when two objects with the same relative distinguished name are moved to the same container. In this case, the globally unique stamp is used; however, it must be used with a GUID. The object that prevails retains the relative distinguished name. The other object is renamed in the following format:

relative distinguished name + "CNF:" + *the object's GUID*

The addition of the GUID ensures that this name is always unique.

Preventing Replication Loops

As explained earlier in this chapter, replication takes place between DCs automatically. On complex networks, this means that replication is unlikely to take place using the same route each time. Sometimes the route might be very direct (and therefore more efficient), whereas other times the route might be more complex. This is to be expected on complex routed networks with WAN links. Network topologies can change as routers are reset, new segments are brought online, or older segments suffer a temporary failure.

Because network topologies can change, replication can sometimes traverse the network in somewhat unpredictable ways. Therefore, a DC can receive a single update from multiple partners. Of course, receiving a single update multiple times would be inefficient, so to take care of this, Windows 2000 uses a process called *propagation dampening*. Propagation dampening is designed to prevent unnecessary data from being pulled across your network.

Propagation dampening is achieved with one piece of data: an update sequence number (USN). This data is used to record the number of updates a system has received from its replication partners. Let's look at update sequence numbers in more detail.

USNs

To calculate which data should be replicated and which data has already been replicated, AD uses USNs. These are stored in memory, in a table called the up-to-dateness table. This table has an entry for every DC in the domain, along with the USN number at the time of the last originating update for that DC. For instance, if DC A performed an originating update to its AD replica that caused its USN to increment to a value of "130", each up-to-dateness table stored on DCs in the domain would record an entry of "A-130."

USNs can be used to prevent unnecessary data being sent across the network. As an example, say that a DC contacts a replication partner and says, in effect, "I have an originating update. When I wrote it to my replica, it made my USN increment to 130. Do you want it?" It is then a simple matter for the receiving DC to read its up-to-dateness table and see whether it already has this update. If it does, no replication is necessary. If it doesn't, it can pull the data. Remember that as previously mentioned, replication in AD is pulled only; data is never pushed across the wire.

Topology for Replication

AD replication is tied to the physical topology of your network. In an ideal Windows 2000 network, the physical topology closely matches the topology that is used to replicate AD data. In Windows 2000, this is achieved automatically by internal mechanisms (which are defined and discussed in this section), using data provided by the system designers/system administrators.

Because replication takes place between DCs, for replication to be efficient, AD needs to take into account the proximity of DCs to each other and the amount of available bandwidth between those DCs. Once it has this information, you can let AD automatically calculate a path between DCs, and it can even determine which DCs should be allowed to talk to each other. Once this setup is in place, you have a *replication topology*.

Note: Replication topologies can change on the fly. If AD finds that a DC has been moved or that the IP subnets on your network have changed, it automatically calculates whether changes should be made to the replication topology in your organization. You should not be worried about this; it is normal AD behavior.

DCs that swap AD data are known as *replication partners.* AD stores information in what is termed a *connection object* that defines these partners. A connection object is a one-way path between DCs, usually created in pairs to facilitate two-way communication between DCs. By having multiple connection objects, you can quickly build an entire replication infrastructure for your Windows 2000 network.

Connection objects can be created automatically or manually. Manually created connection objects override automatic connections. Of course, there is considerable administrative overhead associated with creating these manually. Having them created and maintained automatically is far better. We will look at this process in the "Knowledge Consistency Checker" section later in this chapter.

Replication partners can act as both a source for AD data and as a conduit for data. In other words, a replication partner can be either a *direct replication partner* or a *transitive replication partner.* In the case of a direct replication partner, the partner is acting as a source for originating updates. With a transitive replication partner, data is being obtained indirectly from other replication partners.

 You can force replication to occur immediately by right-clicking on a connection object and selecting Replicate Now. With the Replication Monitor program, you can view transitive replication partners.

Directory Partitions

The data stored within AD is actually broken out into three distinct areas called *directory partitions.* Each of these partitions records and stores a specific type of information. In addition, each can have a different replication topology, largely because not all DCs need to contain the same partitions.

The three directory partitions that exist in AD are as follows:

➤ *Domain partition*—Holds data regarding domain-specific objects, including users, groups, and computers.

➤ *Schema partition*—Contains data that defines which objects can be created within AD and specifies rules regarding these objects, such as mandatory properties.

➤ *Configuration partition*—Contains information about your AD structure, such as the domains and DCs that exist.

DCs do not necessarily contain the same partitions. For instance, each DC in a forest must contain the same schema and configuration partition. However, DCs from different domains store different domain partitions. Each partition has its own replication topology—although most of the time, they end up being the same.

Global Catalog Servers

Clients on a Windows 2000 network perform searches within their local domain and outside their local domain. These include searches for users, groups, or resources such as shared folders. The data the user needs to search is stored in the domain partition. Because DCs in the user's local domain do not hold data from the domain partition of other domains, a special type of server, called a *Global Catalog (GC) server*, is needed to exist to facilitate this function.

A GC stores data about all the domains in a forest. It is not a complete replica of the domain partition; instead, it contains a subset of data from other domains. This subset includes object names and the most commonly searched-for attributes, such as user and group names. GCs are recorded in the configuration partition of the directory so that other DCs are aware of them.

Knowledge Consistency Checker

Creating the replication topology on your own would be a daunting task. Although you can do so, this task is best left to the Knowledge Consistency Checker (KCC).

The KCC is a process that runs on each DC and is used to automatically generate the replication topology for a forest. Each time it runs, it can recalculate the efficiency of routes between DCs and configure the topology accordingly. To do this, it uses the site and subnet information that has been configured within AD. (We look at sites in more detail in the next section.) Because the KCC is constantly checking the efficiency of the connections, it can automatically detect if a problem has occurred and can reconfigure the topology to work around DCs that are down or temporarily unavailable.

As a safeguard against possible problems, the default topology for replication is a two-way bidirectional ring. Also, the KCC ensures that an originating update never takes more than three hops to be replicated.

Optimizing AD Replication with Sites

Before the KCC can do its work, it requires some basic information about your network, including data on the physical aspects of the infrastructure. You supply this data by creating sites. A *site* is an object in AD that includes a list of Transmission Control Protocol/Internet Protocol (TCP/IP) subnets. Sites are parts of your network that enjoy high availability because of fast network connectivity. Once your sites have been created, you must create connection objects between them (these connection objects would imitate the physical connection of your network). The KCC then uses this information to build the necessary replication infrastructure. By creating sites, you are effectively controlling replication on your network—albeit via an automatic process.

By adding subnets to a site, you are implying that these subnets have fast and reliable connectivity among them. You add server objects to site objects. Once a server is part of a site, the KCC can calculate a path through the network in question with the assumption that the servers can talk to each other quickly.

The first site is created automatically when the first server is installed on your Windows 2000 network. Although this site is given the name Default-First-Site-Name, you can assign it a more meaningful name.

DCs in a site do not need to belong to the same Windows 2000 domain. The reason is that there are three partitions of AD to be replicated, and although replicating the domain partition between controllers of different domains does not make sense, this connectivity could be exploited for the schema and configuration partitions.

Sites are used for many different tasks in AD. Aside from their use in AD replication, they are also used to optimize logon traffic and to select shared folders that use the Distributed File System (Dfs). They are also used for the Remote Installation Service (RIS). In all cases, they are used to calculate the local server that can most efficiently provide the service. If a client contacts a server on the same subnet as itself, it is safe to assume processing time will be reduced.

Replication within a Site and between Sites

Although replication occurs both within a site and between sites, there are subtle differences between the two situations. Replication within a site assumes a highly available network with a lot of bandwidth. Therefore, the replicated data is sent uncompressed. Because the DC does not have to take time to compress data, there is less of a load on each DC. However, your network bandwidth suffers because a lot more data goes across the wire. The replication process is triggered by the notification process mentioned earlier in this chapter.

In contrast, replication between sites occurs on a schedule. In addition, the data is compressed before being sent. This means that the load on servers is greater, but the bandwidth requirement is reduced.

You need to be concerned about two parameters:

> ➤ *The schedule*—Defines how often replication takes place. This option allows you to configure replication to take place during off-hours or times when the most bandwidth is available.

➤ *The replication interval*—Defines how often DCs check for changes during periods when replication is allowed to occur

Keep in mind that an incorrectly configured schedule and interval can prevent replication from ever occurring. For instance, if the schedule allows replication to occur only between 6:00 A.M. and 7:00 A.M., replication will only ever occur during a single hour of the day. If the interval is set for every 2 hours, starting at 7:00 A.M., the interval gets checked only on odd hours (7:00 A.M., 9:00 A.M., 11:00 A.M., 1:00 P.M., 3:00 P.M., and so on). Notice that there is no overlap between the schedule and the interval. In this case, the interval is not starting during the scheduled window; therefore, replication would not take place.

 When you are dealing with more than two sites, you have to take into account multiple replicating schedules. Sometimes replication occurs, but it will be very slow. You should be familiar with the delay of replication. For instance, if you have three sites—A, B, and C—if the replication schedule between A and B is 7:00 A.M. to 8:00 A.M., and the replication schedule between B and C is 2:00 P.M. to 4:00 P.M., then the updated data from A won't arrive in C until 2:00 P.M. at the earliest. This will cause it to appear that you have a replication problem.

Bridgehead Servers

Replication between sites occurs from a single point. In other words, data is exchanged between two DCs in each site and then is replicated within the site using normal mechanisms for change. These servers are known as *bridgehead servers* and are chosen automatically.

You can also select a bridgehead server or even a group of preferred servers. The process that chooses bridgehead servers is called the Intersite Topology Generator (ISTG). You simply select the servers you want to use as preferred within the site.

Protocols that Support Replication

It might sound obvious to state that DCs that want to communicate must use the same protocol. However, you should note that in terms of replication, we are referring to the protocol used specifically by AD to achieve our goal.

Two different protocols can be used:

➤ *Remote Procedure Call (RPC)*—This primary protocol is used exclusively for replication within a site.

➤ *Simple Mail Transfer Protocol (SMTP)*—This protocol has a limited implementation and is used when connections between DCs are unreliable. To use SMTP, the DCs must be in different domains and in different sites.

When replicating between sites, you can use RPC or SMTP. The preferred protocol is RPC over IP (which means the RPC calls are wrapped in IP packets for transport across the wire).

In addition to the aforementioned limitations of using SMTP, also note that SMTP cannot be used to replicate all partitions of AD. Because the domain partition has dependencies that fall outside of simply replicating AD data (such as file transfer using the File Replication Service, or FRS), it cannot be used for the domain partition. However, SMTP is useful when a direct connection cannot be made between DCs, because SMTP data can be stored and forwarded by mail servers. This ability can sometimes compensate for poor connections.

Site Links and Their Default Settings

Site links are used to manage replication when it occurs between sites. These settings can be used to configure site links to replicate during certain intervals and to use specific protocols. The options are as follows:

➤ *Transport*—The protocol that you want to use for the site link.

➤ *Member Sites*—Two or more sites that will be part of the site link.

➤ *Cost*—The cost of a link is a value that is used to determine which site link is used if there are multiple site links between different sites. Cost should be based upon the speed and reliability of the link. The better the speed and reliability, the lower the cost (increasing the likelihood that the link will be used). This value can be between 1 and 32,767. The default setting is 100.

➤ *Schedule*—This defines the window in which replication can occur. The range is one-hour increments configured over a seven-day week. The default is for the site link to be available at all times.

➤ *Replication Interval*—This defines how often replication happens within a window. The range is from 15 minutes to 10,080 minutes. The default is 3 hours.

 You should familiarize yourself with the settings that can be configured when creating a site link.

Site Link Bridge

The *site link bridge* is an extension of the sites concept we covered earlier in this chapter. You use site link bridges when your physical network topology requires it. For instance, your corporate network is likely divided by a firewall. In that case, the network is not fully routed—that is, every subnet cannot communicate directly with every other subnet. For AD replication to work, AD must model the normal routing behavior of your network.

A site link bridge is a collection of site links. To create a site link bridge, you first create site links. You then add those sites to a site link bridge. For instance, let's assume you have a site link that contains both London and Houston. The cost of this link is 2. You have a second site link that contains Houston and Dallas. The cost of this link is 6. You could create a site link bridge and add both of these site links to it. This would enable London to communicate with Dallas with a cost of 8.

Note: A site link bridge does not dictate the physical path the network packets take. This aspect of the communication cannot be controlled from within AD.

Notice that the two site links we added to the site link bridge had a site in common—Houston. This is a requirement of creating a site link bridge. If this were not the case, the site link bridge would have no way of working out the total cost of moving a message from London to Dallas.

Because site links are by default transitive, in most cases, you will not have to create site link bridges. However, by creating site link bridges and manually designating DCs that will communicate, you can alleviate some of the problems you may encounter from working on a nonrouted network.

To use site link bridges, you must turn off the Bridge All Site Links feature. Because this is an all-or-nothing affair (sites are either transitive or not), doing so increases the amount of administration you are expected to do yourself.

Note that the KCC and ISTG may become overwhelmed and be unable to build a full replication topology on a regular schedule. This happens when there are many paths on your network, and the KCC must sort through each of them to find the optimal route. In these rare cases, you could disable the Bridge All Site Links option and build site link bridges.

You can also prevent the KCC from building site-to-site topology. However, this increases the overhead of managing your network. One of the best features of the KCC is that it runs on a regular schedule. This means it can recover from sudden changes on your network, such as a site disappearing because a router is down. If the KCC has had its feature set trimmed, you need to take care of these situations yourself. Keep in mind, however, that such situations can be difficult to detect and will take a lot of time to configure. In almost all cases, you are better off using the KCC than performing the task yourself.

Examining Replication Traffic

Although the KCC can be allowed to calculate and configure the topology for your network, you also have to use due diligence in monitoring the efficiency of your AD replication. This can be done through two utilities: Replication Monitor and the Repadmin command-line utility.

By monitoring replication, you can be alerted when you need to make changes to the topology manually. Because monitoring allows you to see replication patterns, you may then decide to step in and make changes to the topology.

Replication Monitor

Replication Monitor is a graphical utility that displays the replication topology of the computers within a site. With this utility, you can view status messages on the state of replication and the current performance of the process. Because you can also view this information at the DC level, you can determine whether a specific pair of replication partners are performing adequately. If not, you might need to trigger the KCC to recalculate the replication topology.

Replication Monitor has a great deal of functionality. Some of the highlights are as follows:

➤ You can see which DCs are direct replication partners with other DCs. This is displayed both directly and transitively.

➤ You can view the USN number on a particular server.

➤ You can view the number of failed replication attempts and the reason replication failed.

➤ You can set defined values that cause Windows 2000 to write to an event log or to send email should a particular condition occur.

➤ You can poll a server to get current statistics and save this data to a log file.

➤ You can view which objects have yet to replicate from a particular server.

➤ You can trigger replication between two DCs.

➤ You can trigger the KCC to regenerate the replication topology.

Replication Monitor can be run on Windows 2000 Advanced Server, whether it is installed as a DC or simply as a member server. This is one of the primary tools at your disposal when troubleshooting replication problems on your network. A typical Replication Monitor screen is shown in Figure 12.1. In this figure, you can see the names of replication partners, along with current USN values.

Repadmin

Unlike Replication Monitor, the Repadmin command-line utility is nongraphical and gives data about only a particular DC. However, it also shares some crossover functionality with Replication Monitor, such as the ability to regenerate the replication topology, force events to occur, and display replication data, including the entries in the up-to-dateness table.

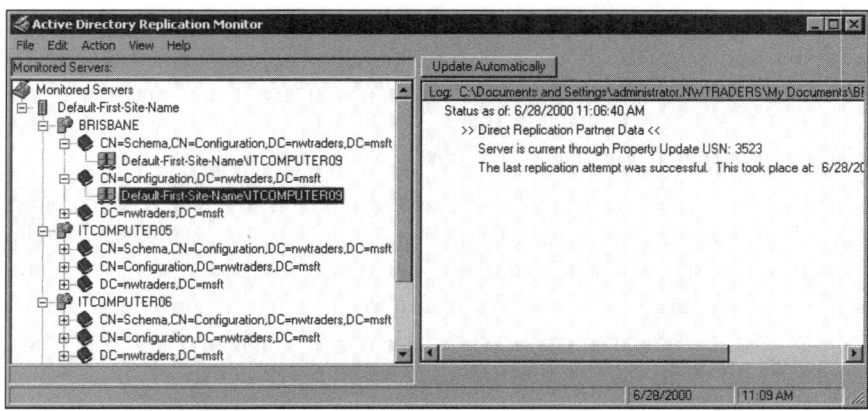

Figure 12.1 Replication Monitor.

If you are checking many different DCs, you are better off using Replication Monitor. However, if you have easy access to a particular controller, Repadmin will likely be sufficient for anything you might need. Because Repadmin is a command-line utility, it has various command switches. These switches are shown in Figure 12.2.

Modifying the Replication Topology

For the most part, replication should occur automatically without intervention from the administrator. Once you have manually created your sites and site links, the KCC takes care of the rest. However, by using the AD Sites and Services tool, along with Replication Monitor and Repadmin, the administrator can make changes to the replication topology.

On rare occasions, you might want to make a change to the replication topology that the KCC has generated. This occurs when an administrator is not happy with the number of hops the KCC uses (as previously mentioned, by default the topology is three hops). If the administrator wants to reduce the number of hops to two or one, the administrator would have to create his or her own topology.

Note that there are some significant downsides to creating the topology yourself. Modifying connection objects or creating your own can prevent the KCC from completing an efficient topology by itself. In addition, it can prevent the KCC from "healing" or reconfiguring the topology should a subnet on the network fail or a DC become unavailable. With these drawbacks in mind, you should take the following into account when creating connection objects manually:

➤ If a DC fails to replicate with its partners, it uses the KCC to make additional connection objects, creating as many new connections as needed to achieve replication.

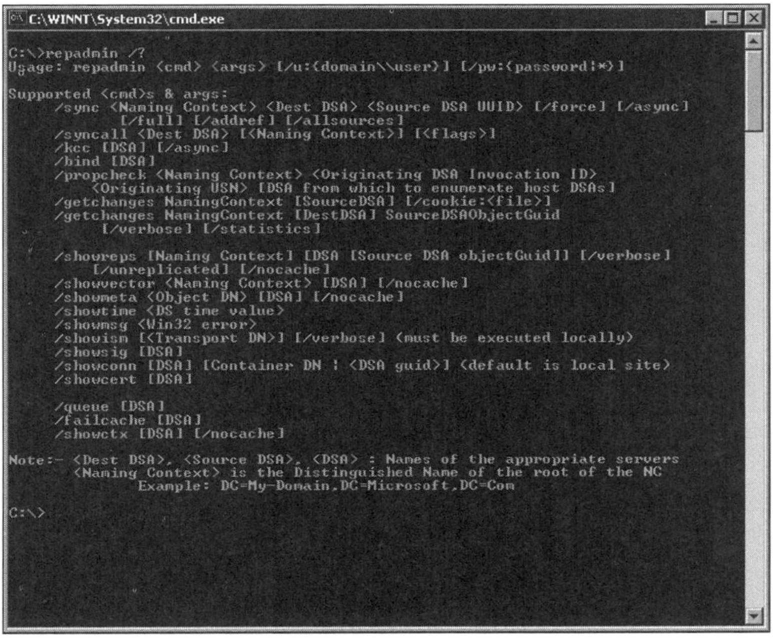

Figure 12.2   Repadmin switches.

➤ The KCC cannot delete manually created connection objects.

➤ If a connection exists between two servers, the KCC won't generate additional connections.

Troubleshooting Replication

Replication problems may occur for many reasons and may manifest themselves in strange ways, such as user accounts that seem to disappear or data being pulled from the directory that is out of date. We'll discuss a few of these problems in this section.

Your replication topology can be quite complex, and the KCC can work only with the data you have provided. If you have not created a sufficient number of site links, the KCC may not be able to connect all sites together with connection objects. This situation can lead to some DCs never being updated. If this occurs, you should create the necessary site links and have the KCC regenerate the topology through the Replication Monitor.

If replication is slow, a scheduling problem may be occurring. As mentioned, the schedule dictates a window of opportunity for replication to occur. If the windows are too small and spread too far apart, you can end up with replication that appears to be slow or even inoperable. This might happen when the schedule for a site link is configured to occur only on Mondays. When you have a string of site links linking DCs together, highly restrictive schedules can cause a lot of latency on your network.

If your physical infrastructure is not sufficient to support AD replication, you can also run into severe problems. For instance, if the bandwidth availability of your network has changed, replication may not be able to occur efficiently. To alleviate this problem, create sites and make sure that only DCs with fast, reliable links are members of it. Once you have done this, you can force the KCC to regenerate the replication topology.

DCs in Windows 2000 are used primarily for authentication. Slow authentication can be caused by several factors. Most likely, however, you have poorly configured sites. Clients are directed to authenticate from sites that are on the same subnet as themselves. If a site has been configured incorrectly, the client might very well be traversing slow connections to get authenticated. Once again, reconfiguring sites on your network will likely solve the problem.

Practice Questions

Question 1

A Windows 2000 network is made up of clients and servers. There are three types of servers: standalone (nonnetworked), member servers, and DCs. DCs authenticate users. Each DC holds a copy of AD. DCs in a Windows 2000 network are peers. They must replicate changes to AD so users can gain access to up-to-date data. What is the name of the type of replication that Windows 2000 DCs use?

- ○ a. Single-master replication
- ○ b. Multiple single-master replication
- ○ c. Multiple-master replication
- ○ d. Peer replication

Answer c is correct. In multiple-master replication, each DC (domain controller) is a peer, which means it is on equal terms with all other DCs. It can accept changes to AD (Active Directory) and will replicate the changes out to its replication partners. Answer a is incorrect because single-master replication is used in NT, not Windows 2000. Answers b and d are invalid answers. Answer a is incorrect because single-master replication is no longer used; Windows NT 4 used this replication method. Answers b and d are incorrect because these are invalid replication types.

Question 2

A system administrator is sitting in a remote office and needs to make a change to AD data. He knows there is a single DC on his local network and would like to use it for these changes because it is closer to his workstation. How can the system administrator choose which DC makes the changes and takes responsibility for replicating data?

- ○ a. You cannot choose the DC that accepts the change.
- ○ b. You must run the administrative utility from the command line and add a switch to specify the DC you want to use.
- ○ c. You always connect to a local DC.
- ○ d. Even if a remote DC receives the change first, it forwards the request to change data in AD to a DC on the same subnet as the administrator.

Answer a is correct. Although Windows 2000 will attempt to connect you to a local DC (domain controller) for authentication, it does not guarantee that this will be the case. Any DC can accept a change; the local DC receives the update from normal replication. Answer b is incorrect because you cannot specify which DC the admin tools will use. Answer c is incorrect because you cannot guarantee that you will always contact the local DC. Answer d is incorrect because data is never forwarded to other DCs except through the normal replication process.

Question 3

You have three distinct subnets on your network. Two of these subnets are in the United States, and they have a 10Mbps connection between them. The third subnet is in England over a 128Kbps link. You want to make sure that replication works efficiently on your network. How many sites would you create on your network?

○ a. You would create three sites: two for the United States and one for England. AD will work out an efficient replication topology.

○ b. You would create a single site and add all DCs to it. AD will then configure replication.

○ c. You would create two sites. One site would include a single subnet from the United States. The second site would include both England and one of the subnets from the Untied States. This allows the subnet in England to replicate with the site in the United States.

○ d. You would create two sites: one in the United States that includes the two subnets in Houston and one for the subnet in England. AD will work out the replication topology based on this data.

Answer d is correct. Sites can be defined as a group of subnets that have fast connectivity. Because the subnet in England is on the other side of a 128Kbps link, this is a slow connection and should therefore be its own site. Answer a is incorrect because three sites are not necessary. All subnets in the United States have fast connectivity, so it would be easier to create a single site in the United States. Answer b is incorrect because a single site would not allow compression of the replication data between the United States and England. Answer c is incorrect because creating a site that included both IP subnets in the United States and England would prevent data from being compressed.

Question 4

> There are two different types of updates to AD. One of these updates occurs when a change is recorded for the very first time. This change is then replicated to all other DCs on the network through normal replication. What is the name of this type of update? [Check all correct answers]
>
> ❑ a. Originating update
>
> ❑ b. Original update
>
> ❑ c. Replicated update
>
> ❑ d. Replicated secondary update

Answers a and c are correct. Answer a is correct because the first time a change is written to AD, this is known as an originating update. This update is then replicated to replication partners, and using the replication topology of the network, it is eventually made in all replicas. Answer c is correct because updates received from replication partners are called replicated updates. Answers b and d are incorrect because they are slightly skewed versions of the actual terms.

Question 5

> When a DC accepts a change, it records it and then begins to replicate the change to its replication partners. This process is always a pull process—that is, a replication partner is informed that changes have occurred and that updates need to be copied. What is the name given to this process?
>
> ○ a. The replication notification process
>
> ○ b. The originating replication process
>
> ○ c. The change notification process
>
> ○ d. The replicated update process

Answer c is correct. This process is known as the change notification process. Once a replication partner is informed that changes have taken place at the replica belonging to a replication partner, those changes are then pulled from that partner. Answers a, b, and d are invalid answers.

Question 6

The replication topology can be created automatically on a Windows 2000 network. An automatic process takes place that generates the topology. It will even regenerate the topology should it become necessary. What is the name of the process that automatically creates the replication topology?

- ○ a. The Replication Topology Generator
- ○ b. The Knowledge Consistency Checker
- ○ c. The Knowledge Constant Changer
- ○ d. The Knowledge Replication Strategy

Answer b is correct. The automatic process is known as the Knowledge Consistency Checker. Although this process can be overridden, doing so is not a good idea. Most of the time, you should let it make decisions about replication partners, because it requires very little configuration and can work in near realtime. Answers a, c, and d are invalid answers.

Question 7

You have two sites that need to be on different subnets. The network connection between these two sites is 128Kbps. Because the connection is slow and these sites contain DCs in different subnets, they will be connected to ensure replication. What is the name of the process that automatically decides which DCs in each of these sites will be replication partners with each other?

- ○ a. The Knowledge Consistency Checker
- ○ b. The Replication Topology Generator
- ○ c. The Internet Site Topology Generator
- ○ d. The Intersite Topology Generator

Answer d is correct. It is the job of the Intersite Topology Generator to decide which specific DCs within a site will replicate with each other. Once these two servers have replicated data, normal replication practices take place to ensure that all other DCs within a site receive the updates. Answer a is incorrect because the Knowledge Consistency Checker is the process that automatically generates the topology. Answers b and c are invalid answers.

Question 8

Because every DC in a Windows 2000 network is a peer, changes can be written to different replicas that might cause conflicts. Siobhan is a system administrator in Cavan, Ireland. Siobhan reads an email that was distributed to the Administrators distribution group that says a user wants his last name changed. She makes the change as soon as she reads the email. An administrator in Basildon, England, also reads the email and makes the change. However, this administrator misreads the email and makes a spelling error in the last name. As replication occurs on the network, a conflict occurs when a DC receives replicated updates for the same property. AD has a built-in mechanism to deal with such conflicts.

From the following, create a list of only the factors that are used in conflict resolution, and put them in the correct order in which they would be checked.

The date/time of the change; the later time prevails.

The status of the user; enterprise administrators override domain administrators.

The GUID of the DCs that made the originating update; the highest GUID prevails.

The time zone. The delegated time zone always prevails.

The site's priority; the site with the highest assigned priority prevails.

The property version number; the highest property version number prevails.

The amount of data in the update; the update with the most data always prevails.

The correct answer is:

The property version number; the highest property version number prevails.

The date/time of the change; the latest time prevails.

The GUID of the DCs that made the originating update; the highest GUID prevails.

If the first piece of data fails to resolve the conflict, AD uses the second piece of data. If that also fails, the third piece—a tiebreaker, which will always resolve the conflict—is used.

Question 9

AD data exists in three different partitions. Two of these partitions exist on every DC within a forest. The third partition exists only on selected DCs. What is the name of the partition that does not exist on every DC in a forest?

- ○ a. The configuration partition
- ○ b. The schema partition
- ○ c. The master partition
- ○ d. The domain partition

Answer a is correct. The configuration partition contains data about the domains and configuration options set within all domains in the forest. Answer b is incorrect because the schema partition includes data regarding the objects that can exist within the directory and any rules that exist for that object. Answer c is incorrect because the master partition does not exist. Answer d is incorrect because the domain partition includes information that is specific for a domain, such as usernames and groups. Therefore, it does not need to exist on every DC within a forest (because a forest is made up of multiple domains).

Question 10

An administrator in Manhattan has created a new group in AD that will be used to combine user accounts from both Manhattan and Houston, Texas. Six hours after creating the account, she receives an email asking her when she is going to have time to create the account. The administrator checks her server log and sees that she created the account earlier in the day. She suspects that she has a problem with replication. Which tool could she use to examine which objects are waiting to be replicated from her local DC?

- ○ a. Replication Monitor
- ○ b. Performance Monitor
- ○ c. The Repladmin command-line utility
- ○ d. The Replication Master Browser

Answer a is correct. The only option that would work in this situation is the Replication Monitor. Answer b is incorrect because Performance Monitor is used for checking overall system performance and does not include counters for specific object replication data. Answer c is incorrect because there is no such utility as Repladmin. Although there is a command-line utility called Repadmin, it is used to examine a local DC. Answer d is an invalid answer.

Need to Know More?

 Boswell, William. *Inside Windows 2000 Server.* New Riders, Indianapolis, IN, 1999. ISBN 1562059297. This book is highly technical and explains the details of using all facets of a Windows 200 Server, including replication.

 Iseminger, David. *Active Directory Services for Microsoft Windows 2000.* Microsoft Press, Redmond, WA, 2000. ISBN 0735606242. This book introduces you to all aspects of working with a Windows 2000 domain, specifically dealing with AD administration.

 Nielsen, Morten Strunge. *Windows 2000 Server Architecture and Planning.* The Coriolis Group, Scottsdale, AZ, 1999. ISBN 1576104362. This book provides assistance with design and migration issues.

 Watts, David V., Will Willis, and Tillman Strahan. *MCSE Windows 2000 Directory Services Exam Prep.* The Coriolis Group, Scottsdale, AZ, 2000. ISBN 1576106241. This book contains more detailed information on replication and how it works with other Windows 2000 components.

  Search the TechNet CD (or its online version through **www.microsoft. com/technet**) and the *Windows 2000 Server Resource Kit* CD using the keywords "replication", "sites", "bridgehead", and "update sequence number".

Operations Masters

Terms you'll need to understand:

✓ Operations masters

✓ Single-master replication

✓ Schema Master

✓ Domain Naming Master

✓ Primary Domain Controller (PDC) Emulator

✓ Relative Identifier (RID) Master

✓ Infrastructure Master

✓ Transferring a role

✓ Seizing a role

✓ Ntdsutil

Techniques you'll need to master:

✓ Displaying the name of the server performing a specific role

✓ Tranferring a role from one server to another

✓ Seizing a role from a server using ntdsutil

✓ Assigning permissions to administer operations masters

Although it's true to say that all domain controllers (DCs) act as peers on a Windows 2000 network when we use Active Directory (AD) replication, at times the peer model does not achieve the desired result. Some functions on a network are best suited to being controlled by a single DC. These functions include implementing security measures, ensuring compatibility with down-level (Windows NT 4) servers, and ensuring that the security identifiers (SIDs) of the clients created in a domain are unique.

To this end, Microsoft has implemented *operations masters*. Operations masters have a unique role to play on your network. Management of operations masters is essential to ensuring that you have a healthy and efficient Windows 2000 network. In this chapter, we define the operations masters and what they do. We also discuss what actions you should take if an operations master fails or becomes unavailable. In addition, we talk about how the role of an operations master can be moved from one DC to another and what you should do if the original operations master comes back online.

Introducing Operations Masters

When replicating AD data, Windows 2000 uses a *multimaster* concept. This means that any DC can accept a change to AD data, and this change will then be replicated to all DCs in the domain and/or forest. Replication conflicts can, and do, occur. Chapter 12 discusses in detail a conflict resolution process that deals with these issues.

Some operations that occur on a Windows 2000 network could be harmful if conflicts were to occur. In the case of these operations, Windows 2000 reverts to using single-master replication. This means that a single DC on the network takes responsibility for performing a specific task. Microsoft has coined the term *role* to describe the task that this DC performs. There are five distinct roles, collectively known as *operations master roles*. When a DC has been assigned a role, it becomes the *operations master* for that role.

Data regarding which DCs are functioning as operations masters is stored in AD. When a client needs to get in touch with an operations master, the client simply queries AD. There are no specific requirements a DC must meet to function as an operations master. This gives you flexibility in deciding which DC takes on the task. It also means that roles can be moved from one DC to another. This becomes more important when a DC acting as an operations master fails.

Note: Although there are no requirements for which DC can act as a specific operations master, pay particular attention to "Recommendations for Operations Masters" at the end of this chapter. For efficiency reasons, it makes sense to assign specific roles to particular DCs.

The Five Operations Master Roles

Each of the five operations master roles that exist on your network has a scope—that is, some of the roles are specific to a domain, whereas others play a role in the entire forest. The five operations masters and their corresponding scopes are set out in Table 13.1. Your Windows 2000 network may have five servers that are acting as operations masters (this would be the case in a single-domain environment), or you could have more.

Knowing this fact becomes important when you are deciding which DC should play a specific role on your network. Once you understand each of the roles, you can decide where best to have this role placed for maximum efficiency.

Because three of the five types of operations masters are domain-wide, you will have several servers in your environment playing that role. Working out the correct placement of the domain-wide roles is easier than doing the same thing for the forest-wide roles. This is because the forest-wide roles must be placed in a location that offers administrators easy and fast access, which can be difficult on wide area networks.

All Windows 2000 installations start with a single server (if this is a migration, it is the first server upgraded). The first server installed takes on all roles. This is unlikely to be optimal for your network, and you should move the roles to other servers as they come online. (We talk about moving roles to other servers in the "Managing Operations Master Roles" section later in this chapter.) Because the first server also operates as a Global Catalog server and DC, the first server installed will be a little overloaded.

When you install a second domain into your Windows 2000 network, the first DC that joins the forest for this new domain assumes the three roles that are domain-based. Once again, this may not be feasible from a performance standpoint. These default behaviors should be considered carefully when you are designing your network.

Now let's define what each role achieves. Once you fully understand why these roles exist, you can better plan their placement on your network.

Table 13.1 Operations masters and their scopes.	
Operations Master	**Scope**
Schema Master	Forest-wide
Domain Naming Master	Forest-wide
Primary Domain Controller (PDC) Emulator	Specific to a domain
Relative Identifier (RID) Master	Specific to a domain
Infrastructure Master	Specific to a domain

Schema Master

AD is a database built up of instances of objects and an object's attributes. The types of objects and the attributes an object can have are defined in the schema for the directory. There must be no conflicts when changes are being made to the schema. For instance, with multimaster replication, any DC can make an update to AD data. If any DC were able to make additions or deletions from the schema, you would end up with replication problems. Let's say an administrator created a new object type called Database Servers. Replication should take care of letting all other DCs know about this change. But what would happen if replication had not yet been able to replicate out this schema change to all DCs? You could end up with a situation where one DC was attempting to replicate AD data, whereas its replication partner didn't even know the object type was possible!

To go one step further, the schema is obviously a very important piece of AD. Because it defines what can exist within the directory, managing the process of updating it with new objects and attributes should be a closely monitored process. To ensure that this process is limited, there is a single read/write copy of the schema on your Windows 2000 network, stored on the Schema Master. In addition, only members of the Schema Admins group can make changes to the schema. Once a change has been made to the schema, the Schema Master then takes on the task of replicating this change to all DCs in the forest.

There is a single Schema Master per forest.

Domain Naming Master

All objects within AD must be unique. That is, you cannot create two objects in a container with the same name. To make sure this is the case, Windows 2000 must ensure that new domains that are added to your Windows 2000 network have unique names. This is the job of the Domain Naming Master.

The Domain Naming Master manages the addition and deletion of domains from the forest. This means that whenever you want to add a domain to your Windows 2000 network, a call must be made to the Domain Naming Master. You will not be able to add or remove a domain if this connection cannot be made. Domains are added to Windows 2000 by running dcpromo.exe. This wizard contacts the Domain Naming Master on your network automatically.

Because the Domain Naming Master needs to be aware of all domains and objects available in the forest, it must also be a Global Catalog server. The Domain Naming Master queries the Global Catalog server before making additions and deletions.

There is a single Domain Naming Master per forest.

Primary Domain Controller (PDC) Emulator

The PDC Emulator plays several important roles on your Windows 2000 network. To understand these roles, remember that a Windows 2000 network can operate in two modes: mixed mode and native mode. Mixed mode means that you have Windows NT 4 servers acting as backup domain controllers (BDCs) alongside Windows 2000 DCs. You cannot change to native mode until these older servers have been eliminated from your network.

 You should not change to native mode if you have older clients on your network. All clients must be compatible with AD before you change to native mode. Otherwise, these clients will be orphaned.

The PDC Emulator acts as a conduit between the newer Windows 2000 DCs and the older-style Windows NT 4 BDCs. The PDC Emulator is, in effect, the PDC for older Windows NT computers. It takes care of replicating AD data to BDCs.

The role of synchronizing older-style DCs with the newer DCs is a two-way street. For instance, if a user object is created within AD, the PDC Emulator makes sure this object is also replicated to older-style DCs. Also, if an older client—a Windows 95 client, for instance—makes a password change, the PDC Emulator accepts the change in the context of being the PDC and replicates that data to AD.

Another area of importance for the PDC Emulator has to do with *replication latency*. Replication latency is the amount of time it takes for a change made in AD to be copied to all replicas. Despite your best efforts, there is no way for this to be done in realtime; it takes time for data to be processed and for packets to travel across the cable. Generally, this is not a problem, but in the case of users' passwords, it can be debilitating. For instance, say a user changes her password. This change is made at a DC in Houston. Before this DC has had a chance to replicate this password change to all other DCs, the user logs off and tries to log on again. This time, the user connects to a different DC. Because this DC does not have a copy of the new password, the logon attempt is declined.

To prevent this from happening, all password changes on a Windows 2000 network are preferentially replicated to the PDC Emulator. Before a DC rejects a logon attempt, it contacts the PDC Emulator to see if any recent changes to the password have taken place. If they have, the PDC Emulator can replicate this data immediately.

The PDC Emulator in a domain also operates as the time synchronization master. All DCs in a Windows 2000 domain synchronize their time with the PDC Emulator. The PDC Emulator in a domain synchronizes its time with the PDC Emulator in the root domain (the first domain installed on your network). The PDC Emulator for the root domain should be synchronized with an external source.

One final area of concern is Group Policy Objects (GPOs). These objects are automatically edited on the PDC Emulator. Although this is not essential for your network, editing these objects on a single server helps eliminate any possible conflicts. This is the default action.

There is a single PDC Emulator per domain.

RID Master

AD is made up of objects known as *security principals*. A security principal is essentially something that can be assigned permissions within a Windows 2000 network. This includes users, groups, and computers. Each security principal is assigned a SID so it can be identified. This descriptor is unique to the object and must always remain unique.

A SID is made up of two components. The first component, the *domain SID*, is common to all security principals in a domain. Because it is common to all objects within a domain, the domain SID alone does not allow objects to have a unique SID. The uniqueness comes from the addition of a second number, the *relative identifier (RID)*. The RID is assigned from a pool of RIDs stored at each DC. The RIDs in this pool are assigned to each DC by the RID Master.

RIDs are assigned to each DC in blocks. Once the block of RIDs is exhausted, the DC requests another block from the RID Master. The RID Master keeps track of which RID blocks have been assigned. This ensures uniqueness.

Note: If the RID pool on a DC is exhausted and the RID Master is not available, you will not be able to create security principals on your network. You can view the pools by using the dcdiag utility.

The RID Master also has a role to play when objects are being moved from one domain to another. In this case, the RID Master ensures that an object is not moved to multiple domains. Further, it deletes the object from the previous domain.

There is a single RID Master per domain.

Infrastructure Master

The domain partition of AD contains data about objects that exist within the domain only. It might also contain references to objects from other domains. This occurs, for instance, when you grant permissions for users that exist in other domains to resources in your domain. Universal groups can be used for this purpose (groups are discussed in detail in Chapter 5).

If a change is made to a referenced object, these changes need to be replicated to all domains. It is the job of the Infrastructure Master to receive these changes and to replicate them to all DCs in its domain.

Let's use an example to clarify this process. A user object named Sam Rao exists in the Asia domain, and it is referenced in the Europe domain. The Sam Rao object is then moved from the Asia domain to the Americas domain. This means the SID for the user changes. (Don't forget, the SID is made up of two components: the domain SID, which in this case will change, and the RID.) This change must be made in both the Asia and the Americas domain, and the reference in Europe must also be updated. The Infrastructure Master will make this change in Europe.

Note: The Infrastructure Master records references to objects that it does not contain in its directory partition. In our example, this means that although it contains a reference to the user object Sam Rao, it does not contain any other object data. It is this distinction that allows the Infrastructure Master to work. If the Infrastructure Master is also a Global Catalog server (which contains a reference to all objects created in a forest), the Infrastructure Master will know about all objects in the forest, and the comparison will not work. This breaks the Infrastructure Master's operation. Therefore, the Infrastructure Master cannot also be a Global Catalog server.

Because there will be no references to external objects in a single domain, there is no need to worry about the Infrastructure Master in a single-domain environment.

There is a single Infrastructure Master per domain.

Managing Operations Master Roles

Because the first DC installed in a domain (or the forest) assumes all of the roles by default, it is highly likely that you will want to change the DCs that perform some of the operations master roles.

Before you can do this, however, you must determine which servers in your environment are currently performing the role. You can then gracefully move the role from one DC to another (known as *transferring* the role), or you can *seize* the role. Seizing a role is the act of taking control away from one DC and assigning it to another without the current operations master relinquishing its role first. You would do this if the DC acting as an operations master had failed and was no longer online. Because the server is not operational, it cannot gracefully give up its role; instead, the role must be seized.

Determining Operations Masters

The tools you use to determine which server is performing a specific role depend upon the scope of the role. Remember that two of the five roles are forest-wide. The remaining three are domain-specific. You can use a single tool to determine the domain-level roles. You must use different tools to figure out the forest-wide roles.

Domain-Level Operations Master Roles

As mentioned, the three domain-level operations master roles are PDC Emulator, RID Master, and Infrastructure Master. You can use the AD Users and Computers tool to find out which server or servers are playing this role. To do this, right-click on Active Directory Users And Computers and select Operations Masters, as shown in Figure 13.1.

When you make this selection, you are presented with the Operations Master dialog box, shown in Figure 13.2. There are three domain-level operations master roles, and each of them are displayed on their own tabs. Along with the name

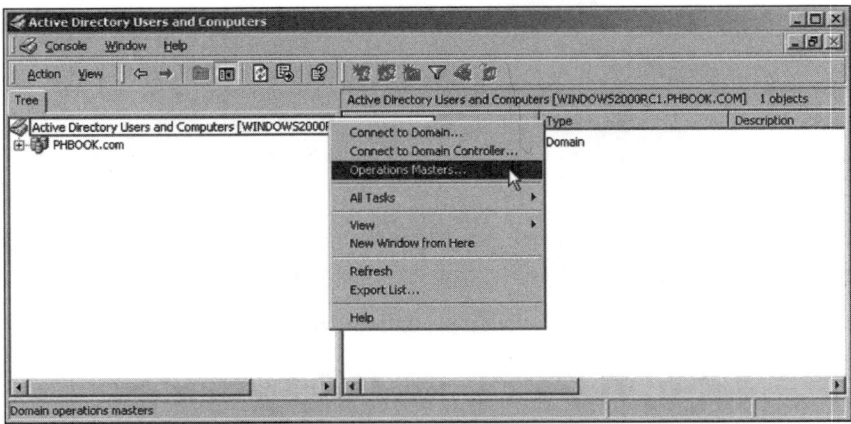

Figure 13.1   Using AD Users and Computers to determine a role owner.

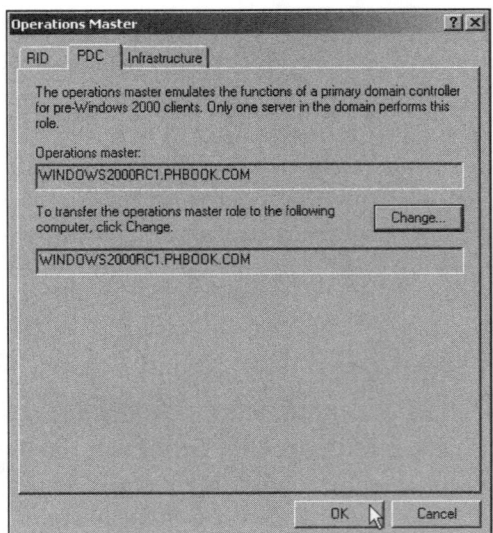

Figure 13.2   The Operations Master dialog box.

of the system playing the role, there is also a Change button. You use this to change the server that is playing the role.

Forest-Level Operations Master Roles

As mentioned previously, two roles are forest-wide: the Domain Naming Master and the Schema Master. You use two different tools to determine which DC is playing these roles. For the Domain Naming Master, you use AD Domains and Trusts. You navigate to the Change Operations Master dialog box, shown in Figure 13.3, in much the same way you reached the Operations Master dialog box in the last section. In this case, right-click on Active Directory Domains And Trusts, and select Operations Master. This brings up the Change Operations Master dialog box. You can change the name of the server that plays the role by clicking on the Change button.

The Schema Master role is a little different. Edits to the AD schema should be a very controlled process, for several reasons. First, when a change is made to the schema, the change must be replicated to all DCs in the forest. This generates a lot of activity on those servers and consumes bandwidth. Second, you can never delete anything from the schema. You can only "deactivate" parts of the schema. That means an object can be deactivated but will still take up space within the schema definition.

To find out which server is playing the role of Schema Master, and also to change the name of the DC that is playing the role, you must use the AD Schema MMC snap-in. By default, this snap-in is not available. To use it, you must first register the schema dynamic link library (DLL). To do this, open a command prompt window and type the following:

```
regsvr32.exe schmmgmt.dll
```

This registers the DLL for use on your system. This command must be run on a Windows 2000 server. If the systemroot (usually c:\winnt folder) is not in your

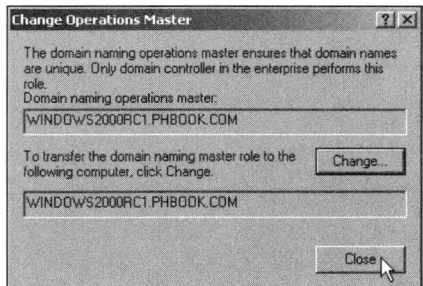

Figure 13.3   The Change Operations Master dialog box.

path, make sure you give the full path to the schmmgmt.dll file. The path should be <systemroot>\system32.

Once you have registered the DLL, you must create a custom MMC console. Follow these steps to create a custom console:

1. Select Start|Run and type "MMC".

2. This brings up an empty console. Click on the Console menu and select Add/Remove Snap-in.

3. This brings up the Add/Remove Snap-in dialog box. Click on the Add button.

4. This displays the Add Standalone Snap-in dialog box. Select Active Directory Schema and click on Add. Click on Close and then on OK.

To display the name of the DC playing the Schema Master role, right-click on Active Directory Schema in the right-hand panel and select Operations Master. This displays the Change Schema Master dialog box, shown in Figure 13.4. You can change the server name by clicking on the Change button.

Note: Each of the methods given in this "Determining Operations Masters" section include an option to connect to an alternative DC on the context-sensitive menu from which you choose the Operations Master option. Use this option to connect to other domains and to view or change the operations master in those domains.

Permissions for Changing an Operations Master Server

Before you can move a role from one server to another, you must make sure that you have sufficient permissions. Table 13.2 details what these permissions should

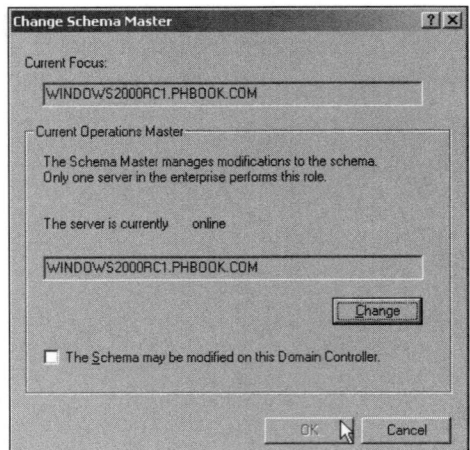

Figure 13.4 The Change Schema Master dialog box.

Table 13.2 Required permissions for changing an operations master role.	
Role	**Group with Permission**
PDC Emulator	Domain Admins group
RID Master	Domain Admins group
Infrastructure Master	Domain Admins group
Schema Master	Schema Admins group
Domain Naming Master	Enterprise Admins group

be. Pay particular attention to the Schema Master, because this is a special group within the domain.

Seizing a Role

Transferring an operations master role from one server to another using the methods outlined in the previous sections is a graceful exchange—that is, an assumption is made that both servers are functioning. With both online, normal AD replication can take care of transferring necessary data from one server to another so it can perform its new role.

This is not always the case, however. If the server playing the role of operations master fails or becomes unavailable, it may be necessary to seize control. Seizing the role forces the transfer from one system to another. It is a last resort and is not recommended.

Note: Seizing a role is a serious matter and should be done in emergencies only. The server currently playing the role must not come back online. If it does, you will have a serious conflict on your network. If you want to reuse a server that previously played a role that has been seized, reformat the partition that contained Windows 2000 and reinstall the operating system.

The method used to seize a role depends on the operations master you are working with. If you need to seize the role for the PDC Emulator or the Infrastructure Master, you can go ahead and use the AD Users and Computers console. Use the method outlined previously when viewing and changing the current DC playing the role.

Things get more complicated if you are changing the Schema Master, Domain Naming Master, or RID Master roles. For these, you must use the ntdsutil command-line utility. This utility is a powerful tool that has many uses. The help screen displaying the various options is shown in Figure 13.5.

As you can see, the **ntdsutil** command has a host of options. The following steps walk you through seizing a role, as well as how to get help with this utility at any time by using the **help** command:

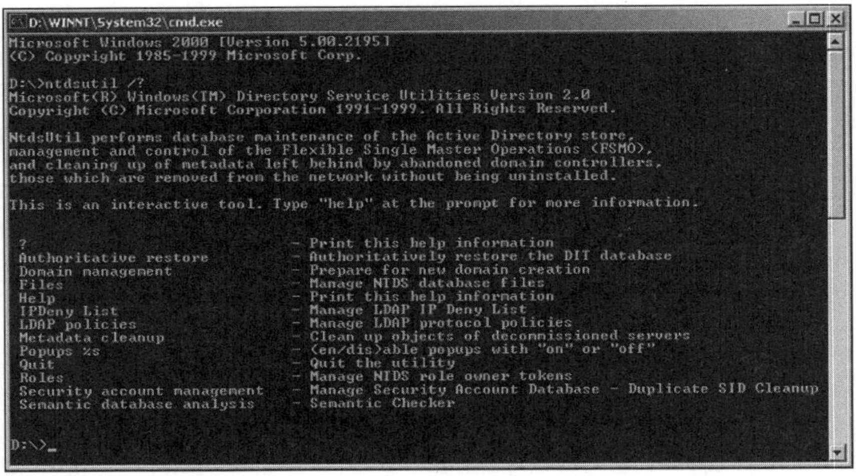

Figure 13.5 The help screen for the ntdsutil utility.

1. Select Start|Run, and type "ntdsutil". Click on OK.

2. At the ntdsutil prompt, type "roles" and press Enter. For help, type "help" and press Enter. Depending on the prompt that is displayed at the time, help information is shown.

3. At the fsmo maintenance prompt, type "connections" and press Enter.

4. At the server connections prompt, type "connect to server" followed by the fully qualified domain name (FQDN) of the DC that will be seizing the role. Press Enter.

5. At the server connections prompt, type "quit" and press Enter.

6. At the fsmo maintenance prompt, type one of the following commands (depending on the role you are attempting to seize):

   ➤ seize PDC

   ➤ seize RID master

   ➤ seize infrastructure master

   ➤ seize schema master

   ➤ seize domain naming master

   Press Enter.

7. At the fsmo maintenance prompt, type "quit" and press Enter.

8. At the ntdsutil prompt, type "quit" and Press Enter.

Once you have completed the command, don't forget to verify that the role has changed by using the method outlined in the "Managing Operations Master Roles" section earlier in this chapter. Don't forget that once a role has been seized, the old server playing the role must never come online again.

Note: Ntdsutil has a host of options. Make sure you experiment with this tool. Also, don't forget to type "help" at each prompt to see a display of available options.

Recommendations for Operations Masters

Losing an operations master does not generally have an immediate impact on your network and its users. The exception to this rule is the PDC Emulator that is used by down-level clients and for password changes. If the PDC Emulator goes down, you may have to seize the role fairly quickly. Protect the server playing this role as best you can.

Always transfer an operations master role rather than seizing it. Only seize a role when it is unavoidable. Make sure you have a process in place that prevents the old operations master from coming back online.

Consider network traffic when deciding which servers on your network should perform each role. For instance, the PDC Emulator is contacted by all down-level clients and by each DC when a password change takes place. This can cause a lot of traffic on an enterprise network. The PDC Emulator should be in a location that allows other servers to have easy access to it. The Infrastructure Master is dependent on the Global Catalog server. Make sure that there is a Global Catalog server in the same site as the Infrastructure Master.

It's a good idea to combine the Schema Master and Domain Naming Master roles. These roles are suited to being on the same server because these tasks are usually performed by the same group within an organization.

Practice Questions

Question 1

> There are five operations master roles on a Windows 2000 network. Where is the data regarding which servers are playing which roles stored?
>
> ○ a. It is stored in the Registry of the server performing the role.
>
> ○ b. It is stored within Active Directory.
>
> ○ c. It is stored in the Registry of the clients.
>
> ○ d. It is stored in a database separate from Active Directory.

Answer b is correct. This data must be in the Registry so clients and down-level servers can query the database when an operations master is required. Answers a, c, and d are incorrect because they are not valid.

Question 2

> Which of the following are the names of the operations master roles? [Check all correct answers]
>
> ❑ a. Schema Master
>
> ❑ b. Infrastructure Master
>
> ❑ c. SID Master
>
> ❑ d. Domain Naming Master

Answers a, b, and d are correct. The operations master roles that are missing are RID Master and PDC Emulator. Answer c is incorrect because there is no such role as the SID Master.

Question 3

David Aldridge is a system administrator at a large company. He is planning his Windows 2000 network with particular attention being given to the placement of the operations masters. He knows that some operations masters have particular requirements. To make his placement decision, he needs to know how many roles will operate forest-wide and how many are domain-wide. How many of the operations master roles are forest-wide and how many are domain-wide?

○ a. Three of the operations master roles are forest-wide and two are domain-wide.

○ b. Four of the operations master roles are forest-wide and one is domain-wide.

○ c. Two of the operations master roles are forest-wide and two are domain-wide.

○ d. Three of the domain master roles are domain-wide and two are forest-wide.

Answer c is correct. The Schema Master and Domain Naming Master are forest-wide roles. Answers a, b, and d are incorrect because the PDC Emulator, RID Master, and Infrastructure Master are all domain-wide.

Question 4

Siobhan Chamberlin is a system administrator for a large company. Siobhan has noticed that she is getting a lot of errors in the system log of Event Viewer. The errors relate to time synchronization on her network. Siobhan knows that this is related to an operations master role. Which role performs time synchronization duties?

○ a. The Infrastructure Master

○ b. The Schema Master

○ c. The Domain Naming Master

○ d. The PDC Emulator

Answer d is correct. The PDC Emulator performs time synchronization within its domain. It in turn synchronizes with the PDC Emulator in the root domain. The PDC Emulator in the root domain should be synchronized with an external source. Answer a is incorrect because the Infrastructure Master is responsible for updating cross-domain references of objects. Answer b is incorrect because the

Schema Master role is to operate as the single location where changes to the schema can be made. Answer c is incorrect because the Domain Naming Master is used to add or remove domains from the forest.

Question 5

Robyn Hitchcock is a member of the Domain Admins group in a Windows 2000 network. He has been asked to add a new object type to AD. However, whenever he tries to access the schema, he is denied access. A new Windows 2000 MCSE named Jaime Rodriguez says this is because of insufficient permissions. However, because Robyn is a member of the Domain Admins group, Robyn doubts this is true. Instead, Robyn thinks it is a network problem. Who is right?

○ a. Jaime is right. Domain Admins do not have sufficient permissions to make changes to the Active Directory schema. You must be at least a Schema Admin to do this.

○ b. Robyn is right. Domain Admins have all permissions on a Windows 2000 network; therefore, he should be able to change the schema.

○ c. Neither is correct. Domain Admins can change schema; therefore, Jaime is incorrect. However, receiving an access denied message indicates a server problem, not a network problem.

○ d. Jaime is right. Domain Admins do not have sufficient permissions to make changes to the Active Directory schema. You must be at least an Enterprise Admin to do this.

Answer a is correct. Only members of the Schema Admin group can make changes to the schema. Answer b is incorrect because Domain Admins do not have all permissions on a Windows 2000 network. Absolute control lies within the Enterprise Admins and Schema Admins groups. Answer c is incorrect because Domain Admins do not have sufficient permissions to change the schema, and an access denied error does not indicate a server problem. Answer d is incorrect because to change the schema, you must be a member of the Schema Admins group, not the Enterprise Admins group.

Question 6

Len Watts is a system administrator. Len's company has just merged with another large organization, and so the company has reorganized the help desk. The help desk used to be dispersed in major cities; now it has been consolidated in London. Since the consolidation, Len has received complaints that some administrative operations on the network are slow. He knows that one reason for the slowdown is that user accounts for the merged company are currently being added to the domain in batches, but that this technique is failing. Len knows the cause of the problem is the placement of an operations master on his network, so he decides to move the role to a location with better network connectivity to the help desk. Which operations master must Len move, and which tool will he use to do it?

○ a. Len must move the Domain Naming Master. This is moved with Active Directory Domains and Trusts.

○ b. Len must move the RID Master. This is moved with Active Directory Users and Computers.

○ c. Len must move the Domain Naming Master. This is moved with Active Directory Sites and Services.

○ d. Len must move the RID Master. This is moved with Active Directory Domains and Trusts.

Answer b is correct. Len must move the RID Master role, and he must use Active Directory Users and Computers to do it. You use this tool to transfer all of the domain-level operations master roles, including PDC Simlulator and Infrastructure Master. Therefore, answer d is incorrect. The Domain Naming Master is the incorrect role, so answers a and c are incorrect, but Active Directory Domains and Trusts is the tool used to move all forest-wide roles.

Question 7

> The Domain Naming Master server has crashed. The word from the hardware techs on site is that it will take a week to order the parts to get it back up and running. Mike DeBussey is the system administrator, and this could not have happened at a worse time. Mike was due to work all weekend creating two new domains. Mike knows that not having a functioning Domain Naming Master will prevent him from creating new domains. So Mike decides to seize the role of Domain Naming Master. Which tool will Mike use to perform this task?
>
> ○ a. Mike will use the ntdsutil command-line utility.
>
> ○ b. Mike will use Active Directory Domains and Trusts to seize the role, because this is a forest-wide operations master.
>
> ○ c. Mike will use the Active Directory Users and Computers tool. This tool is used to seize all roles except that of the Schema Master.
>
> ○ d. Mike will deactivate the current Domain Naming Master with ntdsutil. He will then use Active Directory Domains and Trusts to assign the role to another server.

Answer a is correct. There is no need to use two tools to perform this task. Simply use ntdsutil, a command-line utility with many different options, to seize a role. Answer b is incorrect because Active Directory Domains and Trusts is not used to seize roles. Answer c is incorrect because you cannot use Active Directory Users and Computers to seize forest-wide roles. Answer d is incorrect because Active Directory Domains and Trusts is not used to seize roles.

Question 8

Boyd Collins has just been added to the Schema Admins group so he can make some additions to the schema of Active Directory. Boyd knows that this task is very important and that he must be careful when editing the schema. Fortunately, his development background has prepared him for the task. Boyd knows that he must create a custom MMC in order to edit the schema using the Schema MMC snap-in. However, when Boyd tries to add the snap-in, it is not available on his system. Boyd calls his help desk and asks to be added to all the necessary groups to enable this function, but the help desk tells him that it is not a permissions issue. What must Boyd do to fix this problem?

○ a. Boyd must contact the help desk manager, because the help desk is incorrect; this is a permissions issue. You must be both a member of Schema Admins and Enterprise Admins to edit the schema.

○ b. Boyd is obviously using a Windows 95 computer. The MMC does not work on a Windows 95 box. Boyd must upgrade his system to Windows 2000.

○ c. Boyd must first register schmmgmt with the **regsvr32** command. Boyd will not be able to use the Schema MMC snap-in until this is done.

○ d. Boyd should call the help desk and ask its staff to seize the role of Schema Master. The snap-in not showing on a system is indicative of the server being unavailable.

Answer c is correct. Boyd cannot use the Schema MMC snap-in until he registers schmmgmt with the **regsvr32** command. Answer a is incorrect because the help desk was correct; this is not a permissions issue. Answer b is incorrect because the MMC does work on a Windows 95 box. Answer d is not correct because Boyd would not know that the Schema Master was not available until he tried to make a change to the schema. Because he cannot even find the snap-in, this is not the case.

Question 9

Mona Reed is performing a review of the installation plan for her new Windows 2000 network. Her staff has detailed the placement of all DCs and operations masters. The administrators are in a small building on a single subnet. There are 10 administrators. The network design team proposes that two DCs be placed in their site. Because there are only 10 people, one server would be fairly slow. A more powerful server would be a Global Catalog server and the Infrastructure Master. Mona rejects these plans and asks the network design team to reconsider. What was it about this design that Mona did not like?

○ a. Although two DCs are reasonable in other circumstances, the role of the administrators is too important not to have at least three.

○ b. The Infrastructure Master will not operate on a server that is functioning as a Global Catalog server. Either one of these tasks should be moved to the second DC.

○ c. The Infrastructure Master role does not need to be close to the administrators. Because this role is used only for schema updates, it would be better to move this elsewhere and to replace the role with something more pertinent to the administrators' jobs.

○ d. Mona wants the help desk team to be moved to another site. Having it in a separate site will cause performance issues.

Answer b is correct. Although some of the other answers sound good, only b has it right. Two DCs should give enough redundancy, but three would not be going overboard either. However, answer a is incorrect because not having three would not cause the plan to be rejected. Answer c is incorrect because there are other roles that could be close to the administrators too, but depending on what type of tasks are performed most commonly, it might make sense to make the Infrastructure Master closest. Answer d is incorrect because although the administrators are in a different site, that does not necessarily mean they have a slow connection to the rest of the network. Sites are also sometimes used to manage replication. Regardless of any of this, the Infrastructure Master will not operate correctly on a server that is also a Global Catalog server.

Question 10

> Darrell DeMartino is being left in charge of the network while the full-time administrator goes away for a long weekend. Darrell is confident that he can perform the tasks assigned to him, but he is concerned that in the event of a serious failure of an operations master role, he might not have sufficient permissions to do anything about it. The current administrator has added Darrell to both the Enterprise Admins groups and the Domain Admins Group. Does Darrell have sufficient permissions to perform all tasks that might arise?
>
> ○ a. No, Darrell must also be a member of the Schema Admins group in order to move the Schema Master role.
>
> ○ b. No, Darrell must also be a member of the Schema Operation Admin group in order to move the Schema Master role.
>
> ○ c. Yes, Darrell has all the permissions he could possibly need. The Enterprise Admins group gives him full power on his network.
>
> ○ d. No, Darrell must also be a member of the Operations Masters group on the network. This group has permissions on all forest-level operations master servers.

Answer a is correct. A member of the Domain Admins group can move any of the domain-level operations master roles. Enterprise Admins can move the Domain Naming Master role. However, only Schema Admins can move the Schema Master role. Answer b is incorrect because there is no Schema Operation Admin group; the proper group name is Schema Admins. Answer c is incorrect because Enterprise Admins have all permissions on a network except the ability to work with the schema. Answer d is incorrect because there is no Operations Masters group.

Need to Know More?

 Boswell, William. *Inside Windows 2000 Server.* New Riders, Indianapolis, IN, 1999. ISBN 1562059297. This book gives a lot of detail of the inner workings of various Windows 2000 components.

 Johnson, David and Dawn Rader. *MCSE Windows 2000 Server Prep.* The Coriolis Group, Scottsdale, AZ, 2000. ISBN 1576106969. Because there is some cross-over in the Microsoft exams, this book is a useful complement to help with the 70-217 exam.

 Miller, Chris and Todd Brown. *Microsoft Windows 2000 Server Unleashed.* Sams, Indianapolis, IN, 2000. ISBN 0672317397. This book covers a lot of the administrative tasks you need to master for this exam.

 Minasi, Mark. *Mastering Windows 2000 Server.* 2nd ed. Sybex Computer Books, Berkeley, CA, 2000. ISBN 0782127746. This book does a good job of aiming content at all levels of readers.

 Watts, David, Will Willis, and Tillman Strahan. *Windows 2000 System Administration Handbook.* Prentice-Hall, Upper Saddle River, NJ, 2000. ISBN 0130270105. This book takes a day in the life of an administrator and gives examples of day-to-day tasks you will need to perform.

Active Directory
Database Maintenance

Terms you'll need to understand:

✓ Extensible Storage Engine

✓ ntds.dit

✓ Active Directory (AD) log files

✓ Garbage collection

✓ Tombstoning

✓ Defragmentation

✓ Nonauthoritative restore

✓ Authoritative restore

✓ ADSIEdit

✓ System state data

Techniques you'll need to master:

✓ Performing an authoritative restore of AD data

✓ Using ntdsutil to move the AD data file

✓ Using ntdsutil to move the AD log files

✓ Using the built-in backup utility to perform a backup and restore

Active Directory (AD) is a transactional database. This means that it has built-in recovery techniques that are performed automatically should a system fail because of a hardware problem. It also means that you should know how to both back up and recover the database in the event of failure.

This chapter discusses the structure of the AD, including details of the database and log files that are used to process updates to the data. We examine how data can be backed up and restored. You will see that the AD replication process can be used to update a domain controller (DC) that has been offline for a period of time. It is also possible to force restored data to be propagated throughout the network via AD replication, even if that data is technically out of date.

Introducing AD Maintenance

Because there are so many areas of AD operation that are automatic, you would be forgiven for thinking that there is little reason to be concerned about maintenance tasks. However, this assumption would be incorrect. Maintaining the AD database—on each DC—is an essential task that should be performed regularly. Backing up and restoring data allows you to recover lost or corrupted data.

We will look at four key tasks. Two of these tasks should be scheduled to run on a regular basis. The others should be tested periodically to make sure that you can recover from a problem and that you are enjoying optimal performance.

The tasks are as follows:

➤ Backing up AD data

➤ Restoring AD data

➤ Defragmenting AD data

➤ Moving the AD database

You can use the backup utility that ships with Windows 2000 to back up the AD database. In addition, several third-party utilities are available that can perform the same task. Whichever tool you decide to use, this task should occur on a regular schedule.

It is possible for the AD database to become corrupt or accidentally deleted. When this occurs, you must restore the database. Generally, you use the same tool you used for your backup to do this. However, some tape formats allow you to use different restore software.

There are two instances where the AD database must be moved. The first is during the defragmentation process. This ensures that the process does not corrupt the database. The second is performance-related. If the hard disk that contains AD is becoming full, then performance can be affected. To alleviate this problem, you could move the database.

Defragmentation increases the performance of both writing data to the database and querying the AD data. It can also be used to reduce the amount of disk space the database takes up.

Modifying AD Data

AD uses the Extensible Storage Engine (ESE), which was first pioneered in Microsoft Exchange Server. It uses the concept of *transactions* to ensure that the database does not become corrupted by partial updates and so it can recover in the case of a power failure. Each transaction is a call to modify the database. A modification can be the addition of new data or a change being made to data that is already stored.

For the transactional system to work, the AD database must have associated log files. These log files are used to store modifications before the data is written to the physical database file. We'll look at how this works in a moment. Before we do that, however, we must define which files are used by the database. Five files make up the AD database system:

➤ ntds.dit

➤ edb*.log

➤ edb.chk

➤ res1.log

➤ res2.log

Each of these files has a role to play in ensuring that data can be written to the directory in a safe and recoverable fashion. You should note that these files exist on every DC in your environment. The AD database is not centralized in any way; it exists on each server that is promoted to the role of DC. Each instance must be maintained separately.

Ntds.dit

Ntds.dit is the single file that holds all the AD data, including all objects and the schema information. This file is stored by default in the <systemroot>\NTDS folder, although it can be moved. The ntds.dit file works in conjunction with the log files. The .dit extension stands for "directory information tree."

Edb*.log

The edb*.log file is the transaction log for ntds.dit. The file that is currently being used is called simply edb.log. When that file reaches a specified size (by default, 10MB), the file gets renamed to edb*****.log. The asterisks in this case would be incremented from 1 upward. When the files are no longer needed, they are deleted by the system.

Edb.chk

There can be two copies of changes to AD data. The first copy is kept in log files; these changes occur as data is accepted from an administrative tool. The second copy is the database file itself. This checkpoint file keeps track of which entries in the log file have been written to the database file. In the case of failure, Windows 2000 uses this file to find out which entries in the log file can safely be written out to a database file.

Res1.log and Res2.log

Essentially, res1.log and res2.log are two placeholders that exist to simply take up space. In the event that a DC runs out of disk space, the AD replica can become inoperable. It is far better for the DC to shut down gracefully. These two files, each 10MB in size, exist to prevent a DC from being able to write to the log files. If a DC runs out of disk space, AD can be sure that it has at least 20MB of space to write out any necessary log data.

Garbage Collection

Garbage collection is the process in which old data is purged from the AD. Because all DCs in a Windows 2000 network act as peers, deleting objects is a little more difficult than it might first appear. If an administrator wants to delete a user object from the network, he or she can simply hit the Delete key. However, how will Windows 2000 make sure that all DCs in the enterprise are aware that this deletion is taking place? If the deletion happens in realtime, it can't. Hence, the use of *tombstoning*, explained next.

Data is never immediately deleted from AD. Instead, the object's attributes are deleted and the object is moved to a special container called Deleted Objects. The object is then assigned a tombstone. By default, this tombstone is 60 days, although it can be changed. The tombstone means that the physical deletion of the object will occur by the configured interval. This gives AD replication time to replicate this change to all DCs. It also means that the deletion can take place at around the same time, no matter how distant the DCs may be.

Garbage collection also defragments the database by using the online defragmentation process. We will take a closer look at defragmentation in a moment.

To change the interval for garbage collection, you must use the ADSIEdit tool included with Windows 2000. Connect to the Configuration container and edit the **garbageCollPeriod** and **tombstoneLifetime** attributes. By default, the period is 60 days. This is displayed in ADSIEdit as **<not set>**. Be careful about setting the value too low; this can prevent your system state data restores from working. Microsoft recommends leaving the value set at the default.

Performing Backups

A Windows 2000 DC can be backed up while it is online, thereby minimizing the disruption. It is not enough to back up only the database and log files. Instead, you must backup the system state data.

System state data is a collection of data that makes up a functioning AD infrastructure. It includes the AD database, along with other folders and files. These files collectively can be used to recover from even the most catastrophic failure. System state data includes the following:

➤ AD database files

➤ SYSVOL folder

➤ Registry

➤ System startup files

➤ Class Registration database

➤ Certificate Services database

All of these may not exist on your server; for instance, the Certificate Services database is an optional component. You need all of the available folders because, in one way or another, they support the server.

The SYSVOL folder is a shared folder that exists on all DCs. This folder is used to replicate Group Policy Object (GPO) data and logon scripts. The Class Registration database is composed of component services that are installed on a system.

You can back up the system state data without buying third-party utilities. To do this, simply use the built-in backup utility. Follow these steps:

1. Select Start|Programs|Accessories|System Tools|Backup. When you do this, the backup utility screen shown in Figure 14.1 appears.

2. Run the Backup Wizard, which will walk you through the steps to back up your system, by clicking on the Backup Wizard button.

3. Click on Next on the introductory screen; doing so will bring up the What To Back Up options, which are shown in Figure 14.2.

4. Select the third option, which is Only Back Up System State Data. Click on Next.

5. You will be asked the location and type of backup. If you do not have a tape drive attached to your system, you can save the data to a file. This can be useful because the file will be backed up to tape the next time a tape backup is performed. Figure 14.3 shows you a backup of system state data taking place.

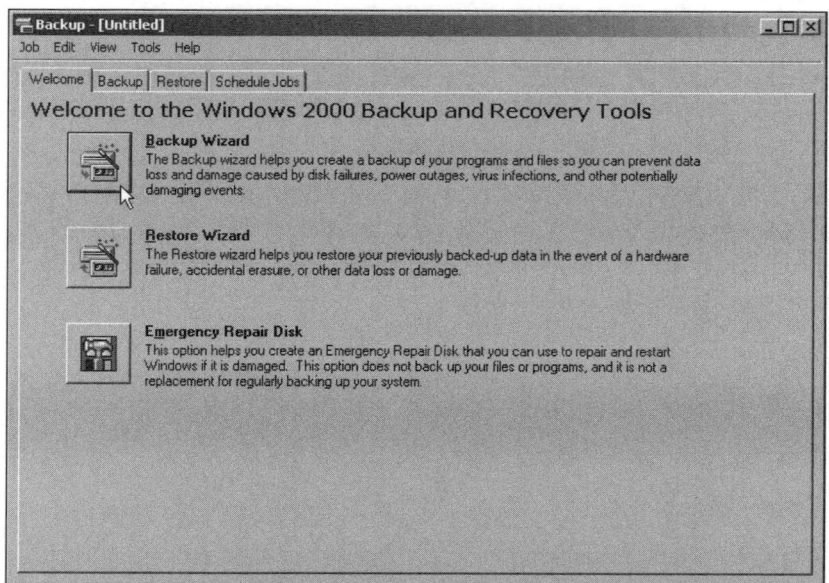

Figure 14.1   The built-in backup utility.

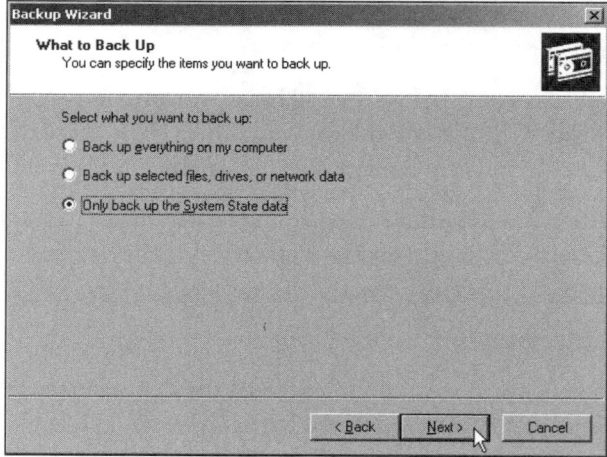

Figure 14.2   The What To Back Up options.

Recommendations for Backing up Data

You can't restore a DC fully if you do not have a backup of the system state data. However, even having that data might not be enough if an entire server has been lost in, say, a flood. Make sure that you are also backing up all other folders and disk drives on the server periodically. To do this, you can use the built-in backup tool or a third-party utility.

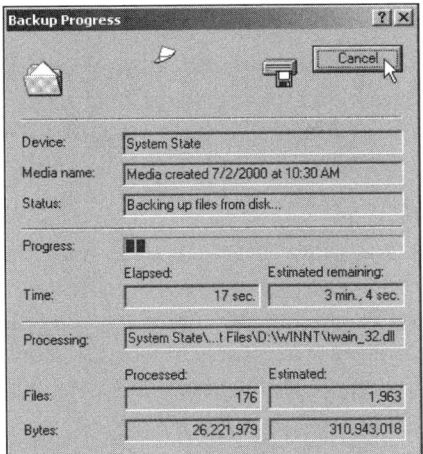

Figure 14.3 A backup taking place.

You must be a member of either the Administrators, Backup Operator, or Server Operators groups before you can back up data. These are built-in groups; if you do not want to use them, you must assign permissions yourself.

The backup utility built into Windows 2000 can only be used locally when backing up system data. This means it cannot be configured from a single server to back up system data on all DCs in your enterprise. For this reason alone, you might want to consider purchasing a utility that offers more features.

Restoring AD

Depending upon the backup options you have implemented in your environment, you might have three methods to choose from when restoring a Windows 2000 DC. If you have a performed a backup by following the steps outlined in the previous section, you could simply perform a restore operation with the built-in backup tool.

When you perform a restore, you have two options: You can perform a nonauthoritative restore or an authoritative restore. We will take a closer look at these two options in a moment.

Alternatively, you can simply rely upon AD replication to take care of updating a new DC. In this scenario, a failed DC is simply reinstalled from scratch. Once the DC is online, it updates itself via normal replication techniques. This would occur automatically and would not require any additional administrative tasks. Because this is a simple process, we won't discuss it any further in this chapter. The AD replication process is discussed in Chapter 12.

Nonauthoritative Restore

The nonauthoritative restore is the simplest form of restore when you are using backup media. A *nonauthoritative restore* is simply a restore of data from backup. Because the data will probably be out of date (presumably, some changes were made to the data in AD after the last backup), normal AD replication processes make sure that the missing data elements are updated.

This would be a common practice if a hard disk failure had taken place. If a hard disk fails, the server might become inoperable. You would simply replace the failed hardware, perform a nonauthoritative restore, and then wait for AD replication to bring the DC up to date. This process is faster than simply reinstalling the server and promoting it to a DC with dcpromo.exe, because less data will have to be replicated to the restored DC.

Performing a nonauthoritative restore is fairly simple. However, you cannot restore AD data while it is in use. For this reason, the server must be taken offline before a restore can happen. To do this, follow these steps:

1. Restart the server, pressing F8 during startup. The Advanced Startup Options are displayed.

2. Select Directory Services Restore Mode. This starts the server, but it does not start AD.

3. Log in to the server using the Administrators account. This is stored locally on each DC and can be different for each DC in your enterprise.

4. Use the backup tool to restore system state data.

5. Restart the DC.

After the server has been restarted, it is updated by its replication partners. An integrity check also takes place, and various indexes on AD data are rebuilt. This places a temporary additional load on the server during boot time.

Restore operations are highly dependent upon the tombstone period discussed in the "Garbage Collection" section earlier in this chapter. If you leave the default tombstone lifetime in place (60 days), you won't be able to restore system state data from tapes that have backups on them older than 60 days. This is because data is deleted once the tombstone lifetime has expired, and introducing a DC with older data that has now been erased from other DCs will cause database inconsistencies. Be careful not to set the tombstone lifetime for too short a time.

Authoritative Restore

The *authoritative restore* can be used to restore individual pieces of AD. This is useful if an error has taken place and an object has been deleted by mistake. Let's look at an example to clarify this process. An administrator is working with the AD Users and Computers tool, and he accidentally deletes an Organizational Unit (OU). The OU contained user objects, and they are deleted as well. Because this change was accepted by a DC, it will be replicated to all AD replicas in the enterprise. Because there is no way to turn off this process, the mistake will soon be widespread on your network.

If the OU contained a small number of accounts, it might not be a problem to simply re-create it; however, if a large number of user objects were involved, it could take some time. An authoritative restore allows an administrator to restore the deleted OU from backup. When an authoritative restore takes place, the property version number (PVN) of the object is, by default, incremented by 100,000. Because the PVN is higher than the copy currently held by the DC's replication partners, the restored object is assumed to be the most up-to-date copy. This change is then forced out to all other DCs via normal AD replication processes.

Note: It is assumed that more than 100,000 changes have not been made to the restored data since the backup took place. You can read about PVNs in Chapter 12.

The process for performing an authoritative restore is somewhat different than that outlined for a nonauthoritative restore. Once you have restored the system state data, you must not restart the computer. Instead, perform these additional steps:

1. Open a command prompt. Type "ntdsutil" and press Enter.

2. Type "authoritative restore" and press Enter.

3. Type "restore subtree *<distinguished name>*", where *distinguished name* is the full path to the object. For an OU called Finance in a domain called HCSNET.COM, this would be **OU=finance,DC=HCSNET,DC=COM**.

4. Type "quit". Type "quit" again and press Enter to exit ntdsutil.

5. Restart the DC.

Moving the AD Database

Because AD is a transactional database, you are able to benefit from some of the standard optimization techniques employed with this type of system. One of the most common suggested techniques is to move the database file to a separate physical hard disk from the log files.

Moving the database to a different physical hard disk than the log files prevents disk contention. The log files are being written to constantly, which means the hard disk heads are fairly busy. When a query is made against the AD database, the heads have to move to read from ntds.dit. This contention reduces performance of the disk subsystem.

Note: Moving ntds.dit does not mean you should pay less attention to the need to protect your data. Your DCs should minimally be running RAID 5. With a single RAID 5 array, you cannot ensure that the database file and log files are on different physical hard disks. If you decide to move the database file to a different disk, make sure that this disk has either RAID 1 (disk mirroring) or RAID 5 enabled.

You can move the database with the ntdsutil command-line utility. For this to work, you must have booted your server in Directory Services Restore Mode. Remember that for most of the major database maintenance tasks (other than performing a backup), you must have booted the server into this mode.

Following are the steps for moving the database file to another hard disk:

1. Restart the server, pressing F8 during startup. The Advanced Startup Options appear.

2. Select Directory Services Restore Mode. This starts the server, but it does not start AD.

3. Log in to the server using the Administrators account. This is stored locally on each DC and can be different for each DC in your enterprise.

4. Open a command prompt. Type "ntdsutil" and press Enter.

5. Type "files" and press Enter.

6. Type "move db to *<drive>\<folder>*", where *drive* and *folder* make up the full path to the new location. Press Enter.

7. Type "quit" and press Enter. Then type "quit" again and press Enter to exit.

8. Restart the DC.

These commands do not simply move the database file; they also update the Registry so it points to the new location. Simply moving the file will cause the DC to fail.

Note: If you want to move the log files, enter "move logs to <drive>\<folder>" instead of "move db to <drive>/<folder>" in the preceding steps. This moves the log files and also updates the Registry.

Defragmenting the AD Database

Fragmentation has existed on personal computers for many years. The AD database suffers from it just like any other file. Fragmentation of the AD database occurs during the normal operation of a DC. Put simply, as database entries are made and then deleted, gaps can occur in the database file. These gaps cause subsequent records to be written randomly across the hard disk sectors, which reduces performance. Read and write operations are much faster if the database reads and writes are made to consecutive sectors of the disk. This is because the disk head moves much less if the sectors are contiguous.

Windows 2000 includes a defragmentation program that works at the file level to make sure each file is written to consecutive sectors of the disk. The defragmentation utility for AD goes one step further and reorders records *within* the database file.

Fragmentation within a database occurs in the same way that fragmentation of files occurs. As an example of how this works, imagine that an object is created within AD. This data is written to 150 consecutive sectors of the hard disk. Two properties of the object are then deleted. The properties' data was stored in sectors 50, 51, 90, and 99. New data is then written to the database. This data requires four sectors. Because it takes the first available sectors, it ends up in sectors 50, 51, 90, and 99. This data is now fragmented. It will take longer to retrieve this data than it would if the sectors that contained the data were consecutive.

AD defragmentation can occur in two modes: online mode and offline mode. These are defined in the following sections.

Online Defragmentation

Online mode means that the server remains online while the process takes place. The online defragmentation method is slower than offline defragmentation, because the DC must service requests while the defragmentation is taking place, and it offers fewer benefits than offline defragmentation.

Online defragmentation is an automatic process that kicks off, by default, every 12 hours. This method is part of the garbage collection process discussed in the "Garbage Collection" section earlier in this chapter. Full defragmentation can take place with this method, but the size of the AD database file will never be reduced. The records in the database are moved so they exist on contiguous sectors, but even if there is a lot of empty space in the database file (for instance, after a mass deletion process), the space will not be returned to the file system.

Offline Defragmentation

Offline mode offers greater benefits, but the DC must be taken offline. Because this process is more vulnerable to being corrupted through an unexpected power failure or hardware issue, an offline defragmentation never occurs on the live database file. Instead, a copy of the database is made, and the defragmentation occurs against it. When defragmentation is complete, you must archive the current version of ntds.dit that is being used and move the defragmented version in its place.

Note: Do not delete the old copy of ntds.dit until the DC has been rebooted and proven to work with the new defragmented file.

Offline defragmentation is the only way to return space from the database to the file system. This is useful after you have performed mass deletions in the database. By default, if you have a database that contains 50MB of data, and 50 percent of that data is deleted, the file remains at 50MB. The only way to return the 25MB to the file system is to perform an offline defragmentation.

Performing an Offline Defragmentation

You must use the ntdsutil command-line utility to perform an offline defragmentation. For the process to run, you must reboot your server and bring it up in Directory Services Restore Mode. The steps for performing an offline defragmentation are as follows:

1. Restart the server, pressing F8 during startup. The Advanced Startup Options are displayed.

2. Select Directory Services Restore Mode. This starts the server, but it does not start AD.

3. Log in to the server using the Administrators account. This is stored locally on each DC and can be different for each DC in your enterprise.

4. Open a command prompt. Type "ntdsutil" and press Enter.

5. Type "files" and press Enter.

6. Type "compact to *<drive>\<folder>*", where *drive* and *folder* are the location where the compacted file will be stored. Press Enter.

7. Once the process is complete, a new ntds.dit will exist at this location. Type "quit" and press Enter. Type "quit" and press Enter again to exit ntdsutil.

8. Copy the new ntds.dit file over the old version of ntds.dit.

9. Restart the DC.

Recommendations for AD Database Maintenance

The first recommendation for maintaining an AD database is to do it! Make sure that you understand which options are available to you and that they are scheduled to be performed on a regular basis. You should be especially careful of changing the default settings for tombstone lifetime. This is 60 days by default, and reducing this time frame can prevent you from being able to restore system state data that is past the tombstone lifetime. (Think of this as a sell-by date; you cannot use the backup if the sell-by date—that is, the tombstone lifetime—has expired.)

You should separate the AD database file from the log files. This prevents disk contention and increases the performance of a DC.

Keep in mind that you do not have to perform an offline defragmentation regularly. Instead, you should rely on the online defragmentation process. You should only perform an offline defragmentation if you think you can compact the database and return a significant amount of space back to the file system. This happens when mass deletions have taken place, or a server used to be a Global Catalog server but will now operate simply as a DC.

Practice Questions

Question 1

Mike Stewart is an administrator in a small branch office of 100 users. He has a single DC to speed up authentication for his users. This server is also used for applications and file and print sharing. He has noticed that disk space will get critical within the next month. He checks the server constantly because he is concerned that he will corrupt the AD database if the disk fills up. He calls the help desk, and its staff tells him that a full disk will not corrupt the database because space has already been allocated to guard against this. What are the names of the file or files that are reserving space on this DC? [Check all correct answers]

❑ a. ntds.dit

❑ b. res1.log

❑ c. res2.log

❑ d. edb.log

Answers b and c are correct. The res1.log and res2.log files are placeholders that are used to reserve space should a DC run out of disk space. If a DC runs out of space, all changes for AD can be written to these files before the server shuts down. They are 10MB each. Answer a is incorrect because ntds.dit is the name of the AD database file. Answer d is incorrect because edb.log is the log file name.

Question 2

Kate Bush is a system administrator for a banking organization. Kate knows that she should back up her DC regularly, but she has not done it for a while because several urgent projects have been going on, and the server could not be taken offline. She places a call to Microsoft's support desk to ask for advice about protecting herself from a server failure. What did the support desk tell Kate?

○ a. Kate was told that she must take the server offline to perform a backup. Suffering from the lack of a server late at night is far better than losing it completely and not being able to get it back.

○ b. Kate was told that she should still perform a backup even if the server is being used. Although she won't be able to back up the log files for AD because they are in use, she can still back up the database and Registry files. This alone would be enough to get the DC functioning again.

○ c. Kate was told not to worry. The database is transactional and can protect itself from failures automatically. Backing up to a file or tape is a precautionary measure that is desirable, but not essential.

○ d. Kate was told to go ahead and perform a backup of system state data. The DC does not have to be taken offline for this process to take place.

Answer d is correct. The built-in Backup utility can be used to perform an online backup. You cannot back up remote servers using this utility; therefore, it must be run on each DC. Answer a is incorrect because it is not necessary to take the server offline to perform a backup. Answer b is incorrect because an online backup can back up log files. Answer c is incorrect because system backup is essential.

Question 3

Duncan Willis is reviewing the files and folders on his server to make sure the system is operating efficiently. When he looks in the folder that contains the AD files, he is surprised to find a group of files with similar names: edb00001.log, edb00002.log, and edb00003.log. Each of these files is taking up 10MB of space. Duncan is tempted to simply delete them because they are wasting space on his system, but he is concerned they might be an important part of AD. Duncan researches the situation and discovers that, indeed, these files should not be deleted. What are these files used for?

- ○ a. These files are checkpoint files, and they store a pointer to the edb.log file. The pointer allows AD to know which entries in the log file have been written out to the database file.

- ○ b. These files are placeholders that exist to prevent AD from failing when the server runs out of hard disk space.

- ○ c. These files are backups of the AD database files. They are created every 60 days on each DC.

- ○ d. These files are old log files. They will be deleted automatically when the system no longer needs them.

Answer d is correct. The AD log file is called edb.log. When this file is full, it is archived using the naming scheme edb*****.log, where the asterisks are replaced by a sequential number. There is no need to delete these files. Answers a, b, and c are invalid answers.

Question 4

> Zevi Mehlman is about to delete 1,000 user objects from his network. He backs up the AD database files and then deletes the records. When he checks the size of the database file to see how much space he has saved, he is disappointed to find that the file has not been reduced in size at all. Zevi decides to wait for a while to see if AD replication reduces the file size. After waiting a week, the file still has not reduced in size. Why is the file the same size it was before the deletions took place?
>
> ○ a. At the same time Zevi is deleting records, someone else has been adding them. The space savings have been offset by the additions.
>
> ○ b. The database will never reduce in size because of deletions.
>
> ○ c. The database will not reduce in size until the tombstone lifetime has expired. Then the database will be compacted.
>
> ○ d. The AD database will not be reduced until AD replication has taken place. Although this will take a variable amount of time, on average it takes 24 hours before all DCs are aware of the deletions and the size of their AD database files is reduced.

Answer b is correct. The database file size will remain static. It can grow automatically, but it does not reduce in size. Answer a is incorrect because deleting a record does not decrease the size of the database file. Answer c is incorrect because tombstoning defines the time before an object is physically deleted from the database, but even this will not physically change the database file size. Answer d is incorrect because replication will not decrease the size of the database.

Question 5

Siobhan Chamberlin has inherited a Windows 2000 network. Siobhan knows that a lot of deletions had been made from the AD database, and she would like to regain the space and have it returned to the file system. Siobhan knows that the garbage collection process performs a defragmentation on a regular schedule (every 12 hours). She decides to wait 12 hours for the defragmentation process to take place and to regain the space. However, when Siobhan checks the next day, she finds to her disappointment that although the garbage collection process took place, the database size has remained the same. Why didn't the defragmentation process reduce the file size?

- ○ a. This is not the job of defragmentation. To recover the disk space, Siobhan must back up and restore the database file.

- ○ b. The garbage collection process performs online defragmentation. This process does not recover disk space. Siobhan must take the DC offline and perform an offline defragmentation for this to take place.

- ○ c. The database file did not have any free space. Because the database file was full, it did not reduce in size.

- ○ d. It is not possible to reduce the size of the database file manually. AD will do this every 60 days if necessary.

Answer b is correct. There are two kinds of defragmentation: online and offline. The garbage collection process uses online defragmentation, and this process cannot reduce the size of the database file. Siobhan must take the DC offline and use the ntdsutil command-line utility to perform an offline defragmentation and return the space to the file system. Answer a is incorrect because reducing the file size is indeed the job of defragmentation. Answer c is incorrect because the database file was not full. Answer d is incorrect because it is possible to reduce the size of the database file manually.

Question 6

> By default, garbage collection takes place on a system every 60 days. The DCs on Leilani Evans' network have plenty of disk space. In addition, she would like to extend the usefulness of her backups. She decides to change the garbage collection process to occur every 90 days. Which tool would Leilani use to do this?
>
> ○ a. Leilani must use ADSIEdit to change the garbage collection period.
>
> ○ b. Leilani must use ntdsutil to change the garbage collection period.
>
> ○ c. Leilani must use both ntdsutil and Active Directory Domains and Trusts.
>
> ○ d. Leilani must make the change using Active Directory Domains and Trusts.

Answer a is correct. Leilani must use ADSIEdit to do this. Answer b is incorrect because, although ntdsutil has many uses, changing the garbage collection interval is not one of them. Answers c and d are incorrect because Active Directory Domains and Trusts is a tool used for domain management.

Question 7

> Moira Chamberlin is a system administrator for an insurance company. Moira accidentally deleted an OU and wants to get it back. Fortunately, she performed a backup of AD just one hour before the deletion. Moira starts the DC in Directory Services Restore Mode and performs a restore using the backup utility. When she is done, she restarts the server. The server comes back perfectly; however, within 30 minutes, the OU she has just restored is once again deleted. Why did this happen?
>
> ○ a. You cannot bring back a deleted object using backup/restore because AD replication mechanisms will cause the object to be deleted.
>
> ○ b. Moira needs to perform the restore on all of her DCs to bring them up-to-date. If she does not do this, AD replication will overwrite any data she restores that had previously been deleted.
>
> ○ c. Moira forgot to check the Authoritative Restore button in the backup/restore utility. If you do not do this, the restore is nonauthoritative, and the deleted data will be deleted when AD replication takes place.
>
> ○ d. Moira cannot use the backup/restore utility alone to perform this task. After the restore is done—but before the DC is brought back online—she must run the ntdsutil command-line utility and mark the OU as an authoritative object.

Answer d is correct. If you want to restore data and have it replicated to all other DCs in the domain, you must perform an authoritative restore. This restore operation is performed by using the backup/restore utility and ntdsutil. Answer a is incorrect because you can restore deleted data. Answer b is incorrect because an authoritative restore means you do not have to restore all DCs. Answer c is incorrect because there is no Authoritative Restore button.

Question 8

Pamela Young is a system administrator for a large enterprise. Pamela would like to increase the performance of AD reads and writes. She remembers reading that to do this she should move the AD database file to a different physical disk than the log files. Her servers are all configured the same way. There is a single disk with the operating system installed on it and a RAID 5 array that includes the AD database files. Pamela decides to move the database file to a single hard disk. During a conversation with her boss, however, she is told that she must not do this. Why did her boss tell her this?

O a. Her boss does not understand AD. He is wrong; the database should be moved.

O b. Although Pamela will gain some benefits from making the move, the lack of data protection in this particular instance means it is not a good idea.

O c. If performance can be gained by moving the database file, Windows 2000 will move it automatically.

O d. RAID 5 is a superior system. Disk writes on a RAID 5 system are substantially faster than any other RAID system; therefore, the files are best left where they are.

Answer b is correct. Although on the surface moving the database file to a single hard disk seems like a good move, the single disk drive offers no data protection. In this case, it is best to leave the database on the RAID 5 volume. Answer a is incorrect because Pamela's boss gave good advice. Answer c is incorrect because Windows 2000 will never move the file automatically. Answer d is incorrect because writes to a RAID 5 array are actually slightly slower than writes to other types of RAID systems.

Question 9

John knows that there is a lot of space being taken up by the AD database, and he wants to return it to the file system. John realizes he must perform an offline defragmentation to achieve this goal. He boots the server into Directory Services Restore Mode and performs the defragmentation. When the defragmentation is complete, he reboots the server. Much to his surprise, the database size did not change. What is the most obvious reason for this?

○ a. In fact, there was no free space in the database file. Although John followed the correct steps, he simply didn't gain anything.

○ b. The defragmentation must have failed. John should check the System log on his Windows 2000 server to find out why and then run the defragmentation again.

○ c. John forgot a step. Once the process had completed, he should have archived the old database file and copied the newly defragmented copy in its place.

○ d. The database always keeps 25 percent of its space available. This helps in case there is a system failure. Although there is space in the database file, there is not enough to maintain this ratio and return space to the file system.

Answer c is correct. In the case of an offline defragmentation, a second copy of the database is made. This copy will be the compressed copy and must be copied to the AD database folder before the server is started up. Answer a is incorrect because John has forgotten a key step in the process; it is not simply a matter of not having any free space. Answer b is incorrect because there is no indication that the defragmentation has failed. With an offline defragmentation, you must look at the second copy of the AD data file to see if space has been saved. Answer d is incorrect because AD does not keep 25 percent as free space. In case of a system failure, AD uses two reserved log files: res1.log and res2.log. Each of these is 10MB in size.

Question 10

Graham Young is a system administrator who has been diligently performing backups of his system state data every 90 days. After 85 days, a server fails because of a hard disk failure. Graham installs a new hard disk and then reinstalls Windows 2000. When this is complete, he reboots to Directory Services Restore Mode, intending to use his last backup. Graham calls a friend to refresh his mind on the steps for restoring AD, and his friend advises him that his backups are too old. Graham doesn't believe this. Who is correct?

○ a. Graham is correct. You can use any backed up data to restore AD files.

○ b. His friend is correct. AD has a limit of 30 days on AD restores. Data that is older than this will be replaced by the AD replication process anyway, so Windows 2000 prevents it from being restored.

○ c. Graham is correct. Although the data is old, he can rely upon the AD replication to clear up any problems he might be causing.

○ d. His friend is correct. Because the backed up data is older than the garbage collection process, Graham could introduce inconsistencies to his DC if he uses this backup.

Answer d is correct. You can adjust the garbage collection process to fit in with your backup schedule. However, you should never attempt to restore data from a backup that is older than the garbage collection process interval (default is 60 days). Answer a is incorrect because the backups are indeed too old to be used. Answer b is incorrect because there is no 30-day limit on restores. Answer c is incorrect because replication would not fix the bad data. Answer a is incorrect because John has forgotten a key step in the process; it is not simply a matter of not having any free space. Answer b is incorrect because there is no indication that the defragmentation has failed. With an offline defragmentation, you must look at the second copy of the AD data file to see if space has been saved. Answer d is incorrect because AD does not keep 25 percent as free space. In case of a system failure, AD uses two reserved log files: res1.log and res2.log. Each of these is 10MB in size.

Need to Know More?

 Blum, Daniel J. *Understanding Active Directory Services*. Microsoft Press, Redmond, WA, 1999. ISBN 1572317213. This resource is a guide to architecture, deployment strategies, and integration.

 Iseminger, David. *Active Directory Services for Microsoft Windows 2000*. Microsoft Press, Redmond, WA, 2000. ISBN 0735606242. This book covers all the new functionality of AD in a clear, concise manner.

 Microsoft Consulting Services. *Building an Enterprise Active Directory: Notes from the Field*. Microsoft Press, Redmond, WA, 2000. ISBN 0735608601. This book is geared toward consultants, system administrators, and other professionals charged with making big AD systems work. It contains lots of valuable datbase sizing information.

 Norris-Lowe, Alistair G. *Windows 2000 Active Directory*. O'Reilly & Associates, Sebastopol, CA, 2000. ISBN 1565926382. This book covers Active Directory Services Interface (ASDI) scripting using Windows Script Host (WSH), Visual Basic, and even ASPs for browser-based administration.

Remote Installation Services (RIS)

Terms you'll need to understand:

✓ IntelliMirror

✓ Preboot execution environment (PXE)

✓ RISetup

✓ RIPrep

✓ Authorizing

✓ Prestaging

Techniques you'll need to master:

✓ Installing RIS on a Windows 2000 Server

✓ Using RISetup to create and configure a RIS server

✓ Using RIPrep to create RIS images for deployment

✓ Creating RIS boot disks

✓ Authorizing a RIS server

✓ Using Active Directory Users and Computers to configure security settings

✓ Understanding the implementation of prestaging

Remote Installation Services (RIS) is a Windows 2000 Server component that allows Windows 2000 Professional to be installed remotely onto systems without requiring a support technician to set the installation options. RIS is a total desktop management solution that combines Folder Redirection, Offline Folders, desktop settings management, roaming profiles, software installation and management, and Group Policy settings that follow a user, group, or computer. These and other technologies make up what Windows 2000 calls *IntelliMirror*. Through these technologies included in Windows 2000, an administrator can effectively deploy new PCs and even reinstall existing PCs from a central location, without having to go out to a user's office.

An Overview of RIS

With IntelliMirror, users no longer have wait unproductively for an IT staff member to show up after they have placed a help desk call. With RIS, even the entire operating system can be reinstalled upon request, with a preconfigured operating system (OS) image applied to the computer. Users need only supply their logon information.

A very important factor of RIS to keep in mind is that the process of applying an OS image to a computer through RIS erases all existing data on the hard drive. For obvious reasons, it is therefore important to ensure that any nonreplaceable user information is backed up prior to reinstalling the OS. Because RIS erases the hard drive, it cannot be used to upgrade an existing OS, such as Windows 98 or NT Workstation 4. Furthermore, RIS can be used to install only Windows 2000 Professional. You cannot install Windows 9x or NT with RIS.

Note: To automate an OS upgrade or install a non-Windows 2000 Professional OS on a client PC, you need to look at a more extensive systems management utility, such as Microsoft Systems Management Server (SMS).

A RIS Scenario

To fully realize the power of RIS and IntelliMirror, imagine a situation where the hard drive in a user's compliant PC has a hardware failure. A desktop support technician would need to go to the user's office and replace the hard drive with a new one. So far, nothing out of the ordinary. However, instead of having to be there for half a day reinstalling the OS and all of the applications, the technician could activate a RIS installation and walk away. The user would only need to type in his or her username and password, and the rest of the process of installing Windows 2000 Professional would proceed automatically.

Once the OS is installed, the user would log on to the network. Group Policy would then run, and through Software Installation and Maintenance settings (assigned and published applications) and desktop settings management, the user would have access to all of his or her applications. In addition, the desktop and Start menu settings would return to the state they were in prior to the hard drive crash. The user could begin productive work immediately, and all of this would take place automatically, without any intervention by an administrator or desktop support technician.

RIS Functionality

RIS works by creating a *preboot execution environment (PXE)* that enables a compliant client PC to gain basic TCP/IP network connectivity. PXE (pronounced "pixie") technology is not integrated into every network card, so you must ensure that you have a PXE-compliant adapter before you can use RIS.

Once network connectivity is established, a series of scripts can be run to bring the client to the point of installing the OS. With RIS, an administrator can choose to have a computer go through the following types of installations:

➤ *RISetup*—A CD-like installation of Windows 2000 Professional, as if a normal installation were taking place off a CD

➤ *RIPrep*—A customized installation to the point of scripting the install with an answer file so that the user would not be required to choose any options during setup

Now that you have a basic understanding of what RIS does, let's discuss the components required for RIS.

RIS Network Requirements

To function, RIS depends on a number of components already being installed and configured on a Windows 2000 network. The following components are absolutely necessary:

➤ Remote Installation Services (RIS) service

➤ Domain Name System (DNS) Service

➤ Dynamic Host Configuration Protocol (DHCP) Server

➤ Active Directory

RIS Service

Windows 2000 includes RIS service as an optional component that can be installed through the Windows Components Wizard of the Add/Remove Programs applet in Control Panel. RIS runs as a service on at least one Windows 2000 Server system on the network, listening for client requests. In addition, the RIS server stores the OS images that the client computer can choose from when it invokes RIS. An administrator can use Group Policy to determine what images should be available to what users.

Domain Name System (DNS) Service

DNS is the service that enables RIS clients to find RIS servers on the network. Windows 2000 RIS servers register themselves in DNS so that when a RIS client establishes network connectivity, it has the name and IP address of a RIS server to pull an image from. Microsoft DNS is not required as long as the third-party DNS server used supports RFCs 2052 (SRV RR) and 2136 (Dynamic Updates).

Dynamic Host Configuration Protocol (DHCP) Server

To establish network connectivity, a RIS client must have an IP address. Because the entire process takes place at the hardware level, it is not possible to provide a static IP address. RIS, therefore, uses dynamic addressing to obtain an IP address and connect to the network. For a RIS client to obtain a dynamic address, a DHCP server must be running on the network. This can be either a Microsoft DHCP server or a third-party DHCP server.

Active Directory

RIS depends on Active Directory (AD) to function for two reasons. First, RIS uses Group Policy, which is dependent on AD, to determine permissions for user accounts and computer accounts prior to supplying RIS image choices to the user. Second, RIS uses network configuration settings stored in AD to determine information such as what RIS server should be used in the case where multiple RIS servers exist on a network. In addition, AD information is used for tasks such as using a standard naming convention for new computers and determining what domain or Organizational Unit (OU) to place the new computer in.

Let's look at the server and client components that make up RIS.

RIS Client and Server Components

In addition to the requirements listed in the previous section, components at both the client and server enable RIS to function.

Client Requirements of RIS

A client computer can meet RIS requirements in one of the following three ways:

➤ The client can meet NetPC or PC98 standards.

➤ The client can have a compliant BIOS.

➤ The client can have a compatible network adapter.

In addition, there are requirements that a client computer must meet to use RIS:

➤ The client must meet the hardware requirements, explained in an upcoming section.

➤ The client must eventually invoke the Client Installation Wizard.

NetPC or PC98 Standards

One way a computer can meet the requirements of RIS is to conform to the NetPC or PC98 standards. A client computer that meets the requirements set forth by either the NetPC or PC98 standards will include PXE functionality. Compliant computers must have version 1.0b at minimum to work with RIS.

Note: Creating a RIS boot disk is necessary if you do not have a PXE-capable network adapter or motherboard, but you do have a network adapter that is supported by the RIS boot disk creation utility Remote Boot Disk Generator (rbfg.exe), which we will discuss later in this chapter.

Compliant BIOS

Another way a PC can meet the requirements of RIS is to have a compliant motherboard BIOS, which will include the necessary PXE functionality for RIS. If you don't currently have a PXE-capable motherboard, contact the manufacturer about a possible flash upgrade, because almost all motherboards are now upgradeable.

Compatible Network Adapters

Additionally, to use RIS, a compliant client computer can simply have a compatible network adapter installed. A compliant network adapter will be PXE-compliant, meaning it supports the preboot execution environment standard. Because of Plug and Play requirements, a compliant network card is also PCI-based. This excludes PCMCIA (Personal Computer Memory Card International Association) network adapters typically found in laptops. Therefore, if you want to use RIS with a laptop system, you must first connect the laptop to a docking station that contains a PCI network adapter that also has PXE functionality.

If the motherboard is not compliant, the computer does not meet NetPC or PC98 standards, and you don't have a PXE-complaint network adapter, it might still be possible to use RIS. Windows 2000 includes a utility, rbfg.exe, that allows an administrator to create a bootable floppy disk that emulates the PXE environment, although few non–PXE-compliant network cards support Windows 2000.

Hardware Requirements

To use RIS on a client computer, the client must meet the following hardware requirements:

➤ Pentium 166 or faster CPU

➤ 32MB of RAM minimum (64MB recommended)

➤ 800MB or larger hard drive

➤ DHCP PXE-based boot ROM or network adapter supported by the RIS boot floppy

Client Installation Wizard

The Client Installation Wizard is the client-side piece for RIS, which is downloaded to the client and communicates with the RIS server. A default set of screens provided by the Boot Information Negotiation Layer (BINL) server-side service is presented to the user. These screens guide the user through the Client Installation Wizard to log on and select Windows 2000 Professional installation options that have been defined by the administrator. The user invokes the Client Installation Wizard by pressing F12 once the PC's POST (power-on self test) process has completed and before the OS starts booting.

Note that the boot process is not secure; information is sent over the network in cleartext that can be read with a packet sniffer. Therefore, you should ensure that only limited RIS servers are on the network, and you should maintain control over who is allowed to set up and configure RIS servers in general.

Server Components of RIS

RIS servers can be either domain controllers (DCs) or member servers. The RIS services on a server are less dependent on specific hardware than client computers are, although there are some hardware requirements to consider. They are as follows:

➤ Pentium 166 or faster CPU (200+ recommended)

➤ 96MB to 128MB of RAM required when running AD, DNS, and DHCP services

➤ 10MB Ethernet adapter (100MB recommended)

➤ Access to Windows 2000 Professional installation files (can be a CD-ROM or network share or a local directory with a copy of the files)

➤ 2GB hard disk for the RIS server's folder tree (devoting an entire hard disk partition to the directory tree for RIS is recommeded)

➤ NTFS-formatted partition for RIS images (RIS cannot be installed on Distributed File System (Dfs) or Encrypting File System (EFS) volumes)

As previously mentioned, the requirements to use RIS from the server end include AD, DNS, DHCP, and the RIS service. When RIS is installed through Add/Remove Programs (RISetup.exe, the program that actually installs RIS, is discussed in the "Configuring RIS with RISetup" section later in this chapter), additional services are installed on the server. These services include:

➤ *Boot Information Negotiation Layer (BINL)*—This service listens for client DHCP/PXE requests. Additionally, BINL redirects clients to the appropriate files needed for installation when using the Client Installation Wizard. It is the BINL service that verifies logon credentials with AD.

➤ *Trivial File Transfer Protocol Daemon (TFTPD)*—This daemon uses TFTP to initially download all files to a client that are necessary to begin the Windows 2000 Professional installation. Included in this download is Startrom.com, which is the bootstrap program that displays the message for the user to press F12 for Network Services. If the user does press F12 within three seconds, the Client Installation Wizard is downloaded through TFTP to the client computer.

➤ *Single Instance Store (SIS)*—The SIS service seeks to reduce disk space requirements for RIS images by combining duplicate files. The service contains an NTFS file system filter (RIS, you'll recall, can be installed only on an NTFS partition) and the service that manages images on the RIS installation partition.

➤ *RIPrep.exe*—This is another server component that is used to create RIS images. We discuss RIPrep.exe later in this chapter in the "Creating RIS Images" section.

Setting up and Configuring RIS

If you perform a typical installation of Windows 2000 Server at the time you run setup, RIS would not be installed. RIS is an optional component that can either be selected in a custom setup or added later through the Windows Components Wizard of the Add/Remove Programs applet in Control Panel.

Installing RIS

The steps for installing RIS are as follows:

1. Select Start|Programs\Administrative Tools|Configure Your Server. Click on Advanced|Optional Components|Start|Windows Components Wizard. Select the Remote Installation Services checkbox and click on Next.

2. Once you click on Next, the installation portion of the wizard begins configuring RIS. Windows 2000 installs RIS services, but it does not actually allow any configuration of RIS during this initial setup. Once RIS is installed, you

will see the completion screen. Click on Finish, and restart your computer when prompted.

Configuring RIS with RISetup

Once RIS is installed and you have restarted your computer, you still need to configure RIS. RISetup.exe is the utility used for this purpose, and it can be invoked by selecting Start|Run and typing "risetup.exe". The Remote Installation Services Setup Wizard, shown in Figure 15.1, prepares the server to be a RIS server.

Once the wizard is initiated, it walks you through the following steps:

1. The first option that you are presented with, shown in Figure 15.2, is the installation directory for RIS. Note that this directory must reside on an NTFS partition with sufficient disk space for your RIS images. If you attempt to install to a non-NTFS partition, the setup wizard returns an error message. Windows 2000 provides a default drive and directory, but the drive may or may not be valid (the wizard does not check the drive for file system type and disk space before offering it as a choice). Therefore, you might have to choose a different drive for your RIS installation. In most cases, however, you should not have to change the default directory name.

 Be aware of the limitations on the location of your RIS default drive and directory. Not only do you need an NTFS partition, but you cannot install the remote installation folder on the same drive as the server's operating system files.

Figure 15.1 The RIS Setup Wizard is invoked through the RISetup.exe command.

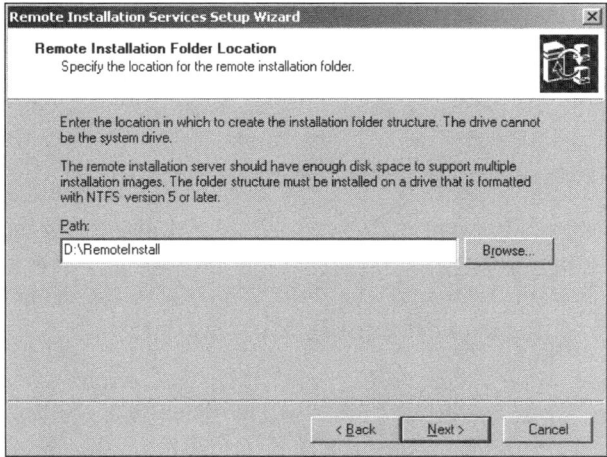

Figure 15.2   The first step in installing RIS is choosing an installation directory.

2. The next screen, shown in Figure 15.3, asks whether you want your RIS server to immediately begin servicing requests once you have completed setup. By default, RIS services do not begin immediately after setup. This is primarily a security measure, and it is best to abide by this safeguard until the server is completely configured. Because you can't use RIS anyway until you've created a RIS image, there is little sense in having the services running when, as mentioned earlier, RIS data is sent to and from the server in cleartext. An unscrupulous individual could exploit your new RIS server if it were online before you were ready to start using it. In addition to deciding whether or

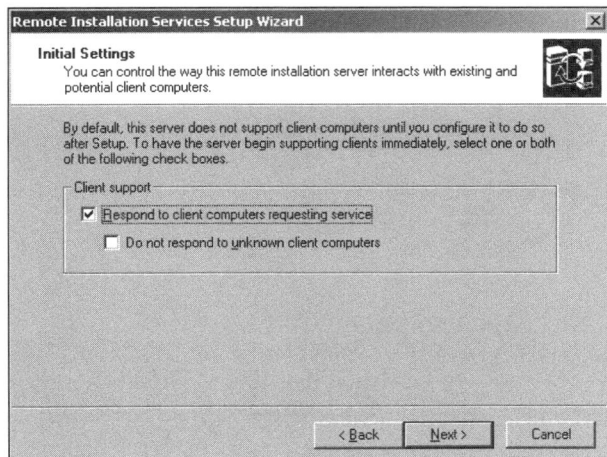

Figure 15.3   You can choose whether to start servicing RIS clients immediately and whether RIS should respond to unknown computers.

not to start RIS, you can choose whether RIS should respond to unknown computers. Select your choices, and then click on Next.

3. The next step in configuring RIS is to point the setup wizard to the installation files for Windows 2000 Professional. This can be a CD or a network path. Once you define your directory, click on Next.

4. Once you define your installation path, the setup wizard prompts you for the name of the folder to copy the Windows 2000 Professional setup files to on the RIS server. Unless you have a specific need to change it, the default directory supplied by RIS setup should be fine. Click on Next.

5. On the next screen, shown in Figure 15.4, type in a "friendly description" for your RIS image, as well as the help text that will be shown in the Client Installation Wizard when the user presses F12 to start RIS on the client. The friendly description makes it easier for users to determine which RIS image to use when they read the choices in the Client Installation Wizard. Click on Next.

6. Before setup actually begins, you are given the chance to review your settings and go back to change any you wish. Make a notation of the installation folder where the image will be placed. Once you click on Finish, installation begins. The RIS setup then begins running through its task list.

7. Once you have completed configuring RIS, you can go into Windows Explorer and look at the new directory structure.

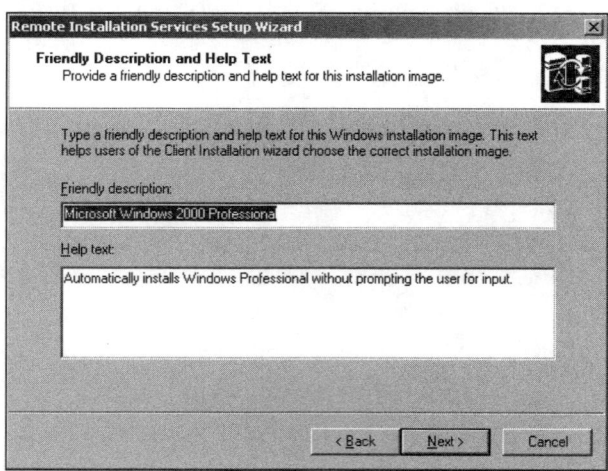

Figure 15.4 Assigning a friendly description to your RIS image.

 It's a good idea for RIS servers to be placed in the same site as the client computers that will be requesting RIS images. This increases performance and lowers the impact of RIS traffic across slow links to other sites.

Now that you have set up and configured RIS, let's look at how to create additional RIS images and RIS boot disks.

Creating RIS Images

As you have seen, CD-based RIS images can be created through the RISetup utility. Additionally, the RIPrep.exe utility allows an administrator to clone a standard corporate desktop for deployment to other systems. In this section, we examine the RIPrep utility and learn about creating RIS boot disks for compatible network adapters.

RIPrep

Unlike RISetup, which allows an administrator to deploy only a CD-based setup of Windows 2000 Professional (even a network-based installation is just a copy of the files from the CD shared on a network drive), RIPrep can be used to deploy the OS, along with customized settings and even locally installed desktop applications. This process is not the true disk cloning that products like Norton Ghost provide; it can be used only with Windows 2000 Professional. Additionally, RIPrep does not support multiple hard drives or multiple partitions on the computer that the image is being created on.

Other limitations of RIPrep include the requirement that a CD-based image that is the same version and language as the RIPrep image also exist on the RIS server, and that the target system must have the same hardware abstraction layer (HAL) as the system used to create the image. By having the same HAL, an image created on a single processor system cannot be installed onto a dual-processor system. Because Windows 2000 does not support Alpha processors like NT 4, you won't have to worry about mixing up Intel (i386) and Alpha images.

Although RIPrep has some limitations, there are advantages to using it over RISetup to create images. Most notably, RIPrep allows an administrator to create a standard desktop image and then use RIS to deploy it to new computers as they come in from an OEM (original equipment manufacturer). Additionally, reinstallation of the OS is much faster from an RIPrep image, because the image is being applied as a copy operation to the target hard drive and not running through an actual Windows 2000 installation, as would happen with a CD or network-based RISetup image.

Creating Images with RIPrep

Creating an image with RIPrep is a two-step process. First, you install and configure a computer with Windows 2000 Professional and the specific applications and settings you want to include in the image. Second, you run RIPrep.exe from the RIS server, but it's important to remember that although the RIPrep.exe utility is located on the RIS server, it is *executed* from the RIS client that the image is being created on.

To execute the RIPrep.exe utility:

1. From the client, click on Start|Run.

2. In the Run box, type the following:

```
\\RISserver\reminst\admin\i386\riprep.exe
```

If you attempt to run RIPrep.exe from a non-Windows 2000 Professional system, you receive an error message stating that the utility will run only on Windows 2000 Professional. When you run RIPrep from a valid system, the Remote Installation Preparation Wizard starts, as shown in Figure 15.5.

Once the wizard is initiated and you have clicked on Next, follow these steps to create an image with RIS:

1. Even though you ran RIPrep.exe from one RIS server, you do not have to necessarily copy the image you are creating to that particular server. As shown in Figure 15.6, you choose which RIS server to copy the image to. After indicating your choice, click on Next.

Figure 15.5   You start the Remote Installation Preparation Wizard by executing RIPrep.exe from a Windows 2000 Professional client computer.

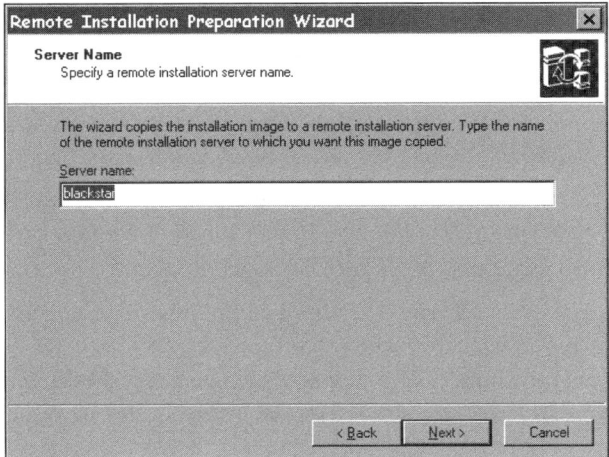

Figure 15.6   If you have multiple RIS servers on your network, you can choose which server should receive the image.

2. Supply the name of the installation folder on the RIS server previously chosen. Typically, you would type the name of an existing folder only if you were replacing an existing image. If this new image will not be replacing an existing image, type in a new folder name, as shown in Figure 15.7, and hit Next.

Note: In this walkthrough example, the image is being created for a corporate Web developer environment. For that reason, we gave the directory a descriptive name— webdev—to identify the image it contains on the RIS server.

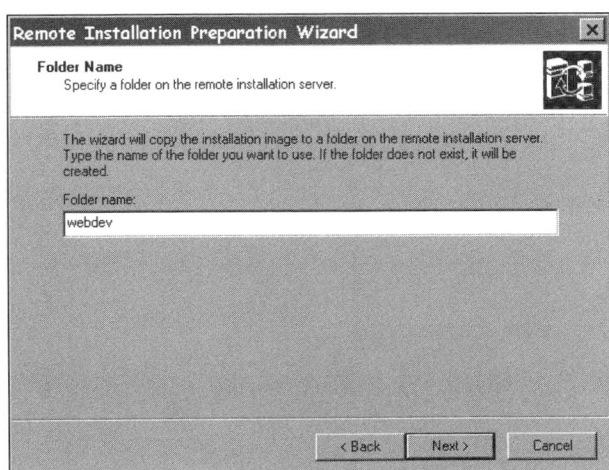

Figure 15.7   Supply a directory name on the RIS server for the Remote Installation Preparation Wizard to copy the image.

3. The next step is to assign a friendly name to the image and create the help text. The friendly name is what displays in the list of available images during the Client Installation Wizard. The help text provides an additional description to help the user identify the correct image to use when acting as a RIS client. In our example RIS image for a Web development system, we list the applications that will be installed on the system, along with the Windows 2000 Professional OS as part of the imaging process. Click on Next.

4. At this point, if you have any programs or services running that could interfere with the imaging process, Windows 2000 warns you. Figure 15.8 lists a number of programs and services that were running on the RIS image source workstation at the time this example image was being created. Once you have closed the programs and stopped the necessary services, click on Next.

5. Before beginning the actual image creation, the wizard allows you to review your choices. Once you have done so and made any necessary revisions, click on Next.

6. The last step is an information dialog box from the Remote Installation Preparation Wizard that describes the process that is about to occur. Once you understand what is about to happen on your system, click on Next to continue. You can watch the wizard image process taking place as various portions are completed.

Images created by the Remote Installation Preparation Wizard are stored in the same subfolder as images created during RISetup. If you did not change the default settings when we examined the RISetup Wizard earlier in this chapter in

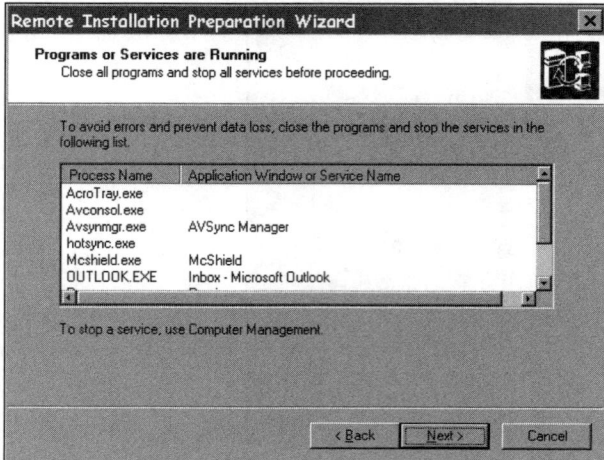

Figure 15.8   The Remote Installation Preparation Wizard prompts you to close any programs and services that might interfere with the imaging process.

the "Configuring RIS with RISetup" section and are using an English-language version of Windows 2000 Server, your RIS directory structure will be as follows:

➤ *\RemoteInstall\Setup\English\Images\win2000.pro\i386*—This is the default image created during the RISetup Wizard earlier. There are subdirectories underneath i386 for this CD-based installation image, for system32, templates, and uniproc.

➤ *\RemoteInstall\Setup\English\Images\webdev\i386*—This is the image directory we just created for our webdev image. A directory called Mirror1 that appears under i386 does not appear in the subdirectories of a RISetup-created image.

Note: It is worth repeating: RIPrep can create images only for single-partition systems. If you want to have Windows 2000 Professional installed to a partition other than the boot partition, the RIS image process will fail.

Creating RIS Boot Disks

Creating a RIS boot disk is necessary if you do not have a PXE-capable network adapter or motherboard, but you do have a network adapter that is supported by the RIS boot disk creation utility, rbfg.exe, which is located under %systemroot%\system32\dllcache. Although we touched briefly upon the Windows 2000 Remote Boot Disk Generator (RBDG) earlier in this chapter, we did not discuss actually creating disks. In this section, you will experience actually creating a RIS boot disk.

There is not much to the RBDG, really. Essentially, as you can see from Figure 15.9, you have the option to view the supported adapter list or create the disk. Most of the selections are fairly self-explanatory (for example, the About selection and the possibility of using a secondary floppy). The RBDG utility erases the floppy

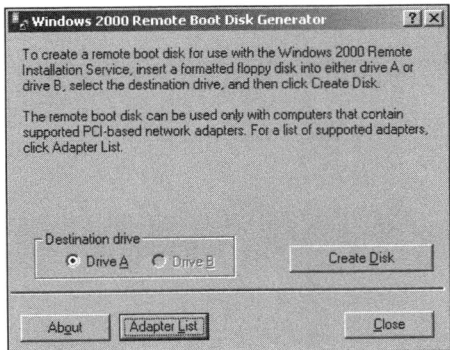

Figure 15.9   The RBDG allows you to create a network-bootable disk for supported network adapters.

in the drive without warning you first, so make sure you have inserted the correct disk and selected the correct drive before continuing.

To see the list of supported adapters, click on the Adapter List button in the utility. The RIS boot disk emulates a PXE environment for these supported non–PXE-capable network adapters, and if you look, you will notice that, once created, the boot disk contains only a single file: RISDISK.

There's no file extension on RISDISK, and the file is only 90KB in size. However, if you have a supported network adapter, this disk is all you need to start the Client Installation Wizard.

Managing RIS Security

Security is always an important issue when discussing networking topics, and it is no different with RIS. What steps can be taken to prevent unauthorized individuals from setting RIS servers, creating images, or even gaining network connectivity through RIS and installing an image? Fortunately, RIS has some built-in safeguards that allow you to maintain some control over who is able to use RIS. Some of these security services include the following:

➤ Requiring RIS servers to be authorized before they can respond to RIS client requests

➤ Using Group Policy to manage RIS client installation options

➤ Editing configuration settings through the AD Users and Computers administrative tool

Authorizing a RIS Server

Before a RIS server can service client requests, it must first be authorized into AD. You can authorize a RIS server in one of the following ways:

➤ In the RIS Setup Wizard, you can choose to have the RIS server start responding to client requests immediately upon completion of the wizard. As discussed previously in this chapter, this is not the recommended method of authorization, and by default, the box to enable immediate authorization is not checked.

➤ If you install RIS onto an authorized DHCP server, you do not have to take any further steps to authorize RIS. The authorization will be passed along from DHCP to RIS because the server is already authorized in AD.

➤ If you install RIS onto a server that is *not* already an authorized DHCP server, you can authorize RIS through the DHCP administrator tool. In the DHCP Microsoft Management Console (MMC), right-click on the DHCP root node of the tree and select Manage Authorized Servers. Click on the Authorize button and type in the fully qualified domain name (FQDN) or Internet Protocol (IP) address of the RIS server. Confirm that this is the server you want to authorize, and you are set.

Similar to the requirements for RIS, Windows 2000 requires DHCP servers to be authorized in AD before they can start distributing IP addresses to clients. Because RIS is dependent on DHCP, it makes sense to use a similar authentication scheme for bringing new RIS servers into an AD network.

Note: To authorize a RIS server, the account you are logged on with must be a member of the Enterprise Admins security group, which resides in the root domain of your organization's forest.

If a RIS server is not responding to client requests, although you have authorized it to do so, the reason might be that the changes haven't yet taken effect in AD. You can speed up the process, though, by opening a command prompt and typing the following:

```
secedit /refreshpolicy /MACHINE_POLICY
```

Managing RIS Client Options with Group Policy

For an additional measure of security, Windows 2000 enables the administrator to configure options that define the behavior of the Client Installation Wizard. Specifically, the options that can be configured are the choices that are presented to the user when they invoke RIS through F12.

The options are configured through the RIS node of the User Configuration container in the Group Policy Editor. Because this is Group Policy, you can apply these settings at the site, domain, or OU level. You might want to use the Default Domain Policy, or you might want to configure different policy options for different OUs. No matter where you choose to apply the policy, editing it is the same. Open the Group Policy Editor and navigate to the RIS node. In the pane on the right side of the editor, right-click on Choice Options and click on Properties. A dialog box like that in Figure 15.10 appears, which shows the following client options:

➤ *Automatic Setup*—Installs by using the computer naming convention and account location already defined by the RIS server. The default setting for this option is Don't Care, which means it inherits its settings from the parent container. Eventually, through inheritance, this policy will be defined as Allow or Deny.

➤ *Custom Setup*—This option allows users to install custom RIPrep-created images. The default setting for this option is Deny.

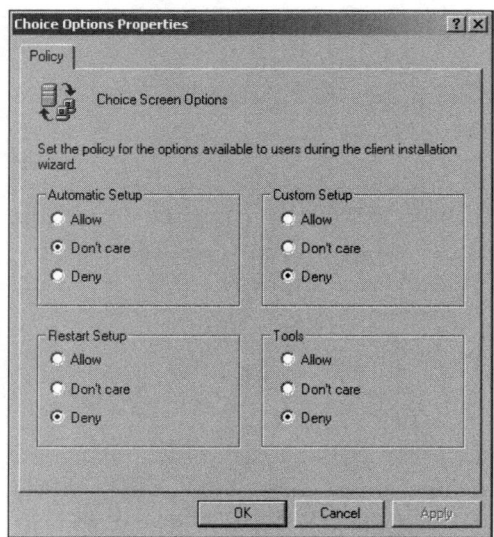

Figure 15.10 An administrator can configure client choice options for additional RIS security.

➤ *Restart Setup*—This option allows a failed installation to restart and will not require any information that has already been provided to be re-entered. The default setting for this option is Deny.

➤ *Tools*—This option allows access to maintenance and troubleshooting tools, such as disk utilities and antivirus software. An administrator might make these types of tools available for troubleshooting purposes. The default setting for this option is Deny.

Managing RIS Settings with the AD Users and Computers Tool

The strongest security settings you can configure for RIS lie within the AD Users and Computers administrative tool. Through this utility, you can perform the following tasks as they relate to RIS:

➤ Configure client support.

➤ Define a computer naming convention.

➤ Grant computer account creation rights.

➤ Prestage computers.

Configuring Client Support

To configure client support, which includes setting whether RIS should respond to clients and whether the RIS server should respond to unknown computers:

1. Open AD Users and Computers.

2. Open either the Domain Controllers or Computers folder (depending on what type of server you installed RIS on), right-click on your RIS server, and click on Properties.

3. Click on the Remote Install tab, which brings up a property sheet like that in Figure 15.11.

4. Configure the desired settings.

Defining a Computer Naming Convention

In addition to configuring client support on the Remote Install tab shown in Figure 15.11, you can click on the Show Clients button to search the AD for known RIS client computers. For more security settings, however, click on the Advanced Settings button, which brings up the property sheet shown in Figure 15.12. Through this property sheet, you can define a computer naming convention for RIS clients. In most cases, you won't want users to come up with their own computer names when installing Windows 2000 Professional, because you would end up with a network full of nonstandard names that make administrative life difficult. Through Advanced Settings, you can determine not only what the naming convention will be, but also where in AD the computer account will be created.

If you choose a naming convention and an AD location for the computer accounts, the user account under which the Client Installation Wizard is run must

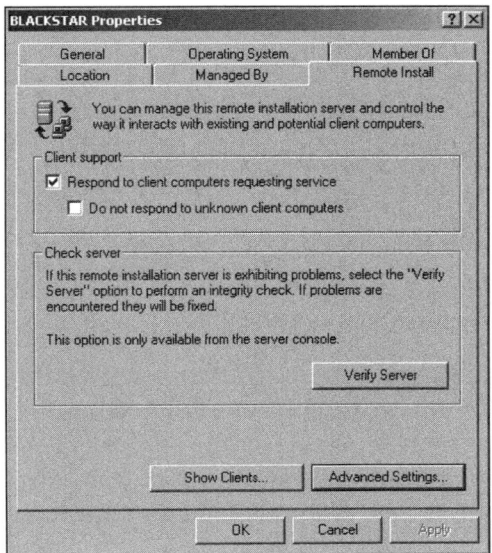

Figure 15.11   The Remote Install property sheet contains RIS server configuration settings.

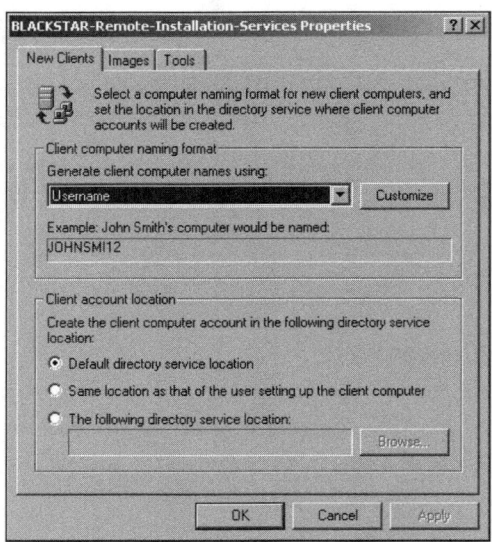

Figure 15.12   The Advanced Settings property sheet contains additional settings to tighten RIS security.

have the necessary permissions to add computer accounts to the domain, which is described next.

Granting Computer Account Creation Rights

To be able to use the Client Installation Wizard to install Windows 2000 Professional into a domain, users must have Read permissions to the OU that has been defined as the AD location for the new computer account, and they must have permissions to create computer objects.

To ensure a user has Read permissions to the required OU:

1. Click on View and select Advanced Features if it is not already selected in AD Users and Computers.

2. Right-click on the desired OU (such as Computers) and click on Properties.

3. Click on the Security tab. Highlight Authenticated Users and verify that the Read Under The Allow Column At Minimum checkbox is selected.

To allow a user permission to create computer objects, you need to use the Delegation of Control Wizard, which is discussed in Chapter 6. With this wizard, you can delegate specific control down to the creation of the computer objects themselves, and you can determine what level of permissions users and groups will have over the creation. This prevents allowing too much control in the hands of users.

Prestaging Computers

If you do not wish to delegate control for users to add their own computers to an OU, you can use a process called *prestaging* to create computer accounts in advance and to ensure that each computer name is unique. Prestaging uses the computer's Globally Unique Identifier (GUID), which is stored in the BIOS of NetPC- or PC98-compatible computers, to identify the computer. The GUID is then stored with the computer account in AD, ensuring that the specific computer that has the correct GUID is the only computer that will use the computer account. With prestaging, an administrator doesn't have to grant computer account creation rights to users; rather, the machine's GUID will be identified by the RIS server.

In addition, by tying the computer's GUID to the computer account, an administrator can ensure that someone doesn't "borrow" a valid computer account for his or her own use, whatever it might be. That way, the administrator knows that a specific computer is using a specific computer account at all times, reducing a potential security risk.

Finding the GUID

To prestage a computer, you must locate the GUID, which is provided by the manufacturer. There are several ways to locate this identifier:

➤ Look for a label inside the computer's case or on the side of the computer.

➤ Check the BIOS of the client.

➤ Start a manual RIS installation and wait for the GUID to appear on the screen during the installation.

Practice Questions

Question 1

> What type of RIS image can be created through the RIS Setup Wizard?
>
> ○ a. CD-based
>
> ○ b. Disk image containing the OS plus any desired custom settings and desktop applications
>
> ○ c. Network-based
>
> ○ d. Both a and c

Answer d is correct. RISetup can be used to create both CD- and network-based installation images. Answers a and c are incorrect because they are only half of the correct answer for this question. Answer b is incorrect because this describes more of an imaging solution, as opposed to a RIS solution with Group Policy.

Question 2

> Which of the following is RIS dependent on to be successfully deployed on a network? [Check all correct answers]
>
> ❑ a. Active Directory
>
> ❑ b. Group Policy
>
> ❑ c. IntelliMirror
>
> ❑ d. DHCP

Answers a, b, and d are correct. Active Directory, Group Policy, and Dynamic Host Configuration Protocol (DHCP) are all necessary to have a successful deployment of RIS on a network. Answer c is incorrect because RIS is not dependent on IntelliMirror, which is simply a collection of change and configuration management utilities that complement the functionality of RIS.

Question 3

Which of the following do not fulfill the client requirements to use RIS?

○ a. PXE-compliant motherboard BIOS

○ b. PC98 or NetPC compliance

○ c. PCI Plug and Play network adapter

○ d. Network adapter supported by a RIS boot disk

Answer c is correct. Although a PCI Plug and Play network adapter is a requirement, that by itself does not fulfill the requirements for RIS. A compliant network adapter would still need to be PXE-compliant. Answers a, b, and d are incorrect because PXE-compliant motherboard BIOA, PC98 or NetPC compliance, and network adapter supported by a RIS boot disk do fulfill RIS requirements.

Question 4

The IT department for Bilka Corporation has decided to utilize RIS for its deployment of desktops. The department's team leader would like to achieve the following goals:

Establish a RIS server on the network.

Create an RIPrep image of Windows 2000 Professional for the RIS server.

Create an RIPrep image of Windows 98 for the RIS server.

Deploy the image to desktop systems.

To accomplish these goals, the department begins by installing a DNS server and Active Directory within the domain. RIS is then installed on a member server of the network. Windows 98 is installed on one client machine and Windows 2000 is installed on another individual client machine. The department goes through the steps of creating images for these client machines. Deployment is attempted as the final step. Which of the following objectives have been met by the solution? [Check all correct answers]

❏ a. Establish a RIS server on the network.

❏ b. Create an RIPrep image of Windows 2000 Professional for the RIS server.

❏ c. Create an RIPrep image of Windows 98 for the RIS server.

❏ d. Deploy the image to desktop systems.

Answers a and b are correct. You can establish a RIS server on a member server within the network, so answer a is correct. Answer b is correct because in creating images, it is possible to create an RIPrep image of Windows 2000. Answer c is incorrect because Windows 98 images are not RIS-compliant; you would need a different deployment solution to deploy Windows 98. Answer d is incorrect because the RIS server will not be functional for deployment with only a DNS server and Active Directory. You still need to establish a Dynamic Host Configuration Protocol (DHCP) server and authorize the RIS server.

Question 5

Under what circumstances can you use RIPrep to create a RIS installation image?

○ a. When you need to create an image that spans multiple partitions

○ b. When you need to be able to support multiple system processors

○ c. When you need to create an image that spans multiple physical drives

○ d. When you already have a CD- or network-based OS image of the same language and version on the RIS server

Answer d is correct. A requirement to use RIPrep is to first have created an RISetup CD-based image. Answers a, b, and c are incorrect because RIS does not support any of these solutions.

Question 6

Here are some common terms having to do with RIS:

RIPrep

RISetup

RISDISK

Active Directory Users and Computers

Prestaging

Match each term with its appropriate definition:

Process by which an administrator ties a computer name to a specific computer's GUID in Active Directory

Utility used to create a CD-like installation of Windows 2000 Professional, as if a normal installation were taking place

File you would find on a RIS boot disk

Utility used by administrators to define a standard computer naming convention for RIS clients

Utility used to create a customized installation to the point of scripting it with an answer file so that the user would not be required to choose any options during setup

The correct answer is:

RIPrep

> Utility used to create a customized installation to the point of scripting it with an answer file so that the user would not be required to choose any options during setup

RISetup

> Utility used to create a CD-like installation of Windows 2000 Professional, as if a normal installation were taking place

RISDISK

> File you would find on a RIS boot disk

Active Directory Users and Computers

> Utility used by administrators to define a standard computer naming convention for RIS clients

Prestaging

Process by which an administrator ties a computer name to a specific computer's GUID in Active Directory

Question 7

From where would you invoke RIPrep.exe to create a RIS installation image?

○ a. At the source client from a RIS server

○ b. At the RIS server

○ c. At the source client from the client

○ d. From the Windows 2000 Server CD-ROM

Answer a is correct. RIPrep.exe is run from the RIS server at the client computer. This is done by selecting Start|Run on the RIS client and typing "*RISserver*\reminst\admin\i386\riprep.exe". Answers b, c, and d do not offer the correct solution to create the image in the proper way, so they are incorrect.

Question 8

What utility do you use to authorize a RIS server?

○ a. DHCP MMC

○ b. DNS MMC

○ c. AD Users and Computers

○ d. RISetup.exe

Answer a is correct. You use the DHCP MMC (Dynamic Host Configuration Protocol Microsoft Management Console) to authorize a RIS server. Answers b, c, and d are incorrect because these each perform unique tasks that do not include the authorization of a RIS server. Answer b is incorrect because the DNS console allows you to administrate your DNS server, which is necessary for RIS. Answer c is incorrect because the AD (Active Directory) Users and Computers tool allows you to configure specific RIS settings for your users. Answer d is incorrect because RISetup.exe kicks off a RIS wizard.

Question 9

What does the Don't Care option mean when you are configuring RIS client choice options?

○ a. The user invoking RIS will determine what image he or she wants to use.

○ b. Permissions will be inherited from the GPO's parent container.

○ c. Users will be allowed to have access because this option means that you don't care if they have access or not.

○ d. Users will not have access because permissions have not been explicitly granted.

Answer b is correct. The Don't Care setting tells Windows 2000 to use the permissions settings from the parent container of the particular GPO. Answer a is incorrect because it describes the Allow option. Answer c is incorrect because the Don't Care option is not a matter of indifference. Answer d is incorrect because users' access will be determined from above; Deny would mean that users won't have access in an absolute sense.

Question 10

How does one go about installing an image on a client computer? [Check all correct answers]

❏ a. The RIS boot floppy automatically kicks off the installation.

❏ b. You must enter the BIOS and select the RIS install option.

❏ c. You must press F12 after the computer is turned on.

❏ d. You must set a jumper on the NIC card to 1-2.

Answers a and c are correct. The RIS boot floppy and pressing F12 after the computer is turned on begins the establishment of a connection with a RIS server; prompts will follow that move the user through the installation. Answer b is incorrect because the BIOS doesn't have a RIS install option. Answer d is incorrect because jumpers on NIC cards aren't used for RIS installation; rather, compatible NIC cards are required.

Need to Know More?

 Boswell, William. *Inside Windows 2000 Server*. New Riders, Indianapolis, IN, 2000. ISBN 1562059297. This is a great resource for clear and in-depth information that strengthens your knowledge of RIS technology, including RIS implementation theory and a complete installation and configuration section.

 Iseminger, David. *Active Directory Services for Microsoft Windows 2000 Technical Reference*. Microsoft Press, Redmond, WA, 2000. ISBN 0735606242. This book focuses on AD but does include some IntelliMirror sections.

 Scrimger, Rob, et al. *Microsoft Windows 2000 Server Unleashed*. Sams, Indianapolis, IN, 2000. ISBN 0672317397. This resource provides an in-depth description of Windows 2000 Server and Advanced Server features, including RIS services and installation and maintenance options.

 Watts, David V., Will Willis, and Tillman Strahan. *MCSE Windows 2000 Directory Services Exam Prep*. The Coriolis Group, Scottsdale, AZ, 1999. ISBN 1576106241. Chapter 13 is the place to go for an in-depth discussion of RIS.

 Search the TechNet CD (or its online version through **www. microsoft.com**) using keywords "RIS" and "IntelliMirror", along with related query items.

Sample Test

Question 1

Sarah is attempting to install Active Directory within a network infrastructure that already has a DNS server in place. The DNS server is running through a Unix box, and it is has been functioning correctly until now. What could be causing a problem that pushes the installation to request that an additional DNS server be established on the new domain controller?

○ a. Unix DNS is not compatible with Active Directory.

○ b. The BIND version needs to be updated.

○ c. Active Directory requires only Windows 2000 DNS.

○ d. Unix uses a different protocol suite than Windows 2000.

Question 2

Your installation of Active Directory halts because the SYSVOL folder does not seem to be placed where you've specified. What is the most likely cause of the problem?

○ a. You've requested it to go on a partition that doesn't have enough space.

○ b. You've formatted the partition with NTFS.

○ c. The drive letter you've specified doesn't exist.

○ d. The partition you are specifying is FAT or FAT32.

Question 3

To allow for backward compatibility with NT 4 domain controllers, what mode should your domains be running in?

○ a. Native mode

○ b. Mixed mode

○ c. RIS mode

○ d. FLIP mode

Question 4

Bob is looking at a diagram of the proposed AD layout for the company. It starts with a parent root of company.com and has several child domains, such as miami.company.com and newyork.company.com. From the following selections, what common feature exists among these domains?

○ a. Common security schemes

○ b. A contiguous namespace

○ c. Shortcut trusts

○ d. Certificate services

Question 5

Cathie is considering her use of DNS under Windows 2000 with Active Directory integrated zones. How will this impact her directory infrastructure?

○ a. This implementation will ensure dynamic updates.

○ b. These zones will automatically replicate to secondary servers.

○ c. These zones will allow for secure updates through the AD.

○ d. AD integrated zones determine the FSMO roles.

Question 6

Maria is a domain administrator who has established a Group Policy Object (GPO), and through inheritance, the GPO's settings have flowed down toward the child OUs beneath. What can Maria do to prevent the flow of inheritance from being blocked by lower-level objects? [Check all correct answers]

- ❑ a. Select the Options button and then choose No Override.

- ❑ b. Select the Allow Inheritable Permissions From Parent To Propagate To This Object checkbox.

- ❑ c. Select the Group Policy tab for the properties of the object and choose Flow Diverted.

- ❑ d. Deselect the Allow Inheritable Permissions From Parent To Propagate To This Object checkbox.

Question 7

Brandon is logging on to a Windows 2000 domain that is in native mode. He is a member of a universal group called Managers. Which of the following will assist in the creation of Daniel's access token?

- ○ a. The PDC Emulator

- ○ b. Global Catalog servers

- ○ c. The Kerberos transaction server

- ○ d. The Infrastructure Master

Question 8

Tom is the owner of a cardboard container corporation that manufactures boxes for shipping computer products. It has a registered namespace of tdboxways.com, which it utilizes for its AD domain. Tom has just purchased an office supply company that currently has no registered namespace, nor an AD domain. In the planning discussions, it has been determined that the combination of both companies will require each to maintain a separate security configuration under a contiguous namespace. Which of the following design types should be implemented?

- ○ a. Single domain

- ○ b. Domain tree

- ○ c. Empty root domain tree

- ○ d. Forest

Question 9

Which two of the following places do GPOs that are created store their information?

❑ a. SYSVOL folder

❑ b. Group Policy Template (GPT)

❑ c. Group Policy Object folder

❑ d. Group Policy Container (GPC)

Question 10

You are working with an IT deployment team that has focused attention on the implementation of RIS within your environment. You've configured a network under DNS with AD installed and functioning. You've created quality CD-based images for your RIS server. When you go to boot from a client's machine that is PXE-compliant, there is a problem locating the RIS server's images. What do you need to implement to correct this problem?

○ a. Terminal Services

○ b. Group Policy

○ c. IntelliMirror

○ d. DHCP

Question 11

Josue has formed a list of AD objects that need to be deleted. He is hoping that this will decrease the size of the database file. After his deletions, he checks the database file and is disappointed to see that the file has not reduced in size. Why is the file the same size it was before the deletions took place?

○ a. These objects are not really being deleted from the database, because once an object is created, it can never be deleted.

○ b. The database will never decrease in size because of deletions.

○ c. The database will not decrease in size until the tombstone lifetime has expired. Then the database will be compacted.

○ d. The AD database will not be reduced until AD replication has taken place. Although this will take a variable amount of time, on average it takes 24 hours before all domain controllers are aware of the deletions and reduces the size of their AD database files.

Question 12

Eve Hackett is the network administrator for a global training corporation. She has created a large number of universal groups with several hundred users in each group. She has noticed that a great deal of network traffic has resulted. What is the recommended way of handling universal groups that Eve should apply?

- ○ a. The universal groups are established properly in the scenario; the traffic is being generated from other sources.

- ○ b. Eve should place the users into local groups and then place the local groups into universal groups.

- ○ c. Eve should place the users into global groups and then place the global groups into universal groups.

- ○ d. Eve should place the users into the universal groups and then place the universal groups into domain local groups.

Question 13

Jenny has consistently saved the system state for the AD domain her company is running. In the process of deleting several objects, it has become necessary to bring these deleted objects back. Jenny has attempted the restore process and the deleted objects return on the DC that she restores the directory to. However, she later notices that these objects are now deleted again. What should be done to correct this problem?

- ○ a. This situation is not resolvable through a restore.

- ○ b. Restore the directory on each domain controller in the domain.

- ○ c. Restore the directory and then set the IsDeleted option of the object to No.

- ○ d. Perform an authoritative restore.

Question 14

You are configuring your OUs through the Delegation of Control Wizard. You establish a No Override policy on a parent OU called Accounting OU. However, you establish a Block Policy Inheritance option on lower-level OUs. Which will take precedence?

○ a. No Override will take precedence.

○ b. Block Policy Inheritance will take precedence.

○ c. Neither will take precedence; they will cancel each other out.

○ d. These options can be set only on parent OU objects.

Question 15

The first domain controller within your domain contains all five FSMO roles. There are several domain controllers within the domain. The first domain controller fails. What allows FSMO roles to continue?

○ a. FSMO roles automatically transfer when the domain controller holding those roles goes down.

○ b. You need to seize the roles by using the ntdsutil tool.

○ c. You can transfer the roles by using the AD Domains and Trusts tool.

○ d. FSMO roles will not be able to continue.

Question 16

To use RIS on a client computer, the client must meet which of the following hardware requirements? [Check all correct answers]

❏ a. Pentium 166MHz processor

❏ b. 16MB of RAM

❏ c. DHCP PXE-based boot ROM or network adapter supported by the RIS boot floppy

❏ d. 300MB of hard disk space

Question 17

You have a primary name server established within your organization, and you have several secondary servers providing load balancing. You want to add another DNS server, yet you don't want to add any extra replication traffic to a network that you feel is already handling too much. What can you do?

○ a. Add another secondary DNS server and configure it not to replicate.

○ b. Add a caching-only server.

○ c. Create an entirely new zone with its own set of primary and secondary zone servers.

○ d. Install a Windows 2000 DNS server and configure it to utilize DDNS (Dynamic DNS).

Question 18

Johnny has designed and implemented a single Windows 2000 domain for his company. The company's headquarters is in Fort Lauderdale, Florida. Smaller branch locations include San Francisco, California, and London, England. Each location has its own DCs and separate subnet configurations, which are connected through ISDN lines that barely support existing traffic. Johnny notices an extreme amount of replication traffic. He checks the Active Directory Sites and Services tool. What will Johnny notice when he checks this tool?

○ a. Johnny will see that the replication topology is incorrectly set, and he will have to run the Knowledge Consistency Checker.

○ b. Johnny will see that the sites configured are missing bridgehead servers.

○ c. Johnny will be able to determine the performance of his ISDN traffic and see which traffic is generating the most harm.

○ d. Johnny will see that all DCs will be contained within the same default site, and he will need to break them up according to subnet.

Question 19

Active Directory replication takes time to occur, and there is a delay before the originating updates are made to every domain controller on the network. What is this delay called?

○ a. Latency

○ b. Constancy

○ c. Change notification process

○ d. Synchronization

Question 20

Chris is a network administrator for Lockworks, Inc. He is implementing a GPO for members of a specific OU and wants the GPO to refresh every 45 minutes. How does Chris go about establishing such a policy? [Choose the best answer]

○ a. Change the policy refresh rate to 30 minutes through the AD Policy Refresh Rate tool.

○ b. Make no policy changes because the default will work.

○ c. Change the policy refresh rate to 30 minutes by using the editing tool and changing the User Configuration through the Administrative Templates and the System options.

○ d. Use the ntdsutil.exe command-line tool to reconfigure the default policy.

Question 21

Chrissy is a senior analyst for Yeats Global Photo. She has configured a design for site replication that takes into consideration the company's five branch offices and their 56Kbps speed connections to the headquarters in Glenn Burnie, Maryland. What further consideration should be given to site design and implementation?

○ a. Her next consideration should be the purchase of faster links between branches.

○ b. Her next consideration should be the establishment of one unique subnet that will work for all sites.

○ c. Her next consideration should be designing subnets for each site where one and only one subnet per site is used.

○ d. Her next consideration should be designing subnets for each site where one or more subnets in a site is used, without using the same subnet in different sites.

Question 22

Steve is the network administrator for a company called DynoTech. He has been designing a directory structure and taking into consideration the many different site configuration options that will be necessary. While Steve is designing his own replication topology for the directory, his administrative assistant Karla reminds Steve that Windows 2000 has an automatically established replication generator. What is this generator called?

○ a. Replication Topology Generator

○ b. Knowledge Consistency Checker

○ c. Uniform Resource Generator

○ d. Globally Unique Stamp Checker

Question 23

Tony is attempting to set up RIS on his server. He installs RIS and then runs RISetup.exe from a command line. The Remote Installation Services Wizard initiates and fails immediately from the first option. What would cause a problem with the establishment of RIS images?

○ a. The RIS server is not enabled to provide services.

○ b. The RIS server doesn't have the path to the Windows 2000 Professional files.

○ c. The RIS server doesn't have a friendly description defined for F12 selection on the client systems.

○ d. The installation directory must reside on an NTFS partition, and he is trying to install it on a different one.

Question 24

To which of the following can Group Policy Objects be applied? [Check all correct answers]

❑ a. Sites

❑ b. Domains

❑ c. Groups

❑ d. Users

❑ e. OUs

Question 25

Which three directory partitions exist in Active Directory? [Check all correct answers]

❑ a. Schema partition

❑ b. AD partition

❑ c. Domain partition

❑ d. Sysvol partition

❑ e. Configuration

Question 26

Which of the following can be used to describe the data involved with an intersite replication scenario? [Check all correct answers]

❑ a. Data is sent uncompressed.

❑ b. Data is sent compressed.

❑ c. Data is sent through a schedule.

❑ d. Data is sent by default replication parameters.

Question 27

Greg has decided to implement a DNS server utilizing Windows 2000. He goes through the process of installing Windows 2000 and makes sure that the installation completes properly. What should be the next step prior to installing the DNS server?

○ a. Begin an installation of AD by using dcpromo.exe and then selecting the option to install the DNS server.

○ b. Begin DNS installation through the AD DNS Configuration utility.

○ c. Change the default IP address that is dynamically assigned to a static IP address.

○ d. Check your network to see if any other DNS servers are necessary.

Question 28

What is the name of the table that exists in memory on each DC and that stores only the update sequence number (USN) value for each DC to which it replicates?

○ a. Replication partner table

○ b. High-watermark table

○ c. Up-to-date vector table

○ d. Up-to-date replication table

Question 29

Which of the following snap-in tools would you find useful to test the level of predefined security that you have established on your domain?

○ a. ADSI Edit

○ b. IP Security Policy Management

○ c. Security templates

○ d. Security Configuration and Analysis

Question 30

A certain application's icons appear in the Start menu or on the desktop of the user's computer according to criteria defined by the administrator. What term can be used to describe this type of application?

○ a. Arranged

○ b. Published

○ c. Assigned

○ d. Inducted

Question 31

By default, which two groups automatically receive the user rights to create OUs?

❑ a. Server Operators

❑ b. Domain Admins

❑ c. Backup Operators

❑ d. Enterprise Admins

Question 32

The IT department for New Horizons Corporation has decided to utilize RIS for its deployment of desktops. The department's team leader would like to achieve the following goals:

Configure pre-RIS Services.

Establish a RIS server on the network.

Create an RISetup image of Windows 2000 Professional for the RIS server.

Deploy the image to desktop systems.

To accomplish these goals, the department begins by installing a DNS server, DHCP, and Active Directory within the domain. RIS is then installed on a member server of the network. The Windows 2000 Professional files are copied off the CD and placed on an NTFS partition. The department goes through the steps of using RISetup to establish the direction toward these files. Deployment is attempted as the final step by booting up with a PXE boot floppy and selecting F11 to choose the RIS description.

Which of the following objectives have been met by the solution? [Check all correct answers]

❑ a. Configure pre-RIS Services.

❑ b. Establish a RIS server on the network.

❑ c. Create an RIPrep image of Windows 2000 Professional for the RIS server.

❑ d. Deploy the image to desktop systems.

Question 33

When deploying software through Group Policy, Gil receives the "Active Directory will not allow the package to be deployed" error message. Which of the following would generally cause this problem?

○ a. Replication latency.

○ b. AD services have stopped as a result of tombstone degradation.

○ c. A corrupt Windows Installer package.

○ d. A misaligned GPO.

Question 34

What administrative template exists under User Configuration but not under Computer Configuration?

○ a. Control Panel

○ b. Network

○ c. Windows Components

○ d. System

Question 35

When adding DCs to your existing domain, what should you take into consideration?

○ a. Nothing. The more DCs on the domain the better.

○ b. Bandwidth usage on the network.

○ c. You can only have three DCs in a domain.

○ d. To promote a server to a DC, you must reinstall the operating system.

Question 36

Shannon wants to make sure that all replication takes place only during the evening hours of the day when nobody is on the network. You can do this by adjusting which portion of the site link?

○ a. Frequency

○ b. Cost

○ c. Transport

○ d. Schedule

Question 37

Which security template would show no regard for performance or functionality with non-Windows 2000 compatibility?

○ a. Basic

○ b. Compatible

○ c. Secure

○ d. High Secure

Question 38

Place the following Windows 2000 scripts in the proper order of execution.

Startup

Shutdown

Logon

Logoff

Question 39

Which Windows 2000 IntelliMirror feature enables user settings (such as desktop wallpaper and customized Start menu settings) to follow a user to whichever computer he or she logs on from? [Choose the best answer]

○ a. Roaming profiles

○ b. Folder Redirection

○ c. My Briefcase

○ d. Offline Folders

Question 40

Maverick Corporation is a multinational company that includes several subsidiaries. It is organized into a single forest with two noncontiguous domain trees, and off one of those trees there are three child domains. What would be the total number of FSMO role servers involved?

○ a. One Domain Naming Master, one Schema Master, one RID Master, one PDC Emulator, and one Infrastructure Master

○ b. One Domain Naming Master, one Schema Master, five RID Masters, five PDC Emulators, and five Infrastructure Masters

○ c. One Domain Naming Master, one Schema Master, three RID Masters, three PDC Emulators, and three Infrastructure Masters

○ d. Three Domain Naming Masters, three Schema Masters, three RID Masters, three PDC Emulators, and three Infrastructure Masters

Question 41

Which of the following are the operations master roles that handle interaction with NT 4 systems?

○ a. Schema Master

○ b. Infrastructure Master

○ c. PDC Emulator

○ d. Domain Naming Master

○ e. RID Master

Question 42

The administrator that handles group policies is trying to perform tests to see if they are working correctly. Rather than wait around until the policy is put in place, what utility can be used to enforce the policy quickly?

○ a. ntdsutil

○ b. secedit

○ c. Recovery Console

○ d. netdom

Question 43

What is the following a view of?

`CN=Arnold Perez,OU=Research,DC=yachtgraphics,DC=COM`

- ○ a. User principal names
- ○ b. Distinguished names
- ○ c. LDAP names
- ○ d. Common names

Question 44

Which of the following is a definition of all objects and their attributes?

- ○ a. Schema
- ○ b. OUs
- ○ c. DNS
- ○ d. Latency

Question 45

Masters.com has a need to implement a DNS structure before the installation of Active Directory. It has five servers to implement DNS on:

Tokyo

Los Angeles

London

Miami

New York

Three of the servers need to have secure updates, one needs to be able to accept updates, and one should not accept updates at all. The ones in Tokyo, Los Angeles, and London are domain controllers, whereas the other two, in Miami and New York, are member servers. In the DNS implementation, there is a need to place the following servers within the five locations; DNS servers can be used more than once:

AD Integrated

Secondary

Caching

Answer Key

For asterisked items, please see textual representation of answer on the appropriate page within this chapter.

1. b	16. a, c	31. b, d
2. d	17. b	32. a, b, c
3. b	18. d	33. c
4. b	19. a	34. a
5. c	20. c	35. b
6. a, c	21. d	36. d
7. b	22. b	37. d
8. b	23. d	38. *
9. b, d	24. a, b, e	39. a
10. d	25. a, c, e	40. b
11. b	26. b, c	41. c
12. c	27. c	42. b
13. d	28. b	43. b
14. a	29. d	44. a
15. b	30. c	45. *

Question 1

Answer b is correct. Most likely, Sarah is using an old version of BIND and needs to upgrade to at least 8.1.2. Answer a is incorrect because Unix DNS can be compatible with an upgrade. Answer c is incorrect because Windows 2000 will work with DNS servers that support RFCs 2052 (SRV Records) and 2163 (Dynamic Updates). Answer d is incorrect because both Unix and Windows 2000 use TCP/IP as their protocol suite of choice.

Question 2

Answer d is correct. The SYSVOL folder structure must be on an NTFS partition. Answers a and c are incorrect because, although these are possible causes of the problem, the question asks for "most likely." Answer b is incorrect because putting the SYSVOL folder on an NTFS partition would have actually been a good thing.

Question 3

Answer b is correct. Mixed mode allows for backward compatibility and synchronization with the Accounts Manager. Answer a is incorrect because native mode would ensure incompatibility with NT 4 domain controllers. Answers c and d are incorrect because they are not really modes.

Question 4

Answer b is correct. The scenario provided is an example of a growing AD tree. The common feature is a contiguous namespace. Answer a is incorrect because common security schemes exist within the same domain, not between domains. Answer c is incorrect because shortcut trusts must be manually established, and they can be formed only between domains that you've selected. Answer d is incorrect because certificate services are not an automatically implemented feature of Windows 2000.

Question 5

Answer c is correct. Active Directory integrated zones allow for the DNS zone files to be replicated with the directory information and also allow for secure updates to be configured. Answer a is incorrect because dynamic updates are resolved between DNS and DHCP in Windows 2000. Answer b is incorrect because AD integrated zones include replication within the Active Directory replication. Answer d is incorrect because AD integrated zones have absolutely nothing to do with FSMO roles.

Question 6

Answers a and c are correct. To ensure the application of that GPO to lower-level objects, you must go into the properties of the object and choose Flow Diverted (answer c), and you must also go into the options for that GPO and select the No Override option (answer a). Answers b and d are incorrect because they involve selections that relate to permissions that are being accepted or denied from upper level OUs.

Question 7

Answer b is correct. Global Catalog servers search for the domain information necessary during logon when an individual uses their user principal name. When a user logs on to a native mode domain (these are the only ones to include universal groups), the GC updates the DC as to the universal group information for that particular user's access token. Answers a and d are incorrect because PDC Emulator and The Infrastructure Master are FSMO roles that are not involved with the generation of the access token. The PDC Emulator is useful in backward compatibility issues with NT 4. Answer c is incorrect because the Kerberos server is used for domain and forest user verification through tickets.

Question 8

Answer b is correct. A domain tree would include one or more domains. In this case, there is a need to maintain separate security policies, which would require two domains under one domain tree. Answer a is incorrect because a single domain would not allow for separate security policies. Answer c is incorrect because an empty root is unnecessary; no guidelines for strict separation of control have been requested. Answer d is incorrect because a forest arrangement would involve two noncontiguous namespaces.

Question 9

Answers b and d are correct. A GPO will store its information within a GPT and a GPC. Answer a is incorrect because the SYSVOL folder, although technically the location of GPO information, is not one of the two best answers. Answer c is incorrect because there is no such thing as a GPO folder.

Question 10

Answer d is correct. To implement RIS correctly, you need to have AD, DNS, and DHCP up and running. Answers a, b, and c are incorrect because Terminal Services, Group Policy, and IntelliMirror do not assist in RIS implementation.

Question 11

Answer b is correct. The database file size will remain static. It can grow automatically, but it does not reduce in size. Answer a is incorrect because objects can be deleted from the database. Answer c is incorrect because tombstoning defines the time before an object is physically deleted from the database, but even this will not physically change the database file size. Answer d is incorrect because deletions are replicated within a relatively quick period of time among domain controllers.

Question 12

Answer c is correct. It is recommended that Eve should place the users into global groups and then place the global groups into universal groups. Because of the replication of universal group content, the user objects are being referenced and creating excess replication. It would be better to place the users into several key global groups and then place those groups into the universal groups. This will reduce the replication load. Answer a is incorrect because this method actually creates tremendous amounts of replication. Answer b is incorrect because local groups would not be available for the domain. Answer d is incorrect because, although this situation is possible, the replication would not be reduced using this step.

Question 13

Answer d is correct. If you want to restore data and have it replicated to all other domain controllers in the domain, you must perform an authoritative restore. This restore operation is performed by using the backup/restore utility and ntdsutil. Answer a is incorrect because you can restore deleted items. Answer b is incorrect because you do not have to update all of the DCs. Answer c is incorrect because there is no way to change the IsDeleted setting for objects.

Question 14

Answer a is correct. No Override will take precedence over all other settings. Answer b is incorrect because Block Policy Inheritance will only work if No Override has not been selected. Answer c is incorrect because answer a is correct. Answer d is incorrect because these options can certainly be set on lower-level OUs.

Question 15

Answer b is correct. Because the server is not operational it will be necessary to seize the roles. Answer a is incorrect because FSMO roles do not automatically transfer. Answer c is incorrect because FSMO roles are transferred smoothly with the AD Domains and Trusts tool only when the DC with those roles is still functional. Answer d is incorrect because there is a method to salvage FSMO roles.

Question 16

Answers a and c are correct. You should have a 166MHz processor and a DHCP PXE-based boot ROM or network adapter supported by the RIS boot floppy. Answer b is incorrect because 32MB of RAM is recommended, not 16MB. Answer d is incorrect because 800MB of hard disk space is recommend, not 300MB.

Question 17

Answer b is correct. The caching-only server doesn't generate traffic but checks in with the DNS servers when it needs help and then holds those resolutions in a TTL (time-to-live) fashion. Answer a is incorrect because although the secondary server sounds tempting, it will add replication traffic. Answer c is incorrect because adding another site with other DNS servers that replicate would certainly devour any remaining network bandwidth. Answer d is incorrect because Windows 2000 is not the cure-all for an existing DNS infrastructure, and the endeavor would be useless.

Question 18

Answer d is correct. All DCs usually go into the default site. In this scenario, it is necessary to establish multiple sites based on subnet and then set replication schedules. Answer a is incorrect because you cannot use the AD Sites and Services tool to determine site topology; you would use it to manage the sites and create new sites based upon your bandwidth capabilities. Answer b is incorrect because there will be no sites unless they are manually established, and there are no such components as bridgehead servers in Active Directory; they are components of Exchange Server. Answer c is incorrect because the AD Sites and Services tool is not for this purpose either.

Question 19

Answer a is correct. *Latency* is the term used to define the replication delay. Answer b is incorrect because *constancy* isn't used with AD at all. Answer c is incorrect because the *change notification process* is the actual process that takes care of replicating data from one domain controller to another. Answer d is incorrect because *synchronization* is used to refer to other portions of AD and the maintenance of similar information.

Question 20

Answer c is correct. By editing the GPO, you can configure a different setting for the refresh rate. Answer a is incorrect because there is no such tool as the AD Refresh Rate tool. Answer b is incorrect because the default refresh rate is 90 minutes. Answer d is incorrect because a command-line tool, such as ntdsutil.exe, is not used to change the refresh rate.

Question 21

Answer d is correct. Sites should be made up of separate subnets, but they can contain more than one subnet per site. Answer a is incorrect because it would not be part of Chrissy's job to purchase faster links. Answer b is incorrect because one subnet would not create separate sites. Answer c is incorrect because you can definitely have more than one subnet per site.

Question 22

Answer b is correct. The Knowledge Consistency Checker is used to automatically generate a replication topology. The administrator can then make changes if necessary according to the needs of the organization. Answers a, c, and d are incorrect because they are all fictitious.

Question 23

Answer d is correct. You must have your RIS files on an NTFS partition, or you will receive an error message and the wizard will fail. Answer a is incorrect because it describes the second step in the process of the RIS Wizard. Answer b is incorrect because it describes the third step in the wizard's process. Answer c is incorrect because it describes the final step in the procedure.

Question 24

Answers a, b, and e are correct. Group Policy Objects can be applied to sites, domains, and OUs. Answers c and d are incorrect because GPOs cannot be applied to groups or users.

Question 25

Answers a, c, and e are correct. The Schema, Domain, and Configuration partitions exist in Active Directory. Answers b and d are incorrect because the AD and Sysvol partitions do not exist in Active Directory; there is no such thing as an AD partition, and the Sysvol partition is one on which the SYSVOL folder must reside (it must be an NTFS partition, but it isn't a directory partition).

Question 26

Answers b and c are correct. Replication that occurs intersite requires data to be compressed and occurs under a schedule. Answer a is incorrect because uncompressed data is utilized in intrasite replication only. Answer d is incorrect because default replication parameters are used for intrasite, non–schedule-based replication, whereas intersite replication requires defined schedules.

Question 27

Answer c is correct. Windows 2000 DNS servers require static IP addresses. Answer a is incorrect because it is not necessary to implement AD with your DNS server; the two can remain separate. Answer b is incorrect because the AD DNS Configuration utility is fictitious. Answer d is incorrect because the question doesn't ask you to perform a search and this is not an automatic next step.

Question 28

Answer b is correct. The high-watermark table stores the update sequence number (USN) value for each DC to which it replicates. Answers a, c, and d are incorrect because these do not match the definition in the question nor are they true words for AD replication.

Question 29

Answer d is correct. The Security Configuration and Analysis tool is used to compare settings between your existing security policy and one of several predefined Microsoft security templates. Answers a, b, and c are all actual snap-in tools within the MMC, although they have different tasks. Answer a is incorrect because ADSI Edit allows you to edit your AD. Answer b is incorrect because IP Security Policy Management is used to implement IPSec policies for your VPN connections. Answer c is incorrect because security templates are static files that need to be used in conjunction with the proper tool provided.

Question 30

Answer c is correct. Assigned applications appear in the Start menu. Answers a and d are incorrect because these refer to fictitious terms for application policy. Answer b is incorrect because published applications do not appear in the Start menu.

Question 31

Answers b and d are correct. The two default groups for creating OUs are the Domain Admins and the Enterprise Admins groups. Answers a and c are incorrect because these groups do not have the rights to create OUs automatically.

Question 32

Answers a, b, and c are correct. These options are met by the solution presented. Answer d is incorrect because the F12 key, not the F11 key, is needed to start the installation and choose your predefined friendly name.

Question 33

Answer c is correct. This error message is usually the result of a corrupt Windows Installer file. To track down the possible problems, you need to establish the connectivity to the DNS server and then connectivity to the DCs within your domain. Answer a is incorrect because replication latency defines the time period when your AD hasn't completed replication of all changes. Answers b and d are incorrect because both are fictitious.

Question 34

Answer a is correct. The only administrative template that exists under User Configuration but not under Computer Configuration is Control Panel. Answers b, c, and d are incorrect because Network, Windows Components, and System do exist under both User Configuration and Computer Configuration.

Question 35

Answer b is correct. When you add DCs to a domain, you improve logon perfor-mance. However, the DCs will cause traffic on the domain because of replication of data between the DCs. Therefore, the more DCs that are on the domain, the more replication that will take place. Replication will use up network bandwidth. Answer a is incorrect because the more DCs that you add, the more this will increase bandwidth usage. Answer c is incorrect because you can have more than three domain controllers in a domain. Answer d is incorrect because promoting a server to be a DC does not require a reinstallation of the operating system.

Question 36

Answer d is correct. By adjusting the schedule of the site link, you can restrict or permit replication to take place at a certain time. Answer a is incorrect because replication frequency is the time interval a DC will wait before checking for changes on other DCs. Answer b is incorrect because replication cost refers to the amount of bandwidth the replication process will use. Answer c is incorrect because there is no such thing as a replication transport value.

Question 37

Answer d is correct. High Secure allows the highest level of security that the templates can provide and, in the process, can hinder performance and non–Windows 2000 compatibility, along with several other possible hindrances. An-swer a is incorrect because Basic templates provide default security policy. Answer b is incorrect because Compatible, which is one level above Basic, still allows for compatibility with applications. Answer c is incorrect because Secure allows for Windows compatibility.

Question 38

The correct answer is:

 Startup

 Logon

 Logoff

 Shutdown

Question 39

Answer a is correct. Roaming profiles allow users to log on to any system and have their personal settings follow. Answer b is incorrect because Folder Redirection redirects certain local folders to a server share without any kind of synchronization. Answer c is incorrect because My Briefcase was a primitive Windows 95 attempt at synchronizing files and folders. Answer d is incorrect because the Offline Folders feature provides the ability to have files and folders synchronized between server copies and local hard drive copies. This feature is used primarily by mobile users who work offline (off the network) frequently.

Question 40

Answer b is correct. You are allowed one Domain Naming Master and one Schema Master per forest. In addition, you need one PDC Emulator per domain, one Infrastructure Master per domain, and one RID Master per domain. In our scenario, we have two domain trees within a single forest and three child domains, a total of five domains. Therefore, b is the only correct answer, and answers a, c, and d are incorrect.

Question 41

Answer c is correct. The PDC Emulator handles backward-compatibility issues. Answer a is incorrect because the Schema Master is necessary to change the schema. Answer b is incorrect because the Infrastructure Master is used to handle reference to objects without them existing in the directory partitions. Answer d is incorrect because the Domain Naming Master enables all objects to be unique.

Question 42

Answer b is correct. The secedit utility enforces the policy change to either the machine or the user. Answer a is incorrect because ntdsutil is used for authoritative restores. Answer c is incorrect because Recovery Console is a command-line interface to help you recover from major problems. Answer d is incorrect because netdom helps you view and establish trust relationships through a command line.

Question 43

Answer b is correct. This is an example of a distinguished name. Answer a is incorrect because a user principal name would be similar to user@company.com. Answer c is incorrect because "LDAP names" is not a true term. Answer d is incorrect because a common name would be similar to Arnold Perez.

Question 44

Answer a is correct. The schema is the definition of all objects and their attributes. Answer b is incorrect because OUs are containers for delegation of authority. Answer c is incorrect because DNS is used for name to IP address mappings. Answer d is incorrect because latency is the delay that exists while directory information is updated.

Question 45

The correct answer is:

Tokyo

AD Integrated

Los Angeles

AD Integrated

London

AD Integrated

Miami

Secondary

New York

Caching

Glossary

· ·

access control entry (ACE)

An entry within an access control list that grants or denies permissions to users or groups for a given resource.

access control list (ACL)

A list that contains a set of access control entries that define an object's permission settings. ACLs enable administrators to explicitly control access to resources.

Active Directory (AD)

The Windows 2000 directory service that replaces the antiquated Windows NT domain structure. Active Directory forms the basis for centralized network management on Windows 2000 networks, providing a hierarchical view of network resources.

Active Directory Service Interfaces (ADSI)

A directory service model implemented as a set of Component Object Model (COM) interfaces. ADSI allows Windows applications to access Active Directory (AD), often through ActiveX interfaces such as VBScript.

Active Directory Users and Computers

The primary systems administrator utility for managing users, groups, and computers in a Windows 2000 domain, implemented as a Microsoft Management Console (MMC) snap-in.

Address (A) record

The most basic type of resource record on a Domain Name System (DNS) server; every client that registers with DNS has an associated A record that maps its name to its Internet Protocol (IP) address.

assigned applications

Through the Software Installation utility in Group Policy, administrators can assign applications to users. Assigned applications are always available to the user, even if the user attempts to uninstall them.

asynchronous processing

Asynchronous processing occurs when one task waits until another is finished before beginning. This type of processing is typically associated with scripts, such as a user logon script not running before the computer startup script has completed. Asynchronous processing is the default behavior in Windows 2000.

attribute

The basic unit of an object, an attribute is a single property that, through its values, defines an object. For example, an attribute of a standard user account is the account name.

auditing

A security process that tracks the usage of selected network resources, typically storing the results in a log file.

authentication

The process by which a user's logon credentials are validated by a server so that access to a network resource can be granted or denied.

AXFR

A Domain Name System (DNS) term that refers to a request from a primary server to one or more secondary servers for a full zone transfer.

backup domain controller (BDC)

A Windows NT 3.x and 4 server that contains a backup copy of the domain Security Accounts Manager (user account and security information). BDCs take the load off of the primary domain controller by servicing logon requests. Periodic synchronizing ensures that data between the primary domain controller (PDC) and backup domain controllers (BDCs) remains consistent.

baseline

A term associated with performance monitoring, a baseline is the initial result of monitoring by which all future results are measured.

bridgehead server

The contact point for the exchange of directory information among Active Directory (AD) sites.

caching

The process by which name resolution query results are stored to speed up future name resolution for the same destinations.

checkpoint file

A file that indicates the location of the last information successfully written from the transaction logs to the database. In a data recovery scenario, the checkpoint file indicates where the recovery or replaying of data should begin.

circular logging

When a log file fills up, it is overwritten with new data rather than having a new log file created. This conserves disk space but can result in data loss in a disaster recovery scenario.

Computer Configuration

The portion of a Group Policy Object (GPO) that allows for computer policies to be configured and applied.

container

An object in Active Directory (AD) that is capable of holding other objects. An example of a container is the Users folder in Active Directory Users and Computers.

convergence

The process of stabilization after network changes occur. Often associated with routing or replication, convergence ensures that each router or server contains consistent information.

counters

The metrics that are used in performance monitoring, counters are what you are actually monitoring. An example of a counter for a Central Processing Unit (CPU) object is %Processing Time.

CScript

The command-line executable for Windows Script Host (WSH).

dcpromo.exe

The command-line utility that is used to promote a Windows 2000 server to a domain controller.

delegation

The process of offloading the responsibility for a given task or set or tasks to another user or group. Delegation in Windows 2000 usually involves granting permission to someone else to perform a specific administrative task, such as creating computer accounts.

directory

A database that contains any number of different types of data. In Windows 2000, the Active Directory (AD) contains information about objects, such as computers, users, groups, and printers, in the domain.

directory service

A service that provides the methods of storing directory data and making that data available to other directory objects.

Directory System Agent (DSA)

The DSA makes data within Active Directory (AD) accessible to applications that want it, acting as a liaison between the directory database and the applications.

disk quota

An administrative limit set on the server storage space that can be used by any particular user.

distinguished name

The name that uniquely identifies an object, using the relative distinguished name, domain name, and the container holding the object. An example is CN=WWillis,CN=Inside-Corner,CN=COM. This refers to the WWillis user account in the inside-corner.com domain.

Distributed File System (Dfs)

A Windows 2000 service that allows resources from multiple server locations to be presented through Active Directory (AD) as a contiguous set of files and folders, resulting in more ease of use of network resources for users.

distribution point

The network shared location for software to be stored for the purpose of making it available for installation to users.

domain

A collection of Windows 2000 computers, users, and groups that share a common directory database. Domains are defined by an administrator.

domain controller (DC)

A server that is capable of performing authentication. In Windows 2000, a domain controller holds a copy of the Active Directory (AD) database.

domain local group

This group can contain other domain local groups from its own domain, as well as global groups from any domain in the forest. Domain local groups can be used to assign permissions for resources located in the same domain as the group.

Domain Name System (DNS)

A hierarchical name resolution system that resolves hostnames into Internet Protocol (IP) addresses and vice versa.

Dynamic Domain Name System (DDNS)

An extension of Domain Name System (DNS) that allows Windows 2000 Professional systems to automatically register their A records with DNS at the time they obtain an Internet Protocol (IP) address from a Dynamic Host Configuration Protocol (DHCP) server.

Dynamic Host Configuration Protocol (DHCP)

A service that allows an administrator to specify a range of valid Internet Protocol (IP) addresses to be used on a network, as well as exceptions (addresses that should be reserved and not given out dynamically). These addresses are automatically given out to computers configured to use DHCP as they boot up on the network, saving the administrator from having to configure static Internet Protocol (IP) addresses on each individual network device.

Encrypting File System (EFS)

A Windows 2000 feature that allows files and folders to be encrypted on NTFS (NT File System) partitions, protecting them from being able to be read by other people.

Extensible Storage Engine (ESE)

The Active Directory (AD) database engine, ESE is an improved version of the older Jet database technology.

File Replication Service (FRS)

A service that provides multimaster replication between specified domain controllers within an Active Directory (AD) tree.

File Transfer Protocol (FTP)

A standard Transmission Control Protocol/Internet Protocol (TCP/IP) utility that allows for the transfer of files from an FTP server to a machine running the FTP client.

firewall

A hardware and software security system that functions to limit access to network resources across subnets. Typically, a firewall is used between a private network and the Internet to prevent outsiders from accessing the private network and limiting what Internet services users of the private network can access.

flat namespace
A namespace that cannot be partitioned to produce additional domains. Windows NT 4 and earlier domains were examples of flat namespaces, as opposed to the Windows 2000 hierarchical namespace.

Folder Redirection
A Windows 2000 feature that allows special folders such as My Documents on local Windows 2000 Professional system hard drives to be redirected to a shared network location.

forest
A grouping of Active Directory (AD) trees that have a trust relationship among them. Forests can consist of noncontiguous namespaces, and unlike domains and trees, they do not have to be given specific names.

forward lookup query
A Domain Name System (DNS) name resolution process by which a hostname is resolved to an Internet Protocol (IP) address.

fully qualified domain name (FQDN)
A Domain Name System (DNS) domain name that unambiguously describes the location of the host within a domain tree. An example of an FQDN is the computer www.inside-corner.com.

Global Catalog (GC)
A catalog that contains a partial replica of every Windows 2000 domain within the Active Directory (AD), enabling users to find any object in the directory. The partial replica contains the most commonly used attributes of an object, as well as information on how to locate a complete replica elsewhere in the directory if needed.

Global Catalog server
The Windows 2000 server that holds the Global Catalog (GC) for the forest.

global group
A group that can contain users from the same domain in which the global group is located. Global groups can be added to domain local groups to control access to network resources.

Globally Unique Identifier (GUID)
A hexadecimal number supplied by the manufacturer of a product that uniquely identifies the hardware or software. A GUID is in the form of 8 characters followed by 4 characters, followed by 4 more, then by another 4, and finally by 12. For example, {15DEF489-AE24-10BF-C11A-00BB844CE637} is a valid format for a GUID (braces included).

Group Policy
The Windows 2000 feature that allows for policy creation that affects domain users and computers. Policies can be anything from desktop settings to application assignment to security settings and more.

Group Policy Editor
The Microsoft Management Console (MMC) snap-in that is used to modify the settings of a Group Policy Object (GPO).

Group Policy Object (GPO)

A collection of policies that apply to a specific target, such as the domain itself (default domain policy) or an Organizational Unit (OU). GPOs are modified through the Group Policy Editor to define policy settings.

hierarchical namespace

A namespace, such as with Domain Name System (DNS), that can be partitioned out in the form of a tree. This allows great flexibility in using a domain name, because any number of subdomains can be created under a parent domain.

host ID

The portion of an Internet Protocol (IP) address that defines the host, as determined by the subnet mask. For example, a host has an Internet Protocol (IP) address of 192.168.1.20 and a subnet mask of 255.255.255.0. The host ID for this would be 20.

HOSTS

A static file that was the primary means for Transmission Control Protocol/Internet Protocol (TCP/IP) name resolution prior to Domain Name System (DNS), the HOSTS file contains a list of host-to-Internet Protocol (IP) address mappings and must exist on every host computer that participates on a network. It has been largely replaced by the more manageable DNS service on all but the smallest of networks.

image

The installation source for Windows 2000 Professional and any optional applications created through the Remote Installation Services (RIS) RIPrep utility.

inheritance

The process by which an object obtains settings information from a parent object.

IntelliMirror

A collection of Windows 2000 technologies that provide for a comprehensive change and control management system.

IXFR

A Domain Name System (DNS) process by which a primary DNS server requests an incremental zone transfer from one or more secondary servers.

JavaScript (JScript)

An ActiveX scripting language that can be used in Windows 2000 with the Windows Script Host (WSH) to run more complicated scripts than what has been available in the past through batch files.

just-in-time (JIT)

Technology that allows software features to be updated at the time they are accessed. Whereas in the past missing application features would need to be manually installed, JIT technology allows the features to be installed on the fly as they are accessed, with no other intervention required.

Kerberos

An Internet standard security protocol that has largely replaced the older LAN Manager user authentication mechanism from earlier Windows NT versions.

Knowledge Consistency Checker (KCC)
A Windows 2000 service that functions to ensure that consistent database information is kept across all domain controllers. It attempts to make sure that replication can always take place.

latency
The delay that occurs in replication from the time a change is made to one replica to the time that change is applied to all other replicas in the directory.

Lightweight Directory Access Protocol (LDAP)
The Windows 2000 protocol that allows access to Active Directory (AD). LDAP is an Internet standard for accessing directory services.

LMHOSTS
A static file used for NetBIOS (Network Basic Input/Output System) name resolution. Similar to a HOSTS file, LMHOSTS needed to exist on every individual computer on a network, making it increasingly difficult to keep up to date as the size of networks grew. LMHOSTS was essentially replaced by Windows Internet Naming Service (WINS) on Windows networks prior to Windows 2000.

local area network (LAN)
A network where all hosts are connected over fast connections (4Mbps or greater for Token Ring, 10Mbps or better for Ethernet).

local Group Policy Objects
Objects that exist on the local Windows 2000 system and take precedence over site, domain, and Organizational Unit (OU) applied Group Policy Objects (GPOs).

Mail Exchanger (MX) record
A Domain Name System (DNS) record that defines an email server.

Microsoft Management Console (MMC)
An extensible management framework that provides a common look and feel to all Windows 2000 utilities.

mixed mode
This mode allows Windows NT 4 domain controllers to exist and function within a Windows 2000 domain. This is the default setting when Active Directory (AD) is installed, though it can be changed to native mode.

multimaster replication
A replication model in which any domain controller will replicate data to any other domain controller. The default behavior in Windows 2000, this contrasts with the single-master replication model of Windows NT 4, in which a primary domain controller (PDC) contains the master copy of everything, and backup domain controllers (BDCs) contain backup copies.

namespace
A collection of resources that have been defined using some common name. A Domain Name System (DNS) namespace is hierarchical and can be partitioned, whereas Windows NT 4 and earlier uses a flat namespace.

name resolution

The process of resolving a hostname into a format that can be understood by computers. This is typically an Internet Protocol (IP) address but could also be a Media Access Control (MAC) address on non-TCP/IP (Transmission Control Protocol/Internet Protocol) networks.

native mode

In this mode, all domain controllers in a domain have been upgraded to Windows 2000 and there are no longer any NT 4 domain controllers. An administrator explicitly puts Active Directory (AD) into native mode, at which time it cannot be returned to mixed mode without removing and reinstalling AD.

Network Basic Input/Output System (NetBIOS)

An application programming interface (API) used on Windows NT 4 and earlier networks by services requesting and providing name resolution and network data management.

network ID

The portion of an Internet Protocol (IP) address that defines the network, as determined by the subnet mask. For example, if a host has an Internet Protocol (IP) address of 192.168.1.20 and a subnet mask of 255.255.255.0, the network ID would be 192.168.1.

network operating system (NOS)

A generic term that applies to any operating system with built-in networking capabilities. All Windows operating systems beginning with Windows 95 have been true network operating systems.

nonlocal Group Policy Objects

Group Policy Objects (GPOs) that are stored in Active Directory (AD) rather than on the local machine. These can be site-, domain-, or Organizational Unit (OU) level GPOs.

NSLOOKUP

A Transmission Control Protocol/Internet Protocol (TCP/IP) utility used in troubleshooting DNS name resolution problems.

NT File System (NTFS)

The Windows NT/2000 file system that supports a much more robust feature set than FAT16 or FAT32 (which are used on Windows 9x). It is recommended to use NT File System (NTFS) whenever possible on Windows 2000 systems.

object

A distinct entity represented by a series of attributes within Active Directory (AD). An object can be a user, computer, folder, file, printer, and so on.

object identifier

A number that uniquely identifies an object class or attribute. In the United States, the American National Standards Institute (ANSI) issues object identifiers that take the form of a x.x.x.x dotted decimal format. Microsoft, for example, was issued the root object identifier of 1.2.840.113556, from which it can create further subobject identifiers.

operations master

A Windows 2000 domain controller that has been assigned one or more of the special Active Directory (AD) domain roles, such as Schema Master, Domain Naming Master, PDC (primary domain controller) Emulator, Infrastructure Master, and Relative ID Master.

Organizational Unit (OU)

An Active Directory (AD) container object that allows an administrator to logically group users, groups, computers, and other OUs into administrative units.

package

A collection of software compiled into a distributable form, such as a Windows Installer (.msi) package created with WinInstall.

parent-child trust relationship

The relationship where a child object trusts its parent object, and a parent object is trusted by all child objects under it. Active Directory (AD) automatically creates two-way trust relationships between parent and child objects.

patching

The process of modifying or updating software packages.

PING

A Transmission Control Protocol/Internet Protocol (TCP/IP) utility that tests for basic connectivity between the client machine running PING and any other TCP/IP host.

policy

Settings and rules that are applied to users or computers, usually Group Policy in Windows 2000 and System Policy in Windows NT 4.

preboot execution environment (PXE)

A set of industry standards that allow for network commands to be run on a client computer before it has booted up in a traditional manner. Used with Remote Installation Services (RIS) in Windows 2000 to install Windows 2000 Professional images on client computers.

primary domain controller (PDC)

A Windows NT 4 and earlier server that contains the master copy of the domain database. Primary domain controllers (PDCs) authenticate user logon requests and track security-related changes within the domain.

public key infrastructure (PKI)

An industry-standard technology that allows for the establishment of secure communication between hosts based on a public key/private key or certificate-based system.

published applications

Through the Software Installation utility in Group Policy, administrators can publish applications to users. Published applications appear in Add/Remove Programs and can be optionally installed by the user.

Registry

A data repository stored on each computer that contains information about that computer's configuration. The Registry is organized into a hierarchical tree and is made up of hives, keys, and values.

relative distinguished name (RDN)

The part of a Domain Name System (DNS) name that defines the host. For example, in the fully qualified domain name (FQDN) www.inside-corner.com, www is the relative distinguished name.

Remote Installation Services (RIS)

A Windows 2000 optional component that allows for the remote installation of Windows 2000 Professional onto compatible client computers.

replica

A copy of any given Active Directory (AD) object. Each copy of an object stored on multiple domain controllers is a replica.

replication

The process of copying data from one Windows 2000 domain controller to another. Replication is a process managed by an administrator and typically occurs automatically whenever changes are made to a replica of an object.

Request For Comments (RFC)

Official documents that specify Internet standards for the Transmission Control Protocol/Internet Protocol (TCP/IP) protocol.

resource records

Standard database record types used in Domain Name System (DNS) zone database files. Common types of resource records include Address (A), Mail Exchanger (MX), Start of

Authority (SOA), and Name Server (NS), among others.

return on investment (ROI)

A business term that seeks to determine the amount of financial gain that occurs as a result of a certain expenditure. Many information technology (IT) personnel today are faced with the prospect of justifying IT expenses in terms of return on investment (ROI).

reverse lookup query

A Domain Name System (DNS) name resolution process by which an Internet Protocol (IP) address is resolved to a hostname.

root server

A Domain Name System (DNS) server that is authoritative for the root zone of a namespace.

router

A dedicated network hardware appliance or server running routing software and multiple network cards. Routers join dissimilar network topologies (such as Ethernet to Frame Relay) or simply segment networks into multiple subnets.

scalability

A measurement (often subjective) of how well a resource such as a server can expand to accommodate growing needs.

schema

In Active Directory (AD), a description of object classes and attributes that the object class can possess.

Schema Master

The Windows 2000 domain controller that has been assigned the operations master role to control all schema updates within a forest.

security identifier (SID)

A number that uniquely identifies a user, group, or computer account. Every account is issued when created, and if the account is later deleted and re-created with the same name, it will have a different SID. Once a SID is used in a domain, it can never be used again.

security templates

Collections of standard settings that can be applied administratively to give a consistent level of security to a system.

Single Instance Store (SIS)

A Remote Installation Services (RIS) component that combines duplicate files to reduce storage requirements on the RIS server.

single-master operations

Certain Active Directory (AD) operations that are allowed to occur only in one place at any given time (as opposed to being allowed to occur in multiple locations simultaneously). Examples of single-master operations include schema modification, primary domain controller (PDC) elections, and infrastructure changes.

site

A well-connected Transmission Control Protocol/Internet Protocol (TCP/IP) subnet.

site link

A connection between sites that is used to join multiple locations together.

slow link

A connection between sites that is not fast enough to provide full functionality in an acceptable time frame. Site connections below 512Kbps are defined as slow links in Windows 2000.

snap-in

A component that can be added or removed from a Microsoft Management Console (MMC) to provide specific functionality. The Windows 2000 administrative tools are implemented as snap-ins.

software installation

A Group Policy component that allows administrators to optionally assign or publish applications to be available to users and computers.

Start of Authority (SOA) record

The first record created on a Domain Name System (DNS) server, the SOA record defines the starting point for a zone's authority.

static IP address

Also called a *static address*, this is where a network device (such as a server) is manually configured with an Internet Protocol (IP) address that doesn't change, rather than obtaining an address automatically from a Dynamic Host Configuration Protocol (DHCP) server.

store

Implemented using the Extensible Storage Engine (ESE), a store is the physical storage of each Active Directory (AD) replica.

subnet

A collection of hosts on a Transmission Control Protocol/Internet Protocol (TCP/IP) network that are not separated by any routers. A basic corporate local area network (LAN) with one location would be referred to as a subnet when it is connected by a router to another network, such as that of an Internet Service Provider.

subnet mask

This defines where the network ID ends and the host ID begins in an Internet Protocol (IP) address. Subnet masks can result in very basic to very complex network configurations, depending on their value.

synchronous processing

Synchronous processing occurs when one task does not wait for another to complete before it begins, but rather runs concurrently. Typically associated with scripts in Windows 2000, such as a user logon script running without waiting for the computer startup script to finish.

system policies

Windows NT 4 Registry-based policy settings, which have largely been replaced in Windows 2000 by Group Policy. System policies can still be created using poledit.exe, however, for backward-compatibility with non-Windows 2000 clients.

Systems Management Server (SMS)

A product in Microsoft's BackOffice server line that provides more extensive software distribution, metering, inventorying, and auditing than what is available strictly through IntelliMirror.

time-to-live (TTL)

The amount of time a packet destined for a host will exist before it is deleted from the network. TTLs are used to prevent networks from becoming congested with packages that cannot reach their destinations.

total cost of ownership (TCO)

A change and control management concept that many information technology (IT) professionals are being forced to become more aware of. TCO refers to the combined hard and soft costs (initial price and support costs) of owning a given resource.

transitive trust

An automatically created trust in Windows 2000 that exists between domain trees within a forest and domains within a tree. Transitive trusts are two-way trust relationships.

Transmission Control Protocol/Internet Protocol (TCP/IP)

The standard protocol for communicating on the Internet and the default protocol in Windows 2000.

tree

A collection of Windows 2000 domains that are connected through transitive trusts and share a common Global Catalog (GC) and schema.

Domains within a tree must form a contiguous namespace.

universal group

A new Windows 2000 security group that can be used anywhere within a domain tree or forest, the only caveat being that universal groups can be used only when Windows 2000 has been converted to native mode.

update sequence number

A 64-bit number that keeps track of changes as they are written to copies of the Active Directory (AD). As changes are made, this number increments by 1.

User Configuration

The portion of a Group Policy Object (GPO) that allows for user policy settings to be configured and applied.

user profiles

These profiles contain settings that define the user environment, typically applied when the user logs on to the system.

Visual Basic Script (VBScript)

An ActiveX scripting language that can be used in Windows 2000 with the Windows Script Host (WSH) to run more complicated scripts than what has been available in the past through batch files. Recently, VBScript has been in the news frequently because of its use in creating email viruses.

well-connected

Description of a network that contains only fast connections between domains and hosts. The definition of "fast" is somewhat

subjective and may vary from organization to organization.

wide area network (WAN)

Multiple networks connected by slow connections between routers; WAN connections are typically 1.5Mbps or less.

Windows Internet Naming System (WINS)

A dynamic name resolution system that resolves NetBIOS (Network Basic Input/Output System) names to Internet Protocol (IP) addresses on Windows Transmission Control Protocol/Internet Protocol (TCP/IP) networks. With Windows 2000, WINS is being phased out in favor of Domain Name System (DNS).

Windows Management Instrumentation (WMI)

A Windows 2000 management infrastructure for monitoring and controlling system resources.

Windows Script Host (WSH)

WSH enables the running of VBScript or JavaScript scripts natively on a Windows system, offering increased power and flexibility over traditional batch files.

WinInstall

An optional utility that ships with Windows 2000 server and can be used to create Windows Installer packages.

WScript

The Windows interface to Windows Script Host.

X.500

A set of standards developed by the International Organization for Standardization (ISO) that define distributed directory services.

zone

A subtree of the Domain Name System (DNS) database that can be managed as a single, separate entity from the rest of the DNS namespace.

zone file

The Domain Name System (DNS) database, traditionally stored as a text file on the primary server and replicated to secondary servers. With Windows 2000, the zone file can be optionally integrated into Active Directory (AD).

zone transfer

The Domain Name System (DNS) process by which zone information is replicated between primary and secondary servers.

Index

Bold page numbers indicate sample exam questions.

A

A records, 58, **66**
Access control entries. *See* ACEs.
Access tokens, 131–132, **150**
Account Lockout security category, **204–205**
Account Policies security category, 191
ACEs, 130–131
Active Directory Domains and Trusts tool. *See* AD Domains and Trusts tool.
Active Directory Installation Wizard. *See* AD Installation Wizard.
Active Directory Sites and Services tool. *See* AD Sites and Services tool.
Active Directory Users and Computers tool. *See* AD Users and Computers tool.
"Active Directory will not allow the package to be deployed" error message, 220
Active Directory. *See* AD.
AD, 24, **34**, **66**, 72, 346
    administrative control delegation, 130
    Allow permission, **146**
    applications published to, 218–219
    attribute alteration conflicts, 275
    authentication, 25
    authoritative restoration, 327, **375**
    Builtin container, **177**
    centralized management, 32
    change notification process, 274
    Computer container, **177**
    contiguous namespaces, **372**

    database file deletions, **335**
    database file placement, **95**
    database log, 73
    database management recommendations, 330–331
    database relocation, 320, 327–328, **338**
    defragmentation, 321–322, 328–330, **339**
    delegation of control, 32–33
    Deny permission, **146**
    distinguished names, 26, **37**
    domain controllers, 28, 30
    domain replication, **42**
    domains, 27–29
    duplicate name conflicts, 275–276
    event logs, 84
    Extensible Storage Engine, 321
    folder publishing, 236–237
    folder structure, 73
    ForeignSecurityPrincipals container, **177**
    garbage collection, 322, **337**, **340**
    Group Policy and, 24
    GuiRunOnce key, 86–87
    installation, 73, 83, **98**, **371**
    installation troubleshooting, 82–83, **94**
    integrated server storage, **67**
    integrated zones, 51–52, 55, **65**, 89–90, **97**, **372**
    IntelliMirror and, 211
    interoperability of, 24, **36**
    latency, **378**
    LDAP support, 25

log file placement, **95**
logical structure, 27–30
LostAndFound container, **177**
naming standards, 26
network administration with, 31–33
nonauthoritative restoration, 326
object deletions, **374**
object ownership, 141
object permissions, 132–140
object relocation conflicts, 275
object security, 130–132
objects, 25
offline defragmentation, **336**
Organizational Units, 28
originating updates, 273, **291**
permissions, 78, **147–148**
physical structure, 30–31
printer publishing with, **238**
printQueue object, 233
records, 108
relative distinguished names, 26
removal of, 84–85
removal troubleshooting, 85
replicated updates, 273, **291**
restoring, 325–327
RIS dependence, **364**
root domains, **40**
schema, 25, **35**, **37**
security boundaries, **38**
security principals, 302
single sign-on, 102, **120**
sites, 31
Software Installation extension and, **224**
standard zones, **65**
System container, **177**
SYSVOL folder, 73, 84, **94**
tombstoning, 322
transaction log, 73
two-way transitive trusts, **41**
unattended installation, 86–89
Users container, **177**
AD Domains and Trusts tool, **96**, 105, **264**
external trust creation, 255
shortcut trust creation with, 252
AD Installation Wizard, 74–79, 84–85, 93, 251–252
preinstallation checks, 80–81
schema directory partition creation, 81
AD Integrated server, **387**

AD Sites and Services tool, 261, **377**
AD Users and Computers tool, 92, **96**, 108, 110, **147**, 168, **178**, **238**, **313**, **367**
publishing folders with, 236
publishing printers with, 233
RIS settings management with, 360–363
taskpad view of, 145
Adaptive testing exams, 13, 17–18
Add/Remove Programs applet, **225**
Address records. *See* A records.
.adm file extension, 182
ADM files, 183–187
Administrative Templates, 182
adding, 187
Computer Configuration container, 189
container, 164
within GPOs, 188–191
removing, 187
User Configuration container, 189
Administrative Tools, **150**
delegation of, 142–145
installation of, 144
MMC consoles, 142–143
taskpads, 144–145
Administrative templates, **384**
adpromo.txt file, **93**
ADSIEdit, **337**
AGDLP acronym, 117
AGUDLP acronym, 118
Allow permissions, 135, **146**
Applications
assigned, **382**
uninstalling from user workstation, 222
Apply Group Policy permissions, **175**
Assigned applications, 218, **225**, **382**
Attribute level replication, 276
Auditing security category, **204–205**
Authoritative primary servers, 49
Authoritative restoration, 327, **375**
AutoConfigDNS key, 88
Automatic two-way trusts, 246

B

Backup domain controllers. *See* BDCs.
Backups, 323–325, **333**
Basic security template, 193, **206**
BDCs, 90
BIND updates, **371**
BINL, 348–349

Block Policy Inheritance, 170, 172, **176**
Boot Information Negotiation Layer.
    See BINL.
Bridgehead servers, 50, 282
Build-list-and-reorder questions, 3, 6–8
Built-in user accounts, 102, **122**
Builtin container, **177**

C

Caching servers, **387**
Caching-only name-servers, 49–50
Caching-only servers, **377**
"Cannot prepare the package for
    deployment" error message, 221
Canonical Name records.
    See CNAME records.
CATEGORY keyword, 185, **202**
Change notification process, 274, **291**
Change Operations Master dialog box, 305
Child domains, **93**, 247–250
    creating, 248–249
    universal group creation in, **264–265**
ChildName key, 88
CLASS keyword, 185, **202**
Client Installation Wizard, 348
CNAME records, 59
Common.adm template, 183, **203**
Compatible security template, 193
Computer Configuration container, 163
    Administrative Templates, **177**, 189,
        204
    Windows Settings node, 191
Computers container, **177**
Conf.adm template, 183
Configuration partitions, 279, **294**, **380**
Contiguous namespaces, 29, 53, **372**
Control Panel template, **384**
Copy Object-User Wizard, 113
Create All Child Objects permission, 132,
    147
Create-a-tree question format, 3, 8–10
CreateOrJoin key, 88
CScript.exe file, 196, **203**
Csvde utility, 106–108, **120**

D

DACL, 130–131, **149**, 172
DatabasePath key, 88–89
dcpromo.exe file, 65, 87, **93**
DCs, 28, 30, **39**, 72, 131, 167, 279–280
    access denied error message, 82
    adding to domains, 244

backing up, 323
bandwidth usage considerations, **384**
fault-tolerant replicas, 81
high-watermark table, **381**
installing, 74–79
replication partners, 279
selecting for replication, **289–290**
DDNS, 59. *See also* DNS.
    dynamic updates, 60
    secure updates, 60
    updates, 60
Defragmentation, 321–322, 328–330, **339**
    offline mode, 329–330
    online mode, 329
Delegation of authority, 135–136.
    See also Permissions.
    documentation of, 136
    Domain Administrators group, 136
    at OU level, **146**
    at property level, 136
    at task level, 136
Delegation of Control Wizard, 168, **178**,
    376
    common task delegation with, 137
    customized task creation in, 137–138
Delete All Child Objects permission, 132,
    147
Deny permissions, 135, **146**
Deploy Software dialog box, 214
Dfs, 281
DHCP, 52, 346, **364**, **374**
DHCP MMC utility, **368**
Direct replication partners, 279
Directory partitions, 279–280
Directory Services Restore Mode, 77
Discretionary access control list. *See* DACL.
Distinguished names, 26, **37**, **387**
Distributed file system. *See* Dfs.
Distribution groups, 115
Distribution points, 216
DNS, 29, 46, 72, 74, 346. *See also* DDNS.
    AD integrated zone replication,
        51-52, 55
    Address records, 58
    BIND updates, **371**
    caching-only name-servers, 49–50
    caching-only servers, **377**
    Canonical Name records, 59
    configuration, **5**, 55–56, **68**
    contiguous namespaces, 53
    domain name creation, 52
    dynamic updates, **67**, 79

forward lookup zones, 56, **65**
forwarding servers, 50–51
full zone transfer, 54
incremental zone transfer, 54–55
installation, **5**, 55, **65**, **68**
IP address host name resolution, 62–63
logging, 62
Mail Exchanger records, 59
Microsoft Management Console, 56
Name Server records, 58
network client types, 52
NSLOOKUP tool, 62–64
Pointer records, 59
preinstallation analysis, 48
primary DNS servers, 49
primary server storage, **67**
recursive queries, **69**
resource records, 57–58
reverse lookup zones, 57
secondary servers, 49, **67**
server type selection, 79
Service records, 59
site structure, 48
standard primary zones, **69**
Start of Authority records, 58
static IP addresses, 52, **65**, **381**
structure, **387**
troubleshooting, 61–64
WINS and, 47
zones, 49, 53–55
Domain Admins group, 136, 142, **148**, **312**, **382**
Domain Controllers. *See* DCs.
Domain-level GPOs, **174**
Domain Name Service. *See* DNS.
Domain Name System. *See* DNS.
Domain Naming Master role, 299–200, 309, **310**, **311**
Domain partition, 279, **380**
Domain SID, 302–303
Domain trees, 245, **268**, **373**
Domain user accounts, 102, **122**
Domain-level operations master roles, 304–305
DomainNetBiosName key, 89
Domains, 72
  automatic two-way trusts, 246
  backward compatibility, **95**
  child domains, **93**, 247–250
  contiguous namespaces, 29

DC additions to, 244
Domains object, **380**
empty root domains, 249–250, **267**
fault-tolerant replicas, 81
forest root domains, 72–73, 247–248
fully qualified domain names, 47
group nesting, **99**
mixed mode, 90, **95**, **372**
multiple DCs in, 81
native mode, 90–91
Organizational Units, 91–92
relative distinguished names, 47
replication, **42**
root domains, 46, 72
schemas, 246
second-level domains, 46
SID history, **99**
top-level domains, 46
trees, 28–29
trusts, 246
two-way transitive trusts, **41**
universal groups, **99**
Drag-and-drop question format.
  See Select-and-place question format.
Duplicate user account names, **123**
Dynamic DNS. *See* DDNS.
Dynamic Host Configuration Protocol
  Microsoft Management Console.
  See DHCP MMC.
Dynamic Host Configuration Protocol.
  See DHCP.

E

edb.chk file, 83, 321–322
edb.log file, 83, **334**
edb*.log file, 321
Empty root domains, 249–250, **267**
END POLICY keyword, **202**
Enterprise Admins group, 250, **382**
ESE, 321
Event Log security category, 191
Event logs, 84
Exam
  adaptive testing, 13, 17–18
  build-list-and-reorder questions, 3, 6–8
  case studies, 13, 15
  create-a-tree question format, 3, 8–10
  exhibits, 4
  fixed-length, 13, 15–16
  guessing, 17–18
  layout, 4

multiple-choice questions, 3, 5
practice exam, 19
question-handling strategies, 16, 18–19
revisiting questions in, 15–16, 19
select-and-place question format, 3,
    11–12
Self-Assessment, 2
short-form, 14–17
simulations, 13
test-taking strategies, 14–19
testing center, 3
testing formats, 12–14
EXPLAIN keyword, 185, **202**
Explicit trust, 252
Extensible Storage Engine. *See* ESE.
External trust, 254–256

F

"The feature you are trying to install
    cannot be found in the source direc-
    tory" error message, 221
File distribution points, 216
File Replication Service. *See* FRS.
File System security category, 192
Find Users, Contacts, And Groups dialog
    box, 114–115
Fixed-length exams, 13, 15–16
Folders
    publishing, 236–237, **240**
    redirection, 199–201, **205**, 211
ForeignSecurityPrincipals container, **177**
Forest root domain, 72–73
Forest-level operations master roles,
    305–306
Forests, 29, 250–253, **269**. *See also* Trees.
    creating, 251–252
    design decisions, 250–251
    Domain Naming Master, 300
    domain trees connected as, **268**
    establishing transitive trust across,
        259–260
    forest root domains, 247–248
    multiple forests, 253–256, **265**
    security boundaries, **269**
Forward lookup zones, 53, 56
Forwarding DNS servers, 50–51
    exclusive mode, 51
    nonexclusive mode, 51
"404 File not found" error, 20
FQDNs, 47
FRS, 199, **207**
FSMO role servers, **386**

Full Control permissions, 132, **147**
Full zone transfer, 54
Fully qualified domain names. *See* FQDNs.

G

Garbage collection, 322, **337**, **340**
GC servers, 29–30, **39**, 260–263, **267**,
    280, **373**
    additions, 261
    logon validation, 260
Global Catalog servers. *See* GC servers.
Global GPOs, 156
Global user groups, 115, **375**
Globally Unique Identifier. *See* GUID.
GPC, **374**
GPOs, 155, **380**
    administrative templates, 188–191
    creating, 158–159, 168
    cross-domain links, 167
    disabling, 172
    disabling unused portions of, 173, **177**
    domain level, **174**
    editing, 160, 169
    flow control, **373**
    global, 156
    linking, 164–165
    local, 157
    multiple links, 165–166
    No Override, **373**
    nonlocal, 156
    refresh rate policy, **378**
    Root container, **174–175**
    site level, **174**
    software deployment and, **228**
    storage domain, 165–166
    SYSVOL folder, 323
    unfiltered, 156
    User Configuration container,
        174–175
GPT, **374**
Group nesting, 90, **99**, 262–263
Group Policy, 155, 158
    Active Directory and, 24
    centralized management with, 32
    Computer Configuration container,
        177, **204**
    containers, 156
    filtering, 172–173
    Folder Redirection feature, 199–201,
        205
    inheritance, 170, **176**
    IntelliMirror and, 211

link management, 168
processing sequence, **176**
RIS client option management with, 359–360
RIS dependence, **364**
script assignment, 197–199
security settings management with, 191–194
Software Installation extension and, **224**
system policy compared to, 157, **179**
task delegation, 167, **178**
troubleshooting, **383**
User Configuration container, **177, 204**
Group Policy Container. *See* GPC.
Group Policy Editor, 160–162
accessing, 163
Administrative Templates container, 164
Computer Configuration container, 163
Root container, 163
security categories, **204**
Software Settings container, 163
User Configuration container, 163
Windows Settings container, 163
Group Policy Objects. *See* GPOs.
Group Policy Template. *See* GPT.
Groups, 102, 115–116
AGDLP acronym, 117
AGUDLP acronym, 118
distribution groups, 115
global groups, 115
local groups, 115
naming scheme, 119
nesting, 116, 118
security groups, 115
in single domain, 117
structured use of, 116–117
type definition, 116
universal groups, 115, **269**
of user accounts, 102
GUID, 276
locating, 363
numbers, 156–157
GuiRunOnce key, 86–87, **97**

H

High Secure security template, 193
High Secure template, **385**
Hops, 274
HOSTS file, 46, **68**

I

Incremental zone transfer, 54–55
Inetres.adm template, 183, **203**
Infrastructure Master role, 299, 302–303, 309, **310, 316**
Inheritance, 138–140, 155, 170, **369**
Block Policy Inheritance, **176**
No Override, **176**
removing, **148**
Integrated zones, 55, **65**, 89–90, **97**
IntelliMirror, **223–224**, 344
Active Directory and, 211
benefits of, 154
Data Management feature, 210
Desktop Settings Management feature, 210
Folder Redirection, 211
Group Policy and, 211
Offline Folders, 211, **227**
Remote Installation Services feature, 211
roaming user profiles, 211
Software Installation and Maintenance feature, 210–213
Windows 2000 support of, **224–225**
Intersite Topology Generator. *See* ISTG.
Invocation ID properties, 276
IP address host name resolution, 62–63
IP Security Policies on Active Directory security category, 192
ISTG, 282, **292**

J

JavaScript, 195
JIT technology, 213
.js file extension, 195
Just-in-time technology. *See* JIT technology.

K

KCC, 280, **292, 379**
Kerberos v5, 256–260, **268**
KEYNAME keyword, 185
Knowledge Consistency Checker. *See* KCC.

L

Latency, 274, **378**
LDAP, 25, 109
Active Directory support of, 25
naming standards, 26
Ldifde utility, 106, 108–109
Lightweight Directory Access Protocol. *See* LDAP.

Links, 283
LMHOSTS resolution method, **68**
Local GPOs, 157
Local groups, 115
Local Policies security category, 191
Local user accounts, 102, **122**
Logoff scripts, 195, **385**
Logon names, **127**
Logon scripts, 195, **385**
Logon validation, 260–261
LogPath key, 89
Loose network consistency, 272
LostAndFound container, **177**

M

Mail Exchanger records. *See* MX records.
Microsoft Certified Professional Web site, 20
Microsoft Management Console. *See* MMC.
Mixed mode domains, 90, **95, 372**
MMC, 56, 142–143
    as AD Editor, 82
    Author mode, 142
    creating, 143
    distributing, 143
    User mode, 142
.msc file extension, **150**, 162
Multiple domains, establishing transitive trust across, 258
Multiple forests, 253–256, **265**
Multiple-choice questions, 3, 5
Multiple-master replication, 272, **289**
MX records, 59

N

Name Server records. *See* NS records.
Native domain mode, 90–91
Negative caching, 50
Nested groups, 116, 118
Nesting, 90
Netdom tool, 255–256, **264**
NetPC standards, 347
Network administration, with Active Directory, 31–33
Network template category, 188
NewDomainDNSName key, 89
No Override, 171–172, **176, 373, 376**
Nonauthoritative restoration, 326
Nonlocal GPOs, 156
Nontransitive trust. *See* External trust.
NS records, 58

NSLOOKUP tool, 62–64
ntds.dit file, 321
ntdsutil utility, 309, 314, **337–338**, 376
nts.dit file, 83

O

Objects
    in Active Directory, 25
    administrative control of, 130
    appropriating ownership of, 141–142
    Domain Admins group ownership of, 142, **148**
    ownership, 141
    permission viewing, 133–135
    permissions, 132–140
    property version numbers, 327
    viewing ownership of, 141
Offline defragmentation mode, 329–330, **336**
Offline Folders, 211, **227**
Online defragmentation mode, 329
Operations Master dialog box, 305
Operations masters, 31, 298
    determining, 303–306
    domain-level roles, 304–305
    forest-level roles, 305–306
    master roles, 298
    role management, 303–309
    role transfer, 307–309
    roles, 299–303, **310**
    server alteration permissions, 306–309
Organizational Units. *See* OUs.
Originating updates, 273, **291**
OUs, 28, 82, 91–92, **96**, 132, **380**
    configuring, **376**
    control delegation, **146**
    creating, 92, **382**
    delegation of control, 32–33, 136
    inheritance, **6**

P

Packages
    configuring, 217–218
    deployment, 216–217
Password Policies security category, **204–205**
Passwords, 111, **127**
PC98 standards, 347
PCI Plug and Play network adapter, **365**
PCMCIA, 347
PDC Emulator, 299, 301–302, 309, **311–312, 386**

Peers, 272
Permissions, 78, 132. *See also* Delegation
  of authority.
    Allow permissions, 135, **146**
    Apply Group Policy permissions, **175**
    Deny permissions, 135, **146**
    flow redirection, 140
    inheritance, 138, **369**
    Read permissions, 175
    viewing, 133–135, **147–148**
Personal Computer Memory Card
  International Association. *See* PCMCIA.
ping command, 220
Pointer records. *See* PTR records.
POLICY keyword, 185, **202**
Preboot execution environment. *See* PXE.
Prestaged computers, 363, **368**
Primary DNS servers, 49
Primary Domain Controller Emulator.
  See PDC Emulator.
Principal logon names, **127**
Printers
    publishing locations, 235–236
    searching for, 235
Printers, as published resources, 232–233
printQueue object, **233**
Program-created shortcuts, 222
Propagation dampening, 278
Property version numbers. *See* PVNs.
PTR records, 59
Published resources, 232, **238, 239, 240**
    keyword and description additions
      to, 236–237, **240**
    location tracking, **239**
    printers, 232–233
    viewing, 234–235
pubprn.vbs script, 234, **238**
PVNs, 276, 327
PXE, 345

R

RAID 1 volume, 328
RAID 5 volume, 328, **338**
RBDG utility, 357
Rbfg.exe utility, 357
RDNs, 26, 47
Read permissions, 132, **147,** 175, 362
Recursive queries, **69**
Registry security category, 192
regsvr32 command, **315**
Relative distinguished names. *See* RDNs.

Relative Identifier Master.
  See RID Master.
Relative identifier. *See* RID.
Remote Boot Disk Generator. *See* RBDG.
Remote Installation Preparation Wizard,
  354, 356
Remote Installation Service. *See* RIS.
Remote Procedure Call. *See* RPC.
Repadmin utility, 284–286
ReplicaDomainDNSName key, 89
ReplicaOrNewDomain key, 89
Replicated updates, 273, **291**
Replication, 272, 273, **381, 384**
    attribute level, 276
    between sites, 281–282
    change notification process, **291**
    configuration partition, **294**
    conflict resolution, **293**
    DC selection for, **289–290**
    direct partners, 279
    latency, 301
    loop prevention, 277–278
    multiple-master concept of, 298
    multiple-master replication, **289**
    partners, 279
    protocol support of, 282–283
    site replication, 280–281
    topology, 278–279, 286–287
    transitive partners, 279
    troubleshooting, 287–288
    within sites, 281–282
Replication Monitor, 284–285, **294**
res1.log file, 83, 321–322, **332**
res2.log file, 83, 321–322, **332**
Resource records. *See* RRs.
Restricted Groups security category, 191
Reverse lookup zones, 53, 57
RFC 1995, 54
RID Master, 299, 302–303, **313**
RIPrep, 349, 353–354, **365–366, 367, 368**
    image creation with, 354–357
    RIS installation image creation, **366**
RIS, 281, 344, **383**
    boot disk creation, 357–358
    client option management, 359–360
    client requirements of, 346–348
    client support configuration, 360–361
    compliant BIOS, 347
    computer account creation rights, 362
    computer naming convention
      definition, 361–362

hardware requirements, 347–348, **376**
image creation, 353–357, **364**
image installation, **369**
installation, 349–350
NetPC standards, 347
PC98 standards, 347
preboot execution environment, 345
prestaged computers, 363, **368**
Read permissions, 362
RIPrep images, **365–366**
RISetup.exe utility, 350–353
security, 358–363
server authorization, 358–359
server components of, 345–346,
348–349
settings management, 360–363
RISDISK, **367**
RISetup.exe utility, 350–353, **367, 380, 383**
Roaming profiles, 211, **385**
Roles, 298–303
seizing, 303
transferring, 303
Root container, 163, **174–175**
Root domains, 28, **40**, 46, 72
Router hops, 274
RPC, 282
RRs, 57–58

S

SACL, 131
Schema, **35, 37, 387**
in Active Directory, 25
directory partition creation, 81
Schema Master role, 299–300, 309, **310,
311, 317**
Schema partitions, 279, **380**
Schemas, 246
Secedit utility, **386**
Second-level domains, 46
Secondary DNS servers, 49
Secondary servers, **66–67, 387**
Secure security template, 193, **206**
Security
AD objects, 130–132
DDNS updates, 60
delegation of control, 32–33
Directory Services Restore Mode
password, 77
domains, 27
High Secure template, **385**
Kerberos, **268**
passwords, 111, **127**

Remote Installation Server, 358–363
templates, 193–194, **206**
terms, **149–150**
Security boundaries, 27, **38, 269**
Security Configuration and Analysis tool,
382
Security descriptor, 130, **149**
Security groups, 115
Security ID. *See* SID.
Security principals, 130, **149**, 302
Select-and-place question format, 3, 11–12
Self-Assessment exam, 2
Server GUID, 276
Servers
bridgehead servers, 282
operations masters, 31
Service records. *See* SRV records.
Short-form exams, 14–17
Shortcut trusts, 252–253, **266**
Shutdown scripts, 195, **205, 385**
SID, 90, **99**, 130, **149**
Simple Mail Transfer Protocol. *See* SMTP.
Single Instance Store. *See* SIS.
Single sign-on, 102
SIS, 349
Site level GPOs, **174**
Sites, 31, 273
DNS design and, 48
links, 283–284
replication, 280–281
subnets, **290, 379**
Sites object, **380**
SMTP, 282
SOA records, 58
Software deployment, 219–220, **223**
troubleshooting, 220–222, **226**
Software Distribution extension
assigned applications, 218–219
published applications, 218–219
Software installation error messages, 221
Software Installation extension, **227**
global properties configuration,
214–215
installation error messages, 221
package deployment, 216–217
prerequisites for, **224**
Windows 2000 support of, **224–225**
Software Settings container, 163
SRV records, 59, **66**
Standard AD zones, 65
Standard primary servers, **66–67**

Standard primary zones, **69**
Start of Authority records. *See* SOA records.
Startup scripts, 195, **205**, **385**
Static IP addresses, **5**, 52, **381**
STRINGS keyword, 185, **202**
Subnets, **379**
System access control list. *See* SACL.
System container, **177**
System policies, Group Policy compared
    to, 157, **179**
System Services security category, 192
System state data, 323
System template category, 189
System.adm template, 183, **203**
SYSVOL folder, 73, 77, 84, **94**, 323
SysVolPath key, 89

T

Taskpads, 144–145, **151**
    customizing, 145
    Taskpad Creation Wizard, 144–145
TCP/IP, 46
Testing center, 3
TFTPD, 349
TGS, 258
Ticket-granting server. *See* TGS.
Timestamps, 276
Tombstoning, 322
Top-level domains, 46
Transactions, 321
Transitive replication partners, 279
Transitive trust, 246–247, **266**
    establishing across forests, 259–260
    establishing across multiple domains,
        258
Transmission Control Protocol/Internet
    Protocol. *See* TCP/IP.
TreeOrChild key, 89
Trees, 28–29, 245, **373**. *See also* Forests.
Trivial File Transfer Protocol Daemon.
    See TFTPD.
Troubleshooting
    A records, **66**
    AD installation, 82–83
    AD removal, 85
    Block Policy Inheritance, 172
    DNS, 61–64
    Group Policy, **383**
    No Override, 172
    shortcuts, 222

software deployment, 220–222, **226**
SRV records, **66**
Trusts, 246
    explicit, 252
    external, 254–256
    shortcut, 252–253, **266**
    transitive, **41**, 246–247, **266**

U

Unfiltered GPOs, 156
Universal groups, 90, **99**, 115, **269**
    creating in child domain, 264–265
    Universal user groups, **124**, **125**, 126,
        375
Update sequence numbers. *See* USNs.
User account names. *See* User logon names.
User accounts, 102, 109–111
    built-in user accounts, **122**
    copying, 113
    Csvde utility, 106–108, **120**
    deleting, 112
    disabling, 113
    domain user accounts, **122**
    duplicate name handling, **123**
    duplicating, 105–109
    enabling, 113
    Ldifde utility, 106, 108–109
    limited access, **121**
    local user accounts, **122**
    locating, 113–114
    logon names, **127**
    naming scheme, 119
    passwords, 111, **127**
    principal logon names, **127**
    renaming, 112
    single sign-on, **120**
    universal user groups, **124**, **125**, 126
    unlocking, 111
    user logon names, **127**
User Configuration container, 163,
    174–175, **177**, **204**
    Administrative Templates, 189
    Windows Settings node, 191
User logon names, 103–104, **127**
    rules for, 104–105
    user principal name, 103–104
User principal names, 260–261
User-created shortcuts, 222
Users container, **177**
USNs, 104, 278

V

VALUENAME keyword, 185
.vbs file extension, 195
VBScript, 195

W

Windows 2000 Resource Kit, 86, 255
Windows 2000 Server installation
  requirements, 73
Windows Components template category,
  188
Windows Internet Naming Service.
  See WINS.
Windows Script Host. *See* WSH.
Windows Settings container, 163
Windows.adm template, 183, **203**

Winnt.adm file, 183
WINS, 47
World Wide Web. *See* WWW.
Write permissions, 132, **147**
WScript.exe file, 196
WSH, 195–197
WWW
  "404 File not found" error, 20
  Microsoft Certified Professional
    Web site, 20
  search tools, 21

Z

Zone database storage, **67**
Zone transfer, 49, 53
Zones, 49

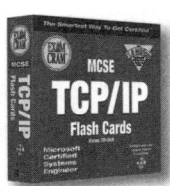

Look for All of the Exam Cram Brand Certification Study Systems

ALL NEW! Exam Cram Personal Trainer Systems

The Exam Cram Personal Trainer systems are an exciting new category in certification training products. These CD-ROM based systems offer extensive capabilities at a moderate price and are the first certification-specific testing product to completely link learning with testing.

This Exam Cram study guide turned interactive course lets you customize the way you learn.

Each system includes:

- A Personalized Practice Test engine with multiple test methods
- A database of nearly 300 questions linked directly to the subject matter within the Exam Cram

Exam Cram Audio Review Systems

Written and read by certification instructors, each set contains four cassettes jam-packed with the certification exam information you must have. Designed to be used on their own or as a complement to our Exam Cram study guides, Flash Cards, and Practice Tests.

Each system includes:

- Study preparation tips with an essential last-minute review for the exam
- Hours of lessons highlighting key terms and techniques
- A comprehensive overview of all exam objectives
- 45 minutes of review questions, complete with answers and explanations

Exam Cram Flash Cards

These pocket-sized study tools are 100% focused on exams. Key questions appear on side one of each card and in-depth answers on side two. Each card features either a cross-reference to the appropriate Exam Cram study guide chapter or to another valuable resource. Comes with a CD-ROM featuring electronic versions of the flash cards and a complete practice exam.

Exam Cram Practice Tests

Our readers told us that extra practice exams were vital to certification success, so we created the perfect companion book for certification study material.

Each book contains:

- Several practice exams
- Electronic versions of practice exams on the accompanying CD-ROM presented in an interactive format, enabling practice in an environment similar to that of the actual exam
- Each practice question is followed by the corresponding answer (why the right answers are right and the wrong answers are wrong)
- References to the Exam Cram study guide chapter or other resource for that topic

CORIOLIS™

Certification Insider Press

The _Smartest_ Way to Get Certified™